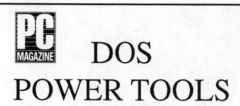 DOS
POWER TOOLS

DOS POWER TOOLS

TECHNIQUES, TRICKS AND UTILITIES

Paul Somerson

Executive Editor, PC Magazine

To the three smartest PC aces I've ever met, who are responsible for much of the programming and technical content of this book — Jeff Prosise, Michael Mefford, and especially PC wizard Charles Petzold; to Bill Machrone and Ken Koppel for saying yes; and to Terry for helping get it right.

Contents

PART II

The DOS Tools   231

Foreword

Computers are terrific power tools. In the right hands they can help you write, calculate, plan, design, even think better. But users typically end up spending far too many hours trying to figure out how to get things done exactly the way they want. Unless someone shows them the right tricks, they can waste hours struggling with tasks that they could have knocked off in a few minutes with the proper techniques.

No matter how experienced you are, you're always a beginner. While you may be a virtuoso at the few programs that you use most often, sit down in front of a brand new software package and you become a fumbling beginner all over again. If you're so smart, as the saying goes, how come you can't do more than two or three things really well with your computer?

Let's face it, computers are incredibly hard to master. Manuals are frequently awful, and good tutorials rare. With a few exceptions, support from manufacturers is pretty much nonexistent. Many users learn just enough to get by, and miss the real power of their systems. They end up doing much of their work by brute force, ignoring techniques for making operation efficient and automatic.

To make matters worse, software isn't the least bit standardized, even on fundamental operations such as starting up, saving files, or getting help. If the controls on your car were as nonstandard as they are on software, you wouldn't even be able to get it out of your driveway.

We Can Help

At *PC Magazine*, the nation's largest and most-respected computer publication, we have two primary goals — to tell you which products are best suited for your needs, and to help you make the best possible use of these products. We show you how to work faster, smarter, and better.

Each issue is packed with how-to columns and articles that give you the kind of hands-on help you need to boost your productivity through the roof. We scour the country to provide the best technical tips, advanced techniques, and ingenious shortcuts that can turn everyone into a true power user.

Several years ago I asked Paul Somerson to put together the very best productivity section on the planet. With the help of experts like Charles Petzold, Michael Mefford, Jeff

Prosise, Jared Taylor, John Dickinson, Neil Rubenking, Ethan Winer, Ray Duncan, Robert Hummel, Craig Stark, the Cobb brothers, and the thousands of readers who provided their favorite tips and tricks, he set out to turn the back pages of *PC Magazine* into a national institution.

And it worked. Grateful readers send us baskets of mail every day thanking us for helping them fully master their computers. With computers becoming increasingly complex, users are starved for this kind of hands-on help. Over the years they're been clamoring for a book that distills the magazine's very best tips and techniques.

Paul has gone well beyond that seemingly simple request. He's taken the most useful step-by-step techniques and how-to explanations from the last few years, enlarged and updated them, and mixed them with a hefty supply of undocumented tricks and ingenious shortcuts. And we added a disk crammed with powerful utilities to fill in the gaps. The result is a package that we're sure will turn even average users into true experts — painlessly.

These expert techniques have already helped hundreds of thousands of *PC Magazine* readers work far more productively. Let them help you too.

Bill Machrone
Editor-in-Chief and Publisher
PC Magazine

Preface

Many PC users think DOS is simply the few seconds of disk grinding between the time they hit the power switch and the time their favorite software pops onto the screen. They've learned how to format a disk and copy a floppy but are ignorant of the genuine magic it can perform in the right hands. Still, even experienced users often miss important shortcuts and tricks. This book and the programs on the accompanying disk will make mastering any DOS system a breeze.

If you've ever wondered why computers aren't easier to deal with, you're not alone. It's really not your fault — the standard DOS manual is a fat, inscrutable alphabetical reference crammed with useless details on how to use Norwegian characters or hook your computer to a nuclear reactor. It doesn't try very hard to help you. If General Patton were alive today he'd slap it.

Worse, the DOS manual makes even the few things that you have to do every day — like print out files — insanely complex. The latest entry on its PRINT command reads:

Format: [d:][path]PRINT[/D:device][/B:buffsiz]
             [/U:busytick][/M:maxtick][/S:timeslice]
             [/Q:quesiz][/C][/T][/P][[d:[path]
             [filename][.ext] . . .]

Clear? And it follows this madness with six pages of dense, oblique prose that would make Hemingway weep. You want to know what /M is for instance? Here's what the manual says: "/M is called maxticks." Maxticks? Huh? So what do they do? According to the manual, /M will "specify how many clock ticks PRINT can have to print characters on the print device." Clock ticks? Print device? Give us all a break.

You don't really have to understand what maxticks are, or what a buffsiz is. But knowing about these details can actually save you time and trouble. In this case, they'll let you print one or more documents without tying up your whole system, so you can start working on other documents right away. We'll explain every one of these PRINT terms later in crisp, understandable English. And in any case we'll give you a handful of PRINT shortcuts you can type in to start speeding up your own work, even if you don't want to learn what it all means.

So Why Do I Need This Aggravation?

Simple. Once you know a few easy techniques and shortcuts you can work far faster and safer. Users flood us with fan mail thanking us for speeding up their daily chores and automating all their drudgework. They tell us that we've taken away the nagging worry that they'll do something stupid, like erase all their files by mistake. And they say we've made life at the keyboard vastly easier and more productive.

Simple? Who's Kidding Whom?

It *is* easy, when someone shows you how, and throws in a few helpful programs to get you through the rough spots. The best way to learn is to have an expert standing over your shoulder pointing out tricks, giving you short, custom-made programs to boost your efficiency, and keeping you out of trouble. That's what we do regularly for over half a million serious readers. We bring relatively new users up to speed quickly, and turn ordinary users into power users.

What's This "We" Business?

A quick plug: *PC Magazine* is the oldest and largest IBM PC and PC-compatible magazine in the world. We not only tell readers what products to buy, but how to use these products (especially DOS) most productively.

Twice each month, *PC Magazine*'s Productivity section prints nearly 50,000 words of helpful, hands-on, how-to advice. Each issue we publish compact but powerful programs you can run on your system to make the whole process painless. And let you do things you never thought possible.

When we need to have a question answered, or a program created, or a comprehensive how-to article written, we rely on a staff of experts and a large stable of specialists around the nation. And each week hundreds of clever readers mail us their favorite discoveries and most ingenious techniques. We publish the most useful ones in our popular interactive columns.

We've taken the best tips, techniques, shortcuts, and actual programs that have appeared in *PC Magazine* over the last few years, added a lot of our own favorite tricks, and put everything in this one package. Our goals were to cover every important area of operation, and to make it all as clear and painless as possible. We wanted to create a single book that would answer every important question and provide truly useful information on every critical area of operation.

So Who's This Book For?

Glad you asked. It's for every serious user who wants to work faster, smarter, and better.

If you're starting out, or if you want a refresher course in the fundamentals, plunge in at the beginning. If you happen to be a black belt expert, you'll still learn plenty; just skim over the first few chapters (we'll bet that even advanced users will find tricks they didn't know).

But no matter where you start, you'll soon find yourself collecting armloads of powerful tips, shortcuts, and advanced techniques. Trust us. Hundreds of thousands of smart readers do on a regular basis.

But a Whole Book On DOS?

This book starts with DOS. But it shows users at every level how to operate their whole systems better. DOS affects every aspect of operation, from keyboards to screens to printers to modems to disk drives.

You can nibble at it and pick up the few techniques you need to get a specific job done, or devour every word and become a true PC guru. If you want the hex numbers and the undocumented commands and the environment variables it's all here. But if all you want to do is master the basics and make your time at the computer so efficient you won't believe you ever did it the hard way, you can do that too.

Okay, So What Exactly Is DOS?

It's easier to start with what DOS isn't. It isn't very easy, friendly, or forgiving. Several years ago IBM responded to such criticism by publishing a booklet with little dancing birds in the margins. This didn't solve the problem. Users still did things the hard way, or avoided doing anything tricky in the fear they'd damage their files (and they were often right to worry).

Sometimes using DOS is a little like manipulating plutonium in the next room through a thick glass window using remote-control robot hands. It's too clumsy. And s-l-o-w. What you really want to do is just get in there and grab what you're working on and knead it into shape. But the mechanisms DOS provides are cumbersome and seemingly difficult to master.

Using a PC means creating, changing, displaying, printing, copying, moving, and storing files. DOS does the really dirty work for you — interpreting and processing the commands you type, loading programs into memory, salting away your work in a semipermanent form that can readily be retrieved and altered, or sending data down a cable to a printer or another computer.

DOS has a truly limited vocabulary of a few dozen commands to handle all of this. Many of these commands are primitive, incomplete, even purposely crippled to protect you from yourself. Some are useless. The trick is to master the important ones, supercharge the incomplete ones, learn the effective DOS shortcuts that can automate your daily chores, and get your hands on a few necessary tools that DOS forgot. We'll show you how, with step-by-step instructions — and we'll provide a slate of powerful little programs to do all the hard work for you.

Keeping Current

One reason DOS is so thorny is that it has to adapt to a rapidly changing technology while remaining compatible with the older hardware and all the original commands. Even so, it should be a whole lot friendlier and easy to get along with. That's where we come in.

Times really have changed. The reason its creators called it DOS (short for *Disk Operating System*) was that it let users work with floppy disks, which were revolutionary two decades ago, but are commonplace to even kindergarteners now. These days optical disks (laser-based storage systems somewhat similar to audio CDs) and even a few hard disks can put a gigabyte — a billion characters' worth — of storage space at your fingertips in a fraction of a second.

(Some system manufacturers are even starting to talk about terabytes — a trillion characters' worth. Sending a terabyte of data to someone over a 1,200-baud modem would take several millenia, give or take a century.)

To put this in perspective, when IBM introduced its first PC in 1981 it actually stuck a plug on the back so users could store data on cassette tape recorders — a method so inefficient it's laughable today.

Impatient?

To be a real power user you should understand what makes your system tick, and be familiar with its evolution and internal structure. This is especially important because DOS comes in so many flavors, revisions, and dialects that you have to know how to handle the important differences between versions.

If you see a term in the early chapters of this book that you don't fully grasp, don't worry. It will all be explained in detail a little later. However, if you just can't wait to plunge in and start boning up on specific tips, jump ahead to the following chapters.

How to Use This Book

The shortest distance between two points may be a straight line, but frankly, we prefer the scenic route. It may take you just a bit longer, but it's a lot more fun. When you travel on an expressway you often miss the sights.

This book will turn anyone into a true power user. But don't be scared by its size. You don't have to start at page 1 and follow it all the way through to the end (although if you do, you'll become an absolute DOS wizard). Most readers tend to jump around from place to place, and this book is designed to accommodate them.

You can use this book and disk several different ways:

- If you're still fairly new at this, you can learn the ropes quickly by glancing at the Up to Speed section.
- If you need the best possible tips on a specific area such as organizing your hard disk, harnessing the color abilities of your new monitor, automating complex file

management tasks, or taming your keyboard, jump directly to that particular chapter.

- If you're interested in wringing the maximum horsepower out of your system, be sure to investigate the advanced techniques in the DOS Tools pages.
- And if you really want to stomp on your system's accelerator, step through every last trick in the Power User Secrets section.

No matter what your level, be sure to try the programs on the accompanying disk. They'll make it a snap to master every aspect of your system. Once you use a utility like Charles Petzold's BROWSE, SWEEP, or ATTR, or Michael Mefford's DR, RN, or CO; or run a powerful application program such as Jeff Prosise's DOSKEY, or IN-STALL/REMOVE, you'll wonder how you ever got anything at all done without them. And the disk contains hundreds more.

Warning!

As with any power tools, be extremely careful when using the programs and tips in this book and on the disk.

Read the appropriate manual entries carefully before running any of the programs. Not all programs will work on all systems (for instance, some are designed for EGAs, ATs, or PS/2 systems only). And just as you wouldn't plug too many power tools into the same outlet, if you want to load lots of different programs into memory at once, experiment with them to see how your hardware configuration handles it before working with any unsaved data.

The final section of this book contains two additional resources — a detailed program manual and a series of handy DOS quick reference charts. The manual is more than just a list of command syntaxes. It's jam-packed with tips, technical explanations, and ingenious customization hints. Both are extremely useful.

No Os

Note that in virtually every example in the text, a 0 is the numeral zero and not a capital o. Similarly, a 1 is a one and not a lowercase L. This book assumes you're using a version of DOS 2.1 or later. If you're not, go out right now and get your hands on the very latest version available.

While virtually all the tricks included here are utterly safe, a few (like those that deal with advanced disk modification techniques) are so powerful that you have to use extreme caution when trying them. The text includes stern warnings about these, but be sure you observe the following rules: read each entire section carefully before attempting the procedures mentioned, don't try modifying any of the procedures, and if you're really nervous, don't execute them. The book contains thousands of other equally useful but less fearsome tips to try.

Finally, the book makes extensive use of a technique called *redirection* to create and modify files. In most cases, this involves creating a small text file that DOS redirects, or feeds, into its DEBUG file-customization program. When creating these small text files or scripts be sure to use a "pure-ASCII" word processor. The DOS EDLIN editor will create such files, as will the ASCII/text modules of popular word processors such as Microsoft *Word*, *WordStar*, *XyWrite*, or *WordPerfect*.

As it's used here, a pure-ASCII file is one that, with just a few exceptions, contains nothing other than the letters, numbers, and punctuation that you can type directly from the keyboard. Most word processors throw in other nontext characters to handle formatting commands such as underlining or margin settings. But just about every word processor lets you create files without these formatting characters.

You can test whether your own word processor is capable of producing such files by using the DOS TYPE command to display them. If you create a file called TEST.FIL, for example, just make sure you're at the DOS A> or C> prompt and type:

```
TYPE TEST.FIL
```

If all you see is clear, unadulterated text, you're probably safe. But if you see odd characters, or if the text jumps and beeps its way across the page, look at your word processor's manual under "DOS files" or "Text files" or "ASCII files" and try again.

Whether you're just starting out, or you're an old hand at DOS, the tips and programs included here will make you the master of your system rather than the other way around. Isn't that why you started using a computer in the first place?

PART I

Getting Up to Speed

Chapter 1

The Development of DOS

Personal computers began appearing in the mid 1970s, initially as hobbyist toys that didn't even have keyboards or screens. The first real one, named Altair by a magazine editor's 12-year old daughter who liked a Star Trek episode that took place in that star system, was built around a jazzed-up calculator chip, the Intel 8080. (Today Intel supplies the state-of-art CPUs for all of IBM's desktop computers.) Produced as a do-it-yourself kit by a company called MITS (for Micro Instrumentation Telemetry Systems), it originally came with 256 bytes of memory, enough to hold only three or four lines of text. Since it lacked a keyboard, you entered information into it by flipping a series of switches on the front panel in binary on-off sequences. Because it had no screen, you had to decode the binary patterns of blinking lights it produced. And it didn't let you store information permanently. Compared to that, DOS is positively telepathic.

Two teenagers, Bill Gates and Paul Allen, who had gotten their digital feet wet by starting Traf-O-Data, a company that made Intel-based computers to measure how many cars rolled over a rubber hose stretched across a road, happened to see a picture of the Altair on the cover of *Popular Electronics* magazine, and developed a version of the BASIC programming language for it. Gates later upgraded Altair BASIC to give it primitive file-management disk-storage abilities, something that would come in handy later. The pair subsequently changed the company name to Microsoft; by 1976 the industry had progressed to the point where Gates was already railing against software pirates (although back then users were making illegal copies of punched paper tape rather than floppy disks). A few years later Gates became the world's youngest billionaire.

Soon after the Altair introduction, a coterie of hard-driving salespeople and "est" devotees became the market leaders with their IMSAI 8080, another Intel-chip machine, and the first computer aimed squarely at small businesses. To let users store data efficiently, IMSAI developed a floppy disk drive whose motors and circuits were run by a program called CP/M (short for Control Program for Microcomputers), which it had licensed from Intergalactic Digital Research — later shortened to Digital Research. Digital Research's Gary Kildall had created CP/M while working for Intel, to scale down the mainframe PL/I programming language into a version that would fit on a microcomputer. Intel hadn't seen much value in this brand new CP/M operating system and had given Kildall all rights to it.

The early versions of DOS owe quite a bit to CP/M. In fact, things like the COM formats of CP/M and DOS and the basic system calls were so similar that programmers could easily switch up from CP/M. CP/M used a command interpreter called CCP (for Console Command Processor), and two fundamental system files called BDOS and BIOS that handled files and I/O. This arrangement is nearly identical to the DOS COMMAND.COM, IBMDOS.COM, and IBMBIO.COM system trio. What was especially remarkable about CP/M was that it took up only 4K of space. DOS 1.0 doubled that, and has been mushrooming ever since.

Chain store magnate and leathercrafter Charles Tandy tried unsuccessfully to buy computers from IMSAI, then ended up creating his own system, the TRS-80, which contained a competing Zilog Z-80 chip, boasted slightly more than 4,000 characters of memory (a page or two of text), and came fully assembled rather than in kit form. To shave a few dollars off the price he designed it to work entirely in uppercase letters. Customers snapped them up as fast as Tandy could make them.

What really kicked the microcomputer business into high gear, however, were a handful of visionary renegades from California and Florida.

In 1976 Steves Wozniak and Jobs, whose early careers included a stint peddling "black box" devices to circumvent AT&T long distance billing computers, bought some MOS 6502 chips and built a few hundred copies of a computer that they christened the Apple I. It too worked in uppercase characters only. Their second-generation Apple II offered an optional floppy disk drive, and sold several orders of magnitude more. One reason for its success was a revolutionary program called *VisiCalc*, which was cobbled together by Dan Bricklin, Dan Fylstra, and Bob Frankston. *Visicalc* turned Wozniak and Jobs's little computer into a powerful financial analysis and planning machine.

But not all operating systems work on all chips. The increasingly popular CP/M ran on chips made by Zilog and Intel but not on the Apple's MOS processor.

Microsoft's Gates and Allen moved to Seattle to write programming languages for computers built around Intel and Zilog processor chips and running CP/M. Dismayed that their languages wouldn't work on MOS-based Apples, they considered translating them all to run on Apple's proprietary operating system, an arduous job. Instead, they joined the crowd, licensed CP/M, and sold it along with an add-in board that had a Zilog chip on it. Apple owners could stick the Microsoft board in their systems and run any CP/M programs.

But Apple was an eight-bit machine and Gates and Allen felt Intel's new 16-bit processors were the wave of the future. So did a local board maker named Tim Patterson who worked for Seattle Computer Products. All earlier processor chips managed data in eight-bit chunks. Intel's new 8088/8086 chip family doubled the processing power.

Patterson's board sported an 8086, and he needed a new 16-bit operating system to take advantage of it. Digital Research had announced that it was planning to tweak CP/M into a 16-bit CP/M-86 version, but Patterson couldn't wait. In early 1980 he started work on one of his own design called QDOS (for Quick and Dirty Operating System) that was to become 86-DOS (or SCP-DOS) and eventually just plain DOS. To make it relatively easy for programmers to translate CP/M software to his system, he retained fundamental CP/M file-management structures and mimicked the way it loaded and ran programs. Patterson then added a device called a File Allocation Table (FAT) which Gates had used in Altair disk BASIC , and a few other refinements.

DOS 1.0

In late 1980, IBM approached Microsoft and revealed that it was considering production of its own eight-bit personal computer. Vast helpings of money, ego, pride, and general corporate paranoia have tempered the details of this exchange, but the popular version is that IBM wanted Microsoft to design a version of BASIC for its new machine that would be delivered on a ROM chip inside the IBM chassis. Gates was happy to oblige and wanted to do a whole raft of languages, as the story goes, but argued that IBM should consider a 16-bit computer instead. When IBM asked who made a 16-bit operating system, Gates is said to have suggested that IBM contact Gary Kildall — and supposedly even dialed the phone to Digital Research himself.

Here the tale gets very fuzzy. According to one telling of it, when IBM trooped down to see Digital Research the next day, Kildall's wife and lawyer were hesitant to sign IBM's strict nondisclosure agreements. Other stories had Kildall out flying his plane while IBM executives waited impatiently for him to land. Microsoft's own publications admit that Gates and Allen had heard rumors that Kildall was about to buy a version of BASIC from a Microsoft competitor and give it away free with every copy of CP/M-86, which didn't exactly endear him to them.

In any event, Gates and Allen bought the rights to Patterson's 86-DOS for around $50,000 and proposed to IBM that Microsoft provide BASIC, FORTRAN, Pascal, COBOL, an 8086 Assembly language, and the 86-DOS operating system for the new computer. IBM agreed in November 1980, and on August 12, 1981 introduced the world to its new PC and its main operating system, Microsoft's DOS 1.0 (which IBM called PC-DOS). At the announcement, IBM mentioned that users would someday be able to buy two competing operating systems: CP/M-86 or the UCSD p-System. But IBM priced these much higher than DOS, and since they were late in reaching the market and received little support from other software vendors, they went nowhere.

Computer hardware (the chips and disk drives and other parts inside the cabinet) isn't useful without software (the programs that put the chips through their paces). And IBM didn't initially offer much software — *EasyWriter*, a bug-filled version of a mediocre word processor; *Adventure*, a mainframe text game adapted for smaller computers; a DOS version of *VisiCalc*; some artless business software; a few Microsoft languages; and one or two other packages.

The most popular and powerful programs back then — *dBASE II* and *WordStar* — ran only on CP/M systems. One of IBM's highest priorities was to make it easy for software vendors to translate programs from CP/M to DOS, and it was smart enough to know that making it easy meant making the two operating systems similar.

Many of the DOS features that today's users truly hate — such as overly brief eight-character filenames with three-character extensions, terse prompts like A>, and unfriendly or missing messages (such as stony silence in response to file deletions) were directly swiped from CP/M. So were underlying structures such as File Control Blocks (FCBs), Program Segment Prefixes (PSPs), and reliance on CP/M's memory loading addresses.

DOS did change a few CP/M quirks. File lengths that were rounded off in CP/M were reported precisely in DOS. Some commands were turned around to be more logical. Programmers could treat input and output to peripheral devices such as printers and screens the same way that they handled files. DOS's variable record lengths made disk storage and retrieval far more efficient. DOS could load and run larger EXE-format files in addition to the smaller standard CP/M-style COM-format files which were limited to 64K. And it could keep a program loaded in memory but inactive so that users could pop it onto their screens whenever they needed it. DOS relied on a FAT, first used by Bill Gates and Tom Patterson, to keep track of where all the various pieces of a file were stored, and could read and write more than one piece of data at a time, which speeded up disk activity significantly.

DOS at least theoretically made it easier for programmers to create their own versions of the COMMAND.COM user interface, although none has ever caught on. But the ability to run scripts of commands called batch files did become very popular. When DOS reported inevitable errors, it did so in a slightly friendlier way than CP/M, and it handled severe hardware errors far better. DOS also sniffed out new disks automatically while CP/M forced users to log such changes manually, and it kept track of the date files were created or changed.

It also split the COMMAND.COM user interface into several parts, a mixed blessing. When the PC was new, and IBM offered it with a maximum 65,536 characters of memory (which is usually rounded off to 64K), this feature was welcome since it let other space-hungry software temporarily steal a few thousand characters of memory space from DOS. When the user was finished with the software he'd have to then insert his DOS disk in drive A: so the part of DOS that hadn't been stolen could reload the part that had. Trouble was that a short time later users were buying systems with ten times that much memory, and the amount of space freed up by this technique was relatively insignificant. But floppy disk users still had to contend with keeping a DOS disk handy to reload the "transient" stolen part.

One of the worst things about the first IBM PC and its operating system was that it could store only 163,840 (160K) characters of data on floppy disks that were clearly capable of squirreling away twice that much. A standard floppy disk has two usable sides, but IBM's original drives (and DOS) took advantage of just one.

And the initial DOS release contained several nasty bugs. In mid-1982 IBM began selling PCs with double-sided drives, and released DOS version 1.1 to handle the new storage abilities and fix several of the early bugs. Microsoft then released its own similar generic DOS upgrade, which it called MS-DOS 1.25.

The initial release of DOS was tiny and relatively crude. Version 1.0 TIME and DATE commands were separate short programs rather than part of the main COMMAND.COM user interface. While the DOS 1.0 directory listing noted the date a file was created or changed, it ignored the time. The MODE command couldn't set communications speeds or protocols, or let the PC's parallel printer adapter work with the many serial printers on the market. You weren't able to have the COPY command join (or *concatenate*) smaller files into larger ones. The onscreen prompts and messages were especially ugly and cryptic.

DOS 1.1 fixed all these problems, or at least made them less irritating. The biggest problem of all was that DOS was still constrained by its CP/M heritage and its clanky internal structure. And although IBM doubled the amount of disk storage space from 163,840 (160K) characters to 327,680 (320K), users found this was far from enough. They demanded disks that were faster and more efficient.

DOS 2.0

In March 1983, IBM announced its PC-XT, a beefed up version of the standard PC that came with three additional internal expansion slots (for a total of eight), a ten-megabyte hard disk, a heftier power supply, and a new version of DOS — 2.0.

The new hard disk (which IBM referred to as a *fixed* disk) could hold the equivalent of more than 31 double-sided floppies. But all that storage space introduced a new problem. DOS 1.0 and 1.1 had crammed all the file information for each floppy disk into a single directory. A single-sided floppy directory had room for a maximum of 64 entries, and you could fit only 112 on a double-sided diskette.

Keeping track of all the files on a hard disk meant coming up with a new DOS file management and directory system. CP/M had dealt with large disks by splitting (or *partitioning*) them evenly into smaller ones, an inelegant and inefficient solution. But UNIX, an operating system developed by the phone company, could handle vast volumes of files with relative style and ease. Microsoft had licensed UNIX, and was offering a version of it called XENIX. At the heart of UNIX/XENIX was a *hierarchical* or *tree-structured* directory system that gave users lots of flexibility in dividing up the available storage space.

Microsoft adapted this tree-structured system as the core of a significantly new incarnation of DOS — version 2.0. But it blundered slightly. UNIX used a slash (/) to identify the hierarchical subdirectory levels that acted as branches on the tree structure. But earlier DOS versions used such slashes as *switches*, command suffixes (such as the /S in FORMAT /S) that turned certain optional features on and off. Microsoft substituted a backslash (\ ) to identify subdirectory levels, which ended up confusing a whole generation of DOS and UNIX users, and caused much consternation abroad where foreign keyboards often didn't come with backslash characters.

IBM and Microsoft also had to find a way to deal with an explosion in the number and type of devices that manufacturers were stamping out for the PC. One of DOS's main roles was to manage the communication between the PC and anything you could hook up to it. If DOS had to contain explicit internal tables and instructions for every possible external device it would end up being absurdly large and cumbersome.

Microsoft designed a new version of DOS with *hooks* in it so that manufacturers of peripheral equipment could supply installable *device driver* programs to hook the new hardware effortlessly into the operating system. Users could load these specific additional sets of instructions into DOS as needed, through a special CONFIG.SYS file. This file also let users customize the configuration of their systems by telling DOS such things as how much memory it should devote to disk buffers (areas of memory that hold disk data for speedy access), how many files could be opened simultaneously, and how frequently DOS should check to see whether a user might be hitting the Ctrl-Break panic button. It also made it easy for users to load a replacement command processor if they weren't planning on using the standard COMMAND.COM, or tell DOS if they were storing COMMAND.COM in an unusual place. And it gave users extended screen and keyboard control with ANSI.SYS, a special device driver supplied by Microsoft in an unsuccessful attempt to standardize certain parts of the user interface across different computer systems.

Version 2.0 introduced several commands most users can't live without. It's hard to believe, but versions 1.0 and 1.1 didn't offer any way to clear the screen. CLS now does it, although unless you're one of the few users taking advantage of ANSI, it will reset your screen colors to drab grey on black. This version was the first to offer batch file commands such as ECHO, IF, FOR, SHIFT, and GOTO. If you haven't yet mastered these, you'll be amazed at how they can help automate drudgework. We'll show you how (and point out tricks for retaining colors when you clear your screen) a bit later.

DOS 2.0 also introduced a raft of commands and utilities to give users control of hard disks, although some, like the pathetic TREE command — designed to "display the entire directory structure" — are a bad joke.

Perhaps to compensate, IBM threw in a gem that has become a power user's best friend — the mini-assembler in DEBUG. You can become an absolute computer whiz without ever having to learn a single thing about hex codes or assembly language. But if you want to climb inside your system and stomp on the gas pedal, there's no better way. It's a lot easier than you think.

One of the most significant changes in DOS 2.0 was the way it dealt with files internally. To remain compatible with CP/M, DOS versions 1.0 and 1.1 kept track of critical file information with a device called a File Control Block (FCB). But as programs became more sophisticated they were forced to manipulate the data stored in FCBs directly, which was awkward and potentially dangerous. And FCBs had no provisions for subdirectory names.

DOS 2.0 introduced *file handles* as an optional way to streamline disk management. Once DOS knew about a particular file in a particular subdirectory, it could act on that file simply by using a two-character shorthand code called a handle. In addition, DOS established five special handles that made it a snap to switch inputs and outputs. Normally the keyboard and screen (which DOS collectively refers to as the console or *CON*) act as both the input and output. But DOS 2.0 let users "redirect" input and output to or from printers, files, or other devices. And it allowed users to *pipe* streams of data through filters to do things like turn uppercase files into lowercase ones, strip out extraneous characters, or sort records in alphabetical order.

The sample filters DOS 2.0 provided are actually pretty useful. They'll let you slog through files and skim out the text you want saved or discarded. They'll sort your directories (or any list of names, numbers, or items that have carriage returns at the end of each entry) lightning fast. And they'll pause your displays for you so you'll never again have text scroll off your screen too quickly to read.

To top it off, DOS 2.0 provided rudimentary background processing. DOS was originally designed as a single-tasking operating system that let users do just one thing at a time. But the designers of version 2.0 threw in a PRINT *spooler* command that could print out one file while a user was actively working on another.

While spoolers are nothing new, this one was. Spoolers normally lop off a big chunk of RAM and trick DOS into sending files to memory that were really destined for the printer. Then they wait for a quiet moment and re-route the files onto your printed page. When they're done printing, however, they still hold onto all the memory they hogged — very inefficient. The DOS PRINT command reads files off your disks and uses your precious memory much more sparingly. It watches how you work, and about 18 times each second, if you're not doing something at that precise moment, it sneaks a few characters at a time to the printer. Your computer is so blazingly fast that this "time slicing" technique makes it appear that it's doing two things at once, when what it's really doing is alternating so quickly you don't notice it. And the best part is that if you happen to be working on something that takes more of your computer's constant attention than usual, you can adjust how frequently the spooler tries to intercede.

In addition, DOS increased the number of 512-byte sectors — the wedge-shaped magnetic pie slices on a floppy disk that actually hold your data — from eight to nine. While DOS kept the number of tracks in each sector at 40, this upped the storage capacity of double-sided floppy disks from 320K to 360K. DOS 2.0 also let users add electronic volume *labels* to their disks, gave them access to a part of memory called the *environment* in which critical system settings were maintained, made memory allocation more efficient, and threw in more than two dozen new commands.

With so many changes and new features, you'd think a brand new version of DOS such as 2.0 would be filled with insidious bugs. And you'd be right. In March 1984, a year after the PC-XT introduction, IBM released DOS version 2.1 to excise these software errors — and to handle a hardware error it produced called the PC*jr*.

The less said about the PC*jr* the better. While it provided more colors onscreen in graphics mode than IBM's real microcomputers, and came with three-voice sound that could play chords, it was utterly nonstandard inside and out. In fact, it used such a cheap, flimsy disk drive that DOS 2.1 actually had to slow down the drive performance so the thing wouldn't crash.

What's especially sad about this is that lots of users still rely on DOS 2.1, which means they have to put up with unacceptably slow drive access times even though they're using machines that could handle much higher speeds. A pity. And one of many good reasons to upgrade to a more recent DOS edition.

Microsoft ended up producing versions 2.05, 2.11, 2.2, and 2.25 with an added modicum of international time, date, keyboard, and currency support. These may come in handy if you need to work with Korean Hangeul or Japanese Kanji characters; today Microsoft sells DOS in more than 60 assorted languages.

DOS 3.0

IBM's PC and PC-XT brought microcomputing into the mainstream of American business. But these machines were both relatively slow and small. In fact, they weren't really even true 16-bit computers. While a 16-bit Intel 8088 central processing unit (CPU) ticked away inside each one, their system *bus* — the connecting pathway of wires that ties the CPU to all the other parts of the system — was a bottleneck that worked in eight-bit chunks only.

IBM introduced its first genuine 16-bit system, the PC-AT. Compared to IBM's earlier releases, this was a rocket ship of a computer. Inside was an 80286 CPU with a trick up its sleeve — it could run everything IBM and Microsoft threw at it and could also accommodate Microsoft's next-generation OS/2 operating system. And it needed a new version of DOS — 3.0.

Engineers measure computer performance in many ways. Two prime indicators are the clock speed of the CPU and the average access time of the hard disk. The faster the clock, the faster a computer processes instructions and the faster just about everything runs. The speedier the hard disk average access time, the speedier it can read and write programs and data. The higher the clock speed and the lower the average access time, the nimbler the system.

Both the PC and the PC-XT run at 4.77 megahertz (MHz). IBM sold many different brands of hard disks for the XT, and the average access time was somewhere between 80 and 115 milliseconds.

The official clock speed of IBM's first AT was 6 MHz, but users quickly found out that by replacing a socketed $4 quartz crystal on the main system board they could boost performance to 8 or even 9 MHz without any ill effects. (IBM is famous for publishing ultraconservative specifications and holding down performance a bit on purpose.) When IBM discovered that users were hot-rodding their systems, they wrote a program that acted as a speed governor and put it onto a system ROM chip to prevent tampering.

All of IBM's AT hard disks ran at speeds of 40 milliseconds or better. Unfortunately, the first big batch of PC-ATs came with CMI-brand drives that crashed in shockingly high numbers. Hard disks — rapidly spinning precision-crafted aluminum platters with magnetic coatings on both sides — need precise feedback on where their magnetic read/write heads are located. If the location mechanism is off by even a tiny bit the heads can write bad data over good or wipe out important tables that tell the computer where files are stored.

Hard disk heads actually "fly" on a cushion of air directly above the surface of the platters themselves. All decent hard disks retract or *park* the magnetic heads when the power goes off so they don't sink down and plow furrows into your data. To save money, CMI disks used what many believe was an unreliable implementation of *wedge servo* technology. Most other hard disks used a dedicated positioning surface, a whole side of a hard disk platter that contained no user data and instead acted as a map to the platters that did. But not CMI's AT drives. And these drives didn't park the heads when you turned the power off. The heads just dropped down onto the data area and scraped against it.

IBM never really admitted doing anything wrong, but tens of thousands of users know differently. If this black episode in microcomputing history had a silver lining, it was that it taught hard disk users how absolutely imperative it is to make frequent and comprehensive backup copies of their work.

In any event, a PC-AT running at 8 MHz was 67 percent speedier than a standard PC or PC-XT. The PC-AT hard disk was twice as fast as the speediest PC-XT drive, which made everything seem a lot more energetic, and ended up turbocharging disk-intensive applications such as database searches. On top of all that, the PC-AT could deal with memory in 16-bit chunks, while the PC and PC-XT had to lumber along with half that amount. Clone makers soon began producing respectable AT imitations that chugged along even faster. To avoid falling behind the competition too much, IBM eventually had to nudge the performance upward slightly each time it refined the AT design.

IBM's newest PS/2 line of hardware and the many high-performance clones on the market make even the fastest IBM PC-AT look like it's standing still. With CPU speeds of 20 and even 24 MHz, hard disk access times in the high teens, and a 32-bit bus that moves information nearly four times as efficiently as the one in the original PC, these hot new microcomputers give refrigerator-sized minicomputers a run for their money.

The PC-AT was originally delivered with a 20-megabyte hard disk, although subsequent versions have enhanced both the AT's speed and the size of its hard disk. Still, 20,480,000 characters' worth of storage meant that backing it all up would take 56 standard 360K *double-density* floppies. The mind reels. Apparently, so did IBM's. It dropped a *quad-density* floppy disk drive, which could hold 1.2 megabytes of data — or the equivalent of nearly four 360K floppies — into each PC-AT. IBM refers to these as *high-capacity* drives. Unhappy users have called them something else, unprintable here.

The PC-AT's new DOS, version 3.0, could handle the increased floppy disk storage. But it also had to understand every other floppy format. In the space of six years IBM had introduced single-sided and double-sided drives, with eight or nine sectors, and in double or quad density, so downward compatibility meant knowing how to deal with:

- 160K single-sided 5-1/4 inch drives
- 180K single-sided 5-1/4 inch drives
- 320K double-sided 5-1/4 inch drives
- 360K double-sided 5-1/4 inch drives
- 1.2M double-sided 5-1/4 inch drives

Well, there's compatibility and there's compatibility. Out of the 25 different possible combinations of using the DISKCOPY command to move information from one to the other, 16 won't work.

What's more, IBM's PS/2 hardware uses 3-1/2 inch diskettes, a whole new ball game. These smaller diskettes are sturdier, easier to transport, and vastly more efficient at storing information. IBM characteristically complicated matters by producing two different and slightly incompatible 3-1/2 inch formats, one that holds 720K and one capable of storing 1.4 megabytes of data. The 5-1/4 inch 320/360K floppy format won't go away very quickly, since so many vendors have made it the standard for program distribution. But the PC-AT's 1.2 megabyte drive and the low-end PS/2 720K diskette are orphans.

All IBM microcomputers gave users a clock and calendar that could stamp DOS directory listings with the time and date files were created or most recently changed. But users had to set the clock each time they started (*booted up*) their systems, unless they had purchased an add-in board with a battery-driven clock on it (and most did). The PC-AT came with its own internal battery-run clock/calendar, although it wasn't until DOS version 3.3 that users could reset it easily.

Figure 1.1 shows the configurations of all of IBM's PCs.

Model	ID Byte	CPU	Speed (MHz)	I/O Bus (Bits)	Maximum RAM	Keyboard	DOS Version
PC	FF	8088	4.77	8	640K	old	1.0
XT	FE	8088	4.77	8	640K	old	2.0
PC*jr*	FD	8088	4.77	8	640K	special	2.1
AT	FC	80286	6/8	16	15M	both	3.0
PC/2	FB	8088	4.77	8	640K	both	–
XT/286	FC	80286	6	16	15M	both	–
Convertible	F9	80C88	4.77	8	640	special	–
Model 30	FA	8086	8	8*	640K	new	–
Model 50	FC	80286	10	16	16M	new	3.3
Model 60	FC	80286	10	16	16M	new	3.3
Model 80	F8	80386	16/20	32	4G	new	3.3

Figure 1.1.   Hardware Configurations of IBM's Personal Computers

*Model 30 has 16-bit memory bus

Program developers live by a rule: "The software is never finished." Each release of DOS or any commercial application is quickly followed by a version with bug fixes, speedups, and forgotten utilities. Market considerations force manufacturers to ship everything at the earliest possible date. Microsoft officially admits that DOS 3.0 "wasn't quite ready" at the introduction of the PC-AT. But it went out the door anyway.

Today, virtually every desk in America has a telephone in one corner. IBM's vision of the future puts a computer terminal next to it, and strings all the terminals together electronically. Networking computers this way does have lots of advantages. It lets users "mail" messages and files to each other, and share centralized data bases of information. Someday when everyone has to send text to everyone else and when it's easier and cheaper to consult a far wider range of databases, this will be attractive.

Networks can also let users share expensive peripherals like plotters or laser printers, but it doesn't make much sense to install three $1,500 network hookups to share one $1,500 printer. Today networks are interesting to a minority of users only — although the number grows as the costs and headaches often associated with using them are reduced. Networks introduce their own special set of problems. Two users may reach for the same data base records at the same time, and something has to mediate the conflict. Worse, giving users access to centralized information means someone has to decide who has the authority to read what files and change which data. And then something has to keep track of the authorization levels and enforce it all, and make sure the right data is routed to the right place.

Microsoft designed DOS version 3.0 to support the official IBM PC network hardware. Unfortunately, the AT was ready before the network features of DOS were, and the Microsoft designers had to deactivate these features in the final product. They finally turned them back on in version 3.1, released in November 1984. But DOS 3.1 was picky; it would handle only certain "well-behaved" networks. ("Misbehaved" products are ones that use undocumented commands, or bypass software safeguards by manipulating hardware directly, or otherwise bend industry rules to enhance performance.)

DOS 3.0 introduced a streamlined method for integrating FCBs and handles. And while it provided a small handful of new features, none was a radical departure from DOS 2.1. In fact, IBM stated in its documentation that "DOS 3.0 does not replace DOS 2.1." But it did fix a nasty 2.1 oversight, by making it harder for users to format their hard disks if they weren't careful. (It wasn't until version 2.0 that DOS asked for confirmation if users tried to delete all the files on their disk with a single ERASE *.* command.) Version 3.0 also let users make files *read-only* to prevent any inadvertent changes or deletions.

Version 3.1 provided better *aliasing* features to combine drives and directories and to trick DOS into treating a subdirectory like a disk drive. DOS 3.2 introduced users to 3-1/2 inch diskettes (although the tools it provided to handle this were downright awful), made it easier for them to upgrade DOS versions, and gave them one of the best, but least-used, new commands, XCOPY.

DOS 3.3, tossed off by IBM pitchmen at the introduction of the PS/2 as an "interim solution" and the operating system for a string of dogs including the PC Convertible, Portable PC, and PC*jr*, deftly excised a heap of user headaches, and added a few sizzling new tricks.

As all seasoned hard disk users are aware, working efficiently on a hard disk machine means pigeonholing related programs and data in electronic file drawers called subdirectories. But users who are currently working in one subdirectory often want to execute a program or look at data stored in another.

Since version 2.0, users had been able to tell the PATH command to check specified subdirectories for executable files (with filenames ending in COM, EXE, or BAT). This let users run programs in other subdirectories, but it didn't let them get at distant data. Nonexecutable files remained immune to even the most comprehensive search, forcing power users to purchase commercial "path extender" programs such as *FilePath* or *File Facility*, or struggle with the DOS 3.1 SUBST command. The DOS 3.3 APPEND command made the process relatively easy — and a lot cleaner.

Serial ports are your system's main gateway to the outside world. Version 3.3 let MODE work with four serial ports rather than just two (OS/2 can juggle up to eight), and cruise along at up to 19,200 baud, double the previous limit. And IBM finally recognized that at least twice a year users need to reset their internal IBM clocks and provided a way to do this without having to hunt down their Diagnostics disks, figure out which option adjusts the time, and then grind through all the irritating preliminary screens. The 3.3 TIME and DATE commands automatically adjusted IBM CMOS memory to reflect the change.

Another improvement was the newfound ability of the DOS 3.3 ATTRIB command to gang-process all files in a directory and its related subdirectories, which made it easier to create backups and prevent inadvertent file deletions or changes. Unfortunately, the same process used by ATTRIB can also "hide" files from casual snooping, but IBM won't show you how. (We will.)

The original DOS architects preferred working with 512-byte disk sectors, and used a FAT to keep track of what data is in which sector. When they designed the FAT they used 16-bit addresses, which allowed a maximum of 65,536 (64K) table entries. This clamped a firm 32 megabyte limit (512 x 65,536 = 33,554,432 bytes) on the size of any physical hard disk. To get around this limit, manufacturers either had to increase the sector size, which made their hardware nonstandard and relatively wasteful, or come up with a whole new file management scheme, which ended up being even more nonstandard.

IBM tuned DOS 3.3 to divide physical hard disks into smaller *logical* drives, and fixed the FDISK command to create *extended* DOS partitions in addition to the *primary* ones users were able to carve out previously. Each extended partition could be further subdivided into logical drives 32 megabytes or smaller, with their own drive letters. Compaq quickly made it even easier to use enormous hard disks, by introducing a DOS version (3.31) that boasted 32-bit FAT addresses.

To expedite directory searches with the new generation of larger hard disks, DOS 3.3 provided a filename *cache* utility called FASTOPEN. Caches keep track of things in memory rather than on disk, speeding up many processes significantly. FASTOPEN notes the location of files and subdirectories (which are really just special classes of files) the first time you hunt for them, and then directs DOS to the exact spot on the disk the next time you have to deal with them.

The DOS BACKUP command had always been so pathetic that an entire industry of third-party backup software has evolved to fill in the gaps. While the version 3.3 enhancements aren't going to put all those developers out of business, they will bring some users back into the fold. Under previous DOS versions you had to format a tall stack of disks before starting the backup process. If you ran out of formatted disks halfway through you had to abort and either find a way to catch up, or start the whole elaborate, time-consuming procedure over again.

In DOS 3.3 the BACKUP command can summon the FORMAT command and prepare unformatted disks if necessary — with certain irritating restrictions. And you have to limit the disks and drives you use; it still can't mix and match. The DOS 3.3 BACKUP works faster and more efficiently than older versions, by copying all smaller files to a single enormous one, and by creating a guide file that tells DOS how to take the big file apart and restore it properly later. It will also create a log file telling you what it did where.

The DOS 3.3 RESTORE gives you added flexibility in restoring backed-up files by date and time, as well as those deleted or changed since you backed them up, or files that are no longer on the target disk. Better yet, while older versions of RESTORE let you accidentally obliterate your current system files (IBMBIO.COM, IBMDOS.COM, and COMMAND.COM or their generic counterparts) with older backed-up versions, DOS

3.3 RESTORE won't. Inadvertently mixing versions of hard disk system files is like replacing a heart surgeon, in the middle of an operation, with a tree surgeon.

Batch files can take much of the anguish out of tricky or repetitive tasks. The first thing most power users do when they create a batch file is turn off the display by issuing an ECHO OFF command. This stops DOS from littering your screen with the frantic prompts, messages, and other electronic graffiti a batch file triggers. But users had no authorized way of preventing this ECHO OFF command from adding to the screen clutter itself. Version 3.3 users can prevent such clutter simply by prefacing any command with a @ symbol.

In addition, DOS 3.3 could CALL one batch file from another, execute it, and then return to the original batch file and continue executing it. Doing this kind of "nesting" under previous editions of DOS meant that each batch file had to load its own separate version of COMMAND.COM, do its work, exit, and drop back to yet another version — which was sort of like restarting a movie each time a latecomer walked into the theatre. DOS 3.3 also documented environment variables for the first time, which let users pass information back and forth from application to application.

DOS 3.0 to 3.2 came in five international flavors. By executing the appropriate KEYBxx command, users could transform the keyboard into British, German, French, Italian, or Spanish modes. With version 3.3, IBM totally revamped the way DOS handled foreign alphabets. IBM's manuals have gotten a bit better over the years, but the three abstruse and seemingly contradictory chunks on this international support virtually defy comprehension. IBM prefaced its long appendix-like treatment of the topic with the caveat "You can use code page switching without fully understanding everything about it." After poring over the text, you'll know why this was included. And if you live in the United States, you'll take one look, put your hand over your heart, and say "Thank God we're Americans."

For the first time, DOS 3.3 set a default number of disk buffers based on your system's configuration. Under previous versions, it assumed every PC and XT user really wanted only two and every AT user only three. DOS will now sniff out what hardware you have available, and allocate from two buffers (minimal RAM and no high density floppies, 3-1/2 inch diskettes, or hard disks) to 15 (any machine with 512K or more of RAM). If you're using a big hard disk you may want more than 15. Better yet, you should try a commercial file cache program.

Figure 1.2 shows the relative sizes of the various versions of DOS. You can use the chart provided to look at the size of COMMAND.COM on diskettes formatted with the /S option and determine the DOS version number. Note that DOS 3.3 is a whopping six times larger than 1.1, and 13 percent fatter than its immediate predecessor.

Figure 1.3 traces the addition of commands through versions of DOS, up to 3.1. Figure 1.4 shows which commands were modified in which versions.

The Future

IBM and Microsoft continue to add and adapt messages and prompts; the infamous and ubiquitous DOS error message "Abort, Retry, Ignore?" became a more chilling "Abort,

Retry, Ignore, Fail?" under DOS 3.3. This isn't exactly friendly. When Microsoft originally designed DOS it published all the specifications so other manufacturers could replace the COMMAND.COM user interface with something different, such as a visual shell. Several amateurs have tried, but nothing much has come of it. Microsoft itself tried an easier interface called *Windows*, but users have resisted, calling it overly large, ungainly, and slow. (Microsoft and IBM adapted *Windows* as a graphic front-end called *Presentation Manager* for the next generation OS/2 operating system.)

DOS needs all sorts of help. Way back when the EGA was first introduced, for instance, users complained that the MODE command couldn't deal with any of the new graphics settings (such as 43 or 50 lines, or the far better color selection). Now that an even jazzier VGA color standard is out, you'd think that DOS could handle at least something past the CGA standard it introduced way back with the original PC. Guess again. But this book/and its accompanying disk provide a dozen utilities to master the EGA. And it will explain in lush detail how to get around most of the other DOS limitations, and provide you with the Utilities DOS Forgot.

DOS 1.0 — 13312 bytes used by system files

COMMAND	COM	3231	8-04-81	12:00a
IBMBIO	COM	1920	7-23-81	12:00a
IBMDOS	COM	6400	8-13-81	12:00a

DOS 1.1 — 14336 bytes used by system files

COMMAND	COM	4959	5-07-82	12:00p
IBMBIO	COM	1920	5-07-82	12:00p
IBMDOS	COM	6400	5-07-82	12:00p

DOS 2.0 — 40960 bytes used by system files

COMMAND	COM	17664	3-08-83	12:00p
IBMBIO	COM	4608	3-08-83	12:00p
IBMDOS	COM	17152	3-08-83	12:00p

DOS 2.1 — 40960 bytes used by system files

COMMAND	COM	17792	10-20-83	12:00p
IBMBIO	COM	4736	10-20-83	12:00p
IBMDOS	COM	17024	10-20-83	12:00p

DOS 3.0 — 60416 bytes used by system files

COMMAND	COM	22042	8-14-84	8:00a
IBMBIO	COM	8964	7-05-84	3:00p
IBMDOS	COM	27920	7-05-84	3:00p

DOS 3.1 — 62464 bytes used by system files

COMMAND	COM	23210	3-07-85	1:43p
IBMBIO	COM	9564	3-07-85	1:43p
IBMDOS	COM	27760	3-07-85	1:43p

DOS 3.2 — 69632 bytes used by system files

COMMAND	COM	23791	12-30-85	12:00p
IBMBIO	COM	16369	12-30-85	12:00p
IBMDOS	COM	28477	12-30-85	12:00p

DOS 3.3 — 78848 bytes used by system files

COMMAND	COM	25307	3-17-87	12:00p
IBMBIO	COM	22100	3-18-87	12:00p
IBMDOS	COM	30159	3-17-87	12:00p

Figure 1.2.   Relative Sizes of All IBM DOS Versions

New External Commands

DOS 1.0	DOS 1.1	DOS 2.0/2.1	DOS 3.0	DOS 3.1	DOS 3.2	DOS 3.3
BASIC.COM	EXE2BIN.EXE	ANSI.SYS	ATTRIB.EXE	BASIC.PIF	DRIVER.SYS	4201.CPI
BASICA.COM		ASSIGN.COM	GRAFTABL.COM	BASICA.PIF	REPLACE.EXE	5202.CPI
CHKDSK.COM		BACKUP.COM	KEYBFR.COM	JOIN.EXE	XCOPY.EXE	APPEND.EXE
COMMAND.COM		FDISK.COM	KEYBGR.COM	SUBST.EXE		COUNTRY.SYS
COMP.COM		FIND.EXE	KEYBIT.COM			DISPLAY.SYS
DATE.COM		GRAPHICS.COM	KEYBUK.COM			EGA.CPI
DEBUG.COM		MORE.COM	KEYBSP.COM			FASTOPEN.EXE
DISKCOMP.COM		PRINT.COM	LABEL.COM			KEYB.COM
DISKCOPY.COM		RECOVER.COM	SELECT.COM			KEYBOARD.SYS
EDLIN.COM		RESTORE.COM	SHARE.EXE			LCD.CPI
FORMAT.COM		SORT.EXE	VDISK.LST			NLSFUNC.EXE
LINK.EXE		TREE.COM	VDISK.SYS			PRINTER.SYS
MODE.COM						
SYS.COM						
TIME.COM						

New Internal Commands

DOS 1.0	DOS 1.1	DOS 2.0/2.1	DOS 3.0	DOS 3.1	DOS 3.2	DOS 3.3
COPY	DATE	BREAK	COUNTRY	*(none)*	*(none)*	CALL
DIR	DEL	BUFFERS	DEVICE			CHCP
ERASE	REN	CD	FCBS			
PAUSE	TIME	CHDIR	LASTDRIVE			
REM		CLS				
RENAME		CTTY				
TYPE		ECHO				
		ERRORLEVEL				
		EXIST				
		EXIT				
		FILES				
		FOR				
		GOTO				

Figure 1.3.   New DOS Commands and Utilities

Note: Files with extensions are predominantly external commands or device drivers. Those without extensions are either internal commands (part of COMMAND.COM) or configuration commands that work specifically with CONFIG.SYS.

Modified External Commands

DOS 1.0	DOS 1.1	DOS 2.0/2.1	DOS 3.0	DOS 3.1	DOS 3.2	DOS 3.3
(none)	(TIME.COM)	CHKDSK.COM	FORMAT.COM	LABEL.COM	ATTRIB.EXE	ATTRIB.EXE
	(DATE.COM)	COMP.COM	BACKUP.COM	TREE.COM	COMMAND.COM*	BACKUP.COM
	FORMAT.COM	DEBUG.COM	RESTORE.COM	LINK.EXE	DISKCOMP.COM	FDISK.COM
	CHKDSK.COM	DISKCOMP.COM	DISKCOMP.COM		DISKCOPY.COM	GRAFTABL.COM
	ERASE.COM	DISKCOPY.COM	DISKCOPY.COM		FORMAT.COM	MODE.COM
	DISKCOMP.COM	EDLIN.COM	GRAPHICS.COM		SELECT.COM	RESTORE.COM
	DISKCOPY.COM	FORMAT.COM				
	LINK.EXE					
	DEBUG.EXE					
	MODE.COM					

*environment
size

Modified Internal Commands

DOS 1.0	DOS 1.1	DOS 2.0/2.1	DOS 3.0	DOS 3.1	DOS 3.2	DOS 3.3
(none)	*(none)*	DIR	DATE	*(none)*	SHELL	ECHO
		DEL	*(external			DATE
		ERASE	command			TIME
			paths okay)*			

Figure 1.4.   Modified DOS Commands and Utilities

Chapter 2

Disk Organization, Files, Filenames

The first thing most users do when they walk over to a computer equipped with a hard disk is type DIR to see what's there. On a well-organized system you'll probably see something like:

```
Volume in drive C is WORKDISK
Directory of C:\

COMMAND   COM      25307    3-17-87    12:00p
CONFIG    SYS         47   10-18-88     7:07a
AUTOEXEC  BAT        256   10-18-88    12:01a
DOS            <DIR>        10-18-88     7:09a
WORDSTAR       <DIR>        11-06-88    12:22a
DBASE          <DIR>         2-11-88    12:00a
LOTUS          <DIR>        12-03-88    12:02a

     7 File(s) 28220672 bytes free
```

However, try this on a disorganized floppy disk system and you'll see a real mess:

```
Volume in drive A has no label
Directory of A:\

TF86_CDY RPT      65387    1-01-80     7:07a
TF86_CDY BAK      54396    1-01-80    12:01a
```

```
RRXWFEB7 4QS        6754   1-01-80    7:07a
FIN_54TT RPT       11239   1-01-80   11:01p
SPELLIT          <DIR>     1-01-80   12:02a
PROSEWIZ EXE       86456   4-17-87    9:54p
FIN_54TT BAK        9437   1-01-80    5:07p
COMMAND  COM       25307   1-01-80   12:00p
AUTOEXEC BAT         256   1-01-80   12:01a
         .
         .
         .
    etc.
```

When you type DIR and press the Enter key, DOS shows you what's in the directory that you happen to be using. Directories are storage bins, like drawers in a file cabinet. Just as some file cabinets prevent you from opening more than one file drawer at once, you can look at the contents of only one directory at a time. Each line in the main part of a DIR listing represents either a single file stored in that directory, or the name of another related directory on the same disk.

And just as some well-organized workers keep their file cabinets in meticulous shape and can find any document in seconds, while others live in the shadow of chaos and can't find anything without tedious searching, disks can be well-organized or in total disarray. Fortunately, once you know the basic techniques and have a few powerful programs handy, your computer can do all the organizing for you. This book will show you the tricks and provide the programs you need.

The Physical Disk

All diskettes and hard disks use the same basic technology. The surface of each is coated with a material that can store lots of isolated magnetic charges. An electromagnetic coil of wire or special "stepping" motor propels a tiny magnetic *read-write head* over the surface of the disk. When you want to store information, you tell a controller circuit to move the magnetic head to an unused part of the disk, then send signals into the head that alter the magnetic charges on a small adjacent area of the surface. When you want to retrieve information, you have the controller move the head to the appropriate area and tell the head to sniff out the pattern of magnetic charges located there.

It's actually a lot more complicated than this. When you issue a command, something has to interpret your typing and figure out what you're trying to do. If it determines that you want to load a program, it has to decipher the name and location of the file, and look on the appropriate disk to make sure it's there. Files are normally stored in small chunks scattered over the surface of the disk, and something has to thread all the chunks together, then find an unused area in memory and copy the chunks there in the right order. At this point things get even more complex, since something has to rope off the area of memory that holds the program, set up other memory areas for storage, see if you entered any parameters after the name of the program that need processing, and pass control to the program.

Fortunately, DOS handles all the details. All you have to do is type in the filename and press Enter.

Individual floppy disks on IBM's earliest PC could hold a mere 64 files, or 160,256 bytes of programs and data. As users began demanding bigger and more efficient systems, manufacturers first tried cramming additional storage space onto the same 5-1/4 inch floppies. But as space needs skyrocketed, vendors started introducing increasingly large hard disks — as well as 3-1/2 inch diskettes that could store as much as 1,457,664 bytes of information — more than nine times the capacity of the first PC diskettes.

IBM's first hard disk, for the XT, held ten megabytes; the first for the AT could store 20 megs. Users accustomed to floppy disks initially wondered how they could possibly fill so relatively enormous a storage space. But having all their programs and files at their fingertips was so seductive that users quickly clamored for more. Stacks of today's muscular hard disks and optical disks can salt away bytes in the gigabyte range (*giga* means billion and is pronounced "jig-guh" the way gigantic is pronounced "jy-gan-tic" — although most users say "giga" with a hard g as in "gargantuan").

But DOS wasn't designed for such massive storage. It doesn't store data in long, continuous, uninterrupted blocks of space. If it did, making additions and deletions to files would become insanely inefficient, since each time you made a file longer, DOS would have to find a brand new uninterrupted amount of disk area to store the enlarged file. So DOS divides files up into little pieces and stores the pieces in small areas called *clusters*.

Clusters are made up of *sectors*. Each sector — the smallest possible user storage area on any DOS disk — is 512 bytes long. On some disks, like the earliest single-sided 160K and 180K floppies, or the high-density 1.2 megabyte 5-1/4 inch and 1.44 megabyte 3-1/2 inch diskettes, each cluster contains just one sector. At the other end of the scale, the absurdly inefficient ten-megabyte XT hard disk allots eight sectors to each cluster, which means it takes 8 x 512, or 4,096 bytes to store even the smallest file on an original XT. And some large, nonstandard hard disks are even worse.

When you store a file on a disk, DOS splits it into cluster-sized chunks and starts looking for vacant parts of your disk to hold these chunks. On a newly formatted hard disk, all these chunks can be continuous and uninterrupted. But on a disk that's seen months or years of heavy use — especially one that's nearly filled with data — DOS has to look long and hard to find empty spaces, and may end up dividing a typical file into dozens of fragmented clusters scattered all over the surface of your disk.

DOS relies on a chart called the File Allocation Table (FAT) to remember which clusters on the disk are temporarily unused, and to keep track of where all the scattered chunks of your files are located. It also uses a special nondisplaying part of the disk's directory to steer itself into each file's very first cluster. But while the directory contains the address of the initial cluster, the FAT maintains the addresses of all the rest of any file's clusters. The FAT is so important that most disks contain two identical copies, and DOS updates both each time it adds, deletes, or changes a file. This way if one copy of the FAT becomes damaged, DOS can consult the other for the vital mapping information it needs.

A raw disk is sort of like a tract of undeveloped land that someone wants to turn into a housing development crammed with one-acre lots. At first the land is just one large uniform property that may have some random buildings, hills, gulleys, and dirt roads on it. The first thing the developer does is flatten out the property, divide the land into lots, and build a grid of roads that lead to each individual lot. He may find that one or two lots contain jagged rocks or swampy areas that can't easily be converted into homes. Then he constructs a main office and puts a map of the development on the wall, displaying the addresses of each lot and marking off the few that have cliffs or quicksand that prevent them from being sold. As buyers start purchasing homes, the developer crosses off these lots one by one.

Fresh from the factory, a disk is just one large uniform surface that has some random information on it (left over from the manufacturing process). The first thing a user has to do with a disk is *format* it, which divides the disk into uniform sectors, evens out the random magnetic hills and valleys in key places, creates the underlying maps and structures, and reports any "bad" sectors that are magnetically unstable or unfit for holding data.

(Actually, hard disks require two kinds of formatting, *low-level* and *high-level*. To continue our analogy, a low-level format is like drawing a map of the land. A high-level format is like actually putting in roads. Most hard disks come from the factory with the low-level formatting already done. And today many dealers even do the DOS high-level formatting to spare users the grief of having to read the manual.)

When the developer first starts hawking his hundreds of homes, the map of available lots is wide open, except for the few that are too craggy or wet to build on. Likewise, when a disk is first formatted, its map of available sectors is wide open, except for the few that are magnetically unsuited to store information. If one huge clan of families approached the developer just as he started selling, and wanted to buy a long string of homes adjacent to each other, the developer could easily put them all in a row, then cross an entire contiguous block of homes off the map. But if the developer sold most of the building lots to unrelated families, the map would start filling up in somewhat random order. Over the years, many of these unrelated families would sell their individual homes and move out, and the development would always contain some homes that were temporarily vacant. If the clan descended on the development a few years after it was built, they probably wouldn't be able to find a string of homes next to each other, and would have to settle for one here, one there, one way over there, etc.

When a disk is newly formatted and empty, you can store files in relatively contiguous clusters. But as you add new files and erase old ones, and make existing files smaller and larger, you end up with pieces of your files all over the disk. It's far faster to load and write files that aren't scattered in many pieces. Hard disk users should periodically make full file-by-file backup copies of all their files, reformat their disks, and then put all the important files back. This has three good effects:

1. It makes sure everything is backed up.
2. It unfragments files so they load faster. When you back up a file, DOS takes all the scattered pieces from the far-flung reaches of your hard disk and puts them all together in one continuous area on the newly formatted backup floppy or tape. When you go

back later and restore your backed up files to the newly formatted hard disk, DOS writes the file in one long, efficient, continuous piece. Of course, as soon as you start editing it again, the efficiency plummets. Because programs don't change much, however, reformatting your disk and then copying programs back to it may speed up loading dramatically.

3. It cleans up unwanted files, giving you lots more free space on your hard disk. You'll be surprised at how many files you'll decide aren't worth copying back to the hard disk once you've backed them up. Having them available on a backup floppy or tape means you can always retrieve them if you need to. But by not copying them back to your hard disk, you'll end up with free space for new files — and you'll prevent the wasteful "churning" DOS is forced to do when it tries to hunt down the few vacant sectors on an overstuffed hard disk.

DOS has a serious design problem when it comes to large hard disks. When you ask it to store a file, DOS consults the FAT to find out where the unused sectors are located. And when you later ask DOS to load a file, it looks up the locations of the bulk of the file's sectors by again examining the FAT.

The engineers who originally designed DOS had to decide how big the FAT should be. Making it too small meant limiting the number of bytes users could store on a single disk. But if they made it too large, they would have ended up with an ungainly FAT that would have taken up too much raw space on each disk. (And remember, this was back in the days when a standard diskette held a trifling 160K, the standard PC came with 16K of RAM, and IBM seriously thought users were going to store their data on cheap tape recorders.) They finally settled on giving the FAT a maximum of 16-bit addresses, which meant that the largest possible table could have 64K worth of entries. Since each entry on the chart was a sector 512 bytes long, the maximum size of any single DOS disk was 64K x 512, or 32 megabytes.

The first IBM hard disk FAT, for the XT, used 12-bit, or 1.5 byte, addresses. Each address was made of three hexadecimal digits (16-bit addresses use four hex digits). But since FAT values are maintained as even pairs of hex digits, and because of the "backwords" storage technique used by the CPU, juggling 12-bit FAT addresses can be a real headache. Fortunately, DOS does all the work.

While 32 megabytes must have seemed enormous in the early 1980s, today it can seem small and cramped. The FDISK command in IBM's PC-DOS 3.3 let users divide (or *partition*) one large physical hard disk into several smaller *logical* drives, each 32 megabytes or less, and each with its own drive letter. DOS version 3.31 extended the idea of logical drives by adding 32-bit FAT addresses, which allow single logical drives as large as half a gigabyte. Other manufacturers have tried increasing the sector size past 512 bytes, which breaks the 32-megabyte barrier but causes all sorts of incompatibility problems.

In any event, all references to disks in this book really mean logical drives 32 megabytes or smaller. If you're using one monster physical drive that you've divided into three logical drives called C:, D:, and E:, this book will treat them as three separate entities. And so will DOS.

File Types

Files are either executable or nonexecutable. Executable files come in two classes — most are *programs* (with COM or EXE extensions) that your system can run, such as *WordStar*, or CHKDSK, or *1-2-3*. But DOS can also execute *batch* files (with BAT extensions), which are sequential lists of DOS commands and program names. DOS churns through batch files a line at a time, executing any DOS commands on each line and running any programs you've specified there.

Most other files store data, in one of two forms. Some data files are in *text* or *low-bit ASCII* format, which means that they contain nothing but the alphanumeric characters you could produce on a conventional typewriter. You can use the DOS TYPE command to read such ASCII files (although the TYPE command can also handle *high-bit* ASCII characters without missing a beat). But such files waste lots of space, and aren't very secure from prying eyes. Many data files are stored in proprietary nontext formats that compress the data more efficiently than ASCII files, and keep the information safe from snoopers. If you try using the DOS TYPE command on these, you'll either see a meaningless mass of what look like random characters, or a few familiar words interspersed with gibberish.

Some special kinds of nonexecutable files, with extensions like SYS or DRV, contain instructions that your operating system uses to control hardware better. The DOS ANSI.SYS device driver gives you enhanced keyboard and screen control. VDISK.SYS turns some of your memory into a virtual disk (as IBM calls it), or RAMdisk. And DRIVER.SYS lets you use some of IBM's external oddball drives.

You may also see files on recent DOS disks that have PIF extensions, which stands for Program Information File. IBM invented the PIF file for use with its *TopView* operating environment. Although *TopView* is now extinct, Microsoft also used PIF files for its *Windows* operating environment. Some programs are specially written to run under Microsoft *Windows*. But many normal programs that run under DOS can still run under *Windows*. Microsoft refers to these programs as either *standard applications* or *old applications*.

Windows looks for a PIF file whenever you want to run an old application. The PIF file contains information about the program and tells *Windows* things like how much memory the application needs and how "well-behaved" the program is. An "ill-behaved" program generally writes directly to the display memory. Virtually all word processors, spreadsheets, and graphics programs do. *Windows* cannot run these programs in a window and may have trouble multitasking them. It has to give up the entire display because it has no way of knowing when the program will write to the screen. A program that does not write directly to display memory, but instead goes through DOS or the BIOS to display everything, can be run in a window, share the screen with other applications, and often be multitasked.)

Program Files

Programs all sport either COM or EXE extensions. The COM stands for *command* and the EXE for *executable* files, but they're really both executable. They're also unreadable.

If you manage to peek inside one (using the COPY /B trick mentioned below) all you'll see is beeping, flashing gibberish punctuated by any error messages and English-language prompts or instructions that happen to be imbedded inside the program code.

The gibberish is really just an artifact. Each byte of every program has a value between 0 and 255; your system interprets strings of these values as instructions that put your programs through their paces. But since IBM's version of the ASCII character set contains 256 separate characters with values between 0 and 255, when you display the contents of a program onscreen your system prints the ASCII characters that happen to represent the value of each byte. These characters generally have nothing to do with the actual program instructions. The beeping and flashing is caused when your system tries to display certain very low values that DOS interprets as *control* characters.

COM files are *memory image* files. The pattern of bytes in the file on the disk is exactly the same as the pattern when the file is loaded into memory, which isn't the case with EXE files. They can't be larger than 64K, and are generally more compact than EXE files. DOS always loads COM files at offset 100H (which is why DEBUG starts COM files at address 100H), and squeezes a 256-byte Program Segment Prefix (PSP) beneath it. The bottom half of the PSP contains a lot of important addresses that tell DOS where to find the things it needs, and the top half contains a copy of the *command tail* — the part of the command line that you entered at the DOS prompt after the filename. Any parameters and switches show up here. DOS also uses this upper area as a default Disk Transfer Area (DTA), a file I/O buffer space.

The COM file extension came from the older CP/M operating system, since the first versions of DOS were heavily based on CP/M. In fact, the COM file formats of CP/M and DOS (including the PSP that DOS builds when it loads a COM file) are practically identical. For software developers, this similarity helped ease the early transition to the PC. Programmers could ignore the segmented addressing scheme of the 8086 and work with just 64K of program and data space, the same as under CP/M.

EXE files are gradually replacing COM files. The mix of code and data in the same segment and the calculation of segment addresses outside the code segment are two of the major stumbling blocks that limit PC programs to one megabyte of addressable memory and prevent them from running under the 80286 extended-memory protected mode. Strictly speaking, COM files no longer exist under OS/2, although you can still run these programs in a "DOS Mode" session. For the millions of older systems running DOS, however, COM programs will still work as advertised.

While programmers once prided themselves on what tight, sleek assembly language COM programs they could write, EXE programs today are often pieced together by teams of coders who use higher-level languages like C and end up with enormous, often sloppy programs that are relative memory hogs.

The EXE format started with DOS and can handle programs larger than 64K; in fact, an EXE file can snatch around 600K in a typical maxed-out system. It does this by using multiple segments for program code, data, and a special storage area called the *stack* (see Chapter 6). Each of these segments can be 64K long. DOS looks at a special *header* at the beginning of any EXE file to figure out how and where to load the individual segments. Every EXE header contains information that DOS needs to load the program into memory correctly, juggle the segment assignments, and allocate space for it to run. You can't see this header information if you load the EXE file directly into DEBUG, because DEBUG uses the header to perform all the space allocation and fix-ups and gets the program ready to run. But you can look at the header if you first rename the file to give it an extension other than EXE and then load it into DEBUG. (But then you won't be able to run it in DEBUG, so don't try.)

Use the following commands to examine the first part of the file header on a sample EXE program called SAMPLE.EXE:

```
RENAME SAMPLE.EXE SAMPLE.XXX
DEBUG
N SAMPLE.XXX
L 0
D 0
Q
```

One value in the header specifies the number of 16-byte paragraphs needed after the end of the loaded program. This extra memory space is used for the *heap* and the *stack*. During calculations, the stack is used to store intermediate results. The heap is used by the program mostly for dynamic storage. If a program executes a STRING$ command or DIMensions an array, the result has to be put somewhere, and it goes in the heap. In a program that does a lot of dynamic string and array allocation, the heap can get pretty cluttered up and disorganized. At times, normal execution can grind to a halt while the program cleans up the heap in a process technically referred to as "garbage collection."

You can examine the PSP by loading the EXE file (not the renamed XXX file) or COM file into DEBUG. To look at SAMPLE.EXE, type:

```
DEBUG SAMPLE.EXE
D 0 L 100
Q
```

In all DOS versions before 3.3 users received a utility called EXE2BIN that can translate certain kinds of EXE files into COM (BIN stands for *binary*) files. (In 3.3 IBM moved EXE2BIN to the *DOS Technical Reference Manual*.) Only EXE files that have been specially prepared, generally in assembly language, can be successfully turned into COM files. These programs must not contain a stack segment, must have no references to relocatable segments, and must begin execution at offset 100H in the file. Since an executable EXE file must have a stack segment and generally uses separate code and data segments, the two formats are essentially incompatible.

(The next few paragraphs are a bit technical, so skip ahead if you'd like.) DOS provides several different ways to exit programs. Under all versions of DOS, the most common method is the:

```
INT 20H
```

command. But you can also use:

```
MOV AH,0
INT 21H
```

The first two bytes of the PSP that DOS builds at the beginning of all programs loaded into memory contains the machine code for an INT 20H (the bytes CD 20). For a COM program, DOS pushes a word of zeroes on the stack before it turns control over to the program. This way, assuming that the stack pointer is the same as it was on entry to the program, a COM program can terminate with a simple:

```
RET
```

This branches to the beginning of the PSP and executes the INT 20H instruction.

Prior to DOS 2.0, interrupt 20H presented some problems for EXE programs. Interrupt 20H requires the value of the CS (Code Segment) register to point to the beginning of the PSP. In general, this is not true for EXE programs. On entry, however, the value of the DS (Data Segment) register points to the PSP. So, to use interrupt 20H, EXE programs have to execute code that looks something like this:

```
PUSH DS
MOV AX,0
PUSH AX
```

This code puts the far address (segment plus offset) of the beginning of the PSP on the stack. The EXE program can then exit with a RET within a far procedure, which effectively branches to the INT 20H instruction at the beginning of the PSP.

DOS 2.0 added interrupt 21H function call 4CH, which has two advantages over interrupt 20H: it doesn't require that the CS register point to the PSP, and it lets a program pass a *return code* or *exit code* (in register AL) back to DOS. You can exploit this return code in a batch file by processing it with IF ERRORLEVEL tests. Or, if the program is executed through function call 4BH as a subordinate process of another program, the parent program can retrieve the return code through function call 4DH.

Aside from these advantages, however, the two methods of termination are about the same. DOS turns an interrupt 20H into an interrupt 21H function call 0. Function calls 0 and 4CH both execute a few lines of code on their own but then share the bulk of the DOS code involved in terminating programs.

It's a similar story for interrupt 27H. By setting register DX to the end of the program and executing an INT 27H, a program can terminate but remain resident. This works for all DOS versions. Interrupt 27H is a problem with EXE programs because CS must again point to the beginning of the PSP.

Beginning with DOS 2.0, interrupt 21H function call 31H can also be used to terminate and remain resident. Here register DX is the size of the program in 16-byte paragraphs. By using a paragraph size rather than a byte size, function call 31H allows a program larger than 64K to remain resident in memory. Like function call 4CH, you can also pass back a return code with function call 31H. But again, interrupt 27H and function call 31H share a lot of DOS code.

Function calls 4CH and 31H are now the "preferred" methods for exiting programs, but only because they are more flexible than interrupt 20H and 27H. The only problem is that these two function calls don't work under DOS 1.1. Not an earth-shaking problem, however.

Nonprogram Files

Programs produce and process data. This data is either in pure-low-bit-ASCII text format or in some compressed proprietary form.

A "pure-low-bit" ASCII file contains only letters, numbers, punctuation, the symbols "#$%&'()*+-/<=>@[\]^_'{|}~, tabs, and variations of the carriage return/line feed combination that tells your system to end one line and start the next one. Such files can't include most characters with ASCII values less than 32 or greater than 127.

Word processors often use special proprietary formats that rely on ASCII characters lower than 32 or greater than 127 to keep track of things like settings (margins, line spacing, etc.) and special printing tricks (underlines, boldfaces, pitch changes, etc.). But most good word processors include a mode that will let you create and edit pure-ASCII files. Or if they don't, they'll usually let you strip out any offending characters from their proprietary formats and leave just the letters, numbers, and punctuation.

Pure-low-bit ASCII files are usually called just ASCII files, text files, or DOS files. You can tell if a file is pure ASCII by using the DOS TYPE command to display its contents onscreen. If it looks like normal everyday text, it's probably pure ASCII or close to it. However, if it's jumbled, or littered with smiling faces, math symbols, crooked lines, and foreign language characters, it's not a pure-ASCII file.

If you have a file punctuated with jumbled characters, you can strip out these nontext characters by passing it through the STRIP.COM filter on the accompanying disk.

To filter a jumbled file called DIRTY.FIL and send the cleaned-up results to the screen, just type:

```
STRIP < DIRTY.FIL
```

If you wanted to take the cleaned-up results and put them in a new file called CLEANED.UP just type:

```
STRIP < DIRTY.FIL > CLEANED.UP
```

On a decently fast hard disk, STRIP.COM can take a messy 100K *WordStar* file and produce a text version in a second or two.

While powerful word processors — with their abilities to move and copy blocks of text, perform formatting magic, and search for and replace strings of characters — are at one end of the editing spectrum, the DOS COPY CON command is at the other. The DOS EDLIN text editor is somewhere in between, although few users ever bother with EDLIN, since everyone either uses word processors, program editors, or even the character handling features of programs like *1-2-3* to create small text files.

All COPY CON can really do is copy characters from the keyboard to a file. The only "editing" it offers is the ability to erase mistakes on the current line with the backspace or left arrow key. But it's fast and convenient, and it lets you create short files without having to leave DOS or have your word processor handy.

COPY CON creates absolutely pure ASCII text files, without any embedded codes, except to indicate the end of the file. It's simple to create a file such as a batch file using COPY CON. First, just pick a filename that ends with BAT, such as DIRSIZE.BAT, type it in after the command COPY CON at the DOS prompt, and press the Enter key:

```
COPY CON DIRSIZE.BAT
```

DOS will drop the cursor down a line and just sit there waiting for you to do something. Start typing up to 127 characters of text per line (126 if it's the last line). If you make a mistake, you can backspace it away *only* if it's on the same physical line of the screen as the cursor. Lines *wrap* down one row on the screen when they reach 80 characters, so if you're typing the 81st and you notice a goof at character 79, you're out of luck. (To abort the process and start again, press Ctrl-Break.) When you're done typing each line, press Enter key to start the next one.

In this case, type in a command to sort the DIR listing in reverse size order and discard extraneous lines:

```
DIR | FIND "-" | FIND /V "<" | SORT /R /+14 | MORE
```

(To make this work, you'll have to have the DOS FIND.EXE, SORT.EXE, and MORE.COM files on the same disk as the batch file you're creating, unless they're in a subdirectory that your PATH command knows about.) Before pressing the Enter key at the end of the line, press the F6 function key. You'll see a ^Z onscreen. This tells DOS you're done. Then press the Enter key and you should see the message:

```
1 File(s) copied
```

Check the directory and you'll see a new file called DIRSIZE.BAT. If you do have the FIND.EXE, SORT.EXE, and MORE.COM files handy, typing DIRSIZE at the DOS prompt will produce a directory listing sorted by file size, with the biggest files at the top.

If for some reason you have changed the meaning of the F6 key (either with ANSI.SYS or a commercial macro-writing program like *ProKey*), you could instead hold down the Ctrl key and press Z. Or you could even hold down the Alt key, type 26 on the number pad (not the top row keys), and then release the Alt key. All three methods will put an ASCII character 26 end-of-file marker at the end of the file.

Most of the time you can put the ^Z end-of-file marker at the end of the last command rather than on an extra line all by itself at the very end of the file. However, certain commands, such as ECHO, require that you follow the command with a carriage return rather than an end-of-file marker. And if you do put the Ctrl-Z on a line by itself, the batch file will usually end up putting two prompts on the screen after it finishes executing.

Creating Filenames

You can't store any information on any disk unless you give it a filename. Unfortunately, because of its CP/M heritage, DOS limits the length of all filenames to 11 characters, just enough to remind you what's inside the file, but far too few if your file contains chart #2 for the fourth quarter income report on the Airframe Division of Amalgamated Electronics, since you'll end up with some cryptic entry like ADAE4QIN.CH2.

Filenames can contain:

- the letters A through Z
- the numerals 0 through 9
- the characters ' ~ ' ! @ # $ % ^ & ( ) - _ { }
- high-bit characters (with ASCII values over 127)

Filenames can't contain:

- spaces
- characters treated as spaces, such as = ; , tab
- the "wildcard" characters ? and *
- characters with special DOS meanings . : " \ / | < > + [ ]
- control characters (with ASCII values less than 33)
- lowercase letters (DOS automatically uppercases these)

Many of the ASCII characters with values between 128 and 165 are foreign language versions of a, e, i, o, u, and y. When creating filenames, the American version of DOS tends to ignore the wide range of accent marks and treat these as the plain old vowels. And DOS turns all lowercase letters into their uppercase versions, which means that you can't have one file called:

```
autoexec.bat
```

and a different one called:

```
AUTOEXEC.BAT
```

(Actually, if you use the brute-force techniques described in Chapter 8 on DEBUG, you can do this, by loading and writing absolute sectors. But while DOS will acknowledge that this lowercase file exists by including it in DIR listings, it won't let you change or delete or examine it — except with DEBUG. This does let you keep the file secure, but fooling around with your directory directly is a bad idea unless you know exactly what you're doing and are sure all your files are backed up. And on a hard disk, where you can really lose big if you make one silly mistake, it's an especially bad idea.)

This capitalized exclusivity also means that upper- and lowercase pairs of special characters such as the ones with values 128/135, 145/146, 148/153, 129, 154, and 164/165 automatically turn into their uppercase versions.

Using some of the more unusual high-bit ASCII characters for filenames can keep prying fingers away, since few users have ASCII charts handy when they snoop inside someone else's system, and even fewer know the Alt-keypad method of generating these odd characters (described in Chapter 5). There's nothing more confounding to a casual snoop than entering a DIR command and seeing an entire screen full of gibberish where the filenames should be.

If you try to create a filename using ASCII 127 (with the Alt-keypad technique), DOS will just backspace the previous character away. But you can use this character in a filename, if you find a way to type it in. BASIC lets you do it. Try typing in the following CHAR127.BAS program:

```
100 'CHAR127.BAS
110 OPEN CHR$(127) FOR OUTPUT AS #1
120 PRINT #1,"It works..."
130 CLOSE:SYSTEM
```

Then, at the DOS prompt, type:

```
BASICA CHAR127.BAS
```

(or GWBASIC CHAR127 if you're using a generic MS-DOS version of BASIC).

The CHAR127.BAS program will create a file with a single ASCII character 127 as the filename. This character will show up in DIR listings as a delta (which looks like a little house).

You can view it by typing:

```
DIR ?
```

because using the single ? wildcard in a DIR command will display all the filenames that are just one character long.

If you try to use an illegal character, such as an asterisk, DOS will discard everything from the asterisk on. So if you type:

```
A>COPY CON NOTE*IT
```

DOS will discard the asterisk and the IT that follows, and create a file called NOTE.

Reserved Filenames

DOS is selfish about its internal names for devices such as printers, communications hardware, the keyboard/screen combination (which is collectively called the console, or CON), and a special dummy device with interesting properties, known as NUL. One reason for this hands-off attitude is that you can use some DOS commands on devices as well as files. For instance, while the COPY command is great for backing up your files to another disk or subdirectory (the more recent XCOPY command is even better), you can also use COPY in conjunction with the CON device to create files:

```
COPY CON FILENAME
```

Using COPY this way tells DOS to take whatever the user is typing at the keyboard and put it in a file called FILENAME (or any other legal filename you specify). And if you type:

```
COPY /B COMMAND.COM CON
```

you'll be able to see the entire contents of COMMAND.COM onscreen, since copying a file to CON reads it from a disk and sends it to your display. You can't do this with a TYPE COMMAND.COM command, since all but the very shortest executable files contain addresses or instructions loaded with ASCII 26 characters. The DOS TYPE command interprets these ASCII 26 characters as end-of-file markers, and grinds to a halt as soon as it stumbles over the first one.

The /B that appears directly after the COPY command in the above example is called a *switch*. Switches turn optional command features on and off (and can also furnish needed values and settings at the same time). In this case, the /B switch tells DOS to look at the directory listing, figure out the exact number of bytes in the file you want copied, and copy them all — including any ASCII 26 characters it sees (which it displays as little arrows). You can slap lots of different switches onto various commands, producing such nightmarish results as:

```
PRINT /D:LPT2 /B:8192 /U:2 /M:4 /S:20 /Q:20 B:\INFO\FIL1 C:\FIL2
```

This particular thorny command would use DOS's *background* printing feature to print two files in a row — one on drive B:, the other on drive C: — using the second of two printers that were attached to your system. And it would let you run another program while the files were printing. (See the next chapter for a full discussion of backslashes and subdirectories.)

DOS refers to the prompt and all the commands, switches, filenames, and miscellaneous parameters following it as the *command line*. Everything after the actual command itself is called the *command tail*. Here's an example:

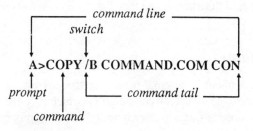

CON isn't the only device that's useful with COPY. You could print out a copy of your AUTOEXEC.BAT file with the command:

```
COPY AUTOEXEC.BAT PRN
```

And COPY isn't the only command that works with devices. If you wanted to send a formfeed command to your printer to advance the paper, you could do it with:

```
ECHO ^L > PRN
```

(You create the ^L by holding down the Ctrl key and typing L. Typing ECHO ^L PRN without the > redirection symbol won't do anything other than printing a ^L PRN onscreen.)

Because DOS has to know when you want it to use PRN or CON as a device, you can't use such *reserved* device names as filenames. Names like:

- CON
- PRN
- PRN.XYZ

are invalid. (PRN.XYZ is no good because DOS interprets the dot after PRN as a space, leaving the filename as just PRN.) However, you could use PRN as the extension, or along with other characters in the filename. These are all legal:

- DRIVER4.PRN
- XYZPRN
- PRN1.CON

But stay away from the following reserved DOS device names:

CON (keyboard/screen)
AUX (first serial port)
PRN (first parallel printer)
NUL (dummy device)
COM1, COM2, COM3, COM4 (serial ports 1 through 4)
LPT1, LPT2, LPT3 (parallel printer ports 1 through 3)

COM1 is pretty much interchangeable with AUX, and LPT1 with PRN. NUL is useful for getting rid of most simple DOS messages — although it can't suppress serious error messages.

If you try copying your COMMAND.COM file to something called ABC.COM, with the command:

```
COPY COMMAND.COM ABC.COM
```

DOS will oblige, and print a:

```
1 File(s) copied
```

message. If you then type DIR to see what's on your disk, you'll see two files with identical sizes:

```
COMMAND   COM    25307   3-17-87   12:00p
ABC       COM    25307   3-17-87   12:00p
```

But if you try copying it to a file called NUL.COM, with the command:

```
COPY COMMAND.COM NUL.COM
```

DOS will interpret this command as

```
COPY COMMAND.COM NUL
```

and discard the .COM part. Copying a file to the NUL device makes DOS go through the motions but not actually copy anything. It will still print a:

```
1 File(s) copied
```

message, but when you type DIR you won't see any file called NUL.COM. Similarly, if you try copying your startup AUTOEXEC.BAT file to one called PRN.BAT, with the command:

```
COPY AUTOEXEC.BAT PRN.BAT
```

DOS will toss the .BAT part and interpret this command as:

```
COPY AUTOEXEC.BAT PRN
```

Since copying any file to the PRN device will cause it to be printed on your default LPT1 printer, this command will either print out your AUTOEXEC.BAT file (if your printer happens to be turned on and connected properly) or freeze your system as DOS tries to print a file to a printer that's not responding.

You can also run into trouble if you try to create a file that has the same name as a subdirectory entry. If you're in a directory that has a subdirectory called BIN branching off of it, typing DIR will produce a listing that includes something like:

```
BIN            <DIR>      12-15-88   10:59p
```

If you then try to create a file called BIN, you'll see a message that makes it look as if you just created a file called BIN even though you didn't.

```
COPY CON BIN
This is a test
^Z
This is a test
        1 File(s) copied
```

This happens because subdirectories are really just special kinds of files, and you can't have two files in the same directory with the same name. When you try to create a file called BIN, DOS looks at the directory and sees there's already a file with that name. However, instead of reporting that it can't create the file, it lies. If you think that's unfriendly, you're right. But you have to very careful with filenames in general. If you've been working on a 100,000-byte file called LIFSTORY that's on drive A: and you type:

```
COPY CON LIFSTORY
Oops
```

and press the F6 function key (to tell DOS you're at the end of the file) and then the Enter key, DOS will wipe out the 100,000 byte file and replace it with the new four-byte file you just created.

Similarly, if you want to print out a short file, such as your startup AUTOEXEC.BAT file, you can type:

```
COPY AUTOEXEC.BAT PRN
```

which will copy the file to your default printer. But if you accidentally switch the order and type:

```
COPY PRN AUTOEXEC.BAT
```

DOS will print a:

```
0 File(s) copied
```

message — and then wipe out your AUTOEXEC.BAT file. Gone. So be very careful with filenames. And make sure you have everything backed up.

The Parts of a Filename

Filenames can be as short as one character, or as long as 11. Once they grow past eight, however, they start encroaching on the filename extension. Most users refer to the entire name of the file as the filename, which isn't technically correct. According to IBM, the whole thing is really called a *filespec* (short for file specification), and has three parts:

d:FILENAME.EXT

where:

d: is the drive the file is on
FILENAME   is the actual filename
EXT   is the optional filename extension

A period separates the filename from its extension, although DOS doesn't display periods in DIR listings. You don't have to use a period when you're dealing with files that don't have extensions, although doing so won't hurt. So you could create a file called TEST by typing either:

```
COPY CON TEST
```

or:

```
COPY CON TEST.
```

Technically you need to include a drive letter in the filespec, since you can have two similarly named files on two drives with utterly different contents — A:DATAFILE can be totally unrelated to B:DATAFILE. However, DOS tries to second-guess you if you omit something it needs. If you're on drive A: and you want to have DOS give you a report on the status of your file and memory use, you can type:

```
A:CHKDSK.COM
```

or simply:

```
CHKDSK
```

In the second version of this command, DOS fills in the missing (A:) drive letter and (COM) extension for you by furnishing *defaults*. Since you were already logged onto drive A: DOS makes drive A: the default. Whenever you issue a command that needs a drive letter, DOS will try using the current drive. And you don't need to supply the COM extension when you're running a command like CHKDSK. The reason for this is a bit complicated:

When DOS sees something on the command line, it tries to figure out, or *parses*, what you typed by first capitalizing it if necessary, then looking for delimiters (spaces, and things like commas and equal signs that act the same as spaces), switches (like /B), drive letters, subdirectory paths, and filenames. It assumes that the very first thing you typed on the command line after the prompt is the main command itself.

This command can be one of four things: an internal command, an external command, the name of the application program, or a typo or missing filename.

Internal commands are the instructions that execute many of the fundamental DOS operations such as DIR and TYPE. They are actually buried inside the main DOS COM-

MAND.COM command processor. DOS first compares what you typed to the list maintained inside COMMAND.COM. In version 3.3 the list contains these commands:

BREAK	INDO (IN DO)
CALL	MD
CD	MKDIR
CHCP	NOT
CHDIR	PATH
CLS	PAUSE
COPY	PROMPT
CTTY	RD
DATE	REM
DEL	REN
DIR	RENAME
ECHO	RMDIR
ERASE	SET
ERRORLEVEL	SHIFT
EXIST	TIME
EXIT	TYPE
FOR	VER
GOTO	VERIFY
IF	VOL

Some of these are just parts of larger commands. EXIST and ERRORLEVEL really only work with IF. FOR and IN DO work together. And NOT doesn't do anything by itself. These few have slightly different properties (which you'll see a bit later) from the others on the list.

If it finds a match, COMMAND.COM then runs the proper instructions, which are also kept inside COMMAND.COM, to execute the command. If it can't find a match, it starts looking in the default directory for an *external* command or applications program with the name you typed. If it can't find the specified filename in the current directory, it will see if you've specified a PATH and start looking in all the directories that this PATH specifies.

External commands are separate programs, outside of COMMAND.COM. DOS version 3.3 contains 36 of these, all of which end in COM or EXE:

ASSIGN.COM	MORE.COM
BACKUP.COM	PRINT.COM
BASIC.COM	RECOVER.COM
BASICA.COM	RESTORE.COM
CHKDSK.COM	SELECT.COM
COMMAND.COM	SYS.COM
COMP.COM	TREE.COM
DEBUG.COM	APPEND.EXE
DISKCOMP.COM	ATTRIB.EXE

DISKCOPY.COM	FASTOPEN.EXE
EDLIN.COM	FIND.EXE
FDISK.COM	JOIN.EXE
FORMAT.COM	NLSFUNC.EXE
GRAFTABL.COM	REPLACE.EXE
GRAPHICS.COM	SHARE.EXE
KEYB.COM	SORT.EXE
LABEL.COM	SUBST.EXE
MODE.COM	XCOPY.EXE

Users sometimes forget that these DOS external commands are actually separate programs, and that they won't work unless the appropriate programs are in the default directory or are in a directory that their PATH command knows about. (And yes, COMMAND.COM, the part of DOS that actually processes the commands you enter, can be an external command itself, and a very useful one as you'll soon see.)

You can also type the name of an application program on the command line. DOS doesn't give its external commands any priority over commercial applications with similar names. It simply tries to run an internal command first and if that doesn't work, it then looks for a file in the current directory that has a matching filename and a COM, EXE, or BAT extension. If it happens to find a DOS program that fits the bill, it runs it. But if you didn't have any external DOS commands handy, and for some reason you renamed your main WS.COM *WordStar* file to CHKDSK.COM, typing CHKDSK would run *WordStar*.

Finally, if DOS doesn't understand what you've entered, you've probably mistyped a command or entered the name of a file that DOS cannot locate. This is usually a PATH problem.

The PATH Command

The PATH command specifies a list of the important directories you want DOS to search when it can't find an executable program in the current directory. DOS keeps this list in a special section of memory called the *environment*.

If you weren't able to use PATHs to tell DOS where to search, you'd either have to keep copies of all your important programs in all your subdirectories, or you'd always have to specify each program's precise location each time you ran it. And if you're wondering why DOS can't just search in every single directory, doing so on even a medium- sized hard disk could take a while each time you typed a command. A typical PATH might look something like:

```
PATH D:\;C:\;C:\BIN;C:\DOS;C:\DOS\BAT;C:\SK;C:\DOS\NORTON
```

which tells DOS to look in the following places for the file you specified, if it can't find it in the current directory:

D:\ (the root directory of drive D:)
C:\ (the root directory of drive C:)
C:\BIN
C:\DOS
C:\DOS\BAT
C:\SK
C:\DOS\NORTON

If you wanted to run a program that wasn't in the current directory or in any of the places listed in your PATH statement, DOS wouldn't be able to run it unless you explicitly entered the name of the directory this file happened to be in. So if the CHKDSK.COM command was in a subdirectory called:

```
C:\LIONS\TIGERS\AND\BEARS
```

and your PATH didn't mention this subdirectory, typing just:

```
C>CHKDSK
```

wouldn't run the program. Even though it was on your disk, if DOS couldn't find it, it couldn't run it. You could run it, however, by typing:

```
C:\LIONS\TIGERS\AND\BEARS\CHKDSK
```

or:

```
\LIONS\TIGERS\AND\BEARS\CHKDSK
```

Here's a fine point but an important one: Note the initial backslash character at the very beginning. By putting this backslash character there, you're telling DOS that the specified PATH for the CHKDSK file started at the root directory. If you omitted this initial backslash:

```
LIONS\TIGERS\AND\BEARS\CHKDSK
```

DOS would assume that the first directory in the list — LIONS — was a directory one level below whatever directory you happened to be in at the time. If you were logged into the root directory, this wouldn't matter. But if you were already in a directory called \WIZ\OZ, and you omitted the initial backslash before LIONS, DOS would think you were really telling it to run:

```
\WIZ\OZ\LIONS\TIGERS\AND\BEARS\CHKDSK
```

And if you happened to be in one called \INCOME\REPORT\4Q, DOS would assume you meant:

```
\INCOME\REPORT\4Q\LIONS\TIGERS\AND\BEARS\CHKDSK
```

When you include an initial backslash in a PATH, you are giving DOS an explicit PATH. When you omit the backslash you give DOS a relative path — one that starts a level down from whatever directory you are in at the time.

If you made a typing mistake when you entered the command, or specified a program that DOS couldn't find, all you'd get would be an error message that told you:

```
Bad command or file name
```

Also, remember that DOS can execute only three kinds of files — those that end in COM or EXE or BAT. So if you had just the following files on your disk:

- CHKDSK
- CHKDSK.WKS
- CHKDSK.BAS
- CHKDSK.DBF
- CHKDSK.SYS
- CHKDSK.DRV
- CHKDSK.PIF

and you typed CHKDSK, all you'd get would be the "Bad command or file name" error message, even though DOS uses extensions such as SYS or PIF (but not on executable programs).

By including the name of a subdirectory in your PATH, you tell DOS to look in that directory for executable files (with COM, EXE, or BAT extensions). But PATHs are for executable files only; DOS won't be able to find nonexecutable files, such as your data files, or *overlay* files that help programs work, in subdirectories specified in your PATH. To have DOS search through your directories to find nonexecutable files, use the AP-PEND command introduced with version 3.3.

DOS will always execute internal commands first, then COM files, then EXE files, and finally BAT files. So if you have these three files on your disk:

- RUNME.COM
- RUNME.EXE
- RUNME.BAT

and you type RUNME, you'll always run RUNME.COM. You'll never get a chance to run either RUNME.EXE or RUNME.BAT, since DOS always tries to run COM files before any other kind of program. If you erased RUNME.COM, you could run RUNME.EXE, but you'd never be able to run RUNME.BAT while either RUNME.COM or RUNME.EXE was in the same directory.

But that's if you try just RUNME without any extension. What if those three RUNME files are on your disk, and you include the extension by typing RUNME.EXE or RUNME.BAT? Sorry, out of luck. DOS will still execute RUNME.COM.

If you have any separate programs on your disk that happen to have the same name as most of the internal DOS commands, you'll never be able to run these at all. This means you can't ever create executable files like BREAK.COM, REM.EXE, DATE.COM, or SET.BAT, since DOS will look inside COMMAND.COM, find a match, and execute the internal command before it has a chance to run the external COM, EXE, or BAT version.

While 34 of the internal commands will indeed preempt external versions, you can actually use four parts of internal command names in external programs: ERRORLEVEL (which under certain circumstances DOS truncates to ERRORLEV), EXIST, INDO, and NOT.

So don't try creating a batch file that has the same basic filename as a program you're using. If you wanted to set up a batch file that logged into your WP subdirectory, activated underlining on an EGA screen, then ran *WordPerfect* (and you had a program called UNDERLIN.COM handy to handle this) you could do it with something like:

```
CD C:\WP
UNDERLIN ON
WP
```

However, you couldn't name this batch file WP.BAT, since typing WP would simply bypass the WP.BAT file and load the WP.EXE program. Instead, name it something like W.BAT.

Well, okay, if you're a stickler, there actually is a way to run a program that has the same name as an internal command.

All you have to do is prefix the similarly named program with a drive letter or path. For example, if you had a special program on your disk that sorted the directory, and you were using something newer than DOS 2.x and just had to name it DIR.COM, you could run it by typing:

```
.\DIR
```

The .\ is DOS shorthand that specifies a file in the current directory. If you omitted this prefix, all you'd get is the normal DOS DIR listing, since COMMAND.COM always gives internal commands priority over external commands with the same name. However, prefacing a command with a drive letter or path designation tells DOS that you want to execute an external file rather than an internal command.

You won't be able to add a .\ prefix like this in DOS versions 2.x, since version 3.0 was the first that let you specify a drive and path before external commands. But if you're logged into a directory called C:\WORK and the DIR.COM program also happens to be in that directory, you could run it by entering:

```
\WORK\DIR
```

You really shouldn't have to worry about this, however, since you can almost always come up with a name that's slightly different from the actual internal DOS command.

Fooling COMMAND.COM's knee-jerk reflex to give internal commands priority can actually save you grief. Say your office is short of PCs, and you have to share your hard disk system with a less sophisticated user. Your worst fear is that your co-worker will try to format a floppy disk, forget to add the drive letter in the FORMAT command, and end up wiping out the contents of the hard disk.

This was all too easy on older versions of DOS. Newer versions of FORMAT.COM won't do anything unless the user specifies a drive letter. And newer versions can also tell if a user is trying to reformat a hard disk, and won't budge unless the user types in the hard disk's volume label. Still, the message DOS prints:

```
Enter current Volume Label for Drive
    (press Enter for none):
WARNING, ALL DATA ON NON-REMOVABLE DISK
DRIVE C: WILL BE LOST!
Proceed with Format (Y/N)?
```

is confounding to someone who has no idea what a non-removable disk is, and if a new or clumsy user has a deadline and needs to format a disk, well, that's what backups are for.

Hard-disk-format victims have devised all sorts of solutions to prevent hard disk format. The best is obviously to remove the FORMAT.COM program from your disk, or rename it to something that would throw beginners off track. But a new user could always bring a floppy disk copy of FORMAT.COM over and copy it onto the hard disk.

If you don't mind patching COMMAND.COM, you can prevent most FORMAT heartache by tricking COMMAND.COM into thinking FORMAT is an internal command. DOS maintains a table of internal commands inside COMMAND.COM and always checks there first when you enter something on the command line. FORMAT is six letters long. Three internal commands — PROMPT, RENAME, and VERIFY — also have six letters in their names. If you replace the six letters in one of these entries with the letters "FORMAT" DOS will see FORMAT on the table when it checks to see if you entered an internal command, and won't execute any external program with the same name.

But putting FORMAT in the table means getting rid of one of the existing six-letter table entries. Fortunately, RENAME has a shorter version, REN. So if you replace the letters RENAME in the table with FORMAT you'll still be able to rename files by using REN. But changing the letters R-E-N-A-M-E to F-O-R-M-A-T in the lookup table won't change the actual instructions that DOS uses to rename files. So if a user enters FORMAT, DOS will see it on the table and execute the rename procedure. Since you can't rename files unless you specify an existing name and a new name, all you'll get is an error. Typing:

```
FORMAT OLDNAME.TXT NEWNAME.DOC
```

will rename a file called OLDNAME.TXT to NEWNAME.DOC. And typing:

```
FORMAT C:
```

will just produce an "Invalid number of parameters" message.

But this won't work if a user boots off a diskette and executes the FORMAT command that's on the floppy. And patching COMMAND.COM isn't always such a good idea. If you do it, be sure that all versions of COMMAND.COM on your disk are identical. Otherwise DOS can become confused.

You could use either the *Norton Utilities* or DEBUG to change RENAME to FORMAT. Once you've patched COMMAND.COM, use REN to rename FORMAT.COM to FORMAT[].COM (where [] stands for an ALT+255 null). To do this, type:

```
REN FORMAT.COM FORMAT
```

but don't press the Enter key yet — hold down the Alt key and type 255 on the numeric keypad, then release the Alt key. The cursor will move over one space. Then type:

```
.COM
```

and press the Enter key.

Finally, create a batch file called F.BAT:

```
ECHO OFF
CLS
ECHO Insert disk in drive A: and
PAUSE
FORMAT[] A: /V /S
```

Remember to type in FORMAT[] (where [] represents Alt+255) when creating your batch file, or this won't work.

To patch COMMAND.COM with DEBUG, first make a backup copy of COMMAND.COM called COMMAND.OLD so that if you make a mistake you can start over. Then type:

```
DEBUG COMMAND.COM
```

Find out how long your version is by typing:

```
RCX
```

and pressing the Enter key twice. You'll see something like:

```
CX 62DB
```

Take the four-digit hex number following the CX and type:

```
S 100 L62DB "RENAME"
```

(substituting the four-digit hex number if yours is different from 62DB). Press the Enter key and you should see something like:

```
61B2:547B
```

Ignore the leftmost four digits, preceding the colon. Take the rightmost four digits and type:

```
E 547B "FORMAT"
```

(substituting the four-digit hex number if yours is different from 547B). Press the Enter key. Then press W (and Enter) to write the new version back to disk, and Q (and the Enter) to quit DEBUG. Once you've patched COMMAND.COM, reboot.

Another simple way to prevent unwanted formatting is to rename FORMAT.COM to something innocuous like DATA.COM and then insert a simple reboot routine at the beginning of your old FORMAT.COM file. Type in FORMAT and the system will reboot. Type in DATA and you can format disks. Make sure you have DEBUG.COM handy, and type in the following ten lines to create both files.

```
DEBUG
N FORMAT.COM
L
N DATA.COM
W
N FORMAT.COM
E 100 B8 40 00 8E D8 B8 34 12
E 108 A3 72 00 EA 00 00 FF FF
W
Q
```

Be sure to press the Enter key at the end of each line. You could of course create a tiny 16-byte reboot file called FORMAT.COM, but the short length would be a tipoff to an unauthorized user that something was amiss.

If you try this, you can format a floppy in drive A: by typing:

```
DATA A:
```

And if you type FORMAT at the DOS prompt your system will do a warm reboot. If you really want to be safe, change the 34 12 at the end of the line that begins E 100 to 7F 7F, so the line looks like:

```
E 100 B8 40 00 8E D8 B8 7F 7F
```

This will make your system do a long cold boot with all the slow memory diagnostics.

Some users create a file on every disk that contains a sorted DIR listing. You can do this easily if you have the DOS programs MORE.COM, FIND.EXE, and SORT.EXE handy. (It's best to have them on a hard disk in a subdirectory that your PATH knows about.) Just type:

```
DIR | SORT | FIND "-" | FIND /V "<" > DIRFILE
```

The DIR command produces a list of files as well as a report on how many bytes are free, how many files are there, and what the volume label is, if one exists. The | is the *pipe* sign, and the > is a *redirection* sign. The default devices for input and output (*I/O*) are obvious: input usually comes from the keyboard; output usually goes to the screen. But starting with version 2.0, DOS let you mix and match I/O. You can take output that would normally appear on your screen, and instead reroute it to you printer or modem — or capture the characters by turning them into a file on your disk. Similarly, you can take characters in a file on your disk and feed them into a program just as if you were typing them at the keyboard. And you can *filter* files through pipes on the way from one place to another. This lets you do things like search for or screen out certain characters, or sort jumbled lists into orderly ones. Piping and redirection of I/O are extremely powerful tools that you'll use often.

Using the SORT command as shown above will arrange the DIR listing in rough alphabetical order. The first FIND command will screen out all the miscellaneous DIR information and leave just the filenames, since files all have hyphens in their creation dates but miscellaneous "bytes free" or "Volume in" reports rarely use hyphens. The second FIND will weed out any subdirectory listings, because each contains a <DIR> instead of a size:

```
Volume in drive C is WORKDISK
Directory of C:\

COMMAND   COM     25307    3-17-87   12:00p
CONFIG    SYS        47   10-18-88    7:07a
AUTOEXEC  BAT       256   10-18-88   12:01a
DOS             <DIR>     10-18-88    7:09a
WORDSTAR        <DIR>     11-06-88   12:22a
DBASE           <DIR>      2-11-88   12:00a
LOTUS           <DIR>     12-03-88   12:02a

      7 File(s)    28220672 bytes free
```

Miscellaneous DIR information filtered out by first FIND command

Subdirectory listings filtered out by the second FIND command

Miscellaneous DIR information filtered out by first FIND command

The final redirection command sends the output to a file called DIRFILE. You could then view the sorted list of files on your disk by typing:

```
TYPE DIRFILE
```

If your list was longer than 24 files, you could type:

```
MORE < DIRFILE
```

which would show you a screenful at a time (assuming you were using a monitor that displayed the standard 25 lines), then pause and prompt you to press any nonshift key to view another screenful.

If you do this to all your disks, you'll end up with a different version of DIRFILE on each one. The one on drive A: is really A:DIRFILE, the one on B: is B:DIRFILE, etc. And when you do just about anything with these files you have to use the appropriate drive letters, so they really are part of the filespec.

Even though IBM's various manuals don't seem to agree in their definition of the filespec, a file's PATH is just as important as its drive letter, especially on a hard disk, and should be thought of as a fourth filespec component. Just as you can have two similarly named files called A:DIRFILE and B:DIRFILE, you can also create C:\DOS\DIRFILE and C:\WORD\DIRFILE on the same physical disk.

Wildcards

You don't have to specify the PATH if you're referring to files in the current — or default — subdirectory. If you're logged into a subdirectory called \DOS and you want to check out your COMMAND.COM file, all four commands below will produce the same result:

```
DIR COMMAND.COM
DIR C:\DOS\COMMAND.COM
DIR \DOS\COMMAND.COM
DIR .\COMMAND.COM
```

DOS is very flexible, and provides even more ways to ferret out just the COMMAND.COM file entry. You could simply type DIR and use a DOS filter to screen out everything that didn't have the character string "COMMAND COM" in it:

```
DIR | FIND "COMMAND COM"
```

Unfortunately, you'd have to specify "COMMAND COM" rather than "COMMAND.COM" because that's how the DIR listing displays it. DOS is flexible, but consistently inconsistent.

You could also isolate COMMAND.COM in directory searches by looking for a part of its filename:

```
DIR | FIND "COMMAND"
```

However, if you had a game on your disk called COMMANDO.EXE, and a list of *Word-Perfect* commands called WCOMMAND.LST, this filtering technique would find all three files with the characters "COMMAND" in their names.

Finding one file is easy. However, you might want to look at an entire class of related files, such as all the COM files on your disk, at one time. Or you may have several customized versions of COMMAND.COM, such as COMMAND1.COM and COMMAND2.COM on your disk and want to look at the date you created each version.

DOS makes it easy to list such groups of files, by using one of two special symbols on the command line. IBM calls this pair — an asterisk (*) and a question mark (?) — *global file name characters*. Everyone else calls them *wildcards*.

A question mark can stand for any single character (including a blank, or no characters). An asterisk can represent up to eleven characters. If you apply this rule to the character string:

    ?UN

you could substitute ten single characters in place of the ? and end up with English words — BUN, DUN, FUN, GUN, HUN, NUN, PUN, RUN, SUN, TUN (a big barrel).

If you tried this with the character string:

    SYL*

you could substitute all sorts of character combinations of varying lengths in place of the * and end up with words like SYLLABLE, SYLLABUB, SYLLABUS, SYLLOGISM, SYLPH, and SYLVAN. Of course, not all of these could be filenames, because some are longer than eight characters. If you tried to create a file called SYLLOGISM, DOS would end up calling it SYLLOGIS.M since it allows a maximum of eight characters to the left of the extension.

Assume your disk contained the following files:

- COMMAND.COM
- COMMAND.CO
- COMMAND.EXE
- C.COM
- COMMAND1.COM
- COMMAND.C
- ZOMMAND.COM
- COMMAND.ZOM
- COMMA.COM
- COMMAND
- COMM.AND
- ZZZ.1
- REDLINE.DBF

The broadest possible wildcard directory search would be:

```
DIR *.*
```

which is really the same as:

```
DIR
```

or:

```
DIR *
```

or:

```
DIR ????????.???
```

An asterisk to the left of a period lets DOS substitute from one to eight characters there. An asterisk to the right of a period lets DOS substitute from zero to three characters there. A filename needs at least one character to the left of the period, but can get by just fine with no characters after the period. One asterisk used by itself can stand for all 11 possible characters. When you issue a DIR command without anything after it, DOS internally puts *.* after it. And it then turns all the asterisks into the correct number of question marks. So when you type DIR, DOS first translates it to DIR *.* and then finally to DIR ????????.??? (both of which will show all your files).

Incidentally, you could also see the complete set of files in any directory by typing:

```
DIR .
```

but this technique doesn't have anything to do with wildcards. Used this way, the period following DIR is shorthand for the current subdirectory itself, just as a double period represents the parent directory. You can see these special directory entries by logging into any subdirectory and typing DIR. You'll see, for example,

```
Volume in drive C is WORKDISK
Directory of C:\DOS

    .           <DIR> 3-15-88 5:15p
    ..          <DIR> 3-15-88 5:15p
```

Wildcards really come in handy when you use them to isolate certain parts of filenames. For instance, you could limit your search to files that end in COM only with the command:

```
DIR *.COM
```

This tells DOS to accept anything on the left side of the period, but to screen out all files that have something other than a COM to the right of the period. This command would display every file on the above sample list that ended in COM, and no others:

- COMMAND.COM
- C.COM
- COMMAND1.COM
- ZOMMAND.COM
- COMMA.COM

If you put the asterisk on the other side of the period:

```
DIR COMMAND.*
```

DOS wouldn't care what was after the period, but would list only those files with the precise letters "COMMAND" — and only those letters — before the period:

- COMMAND.COM
- COMMAND.CO
- COMMAND.EXE
- COMMAND.C
- COMMAND.ZOM
- COMMAND

This variation would list plain old COMMAND (with no extension) because an asterisk to the right of a period can stand for three, two, one, or no characters. COMMAND with no extension is really the same as:

```
COMMAND.
```

but you rarely see it listed that way.

However, this particular search won't list COMMAND1.COM, since COMMAND1 is not equal to COMMAND, and you told DOS to list only those files with the exact string "COMMAND" to the left of the period. If you wanted to include COMMAND1.COM in the list, you'd have to broaden the previous command either with:

```
DIR COMMAND*.*
```

or:

```
DIR COMMAND*
```

or even with:

```
DIR COMMAND?.*
```

Remember, asterisks can represent from one to 11 letters, but a question mark always represents just one character. All three of the above commands would produce the same result:

- COMMAND.COM
- COMMAND.CO
- COMMAND.EXE
- COMMAND1.COM
- COMMAND.C
- COMMAND.ZOM
- COMMAND

You should always try to limit wildcard searches by making them as explicit as possible. A command like:

```
DIR C*.COM
```

would list any file that started with C and ended with COM:

- COMMAND.COM
- C.COM
- COMMAND1.COM
- COMMA.COM

You could limit the search to list only files that ended in COM and that started with the letter C but had five or fewer characters to the left of the period, with:

```
DIR ?????.COM
```

which would yield:

- C.COM
- COMMA.COM

If you wanted files that started with the letter C and had extensions that started with the letter C, you could try:

```
DIR C*.C*
```

or:

```
DIR C*.C??
```

which would both list:

- COMMAND.COM
- COMMAND.CO
- C.COM
- COMMAND1.COM
- COMMAND.C
- COMMA.COM

To narrow this search to files that started with the letter C and had extensions shorter than two characters long, this would do it:

```
DIR C*.??
```

You'd see just:

- COMMAND.CO
- COMMAND.C

You get the idea. One thing to watch out for is that once DOS sees an asterisk, it ignores everything following the asterisk up to the next period or the end of the filename. So:

```
DIR C*QQQ.COM
```

will list

- COMMAND.COM
- C.COM
- COMMAND1.COM
- COMMA.COM

just as if you had typed:

```
DIR C*.COM
```

And trying:

```
DIR *OMMAND.*OM
```

or even:

```
DIR *HELLOTHERE
```

will list every file on your disk, since DOS ignores what comes after the asterisks and treats these two commands as:

```
DIR *.*
```

and:

```
DIR *
```

What you probably meant to type rather than DIR *OMMAND.*OM was:

```
DIR ?OMMAND.?OM
```

which will yield:

- COMMAND.COM
- ZOMMAND.COM
- COMMAND.ZOM

since all three of these are the same except for the very first letter and the first letter of the extension. The more specific you make the command, the more you'll limit the search.

Wildcards are especially useful in deleting groups of files and in making backups. Many word processors create backup files with BAK extensions, and these can eat up lots of space. Once you've determined that you don't need these files any longer, you can wipe out the whole gang of them with a simple command:

```
DEL *.BAK
```

And wildcards can take the drudgery out of backups. If you spent all day working on the fourth quarter projections, and all the files have 4Q9 extensions (for fourth quarter of 1989), you can copy them all from your hard disk to a floppy with the command:

```
COPY *.4Q9 A:
```

(or the even better DOS 3.2 and later XCOPY *.4Q9)

Of course, many applications use their own extensions, so you may have to put identifying codes at the beginning rather than the end of the filename. If you were working on the Sturm and Drang accounts, you might want to give these files names like:

- 4Q9STURM.WK1
- 4Q9DRANG.WK1

The problem with naming files this way is that you later might want to copy all your Drang accounts to one disk, and they might have names like:

- 4Q9DRANG.WK1
- DRANG.RPT
- 89DRANG.MEM

You could put the DRANG part at the beginning of the filenames:

- DRANG4Q9.WK1
- DRANG.RPT
- DRANG89.MEM

which would let you handle them with a DRANG*.* wildcard. But this way you wouldn't necessarily be able to use wildcards to find all the files with 4Q9 in them. STURM4Q9 and DRANG4Q9 have the same number of letters, which would let you use ?????4Q9, but a filename like GUB4Q9 would throw the process off.

DOS doesn't make it easy to use wildcards when the string of characters you want to isolate is in different places in the filenames. But you can employ a combination of sophisticated DOS tricks to do it, as long as the DOS FIND.EXE program is either in your current directory or is in a directory that your PATH knows about. It gets a little complicated (no one ever said DOS would be easy) so you may want to refer to Chapter 10 on batch files before you tackle this:

Use your pure-ASCII word processor, EDLIN, or the DOS COPY CON command to create two BAT files. (Before you try this, be sure you don't already have a file on your disk called DOIT.BAT, because this process will erase it. If you do, either rename the existing file, or change all the references in COPYSOME.BAT and NEXTFILE.BAT from DOIT.BAT to something else.)

First, COPYSOME.BAT:

```
ECHO OFF
IF %2!==! GOTO OOPS
IF EXIST DOIT.BAT DEL DOIT.BAT
FOR %%A IN (*.*) DO COMMAND /C TESTTHEM %%A %1 %2
COMMAND /C DOIT
DEL DOIT.BAT
GOTO END
:OOPS
ECHO Enter a string to search for, and a drive
ECHO or directory to copy the matching file to
:END
```

Then, TESTTHEM.BAT:

```
ECHO OFF
ECHO COPY %1 %3 | FIND "%2" >> DOIT.BAT
```

Then, to copy any filename with the string DRANG in it to drive A:, just type:

```
COPYSOME DRANG A:
```

Or to copy the files to \WORK\ACCT\1989, type:

```
COPYSOME DRANG \WORK\ACCT\1989
```

The COPYSOME.BAT batch file will first make sure that you entered both a string of characters to search for and a drive or directory to copy the matching files to. If you forget one or the other it will abort the process and print an error message.

Be sure you enter the string first and the drive or directory second. And make certain that you enter the string in all uppercase letters, and that you don't put quotation marks around the string.

COPYSOME will then use a FOR batch command to take all the filenames in your directory one by one and feed them into the second TESTTHEM.BAT batch file. The:

```
%%A %1 %2
```

at the end of the FOR command will pass three parameters to TESTTHEM.BAT. Each time the FOR command cycles through, this will replace %%A with the name of the file, %1 with the character string you're trying to match, and %2 with the drive or directory you want to copy everything to. But by the time these parameters reach TESTTHEM.BAT, the parameters shift slightly:

%%A in COPYSOME becomes %1 in TESTTHEM
%1 in COPYSOME becomes %2 in TESTTHEM
%2 in COPYSOME becomes %3 in TESTTHEM

Each time COPYSOME passes these parameters to TESTTHEM, TESTTHEM translates the:

```
ECHO COPY %1 %3 | FIND "%2" >> DOIT.BAT
```

line to something like:

```
ECHO COPY 89DRANG4.MEM A: | FIND "DRANG" >> DOIT.BAT
```

The command at the beginning of this line would normally use ECHO to display the text following the word ECHO. But this batch file pipes this text through the FIND filter. FIND will look at the text to see if it contain the specified string (in this case "DRANG").

If the text doesn't contain the specified string, nothing else will happen and the process will continue with the next filename. But if FIND does locate the string it passes the string through to the very end of the command. Here, the final:

```
>DOIT.BAT
```

command takes any text that survived the FIND test and adds it to a file called DOIT.BAT. Note that a single > sign creates a new file and redirects data into it. A double >> sign will create a file if none exists, and will append data to the file if it's already there. You have to use a double >> sign here because each time you find a filename with the characters DRANG in it, you're going to add an additional line to DOIT.BAT, and you don't want each new line to wipe out the old one.

So if COPYSOME.BAT passes TESTTHEM.BAT parameters like:

```
%%A = 89DRANG4.MEM
 %1 = DRANG
 %2 = A:
```

TESTTHEM plugs these into its main command and ends up with:

```
ECHO COPY 89DRANG4.MEM A: | FIND "DRANG" >> DOIT.BAT
```

Since the characters "DRANG" are indeed in the string:

```
COPY 89DRANG4.MEM A:
```

the FIND filter passes this string through to the:

```
>DOIT.BAT
```

command, where the string is appended to the DOIT.BAT file.

However, if COPYSOME passes TESTTHEM parameters that don't include the specified characters, such as:

```
%%A = 89STURM4.MEM
 %1 = DRANG
 %2 = A:
```

TESTTHEM will turn this into:

```
ECHO COPY 89STURM4.MEM A: | FIND "DRANG" >> DOIT.BAT
```

The FIND test won't pass anything through, since the characters "DRANG" aren't in the COPY 89STURM4.MEM A: string.

When the FOR command in the COPYSOME.BAT file has worked all the way through the (*.*) set of files, COPYSOME will execute the command in the next line:

```
COMMAND /C DOIT
```

This will run the DOIT.BAT file you just created, and make all the copies. When DOIT has made its last copy, DOS will delete DOIT.BAS and the process ends.

Whew. Okay, it's convoluted, but it shows what you can do by slapping together a few DOS commands. And once you have both the COPYSOME.BAT and TESTTHEM.BAT batch files on your disk, you don't have to worry about how they work. You just use them. It's a whole lot easier than sitting down with (shudder) paper and pen and making a list of all the files you have to copy and then typing in the COPY commands one by one.

Incidentally, if you're using a version of DOS 3.3 or later, replace the:

```
FOR %%A IN (*.*) DO COMMAND /C TESTTHEM %%A %1 %2
```

line in COPYSOME.BAT with:

```
FOR %%A IN (*.*) DO CALL TESTTHEM %%A %1 %2
```

Do the same thing with the COMMAND /C DOIT line that follows. Prefix the initial ECHO OFF with a @ sign (so it looks like @ECHO OFF), which will prevent it from displaying onscreen.

Using CALL will expedite things a bit and get rid of some screen clutter. The COPYSOME.BAT batch file turns ECHO OFF to prevent commands from showing up on the screen as they execute. But when you use COMMAND /C to run another batch file, DOS loads a second copy of COMMAND.COM, which turns ECHO on again for the second batch file. CALL leaves the ECHO state alone. If it's off in the first batch file, CALL leaves it off.

Be careful when you're using a command such as REN (or its longer version RENAME) or DEL (or its longer cousin ERASE) with wildcards, since the wildcard may end up including more files than you intended.

If you tried to delete all your BAK backup files by typing:

```
DEL *.BA*
```

you would erase anything with an extension beginning with BA. Since this includes batch files (which end in BAT) and BASIC program files (which normally end in BAS), you'd delete far more than you wanted. The safe way to delete or rename is to use the DIR command with the wildcard structure first, and then to use the DEL or REN. DOS makes this easy, since it lets you use the F3 key to duplicate any or all of what you typed in the previous command.

So if the only files in your directory that had extensions beginning with BA were indeed backup files, you could type:

```
DIR *.BA*
```

and see something like:

```
Volume in drive C is WORKDISK
Directory of C:\ACCOUNT

SCHEDULE BAK     16256   10-17-88   12:01a
4Q9DRANG BAK     21256   10-24-88    6:32a
DRANG    BAK     32932   11-12-88   11:40a
```

```
89DRANG   BAK        9674  11-15-88    1:23p

4 File(s) 4122624 bytes free
```

you could then just type DEL and press F3:

```
DEL *.BA*
```

However, if you tried typing DIR *.BA* and you saw:

```
Volume in drive C is WORKDISK
Directory of C:\ACCOUNT

AUTOEXEC BAT       256   2-11-88    3:15p
SCHEDULE BAK     16256  10-17-88   12:01a
RUN      BAT       128   2-12-88    7:28a
4Q9DRANG BAK     21256  10-24-88    6:32a
DRANG    BAK     32932  11-12-88   11:40a
CHART    BAS     28932   8-22-88    8:32p
89DRANG  BAK      9674  11-15-88    1:23p

7 File(s) 4122624 bytes free
```

you could see that the DEL *.BA* would have erased too much. If this happens, just narrow the focus of the wildcard by changing the command to DEL *.BAK instead.

DOS is a little protective of your files. If you type just:

```
DIR C*
```

DOS will display everything beginning with the letter C (such as COMMAND.COM). But if you type:

```
DEL C*
```

DOS won't erase COMMAND.COM or anything else that has an extension of any kind. (It will, however, erase files that begin with C but don't have extensions.) It's decent of DOS to make the directory search wildcards broader than the deletion wildcards.

One place that a wildcard can come in very handy is in fixing filenames with spaces in them. DOS won't let you put a space in a filename, but some programs (and even BASIC) will. If you try to create a file called

```
SPACE IT
```

DOS will get confused and print an error message that warns:

```
Invalid number of parameters
```

But you can create such a file with BASIC. Type in the following short BADNAME.BAS program:

```
100 ' BADNAME.BAS
110 OPEN "SPACE IT" FOR OUTPUT AS #1
120 PRINT #1,"Ooops..."
130 CLOSE:SYSTEM
```

Then, at the DOS prompt, type:

```
A>BASICA BADNAME
```

(or GWBASIC BADNAME if you're using a generic MS-DOS version of BASIC). The BADNAME.BAS program will create a file with a space in it called SPACE IT. To see this file, just type:

```
DIR S*
```

and sure enough you'll see:

```
SPACE IT 11 11-17-88 5:31p
```

If you try to rename or copy or delete the file, you won't be able to, since DOS will interpret the space as the end of the filename, not a character in the middle. Depending on what you're trying to do all you'll get is error messages like:

- Invalid number of parameters
- Duplicate file name or File not found
- Invalid parameter
- File not found

You could remove the space by loading your disk's directory sectors into DEBUG and changing the name with the DEBUG E command. But why bother, when a simple wildcard operation can do it for you? Just type:

```
REN SPACE?IT SPACEIT
```

and you'll end up with something called SPACEIT that will respond to all normal DOS commands.

Filename Extensions

Filenames can contain from one to eight characters. Extensions can have from zero to three characters. You don't have to use extensions, but they help you organize or search for data. However, you can't use an extension without a filename preceding it. These are all valid filenames:

- A
- A.B
- A.BB
- A.BBB
- AAAAAAAA
- AAAAAAAA.B
- AAAAAAAA.BB
- AAAAAAAA.BBB
- {(_)}
- '~'!@#%$.^&-
- $

These aren't:

- AAAAAAAAA   (more than eight characters in the filename)
- .AAA   (no filename)
- AAAAAAAA.AAAA   (more than three characters in the extension)
- AAAAAA A   (space in the filename)
- AA+AA/A   (illegal characters + and / in filename)
- ?   (illegal character)

If you do try creating a file such as:

ABCDEFGHIJKLM.NOPQRSTUVWXYZ

filename   *.ext*

DOS will truncate the filename to the first eight characters before the dot, and the extension to the first three characters after the period, producing:

```
ABCDEFGH.NOP
```

Extensions are important, since they tell DOS which files it can try to execute and which it can't, and how in memory to load the executable ones. You and your programs can use extensions to organize your files. Most applications keep track of their specialized data files by giving them extensions, such as WKS for old-style *1-2-3* worksheets and DBF for old-style dBASE database files.

And by using extensions you can exploit DOS's formidable wildcard abilities. Without this wildcard magic it would be a real headache to do simple everyday chores like copying all your database files from drive C: to drive B:. First you'd have to type DIR to see all the files in your logged subdirectory, and then write down the names of each one that you thought was a database file. Then you'd have to copy them one by one. Instead, assuming you're on drive C: and that all your database files end with a DBF extension, you can simply type:

```
COPY *.DBF B:
```

Normally DOS will print a message when it's done, reporting how many files it copied. If you want to suppress this message, just stick a > NUL on the end of the command. This redirects the output of the command (which in this case is just the "File(s) copied" message) into a special DOS device called NUL that simply discards the characters. Typing:

```
COPY *.DBF B: > NUL
```

will make the copies and avoid screen clutter. Doing this isn't such a good idea when you're making important backup copies, since you want to know the number of files that DOS actually was able to copy. If you have 30 files on your disk that have a DBF extension and DOS reports:

```
2 File(s) copied
```

you can tell something is wrong, and go back and fix the problem before it's too late.

However, most serious users have to issue so many commands to set things up properly when they start working that they put all these commands in a special startup file called AUTOEXEC.BAT. DOS executes this startup file automatically when you power up each day. These users also know that they can improve performance by lopping off a chunk of memory and convincing DOS to treat this memory as a super-fast disk called a RAMdisk. So their AUTOEXEC.BAT files are filled with commands to copy files from floppies or hard disks to RAMdisks. This normally produces a long cascade of "1 File(s) copied" messages. Adding a > NUL to each COPY command in your AUTOEXEC.BAT will do away with these unsightly messages.

(Incidentally, IBM and Microsoft have had more than half a decade to cram sophisticated tricks into DOS and generally refine it. It's hard to believe that they still have DOS printing and idiotic message like "1 File(s) copied." Or refusing to tell you how many files DOS erased when you use a wildcard with the DEL or ERASE commands.)

In this chapter we described the basic principles of data storage and the physical properties of the disk. While the PC will place data in its own convenient locations, it's up to you to impose a structure on that data by organizing it into files and assigning those files unique and descriptive names. DOS has some inflexible rules that define what it will and will not recognize in a filename. We've presented those rules here, as well as some simple tips to help you create workable filenames.

In the next chapter we'll take a closer look at how to manage these files on a hard disk.

Chapter 3

Hard Disks Made Easy

The single most important productivity enhancement for most users is a fast hard disk. A hard disk gives you instant access to all your files, speeds up operation dramatically, and makes "disk full" errors a lot less common. Floppies are how new software products are packaged, and how you back up your files — unless you use a tape drive or Bernoulli Box. They're also for the birds. Hard disks used to be expensive and unreliable. That's all changed. Today they're inexpensive and unreliable. I've personally replaced seven hard disks over the past three years, and have to perform tedious daily ministrations to keep my current one purring.

Even the most expensive hard disks are frail and transitory. Many users wedge PC-ATs or PS/2s into floor stands beneath their desks, which is fine until they start playing knee-hockey with their systems. Others blithely slide working XTs back and forth across their desks to make room for paperwork, or routinely lift a corner of the chassis to retrieve something that's burrowed beneath it.

You've all probably seen versions of the famous illustration where a human hair, a smoke particle, and even the greasy schmutz of a fingerprint seem enormous compared to the gap between the magnetic head of a hard disk and the rotating disk platter itself. With tolerances slightly above the angstrom level, dropping a chassis a quarter inch, or tapping it with your toe, is the hard disk equivalent of an atom bomb going off directly overhead.

It's true that packages like the *Norton Utilities* and *Mace Utilities*, and even the dangerous DOS RECOVER command, can rescue parts of text files that remain intact after a bounced magnetic head has plowed little oxide furrows into the disk surface. But these programs aren't very good at resurrecting program files, or chunks of data stored in binary format. And when you see a message like:

```
General Failure error reading drive C
Abort, Retry, Ignore?
```

well, that's what backups are for.

If you set up your hard disk properly, you'll not only take the anguish out of daily backups, but you'll also end up working a whole lot smarter and more efficiently. While you'll have to learn how to handle subdirectories, the tips and utilities provided here should make it a breeze. Once you learn the basics — and install the tools you'll find in this chapter — you'll be able to solo with the best of them.

Formatting the Hard Disk

Hard disks require two kinds of formatting, *low-level* and *high-level*. These days the fundamental low-level formatting is done at the factory. You or your dealer have to do the high DOS-level formatting.

Dealers nowadays test and set up hard disks before shipping them to purchasers. Unfortunately, they also usually follow the questionable advice in the DOS manual and copy all the files from the two DOS floppy disks onto the root directory. For best performance, you should clean things up if you log into a brand new hard disk, type DIR, and see the listing scroll off your screen. But you can't just erase or move all the files there; you'll learn which ones have to stay in a moment.

If your dealer or MIS department didn't set up your system, and you have a single 30 megabyte or smaller hard disk, it's fairly straightforward.

(If you have a hard disk that no one has touched, and all you see when you try to start is a "161 — System Options Not Set" message, hunt for the SETUP program, which on older systems IBM perversely buried on its Diagnostics disk. Put this disk in drive A:, turn the computer on, press F1 when prompted, and answer the questions about date, time, hard disk type, floppy disk type(s), and memory size. If you need to know the drive type, check to see that it's not in the documentation that came with your system. If it's not, take the cover off the computer and look for the number on the label on the front of the drive. If all else fails, call your dealer.)

Once the setup program has run, insert your DOS disk in drive A: and turn your system on. Press the Enter key twice when asked for the date and time. Type in:

```
FDISK
```

and press the Enter key, and when you see the "Fixed Disk Setup Program" screen, accept the defaults by pressing the Enter key again to create a DOS partition, and then once more to tell the program you want to devote the entire hard disk to DOS.

You can slice up a standard hard disk into as many as four partitions, and jump from one to the other by using FDISK. Take our word for it, unless you have a penchant for dabbling in other operating systems, you don't want to.

After you've answered the partitioning questions, press any key and your system should reboot. This time, unless you're using an AT or XT-286 or PS/2 with a battery-operated clock, enter the correct date and time when asked. Assuming you're installing your first 30 megabyte or smaller hard disk in an XT or AT, type:

The Low-Level Format

Many systems come with their own built-in low-level formatters. If you've installed third-party hard disks driven by Western Digital controller cards (ROM version 6.0 or earlier) and either wish to experiment or did not receive adequate instructions on how to low-level format your hard disk, it's easy to do so. But don't even think of trying this unless you're installing a brand new hard disk and feel adventurous.

These procedures will also let you change other hard disk specifications if you want, such as the drive designation and the *interleave* factor, a measure of how physically close to one another the controller writes consecutive sectors. However, fooling with these will wipe out everything on your hard disk. Be absolutely sure this is what you want to do before trying it. And it won't work on systems with other controller cards.

First, load DEBUG.COM by typing DEBUG, and at the "-" prompt enter:

```
RAX
```

When DEBUG responds with a ":" enter the drive designation and the interleave you want. For example, for a hard disk designated as drive D: with an interleave of 4 you would enter:

```
0104
```

since drives are designated 0 through 7 with drive C: equal to 0. (The relative drive number goes into register AH, and the interleave factor into AL.)

Then, at the DEBUG prompt, enter:

```
G=C800:5
```

Answer Y to the question onscreen if you wish to begin low-level formatting.

Finally, use FDISK and FORMAT to complete the setup of your newly configured drive. Remember — this will erase all information already on your hard disk, so most of you won't want to try it. If you do, first, make sure your backups are absolutely current, and, second, jot down the default settings so you can reset everything to normal when you're done. You obviously will know what the original relative drive number is, and the low-level formatter should print out the standard interleave factor in its prompt.

```
FORMAT C:/S/V
```

and, if necessary, verify that you want to proceed by entering Y.

The /S suffix, or *switch* tells DOS you not only want to format the hard disk, but want to add the three system files — IBMBIO.COM, IBMDOS.COM (or their non-IBM-specific cousins), and COMMAND.COM — to it so you can boot without having to stick a DOS floppy disk in drive A:.

If you forgot to add the /S, or if your system is delivered with a hard disk that's been FDISKed and formatted but without these three system files, turn your system on with your main DOS disk in drive A:, enter the correct date and time, and then type:

```
SYS C:
COPY COMMAND.COM C:
```

The /V switch tells DOS to let you add a volume name. This doesn't really do much except let you personalize your directory listings and CHKDSK reports, and avoid the pesky "Volume in drive C has no label" messages. With recent versions of DOS you can always go back and use the LABEL command to add or revise the volume label.

It's becoming increasingly common to add additional hard disks, especially monstrous ones that hold vastly more than IBM's original issue 10s, 20s, and 30s. Current DOS versions limit individual drives to a maximum of 32 megabytes. Manufacturers of larger hard disks usually add small driver programs to get around this restriction. However, starting with version 3.31, Microsoft fixed this problem.

Subdirectory Structure

Many users who are either lazy or are befuddled by the terse explanation of subdirectories in the DOS manual end up dumping all their files into the main, or *root* directory. It's called a root directory because all other subdirectories branch off of it in a shape vaguely resembling an upside-down tree, or more accurately, a family tree, with the progenitor planted at the top and all the descendants fanning out beneath him. A simple representation looks likes this:

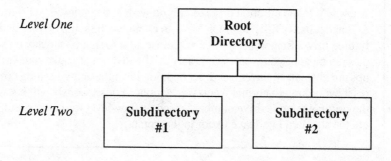

You could make the tree much more complex, with third, fourth and fifth levels dangling below the second, each one bristling with additional subdirectories. Too few subdirectories and you end up with unmanageable numbers of files in each; too many and you can run into PATH problems (more about that later).

Note that the schematic representation of your subdirectory structure doesn't have to be in the form of a symmetric tree. An equally valid way to describe the above setup is:

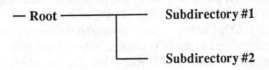

Note also that the root of the tree is at the top, so it's really an upside-down tree. A lower level is one farther away from the root. As you go higher in the tree you get closer to the root. This sounds confusing, and it is. Just be thankful that IBM didn't choose UNIX instead of DOS.

IBM's XT and AT hard disks (which in its typically contrary way IBM calls *fixed* disks because they're fixed in place and not removable like floppies) can hold between ten and 30 million characters; its loaded PS/2s and the killer systems from other manufacturers can squirrel away as many as half a billion. With storage space so capacious, keeping similar files grouped together is a necessity. Otherwise, you (and DOS) would have to sort through hundreds or thousands of files each time you wanted to find a single program to run.

Just as you can't be at two places at the same time (unless you have a good lawyer), DOS lets you log into only one subdirectory at a time. When you first boot up, DOS logs you into the root directory of either your hard disk or the diskette in drive A:. If you installed the necessary DOS system files on your hard disk, and if you either didn't have a floppy disk in drive A: or had one there but left the drive A: door open, you'll boot off the hard disk. If this doesn't happen it's probably because you either have some bizarre brand-X hard disk or an early PC with an old ROM chip that doesn't understand hard disks.

You really need only three files in your root directory:

- COMMAND.COM
- AUTOEXEC.BAT
- CONFIG.SYS

Actually, a root directory formatted with the /S/V option will contain two additional, *hidden* files, IBMBIO.COM and IBMDOS.COM (or Microsoft's generic versions of these), plus the volume label, which is also stored in a small hidden file. They're called hidden files since they won't show up in normal directory searches. But they're there, and you can see at least the system files at the top of the list when you type:

```
CHKDSK C:/V
```

IBMBIO.COM contains additions and corrections to the gut-level device-handling BIOS routines that come with your system on ROM chips. IBMDOS.COM provides other fundamental services for things like copying and deleting files, searching through the directory, or reading the keyboard.

Technically, you can patch these system files and put the COMMAND.COM, AUTOEXEC.BAT, and CONFIG.SYS files in other places than the root directory. But playing with your hidden files is like playing with fire.

COMMAND.COM is the primary command interpreter, processor, and loader that watches what you type at the DOS prompt. When it sees you trying to execute an *internal* command such as DIR, TYPE, RENAME, COPY, or ERASE, it can dispatch these right away, since the main routines for these are stored inside COMMAND.COM (which is why they're called internal commands). When it can't find an internal command to match what you typed — such as FORMAT, SORT, or 123 — it looks in a set of directories you specify, called a *path*, for files with COM, EXE, or BAT extensions, and tries to load or execute these *external* commands. In addition, a disposable part of COMMAND.COM looks for the startup AUTOEXEC.BAT file to execute immediately after bootup.

Every hard disk system should have an AUTOEXEC.BAT file, if only to set the proper system prompt. But it's also handy for loading resident pop-up programs like *SideKick* into memory, changing screen colors, setting operating modes (to switch monitors or specify communications protocols, for instance), copying files into RAMdisks, and otherwise automatically configuring your system the way you like it.

Actually, AUTOEXEC.BAT doesn't have to be located in the root directory, and doesn't even have to have a BAT extension, even though it's a batch file. (See the sidebar "Booting Up With BERNIE.")

The normal DOS hard disk prompt is a cryptic:

```
C>
```

which tells you only that at that moment DOS recognizes drive C: — rather than the other drives in your system — as the active drive. Once you start creating subdirectories and jumping around from one to another, you'll want to know which subdirectory you're currently logged into. By issuing the command:

```
PROMPT $P$G
```

you'll tell DOS to report the name of the subdirectory along with the drive that's active, each time you finish executing a command or program. The root directory prompt will change to:

```
C:\>
```

The solitary backslash is DOS's shorthand for indicating the root directory. If the back-slash-greater-than-sign combination is too visually jarring, you could adapt the prompt to:

```
PROMPT $P:
```

which will make the root directory appear as:

```
C:\:
```

Remember, the \ sign all by itself stands for the root directory. You can always see what's in the root directory, for instance, by typing:

```
DIR \
```

Later, when you add other subdirectories, you'll connect subdirectory names and their files with \ characters. So a subdirectory called PCMAG that's one level down from the root directory would actually be called \PCMAG. And if you were to branch an additional subdirectory off of \PCMAG, and called it \UTIL, the actual name of this new subdirectory would be \PCMAG\UTIL. A file called TOOLS.DOC in this new subdirectory would then be called \PCMAG\UTIL\TOOLS.DOC.

One of the handiest, but most confusing, aspects of naming files in subdirectories is that you could pepper your hard disk with other TOOLS.DOC files. So a TOOLS.DOC file on drive C: in the \PCMAG subdirectory would really be C:\PCMAG\TOOLS.DOC, while a different version in the root directory would be C:\TOOLS.DOC. The full name of any file has three parts — drive letter, path, and the actual filename-plus-extension.

A representation of this structure would be:

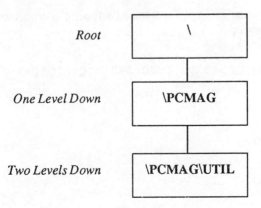

Root   \

One Level Down   \PCMAG

Two Levels Down   \PCMAG\UTIL

The root directory doesn't have a user-defined name such as PCMAG, so DOS designates it as just \ with nothing following it. The DOS manuals clearly state that the maximum length of any subdirectory path — the list of directory names from the top (root) to the deepest level — may be no longer than 63 bytes, measured from the beginning of the first name to the end of the last name, excluding slashes in front or at the end.

DOS function call 47H (Get Current Directory) requires a 64-byte area in memory to return the current directory path. It is not preceded by a backslash but it is terminated by a hex 0, so this is consistent with the 63 character restriction.

How many nested levels are allowed in a directory structure? Although the manuals never say so, the answer is obviously 32. If each of the subdirectory names is one letter long and they are separated by backslashes, then 32 levels would make the total length 63.

Of course, 32 nested levels of subdirectories would place an enormous drain on DOS as well as on the human user's mental faculties. What happens if you attempt to go beyond 32? Don't even try. You may get away with it but DOS will make life hard after that and you'll have difficulty just removing that snarl of subdirectories.

Customizing Your Prompt

The PROMPT command can do all sorts of tricky things, such as reporting the time and date, or the DOS version. If you ask it to, it will print the current time whenever you do something that summons another DOS prompt, such as press the Enter key again, or finish executing a program. It will not act as a clock and display the continuously changing time. And it will display time in hundredths of seconds based on a 24-hour clock. If you want it to print just the hours and minutes, you can backspace away everything else, with the command:

```
PROMPT It's now $T$H$H$H$H$H$H
```

Users who discover the PROMPT command's flexibility invariably end up creating strange prompts such as:

```
PROMPT +$Q$Q$Q$Q+$_$B  $N$G $B$_+$Q$Q$Q$Q+$_
```

which produces:

```
+====+
|  C> |
+====+
```

or:

```
PROMPT $L$N$G $L$N$G$_     $B$_    $Q$Q$Q$_
```

which yields:

```
<C> <C>
    |
 ___|___
```

A less frivolous use of the PROMPT command is in sending escape sequences to the ANSI.SYS extended screen driver, which can give you precise control over the way your monitor looks and works. The real strength of including $P in any PROMPT command is that when you log into a subdirectory, DOS will display the name of that subdirectory. So if your PATH setting is $P: and you create a subdirectory called STAR in which you keep all your *WordStar* files, and you move from the root directory into that subdirectory, your prompt will change from:

```
C:\:
```

to:

```
C:\STAR:
```

To see the command that most recently configured your prompt, type SET on a line by itself, which displays the system's environment — the fundamental settings that tell DOS where to look for key files and how to prompt the user. To restore the prompt to its original C> just type PROMPT with nothing following it.

Customizing your prompt isn't all roses. Once you tell DOS to include the subdirectory name in the prompt, it will relentlessly seek one out. So if you have a $P in your PROMPT command and log into a floppy drive, then remove the disk from that floppy drive and do something that generates an "Abort, Retry, Ignore?" message, DOS won't budge until you stick the diskette back in the floppy slot. Newer versions of DOS give you the additional option to "Fail" which actually lets you succeed here. If you are offered this option, type F, then enter the drive letter of your hard disk.

A second disadvantage is that if you have tons of multilayered subdirectories with long directory names, and you're logged into one five levels deep, the prompt may be so long that your commands wrap around the right edge of your screen. The best solution is to keep subdirectory names short. In addition to preventing wraparound problems, this makes it far easier to switch between subdirectories. It's a lot simpler to type \WST\UT than \WORDSTAR\UTILITY, especially when you're doing it several times a day. (While you're at it, truncate the names of programs you use every day. Why type EDITOR when you could just key in ED? If you don't like the idea of renaming your files you can always create batch files with short names that can run programs with longer ones.) Also, resist the temptation to use extensions in subdirectory names since they'll just make the whole process more cumbersome and prone to error.

Another solution to wraparound ills is to end all your prompts with a $_ which jumps the cursor down to column 1 of the line below. Unfortunately, doing this will confuse certain DOS utilities like MORE that are designed for single-line prompts and will end up scrolling information off the screen before you can read it.

The CONFIG.SYS File

Apart from AUTOEXEC.BAT, the only other file that normally has to be in the root directory is CONFIG.SYS. Your system will run without a CONFIG.SYS file, but will work better with one. And certain programs demand one. If you're using a database manager, for instance, that handles more than eight open files at once, you have to prepare DOS for juggling the extra ones with a FILES= command in CONFIG.SYS.

But where CONFIG.SYS really shines is in increasing disk-read buffers, loading device drivers, and adding logical drives to your system.

For some odd reason, IBM specified a default of two buffers for the XT, and a paltry three for the AT. Buffers are simply chunks of memory set aside to store the data your system most recently read from or wrote to your disk, although some buffers don't store written data. If you have to go back and read or write the same data, it's far speedier to do so via these memory buffers than to have to move the magnetic heads again and slurp up or slap down the information on the physical disks one more time.

Buffer needs vary from system to system, and the number of buffers is often a topic of heated discussion when tech types get together. Virtually everyone agrees that three is a joke. Somewhere around ten or 15 seems right for XT users, and 20 or 30 for AT users and other power users. Specifying too many is as detrimental to performance as too few, since your system will end up wasting time as it churns through endless reams of data it will never use.

If you currently have a directory crammed with hundreds of files, it's easy to demonstrate how increasing the number of buffers can help boost performance. First, make sure you don't have a CONFIG.SYS file, or if you do, that it doesn't contain a BUFFERS= command. If yours does, rename it temporarily.

Reboot, and issue a DIR command. The first few dozen files scroll rapidly by, but eventually the buffers fill, and the display suddenly turns balky. If you get tired of watching your files bounce slowly upward, interrupt the directory listing by holding down the Ctrl key and tapping either the C key or the ScrollLock key. Then, when you're back in the root directory at the DOS prompt, create a CONFIG.SYS file by typing:

```
COPY CON CONFIG.SYS
```

and then pressing the Enter key. The cursor will drop down a line. Type:

```
BUFFERS=15
```

and then press Enter, the F6 function key, and then the Enter key again. You'll see the message:

```
1 File(s) copied
```

Reboot and reissue the DIR command. Now virtually all the files will fly by, not just the first few, since your system can load a giant chunk of directory data from your disk into memory at one pass and not have to keep reading the disk in little sips.

CONFIG.SYS is also where you instruct your system to load device drivers such as the DOS VDISK.SYS *virtual disk* (RAMdisk), or drivers to link your basic hardware with mice, nonstandard external storage devices, 3-1/2 inch outboard floppy drives, or giant hard disks.

And it's where you tell DOS how many drives you're going to want to use. When you boot up, DOS assumes a maximum of five (drives A: through E:). But if your system is loaded to the gills with hard disks, half-heights, microfloppies, and other exotica, you might need more. And if you use the SUBST command to fool your system into treating a subdirectory like a disk drive to get around PATH or environment limitations, you'll have to prearrange it with a LASTDRIVE= CONFIG.SYS command.

Apart from the hidden DOS system files, COMMAND.COM, AUTOEXEC.BAT, and CONFIG.SYS, a well-organized disk's root directory should contain no other nonhidden files.

Some users don't mind having their important DOS utilities in their root directory, and cut through the clutter of a messy directory with a DIR/P (paused directory) or DIR/W (wide directory) command. This won't radically degrade performance, and may actually be a hair faster than storing the utilities in a separate \DOS subdirectory, if the files are kept at the very beginning of the hard disk directory. But it's even faster to keep them on a RAMdisk. And clutter gets to be a bad habit. Soon you start dumping files anywhere. Users who run the REPEATS.COM duplicate file finder on the accompanying disk are always amazed at the large number of misplaced and misfiled programs and data.

As mentioned earlier, it's a good idea to clean up a root directory cluttered with extraneous files. If all a dealer or corporate systems installer did when setting up your brand new system was copy all the DOS files from their original floppies to your root directory, you can go ahead and erase everything except COMMAND.COM (which is required to reboot the computer).

You can see if all the files in your root directory are also on your DOS disk either by putting the DOS disk in drive A: and then typing:

```
DIR C:/W
```

and then:

```
DIR A:/W
```

for a wide-display filenames-only listing. Or, turn on your printer and either type:

```
DIR C: > PRN
```

and then:

```
DIR A: > PRN
```

or hold down the Ctrl key and press P (or PrtSc) to toggle your printer on so that it echoes everything simultaneously to the printer and the screen, and type DIR C: and then DIR A: for a printed copy of your directory listing. If you used the Ctrl-P (or Ctrl-PrtSc) technique to turn simultaneous printing on, hold down the Ctrl key and type P (or PrtSc) once more to toggle it off.

You can also see what's on your disk by sorting the files in order of their extension. The command:

```
DIR | SORT /+10 | MORE
```

will make it easy. For this to work, the DOS SORT.EXE and MORE.COM files must be on the current directory, or be in directories that you've included in your PATH command.

The DOS COMP utility can also come in handy here. If your DOS disk is in drive A:, type:

```
COMP . A:
```

(The period used in this example is a shorthand way to indicate whatever directory you are currently in.)

Any way you do it, if you see that all you have on your root directory is DOS files, erase all the files except COMMAND.COM (you'll put them back in their proper places later). If you have AUTOEXEC.BAT or CONFIG.SYS files, examine their contents by using the TYPE command. To see what's inside CONFIG.SYS, just type:

```
TYPE CONFIG.SYS
```

If you see other files listed, such as:

```
DEVICE=VDISK.SYS 360
DEVICE=ANSI.SYS
DEVICE=MOUSE.SYS
```

you'll want to leave VDISK.SYS, ANSI.SYS, and MOUSE.SYS where they are on the root directory. Later you can move them out of the root directory to a subdirectory called \BIN (so named because that's where you store your programs, which are in binary, non-text format), and change the CONFIG.SYS file so that it says:

```
DEVICE=\BIN\VDISK.SYS 360
DEVICE=\BIN\ANSI.SYS
DEVICE=\BIN\MOUSE.SYS
```

Similarly, if you use the TYPE command to examine AUTOEXEC.BAT and see that it loads *SideKick* with the command SK, leave SK.COM in the root directory for now.

Later, if you create a third-level subdirectory below \BIN called \BIN\KICK, and move your *SideKick* files there, you would change the line in your AUTOEXEC.BAT file from:

```
SK
```

to:

```
\BIN\KICK\SK
```

The TYPE command is terrific for peeking into short text files. But if a file is longer than 24 lines, the beginning will scroll off the screen before you can read it. To prevent this, use the MORE.COM utility, which shows you the contents of files a screenful at a time. If your AUTOEXEC.BAT is getting long, type:

```
MORE < AUTOEXEC.BAT
```

You could also enter:

```
TYPE AUTOEXEC.BAT | MORE
```

but the first method is more efficient and easier to type.

Directory Limits

You can store up to 64 files in the root directory of a single-sided floppy disk (if you can still find one), and 112 files in the root directory of a more common 360K floppy. The root directory on the unpopular 1.2 megabyte floppy holds 224. And there's space on most hard disk root directories to store 512 files.

But don't test this out on your hard disk. If you do, you'll end up after the 509th with a "File creation error" message (the 510th, 511th, and 512th are the two hidden system files and the hidden volume label). Any subdirectory entries you may have in the root directory are really just special types of files, so they're included in the count too. So you may run out of room well before you actually have a chance to create the 512th file.

The number of directory entries in a subdirectory is limited only by available space on the disk. That's because each subdirectory is really just a special kind of file that keeps track of other files. Because the subdirectory itself is a file, it can grow the same way a data file grows when you add information to it.

Remember — if you really want to organize your hard disk properly, don't put any other files on your root directory than the ones mentioned above. Then, when you type:

```
DIR C:\
```

all you'll see is one screenful of your bootup files and main subdirectory listings. It'll be an index into your hard disk.

Disk Tools

When IBM introduced its hard disk XT, it added several UNIX-like *hierarchical* subdirectory features (as well as a UNIX-like tree structure) to the new release of DOS that accompanied it (version 2.0). Among these powerful new commands were:

- MKDIR (and MD)
- RMDIR (and RD)
- CHDIR (and CD)
- PATH

Nobody anywhere ever uses the command names MKDIR, RMDIR, and CHDIR, since the shorthand versions MD, RD, and CD will do just fine. Of course, since the IBM DOS manual is not exactly what you'd call friendly, you can't look up these commands by hunting for the shorter versions in the alphabetical reference section. MD, CD, and RD aren't even in the manual's index. Nice touch, IBM.

The MD command creates a new subdirectory. The first thing you should do after running FDISK and FORMAT is create a DOS subdirectory. To do this, type:

```
MD \DOS
```

If you are sure you are in the root directory, you can also type:

```
MD DOS
```

since both commands will do the same thing — create a subdirectory one level down from where you currently are, in the root directory.

By omitting the backslash (as in MD DOS) you're saying "create a directory called DOS that's one level down in the subdirectory tree from where I currently am." By including the backslash (as in MD \DOS) you're saying "create a directory called DOS that is one level down from the root directory," since the single backslash specifies the root directory.

The method that *omits* the backslash uses relative locations. The technique that *includes* the backslash uses absolute locations. Both have their advantages. We'll discuss this in more detail later. This is a critical distinction, and a point of real confusion among new hard disk users. (Many DOS commands allow alternate phrasings. For instance, you can use several different syntaxes to perform the same COPY command, depending on what you want to do and where you currently are.)

Once you've created the \DOS subdirectory, log into it (or Change Directories) from the root directory by issuing the CD DOS (or CD \DOS) command. Here's a shortcut — once you've typed MD \DOS to create the subdirectory, type the letter C and then press

F3. F3 repeats the previous command, so it will fill in the command line with the rest of what you typed at the previous DOS prompt. So at the C> prompt you'd type:

```
MD \DOS
```

then press the Enter key. Then you'd type:

```
C
```

and press F3. As soon as you did you'd see:

```
CD \DOS
```

Press the Enter key and DOS will log you into your new \DOS subdirectory, and you'll see:

```
C>
```

How do you know you're in the \DOS subdirectory? If you type in DIR you'll get something like:

```
Volume in drive C is PC MAGAZINE
Directory of C:\DOS

   .          <DIR>        6-10-88  10:48p
   ..         <DIR>        6-10-88  10:48p
       2 File(s)   20840448 bytes free
```

You can see the current directory in the second line of the DIR report. But if you remembered to set your prompt to $P: you could automatically tell which directory you were logged into, since instead of:

```
C>
```

as soon as you typed CD \DOS you'd see:

```
C:\DOS:
```

Typing CD by itself will also display the current subdirectory. But that's an extra step.

Notice that DOS already thinks you have two files in the \DOS subdirectory with the peculiar names . and .. and with <DIR> where the file size usually goes. Dot notation will be covered a bit later. The <DIR> tells you you're dealing with subdirectory entries. Now go back to the root directory. You can do this one of two ways.

You can use the absolute location technique and issue a command that says "move to the root directory":

```
CD \
```

or you can say "move one level up from where I am" with the command:

```
CD ..
```

You could have typed CD\ rather than CD \ , and CD.. rather than CD   .. since in this case DOS isn't picky about extra spaces (unless you're using one of the older DOS versions, in which case the space between the CD and the .. is mandatory). The double dot stands for the *parent* directory of the one you're currently logged into — the directory (or subdirectory) directly one level up toward the root. In this case the only level up is the root.

If you're curious, the single dot stands for the directory you're currently in. This shorthand actually comes in handy when you're prompted for a subdirectory name and you're in one five levels deep and would rather type a single period than a long, elaborate pathname — although just pounding on the Enter key sometimes works in such situations.

If you're deep inside one subdirectory like A/B/C/D/E/F/G and you're using the DOS COMP utility to compare a file there with another file deep within another directory like /1/2/3/4/5/6, you can enter:

```
COMP /1/2/3/4/5/6/PROGRAM
```

COMP will respond with a message to enter the directory the other version of the file is in. Just type a period, which tells DOS to look at the subdirectory you're currently logged into. Or, you could specify the period on the command line, as was done earlier:

```
COMP /1/2/3/4/5/6/PROGRAM .
```

or:

```
COMP . /1/2/3/4/5/6/PROGRAM
```

You can also use the dot to simplify erasing all the files in a subdirectory. Instead of typing:

```
DEL *.*
```

all you really have to type is:

```
DEL .
```

This technique can be potentially dangerous, however. If you let someone who doesn't understand subdirectories use your system you can run into trouble. If a novice user doesn't have a clue what the . and .. represent in a directory listing but does know about the DIR and ERASE commands, and somehow logs into a directory one level down from the root, he or she may be tempted to erase these mysterious double dot entries and end up deleting all the files in the current and root directories.

DOS will respond with a:

```
Are you sure (Y/N)?
```

warning when you try to erase an entire subdirectory like this, but that's not a threatening enough message to a novice. You can make this message meaner by patching COMMAND.COM, but many users feel COMMAND.COM is sacrosanct and shouldn't be touched. If you're not one of these, here's how to avoid potential mass-erasure problems like this by changing the message from:

```
Are you sure (Y/N)?
```

to:

```
Now hit the N key!!
```

First, make sure you have a copy of DEBUG.COM handy, and then make a backup copy of COMMAND.COM called COMMAND.OLD so that if you make a mistake you can start over. Then type:

```
DEBUG COMMAND.COM
```

Find out how long your version is by typing:

```
RCX
```

and pressing the Enter key twice. You'll see something like:

```
CX 62DB
```

Take the four-digit hex number following the CX and type:

```
S 100 62DB "Are you sure"
```

(substituting the four-digit hex number if yours is different from 62DB). Press the Enter key and you should see something like:

```
61B2:5158
```

Ignore the first four digits preceding the colon. Take the rightmost four digits and type:

```
E 5158 "Now hit the N key!!"
```

(substituting the four-digit hex number if yours is different from 5158). Press the Enter key. Then press W (and Enter) to write the new version back to disk, and Q (and Enter) to quit DEBUG. Once you've patched COMMAND.COM, reboot.

If you do this, make sure you don't mix patched and unpatched versions of COM-MAND.COM on the same disk, or you'll confuse DOS.

In any event, once you've used the CD\ or the CD .. command, and you're back in the root directory, type DIR and you'll see a new listing along with:

```
Volume in drive C is PC MAGAZINE
Directory of C:\
COMMAND  COM    25307   3-17-87  12:00p
CONFIG   SYS      128   1-11-88   3:27p
AUTOEXEC BAT      640   2-22-88   8:12p
DOS           <DIR>     6-10-88  10:48p
```

The <DIR> tells you that you now have a subdirectory one level down from the root directory.

Important Files

You should now copy all the important files from your DOS floppy disks into your new DOS subdirectory. You can log onto drive A: and type:

```
COPY *.* C:\DOS
```

or, while in the root directory in drive C:, type:

```
COPY A:*.* \DOS
```

Or you could log into C:\DOS (with the CD DOS or CD \DOS command) and simply type:

```
COPY A:*.*
```

or:

```
COPY A:.
```

Even better is to use the XCOPY command introduced with DOS 3.2. COPY works one file at a time. XCOPY will read in as many commands in one gulp as memory allows, then spit them out in one continuous stream without bouncing back and forth repeatedly the way COPY does. XCOPY is also a terrific backup tool.

If you're logged into C:\DOS and you have XCOPY handy, just type:

```
XCOPY A:
```

Make sure you copy the important files from both the main DOS floppy disk and the supplemental one. (Starting with DOS 3.3, these are called "Operating" and "Startup" disks.)

However, you can skip some of the files nobody ever uses, such as VDISK.LST (a long assembly language source code file for programmers), anything that ends with a BAS extension (unless you think DONKEY is an exciting and challenging game), and some of the stranger utilities such as KEYBIT.COM and KEYBFR.COM which load in foreign keyboard templates (in this case Italian and French). These foreign utilities were all combined into one file called KEYB in version 3.3.

You can also toss BASIC, since BASICA does everything BASIC does and more. In fact, with version 3.3, BASIC just loads BASICA. It's hard to believe, but some of the programs on even the most recent version of DOS will work only on the PC*jr*; try running MUSICA.BAS for instance. Do however copy DEBUG.COM, which, for some bizarre reason is not on the main DOS disk. Incidentally, while IBM removed the documentation for DEBUG from the 3.3 manual, it left the program on the disk.

Now that you've created a subdirectory (called \DOS) one level down from the root directory, go ahead and create another subdirectory on the same level as \DOS, called \BIN. But be careful. Why?

If you're currently logged into either the root directory or the \DOS directory, you could create \BIN with the absolute command:

```
MD \BIN
```

This command in effect says "create a subdirectory one level down from the root directory and call it BIN." The single \ prefix means "one level down from the root directory."

However, if you forget the backslash and try the command:

```
MD BIN
```

two different things will happpen, depending on where you currently are on your hard disk, since omitting the backslash makes this a relative command rather than an absolute one.

Typing MD BIN will create a subdirectory that's one level down from where you currently are. So if you're currently logged into the root directory, MD BIN will create a subdirectory called \BIN that's one level down from the root.

But if you're currently logged into \DOS, which is already one level down from the root, and you type MD BIN, you'll end up creating a subdirectory called \DOS\BIN that's one level down from \DOS and two levels down from the root. That's because leaving out the backslash in the MD command makes it a relative rather than an absolute command .

To recap, if you already have a subdirectory called \DOS, but you're currently logged into the root directory:

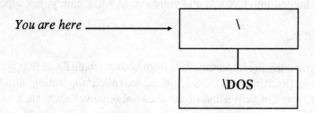

You are here ────────▶   \

\DOS

and you type MD BIN, you'll end up with:

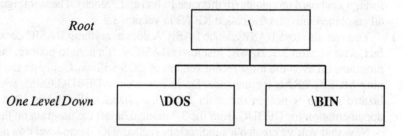

Root   \

One Level Down   \DOS   \BIN

which is what you want. But if you're already one level down, in \DOS:

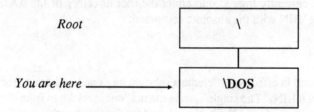

Root   \

You are here ────────▶   \DOS

and you type MD BIN, you'll get:

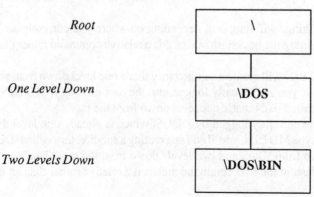

Root   \

One Level Down   \DOS

Two Levels Down   \DOS\BIN

Actually, it really doesn't matter which way you set up your subdirectories. Most users aren't really comfortable creating tree structures any more complex than one or two levels deep. A few prefer intricately filigreed systems. For best results, *keep it simple.* The only real reason to create lots of subdirectories branching off of each other is if your work demands it.

For instance, if you're a CPA with many clients, each one deserves its own subdirectory, and each will require still deeper subdirectory levels of organization. It's good practice to keep records separated by year or quarter or even month, depending on the quantity of files. But while it might make sense to keep expenses in one subdirectory and income in another, it would be ridiculous to have one called:

```
\SMITHCO\1987\JUNE\EXPENSES\OFFICE\PENCILS
```

and another:

```
\SMITHCO\1987\JUNE\EXPENSES\OFFICE\STAPLES
```

If you've followed the earlier instructions properly, you now have two subdirectories called \DOS and \BIN, each one level down from the root directory. \DOS contains all the important files you copied from your two main DOS disks. \BIN should contain all the smaller non-DOS utilities and batch files you use every day.

You should absolutely positively copy many of the utilities from the accompanying disk to \BIN. Tops on the list are VTREE.COM, BROWSE.COM, DR.COM, RN.COM, and CO.COM. But other winners such as CARDFILE.COM and SETUP.COM belong there too. If you have the space, copy them all.

VTREE.COM displays a pictorial representation of the tree structure of the subdirectories on your hard disk. BROWSE.COM is a replacement for the DOS TYPE command that lets you scan rapidly through your files. DR.COM is a sensational file manager. RN.COM manages whole subdirectory structures, and lets you run DR from within it. CO.COM makes copying, moving, or deleting selected files a breeze. CARDFILE is a pop-up name and address filer and phone dialer. While it isn't strictly a DOS utility, it's one of the most popular programs we've published. SETUP tames your printer. Dozens of others will make your life at the keyboard a joy rather than a chore, and really streamline your hard disk operation.

Once you've created your \BIN subdirectory, copy these utilities into it (by adapting any of the syntaxes you used to copy your DOS files into \DOS, above). Log into \BIN by typing:

```
CD \BIN
```

and run VTREE by typing:

```
VTREE
```

You should see something that looks like:

DOS

BIN

This may not be a very impressive graphic representation, but it's vastly better than the nearly useless output produced by the DOS TREE.COM utility. All TREE.COM does is grind out a long, slightly confusing textual description. With just two subdirectories it's not so terrible, but with 20 or 30 all you get is an unmanageable scrolling mess. And displaying such a graphic object as a hierarchical tree with words alone is like trying to describe colors to someone who's congenitally blind.

TREE's version of the above subdirectory structure is:

```
DIRECTORY PATH LISTING FOR VOLUME PC MAGAZINE

Path: \DOS

Sub-directories: None


Path: \BIN

Sub-directories: None
```

You can make TREE slightly more useful by adding an /F switch, which will display all the files in all the subdirectories. But even this use of TREE is overshadowed by the far better CHKDSK /V, which also lists all the files on your disk. CHKDSK /V displays full pathnames; TREE /F doesn't. And TREE pads all its listings with unnecessary spaces, which makes it scroll rapidly off your screen. As a bonus, CHKDSK /V adds the standard CHKDSK report detailing the number of files, bytes free, etc. And it displays the hidden files; TREE /F doesn't. Finally, CHKDSK /V is far faster. Chugging through slightly more than 2,000 files on an AT took CHKDSK /V 98 seconds. TREE /F produced an inferior report and took 123 seconds, or 25 percent longer.

When you copy our program, VTREE.COM, into your \BIN directory, the very next thing you should do is type:

```
ERASE \DOS\TREE.COM
```

Incidentally, early versions of TREE contain a nasty bug. When the TREE command in PC-DOS 2.0, 2.1, and 3.0 encounters a directory with an extension, such as UTILS.NEW, it stops in its tracks after it has finished listing any directories below the one with the extension. DOS didn't get around to fixing it until version 3.1.

Earlier TREE versions also don't list files in the root directory when you specify the /F parameter after TREE. The upgraded TREE in DOS versions 3.1 and later also fixes this problem.

Note that in the above example, the full name of the primitive DOS utility that you just expunged was \DOS\TREE.COM rather than just TREE.COM. That's because you can have different versions of similarly named files in different subdirectories. You can even have similarly named subdirectories; if you wanted to (but trust us, you don't) you could have a subdirectory called \DOS and one called \BIN\DOS on the same disk.

For instance, you could rename VTREE.COM to TREE.COM and put it in \BIN. So if you keep the original DOS version in the \DOS subdirectory, your hard disk would then contain files called \DOS\TREE.COM (which is the original DOS version) and \BIN\TREE.COM (which is the renamed version of VTREE.COM). To run the original DOS version, you'd type:

```
\DOS\TREE
```

To run VTREE.COM, which for this example you renamed to TREE.COM, you'd type:

```
\BIN\TREE
```

If you were in the root directory, and you hadn't yet used the PATH command to tell DOS where to look for executable files, and you typed:

```
TREE
```

you wouldn't run either \DOS\TREE or \BIN\TREE; all you'd get is a "Bad command or file name" message. As discussed above, when you type a command like TREE at the DOS prompt, COMMAND.COM first checks whether it's an internal command, and when it discovers it's not, checks the current directory and then a PATH — a specified set of directories — for a file by that name with a COM, EXE, or BAT extension. If \DOS and \BIN aren't yet included in the path, COMMAND.COM won't check in those subdirectories, and won't run either version of TREE.COM.

You can tell COMMAND.COM to check in both of these subdirectories with the command:

```
PATH C:\DOS;C:\BIN
```

or:

```
PATH C:\BIN;C:\DOS
```

The difference between these two is that if the top path is active, DOS will look in the \DOS subdirectory before it looks in \BIN. In the second example it will examine \BIN before \DOS. If DOS finds a TREE file ending in COM, EXE, or BAT, it will stop looking and execute the file. So if the first path is in use, typing TREE will run the DOS version of TREE. If the second path is in use, DOS will find the renamed versic.. of VTREE and run it. If you had files called TREE.COM, TREE.EXE, and TREE.BAT in either subdirectory, DOS would run TREE.COM. It always looks for COM files first, then

EXEs, and finally BATs. But it won't look for filenames with any other extensions, such as data files or program overlays. If you have a version of DOS 3.3 or later, you can use the APPEND command to mimic the PATH command and find any kind of file. If you're using an earlier version, you can purchase a commercial PATH extender like *Filepath* or *File Facility*. But save yourself heartache and upgrade to the most current DOS version available.

It's best to include a PATH command like either of the ones above in your startup AUTOEXEC.BAT file. And if you're using a PATH extender or APPEND, add a separate line in your AUTOEXEC.BAT for it too.

As mentioned above, the SET command can show you the command you entered to customize your prompt. Typing SET on a line by itself will also display the current path setting, as will typing PATH by itself. You can always modify your existing path setting by following the PATH command with the new list of subdirectories, joined together with semicolons.

A smarter technique for adding path settings is to use environment variables. These variables weren't documented until version 3.3, and they don't work at all in version 3.0. And you have to make sure you have enough environment space to accommodate these variables.

The environment is a special area of memory that DOS uses to store important settings like your current PROMPT setting, what directories your path includes, and where to look for your main copy of COMMAND.COM. You can also park variables there by using the SET command, and retrieve them in batch files by wrapping the variable name in percent signs. So if you wrote a small batch file that included just the lines:

```
SET COLOR=BLUE
ECHO %COLOR%
```

the first line of the batch file would insert the string:

```
COLOR=BLUE
```

into the environment, and the second line would look in the environment for the value, replace %COLOR% with BLUE, and display the word:

```
BLUE
```

on screen. If you later typed:

```
SET COLOR=RED
```

and ran a batch file that included the line:

```
ECHO %COLOR%
```

it would print:

RED

To get rid of the COLOR environment variable, just type:

```
SET COLOR=
```

with nothing after the equals sign. At any point you can see all your environment settings by typing:

```
SET
```

at the DOS prompt.

However, DOS sets up a default environment that's only 160 bytes long, and this space fills up quickly. You can make it bigger, but the method varies with the DOS version you're using. Under DOS 2.0 and 2.1 you can patch COMMAND.COM at address ECF to represent the number of 16-byte memory paragraphs that will make up your new environment. (For DOS 2.11 the address is DF3.) DOS 3.0 and 3.1 lets you put a:

```
SHELL [d:][path]COMMAND.COM /E:n /P
```

command in your CONFIG.SYS file, where n is the number of 16-byte *paragraphs*. For versions 3.2 and later, use the same SHELL command but specify the actual number of bytes rather than paragraphs. You can increase the size from the default of 160 bytes up to 32K in DOS 3.2 and 3.3, but the maximum size in earlier versions is 62 paragraphs, or 992 bytes.

Once you've made sure you have enough environment space, create a small batch file called ADDPATH.BAT by getting into DOS, typing in the lines below, pressing the Enter key at the end of each one, and then pressing the F6 key and the Enter key one final time when you're all done. Do it right and you'll get a "1 File(s) copied" message afterwards:

```
COPY CON ADDPATH.BAT
ECHO OFF
IF %1!==! GOTO OOPS
PATH=%PATH%;%1
GOTO END
:OOPS
ECHO Enter the new directory after %0
ECHO that you want to add to your PATH
:END
```

To test it out, assuming you don't already have PATH set, create a simple PATH to your C:\DOS directory with the command:

```
PATH=C:\DOS
```

Then type either PATH or SET to make sure you typed it in properly. To extend the path so it included C:\BIN, you'd ordinarily have to type:

```
PATH=C:\DOS;C:\BIN
```

But if you have ADDPATH.BAT handy, all you have to do is type:

```
ADDPATH C:\BIN
```

Then type SET or PATH again and you'll see the path setting has indeed been extended.

When the PATH statement is short, this doesn't save much typing. But when your path goes all the way across the screen, you'll appreciate it. It works by using an environment setting as a variable. The %PATH% is a variable that tells DOS "look inside the current environment setting and substitute, in place of the %PATH% in the batch file, whatever follows the word PATH=." The technique also uses what is called a replaceable parameter — the %1. When DOS sees this in a batch file, it replaces the %1 with the first word or string of characters you typed on the command line immediately following the name of the batch file.

So if the batch file is called ADDPATH, and at the DOS prompt you typed:

```
ADDPATH HELLO
```

it would replace the %1 with HELLO.

The "IF %1!==! GOTO OOPS" (note the double equals sign) tests to see whether you typed anything in after the name of the batch file. If you did type something in, like C:\BIN, DOS replaces the %1 with C:\BIN and turns the test into:

```
IF C:\BIN!==! GOTO OOPS
```

Now C:\BIN! is clearly not equal to !, so the test fails. However, if you entered nothing after the name of the batch file, %1 would be equal to nothing, and DOS would turn the test into:

```
IF !==! GOTO OOPS
```

Sure enough, ! does equal !, so the batch file will jump to the "label" called :OOPS, where it prints a message providing instructions. (Labels are preceded with colons and don't execute.) This effectively jumps around the "PATH=%PATH%;%1" command if you forgot to enter an additional path extension. DOS will replace the %0 in the line that says "ECHO Enter the new directory after %0" with the name of the batch file itself. This way, if you change the name of the batch file from ADDPATH.BAT to something else, DOS will always display the current name in the instructions.

If you did enter a new subdirectory that you wanted tacked onto the end of your path, DOS would *concatenate* it when it came to the "PATH=%PATH%;%1" line. It would replace the %PATH% with the current path and the %1 with the new subdirectory you just typed in. And it would tack on the semicolon DOS uses to separate subdirectories. If the current path was:

```
PATH C:\DOS
```

and you typed in:

```
ADDPATH C:\BIN
```

you'd end up with:

```
PATH C:\DOS;C:\BIN
```

The equals sign sometimes used after PATH is optional; DOS treats it as a space. Typing:

```
PATH C:\DOS
```

or:

```
PATH=C:\DOS
```

will produce identical results. If you do like to experiment with your path settings, you can always make it easy to reset everything by typing:

```
PATH > OLDPATH.BAT
```

at the DOS prompt before you make any changes. This redirects the environment string into a batch file called OLDPATH.BAT. When you're done changing the PATH, just type:

```
OLDPATH
```

at the DOS prompt to put things back to normal. Sometimes you may need to add directories to your PATH setting temporarily, then get rid of the additions when you're done. You can adapt the process described above by modifying ADDPATH slightly:

```
COPY CON ADDPATH.BAT
ECHO OFF
IF %1!==! GOTO OOPS
SET P1=%PATH%
PATH=%PATH%;%1
GOTO END
:OOPS
ECHO Enter the new directory after %0
```

```
ECHO that you want to add to your PATH
:END
```

Then create another called PATHOLD.BAT that restores the original PATH:

```
ECHO OFF
PATH=%P1%
SET P1=
```

For instance, if you want to add C:\BIN to your existing PATH temporarily, type:

```
ADDPATH C:\BIN
```

just the way you did before. But when you're done, to restore things the way they were before you made the addition, just type:

```
PATHOLD
```

The new "SET P1=%PATH%" line simply creates a dummy variable called P1 that stores the contents of the old PATH, before you make any PATH changes. PATHOLD.BAT then takes the original PATH — stored under the P1 environment variable — and puts things back the way they were, then gets rid of the dummy P1.

The only problem with this is that you have to single-step your way through. If you add one directory and later want to get rid of it and add another one, you have to run PATHOLD before you add the second one. If you don't, ADDPATH will add the second new one onto the first.

PATH Magic

Just about every hard disk user ends up battling the DOS PATH. Since many users keep data directories one level down from the programs that use the data, one way to make life easier is to include a ".." in your PATH. Some users even try starting their own PATH with D:\; .. ; C:\; so DOS can always try to look one level higher no matter where they are in their subdirectory structure.

But what users really need is a PATH editor to let them add or remove subdirectories temporarily. You can create a series of batch files to do just that. To use them, simply type:

```
[d:][path]CHPATH SUBDIR [-B|-E|-DB|-DE|-I]
```

where:

[d:][path]CHPATH is the name of the main batch file
SUBDIR is the subdirectory on which to act

-B will add the specified subdirectory to the beginning of the existing PATH

-E will add the specified subdirectory to the end of the existing PATH

-DB will delete from the current PATH all subdirectories up to and including the specified subdirectory

-DE will delete from the current PATH all subdirectories after the specified subdirectory

-I will let you remove a single subdirectory inside the current PATH

For example, if your PATH is C:\111;C:\222;C:\333; and you entered:

```
CHPATH C:\444 -E
```

you'd end up with C:\111;C:\222;C:\333;C:\444;. If you started with the same PATH but entered:

```
CHPATH C:\444 -B
```

you'd end up with C:\444;C:\111;C:\222;C:\333;. If you started with C:\111;C:\222;C:\333;C:\444; and you entered:

```
CHPATH C:\222 -DB
```

you'd end up with C:\333;C:\444;. If you started with the same C:\111;C:\222;C:\333;C:\444; and you entered:

```
CHPATH C:\222 -DE
```

you'd end up with just C:\111. If your current PATH was C:\111;C:\222;C:\333;C:\444; and you entered

```
CHPATH C:\333 -I
```

you'd end up with just C:\111;C:\222;C:\444;.

You'll need four batch files, the main CHPATH.BAT, CPSET1.BAT, CPSET2.BAT, and CPSET3.BAT to handle the trickier delete-to-beginning and delete-to-end operations. First, CHPATH.BAT:

```
ECHO OFF
REM CHPATH.BAT
IF %2!==! GOTO ERROR
PATH > RESET.BAT
SET M=%1
SET P=%2
IF !%2==!-DB CPSET1 %PATH%
IF !%2==!-db CPSET1 %PATH%
```

```
IF !%2==!-DE CPSET2 %PATH%
IF !%2==!-de CPSET2 %PATH%
IF !%2==!-I CPSET3 %PATH%
IF !%2==!-i CPSET3 %PATH%
SET P=
SET M=
IF !%2==!-B PATH=%1;%PATH%
IF !%2==!-b PATH=%1;%PATH%
IF !%2==!-E PATH=%PATH%;%1
IF !%2==!-e PATH=%PATH%;%1
PATH
GOTO END
:ERROR
ECHO Current path is:
PATH
ECHO Proper syntax is:
ECHO %0 DIRECTORY [-B -E -DB -DE -I]
:END
```

Next, CPSET1.BAT, whose only purpose is to invert the order of the PATH entries:

```
REM CPSET1.BAT
CPSET2 %9;%8;%7;%6;%5;%4;%3;%2;%1;
```

Then CPSET2.BAT:

```
ECHO OFF
REM CPSET2.BAT
SET PATH=
:LOOP
IF !%P%==!-DB PATH=%1;%PATH%
IF !%P%==!-db PATH=%1;%PATH%
IF !%P%==!-DE PATH=%PATH%%1;
IF !%P%==!-de PATH=%PATH%%1;
SHIFT
IF NOT !%1==! IF NOT !%1==!%M% GOTO LOOP
SET M=
SET P=
PATH
```

And finally, CPSET3.BAT:

```
ECHO OFF
REM CPSET3.BAT
SET PATH=
```

```
:LOOP
IF NOT %1==%M% PATH=%PATH%%1;
SHIFT
IF NOT !%1==! GOTO LOOP
SET M=
SET P=
PATH
```

About the only drawback to using the batch programs is that when you want to delete subdirectories you have to type them uppercase exactly the way they appear in the path. So if a subdirectory is C:\SK and you type c:\sk or just \SK they won't work properly. Also note that as the programs are currently written you can't use the delete-to-end or delete-to-beginning functions successfully if you have more than nine subdirectories in your PATH.

Note: CHPATH.BAT creates a file called RESET.BAT. To reset your PATH the way it was before you made any changes, just type RESET.

Some of the assembly language utilities on the accompanying disk can make the process a bit easier. But DOS can do it all for you too.

Keeping subdirectory names short saves environment space and wear and tear on your typing fingers. It's also a good idea because the CD command can't handle more than 63 characters. If you absolutely can't live without long subdirectory names, and you run out of environment space, you can always use the SUBST command as shorthand in your AUTOEXEC.BAT file. Subdirectories really work pretty much like individual disk drives. SUBST blurs the distinction.

If you have a tangle of subdirectories like:

```
C:\ABLE\BAKER\CHARLIE\FOXTROT
```

you could issue the SUBST command:

```
SUBST E: C:\ABLE\BAKER\CHARLIE\FOXTROT
```

before you issue the PATH command. Then, the short path command:

```
PATH E:
```

will actually tell DOS to include C:\ABLE\BAKER\CHARLIE\FOXTROT in its path searches. This method cuts down on your typing and lets you treat long subdirectories the exact same way you'd treat drives. If you type:

```
DIR E:
```

you'll see what files are in C:\ABLE\BAKER\CHARLIE\FOXTROT. You can also use this trick to copy files in and out of that subdirectory. And you can log into it just by typing E: at the prompt. Note that you can't use a higher drive letter than E: unless you warn DOS beforehand in your CONFIG.SYS file with the LASTDRIVE= command. And you can create such drives temporarily. The command:

```
SUBST E: /D
```

will undo the substitution. But, if you're going to use this trick, read all the warnings in the SUBST section of the DOS manual. Commands like LABEL and BACKUP can cause problems with it. And SUBST is magic with programs like *WordStar* 3.x that can find their overlays on specified drives but not subdirectories. Notice that each of the subdirectories is preceded by a drive letter, C:. If all you ever do is use your C: hard disk, and never log onto a RAMdisk or a floppy, you can omit this. A path such as:

```
PATH \DOS;\BIN
```

would work just as well.

You should include the drive letters, however, because if you really want to boost performance you'll create a RAMdisk and copy your most frequently used programs — and all your long batch files — into it.

The DOS RAMdisk

As every power user knows, a RAMdisk is a section of memory that some software has tricked DOS into treating like an additional physical disk drive. RAMdisks are far faster than even the fastest hard disks, since they contain no moving parts. The tradeoff, of course, is that RAMdisks are volatile; all data stored on them vanishes when you turn the power off or when the current in your wall socket hiccups.

To install the free RAMdisk that comes with later versions of DOS, make sure the DOS VDISK.SYS program is in your C:\DOS subdirectory, and include this line in your CONFIG.SYS file:

```
DEVICE=C:\DOS\VDISK.SYS
```

This command will set up a virtual drive D: with 64K of available space. If you want a larger RAMdisk, you can specify the number of bytes at the end of the command. For example,

```
DEVICE=C:\DOS\VDISK.SYS 360
```

would set up a drive D: that's the same size as a standard double-sided floppy. However, IBM won't let you DISKCOPY into it. RAMdisk software from other manufacturers, such as AST's *SUPERDRV*, will let you use the DISKCOPY command. IBM's VDISK driver will let you create multiple virtual disks, configure the sector size and number of directory entries, and, in the most recent versions of DOS, use extended memory.

The trick is to figure out which major programs, batch files, and utilities you use frequently and insert a cascade of commands in your AUTOEXEC.BAT file to copy those files to the RAMdisk. Then make sure your path includes this new drive. In the example used above, the path would now look like:

```
PATH=D:\;C:\DOS;C:\BIN
```

Putting D:\ first means that the root directory of the RAMdisk is the first place DOS will look.

It's smart to put all your batch files except the tiniest ones into a RAMdisk, since batch files execute one slow line at a time. Watching even a hard disk grind its way through a medium sized batch file is no fun.

Let's say you use three programs very often — CHKDSK.COM, a color-setting and screen-clearing program called C.COM, and BROWSE.COM. Your AUTOEXEC.BAT file would contain the lines:

```
COPY C:\CHKDSK.COM D: > NUL
COPY C:\C.COM D: > NUL
COPY C:\BROWSE.COM D:Z.COM > NUL
```

The > NUL at the end of each line gets rid of the "1 File(s) copied" messages. Notice that the third line not only copies BROWSE.COM to D: but also renames it to Z.COM. That's because Z is a lot easier to type than BROWSE since Z is one letter long and happens to be at the lower lefthand corner of the keyboard.

Protecting AUTOEXEC.BAT and CONFIG.SYS

Most software packages these days either come with instructions that suggest creating one or more dedicated subdirectories, or have their own installation programs that do it automatically.

However, these automatic installers can be downright dangerous. Some replace your versions of AUTOEXEC.BAT and CONFIG.SYS with their own, when they really ought to modify yours rather than trashing them. Others hide files, which makes it difficult to remove subdirectories.

You can prevent your AUTOEXEC.BAT and CONFIG.SYS files from being written over by using the TYPE or BROWSE commands or your word processor to examine the program's BAT and installation programs. If you see a command that simply copies that program's versions of AUTOEXEC.BAT and CONFIG.SYS to your hard disk, you can use your word processor to adapt your existing files rather than watch them get trashed.

A smart idea is to maintain a small subdirectory called \BAKUP containing nothing but your current versions of COMMAND.COM, AUTOEXEC.BAT, and CONFIG.SYS. Every time you update one of these, copy it to the \BAKUP subdirectory. Then when a program installs itself destructively you can type:

```
COPY \BAKUP \
```

This is shorthand — you could have said:

```
COPY \BAKUP\*.* \
```

Or, you can log into the root directory and just type:

```
COPY BAKUP
```

DOS thinks that when you tell it to perform a task such as copying or deleting and you specify just the name of the subdirectory, you are asking it to do something to all the files in the subdirectory. So if you have a \BIN directory and you type:

```
DEL \BIN
```

DOS assumes you want to wipe out every file in the subdirectory just as if you had typed:

```
DEL \BIN\*.*
```

In both cases it will warn you in its quirky way with the message:

```
Are you sure (Y/N)?
```

Keeping duplicates of your important root directory files in a \BAKUP subdirectory is also a good idea if you try to get too tricky. While DOS usually pauses to warn you if you try to delete all the files in a directory, you can sidestep the protection. Execute either of the commands:

```
FOR %A IN (*.*) DO DEL %A
```

or:

```
ECHO Y | DEL *.*
```

and DOS will merrily wipe out every last nonhidden file. The syntax for the above FOR command is correct if you type it in at the DOS prompt (be careful if you try this). But if you want to use it in a batch file replace both single % signs with double %% signs (and be even more careful).

Hidden Files

Hidden files can be a real problem with subdirectories. Few users keep the same subdirectory structure for very long. Most end up cutting and pasting branches of the tree as they get more sophisticated or desperately short of space, or when they replace applications packages with newer ones.

The RD command removes subdirectories, but only when they're empty. If you've left even one file or lower-level subdirectory in them, you won't be able to expunge the subdirectory.

Some programs, in spiteful attempts at copy protection, install hidden files that you can't see in normal directory searches. If you try to remove a subdirectory that you think is empty, and you see this message:

```
Invalid path, not directory,
or directory not empty
```

first check to see if you've left any subdirectories branching off the one you want to get rid of. If so, you have to move or erase the contents of those lower-level subdirectories first, then use the RD command to remove them.

If there aren't any files or lower-level subdirectories, some nasty application has probably planted a hidden file there. You can check on this by executing the CHKDSK /V | MORE command, which will show all the files on your disk a screenful at a time, including the hidden ones. Then use the ATTR.COM or UNHIDE.COM programs on the accompanying disk to unhide the file. You can also use ATTR.COM or the accompanying HIDE.COM programs to make any program hidden.

To hide a file like AUTOEXEC.BAT, type:

```
HIDE AUTOEXEC.BAT
```

To unhide it, type:

```
UNHIDE AUTOEXEC.BAT
```

Warning: Some commercial software packages not only hide files but scramble the arrangement of DOS sectors beneath the hidden file. If at all possible, always try to use the deinstallation program that came with the software package before using a utility like UNHIDE or ATTR to reveal the program so you can erase it.

Changing the file attributes to "hidden" or "read-only" will prevent programs from overwriting them. These utilities use function 43H of INT 21 to first check the existing attribute byte, and change only the bits that need modification. ORing the existing value with 1 makes it read-only; ORing it with 2 makes the file hidden. ANDing it with FE takes away the read-only attribute; ANDing it with FD unhides the file. This way it leaves other attributes (system or archive) as they were.

Unfortunately, you can't use function 43 to change the attribute byte of subdirectories or volume labels, so this won't let you meddle with those.

Be careful when hiding files *en masse*. If you issued a command such as:

```
FOR %A in (*.*) DO HIDE %A
```

you'd end up with a whole directory of hidden files. You won't be able to use a similar command to unhide them all at once, since DOS won't see any files to unhide. You'll have to unhide all your files individually. The safest thing to do if you hide lots of files is first create a master file listing all the filenames, and put this master file in another directory or on another disk. If you're on drive C: you could use a command like:

```
DIR > B:C-HIDDEN.LST
```

Making all your root directory files hidden may look interesting, but it can confuse anyone else who tries to work with your system. Making them read-only will prevent other programs from changing (or deleting) them, but you'll still see them in normal DIR searches.

Some awful installation programs change things as they proceed. They may rename a driver file on the original disk or delete files once they've copied them to a hard disk. If the installation process is interrupted, or if it's so dumb that it doesn't know when something's gone wrong, you may have trouble reinstalling things later.

Another clever way to prevent having software packages replace or otherwise modify AUTOEXEC.BAT is to make your AUTOEXEC.BAT tiny and have it run another start-up batch file with a different name that does all the real work. This way if something clobbers the file on your disk named AUTOEXEC.BAT, it won't hurt your real startup file.

To do this, just put the following two lines in your AUTOEXEC.BAT:

```
ECHO OFF
SETPATH STARTUP
```

All this does is execute another batch file called SETPATH.BAT:

```
SET NORMPATH=C:\DOS;C:\UTIL;C:\
PATH %NORMPATH%
%1
```

SETPATH.BAT sets the path, and then executes the STARTUP.BAT file, since its %1 replaceable parameter refers to the word STARTUP in the last line of the AUTOEXEC.BAT file.

The STARTUP.BAT file contains all commands you normally would have placed in an AUTOEXEC.BAT file:

```
PROMPT $P$G
PRINT /D:PRN /Q:32
CARDFILE C:\UTIL\CARDFILE.TXT
DOSKEY
CTYPE /MA
SPEEDUP
```

There are several advantages to this technique:

- The AUTOEXEC.BAT file is simple to recreate if it is destroyed or inadvertently modified.
- The PATH command is in its own separate batch file, making it easy to change if directories are added or removed.
- The SETPATH.BAT file can quickly restore the default path if it has been changed.
- By creating a batch file like ADDPATH.BAT:

```
PATH %NORMPATH%;%1
```

  it's easy to add a new directory to the path temporarily, and then restore it later with SETPATH.BAT. Don't try this with buggy DOS 3.0 however.

- If all memory resident programs are removed by utilities such as IN-STALL/REMOVE, running STARTUP.BAT restores the memory resident programs as they were at power-on time.

Another ingenious protection solution is to change COMMAND.COM so it looks for a file with a name other than AUTOEXEC.BAT. In fact, the first file COMMAND.COM tries to execute doesn't even have to end in .BAT. See the sidebar "Booting Up With BERNIE" for details.

Subdirectory Navigation

It's easy to create new subdirectories and move around inside existing ones if you have the right tools handy and follow a few simple rules.

The first rule is to remember that when you want to move up — toward the root directory — all you have to do is type:

```
CD ..
```

(or CD ..) to jump to each successive parent directory. However, when you finally land in the root directory, you can't move up any more levels, trying to do so will produce an "Invalid directory" message.

It is especially easy to back out to the root directory by using the F3 key. If you're in a subdirectory five levels deep called:

```
LEV1\LEV2\LEV3\LEV4\LEV5
```

(you of course will be able to tell this by looking at the C:\LEV1\LEV2\LEV3\LEV4\LEV5: prompt that your PROMPT $P: command displays) and you want to jump back to the root directory, you can do this the easy way, by typing:

```
CD \
```

or, you can jump upward a level at a time by typing:

```
CD ..
```

once and then tapping the F3 key four more times. Each time you do, DOS will repeat the earlier command, and since that command is CD .. it will bounce you rapidly root-ward.

To move in the other direction, down from the root directory to LEV5, you could of course simply type:

```
CD \LEV1\LEV2\LEV3\LEV4\LEV5
```

However, you can't type:

```
CD \LEV5
```

because that would tell DOS to jump you into a subdirectory called \LEV5 that was just one level down from the root directory. The real name of the \LEV5 subdirectory above is not just \LEV5; it's \LEV1\LEV2\LEV3\LEV4\LEV5.

Another way to get from the root directory to there is by using the relative version of the CD command to bounce you down one level at a time. Note that since DOS keeps track of each subdirectory by its full pathname rather than by just its particular branch on the tree, you could have a path like:

```
C:\SHARE\AND\SHARE\ALIKE
```

since the subdirectory:

```
C:\SHARE
```

is utterly different from:

```
C:\SHARE\AND\SHARE
```

One is a single level down from the root directory, while the other is three levels down. However, having similar names like this is confusing, and is a bad idea for an important reason you'll see later.

To go from the root to the lowest branch one level at a time, you'd type:

```
CD SHARE
CD AND
CD SHARE
CD ALIKE
```

When you're on one branch of a tree it's easy to bounce around from one subdirectory to another on the same level. If you have a tree that looks like this:

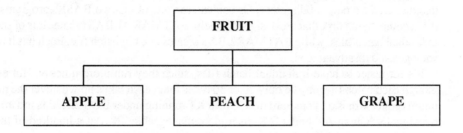

and you're currently in \FRUIT\APPLE and you want to jump to \FRUIT\GRAPE, you can type in:

```
CD ..\GRAPE
```

since the .. is shorthand for the parent directory (\FRUIT). But jumping from one deep branch of your subdirectory structure to a completely different branch can be a bad typist's nightmare.

If you're currently logged into:

```
\FRUIT\PEACH
```

and you want to jump to:

```
\PROGS\STAR\VER3\MEMOS\MERGER
```

you'd normally have to type in:

```
CD \PROGS\STAR\VER3\MEMOS\MERGER
```

Awful. But there's a far easier trick. If your hard disk is set up properly you can simply type:

```
MERGER
```

and DOS will zap you there.

The trick is to create either a slate of small batch files — or one huge batch file — to do all the switching. If you had a batch file called MERGER.BAT on your hard disk, in a subdirectory included in your path, with the contents:

```
CD \PROGS\STAR\VER3\MEMOS\MERGER
```

typing MERGER would execute that batch file, which would in turn execute the proper thorny CD command. This is why it's a good idea to have subdirectories that avoid confusingly similar names. You can create a new batch file every time you issue an MD command to create a new subdirectory. Or you can run one of the two BASIC programs on the accompanying disk that are designed to help. BATMAKR1.BAS creates lots of small individual batch files, while BATMAR2.BAS creates one big batch file. Each has its advantages and disadvantages.

It's far faster to have individual batch files, since they run more quickly. But even though each batch file may be only 20 or 30 bytes long, each takes up whatever the minimum cluster size is on your hard disk. On an XT running under DOS 2.X, this is a mind-bending 4K. On an AT under 3.X, its a more manageable 2K. Put a hundred of these small files on your hard disk and you start chewing up valuable real estate.

The advantage of using one big file is that it takes up far less space. The severe disadvantage is that it executes ponderously. This is because one big batch file has to test your input and match it against all the subdirectories on your disk to see which one to switch to. Batch files execute one slow line at a time, so on a slow XT hard disk the process can take ten or 20 seconds if the subdirectory you want is at the very bottom of the list of tests. If you are tight for space and want to use the one-big-file method, put a command in your AUTOEXEC.BAT file to copy this subdirectory switcher to a RAMdisk, and run it from there.

The other real advantage of having small individual files is that they're more forgiving of typing mistakes. If you tell the long batch file to switch to a subdirectory that doesn't exist, it has to check the one you entered against its entire list, which means chugging its way one line at a time through every test. And, while the one long batch file does at least check for all uppercase and all lowercase entries, it doesn't test for mixtures of upper- and lowercase. It could handle user input such as:

```
merger
```

or:

```
MERGER
```

but not Merger, or MErger (a common typing mistake) or something like MeRgEr. That's because this method uses replaceable parameters, and DOS retains the case of your typing exactly. With the individual file technique, you're typing in a command (the name of a file actually) rather than a replaceable parameter. DOS automatically translates commands into all uppercase for you. Use the shorter individual system if at all possible.

Both versions work from a list of subdirectories you create by typing:

```
CHKDSK /V | FIND "Dir" > TEMPFILE
```

The /V switch tells CHKDSK to list all the files on your disk, including subdirectories (which are simply files that DOS codes a special way). DOS then pipes the CHKDSK output through its FIND filter, discarding every line that doesn't have the letters "Dir" in them. This eliminates all conventional files and blank lines, as well as the normal CHKDSK report on the number of hidden files and bytes free.

The longer version creates a single BAT file to handle all the subdirectory switching. If all you had on your hard disk were a root directory and two subdirectories one level down, \DOS and \BIN, the contents of S.BAT would look something like:

```
ECHO OFF
IF %1!==! GOTO ERROR2
IF %1==DOS goto DOS
IF %1==dos goto DOS
IF %1==BIN goto BIN
IF %1==bin goto BIN
GOTO ERROR1
:DOS
CD C:\DOS
GOTO END
:BIN
CD C:\BIN
GOTO END
:ERROR1
ECHO Subdirectory %1 not found.
ECHO Try again.
GOTO END
:ERROR2
ECHO You must enter a subdirectory
ECHO name after %0
:END
```

Both versions require that you have CHKDSK.COM and FIND.EXE on your current directory, or in a subdirectory that you've included in your path. Once you've run the CHKDSK/V command mentioned above, run BATMAKR2.BAS to create the long S.BAT file. If you enter only the name of the batch file you just created, S, with no sub-directory after it, the line:

```
IF %1!==! GOTO ERROR2
```

will jump to to the ERROR2 error message. The %0 in this message is a special replaceable parameter that prints the name of the batch file itself in place of the %0. If you change the name of the batch file to something like SWITCH.BAT, this device will handle the new name.

BATMAKR2 automatically creates both a lowercase and an uppercase test. If you entered:

```
S DOS
```

or:

```
S dos
```

either would jump the program to the :DOS label. The line immediately following the label switches to the \DOS subdirectory and then jumps the program to the :END label so it exits. There are other faster ways to exit, such as having the batch file execute another short batch file, but the delay isn't all that bad on a RAMdisk, and you really shouldn't run this on anything else.

If you enter a subdirectory name that's not in the list of tests at the beginning of the program, you'll jump to the :ERROR1 label, which uses the %1 replaceable parameter to tell you it couldn't find the directory you specified.

You could adapt this process so that you jump directly to labels that are the same as your subdirectory names. Batch file labels are not case-sensitive, so you don't have to use any case tests at all. The problem with these is that if you make a typing mistake or enter a directory for which there is no label, DOS just prints a "Label not found" message and aborts the batch file. See the Chapter 10 on batch files for details.

BATMAKR1.BAS is shorter, and creates shorter files that work far faster than the long S.BAT. After you run it, to change to \BIN you'd just type BIN.

These programs don't offer any fancy way to jump back to the root directory. After all, CD\ isn't that hard to type. And if you're really rabid about it, you can always create a ROOT.BAT batch file that executes this for you.

But how do you know what directories are on your disk? Simple. Just redirect the output of VTREE into a file called VTREE.PIC with the command:

```
VTREE > VTREE.PIC
```

and then create a small batch file called V.BAT:

```
COPY CON V.BAT
BROWSE VTREE.PIC
```

Press the Enter key after each line, and when you're finished, press the F6 function key and then the Enter key one more time.

Redirect the output of VTREE into VTREE.PIC every time you create a new subdirectory or remove an existing one. Then, assuming BROWSE.COM and V.BAT are in a subdirectory that you've included in your PATH, each time you type:

```
V
```

you'll see an instant graphic representation of your subdirectory tree structure. You can use the arrow and PgUp/PgDn keys to move around in the tree. Pressing Esc will return you to DOS where you can switch to the target subdirectory by using one of the BAT-MAKR programs described above.

If you have *SideKick*, an even better adaptation of this method is to use *SideKick*'s notepad as a window that displays the VTREE.PIC file as the default. Store VTREE.PIC in your \BIN subdirectory. Bring up *SideKick*'s main menu, and type F7 or S for the setup menu. Type in \BIN\VTREE.PIC as the new Notefile name and press F2 to save this as the default. Then whenever you pop up *SideKick* and select the notepad, the graphic representation will jump onto the screen. Press QG to turn on the graphics line characters that connect the subdirectories.

Once you've created a lot of individual switcher files, make sure that whenever you create a new subdirectory, you also create a batch file (which goes in \BIN or \BAT) that simply contains the full pathname of the subdirectory with a CD\ prefix. So if you're adding a new directory called 1\2\3\4\5, create a batch file called 5.BAT:

```
CD \1\2\3\4\5
```

and put this batch file into \BIN or \BAT. Then, just type 5 to jump directly into your \1\2\3\4\5 directory.

You'll obviously have a problem with this if your disk contains two subdirectories with similar names, such as \ACCOUNT\1989\TAX and \ACCOUNT\1990\TAX. In this case you'd have to either change one of the names slightly, or forego this technique.

Some users feel this is too wasteful, since each file, no matter how small, can take up 4K on an XT or 2K on an AT. However, this is a small price to pay for ease of tree-hopping. You could also use the short utilities UP.COM, DOWN.COM, and NEXT.COM on the accompanying disk to move you effortlessly around your subdirectory tree.

UP.COM is a lot like the command CD.. except that if you keep tapping CD.. you'll eventually get to the root directory and receive the "Invalid directory" message mentioned earlier. When UP.COM reaches the root directory it just sits there silently. DOWN.COM takes you in the other direction, away from the root. NEXT.COM moves you sideways. Try them. You'll like them. NEXT is especially useful when you type it in once and then just lean on the F3 and Enter keys to meander up and down the branches of your subdirectory tree.

You can also create four batch files that work almost as well — UP.BAT, DOWN.BAT, NEXT.BAT, and ROOT.BAT. UP.BAT lets you move to a parent directory — the one above the current directory — by typing UP and pressing Enter. DOWN.BAT moves you down one level. For example, to go to a subdirectory called DOS located one level below the current directory, just type DOWN DOS. Type NEXT if you want to move over to another directory on the same level — one that branches off the same parent directory that you're currently logged into. Finally, type ROOT to return to the root directory.

Here's UP.BAT:

```
ECHO OFF
CD..
```

DOWN.BAT is a little more complex:

```
ECHO OFF
IF %1!==! GOTO OOPS
CD %1
GOTO END
:OOPS
ECHO You have to specify where you want to move down.
:END
```

This is NEXT.BAT:

```
ECHO OFF
IF %1!==! GOTO OOPS
CD..\%1
GOTO END
:OOPS
ECHO You have to specify where you want to move over.
:END
```

And this is ROOT.BAT:

```
ECHO OFF
CD\
```

When using DOWN.BAT or NEXT.BAT, be sure to enter the names of the subdirectory where you want to end up. If you don't specify one, the batch file will ask where you want to go.

If you're a diehard power user, you may think these programs are silly. All these batch files really do is type in the CD commands that you can rattle off in your sleep. But they can be helpful for new or casual users. On the other hand, unless something is unusually complex and bizarre, it's always better to learn how to do something the real way than to learn just the shortcut. If all you learn is to type UP and you have to move to someone else's system, all typing UP will do is produce an error message. The bottom-line answer is that these programs may help someone get started, but once he or she becomes proficient, it's better to master the the real thing.

The following HOME.BAT batch file does a very interesting trick:

```
ECHO OFF
IF %1!==! GOTO CHANGE
SET HOMEDIR=%1
:CHANGE
IF %HOMEDIR%!==! GOTO OOPS
CD %HOMEDIR%
GOTO END
:OOPS
```

```
ECHO Enter a full path after %0
:END
```

If you specify a subdirectory path after the word HOME, it will set the environment variable HOMEDIR to that path and change to that directory for you. Then if you go wandering off through your tree structure you'll move back to the subdirectory you specified earlier simply by typing HOME by itself.

The main problem with this is that you have to specify an absolute path rather than a relative one. If you're in \DOS and you want to jump to \DOS\BAT you can normally do it with the command:

```
CD BAT
```

But if you want to specify this directory with HOME.BAT, you have to do it by typing:

```
HOME \DOS\BAT
```

You can't just type:

```
HOME BAT
```

This is because typing CD BAT will move you from \DOS to \DOS\BAT only when you happen to be in \DOS. If you're in \BIN and you type CD BAT, DOS will think you want to switch to \BIN\BAT and this directory probably doesn't exist.

You also have to make sure that a copy of HOME.BAT is in a subdirectory that your path knows about. And you have to set it properly the first time you use it. If you haven't entered anything after HOME and you type HOME by itself, the batch file will simply print a message telling you to enter something next time.

Also, because of a DOS bug, you can't use HOME.BAT with version 3.0, because it has trouble with environment variables.

Of course the best navigation tool of all is RN.COM, especially when coupled with DR.COM. To use RN and DR, just type RN/I to install the program. Then, whenever you want to see, change, or move around your subdirectory structure, type RN at the DOS prompt and follow the directions onscreen. Pressing F10 will load DR.COM (if it's handy), which makes this even more useful, since DR will let you examine, rename, move, or delete any file.

Finding Files

Users have their own favorite ways to find files buried deep inside a long-forgotten subdirectory. The SEARCH and WHERE programs on the accompanying disk can help. But by executing a simple FINDFILE.BAT batch file you can have DOS do it:

```
ECHO OFF
IF %1!==! GOTO OOPS
ECHO NOW SEARCHING DIRECTORIES FOR "%1"
CHKDSK /V | FIND "%1" | MORE
GOTO END
:OOPS
ECHO Enter a filespec (or part of one) after %0
:END
```

FINDFILE exploits the /V feature of CHKDSK.COM. The /V option lists all files in all subdirectories, but you wouldn't know this from some of the early DOS manuals, which describe it with meaningless remarks like saying it will "display a series of messages indicating its progress, and provide more detailed information about the errors it finds." The more recent editions of the manual are a little clearer.

Adding a /V switch makes it a snap to search for a particular file. FINDFILE pipes the output of CHKDSK /V through the FIND.EXE and MORE.COM filters, so you have to have these DOS utilities on the same subdirectory as FINDFILE.BAT or in a directory your path knows about.

If you wanted to search for BASICA.COM, for instance, you would simply type:

```
FINDFILE BASICA
```

If you typed:

```
FINDFILE BASIC
```

the batch file would locate both BASIC.COM and BASICA.COM, and any other filename with the capital letters BASIC in it. You may also use parts of names. Typing:

```
FINDFILE ASICA
```

would find BASICA.COM. This comes in handy if you want to look for files with the same extensions. Enter:

```
FINDFILE .COM
```

and you'll see all your COM files. Remember to enter capital letters only. And don't put quotes around the filenames or parts of filenames you want to find — the batch file will do this for you automatically. FINDFILE won't display a special message telling you no matches were found if it comes up empty. But this will be obvious when no matches are displayed on your screen. The only real problem with this is that FINDFILE.BAT is slow, especially on a nearly full hard disk, since it has to pipe hundreds or thousands of filenames through a filter, and create temporary files while it does so. You could redirect the output of CHKDSK /V into a file and adapt FINDFILE so it looks at the existing list of filenames instead of having to recreate the list each time. The tradeoff is that such a list has to be updated frequently, and ends up always being at least a bit out of date.

Moving Files

When users normally move a file from one subdirectory to another, they first copy the file with the COPY command and then use ERASE to delete the original. Or they write a short batch file to do it:

```
COPY %1 %2
ERASE %1
```

The problem with such a batch file is that if an incorrect destination is specified, it can fail to make the copy but then go ahead and erase the original anyway. A better way is to use one of the utilities on the accompanying disk. Or you could try the following MOVEIT.BAT batch file:

```
ECHO OFF
IF NOT %2! == ! GOTO TEST
ECHO You must specify what to move
ECHO and where to move it to, eg:
ECHO %0 CHKDSK.COM \DOS
GOTO END
:TEST
IF NOT EXIST %2\%1 GOTO COPY
ECHO %1 is already in %2
ECHO To prevent overwriting %1, press
ECHO Ctrl-Break right now. Otherwise
PAUSE
:COPY
COPY %1 %2\%1>NUL
IF NOT EXIST %2\%1 GOTO ERROR
ERASE %1
GOTO END
:ERROR
ECHO Error in destination specified, or
ECHO the file to be moved is not in
CD
:END
```

MOVEIT.BAT starts by checking to see if you entered the correct number of parameters, and gives you a help message if you didn't. It then copies the file, using

%2\%1 so you don't have to spell out the name of the file in both locations (wildcards will work). However, this limits you a bit, since you have to be in the directory of the file you are trying to copy. (You could modify it to COPY %1 %2 if you like, which would allow you to copy files without having to first log into those files' subdirectory — but you would have to spell out the name of the file in both places.) Finally, it erases the original file only if it finds the new one.

It's smart to confirm that the copy was indeed made before deleting the original. But versions of DOS earlier than 3.0 will have problems with IF EXIST tests and paths.

MOVEIT.BAT checks to make sure the file isn't already at the destination subdirectory before you copy it, which prevents you from accidentally overwriting files. If you see a message warning you that you're about to obliterate an existing file, just press Ctrl-Break and then the Y key to abandon the process. Otherwise, press any key to proceed.

Fine-Tuning Your Hard Disk System

While DOS limits the number of files you can shoehorn into the root directory, and smart users know to keep their root directories small, the number of files in each of your subdirectories is limited only by the amount of space on your disk.

But it's not wise to let your subdirectories get too big, unless you have an easy way to back them up.

The DOS BACKUP and RESTORE commands aren't very slick, but they're free and can split large files up and spread them over several disks. You can back up incrementally, by having BACKUP copy only files created or changed after a certain date, or modified since the last time you backed up. You can tell BACKUP to dig down into your subdirectory structure and overwrite earlier versions or add a new version along with the old.

But, BACKUP should format brand new disks automatically. And it changes backed-up programs slightly so you can't just run them unless you first RESTORE them. You have to be careful (and use the /P switch) when you're restoring files backed up with earlier DOS versions so you don't write the wrong system files onto your hard disk. DOS 3.3 and later versions are careful about this; earlier ones weren't.

Because of all these potential problems, many users keep their subdirectories small enough so each can be copied onto a single floppy disk. And they're starting to discover the terrific DOS 3.2 XCOPY command as a better way to create backups. This obviously won't work with giant files. If you work with large files, you have to either grit your teeth and use BACKUP, or buy a tape drive or Bernoulli Box.

Do get into the habit of backing up regularly. The morning you turn your system on and hear a sound like a wrench in a blender, you'll be glad you did.

Backing up just the files you changed or added recently is better than not backing up at all, but when your hard disk goes south, you'll have to spend days putting all the little puzzle pieces back together. It's a good stopgap measure, but nothing beats making complete archive copies of the whole disk.

A real advantage to backing up everything at once is that you'll be able to streamline your file structure and end up working far faster. The routine process of adding to and editing down your files each day ends up sowing little file fragments more or less at random over the surface of your disk.

You should periodically copy all your files to a backup medium (and get rid of the duplicates, BAK versions, and dead data in the process), reformat your hard disk, and then copy everything back. You'll notice an immediate improvement in speed. When you do this, put the subdirectories that you path to at the very beginning of your directory by making sure they're the first ones you copy to the newly formatted disk.

One final pearl is obvious, but bears repeating. Think before you FORMAT. Even though the latest versions of DOS make you type in a Y and then press the Enter key before going ahead and wiping everything out, late at night you may misinterpret the question or press a Y when you meant N, or have some aberrant and lethal combination of JOIN, APPEND, and SUBST bubbling away under the surface that steers an innocent floppy request into a jolt of panic. (And never run RECOVER, unless you're really desperate, since this will bollix up everything and turn your hard disk structure and all the files on it into anonymous mush.)

A few seconds into the formatting process the hard disk FATs and directories get zeroed out, and any attempt at resurrection is only a best guess. It is possible to bring much of your data back to life with a utility like Mace's or Norton's, especially if you let Mace park a copy of your FAT ahead of time. But don't tempt fate.

If you're working on something time-sensitive and critically important, stop frequently while you're working and make a working copy to a floppy. It is possible to corrupt a hard disk if you're writing to it and the local power company decides that moment would be a good one to switch generators. You can set up a batch file to automate the process. Otherwise you might end up spending the rest of the evening patching together little shards of your work that you've fished out of the magnetic murk.

If you notice that performance is degrading, or hear the percussive rhythm of repeated read retries, run Norton's DISKTEST program. This takes a few minutes, but can ferret out developing programs and zap out bad sectors better than DOS can. And if Norton reports grief, back up everything pronto and hie down to your dealer. When hard disks start whimpering they go downhill real fast. Hard disk problems never just go away.

Caveat Emptor

If you don't yet own a hard disk, remember, no matter what kind of hard drive you're considering, don't buy yourself trouble. Make sure it's (1) safe, and (2) fast. While no hard disk is immune to potential disaster, some are more fragile than others. Since most users back up their data infrequently, a hard disk problem can wipe out weeks of work.

Don't buy a hard disk unless its heads *retract* automatically when you turn the power off. Otherwise, they'll just drop down to the disk and take a bite out of whatever data's there.

And don't get stuck with a low-speed disk in a high-speed system. While you can measure hard disk performance many different ways, the most common single gauge is *average access time* in milliseconds. The lower the number, the faster the drive. IBM's several different low-performance PC-XT drives score anywhere from 80 to 115 ms. IBM's specification for its far faster PC-AT is 40 ms. or less. Some speed demons are down in the teens.

While other factors can influence speed, average access time is a fairly reliable performance indicator. Take pains *not* to buy a hard drive that's dragging its foot, especially in a computer that runs at a relatively high clock speed.

Booting Up with BERNIE

Everyone knows the first thing DOS does after turning itself on is look for a batch file called AUTOEXEC.BAT and try to run it if it's there, right?

Not if it's busy booting BERNIE.

The mechanism that tries to sniff out the existence of a bootup file is buried in COMMAND.COM. This bootup file doesn't have to be called AUTOEXEC.BAT. In fact, it doesn't even have to end in BAT.

It's easy to change the name of this bootup file to something innocuous like BERNIE. This will prevent others from using the TYPE command to look inside AUTOEXEC.BAT to see what files you use when you start your system. And it will keep snoops at bay by displaying a special message. Here's how:

First, make sure you have copies of COMMAND.COM and AUTOEXEC.BAT stashed safely away, since the process described below alters COMMAND.COM slightly. If you try this and want to put things back to the way they were, all you'll have to do later is copy your old original COMMAND.COM over the patched one, and then copy it and the original AUTOEXEC.BAT back to the root directory.

Put DEBUG.COM and a copy of COMMAND.COM in your root directory. If you've never used DEBUG.COM before, it's on your Supplemental DOS disk, not the main disk.

This process assumes that you normally boot from a system with a C: hard drive, and that you have a subdirectory called C:\DOS. If not, it's pretty simple to figure out how to adapt it. To get the ball rolling, enter:

```
DEBUG COMMAND.COM
```

You should see a hyphen at the left edge of your screen. This is the DEBUG prompt. Type:

```
S 100 5000 "AUTO"
```

and DEBUG should print two pairs of four-digit hexadecimal numbers (hex numbers can be made up of the numerals 0-9 plus the letters A-F), separated by a colon. Ignore the leftmost four digits; they'll vary from system to system and they don't matter here. But note the rightmost four digits; this is where the name \AUTOEXEC.BAT is located inside COMMAND.COM. Now enter:

```
E **** "DOS\BERNIE "
```

but substitute those rightmost four digits in place of the ****. For instance, if DEBUG responded earlier with:

```
   54BA:130F
```

after you entered the line beginning with the S, you would enter E 130F
"DOS\BERNIE   " there.

Note that you must include two blank spaces between BERNIE and the
rightmost quote mark. This is because \DOS\BERNIE is two characters shorter
than the \AUTOEXEC.BAT that appears inside COMMAND.COM. You have
to pad over all existing letters in AUTOEXEC.BAT with spaces if your new
name isn't as long.

Then type W and press the Enter key, and type Q and press the Enter key.

Finally, copy your AUTOEXEC.BAT routine to your \DOS subdirectory and
name it BERNIE, and then delete it from the root directory, with the commands:

```
   COPY AUTOEXEC.BAT \DOS\BERNIE
   DEL \AUTOEXEC.BAT
```

You can then create a phony AUTOEXEC.BAT file in your root directory that
contains the line:

```
   PROMPT Access Denied$_
```

If another user tries to run AUTOEXEC.BAT, all he'll get is a screen full of
"Access Denied" prompts. You can even adapt the above technique to patch
COMMAND.COM so that it changes the DIR command most people will try to
use to see what's on your disk. Enter:

```
   DEBUG COMMAND.COM
```

and then:

```
   S 100 5000 "DIR" 3
```

(The 3 is important, since the letters DIR are in COMMAND.COM several
times, but you're looking for the only one that's followed immediately by a 3).
DEBUG will print two more pairs of hex numbers separated by a colon. Then
enter:

```
   E **** "DUR"
```

but again, substitute the four rightmost hex digits for the ****. Then type W and
press the Enter key, then Q and Enter, and then reboot. If you type in DIR you'll
get a "Bad command or filename" error. If you type in DUR you'll see your normal directory listing.

A word of caution though — don't mix versions of COMMAND.COM. DOS checks to make sure the version it dealt with originally is not different from one you're trying to use later. That's why you made copies of your originals before you started.

Chapter 4

Hex Class

Ok, this is your chance. If you're fairly new to all this, or if all you want is a thorough mastery of the DOS commands, with a double armload of time-saving tricks and ingenious shortcuts thrown in, turn to the next chapter. Because it's time to talk about binary and hex. You can get by just fine without them. But if you really want to make your system hum, you should know your way around inside. And inside means hex numbers.

It's really not all that difficult; it's just that discussions of 1s and 0s are not inherently absorbing. Still, being a power user means knowing at least a little about all this so that later when we talk about things like binary bit masks (to give you total control over the shift keys on your keyboard) and hexadecimal addresses (to help you recover lost data) you don't just scratch your head and turn on HBO. So here goes. We'll try to make it as painless as possible. And we'll throw in a few surprises you'll like.

There's no such thing as a little bit pregnant, or a little bit dead. You either are or you aren't. Life offers few such absolutes. A hundred people look at a sculpture in an art museum. A third love it. A third hate it. A third look at their watches.

If you watch old Fred Astaire movies you rarely see objects that are all black or all white. Some things are close, but if you look carefully you'll admit that they are 2 percent grey or 98 percent grey. And most things are closer to the middle of the scale.

High-contrast photographic paper, on the other hand, is designed to produce a stark black-on-white image without any greys whatsoever. You put it into a darkroom enlarger and project a normal photographic negative with lots of shadows and grey shades onto it. Anything that's 49.99 percent grey or lighter doesn't trigger the silver salts and remains bright and white; wherever anything is 50 percent grey or darker, however, the paper turns jet black.

The world is analog. A dot of color on a TV screen is produced by a fast-changing wave-shaped signal and can be one of hundreds of thousands of hues and tints. However, the waveform is subject to all kinds of distortion and deterioration; make a copy of a TV show on a VCR and then a copy of the copy, and after a few generations play it back on the same TV set and you'll see the colors and the general sharpness are very different from the original. Each copy chews up the shape of the wave a little; after thousands of copies all you'd have is hissy static and a demonstration of entropy in action.

Computers are digital. A dot on a computer screen is produced by a hard, cold, unchanging numeric value. Create a graphics image on a digital computer and make hundreds of successive copies of it and display the 500th one on the same computer and it will have the exact same colors as the original. When you copy a file containing the data that make up the picture, all the mechanisms involved make sure if the value of the first dot in the file was a 69, it remains a 69. It's easier to pack more information into an analog signal. But if you need precision, you have to sacrifice a little quantity for quality. And when you're dealing with computers, the integrity of your data is sacrosanct.

The fundamental building block of digital information is a *bit* (short for *binary digit*). One bit can't store much information by itself; it has a short menu — on or off, 1 or 0, "high" or "low." But in the right chip at the right time, a single bit can trigger instructions that change or move lots of other bits, and when you start stringing millions of them together incredibly fast, you can get some real work done.

Some people are adept at fudging their way through life, laying down dense fog like a PT boat. But you can't fudge a bit. It's either in one state or the other — one of life's few absolutes. Binary numbering makes a lot of sense on a digital computer, a system made up of hundreds of thousands of interconnected switches that are either on or off. Simple two-position switches can indicate the status of something (like an "occupied" sign on a jet), store data (a W or L is what you really want to know about what your local baseball team did the night before), or execute important decisions (like switching tracks to send Chicago trains either north to Boston or south to Washington). But bits are most useful when arranged in groups of eight called *bytes*. A byte is a convenient way to store eight related pieces of information, such as the condition of eight different status indicators deep in the heart of your main chips. It's also handy for representing a letter, number, or special character such as 1/2 or the symbol for pi. And while chips deal with long binary streams of 1s and 0s, humans prefer friendlier alphabets.

Your system is built to move information in one, two, or four byte chunks — depending on whether you're using an eight-bit, 16-bit, or 32-bit computer — rather than in lots and lots of individual bits. (Actually, some second-level processors, like those used by display adapter boards for EGA-compatible monitors, even work with halves of bytes called *nibbles*, and a base-8 numbering system called *octal*. If you're genuinely interested in EGA sleight-of-hand, you may want to dabble in octal a little later.)

If you noticed that everything so far seems to be divisible by the number 2, you're right. It all leads back to binary. EGAs use four bits to specify colors. PCs rely on a mixture of eight and 16. Systems based on Intel's 80286 chip, such as the PC-AT, can handle 16 from stem to stern. And the latest crop of 80386 powerhouses devour 32 at a single gulp. Users once added extra computer memory in packages of about 64,000 bytes. Today the number has jumped to roughly 256,000 or even four times that.

We all like round numbers. Folks who make it to 100 get on the evening news. The advent of a decade is important enough; we're on the verge of a new century and millenium, and the celebration will undoubtedly be eye-popping, all because of a few well-placed zeros.

The computer industry likes round numbers too. But in this business they should really be called "around" numbers, since the two most common big ones — a K for kilobyte (around a thousand bytes) and M for megabyte (around a million bytes) are actually 1,024 and 1,048,576 respectively.

Inflation is affecting even these numbers. Huge storage devices (optical disks and monstrous hard disks) that can salt away a *gigabyte* (around a billion characters) are appearing on the scene. (Incidentally, the word is pronounced JIG-uh-byte, not GIG-uh-byte, since it comes from the same root as giant and gigantic rather than gargantuan.) And chip makers love to see our reaction when they start talking about the 80386's ability to address a terabyte (around a trillion bytes). (The root for this word, which means monster, was last in the news as "teratogenic" when it described the property of the drug thalidomide to deform offspring.)

One kilobyte is 2^{10} (2 x 2 x 2 x 2 x 2 x 2 x 2 x 2 x 2 x 2). One megabyte is 2^{20}. So when you see a memory board that holds 64K, it actually can juggle 64 x 1,024, or 65,536 bytes. And when someone tells you a PC's 8088 chip can directly handle a megabyte of memory, they mean 1,048,576 rather than just a paltry one million memory locations. However, it's far easier to call these amounts Ks and megs, which everyone does anyway.

Working with binary or hex numbers isn't intrinsically harder than dealing with decimals; it's just that we've all had so much practice with decimal calculations that we're pretty handy with them by now. But play with binary and hex for a while and you'll pick it up pretty fast.

Odds are that we use a decimal (base-10) system because human have ten fingers and toes. So let's count toes. In decimal it's easy. But start with 0 instead of 1 to make it a little less dull.

0
1
2
3
4
5
6
7
8
9

Ten toes, ten digits. At this point you run out of both. Any more and you have to go to double-digits.

Counting in binary is easy too. The decimal system has ten digits to play with. When you run out, you have to start using more than one digit, and you do it by putting a 0 in the column where the single digits were, and a 1 in the next column.

The binary system has two digits to play with, 0 and 1. When you run out, you also put a 0 in the column where the single digits were, and a 1 in the next column. Only you run out a lot sooner. So you have to keep putting 0s in the columns where you just ran out and 1s in the next column over to the left. Counting toes in binary looks like this:

0	(the first number, just as with decimal)
1	(ran out of single digits; shift over one column)
10	
11	(ran out of double-digits; shift again)
100	
101	
110	
111	(that's all the triple-digits; shift one more time)
1000	
1001	(last toe)

People often pad binary numbers out with 0s, so the same counting process could just as easily look like:

```
0000
0001
0010
0011
0100
0101
0110
0111
1000
1001
```

How do you translate a decimal number into binary format? The key is to become comfortable with the first nine powers of 2. Remember that 2^0 is equal to 1.

$$2^8 = 256$$
$$2^7 = 128$$
$$2^6 = 64$$
$$2^5 = 32$$
$$2^4 = 16$$
$$2^3 = 8$$
$$2^2 = 4$$
$$2^1 = 2$$
$$2^0 = 1$$

Look at the binary version of this chart and you'll see an interesting pattern that will make sense in a moment:

$$2^8 = 100000000$$
$$2^7 = 010000000$$
$$2^6 = 001000000$$
$$2^5 = 000100000$$

2^4 = 000010000
2^3 = 000001000
2^2 = 000000100
2^1 = 000000010
2^0 = 000000001

Now pick a number to translate: 13.

The goal is to see which of the powers of 2 make up this number. Consult the chart and look for the biggest number that's equal to or smaller than the one you've picked (13). Obviously the number that fits this description is 8. Since 8 is the fourth one in the chart, the binary version of 13 will have four binary digits, and the leftmost one will be a 1 (although you could stick 0s on the left, since leading 0s don't mean anything in binary just as they don't in decimal; 00000027 is the same in decimal as just plain 27). Then, since you already considered the 8, get rid of it. Subtract it from 13.

1 _ _ _

After subtracting 8 from 13, you're left with 5. Look at the chart again. The next number under 8 is 4. Since you can safely subtract 4 from 5 without ending up with a negative number, put another 1 in the next position over to the right, and subtract the 4 from 5 to leave a remainder of 1.

1 1 _ _

Consult the chart again. The next lower number after 4 is 2. But you can't subtract the 2 from 1 or you'd end up with a negative number. So you'll put a 0 in the next position over.

1 1 0 _

The last number on the chart is 1. You can subtract 1 from the remainder of 1 and still not have a negative number, so put a final 1 in the rightmost position.

1 1 0 1

Decimal 13 is equal to binary 1101.

Another way to look at what you just did is to say 13 is made up of 1 1 0 1

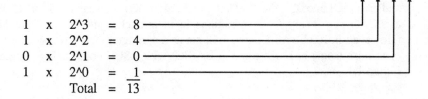

```
1   x   2^3   =   8
1   x   2^2   =   4
0   x   2^1   =   0
1   x   2^0   =   1
        Total =  13
```

Going from binary to decimal is easier. Pick a number: 00110100. Ignore the 0s on the left side (remember, 00000027 in decimal is equal to plain old 27). This leaves a six-digit binary number, 110100. Turn it on its side and put it next to the lowest six entries on the chart. Mutiply as indicated, then add up the result:

$$
\begin{array}{ccccc}
1 & x & 2^5 & = & 32 \\
1 & x & 2^4 & = & 16 \\
0 & x & 2^3 & = & 0 \\
1 & x & 2^2 & = & 4 \\
0 & x & 2^1 & = & 0 \\
0 & x & 2^0 & = & \underline{0} \\
& & \text{Total} & = & 52
\end{array}
$$

You don't really need the chart. You do need to remember the sequence of 1, 2, 4, 8, 16, 32, 64, 128, 256. Then whenever you see a binary number, just count over from the right, and in your head say "that's no 1s plus no 2s plus a 4 (subtotal=4) plus no 8s plus a 16 (subtotal 20) plus a 32 (total 52)." It's easier than it sounds.

Pattern Recognition

While your system can deal with 256 different characters, all it's really doing is handling 256 different numeric values. In one of the only fairly successful attempts to standardize anything on the PC, IBM adopted (and added to) a character-numbering system called ASCII (pronounced as-kee, and standing for the American Standard Code for Information Interchange). In every ASCII file a capital A has a value of decimal 65, a capital B 66, a lowercase a 97, a lowercase b 98, etc.

Your keyboard lets you type 95 characters directly — 26 uppercase and 26 lowercase letters, ten digits, a space, and 32 punctuation marks:

!"#$%&'()*+,-./:;<=>?@[\]^_'{|}~

In addition, your keyboard and computer have to agree on codes for other important operations such as tabs, backspaces, escapes, carriage returns, line feeds, form feeds (otherwise known as page breaks), and so on. You can generate these codes by holding down the Ctrl key and pressing letter keys; to generate a 3 you'd hold down the Ctrl key and press a C (since C is the third letter in the alphabet). You can use a Ctrl-C, abbreviated as ^C, to stop many DOS operations in their tracks, just as with Ctrl-ScrollLock. (However, in IBM BASIC, a ^C will act as a carriage return.) A few of the important operations (some in DOS; some in BASIC) with ASCII codes below 32 are shown in Figure 4.1.

Ctrl Code	ASCII Value	What it does in DOS and/or BASIC
	0	Nul
^B	2	Jump to previous word
^C	3	Break; carriage return in BASIC
^E	5	Erase to end of line
^F	6	Jump to next word
^G	7	Beep
^H	8	Backspace
^I	9	Tab
^J	10	Line feed
^K	11	Home (sometimes)
^L	12	Form feed
^M	13	Carriage return
^N	14	End of line
^P	16	Toggle echo to printer on and off
^Q	17	Restart scrolling in CP/M type operations
^R	18	Toggle Insert/overtype
^S	19	Toggle scrolling on and off
^Z	26	End of file
^[	27	Esc
^\	28	Cursor right
^]	29	Cursor left
^^	30	Cursor up
^_	31	Cursor down

Figure 4.1. Control Code Operations

You can fit all the letters of the alphabet, digits, punctuation, and control codes (with ASCII values lower than 32) into 128 characters. Early seven-bit systems could address only 128 characters, since 2^7 is 128. IBM added one bit to this system and doubled the number of characters to 256.

The leftmost side of a number is the *high order* side and the rightmost side the *low order* one. This is obvious; for the decimal number 567, for instance, the 5 stands for how many hundreds and the 7 for how many ones. Hundreds are higher than ones in any system, so the 5 is on the high side and 7 on the low side.

Because adding this additional bit meant slapping it onto the leftmost side, ASCII numbers over 128 — which all have a 1 as the leftmost digit — are sometimes referred to as *high-bit* characters.

IBM's high-bit characters let you use foreign languages, create mathematical formulas, and draw box-character pictures and borders. IBM also added a few printable symbols to the ASCII characters with values under 32 (for instance, decimal ASCII character 11 produces the biological male sign and character 12 the female sign).

To see all the ASCII characters, run the tiny demonstration program called SHOW-CHAR.COM on the accompanying disk. BIOS provides many different methods for writing characters. You could use something like BIOS service hex 0E, which treats the screen like a teletype, advancing the cursor automatically each time it prints a character, and wrapping text down to the next line when necessary.

However, this service gives special treatment to four ASCII characters:

- decimal 7 — beep
- decimal 8 — backspace
- decimal 10 — linefeed
- decimal 13 — carriage return

If you use it to print these four, you won't see their character symbols onscreen. Try to write an ASCII 7 with service 0E, for instance, and instead of displaying the small centered dot character that IBM assigned to a character 7, all you'll get is a beep.

BIOS services 09 and 0A will print the characters IBM assigned to all 256 ASCII values, including the troublesome four above. All three services, 09, 0A, and 0E, will display three ASCII characters as blanks:

- decimal 0 — null
- decimal 32 — space
- decimal 255 — blank

The difference between services 09 and 0A is that service 09 can change the attribute as it writes each character, while service 0A can't. But with both of these you have to advance the cursor yourself, since BIOS won't do it for you.

The SHOWCHAR.COM program will first use BIOS service 08 to read the attribute at the current cursor position, and will then use service 06 to clear the screen to that position. Then it will display all 256 characters in rows of 32.

```
MOV    AH,8       ; read attribute at cursor
INT    10         ; do it
MOV    BH,AH      ; move attribute into BH
MOV    AX,0600    ; clear screen
XOR    CX,CX      ; starting wth upper lefthand corner
MOV    DX,1849    ; and using whole 25 x 80 screen
INT    10         ; do it
XOR    DX,DX      ; put cursor in upper left corner
XOR    BH,BH      ; of page 0
MOV    CX,1       ; just print one character at a time
PUSH   AX         ; save value of character
```

```
MOV    AH,02      ; set cursor position
INT    10         ; do it
POP    AX         ; restore value of character
MOV    AH,0A      ; write character to screen
INT    10         ; do it
INC    AL         ; get ready for next character
ADD    DL,2       ; two columns over
CMP    DL,40      ; is cursor at end of row?
JNZ    12F        ; no, so skip next routine
INC    DH         ; otherwise move down a line
XOR    DL,DL      ; and back to beginning of line
CMP    AL,FF      ; is it last character?
JNZ    0117       ; no, go back and print next one
RET               ; yes, bye
```

You can run the SHOWCHAR.COM program on the accompanying disk or create a script file that will produce the program for you. Create a script file called SHOW-CHAR.SCR that contains the following nine lines:

```
E 0100 B4 08 CD 10 88 E7 B8 00 06 31 C9 BA 49
E 010D 18 CD 10 31 D2 30 FF B9 01 00 50 B4 02
E 011A CD 10 58 B4 0A CD 10 FE C0 80 C2 02 80
E 0127 FA 40 75 04 FE C6 30 D2 3C FF 75 E4 C3
N SHOWCHAR.COM
RCX
34
W
Q
```

Be certain you press the Enter key at the end of each line, especially the last one with the Q. Then make sure DEBUG.COM version 2.0 or later is handy at the DOS prompt, type:

```
DEBUG < SHOWCHAR.SCR
```

Displaying the ASCII characters in rows of 32 shows that the lowercase alphabet letters have values that are decimal 32 (hex 20) higher than their uppercase cousins.

You can experiment with this program to change the way it displays characters. For instance, once you've created it, you can type:

```
DEBUG SHOWCHAR.COM
E 115 D0 07
E 123 EB 0A
```

```
N  SHOWFULL.COM
W
Q
```

The basic SHOWCHAR.COM program displays only one of each character at a time. SHOWFULL.COM will display 2,000 (hex 7D0) characters at a time — a full 25 x 80 screenful. BIOS will flash through all 256 full screens of characters in a few seconds.

Or, to see the difference between services 09 and 0A, first use a pure-ASCII word processor or EDLIN to create the following ADDCOLOR.SCR script file. Be sure to press the Enter key at the end of each line, especially the last one with the Q:

```
E  11D 88 C3 B4 09 CD 10 FE C0 80 C2 01 80 FA
E  12A 40 75 04 FE C6 30 D2 3C FF 75 E2 C3
N  SHOWCOLR.COM
RCX
36
W
Q
```

Then, at the DOS prompt, type:

```
DEBUG SHOWCHAR.COM < ADDCOLOR.SCR
```

and you'll end up with a variation of SHOWCHAR.COM called SHOWCOLR.COM that displays each character using the ASCII value of the character as the attribute. If you're using a color monitor, you'll see all 256 possible attributes.

SHOWCOLR.COM will display four rows of characters, rather than the eight produced by SHOWCHAR.COM. All four rows will be in color, and because of the BIOS color numbering system, the foreground colors in the bottom two rows will be blinking. The four rows will be divided into four chunks of background colors that are each 16 characters wide. Within these chunks, each of the 16 characters will have a different foreground color. The leftmost eight will appear in normal colors, while the rightmost eight will appear as high-intensity (bright) colors.

Here's why:

It's easiest to see how this works by using the hex value of each attribute. All attributes can be expressed as two-digit hex numbers. The lefthand and righthand digits can each range from 0 to F, which yields decimal 256 possible values from 00 through FF.

The lefthand digit represents the background color, and the righthand digit the foreground color. So on a color system, a number like 71 will produce blue (1) text on a white (7) background, while 17 will yield white text on a blue background. The hex color assignments are shown in Figure 4.2.

Value	Color	Value	Color
0	Black	8	Grey
1	Blue	9	Bright blue
2	Green	A	Bright green
3	Cyan (Lt Blue)	B	Bright cyan
4	Red	C	Bright red
5	Magenta	D	Bright magenta
6	Brown	E	Bright yellow
7	White	F	Bright white

←—— background only ——→

←——————— foreground ———————→

Figure 4.2. Hex Color Assignments

However, a value like 4E will produce bright yellow text (E) on a red (4) background, while E4 will produce bright blinking yellow text on a red background. Any value that has a lefthand digit higher than 7 will blink. So a number like 71 won't blink, while a number like 81 will.

Any value that has a righthand digit higher than 7 will appear as a high-intensity color. So a number like 47 will produce a normal, low-intensity color, while 48 will display something in high-intensity.

When you type something like:

```
DEBUG SHOWCHAR.COM < ADDCOLOR.SCR
```

what you're doing is using the redirection abilities of DOS (versions 2.0 and later) to take characters in a file and treat them as keystrokes that DEBUG uses to create a file. DEBUG doesn't care where its keystrokes are coming from — a live user at the keyboard or a file that contains keystrokes that the user put there long ago.

Redirecting script files like this makes a lot of sense when you're using DEBUG to create files, since it lets you check your typing, and since you can often adapt script files so DEBUG can create customized variations of programs for you.

To create files using this technique, make sure you use a pure-ASCII word processor, the DOS EDLIN line editor, or the DOS COPY CON command. If you're not sure whether your word processor can produce pure ASCII text (a file composed of just letters and numbers and punctuation, and not containing anything else), just load it up and type a paragraph and save it as a short file called TEST. Then exit your word processor and get into DOS and type:

```
TYPE TEST
```

You could also use lowercase letters, by typing:

```
type test
```

since DOS translates all characters into uppercase before trying to do anything serious with them, except in a few rare examples such as the with ANSI.SYS keyboard and screen extender that are discussed in Chapter 9.

Either way, if all you see is the text you typed and nothing else, your word processor should do just fine for creating script files. But if your screen fills with "garbage" characters that jump around and beep and clear the screen, you'll have to use another method. Most word processors have a way to create pure-ASCII files; check your manual under "text files" or "ASCII" or "DOS files" or "program editing."

To create the file directly in DOS, make sure you're at the DOS prompt, and type:

```
COPY CON SHOWCHAR.SCR
```

and press the Enter key. The cursor should do nothing except drop down a line and blink dully at you.

Start typing the script, line by line. Make sure each line is absolutely correct before you press the Enter key at the end of it; if you make any mistakes use the backspace key to erase them and then type in the right characters.

Be sure to press the Enter key at the end of each line, especially the last one (with the lonesome Q).

When you're all done, and you're sure you've pressed the Enter key after the final Q, the cursor should be directly below the Q. Press the grey F6 function key and then press the Enter key one last time. When you press the F6 key you'll see a ^Z appear, and then when you press the final Enter key you'll see a "1 File(s) copied" message. You'll then be back at the DOS prompt again. If you want, type DIR SHOWCHAR.SCR and you should see the file you just created with a number just under a thousand beside it, and a date and time. If you don't, you did something wrong and should start the whole process over again.

The COPY CON FILENAME (where FILENAME stands for the name of the file you want to create and not the word "FILENAME" itself) command tells DOS to take the information you're typing at the console (the keyboard and screen) and copy it into a file with the name you entered after the word CON. Pressing the F6 function key when you're all done puts a special character at the end of your file called (surprise) an *end-of-file-marker*. This special character has an ASCII value of 26, and there are several other ways you could put this character there. The easiest is to hold down the Ctrl key and press the Z key while you're holding it down. The ^Z that shows up on the screen when you do either is shorthand for Ctrl-Z.

DOS generally stops in its tracks when it sees an end-of-file marker, as do many commercial software products. So, when creating text files, be careful not to let a stray ^Z wander into your file or DOS will ignore everything that follows.

The only real problem with using the COPY CON technique is that you can't back up and correct a line above the one you're working on. You can fix problems only in the

current line. If you make a mistake and don't catch it in time, you have to start over, or go in and edit the file later with EDLIN or a real word processor. And if you have one of those handy, you might as well create the whole file on it.

Anyway, once you've created the SHOWCHAR.SCR script file, locate your supplemental DOS disk and look for DEBUG.COM on that disk. (You have to be using a version of DOS that starts with a 2 or a 3 to make this work; if you're still using 1.1 stop right now and go to your dealer and upgrade.)

Copy DEBUG.COM onto the disk that has SHOWCHAR.SCR on it. If you're way ahead of this discussion and have a hard disk with DEBUG in a subdirectory that you've included in your path, fine. If you don't understand a word of that last sentence, go back to Chapter 3 to review the PATH command.

Finally, to create the final program, make sure both SHOWCHAR.SCR and DEBUG.COM are on the disk you're currently using, and at the DOS prompt type:

```
DEBUG < SHOWCHAR.SCR
```

You'll see the SHOWCHAR.SCR scroll down your screen. You don't want to see anything that says "error." If you do see any error messages, use the DOS TYPE command (as mentioned above) to make sure you actually did create a pure ASCII file. If the file goes by too quickly, you can stop and start it from scrolling by holding down the Ctrl key and pressing the S key. Also, be sure you left a blank line above RCX; if you didn't you'll see a string of error warnings.

If your whole system locks up, it's because you forgot to press the Enter key after the final Q. Reboot, then go back and retype the SHOWCHAR.SCR file and press the Enter key twice for good measure at the end. What the "DEBUG < SHOWCHAR.SCR" command does is take the script file you just created and redirect it into the DEBUG.COM program. Essentially, it takes the keystrokes that you typed in earlier when you created the file and feeds them into DEBUG. Those keystrokes contain data and DEBUG commands to assemble the data into a file called a COM file or command file (one that you can run in DOS and that ends in .COM). Script files like this are handy, especially when you create them with a real word processor, because they let you correct previous mistakes and it's easy to modify them slightly and create improved versions of the COM files.

When you're all done, just be sure you're looking at a DOS prompt, and type:

```
SHOWCHAR
```

and you'll see every ASCII character.

Chip Logic

Dealing with all the binary 1s and 0s is a nuisance. But they really come in handy when you have to do *logical operations*.

Why is the ASCII value for *A* 65 and for *a* 97? Look at the binary representations of the first few letters of the alphabet:

A	65	1000001	B	66	1000010	C	67	1000011
a	97	1100001	b	98	1100010	c	99	1100011
		↑			↑			↑
		sixth			sixth			sixth
		bit			bit			bit
		(2^5)			(2^5)			(2^5)
		=32			=32			=32

The lowercase version of each is identical to the uppercase version, except that in all cases the sixth binary digit over from the right is a 1 in the lowercase version and a 0 in the uppercase one.

The easy way to find out the decimal value of a binary bit is to count over from the right "1, 2, 4, 8, 16, 32, 64...." Do this and you'll reach 32 when you get to the sixth binary digit. You could also try to remember that the sixth bit over is 2^5, since computer numbering systems generally start with 0 rather than 1 and since the rightmost bit is 2^0. But some users forget, and make the sixth bit 2^6, which is wrong.

Subtract 65 (the value of uppercase A) from 97 (the value of lowercase A) and you'll get 32. So you can instantly calculate the value of any capital letter by subtracting decimal 32 from the value of the lowercase letter. And, of course, you could add 32 to the value of the uppercase letter to obtain the ASCII value of the lowercase letter.

If you wanted to convert every lowercase character in a typical text file to uppercase you couldn't just subtract 32 from the ASCII value of every letter, since files contain mixtures of uppercase and lowercase letters. Subtracting 32 from all the lowercase letters would indeed yield uppercase ones. But if you did this blindly, you'd also end up subtracting 32 from the letters that were already uppercase, which would turn them into something unrecognizable.

Here's a short sentence, with the decimal ASCII value of each character shown beneath it:

I	.	L	o	v	e	N	Y
73		76	111	118	101	78	89

Subtract 32 from each and you get:

)	,	O	V	E	.	9
41	44	79	86	69	46	57

As you can see from the "ABC" and "abc" examples above, subtracting 32 from the value of a number is the same as turning the sixth bit (2^5) from a 1 to a 0. So what you really want to do is find a way to look at the sixth bit and turn it into a 0 only if it's currently a 1.

Your computer can do this instantly, by using logical operations. In this case, you would use the logical AND operation to make letters uppercase, and the logical OR operation to make them lowercase.

The most useful logical operations are AND, OR, NOT, and XOR. They're fairly intuitive, but as with binary numbers, they take some getting used to. Think of them as miniture legal contracts.

If a contract says you will be paid if you:

write a novel
AND
write greeting cards

obviously you'll get paid only if you write both. If a contract says you will be paid if you:

write a novel
OR
write greeting cards

you have to write only one of these to get paid (what a choice). If a contract says you will be paid if you:

do NOT grow crops this year

you'll fatten your bank account only if your back 40 sit idle.

We all deal with AND, OR, and NOT operations regularly. XOR, which stands for *eXclusive OR*, simply flips one binary state to another, but can also add binary numbers together (see "Chomping at the Bit"). Flipping twice brings you back to the original state.

Computers use XOR operations for all sorts of things. If you XOR a value with itself, you cancel it out and end up with 0. And if you want to produce graphic animations, you first XOR one image onto the screen to draw something at a certain location, and then XOR the same image at the same location again to restore the screen to the way it was originally. Since the second XOR effectively erases the image (by canceling out the changes), you can move an image across your screen by having XOR repeatedly draw it and then erase it.

Bit Masks

ANDing any ASCII value with decimal 223 will capitalize lowercase letters and leave uppercase letters alone. AND works by comparing two values (the example below will compare one bit at a time) and returning a 1 only when both values are nonzero.

	AND Table			
1	AND	1	=	1
1	AND	0	=	0
0	AND	1	=	0
0	AND	0	=	0

In binary notation, 223 is 11011111, and this number works as a *bit mask*. ANDing any binary number of eight digits or less with it will leave things the way they were in every position except the sixth over from the right, where it will leave 0s alone and change 1s to 0s. This forces the digit in that position to become a 0, which is the same as subtracting 32. But it does this only when there's a 1 in that position. In other words, it subtracts 32 only when there's a 32 there to subtract. It's called a mask because it masks out any changes except in the one place where we want the change to happen — the 0 in the 2^5 position.

Since A (decimal 65) is binary 01000001, while a (decimal 97) is binary 01100001, ANDing these numbers with 11011111 could be represented as:

$$
\begin{array}{rll}
 & 01000001 & (65) \\
\text{AND} & \underline{11011111} & (223) \\
 & 01000001 & (65)
\end{array}
$$

$$
\begin{array}{rll}
 & 01100001 & (97) \\
\text{AND} & \underline{11011111} & (223) \\
 & 01000001 & (65)
\end{array}
$$

ANDing either a 0 or a 1 with 1 in effect leaves the value alone, and ANDing both a 0 and a 1 with 0 in effect turns the value into a 0. The binary number 11011111 forces the 2^5 bit — the sixth one from the right — to become a 0 and leaves all the other bits the way they were.

Changing a bit from 0 to 1 is often referred to as *setting* the bit, and changing it from a 1 to a 0 as *unsetting* the bit. The only difference between a lowercase letter and its capital counterpart is that the 2^5 bit is *set* (=1) in the lowercase version. ANDing it with 11011111 *unsets* the bit, changing it to a 0 and lowering the ASCII value by 32.

To reverse the process and turn capital letters into lowercase ones, use the logical OR operation to OR a value with 32.

	OR Table			
1	OR	1	=	1
1	OR	0	=	1
0	OR	1	=	1
0	OR	0	=	0

32 equals binary 00100000. Since ORing either a 1 or a 0 with 0 in effect leaves the value alone, and ORing either a 1 or a 0 with 1 in effect turns the value into a 1, the binary num-

ber 00100000 forces the 2^5 bit to become a 1 and leaves all the other bits the way they were.

This sets the unset 2^5 bit in an uppercase letter, changing it to a 1 and raising the ASCII value by 32. But it leaves already set bits just the way they were.

$$
\begin{array}{llr}
      & 01000001 & (65) \\
\text{OR} & \underline{00100000} & (32) \\
      & 01100001 & (97)
\end{array}
$$

$$
\begin{array}{llr}
      & 01100001 & (97) \\
\text{OR} & \underline{00100000} & (32) \\
      & 01100001 & (97)
\end{array}
$$

Hex Marks the Spot

Nobody likes dealing in cumbersome eight-bit binary numbers. But our more comfortable decimal (base-ten) system doesn't really lend itself to the base-two world of computers. A base-16 number system does, since every eight-bit binary number can be expressed as two single-digit base-16, or *hexadecimal*, numbers strung together. In fact, it's easier to translate binary numbers into hexadecimal and back than to translate binary into decimal and back.

Hexadecimal (hex for short) numbering works just like decimal numbering except that it provides six additional digits. The first ten digits are the same as the ten decimal ones you use every day. But you run out of digits after you get to 9. Hex then tacks on the first six letters of the alphabet. So, you count to 10 in hex like this (decimal values are shown in parentheses):

0 (0)
1 (1)
2 (2)
3 (3)
4 (4)
5 (5)
6 (6)
7 (7)
8 (8)
9 (9)
A (10)   *line feed is Ascii 10 or ^J*
B (11)
C (12)
D (13) <   *carriage return is ASCII 13 or ^M*
E (14)
F (15)
10 (16)

How do you tell a hexadecimal 10 (which is really equal to decimal 16) from a garden-variety decimal 10? Hex numbers usually end with an H (or an h), or have a &H (or &h) prefix attached. So,

```
10h
10H
&H10
&h10
```

are all the same number.

Programmers often like working with two-digit hex numbers, so they'll stick zeros onto the left side. 0D is the same as D; 0A the same as A. Scripts often use ",0D,0A" at the end of the messages to tell the program to insert a carriage return (an 0D character) and a linefeed (an 0A character) at the end of the text.

Hex is handy because you can squeeze lots of values into a compact amount of space. Using decimal numbers takes three digits to write 156 of the ASCII characters (all the ones greater than 99). But every ASCII character can fit into two hex digits (decimal 255 is the same as hex FF).

Your system comes from the factory containing certain important gut-level tools and programs already loaded on ROM chips (which will be discussed in the next chapter), and each generation of these chips has important changes from previous versions. You can figure out which set of chips is in your system by peeking at a specific memory location, or address. The address that tells you the date your system ROM was released is 61440:65525 in decimal, but is F000:FFF5 in hex.

To see this date yourself, get into DOS, make sure DEBUG.COM is on your disk, and type:

```
DEBUG
```

You'll see a (-) at the left edge of your screen; this is DEBUG's prompt the same way that "OK" is BASIC's prompt and A> or C> is DOS's default prompt. Type:

```
D F000:FFF5 L8
```

and press the Enter key. The date will appear at the right edge of your screen. Then press Q and then Enter to quit DEBUG and return to DOS.

You could also retrieve the date by plugging the numbers into a short BASIC program:

```
100 DEF SEG=61440!
110 FOR A=0 TO 7
120 PRINT CHR$(PEEK(65525!+A));
130 NEXT
```

The hex version of this program doesn't save much typing, though:

```
100 DEF SEG=&HF000
110 FOR A=0 TO 7
120 PRINT CHR$(PEEK(&HFFF5+A));
130 NEXT
```

Hex also makes binary translations a dream. For instance, what is the binary equivalent of FF? Well, that one's too easy, since it's equal to 255, and 255 is the highest number you can make out of 1s and 0s, which means it must be made up of all 1s:

11111111

But pick any other hex number: &H3D (61 in decimal notation). Each hex digit stands for half of an eight-digit binary number. Remember that one binary digit is a bit and that eight bits make a byte. And that half a byte is called a nibble. (Get it? Byte? Nibble?)

In &H3D, the 3 stands for the lefthand (or *high*) nibble, and the D for the righthand (or *low*) nibble. In binary notation, decimal 3 is 0011, while decimal 13 — which is what hex D is equal to — is 1101. We figured that out above.

So hex 3D is equal to 00111101. This is easier to see if you put a space in the middle: 0011 1101.

Going from binary to hex is also easy. What's 10100101? First break it in half: 1010 0101. The left half (or high nibble) is 1010:

$$
\begin{array}{rcccl}
1 & x & 2^3 & = & 8 \\
0 & x & 2^2 & = & 0 \\
1 & x & 2^1 & = & 2 \\
0 & x & 2^0 & = & \underline{0} \\
  &   & \text{Total} & = & 10 \quad \text{decimal, or A in hex}
\end{array}
$$

The right half (low nibble) is 0101:

$$
\begin{array}{rcccl}
0 & x & 2^3 & = & 0 \\
1 & x & 2^2 & = & 4 \\
0 & x & 2^1 & = & 0 \\
1 & x & 2^0 & = & \underline{1} \\
  &   & \text{Total} & = & 5 \quad \text{decimal, or 5 in hex}
\end{array}
$$

Therefore, 10100101 is A5 in hex, or 165 in decimal. Note that the numbers 1 through 9 are the same in decimal and hex. Most new users get the hang of it pretty quickly, but they all make a common mistake of putting 10 after 9 in hex, when everyone knows hex 9 is followed by hex A. Don't worry, you'll get used to it. It's not really all that hard to convert two-digit hex numbers into decimal. First, convert each digit into decimal. From the above example, A is equal to 10, and 5 is equal to 5. Multiply the value of the left-hand digit by 16 and add the righthand digit to it:

$(10 \times 16) + 5 = 165$.

Converting a decimal number 256 or less to hex is only a little harder. First divide the number by 16. You'll probably end up with a whole number quotient and a remainder. Convert them each to single digit hex numbers. Put the whole number on the left and the remainder on the right:

165 / 16 = 10 with a remainder of 5
    10 = A
     5 = 5

So the hex representation is A5.

Hex is the language of DEBUG. And DEBUG is an incredible power tool. It lets you rip open the DOS covers and repair, examine, or customize anything. And it makes it easy to create and customize short assembly language programs like SHOWCHAR.COM above.

Multiplying and Dividing Hex Numbers

Translating numbers into and out of hex is hard enough, and adding or subtracting them is no picnic, but multiplying and dividing is out of the question. Lots of books show you how; we'll spare you the grief. Actually, we will tell you how: just install a copy of Borland's *SideKick* on your system. Even the older version of the software comes with an ASCII chart, a powerful notepad/clipboard that can lift text off your screen and move it to another program or store it in a file, and a terrific decimal/hex/binary calculator. Some of our programmers even use the *WordStar*-like notepad as their main program editor.

BASIC makes it a snap to translate most integer values in and out of hex. And it can simplify working with ASCII values. Type either BASICA or GWBASIC to get the ball rolling. To have it figure out the decimal value of the hex number 7ABC, just type:

```
PRINT &H7ABC
```

and press the Enter key. BASIC will print out:

```
31420
```

Unfortunately, since BASIC has to work with both positive and negative integers, the largest positive integer it can deal with is 32,767 (7FFFH). Tell it to PRINT &H7FFF and you'll indeed get 32767 (without the comma). But since BASIC can handle only 65,536 possible integers, it has to rope off the half starting with 32,768 and pretend they're negative numbers. So entering:

```
PRINT &H8000
```

will get you

```
-32768
```

Note that while you may use either &H or &h as a prefix, BASIC won't understand H or h suffixes on hex numbers. If you tried to type PRINT 7FFFH you'd get:

```
7 0
```

since BASIC would think you were asking it to print the value of 7 (which is 7) and then print the value of the variable FFFH, which would be zero unless you had by chance assigned it another value previously.

However, if you treat this operation as a calculation, BASIC will oblige with higher numbers. Enter:

```
PRINT &H7FFF+1
```

and BASIC will return:

```
32768
```

Try:

```
PRINT &H7FFF+&H7FFF
```

and you'll get:

```
65534
```

You can go the other way, from decimal to hex, without such headaches. Type in:

```
PRINT HEX$(64206)
```

and BASIC will respond with:

```
FACE
```

(&HFACE is a valid hex number). You can go all the way up to:

```
PRINT HEX$(65535)
```

which will produce:

```
FFFF
```

Try anything higher, such as:

```
PRINT HEX$(65535+1)
```

and BASIC will simply print the error message "Overflow."

To figure out the ASCII value of any character, nestle it inside parentheses and quotes, and preface it with ASC. Type:

```
PRINT ASC("A")
```

and you'll get its decimal ASCII value:

```
65
```

To convert numbers from 0 to 255 into their respective ASCII characters, put the decimal ASCII value inside parentheses and preface it with CHR$. Enter:

```
PRINT CHR$(65)
```

and you'll see:

```
A
```

You can also use hex notation when producing ASCII characters. You could have typed:

```
PRINT CHR$(&H41)
```

to produce the same:

```
A
```

since hex 41 is equal to decimal 65.

But if all you have to do is add or subtract hex numbers, which is usually the case, you can do it for free by using DEBUG. Just get into DOS, type DEBUG, and at the DEBUG hyphen (-) prompt, type in the letter H followed by any two hex numbers of four digits or less, and press the Enter key. DEBUG will print out the sum of your numbers and the difference.

It might look something like this:

```
-H FFFF 0001
0000 FFFE
```

DEBUG reports sums in four digits only, as you can see from the example above, since FFFFH + 1 equals 10000H, not 0000H. But that doesn't matter much, because four digits is plenty for what you'll have to do with hex.

Chomping at the Bits, or How Transistors Add

Logical operations such as AND and OR are fundamental building blocks of digital computers. Virtually every hardware interconnection in the PC is a *bit carrier*. The wires, the connections between chips on the circuit boards, and the connections within the chips themselves all carry signals in the form of voltages. In most cases a 1 bit is represented by a five-volt signal and a 0 bit is represented by a zero-volt signal. The 8088 CPU in the PC and PC-XT uses 20 pins to address its memory chips. If you could freeze the operation of the PC and measure the instantaneous voltage of these 20 pins, you would find that each would be very close to either zero volts or five volts. If you were real fast, and handy with a voltmeter, you could figure each 20-bit address the 8088 was outputting to memory. All chips inside a PC manipulate data in the form of bits. Regardless of the complexity of the chips, all contain transistors that are wired together into small fundamental *logic gates*. These gates receive two input signals (two bits) and use them to create one output signal (another bit).

The input to an OR gate is two signals (here called A and B), each of which can be either a 0 or a 1. The output is a 1 if either A or B is a 1. You can represent this by the formula:

A OR B

and can show all the possible results in the table:

A	B	A OR B
0	0	0
0	1	1
1	0	1
1	1	1

In theory, you need only two transistors to construct an OR gate within an integrated circuit. Think of the transistors as light switches — one for each input — wired in parallel so that the output is "on" (a 1 bit) if either switch is turned on.

The output to an AND gate is a 1 only if both inputs are 1. The formula looks like:

A AND B

and you can show all the possible results in the table:

A	B	A AND B
0	0	0
0	1	0
1	0	0
1	1	1

You could (at least in theory) construct this gate from just two transistors wired in series. Just as with light switches wired in series, the output will be "on" (a 1 bit) only if both are turned on.

The important, although seemingly trivial, NOT operator takes just one input (here called A). If A is a 0, NOT changes it to a 1. If A is a 1, then NOT changes it to a 0. Within a circuit, the output from an OR gate can be the input to a NOT, so they can function together, as represented by the formula:

NOT (A OR B)

Incidentally, since operations work from left to right, you need to put parentheses around A OR B in the above example. If you didn't, what you'd be saying is (NOT A) OR B.

This is called a NOR gate, which you can represent as:

A NOR B

Here's what the table looks like:

A	B	A NOR B
0	0	1
0	1	0
1	0	0
1	1	0

You may have noticed that the NOR table is simply the inverted result shown in the OR table — the 0s in the OR table are 1s in the NOR table, and 1s in the OR table become 0s in the NOR table.

Similarly, an output from an AND gate can feed into a NOT to construct a NAND gate. The formula:

A NAND B

is the same as:

NOT (A AND B)

with the following table:

A	B	A NAND B
0	0	1
0	1	1
1	0	1
1	1	0

You may start to see some relationships between all these tables. For instance, if you turn the third column of the OR table upside down, it looks like the third column of the NAND table. Therefore:

A OR B = (NOT A) NAND (NOT B)

Similarly:

A AND B = (NOT A) NOR (NOT B)

These logical operations are not just mathematical exercises; they perform vital functions in the PC's hardware, where transistors are wired together to form tiny logic gates. The individual logic gates are then wired together to do more complex tasks, often within the same chip.

As everyone knows, computers can add two numbers together. And while we take this for granted nowadays, once you start looking at the computer in terms of logic gates, it no longer seems trivial. How can transistors add?

First you have to wire together an OR gate, an AND gate, and a NAND gate. You start with two inputs and run them into both the OR gate and the NAND gate. The output from the OR gate and the output from the NAND gate become the inputs to the AND gate. This connection can be symbolized by the formula:

(A OR B) AND (A NAND B)

This is called an *exclusive OR* gate, often abbreviated XOR. Instead of writing the whole expression, we can simply use:

A XOR B

The table for the XOR gate is shown below:

A	B	A XOR B
0	0	0
0	1	1
1	0	1
1	1	0

This table is similar to the OR gate except that when both A and B are 1, the result is a 0. What makes the XOR gate interesting is that it adds the two bits together, producing the following results:

$$
\begin{array}{cccc}
0 & 0 & 1 & 1 \\
\underline{+0} & \underline{+1} & \underline{+0} & \underline{+1} \\
0 & 1 & 1 & 10
\end{array}
$$

This lets you create a formula that says:

SUM = A XOR B

To demonstrate this, trying adding two four-bit numbers together, such as 3 and 6. The addition (shown in both decimal and binary form) is shown below:

$$
\begin{array}{cc}
3 & 0011 \\
\underline{+6} & \underline{+0110} \\
9 & 1001
\end{array}
$$

To add multidigit binary numbers together, start at the right most or *least significant* pair of bits and proceed to the left, just as you do when you add together multidigit decimal numbers.

Since adding 1 + 1 produces a two-digit binary number (10), you end up with a *carry-out* bit that you have to include in the next calculation over to the left as a *carry-in* bit. Because of this carry bit, the formulas become a little more complex:

SUM =   (A XOR B) XOR (CARRY-IN)
CARRY-OUT =   (A AND B) XOR ((A XOR B) AND (CARRY-IN))

If you want to verify that these formulas work for the calculation shown above, you can put together a table that shows the bits to be added, the SUM from each calculation, the CARRY-OUT from the calculation, and the CARRY-IN from the previous calculation. Start with the rightmost column and proceed toward the left:

A:	0	0	1	1
B:	0	1	1	0
CARRY-IN:	1	1	0	0
CARRY-OUT:	0	1	1	0
SUM:	1	0	0	1

Humans may require several minutes to plug the bits into the formulas and determine the final result. Transistors do it in well under a millionth of a second.

— Charles Petzold

Chapter 5

The Keys to the Kingdom

Sure, sure. You're an old hand at the keyboard, and your fingers automatically reach for the home row when you climb out of bed in the morning. But you may not know all the PC keyboard's basic tricks.

First, a quick history: the earliest PC sported an 83-key keyboard that divided the user community into two camps. Most of us loved it, since it had the best "feel" of any keyboard ever made. IBM spends a lot of time sticking people in chairs and watching them work, and all this ergonomic research paid off handsomely.

The few ragtag complainers and malcontents who hated it did have one valid point — the placement of some of the keys was nonstandard. The Enter key was somewhat small and too far to the right. The left Shift key was a little far to the left. The whole right side of it was a bit crowded. And you couldn't tell what state the Shift keys happened to be in.

The original 84-key PC-AT keyboard fixed all these woes, and bcame an instant and absolute classic. However, IBM didn't know when to stop, and ended up moving the function keys from the left side to the top, doing random damage to the Ctrl and Alt keys, and using a slightly cheaper mechanism to pop the keys up after you press them down.

The subsequent generation of 101/102-key keyboards featured separate number and cursor pads, stuck on a handful of new keys, and were as wide as your desk. They also made it difficult to use some software products. For example, millions of *WordStar* users depended on having the Ctrl key beside the A key. When IBM hid the Ctrl key these users either had to retrain their fingers, or run a program like IBMFIX.COM (on the accompanying disk) to put things back to normal.

But all the IBM keyboards shared the same glorious feel. Each had exactly the right amount of "overstrike" so that you had to build up a certain amount of pressure to reach a trigger point before the key sprang into action. Each clicked on the way down and on the way up, giving users unparalleled tactile feedback and boosting their morale by subconsciously making them think they were typing twice as fast. Every key was bounce-

147

free; pallid plastic clone keyboards commonly stuttered extra characters onto the screen, but not IBM's. IBM's was angled perfectly, and expertly scooped and dished so that your fingers fit precisely onto the wide keytops. It was also heavy, so that muscular typing wouldn't chase it around the desktop.

Some users liked competitors' keyboards because they were silent. That's like preferring beer to vintage champagne because the bottles are easier to open. The IBM keyboard is so good that it's almost reason enough to stick with IBM (unless you can't resist increased power from a company like Compaq or low price from a mail order vendor). Using anything else is like kneading gummy marshmallows or typing on a pocket calculator.

Users switching from typewriters to computers are often stymied by the welter of extra PC keys. After all, four separate ones have left arrows on them. Function keys are intimidating to new users, as are such foreign-looking characters as:

^ { } |\~ ' < >

And labels like SysReq, PgDn, and PrtSc can initially confound anyone. However, until someone comes up with a flawless voice recognition device, IBM's crisp, solid, elegant keyboards will remain the best ways to digitize your thoughts and data.

The keys to the kingdom come in four families:

1. The normal typewriter keys (and their less familiar cousins such as <, >, and |).
2. The shift and special purpose keys.
3. The cursor-movement and number-pad keys.
4. The grey function keys (F1 through F10 on older models, F1 through F12 on newer ones).

Typewriter Keys

Nothing is really different about these on the PC keyboard except that you get a few extras thrown in — and some common keys, such as the cents sign, are missing.

This is because computer keyboards are designed to work with the ASCII character set. As mentioned earlier, IBM adopted (and enhanced) a character-numbering system called ASCII (American Standard Code for Information Interchange). Deep down, computers don't know anything about letters. But they're terrific at juggling numbers. So when it has to move an A from one place to another, your computer actually uses the number 65 to represent the A. Programs in your ROM chips translate these values into the dot patterns that draw the actual characters on your screen. But to the computer, an A is always a 65 (unless it's a lowercase a, in which case it's a 97).

You can type in 95 of the ASCII characters shown in Figure 5.1 from your keyboard. In the chart, the number in each lefthand column is the ASCII value of the character beside it.

ASC	CHR	ASC	CHR	ASC	CHR	ASC	CHR	ASC	CHR	ASC	CHR
*32	(SPC)	48	0	64	@	80	P	96	'	112	p
33	!	49	1	65	A	81	Q	97	a	113	q
34	"	50	2	66	B	82	R	98	b	114	r
35	#	51	3	67	C	83	S	99	c	115	s
36	$	52	4	68	D	84	T	100	d	116	t
37	%	53	5	69	E	85	U	101	e	117	u
38	&	54	6	70	F	86	V	102	f	118	v
39	'	55	7	71	G	87	W	103	g	119	w
40	(	56	8	72	H	88	X	104	h	120	x
41	)	57	9	73	I	89	Y	105	i	121	y
42	*	58	:	74	J	90	Z	106	j	122	z
43	+	59	;	75	K	91	[	107	k	123	{
44	,	60	<	76	L	92	\	108	l	124		
45	-	61	=	77	M	93	]	109	m	125	}
46	.	62	>	78	N	94	^	110	n	126	~
47	/	63	?	79	O	95	_	111	o	**127	Δ

Figure 5.1. ASCII Typewriter Keys

* Character 32 is a space, and is generated when you tap the spacebar.
** IBM calls character 127 a *delta* but it's actually shaped like a small house.

The characters you see onscreen will differ slightly from system to system. Characters on IBM monochrome screens are made up of lots of dots. Those on EGA displays are nearly as sharp and clear as monochrome characters. But CGA character sets are crude. The dot patterns for each monitor are contained on special ROM chips attached to the respective display adapters. But IBM keeps a set of these CGA patterns in the main system ROM so it can draw characters when you're in BASIC graphics screens 1 and 2. The characters are crude because they're drawn in a grid eight dots wide and eight dots high — not very conducive to graceful curves and tricky angles.

You can't easily look inside your main system ROM but the BASIC ROMPRINT.BAS program below can (starting at address F000:FA6E). It reads the values stored there and interprets them as light and dark blocks on your screen. The main ROM stores the patterns for each character as a sequence of eight binary numbers, one per row. ROMPRINT retrieves the decimal value of each number and translates it into the binary pattern for each row. It lets you strike actual keys from the keyboard, or enter ASCII values between 0 and 127 from the chart shown in Figure 5.1. If you want to see the dot patterns for the digits 0–9, enter their ASCII values (0 = 48, 1 = 49 ... 9 = 57). If you do type in ASCII numbers, press the Enter key after entering any values with fewer than three digits. When you're all done, press the F10 function key to end the program.

```
100 'ROMPRINT — displays ROM ASCII dot patterns
110 SCREEN 0:COLOR 2,0,0:LOCATE ,,0:KEY OFF:DEFINT A-Z:CLS
120 DEF SEG=0:POKE 1047,PEEK(1047) OR 32:KEY 10,""
130 ' --- points to ROM; sets up print characters ---
140 DEF SEG=&HF000:A$=STRING$(2,219):B$=STRING$(2,176)
150 ' --- gets ASCII value ---
160 PRINT "Type a key, or enter any number between"
170 PRINT "000 and 127 (press the <F10> key to end): ";
180 I$=INKEY$:IF I$="" THEN 180 ELSE IF I$=CHR$(0)+"D" THEN END
190 IF I$=CHR$(13) THEN IF C$="" THEN D=13:GOTO 240 ELSE 220
200 IF I$>CHR$(57) OR I$<CHR$(48) THEN D=ASC(I$):GOTO 240
210 C$=C$+I$:PRINT I$;:IF LEN(C$)<3 THEN 180
220 IF VAL(C$)>127 THEN C$="":CLS:GOTO 160 ELSE D=VAL(C$)
230 ' --- draws dot pattern row by row ---
240 CLS:FOR E=1 TO 8
250 F=PEEK(&HFA6D+(8*D)+E)
260 IF F=0 THEN PRINT STRING$(16,176):GOTO 300
270 FOR G=7 TO 0 STEP -1
280 IF F<2^G THEN PRINT B$; ELSE PRINT A$;:F=F-2^G
290 NEXT:PRINT
300 NEXT:PRINT:IF D<>11 AND D<>12 THEN PRINT TAB(8);CHR$(D)
310 PRINT:C$="":GOTO 160
```

The program also displays the actual life-size character beneath the enlarged dot pattern. It won't display the whole character set, since the system uses some with values like 7, 10, 12, and 13 to control the position of the cursor, clear the screen, beep, and manage other display chores. But ROMPRINT will show you the actual patterns stored in ROM for every single one.

High-Bit Characters

Display adapters are designed to zap the appropriate character dot patterns onto the screen very rapidly. BASIC's graphics modes have to go in and draw text characters a dot at a time. And in all 1.x and 2.x versions of DOS, users couldn't put any of the *high-bit* foreign language, math, and border-drawing characters (with ASCII values over 127) onto BASIC graphics screens, since the patterns for these weren't stored on the system ROM chips.

But DOS version 3.0 offered a new utility called GRAFTABL.COM that made it possible to display the high-bit characters. All you had to do was type in GRAFTABL before loading BASIC and DOS would create a memory-resident lookup table containing the proper values. GRAFTABL.COM remained the same in versions 3.1 and 3.2, but when IBM introduced its confounding foreign language features in version 3.3 it made GRAF-

TABL.COM five times larger to accommodate slight differences in foreign character sets.

The GRAFPRNT.BAS program below looks inside GRAFTABL.COM, reads the character patterns into an array, and uses ROMPRINT's binary pattern printer to display an enlarged version of any ASCII character from 128 through 255. It checks to make sure you have a proper version handy, and automatically sniffs out whether it's dealing with an older GRAFTABL.COM or a fat new one, since the internal structures are different.

```
100 ' GRAFPRNT - prints GRAFTABL.COM hi-bit ASCII patterns
110 SCREEN 0,0:KEY OFF:COLOR 2,0,0:CLS:DEFINT A-Z
120 DEF SEG=0:POKE 1047,PEEK(1047) OR 32:DEF SEG:KEY 10,""
130 DIM H(128,8):M$=STRING$(2,176):N$=STRING$(2,219)
140 ' --- open GRAFTABL, get version, validate, fill array ---
150 OPEN "GRAFTABL.COM" AS #1 LEN=1:FIELD #1,1 AS A$
160 IF LOF(1)=1169 THEN S=4 ELSE S=48
170 GET #1,1+S:IF ASC(A$)<>120 THEN CLOSE:GOTO 360
180 FOR B=1 TO 128:LOCATE 1,1,0:PRINT 128-B:FOR C=1 TO 8
190 GET #1,(B-1)*8+C+S:H(B,C)=ASC(A$):NEXT:NEXT:CLOSE:CLS
200 ' --- gets ASCII value ---
210 PRINT "Enter any number between 128 and 255"
220 PRINT "or (press the <F10> key to end): ";
230 I$=INKEY$:IF I$="" THEN 230 ELSE IF I$=CHR$(0)+"D" THEN END
240 IF I$>CHR$(57) OR I$<CHR$(48) THEN BEEP:GOTO 230
250 C$=C$+I$:PRINT I$;:IF LEN(C$)<3 THEN 230
260 IF VAL(C$)<128 OR VAL(C$)>255 THEN C$="":CLS:GOTO 210
270 ' --- draws dot pattern row by row ---
280 CLS:FOR E=1 TO 8
290 F=H(VAL(C$)-127,E)
300 IF F=0 THEN PRINT STRING$(16,176):GOTO 340
310 FOR G=7 TO 0 STEP -1
320 IF F<2^G THEN PRINT M$; ELSE PRINT N$;:F=F-2^G
330 NEXT:PRINT
340 NEXT:PRINT:PRINT TAB(8);CHR$(VAL(C$)):PRINT:C$="":GOTO 210
350 ' --- if correct file is not found ---
360 PRINT "Put DOS 3.0 or later GRAFTABL.COM on disk and restart"
```

If you want to see the cents sign that's missing from the IBM keyboard, just run GRAFPRINT and type in 155. (If your printer can handle it, you can insert this character into your documents where needed, by using the Alt-key method described below.) The nonalphanumeric typewriter keys have their own ASCII codes:

- Backspace 8
- Tab   9
- Enter   13

You can see the characters produced by these three by pressing the actual keys. Or you could press Ctrl-H to print a backspace, Ctrl- I to print a tab, and Ctrl-M to print a backspace. (Pressing Ctrl-H means holding down the Ctrl key and pressing the H key.) In fact, you could also see the lower 26 ASCII characters by running ROMPRINT, and holding down the Ctrl key while you type the letters of the alphabet.

Why?

Shift and Special Purpose Keys

A typewriter contains just one set of Shift keys, in which both keys do the exact same thing and are duplicated just to make two-handed typing easier. The PC keyboard contains three different sets of Shift keys, not just one. Each changes the meaning of an alphanumeric key just as pressing the A key by itself produces an "a" but pressing it while holding the Shift key down produces a capital A. To your computer, a and A are totally different characters with different ASCII codes (although certain programs, such as DOS and BASIC, automatically translate most lowercase keys to their uppercase versions).

When you type an A, the keyboard sends two special codes to the CPU — the first a hardware interrupt telling it to wake up because a key has been struck, and the second a *scan code* telling it that this particular key happened to be a capital A. Then, when you lift your finger off the A, the keyboard actually sends a third *release code* telling the CPU you're all done, which comes in handy when you're holding down a key to repeat a whole row of the same character, such as an underline.

But your PC needs to keep track of more than just letters, numbers, and punctuation. It has to know when you want to go to the next line, or the next page, or tab over to the right — or when to beep to get your attention, or to stop when you press the panic button because something is going wrong. And the programs you run have to know lots more, such as when text should be underlined or boldfaced.

To make it easy for you to generate these additional codes, your PC gives you two extra Shift keys, Ctrl and Alt. All these extra Shift keys really do is change the codes generated by your normal alphanumeric typewriter keys. It's up to the program you're running to interpret the special codes that you type into meaningful commands. Unfortunately, there's virtually no standardization of codes today; just about every program uses its own completely unique set. The code that tells one word processor to shift into boldfaced text might tell another word processor to change the right margin.

When you type any letter, your computer looks at a special pair of *status bytes* at locations 417 and 418 in the very bottom (0000) segment of memory to see if any of the Shift keys are engaged. Whenever you hold down a Shift key or toggle one on, your computer "sets" (turns from 0 to 1) an individual bit in one of these two bytes to keep track of every shift state in the system. It then resets (turns back to 0) the relevant bits when you lift your finger or toggle a Shift key off. Later we'll provide tools that give you control over these bytes and let you set them in any state you want.

If the status bytes show that no Shift keys are active, your computer translates the scan code sent by the letters on your keyboard into ASCII values somewhere between 97 (an a) and 122 (a z).

If you're holding down the normal Shift key, your computer knows you want a capital letter, and translates the keystroke into an ASCII value between 65 (A) and 90 (Z). The ASCII value for each uppercase letter is the same as the value for the lowercase letter minus 32, and your computer can instantly turn a lowercase letter into its uppercase version simply by turning the sixth bit from a 1 to a 0. In the binary representation of the ASCII code for every lowercase letter, the sixth bit over from the right is always on (set to 1). In every uppercase letter, this bit is turned off (set to 0). When this bit is on, it adds a value of 2^6 (or 32) to the ASCII code. Turning the bit on adds 32 and lowercases any letter; turning it off subtracts 32 and uppercases the letter.

You can verify this by looking at Figure 5.1 above, which is conveniently arranged in columns 16 entries long. The uppercase letters in columns 3 and 4 are in the same relative positions as the lowercase versions in columns 5 and 6. Each is just shifted 32 table entries (or exactly two columns) over.

When you type in letters while holding down the Ctrl key, your computer generates codes between 1 (for both A and a) and 26 (for both Z and z). The ASCII value for these is the same as the value for the corresponding uppercase letter minus 64.

Typing Ctrl-A is the same to your computer as typing Ctrl-a; the Ctrl key takes precedence over the normal Shift key. (When manuals refer to Ctrl-shifted keys they always use capital letters, so you'll see Ctrl-A and Ctrl-B but never Ctrl-a and Ctrl-b.)

If you're in DOS, typing Ctrl-A will put a ^A onscreen. The caret (^) as a prefix is shorthand for Ctrl. As mentioned earlier, some of the Ctrl-shifted keys trigger DOS or BASIC operations. You can tell DOS you're done creating a file by typing Ctrl-Z. You can make DOS beep by telling it to ECHO a ^G. To see this in action, get into DOS, type the following line, and press the Enter key. To generate the ^G, hold down the Ctrl key and type G while the Ctrl key is down:

```
ECHO ^G
```

You could also have typed:

```
COPY CON BEEP
^G^Z
```

which would have created a file called BEEP. (To create the ^G and the ^Z, hold down the Ctrl key and press GZ.) Then type:

```
TYPE BEEP
```

and you'd hear the familiar tone. If you try this, erase the BEEP file you just created by typing ERASE BEEP, or else you'll clutter up your disk.

The important DOS Ctrl and alphabetic key combinations are:

| Ctrl | C | Generally breaks out of whatever you happen to be doing at the time. Interchangeable most of the time (not in BASIC) with Ctrl-Break. |

| Ctrl | G | Beep (only when used in certain ways). |

| Ctrl | H | Same as backspace. |

| Ctrl | I | Same as Tab. |

| Ctrl | M | Same as Enter. |

| Ctrl | P | Acts as a "toggle" to turn a feature on and off that sends whatever is appearing onscreen simultaneously to your printer. Be sure your printer is on before trying this. If your system "hangs" and all you get is an error message, press Ctrl-P again to toggle it off. Typing in Ctrl-PrtSc is usually the same as typing Ctrl-P, although Ctrl-PrtSc works in BASIC while Ctrl-P doesn't. This shouldn't be confused with Shift-PrtSc, which dumps an image of whatever is onscreen to your printer one whole screen at a time. |

| Ctrl | S | Freezes and restarts some DOS operations (like scrolling DIR listings); similar to Ctrl-NumLock except that Ctrl-Numlock will only suspend things while Ctrl-S will pause and restart them |

| Ctrl | Z | DOS end-of-file marker. |

You can see the characters IBM uses to represent all the ASCII codes below 32 by running ROMPRINT and typing in Ctrl-A for ASCII character 1, Ctrl-B for character 2, etc. Figure 5.2 shows the ASCII Ctrl characters. To extend the ASCII chart, shown in Figure 5.1, attach these two columns to the left side:

ASCII	Crtl	CHR	ASCII	Ctrl	CHR
0	^@		16	^P	►
1	^A	☺	17	^Q	◄
2	^B	☻	18	^R	↕
3	^C	♥	19	^S	‼
4	^D	♦	20	^T	¶
5	^E	♣	21	^U	§
6	^F	♠	22	^V	▬
7	^G	•	23	^W	↨
8	^H	◘	24	^X	↑
9	^I	○	25	^Y	↓
10	^J	◙	26	^Z	→
11	^K	♂	27	^[	←
12	^L	♀	28	^\	∟
13	^M	♪	29	^]	↔
14	^N	♫	30	^^	▲
15	^O	☼	31	^_	▼

Figure 5.2. ASCII Ctrl Characters

Some of the characters in Figure 5.2 may look a little strange. The ^^ means Ctrl-caret and the ^_ means Ctrl-underline, which look odd, but don't worry, since you'll never really have to use them. The ^[represents ASCII character 27, or Esc, and you definitely will have lots of reasons to use this one. It plays a critical role in issuing *escape codes* or *escape sequences* that can put your printer through its paces or help send DOS commands to set screen colors or redefine keys using ANSI.SYS.

The ^@ (ASCII character 0) is a *null* that your system uses to identify plain old function keys, function keys you press while holding down Shift keys (Shift, Ctrl, Alt), or various keys you press while holding down the Alt key (such as Alt-A, Alt-5, or Alt-=). Some programs, especially communications software, insert nulls as placeholders in data files, which can play havoc with noncomprehending applications like old-fashioned word processors.

As mentioned above, the Ctrl key has a special role when used with some of the non-alphabetic keys:

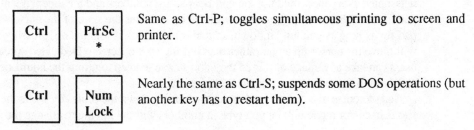

Ctrl **PtrSc** *	Same as Ctrl-P; toggles simultaneous printing to screen and printer.
Ctrl **Num Lock**	Nearly the same as Ctrl-S; suspends some DOS operations (but another key has to restart them).

Ctrl	Scroll Lock

Nearly the same as Ctrl-C; breaks or stops many DOS operations. Stops BASIC operations while Ctrl-C won't.

Ctrl	Alt	Del

Performs "warm" reboot that restarts system but bypasses time-consuming diagnostic tests. Hold Ctrl and Alt down first and then press Del.

interchangeable in DOS, but only Ctrl-PrtSc will echo what's on the screen to the printer; Ctrl-NumLock will pause the display but Ctrl-S won't, and Ctrl-Break will stop BASIC in its tracks but Ctrl-C won't.

However, BASIC throws in a few Ctrl-key gifts of its own. Ctrl-Home clears the screen, Ctrl-left arrow (or Ctrl-B) moves the cursor to the previous word, Ctrl-right arrow (or Ctrl-F) moves the cursor to the next word, and Ctrl-End (or Ctrl-E) erases to the end of the current line. Ctrl-K moves the cursor to the home position at the screen's upper left corner, Ctrl-L clears the screen (just like Ctrl-Home), Ctrl-N moves the cursor to the end of the current line (like the End key), Ctrl-G really does beep, Ctrl-R toggles between insert and overwrite modes, and Ctrl-[simulates an Esc. The odd quartet of Ctrl-\, Ctrl-], Ctrl-caret, and Ctrl-underline move the cursor right, left, up, and down respectively.

If you want to prevent users from breaking out of programs by pressing Ctrl-C or Ctrl-ScrollLock, or resetting your system by pressing Ctrl-Alt-Del, you can run the CTRLLOCK.COM Ctrl-key disabler on the accompanying disk.

This program effectively prevents anyone from rebooting the system by using Ctrl-Alt-Del, so if you do want to reboot you have only two choices. You can turn the main power switch off and then on again. Or you can run the WARMBOOT.COM program on the accompanying disk.

Both Shift keys work exactly alike, although your computer can tell whether you've pressed the left or right one. Game designers often use the different Shift keys to perform different tasks, such as triggering left or right flippers in pinball games. Each Shift key doesn't do much more than flip the case of letters. It turns lowercase letters into uppercase ones, just like the Shift on a typewriter. It also works backwards when the Caps-Lock key is toggled on, so that uppercase keys turn into their lowercase cousins.

The Shift key also temporarily reverses the state of the cursor/number pad. The Num-Lock toggle is normally off so the pad works in cursor mode when you first boot up (although IBM turned it back on when it delivered the 101-key wide-load keyboard, since it assumed everyone would use the number pad for numbers and the independent cursor pad to move the cursor). Pressing the Shift key switches the state of the cursor/number pad for as long as you hold it down, so that if NumLock is toggled on, pressing Shift-8 will move the cursor up a line rather than putting an 8 onscreen. Dedicated spreadsheet users can take advantage of this so they don't have to keep toggling the NumLock back and forth to move the cursor between numeric entries.

And of course, the reverse is also true — holding down the Shift key while the cursor pad is in cursor mode will let you type in numbers without having to change the state of the pad. This is especially handy on machines that don't have shift indicator lights, since it lets users stay in one mode all the time and use the Shift key only when they have to switch temporarily to the other mode and back.

Shift does have one special trick up its sleeve. You can use it to make *hard copies* on your printer of whatever text happens to be on your screen, simply by pressing Shift-PrtSc. This is referred to as a *screen dump*. The dump will show only the current screen; if you want to take every single line on your screen and "echo" it simultaneously to your printer, use Ctrl-PrtSc or Ctrl-P instead. (While Ctrl-P will toggle simultaneous printing, all Shift-P will do is print a capital S on your screen.)

The problem with Shift-PrtSc is that if you trigger it inadvertently it will either waste a sheet of paper if your printer is currently turned on and *online* (connected to your PC and ready to receive characters), or freeze your system if the printer is either turned off or *offline*. If this happens, the easiest thing to do is turn the printer on, let it print the screen dump, and then turn it off. If you don't have a printer connected, you may have to wait for the system to *time out* since it will give up and unfreeze the system after a good long wait.

It's fairly simple to deactivate the screen dump feature, since a screen dump is an interrupt (INT 5). The first thing such an interrupt does when triggered is look in the Interrupt Vector Table to find the address of the actual dumping program. You could poke around in the table and change the address to something harmless, but this would disable the feature the whole time your system was running, unless you went back and restored it. A better way is to use the utility we provide, which puts a message on your screen after you press Shift-PrtSc and asks if you really want to go ahead or if you just pressed the keys by mistake. If you did press them accidentally, the utility will go away and give you back control of your system before it has a chance to lock up.

Screen dumps don't always work. Text screens often contain high-bit ASCII border and box-drawing characters that many printers don't understand. While your screen may display a very fancy menu box with shadows on two sides giving it a classy 3-D effect, dumping the image to your printer may produce an ugly mess. And true graphics images often send printers into fits. If you want to dump unusual characters or fancy graphics images to your IBM-compatible printer, load the memory-resident DOS GRAPHICS utility first (simply by typing GRAPHICS at the DOS prompt). Then type Shift-PrtSc. If you don't have an official IBM printer, this may not work. Some printer manufacturers who persist in using nonstandard codes may supply their own graphics screen dump programs. And just about every non-IBM Shift-PrtSc graphics dump will have little white horizontal stripes on it, since IBM's official graphics resolution is — surprise — different from most other manufacturers'.

| Shift | Temporarily reverses whatever shift state the keyboard is in. Normally, all this does is turn lowercase letters into capital letters. But if CapsLock is on and everything you're typing is capitalized, holding either Shift key down lets you type a few lowercase letters. Even better, it flips the state of the cursor/number pad, to let you move the cursor while in numeric mode or enter numbers while in cursor mode. |

Shift	PrtSc *

Prints a screen dump — a copy of whatever is currently on the screen. If you want a graphics image printed, you have to execute the external DOS GRAPHICS command first, and hope when your salesman sold you that "IBM compatible" printer he wasn't just blowing smoke.

The Alt key doesn't really do much on its own, but team it up with the number pad and you get a powerful tool. About the only thing the Alt key does, in fact, is provide a shorthand way of writing and editing BASIC programs. When you're using the BASIC editor, instead of having to type SCREEN, you can just press Alt-S and the word SCREEN will pop onto the screen. BASIC supplies Alt-key shortcuts for every letter of the alphabet except J, Q, Y, and Z. But not too many programmers really use these. Figure 5.3 shows the Alt-key combinations that can be used in BASIC.

Alt-A	AUTO	Alt-M	MOTOR
Alt-B	BSAVE	Alt-N	NEXT
Alt-C	COLOR	Alt-O	OPEN
Alt-D	DELETE	Alt-P	PRINT
Alt-E	ELSE	Alt-R	RUN
Alt-F	FOR	Alt-S	SCREEN
Alt-G	GOTO	Alt-T	THEN
Alt-H	HEX$	Alt-U	USING
Alt-I	INPUT	Alt-V	VAL
Alt-K	KEY	Alt-W	WIDTH
Alt-L	LOCATE	Alt-X	XOR

Figure 5.3. BASIC Alt-Key Shortcuts

Note: No Alt-key combinations for J,Q,Y,Z

Although these shortcuts are currently built into IBM hardware, they're really out of date. The MOTOR command, for instance, is used only to start and stop tape cassette operation, and the mechanism for this was discontinued years ago. But the command remains. (Actually, early BASIC programmers found a legitimate use for this command. All it really did was turn a mechanical switch called a solenoid on or off, and programmers found that by repeatedly and rapidly turning it on and then off, they could generate a motorboat sound.)

The Alt key's real magic is in generating ASCII characters. By holding down the Alt key, typing in a decimal ASCII value on the number pad, and then releasing the Alt key, you can make any character appear at the cursor except one — a null, or ASCII character 0. Null identifies shifted key combinations or nonalphanumeric keys such as Home, End, or F1. (IBM claims you can generate this null character by typing in Alt-2, but that doesn't work. However, pressing the F7 function key in DOS will generate an ASCII 0 and put a ^@ onscreen; if you're using the DOS COPY CON technique to create a small file, just tap F7 to insert a null.) This technique works only with the number pad. Holding down the Alt key and typing the numbers on the top-row typewriter keys just won't do it.

The Alt-number pad technique is extremely useful for creating fancy borders, boxes, math formulas, foreign language characters, and anything else you can construct out of the high-bit ASCII characters — those with values greater than 127. It's also handy for exercising the ASCII characters with very low values — less than 32.

Want to see a smiling face in DOS? Just type ECHO and a space, hold down the Alt key, type 1 (or 2), release the Alt key, and press the Enter key. Then have a nice day. You could have also typed Ctrl-A in place of Alt-1, or Ctrl-B instead of Alt-2, to generate the face character. It's easy to remember that A is the first letter of the alphabet, B the second, C the third, and Z the 26th. But quick — which letter do you hold down for V? It's far easier to type Alt-22.

And while you can use the Ctrl-key combinations as well as the Alt- key ones for very low characters, once you get past Z, you're strictly in Alt territory.

To generate little boxes in DOS, type the two sets of keystrokes that follow. An instruction like ALT-201 means:

1. Hold down the Alt key.
2. Type 201 on the number pad, not the top row.
3. Release the Alt key.

An "Enter" means press the Enter key, "space" means tap the spacebar, and "F6" means lean on the grey F6 function key.

For a small single-line box

```
COPY CON SINGLE
Enter
ALT-218
ALT-196
ALT-196
ALT-191
Enter
ALT-179
space
space
ALT-179
Enter
ALT-192
ALT-196
ALT-196
ALT-217
Enter
```

For a small double-line box:

```
COPY CON DOUBLE
Enter
ALT-201
ALT-205
ALT-205
ALT-187
Enter
ALT-186
space
space
ALT-186
Enter
ALT-200
ALT-205
ALT-205
ALT-188
Enter
```

```
F6                          F6
Enter                       Enter
```

When you're done, type:

```
TYPE SINGLE
```

for a single-line box, and

```
TYPE DOUBLE
```

for a double-line box.
The boxes look like this:

Once you have the basic box parts — the four corners, the horizontal line, and the vertical line — created, you can work on the files with your word processor and use the block copy feature to expand it and change its shape. Some word processors may be confused by the high ASCII values, however.

You can combine single and double-line boxes in four possible ways. The ASCII values you need to know to draw these are as follows:

Single horizontal, single vertical:

```
    218     196     194     191
     ┌       ─       ┬       ┐
179  │                       │ 179
195  ├       197─   ┼       ┤ 180
     └       ─       ┴       ┘
    192     196     193     217
```

Double horizontal, double vertical:

```
    201     205     203     187
     ╔       ═       ╦       ╗
186  ║                       ║ 186
204  ╠       206─   ╬       ╣ 185
     ╚       ═       ╩       ╝
    200     205     202     188
```

Single horizontal, double vertical:

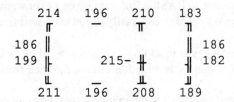

Double horizontal, single vertical:

```
     213    205    209    184
      F      =      T      ]

179  |                     |   179
198  |=     216-   +     =|   181

      L      =      ⊥      ]
     212    205    207    190
```

You can also use the high-bit solid and shaded characters to draw pictures onscreen. You may want to use the GRAFPRNT.BAS program to look at these in more detail. IBM provides a kit of eight:

219	solid box
178	75% grey
177	50% grey
176	25% grey
220	bottom half
223	top half
221	left half
222	right half

These may not seem like a flexible enough arsenal, but with a little ingenuity you can use these and other high-bit characters to draw charts, tables, graphs, and even animated pictures.

You use the Alt key in BASIC instead of the usual CHR$(n) notation. If you wanted to print a capital A you could tell BASIC:

```
PRINT CHR$(65)
```

Or you could say:

```
PRINT "A"
```

The same is true with high-bit characters. Just type in PRINT and the left quotation mark, use the Alt-number pad technique to generate the character you want, and then type a closing quotation mark. It's all the same to BASIC. But even if you never want to touch a line of BASIC, the Alt key can be very useful, especially if you keep sensitive files on your disks.

One of the very best uses of the Alt key is in adding a special kind of blank character in your filenames that can prevent casual users who don't know the trick from gaining access to your sensitive files.

If you keep a file on your disk that you don't want anyone to see, you can do several things to keep it out of harm's way:

1. Lock your system whenever you walk away from it for even a few seconds.
2. Hide the file from normal directory searches.
3. Hide the subdirectory in which the file is stored.
4. Give the file an incomprehensible name such as LVX_1TQY or an innocent one like DIAGNOST.PRG.
5. If your applications software can handle it (some can't), put a Ctrl-Z DOS end-of-file marker as the first character in the file, to prevent casual snoops from using the DOS TYPE command to view the contents.
6. Slap (mostly) invisible character on the end of it that most users won't figure out.

Actually, there's only one way to keep your data safe, and that's to maintain it on removable media such as floppy disks or Bernoulli cartridges, and keep these locked up. (To edit or consult such secret files, security-conscious users frequently copy them from floppies to their hard disks and then put them back on floppies when they're done. Then they erase the sensitive files from their hard disk. Programs like the *Norton Utilities* make it easy for someone to come along and "unerase" these files. But Norton also provides a utility called WIPEFILE that can totally obliterate any traces of your secret data. If you do use a program like WIPEFILE, be sure to check your hard disk for all erased files, since many applications create temporary work files without your knowledge that remain hidden on your disk. These can be just as dangerous in the wrong hands as the originals.)

Trick #6 above is easy. To try it, create a dummy file called DUMMY.BAT by typing the program below and pressing the Enter key at the end of each line. Press the F6 function key where it says <F6>, and then press the Enter key again at the very end. Note — don't actually enter the @ sign shown in the filename. In place of the @ after the word DUMMY, enter Alt-255 by holding down the Alt key, typing 255 on your number pad, and then releasing the Alt key. What looks like a space will appear above the cursor. Then continue typing the letters .BAT that follow this character.

```
COPY CON DUMMY@.BAT
ECHO OFF
ECHO Most users couldn't get this far
<F6>
```

Verify that the file is on your disk by typing:

```
DIR DUM*.*
```

and you'll see something like:

```
DUMMY BAT 49 9-08-89 10:59p
```

Since this is a batch file, you should be able to execute it simply by typing the part of the filename before the BAT extension. But if you type just:

```
DUMMY
```

all you'll get is an error message that says:

```
Bad command or filename
```

This is because the name of the file isn't DUMMY.BAT; it's DUMMY@.BAT, where the @ represents the ASCII 255 blank character. Now press the F3 key, which will dredge up the last command you typed, and put the letters DUMMY at the DOS prompt — but don't press the Enter key yet. Instead, use the Alt-key trick to type in the Alt-255 character, and then press the Enter key. You should see:

```
ECHO OFF
Most users couldn't get this far
```

Remember, this filename has six characters before the BAT extension, not five. The sixth is ASCII character 255, which is a blank. It may be annoying to have to use the Alt-255 technique every time you want to do anything with the file, but it will keep the honest people from snooping into it.

Unscrupulous users will always find a way. They may know the Alt-key trick. If they don't, they'll realize something is fishy when they try the DOS TYPE command:

```
TYPE DUMMY.BAT
```

and nothing happens. If they're smart, they'll know another way to display the contents of files. All they have to do is type:

```
COPY DUM*.* CON /B
```

This command tells DOS to display the full contents every file beginning with the letters DUM. Adding a /B at the end gets around the trick of putting a Ctrl-Z as the first character of the file.

This trick works fairly well with directory listings, since DOS puts spaces between the left half of the filename and its extension rather than a period. But if you copied a file that had an Alt-255 character in its filename, DOS would tip its hand. If this file were the only one on your disk that started with the letters DUM, and you typed:

```
COPY DUM*.* ZUM*.*
```

DOS would print:

```
DUMMY .BAT
       1 File(s) copied
```

which would reveal the extra blank character before the period. Still, it will keep casual users from causing problems.

If you already know what subdirectories are, you might want to use this Alt-255 trick the next time you create one. (If you don't, refer to Chapter 3, and then come back here and try this.) When you type MD (or MKDIR) to create a subdirectory, add an Alt-255 to the end of the subdirectory name just as you did with the DUMMY filename above. Once you've created it, you won't be able to log into it, or remove it, or do anything to it unless you tack on the Alt-255. The only problem with this is that if you change your DOS prompt (with a command like $P:) the blank space will look odd. If you created a subdirectory called C:\DOS* (again, where the * represents an Alt-255), and your prompt was indeed $P:, when you logged into it you'd see:

```
C:\DOS :
```

Still, casual users would think the blank was a space, and wouldn't be able to log into the subdirectory unless they knew how to generate an ALT-255.

Alt

1 End	7 Home	3 PgDn

Holding down the Alt key and typing an ASCII code on the number pad, and then releasing the Alt key produces an ASCII character for that code, here an upside down ¡for ASCII character 173.

You don't have to type in all three numbers; Alt-1 works just like Alt-001. And if you type more than three numbers, the PC first does a mod 256 operation on the it (converts it to an integer between 0 and 255). One interesting note about the Alt key — if you press it and the Ctrl key and either Shift key at the same time, the PC gives the Alt key priority, and then Ctrl. It works alphabetically.

While you can't use the top row numbers to generate Alt-key ASCII codes, they'll work just as well as the number pad when it comes to entering numbers in most applications. But numbers aren't the only characters that you can enter in different ways.

Cursor Movement and Number Pad Keys

Your keyboard sports two pluses and two minuses, as well as two periods and two asterisks. This redundancy makes sense, since IBM had to keep users happy who were accustomed to typewriter layouts, while appealing to green eyeshade types who use adding machine keypads all day long. IBM's new wide-body keyboard goes even further in this direction.

One thing that confuses legions of new users are the four keys with arrows on them pointing left. These do four very different things:

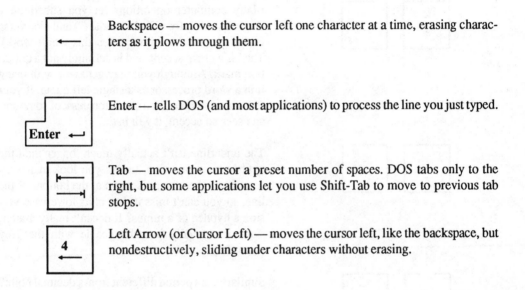

Backspace — moves the cursor left one character at a time, erasing characters as it plows through them.

Enter — tells DOS (and most applications) to process the line you just typed.

Tab — moves the cursor a preset number of spaces. DOS tabs only to the right, but some applications let you use Shift-Tab to move to previous tab stops.

Left Arrow (or Cursor Left) — moves the cursor left, like the backspace, but nondestructively, sliding under characters without erasing.

But these aren't the only potentially troublesome pairs or trios of keys.

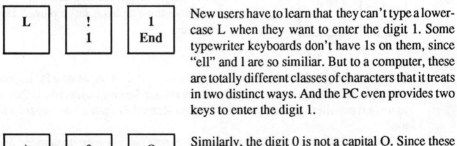

New users have to learn that they can't type a lowercase L when they want to enter the digit 1. Some typewriter keyboards don't have 1s on them, since "ell" and 1 are so similiar. But to a computer, these are totally different classes of characters that it treats in two distinct ways. And the PC even provides two keys to enter the digit 1.

Similarly, the digit 0 is not a capital O. Since these are often hard to distinguish on some systems, experienced users put a slash through zeros whether entered from the top row or the number pad.

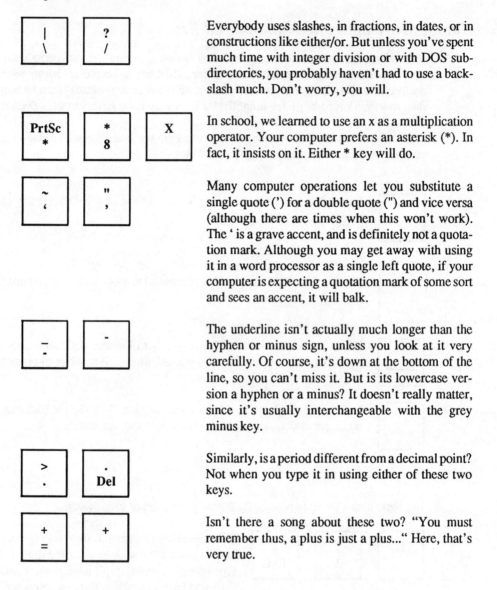

Everybody uses slashes, in fractions, in dates, or in constructions like either/or. But unless you've spent much time with integer division or with DOS subdirectories, you probably haven't had to use a backslash much. Don't worry, you will.

In school, we learned to use an x as a multiplication operator. Your computer prefers an asterisk (*). In fact, it insists on it. Either * key will do.

Many computer operations let you substitute a single quote (') for a double quote (") and vice versa (although there are times when this won't work). The ' is a grave accent, and is definitely not a quotation mark. Although you may get away with using it in a word processor as a single left quote, if your computer is expecting a quotation mark of some sort and sees an accent, it will balk.

The underline isn't actually much longer than the hyphen or minus sign, unless you look at it very carefully. Of course, it's down at the bottom of the line, so you can't miss it. But is its lowercase version a hyphen or a minus? It doesn't really matter, since it's usually interchangeable with the grey minus key.

Similarly, is a period different from a decimal point? Not when you type it in using either of these two keys.

Isn't there a song about these two? "You must remember thus, a plus is just a plus..." Here, that's very true.

The funny thing is that when most new users first get their hands on a PC keyboard, they complain about all the extra keys. Once they master the new keyboards, if they ever have to use a typewriter again they end up echoing Ronald Reagan's line "where's the rest of me?"

The NumLock key — which toggles the cursor pad between its numeric and cursor-moving states — is the source of much user consternation. Somehow it always seems to wriggle itself into the opposite state from the one you want. If you're trying to move your cursor up the screen, for instance, you may end up with a row of 888888s instead, since Up Arrow and 8 share the same key.

The disk that accompanies this book contains three programs that help you work with Shift Lock keys. For example, it's possible to set the state of a Shift Lock key more or less permanently, and then run a short program that disables it for as long as you want. A second program is for users who don't ever enter numbers on the cursor pad and causes the PC to beep if NumLock is set wrong. A third program can change any shift state with a single command. But most users want the flexibility to shift it back and forth, and they don't need any extra beeps. If you want to take our word for this, and skip the slightly technical explanation that follows, jump ahead in this chapter right now to the section on freezing your display.

Since IBM's 101/102-key keyboard provides a number pad and a separate cursor pad, it designed the keyboard to start operating with the number pad already in numeric mode. Some users hate this. If you're among them, you can create a tiny program that will reset the NumLock state for you. You can add the name of this tiny file to your AUTOEXEC.BAT program to do the resetting right after you boot up. Figure 5.4 shows you how.

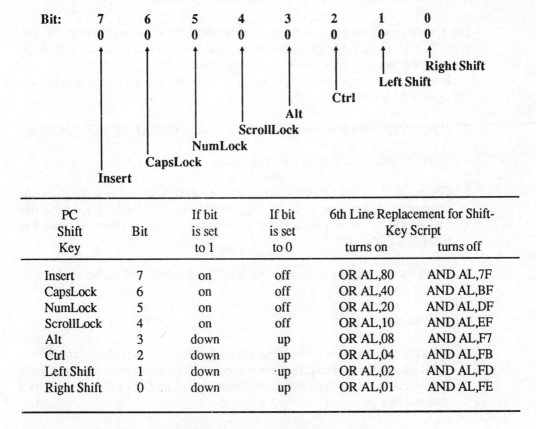

PC Shift Key	Bit	If bit is set to 1	If bit is set to 0	6th Line Replacement for Shift-Key Script	
				turns on	turns off
Insert	7	on	off	OR AL,80	AND AL,7F
CapsLock	6	on	off	OR AL,40	AND AL,BF
NumLock	5	on	off	OR AL,20	AND AL,DF
ScrollLock	4	on	off	OR AL,10	AND AL,EF
Alt	3	down	up	OR AL,08	AND AL,F7
Ctrl	2	down	up	OR AL,04	AND AL,FB
Left Shift	1	down	up	OR AL,02	AND AL,FD
Right Shift	0	down	up	OR AL,01	AND AL,FE

Figure 5.4. Keyboard Status Control Bytes at Address 0000:0417

The PC keeps track of the state of each Shift key by setting (turning to 1) and unsetting (turning to 0) individual bits in the Keyboard Status Control Byte at address 0000:0417 in RAM. It's easy to adapt an all-purpose assembly language program to set or unset any of these Shift keys. The basic framework is a file called SHIFTKEY.SCR:

```
N UNAMEIT.COM           <— 1. REPLACE THE FILENAME.
A
MOV DX,0040
MOV DS,DX
MOV AL,[0017]
AND AL,DF               <— 2. CHANGE THIS LINE.
MOV [0017],AL
INT 20

RCX
F
W
Q
```

Use a word processor to create the basic SHIFTKEY.SCR, starting with the N UN-AMEIT.COM line and ending with the Q. Be sure to leave the blank line above the RCX, and press the Enter key after each line, especially the last line.

Then, to create a particular assembly language file to set one of the Shift keys the way you want it, all you have to do is:

1. Make a copy of the SHIFTKEY.SCR file and call it WORKFILE.SCR, by typing:

    ```
    COPY SHIFTKEY.SCR WORKFILE.SCR
    ```

2. Change the UNAMEIT.COM in the top line to reflect what you're going to use the program for. If you want to set the CapsLock key on, you might pick a name like CAPSON.COM. If you want to set the NumLock key off, choose a name like NUMOFF.COM.

3. Here's the only slightly tricky part. Replace the entire sixth line — the one that now says

    ```
    AND AL,DF
    ```

    with a line from the chart above. If you look at the two righthand columns in the chart, you'll see that the AND AL,DF turns NumLock off (if this is what you want, leave it alone). If you want to do something like turn the CapsLock on, however, you'd change it to

    ```
    OR AL,40
    ```

4. Then save this WORKFILE.SCR file with the changes you just made, and put it on the same disk as DEBUG.COM version 2.0 or later. To create the file, type:

```
DEBUG < WORKFILE.SCR
```

Obviously, this isn't much use in changing the status of a key like Alt or Ctrl. But these individual files are very useful for toggling the shift locks on your keyboard the exact way you want just as if you manually leaned on them yourself. You can put these in batch files that first set the appropriate shift state and then load your favorite commercial software, so the program comes up with all the shifts properly set and ready to go.

The assembly language utilities that you create this way all use the same technique. First they load the segment (0040) and the offset (0017) addresses. As mentioned earlier, you can express just about every address in many different ways. The address 0040:0017 is the same as 0000:0417, which is the same as absolute address 417. IBM calls the byte at this address the Keyboard Status Control Byte, or the Status Byte, and you'll often hear this important location referred to as the byte at address 417.

The utility then looks up the value at this address, and puts it into a workspace called a register. It performs a logical bit-mask operation on this value, forcing one particular bit to turn on or off, and then moves the newly changed value back to its old 417 address.

All a bit mask does is turn a single specified bit on (so it's a 1) or off (so it's a 0) while making sure the other seven bits in the byte aren't disturbed. The logical operation process itself is interesting since it has to be smart enough to switch the state of a bit when the bit is set incorrectly, but leave the state of the bit alone if it's already set properly. (Bit masks are explained in detail in Chapter 4.)

Remember that either Shift key will temporarily switch the state of the cursor/number pad. So if you're entering a series of numbers with NumLock set on, and you see a mistake and want to move the cursor up a few rows, just hold down either the left or right Shift and tap the Up Arrow key a few times. When you're done, release the Shift and you're back in numeric mode. And this works just as well the other way around.

But be careful. If NumLock is on and you're entering figures into the number pad, and you decide to hold down the Shift key to move the cursor, don't type in a period, since a shifted period is the same as a tap of the Delete key and something will vanish.

Incidentally, you can perform several bit mask operations at once. If you want to turn CapsLock and NumLock on at the same time, just add the two hex numbers in the OR column.

CapsLock	OR AL,40
+ NumLock	OR AL,20
Both	OR AL,60

(Remember that these are hex numbers. Adding 40 + 20 equals 60 both in decimal and hexadecimal notation. But adding 80 + 20 equals A0 in hex.)

Figuring out the combination AND numbers to turn shift states off isn't really all that hard. If you'll notice, the numbers in the AND column are just hex FF minus the numbers in the OR column. If OR AL,60 turns both the CapsLock and NumLock on, you can figure out which values will turn them off when used with a logical AND:

$$
\begin{array}{r}
FF \\
- \ 60 \\
\hline
9F
\end{array}
$$

So to turn CapsLock and NumLock off with the same command, use:

    AND AL, 9F

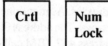 And of course you freeze DOS displays in mid-scroll by pressing Ctrl-NumLock. But to restart things you have to press a letter or number key. Ctrl-S is a better bet because the two keys are close together and because you can unfreeze the paused display just by pressing Ctrl-S again.

Freezing the Display

"Now hold on a minute," you might say, "let me get this straight. If I want to freeze my display while it's scrolling I have to hold down the Ctrl key and press NumLock? The key right next to NumLock on most systems is ScrollLock, but it doesn't seem to have anything to do with scrolling. You mean IBM named one key ScrollLock but didn't give it any connection with scrolling, and then went ahead and assigned a key the power to stop scrolling, but called it NumLock? Does IBM make up this stuff as it goes along?"

Well, you said it, we didn't.

To make matters worse, written below the ScrollLock label almost as an afterthought, and invisible in poor light, is the word "Break." Now ask yourself this: If you're new at this, and someone's just spent a pile of money on a system that's taken you and an installer a week to get working, and you already have a deadline staring you in the face, are you going to let any of your fingers even close to a key named Break? Especially a key that's somehow supposed to lock scrolling but doesn't do anything of the sort?

If you think about it for a second or two you'll realize that a panic button key isn't such a bad idea, since it's so easy for a computer to start running madly off in the opposite direction, and you need a device to get its attention again. But when your system is cranking madly away processing something you don't want it to, or scrolling through a long list that suddenly reveals the items you were searching for, the last thing you want to have to do is grope for two different keys. Imagine if a huge stamping press had a two-part red emergency stop button. If OSHA ever bought a PC they'd have the guy who designed the Break feature making little rocks out of big ones.

But remember, IBM provides an easier way to hit the brakes, with Ctrl-C, even through Ctrl-C and Ctrl-ScrollLock aren't exactly the same. The one thing they both may do is put a ^C on the screen if they manage to bring a process to its knees. Why didn't IBM use the far more mnemonic Ctrl-B to trigger this? They thought Ctrl-C was easy to remember, since by the time you find the two proper keys to press you're screaming "Come on already, break!"

The worst thing about having to grope blindly for Ctrl-ScrollLock or Ctrl-NumLock is that if your fingers slip a bit you may end up pressing Ctrl-PrtSc, which may indeed stop everything in its tracks as your system tries to send output to a printer that's turned off.

Break isn't just for emergencies. Some programs, like the current versions of EDLIN distributed along with DOS, are so primitive that they make you use Ctrl-ScrollLock to stop normal editing commands. Give us a break.

Pawing at Ctrl-ScrollLock or Ctrl-break won't always stop what you're doing. Some programs use these key combinations to trigger their own commands. Typing Ctrl-C in *WordStar* is the same as pressing the PgDn key. And if you press Ctrl-ScrollLock all *WordStar 3.3* will do is put a

```
(Vp6w6n?
```

on your screen.

Programmers can write software using a variety of keyboard-reading techniques that explicitly check or refrain from checking to see whether the user pressed Ctrl-C. DOS checks to see whether a user typed Ctrl-C only during standard input/output such as accepting keystrokes or displaying a file using the TYPE command, and when it's in control of printing or communications. But version 2.0 let users add the command:

```
SET BREAK=ON
```

to their CONFIG.SYS system configuration file, which forces DOS to check for this combination of keystrokes more frequently. However, forcing DOS to do anything usually slows it down a bit, and increased break-checking is no exception.

You can turn the extra break-checking on and off at the DOS prompt. Just type BREAK ON to enable the additional checks and (surprise) BREAK OFF to disable them. Typing just BREAK by itself will report the current ON or OFF status.

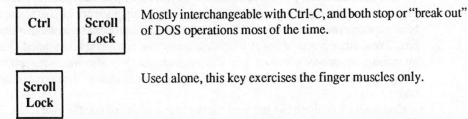

| Ctrl | Scroll Lock | Mostly interchangeable with Ctrl-C, and both stop or "break out" of DOS operations most of the time. |

| Scroll Lock | Used alone, this key exercises the finger muscles only. |

Caps Lock

New users often gripe that the CapsLock key doesn't work properly. On typewriters it usually hunkers down a quarter inch or so and stays there to let you know it's set. Early

PCs offered a feature to let you know as well. It was called looking at the screen to see whether everything you were typing was iN tHE wRONG sTATE. (We'll provide a utility later that educates the CapsLock key to smarten it up so it never does this to you again.)

The AT changed all this, by providing status lights to display the current state of the CapsLock, NumLock, and ScrollLock shifts. For some inexplicable reason, IBM left these off some of its later keyboards, even though the spaces for them were clearly visible. And with enough fancy fingerwork, you can knock these status lights out of synch, so they blink on when they should be off and vice versa. We'll explain how to reset them later.

The other complaint most often voiced by novices is that CapsLock doesn't shift "uppercase" punctuation marks properly. Toggle the CapsLock on and press the comma key expecting to see its upstairs < sign, or type the top row 1 when you want a ! and all you get is the unshifted version of each. Presumably IBM either felt the downstairs keys were more important, or thought that the only keys the CapsLock should adjust were the ones with just one character stamped on them — the alphabetic keys. Any key with two characters on it needs a tap on the Shift key to produce its upper version.

Esc

The Esc key is another (smaller scale) panic-button. In DOS, it stops what you're typing, prints a backslash, drops the cursor down to the next line, and gives you a chance to start over. It won't give you back your DOS prompt though, because it figured if you wanted to do that you'd pound on Ctrl-C. Instead, it assumes you interrupted your earlier command and want to try entering it again.

In most commercial applications, Esc steps you backwards through a succession of hierarchical menus or commands, or cancels operations. It's one of the few conventions adopted by a large number of program designers; the only other one is that F1 will summon some sort of help screen. If you're ever using a new application and the manual isn't handy or isn't indexed (hard to believe but true) or was written by the programmer and not a professional manual writer, and you're stuck, try drumming on the Esc key until you land in a familiar place.

ASCII character 27, generated by the Esc key, wakes up certain printers and screens. When you print a page all you're really doing is sending a stream of characters out the back of your system and down a cable to another set of processors in another hardware box. These other processors watch the data go by and convert it into printed characters by moving the printer's motors, gears, or mirrors. But they also watch for special *control* or *escape* codes that trigger the printer's processor to change the current configuration.

Commands like these can tell your printer to use larger or smaller characters, change paper trays or ribbon colors, adjust spacing measurements, shift to different type fonts, even print sideways (in *landscape* mode rather than *portrait* — these terms were borrowed from the art world where portraits are generally taller than they are wide and landscapes the other way around).

Escape sequences can also tell DOS you're trying to send it a special ANSI.SYS command. Few users take advantage of ANSI (which stands for the American National Standards Institute and is pronounced ANN-see), since its commands are nasty to deal with and don't work all the time. When everything is properly set, they can turn drabs screens into lush, colorful ones. But if you're not expecting an ANSI file brimming with escape characters and left brackets, and you try to do anything with it, you end up with a mess.

DOS screens are usually a dull grey on black, and work only one line at a time. And even if you've set your screen colors using a small utility like any of the ones we provide later, as soon as you type CLS to clear the screen, DOS jumps back to grey on black. The ANSI screen commands can position your DOS cursor anywhere you want it and set any character to any color. And the colors stick, so that CLS simply erases characters but doesn't meddle with any colors you've chosen.

You can also use the ANSI codes to redefine and add primitive macro features to your keyboard. And you can get at much of its magic through the underused DOS PROMPT command.

Function Keys

Function keys (F1 through F10 on older systems, F1 through F12 on newer ones) fall neatly into two categories — underused and overused. Some software, like *WordPerfect*, makes such extensive use of the these keys that it can be hard to remember whether to press F8, Ctrl-F8, Shift-F8, or Alt-F8 to get something done. Other software, like DOS, makes such feeble use of function keys that a few keys remain unassigned and most that are assigned remain unpopular with users.

Actually, function keys can be helpful in two ways. They can compress lots of hard-to-remember or tricky-to-type keystrokes onto one single key. And they can act as dedicated command keys so that pressing F1 brings up a help screen, or striking F9 jumps you to the beginning of a file and F10 to the end.

DOS uses the first seven function keys, F1 through F7, to make life a little easier at the keyboard. One key, F3, is indeed a terrific tool. The others are occasionally handy. (BASIC gives function keys far more intrinsic power.) You can harness ANSI's redefinition abilities to make function keys more useful, but few users bother. Most either don't use function keys much, or else purchase a full-fledged keyboard macro package like *ProKey* or *SuperKey* to redefine keys.

The majority of DOS's built-in function keys let you re-execute the previous DOS command you just entered, either exactly as you entered it earlier, or with changes. DOS puts all the keystrokes you type for each command into a *template*. If you typed in:

```
DIR
```

the template would contain just the letters D, I, and R. If you typed:

```
COPY C:\DOS\UTILITY\*.PRG B:\BACKUP\DOS\PROGS *.PBK /V
```

that whole long string of characters from the intial COPY to the final /V would be in the template. The ability to re-execute commands isn't such a big deal when all you're doing is typing DIR repeatedly. But even then, it's easier to press one key than three, and when you're dealing with long and thorny commands this can be an absolute blessing.

Some of the examples below use the same sample template, and assume you are logged onto drive C:

```
COPY A:ABCD B:WXYZ
```

Both of these take one key at a time from the previous command and copy it to the current command. So if you had finished executing the sample COPY command shown here, and were back again at the DOS prompt, the first time you press either of these keys, you'd see:

```
C
```

Press either key once again and the screen would look like:

```
CO
```

Press either one of these seven more times and you'd see:

```
COPY A:AB
```

So if you wanted to repeat the previous command, you could simply hold down the F1 or right-arrow key until DOS displayed the entire previous template. If you then press the Enter key, DOS would execute this command just as if you had typed it in. But there's a far easier way than dredging up all the keystrokes one at a time.

F3 One tap on F3 zaps the last command entered back onscreen. This is one of the best things the designers of DOS ever did. Since users frequently find themselves repeating DOS commands, and since many commands involve hard-to-type combinations of slashes, backslashes, colons, and hierglyphic filenames, F3 is a genuine boon.

Even better, you can use these keys to "fill out" the rest of a command. Here's a good example: Once you copy critical files, you may want to check the validity of the copies by using the COMP command to compare them to the originals. Both COPY and COMP are four letters long, and both share the same basic syntax. So once you type in:

```
COPY A:ABCD B:WXYZ
```

and press the Enter key to make the copies, you can simply type in:

```
COMP
```

and then press the F3 key. DOS will fill in the rest of the template for you, supplying drives and filenames of both the original files and the copies:

```
COMP A:ABCD B:WXYZ
```

You may have to edit the command slightly. If you used a /V suffix, or *switch*, at the end of the original COPY command to verify the accuracy of your copies, you'll have to delete it from the COMP command. But this is simple; just backspace it away. (Incidentally, adding a /V to verify the copying process — which is the same as giving DOS a VERIFY ON command — doesn't compare the two files byte by byte. Instead, it simply makes sure that DOS can read the appropriate sectors that contain the copy of your file, and then does a CRC check — a crude test for errors that catches flagrant mistakes but can be fooled. To compare two files more precisely, use the limited PC-DOS COMP or the better MS-DOS FC commands.)

Pressing F3 to COMP a file after you COPY it isn't really necessary unless your drives are acting up and generating error messages. But it doesn't hurt, especially when you're copying a vitally important file from a RAMdisk or hard disk to a single backup floppy. We've had lots of trouble with IBM's awful 1.2 megabyte floppy drives, where COPY /V bubbles blithely along without reporting any errors but COMP catches them by the fistful.

F1/right arrow and F3 can also turn a:

```
DISKCOPY A: B:
```

command into a:

```
DISKCOMP A: B:
```

with a few simple keystrokes. Just tap F1 six times, type in MP to replace the final two PY characters of DISKCOPY, and then press F3. (You really shouldn't use DISKCOPY to back up your files, for reasons we'll get to later.) But again, DOS provides an easier way.

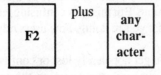

The first six letters of DISKCOPY and DISKCOMP are identical. You can have DOS copy those six letters from the old template into the new one by entering F2 and the seventh letter (in this case, the P in DISKCOPY). Typing F2 and the P would produce:

```
C>DISKCO
```

You could then type MP and then press F3 to finish changing the DISKCOPY A: B: into a DISKCOMP A: B:.

Typing F2 and then a character will look inside the template created by the previous command and copy everything up to (but not including) that character onto the screen.

In the unlikely event that you want to do the reverse — copy everything *after* a specific character — DOS will happily oblige.

SWEEP.COM, a program on the accompanying disk, lets you execute commands in all the subdirectories on your disk. You can see all the backup files that end with a .BAK in all of your subdirectories, by typing:

```
SWEEP DIR *.BAK
```

While this will display the backup files in every subdirectory, you might want to focus on the ones in the subdirectory you're currently working in (you can be in only one subdirectory at a time). You could re-enter the command:

```
DIR *.BAK
```

but DOS provides a slightly easier way.

| F4 | plus | any char-acter | Just type F4 and then D, and DOS will skip over all the characters up to the D in the word DIR. However, you won't see anything onscreen. But then press F3 and DOS will put the rest of the previous command onscreen, from the D onward. The F4 key works like the F2 key in reverse. |

So, if the previous command was:

```
SWEEP DIR *.BAK
```

and you typed F4, then D, then F3, you'd see:

```
DIR *.BAK
```

The F2 and F4 keys will always jump over or to the first occurrence of the character you specify. If you want to jump over or to a second or third occurrence of that character you can repeat the command a second or third time. But this gets confusing, especially when you're working with F4 and can't see what you're doing. Few users rely on the F2 key, and virtually nobody uses F4.

If you're trying any of the above tricks and you get hopelessly lost or confused, you can always press Ctrl-ScrollLock or Ctrl-C to abort, and start again on the next line. However, if you want to make some corrections in the current line, and keep working on it, you can do so.

| F5 | Pressing F5 replaces the old template from the previous command with the new one you're working on. You can then continue to edit this new one, using the F1, F2, F3, and F4 keys. This is another fairly useless and unpopular function key. |

While DOS provides the F1 through F5 keys to edit the command line template, it tosses in two more simple tools.

When you create files in DOS you have to tell it when you're done. You do this by adding an *end-of-file marker* as the very last character. This special character is a Ctrl-Z, with an ASCII value of 26 — easy to remember since Z is the 26th letter of the alphabet. You can generate this character using three different techniques. First, you could hold down the Ctrl key and press Z. Second, you could hold down the Alt key, type 26 on the number pad (not the top row number keys), and then release the Alt key. Or third, you could simply press F6. Each will put a ^Z onscreen and an end-of-file marker (which may show up under certain circumstances as a small right-pointing arrow) in your file.

Pressing F6 isn't much more efficient than typing Ctrl-Z. But it's there, and lots of users are accustomed to ending files by pressing F6 and then the Enter key.

F6	Puts an ASCII character 26 (Ctrl-Z end-of-file marker) onto the screen at the current cursor position.

The only other function key that does anything at all is F7, which sticks a null — with an ASCII value of 0 — onto the screen at the current cursor position. Pressing F7 prints a ^@ and can generate a CHR$(0) if you need one. You probably won't. But if you do, be glad F7 is there, since this null character is the only one you can't create using the Alt-key-plus-number-pad technique.

F7	Puts an ASCII character 0 (null) onto the screen at the current cursor position.

Several other keys can help you edit in DOS:

Esc	Pressing the Esc key cancels whatever you're doing, prints a backslash (\), and drops the cursor down one line without disturbing the contents of the old template. You can often get a similar interrupted result by pounding on Ctrl-ScrollLock or Ctrl-C.

Ins	Pressing the Ins key lets you insert characters at the cursor position without wiping out any characters in the template. DOS is normally in *overstrike* or *overwrite* mode, which means that if you put the cursor in the middle of a word and start typing, DOS will obliterate the old characters with any new ones you type. The Ins key will tell DOS to go into *insert* mode, which pushes existing text to the right as you type in new characters.

You'll find yourself using the Ins key often. If you were currently logged into drive C: and you tried to execute the example mentioned earlier:

```
COPY A:ABCD B:WXYZ
```

but you forgot the A: before ABCD, you'd end up with:

```
COPY ABCD B:WXYZ
```

This would tell DOS to copy the file ABCD from your current drive (which in this case would be C:) to drive B: and rename it WXYZ. What you really wanted to do however was copy the ABCD file on drive A:, but you forgot to specify the A:. If DOS found a file on drive C: called ABCD it would copy C:ABCD to B: and rename it during the process. But if DOS couldn't find it (which was probably the case) it would print an error message. To fix the command, you'd either lean on the F1 or the right arrow key to read the:

```
COPY
```

out of the old template, or you'd press F2 A, which would do the same thing a little faster. Then, press Ins to put DOS into insert mode and type A:

```
COPY A:
```

and finally, press F3 to put the rest of the old template onscreen:

```
COPY A:ABCD B:WXYZ
```

Del	Del simply deletes keys from the template one by one. If you spelled COPY COPPY, you'd just position the cursor on one of the Ps and press Del to erase it. You need to use the Del key when dealing with characters inside words. (COP Y isn't the same thing as COPY.) The Del key lets you close up the word and get rid of the extra space.

However, if the letter you have to erase happens to be at the beginning or end of a word, you can usually just press the space bar to get rid of it, since DOS interprets one space the same way it treats many continuous spaces. So:

```
C> COPY A:ABCD B:WXYZ
```

will do the same thing as the original example. If you spelled COPY mistakenly as COPYY, you could simply position the cursor on the second Y and press the spacebar.

If you realize you've made a typing mistake while you're working on the same line, you could either press F5 to replace the old template with the new one, and then move to the offending character and write over it, or you could backspace to the mistake, correct it, and then re-enter the rest of the command. The left arrow key will do the same thing. Both backspace "destructively" since they erase everything as they move.

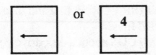 or Erases characters and moves the cursor to the left.

Of all the DOS function keys, the best is clearly F3. You'll find yourself using it all day long. One of the handiest F3 tricks lets you verify wildcard deletions. If you're working on a corporate contest, and have a lot of old files on your disk like CONTEST.RUL, CONTEST.TXT, CORP.LOG, and CORP.TXT, and you want to delete them all with the command:

```
DEL CO*.*
```

you'd better be careful, since this command would also erase files such as COMMAND.COM and COMP.COM. To see what files you would erase with such a wildcard command, first type:

```
DIR CO*.*
```

If all you see is something like:

```
CONTEST   RUL   1920    8-17-87   8:00p
CONTEST   TXT   26624   9-08-87   3:07p
CORP      LOG   3968    9-12-87   9:03p
CORP      TXT   7552    8-21-87   1:02p
```

Then just type:

```
DEL
```

and press the F3 key, which will add the remaining characters from the previous template:

```
DEL CO*.*
```

However, if you see files like COMMAND.COM in the directory listing, you can avoid potential trouble by making the DEL command more specific. In this case you might want to try it in two stages, first:

```
DEL CON*.*
```

and then:

```
DEL COR*.*
```

But even then it doesn't hurt to try DIR CON*.* and DIR COR*.* first and then use F3 when you're satisfied you won't erase any unexpected files.

F2 can be a real lifesaver as well. Whenever you tell DOS about a disk drive you have to use a colon. Unfortunately, the colon is a shifted character, and it's common when typing rapidly or working late to press the lowercase semicolon instead. If you end up with a command such as:

```
COPY A;ABCD B:WXYZ
```

DOS will become confused, since it treats a semicolon like a space (tabs, equals signs, and commas are also turned into *delimiters* that work like spaces). It will think that you're trying to copy a file called A on your current drive and rename it to ABCD in the process. But it won't understand the B:WXYZ and will print an "Invalid number of parameters" message.

To fix this, simply press F2 and then a semicolon, which will put a:

```
COPY A
```

onscreen. Then type a colon and press F3 and the command will be ready to go.

Figure 5.5 summarizes the keys that will execute certain DOS functions.

Key	DOS Function
F1[*]	Copies characters one by one from old template to new
F2	Copies up to specified character from old template
F3	Copies all remaining characters from old template
F4	Skips up to specified character from old template
F5	Replaces old template with existing one
F6[**]	Generates ASCII 26 end-of-file marker (^Z)
F7	Generates ASCII 0 null (^@)
Esc	Interrupts and cancels changes in current line
Ins	Switches DOS from overwrite mode into Insert mode
Del	Erases character at cursor and skips over it in template
Bksp[***]	Erases one character to the left

Figure 5.5.   Keys that Produce Selected DOS Functions.

[*] Same as right arrow key
[**] Same as Ctrl-Z
[***] Same as left arrow key

Assuming that you're logged onto drive C: and that the previous command was COPY A:ABCD B:WXYZ, here's what you can do with function keys:

Pressing	Produces
F1	C
F2 + W	COPY A:ABCD B:
F3	COPY A:ABCD B:WXYZ
F4 + W + F3	WXYZ

If you then press F5, DOS would replace the old COPY A:ABCD B:WXYZ template with these.

AT Keyboard Tricks

IBM started letting users program their keyboards with the first AT. By issuing a few simple BASIC commands you can experiment with IBM's programmable keyboards to see how they work, or to customize the key action.

To change the keyboard's LED shift-lock indicators, just issue an OUT &H60,&HED (the SET/RESET LEDS command), and follow this immediately with an OUT &H60,nn (where nn is a binary value indicating which LEDs to turn on). Bit 0 is for the ScrollLock indicator, bit 1 is for NumLock and bit 2 is for CapsLock. The LEDCYCLE.BAS program below cycles the AT's LEDs through a binary counting sequence:

```
100 ' LEDCYCLE.BAS — by Dan Rollins
110 DEF SEG=&HFFFF:IF PEEK(14)=252 THEN 130
120 PRINT "Try this on an AT only!":END
130 FOR J=0 TO 7
140 OUT &H60,&HED:OUT &H60,J
150 FOR DELAY=1 TO 1000:NEXT
160 IF INKEY$ > "" THEN STOP
170 NEXT
180 GOTO 130
```

However, turning an LED on or off does not change the ScrollLock, NumLock, or CapsLock keyboard shift states. These actual shift states are controlled by bits 4, 5, and 6 of the BIOS KB_FLAG at address 0040:0017. To see this in action, run the TOGGLE.BAS program below, which turns on the NumLock LED and sets the NumLock state:

```
100 ' TOGGLE.BAS — by Dan Rollins
110 DEF SEG=&HFFFF:IF PEEK(14)=252 THEN 130
120 PRINT "Try this on an AT only!":END
130 NUM.LED=4:NUM.FLG=&H10
```

```
140 CPS.LED=2:CPS.FLG=&H20
150 SCR.LED=1:SCR.FLG=&H40
160 DEF SEG=&H40
170 POKE &H17,PEEK(&H17) OR NUM.FLG
180 OUT &H60,&HED:OUT &H60,NUM.LED
```

It's simple to program any AT or later keyboard to change the amount of time to wait before sending the first repeat (the delay) and the time between repeats (the rate).

First, output a command (&HF3), then output a delay-and-rate value. Bits 5 and 6 control the delay, ranging from 250 ms up to 1 second. The lowest five bits (bits 0 through 4) identify the repeat rate, ranging from about 30 repeats per second to two repeats per second. The following two commands set the keyboard to a one-quarter second delay and 20 repeats per second:

```
OUT &H60,&HF3:OUT &H60,4
```

Important: Be sure to enter both commands on the same line.

After receiving the &HF3 command, the keyboard locks up until it receives the rate and delay data byte.

You can use the KEYRATE.BAS program below to set the keyboard typematic parameters. It includes the logic to display the exact delay and rate you select:

```
100 ' KEYRATE.BAS — by Dan Rollins
110 DEF SEG=&HFFFF:IF PEEK(14)=252 THEN 130
120 PRINT "Try this on an AT only!":END
130 PRINT "=low values are fastest="
140 INPUT "initial delay (0-3): ,"ID
150 INPUT "repeat rate (0-31): ,"RR
160 OUT &H60,&HF3:OUT &H60,(ID*32) OR RR
170 PRINT "initial delay is";
180 PRINT (ID+1)*.25;"seconds"
190 A=(RR AND 7):B=(RR AND 24)\8
200 P=(8+A)*(2^B)*.00417
210 PRINT "repeat rate is";
220 PRINT 1/P;"per second"
```

The default power-on settings are a one-half second delay and a repeat rate of ten per second. A better setting is a one-quarter second delay and 15 to 20 repeats per second. You can set the keyboard to output up to 30 repeats per second which after a little practice is perfectly manageable and a boon to your throughput.

You can also create two assembly language files, FAST.COM and SLOW.COM, that will set the rates without forcing you to use BASIC. Just make sure DEBUG.COM is handy and type in the following ten lines, pressing Enter at the end of each one.

```
DEBUG
E 100 B0 F3 E6 60 B9 00 10 90 E2 FD B0 00 E6 60 C3
N FAST.COM
RCX
F
W
E 10B 7F
N SLOW.COM
W
Q
```

When you're done, you'll have two new files on your disk. For a laugh, type:

```
SLOW
```

and press Enter. See what your typematic rate is like. You won't believe it. Then, to speed things up considerably, type:

```
FAST
```

and press Enter. If you've never speeded up your keyboard before, you won't believe this either.

To change the rates, patch the byte in either SLOW.COM or FAST.COM at address 10B.

Keyboard Operation

The standard IBM keyboard contains a dedicated Intel 8048 microprocessor that monitors all key action and reports any activity to the CPU. When a key is pressed, the keyboard generates an interrupt 9 and puts a *make* code — the scan code of the key just struck — in the keyboard data port. Releasing a key generates a break code. The break code is simply the scan code with its high bit set (which is equal to the value of the make code plus 128). For the most part, keyboard scan codes are numbered sequentially from left to right, beginning at the top row of the old PC keyboard. Exceptions include the function keys and cursor keys.

The 8048 also issues repeated make codes when a key is held down. After key contact has been maintained for about a half second, interrupts are generated several times per second just as if the key were being alternately pressed and released. This results in the keyboard's *typematic* action. BIOS masks out the repetition both of Shift keys (e.g., Ctrl and Alt), and of those (like Ins) that toggle a state. Starting with the AT, users could change both the delay before any typematic effect started, and the typematic rate itself.

Instead of using interrupts to process keystrokes, some non-PC systems detect keystrokes by having the CPU *poll* or periodically check the keyboard to see if a key has been typed. Since it has to poll the keyboard many times per second to make sure nothing is missed, a significant portion of the CPU's time is diverted from other tasks. Thanks to the architecture of the PC and its smart keyboard, the 8048 can sit quietly in the background and grab the attention of the 8088 only when keyboard action is detected.

When you press a key, the keyboard's microprocessor generates a keyboard interrupt called IRQ1, which normally has the second highest priority of all the PC hardware interrupts. (The highest priority interrupt is IRQ0, which is the clock timer. Some of the other hardware interrupts are used by the serial ports, the parallel port, and the disks on your system.)

The PC's 8259 interrupt controller translates IRQ1 into interrupt 9. When the microprocessor receives a hardware interrupt it stops what it's doing and jumps to the interrupt service routine. For interrupt 9, this routine is located at hex address 0000:0024. If you boot up without loading any resident programs this address points to a routine in the ROM BIOS.

The BIOS interrupt 9 routine reads the scan code of the key from the hardware. This routine is responsible for converting the scan code into an ASCII code, maintaining shift state information, pausing on Ctrl-NumLock, executing an interrupt 5 (print screen) when it detects a Shift-PrtSc, and rebooting on Ctrl-Alt-Del.

The assembly language code for interrupt 9 (including the several tables it uses) takes up about nine pages in the listing of the BIOS contained in the *IBM Technical Reference* manual.

After decoding the keystroke, interrupt 9 stores both the scan code and the ASCII code in a circular buffer located in the BIOS data area. The buffer is 16 words (32 bytes) long and can hold 15 keystrokes (since each keystroke requires two bytes), which lets you type up to 15 characters ahead of what your program has pulled from the buffer.

BIOS maintains four parameters in its own data area that pertain to the buffer: the address of the buffer head, the address of the buffer tail, and the starting and ending addresses of the buffer itself. The tail is where the next character will be written to; the head is where the next character will be read from. The BIOS routines that handle a call to interrupt 9 place characters into the buffer. Entries are read when a program invokes interrupt 16H with the AH register set to zero.

The buffer is empty when the address of the head is the same as that of its tail. It's full when the tail lags behind the head by only two bytes. If you type a character with the buffer full, a short beep warns you that the PC can't accept another character until one is read to make room. When interrupt 16H is requested to perform a read, it effectively deletes the entry after reading it by adding two to the head address. When a character is inserted, the tail address is incremented by two so that the next entry won't overwrite the last. The tail and head wrap around to the start when the most recent advance causes one of them to overshoot the end of the buffer. Thus the tail forever chases the head but is never allowed to overtake it.

The BIOS uses the starting and ending buffer addresses when it wraps the head or tail around to the beginning. But rather than being hardwired into the code, these values are maintained in a memory location where they can be altered by the user. Such a design allows the buffer to be modified. By changing the starting and ending addresses, a program can relocate the buffer to any free area of memory (including inside its own allocated area) and can make it as short or as long as it chooses. There are many utilities available that extend the buffer's 16-character capacity to something greater. That's useful if you want to type ahead when the computer is involved in another task (like compiling a program to disk) and, for the moment, can't take time out to process keystrokes.

Programs can directly manipulate the keyboard buffer, but only with caution. Interrupts must be disabled so that one routine won't attempt to insert an entry at the same time that another routine is involved in modifying the head and tail addresses. Hardware interrupts like the one generated by the keyboard are funneled through a chip called the 8259 Programmable Interrupt Controller (PIC for short). The 8259 acts as a sort of secretary for the main microprocessor, screening its calls and holding those that come while another interrupt is being processed. A pending interrupt 9 is delayed until the current interrupt 9 routine formally ends the interrupt hold state by OUTing the value 20H to port 20H.

If the keystroke is a "shift" key (Ctrl, Alt, left and right Shift keys) or a toggle key (CapsLock, NumLock, and Scroll Lock), the interrupt 9 routine does not store the key in the buffer, but instead adjusts two other bytes in lower memory to reflect the current shift states. If the key you've pressed has no ASCII value (e.g., if it's a function key or a cursor key), the ASCII code stored in the buffer will be zero, and the scan code registered will either be an actual scan code (if the key was struck without shifts), or an extended key code. If the BIOS interrupt 9 routine detects a keystroke that is not defined, such as the number pad 5 key when NumLock is off, it simply ignores it. The two-byte keystroke code will stay in this buffer until some other program removes it.

If you program in BASIC or another high-level language, you probably use statements such as INPUT or INKEY for reading the keyboard, without worrying much about how the program gets the actual keystrokes. Assembly language programmers, however, know about several ways to read the keyboard. The easiest way is to use one of the several DOS function calls for keyboard input that are documented in the *IBM Technical Reference* manual.

When DOS receives a request to read the keyboard through one of the DOS function calls, it usually calls a routine in the CON device driver. (CON stands for "console," and refers to the keyboard and display.) The CON device driver is loaded automatically when DOS is booted.

However, if you've executed a command on the DOS command level that uses redirection of standard input (to get input from a file, for example), DOS will not call a routine in CON, but will instead call a routine in the device driver that accesses your disk. Similarly, if you've executed the CTTY command to use a terminal connected to a serial port as your console, DOS will instead call a routine in the AUX device driver.

Under normal conditions, however, DOS calls the CON device driver, and the CON device driver calls the interrupt 16H routine in the ROM BIOS. The code for BIOS interrupt 16H is very short. Its main functions are to retrieve the keystroke from the buffer where it's been since interrupt 9H put it there, and to return it to the calling program. All the real work has already been done by interrupt 9H.

The BIOS interrupt 16H returns two bytes, one for the ASCII code and one for the scan code. If the keystroke is a non-ASCII extended key, the ASCII code will be zero. For ASCII keys, the CON device driver simply ignores the scan code and returns the ASCII code to DOS, which then passes it on to the program that made the DOS call. For extended keys, the CON device driver returns a zero and saves the extended keyboard code. It returns the scan code when it is called a second time. So reading extended keys through DOS requires calling DOS twice.

Many large application programs, such as spreadsheets and processors, don't use DOS to read the keyboard; instead, they bypass DOS and use the BIOS interrupt 16h directly, for several reasons.

For one thing, interrupt 16H can also return shift information and DOS cannot. Many large programs display shift information on the screen; if they use the BIOS to get this information, they might as well use the BIOS to get other keyboard information as well. Again, for reading function keys and cursor keys, using the BIOS is somewhat easier because it requires only one call instead of two.

Again, some programs need to distinguish between the plus and minus keys on the top row of the keyboard and the plus and minus keys to the right of the cursor pad. Using DOS calls to get keyboard information makes this distinction impossible, since the CON device driver returns the same ASCII plus and minus codes for both pairs of keys. The BIOS interrupt 16H, however, returns unique scan codes for these two sets of keys, so programs can treat them differently, if desired.

Some programs use the keyboard on a more fundamental level, by redirecting the hardware keyboard interrupt (interrupt 9) and interpreting keystrokes themselves. There are certainly some advantages to doing this. First, the program gets keyboard information faster, since it doesn't have to keep checking if a keystroke has been typed. Second, as mentioned earlier, interrupt 9 ignores keystrokes that are not defined, so programs can use undefined keystrokes (such as Alt-Tab) for their own purposes.

Some programs use their own interrupt 9 handlers to supplement the one in the BIOS, and just add their own decoded keystrokes to the normal buffer that the BIOS maintains. They can then read the keystrokes through interrupt 16H. Other programs take over interrupt 9 completely.

Many pop-up resident programs intercept interrupt 9 and check each keystroke that you type. If your keystroke is anything but the special key that has been defined to trigger the pop-up, the program simply lets the regular BIOS interrupt 9 process the key. The keyboard hardware of the PC is quite amenable to this procedure, since a program can read a key through an input port (60H) without actually removing it from the hardware. This lets the interrupt 9 routine still process the key even though another program has already taken a look at it.

There are several places where a resident program could insert itself, to change one key into another or to define a whole string of characters that are to be triggered by a single keystroke. The choice of where to insert the keyboard redefinition routine depends on what programs are to be affected by the redefined keys. For instance, with a high-level keyboard redefiner that works at the DOS level, programs that use the BIOS for getting keystrokes will not be affected by it.

Indeed, the fact that many application programs bypass DOS can be an advantage, since this lets you define function keys for use at the DOS command level without having to worry that they'll maintain those functions within an application program. For example, if you define F10 to be "DIR," you don't want it to replace the "Graph" function in Lotus 1-2-3.

All DOS versions since 2.0 have included a replacement for CON that makes it easy to redefine the keyboard for programs that use DOS to obtain keyboard information — the ANSI.SYS device driver. DOS uses the CON device driver to obtain keystrokes, and the CON device driver uses the BIOS interrupt 16H. The CON device driver is also used by DOS for console output, which is the video display.

ANSI.SYS replaces the normal CON device driver with one that provides extended screen and keyboard control. It implements a subset of American National Standards Institute (ANSI) document X3.64-1979, entitled *American National Standard Additional Controls for Use with American National Standard Code for Information Interchange*. The acronym ASCII is derived from this. Essentially, the X3.64-1979 standard defines the control sequences that allow programs to control a video display (e.g., position the cursor or set high intensity) in addition to just writing to it.

Once you've loaded ANSI.SYS by including it in your CONFIG.SYS file, all you have to do to redefine a keystroke or create a keyboard macro is send an ANSI control sequence to the display through DOS.

These ANSI redefinitions work on the DOS command level and within programs that use DOS for keyboard input (such as EDLIN and DEBUG), but they will not work in BASIC or in most large applications. Programs that are not affected by these redefined keys use BIOS rather than DOS to obtain keyboard input. If you tried turning your grey plus key into an Enter key by issuing the ANSI redefinition command, this will redefine both of your plus keys as Enter:

```
ESC[43;13p
```

(43 is the decimal ASCII code for the plus sign, 13 is the ASCII code for Enter, and ESC means the ESC character and not the actual letters E-S-C.) Moreover, it probably wouldn't work in a spreadsheet program where it would be of most use.

But it's possible to create a dedicated program that will redefine the grey plus key as an Enter key.

The NEWENT program intercepts interrupt 9, which is the hardware keyboard interrupt routine. It reads the keystroke from an input port and also checks the shift status states stored in lower memory. It converts the key only if NumLock is toggled, or if either the left or right Shift key is depressed. Like the number pad, NEWENT will not convert the key if NumLock is toggled and a Shift key is down.

To create NEWENT.COM, type in the following NEWENT.SCR script file using a pure-ASCII word processor or EDLIN. Omit the semicolons and the comments following them. Be sure to leave a blank line above RCX, and to press the Enter key at the end of each line, especially the last one with the Q:

```
A JMP     0164            ; Jump to Initialize
DW        0,0
STI
PUSH      AX
PUSH      DS
IN        AL,60           ; Read key
CMP       AL,4E           ; Check if grey-plus
JNZ       015D
MOV       AX,0040
MOV       DS,AX           ; Segment at 40H
MOV       AL,[0017]       ; Get shift states
AND       AL,2F           ; Check if Num Lock
JZ        015D            ; or Upper Shifts
CMP       AL,20
JZ        0123
CMP       AL,03
JA        015D
IN        AL,61           ; Reset keyboard
MOV       AH,AL
OR        AL,80
OUT       61,AL
MOV       AL,AH
OUT       61,AL
PUSH      BX
PUSH      DI
MOV       AX,1C0D         ; Set key to Enter
MOV       BX,[001C]       ; Get buffer tail
MOV       DI,BX
ADD       BX,+02          ; Increment
CMP       BX,[0082]       ; See if wrap around
JNZ       0147
MOV       BX,[0080]       ; If so, set to beg
CMP       BX,[001A]       ; See if buffer full
JZ        0153
MOV       [DI],AX         ; If not, save key
MOV       [001C],BX       ; And new pointer
POP       DI
POP       BX
CLI
MOV       AL,20           ; Re-enable interrupts
```

```
OUT          20,AL
POP          DS
POP          AX
IRET                           ; And exit
POP          DS
POP          AX
CS:
JMP          FAR [0102]
MOV          AX,3509           ; Get Int. 9H address
INT          21
MOV          [0102],BX
MOV          [0104],ES
MOV          DX,0106           ; Set a new one
MOV          AX,2509
INT          21
MOV          DX,0164           ; Terminate and
INT          27                ; stay resident
RCX
7E
N NEWENT2.COM
W
Q
```

Then enter:

```
DEBUG < NEWENT.SCR
```

and run the program by typing:

```
NEWENT
```

When NEWENT converts a key, it has to clear the keyboard I/O ports, store the key in the the keyboard buffer in lower memory, and re-enable interrupts. The only place this is documented is in the assembly language code for the BIOS interrupt 9H in any of the *IBM Technical Reference* manuals for the PC family. However you'll find some of the same code in any keyboard macro program and in many resident pop-up programs.

If you're using an older version of DOS, there's even a third method to convert one key to another. PC-DOS 3.0 through 3.2 included several resident programs called KEYBUK.COM, KEYBGR.COM, KEYBFR.COM, KEYBIT.COM, KEYBSP.COM designed for foreign keyboards, that entirely replace the BIOS interrupt 9 keyboard handler. These were removed in version 3.3 and turned into a master keyboard loading routine called KEYB.

The KEYBxx programs took over interrupt 9 completely and let you flip to the U.S. keyboard by typing Ctrl-Alt-F1 or to the foreign language version by typing Ctrl-Alt-F2. You can use DEBUG to peek inside these, look at the chart of key arrangements, and move the keys around. However, all three versions worked a bit differently.

You can do other interesting things with this like replace a whole set of normal keys with high-bit box and border characters and then toggle back and forth between the normal alphabet and the box drawing keys by typing Ctrl-Alt-F1 and Ctrl-Alt-F2. Or you could patch the keyboard mapping tables to switch back and forth between QWERTY and Dvorak layouts.

— Charles Petzold and Jeff Prosise

40:17 (one byte)

Bit 0	Right Shift pressed	Bit 4	ScrollLock locked
Bit 1	Left Shift pressed	Bit 5	NumLock locked
Bit 2	Ctrl pressed	Bit 6	CapsLock locked
Bit 3	Alt pressed	Bit 7	Insert locked

40:18 (one byte)

Bit 0	Left Ctrl pressed	Bit 4	ScrollLock pressed
Bit 1	Left Alt pressed	Bit 5	NumLock pressed
Bit 2	SysReq pressed	Bit 6	CapsLock pressed
Bit 3	Pause locked	Bit 7	Insert pressed

40:1A (two bytes) — pointer to keyboard buffer head
40:1C (two bytes) — pointer to keyboard buffer tail
40:1E (32 bytes) — keyboard buffer
40:80 (two bytes) — pointer to keyboard buffer start offset
40:82 (two bytes) — pointer to keyboard buffer end offset

40:96 (one byte)

Bit 0	Last code was E1 hidden
Bit 1	Last code was E0 hidden
Bit 2	Right Ctrl key pressed
Bit 3	Right Alt key pressed
Bit 4	101/102-key keyboard attached
Bit 5	Force NumLock if read ID and KBX
Bit 6	Last character was first ID character
Bit 7	Read ID in progress

40:97 (one byte)

Bit 0	Keyboard LED state
Bit 1	Keyboard LED state
Bit 2	Keyboard LED state
Bit 3	Reserved (0)
Bit 4	Acknowledgment received
Bit 5	Resend receive flag
Bit 6	Mode indicator update
Bit 7	Keyboard transmit error flag

Figure 5.6.   Important PC and PS/2 Keyboard BIOS Addresses

Chapter 6

Chips and Memory

Deep down, all people are pretty much alike. True, some have blue eyes and some have brown, some are well over six feet tall and others short and stumpy, and one may pick up the Unified Field Theory where Einstein left off while another becomes the nation's latest celebrity thrill killer. But their internal parts are basically similar. The same is true with PCs.

The CPU — The Brains of the PC

At the heart of every microcomputer is a microprocessor, a skinny sliver of purified crystaline silicon that has been *doped* — coated with impurities that give it electronic switching abilities — etched with a witch's brew of poisonous gasses, and then entombed in a small ceramic block. When people talk about "the chip" inside a PC they mean this one. It's often referred to as a CPU or *central processing unit*, although you never hear anyone say "hey, nice unit in that computer."

The two most popular microcomputer CPUs these days are made by Intel and Motorola in "clean rooms" straight out of science fiction movies, where workers pad the halls wearing sneeze masks and special dust-free booties. (Chips are fast because they're so small and densely packed that signals can move from one place on them to another a few millionths of an inch away in a few billionths of a second. The scale is so infinitesimal that a dust speck on a chip would be like an aircraft carrier in your bathtub.) The two biggest microcomputer companies are Apple and IBM. Apple switched from chips made by MOS Technology to the Motorola 68000 family of CPUs. IBM has stuck with the Intel 8088/8086 line of chips from the beginning.

What distinguishes a CPU from humbler chips is its ability to do arithmetic and logical operations, decode special instructions, and issue appropriate controlling signals to other chips in the system. One typical instruction might store a character in the computer's main memory, while another instruction will fetch the character back when needed. The CPU can communicate with the rest of the system through numbered *ports*. And it comes from the chip foundry with a tiny amount of memory aboard, located in places called *registers*. An 8088 CPU has a scant 14 registers, each capable of storing two bytes. A byte can hold any eight-bit binary address or a single character like an A or a 4. When two bytes are strung together, as they are in registers, they're called a *word*. Virtually everything your computer does is in one form or other shuttled in and out of those registers at incredible speeds.

For their tiny size, registers are power-packed. They do things like store memory addresses (the PC's 8088 registers can handle up to a million different ones), hold data, keep track of which instructions to execute next, and maintain status and control indicators called *flags* that report on the success or failure of previous instructions and can control how the CPU executes current and future ones.

The CPU sits astride the computer's *bus*, a multilane highway of wires that carries data, controlling signals, and electrical power to all the major parts under the hood. The wider the bus the greater the amount of data a computer can move in a single operation. A PC or PC-XT has eight data lines, a PC-AT 16, and a high-end PS/2 a whopping 32. (The models 25 and 30 have a 16-bit data bus.)

The original PC is classed as a 16-bit machine, since its 8088 CPU does indeed manipulate information in 16-bit chunks — but only inside the CPU itself. When its CPU needs raw data to work on, or when it finishes processing some information and wants to store it back in memory, it has to break the data into eight-bit pieces so it can squeeze through the narrow eight-bit bus. A timer circuit commonly called the *clock* sends pulses down one of the bus lines several million times each second to keep everything synchronized. In a PC the timer ticks at 4.77 megahertz (MHz). Since *mega-* means million and *Hertz* means cycles-per-second, that may seem pretty fast. Well, compared to a postal worker maybe, but these days 4.77 MHz is a real crawl. Current hardware runs at from two to five times the original PC's clock speed.

A clock is like the big sweaty guy on a galley slave ship in a gladiator movie beating out the rowing tempo on a drum. The more energetic his drumming the faster the ship moves. However, no microcomputer actually performs calculations at anywhere near the clock rate. The PC, like virtually every other computer, is a *Von Neumann* machine (named after mathematician John Von Neumann who contributed to the design of early room-sized computers such as ENIAC). Von Neumann machines execute all instructions one at a time. Some state-of-the-art supercomputers, like those made by Cray, can process similar groups of instructions concurrently in what is called *parallel processing*. Every Von Neumann CPU wastes lots of time waiting for the current instruction to finish so it can trigger the next one. And instructions can hog lots of timer cycles. Even the PC's NOP (pronounced no-opp) instruction, a placeholder that is expressly there to do nothing except wait, takes three clock cycles to execute.

(The clock in the PC is actually a special Intel chip that oscillates at 14.31818 MHz, or three times as fast as the often-quoted 4.77 MHz clock speed. This is too fast for most circuits, so other timer chips inside the PC use every third or fourth or fifth of these ticks to slow down the pace for their own needs.)

Most CPUs are pretty capable at doing basic integer arithmetic (remember, they were first designed as calculator chips) but stumble over *floating point* operations, which require juggling of decimal points and so take longer and demand more precision than working with whole numbers. Normally, when software has to work with decimal numbers it uses relatively slow brute-force tricks, and can end up dragging its feet and rounding off calculations crudely.

When IBM first introduced the PC it left a large empty socket next to the CPU that it eventually filled with a *numeric coprocessor* chip called an 8087. This number-crunching chip was designed to perform the complex calculations Intel's main 8088 and 8086 CPUs couldn't handle efficiently. And it included special built-in circuitry to zip through things like trigonometric operations in the blink of an electronic eye. As Intel re-engineered its 8088/8086 into an 80286 and then an 80386, it made sure the companion math coprocessors (80287s and 80387s) kept pace.

However, just sticking a math chip in the empty socket doesn't make every software application run faster. Some applications, such as word processors or data base managers, don't do much tricky math. And while some applications, such as CAD (computer aided design) packages, engineering programs, and spreadsheets, could run far faster by using such a number cruncher, unless the software includes special instructions to wake up the math chip and send data to it, the chip will just sit idly by.

Computers can get things done one of two ways. They can actively and repeatedly go out and check whether something has happened yet, or they can lie back and wait for events to announce themselves. Continuously *polling* the hardware to see whether the user has hit a key, a disk drive has stopped spinning, or a printer is turned on is incredibly wasteful. Today's CPUs are *interrupt-driven*, somewhat like a hospital emergency room staff that's normally in low gear doing routine record keeping but can spring into action when necessary. And as in an emergency room, certain interrupts have priority over others. If a physician is adjusting one patient's bandage and the local rescue crew wheels in a sword swallower who tried shoplifting a chain saw, the focus of attention changes instantly. If your computer is leisurely printing out a document and you happen to start typing, its attention has to shift quickly or the keystrokes will be lost forever.

When a computer detects an incoming interrupt, it parks or "pushes" critical information about what it was originally doing into a section of memory called a *stack* and attends to the interrupt. Then when the CPU is finished handling the interrupt, it retrieves or *pops* the critical information it temporarily stored so it can get back to what it was originally working on. And it can stack such information many levels deep, so that if a second, more urgent interrupt barges in, the CPU parks information about the first interrupt while it works on the second, and so on.

This temporary storage device is called a stack because it resembles a box-shaped device in a cafeteria with a hole in the top for dishes and a spring at the bottom to push the dishes upward. Both the cafeteria and the computer stacks are designed so that only the top item on the stack is accessible; as you push each new item onto it, it presses all the items beneath it down one level each time. And when you remove an item from either stack, the one directly under it pops up and rises to the top. It's like a union seniority system when times are hard: LIFO — last in, first out.

If you were very methodical and had just finished washing a pile of dishes with the letters of the alphabet painted on them, and you wanted to store them in the right order, you'd put dish labeled Z in the cafeteria storage device first.

— Z —   — Y —   — X —
Dish Z   Dish Y   Dish X

Empty
Dish Stacker
(X-ray view)

Dish Z would then be at the very top of the stack, since it was the only one in the stack.

— Z —

— Y —   — X —

Dish Stacker   Dish Y   Dish X

Then, you'd put dish Y on top of dish Z. Dish Y would push dish Z down inside the storage box and then would become the top dish.

— Y —
— Z —

— X —
Dish Stacker   Dish X

Continue by putting dish X on top of dish Y, which then disappears down the stack along with dish Z. Only dish X is visible.

— X —
— Y —
— Z —

Dish Stacker

To get to dish Z at this point, you'd have to first pop dish X off, and then pop off dish Y.

As any harried office worker knows, processing interrupts is a tricky business. You have to be able to respond quickly to genuine crises, ignore persistent but trivial ones, put all such interruptions in proper priority order, and make sure that everything is eventually dispatched. To take pressure off the main CPU, IBM routed all interrupt requests through a chip cleverly named an *Interrupt Controller*. In the PC and PC-XT this chip can juggle as many as eight interrupts at once; by daisy-chaining two of these chips together, the PC-AT's designers were able to have it handle up to 15 simultaneously.

Other semi-intelligent chips control other important aspects of operation, leaving the CPU free to chew its way through programs and data while leaving the actual dirty work to specialists. Instead of filtering every last byte of your data through its registers, the CPU knows how to delegate. Handling data on disks is painfully slow since the system has to make sure the disks are spinning at the proper rate, move a magnetic head to a directory table to figure out where the data is, wait for that area of the disk to come spinning around, move the heads to read it, and maybe even go back and repeat the process if the data is scattered over several locations (as it often is). Shuffling data around in memory is fast; there are no moving parts.

One common CPU chore is to move large amounts of information from slow disks to fast memory and back. Passing it all through the CPU's skimpy registers would be ridiculously inefficient (as it was on the PC*jr*). The PC's DMA (direct memory access) controller can bypass this potential bottleneck; it's like an interstate beltway that skirts a city while the main highway chugs its way downtown. When IBM gave the PC-AT a 16-bit data bus it had to stick in a second DMA controller to help it move data around in 16-byte chunks.

Other controller chips manage the disk drives, the keyboard, the video output, and some of the input and output. Fortunately, DOS — with the help of some gut-level BIOS (basic input/output software) programs built into the PC — takes care of all the messy details so you don't have to.

RAM

Some chips, like the CPU and the DMA controller, contain small amounts of onboard memory for temporary storage. But all the garden-variety day-to-day storage and retrieval activities take place in the main system RAM.

Every microcomputer comes with two kinds of memory, RAM and ROM. RAM originally stood for *random access memory*, but it really should be called RWM for read/write memory. ROM stands for *read only memory*, which is correct. RAM, ROM, and disks are all random-access storage devices since they let you jump directly to any point on them to store or look up information. You don't have to slog through storage areas 1 and 2 to get to storage area 3. But RAM and ROM chips have several important differences. ROM chips contain vital, permanently stored information put there by your computer manufacturer. Turn the power off and this information remains intact. You can't change, or "write" over this information directly (although IBM provided a clever way to update it). But you can retrieve, or "read" it. That's why it's called read-only.

When you turn your system on, programs stored on a ROM chip tell the hardware how to begin operating. After sniffing around to figure out what hardware happens to be hooked up to your system, a special program on a ROM chip tests your RAM to make sure it's working properly. In all but the earliest PCs, as it checks memory, this POST (Power On Self Test) diagnostic program displays the amount of RAM it has tested and approved. This is the slowly changing number you see in the upper lefthand corner of your screen when you start. The POST tests memory by writing information into RAM and then reading it back and comparing it with the original information to make sure RAM hasn't mangled it. You can read from both ROM and RAM. But you can write only to RAM.

ROM never changes. The information on it always stays the same, whether the power is on or off. The only way to fix serious bugs on them is to yank them out and replace them with newer models. IBM's early PC ROM chips had several annoying deficiencies. One chip couldn't divide properly by 10, but that was corrected in a hurry. And the early PC ROMs made it hard for users to stuff the maximum 640K of RAM into their systems, or to boot up from hard disks.

We'll get to where all this memory is located a little later in this chapter. For now, think about memory as a concert hall, with several sections, and numbered seats in each section. ROM is all the way in the back of the hall. RAM hogs all the good seats, from the first row to about two-thirds of the way toward the rear.

Each new version of DOS contains patches to some of the gut-level programs and tables delivered on ROM chips. These patches can't alter the ROM chips themselves. But when the PC starts up each day, it takes some of the permanent ROM information and copies it into "low" RAM memory — the first rows of theatre seats — and then goes to the copy of the information rather than the original ROM chip when it needs to look something up. (The million or so characters of memory in a PC are arranged in regions called *segments* that will be discussed soon; ROM data is stored in a distant Siberia far from the "lower" 640K of RAM where most of the computer's action takes place.) The patches provided with each new DOS version can and regularly do overwrite the older ROM information that's been copied into low memory.

As you use your system, you write information into RAM. When RAM fills up, you have to erase unwanted information to make room for new data. And, when you turn your system off, all the information stored in RAM vanishes forever. Sometimes your local power company or a fellow employee turning on an air conditioner or heater that's plugged into the same outlet accidentally does this for you while you're working, so you have to be fanatical about taking the data stored in memory and copying it onto a more or less permanent storage medium like a disk frequently.

RAM and ROM are both memory chips that store information. The important similarities and differences in storage devices are shown in Figure 6.1.

Storage Devices	RAM	ROM	Disks
Data already on it when you turn computer on	No	Yes	Maybe
Data remains on it when you turn computer off	No	Yes	Yes
Can read information from it	Yes	Yes	Yes
Can write information to it	Yes	No	Yes
Can change the information on it	Yes	No	Yes
Can handle information very quickly	Yes	Yes	No

Figure 6.1. Characteristics of Storage Devices

Here's an easy way to remember the difference between memory chips. Let's say you walk into a classroom, and see an empty blackboard at one end of the room (RAM), and a bulletin board inside a glass display case at the other (ROM).

The bulletin board may contain schedules, fire drill codes, and lists of telephone numbers. The blackboard has nothing on it. You can write on the blackboard. But you can't write on the glass-covered bulletin board. You can read information from both. When you fill the blackboard, you have to erase some older information so you have room to write down the newer data. When class is over, you erase the blackboard, turn out the lights, and leave. The blackboard is again empty. But the bulletin board at the other end of the room still contains the information that was on it when you entered. And it will be there tomorrow.

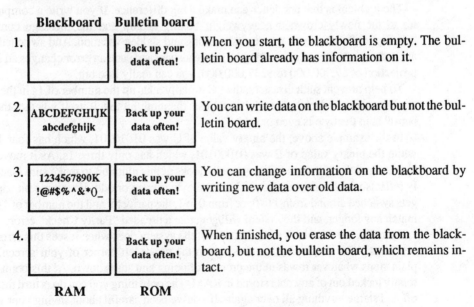

Blackboard   Bulletin board

1. [ ] / Back up your data often! — When you start, the blackboard is empty. The bulletin board already has information on it.

2. ABCDEFGHIJK abcdefghijk / Back up your data often! — You can write data on the blackboard but not the bulletin board.

3. 1234567890K !@#$%^&*0_ / Back up your data often! — You can change information on the blackboard by writing new data over old data.

4. [ ] / Back up your data often! — When finished, you erase the data from the blackboard, but not the bulletin board, which remains intact.

RAM   ROM

All data stored in RAM vanishes when you turn the power off; such storage is *volatile*. Information on ROM chips remains intact when the power snaps off; this kind of storage is *non-volatile*.

Parity Problems

While there are eight bits in a byte, the PC's RAM normally handles small packages of information nine bits at a time rather than eight. The extra bit is called a *parity* bit and it's a crude way to insure the integrity of your data. One bit can make a whale of difference. Here's why:

To your CPU, the letter U is a just the decimal number 85. The binary representation of 85 is:

01010101

(If you skipped ahead to here, and you're mystified by all those 1s and 0s, go back two chapters and read how binary numbers work. It's actually pretty simple.)

Change just a single bit from one state to the other — say the fourth one over from the left — and the binary number becomes:

01000101

which translates to decimal 69, or the value of E.

The problem is that one letter can make a big difference. If you write a computer letter to the newly crowned heavyweight boxing champ and the message comes out "chump" or "chimp" you'd better take a long and sudden vacation. And switched letters are bad enough. If you're working on a spreadsheet and such an error changes an income projection of $7,000,000 to $237,000,000, you can really lose big.

To help prevent such disasters, the PC initially adds up the number of 1s in the binary representation of each byte and then adjusts the ninth bit to tell itself whether the number of 1s in the byte is even or odd.

In the example above, the binary value of U was 01010101, which has four 1s in it, while the binary value of E was 01000101, which has only three 1s. As it moves each byte around the system, a PC continually looks at this ninth bit to make sure it accurately reflects whether the number of 1s in the byte is even or odd. If a single bit somehow gets switched around from 1 to 0, or from 0 to 1, the parity bit and the number of 1s won't match any longer, and the system will generate a dreaded "Parity Check" error.

Actually, the error isn't so bad, it's what the system does when it sees this error that's insidious. After displaying the message in the upper left corner of your screen, it just plain stops whatever it was in the process of doing and shuts down. At this point you're totally locked out of any data stored in RAM. The only thing you can do is turn the power off and start everything all over again. If you've been careful about saving your work to a disk every few minutes, all you lose are the few changes you made since the last disk save. If you haven't saved anything, you say "darn" and learn to save next time.

The parity error may have occurred because a RAM chip failed — they do mysteriously break from time to time. Or a stray cosmic ray may have zapped the chip as it passed through you and the earth on its way to Neptune. Or a balky generator at your local power company may have burped out some fluctuation in the line voltage that got past your computer's power supply. If it was a bad chip you'll get the same message again after you reboot, and you either have to figure out which chip went south, yank it out, and replace it, or pay your dealer to do it. If a chip on your main system board — the one that the CPU is attached to — fails, the system will display PARITY CHECK 1. If it senses a broken chip on an add-in board it will display PARITY CHECK 2. While the PC-AT is a little less terse, if this happens to you, a cheerier message is not what you want or need.

You'll know you have a bad chip if you reboot and see an error message beginning with a string of numbers followed by 201. The four hexadecimal digits that precede the 201 can pinpoint the exact chip that failed. On a PC, the machine will boot and you'll get an instant PARITY CHECK message that overwrites the 201 numbers, so you have to look quickly. On an XT, the message is not overwritten. On the newer PS/2 systems, IBM replaced the PARITY message with two numerical error codes:

- 110 for PARITY CHECK 1
- 111 for PARITY CHECK 2

These are two numbers you won't want to see.

What the PC really should do when it detects such an error is put the offending data onscreen (if it's still able to) with the message: "Error detected in this data. Should I continue (Y/N)?" If the error was in the programming code that puts your software through its paces, or in a long list of numbers, you may want to quit and restart. But if all you see is the message:

The bank robber's holdup note said "I have a gub."

you can fix the error and continue without losing any work.

What is particularly irritating about parity errors is every one out of nine (11.11%) times such errors occur it's the result of the error-detecting mechanism and not incorrect data. All a parity error detector does is compare eight bits to one bit. If the chip with the one parity bit on it fails, your data — the other eight bits — may be perfectly fine, but the comparison test will indicate a problem and shut down your system.

Parity-checking can prevent data integrity problems. But only some of them. If one bit gets changed in a byte, the system will ferret out the problem. But if two bits in a single byte change, the parity detection bit will accurately reflect the oddness or evenness of the number of 1s. If the original byte was U or 01010101, the number of 1s is four, which is even. If you flip any two bits from 1 to 0 or from 0 to 1, you'll still have an even number of bits, although the new number won't represent a U anymore.

ROM is not parity checked. Some clone makers let you flick a switch to disable RAM parity checking. And some portable computers don't check parity, since that lets the manufacturers put in fewer chips that consume less power, and power sipping is the name of the game with laptops. If you have the option of turning parity checking on or off, you should probably leave it on anyway. But in any case you should save your work to disk often.

Larger computers that can't afford to stop dead in their tracks use a more sophisticated system called error correction. But this takes even more space, and incorporating error corrections into the PC would mean changing the underlying system architecture. And it's not perfect. The common error correcting scheme used today can fix one-bit errors, but it can only detect — not fix — errors of two or more bits in a single byte. All PCs will have error correction abilities someday, but they don't yet.

Future microcomputers may also have *static* RAM. All but a few of today's PCs use *dynamic* RAM that needs to be recharged or "refreshed" hundreds of times each second, which limits memory speeds. Static RAM doesn't need to be continually recharged, and is faster than dynamic RAM, but far more expensive.

ROM — Free Programs

When you buy a PC you get two sets of free programs. One set, called microcode, is permanently *hard-wired* into the circuitry of the CPU and tells it (in the tersest, most inscrutable *machine code* possible) how to operate. The other set comes on a few ROM chips and provides software routines that help the system function. Programs that are delivered on chips are in a netherworld somewhere between hardware and software. Hardware is the machinery itself. Software is the list of instructions that tell the hardware what to do.

Your home phonograph, tape deck, or CD player is hardware. The records, disks, and tapes contain software. The general rule is if it has a wire coming out of it, it's hardware. If it doesn't do anything until you memorize a manual that sounds as if it was translated from a foreign language by a bored high school student, it's software.

Programs (software) that come delivered on ROM chips (hardware) are called *firmware*. Firmware includes copyright information, tests, tables, error messages, and a toolkit of useful routines that display characters on the screen in the colors of your choice, read information from a disk or keyboard, or send a copy of what's on your screen to your printer. ROM chips on IBM computers also include a stripped down version of the BASIC language.

Every piece of commercial software on the market uses at least some of these routines, by issuing what are called *software interrupts*. Software interrupts are different from the hardware interrupts mentioned earlier, which let the computer know you're pressing a key or that the printer just ran out of paper. And they're also different from the panicky interrupts triggered inside the CPU when something truly bizarre or unexpected happens like when something tries to divide by zero.

All programs have to perform the same basic operations such as interpreting keystrokes, displaying characters on a screen, or reading information from disks. The routines on ROM chips handle the hard part. Some programs, in a mad quest for extra speed or control, bypass these routines and control the hardware directly. But most programs are content to use the toolkit IBM (and its copycat clone makers) provided.

To see one of these routines in action, walk over to any IBM computer and turn the power on without putting a disk in the drive. If the computer doesn't have a hard disk, BASIC will appear onscreen. If it does have a hard disk, load BASIC by typing:

```
BASIC
```

and then pressing the Enter key. Then type the following line exactly as it appears:

```
DEF SEG=61440:R=57435:CALL R
```

Press the Enter key and your system will reboot. What this command does is use the BASIC language that comes on one IBM ROM chip to run a little firmware program on another ROM chip that restarts your system.

The PC's 8088 CPU can keep track of, or *address*, slightly more than a million memory locations. Just about everything the CPU does use addresses in one form or another. It's either looking in one location to see what's there, parking data temporarily in another location so it can process other data, or running short programs that are kept at certain addresses.

But a million is a big number, and it's sometimes easier to work with smaller numbers. If you're in New York City, which has a telephone area code of 212, and you have to call someone nearby, you want to be able to dial just the seven-digit phone number and not have to punch in a 1 and the extra three digits of the area code each time you make a local call. If most of your calls are indeed local, this saves time as well as wear and tear on the dialing finger. When you dial any seven digits (that don't start with a 1), the phone company assumes you're calling a number in the immediate vicinity.

If you want to talk to someone in Seattle, you can add the extra area code numbers, and the phone company knows you're not placing a local call.

The 8088 CPU addresses memory locations in a similar way. It divides the whole one-megabyte range of possible addresses into 16 regional sections called segments that are each 64K bytes long.

The DEF SEG in the example that appeared earlier switches BASIC to one of these segments (in this case the very topmost one), which happens to be where IBM keeps track of the ROM chip routines that make up its main BIOS input/output toolkit.

This kind of memory segmentation can be useful, since it can let programs use smaller numbers to keep track of important local addresses. Working with most smaller numbers is faster than struggling with bigger ones. But they can also be the bane of programmers, since the advantage in using smaller, local numbers applies only to whatever 64K segment the programmer happens to be using at that time. Most programs these days are considerably larger than 64K, which means jumping repeatedly from one 64K segment to another.

Remember, computers are built around chips that have a really limited perspective. The fundamental piece of information in any chip is a bit. And a bit can be in only one of two states, on or off. So a one-bit chip (if one existed) could theoretically keep track of only two possible locations, at address 0 or address 1. Not very useful.

A two-bit chip — one with room for twice as many binary digits as a one-bit chip — could theoretically keep track of 2^2 (2 x 2, or four) locations, at binary addresses:

00 (decimal 0)
01 (decimal 1)
10 (decimal 2)
11 (decimal 3)
| |
two
bits

If you kept on adding bits to the addressing mechanism, you would double the number of locations each time. A three-bit system could handle 2^3 (2 x 2 x 2, or eight) locations:

000 (decimal 0)
001 (decimal 1)
010 (decimal 2)
011 (decimal 3)
100 (decimal 4)
101 (decimal 5)
110 (decimal 6)
111 (decimal 7)
|||
three
bits

A 16-bit chip like the 8088 can address only 2^16 (65,536) bytes directly. So 17 bits could address 2 x 65,536 (131,072) bytes; 18 bits 2 x 131,072 (262,144) bytes; 19 bits 2 x 262,144 (524,288) bytes; and 20 bits 2 x 524,288 (1,048,576) bytes — the "megabyte" used as the standard measure of memory.

Now hold on . . . . It says here that the PC can address one megabyte of memory. But the calculations above show that it would take 20 bits to address a full 1,048,576 bytes. The CPU inside the PC is a 16-bit 8088, and with 16 bits all you can address is 65,536 bytes. How does a 16-bit CPU handle 20-bit addresses?

Easy. Well, not exactly. It uses two addresses for each memory location, one for the segment itself and one for the *offset* into that segment. If you use the concert hall metaphor mentioned earlier, the segment is the section and the offset is the seat. So you could have two seats numbered 27 — one in the orchestra and one in the balcony. Just as the full number of the seats might be something like O27 and B27, you can express the address of any byte in your PC as SEGMENT:OFFSET.

In the DEF SEG statement, the number 61440 was the segment address. The other number, 57435, was the offset. So:

```
DEF SEG=61440:R=57435:CALL R
```

was the same as saying "look at the 57,435th byte in from the beginning of the segment that begins at address 61440 and run the program that starts there."

If you think this sounds confusing, you're right. Instead of having to wrestle with segmented addresses, programmers would much rather have had a chip that could do direct *linear* addressing, where each byte had an address from 0 to 1,048,576. If the PC had a linear addressing system, the BASIC program could have said "run the program at address 1,040,475."

You may be scratching your head now and wondering two things. First, how did 61440 and 57435 become 1,040,475? Second, do you really have to know all this?

The answer to the second question is a qualified no. PC users should really never have to take the tops off their computers and fiddle with the boards inside. Their systems should figure out what equipment is attached and then configure all the important settings automatically. DOS should be smart enough to anticipate what the user wants to do next, and deal with the user in a far friendlier and more intelligent way. Software should be infinitely flexible and understanding, and continually customize itself to the user's changing needs and abilities.

But we're still in the frontier of this business. We're pioneers (although at least we don't have to load programs from paper tape and read blinking lights to get our work done like the computer scouts who blazed the early trails in the 70s.) It's still the Wild West out there. Each new software company gallops onto the scene yelling "My standard is better than your standard." The ensuing Darwinian gunfights weed out the real losers but wound a lot of bystanders like us in the process.

You can have someone else set up and repair your system, and can struggle through your favorite software without ever knowing about memory segments. But the more you know about your system the better off you'll be. Most users discover that the longer they spend at their systems the more proficient they get and the more they want to be able to do. If you know the basics you'll be able to adapt your system and get it to do far more things far faster and far more easily. And prevent disasters.

Here's a specific example: Once a week like clockwork we get a panicky phone call from someone who inadvertently exited a word processor without ever having saved the file to disk. If the caller was using mainstream word processing software, and didn't touch the computer after realizing what happened, it's usually fairly simple to look inside the user's RAM, find the file, and copy it from memory to a disk.

A rescue job like this starts by having the DOS DEBUG.COM program search through memory for the first few words of the user's file. DEBUG is very good at this, but can search only one segment at a time. If you know how segments work, finding unsaved files is a snap. The "Ooops" sidebar at the end of this chapter will show you how.

As mentioned earlier, the 14 registers inside the CPU are each two bytes long. A two-byte register can hold 16 bits, so the biggest number any of its registers can manipulate is 2^{16}, or 65,536. (If you want to use *signed* numbers that could be either positive or negative, the largest value would be 32,767 and the smallest -32,768. But take it from us, for the purposes of this book you don't want to.)

"Since there are 16 64K memory segments," you might argue, "the CPU could have used a kind of shorthand and called the first segment 0, the second segment 1, the third 2, and the last one 15. Then our BASIC reboot program could have been written DEF SEG=15:R=57435:CALL R." But that won't work.

The reason is that while the addressable memory in a PC is indeed split into 16 segments each 64K long for certain purposes, programmers need to divide available RAM into much finer slices than in such whopping chunks.

Just about all programs use memory in several standard ways. Some RAM has to store the actual program instruction code itself — the part that "runs." Some is needed to store the data that the program creates or changes. A little is needed for the stack, a storage area that holds addresses and miscellaneous amounts of temporary information. And sometimes programs have to work with so much data that they need a little extra room for it.

The 8088 CPU has four different segment registers to keep track of these four kinds of segments:

- Code segment (CS)
- Data segment (DS)
- Stack segment (SS)
- Extra segment (ES)

Since registers control segment addresses, the maximum number of addresses can't be greater than the largest number a 16-bit register can hold — 65,536, or 64K. In dealing with PCs you keep coming across that 64K number. 64K is the:

- number of possible segment addresses
- maximum number of bytes in a segment
- number of port addresses the CPU can use for I/O
- maximum size of a COM program
- maximum size of a BAS (BASIC) program

all because:

- the 8088 is a 16-bit chip
- each bit can be in two states (0 or 1)
- so $2^{16} = 65,536$ (64K)

But while the maximum size of each segment is 64K, the segments can (and do) overlap each other. And they can be far smaller than 64K.

A stack segment can be fairly tiny. Unless you change it with a CLEAR command, for instance, the default size of the stack in BASIC is either 512 bytes or one-eighth of the available memory, whichever is smaller. If you're not nesting lots of short routines, or trying to fill in or "paint" complex pictures (both of which need more than the usual amount of stack space so BASIC can interrupt operations and jump to other operations repeatedly and then get back to what it was doing) this 512 bytes will do just fine. If programmers had to lop off 64K for each segment, they'd end up wasting tons of space.

If each segment had to be 64K, it could start at only one of 16 fixed places in memory. So to make things more flexible, the CPU lets programmers deals with any one of 65,536 different segment addresses. The only restriction is that each segment has to start at the beginning of a *paragraph*.

Paragraph?

In computer parlance, a paragraph is simply a number that is evenly divisible by 16. The reason for this is that while the 8088 CPU can address 1,048,576 total bytes, its segment registers can handle only 65,536 possible segment starting addresses. Divide 1,048,576 by 65,536 and you get 16. You can have a segment start at the very first paragraph (0), or at paragraph 1, or at paragraph 65,535. But it can't start at paragraph 1.5.

It's sort of like talking about fingers. You like to deal with whole hands, not fractions like 1.5 hands. And just as each set of hands is made up of ten smaller parts (fingers), each paragraph is made up of hexadecimal 10 smaller parts (bytes). What is written as 10 in hex notation is equal to 16 in our more familiar decimal system.

The idea of paragraphs is familiar to anyone who has used DEBUG. If the lower 128 ASCII characters were loaded into the very bottom part of your system's memory (and there's a good reason why they aren't, since other important things are kept there), and you used the DEBUG D command to display them, you'd see something like:

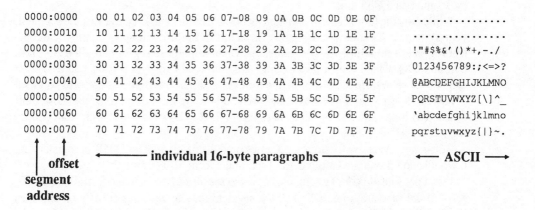

```
0000:0000   00 01 02 03 04 05 06 07-08 09 0A 0B 0C 0D 0E 0F    ................
0000:0010   10 11 12 13 14 15 16 17-18 19 1A 1B 1C 1D 1E 1F    ................
0000:0020   20 21 22 23 24 25 26 27-28 29 2A 2B 2C 2D 2E 2F     !"#$%&'()*+,-./
0000:0030   30 31 32 33 34 35 36 37-38 39 3A 3B 3C 3D 3E 3F    0123456789:;<=>?
0000:0040   40 41 42 43 44 45 46 47-48 49 4A 4B 4C 4D 4E 4F    @ABCDEFGHIJKLMNO
0000:0050   50 51 52 53 54 55 56 57-58 59 5A 5B 5C 5D 5E 5F    PQRSTUVWXYZ[\]^_
0000:0060   60 61 62 63 64 65 66 67-68 69 6A 6B 6C 6D 6E 6F    `abcdefghijklmno
0000:0070   70 71 72 73 74 75 76 77-78 79 7A 7B 7C 7D 7E 7F    pqrstuvwxyz{|}~.
```

↑   ↑   ←——— **individual 16-byte paragraphs** ———→   ←— **ASCII** —→
offset
segment
address

Each horizontal line is one paragraph, and contains 16 bytes. The two groups of four-digit numbers on the left, separated by the colon, are the segment and offset addresses. (Each is only four digits long because DEBUG works exclusively in hexadecimal notation and can cram any number from 0 to 65,536 into four hex digits.) The numbers in the middle are the hexadecimal representations of the bytes in each paragraph. DEBUG will display the actual characters each byte represents at the right side of its display, if the characters have ASCII values greater than 31 (1F in hex) and less than 127 (7F in hex). Otherwise it prints dots.

The decimal number for the segment 61440 is actually F000 in hex. And the decimal 57435 offset is hex E05B. The conventional notation for memory addresses is SEGMENT:OFFSET, so this address is really F000:E05B.

To translate a two-part address like F000:E05B into a single linear or *absolute* address that actually points to the precise one byte in the PC's megabyte of memory that you want, just shift and add.

In this case, shifting means bumping the number up by one decimal place, or order of magnitude. The decimal orders of magnitude start with 1, 10, 100, 1000, 10000; each time you add a zero. What you're really doing is multiplying the previous number by 10, since we use a base-10 number system.

Shifting over a digit in hex means multiplying by 16. The decimal equivalents of the first few hex orders of magnitude are 1, 16, 256, 4096, 65536. In hex, these are 1H, 10H, 100H, 1000H, 10000H; multiplying by 16 is really multiplying by 10H. So first, multiply the segment address by 16 to shift it up a notch. This is simple; stick a 0 on the end of F000 and you get F0000. Then add the offset to it:

```
    F0000
+   E05B
    FE05B
```

Hex FE05B is indeed equal to decimal 1,040,475. To check it, multiply decimal 61440 by 16 and add 57435 to it.

While only the four segment registers mentioned earlier can keep track of the segment, your system can calculate and juggle offsets in lots of different ways. Segment and offset registers deal with two-byte addresses. General purpose registers (called AX, BX, CX, and DX), which can be pressed into action to hold two-byte offsets, can also store single byte values. Because of this, the four general purpose registers are often divided in halves. If you looked inside AX and found it holding the value E05B, the "low" half of that two-byte pair (5B) would be in register AL (L = Low) and the "high" half (E0) in register AH (H = High).

But — are you ready for this? — if you stored the offset address E05B in register AX, it would end up switched around, tail first, in the form 5B E0. Why?

Don't peek inside your system and expect to see all addresses in the form F000:E05B. Most of the time programs establish the segment they're working in early on and then just specify offsets inside that segment — like dialing local phone numbers without the area codes.

But if the segment you're using is F000, you'll never see it written that way. F000 is really two bytes, F0 and 00. A pair of bytes joined like this is called a word. Your PC uses a backwards (or "backwords") method for storing each of these, so F000 is actually stored 00F0.

In the word F000 (or any hex number bigger than a single byte), the *most significant* byte is the larger one (F0) and the *least significant* byte is the smaller one (00). The PC stores such two- byte addresses with the least significant byte first. It stores *strings* of letters such as error messages in the normal non-backwards way, however.

That's because the PC puts the upper half of the number higher in memory and the lower half lower in memory, which makes perfect sense. When you scan through memory, you generally start from near the bottom and move upward, which also makes sense, so you hit the low byte first. When you refer to the address of a word, you always mean where the word starts, and it starts at the lower half.

To simplify things, say you're storing the word F000 at absolute memory address 1. The normal way to map out on paper how memory works is to put the very bottom part at the top of the page and work downward:

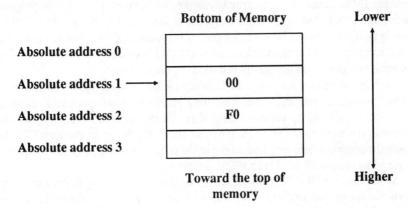

Confusing? At first. It's especially diabolical when dealing with the 12-bit addresses that the PC-XT File Allocation Table (FAT) uses to keep track of clusters. But for now, just remember that if you're using DEBUG to search for segment F000, you'll have to tell it to hunt for 00 F0.

One more note about addresses — the same absolute address can be expressed in many different ways. This is sort of like saying you could express the decimal number 10 as (5 + 5) or (8 + 2).

The very bottom of memory is at relative address 0000:0000, and absolute address 00000. (The very top is F000:FFFF or FFFFF.) The absolute hex address one paragraph up from the bottom of memory (10H bytes up in hex; 16 bytes up from the bottom in decimal) would be 00010. You could express this as 0000:0010. But you could just as easily write it as 0001:0000. All three refer to the same location in memory.

To test this, use the shift-and-add technique mentioned earlier:

```
for 0000:0010 ┐                for 0001:0000 ┐
      |       |                      |       |
   00000      |                   00010      |
 +  0010 ◄────┘                 +  0000 ◄────┘
   00010                          00010
```

Obviously, the higher up you go into memory the more ways you have of referring to paragraph addresses (sometimes called paragraph *boundaries*) using relative SEG-MENT:OFFSET notation. One is just as good as another in telling your CPU how to behave.

Mapping the Meg

But you can't get your hands on the whole megabyte of memory. IBM originally divided the available megabyte into 16 blocks, each one 64K long, and reserved some for ROM, and some for the displays, some for expansion room, which was used eventually by gut-level BIOS *extension* programs to handle things like hard disks that weren't offered originally. It left the remaining ten blocks, or 640K, for your programs.

Well, almost 640K. DOS takes up a good chunk, and the amount grows with each release. BIOS needs a little, to store keystrokes when you type so fast the program you're using can't soak them all up right away, and to keep track of things like whether the Ctrl key is being held down, how much memory is installed, the current video mode, the current time (expressed in clock ticks since midnight), how many lines can fit on your screen, or what equipment is supposedly installed in your system.

Each PC maintains a sort of travel agency called the *Interrupt Vector Table* at the absolute bottom of memory. When something generates an interrupt, it checks this table to see where it should go for the routine that will do the actual work. This table is very popular; it's used by BIOS, DOS, the interrupt controller chip, the main CPU itself, and even the programs you may be running at the time. It's really just a list of up to 256 four-byte addresses, in SEGMENT:OFFSET form.

When interrupt 0 ("Divide by Zero") needs to know where in the total megabyte to look for the special routine to deal with such an error, it checks the first four bytes (table entry #0) for the address or *vector*. When interrupt 1 (used by DEBUG) drops in, it checks the next four byte address (table entry #1). When INT 2 (which is usually how interrupts are abbreviated) is involved, you have problems, because odds are that's a parity error lurching toward its fatal nonmaskable interrupt goodnight kiss. If you poke around in this table and replace an existing entry with the address of your own program, the table will send the respective interrupt to your program rather than the old one.

The top segment of the megabyte is taken up by your system ROM, which needs this space to store the tests that are performed during the initial power-on diagnostic check to make sure things are working properly, and the gut-level BIOS routines that take care of the nitty-gritty details in controlling your drives, keyboard, clock, displays, printer, serial port, and memory.

The middle B000 segment was originally allocated for video. PC displays are *memory-mapped*, which means that each video memory address corresponds with a small but specific area of the screen. If you have a color system, running this program:

```
100 DEF SEG=&HB800
120 POKE 1,78
130 POKE 0,1
140 POKE 3999,100
150 POKE 3998,2
```

will put four values into memory at segment B800H that your CRT controller will turn instantly into characters and colors onscreen. This particular program will put a small yellow-on-red face in the upper lefthand corner of your screen and a red-on-yellow one in the lower righthand corner. (If you're using a monochrome screen, omit lines 120 and 140, and change the &HB800 in line 100 to &HB000.)

A rough map of the entire megabyte would look something like:

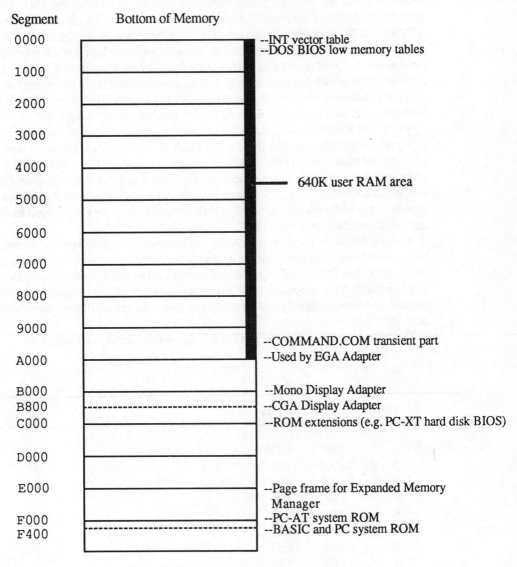

Segment	Bottom of Memory
0000	--INT vector table / --DOS BIOS low memory tables
1000	
2000	
3000	
4000	
5000	640K user RAM area
6000	
7000	
8000	
9000	
A000	--COMMAND.COM transient part / --Used by EGA Adapter
B000	--Mono Display Adapter
B800	--CGA Display Adapter
C000	--ROM extensions (e.g. PC-XT hard disk BIOS)
D000	
E000	--Page frame for Expanded Memory Manager
F000	--PC-AT system ROM
F400	--BASIC and PC system ROM

Top of Memory

The lower 640K (segments 0000 through 9000) can get pretty crowded. Users commonly wedge in the Interrupt Vector Table, the low-memory BIOS control area, the updated IBMBIO.COM and IBMDOS.COM system file patches and services (or their generic Microsoft equivalents), the guts-level DOS *kernel* (which manages system functions such as file and memory management), any device drivers (such as MOUSE.SYS or ANSI.SYS), disk buffers, stacks, environment and file control blocks, the resident slice of COMMAND.COM (the part that prints the friendly "Abort, Retry, Ignore, Fail?" message when your drive door is open), and the transient slice (the part that's responsible for the friendly A> prompt and that parses and executes your commands), as well as any commercial programs that are currently running or are resident but inactive (such as *SideKick*), the stack and data for these programs, and any DOS TSRs (Terminate-and-Stay-Resident programs) such as MODE and PRINT that lurk in the background.

When IBM first introduced the PC, it left several gaps in the megabyte. The first was at segment A000, the one directly after the 640K of user memory. Since the next hunk of RAM real estate wasn't officially claimed until segment B000 or B800, this left 64K of prime memory for the taking. Users quickly figured out that they could set the tiny and inaccessible DIP switches (which supposedly stands for "dual in-line package switches" but really means "damned invisible plastic" since they're so hard to see) to turn 640K into 704K or even more.

The next 64K memory block after A000 was for extended video displays, among other things. IBM's common monochrome adapter locked up the first available address in this block, B000. But CGAs (color/graphics adapters) used a starting address halfway up the block, at B800. This meant that enterprising memory hounds could squeeze out the additional 32K between B000 and B800 and use it above the extra 64K they already swiped at A000.

The settings on block 2 of PC and PC-XT dip switch blocks to do this were:

Switch	704K	736K
1	ON	OFF
2	ON	ON
3	OFF	OFF
4	ON	ON
5	OFF	OFF
6	OFF	OFF
7	OFF	OFF
8	OFF	OFF

Users who had IBM's original ROM chip set found it wouldn't recognize more than 544, but IBM sold a replacement part up until the middle of 1987. And memory hungry users had to purchase expansion RAM boards sophisticated enough to let them set the addresses of such additional RAM to A000 and B000, so it wouldn't conflict with existing memory, and so that DOS could find it. This undocumented memory enlarger worked fine for a few years. The POST memory diagnostic routine would examine this additional user memory, and the DOS CHKDSK.COM utility would report it.

But a new generation of IBM displays created a new problem. IBM's outdated CGA was, in a word, pathetic. It produced an image so grainy you thought you were looking at it through a screen door.

Display adapters draw letters and numbers out of dot patterns in a grid called a character box. The monochrome adapter's relatively detailed character box measures 9 dots x 14 dots. However, this really works out to 7 x 11 since the leftmost and rightmost columns and the top two rows and bottom row are blank, and serve as *character separators* to keep nearby letters from touching. And the bottom two rows are reserved for descenders on characters such as q, y, j, g, and p.

The CGA character box is a crude 8 x 8. The only character separators are the rightmost column and the bottom row, so this produces 7 x 7 dot characters. However, the bottom row also doubles as space for descenders, so the lower parts of letters such as q and y actually touch the tops of tall letters below them.

Worse, the CGA adapter didn't have enough memory on it, so that each time it scrolled up one line the entire display would go dead and turn black for a fraction of a second and then flash back into life. Repeated scrolling meant an extremely disturbing flicker. And to top it off, while the memory on the monochrome adapter was *dual ported* so you could write data to it at the same time you were reading other data from it without disturbing the onscreen image, trying this on a monitor attached to a CGA card produced a jarring burst of visible static called "snow." The monochrome adapter put a total of 720 x 350 dots onscreen (and came with a long-persistence phosphor that removed any hint of flicker, and blurred the last traces of dots into what looked like solid lines), while all the CGA could muster was 640 x 200. And the mono adapter could form characters faster and pump data onto the screen faster. IBM really seemed to have designed the CGA to hook up to television sets. As proof, its CGA characters were all constructed of double-dot patterns to overcome the inherent fuzziness and imprecision of home TVs. Users could change jumper J3 on the CGA itself so that it would produce slightly sharper single-dot characters in a 5 x 7 grid. But to do this you had to rip open your system, pull out the board, and solder in a wire! Would you?

IBM wasn't interested in color back then, and still makes life hard for users of color systems. The CLS clear screen command still resets any existing colors to grey on black, unless the user happens to have ANSI.SYS loaded and properly configured, and ANSI can be a pain in the neck, since not all software can handle it.

However, when IBM introduced the PC-AT it realized it had to upgrade the color display, and eventually introduced an interim color (and monochrome) system called the EGA. Chapter 13 covers the EGA, and provides a fat arsenal of color tools.

The EGA devoured memory, and claimed the block at A000 for its high-resolution graphics modes, which conflicted with users who had reset their system switches to push RAM past 640K.

The Official Way to Expand Memory

IBM's very first PC came standard with a tiny 16K of RAM, on 16K memory chips. One reason DOS was so scrawny back then is that it had to squeeze inside this small scrap of RAM. If you were really adventurous you could expand it all the way up to 64K, but all that extra memory wasn't cheap back then.

Several years later IBM started putting 64K RAM chips on its system board, and just about everyone bought multifunction/memory expansion cards and shoved the full complement of 640K into their machines. Eventually IBM would move to 256K and one megabyte chips and let users play with eight megs or more.

But users quickly found 640K wasn't enough.

First, programmers who had written very tight, compact assembly language applications software soon found that they could crank out programs faster, and maintain them more easily, if they wrote them in a compiled language that ended up taking more disk space. And programs began getting feature-crazy, so that software vendors could crow about how their packages offered fancy but useless chrome strips and tailfins that competitor's products didn't.

Second, users began creating larger data files. Instead of keeping separate yearly spreadsheets on company performance, for instance, they found they could combine the last five years into one massive whopper.

Finally, users discovered memory-resident, or TSR, programs. You'd load these into memory and they'd sit idly in the background waiting to spring into the foreground. TSR (Terminate-and-Stay-Resident) programs like these turned out to be so useful and popular that many users couldn't get any work done unless three or four of them were stuffed into RAM.

SideKick, the grandddaddy of them all, provided a pop-up calculator, ASCII table, clipboard/notepad, dialer, and calendar. Others let you create keyboard macros, so that one or two keystrokes could trigger hundreds more and pare repetitive tasks down to size; or would kick your modem into action periodically to download your electronic mail; or back up your hard disk onto a tape drive every night at 5:00.

All PCs shared three space problems. You couldn't run programs that were larger than 640K, and even that figure was low, since you also had to take into account the overhead required by DOS and BIOS. You couldn't put more than 640K of data into memory, and again, you had to leave space for DOS, BIOS, and at least part of your program. And you couldn't have DOS handle individual hard disks that were larger than 32 megabytes.

Lotus Development Corporation, the makers of *1-2-3*, finally got tired of listening to their customers scream that they couldn't create enormous spreadsheets. So together with chip-maker Intel, they developed a variation of an old "bank switching" technique and named it the Expanded Memory Specification 3.0. Later, they twisted Microsoft's arm to endorse a 3.2 mutation of it and called the result the Lotus/Intel/Microsoft (LIM) Expanded Memory Specification 3.2, or "LIM spec memory" for short.

Shortly afterward, board manufacturer AST enlisted two other industry heavyweights, Quadram and Ashton-Tate, and published a much more flexible EMS version they called EEMS (Enhanced EMS). EEMS was a superset of EMS, which caused problems since software designed for EMS boards would run on EEMS hardware but it wouldn't always work the other way around. Both gave users up to eight megabytes of additional memory, although various headaches with drivers and multiple memory boards prevented the spec from being exploited fully.

The Lotus/Intel/Microsoft trio then enhanced some of AST's ideas and added a few of their own and announced an improved version called LIM 4.0. This new LIM spec quadrupled the potential amount of expanded memory in a system from eight megs to 32, gave developers a whole new set of programming tools, and added better support for multitasking and program execution in high memory. This solved the "large data" problem temporarily. It didn't solve the "large program" problem. Recent operating systems such as OS/2 and hot chips like the 80386 make short work out of memory problems. And both Microsoft and IBM have tricks up their sleeves as larger hard disks become common. Compaq was first to smash the 32 meg hard disk barrier with DOS 3.31, although other vendors had done it in a wasteful way by increasing sector size past 512 bytes.

The original LIM bank switcher used expanded memory that wasn't a part of the PC's addressable one megabyte. Just add a bank-switching memory expansion board to your system, tell your CONFIG.SYS bootup configuration file about a program called an Expanded Memory Manager (EMM), and any LIM-aware software could toss enormous data files around in RAM with abandon.

The trick was to grab (or *map*) one unused 64K segment near the top of the PC's addressable megabyte of RAM and use it as a narrow doorway into the far greater amount of memory on the bank switching card itself. This doorway was called a *page frame* and contained four smaller 16K sections called *windows*.

While the original spec demanded one contiguous 64K chunk of RAM, later enhancements eased the requirements slightly, and made the mapping process far more accommodating.

When a program like *1-2-3* needed more space in RAM for a growing spreadsheet, it could put information into expanded memory, and retrieve it later, by shuttling it up and back 16K at a time through one of the windows. The EMM had to be smart enough to know when *1-2-3* needed something that wasn't currently in one of these little windows, and shuffle things around to snag it and bring it down to the page frame.

Expanded memory is like a research department in a small office using a bank of four elevators connected to a vast warehouse of archives. Whenever they need a single document from the warehouse, they can send the elevator up to retrieve it. But if they want several hundred volumes, they're going to have to use all the elevators and make several trips. The elevators are all one size, which makes it wasteful to get just one scrap of paper, and slow to retrieve large amounts of data. Since the warehouse manager doesn't want his precious data to get lost, and since there isn't much room to spare in the research department office, when the researchers want something new they have to send some of the older stuff back.

Expanded vs. Extended

Who names these things? Few enough users really understand what's going on under their hoods anyway, and you'd think the folks who invent all this stuff would go out of their way to make it clear and unconfusing. Then again, these are the same people who created a multibillion dollar industry based around a computer system so hostile to novices that if brand new users somehow manage to get their systems hooked up properly and figure out which one of eight possible ways to insert their DOS floppy disks is right, their reward is a black screen with nothing on it but an A> in the corner.

Some rascals decided to call bank-switched RAM *expanded memory*, while calling the special kind of RAM available in 80286 and 80386 machines (like the PC-AT and most PS/2s) *extended memory*. These even sound the same if you say them both fast enough.

Working on one of today's hot chips in a normal everyday one-megabyte configuration with 640K or less of usable RAM is called running in *real mode*. However, you can tweak chips like the 80286 to run in a special, enhanced state called *protected mode*. A protected mode system lets users directly address more than one megabyte of memory, and lets them *multitask*, or run several programs simultaneously.

Previous attempts at multitasking ran into lots of trouble. The usual bugaboo was that if three programs were churning through their paces at the same time and one crashed, the whole house of cards would tumble down. That's bad enough in real mode when one program with one set of data crashes and burns; it's downright evil when a crashed multitasking system does two or three times the normal damage. Protected mode protects the user from this nightmare — when one program crashes, the others keeping humming blithely away.

When people mention the bit-size of a computer, they're really talking about the microprocessor register size used for storing data within the CPU. (However, if they mention two numbers, the second one is the width of the bus.) The register size was eight bits (one byte) for the ancient generation of 8080 and Z-80 chips popular before the PC was introduced; 16 bits (one word) for the 8088, 8086 chips, and 80286, which are used in the PC, AT, and some of the PS/2 systems; and 32 bits (a *long word* or *double word*) for the 80386. These chips can often divide larger registers into several smaller ones.

The CPU includes an *arithmetic logic unit* (ALU) that can do addition and subtraction, logical ANDs and ORs, bit shifts, and negation on the data in the registers. To be efficient, the ALU has to operate on whole registers at once. Microprocessors also generate addresses to access data from memory, and perform arithmetic operations on these addresses. Ideally, the microprocessor should use the same ALU to operate on both data and addresses.

The early eight-bit 8080 chip would have been simpler if it had used only eight bits for addressing. But this would have limited its addressing abilities to just 256 bytes (2^8). Instead, the 8080 forms addresses by sticking two bytes together. This chip has minimal 16-bit arithmetic capabilities.

Both the 8086 and 8088 CPUs handle data internally in 16-bit chunks, although the 8088 used in the PC and XT accesses memory externally only eight bits at a time. The easiest way for the designers of the PC to handle memory addresses would have been to limit the machine to 64K (2^16) so the CPU could address everything directly. But 64K is just too small. Instead, they had the CPU in the PC and XT calculate physical addresses by adding a 16-bit offset register to a 16-bit segment register that has been shifted to the left four bits. The result is a 20-bit address that can access one megabyte. But the chip is really only working with 16 its for both data and address.

With the advent of the 80286 chip things got even more complex. In real mode, the 80286 works the same as the 8086 and 8088. In protected mode, however, the segment registers are *selectors* for accessing a 24-bit *base address* from memory. The chip then adds this to the 16-bit offset address. This yields a 24-bit address that can handle 16 megabytes of memory.

The 80386 is a full-fledged 32-bit microprocessor. It stores data in 32-bit registers and can do full 32-bit arithmetic. It uses a 32-bit address that can directly access four gigabytes (four billion bytes) of memory. Like the 80286 in protected mode, the 80386 uses a selector to reference a base address that it adds to an offset address, but the base address and offset address are both 32 bits. The only time the 80386 uses 64 bits is when doing double word multiplication and division.

The 80286 chip at the heart of the PC-AT can theoretically address 16 megabytes of RAM directly. Anything past the normal one megabyte is extended. The PC-AT's designers figured that three megabytes would be enough, but recent developments have given power users several times that amount. Still, there really aren't very many programs that can take advantage of this extended RAM. The most common is the DOS 3.x VDISK RAMdisk.

Because of significant differences between real mode and protected mode, current versions of DOS and most application programs cannot use this additional 15 megabytes of extended memory. Getting access to it requires OS/2 or one of the many protected mode operating systems trying to compete with it.

Lots of clones these days brag about how they come straight from the factory with a megabyte of RAM while IBM's machines sport a relatively meager 512K or 640K. What they don't explain is that this additional 384K can't be addressed directly. In fact, about all you can do with the excess RAM is make a large RAMdisk out of it, which isn't such a bad idea.

RAMdisks are nothing more than areas of memory that your system treats just like physical disk drives. You don't have to format them, and at least with the VDISK version supplied by IBM, you can't use the DISKCOPY or DISKCOMP utilities with them (although you can do this with RAMdisk software supplied by other manufacturers such as AST). RAMdisks are extremely fast, since they have none of the arms and motors and other moving parts that slow down mechanical disk drives. But they're volatile, so that you have to take any information temporarily stored on a RAMdisk and copy it to a floppy or hard disk before you turn your system off or you'll lose it all.

You can use this kind of extra clone memory for a RAMdisk by making sure the DOS 3.x VDISK.SYS device driver is on your disk in a subdirectory called \DOS. Then put this line in your CONFIG.SYS file:

```
DEVICE=\DOS\VDISK.SYS 384 /E
```

The VDISK driver uses a BIOS call that temporarily switches to protected mode, accesses the extended memory, and then switches back to real mode.

To make things even more confusing, vendors eventually introduced products to use extended memory that emulated LIM expanded memory. Clear?

Memory and the Bus

One last note about chips and memory: The PC used a 16-bit chip but an eight-bit bus. The PC-AT came with an interim 16-bit chip that used 16-bit bus (Intel later revealed that it was sort of a mistake and that the 80386 was really the chip the 80286 should have been). The new top-level generation of PS/2s use a 32-bit chip and a 32-bit bus.

One of the big speed advantages of the PC-AT was that it could move memory around on the bus twice as efficiently as the PC. New 16-bit memory boards came with a small stub that fits into a special plug on the system board to handle the extra data lines. And users who upgraded from PCs to PC-ATs thought that they'd have to throw their old memory boards away when they switched. Well, it turns out that they didn't have to. But maybe they should have.

The PC and XT expansion board bus connectors carry 62 signals including the 20 address lines (which allow the 8088 microprocessor to access one megabyte of memory) and eight bidirectional data lines. The PC-AT has eight expansion board slots. Six of these have a second bus connector with 36 signals, including four additional address lines (for the total 16-megabyte memory space) and eight more bidirectional data lines, because the 80286 accesses data in words rather than bytes.

The 62-signal connector on the PC-AT is highly compatible with that on the PC and XT. The two PC-AT expansion board slots that have only the old 62-signal connector are designed for older boards with byte-accessible memory and I/O. Existing video cards work in these slots, for instance. However, the 62-signal connectors on the other six slots are wired exactly the same as these two. Here's the catch: The 36-signal bus connector on the PC-AT has two signals called "MEM CS16" and "I/O CS16." These signals must be generated by any AT board that can handle 16-bit memory or I/O transfers. If these signals are not present — and they won't be if the board doesn't use this second connector — the AT will access memory (or I/O) with eight-bit transfers.

This means the PC-AT can indeed handle old memory boards. But users will notice a significant speed penalty for programs that run in this memory space or use data in it. It's just not worthwhile to spend the money for a PC-AT and then slow it down by inhibiting 16-bit memory transfers, which is one of the major speed advantages of the 80286 over the 8088.

Resurrecting "Lost" Files from RAM

It happens to everyone. It's well after midnight and you're typing furiously to meet a critical deadline. The muscles in your back stopped throbbing hours ago and have now tied themselves into an icy clove hitch. Your fingertips are flattened and numb, and you're so bleary-eyed you can't tell whether you're staring at a color or a mono screen.

Then your system starts making a dry wheezing sound and you realize you had better save your last few hours of work to disk, so you punch in a series of commands. One of three things happens:

- You entered the command properly and your system copied the file safely from RAM to a more permanent storage medium.
- You entered the command properly but your disk was nearly full and your word processor became angry at you for trying such a pinheaded move and decided to quit and drop you out of the program and back into DOS without saving anything.
- You entered some thick-fingered command from out of the Twilight Zone that your software interpreted as "quit without saving" and happily obliged, leaving you at the DOS prompt with a funny expression on your face.

If either of the latter two scenarios ever spoiled an evening for you, you probably thought that all your work was forever lost. But unless you were using some oddball word processor with a proprietary non-ASCII format, you could have saved most or all of your file. The most important rule if this ever happens is don't turn your system off or run any other programs. Then follow the instructions below.

Word processors generally keep a large dollop of your file in RAM, and *spill* or move parts of it to disk when RAM fills up. These temporary spill files usually have extensions like $$$ or TMP, and your word processor combines, renames, erases, and cleans up such files when you tell it to save things and quit. (Temporary files are sometimes "hidden" from normal directory searches, and since they vanish when you exit, you don't normally see them.) But while applications erase temporary disk files when you exit, they don't usually get rid of the parts of your file they keep in memory.

So if you ever find yourself staring at a DOS prompt with an unsaved file floating around somewhere in the electronic ether, don't panic. It's fairly simple to retrieve most of the file from memory, and the rest of it from hidden or erased $$$ files on your disk.

Here's how: Open your desk drawer and take out your emergency file resuscitation kit, which consists of:

- A copy of your DOS disk with DEBUG.COM on it
- Two blank, formatted disks
- The *Norton Utilities* (or equivalent)
- A pencil and pad of paper

Your first and most important job is to rescue your file from memory. Once that's done you can begin looking for other parts of it that may be scattered across your disk. Again, if you ever do find yourself unexpectedly back in DOS without having saved your file to disk, be absolutely sure you *do not* run any other programs, or turn your system off.

This example assumes you save your files periodically, and that you don't have some enormous unsaved whopper file sprawling across several memory segments. The process isn't really difficult, but it can be tricky enough to someone who has never seen a hex number or used DEBUG. If your file does extend across two or more segments, the process gets a lot more complicated.

It is convenient here to slice up the PC's one megabyte (1,048,576 bytes) of RAM into 16 segments, each 64K (65,536 bytes) long. You can normally address only the lower ten 64K segments (for a total of 640K). The other six are for ROM programs, video displays, hard disk interfaces, network connections, and other special functions provided by your system. A map of these ten segments of "user memory" would look like this:

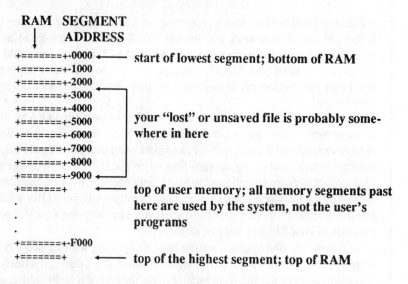

Follow these instructions carefully:

1. If DEBUG.COM is on your hard disk, just type DEBUG. If it's not, stick the floppy with DEBUG.COM on it in drive A:, type DEBUG, and press the

Enter key. In either case all you'll see is the DEBUG prompt, which is just a
hyphen at the left edge of your screen. (Note: type in the following DEBUG instructions exactly as they appear, carefully substituting the addresses that apply
to your system for the ones used in the examples. Using the S (Search) and D
(Dump) commands can't really do any damage, but other DEBUG commands
can. If you're careful, you'll be fine. But don't start playing indiscriminately
with DEBUG tools like E (Enter) or M (Move) unless you know what you're
doing. Also note that you can enter DEBUG commands in uppercase or lowercase, although all the examples here will be in uppercase to avoid confusion between characters like l and 1.)

2. Think hard and try to remember a keyword near the very beginning of
your file. If you were writing a report on Yamigazi Industries, the word
"Yamigazi" will do just fine. If it's on platinum futures, use "platinum." Pick a
word that's distinctive and not too short. Chop off the last letter, since some
word processors modify final letters slightly. (This would leave you with
Yamigaz and platinu.)

3. Give DEBUG the command to search for this word, memory segment by
memory segment. DEBUG will search every nook and cranny of each 64K segment (and help you extract the file when you find it), but it can't handle more
than one segment at a time. For the purposes of this example, use the word
"platinu" (remember, without the final letter, and in lowercase unless you're
sure all references to the word were in uppercase). And start at the top of your
640K workspace and work downward; the order doesn't really matter so long as
you try every segment. Type in everything below except the hyphen:

```
-S 9000:0 LFFFF "platinu"
```

and then hit the Enter key. (Obviously, substitute the particular word you want
to find in place of "platinu" in the example above.) What this command says is
"search through memory starting at the beginning of segment 9000, and continuing for 65,535 (hex FFFF) bytes, and report the address each time it finds the letters 'platinu.'"

DEBUG will zip all the way through segment 9000 searching for this exact
string of letters. If it finds the string it will print one or more eight-digit hex numbers with a colons in the middle, something like this:

```
9000:2F3D
9000:301E
9000:317F
-
```

These hex numbers would represent the addresses in memory segment 9000 of
any occurrences of the letters "platinu." DEBUG may print one of these num-

bers or a whole list of them. Or it may print nothing except another hyphen. If it prints one or more of these hex numbers, go to step 5. If it doesn't print anything except another hyphen, it didn't find anything, so you have to tell it to search the next lower segment of memory.

4. Since DEBUG didn't find the word in segment 9000, work your way down the following commands one by one (remembering not to type the hyphen):

```
-S 8000:0 LFFFF "platinu"
-S 7000:0 LFFFF "platinu"
-S 6000:0 LFFFF "platinu"
-S 5000:0 LFFFF "platinu"
-S 4000:0 LFFFF "platinu"
-S 3000:0 LFFFF "platinu"
-S 2000:0 LFFFF "platinu"
-S 1000:0 LFFFF "platinu"
-S 0000:0 LFFFF "platinu"
```

It's extraordinarily unlikely that it would find something in the lowest segments, but when you're desperate, you can't lose and should try anything legal. Here's a shortcut — after typing:

```
S 9000:0 LFFFF "platinu"
```

just type in:

```
S 8
```

but don't press Enter yet — instead, press the grey F3 function key. DOS will fill in the rest of the line for you. Then press Enter. If DEBUG doesn't find anything in segment 8000, type in

```
S 7
```

and press F3, and then Enter, etc.

(If you work your way down the ladder far enough DEBUG will definitely find something, since it will stumble over itself. When you tell DEBUG to do something, it uses a part of memory to hold the instructions you gave it, and at some point it will find these instructions and end up telling you its own address.)

If you get to the end of the list without having DEBUG print out any hex addresses, something is wrong. Make sure you removed the last letter of the word you're searching for, that you spelled the word properly, and that you entered it in the exact uppercase or lowercase form in which it originally appeared in your document. If you swear that you followed every instruction to the letter, pick another word and try the whole process again.

5. It's a good idea to work all the way down the list for two reasons (and it's easy when you use the F3 trick mentioned in step 4). First, one of the addresses DEBUG reports will be an artifact of the search itself, since it will uncover its own workspace and find the search command that you just typed in. Second, it's possible that a duplicate copy of the word might be lurking in memory from another file you created earlier. Jot down the addresses DEBUG reports. If it prints out a whole long string of them, the first in the list is the most important. If it scrolls the list off the screen too fast for you to note the first few, use the following pause technique:

- Position your left hand on the Ctrl key and your right hand over the letter S. Holding down the Ctrl key and pressing S will alternately freeze and unfreeze the display. (The first Ctrl-S will freeze it, the next will start it up again, the third will freeze it again, etc.)
- Then press F3 and then the Enter key, and punch Ctrl-S as soon as the addresses start to scroll. This will pause the display so you can write the first address in the list down. Press Ctrl-S when you're done to start scrolling again.

6. Once you've written down the list of addresses that DEBUG reported, you have to figure out which one represents the address of the first occurrence in your file of the word you are seeking. Look at the list and pick the lowest address. Each address comes in two halves. The segment is on the left and the offset on the right. In the example above,

9000:2F3D

SEGMENT : OFFSET

9000 is the segment and 2F3D is the offset. (Think of the segment as an area code and the offset as a local phone number.) It's easy to put the segments in order, since 9000 is the highest and 0000 is the lowest. If you wrote down the addresses inside each segment in the order in which DEBUG reported them, the lowest should be at the top.

7. Now that you've identified the lowest address reported by DEBUG, examine the area in memory specified by that address. If the lowest address you found was 4000:D1F6, you would change the rightmost digit (here it's a 6) to a 0, then type in everything below except the hyphen:

```
-D 4000:D1F0
```

and press the Enter key. (The DEBUG D command stands for Dump and will display the contents of the 128 bytes of memory immediately following the hex address you specified.) Again, you would substitute the lowest address you found in your own search for the 4000:D1F0 used above. You should see a three-part display that looks something like this:

```
4000:D1F0 57 68 69 6C 65 20 70 6C-61 74 69 6E 75 6D 20 73 While platinum s
4000:D200 68 61 72 65 73 20 6D 61-6E 79 20 6F 66 20 74 68 hares many of th
4000:D210 65 20 70 72 6F 70 65 72-74 69 65 73 20 6F 66 20 e properties of
4000:D220 67 6F 6C 64 2C 20 69 74-20 68 61 73 20 6E 65 76 gold, it has nev
4000:D230 65 72 20 8D 0A 62 65 65-6E 20 61 20 70 6F 70 75 er ..been a popu
4000:D240 6C 61 72 20 6D 61 74 65-72 69 61 6C 20 66 6F 72 lar material for
4000:D250 20 6A 65 77 65 6C 72 79-20 6F 72 20 65 78 70 65  jewelry or expe
4000:D260 6E 73 69 76 65 20 74 61-62 6C 65 77 61 72 65 2C nsive tableware,
 address          hex values of the actual bytes         ASCII version
```

The lefthand column shows the address of each paragraph — 16-byte section of memory — which is represented by one horizontal row in the DEBUG desplay above. The middle column contains the actual hex values of each of the 16 bytes in the paragraph. The righthand column displays the ASCII text representation of what's in memory at those addresses. When DEBUG finds any value that isn't a letter, number, or punctuation symbol, it will print a period in the righthand column. The two periods before the word "been" above are examples of this, since DEBUG couldn't easily print the characters that 8D and 0A — a high-bit carriage return and line feed — represent.

If you do see something like this display, congratulations. The hard part is over. Now you simply have to find the beginning and ending addresses of your file and copy the information from the memory area between these two addresses to a disk.

(If all you see is something like:

```
4000:6FC0 00 00 00 00 00 00 00 00-00 00 00 00 00 00 00 00 ................
4000:6FD0 00 00 00 00 00 00 00 00-44 0D 34 30 30 30 3A 36 ........D.4000:6
4000:6FE0 46 30 30 0D 46 46 20 22-70 6C 61 74 69 6E 75 22 F00.FF "platinu"
4000:6FF0 0D 00 00 00 00 00 00 00-00 00 00 00 00 00 00 00 ................
```

keep looking, since that's just a partial regurgitation of the DEBUG command you typed in. It means DEBUG just found itself.)

But for our example assume you did find what you think is the actual beginning of the text, at address 4000:D1F0. Make sure this indeed is the beginning, and that you checked all the lower addresses to see if there were any earlier occurrences of the word platinum.

Then, tiptoe backwards in memory a bit just to see where your text actually starts. You may not have used the word "platinum" until the second or third sentence, and the goal here is to recover as much of your file from memory as possible. This means figuring out increasingly lower hex offset addresses (the four hex numbers to the right of the colon). If you're utterly befuddled by hex numbers see Chapter 4 or try this:

- Leave the four hex numbers to the left of the colon alone. Don't change them. And leave the first two hex numbers to the right of the colon alone as well.
- But replace the rightmost two hex numbers with 0s. In the example above, you would change:

```
4000:D1F6
```

to:

```
4000:D100
```

(The two rightmost zeros were changed from F6 to 00.)
Then type in everything except the hyphen:

```
-D 4000:D100
```

and press the Enter key. Look at the rightmost column. If it's still filled with your text, you may want to subtract 1 from the third digit over from the right (in the above example this would be the 1 directly after the 4000:D) and start the process again. In this case if you want to keep moving backward you'd change 4000:D100 to 4000:D000.

If the righthand column of the DEBUG display is filled with gibberish, type in just:

```
D
```

and press the Enter key. Keep typing D and pressing Enter repeatedly and DEBUG will work its way upward through memory 128 characters at a time. It's tedious, but worth it. Stop when you see the very beginning of your text. Look at the eight-digit hex address at the left edge of your screen in the same row as the beginning of your text and write it down on your notepad next to the word "START." Here it was 4000:D1F0.

Then, to find the end of your text, keep hitting D and Enter and checking the righthand column of the DEBUG display. So long as you see your text there, keep typing D and pressing Enter.

When you do finally reach the end, look at the eight-digit hex address at the left edge of your screen that's in the row directly after the very last sentence of your text and write down the rightmost four digits on your notepad next to the word "END." (You needed all eight digits for the starting address but only four digits are significant here.) In this example your text ends in the line with the address 4000:FB60, so you'd write down the rightmost four digits of the address of the following line, FB70.

```
4000:FB30 73 20 61 20 76 65 72 79-20 61 74 74 72 61 63 74  s a very attract
4000:FB40 69 76 65 0D 0A 61 6E 64-20 63 75 72 72 65 6E 74  ive..and current
4000:FB50 6C 79 20 75 6E 64 65 72-70 72 69 63 65 64 20 6D  ly underpriced m
4000:FB60 65 74 61 6C 2E 1A 1A 1A-1A 1A 1A 1A 1A 1A 1A 1A  etal............
4000:FB70 1A 1A 1A 1A 1A 1A 1A 1A-1A 1A 1A 1A 1A 1A 1A 1A  ................
```

Still, try typing D and pressing Enter a few more times to make sure there isn't any text hiding a little farther up in memory.

8. Now you know the starting and ending addresses of your file. It may be a little chopped up, and the entire file may not be there, but you can breathe easier knowing you're about to recover everything you just found.

But first you have to do a little hex math. DEBUG's free built-in hex calculator can help. For the time being, ignore the segment portion of the two addresses you found (they should be the same). Type in the letter H, then the last four hex digits of the ending address, and finally the last four hex digits of the starting address, so it looks like:

```
-H FB70 D1F0
```

(Again, don't type in the hyphen.) Press the Enter key and DEBUG will respond with:

```
CD60 2980
-
```

The first number is the sum of the two hex numbers you typed in; the second is the difference. You're interested in the second one, the difference between the ending address and the starting address — because this is equal to the length of the file in RAM. Jot down this second number (2980) on your notepad next to the word "LENGTH."

9. Now that you know the length of the file, the starting address in memory, and the ending address in memory, you're ready to copy, or "write" the file from memory to a disk.

Always be extremely careful in using the DEBUG W (Write) command, since writing files to the wrong place can destroy good data by writing bad data over it. Check your typing carefully before you press the Enter key.

It's best to copy your file to a floppy disk, especially if you're a hard disk user. This is because your word processor may have "spilled" some of the file from RAM to your hard disk when memory began to get a little crowded. Later you might want to try using a program like the *Norton Utilities* to browse around on your hard disk and find $$$ or TMP files that your word processor had hidden there or created and then erased. If you were to write to your hard disk (under certain older versions of DOS) you might obliterate these files and ruin your chances of recovering them. So use floppies instead.

Put a blank formatted disk in drive A:. Since you're going to create a file on this disk, you have to give it a name, like PLATINUM.TXT. Be sure to put the drive letter in front of the name, so it's really A:PLATINUM.TXT. To have DEBUG assign this name, type:

```
-N A:PLATINUM.TXT
```

(but omit the hyphen). Press the Enter key.

Next you have to tell DEBUG how much memory to copy to this file, and where to start. Telling it how much is a two-step operation. First type in (without the hyphen):

```
-RBX
```

and press the Enter key. DEBUG will respond with:

```
BX 0000
:
```

Since this example assumes your entire file was within a single 64K segment, you want the value in BX to be 0000 as shown. Just press Enter. Otherwise enter 0 then press Enter.

Then type (no hyphen):

```
-RCX
```

and press the Enter key. When DEBUG responds with:

```
CX 0000
:
```

type in the four-digit hex length, 2980, after the colon and press the Enter key. It will look like:

```
CX 0000
:2980
_
```

Remember — the 2980 is just for the purpose of this example. You would actually type in the length of the file you were trying to restore.

10. One more step and you're done. When you see the DEBUG prompt again, type in a W followed by the starting address. In this example the starting address was 4000:D1F0 so you would type everything but the hyphen:

```
W 4000:D1F0
```

and press the Enter key.

Now exit DEBUG by typing Q and then pressing the Enter key, and look at the PLATINUM.TXT file on drive A:. You can use the DOS TYPE command to do this:

```
TYPE A:PLATINUM.TXT
```

Or you can copy it to your printer with the command:

```
COPY A:PLATINUM.TXT PRN
```

Don't use any programs to examine the file, since these may overwrite part of memory, and you want to be sure you recovered everything before disturbing what's in memory. If you made a mistake, and the PLATINUM.TXT file contained gibberish, you can go back and step through the instructions again.

After what it's been through, the file will probably will need some fussing and cleaning up. Once you've determined that you rescued as much of it as you can, you can load your word processor and comb through the file to remove extraneous characters, fill in gaps, move the parts around to their proper positions, and generally spruce things up. You may not recover every last word (especially if the file in memory was very long) but you'll be far better off than you were when you first realized what had happened.

Note: if you are repeatedly typing D and pressing Enter (step 7) to find out where your text ends, and you suddenly see that the rightmost four digits change from FFF0 to 0000, this means that your file crosses a segment boundary. If this happens, the easiest thing to do is to extract your file from memory and save it to disk in separate chunks (such as A:PLATINUM.1 and A:PLATINUM.2) and then use your word processor later to combine these individual files into one big file. Use FFFF as the ending address for the first chunk and step through the whole rescue process described above, saving the file as PLATINUM.1. Then increase the segment by 1000 (in the above example you would change 4000 to 5000), and use 0000 as the starting address. To resume the search for the end of your file you would then type:

```
D 5000:0
```

and press the Enter key, and then keep typing D and pressing Enter until you find the end of your text. Then you'd save this second part as PLATINUM.2.

While this should work with word processor and other text files, it probably won't do very well with spreadsheet or database files, since these are often in non-ASCII formats with non-text control information hopelessly interspersed with the data. The rule is back up such files early and often.

If you didn't recover your entire file, and you walked through the above process a second time to make sure you didn't miss anything, load a copy of a program like the *Norton Utilities* and search through your original disk for spill files. It's a fairly straightforward process and is worth your time; the programs will do all the work once you've given them proper instructions.

One more point — the fact that you can go in and retrieve files from memory or from parts of a disk that you thought were empty means that others can walk over to your system and do the same thing when you're not there. Programs like the *Norton Utilities* can uncover and obliterate any unwanted hidden or previously "erased" files that are actually still intact. If you are security conscious, turn your system off when you walk away from it, or lock the keyboard and remove any mice that may be connected, to prevent unauthorized users from looking in your system's RAM and recovering data the way you just did.

PART II

The DOS Tools

Chapter 7

EDLIN

The single most popular microcomputer application is word processing. Nearly every serious user has one handy, and the people who don't own one use text entry functions of programs such as *1-2-3* to create memos and batch files. Virtually no one uses EDLIN, the text editor that comes with DOS, and with good reason. EDLIN is a line editor rather than a full-screen editor, which means you can edit only one line at a time rather than jumping all over the screen. And it's far from friendly. But if you're accustomed to one word processor, and you find yourself on someone else's system and all that's handy is a word processor you've never used, you can always boot up EDLIN to create or change ASCII files. We'll let you in on some interesting things you can do with EDLIN, and provide an armload of shortcuts.

Don't get us wrong, however. EDLIN won't do any fancy text formatting. It doesn't have an adjustable right margin that will automatically wrap your text down to the next line the way every word processor does. You can't use it to create double-spaced documents. It makes you use truly awful DOS brute-force commands such as Ctrl-Z and Ctrl-Break to get serious work done. It can't handle any lines longer than 254 characters (the manual says 253 but 254 works on our systems), or any file with more than 65,529 lines in it. It can't back up to the previous screen line once you've wrapped the cursor around from the right edge of your screen to the next line. And you have to switch constantly back and forth from command mode to editing mode. But you can copy or move groups of lines, search for particular strings of characters, or even replace one chunk of text with another. And the price is right.

You need to specify a filename when starting EDLIN from DOS. EDLIN has two modes, command mode and edit/insert mode. When you're in command mode the EDLIN prompt — an asterisk (*) — hugs the lefthand screen margin; when you're in edit/insert mode this prompt is indented eight spaces. To switch from command mode to edit/insert mode, enter a command such as I, to add new text, or a valid line number, to edit the line with the number you specified. The easiest way to switch from edit/insert mode to command mode is to hit Ctrl-Break or Ctrl-C.

Every example below starts with an asterisk to show you what the screen should look like. However you don't ever have to type an asterisk; EDLIN will take of that for you.

EDLIN numbers all lines only for your and its own convenience; the line numbers that appear before each line aren't put into the actual file. Since EDLIN is a line editor rather than a full-screen editor it can really edit only one line at a time. It refers to the line it's working on as the *current* line, and puts an asterisk on this single line, after the line number and before the text. This current-line asterisk is different from the asterisk EDLIN uses as a prompt.

In virtually all cases you may enter EDLIN commands in uppercase or lowercase (or a combination of the two), and you can usually insert spaces inside the command. These three commands will all do the same thing:

```
*1,2P
*1,2p
* 1 , 2 P
```

However, EDLIN's Search (S) and Replace (R) commands are pickier about extra spaces, since they let you search for spaces and replace them. And when using these commands you have to make sure that you specify the exact strings you want to search for — if you ask EDLIN to find "HELLO" it will catch every HELLO but ignore variations such as "Hello" and "hello."

With commands that can work with ranges of lines, EDLIN lets you omit the actual line numbers and accept default settings.

However, with operations such as Move or Copy, you still have to include the comma separating the beginning and end of the range, even if you omit the line numbers themselves. Other EDLIN commands such as List, Page, Delete, Search, and Replace, are less fussy, and don't require either line numbers or commas. You can specify lines one at a time or in ranges, or you can refer to them in relative terms. To edit line 3, just type:

```
*3
```

To list just line 3 you could type:

```
*3,3P
```

(which tells EDLIN to start and stop with just line 3). Once you issue either of these commands, EDLIN makes line 3 the current line. If you then wanted to edit line 5, you could type either:

```
*5
```

or:

```
*+2
```

as the +2 tells EDLIN to edit the line with a line number two higher than the current line. Or if you had just listed line 3, and wanted to broaden the display one line on either side, you could either type:

```
*2,4P
```

or:

```
*-1,+1P
```

To exit prematurely from a long process (such as a Replace Text command) hit Ctrl-Break or Ctrl-C. To quit and save your changes, type E. To quit without saving your changes, type Q and then tell EDLIN you're sure you want to abort your file, by typing Y. Be careful when using Ctrl-Break or Ctrl-C when inserting or editing text, since this tells EDLIN to cancel any changes made in the line. To register a change, you have to press the Enter key. If you want to insert a special control character, preface it with a ^V. Normally you can't enter an Escape character in your file, since DOS interprets this as a signal to interrupt what you're doing. But if you're trying to create an ANSI file that needs a CHR$(27) Esc prefix, simply type:

```
^V[
```

If you need to put any other control character (such as ^A or ^B) into your file to trigger a special effect on your printer, just enter the uppercase version of the letter after ^V (or the Ctrl- shifted version). Be sure not to enter the lowercase version. To put a ^A in your file, you could type either:

```
^VA
```

or:

```
^V^A
```

If you want to put high-bit ASCII math, border, or foreign language characters into your file, use the Alt-plus-number-pad technique: Just hold down the Alt key, type the ASCII value on the number pad (not the top row number keys), and release the Alt key. If you wanted to put the pi symbol in your text, you'd simply hold down Alt, type 227 on the number pad while holding it down, and then release the Alt key. A pi sign would then appear at the cursor. Unfortunately, not all printers can reproduce such high-bit characters accurately. Nor will this Alt key technique let you put a CHR$(0) null in your text. If you need to do this, just press the F7 key. A ^@ will appear at the cursor, and an ASCII character 0 will be inserted into your text.

It's possible to put more than one command on a single line by separating the commands with a semicolon. If you wanted to display lines 7-8 and lines 12-14 together, you could do it with the single command:

```
7,8L;12,14L
```

If you want to add a second command to the same line as a search, you have to separate the commands with a Ctrl-Z or else EDLIN will think that the second command, semicolon and all, is part of the string involved in the search.

While EDLIN can help you put your files into shape, it's not designed to print anything. You could use your word processor to print the file, or you could use the DOS PRINT or COPY commands. To use the PRINT command, make sure the DOS PRINT.COM file is on the disk you're using, or is in a drive or subdirectory that your PATH command knows about. Then just type PRINT FILENAME (substitute the name of your own file for FILENAME). Or just type COPY FILENAME PRN.

Finally, one simple tip that can save lots of keystrokes — make a copy of EDLIN.COM and call it E.COM. You could simply rename EDLIN.COM to E.COM, but it's a good idea to keep all the files on your \DOS subdirectory intact if someone else has to use your system, and doing so makes it easier to upgrade from one version of DOS to the next. You may decide EDLIN is so clanky and unintuitive that you'd rather use your word processor or a vastly better quick editor like *SideKick*'s notepad instead. But if you do plan to use EDLIN, it's a lot easier and faster to type:

```
E CONFIG.SYS
```

than:

```
EDLIN CONFIG.SYS
```

especially if you use it all day long. If you try this, either keep E.COM on your main floppy disk (the file is so small you should be able to squeeze it on), or put it in your hard disk \BIN subdirectory along with the rest of your important utilities.

All examples below assume the file you started out with consists of the following five lines. The current line is always line 1, unless otherwise specified:

```
1:*line 1
2: line 2
3: line 3
4: line 4
5: line 5
```

Starting EDLIN

Format: **EDLIN FILENAME**

You can't start EDLIN without specifying a filename. If you enter the name of an existing file, EDLIN will try to load the whole file into memory. However, EDLIN will stop loading a file if it determines that RAM is filling up so fast that only 25 percent of available memory is free. If this happens, you'll have to edit the file in pieces, then use the Write Lines (W) and Append Lines (A) commands to write the beginning of the edited file to disk and load the unedited part of the file into memory. You really shouldn't have to worry about this, since you shouldn't be editing long files with EDLIN. It's really best for batch files, short memos, and other miscellaneous DOS tasks, like changing your CONFIG.SYS system configuration file or creating an ANSI string to change colors. For longer files, use your word processor instead.

EDLIN is actually an *external* DOS program called EDLIN.COM. Some commands such as DIR or TYPE are *internal*, which means they're part of COMMAND.COM and are always available to you whenever you see the DOS prompt. But you have to tell DOS where the EDLIN.COM program is on your disk, so DOS can find and load it if you are currently in a subdirectory that doesn't contain a copy of EDLIN.COM. If you're using a hard disk, the best way to handle this is to have a dedicated \DOS subdirectory that contains all your DOS files, including EDLIN.COM, and nothing else. To make sure DOS knows where all its important files are kept, include the \DOS subdirectory in your PATH command. By setting your disk up this way, you'll be able to use EDLIN no matter what subdirectory you happen to be using. Either issue this PATH command at the DOS prompt, or include a variation of it in your AUTOEXEC.BAT bootup file.

If you start EDLIN by specifying the name of a file that's not on your disk, EDLIN will create a new one, and tell you so, with a "New file" message. This means that if you're trying to edit an existing file and you see the "New file" message you either made a typing mistake when you entered the filename, or you're in the wrong subdirectory. Quit (by typing Q and then Y) and when you're back at the DOS prompt, type DIR FILENAME and press the Enter key (but of course substitute the actual name of your file). If you see the file, restart EDLIN and watch your typing. If you don't see the file, you're probably in the wrong subdirectory. Use the CD (Change Directory) command to log into the correct one.

Even if there's plenty of free memory in your system, EDLIN will stop loading any existing file when it sees a special character (with an ASCII value of 26) called a Ctrl-Z end-of-file-marker. EDLIN makes sure this special character is at the end of each file it edits, and puts one there if none exists, along with an extra carriage return and line feed. It doesn't expect to stumble over this character in the middle of a file.

But EDLIN can remove such nasty Ctrl-Z end-of-file characters that have somehow crept into your files by mistake. If you know you have a file that's 100 lines long, but EDLIN will display only the first three lines, odds are that an ASCII character 26 mysteriously found its way into the beginning of line 4. Other DOS commands such as TYPE will also screech to a halt when they see this end-of-file character, as will some commercial products such as *WordStar*.

If you think this has happened, add a /B to the end of the EDLIN FILENAME command. So if you have a file called PHONE.LST and EDLIN seems to be loading only the beginning of it, type Q and then Y to quit, and then reload the file with the command:

```
EDLIN PHONE.LST /B
```

(DOS almost always lets you enter switches such as /B either in uppercase or lowercase. But version 3.3 contains a bug that doesn't recognize /b, so it's always safe to use /B. In fact, version 3.3 has a hard time with uppercase and lowercase commands in general. Normally, if you try to edit a backup file that ends in BAK, EDLIN will refuse to load it and will just print a "Cannot edit .BAK file — rename file" message. If you try this with version 3.3 and enter a filename that ends in BAK you'll indeed get such an error message, and EDLIN will drop you back into DOS. But enter the extension using lowercase characters (bak) and EDLIN will blithely edit and save the file.)

You can either page through your document using the Page (P) command to see if any lines contain a stray ^Z, or you can have EDLIN's Search (S) hunt for it. To have EDLIN do the work, as soon as you load the file type:

```
*S^V^Z
```

When you first load a file, EDLIN makes line 1 the current line. Using the S command without line numbers will search from the line immediately following the current one (since the current line is 1, the search would start with line 2), and continue all the way to the last line loaded in memory. This won't catch any Ctrl-Z characters in line 1, but there probably wasn't an end-of-file marker there since in the above example EDLIN managed to display the first few lines. If you wanted to broaden the search to include the first line, just add a 1, prefix to the command right before the S.

You couldn't just enter the command as *S^Z since EDLIN uses ^Z in search commands to mark the end of the command, and not as a literal keystroke to hunt for. Fortunately, EDLIN lets you enter control characters by prefacing them with a ^V. So when you tell it to search for ^V^Z you're really saying "try to find a ^Z character."

If you do find a Ctrl-Z character in your file you can edit the line to remove it, and then continue searching for others. Or you can simply use the Replace (R) command to delete every Ctrl-Z in your file. The command:

```
*R^V^Z^Z
```

will do just that. (Again, to include line 1 in the search, add a 1, at the beginning of the command.) Then save and exit the file with the E command.

Let's get right into EDLIN's commands. Then, at the end of the chapter you'll find more advice on using EDLIN.

The EDLIN Commands

Append Lines

Format: [n] A

This command loads additional lines from disk to memory. You need to do this only when EDLIN wasn't able to load your entire file into memory when you started. EDLIN will stop loading your file if it figures out that 3/4 of your available memory is full. If this happens, and you want to edit the rest of your file, first use the Write Lines command (W) to write the beginning of your file from memory to a disk. Then use Append to read in [n] additional lines from your disk to the end of the file in memory. You probably won't have to use this, since you should edit large files with your word processor rather than EDLIN. (See Write Lines.)

Copy Lines

Format: [line],[line],line[,count]C

This command copies one line or a block of lines from one place in your file to another. Copying lines leaves the original lines alone and simply duplicates them elsewhere. If you want to copy lines from one place to another and delete the originals, use the Move command instead. The optional [,count] lets you make multiple copies of the block of lines you specified — if you omit this number EDLIN will make only one copy. If you omit either of the first two [line] numbers, EDLIN will assume you want to copy the current line (but you have to type in the commas even if you omit the numbers). And you have to specify where you want the copied block to go. The line number you want the block copied to has to be outside the range of the block you want copied, so you can't tell EDLIN to take lines 3 through 5 and copy them to line 4.

For example:

```
*3,4,5c
```

makes one copy of lines 3 and 4 and puts these two lines before line 5. It will then make the second line 3 the current line and renumber all the lines:

```
1: line 1
2: line 2
3: line 3
4: line 4
5:*line 3
```

```
6:  line 4
7:  line 5
```

```
*,,6,3c
```

makes three copies of the current line (here it's line 1) and adds these after line 5. It will
then make the first of these three copied lines the current line, and renumber all your
lines:

```
1:  line 1
2:  line 2
3:  line 3
4:  line 4
5:  line 5
6:*line 1
7:  line 1
8:  line 1
```

Delete Lines

Format: **[line][,line]D**

This command deletes the current line and moves all following lines up a notch, when
used without any line numbers. Specifying just one line number deletes that particular
line. Omitting the first parameter (but leaving in the initial comma) deletes all lines from
the current one to the one specified. Specifying two numbers deletes everything between
them, including the specified lines themselves. EDLIN then makes the line immediately
following the deletion the current one.

If you want to get rid of several lines in a row, it's best to specify the beginning and
end of the range you want deleted rather than erasing them one at a time. Users often forget that EDLIN renumbers their documents each time a line is deleted. So if you use the
P or L command to view your text, and see that you want to erase lines 10 and 11, issuing the commands:

```
*10D
*11D
```

won't do it. After the first command (10D) gets rid of line 10 it will then move the old
line 11 down a notch and turn it into the new line 10, move the old line 12 down and
make it the new line 11, etc. The second command (11D) would mistakenly end up erasing what used to be line 12, since everything moved down a notch after the first deletion.
If you did want to erase lines 10 and 11 one at a time you could type:

```
*10D
*10D
```

An easy way to do this is to type in the command the first time and press Enter, then press F3 to repeat the previous command, and then press Enter.

For example:

```
*,3D
```

deletes everything from the current line (in this case line 1) up to and including line 3:

```
1:*line 4
2: line 5
```

```
*2,4D
```

deletes everything from lines 2 through 4, including lines 2 and 4:

```
1: line 1
2:*line 5
```

```
*2D
```

deletes line 2:

```
1: line 1
2:*line 3
3: line 4
4: line 5
```

```
*D
```

deletes the current line only (in this case line 1):

```
1:*line 2
2: line 3
3: line 4
4: line 5
```

Edit Line

Format: **[line]** *or* **[special symbol]** *or* **[Enter key alone]**

This command lets you edit any existing line. If you're in the command mode (with the asterisk hugging the left margin) and you simply press the Enter key without specifying a number, EDLIN will assume you want to edit the line *following* the current one. If you're not at the end of the file, it will take the line following the current one and display it in edit mode (indented eight spaces), and treat this new line as the current one. So if the current line happens to be line 2, and you simply press the Enter key in command mode, EDLIN will display line 3 in edit mode and turn line 3 into the current line. Typing a question mark (?) and then pressing the Enter key is the same as pressing the Enter key by itself.

If you're in command mode and you want to edit the current line, just type a period (.), a minus sign (-), or a plus sign (+) and then press the Enter key. If you want to edit a specific line, just enter the number of that line and press Enter. Although it's not documented, if you want to edit the next two lines, just type a semicolon (;) and press Enter. Typing a pound sign (#) and then pressing Enter will take you past the last line of your file; if you then type I and press the Enter key to go into insert mode, EDLIN will let you append text to the end of your file.

Once you've edited a line, pressing the Enter key replaces the original version of the line with the edited version. Once you've switched from command mode to edit mode, if you want to abort the process and leave the original line intact, either press the Enter key before making any changes, or press either Ctrl-Break or Ctrl-C. You can also press Esc and then the Enter key to avoid making any changes.

When you're in edit mode you can use all the familiar DOS editing keys, such as F2 plus a character to display everything from the beginning of the original version of that line to the first occurrence of the specified character in the line.

If you're not comfortable with the F2-plus-a-character technique, you can edit an existing line simply by pressing F3 to have DOS type in the previous version of the line automatically for you, and then use the backspace or left arrow keys to erase the part of the line you want to change. Or instead of hitting F3 to reproduce the entire line, you can hold down the F1 or right arrow keys to retype the previous version of the line one character at a time. If you're careful about it, you can use the Insert and Delete keys to add and remove individual characters in the middle of the line, and then press F3 when you're done, to type in the rest of the line for you.

For example:

```
*.
```

or:

```
*+
```

or:

```
*-
```

brings the current line (in this case line 1) into edit mode:

```
1:*line 1
```

```
*
```

Just pressing the Enter key by itself when in command mode brings the following line into edit mode. In this case the current line is line 1, so the following line is line 2:

```
2:*line 2

*3
```

Specifying any valid line number brings that line (in this case line 3) into edit mode:

```
3:*line 3

*;
```

Typing a semicolon and then pressing the Enter key brings the two following lines into edit mode. In this case the current line is line 1 so the two following lines are 2 and 3. This example assumes you then press the Enter key twice and didn't make any changes:

```
2:*line 3
2:*
3:*line 3
3:*
```

End Edit

Format: E

This command saves the file to disk and exits. (If you want to exit without saving any changes you made, type Q to quit.) If you're editing an existing file called OLDFILE.TXT and exit EDLIN with an E command, EDLIN will save the newly edited version as OLDFILE.TXT and tack a BAK extension onto the old, unchanged version, renaming the old version to OLDFILE.BAK. If you're just starting a file, EDLIN won't create such a backup file. Each subsequent time you edit the file, EDLIN will get rid of the previous BAK version of it and create a new BAK version. EDLIN makes sure there is a carriage return/line-feed/end-of-file marker trio of characters (ASCII characters 13, 10, and 26) at the end of any file it saves.

If your disk doesn't have enough room to save all the changes you made, EDLIN will save as much as it can onto your disk, and discard the rest. If this happens, EDLIN will give the partially saved version a $$$ extension, and it won't give the original version of your file a BAK entension.

(See Quit Edit.)

Import Files

See Transfer Lines.

Insert Lines

Format: [line]I

This command lets you start adding text to a new file, or insert new text in an existing file directly before the line you specified. When you type I, EDLIN assumes you want to insert multiple lines, and will keep displaying the next higher line number each time you press the Enter key. If you want to stop inserting lines, you have to press Enter to lock in the last line you inserted, and then press either the Ctrl-Break or Ctrl-C keys to abort the insertion process. If you don't press the Enter key at the end of your last line of inserted text before aborting, EDLIN will think you want to abort this last line, and discard it.

If you type I by itself and then press Enter, or type a period (.), and then I, and then press Enter, EDLIN will start inserting text directly before the current line. If you type a valid line number, then I, and then Enter, EDLIN will insert any text you type directly before the line number you specified. If you type a pound sign (#) and then I and press Enter, or a ridiculously high number such as 65000 and then I and Enter, EDLIN will move to the end of your file and start appending text there.

If you type a semicolon (;), then I, and then press Enter, strange things will happen depending on what you do next. In all cases, EDLIN will increase the number of the current line by 1. If you press the Enter key without entering any text, EDLIN will give you a second chance to insert text on that same line. Type in a line of text at that point and EDLIN will accept it and move on to the next line. But if you enter text at the first opportunity, EDLIN will accept it, make it look as if you have a second chance to enter text on that same line, accept that as well, and put the second line before the first.

In fact, the insert function gets confused and will do all sorts of odd things if you follow I with a plus (+) or minus (-) sign before pressing Enter, or type several IIIIs in a row before you press Enter. None really helps you very much.

The following examples assume the new single line you insert is always "This is a new line" and ignore the curious but useless variations such as I+ and ;I:

```
*.I
```

or:

```
*I
```

lets you insert new lines before the current line. In this case the current line is line 1:

```
1:*This is a new line
2:*^C
```

produces:

```
1: This is a new line
2:*line 1
3: line 2
4: line 3
5: line 4
6: line 5

*3I
```

lets you insert new lines directly before line 3:

```
3:*This is a new line
4:*^C
```

produces:

```
1: line 1
2: line 2
3: This is a new line
4:*line 3
5: line 4
6: line 5

*65000I
```

or:

```
*#I
```

lets you append new lines at the very end of your file, assuming your file is smaller than 65000 lines:

```
6:*This is a new line
7:*^C
```

produces:

```
1: line 1
2: line 2
3: line 3
4: line 4
5: line 5
6: This is a new line
```

List Lines

Format: [line][,line]L

This command lists, or displays, one or more lines without changing which line EDLIN thinks is the current one. If you type L by itself and then press Enter, EDLIN will try to display a screenful (23) of lines, with the current line in the middle of the screen. The 11 lines preceding the current line will appear above the current line, and the 11 lines following the current line will appear below it. If EDLIN can't find 11 lines that precede the current line, it will try to add extra lines at the end until it can display a total of 23.

If you type one valid line number followed by L, and then press Enter, EDLIN will try to display 23 lines beginning with the line you specified. Type a single line number, and then a comma, and then L and press Enter, and EDLIN will do the same thing. Both variations of this command tell EDLIN to display the specified line and up to 22 lines that follow it.

If you type a comma, and then a valid line number, and then press Enter, EDLIN will try to display the 11 lines preceding the current one, and all the lines following the current one up to and including the specified line. However, if you try this and the specified line is very far after the current line, EDLIN will end up displaying too many lines and will scroll the display off the screen. Worse, if the specified line is more than 11 lines before the current line, EDLIN will ignore your numbers and treat the command as if you had simply typed in a naked L.

If you type two valid line numbers separated by a comma and followed by an L, and then press Enter, EDLIN will display the lines starting with the first line number and going up to and including the second line number. Since EDLIN uses a pound sign (#) to mean "the last line in the file," you can view a 60-line file in one big continuous gulp by typing:

```
*1,#L
```

to produce:

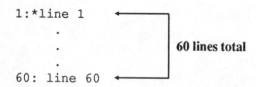

```
1:*line 1
    .
    .                        60 lines total
    .
60: line 60
```

The following examples assume a 60-line file in which each line is simply the word "line" followed by the appropriate line number, and where line 30 is the current line:

```
*L
```

lists the 11 lines before the current line (30), plus the current one itself, and then the 11 lines after the current line. If EDLIN finds fewer than 11 lines before the current line it will try to display more than 11 lines after the current line. However, if you had just started to edit, and hadn't yet identified a current line, typing L would list the first 23 lines of your file.

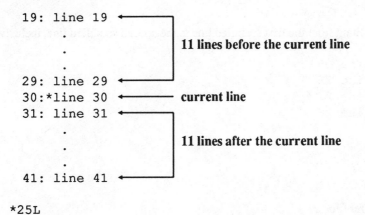

```
19: line 19
     .
     .
     .
29: line 29
30:*line 30
31: line 31
     .
     .
     .
41: line 41
```

11 lines before the current line

current line

11 lines after the current line

```
*25L
```

displays the line specified (25) plus the 22 lines that follow it.

```
25: line 25
     .
     .
     .
29: line 29
30:*line 30
31: line 31
     .
     .
     .
47: line 47
```

```
*,25L
```

displays lines starting 11 lines before the current one, and ending at the line specified (25). Since the current line in this case is line 30, the display begins 11 lines earlier (line 19). If you had just started to edit, and hadn't yet identified a current line, typing ,25L would list the first 25 lines of your file (scrolling the first few off the top of your screen):

```
19: line 19
20: line 20
21: line 21
22: line 22
23: line 23
```

```
24: line 24
25: line 25
```

```
*25,28L
```

lists everything from the first specified line to the second specified line, inclusive:

```
25: line 25
26: line 26
27: line 27
28: line 28
```

See Page.

Merge Files

See Transfer Lines.

Move Lines

Format: **[line],[line],lineM**

This command moves a line or lines, in the range defined by the first two numbers, to a position in your text directly before the third line number. The new location (the third number) must be outside the range defined by the first two numbers, so you can't move lines 3 through 5 to a position directly before line 4. If you omit either of the first two numbers, EDLIN will assume you want to move the current line — but you'll still need to type in the commas, and you must specify a third (destination) line number.

For example:

```
*3,5,1M
```

moves all the lines from 3 through 5 to a new location directly before line 1:

```
1:*line 3
2: line 4
3: line 5
4: line 1
5: line 2
```

```
*5,5,1M
```

moves the single line 5 directly before line 1:

```
1:*line 5
2: line 1
3: line 2
4: line 3
5: line 4
```

```
*1,1,5M
```

or:

```
*,,5M
```

moves the single line 1 directly before line 5. Omitting the first two numbers tells EDLIN to assume that you want to move the current line, which in this case is line 1:

```
1: line 2
2: line 3
3: line 4
4:*line 1
5: line 5
```

```
*1,1,6M
```

or:

```
*1,1,#M
```

or:

```
,,#M
```

moves line 1 to the end of the file, since in this case line 1 is the current line and line 5 is the last line:

```
1: line 2
2: line 3
3: line 4
4: line 5
5:*line 1
```

Page

Format: [line][,line]P

This command displays lines, and changes the number of the current line. The similar List Line (L) command also displays lines — though according to slightly different rules — but doesn't alter the number of the current line. When you use the P command without any line numbers, EDLIN will display the 23 lines following the current line (but won't show the current line itself), and will change the current line in the process. This is very handy for examining your file a screen at a time; when you start EDLIN if you just keep tapping P and Enter you'll page all the way through from beginning to end. You can't do this with repeated L commands, since L won't change the number of the current line and will keep displaying the same screen over and over. (See List.)

The following examples assume a 60-line file where each line is simply the word "line" followed by the appropriate line number, and where line 30 is the current line. The examples are identical to those presented for the List command, to make it easy for you to compare the Page and List commands:

```
*1,#P
```

displays the entire file just as List (L) does, except that P will turn the last line in the file into the current one, while L will leave the current line alone.

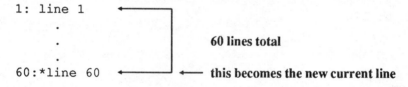

```
1: line 1                          60 lines total
      .
      .
      .
60:*line 60                        this becomes the new current line
```

```
*P
```

displays the line immediately after the original current line plus the 22 lines following it, and will then turn the last line displayed into the new current line. While List (L) will also display 23 lines, it will try to show the 11 lines before and after the current line, and will not change the current line.

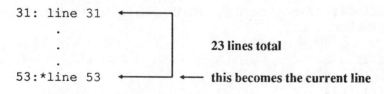

```
31: line 31                        23 lines total
      .
      .
      .
53:*line 53                        this becomes the current line
```

```
*25P
```

displays the line specified (in this case it's line 25) and the 22 lines following it, and will make the very last line displayed (in this case 25 + 22, or line 47) the current one. Here, Page (P) works about the same as List (L) except that L doesn't change the current line.

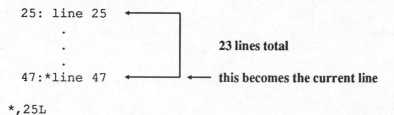

```
25: line 25
     .
     .                      23 lines total
     .
47:*line 47                 this becomes the current line
```

```
*,25L
```

produces only an "Entry error" message if the current line is 30, since in effect you're asking it to display from lines 30-25, and EDLIN can't page backwards. However, the List (L) command can indeed handle such a command, since it tries to start displaying text starting 11 lines before the current one, and ending at the line specified. So if the current line is 30, the command ,25L will display from line 19 (30 - 11) through 25. If the current line was line 1, both the ,25L and ,25P commands would display the first 25 lines of your file, and would end up scrolling the first few off the top of your screen. The only difference would be that the P version would make line 25 the current line, while the L version would leave the current line as line 1.

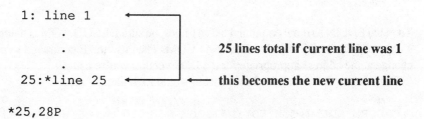

```
 1: line 1
     .
     .                      25 lines total if current line was 1
     .
25:*line 25                 this becomes the new current line
```

```
*25,28P
```

lists everything from the first specified line to the second specified line, inclusive. In this case P works just like L except that P will turn the last displayed line into the current one.

```
25: line 25
26: line 26
27: line 27
28:*line 28
```

Note: The EDLIN P (Page) command displays just 23 lines when arguments are not specified. By changing the line count byte it's possible to have EDLIN display any number of lines from 1 to 128. For instance, since 43-line screens are becoming more popular, you may want to patch EDLIN so the P command displays 41 lines rather than just 23.

The hex offset address of the line count byte varies according to the DOS version:

Version	Offset
2.0	700
2.1	700
3.0	102B
3.1	105C
3.2	105C
3.3	105C

The default value at this address is 16, since this is part of the instruction:

```
ADD DX,+16.
```

The value of this byte cannot exceed 7F hex, unless you want your whole document to streak past. Values lower than hex 16 will cause the P command to display fewer than 23 lines. Note that the actual number of lines EDLIN will display is one greater than the value at this byte.

Screen Size	Hex Value at Offset
25	16
35	20
43	28

To patch EDLIN so the P command lists 41 lines, be sure DEBUG.COM is handy. Make a copy of EDLIN.COM called EDLIN41.COM. Then use the E command to make the change at the address appropriate for the DOS version you're using.

For versions 3.1 through 3.3 the process would look like:

```
C>COPY EDLIN.COM EDLIN41.COM
        1 File(s) copied
C>DEBUG EDLIN41.COM
-E 105C
30F9:105C 16.28
-W
Writing 1D66 bytes
-Q
```

Once you've copied EDLIN.COM to EDLIN41.COM, DEBUG prints the hyphens, this line (the 30F9 right before the colon is a hex number that will vary from system to system and doesn't matter here):

```
30F9:105C 16.
```

and the "Writing 1D66 bytes" message. You type everything else.
    See List.

Quit Edit

Format: Q

This command lets you abort a file — quit EDLIN without saving any changes you may have made — and return to DOS. To make sure you don't lose your work inadvertently by typing Q when you don't mean it, EDLIN displays an "Abort edit (Y/N)?" message to allow you to confirm the action. If you type Y, EDLIN will quit and all your changes will be lost. Type N (or any character other than Y or y) and EDLIN returns you to command mode with your file intact.

Read In Files

See Transfer Lines.

Replace Text

Format: [line][,line][?]R[oldstring][<F6>newstring]

This command replaces one string of characters with another. EDLIN can replace strings in just one line or throughout your entire document, with confirming prompts or without, and can handle multiple occurrences of a string in the same line. (Each time it replaces a string it will print the entire revised line, so if it's making multiple changes in the same line you'll see that line onscreen several times.) EDLIN identifies the last line that it changes as the current line.

The R command can replace one single character or a whole series of words, but as with the Search Text (S) command, the matches have to be exact. If you tell EDLIN to find every "the" it will skip over "THE" and "The" — but it will find imbedded strings such as the letters t-h-e inside "them" and "whether" and "Goethe." If you want to find whole words only, you can try putting a space on either side of the word when you specify it in the R command. This will work most of the time with a word like "the" which is almost never followed by punctuation. But many words could be followed by commas, periods, or question marks, so this technique is far from foolproof. And since EDLIN can't ignore cases, you may have to search through once for each "the" and repeat the command to catch any "The" that happens to start a sentence. If you do try putting a space on either side of the old string, remember to put spaces on either side of the replacement string as well. Note that quotes are used here to make the examples clearer — don't use quotation marks in the actual EDLIN commands unless a quote mark is indeed part of the string you're replacing.

You can ask to preview each potential replacement, with the change already in place, by putting a question mark (?) before the R. If you do this, EDLIN will show you what the replacement would look like and then print a very terse "O.K.?" prompt. If you type either Y or y or press the Enter key, EDLIN will make the change. If you type any other character EDLIN will leave that particular string alone. In either event it will then continue searching. If you use this prompt feature, make sure you put the ? before the R, not after it, since EDLIN interprets anything after the R as part of the old string you want to replace, and will end up hunting for a string beginning with a question mark.

EDLIN uses a Ctrl-Z to separate the old string from the new one. You can generate a Ctrl-Z either by tapping once on the F6 function key; by holding down the Ctrl key and typing Z; or by holding down the Alt key, typing 26 on the number pad (not the top row keys), and then releasing the Alt key. Be sure not to put any extra spaces on either side of the Ctrl-Z or EDLIN will interpret them as part of the string to replace.

You may use this feature to delete strings of text. After the R in the command, simply enter the old string you want deleted, press the F6 function key, and then press Enter instead of specifying a new string. In effect you're telling EDLIN to replace something (the old string) with nothing. If you try this, be sure to consider any leading or trailing spaces around the string you're deleting.

If you omit the first line number, EDLIN will start trying to replace strings in the line immediately following the current line. Omit the second line number and EDLIN will scan through to the end of the document, or at least as much of it as is currently in memory. Omit both line numbers and EDLIN will start the replacement process with the line following the current one and stop only when it reaches the final line in memory.

Each time you specify a Search string or a Replace string, EDLIN stores it in a special buffer. If you omit either string the next time you issue the command, EDLIN will use the strings from the previous command. If you wanted to find every occurrence of the word "flower" and replace it with "Zantedeschia aethiopica" between lines 1 and 50 of your document, you would type:

```
*1,50Rflower^ZZantedeschia aethiopica
```

(where ^Z represents a Ctrl-Z character, not a ^ and a Z). If you then wanted to replace the same old string with the same new one in lines 51 through 100, all you'd have to type is:

```
*51,100R
```

If you omit the first string (the old text that you want to replace), EDLIN will look in its buffers and try to dredge up either the previous initial R (Replace Text) string, or the previous S (Search Text) string, whichever is more recent. But if you omit the second string (the new text that replaces the old), EDLIN will try to hunt down the last R string.

Since EDLIN can't work with lines longer than 254 characters, it won't be able to handle such lengthy lines when you're replacing a short string with a longer one.

The following examples assume the file is the simple five-line file used above, and that the current line is line 1. And don't forget that the ^Z represents a Ctrl-Z character, not a ^ and a Z. See the text above for the three ways to generate this character:

```
*Rline^ZLINE
```

starts the replacement process on the line following the current one (line 2 in this case, since the current line is line 1), and replaces each "line" it finds with a new "LINE" string.

```
2: LINE 2
3: LINE 3
4: LINE 4
5: LINE 5
```

```
*1,3Rline^ZLINE
```

limits the replacement process to all lines between 1 and 3, and changes each "line" it finds there to "LINE."

```
1: LINE 1
2: LINE 2
3:*LINE 3
4: line 4
5: line 5
```

```
*,3Rline^ZLINE
```

since no beginning line is specified, EDLIN starts the replacement process with the line following the current one. The current line is line 1, so this starts at line 2 and ends with line 3, changing each "line" it finds to "LINE."

```
1: line 1
2: LINE 2
3:*LINE 3
4: line 4
5: line 5
```

```
*1,#Rline^Z
```

searches through the entire document from line 1 to the final line loaded in memory and replaces every "line" string with a null string, effectively deleting the word "line" throughout the document.

```
1:* 1
2:  2
3:  3
4:  4
5:  5
```

```
*1,#?Rline^ZLINE
```

searches through the entire document from line 1 to the final line loaded in memory and asks whether or not to replace every occurrence of "line" that it finds with "LINE." When EDLIN prompts the user in this way it displays what the replacement would look like if the user answered the prompt with Y or y or Enter. It interprets any other character keypress as a No. In the example below, the user responded to the five prompts with: Y N y A Enter. EDLIN replaced strings in the first, third, and fifth lines, but not the second and fourth, since only Y or y or Enter tells EDLIN to go ahead with the change.

```
                    1:*LINE 1
        O.K.? Y
                    2: LINE 2
        O.K.? N
                    3: LINE 3
        O.K.? y
                    4: LINE 4
        O.K.? A
                    5: LINE 5
        O.K.?

                    1: LINE 1
                    2: line 2
                    3: LINE 3
                    4: line 4
                    5:*LINE 5
```

Search Text

Format: [line][,line][?]S[string]

This command scans through the file for occurrences of a specified string. Just about all the tricks and caveats that apply to the Replace Text command also apply here. Since searches are case-sensitive you have to specify search strings exactly. You can often isolate words by specifying spaces before and after. If you omit line numbers EDLIN starts with the line immediately following the current one and searches until it finds the last line in memory. Once you've specified a search string using the S or R commands, you can repeat the search without having to type in that string.

And, as with the Replace command, you can insert a question mark (?) in the command to have EDLIN prompt you by asking "O.K.?" when it finds a match. At that point if you do anything other than type Y or y or just press Enter, EDLIN will search for the next occurrence of the string. If you don't use a question mark, EDLIN will stop the first time it finds the string and make the line with the string the current one. If you do use a prompt EDLIN will turn the first line you accept into the current one.

EDLIN will print a "Not found" message if it can't locate the string you specified, or if you ask it to prompt you and it finishes searching through a range without having you accept any of the matches it uncovered.

It's possible to add a second command to Search Text, by tacking a Ctrl-Z and then the new command (with no intervening spaces) onto the end. For instance, if you knew you had used the word "banana" only once in your document and wanted to see the line it was in along with the 23 lines following it, you could issue the command:

```
1,#Sbanana^ZP
```

and EDLIN would execute a P (Page) command as soon as it found the word banana.

The following examples assume the file is the simple five-line file used above, and that the current line is line 1:

```
*S3
```

searches from the line after the current one to the last file in memory for the first occurrence of the string "3." Here the current line is line 1, so the search begins at line 2:

```
   3: line 3
```

```
*Sline
```

searches from the line after the current one to the last file in memory for the first occurrence of the string "line." Here the current line is line 1, so the search begins at line 2:

```
   2: line 2
```

```
*1Sline
```

or:

```
*1,Sline
```

or:

```
*1,#Sline
```

searches from line 1 to the last file in memory for the first occurrence of the string "line."

```
   1:*line 1
```

```
*,3Sline
```

since no beginning line is specified, EDLIN starts the replacement process with the line following the current one. In this case the current line is line 1, so this starts at line 2. As specified, EDLIN would continue searching until line 3, but it stumbled over the string it was looking for in line 2.

```
2: line 2
```

```
*1?Sline
```

searches through the entire document from line 1 to the final line in memory for occurrences of the string "line" and asks whether each is the one the user wants. In the example
below, the user responded to the four prompts with: N n A Enter. EDLIN will stop searching only when it reaches the end of the range specified, or when the user types a Y or
y or presses Enter in response to the "O.K.?" prompt. In this case, the user didn't respond
positively until the fourth request:

```
            1:*line 1
    O.K.? N
            2: line 2
    O.K.? n
            3: line 3
    O.K.? A
            4: line 4
    O.K.?
```

See Search Text.

Transfer Lines

Format: [line]T[d:]filename

This command merges an existing file from disk into memory directly before the
specified line, or before the current line if no line number is specified.
    The following examples assume that the current line is line 1 and that you have a file
on drive A: called ONELINE.TXT that contains the single line "IBM keyboards are the
best:"

```
*3TA:ONELINE.TXT
```

merges the file ONELINE.TXT from drive A: into the current file directly before line 3.

```
    1: line 1
    2: line 2
    3:*IBM keyboards are the best
    4: line 3
    5: line 4
    6: line 5
```

```
*TA:ONELINE.TXT
```

merges the file ONELINE.TXT from drive A: into the current file directly before the current line. In this case the current line is line 1, so EDLIN reads the new file in at the very beginning of the existing one.

```
1:*IBM keyboards are the best
2: line 1
3: line 2
4: line 3
5: line 4
6: line 5
```

```
*#TA:ONELINE.TXT
```

merges the file ONELINE.TXT from drive A: into the current file at the very end of the current file.

```
1: line 1
2: line 2
3: line 3
4: line 4
5: line 5
6:*IBM keyboards are the best
```

Write Lines

Format: [n]W

This command writes lines to disk to provide space for EDLIN to load an additional part of a file that was originally too large to fit into memory. If you tried to edit a file that EDLIN couldn't load in one gulp, you have to edit the part that it could load, use this command to write the beginning of the file to disk and automatically renumber the remaining part of the file, and then read in more of the file from disk using the Append (A) command. This command won't work if more than 25 percent of memory is available. If needed, EDLIN will write lines to disk starting with line 1 and continue until 25 percent of memory is free. (See Append Lines.)

Using EDLIN

Be careful when mixing EDLIN output with redirected DOS output. For instance, if you redirect the output of ECHO to create a sample TEST.TXT file:

```
ECHO Line 1 > TEST.TXT
ECHO Line 2 >> TEST.TXT
ECHO Line 3 >> TEST.TXT
```

and then enter:

```
TYPE TEST.TXT
```

to see what's in the new file, DOS will display:

```
Line 1
Line 2
Line 3
```

Load TEST.TXT into EDLIN and save it with the E command. Now append another line onto the file:

```
ECHO Line 4 >>TEST.TXT
```

and do another TYPE command:

```
TYPE TEST.TXT
```

and all you'll see is the first three lines:

```
Line 1
Line 2
Line 3
```

What happened here was that EDLIN added an end-of-file marker to the file, and the next redirection command appended the line after that end-of-file marker. Line 4 was still in the file, but was located after the end-of-file marker. When the DOS TYPE command hit the end-of-file marker it quit before it reached the new line. DOS lets you get around this by using a /B switch (the /B stands for *binary* since binary, or nontext, files treat ASCII character 26 as just another character and not a signal to quit).

Programs written for DOS should not really need an end-of-file marker because the exact size of the file is contained in the directory entry. This was not always the case. Before DOS, the most popular eight-bit microcomputer operating system was CP/M, which stored files in blocks of 128 bytes. The CP/M directory entries indicated only the number of 128-byte blocks and not the exact size of the file. ASCII text editors needed an end-of-file marker to determine what was actually part of the file and what was junk. When you redirect standard output to a file, DOS does not append an end-of-file marker to the file it writes. And if the file already contains an end-of-file marker, DOS does not remove it. However, EDLIN always adds an end-of-file mark to files it saves. And the DOS TYPE command always stops at the first end-of-file marker it finds.

To see what's going on, add a /B when you load the file into EDLIN:

```
EDLIN TEST.TXT /B
```

(Some versions of EDLIN contain a bug that won't let EDLIN recognize a lowercase /b switch. To be safe, make sure any /B you enter is a capital letter.) This tells EDLIN to load in the entire file regardless of imbedded end-of-file marks. You'll see the whole file with the fourth line if you do an L (list) in EDLIN. You can also see the whole file by entering:

```
COPY /B TEST.TXT CON
```

or:

```
COPY TEST.TXT CON /B
```

both of which do a *binary mode* copy of the file to CON (the screen, or *console*). The end-of-file markers show up as little right arrows.

But even if you use EDLIN in binary mode, it will still append an end-of-file marker to the end of the file. To get rid of it you could execute the following commands right after you exited EDLIN:

```
TYPE TEST.TXT >TEMPFILE
DEL TEST.TXT
REN TEMPFILE TEST.TXT
```

The TYPE command normally displays the file TEST.TXT up to (but not including) the end-of-file marker. Redirecting the output of this TYPE process into a temporary file like TEMPFILE will copy everything in the TEST.TXT file except the end-of-file marker. Then just delete the original TEST.TXT file, rename the new TEMPFILE to TEST.TXT, and then delete TEMPFILE. You could automate the whole process with a batch file:

```
ECHO OFF
IF %1!==! GOTO OOPS
EDLIN %1
TYPE %1 >TEMPFILE
DEL %1
REN TEMPFILE %1
GOTO END
:OOPS
ECHO Enter a filename after %0
:END
```

You can try using EDLIN to remove end-of-file characters one at a time. If there aren't too many in your file you may be able to get away with a global replacement operation. Since you can't specify a Ctrl-Z directly, you have to enter it as Ctrl-V Ctrl-Z, which looks like ^V^Z.

However, EDLIN will choke if you try a R (Replace) command and the end-of-file markers are too thick. If this happens, use DEBUG to ferret out the offending ASCII 26 characters. (The process described here is for files less than 64K in length; for longer ones you'll have to work with the CX and BX registers. See Chapter 8 on DEBUG for details.) DEBUG works exclusively in hex, so use the hex 1A notation for decimal ASCII 26. First, make a copy of the file, and work with the copy of the file rather than the original. If you make a mistake you can start the whole process again.

Load the file into DEBUG. See how large it is by typing RCX and pressing Enter twice. Then take the hex number that DEBUG prints out in response, and plug it into a S (Search) command. The whole process will look something like:

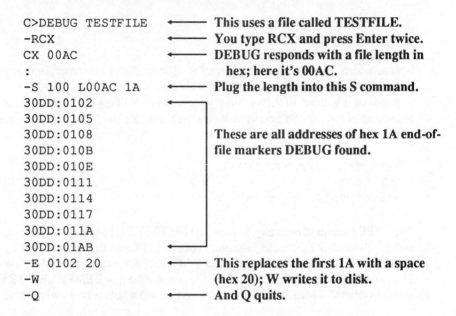

```
C>DEBUG TESTFILE      ◄─────  This uses a file called TESTFILE.
-RCX                  ◄─────  You type RCX and press Enter twice.
CX 00AC               ◄─────  DEBUG responds with a file length in
:                                hex; here it's 00AC.
-S 100 L00AC 1A       ◄─────  Plug the length into this S command.
30DD:0102     ◄─
30DD:0105
30DD:0108             These are all addresses of hex 1A end-of-
30DD:010B             file markers DEBUG found.
30DD:010E
30DD:0111
30DD:0114
30DD:0117
30DD:011A
30DD:01AB     ◄─
-E 0102 20            ◄─────  This replaces the first 1A with a space
-W                           (hex 20); W writes it to disk.
-Q                    ◄─────  And Q quits.
```

The example used only one E command to fix just the first occurrence of the hex 1A. To get rid of all the end-of-file markers you'd have to repeat the E command with every address DEBUG reported.

Note: If you're good at hex, and you see that all the addresses of the 1A characters are in one continuous block, you can use a single DEBUG F (Fill) command to repair the damage. So if you see something like:

```
30DD:10C9
30DD:10CA
30DD:10CB
30DD:10CC
30DD:10CD
30DD:10CE
30DD:10CF
```

You can issue the command:

```
F 10C9 10CF 20
```

which will fill the range of addresses from 10C9 (the first one on the list) to 10CF (the last one on the list) with hex 20 characters — spaces. Then type W (and press Enter) and Q (and press Enter) to save the changes. However, in the main example above, the addresses aren't in one continuous block.

Ignore the four digits to the left of the colon in the long list of addresses DEBUG prints out (here it's 30DD). This will vary from system to system and doesn't matter here. The four hex numbers to the right of each colon are the DEBUG offsets of each hex 1A character (remember, DEBUG works in hex — a hex 1A is the same as a decimal 26).

Then, use the E command with each address to replace the 1A with a 20 (a hex 20 is a space):

```
E 0102 20
```

and work your way through. When you're done, enter W to write the changes to disk and Q to quit. Again, work only on a copy of your file, not the original. And note that the above procedure is for files 64K or less in length only.

ECHO Version Madness

If you created batch files before DOS version 3.1 and used the trick of printing a blank line by following the ECHO command with two spaces, when you upgrade to a newer DOS version these ECHO commands will simply print "Echo is off" messages rather than blank lines. A batch file and EDLIN can fix the problem. ECHO will print a blank line if you follow it with a space and then an ASCII 255 character rather than with two spaces. ASCII 255 shows up as a blank on the PC screen, but to DOS, it's nonblank, so you won't get the "Echo is off" message. You can enter an ASCII 255 by holding down the Alt key, typing 255 on the number pad (not the top row number keys), and then releasing the Alt key.

Some text editors and word processors will have trouble with this ASCII 255, but the DOS EDLIN editor can handle it without any problems.

To fix the double space problem with EDLIN, use the R command to replace the final space with the a character 255,by entering this line:

1. Type: 1,RECHO (with two spaces after the ECHO).
2. Press the F6 function key.
3. Type just: ECHO.
4. Generate a character 255 by holding down the Alt key, typing 255 on the number pad, then releasing Alt.

The line looks like this:

```
*1,RECHO   ^ZECHO
```

The first number tells EDLIN to start at line 1. Since you didn't enter a second number after the comma, this tells EDLIN to repeat the operation on every line loaded in memory. The R is EDLIN's Replace command, and here it's followed immediately by the old string — ECHO and two blanks. When you press the F6 key after entering the old string, you'll see a ^Z. Then type the new string — ECHO followed by a blank followed by the ASCII code 255. Character 255 will appear as a blank on your display. EDLIN's search and replace is case-sensitive, so you'll have to repeat the command for occurrences ECHO, echo, and Echo.

Since EDLIN gets keyboard input through DOS (unlike most word processors and text editors), you can use it with redirection of standard input. Begin by creating a small script file (in EDLIN, of course) called REPLACE that looks like:

```
1,RECHO  <F6>ECHO<255>
1,REcho  <F6>Echo<255>
1,Recho  <F6>echo<255>
E
```

To enter the above four lines, first enter:

```
I
```

to put EDLIN into Insert mode. Then type each line, but press the F6 key where each one has an <F6> and generate a character 255 where each has a <255>. Be sure to observe the capitalizations carefully.

If you ever have to edit REPLACE after you create it, use the /B option with EDLIN. Since F6 is the same as a Ctrl-Z, which normally means "end of file," EDLIN will stop reading the file at the first Ctrl-Z unless it has the /B flag.

After typing the fourth line (with the solitary E), press Ctrl-C to get back to command mode and then enter E to save the file and quit.

To change a particular batch file (here called OLDFILE.BAT), all you have to do is enter the command:

```
EDLIN OLDFILE.BAT < REPLACE
```

DOS will take its input from REPLACE to do the search-and-replace operations automatically for you.

If you have lots of batch files with two spaces after ECHO, you can change them all with a pair of one-line batch files. First, create a one-line batch file called CHGBAT.BAT:

```
EDLIN %1 < REPLACE
```

Then create another one-line batch file call CHGALL.BAT that looks like:

```
FOR %%X IN (*.BAT) DO COMMAND /C CHGBAT %%X
```

If you run CHGALL.BAT, it will execute CHGBAT.BAT for every batch file on the disk (or subdirectory). Each time CHGBAT runs, it loads another batch file into EDLIN and uses REPLACE for the keystrokes to do the search-and-replace.

One interesting side effect of this process is that some batch files get edited twice. EDLIN renames the old version of an edited file with an extension .BAK, and creates a new directory entry to save the new version. Because of this, the FOR command in CHGALL.BAT stumbles over the file a second time. Note that CHGALL.BAT and CHGBAT.BAT will themselves be edited by EDLIN during this process. Neither of these peculiarities should cause a problem.

Chapter 8

DEBUG

Don't be put off by the name or the formidable set of commands: DEBUG is a serious computer user's best friend. Those of you who are already familiar with DEBUG may wish to go directly to the summary of commands in the second part of this chapter.

IBM and Microsoft need some real help when it comes to being friendly. They shouldn't have called this wonderful program DEBUG, which sounds as if it's for programmers only and that it involves something that's broken. Instead, they should have named it something like POWERUSR, or SLIKTOOL, or DOITALL. Well, maybe not.

It's almost as if these two companies tried to scare users away. Okay, DEBUG can be used as a high-level tool for fixing broken programs. But most real programmers have moved on to more powerful debugging aids produced by Microsoft and others. IBM would like us to believe that DEBUG is there mostly to "provide a controlled testing environment so you can monitor and control the execution of a program to be debugged" and "execute object files." Lost in the shuffle is a fragment admitting that it can "load, alter, or display any file." Totally ignored is its crude but useful ability to assemble and unassemble code — to translate assembly language instructions used by programmers into the *machine language* your CPU speaks, and back again.

Actually, DEBUG is for two sets of users. It's true that a handful of its commands are only for hard-core programmers who really need to trace though the underlying chip instructions one step at a time, or set *breakpoints* so that a program will screech to a halt and display the contents of the main CPU registers, or suck in data from a computer port.

But to the average power user, DEBUG is the ultimate program generator, analyzer, and customizer. Once you learn its few simple rules you can create short, powerful new programs and add flash to existing ones.

Unfortunately, because DEBUG is so incredibly powerful, it's also incredibly dangerous. (And, like every other part of DOS, it's frequently counterintuitive.) It's sort of like a carpenter's shop — filled with sharp tools you can use to build or fix just about anything safely, so long as you wear goggles and watch out for your fingers.

Most users are smart enough to work with copies of their programs rather than the originals when trying any sort of customization, so they won't end up ruining a $500 program with an errant keystroke. But certain madcap copy protection schemes can cause trouble because the programs they "protect" often don't play by the rules even if you and DEBUG do. Worse, because DEBUG lets you write information to absolute addresses on your disk rather than forcing you to have DOS take care of this safely for you, you can wipe out an entire hard disk with one simple erroneous command.

The general DEBUG safety rules are:

1. Always work with copies of your programs, *never* the originals.
2. Don't fool around with copy protected programs unless you're positive you know exactly what you're doing.
3. Whenever you are about to write sector information (with the W command) stop and triple-check your typing and your intentions. If you had read information from drive B:, had changed it slightly, and are about to write it back to the same drive, be sure your drive specification is correct. DEBUG uses a 0 to represent drive A:, a 1 to represent drive B:, and a 2 to represent drive C:. If you're trying to alter the disk directory, or (heaven forbid) the File Allocation Table (FAT) on drive B:, and it's late at night, and you inadvertently write the new information to drive 2, well, that's what backups and four-letter words (like "oops") are for.
4. If you have any doubt whatsoever about what you're doing, get back to the DEBUG prompt (by hitting Ctrl-Break or Ctrl-C), type Q on a line by itself to quit, and then press the Enter key to return to the main DOS prompt. You can always go back later and try your DEBUG work again. If you're at all hesitant about a change you made or a value you entered, make absolutely sure that you *don't* enter the W (Write) command. And avoid using the DEBUG G (Go) command to execute the program you're fiddling with, since unpredictable things can happen if you haven't reset all the registers properly, or if you've entered some but not all the changes you're working on.
5. While it may be tempting to change real gut-level aspects of the program, such as timing settings, again, don't, unless you're an expert. It's true that you can goose up the performance of your system by altering table settings that control such things as floppy disk head movement. It's also true that putting the wrong value in the wrong part of a table can send a disk head mechanism careening into someplace noisy and destructive.
6. There's a saying that "software can't destroy hardware." Unfortunately, it's not true. Apart from sending sensitive disk drive mechanisms into never-neverland, it's possible to blow out monitors or transformers. Again, if you simply follow reliable instructions to the letter and heed all of the warnings, you should be safe.

If you're in doubt about a particular DEBUG trick, *don't try it.* We hear lots of horror stories where users say "I know the instructions said 'for IBM hardware only' but my salesman told me this Yamagazi AT was virtually identical to an IBM." Or where the user says "I know it said 'for color monitors only' but my monochrome was a color — green. Now it's black."

Every DEBUG technique discussed in this book has been tested extensively on IBM equipment. However it is impossible to test every technique presented here on every single nonstandard system, given all the combinations and permutations on the market. Again, if you're not using an IBM system and you have any doubts whatsoever, *don't even think of trying these!*

At *PC Magazine* we receive barrels of potentially dangerous tips and tricks for IBM machines, some of which are quite useful, if a bit flashy. But if a tip appears at all troublesome we don't print it. The tips that make it into print are the ones we feel are safe. Most of the tips we publish simply create assembly language programs that use combinations of standard DOS and BIOS instructions to search for files, change colors, convert lowercase text to uppercase, etc. Others change harmless settings — to suppress screen clutter in batch files, or allow more than ten mismatches when DOS is comparing two files, for example.

Now that that's out of the way, we have to mention one more nasty thing — DEBUG works exclusively in hex. Hexadecimal notation is pretty basic stuff, and it's not hard to master. If you're uncomfortable with it, see the earlier chapter on hex and binary.

Addresses

The smallest four-digit hex number is 0000 (same as decimal 0). The largest is FFFF (same as decimal 65,535). This means that four hex digits can represent 65,536 different decimal values (1 through 65,535, plus 0). Decimal 65,536 is often abbreviated as 64K. 1K is equal to 2^10, or 1024 (not 1000, as some users think). 64 * 1024 = 2^16, or 65,536.

The PC can address one megabyte of memory. One megabyte is equal to 2^20, or decimal 1,048,576. 16 * 65,536 is also equal to 1,048,576. The lowest address is address 0. The highest is 1,048,576.

For many common tasks it's easier and quicker to work with smaller numbers rather than larger ones. Anyway, the original PC came with a 16-bit chip, and the biggest number this chip could address "directly" was 2^16, or 65,536.

But since 65,536 is 1/16th of 1,048,576, being able to handle only 65,536 addresses directly meant working with only 1/16th of the available memory at any one time. To give users access to the rest, IBM designers employed relative addressing. They chopped the one megabyte into 16 chunks called segments, each 64K long. Once you specified which of the 16 segments you wanted to work with, you could address any of the 65,536 bytes in that segment directly.

If you have to know what's at address 5, you can tell DEBUG simply to report the value at address 5. Because you didn't mention any particular segment, it will tell you the value at address 5 of whatever segment you're in at the time. If you want to look at address 5 in another segment, you have to specify both the address and the segment you want.

Manuals sometimes provide maps that show the one meg of memory divided neatly into 16 even chunks 64K apart from each other, starting out:

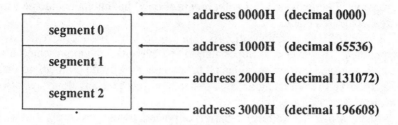

It doesn't really work like that. Segments can have any starting absolute address from 0 to 1048560, so long as the address is evenly divisible by 16. So 16 and 32 and 524288 are all valid absolute addresses, but 1 and 17 are not. And segments can overlap, either partially or totally.

Relative, or segmented, addresses are usually expressed as a pair of two four-digit hex numbers separated by a colon:

XXXX:YYYY

The XXXX represents the segment. The YYYY stands for the *offset* into that segment.

Once you've mastered hex, start putting it into action. DEBUG.COM is usually on the DOS Supplemental or Operating disk, depending on the version. If you have a hard disk, be sure to copy it into your main DOS subdirectory, and be sure you're using a PATH command that includes this DOS subdirectory. This will let you use DEBUG anywhere on your hard disk. If you don't have a hard disk, you should put DEBUG.COM on your main bootup or utilities disk and keep it handy at all times.

The DEBUG prompt is simply a hyphen hugging the left edge of your screen:

-

All of DEBUG's commands are single letters. You may enter them in upper- or lower-case, or a mixture of both. The examples here will use uppercase text to avoid confusing 1 with "ell." And you don't have to separate the single-letter commands from the parameters that follow them. Typing:

RCX

to see what's in the CX register (this will be covered shortly) is the same as typing:

R CX

Similarly, you can use either:

D120

or:

```
D 120
```

to display the values of the 128 bytes of memory starting at offset 120H (again, we'll get to displaying memory a bit later).

When entering a lot of information or making extensive changes using DEBUG, it's often best to create pure-ASCII *scripts* and then redirect these scripts into DEBUG. DOS versions 2.0 and later treat such redirected files as if they were actual keystrokes.

Scripts are handy because they make it easy for you to proofread your typing before executing actual DEBUG commands. If you find a typo in your script it's a whole lot easier to correct it with a word processor or EDLIN than to end up with a real mess that you created while in DEBUG because you typed something incorrectly.

Scripts are also valuable because in some cases you can add nonexecutable comments that DEBUG ignores but that can remind you much later of what you did. And if you store your scripts on disk, you can cannibalize them and use them to create other slightly different scripts. They're also handy for transmitting via modem. Many telecommunications services work with text files only, and won't let you send programs. But you can send scripts, since they're just ASCII files, and have the recipient redirect these scripts into DEBUG to create the program you wanted to send.

Redirectable scripts have to be pure-ASCII files, without any extra word processing formatting commands imbedded in them. The easiest way to create them is with a pure-ASCII editor like *SideKick*'s notepad, or with a word processor that can export DOS files (such as *WordPerfect* or *Word*), or with a word processor that has a built-in ASCII mode (such as *WordStar* in nondocument mode). EDLIN isn't bad for shorter scripts, and you could even use the DOS COPY CON command.

DEBUG doesn't execute a command until you press the Enter key. So any script you create has to have a carriage return at the end of every line — especially the last one, which is always Q on a line by itself to quit. If you don't end every script file with a Q that has a carriage return after it, redirecting it will hang your system. *So be sure you press the Enter key at the very end of any DEBUG script, or you'll have to reboot.*

Most DEBUG commands perform just one task and then return you to the DEBUG prompt. If the task takes too long to execute (displaying the contents of a huge chunk of memory, for instance), you can hit Ctrl-Break or Ctrl-C to interrupt it and return to the DEBUG prompt. If you're using the DEBUG mini-assembler to turn assembly language statements into machine readable code, press the Enter key twice after you enter your final statement, to return to the DEBUG prompt.

Since many DEBUG scripts contain assembly language commands and statements, you can simulate pressing the Enter key at the end of the final statement by leaving a blank line after that statement. If you don't do this, DEBUG will try to interpret everything that follows as additional assembly language statements. If you try typing in the example scripts that follow, be sure to copy them exactly as they appear, blank lines and all.

Here's an example of a DEBUG script file, called BEEP.SCR:

```
N BEEP.COM        ; gives the file a name
A
MOV DL,7          ; ASCII 7 is the beep character
MOV AH,2          ; the DOS "display output" function
INT 21            ; kicks DOS into action
RET               ; return to DOS — next line is blank!

RCX
7
W
Q
```

DEBUG ignores any text following semicolons, and the semicolons themselves. They're included just to remind you later what the program is doing. You have to be careful when you use them, since DEBUG may interpret such comments as part of a command to execute, and get thoroughly confused. It's pretty safe to use them with assembly language instructions like the ones above, and very unsafe when you're entering single letter commands.

You can type this script in using any of the tools mentioned above. If by some crazy circumstance you don't have a word processor handy and refuse to learn EDLIN, you could create the script by adding a COPY CON BEEP.SCR line before the first "N BEEP.COM" line, and pressing Enter, then the F6 function key, and then Enter when you're done.

In any case, be sure to leave the blank line above RCX. You can do this by pressing the Enter key twice after RET. And double check that you press the Enter key at the very end, after the Q. If you did, the cursor will be on the line below the Q. Call the file BEEP.SCR. When you're all done, get back to your main DOS prompt and type:

```
DEBUG < BEEP.SCR
```

DOS will feed the BEEP.SCR commands into DEBUG a line at a time, and you'll be able to see DEBUG processing them one by one. If everything goes the way it should, near the bottom of the screen you'll see the message:

```
Writing 0007 bytes
```

If you make a typing mistake, DEBUG will show you where the trouble is by pointing to it and printing the word Error. If you had typed "MOV LD,7" instead of "MOV DL,7," you'd see:

```
33DB:0100 MOV LD,7
                ^ Error
```

If DEBUG detects such a syntax error, it may or may not continue and create the file, depending on the severity of the problem. Watch the screen closely as DOS redirects the script file into DEBUG. If you see any error messages do not try to execute the program you were trying to create! Instead, erase any erroneous file it may have created, check your typing, and try again.

If you type the BEEP.SCR file correctly and redirect it properly into DEBUG, you'll end up with a seven-byte program on your disk called BEEP.COM. Type BEEP to run it and DOS will beep. Here's how it works:

The first "N BEEP.COM" line tells DEBUG to give the file a name. DEBUG can't create a file unless you specify a filename. Since you want to create an executable file, you have to give the file a COM or EXE extension. When creating any kind of files with DEBUG, use COM extensions only.

The "A" command turns on DEBUG's mini-assembler, which will convert any assembly language statement(s) that follow into a machine-level form your CPU can readily understand. If you haven't used the Assemble command previously and you enter an A without specifying an address after it, DEBUG will start assembling these machine-level instructions at address 100. If you're using the A command more than once in a particular DEBUG session, or you want to have DEBUG put the assembled code at an offset higher than 100, be sure to include the proper addresses.

The next four lines are the actual assembly language statements. "MOV DL,7" moves, or puts, the value 7 into the register DL. "MOV AH,2" moves, or puts, the value 2 into the register AH. INT 21 is the main interrupt that kicks DOS into action. When your program invokes INT 21, DOS looks at the value in the AH register to figure out which of its dozens of function calls it's supposed to execute. Other values in other registers provide the raw material for the specific DOS function call to process, or narrow how some of the more flexible function calls should act. In this example, the value of 2 in register AH tells DOS to use function call 2 to print one character onto the screen. When you trigger DOS with an INT 21 and it sees a 2 in AH, it looks in the DL register for a number and displays onscreen the ASCII character represented by that number. Printing an ASCII 7 character beeps. As it's used here, the final "RET" will jump control of the system back to COMMAND.COM when the program finishes executing.

Registers are tiny storage areas inside the main CPU chip, and virtually every instruction or slice of data in your computer either passes through these registers or is in some way controlled by what's temporarily stored there. Chips in the Intel 8088 family contain 14 registers, each of which is 16 bits (two bytes) long. Four of these are general purpose, or *scratch-pad* registers: AX, BX, CX, and DX. Each of these four two-byte scratch-pad registers can be divided into high and low bytes. Remember, one byte contains eight bits. Two bytes together form what's called a *word*, so each of these 16-bit registers is actually a word. And each word has high and low halves, the way the decimal number 27 does — in this case the 2 would be the high half since it's actually 2 x 10 (or 20), while the 7 is the low half, since it's actually 7 x 1 (or 7). The number on the left, in the tens column, is always higher, or worth more than, the lower number on the right, in the ones column.

The high bytes are referred to as AH, BH, CH, and DH, and the low bytes as AL, BL, CL, and DL. Each of these high and low registers can store a single byte; the full AX, BX, CX, and CX registers can store two bytes (one word) in a single gulp. If you need to manipulate just one byte, you generally use the high or low registers. If you have to handle two bytes together, you use the full-size registers. The above example used AH to tell DOS which function call you wanted, and DL to store the value of the character you wanted to display.

Four additional segment registers tell the CPU the starting address of four important 64K memory segments: the code segment (CS), data segment (DS), stack segment (SS), and extra segment (ES). Another five registers provide the necessary offsets: the instruction pointer (IP), stack pointer (SP), base pointer (BP), source index (SI) and destination index (DI). The final one, called the *flags* register, maintains the on-off status of 16 individual bits. Processes can change individual bit settings to keep track of events, or refer to the settings changed by other processes or events and act accordingly.

When you initially load DEBUG, it sets the addresses of the CS, DS, ES, and SS segments so they're all located in memory directly after the space taken up by the DEBUG program itself. It also normally sets the values of the main registers you'll be using — AX, BX, CX, and DX (as well as some of the others) to zero. If you loaded a file shorter than 64K bytes from the DOS command line at the same time that you started DEBUG, DEBUG will set the CX register to reflect the length of this file. If the file is larger than 64K, DEBUG will use both the CX and BX registers to maintain the file length. If you later load a file using the N (Name) and L (Load) commands, DEBUG will then put the file's length into the CX register (and the register BX if necessary).

The last four lines of the example above reset the CX register to 7 (since CX is a two-byte register, this actually set CX to 0007 — the high byte is 00 and the low one 07), write the file to disk (W), and then quit (Q). When you ask DEBUG to write a file, you have to specify a filename and a file length. You tell it the filename either by using the N (Name) command, or by including the name on the command line when you first start DEBUG (as in C>DEBUG BEEP.COM). You specify the file length by putting a value in the CX register.

At times you may want DEBUG to process strings of characters. When entering such strings, you can use pairs of either single quotes (') or double quotes ("). This lets you include the opposite kind of quote in the string you're entering. So if you entered "The word 'gub' will appear in quotes" or 'The word "gub" will appear in quotes,' sure enough both statements will be true. It gets tricky, but you can also use the same type of quotation marks inside and outside the string, if you double them inside: "This uses the ""double quote"" mark twice."

The purpose of the DEBUG examples in this chapter is not to teach you every last thing you have to know about assembly language, but to familiarize you with the kinds of things DEBUG can do. If you really want to learn about assembly language, purchase the IBM or Microsoft MASM programs and read the manuals. The programs you'll learn to create here are all very short and single-minded, and they use a lot of shortcuts and defaults.

Also, unless you're a serious assembly language programmer, you don't really have to know every last command in DEBUG. All you need to learn are the basic commands to create and modify programs. For the purpose of working more productively you don't have to learn how to use DEBUG as a "controlled testing environment." Commands that execute programs from within DEBUG, or trace through them one instruction at a time are extremely helpful to professional programmers, but they're not necessary here. And virtually all the following examples will concentrate on creating and customizing files rather than tearing into your disk sectors and fooling around with underlying system structures.

You can make a permanent record of any DEBUG activity either by redirecting your efforts to a file, or by *echoing* them simultaneously to your printer. To get a printed copy of your DEBUG session, turn your printer on, then type Ctrl-P or Ctrl-PrtSc. Anything that appears onscreen will also be sent to your printer a line at a time, although your printer may have a hard time trying to reproduce some of the nontext characters that your screen can handle with ease. To turn this printer echo feature off when you're done, just type Ctrl-P or Ctrl-PrtSc one more time.

While it's often useful to redirect a DEBUG output to a file, this can be a bit tricky since you won't be able to see what you're doing. Redirecting output to a file is the opposite of the script file process mentioned earlier. When you redirect input (such as a script file) into DEBUG, DOS feeds characters from the script file into DEBUG just as if you were typing at the keyboard. When you redirect the output from DEBUG into a file, DOS takes all the characters that would normally show up on your screen and instead reroutes them into a file on your disk. Because DOS will intercept each character before it gets to your monitor, you won't see be able to see what's going on until you finally type Q to quit, press Enter, and return to the main DOS prompt. So if you try redirecting the DEBUG output with the simple command:

```
DEBUG > OUTPUT.FIL
```

you have to know exactly what you want to type, because you'll be flying blind.

A better way to end up with a DEBUG output file on disk is to first step through the exact DEBUG process you want — without worrying about redirection. Write down every keystroke you use, or have a screen-capture utility like *SideKick*'s notepad record your keystrokes for you. Then type all these keystrokes into a script file called DEBUG.SCR (or edit the file *SideKick* created). Remember to insert blank lines in the script file if necessary, and be absolutely sure to press the Enter key at the very end after the final Q.

Then review the DEBUG.SCR file carefully. It should contain all the keystrokes you would normally enter in the particular DEBUG session you want to capture on disk, and nothing else. Put this script file on the same disk as DEBUG and type:

```
DEBUG < DEBUG.SCR > DEBUG.OUT
```

Your disk will churn for a second or two as DOS feeds the DEBUG.SCR keystrokes into DEBUG and then creates a file on your disk called DEBUG.OUT that contains everything DEBUG would have displayed on your screen.

For example, let's say you wanted to see the text parts of the main DOS command processor, COMMAND.COM. These include internal commands, error messages, prompts, etc.

As we've seen, DOS commands come in two flavors — internal and external. External commands are individual programs (with COM or EXE extensions) delivered on your DOS disks. Commands like CHKDSK and SORT are external commands, since you execute them by running programs called CHKDSK.COM and SORT.EXE. However, the instructions for executing commands like DIR and TYPE are internal, since they're actually imbedded inside COMMAND.COM.

When you enter something at the DOS prompt, DOS first looks inside COMMAND.COM to see if what you typed is an internal command. If not, it tries to find a file with the name you specified ending with COM, then EXE, or finally BAT in the current subdirectory. If it doesn't locate one, it will scan through all the other subdirectories listed in your PATH statement for COM, EXE, or BAT files, in that order. As soon as it finds one it will stop looking and execute it. If it doesn't, it will issue a "Bad command or filename" error message.

So, let's look inside COMMAND.COM. The following example uses version 3.3 of DOS, but any version 2.0 or later will work the same way. If you are using a DOS version other than 3.3, some of the numbers shown below will be different. And while it assumes you're on drive C:, the process is the same on any drive so long as COMMAND.COM and DEBUG.COM are on a disk in that drive.

First, at the main DOS prompt, start DEBUG and tell it you want to load the COMMAND.COM program into memory:

```
DEBUG COMMAND.COM
```

Then, when you see the DEBUG hyphen prompt, find out how long the program is by typing:

```
RCX
```

DEBUG will respond by printing:

```
CX 62DB
:
```

(The hex number after CX will be different if you're trying this on a version other than DOS 3.3. Note this number, since you'll have to use it shortly.)

Typing RCX (or R CX, or r cx, or rcx) tells DEBUG to display the value currently in register CX and then pause and wait to see if you want to change this value. If you do want to enter a new value, type a hex number immediately after the colon and then press the Enter key. If you don't want to change the value, but just wanted to see what the value was, just press the Enter key without entering a new value.

You could also type just an R by itself, and then press the Enter key. Doing this right after you typed DEBUG COMMAND.COM would print:

```
AX=0000  BX=0000  CX=62DB  DX=0000  SP=FFFE  BP=0000  SI=0000  DI=0000
DS=33F7  ES=33F7  SS=33F7  CS=33F7  IP=0100   NV UP EI PL NZ NA PO NC
33F7:0100 E92D0D         JMP      0E30
```

Entering R without anything after it will display the contents of all your system's registers, the state of all its flags, and the actual instruction that will be executed next. In the above display, the registers are the 13 blocks of characters with equals signs in the middle, the flags are the eight pairs of letters, and the bottom line indicates that the JMP 0E30 instruction at address 100 is the next one to execute. For the purpose of this example, all you need is the value in register CX. The third number in the top row tells you this value is 62DB.

Once you learn the file's length, have DEBUG search all the way through the COMMAND.COM file that's currently loaded in memory for the string "Batch." COMMAND.COM stores its main messages, commands, and prompts in a lump near the very end of the file. The first bit of text stored there is a "Batch file missing" error message, so if you find the address of this particular message you can jump to this address and browse through all the text that follows.

DEBUG needs to know where it should start and stop searching for something (in this case the "Batch" string). You can specify the search parameters one of two ways. Either give DEBUG explicit starting and stopping addresses, or tell it the starting address and then provide a number representing how many bytes after this address DEBUG should scan through.

The starting address is simple; DEBUG always loads COM files so they start at memory offset 100 (remember, all these numbers are in hex, not decimal). Since you want to search a file from beginning to end that is 62DB bytes long, starting at 0100, the ending address is 63DB. So you would specify explicit starting and stopping addresses by typing:

```
-S 100 63DB "Batch"
```

In the procedure above, you snooped inside the R register to learn how long the COMMAND.COM file was. DOS version 3.3 DEBUG will report 62DB; this number will be different if you're using a different version of DOS. But notice that while the length of the file is 62DB bytes, you have to enter 63DB as the explicit ending address. Why?

The number 63DB is 100 higher than the actual file length 62DB. DEBUG normally loads files at address 100, not at address 0 (unless they're EXE files), and this moves all the addresses in the file up by 100. If you want to look at the first two bytes in a file — bytes 0 and 1 — you actually have to tell DEBUG to look at the contents of addresses 100 and 101.

The first byte in the file is loaded into address 100, the second byte at address 101, and the 62DBth byte at 63DB. So you have to add 100 to the length of the file if you want DEBUG to search all the way through to the last byte loaded in memory. To do this, just add 1 to the third hex digit over from the right. The third digit from the right in this example is 2, so you add 1 to it and it becomes 3.

The process of adding 100 like this is trivial unless the third digit over is hex F. In the decimal number system, if you add:

```
  1
+ 9
```

you end up with a 0 in the column that has the 9 in it, and you carry a 1 over to the column immediately to its left. In the hexadecimal number system, if you add:

```
  1
+ F
```

you end up with a 0 in the column that has the F in it, and you carry a 1 over to the column immediately to its left. If DEBUG had reported a file length of 1111, adding 100 to it would give you 1211. But if the file length were 1F11, adding 100 to it would produce 2011. And if the file length were 9F11, adding 100 would yield A011. Don't mix hex and decimal numbers when in DEBUG; be careful to work exclusively in hex.

If you feel squeamish about adding hex numbers, let DEBUG do it for you. If you wanted to add 100 to 62DB, all you have to do is make sure you see the DEBUG hyphen prompt and then type:

```
H 62DB 100
```

DEBUG will respond by printing:

```
63DB  61DB
```

The first number (63DB, the one you're looking for) is the sum of 62DB + 100. The second number (61DB) is the difference of 62DB - 100. You don't need to use the subtraction feature of this H (hex math) command here, but if you ever do, make sure you enter the numbers in the proper order. Adding numbers in either order will produce the same result (3 + 5 and 5 + 3 will both yield 8). But this even-handedness doesn't apply to subtraction; 3 - 5 is definitely not the same as 5 - 3.

DEBUG makes it even easier to specify a search range. All you really have to do is enter the starting address and the number of bytes to search. Since you want to scan through the entire COMMAND.COM file, the number of bytes to search is equal to the length of the file. So instead of entering explicit starting and stopping addresses, you could issue a variation of the search command used earlier:

```
-S 100 L 62DB "Batch"
```

This command tells DEBUG to start a search for the string "Batch" at address 100 and continue searching for a length of 62DB bytes. You'll get the same results whether you use an "L" like this to specify the search length, or instead specify the explicit starting and stopping addresses. But this way you don't have to do any hex math.

DEBUG will search through the file and report all occurrences of the "Batch" string. Since searches are case sensitive, DEBUG will ignore any "batch" or "BATCH" strings it may find. It's important in this example to specify all lowercase letters except for the initial capital B, since COMMAND.COM does indeed contain other "batch" strings that you don't want to examine.

If you had wanted DEBUG to locate every occurrence of this word including all-lower-case versions ("batch") as well as lowercase versions with initial capital letters ("Batch") you could have changed the search command to:

```
-S 100 L 62DB "atch"
```

or:

```
-S 100 63DB "atch"
```

Of course, this would also find words like patch, or snatch, or potlatch if any existed in the file you were scanning. However, COMMAND.COM contains only three strings with "atch" in them. If you tried either of these "atch" search commands in version 3.3, DEBUG would report something that looked like:

```
33F7:0A51
33F7:4DCA
33F7:4DF4
```

Try this yourself with version 3.3 and you'll see the same three numbers to the right of the colons, but different numbers to the left. The number to the left (in this case 33F7) is the segment address, and it will vary from system to system depending on how much memory your computer has and what else you currently have loaded in memory. Manuals sometimes replace the varying segment addresses with a row of "xxxx" characters, so if you see something that looks like:

```
xxxx:0A51
xxxx:4DCA
xxxx:4DF4
```

all it really means it that any four-digit hex number can appear where the xxxx characters are.

But since you really wanted DEBUG to look for just the string "Batch" it will find just one occurrence:

```
33F7:4DC9
```

Jot down the offset address — the rightmost four bytes, or 4DC9 — because you'll need it for the next process.

To make sure you've found the proper string, use the DEBUG Display (D) command. You can use the same basic syntax rules for the Display command that you used with the search command. The display range can either be an explicit starting and stopping address, or a starting address and a length of bytes for DEBUG to display. Since the word "Batch" is five characters long, both of the following commands will display the string at the offset address the above search command located:

```
D 4DC9 4DCD
```

or:

```
D 4DC9 L 5
```

The top command first lists the starting address and then the stopping address. Note that the stopping address is the starting address + 4, not the starting address + 5. This is because you want DEBUG to display the value of the byte at address 4DC9 (the "B" in "Batch") plus the next four characters ("atch"). Again, if you're a little shaky on hex math (hex 9 + 4 = D, not 13), you can use the DEBUG H command to add the two numbers together for you.

The bottom command first lists the starting address and then tells DEBUG to display five bytes starting with that address. In this case you specify five rather than four, since you're asking DEBUG to display a total of five bytes.

Either way, you'll see something like:

```
33F7:4DC0              42 61 74 63 68           Batch
```

Every DEBUG D display has three parts. The first part, at the lefthand edge of your screen, is the address of the memory that DEBUG is displaying, in SSSS:OOOO segment:offset format. The second, in the middle of your screen, are the individual values of the chunk of memory DEBUG is displaying, in hexadecimal notation. The third, at the righthand edge of your screen, is the ASCII representation of what's in memory at the addresses you specified. To avoid cluttering up this part of the display with things like happy faces, musical notes, or Greek and math characters, DEBUG will print a period (.) when it sees any value below hex 20 (decimal 32) or above hex 7E (decimal 126).

DEBUG will often display what looks like random letters, numbers, and punctuation in the rightmost third of the screen. These are just artifacts, and don't mean anything. DEBUG isn't smart enough to know what parts of a program are text that should be displayed and what parts are actually meachine-level instructions that shouldn't be displayed. Whenever it sees a hex value of 50 (decimal 80), for instance, DEBUG will display a "P." If this value of 50 happens to be in a message such as "Path not found" you'll be glad it did. But the 50 could just as easily have been part of an address or value in a gut-level instruction.

For instance, if the internal code of a program moved a value of 5000 into register AX (with the command MOV AX,5000), the actual machine-level version of this instruction would be:

```
B80050
```

DEBUG would display the B8 and the 00 as periods, since B8 is above hex 7E and 00 is below hex 20. But it would display the 50 in the righthand third of the screen as a P. In fact, one particular assembly language command (PUSH AX) is represented in machine-level code as the single value:

```
50
```

which would show up in a DEBUG display as a solitary P.

Artifacts like these occur because your system has a small, 256-unit vocabulary. Every message, prompt, command, instruction, and address has to be made up of single-byte values between 0 and 255. Your CPU is smart enough to sort it all out when it processes the stream of bytes, but DEBUG isn't. So ignore these random characters in DEBUG displays.

You can't use the Search (S) command without specifying an address range and something to search for. So typing S by itself at the DEBUG prompt would be meaningless, and would only generate an error message. But you can (and will frequently want to) issue a Display (D) command on a line by itself.

If you start DEBUG, load COMMAND.COM into it, then type D by itself and press Enter, DEBUG will display the first 128 bytes of the file, from address 100 through address 17F. Each subsequent time you type D without any parameters after it and press Enter, DEBUG will display the next 128 bytes in memory immediately following the previous block. If you keep pressing just D and then Enter enough times — 512 to be exact — you'll work all the way to the end of the current segment and start over again at the beginning of the segment.

DEBUG displays such blocks of memory information in a grid 16 bytes wide, and either eight or nine rows tall. (If you specify a starting address at the beginning of a paragraph — one that ends in a 0 such as 100 or 3D0 — you'll see a tidy block of bytes eight rows high. But if you specify any other address DEBUG will stagger the display into a ninth row.) So if you type the following two lines to display the beginning of COM-MAND.COM version 3.3:

```
C>DEBUG COMMAND.COM
-D
```

(don't type the DOS C prompt or the DEBUG — prompt; these are just included to illustrate what your screen should look like) you'll see:

```
33F7:0100   E9 2D 0D BA DA 0A 3D 05-00 74 1B BA BF 0A 3D 02   .-....=..t....=.
33F7:0110   00 74 13 BA 85 0A 3D 08-00 74 0B BA 71 0A 3D 0B   .t....=..t..q.=.
33F7:0120   00 74 03 BA 62 0A 0E 1F-E8 6A 06 EB 0C CD 21 72   .t..b....j....!r
33F7:0130   D2 B4 4D CD 21 2E A3 EA-0B E9 76 01 2E F6 06 59   ..M.!.....v....Y
33F7:0140   0C 01 74 0C 2E F6 06 59-0C 02 74 03 E9 01 13 CF   ..t....Y..t.....
33F7:0150   2E F6 06 59 0C 04 74 11-80 FC 01 72 F2 80 FC 0C   ...Y..t....r....
33F7:0160   77 ED 83 C4 06 F9 CA 02-00 2E 80 0E 59 0C 04 FB   w...........Y...
33F7:0170   0E 1F A1 F3 0B 0B C0 75-06 50 B4 0D CD 21 58 F7   .......u.P...!X.
```

Again, if you try this on your own DOS 3.3 version of COMMAND.COM the only difference will be the 33F7 segment at the left edge of the display.

Each row of 16 bytes is called a paragraph. DEBUG doesn't label the individual columns, but if it did, you'd see something like:

```
            0  1  2  3  4  5  6  7- 8  9  A  B  C  D  E  F
            -------------------------------------------------
33F7:0100   E9 2D 0D BA DA 0A 3D 05-00 74 1B BA BF 0A 3D 02   .-....=..t....=.
33F7:0110   00 74 13 BA 85 0A 3D 08-00 74 0B BA 71 0A 3D 0B   .t....=..t..q.=.
```

It's simple to find a value at a particular address. First, locate the paragraph (the row) with the offset address at or just below the precise address you're seeking. Then count over from left to right one byte at a time. As you can see from the column labels above, the address of the first byte in each paragraph ends with 0, the second byte with 1, the third with 2, and the last (16th) byte with F. (Remember, these labels don't actually appear in DEBUG displays. Neither do the pairs of xx characters below; they simply mean that here you should ignore everything marked xx.) In the above example the value at address 100 is E9 since this is the number at the intersection of the row starting with 0100 and the column with the label of 0:

```
            0  1  2  3  4  5  6  7- 8  9  A  B  C  D  E  F
            -------------------------------------------------
33F7:0100   E9 xx xx xx xx xx xx xx-xx xx xx xx xx xx xx xx   .-....=..t....=.
33F7:0110   xx xx xx xx xx xx xx xx-xx xx xx xx xx xx xx xx   .t....=..t..q.=.
```

The value at address 112 is 13, since this number appears at the intersection of the row beginning 110 and the column with the label 2:

```
            0  1  2  3  4  5  6  7- 8  9  A  B  C  D  E  F
            -------------------------------------------------
33F7:0100   xx xx xx xx xx xx xx xx-xx xx xx xx xx xx xx xx   .-....=..t....=.
33F7:0110   xx xx 13 xx xx xx xx xx-xx xx xx xx xx xx xx xx   .t....=..t..q.=.
```

While DEBUG doesn't show column labels, it does make the process of counting over somewhat easier by putting a hyphen halfway across the display, between columns 7 and

8. So if you want to see the value at an address ending with a 7, find the appropriate row and look at the number directly to the left of the hyphen. The value at 107 is 05:

```
           0  1  2  3  4  5  6  7- 8  9  A  B  C  D  E  F
          -----------------------------------------------
33F7:0100 xx xx xx xx xx xx xx 05-xx xx xx xx xx xx xx xx   .-....=..t....=.
33F7:0110 xx xx xx xx xx xx xx xx-xx xx xx xx xx xx xx xx   .t....=..t..q.=.
```

Once you've used the D command to verify that the "Batch" search address is correct, start displaying the next few 128-byte blocks of memory following that address. Your displays will be neater if you round the address down to an even paragraph address. To do this just replace the rightmost digit with a 0.

Since the Search command found the "Batch" string at address 4DC9, replace the rightmost 9 with a 0 and enter the command:

```
D  4DC0
```

You should see a chunk of memory that contains DOS error messages:

```
33F7:4DC0  37 6E 44 09 00 63 37 0D-0A 42 61 74 63 68 20 66   7nD..c7..Batch f
33F7:4DD0  69 6C 65 20 6D 69 73 73-69 6E 67 0D 0A 00 67 37   ile missing...g7
33F7:4DE0  0D 0A 49 6E 73 65 72 74-20 64 69 73 6B 20 77 69   ..Insert disk wi
33F7:4DF0  74 68 20 62 61 74 63 68-20 66 69 6C 65 0D 0A 61   th batch file..a
33F7:4E00  6E 64 20 70 72 65 73 73-20 61 6E 79 20 6B 65 79   nd press any key
33F7:4E10  20 77 68 65 6E 20 72 65-61 64 79 0D 0A 00 80 37    when ready....7
33F7:4E20  42 61 64 20 63 6F 6D 6D-61 6E 64 20 6F 72 20 66   Bad command or f
33F7:4E30  69 6C 65 20 6E 61 6D 65-0D 0A 00 C0 37 44 75 70   ile name....7Dup
```

Ignore the segment addresses, which will be different on your system. Keeping pressing just D and the Enter key a few times and you'll see more error messages:

```
33F7:4E40  6C 69 63 61 74 65 20 66-69 6C 65 20 6E 61 6D 65   licate file name
33F7:4E50  20 6F 72 20 46 69 6C 65-20 6E 6F 74 20 66 6F 75    or File not fou
33F7:4E60  6E 64 0D 0A 00 DD 37 46-69 6C 65 20 6E 6F 74 20   nd....7File not
33F7:4E70  66 6F 75 6E 64 0D 0A 00-07 38 50 61 74 68 20 6E   found....8Path n
33F7:4E80  6F 74 20 66 6F 75 6E 64-0D 0A 00 1A 38 41 63 63   ot found....8Acc
33F7:4E90  65 73 73 20 64 65 6E 69-65 64 0D 0A 00 2D 38 49   ess denied...-8I
33F7:4EA0  6E 73 75 66 66 69 63 69-65 6E 74 20 64 69 73 6B   nsufficient disk
33F7:4EB0  20 73 70 61 63 65 0D 0A-00 3F 38 4F 75 74 20 6F   space...?8Out o
```

and then, later, some prompts, and finally a list of internal DOS commands:

```
33F7:5440  5F 86 19 24 0B 14 00 03-4E 4F 54 84 09 0A 45 52   _..$....NOT...ER
33F7:5450  52 4F 52 4C 45 56 45 4C-48 0A 05 45 58 49 53 54   RORLEVELH..EXIST
```

```
33F7:5460  DB 09 00 03 44 49 52 03-CB 0E 04 43 41 4C 4C 02   ....DIR....CALL.
33F7:5470  BD 0A 04 43 48 43 50 02-D2 15 06 52 45 4E 41 4D   ...CHCP....RENAM
33F7:5480  45 01 0B 12 03 52 45 4E-01 0B 12 05 45 52 41 53   E....REN....ERAS
33F7:5490  45 01 A2 11 03 44 45 4C-01 A2 11 04 54 59 50 45   E....DEL....TYPE
33F7:54A0  01 83 12 03 52 45 4D 02-04 01 04 43 4F 50 59 03   ....REM....COPY.
33F7:54B0  15 2A 05 50 41 55 53 45-02 95 11 04 44 41 54 45   .*.PAUSE....DATE

33F7:54C0  02 20 21 04 54 49 4D 45-00 38 22 03 56 45 52 00   . !.TIME.8".VER.
33F7:54D0  79 13 03 56 4F 4C 01 23-13 02 43 44 01 C2 18 05   y..VOL.#..CD....
33F7:54E0  43 48 44 49 52 01 C2 18-02 4D 44 01 05 19 05 4D   CHDIR....MD....M
33F7:54F0  4B 44 49 52 01 05 19 02-52 44 01 49 19 05 52 4D   KDIR....RD.I..RM
33F7:5500  44 49 52 01 49 19 05 42-52 45 41 4B 00 F5 28 06   DIR.I..BREAK..(.
33F7:5510  56 45 52 49 46 59 00 27-29 03 53 45 54 02 AA 16   VERIFY.').SET...
33F7:5520  06 50 52 4F 4D 50 54 02-90 16 04 50 41 54 48 02   .PROMPT....PATH.
33F7:5530  93 14 04 45 58 49 54 00-62 16 04 43 54 54 59 03   ...EXIT.b..CTTY.

33F7:5540  6D 15 04 45 43 48 4F 02-B2 28 04 47 4F 54 4F 02   m..ECHO..(.GOTO.
33F7:5550  F1 0A 05 53 48 49 46 54-02 76 0A 02 49 46 02 34   ...SHIFT.v..IF.4
33F7:5560  09 03 46 4F 52 02 4E 0D-03 43 4C 53 00 02 15 00   ..FOR.N..CLS....
33F7:5570  41 7C 3C 3E 24 28 29 29-00 49 4E 44 4F 2A 2D 2B   A|<>$()).INDO*-+
33F7:5580  4C 6C 61 7A 44 43 53 58-2E 3F 2E 2C 3A 2E 70 00   LlazDCSX.?.,:.p.
33F7:5590  00 2E 43 4F 4D 2E 45 58-45 2E 42 41 54 56 42 41   ..COM.EXE.BATVBA
33F7:55A0  50 57 20 00 00 00 00 00-00 00 00 00 00 00 00 00   PW .............
33F7:55B0  00 00 00 00 00 00 00 00-00 00 00 00 00 00 00 00   ................
```

As you can see, the interesting text parts of DOS 3.3 COMMAND.COM start at the even paragraph address 4DC0 and end at address 556B. Now you can create a script file called DEBUG.SCR that contains the commands:

```
D 4DC0 556B
Q
```

Be sure to press the Enter key after the final Q. Put this DEBUG.SCR script file on the same disk as DEBUG.COM and type:

```
DEBUG COMMAND.COM < DEBUG.SCR > DEBUG.OUT
```

Since this process creates a file, make sure you have room on your disk for a new file and that if you're using a floppy disk the write-protect notch isn't covered. When DOS finishes redirecting the files in and out of DEBUG it will simply print a new DOS prompt onscreen. It won't tell you that it created a new file, but you can verify that it did by typing:

```
DIR DEBUG.OUT
```

You'll see something like:

```
DEBUG    OUT    9733  10-14-88   4:52p
```

You can examine this file with your word processor, or with the EDLIN text editor on your DOS disk. Or you could simply type:

```
MORE < DEBUG.OUT
```

This command will redirect the DEBUG.OUT output file into MORE.COM, which will display a screenful of the file at a time. You can either type any character key to see each additional screenful, or press Ctrl-Break or Ctrl-C to abort the display and return to the DOS prompt.

Notice that the command:

```
DEBUG COMMAND.COM < DEBUG.SCR > DEBUG.OUT
 (1)         (2)           (3)          (4)
```

had four parts. The first part started running DEBUG. The second had DEBUG load COMMAND.COM into memory. The third provided the necessary DEBUG Display and Quit commands, and the fourth told DOS to send the output to a file rather than to the screen.

You could remove the second step and shorten the process a bit, by changing the DEBUG.SCR file. Add two lines to the beginning and call this new file DEBUG-NEW.SCR:

```
N COMMAND.COM
L
D 4DC0 556B
Q
```

Then then issue the shorter command:

```
DEBUG < DEBUGNEW.SCR > DEBUG.OUT
```

The N (Name) command in the first line of DEBUGNEW.SCR tells DEBUG that a future Write or Load command will apply to the file whose name follows. The L (Load) command on the second line loads that file into memory just as if you had typed it in after the word DEBUG at the DOS prompt.

Be careful when dealing with files that end in EXE. Both DOS and DEBUG have to shuffle things around a bit in memory when working with EXE files. You'll notice a difference right away if you load one (try the DOS SORT.EXE file, for instance) into

DEBUG and type D. Instead of starting the display at address 100, DEBUG will begin at address 0. And if you try to change the file and write it back to disk, DEBUG won't let you.

It is possible to change the contents of an EXE file with DEBUG. If you read about an interesting patch for an EXE file, copy the file and give the copy an extension other than EXE, such as XXX. (Put the original safely away on another disk or in another subdirectory so you don't accidentally write over it later.) Then load this copy into DEBUG, and treat it like any other file. After you make the changes in the file with the XXX extension, write them to disk and quit. When you're back at the main DOS prompt, make sure you put the original EXE file on another disk or in another subdirectory, and use the RENAME (or REN) command to change the extension from XXX to EXE. Then run it to check your changes. Finally, decide whether you want to use the newer version or the older version of the program — don't keep two similarly named versions of a file on any hard disk. If you prefer the older version, erase the newly changed one. If you like the new, patched version better, rename the old one by giving it an OLD suffix, or copy it to an archive floppy disk and make sure it's gone from your hard disk.

As was shown earlier with the BEEP.COM program, DEBUG makes it a snap to create small programs. All BEEP.COM really does is use DOS function call 2 to display a single character onscreen. It just so happens that printing this ASCII 7 character onscreen makes your system beep.

But printing one character isn't very dramatic. Fortunately, it's nearly as easy to print a whole screenful. You wouldn't actually want to fill the entire screen, since the DOS prompt that appears after such a program finishes running will scroll some of the lines off the top. So we'll settle for 23 lines. And we'll fill these lines with hearts.

One of the hallmarks of topnotch programming these days is the ability to make screens "pop." It's much more dramatic to have a screenful of information flash instantaneously onto your screen than to watch it flicker slowly down the glass a line at a time. However, speedy displays and DOS don't mix. Virtually all the fast screen techniques involve low-level BIOS or memory-shuffling routines. The HEART.COM program below is designed to extend the DOS-based BEEP.COM example, not break any speed limits. Type in the following HEART.SCR script file:

```
N HEART.COM
A
MOV CX,730    ; repeat 1,840 times (23 lines x 80 chars)
MOV DL,3      ; ASCII 3 is a heart character
MOV AH,2      ; DOS "display output" function
INT 21        ; gets DOS rolling
LOOP 107      ; jumps back a line 1,839 times
RET

RCX
C
W
Q
```

(If you don't have a word processor or EDLIN available, you can create this file in DOS by adding a line at the very top that says:

```
COPY CON HEART.SCR
```

Then type the above script, omitting the comments after the semicolons and the semicolons themselves. When you're all done, press the Enter key an extra time, then press the F6 function key, then Enter again.)

Once you've created the script file, put it on the same disk as DEBUG and type:

```
DEBUG < HEART.SCR
```

This will create a slightly enhanced version of the BEEP.COM file called HEART.COM. It prints a heart-shaped character instead of a character that beeps, and does it 1,840 times (23 rows x 80 characters per row). Run it and 92 percent of your screen will fill up with hearts. Put it in someone's AUTOEXEC.BAT file on Valentine's Day.

(Okay, nobody likes slow programs. If you really want to see how must faster it can be to use BIOS services than DOS routines, type in the following script:

```
N FILLFAST.COM
E 100 B4 02 BA 00 00 B7 00 CD 10 B4 08 CD 10 88 E7 B8
E 110 00 06 B9 00 00 BA 4F 18 CD 10 B4 02 BA 00 00 B7
E 120 00 CD 10 B9 30 07 B8 03 0A B7 00 CD 10 B4 02 BA
E 130 00 17 B7 00 CD 10 C3
RCX
37
W
Q
```

This program, FILLFAST, reads the attribute in the upper lefthand corner of the screen and fills most of the screen instantly with hearts in that color.)

Let's look at the original HEART.COM program closely to see what's going on. To do this, use DEBUG's U (Unassemble) command. Get the ball rolling by typing:

```
DEBUG HEART.COM
```

When you see the familiar DEBUG prompt, find out how long the file is by typing:

```
RCX
```

and pressing the Enter key twice. Or, cheat by looking at the line in the HEART.SCR script between RCX and W. Either way, you'll figure out that it's 0C bytes (decimal 12) in length.

As with most of DEBUG, you could issue an Unassemble command using one of two syntaxes. The easy way is entering the starting address and the length:

```
U 100 L C
```

This looks cryptic, but it simply means "try to convert the 12 (hex C) bytes of machine-level code starting at memory offset 100 into recognizable assembly language commands." Finally, type Q to quit and press Enter. The whole process look like:

```
C>DEBUG HEART.COM
-RCX
CX 000C
:
-U 100 L C
33F7:0100 B93007            MOV      CX,0730
33F7:0103 B203              MOV      DL,03
33F7:0105 B402              MOV      AH,02
33F7:0107 CD21              INT      21
33F7:0109 E2FC              LOOP     0107
33F7:010B C3                RET
-Q
```

(Ignore the 33F7 segment address, as always.) The harder way to issue the Unassemble command is to enter explicit starting and stopping addresses. The starting address is easy since DEBUG loads all COM files at offset 100. And since the file is 0C bytes long, the ending address is starting address + length - 1, or:

$$100 + C - 1 = 10B$$

Technically you don't have to subtract the 1, since all leaving it in will do is stretch out the display one extra line. But the file starts at address 100, not address 101. The first byte of the file is at address 100, the second at 101, the third at 102, and the last (12th) at address 10B. So the command:

```
U 100 10B
```

would have produced the same display as U 100 L C.

You may have noticed that the display produced by the U command is almost identical to the HEART.SCR script file that created it. The Unassemble command usually produces a reasonable facsimile of the original, although since certain assembler programs turn slightly different assembly language instructions into the same machine-level code, DEBUG may not be able to turn things back exactly the way they were. But it'll almost always be close enough.

DEBUG's U display does provide something very useful that wasn't in the script — the addresses of each instruction. In this case you really need to have the addresses handy to see what's going on.

The middle of both the BEEP.COM and HEART.COM programs are pretty much the same:

```
BEEP.COM            HEART.COM
       .                   .
       .                   .
       .                   .
    MOV DL,7            MOV DL,3
    MOV AH,2            MOV AH,2
    INT 21             INT 21
       .                   .
       .                   .
       .                   .
```

Both programs use the DOS "display output" function call 2, which looks at the value in the DL register and prints the ASCII character with that value onscreen. With BEEP.COM the value here is 7; with HEART.COM it's 3. And both programs use the RET instruction to jump control back to COMMAND.COM when they're finishing executing.

But HEART.COM adds two additional lines that work hand in hand:

```
MOV CX,730
     .
     .
     .
LOOP 107
```

If you're handy with BASIC, the MOV CX and LOOP instructions are similar to BASIC's FOR...NEXT commands. Both tell your program to repeat a process a certain number of times. The BASIC version of HEART.COM would look something like:

```
100 FOR A=1 TO 1840
110 PRINT CHR$(3);
120 NEXT A
130 SYSTEM
```

In assembly language you can specify how many times you want something to repeat by moving that number into the CX register. Filling 23 lines, each 80 characters long, means printing the heart character 1,840 times (730 in hex). The first time the HEART.COM program executes, it stuffs this hex 730 value into CX, displays the ASCII 3 character, and then executes the LOOP 107 instruction. At this point LOOP does two things. First, it subtracts 1 from the number in the CX register, turning the original 730 into 72F (since hex 730 - 1 = 72F). Then it checks to see if this number is equal to 0 (after subtracting 1 from the current value enough times it will be). Since 72F is greater than 0, LOOP tells the program to loop back to the address specified after the word LOOP — offset 107.

As you can see from the unassembled listing, address 107 contains the instruction INT 21, which tells DOS to execute a function call again. Nothing has changed in any of the registers, so DOS looks in register AH, sees the 2 that was there earlier, and starts executing the same "display output" function call 2. It looks in register DL to see which character to display, finds the 3 that was there before, and prints a character 3 heart. Then it reaches the LOOP instruction once more, reduces the value in the CX register by 1 from 72F to 72E, sees that this number is not yet equal to 0, and loops back to address 107.

After 1,839 loops the value in the CX register will be 1. This time (after printing the 1,840th heart), when the program hits the LOOP instruction, LOOP will subtract 1, check and see that the value in the CX register is finally 0, and end the looping process. The program will have its first opportunity to execute the instruction on the line following the LOOP 107; each previous time LOOP jumped it back to address 107. Since this instruction is RET, the program finishes running and hands control back to COM-MAND.COM.

But this program gets boring after you run it a few times. So to spice it up, change the character it prints. If you like music, you might want to see a screen full of notes. All you have to do is change the value in the DL register from 3 to E (decimal 14). You can change this value one of two ways. But first you have to figure out where in memory the value is. By looking at the Unassemble listing you can spot it in a second:

```
33F7:0103 B203          MOV     DL,03
```

The Unassemble listing is made up of three parts. The lefthand column contains the address of the instruction in memory, in segment:offset form. (Yes, ignore the 33F7 segment address. But jot down the 103 offset address.) Immediately after the address is the second part of the listing — a hexadecimal representation of the actual machine-level code that puts the CPU through its paces. In this case it's B203. B2 is shorthand that tells the CPU to move a value into the DL register. The 03 is the value it moves. At the right edge of the listing is DEBUG's best guess at what the programmer's original assembly language instruction was.

Each address in memory contains a single byte that DEBUG displays as a two-digit hex number (it pads a single digit value like A with a 0, turning it into 0A). The B203 machine-level code actually represents two bytes, B2 and 03. Since the two-byte B203 code begins at offset 103, the actual hex value at address 103 is B2. The address of the 03 value is 104.

So to change the HEART.COM program so it displays musical notes instead of hearts, all you really have to do is put a value of 0E at address 104, and then use the Write command to make the change stick. You'll probably also want to give the file a new name like MUSIC.COM or NOTE.COM.

The easiest way to do this is to use the E (Enter) command (although you could also manage with the somewhat similar F (Fill) command). You can use the Enter command in expert or nervous mode. In expert mode you enter the address and the new value blindly at the same time and then write the changed file to disk. In nervous mode you first enter just the address and have DEBUG report what's there before you make the change. If you see a value there that tells you you're at the wrong address, you just press the Enter key to cancel the command and return to the DEBUG prompt.

Here's what the process would look like in expert mode, assuming you're absolutely sure the value you want changed is at address 104, and assuming you want to save the new file as MUSIC.COM:

```
C>DEBUG HEART.COM
-E 104 0E
-N MUSIC.COM
-W
Writing 000C bytes
-Q
```

You would type everything shown except the C and - prompts and the "Writing 000C bytes" message. And you could enter the new value after the 104 as E instead of 0E if you liked.

Because you specified a new name with the N command, DEBUG will create a brand new file called MUSIC.COM the same length as the HEART.COM program you started out with, and otherwise identical except for the one change at address 104. It won't alter the original HEART.COM program; all it did was borrow HEART.COM's code. You'll end up with two programs on your disk, HEART.COM and MUSIC.COM.

If you're the cautious type, you'll probably want to use the nervous mode. Type DEBUG HEART.COM to get the ball rolling, and when you see the DEBUG - prompt, just type:

```
E 104
```

and press the Enter key. When you specify an address after the E command but not a new value, DEBUG displays the address and the value that's currently there and then prints a period (.). It parks the cursor directly to the right of the period, ready for you to enter a new value that will replace the existing one:

```
33F7:0104  03._
```

If you're satisfied that this is where you want to make the change, just type in the new value and press Enter. If you realize you're at the wrong address, you can press Enter without putting in a new value, to abort the process.

If you do type in a new value at this point and then lock it in by pressing the Enter key, you can check to make sure you entered the correct number at the correct address by pressing F3. DEBUG uses the same function key tricks as DOS and EDLIN. So whenever you hit the F3 key, DEBUG will type in the previous command for you automatically. If you did enter a new value, pressing the F3 key will display the address and the new value, and a period, and sit there waiting to see if you want to change it again. Since you probably don't, just tap the Enter key and you'll be right back at the DEBUG prompt.

If you entered the new value in nervous mode, and then pressed F3 to check on your handiwork, the screen would look like this:

```
C>DEBUG HEART.COM
-E 104
33F7:0104  03.0E
-E 104
33F7:0104  0E.
-N MUSIC.COM
-W
Writing 000C bytes
-Q
```

The E command is actually far more flexible than these simple changes indicate. The following few examples are just dummies; don't try typing them in since they won't do anything except illustrate the proper E command syntax.

You can use E to enter a new string of characters:

```
E 4D3 "This is a test"
```

Or you can enter a series of bytes in hex notation:

```
E A27 41 7C 3C 3E 24 28 29 29
```

Or you can mix strings and bytes:

```
E 2F0 41 7C "A test" 3C 3E 24 28 29 29
```

If you use the E command in nervous mode (okay, it's not actually called nervous mode) instead of working a single byte at a time, you can move forward and backward through your entire file by pressing the space bar or the minus key. Each time you tap on the space bar DEBUG will print the value of the next higher address onscreen and skip to it. When it has printed eight values onscreen it will jump down to the next line and start to print another eight. If you hit either of the minus keys, DEBUG will start marching in the other direction and print the next lower address onscreen, one to a line. (If you lean on the space bar or minus key long enough, you'll reach the top or bottom of the segment and DEBUG will cycle through the entire segment again.)

To try scanning forward and then backward through the NOTE.COM file, load it into DEBUG with the command:

```
DEBUG NOTE.COM
```

and then type:

```
E 100
```

to get the ball rolling. Then start tapping on the space bar and minus keys to navigate your way through. The following example steps all the way through the 12-byte file from front to back (by pressing the space bar 11 times) and then from back to front (by hitting the minus key 11 times):

```
-E 100
33F7:0100   B9.    30.    07.    B2.    0E.    B4.
02.   CD.
33F7:0108   21.    E2.    FC.    C3.-
33F7:010A   FC.-
33F7:0109   E2.-
33F7:0108   21.-
33F7:0107   CD.-
33F7:0106   02.-
etc.
```

When you're all done, press the Enter key by itself, or Ctrl-Break or Ctrl-C to return to the DEBUG prompt.

DEBUG's Fill (F) command is especially handy for replacing a large chunk of memory with one repeating character. If you wanted to put a 0 in every memory address from offset 100 to offset D000 — nearly 53,000 (decimal) zeros — you could do it instantly with the command:

```
F 100 D000 0
```

You could also use the Fill command to change the one value at address 104 so the program displays a musical note rather than a heart. The command:

```
F 104 L 1 0E
```

would do it. This tells DEBUG to start at address 104 and fill a range of memory 1 byte long with the value 0E.

DEBUG provides another way to change BEEP.COM. When you originally created the file you used a script file that turned on DEBUG's mini-assembler with an A command and then fed assembly language instructions (such as MOV AH,2 and INT 21) into it. You can use the A command to make selective patches as well. The assembly language instruction that tells the DOS "display output" function call 2 which character to display is:

```
33F7:0103   B203              MOV    DL,03
```

As you can see from the Unassemble (U) listing, this instruction is located at address 103 in memory. To insert one or more new assembly language instructions in memory, enter the A command followed by the address where the new instructions will start, and then enter the new lines. When you're done, just press the Enter key by itself to exit the mini-assembler and return to the DEBUG prompt. Finally, use the Unassemble command to check your work. To turn HEART.COM into MUSIC.COM using this technique, first

Unassemble the code to see which address to alter, then enter the A command along with this address to make the change, then use Unassemble again to check your typing. Enter the new name (with N), write the new file to disk (with W), and quit (Q). The whole process would look like:

```
C>DEBUG HEART.COM
-U 100 L C
33F7:0100 B93007       MOV       CX,0730
33F7:0103 B203         MOV       DL,03
33F7:0105 B402         MOV       AH,02
33F7:0107 CD21         INT       21
33F7:0109 E2FC         LOOP      0107
33F7:010B C3           RET
-A 103
33F7:0103 MOV DL,0E
33F7:0105
-U 100 L C
33F7:0100 B93007       MOV       CX,0730
33F7:0103 B20E         MOV       DL,0E
33F7:0105 B402         MOV       AH,02
33F7:0107 CD21         INT       21
33F7:0109 E2FC         LOOP      0107
33F7:010B C3           RET
-N MUSIC.COM
-W
 Writing 000C bytes
-Q
```

If you're not crazy about hearts or notes, you can substitute just about any character at address 104. For an interesting effect, try values B0, B1, or B2 (which produce interesting textures), or F8, F9, or FA, which will fill your screen with dot patterns. The IBM character set has some other interesting possibilities as well. Once you've created HEART.COM, type in the following PICTURE.SCR script file to see some of the possibilities:

```
N HEART.COM
L
E 104 B0
N PATTERN1.COM
W
E 104 B1
N PATTERN2.COM
W
E 104 B2
```

```
N PATTERN3.COM
W
E 104 F8
N DOT1.COM
W
E 104 F9
N DOT2.COM
W
E 104 FA
N DOT3.COM
W
E 104 0B
N MAN.COM
W
E 104 0C
N WOMAN.COM
W
E 104 01
N FACE1.COM
W
E 104 02
N FACE2.COM
W
Q
```

To create the files, make sure HEART.COM, PICTURE.SCR, and DEBUG.COM are on your disk, that your disk has room on it for a few files, and that if you're using a floppy disk, that the write-protect notch isn't covered. Then type:

```
DEBUG < PICTURE.SCR
```

When it finishes, run PATTERN1, PATTERN2, PATTERN3, DOT1, DOT2, DOT3, MAN, WOMAN, FACE1, and FACE2 to see what these look like.

While DEBUG offers a handful of additional commands, the only other one serious power users probably need to know about is Move (M). Microsoft and IBM misnamed this command since it really copies memory values instead of moving them. The term "move" incorrectly suggests that DEBUG gets rid of the original after relocating it to a new place. In fact, DEBUG leaves the original alone, unless the new place you move it to overlaps itself.

If your file contains the message "This is a test" at address 100 and you move (copy) this block of 14 characters to a new location 15 bytes later (at address 10E), you'll end up with:

```
"This is a testThis is a test"
```

at address 100. But if you take the same block of text and instead move it up just five bytes (to address 104), you'll get:

```
"ThisThis is a test"
```

since the new address overlaps most of the old one.

Moves can be a bit tricky, because you have to make sure you don't accidentally obliterate any existing parts of your program, and because you have to remember to adjust the value in the CX register to compensate for any change in length.

To see Move in action, first create a small file called MOVETEST.COM, by typing in the following MOVE1.SCR:

```
N MOVETEST.COM
A
MOV AH,09
MOV DX,0108
INT 21
RET

E 108 "DEBUG is",D,A
E 112 "very",D,A
E 118 "powerful.",D,A,24
RCX
24
W
Q
```

Be sure to leave the blank line after RET, and to press the Enter key after the final Q. Then redirect this script file into DEBUG with the command:

```
DEBUG < MOVE1.SCR
```

When you run MOVETEST.COM (by typing MOVETEST at the DOS prompt), all it will do is print:

```
DEBUG is
very
powerful.
```

MOVETEST.COM takes advantage of the DOS "display string(s)" function call 9. When DOS sees a value of 9 in the AH register, it looks in the CX register for an address that tells it where the text strings are located. Then it displays any ASCII strings it finds starting at that address and continuing until a character 24 ($) tells it to stop. (If you try this yourself, remember that you need to put an:

```
,0D,0A
```

or simply:

```
,D,A
```

at the end of each string when you want a carriage return and line feed.)

When you use the Move command you have to give DEBUG two pieces of information — what you want copied, and where you want it copied to. You can tell DEBUG what part of memory you want copied either by specifying explicit starting and stopping addresses, or by listing the starting address and telling it how many bytes to copy. In either case you then have to specify the new destination address (where you want this copied chunk of memory to go).

All of the examples below use starting addresses and lengths rather than explicit starting and stopping addresses, but either technique will work. The number immediately following each M is the starting address. The number following each L is the length — the number of bytes to move. The final number in each line is the new destination address.

Let's say that after looking at everything DEBUG can do, you want to change the MOVETEST.COM message to be more emphatic. To do this, create the following MOVE2.SCR script file:

```
N MOVETEST.COM
L
M 118 L C 130
M 112 L 6 118
M 112 L 6 11E
M 112 L 6 124
M 112 L 6 12A
RCX
3C
W
Q
```

Then redirect the file into DEBUG with the command:

```
DEBUG < MOVE2.SCR
```

Finally, run the changed version MOVETEST and you'll see the new message:

```
DEBUG is
very
very
very
very
```

```
very
powerful.
```

The MOVE2.SCR script file contains five Move instructions that copy small blocks of information from one place to another in memory. First it summons the old MOVETEST.COM file by using the N command to tell DEBUG which file you want to work on, and then the L command to load this file into memory. Then it uses the Move command to insert an additional copy of the line:

```
"powerful.",D,A,24
```

18 hex (24 decimal) bytes higher (later) in memory. Here's a step-by-step scorecard of what happens:

Original arrangement of MOVETEST.COM text:		After the first Move instruction:	
Address	Text starting at this address	Address	Text starting at this address
108	"DEBUG is",D,A	108	"DEBUG is",D,A
112	"very",D,A	112	"very",D,A
118	"powerful.",D,A,24	118	"powerful.",D,A,24
		.	
		.	
		.	
		130	"powerful.",D,A,24

MOVE2.SCR has to copy the line containing "powerful" before it makes any other moves, to get it safely out of the way. The second Move instruction copies the word "very" (plus the 0D and 0A carriage return and line feed characters) on top of it. This obliterates the first six letters of the original "powerful" at address 118:

After the second Move instruction:

Address	Text starting at this address
108	"DEBUG is",D,A
112	"very",D,A
118	"very",D,A,"ul.",D,A,24
.	
.	
.	
130	"powerful.",D,A,24

The third Move instruction finishes wiping out the tail end of the original "powerful" at address 118:

After the third Move instruction:

Address	Text starting at this address
108	"DEBUG is",D,A
112	"very",D,A
118	"very",D,A,
11E	"very",D,A,
	.
	.
130	"powerful.",D,A,24

The final two Move instructions fill in the gap:

After the fifth Move instruction:

Address	Text starting at this address
108	"DEBUG is",D,A
112	"very",D,A
118	"very",D,A,
11E	"very",D,A,
124	"very",D,A,
12A	"very",D,A,
130	"powerful.",D,A,24

All these five Move commands really do is push the word "powerful" up to a higher address in memory, and then fill in the gap by making four additional copies of the word "very" (plus the 0D and 0A carriage return and line feed characters that follow it). Each of the four new occurrences of "very" (and its 0D,0A) takes up six characters. So the file has to be 4 x 6 = 24 bytes longer (decimal 24 = 18 in hex notation). The old MOVETEST.COM file was 24 (hex) bytes long. MOVE2.SCR reset the CX register to 3C to reflect the increased length (hex 24 + 18 = 3C).

Now that you lengthened the file, what about making it smaller? Shortening a file with the Move command is even easier than stretching it out. Let's say you want to change the display so it says simply:

```
DEBUG is
powerful.
```

All you have to do is move the "powerful" line down from its 130 address so it overwrites the first "very" at address 112. Actually, since the string "powerful" (along with the 0D,0A,24 characters that follow it) is twice as long as each "very" string (and its 0D,0A characters), this will overwrite the first two occurrences of "very."

This short MOVE3.SCR script file will do it:

```
N MOVETEST.COM
L
M 130 L C 112
RCX
1E
W
Q
```

Once you've created MOVE3.SCR, redirect it into DEBUG with the command:

```
DEBUG < MOVE3.SCR
```

Moving the line "powerful" (and its 0D,0A,24 suffix) from address 130 down to address 112 actually leaves a lot of unneeded text still in memory — three orphaned occurrences of "very" at addresses 11E, 124, and 12A as well as the original "powerful" at address 130. The DOS display string function call won't even get to all this extra text, because it will stop printing when it hits the first character 24 ($). When you moved the "powerful" line down from address 130 to address 112, you brought the $ with it. DOS will stop dead in its tracks when it reaches this $, even though more text is in memory beyond it.

In order to get rid of all this unneeded MOVETEST.COM text, the MOVE3.SCR script file adjusted the value in the CX register from 3C (decimal 60) bytes down to 1E (decimal 30) bytes. Technically it really didn't have to make the file any smaller. Because of the way DOS allocates disk space, even a one-byte file takes up a minimum of 2,048 (2K) bytes, and can hog as much as 8,192 bytes (8K) on an XT. So making the file 30 bytes shorter isn't going to save any disk space. And since the DOS display text function call will stop working as soon as it reaches the first $, it will ignore the unneeded text that follows. But why be sloppy?

Here's what your system's memory looked like after MOVE3.SCR shortened the MOVETEST.COM file:

After the single MOVE3.SCR
Move instruction:

Address	Text starting at this address	
108	"DEBUG is",D,A	
112	"powerful.",D,A,24	
11E	"very",D,A,	
124	"very",D,A,	All of this is unused.
12A	"very",D,A,	
130	"powerful.",D,A,24	

Starting Up DEBUG

Format: **DEBUG** *or* **DEBUG d:[path]FILENAME**

To start DEBUG, type either:

```
DEBUG
```

or:

```
DEBUG [d:][path]filename[.ext]
```

substituting the name of the file you want to examine or change in place of [d:][path]filename[.ext].

If you type just DEBUG and press Enter all you'll see is the DEBUG - hyphen prompt. If you type DEBUG and then the name of a file DOS can locate, you'll still see nothing but the DEBUG hyphen prompt. However, when you specify a filename on the DOS command line (e.g., DEBUG COMMAND.COM), DEBUG will load that file into memory. You can then display or modify any part of that file. If you do make any changes you can then write the modified file back to disk. You can start DEBUG without including a filename on the command line, and then later use the N (Name) and L (Load) commands to load a file for DEBUG to examine or change.

Most of the time you'll want to start DEBUG by specifying a filename on the DOS command line. The only times you wouldn't want to are when you need to examine what's already loaded in memory or create a brand new file. But even then you still may want to include a filename on the command line.

If you specify a file DEBUG can't locate, such as a brand new file you're trying to create, you'll see a "File not found" message, followed on the next line by the normal hyphen prompt. If you're trying to load an existing file and you see this message, you either typed in the filename incorrectly or you were trying to load a file in another subdirectory or on another disk that DOS couldn't locate. If this happens, type Q and hit Enter to quit, then make sure that file is handy and restart.

If you are trying to create a brand new file, you have to tell DEBUG what to name it. While you can do this with the N (Name) command, specifying the new name on the DOS command line will have the same effect. You'll still see the "File not found" message, but this will let you Write (W) the new file to disk later without having to re-enter it with the DEBUG N command.

For example, if you were on drive C: and you wanted to look inside your system ROM to see the copyright date, or if you wanted to examine any other part of memory, you'd start by typing simply DEBUG. All you'd see is the DEBUG prompt:

```
C>DEBUG
-
```

If you then entered D to display the contents of memory, DEBUG would show you whatever happened to be loaded at offset 100 (hex) of DEBUG's data segment.

If you wanted to examine the copy of COMMAND.COM in your \DOS subdirectory, you'd type DEBUG and the path and filename:

```
C>DEBUG \DOS\COMMAND.COM
-
```

Type D and then press Enter at this point and you'd see the first 128 bytes of COMMAND.COM.

If you wanted to create a brand new file called NEWHEART.COM, you could either specify it on the command line:

```
C>DEBUG NEWHEART.COM
File not found
-
```

or you could use the N (Name) command:

```
C>DEBUG
-N NEWHEART.COM
-
```

Naming a File for Loading or Writing

Format: N [d:][path]filename[.ext]

You can't load or write a file unless you first specify a filename one of two ways. You can either enter a filename on the DOS command line (e.g., DEBUG COMMAND.COM), or you can use the N command to do it later. For example,

```
DEBUG GREEN.COM
```

or

```
-N GREEN.COM
```

If you try to use the W command to write a file without having first specified a name, DEBUG won't oblige, and will simply print the error message "(W)rite error, no destination defined."

If you start DEBUG without specifying a filename, and want to load an existing file (like YELLOW.COM) later, you have to use the N command to give DEBUG the filename you want it to load:

```
C>DEBUG
-N YELLOW.COM
-L
```

The N command comes in very handy when you're modifying a file and you want to save the modified version without destroying the original. Let's say you had a file on your disk called RED.COM that cleared your screen, set the colors (on a CGA, VGA, or EGA only) to red text on a white background, and even set the border to red if you were using a CGA (and did nothing if you weren't). Don't have such a file handy? Then make sure DEBUG is on your disk, and at the DOS prompt type:

```
DEBUG RED.COM
E 100 B8 00 06 B9 00 00 BA 4F 18 B7 74 CD 10 B4 02
E 10F BA 00 00 B7 00 CD 10 B0 04 BA D9 03 EE C3
RCX
1D
W
Q
```

Ignore the "File not found" message DEBUG prints when you start. If you wanted to change the file slightly so it set the text and border colors to blue instead of red, you could patch the program at locations 10A for the text color and 117 for the border. To do this, you'd use the E command and type the following:

```
DEBUG RED.COM
E 10A 71
E 117 01
N BLUE.COM
W
Q
```

Notice that after entering the patches with the E command, you used the N command to give the modified file a new name. By doing this you created a second file called BLUE.COM and left the first RED.COM file alone. If you hadn't done this you would have saved the changed file as RED.COM — and RED.COM would have set your colors to blue.

You could also have created a file called PURPLE.COM at the same time you created RED.COM, by adding two new E instructions and another N and W command. If you had typed:

```
DEBUG RED.COM
E 10A 71
E 117 01
N BLUE.COM
```

```
W
E 10A 75
E 117 05
N PURPLE.COM
W
Q
```

the first W would have written the changes to a file called BLUE.COM that set your colors to blue on white. The second W would have written the second set of changes to a file that the second N named PURPLE.COM.

Displaying Memory Contents

Format: **D [address][address]** *or* **D address length**

Microsoft and IBM call the D command "Dump" but you may want to think of it as "Display." Use it to examine from 1 to 65,536 bytes of memory at a time.

Issuing a D command on a typical 80-column screen will display three things:

1. *At the left edge of your screen*, the segment and offset addresses of the memory you want to examine, in even-paragraph chunks. A paragraph is a slice of memory 10 hex (decimal 16) bytes long that is evenly divisible by hex 10; in other words a chunk of memory that starts at an offset address ending in a 0. 100 and 110 and FE0 and CC0 are all paragraph addresses. 101 and 112 and FE9 and CCF are not.
2. *In the middle part of your screen*, the hex values of the bytes in that paragraph. If you ask DEBUG to display the whole paragraph, you'll see decimal 16 bytes. If you ask it to start displaying memory at an address that's not a paragraph boundary, you'll see fewer than decimal 16. DEBUG will insert a hyphen between bytes 7 and 8. (Since the first byte in each paragraph is byte 0, the hyphen is smack in the middle, between the 8th and 9th byte in each row.)
3. *At the right edge of your screen*, the ASCII representation of any values between hex 20 and 7E (decimal 32 and 126). DEBUG displays a period (.) for any value below hex 20 or greater than hex 7E.

If you issued the command:

```
-D F000:0 L 30
```

to display the hex 30 (decimal 48) bytes starting at offset 0 of segment F000 on an IBM AT (this address happens to be the beginning of the AT's BIOS), you'd see:

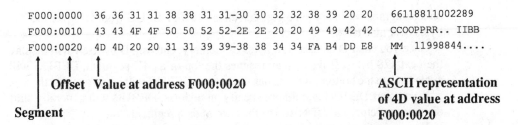

```
F000:0000   36 36 31 31 38 38 31 31-30 30 32 32 38 39 20 20   66118811002289
F000:0010   43 43 4F 4F 50 50 52 52-2E 2E 20 20 49 49 42 42   CCOOPPRR.. IIBB
F000:0020   4D 4D 20 20 31 31 39 39-38 38 34 34 FA B4 DD E8   MM 11998844....
```

Offset Value at address F000:0020

Segment

**ASCII representation
of 4D value at address
F000:0020**

Note that in this case DEBUG displayed periods after 11998844 because the values there (FA B4 DD E8) are higher than 7E. But it displayed periods after CCOOPPRR because the values there (2E 2E) are the hex representation of actual periods.

The double letters in the message are there because of the way display memory is arranged, in odd- and even-address chunks. To see what this really says, you can copy this message from the part of memory where it normally sits — the very beginning of segment F000 — to the part of memory that controls your video display. On a color system the beginning of video memory is located at address B800:0. On a monochrome system it's B000:0. (If you have a mono system, substitute B000 for B800 in the statement below.) Load DEBUG and type:

```
-M F000:0 L 2C B800:0
```

The M command (Move) copies the first 2C (decimal 44) bytes of memory from offset 0 of segment F000 — the beginning of the AT ROM BIOS — to offset 0 of segment B800 (the beginning of color video memory, and the upper lefthand corner of a color screen). On the upper lefthand corner of either screen you'll see a crazy-quilt of attributes and the letters:

```
6181028 COPR. IBM 1984
```

The long number is the part number for the ROM chip that contains the message. The rest is IBM's copyright notice. The unusual colors (or mono attributes on a mono system) are artifacts.

Video memory is arranged so that the even-numbered bytes contain the values of the characters you want to display, and the odd-numbered ones hold the attributes. Since each value appears twice, the system will display the even-numbered ones as the characters these represent, and then translate the odd-numbered versions of each into the attributes for these characters. You may enter D commands in four slightly different ways:

1. If you enter D by itself, DEBUG will display 128 bytes of memory. If you begin the display on an even paragraph boundary, as you would if you had just loaded DEBUG and issued no other commands, DEBUG will display these 128 bytes in eight even rows (paragraphs). If you had previously displayed a part of memory that didn't start

on a paragraph boundary (an offset that ends in a 0), DEBUG would stagger the 128 bytes over nine rows.

Once you enter D and see 128 bytes of memory, entering D by itself will display the next 128 bytes. If the display reaches the top of a 64K segment, DEBUG will cycle back to the bottom; if it reaches the bottom DEBUG will begin again at the top.

If you start DEBUG and do not specify an address, DEBUG will generally start displaying memory at offset 100 of the current data segment.

However, if you enter a D without any address after it, and display a few successive memory blocks by entering just D a few more times, and then later load a COM file (by entering an N and a filename that ends with .COM and then an L), and then enter a D all by itself, DEBUG will start displaying bytes at 100 again, instead of remembering the last address it displayed.

2. If you enter a D with a single address after it, DEBUG will display the 128 bytes beginning with that address. If you follow this immediately by entering just a D with no address after it DEBUG will show you the very next 128 bytes after the first 128 that you specified.

If you enter an address in segment:offset form, DEBUG will show you the contents of memory in the segment you specified. If you omit the segment and simply enter the offset, DEBUG will assume you want it to look inside its default data segment — the one it will load your programs into if you ask it to.

You can also enter segment:offset addresses by using the alphabetical shorthand form of the segment (such as DS:100 when you want to specify offset 100 of the data segment), but this is really just for serious programmers.

3. If you enter a D followed by an address, then an L and a hex number range from 1 to 0000 (0000 is shorthand for 10000), DEBUG will display the number of bytes in the range specified, starting at the address specified. This will let you examine just one single byte (if the range number is 1), or an entire 64K segment (if the range number is 0000 and you're starting at offset 0) in one continuous scrolling list. If you want to break out of an overly long display, just type Ctrl-Break or Ctrl-C.

4. If you enter a D followed by two addresses, DEBUG will display the contents of memory starting at the first and continuing to the second. You may specify a segment and offset for the first address, but only an offset for the second.

For example, to display the single byte of memory starting at offset 0 of segment F000, you could enter either:

```
-D F000:0 0
```

which tells DEBUG to display memory starting and stopping at offset 0 of segment F000, or:

```
-D F000:0 L 1
```

which tells DEBUG to display one byte of memory starting at offset 0 of segment F000.
To display the entire F000 64K segment of memory, you could enter either:

```
-D F000:0 FFFF
```

or:

```
-D F000:0 L 0000
```

Or you could type:

```
-D F000:0
```

and press the Enter key 512 times. The first two examples will scroll the display in one continuous gulp. The third will do it in 128-byte slices.

All of the following examples assume you loaded COMMAND.COM version 3.3 into memory either by typing DEBUG COMMAND.COM at the DOS command line, or by entering DEBUG, then using successive N COMMAND.COM and L commands to take care of it.

To view COMMAND.COM from the beginning of the file in even eight-paragraph chunks, you'd simply keep typing D and pressing the Enter key:

```
-D
30F9:0100  E9 2D 0D BA DA 0A 3D 05-00 74 1B BA BF 0A 3D 02   .-....=..t....=.
30F9:0110  00 74 13 BA 85 0A 3D 08-00 74 0B BA 71 0A 3D 0B   .t....=..t..q.=.
30F9:0120  00 74 03 BA 62 0A 0E 1F-E8 6A 06 EB 0C CD 21 72   .t..b....j....!r
30F9:0130  D2 B4 4D CD 21 2E A3 EA-0B E9 76 01 2E F6 06 59   ..M.!.....v....Y
30F9:0140  0C 01 74 0C 2E F6 06 59-0C 02 74 03 E9 01 13 CF   ..t....Y..t.....
30F9:0150  2E F6 06 59 0C 04 74 11-80 FC 01 72 F2 80 FC 0C   ...Y..t....r....
30F9:0160  77 ED 83 C4 06 F9 CA 02-00 2E 80 0E 59 0C 04 FB   w...........Y...
30F9:0170  0E 1F A1 F3 0B 0B C0 75-06 50 B4 0D CD 21 58 F7   .......u.P...!X.
-D
30F9:0180  06 97 0B FF FF 74 4B 0B-C0 75 47 E8 5F 02 E8 A8   .....tK..uG._...
30F9:0190  03 73 39 53 8E 06 97 0B-26 8B 1E 04 00 83 FB 00   .s9S....&.......
30F9:01A0  74 08 06 8E C3 B4 49 CD-21 07 26 8A 0E 01 00 26   t.....I.!.&....&
30F9:01B0  8B 1E 02 00 B4 49 CD 21-89 1E 97 0B FF 0E FC 0B   .....I.!........
30F9:01C0  75 D2 5B 88 0E ED 0B C6-06 5A 0C 00 E8 C3 05 E8   u.[......Z......
30F9:01D0  40 02 33 C0 8B E8 A2 F8-0B A2 F9 0B E8 1C 00 39   @.3............9
30F9:01E0  06 F3 0B 74 06 C7 06 F3-0B FF FF 80 26 59 0C FB   ...t.........&Y..
30F9:01F0  38 06 E9 0B 75 03 E9 25-01 F9 CB 50 33 C0 2E 86   8...u..%...P3...
```

and so on. Not really much to look at here.
To view a continuous list of internal DOS commands, you would enter:

```
-D 5448 556B
```

which tells DEBUG to display everything from offsets 5448 through 556B:

```
30F9:5440                     4E 4F 54 84 09 0A 45 52        NOT...ER
30F9:5450  52 4F 52 4C 45 56 45 4C-48 0A 05 45 58 49 53 54   RORLEVELH..EXIST
30F9:5460  DB 09 00 03 44 49 52 03-CB 0E 04 43 41 4C 4C 02   ....DIR....CALL.
30F9:5470  BD 0A 04 43 48 43 50 02-D2 15 06 52 45 4E 41 4D   ...CHCP....RENAM
30F9:5480  45 01 0B 12 03 52 45 4E-01 0B 12 05 45 52 41 53   E....REN....ERAS
30F9:5490  45 01 A2 11 03 44 45 4C-01 A2 11 04 54 59 50 45   E....DEL....TYPE
30F9:54A0  01 83 12 03 52 45 4D 02-04 01 04 43 4F 50 59 03   ....REM....COPY.
30F9:54B0  15 2A 05 50 41 55 53 45-02 95 11 04 44 41 54 45   .*.PAUSE....DATE
30F9:54C0  02 20 21 04 54 49 4D 45-00 38 22 03 56 45 52 00   . !.TIME.8".VER.
30F9:54D0  79 13 03 56 4F 4C 01 23-13 02 43 44 01 C2 18 05   y..VOL.#..CD....
30F9:54E0  43 48 44 49 52 01 C2 18-02 4D 44 01 05 19 05 4D   CHDIR....MD....M
30F9:54F0  4B 44 49 52 01 05 19 02-52 44 01 49 19 05 52 4D   KDIR....RD.I..RM
30F9:5500  44 49 52 01 49 19 05 42-52 45 41 4B 00 F5 28 06   DIR.I..BREAK..(.
30F9:5510  56 45 52 49 46 59 00 27-29 03 53 45 54 02 AA 16   VERIFY.').SET...
30F9:5520  06 50 52 4F 4D 50 54 02-90 16 04 50 41 54 48 02   .PROMPT....PATH.
30F9:5530  93 14 04 45 58 49 54 00-62 16 04 43 54 54 59 03   ...EXIT.b..CTTY.
30F9:5540  6D 15 04 45 43 48 4F 02-B2 28 04 47 4F 54 4F 02   m..ECHO..(.GOTO.
30F9:5550  F1 0A 05 53 48 49 46 54-02 76 0A 02 49 46 02 34   ...SHIFT.v..IF.4
30F9:5560  09 03 46 4F 52 02 4E 0D-03 43 4C 53               ..FOR.N..CLS
```

Remember that since DEBUG loads COM files at address 100, these offsets are hex 100 bytes higher than they actually appear in the file. Here's a BASIC program to display the internal commands for any IBM COMMAND.COM version from 2.0 through 3.3. Note that the offsets the BASIC program uses are hex 100 lower than the ones you'd enter in DEBUG:

```
100 ' DBUGLIKE.BAS — Displays internal DOS commands
110 ' (for IBM COMMAND.COM versions 2.0-3.3 only)
120 DEFINT A-Z:CLS:DIM T(16),W(6),X(6),Y(6),Z$(6)
130 FOR A=1 TO 6
140 READ W(A):READ X(A):READ Y(A):READ Z$(A):NEXT
150 OPEN "COMMAND.COM" AS #1 LEN=1:FIELD #1,1 AS A$
160 FOR B=1 TO 6:IF LOF(1)=W(B) THEN 180 ELSE NEXT
170 PRINT "For IBM versions 2.0-3.3 only!":CLOSE:END
180 PRINT "COMMAND.COM VERSION ";Z$(B)
190 PRINT "(DEBUG addresses are &H100 bytes higher!)"
200 PRINT:FOR C=X(B) TO Y(B) STEP 16
210 PRINT "XXXX:";HEX$(C);SPC(2);
220 FOR D=0 TO 15:GET #1,C+D+1
230 H$=HEX$(ASC(A$)):T(D)=ASC(A$)
240 IF LEN(H$)=1 THEN H$="0"+H$
250 PRINT H$;
260 IF D=7 THEN PRINT "-"; ELSE PRINT " ";
```

```
270 NEXT:PRINT SPC(2);
280 FOR E=0 TO 15
290 IF T(E)<32 OR T(E)>127 THEN PRINT ".";:GOTO 310
300 PRINT CHR$(T(E));
310 NEXT:PRINT:NEXT:CLOSE:END
320 DATA 17664,&H39A0,&H3AC0,2.0
330 DATA 17792,&H39C0,&H3AD0,2.1
340 DATA 22042,&H4940,&H4A60,3.0
350 DATA 23210,&H4BF0,&H4D00,3.1
360 DATA 23791,&H4E10,&H4F20,3.2
370 DATA 25307,&H5340,&H5460,3.3
```

You could have viewed the same list of version 3.3 internal commands by typing:

```
-D 5448 L 124
```

This would display hex 124 bytes of memory starting at offset 5448.

Or, you could examine these commands simply by typing:

```
-D 5448
```

and pressing Enter, and then typing just D and pressing Enter twice. Entering D and a single address will display 128 bytes starting at that address. Typing D by itself after that will keep displaying consecutive 128-byte chunks following the one you specified.

Note that while you can enter a range (using the L command to specify a length of bytes to display) after you enter an address, you can't just enter a range by itself. The command:

```
-D L124
```

will produce an error message.

DEBUG remembers which addresses you specified most recently when using the D command. If you use D to view memory between offsets 100 and 200, then use the U command to unassemble the code between offsets 600 and 700, and then enter D by itself, DEBUG will display memory starting at 201 rather than 701, because the last byte the D command displayed was at offset 200.

Entering New Memory Contents

Format: **E address [list]**

The versatile Enter command lets you insert new memory values and modify existing ones. You can use it in one of two modes:

1. You may specify an address and a value and have DEBUG blindly enter that value at that address.

2. Or you may enter an address, have DEBUG display the value currently stored at that address, and change the value only if you want to.

The first brute-force technique lets you enter a block of new information at one time. This comes in handy when you're entering strings of characters, or when you're following a script.

The second technique lets you confirm your modifications by verifying the current values before you make any changes. And it lets you jump forward or backward through the file a byte at a time. For example, many users rely on the E command to enter small COM programs. Try typing in the following REMINDER.SCR file using a pure ASCII word processor:

```
N REMINDER.COM
E 100 B4 09 BA 08 01 CD 21 C3 42 61 63 6B 20 75 70 20
E 110 79 6F 75 72 20 77 6F 72 6B 20 64 61 69 6C 79 21
E 120 0D 0A 24
RCX
23
W
Q
```

Of course, since all this program does is print a message that says:

```
Back up your work daily!
```

it's actually easier to use the E command to enter the message directly than to type in the individual hex values of the letters in the string:

```
N REMINDER.COM
E 100 B4 09 BA 08 01 CD 21 C3
E 108 "Back up your work daily!"
E 120 0D 0A 24
RCX
23
W
Q
```

In both cases you're creating a new file, so you really don't care what memory values your brand new program is overwriting. And since you're following a published script you can pretty much enter the values without worrying about damaging anything.

But when you're changing values inside an existing file you really should verify that you're modifying the proper bytes.

Let's make a simple change in the REMINDER.COM file so it beeps at you to drive the "Back up..." message home. One easy way is to replace the exclamation point (character 21 hex) with an ASCII character 7. Printing a character 7 onscreen causes a beep.

To do this you have to find the memory address that currently stores a value of 21, and enter a 7 at that address. You can see from looking at the script file you typed previously that the file is hex 23 bytes long (this is the value entered below the RCX command that sets the file length), and that the exclamation point is very near the end of the file.

To figure out the exact address, look at the middle of the second script file:

```
E 108 "Back up your work daily!"
E 120 0D 0A 24
```

Notice that the actual message starts at address 108, and that the three characters that follow the message begin at address 120. Since the exclamation point is the last character in the string, its location is right before the three characters that start at offset 120.

(You could, of course, zero in on the exact address by counting from the "B" in "Back" — at address 108 — and working your way one byte at a time across to the "!" at the end. Each character represents one byte, so you'd simply count 108...109...10A etc. But it's easier to assume that the exclamation point is at the address directly before the three characters starting at 120.)

Here's where the the interactive mode of the E command comes in handy: New DEBUG users sometimes forget that in hex the number right before 20 is 1F, not 19. So if you used the interactive E mode to change 21 to 7 and you thought the right address was 119, when you entered the 119 address you'd see:

```
-E 119
30F9:0119  20.
-Q
```

(If you try this yourself, remember that you'll see another number in place of the 30F9 to the left of the colon, because this is the segment address, which will vary depending on your system configuration.)

Notice that the E 119 command reported that the value at address 119 was 20. Since you wanted to replace an existing value of 21, not 20, offset 119 is the wrong address.

Fortunately, the interactive E mode lets you scan ahead in the file byte by byte until you reach the proper value. To scan ahead, just tap the space bar until you see the value you're looking for. This would look like:

```
-E 119
30F9:0119  20.   64.   61.   69.   6C.   79.   21.
```

The value of 21 is actually located six bytes later, at address 11F. Once you found it by leaning on the space bar, you could enter a new value of 7 to the right of the period DEBUG displays, then use the W and Q commands to write the changed file to disk and quit:

```
-E 119
30F9:0119  20.    64.    61.    69.    6C.    79.
21.7
-W
Writing 0023 bytes
-Q
```

If you wanted to keep the original REMINDER.COM file (with the exclamation point) intact and create an additional file that beeped, you could add a line to give the modified file a new name like REMINDR2.COM:

```
-E 119
30F9:0119  20.    64.    61.    69.    6C.    79.
21.7
-REMINDR2.COM
-W
Writing 0023 bytes
-Q
```

It's easy to get too far ahead in the file when jumping byte by byte by tapping the space bar. If this happens you can move backward by hitting the minus (hyphen) key. You'll know you went too far if you see the three final characters — the 0D, 0A, and 24. If this happens, hit the minus key several times to back up to the 21, enter the new value, then execute the same closing commands as above.

```
-E 119
30F9:0119  20.    64.    61.    69.    6C.    79.    21.
30F9:0120  0D.    0A.    24.-
30F9:0121  0A.-
30F9:0120  0D.-
30F9:011F  21.7
-REMINDR2.COM
-W
Writing 0023 bytes
-Q
```

The interactive E command also comes in handy when you have to replace several characters in a row.

Some commercial word processing programs stick hex 1A (decimal 26) end-of-file markers onto the back of text files to pad out their lengths. If you combine two such files into one, it's possible to end up with end-of-file markers in the middle of the file — which will confuse these programs (and DOS as well) into thinking the files end prematurely. If this happens, you can use DEBUG to scan through the file byte by byte. Whenever you see a value of 1A in the middle of your text, you can replace it with a space (a hex 20).

Whenever you see any other value you can press the space bar to skip over it and leave it untouched.

If you know that you combined two files, but when you try to load them into your word processor or examine them with the DOS TYPE command, the file seems to end with:

```
This is the end of the first little file.
```

Examine the file with DEBUG. Figure out the hex file length by typing RCX, and then use the Search (S) command to look for any 1A characters that aren't right at the end. You may see something like:

```
-RCX
CX 0780
:
-S 100 L 780 1A
30DD:062B
30DD:062C
30DD:062D
30DD:062E
30DD:062F
30DD:087C
30DD:087D
30DD:087E
30DD:087F
```

The four addresses at the end (087C, 087D, 087E, and 087F) are where they belong — at the end. Remember, if RCX tells you the file is hex 780 bytes long, the file will actually end 100 hex bytes highter, since DEBUG loads files at address 100, not address 0. So these are the last four addresses in the file.

The other five occurrences of 1A that DEBUG's Search command uncovered — 062B, 062C, 062D, 062E, 062F — shouldn't be there, since 1A characters don't belong anywhere in a text file except at the very end. You can see them by using the D command. Here these 1A characters are at the end of the third paragraph (row):

```
-D 600
30DD:0600  54 68 69 73 20 69 73 20-74 68 65 20 65 6E 64 20   This is the end
30DD:0610  6F 66 20 74 68 65 20 66-69 72 73 74 20 6C 69 74   of the first lit
30DD:0620  74 6C 65 20 66 69 6C 65-2E 0D 0A 1A 1A 1A 1A 1A   tle file........
30DD:0630  41 6E 64 20 74 68 69 73-20 69 73 20 74 68 65 20   And this is the
30DD:0640  62 65 67 69 6E 6E 69 6E-67 20 6F 66 20 74 68 65   beginning of the
30DD:0650  20 73 65 63 6F 6E 64 20-6C 69 74 74 6C 65 20 6F    second little o
```

It's easy to get rid of them. You could use the E or Fill (F) commands to do it without confirmation, but if you're the cautious type you might want to make sure you're making changes at the proper addresses. To do so, type:

```
-E 620
30DD:0620  74.    6C.    65.    20.    66.    69.
6C.    65.
30DD:0628  2E.    0D.    0A.    1A.20  1A.20  1A.20
1A.20  1A.20
30DD:0630  41.
-W
Writing 0780 bytes
-Q
```

When DEBUG displayed any character other than 1A, simply press the Enter key to leave it unchanged and skip to the next one. When you do finally see the string of 1A characters, change them by entering hex 20 values (spaces) beside the periods DEBUG prints. Then write the modified file to disk and quit, using the W and Q commands.

If you used the DOS TYPE command now, you'd see something like:

```
This is the end of the first little file.
     And this is the beginning of the second little one.
```

The second line is pushed over several spaces to the right because you changed the end-of-file characters separating the two lines into space characters. You can use your word processor to remove these extra spaces, or you could have used the DEBUG Move (M) command to wipe them out by moving everything five addresses lower from the word "And" on up.

Filling a Block of Memory

Format: **F range list**

The Fill command can double as a brute-force, noninteractive Enter command.

Here are two similar ways to create a program called FOOTBALL.COM. The first uses the Enter (E) command:

```
N FOOTBALL.COM
E 100 B4 09 BA 08 01 CD 21 C3 "Hi Mom!" 0D 0A 24
RCX
12
W
Q
```

The second uses the Fill (F) command:

```
N FOOTBALL.COM
F 100 L 12 B4 09 BA 08 01 CD 21 C3 "Hi Mom!" 0D 0A 24
```

```
RCX
12
W
Q
```

You can see that these two programs are almost identical.

The Fill command is useful for converting data files to text files. Many database managers produce ASCII files that contain nontext information in a "header" at the beginning of the file. If you try to read this file into your own database program, word processor, or spreadsheet, you'll end up with a mess. Sometimes database programs even put end-of-file markers at the beginning of such files to prevent nonauthorized users from peeking at the contents of the file. But you can have DEBUG examine the beginning of the file to see where the ASCII data actually starts, then cover over any nontext information. Just use the Fill command to put spaces (hex 20 characters) over anything before your data. Then use your word processor to remove the spaces. (An even better way is to use the DEBUG Move command to move the part of the file with your data over the nondata part, obliterating anything non-ASCII.)

You can also use the Fill command to wipe out a whole block of troublesome repeating characters in a file. Some word processors insert large numbers of end-of-file markers into text files. And some communications programs stick nulls — character 0s — into files. Both can confound certain commercial programs.

To get rid of these, browse through the file with the Display (D) command or scan through with the Search (S) command to find out where the block of 00 or 1A characters is located. Then use the Fill command to change these characters into something harmless like spaces. (Again, the Move command does this even better.)

If nulls creep into a text file, you might load a file and see nothing but:

```
^@^@^@^@^@^@^@^@^@^@^@^@^@^@^@^@^@^@^@^@^@^@^@^@^@^@^@^@^@^
```

signs. Worse, once your cursor hits these null signs your word processor may choke to a halt and force you to reboot. To get rid of these, figure out where they start and stop:

```
C>DEBUG EXPAND.RPT
-D
3482:0100  00 00 00 00 00 00 00 00-00 00 00 00 00 00 00 00   ................
3482:0110  00 00 00 00 00 00 00 00-00 00 00 00 00 00 00 00   ................
3482:0120  00 00 00 00 00 00 00 00-00 00 00 00 00 00 00 00   ................
3482:0130  00 00 00 00 00 00 00 00-00 00 00 00 00 00 00 00   ................
3482:0140  00 00 00 00 00 00 00 00-00 00 00 00 00 00 00 00   ................
3482:0150  00 00 00 00 00 00 00 00-00 00 00 00 00 00 00 00   ................
3482:0160  00 00 00 00 00 00 00 00-00 00 00 00 00 00 00 00   ................
3482:0170  00 00 00 00 00 00 00 00-00 00 00 00 00 00 00 00   ................
-D
3482:0180  00 00 00 00 00 00 00 00-00 00 00 00 00 00 00 00   ................
3482:0190  00 00 00 00 00 00 00 00-00 00 00 00 00 00 00 00   ................
```

```
3482:01A0  00 00 00 00 00 00 00 00-00 00 00 00 00 00 00 00   ................
3482:01B0  00 00 00 00 00 00 00 49-74 20 73 65 65 6D 73 20   .......It seems
3482:01C0  74 68 65 20 66 69 67 75-72 65 73 20 77 65 27 76   the figures we'v
3482:01D0  65 20 62 65 65 6E 20 75-73 69 6E 67 20 74 6F 20   e been using to
3482:01E0  70 6C 61 6E 20 6F 75 72-20 77 65 73 74 65 72 6E   plan our western
3482:01F0  20 65 78 70 61 6E 73 69-6F 6E 20 61 72 65 20 6F   expansion are o
```

When you tell DEBUG to fill an area of memory you can specify explicit starting and stopping addresses. Or you can enter a starting address and then tell DEBUG how many bytes it should fill beginning with that address.

The 00 null characters start at address 100 and continue to address 1B6. You could change these to asterisks (hex 2A) with either of the following Fill commands:

    -F 100 1B6 2A

or:

    -F 100 L B7 2A

In either case, if you used the:

    -D 100

command to examine the changes, you'd see:

```
-D 100
3482:0100  2A 2A 2A 2A 2A 2A 2A 2A-2A 2A 2A 2A 2A 2A 2A 2A   ****************
3482:0110  2A 2A 2A 2A 2A 2A 2A 2A-2A 2A 2A 2A 2A 2A 2A 2A   ****************
3482:0120  2A 2A 2A 2A 2A 2A 2A 2A-2A 2A 2A 2A 2A 2A 2A 2A   ****************
3482:0130  2A 2A 2A 2A 2A 2A 2A 2A-2A 2A 2A 2A 2A 2A 2A 2A   ****************
3482:0140  2A 2A 2A 2A 2A 2A 2A 2A-2A 2A 2A 2A 2A 2A 2A 2A   ****************
3482:0150  2A 2A 2A 2A 2A 2A 2A 2A-2A 2A 2A 2A 2A 2A 2A 2A   ****************
3482:0160  2A 2A 2A 2A 2A 2A 2A 2A-2A 2A 2A 2A 2A 2A 2A 2A   ****************
3482:0170  2A 2A 2A 2A 2A 2A 2A 2A-2A 2A 2A 2A 2A 2A 2A 2A   ****************
-D
3482:0180  2A 2A 2A 2A 2A 2A 2A 2A-2A 2A 2A 2A 2A 2A 2A 2A   ****************
3482:0190  2A 2A 2A 2A 2A 2A 2A 2A-2A 2A 2A 2A 2A 2A 2A 2A   ****************
3482:01A0  2A 2A 2A 2A 2A 2A 2A 2A-2A 2A 2A 2A 2A 2A 2A 2A   ****************
.3482:01B0  2A 2A 2A 2A 2A 2A 2A 49-74 20 73 65 65 6D 73 20   *******It seems
3482:01C0  74 68 65 20 66 69 67 75-72 65 73 20 77 65 27 76   the figures we'v
3482:01D0  65 20 62 65 65 6E 20 75-73 69 6E 67 20 74 6F 20   e been using to
3482:01E0  70 6C 61 6E 20 6F 75 72-20 77 65 73 74 65 72 6E   plan our western
3482:01F0  20 65 78 70 61 6E 73 69-6F 6E 20 61 72 65 20 6F   expansion are o
```

Later you can use your word processor to get rid of these extra asterisks.

You can also use Fill to clean out a block of memory. If you want to do some serious DEBUG string moving on a file called FIXIT.TXT, it's hard enough to figure out where all the important strings start and stop. If you load a file into a part of memory that already contained similar strings you can get hopelessly lost. To prevent this, you can wipe out any existing values by filling the whole bottom of DEBUG's data segment with uniform background characters. If you wanted to fill the entire workspace with 00 characters, you'd load DEBUG without specifying a filename, fill a large chunk of memory with 00 characters, then Name and Load the file:

```
C>DEBUG
-F 100 7000 00
-N FIXIT.TXT
-L
```

Since IBM and IBM-compatible video displays are memory-mapped, you can see how fast DEBUG fills memory. If you stick decimal 4000 (hex FA0) characters into the right part of memory (address B800:0 for color systems; B000:0 for mono), your screen will instantly fill with the characters you entered. If you have a color system, type:

```
C>DEBUG
-F B800:0 L FA0 "q"
```

and 2,000 blue lowercase "q" characters will appear in a flash. Or substitute a lowercase "t" to end up with 2,000 red lowercase "t" characters. (Use B000:0 instead of B800:0 on mono systems, and forget about colors. Using "q" will underline the entire screen, however.)

A typical 80-column screen holds 2,000 characters. But hex FA0 is equal to decimal 4,000, not 2,000. Why? The PC video memory is divided into even and odd halves. Putting a value at an even address (B800:0, B800:2, etc.) will display the ASCII representation of that character onscreen. Putting a value at an odd address (B800:1, B800:3, etc.) provides the attribute for the character at the next lower address. The hex value for "q" is 71, which produces blue text (blue = 1) on a white background (7 = white). The hex value for "t" is 74, which produces red text (red = 4) on a white background. On mono screens, blue text ends up as underlined text.

Moving a Block of Memory

Format: **M range address**

The Move command is misnamed. It really should be called the Copy command, since it copies data from one place in memory to another rather than moving it. The term "Move" suggests that DOS deletes the original. It doesn't, unless you intentionally overlap the areas involved so the new location overwrites the old one.

You can end up with some strange effects by moving strings into video memory. If you try this, remember that to be recognizable, text has to load at even bytes and attributes for the text at odd bytes.

To see this in action, create the following three short files. First SCRNTST.BAT:

```
ECHO OFF
DIR
PAUSE
DEBUG < SHIFT1
PAUSE
DEBUG < SHIFT2
```

Then SHIFT1:

```
M B800:0 L FA0 B800:52
Q
```

And finally, SHIFT2:

```
M B800:52 L FA0 B800:0
Q
```

Remember to press the Enter key after typing the Q in SHIFT1 and SHIFT2, or your system will hang and you'll have to reboot. Also, these files are written to work on color systems. For mono screens, change the each of the four B800s to B000.

All this will do is fill your screen with a directory listing, then move one 80 x 25 screenful — 4,000 bytes (hex FA0) — of video memory to a slightly higher address and then back. The DIR display will shift over to the right side of the screen and then return to its normal position. If you change the 52 in both SHIFT1 and SHIFT2 to an odd number like 51 or 53, DEBUG will move the even numbered part of memory, your text, into the odd part, turning it into attributes. Then it will move it back to text.

Move is very useful when it comes to eliminating headers on data files. Many database managers create pure ASCII fixed-length files that you can import into a word processor or spreadsheet, except that these files begin with coded information that tells the database the record structure, number of entries, and so on. You can get rid of this header with a few simple DEBUG instructions. Here's a simplified example, using a very small file:

Let's say someone gives you a file called ADRSBOOK containing names and addresses that you need. If you don't have the database program that created the file, and your own database program won't import it, you can't really do much with it. Unless you fix the problem with DEBUG.

First, load the file into DEBUG. Use the RCX command to see how long it is, then plug this length into the Search (S) command to see if it contains a hex 1A end-of-file marker:

```
C>DEBUG ADRSBOOK
-RCX
CX 0400
:
-S 100 L 400 1A
30DD:03B4
```

Now you know that the file is 400 bytes long and that it may end at offset 3B4. (Obviously, not all database file formats will be this easy. But this example uses a genuine database file.) Type D and press the Enter key a few times until you see where the actual data begins:

```
-D
30DD:0100  02 03 00 06 06 58 39 00-4C 41 53 54 00 00 00 00   .....X9.LAST....
30DD:0110  00 00 00 43 0F D9 AA 00-46 49 52 53 54 00 00 00   ...C....FIRST...
30DD:0120  00 00 00 43 08 E8 AA 00-53 54 52 54 41 44 52 53   ...C....STRTADRS
30DD:0130  00 00 00 43 12 F0 AA 00-43 49 54 59 00 00 00 00   ...C....CITY....
30DD:0140  00 00 00 43 08 02 AB 00-53 54 00 00 00 00 00 00   ...C....ST......
30DD:0150  00 00 00 43 02 0A AB 00-5A 49 50 00 00 00 00 00   ...C....ZIP.....
30DD:0160  00 00 00 4E 05 0C AB 00-0D 00 00 00 00 00 00 00   ...N............
30DD:0170  00 00 00 00 00 00 00 00-00 00 00 00 00 00 00 00   ................
-D
30DD:0180  00 00 00 00 00 00 00 00-00 00 00 00 00 00 00 00   ................
30DD:0190  00 00 00 00 00 00 00 00-00 00 00 00 00 00 00 00   ................
30DD:01A0  00 00 00 00 00 00 00 00-00 00 00 00 00 00 00 00   ................
30DD:01B0  00 00 00 00 00 00 00 00-00 00 00 00 00 00 00 00   ................
30DD:01C0  00 00 00 00 00 00 00 00-00 00 00 00 00 00 00 00   ................
30DD:01D0  00 00 00 00 00 00 00 00-00 00 00 00 00 00 00 00   ................
30DD:01E0  00 00 00 00 00 00 00 00-00 00 00 00 00 00 00 00   ................
30DD:01F0  00 00 00 00 00 00 00 00-00 00 00 00 00 00 00 00   ................
-D
30DD:0200  00 00 00 00 00 00 00 00-00 00 00 00 00 00 00 00   ................
30DD:0210  00 00 00 00 00 00 00 00-00 00 00 00 00 00 00 00   ................
30DD:0220  00 00 00 00 00 00 00 00-00 00 00 00 00 00 00 00   ................
30DD:0230  00 00 00 00 00 00 00 00-00 00 00 00 00 00 00 00   ................
30DD:0240  00 00 00 00 00 00 00 00-00 00 00 00 00 00 00 00   ................
30DD:0250  00 00 00 00 00 00 00 00-00 00 00 00 00 00 00 00   ................
30DD:0260  00 00 00 00 00 00 00 00-00 00 00 00 00 00 00 00   ................
30DD:0270  00 00 00 00 00 00 00 00-00 00 00 00 00 00 00 00   ................
-D
30DD:0280  00 00 00 00 00 00 00 00-00 00 00 00 00 00 00 00   ................
30DD:0290  00 00 00 00 00 00 00 00-00 00 00 00 00 00 00 00   ................
30DD:02A0  00 00 00 00 00 00 00 00-00 00 00 00 00 00 00 00   ................
30DD:02B0  00 00 00 00 00 00 00 00-00 00 00 00 00 00 00 00   ................
30DD:02C0  00 00 00 00 00 00 00 00-00 00 00 00 00 00 00 00   ................
```

```
30DD:02D0   00 00 00 00 00 00 00 00-00 00 00 00 00 00 00 00    ................
30DD:02E0   00 00 00 00 00 00 00 00-00 00 00 00 00 00 00 00    ................
30DD:02F0   00 00 00 00 00 00 00 00-00 00 00 00 00 00 00 00    ................
-D
30DD:0300   00 00 00 00 00 00 00 00-00 20 54 65 6E 6E 79 73    ......... Tennys
30DD:0310   6F 6E 20 20 20 20 20 20-20 41 6C 20 20 20 20 20    on       Al
30DD:0320   20 31 38 20 48 6F 67 62-6F 6E 65 20 4C 61 6E 65     18 Hogbone Lane
30DD:0330   20 20 20 54 68 75 64 77-65 6C 6C 47 41 33 30 32       ThudwellGA302
30DD:0340   37 33 20 41 72 6E 6F 6C-64 20 20 20 20 20 20 20    73 Arnold
30DD:0350   20 20 4D 61 74 74 20 20-20 20 31 31 31 20 57 69      Matt       111 Wi
30DD:0360   6E 65 64 61 72 6B 20 53-74 2E 20 20 54 68 69 72    nedark St. Thir
30DD:0370   73 74 79 20 54 58 37 37-36 31 39 20 44 75 6E 6E    sty TX77619 Dunn
```

The data starts at address 30A. And it presumably stops at the end-of-file marker at
address 3B4. (Remember, it's a short file.) What you then have to do is move this block
of data down into memory to the beginning of the file so the data overwrites the header:

```
-M 30A 3B4 100
```

You can use the D command to display the new memory contents at address 100:

```
-D 100
30DD:0100   54 65 6E 6E 79 73 6F 6E-20 20 20 20 20 20 20 41    Tennyson       A
30DD:0110   6C 20 20 20 20 20 20 31-38 20 48 6F 67 62 6F 6E    l       18 Hogbon
30DD:0120   65 20 4C 61 6E 65 20 20-20 54 68 75 64 77 65 6C    e Lane    Thudwel
30DD:0130   6C 47 41 33 30 32 37 33-20 41 72 6E 6F 6C 64 20    lGA30273 Arnold
30DD:0140   20 20 20 20 20 20 20 20-4D 61 74 74 20 20 20 20            Matt
30DD:0150   31 31 31 20 57 69 6E 65-64 61 72 6B 20 53 74 2E    111 Winedark St.
30DD:0160   20 20 54 68 69 72 73 74-79 20 54 58 37 37 36 31      Thirsty TX7761
30DD:0170   39 20 44 75 6E 6E 65 20-20 20 20 20 20 20 20 20    9 Dunne
```

Now you want to write this new file to disk. You don't want to destroy the old one, in
case you made a mistake, so give the new file a name like NEWDB.FIL:

```
-N NEWDB.FIL
```

If you want, you can adjust the length. The data used to start at address 30A, but you
moved it down to address 100. So you can now make the file 30A minus 100, or 20A
bytes shorter. The old file length was 400. If you subtract 20A from 400, you get a new
length of 1F6. Use the DEBUG H (Hex math) command if you're shaky about hex calculations:

```
-H 30A 100
040A  020A
```

```
-H 400 20A
 060A  01F6
```

(After you type in the numbers after the H, DEBUG prints first the sum of the two numbers and then the difference.)

If you've been paying close attention, you might think this file length of 1F6 is too long. After all, if the data started at address 30A and stopped at the end-of-file marker at address 3B4, 3B4 minus 30A is 0AA bytes. Actually, the data in this example is just about this short. What happened was that the database manager padded out the end of the file.

Finally, use the W command to write the new NEWDB.FIL file to disk and the Q file to quit. In this case you were fortunate — the process got rid of the header and left you with a perfectly readable ASCII file. You won't always be so lucky. Sadly, the structure of every database file is different. Some don't even contain ASCII text. But in most cases you can use DEBUG to extract the important data. The critical thing here is to give any files you write to disk a new name so you don't wipe out the old. (Instead of using the N command, you could copy the file before you started working with DEBUG, then load, modify, and write the copy to disk.)

While you can use the Move command to copy text, you may have a harder time moving program instructions. Unless you're really sure you know what you're doing, don't start slicing and dicing your programs by moving blocks of instructions around. For example, if you're starting out with a file that looks like this when displayed with the D command:

```
30DD:0100  41 42 43 44 45 46 47 48-49 4A 4B 4C 4D 4E 4F 50   ABCDEFGHIJKLMNOP
30DD:0110  51 52 53 54 55 56 57 58-59 5A 31 32 33 34 35 36   QRSTUVWXYZ123456
30DD:0120  00 00 00 00 00 00 00 00-00 00 00 00 00 00 00 00   ................
30DD:0130  00 00 00 00 00 00 00 00-00 00 00 00 00 00 00 00   ................
30DD:0140  00 00 00 00 00 00 00 00-00 00 00 00 00 00 00 00   ................
30DD:0150  00 00 00 00 00 00 00 00-00 00 00 00 00 00 00 00   ................
30DD:0160  00 00 00 00 00 00 00 00-00 00 00 00 00 00 00 00   ................
30DD:0170  00 00 00 00 00 00 00 00-00 00 00 00 00 00 00 00   ................
```

you could copy this text by specifying explicit starting and stopping addresses (100 and 11F respectively) and then telling DEBUG where to put the copy (120). After issuing this command, check your work by using the Display command (but tell it to start displaying at address 100):

```
-M 100 11F 120
-D 100
30DD:0100  41 42 43 44 45 46 47 48-49 4A 4B 4C 4D 4E 4F 50   ABCDEFGHIJKLMNOP
30DD:0110  51 52 53 54 55 56 57 58-59 5A 31 32 33 34 35 36   QRSTUVWXYZ123456
30DD:0120  41 42 43 44 45 46 47 48-49 4A 4B 4C 4D 4E 4F 50   ABCDEFGHIJKLMNOP
30DD:0130  51 52 53 54 55 56 57 58-59 5A 31 32 33 34 35 36   QRSTUVWXYZ123456
30DD:0140  00 00 00 00 00 00 00 00-00 00 00 00 00 00 00 00   ................
```

```
30DD:0150   00 00 00 00 00 00 00 00-00 00 00 00 00 00 00 00   ................
30DD:0160   00 00 00 00 00 00 00 00-00 00 00 00 00 00 00 00   ................
30DD:0170   00 00 00 00 00 00 00 00-00 00 00 00 00 00 00 00   ................
```

You can also give DEBUG a starting address and a range of bytes to copy. The first M command took 20 (hex) bytes and copied them without any overlap, yielding 40 bytes. To copy these 40 bytes (again without any overlap) by using an address and a range length, specify the starting address (100), the range length (40), and the destination address (140). The use the D 100 command to view your work:

```
-M 100 L 40 140
-D 100
30DD:0100   41 42 43 44 45 46 47 48-49 4A 4B 4C 4D 4E 4F 50   ABCDEFGHIJKLMNOP
30DD:0110   51 52 53 54 55 56 57 58-59 5A 31 32 33 34 35 36   QRSTUVWXYZ123456
30DD:0120   41 42 43 44 45 46 47 48-49 4A 4B 4C 4D 4E 4F 50   ABCDEFGHIJKLMNOP
30DD:0130   51 52 53 54 55 56 57 58-59 5A 31 32 33 34 35 36   QRSTUVWXYZ123456
30DD:0140   41 42 43 44 45 46 47 48-49 4A 4B 4C 4D 4E 4F 50   ABCDEFGHIJKLMNOP
30DD:0150   51 52 53 54 55 56 57 58-59 5A 31 32 33 34 35 36   QRSTUVWXYZ123456
30DD:0160   41 42 43 44 45 46 47 48-49 4A 4B 4C 4D 4E 4F 50   ABCDEFGHIJKLMNOP
30DD:0170   51 52 53 54 55 56 57 58-59 5A 31 32 33 34 35 36   QRSTUVWXYZ123456
```

Both of the examples above assumed you wanted to move text without overlapping anything. Let's assume you wanted to copy just the first line (ABCDEFGHIJKLMNOP) and get rid of the second (QRSTUVWXYZ123456). The Move command makes it easy. First, start with the original file again:

```
30DD:0100   41 42 43 44 45 46 47 48-49 4A 4B 4C 4D 4E 4F 50   ABCDEFGHIJKLMNOP
30DD:0110   51 52 53 54 55 56 57 58-59 5A 31 32 33 34 35 36   QRSTUVWXYZ123456
30DD:0120   00 00 00 00 00 00 00 00-00 00 00 00 00 00 00 00   ................
30DD:0130   00 00 00 00 00 00 00 00-00 00 00 00 00 00 00 00   ................
30DD:0140   00 00 00 00 00 00 00 00-00 00 00 00 00 00 00 00   ................
30DD:0150   00 00 00 00 00 00 00 00-00 00 00 00 00 00 00 00   ................
30DD:0160   00 00 00 00 00 00 00 00-00 00 00 00 00 00 00 00   ................
30DD:0170   00 00 00 00 00 00 00 00-00 00 00 00 00 00 00 00   ................
```

Then move just the first line down so it overwrites the second one. Both of the following commands would do it:

```
-M 100 10F 110
```

or:

```
-M 100 L 10 110
```

The first tells it to take everything from addresses 100 through 10F and copy it to address 110. The second says to take the hex 10 bytes starting at address 100 and copy them down to address 110. In either case, use the D 100 command afterward and you'd see:

```
30DD:0100  41 42 43 44 45 46 47 48-49 4A 4B 4C 4D 4E 4F 50   ABCDEFGHIJKLMNOP
30DD:0110  41 42 43 44 45 46 47 48-49 4A 4B 4C 4D 4E 4F 50   ABCDEFGHIJKLMNOP
30DD:0120  00 00 00 00 00 00 00 00-00 00 00 00 00 00 00 00   ................
30DD:0130  00 00 00 00 00 00 00 00-00 00 00 00 00 00 00 00   ................
30DD:0140  00 00 00 00 00 00 00 00-00 00 00 00 00 00 00 00   ................
30DD:0150  00 00 00 00 00 00 00 00-00 00 00 00 00 00 00 00   ................
30DD:0160  00 00 00 00 00 00 00 00-00 00 00 00 00 00 00 00   ................
30DD:0170  00 00 00 00 00 00 00 00-00 00 00 00 00 00 00 0A   ................
```

Searching for Characters

Format: **S range list**

The Search command will scan through up to 64K of memory at a time for a list of specified characters and report the starting addresses of any it finds. If DEBUG stumbles over lots of occurrences, it will scroll the addresses off the screen. If it doesn't find any matches it will simply print another DEBUG - prompt.

You can search for individual hex values such as 49 42 4D or for text strings "IBM" or for combinations of both such as "IBM" 41 54. Make sure you specify the precise characters you want DEBUG to find. Looking for "IBM" won't find "I.B.M." and "DIR" won't find "Dir" or "dir" or any other inexact match. To look for such variations, execute multiple searches.

What you see onscreen is not necessarily what you get. *WordStar*, for instance, adds decimal 128 to the ASCII value of the last character in most words. If you search for the word "bullnose" in a *WordStar* file, you may never find it. But if you lop off the last letter, and search for "bullnos" you probably will.

If you're searching all the way through your main 640K of memory, you'll end up seeing reports of phantom matches. When you type in the Search command, DOS enters the command itself in memory, and DEBUG will find occurrences like these as it scans through. So if you make an extensive all-sector search and then go back and use the D command to verify the occurrence, you may not see why DEBUG reported it in the first place. For example, to search through the top segment of memory (ROM BIOS segment F000) for the string "/84" — the copyright date of an early AT — you could use explicit starting and stopping addresses:

```
-S F000:0 FFFF "/84"
```

This tells DEBUG to start searching at address F000:0000 for the string "/84" and continue the search until offset FFFF in that same segment. You could also use a starting address and a range to perform the same search:

```
-S F000:0 L 0000 "/84"
```

This has DEBUG scan 10,000 bytes for the same string, starting at address F000:0000. When searching for text, it's easiest to wrap it in quotes. But you could have specified the actual hex representation for the characters / and 8 and 4 ("/" = 2F; "8" = 38; and "4" = 34):

```
-S F000:0 L 0000 2F 38 34
```

And, obviously, you don't have to scan through an entire segment each time. To search for this string in the first hex 100 bytes of segment F000, you could enter:

```
-S F000:0 FF "/84"
```

or:

```
-S F000:0 L 100 "/84"
```

DEBUG searches through memory very quickly. If it finds lots of occurrences of the string you're looking for, it will scroll the addresses rapidly off the top of the screen. You can get around this problem by echoing everything to your printer, or by redirecting the output to a file.

To send the output to both your screen and printer, turn on your printer and type Ctrl-P or Ctrl-PrtSc. To stop this echoing process, type Ctrl-P or Ctrl-PrtSc again.

To redirect the output to a file, type:

```
DEBUG > OUTPUT.FIL
```

then type in the command that produced the overly large output and press Enter. (Be careful; since DOS is redirecting all of DEBUG's output, you won't be able to see what you type.) Then type Q and press Enter. You should see the DOS prompt again. To view the list of addresses, load the OUTPUT.FIL into your word processor, or use the DOS TYPE command (TYPE OUTPUT.FIL). If the file is long, make sure the DOS MORE.COM utility is handy and type:

```
MORE < OUTPUT.FIL
```

You could also create a tiny file with the single DEBUG command and a Q (to quit) and call the file INPUT.FIL. It might look like:

```
S F000:0 L 100 "/84"
Q
```

(Be sure to include the Q and to press the Enter key after typing the Q or your system will freeze and you'll have to reboot.) Then get into DOS and type:

```
DEBUG < INPUT.FIL > OUTPUT.FIL
```

To search through version 3.3 COMMAND.COM for the DIR command, load COM-MAND.COM into DEBUG, use the RCX command to find out how long the file is, then specify this length in the Search command:

```
C>DEBUG COMMAND.COM
-RCX
CX 62DB
:
-S 100 L 62DB "DIR"
30FB:5170
30FB:5464
30FB:54E2
30FB:54F1
30FB:5500
```

You can check to see exactly what the Search command found by using the D command. To make the screen tidy, replace the very last digit in the addresses DEBUG reported with a 0. So if DEBUG reported a match at 30FB:5464, ask it to look for the hex 10 bytes starting with 5460. (When you're searching through a file and then using the D command to verify the matches, you don't have to specify the segment — the offset address will do fine by itself.)

```
-D 5170 L 10
30FB:5170  44 49 52 3E 20 20 20 00-0E 3B 49 42 4D 20 50 65   DIR>   ..;IBM Pe
-D 5460 L 10
30FB:5460  DB 09 00 03 44 49 52 03-CB 0E 04 43 41 4C 4C 02   ....DIR....CALL.
-D 54E0 L 10
30FB:54E0  43 48 44 49 52 01 C2 18-02 4D 44 01 05 19 05 4D   CHDIR....MD....M
-D 54F0 L 10
30FB:54F0  4B 44 49 52 01 05 19 02-52 44 01 49 19 05 52 4D   KDIR....RD.I..RM
-D 5500 L 10
30FB:5500  44 49 52 01 49 19 05 42-52 45 41 4B 00 F5 28 06   DIR.I..BREAK..(.
```

If you want to scan all the way through a segment such as 3000 for a string like "IBM" you can issue the command:

```
-S 3000:0 0000 "IBM"
```

If you want to scan through every one of the ten segments in main memory (the main 640K is made up of ten individual 64K segments), you can use the DOS function keys to streamline the process of entering so many similar commands. First look through the lowest segment (0000):

```
-S 0000:0 0000 "IBM"
```

Then tap either the right arrow key or the F1 key twice, which repeats the S and the space that follows it from the previous command. Assuming DEBUG didn't find any matches in segment 0000, the screen will look like:

```
-S 0000:0 0000 "IBM"
-S
```

Type in a 1 and press F3, which fills in the rest of the previous command. The screen will look like:

```
-S 0000:0 0000 "IBM"
-S 1000:0 0000 "IBM"
```

You can also use the DOS F2 key plus a character, which repeats the previous command up to the specified character. Pressing F2 and the 1 at this point would print the previous S and space and stop before the 1. You could then enter a 2 and press F3 to complete the command.

An easier way to search through all 16 of your system's segments (including things like ROM BIOS and video areas) is to use a SCAN.BAT batch file:

```
ECHO OFF
IF %1!==! GOTO OOPS
ECHO S 0000:0 L0000 %1 %2 %3 %4 %5 %6 %7 %8 %9 >  RAWFILE
ECHO S 1000:0 L0000 %1 %2 %3 %4 %5 %6 %7 %8 %9 >> RAWFILE
ECHO S 2000:0 L0000 %1 %2 %3 %4 %5 %6 %7 %8 %9 >> RAWFILE
ECHO S 3000:0 L0000 %1 %2 %3 %4 %5 %6 %7 %8 %9 >> RAWFILE
ECHO S 4000:0 L0000 %1 %2 %3 %4 %5 %6 %7 %8 %9 >> RAWFILE
ECHO S 5000:0 L0000 %1 %2 %3 %4 %5 %6 %7 %8 %9 >> RAWFILE
ECHO S 6000:0 L0000 %1 %2 %3 %4 %5 %6 %7 %8 %9 >> RAWFILE
ECHO S 7000:0 L0000 %1 %2 %3 %4 %5 %6 %7 %8 %9 >> RAWFILE
ECHO S 8000:0 L0000 %1 %2 %3 %4 %5 %6 %7 %8 %9 >> RAWFILE
ECHO S 9000:0 L0000 %1 %2 %3 %4 %5 %6 %7 %8 %9 >> RAWFILE
ECHO S A000:0 L0000 %1 %2 %3 %4 %5 %6 %7 %8 %9 >> RAWFILE
ECHO S B000:0 L0000 %1 %2 %3 %4 %5 %6 %7 %8 %9 >> RAWFILE
ECHO S C000:0 L0000 %1 %2 %3 %4 %5 %6 %7 %8 %9 >> RAWFILE
ECHO S D000:0 L0000 %1 %2 %3 %4 %5 %6 %7 %8 %9 >> RAWFILE
ECHO S E000:0 L0000 %1 %2 %3 %4 %5 %6 %7 %8 %9 >> RAWFILE
ECHO S F000:0 L0000 %1 %2 %3 %4 %5 %6 %7 %8 %9 >> RAWFILE
ECHO Q >> RAWFILE
DEBUG < RAWFILE | FIND /V "-" > HITLIST
DEL RAWFILE
ECHO The results are in a file called HITLIST
GOTO END
```

```
:OOPS
ECHO Specify something for %0 to search
ECHO such as hex bytes, eg :  %0 45 3B 61 FF
ECHO or text in quotes, eg:  %0 "qwerty"
ECHO or both, eg:            %0 "qwerty" 45 61
END
```

Be sure to include the line:

```
ECHO Q >> RAWFILE
```

If you omit this, the script won't execute the proper instruction to quit DEBUG, and your system will freeze, forcing you to reboot.

The SCAN.BAT batch file starts out by using the line:

```
IF !%1==! GOTO OOPS
```

to make sure you entered a string to search for. DOS substitutes the first thing that you typed on the command line after the name of the batch file, in place of each %1 replaceable parameter that it sees inside the batch file. If you typed:

```
SCAN "IBM"
```

DOS will replace every occurrence of %1 in the batch file with the string "IBM". If you typed:

```
SCAN "IBM" 20 31
```

DOS would still replace every %1 with "IBM". But it would also replace any %2 it finds with the hex value 20, since 20 is the second thing you typed after the name of the batch file, and any %3 with 31. It replaces any %0 in the batch file with the name of the batch file itself. So in:

```
SCAN "IBM" 20 31
```

DOS would replace any occurrences of %0, %1, %2, and %3 as follows:

```
SCAN    = %0
"IBM"   = %1
20      = %2
31      = %3
```

If you entered just:

```
SCAN
```

the %1 replaceable parameter would be equal to (nothing), since you didn't type anything in after SCAN. The test:

```
IF !%1==! GOTO OOPS
```

means that if you did type something in after SCAN (such as SCAN "IBM"), the %1 would be replaced by "IBM" and the test would become:

```
IF !"IBM"==! GOTO OOPS
```

Now since !"IBM" is clearly not equal to ! the test fails. (Remember, you have to use a double equals sign in batch file tests.) If you didn't enter anything, the test becomes:

```
IF !==! GOTO OOPS
```

This test is true since ! does equal ! and the batch file then executes the rest of the command, jumping to a label named OOPS. Labels are short words starting with colons. When the batch file jumps to the OOPS label it executes the three lines following it, printing a message onscreen that tells the user to enter a parameter next time.

You don't have to specify the colon before the label in a GOTO command (although it won't hurt), but you do have to include it at the point in the batch file where it actually serves as a label. Labels and conditional GOTO commands let you jump around, or *branch*, inside a batch file, adding tremendous power and flexibility.

If you entered just a single parameter, such as "IBM", the batch file would replace every %1 it finds with it, turning a line such as:

```
ECHO S 0000:0 L0000 %1 %2 %3 %4 %5 %6 %7 %8 %9 >  RAWFILE
```

into:

```
ECHO S 0000:0 L0000 "IBM" >  RAWFILE
```

(If your batch file included a line such as:

```
ECHO %1 %1 %1
```

DOS would translate this to:

```
ECHO "IBM" "IBM" "IBM"
```

since it would replace all three instances of %1.)

If you entered only one parameter on the command line after the name of the batch file, DOS would make the rest of the replaceable parameters — %2 through %9 — equal to (nothing) and would effectively discard them.

The single > redirection sign followed by a filename (RAWFILE) tells DOS to send the characters following the ECHO command into the file specified instead of printing them on the screen. A single > command will wipe out an existing file with the name specified; a double >> sign will append the new information without destroying the old one. By starting out with a single > sign you erase any old RAWFILE file that happens to be on your disk. And by following this with a succession of double >> signs, you build up the new RAWFILE file one line at a time.

The SCAN.BAT batch file creates a new script file called RAWFILE. RAWFILE contains instructions to search through all 16 memory segments one by one for the string or hex characters that you entered. In this particular case the file will look like:

```
S 0000:0 L0000 "IBM" 20 31
S 1000:0 L0000 "IBM" 20 31
S 2000:0 L0000 "IBM" 20 31
S 3000:0 L0000 "IBM" 20 31
S 4000:0 L0000 "IBM" 20 31
S 5000:0 L0000 "IBM" 20 31
S 6000:0 L0000 "IBM" 20 31
S 7000:0 L0000 "IBM" 20 31
S 8000:0 L0000 "IBM" 20 31
S 9000:0 L0000 "IBM" 20 31
S A000:0 L0000 "IBM" 20 31
S B000:0 L0000 "IBM" 20 31
S C000:0 L0000 "IBM" 20 31
S D000:0 L0000 "IBM" 20 31
S E000:0 L0000 "IBM" 20 31
S F000:0 L0000 "IBM" 20 31
Q
```

(You'll never see RAWFILE, since the batch file erases it before it exits.)

SCAN.BAT uses two kinds of redirection — sending a file into DEBUG and capturing the output from DEBUG. First, it redirects the contents of RAWFILE into DEBUG just as if you had typed in all the search instructions yourself. Then, it redirects the DEBUG output to a file called HITLIST. When it's all done, all you have to do to see the address of each occurrence of the information you were hunting for is look at HITLIST. The best way to do this is to load HITLIST into your word processor or, use the DOS TYPE command. If HITLIST is long, use the MORE command; make sure the DOS MORE.COM program is handy and type:

```
MORE < HITLIST
```

The SCAN.BAT batch file also pipes the DEBUG output through a FIND filter with the line:

```
DEBUG < RAWFILE | FIND /V "-" > HITLIST
```

As DOS sends each line of output through its FIND.EXE filter utility, it checks to see if the line contains a specified character or string of characters. In this case the specified character it looks for is a hyphen (-). The /V switch after the FIND tells DOS to discard any line it finds that happens to have a hyphen anywhere in it. The FIND utility can either screen out lines that do contain the specified string, or those that don't contain it. (As it's used here the command excludes anything with a hyphen. All DEBUG commands have a hyphen as the first character in each line and you don't want your file cluttered with these commands — you want just the results.) However, filtering the text this way takes a bit more execution time and means you have to have the DOS FIND.EXE program handy. If you don't mind seeing the actual commands in the output, and you want to speed things up slightly, change the line to:

```
DEBUG < RAWFILE > HITLIST
```

This means that once you put the SCAN.BAT file and DEBUG.COM in the same directory you can search all the way through memory for any string, or (up to 9) hex values, or combinations of both simply by typing the word SCAN and the information you're looking for. Make sure that you enclose any text you're hunting for inside quotation marks, and that any values you enter on the command line are in hex notation rather than decimal.

As mentioned earlier, DEBUG will report some phantom addresses where it or DOS temporarily puts copies of the string you specified.

Assembling ASM Instructions

Format: **A [address]**

DEBUG's mini-assembler is an extremely powerful tool. As with all power tools, however, you have to be careful how you use it. If you're carefully copying a program out of a book or magazine, or you're an old hand at assembly language, this DEBUG feature can be incredibly useful. Otherwise, don't experiment, unless you're absolutely sure every last file on your system is backed up — and be especially wary about fooling around with anything that deals with disks, and especially anything that writes.

Serious assembly language programmers will use the IBM/Microsoft full-fledged assembler, which is far more powerful and sophisticated. The mini-assembler is for creating and fixing short programs like the ones in this book.

You can use most of the standard 8086/8088 assembly language syntax in DEBUG. But DEBUG's mini-assembler is not built to handle complex programs. For instance when you want the program flow to jump from one place to another you have to furnish precise addresses of where to go; with full-fledged assemblers you can use "labels" instead of addresses. And DEBUG isn't as flexible or understanding about certain kinds of instructions. But for quick-and-dirty programs it's just what the doctor ordered.

To figure out what to do with it, you'll have to get your hands on a book specially written for serious users who want to pick up the fundamentals of programming. One of the best for beginners is Peter Norton's *Programmer's Guide to the IBM PC* from Microsoft Press.

To use the mini-assembler for the first time, just get into DEBUG and type A at the main DEBUG - prompt. DEBUG will print an address in segment:offset form starting with offset 0100:

```
C>DEBUG
-A
30DD:0100
```

(Ignore the four hex digits to the left of the colon. This will vary from system to system and won't affect what you're doing.)

At this point DEBUG expects you to enter an assembly language instruction. If you don't want to, just press the Enter key and you'll return to the DEBUG prompt. If you do want to, go ahead and enter it. Type MOV AH,05 and press the Enter key:

```
C>DEBUG
-A
30DD:0100 MOV AH,05
30DD:0102
```

DEBUG will accept what you typed, assemble the instruction into machine-readable code at that address, and skip ahead the proper number of bytes to the next free space in memory waiting for you to enter another instruction. Here it translated the MOV AH,05 instruction into something two bytes long, since the next address it displayed was 0102. If you type something DEBUG doesn't understand, it prints an error message and lets you try again at the same address. For instance, if you had accidentally typed:

```
C>DEBUG
-A
30DD:0100 MOV HA,05
                 ^ Error
30DD:0100
```

DEBUG would have caught the mistake and indicated where it was by pointing to it. Then it would put the same 0100 address onscreen a second time to let you enter the corrected version of this instruction.

But since DEBUG liked the MOV AH,05 (you could have just as easily typed MOV AH,5 by the way), it asked you to enter another instruction at address 102. So type in MOV DL,0C:

```
C>DEBUG
-A
30DD:0100 MOV AH,05
```

```
30DD:0102 MOV DL,0C
30DD:0104
```

Again, you can tell it liked what you typed, since it dropped down a line and offered you the chance to enter another instruction at an address two bytes higher, 0104.

(DEBUG is smart enough to know what's legal and what isn't. But it obviously can't tell what's ridiculous. So long as you enter the proper syntax, it will blithely let you create a program to wipe out all the files on your hard disk, or spin into an endless loop that will crash your system. Be extremely careful about all this; one mistyped digit can have catastrophic results. For instance, BIOS interrupt 13 lets you read disk sectors by putting a value of 2 in the AH register. But it lets you write disk sectors by putting a value of 3 in AH. If you accidentally type a 3 instead of a 2, you can kiss your data goodbye.)

To finish the sample program, enter INT 21 to launch DOS into action, and then RET to return to the DOS prompt. You could use INT 20 instead of RET to end short COM programs, but they'll both have the same effect, and RET is easier to type:

```
C>DEBUG
-A
30DD:0100 MOV AH,05
30DD:0102 MOV DL,0C
30DD:0104 INT 21
30DD:0106 RET
30DD:0107
```

When you've entered the last assembly language instruction, you'll see the next address — 0107. Just press the Enter key and you'll return to the main DEBUG prompt. Note the 0107 address, however, since you'll need it for the next step.

You can check your typing by using the Unassemble (U) command. DEBUG will look at the machine-readable code it just assembled, and try to take it apart and reproduce the assembly language instructions you typed in. Since you just started entering instructions at address 0100 and stopped right before 0107, you could type either:

```
-U 100 106
```

or:

```
-U 100 L 7
```

Since you stopped entering instructions right before address 0107, the assembled code occupies seven bytes of memory, not six. Remember that the first byte is at address 100, not 101. And the last byte is at address 106. The first version of the Unassemble command above tells DEBUG to unassemble everything from addresses 100 through 106. The second tells it to unassemble the seven bytes starting at address 100. Both will generate the same display:

```
30F9:0100 B405          MOV AH,05
30F9:0102 B20C          MOV DL,0C
30F9:0104 CD21          INT 21
30F9:0106 C3            RET
```

The leftmost column contains the segment:offset memory addresses that you wanted to examine. The next column shows the hexadecimal representations of the actual machine-level code that DEBUG translated the assembly language instructions into. Sending the two bytes B4 and 05, here stuck together as B405, to the CPU tells it to put a value of (MOV) 05 into register AH. The rightmost column is DEBUG's best guess about which instructions you originally typed.

If you saw at this point that you had made a mistake, you could use the A command to correct it. The program you're in the process of creating will send an ASCII decimal character 12 to the printer, which should generate a form feed. Since DEBUG works exclusively in hex, you have to enter the character in its hex form, 0C (or just plain C). If you forgot this, and entered a decimal 12 instead of a hex C, you'd be telling the program to send a hex 12 (decimal 18) to the printer. If you unassembled your typing, you'd see something like:

```
30F9:0100 B405          MOV AH,05
30F9:0102 B212          MOV DL,12
30F9:0104 CD21          INT 21
30F9:0106 C3            RET
```

To fix this, tell DEBUG you want to re-assemble the instruction beginning at address 102, since you'll have to re-enter the entire MOV DL,0C and this starts at offset 0102:

```
-A 102
```

DEBUG will respond with:

```
30F9:0102
```

Just type in the correct instruction:

```
30F9:0102 MOV DL,0C
```

and press the Enter key. DEBUG doesn't know if you wanted to fix just one instruction or enter several new ones, so it will print the next memory address and offer you the chance to change it as well:

```
30F9:0102 MOV DL,0C
30F9:0104
```

Since all you wanted to re-enter was the single instruction at address 102, press the Enter key to exit the mini-assembler and return to the main DEBUG prompt. Then repeat the unassemble command to verify the correction.

(You could have also used the Enter (E) command to make the change. By looking at the unassembled code you could see that the erroneous value of 12 was at address 103:

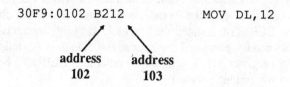

```
30F9:0102 B212          MOV DL,12
```

               address   **address**
                 102   **103**

You could then have typed:

```
-E 103
```

and pressed the Enter key. DEBUG would have responded with:

```
30F9:0103  12.
```

Then enter the correct value of 0C by typing it in and hitting Enter. Use either the Unassemble or Enter commands to verify the change.)

To create the program you just entered, you have to name it, using N FF.COM. First tell DEBUG how long it is, by typing RCX and pressing Enter, then enter 7 when DEBUG displays the colon, and write it to disk (with W), and quit (Q):

```
-N FF.COM
-RCX
CX 0000
:7
-W
Writing 0007 bytes
-Q
```

This program will send a form-feed character (decimal 12, hex 0C) to LPT1:, unless you rerouted printer output somewhere else.

If you go back later to work with the mini-assembler again in the same DEBUG session, DEBUG will remember the last address you used. If you type A without specifying an address after it, DEBUG will assume you want to continue entering new instructions where you left off. Since you left off at address 107 in the above example, you can do some other DEBUG chores and then type:

```
-A
```

to have DEBUG would respond with:

```
30DD:0107
```

Keeping track of the last memory address is handy if you want to continue working on a program in progress. But if you want to create a brand new, unrelated program, you'll have to tell the mini-assembler to start again at address 100:

```
-A 100
```

The mini-assembler is terrific at handling text. To do so, just prefix the text with a DB opcode:

```
C>DEBUG
-A
30DD:0100 MOV AH,09
30DD:0102 MOV DX,108
30DD:0105 INT 21
30DD:0107 RET
30DD:0108 DB "Common sense is not so common.",0D,0A
30DD:0128 DB "                 — Voltaire",0D,0A,24
30DD:0149
-RCX
CX 0000
:49
-N HOWTRUE.COM
-W
Writing 0049 bytes
-Q
```

DEBUG will calculate how long each string is and automatically start the next instruction (or string) at the next available location. So after you entered:

```
30DD:0108 DB "Common sense is not so common.",0D,0A
```

DEBUG figured out that the next string would begin at address 128, and printed:

```
30DD:0128
```

Each line of text is followed by an 0D,0A (or D,A) carriage-return and line-feed combination. The commas separating these from the text are optional; spaces will work just as well. Note also that when you use function 9 of interrupt 21 you have to put a final "$" after the end of the last string. You could have just as easily entered:

```
30DD:0108 DB "Common sense is not so common." D A
30DD:0128 DB "                          — Voltaire" D A "$"
```

If you put your strings at the end of the program, DEBUG makes it a snap to figure out how many bytes to tell the CX register to write. Just look at the address the mini-assembler prints after you enter the last string. In this case it's 149. Since DEBUG began assembling instructions at offset 100, subtract 100 from 149 and tell the CX register to write 49 bytes.

Unassembling Instructions

Format: **U [address]** *or* **U [range]**

Just as DEBUG lets you translate assembly language instructions into machine-readable code (with the Assemble (A) command), it will reverse the process and turn a stream of hex bytes only a CPU can understand back into recognizable assembly language statements. Or at least it will try to.

One of the main problems is that the Unassemble command can't distinguish program instructions from data, and will try to translate the data back into assembly language statements instead of roping it off and indentifying it as something other than program instructions. Another problem is that different assembler programs can turn different variations of assembly language instructions into the same basic code. The DEBUG Unassembly command has no idea which one of the original variations the programmer used, and may not translate every byte back to the exact source code used to create the program. A third problem is that if you give the Unassemble command the wrong starting address, it will start translating things in mid-instruction, and end up with gibberish. And finally, it's best at translating the kinds of short and sweet COM programs DEBUG can create. Long complex programs, and code created by compilers jump around so much and use so many intertwined libraries of subroutines that you really won't be able to make much sense of most Unassembled output.

But this command can be extremely useful in fixing short programs you or someone else created with DEBUG's mini-assembler. Let's say that someone put a program called WARNING.COM on your disk that was supposed to print the message "DO NOT ERASE YOUR FILES NOW!" Unfortunately, the programmer goofed. When you run it, the program prints "ERASE YOUR FILES NOW!"

The first thing to do is load WARNING.COM into DEBUG, see how long it is (by typing RCX and hitting Enter twice), and display the program using the D command:

```
-RCX
CX 0027
:
-D 100 L 27
30F9:0100  B4 09 BA 0F 01 CD 21 C3-44 4F 20 4E 4F 54 20 45   ......!.DO NOT E
```

```
30F9:0110   52 41 53 45 20 59 4F 55-52 20 46 49 4C 45 53 20    RASE YOUR FILES
30F9:0120   4E 4F 57 21 0D 0D 24                                NOW!..$
```

What this tells you is that the actual message inside WARNING.COM is accurate, but that something is wrong with the program portion. You can see by looking at the ASCII display and counting over that the text begins at address 108. But the machine-readable program code from addresses 100 to 107 is inscrutable. Until you use the Unassemble command:

```
-U 100 107
30F9:0100   B409         MOV  AH,09
30F9:0102   BA0F01       MOV  DX,010F
30F9:0105   CD21         INT  21
30F9:0107   C3           RET
```

Now you have to do a little detective work. How does the program work? The first thing to do is look for the workhorses of the programming world — interrupts. In this case the program contains just one instruction that begins with INT. The 21 after the INT tells you the program uses the main DOS interrupt.

By consulting a book such as Norton's *Programmer's Guide to the IBM PC* or IBM's *DOS Technical Reference Manual*, you can look at the description of INT 21 and see that this key interrupt executes dozens of individual function calls and identifies which one to execute by putting the hex value of that function call into the AH register. Sure enough, the very first instruction puts a value of 09 there.

If you then jump to the section detailing function call 09H, you'll see all the important facts that govern its operation. DOS refers to this function call as "Print String" while Norton cautions that it really should be called "Display String." Both sources provide the following information:

1. The string must end in a $ (hex character 24).
2. DOS will send the string to the standard output device (Norton adds that the default is the screen).
3. The value in the data segment's DX register "points" to the beginning of the string.

The second line of the unassembled code shows that the value in DX is 010F. But when you used the D command to display the contents of the program you saw that the text actually started at address 108. So in the erroneous WARNING.COM program, the DX register is pointing somewhere inside the text string rather than at the very beginning of it:

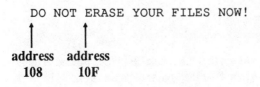

```
DO NOT ERASE YOUR FILES NOW!

    ↑       ↑

address address
  108     10F
```

To fix the problem, change the value in the DX register from 10F to 108. You can do this by using the Assemble (A) command to create a whole new MOV DX,010F instruction at address 102:

```
-A 102
30F9:0102 MOV DX,0108
30F9:0104
```

and then pressing the Enter key when DEBUG prints the following 104 address. Or you can look at the actual machine-level hex byte code, figure out which bytes store the incorrect 010F value, and use the Enter (E) key to replace the old incorrect number with the correct one.

Using the E command on two-byte addresses is a bit tricky. If you look carefully at the unassembled line beginning at address 102:

```
30F9:0102 BA0F01         MOV DX,010F
```

you'll notice that the BA0F01 machine-level code seems to have scrambled the 010F address into 0F01. This happens because of the seemingly backwards (or "backwords") way your computer stores two-byte numbers, *words.*

Each offset address is two bytes long. Two bytes together make up what is called a word. In any word, one byte is higher, or worth more than, the other, just as in the decimal number 39, the 3 is worth more than the 9, since the 3 digit actually stands for 30, not 3. The byte that is worth more is called the *most-significant byte* and the one that's worth less is the *least-significant byte*. These are sometimes abbreviated as MSB and LSB. Grammarians might quibble that these should really be called "more-significant" and "less-significant" but engineers designed this system, not grammarians.

Here's the important part: It takes two bytes in memory to store a word. One byte has a higher address than the other. Your computer stores the most-significant byte of any word at the higher address of the two (and, obviously, the least-significant byte at the lower address).

The word 010F is actually made up of two individual bytes, 01 and 0F. The 01 byte is the most significant, and the 0F the least significant. So the higher 01 byte is at the higher address and the lower 0F at the lower address.

By looking at the output of the D command you issued earlier:

```
30F9:0100  B4 09 BA 0F 01 CD 21 C3-44 4F 20 4E 4F 54 20 45    ......!.DO NOT E
             ↑  ↑  ↑  ↑
address:   100 | 102 | 104
             101   103 |
                     | MSB
               LSB
```

you can count over from the left and see that the lower 0F byte is indeed at the lower address (103) and that the higher 01 byte is at the higher (104) address.

To replace the old incorrect 010F value with the proper 0108 value, first divide the 0108 word in half. Then enter the least-significant byte (the 08 part) at the lower address (103) and the most-significant byte (the 01 part) at the higher address (104). Since the value at address 104 is already 01, you can just replace the 0F at address 103 with 08.

It doesn't matter whether you use the Assemble (A) or Enter (E) command to change the MOV DX,010F instruction to MOV DX,0108. Each has its advantages. In any case, go back and unassemble the beginning part of WARNING.COM again. This time you should see:

```
-U 100 107
30F9:0100 B409          MOV AH,09
30F9:0102 BA0801        MOV DX,0108
30F9:0105 CD21          INT 21
30F9:0107 C3            RET
```

Use the W command to write the changed program to disk and the Q command to quit. If you're nervous about all this, you may want to add another line:

```
-N WARN.COM
```

before you write the modified version. This will create a new file called WARN.COM that won't overwrite the existing WARNING.COM program. If you goofed when modifying the original program, you can erase WARN.COM and try again on the un-damaged original. Another way to safeguard the original is to make a copy of WARN-ING.COM called WARN.COM (or whatever) before making any changes, and then load the WARN.COM copy into DEBUG rather than the WARNING.COM original.

If you had used the Unassemble command on the text part of WARNING.COM (the part that started at address 108), DEBUG would have ended up displaying a meaning-less series of instructions. First figure out how long the program is, by typing RCX and pressing Enter twice. Then use the D command to display everything from address 108 (where you know the text starts) to the end:

```
-RCX
CX 0027
:
-D 108 126
30F9:0100                       44 4F 20 4E 4F 54 20 45          DO NOT E
30F9:0110 52 41 53 45 20 59 4F 55-52 20 46 49 4C 45 53 20   RASE YOUR FILES
30F9:0120 4E 4F 57 21 0D 0D 24                              NOW!..$
```

Then Unassemble the same range of addresses:

```
-U 108 126
30F9:0108 44            INC SP
30F9:0109 4F            DEC DI
```

```
30F9:010A 204E4F        AND  [BP+4F],CL
30F9:010D 54            PUSH SP
30F9:010E 204552        AND  [DI+52],AL
30F9:0111 41            INC  CX
30F9:0112 53            PUSH BX
30F9:0113 45            INC  BP
30F9:0114 20594F        AND  [BX+DI+4F],BL
30F9:0117 55            PUSH BP
30F9:0118 52            PUSH DX
30F9:0119 204649        AND  [BP+49],AL
30F9:011C 4C            DEC  SP
30F9:011D 45            INC  BP
30F9:011E 53            PUSH BX
30F9:011F 204E4F        AND  [BP+4F],CL
30F9:0122 57            PUSH DI
30F9:0123 210D          AND  [DI],CX
30F9:0125 0D2461        OR   AX,6124
```

```
          ↑ ↑ ↑
         125 | |
           126 |
             127
```

Junk. That's why when you're trying to fix a program you have to use the D and U commands together. In many cases neither the U or D will help, since programs often insert (or *hard-wire*) important data into the program code. Programmers use such data to set defaults, provide lookup tables, etc.

Incidentally, you may have noticed that in the above example even though you asked DEBUG to unassemble memory between addresses 108 and 126, DEBUG went all the way to address 127. If you didn't notice, look at three bytes in the unassembled listing at address 125. (They're all lumped together here, but the first is 0D, the second 24, and the third 61. The second value — 24 — is the actual end of the program. Hex 24 is the code for the final "$" you used to mark the end of the string.")

So why did DEBUG display more memory than you specified? It interpreted the 0D2461 clump of bytes that started at address 125 as one big instruction, and displayed the entire instruction rather than lopping the end of it off prematurely. In fact, the Unassemble listing would have been the same if you had used any of the three following ranges:

```
-U 108 125
```

or:

```
-U 108 126
```

or:

```
-U 108 127
```

In each case, once the Unassemble command sniffs out what it thinks is even a single byte of an instruction it will print the entire instruction.

The Unassemble command can interpret the same stream of hex codes in different ways depending on where you tell it to start. Begin at the beginning, and DEBUG will get it right:

```
-U 100 L8
30F9:0100 B409          MOV   AH,09
30F9:0102 BA0801        MOV   DX,0108
30F9:0105 CD21          INT   21
30F9:0107 C3            RET
```

But start at an address one byte too high and DEBUG will turn the first two instructions into mush:

```
-U 101 L8
30F9:0101 09BA0801      OR    [BP+SI+0108],DI
30F9:0105 CD21          INT   21
30F9:0107 C3            RET
30F9:0108 44            INC   SP
```

Start even farther up and you get equally meaningless results:

```
-U 104 L8
30F9:0104 01CD          ADD   BP,CX
30F9:0106 21C3          AND   BX,AX
30F9:0108 44            INC   SP
30F9:0109 4F            DEC   DI
30F9:010A 204E4F        AND   [BP+4F],CL
```

If you're trying to unassemble something and you just know the program is in there somewhere, try a few different starting addresses until you see a display that contains recognizable instructions. It can be especially confusing when you're just a byte or two off. If you're looking for a specific address, start a dozen or so bytes earlier so the Unassemble command has a chance to get properly on track.

When you first start DEBUG, if you enter the U command without any address or range after it, DEBUG will unassemble the first 32 bytes starting at offset 100 (and possibly a few more than 32, if the 32nd byte is in the middle of a single instruction it's trying to display). Each successive time you then hit U without any parameters after it, DEBUG will unassemble the next 32 or so bytes. DEBUG will always remember the last byte it unassembled. If you enter another command, such as D, between two U commands, the second U command will start displaying code right after the address where the first U command stopped — ignoring whatever you happened to do with D. For example, if you want to unassemble the first 32 bytes of COMMAND.COM (version 3.3):

```
C>DEBUG COMMAND.COM
-U
30F9:0100 E92D0D          JMP   0E30
30F9:0103 BADA0A          MOV   DX,0ADA
30F9:0106 3D0500          CMP   AX,0005
30F9:0109 741B            JZ    0126
30F9:010B BABF0A          MOV   DX,0ABF
30F9:010E 3D0200          CMP   AX,0002
30F9:0111 7413            JZ    0126
30F9:0113 BA850A          MOV   DX,0A85
30F9:0116 3D0800          CMP   AX,0008
30F9:0119 740B            JZ    0126
30F9:011B BA710A          MOV   DX,0A71
30F9:011E 3D0B00          CMP   AX,000B
```

DEBUG will actually display the first 33. If you then entered U again without any parameters after it, DEBUG would continue the unassembly process with address 121.

You don't ever have to specify a stopping address. And you can tell DEBUG to start anywhere. If you entered:

```
-U 121
```

DEBUG would display the 32 bytes (and actually end up showing you 33) starting at address 121 and stopping at address 141. If for some perverse reason you wanted to unassemble all of COMMAND.COM version 3.3 you would first find out how long the program is by typing RCX and pressing Enter twice. DEBUG would report a length of 62DB bytes. Then you'd enter the command:

```
-U 100 62DB
```

and sit back and watch for a long while. To stop the display, just hit Ctrl-Break or Ctrl-C.

If you wanted to see the assembly language code for the first two instructions, you could type either:

```
-U 100 105
```

or:

```
-U 100 L 6
```

Both would display the same unassembled code:

```
30F9:0100 E92D0D        JMP  0E30
30F9:0103 BADA0A        MOV  DX,0ADA
```

Fine, fine, you may be saying. But what can you really do with this command that's useful?

Here's something:

It's really incredible that DOS is still back in the dark ages (well, maybe the black and white ages) when it comes to color. Even after half a decade of changes, DOS still clears the screen to grey on black. But it doesn't have to. In fact, the code to set the foreground and background colors to anything you want is already in COMMAND.COM. It's just that the folks who maintain the code have decided they want you to see everything in attribute 07 — and that translates to whitish-grey (the 7) on a black (0) background.

Some programmers feel that you should never patch COMMAND.COM. They say that if you start getting patch-happy you may change something that will have unexpectedly awful results later. But the truth is that if you keep your patches to the barest minimum, it's not so terrible. The only thing you do have to guard against, however, is mixing versions of COMMAND.COM on the same disk, which confuses DOS.

DOS and most other programs do video tasks such as clearing the screen by using BIOS interrupt 10 (hex). Some fancy programs come with their own proprietary screen utilities. But not DOS. When you type CLS, COMMAND.COM scans its list of internal commands, sees that CLS is indeed an internal command, then executes the screen-clearing routine inside itself.

BIOS interrupt 10 provides two similar services called Scroll Window Up (Service 6) and Scroll Window Down (Service 7). These will both open just about any size window onscreen and insert blank lines at the top or bottom to scroll the existing text away. You can tell it exactly how big a window to scroll and what color to make the blank lines by using the following registers:

- AH = the service itself (6 means up, 7 means down)
- AL = how many lines to scroll (a 0 here clears the window)
- BH = the color of the blank lines
- CH = upper lefthand window row
- CL = upper lefthand window column
- DH = lower righthand window row
- DL = lower righthand window column

To clear an entire 25 x 80 screen to blue text on a white background using Service 6, you could create the following code fragment:

```
MOV AX,0600    ; AH=6 means up; AL=0 means clear screen
MOV BH,71      ; color (7=white bkgnd; 1=blue frgrnd)
```

```
MOV CX,0000 ; start at row 0, column 0 (top left corner)
MOV DX,184F ; stop at row 18 (dec 24; col 4F (decimal 79)
INT 10
```

(The reason this fragment tells interrupt 10 to stop the window on the 79th column of the 24th row is that since the screen actually begins on column 0 of row 0, the lower right-hand corner is indeed column 79 of row 24. In wouldn't hurt anything to specify row 25 and column 80 unless you're doing something fancy such as using more than one screen "page." You're probably not.)

This code fragment uses a sort of shorthand in filling the appropriate registers. Instead of putting two separate byte values into the AH and AL registers, it combined the single-byte values (06 and 00) into one double-byte word (0600) and moved this word into the AX register. In this example:

```
MOV AX,0600
        ↑ ↑
       AH AL
```

the 06 fills the AH register and the 00 fills the AL register. This is the same as saying:

```
MOV AH,06
MOV AL,00
```

except that the first way is shorter. The example fills the CX and DX registers using the same kind of shorthand.

You can even assemble this if you want. If you do, be sure to stick a RET command onto it below the INT 10. Tell DEBUG it will be 0E bytes long (with the RCX command). Name it BLUE.COM. Then write it and quit, and when you're back at the DOS prompt type BLUE. To make this really effective you'd have to add some cursor positioning code too, but that's not the point of this exercise.

COMMAND.COM uses a variation of this code fragment to do its screen clearing. To find this COMMAND.COM screen clearing mechanism, use DEBUG's Search (S) command to look for interrupt 10. Load COMMAND.COM into DEBUG. Find out how long your version is by typing RCX and pressing Enter twice (this example uses version 3.3). Then search the whole file for all occurrences of CD 10, the machine-readable code for interrupt 10:

```
C>DEBUG COMMAND.COM
-RCX
CX 62DB
:
-S 100 L 62DB CD 10
```

```
30F9:2B88
30F9:2B94
30F9:2B9B
30F9:2B9F
30F9:2BB0
30F9:2BB8
```

Fortunately these addresses are clumped closely together, which makes it easy to display them all with the Unassemble command in one gulp. Start a few bytes before the first match that the Search command found, and continue a bit past the last one:

```
-U 2B80 2BC0
30F9:2B80  8CC0       MOV  AX,ES
30F9:2B82  3BD0       CMP  DX,AX
30F9:2B84  7735       JA   2BBB
30F9:2B86  B40F       MOV  AH,0F
30F9:2B88  CD10       INT  10
30F9:2B8A  3C03       CMP  AL,03
30F9:2B8C  7609       JBE  2B97
30F9:2B8E  3C07       CMP  AL,07
30F9:2B90  7405       JZ   2B97
30F9:2B92  B400       MOV  AH,00
30F9:2B94  CD10       INT  10
30F9:2B96  C3         RET
30F9:2B97  B40B       MOV  AH,0B
30F9:2B99  33DB       XOR  BX,BX
30F9:2B9B  CD10       INT  10
30F9:2B9D  B40F       MOV  AH,0F
30F9:2B9F  CD10       INT  10
30F9:2BA1  8AD4       MOV  DL,AH
30F9:2BA3  FECA       DEC  DL
30F9:2BA5  B618       MOV  DH,18
30F9:2BA7  33C0       XOR  AX,AX
30F9:2BA9  8BC8       MOV  CX,AX
30F9:2BAB  BB0007     MOV  BX,0700
30F9:2BAE  B406       MOV  AH,06
30F9:2BB0  CD10       INT  10
30F9:2BB2  33D2       XOR  DX,DX
30F9:2BB4  B700       MOV  BH,00
30F9:2BB6  B402       MOV  AH,02
30F9:2BB8  CD10       INT  10
30F9:2BBA  C3         RET
30F9:2BBB  BEBA3D     MOV  SI,3DBA
30F9:2BBE  AC         LODSB
30F9:2BBF  8AC8       MOV  CL,AL
```

This display may look a bit daunting, but you'll see how easy it is to map it out. Incidentally, this whole process is easier when you do it on paper. To get a printout of it, turn your printer on and type either Ctrl-P or Ctrl-PrtSc before you issue the U 2B80 2BC0 command. DOS will print each line both on the screen and on the printer. Then type Ctrl-P or Ctrl-PrtSc one more time to turn this printer "echoing" feature off.

The first thing to do is to figure out what each of the six INT 10s does. Get out your copy of Norton's *Programmer's Guide to the PC* or any other reference book that lists the various BIOS services. Scan through the instructions right before each INT 10 until you see a MOV AH. In some programs you may have to look for a MOV AX, since it may use the same kind of "shorthand" mentioned earlier. When the program gets to an INT 10 it looks at the value in the AH register to figure out which interrupt 10 service to execute. Here's an annotated version of the unassembled listing, trimmed on the top and bottom:

```
30F9:2B86 B40F          MOV AH,0F    ; Service 0F =
30F9:2B88 CD10          INT 10       ; get video mode
================================================================
30F9:2B8A 3C03          CMP AL,03
30F9:2B8C 7609          JBE 2B97
30F9:2B8E 3C07          CMP AL,07
30F9:2B90 7405          JZ  2B97
30F9:2B92 B400          MOV AH,00    ; Service 00 =
30F9:2B94 CD10          INT 10       ; set video mode
================================================================
30F9:2B96 C3            RET
30F9:2B97 B40B          MOV AH,0B    ; Service 0B =
30F9:2B99 33DB          XOR BX,BX    ; set palette
30F9:2B9B CD10          INT 10
================================================================
30F9:2B9D B40F          MOV AH,0F    ; Service 0F =
30F9:2B9F CD10          INT 10       ; get video mode
================================================================
30F9:2BA1 8AD4          MOV DL,AH
30F9:2BA3 FECA          DEC DL
30F9:2BA5 B618          MOV DH,18
30F9:2BA7 33C0          XOR AX,AX
30F9:2BA9 8BC8          MOV CX,AX
30F9:2BAB BB0007        MOV BX,0700
30F9:2BAE B406          MOV AH,06    ; Service 06 =
30F9:2BB0 CD10          INT 10       ; scroll window up
================================================================
30F9:2BB2 33D2          XOR DX,DX
30F9:2BB4 B700          MOV BH,00
30F9:2BB6 B402          MOV AH,02    ; Service 02 =
30F9:2BB8 CD10          INT 10       ; set cursor position
```

The one we're hunting for is the large Service 06 near the bottom. This doesn't look exactly like the BLUE.COM example mentioned above, but all the necessary values and settings are there, even if COMMAND.COM does things differently. For instance, when BLUE.COM put a 00 in register AL to tell interrupt 10 to clear the window it did it with the instruction:

```
MOV AX,0600
```

(The 00 at the end of 0600 filled AL.) COMMAND.COM does it with the command:

```
XOR AX,AX
```

since using a XOR operation on any value cancels out that value and turns it into 0. It followed this with a MOV AH,06 instruction to put the 6 into AH.

The register that controls color settings for Service 06 is BH. BLUE.COM put a 71 there:

```
MOV BH,71
```

The left digit of the value in BH (here it's 71) controls the background. The right digit controls the foreground (text). The basic IBM color scheme is:

0 Black	8 Dark grey
1 Blue	9 Bright blue
2 Green	A Bright green
3 Cyan (light blue)	B Bright cyan
4 Red	C Bright red
5 Magenta (purple)	D Bright magenta
6 Brown (dark yellow)	E Yellow
7 White (light grey)	F Bright white

So 71 will produce blue text on a white background.

COMMAND.COM puts a value of 07 into this register, which means grey-white text on a black background. All you have to do to patch this permanently is to change the value to something more colorful. A value of 4E will clear your screen to bright yellow text on a red background, so try it. Once you know the technique you can always change it to something else.

Look at the annotated listing again. The 07 byte is at address 2BAD (easy to remember for version 3.3 — "too bad"). So to patch COMMAND.COM so that it will clear the screen and print bright yellow text on a red background in version 3.3, type:

```
C>DEBUG COMMAND.COM
-E 2BAD
```

and press the Enter key. Make sure you see something like:

```
30F9:2BAD   07.
```

(Remember, ignore the first four hex digits to the left of the colon; they'll vary from system to system and don't affect anything here.) If you don't see an 07, press Enter to return to the DEBUG prompt, then type Q and Enter to quit and make sure you're using version 3.3. Then start again. If you do see an 07, type in the new value (4E) next to the period and press Enter.

Then, give the file a new name. Use the N command to name it COMMAND1.COM. Then type W and Enter to write the file and then Q and Enter to quit:

```
-N COMMAND1.COM
-W
Writing 62DB bytes
-Q
```

Type CLS and the screen will still clear to an ugly grey on black. But load the new COMMAND1.COM by typing:

```
COMMAND1
```

at the DOS prompt. You'll see the familiar DOS sign-on message: Then type CLS and the screen should clear to the colors you wanted.

You can get back to your boring old grey on black CLS by exiting this secondary command processor. Just type:

```
EXIT
```

at the DOS prompt. Now try CLS and you'll be back to grey on black.

Once you're convinced you like the new colors, you can rename the patched COMMAND1.COM to COMMAND.COM and put it on your start-up disk to replace the older version. Boot up with the patched version and type CLS to set the colors properly. You can also set colors by using ANSI.SYS (see Chapter 9).

The instructions above are for DOS 3.3 only. For other versions of DOS use these addresses to patch COMMAND.COM to add color to CLS:

DOS Version	Address
2.0	2346
2.1	2359
3.0	2428
3.1	2642
3.2	282E
3.3	2BAD

If you have a CGA system these patches won't set the border color. EGA and VGA screens don't have borders that can be set, and, anyway, adding code to set CGA borders is far more complex than just changing a byte value.

Displaying Register and Flag Contents

Format: **R [registername]**

This command is primarily for hard-core programmers, but all users need to understand one very important aspect of it: it shows the current state of the CPU registers and flags and lets you change them.

The R command can work three different ways:

1. Typing R by itself will print the hex values in all 14 of the system registers, show all eight flag settings, and display the next instruction DEBUG is poised to execute.

2. Typing R with an F after it will display just the flag settings.

3. Following R with the name of a specific register will display the contents of that single register and let the user either enter a new value or just press the Enter key to keep the old one.

If you're not a serious programmer you never really have to see the state of your system flags. And while you do need to examine and change one or two system registers, you really don't need to see them all at once. So you can pretty much ignore modes 1 and 2 above. But here's what they look like, if you're curious:

```
C>DEBUG COMMAND.COM
-R
AX=0000  BX=0000  CX=62DB  DX=0000  SP=FFFE  BP=0000  SI=0000  DI=0000
DS=30F9  ES=30F9  SS=30F9  CS=30F9  IP=0100    NV UP EI PL NZ NA PO NC
30F9:0100 E92D0D        JMP 0E30
-R F
NV UP EI PL NZ NA PO NC  -
```

DEBUG initially sets the value of the four general-purpose or scratch-pad registers (AX, BX, CX, and DX) to zero. However, when you tell DEBUG to load a typical (short) program into memory it moves the program's length into register CX. COM-MAND.COM version 3.3 is decimal 25307 bytes long, or 62DB in hex, so these four registers would look like:

- AX = 0000
- BX = 0000

- CX = 62DB
- DX = 0000

Each register can hold two-byte values from hex 0000 (0 decimal) to FFFF (65535 decimal — or 64K). If a program is larger than 64K, DEBUG uses both the CX and BX registers to store the length.

Remember, a pair of bytes together is word. You can manipulate each of these registers one word (two bytes) at a time by referring to them as AX, BX, CX, and DX. Or you can chop each in half and manipulate just a single byte at a time: the high half and the low half. The high halves are called AH, BH, CH, and DH. The low halves are AL, BL, CL, and DL.

AH	AL	=	AX
BH	BL	=	BX
CH	CL	=	CX
DH	DL	=	DX

1 byte   **1 word**

If the two-byte value in CX is 62DB, then CH holds the high 62 byte and CL the low DB byte. Used by itself, DEBUG's R command will show you all the two-byte registers. And it will let you examine, and change, any single two-byte register. But you can't use it to see just the high or low halves; you have to look at the value of the whole word.

Virtually all the examples in this book use the CX register to set or change program lengths. Many of the programs use one or more of these general-purpose registers to feed parameters into interrupts. For instance, if you're using Service 6 of BIOS interrupt 10 to clear the screen (or scroll a window of any size upward) you put the following values into the following registers:

- The number of the service itself   into   AH
- The number of lines to scroll   into   AL
- The color of the new blank lines   into   BH
- The upper lefthand row number   into   CH
- The upper lefthand column number   into   CL
- The lower righthand row number   into   DH
- The lower righthand column number   into   DL

In this case you simply put the appropriate values' inputs into the proper registers and execute the interrupt without having to worry about the state of the registers afterward.

In other cases, interrupts perform operations for you and leave the results in certain registers.

For instance, to find out what character and color are at the current cursor position (with Service 8 of BIOS interrupt 10) you put the following numbers into the following registers:

- The number of the service itself   into   AH
- The video page number   into   BH

(In most cases, the *page* — the slice of video memory that displays the image — is 0.) After you execute this interrupt you can look into two registers to get the information you need:

- The ASCII value of this character   is in   AL
- The attribute of this character   is in   AH

To master most of the techniques in this book you won't have to work much (or at all) with the other registers. The PC's one megabyte of main memory is segmented (divided) into slices 64K bytes or smaller. Segment registers tell the system which slice you're working with. Offset registers specify the precise location in each segment slice.

If you want to look at the value at offset 62DB, you have to tell the system which 62DB address you want to examine. If you don't specify a distant segment, the system will assume you're talking about the one you've been using, the one you're currently in, or the one it normally checks for similar requests.

Each of the four segment registers (CS, DS, SS, and ES) has a special role. CS tells the system where to find the *code* segment, the slice of memory where your program is loaded. DS contains the address of the *data* segment, the place your program stores its data. SS points to the *stack* segment, a special storage area where the program can temporarily park information it needs to function properly. And ES lets the system know where to find an *extra* segment it can use to squirrel away working data.

These CS, DS, SS, and ES segments may be at different parts of memory, or they may overlap. When DEBUG loads a program like COMMAND.COM, all four of these segments share the same exact area of memory, starting at the first unused memory space — in this case right after where DEBUG itself is loaded:

- DS=30F9
- ES=30F9
- SS=30F9
- CS=30F9

While you'll use the four general-purpose registers frequently, and the four segment registers on occasion, you probably won't need to worry about the other five — the segment registers. One special offset register, the *instruction pointer* (IP), specifies where inside the code segment to find the very next executable instruction. The other offset registers are divided into *pointer* and *index* registers.

The *stack pointer* (SP) and *base pointer* (BP) help programs manage the flow of information onto and off of the stack. A computer like the PC can handle only one tightly focused task at a time. A seemingly simple task such as printing one character onscreen can actually be made up of lots of smaller, discrete ones such as moving values around in memory, checking modes, looking up dot patterns, setting attributes, deciding whether or not to scroll the screen, advancing the cursor, and doing other miscellaneous housekeeping. As your computer executes one main task it frequently has to pause and execute others, and then return to the original task at hand. When it puts one thing on hold so it can do another, it stores the values, addresses, and other settings needed by the first task temporarily in the chunk of memory called the stack. Then when it's done with the second task, it can retrieve all this needed information from the stack and resume working on the first task. Pointer registers keep track of offsets in the stack segment.

The *source index* (SI) and *destination index* (DI) registers work somewhat like the pointer registers, except that index registers normally maintain offsets into the current data segment rather than the stack segment. They're used for things like moving strings from one place in memory (the source) to another (the destination).

DEBUG initially sets the index registers and base pointers to zero. Unless it's working with an EXE file, DEBUG sets the stack pointer to FFFE, or as high as the available memory allows. And it usually puts a value of 100 in IP, since the instruction pointer initially stores the address of the first executable instruction at the very beginning of the program. After DEBUG loaded COMMAND.COM (at offset 100), these looked like:

- SP=FFFE
- BP=0000
- SI=0000
- DI=0000
- IP=0100

Apart from the four general-purpose registers, four segment registers, and five offset registers, the PC maintains a special two-byte storehouse of data called the *flags* register. A flag is an individual bit (a 1 or a 0) that can show the status of — or control — gut-level operations. Six of these are *status* flags that act as a scoreboard to report what happened during recent arithmetic and logical operations. Three are *control* flags that influence the behavior of certain processes. (In Intel's early CPUs, the other seven bits in the flag register remain unused; more advanced chips take advantage of a few other flags.)

The status flags report on the outcome of events. Programs constantly test to see whether two numbers have the same value, or whether numbers are equal to zero. If they are, the system sets the zero flag bit; turns it "on" by giving it a value of 1. If they're not, the system clears the zero flag, turns it off by giving it a value of 0. Flags can also tell whether the result of an arithmetic process was so big that the system had to *carry* a digit out of a register. And they can specify whether a number is negative, or so huge that it totally overflows the system's working range. The system also monitors *parity* by setting a flag if the binary number representing a value has an even number of 1s in it. And it maintains a special *auxiliary carry* flag to help straighten out the messy conversions required when dealing with *binary-coded decimal* (BCD) calculations. (Take our word for it — you don't want to know.)

Control flags can send certain repeated operations in one direction or another, or tell the system whether or not it may use external interrupts, or let programmers step through (*trap*) executable code one instruction at a time.

Packing all these flags into a single register lets you treat them as a single unit. This makes it easier to save, examine, or change the state of your system with special flag instructions. When you first load a program such as COMMAND.COM into DEBUG and enter R all by itself, or R followed by F, all you'll see is:

```
NV UP EI PL NZ NA PO NC
```

The abbreviations are vaguely mnemonic. NV, the least obvious abbreviation, stands for "No oVerflow" (the reverse OV would spell trouble). UP reveals that the direction is UP (the opposite is DN for DowN). EI stands for "Enable Interrupts" (DI would indicate that external interrupts were temporarily DIsabled). PL is used when the sign of a number is a PLus; if the number were NeGative the abbreviation would be NG. NZ obviously says "Not Zero" (and ZR would mean a number was equal to ZeRo or that two numbers were equal to each other). NA tells us "No Auxiliary" carry correction is necessary (AC would let us know one was needed). PO spells out "Odd Parity;" even would trigger a PE. And NC informs us "No Carry" was involved; a CY would tell us a CarrY did occur. The codes are summarized in the following chart:

Flag	*Set (=1)*	*Clear (=0)*
Overflow (yes/no)	OV	NV
Direction (down/up)	DN	UP
Interrupt (enabled/disabled)	EI	DI
Sign (negative/positive)	NG	PL
Zero (equal/not equal)	ZR	NZ
Auxiliary carry (yes/no)	AC	NA
Parity (even/odd)	PE	PO
Carry (yes/no)	CY	NC

DEBUG's R command will display the state of all six status flags, and two of the three control flags (direction and interrupt). If you want to single-step your way through a program, you have to turn the trap flag on by invoking DEBUG's Trace command.

At any point you can examine the state of all the registers and flags by typing R and pressing Enter:

```
-R
AX=0000  BX=0000  CX=62DB  DX=0000  SP=FFFE  BP=0000  SI=0000  DI=0000
DS=30F9  ES=30F9  SS=30F9  CS=30F9  IP=0100   NV UP EI PL NZ NA PO NC
30F9:0100 E92D0D        JMP 0E30
-
```

If you want to display just the flags, add an F:

```
-R F
NV UP EI PL NZ NA PO NC   -
```

(The spaces between the R command and any register after it are optional. R F is the same as RF. RCX and R CX will both work.) If you issue an R F command, DEBUG will wait for you to change one or more flag settings. If you want to leave things exactly as they were (and most of the time you probably should), just press the Enter key. If not, enter the opposite code(s), shown in the table above.

For example, if you wanted to disable external interrupts and switch parity from odd to even, you could type:

```
NV UP EI PL NZ NA PO NC   -  DI PE
```

or:

```
NV UP EI PL NZ NA PO NC   -  PE DI
```

or:

```
NV UP EI PL NZ NA PO NC   -  PEDI
```

or:

```
NV UP EI PL NZ NA PO NC   -  DIPE
```

and then press Enter. The order, spacing, and uppercasing are optional. To check your typing, enter R F again and you should see:

```
-R F
NV UP DI PL NZ NA PE NC   -
```

The only time you'll probably ever have to use the R command is when you create or modify a program. If you used the Assemble (A) command to create a tiny program called AMERICA.COM:

```
C>DEBUG
-A
30DD:0100 MOV AH,9
30DD:0102 MOV DX,108
30DD:0105 INT 21
30DD:0107 RET
30DD:0108 DB "Back in the US" 0D 0A 24
30DD:0119
```

```
-N AMERICA.COM
-W
```

and tried to write the file to disk without specifying a length, DEBUG would create a file zero bytes long:

```
Writing 0000 bytes
```

To have DEBUG create the file you wanted, you have to tell it how many bytes to write. Whenever you use its mini-assembler to assemble a program, DEBUG figures out how many bytes the machine-level version of the previous command would fill in memory and prints the very next address onscreen as a prompt. In this case the last line of the program was:

```
30DD:0108 DB "Back in the US" 0D 0A 24
```

so DEBUG assembled that line and then printed:

```
30DD:0119
```

To exit the mini-assembler and return to the main DEBUG prompt, you would note this address (119) and press the Enter key. Then, since the file starts at offset 100, tell DEBUG how long the file is by subtracting 100 from 119 and entering the result, 19, in the CX register:

```
-RCX
CX 0000
:19
```

Now use the W command to write the file to disk (and then Q to quit). You should see:

```
-W
Writing 0019 bytes
-Q
```

New users sometimes forget to subtract the 100. It usually won't hurt a program to make it a bit longer, since programs stop when they reach instructions like INT 20 or RET, and anything past that is ignored. The AMERICA.COM program uses the DOS "Display String" function call 9, which stops when it sees a $ (here this is entered as a hex 24). So DOS would ignore anything after the equals sign.

However, it can be dangerous to make programs too short. If the final instruction were INT 20 or RET (to quit the program and return to the main COMMAND.COM prompt), and you entered a length in the CX register that was one byte too short, DOS wouldn't be able to execute this last instruction, and would never be able to exit the program. You'd then have to reboot.

You also may have to use the RCX command when you modify a program. If you run the AMERICA.COM program, it will simply print:

```
Back in the US
```

To add a few characters to the string this program displays, load AMERICA.COM into DEBUG, type RCX and press the Enter key twice to find out how long the program is, then use the Display (D) command to show you the contents:

```
C>DEBUG AMERICA.COM
-RCX
CX 0019
:
-D 100 L 19
30F9:0100  B4 09 BA 08 01 CD 21 C3-42 61 63 6B 20 69 6E 20    ......!.Back in
30F9:0110  74 68 65 20 55 53 0D 0A-24                         the US..$
```

The actual string that AMERICA.COM displays ends at address 115, and is followed at addresses 116 through 118 by an 0D 0A 24 — a carriage return, a line feed, and a $ string terminator. So add two more letters to the existing string, starting at address 116, and then slap on the required 0D 0A 24:

```
-E 116 "SR" 0D 0A 24
```

If you tried to write the program to disk at this point, you'd end up with a mess, since DEBUG still thinks the program is 19 hex bytes long and will truncate it prematurely, omitting the final two characters from the file. The final few characters of the original and new programs would look like:

	Address 114	Address 115	Address 116	Address 117	Address 118	Address 119	Address 11A
Original	U	S	(CR)	(LF)	$		
New	U	S	S	R	(CR)	(LF)	$

(CR) = carriage return
(LF) = line feed   **end of program**

(Remember, the program starts at address 100, not address 101. So the last — hex 19th — byte is at address 118, not 119.)

In the original program, the final character was a $ that DOS needed to terminate the string. But in the modified version, the two new bytes of text pushed the final two characters — the line feed and the $ — into addresses 119 and 11A. The new program is 1B bytes long (hex 19 + 2 = 1B), but since you didn't tell DEBUG the program was larger, it wrote only the first 19 bytes to the new file. So when DOS executes the new one, it won't find a $ to tell it to stop, and will keep printing whatever garbage is in memory until it inevitably stumbles onto a random value of 24 that just happens to be in memory.

To prevent this from happening, tell DEBUG the program is now 1B bytes long instead of 19. And since you're modifying an existing file, give the new one a new name so you don't wipe out the old one. Then write the file and quit:

```
-RCX
CX 0019
:1B
-N BEATLES.COM
-W
Writing 001B bytes
-Q
```

This time when you run BEATLES.COM you'll see:

```
Back in the USSR
```

If all you want to do is examine the contents of a register like CX, you can type RCX and press the Enter key twice, or you can just type R and press Enter once. The second way involves a bit less typing, but it clutters up your screen by showing you the contents of all the registers and flags. Either way will work.

Performing Hexadecimal Arithmetic

Format: **H value value**

Counting in hex is daunting for beginners, who commonly forget that the number after 19 is 1A, not 20, and that the number right before 20 is 1F, not 19. Doing even simple math, especially with hex numbers several digits long, can be hair-raising.

But the only real math you have to do is add and subtract hex numbers. To help, DEBUG gives you a free hex calculator. Just get to the DEBUG prompt, type H and two numbers, and DEBUG will print first the sum and then the difference.

You can't enter numbers larger than FFFF (about 65,000 decimal). And DEBUG can't handle sums larger than FFFF, or negative numbers. If you ask it to add FFFF and 1 it will print 0000:

```
-H FFFF 1
0000  FFFE
```

Tell it to subtract 1 from 0 and you'll get FFFF:

```
-H 0 1
0001  FFFF
```

While these examples are trivial, this command really comes in handy when you're fumbling with two thorny numbers such as:

```
-H C79B E8AF
B04A  DEEC
```

Note that the order in which you specify the raw hex numbers is critical. Entering:

```
-H 2 3
```

will produce:

```
0005  FFFF
```

while switching the numbers around:

```
-H 3 2
```

will print:

```
0005  0001
```

The additions will always be the same, but subtracting 3 - 2 is far different from subtracting 2 - 3.

If you keep DEBUG.COM and the DOS FIND.EXE filter on your disk, you can write a small batch file to do hex addition and subtraction for you automatically. Create the following batch file using a pure ASCII word processor, or EDLIN:

```
ECHO OFF
IF !%2==! GOTO OOPS
ECHO H %1 %2 > DEBUG.SCR
ECHO Q >> DEBUG.SCR
ECHO The sum and difference of %1 and %2 are:
DEBUG < DEBUG.SCR | FIND /V "-"
DEL DEBUG.SCR
GOTO END
```

```
:OOPS
ECHO You have to enter %0 followed by
ECHO 2 hex numbers each FFFF or less
ECHO (e.g. %0 4D7F 5A4)
:END
```

(You can also create this file by using the DOS COPY CON command. To do so, add a line at the top that says:

```
COPY CON HEX.BAT
```

When you're done typing the last line, press the Enter key, then press the F6 function key, and then press the Enter key a final time.)

To use it at the main DOS prompt, make sure you have DEBUG.COM, FIND.EXE, and this HEX.BAT batch file handy. Then type the word HEX followed by the two hex numbers (hex FFFF or smaller) that you want to add or subtract.

After issuing the ECHO OFF command to suppress screen clutter, the batch file first makes sure you entered two hex numbers. When you execute a batch file, DOS looks for any delimiters such as spaces or commas that separate what you typed into groups of characters. It then takes these groups and uses them to set the values of up to ten replaceable parameters.

The first replaceable parameter is always the name of the batch file itself, and DOS refers to this as %0. DOS calls the second discrete thing you type %1, the third one %2, etc. If you put a %0 or %1 in your batch file, DOS will replace these with what you typed on the command line. So if you execute the batch file HEX.BAT by typing:

```
HEX 1A 3B
```

DOS will make the following substitutions:

%0	HEX
%1	1A
%2	3B

To make sure you entered two hex numbers after the word HEX on the command line, the batch file checks to see if parameter %2 contains something or not. If you entered just one hex number on the command line after the word HEX, or didn't enter any hex numbers at all after the word HEX, %2 would be equal to nothing. The test:

```
IF !%2==! GOTO OOPS
```

would replace the %2 with nothing, leaving:

```
IF !==! GOTO OOPS
```

Since ! is indeed equal to ! (you could have used another symbol such as @ if you don't like exclamation points), the test is true, and the batch file executes the command following the test (GOTO OOPS). The batch file will look for a label called :OOPS and jump directly there without executing any intervening instructions. In this batch file, the commands following the :OOPS label will provide a reminder about the proper syntax.

If you did enter two hex numbers, such as 1A and 3B, DOS will replace the %2 with 3B and make the test:

```
IF !3B==! GOTO OOPS
```

Since !3B is clearly not the same as !, the test will fail (which is what you want), and the batch file will grind into action.

The lines:

```
ECHO H %1 %2 > DEBUG.SCR
ECHO Q >> DEBUG.SCR
```

will first redirect the letter H, plus the two hex numbers you entered on the DOS command line after the word HEX, into a file called DEBUG.SCR. (The double >> symbol appends the redirected characters to an existing file rather than creating a new one.)

What this will end up doing is creating a temporary file called DEBUG.SCR that contains two DEBUG commands and the hex numbers you entered. If these hex numbers were 1A and 3B, the contents of the DEBUG.SCR file would be:

```
H 1A 3B
Q
```

The batch file will then display a message onscreen to clarify what's happening. DEBUG will replace the %1 and %2 here as well, and end up printing:

```
The sum and difference of 1A and 3B are:
```

It then takes the DEBUG.SCR file it just created and redirects the characters in this file into DEBUG just as if you had typed them at the keyboard. These characters issue the DEBUG commands to perform hex arithmetic on the numbers you entered. The same batch file line then sends the resulting DEBUG output through a FIND filter to get rid of the actual DEBUG commands. If you didn't use this filter, you'd see

```
The sum and difference of 1A and 3B are:
-H 1A 3B
0055  FFDF
-Q
```

However, the:

```
/V "-"
```

at the end of the FIND command tells DOS to display only those lines that do *not* contain a "-." Since all DEBUG commands contain a hyphen, this filters out the actual commands and cleans up the display. All you see is:

```
The sum and difference of 1A and 3B are:
0055  FFDF
```

Finally, the batch file deletes the temporary DEBUG.SCR file and exits. While HEX.BAT can check to make sure you entered two hex numbers, it can't check to see if these numbers are valid. So if you enter something DEBUG can't handle, you'll see an error message.

Comparing Two Blocks of Memory

Format: **C range address**

This command is useful in isolating file differences, though you probably won't use it much (if at all). The pathetic PC-DOS COMP command (Microsoft's MS-DOS FC is far superior) will refuse to work if you ask it to examine two things of unequal length. And, the DOS COMP utility will stop in its tracks after ten mismatches, while the DEBUG C command will grind merrily away reporting them by the screenful.

To use the C command, type in C, then a first range of memory, and then a second starting address. When entering the first range you can use explicit starting and stopping addresses, or you can specify a starting address and a length of bytes to check. When specifying the second block of memory you want to check, all you have to enter is the starting address. DEBUG will calculate the length of the first block and apply that length to both comparisons.

The two commands below will each direct DEBUG to compare two blocks of memory each 10 hex (16 decimal) bytes long — one starting at address 100 and the other at address 110:

```
-C 100 L 10 110
```

and:

```
-C 100 10F 110
```

If you had used the E command to enter the following values into addresses 100 and 110:

```
-E 100 0 1 2 3 4 5 6 7 8 9 A B C D E F
-E 110 0 1 2 3 4 5 6 8 7 9 A B C D E F
```

you could then view these values by using the D command:

```
-D 100 L 20
30DD:0100 00 01 02 03 04 05 06 07-08 09 0A 0B 0C 0D 0E 0F
30DD:0110 00 01 02 03 04 05 06 08-07 09 0A 0B 0C 0D 0E 0F
```

Notice that the seventh and eighth bytes are switched. The C command tells DEBUG to look at every byte in the first range you specified and compare it to the corresponding byte in the second chunk. If it finds mismatches, it will sandwich them between the two addresses of the differing bytes, so the two Compare commands above would each yield the report:

```
30DD:0107   07   08   30DD:0117
30DD:0108   08   07   30DD:0118
```

If DEBUG doesn't find any mismatches it will simply print another hyphen prompt.

If you had two programs on your disk of the same length called REDWHITE.COM and WHITERED.COM that cleared the screen to different colors (red on white vs. white on red), to find the differences in the files; you could use the DOS COMP utility

```
C>COMP REDWHITE.COM C:WHITERED.COM
C:REDWHITE.COM and C:WHITERED.COM
Compare error at OFFSET A
File 1 = 74
File 2 = 47
```

Or you could use the DEBUG C command. But since DEBUG will load any file with a COM extension at address 100, you'd have to rename one of the files. Then get into DEBUG, Name (with N) and Load (with L) the file that still had the COM extension, and find out its length by entering RCX and pressing the Enter key twice. DEBUG will load this COM file at address 100. Then load the other file (without the COM extension) at address 200. Issue a Compare command that tells DEBUG to check two blocks of memory 1D bytes long, starting at addresses 100 and 200. Then enter Q to quit:

```
C>RENAME WHITERED.COM WHITERED
DEBUG
-N REDWHITE.COM
-L
-RCX
CX 001D
:
-N WHITERED
```

```
-L 200
-C 100 L 1D 200
30F9:010A   74   47   30F9:020A
-Q
```

The COMP command reported that the files were the same except for the bytes at offset A. Since DEBUG loaded the files at offsets 100 and 200, it found the same mismatches at addresses 10A and 20A.

(If you want to try this, you can create the two color setting files with the following DEBUG script. Type it in using a pure-ASCII word processor or the DOS EDLIN utility. Name the script COLOR.SCR:

```
N REDWHITE.COM
E 100 B8 00 06 B9 00 00 BA 4F 18 B7 74 CD 10 B4 02
E 10F BA 00 00 B7 00 CD 10 B0 04 BA D9 03 EE C3
RCX
1D
W
E 10A 47
N WHITERED.COM
W
Q
```

Be sure to press the Enter key at the end of each line, especially the last one, with the Q. Then put COLOR.SCR and DEBUG on the same disk and type:

```
DEBUG < COLOR.SCR
```

(If you don't have a pure-ASCII word processor handy, use the DOS COPY CON command. Add a line to the very beginning of the program that says:

```
COPY CON COLOR.SCR
```

When you're all done, press the Enter key after the final Q, then press the F6 function key, and then press Enter again.)

Loading Disk Information into Memory

Format: **L [address [drive sector sector]]**

This powerful command lets you take just about any information from any part of a disk and put a copy of it in memory. You can then use DEBUG's editing commands to modify it and very carefully write the new information back to the disk.

DEBUG lets you load information in two forms — files and disk sectors.

Loading files is safe and easy. Loading sectors is trickier. Users often load something so they can change it and then write the changes back to disk, so working with sectors is *playing with fire*:

WARNING!
**Unless you know exactly what you're doing, are sure your disks are complete-
ly backed up, take every possible prudent measure to safeguard your system,
and triple-check every command before you execute it, be extraordinarily
careful when loading and working with sectors, and utterly paranoid and
overcautious when writing them. Be sure you always work on copies of your
files, *never* the originals. If you're the least bit nervous or uncertain about this
kind of activity, *don't do it*. Just type Q and press the Enter key to Quit.**

Loading Files

The easiest way to load a file is to specify it on the DOS command line after the word DEBUG. To load a copy of the DOS MODE.COM utility that's in your \DOS subdirectory on drive C: you could do it from any subdirectory on any disk by typing:

```
DEBUG C:\DOS\MODE.COM
```

(This of course assumes that DEBUG.COM is itself in the current subdirectory or is in a directory that your PATH command knows about.)

If you're loading a copy of MODE.COM that's in the subdirectory you're currently logged into, just type:

```
DEBUG MODE.COM
```

If DEBUG can locate the file it will usually load it into memory at offset 100 and then just print the DEBUG hyphen prompt to tell you it's ready for a command. If DEBUG can't find the file it will print the "File not found" error message to let you know it had trouble, and then display the hyphen prompt. It won't be able to find files in other directories unless you specify the precise subdirectory the file is in, even if it's in a subdirec-
tory you've included in your system's path. While you can run any executable file in any subdirectory that your path knows about, DEBUG won't let you load a file in another directory unless you explicitly include the file's path on the DOS command line.

So if your normal PATH command is:

```
PATH C:\BIN;C:\DOS;C:\;D:\
```

and you're currently in a subdirectory called C:\WORK and you want to load C:\DOS\MODE.COM into DEBUG, just typing:

```
DEBUG MODE.COM
```

won't do it. But:

```
DEBUG \DOS\MODE.COM
```

would.

Incidentally, when you want to write a file to disk, you have to make sure DEBUG knows the file's name beforehand. You can load a file from the DOS command line (by putting the filename after DEBUG), or you can use the N and L commands together:

```
DEBUG
-N \DOS\MODE.COM
-L
```

If DEBUG can't find the file you specified using this Name and Load technique, it will tell you so by printing a "File not found" message. But be careful — even if DEBUG prints this message, it will use the name of this file that it couldn't find the next time you issue a Write (W) command, unless you enter a new name later.

So if you type:

```
DEBUG PI.FIL
```

and it comes back and tells you:

```
File not found
-
```

it will still register the name "PI.FIL." If you forget to enter a different name later, and you use the W command to Write some information to disk, DEBUG will use the filename PI.FIL for the file it creates.

So if you originally loaded DEBUG by typing DEBUG PI.FIL, and had DEBUG tell you it couldn't find a file with that name, but you went ahead anyway and entered some information and then told the CX register how many bytes to write, and used the W command to write it:

```
-E 100 "PI=3.14159265"
-RCX
CX 0000
:D
-W
Writing 000D bytes
-Q
```

DEBUG will create a brand new file called PI.FIL. If you later issue the DOS command:

```
TYPE PI.FIL
```

you'll see:

```
PI=3.14159265
```

Loading any file is easy. Just type an N and then the filename (and its path, if the file is located in another subdirectory) and then an L. You can see if DEBUG knows the filename by peeking at the address where DEBUG stores it — offset 82 of the code segment. To check, just type:

```
D CS:81
```

DOS uses the area at this offset in its Program Segment Prefix control block to store the characters you entered on the command line after the main program name — often called the command tail. When you type CHKDSK /F, for instance, everything after the final K in CHKDSK — the space, the slash, and the F — goes here. When you load a file into DEBUG by specifying it after the DEBUG name on the command line, DOS puts this filename at offset 81, and it uses the single byte at offset 80 to tell it how many characters you typed after the main program name. Using the DEBUG Name (N) command also puts the name you entered at this offset.

If you load one file and then later load a different one, DEBUG will load them both at offset 100, and the second one will overwrite the first. DEBUG normally loads files at offset 100, so if you want to load two files at different addresses, you can do so by including the addresses after the L command.

If you also have a file on your disk called E.FIL that contains the text E=2.71828, you could load both PI.FIL and E.FIL into memory at the same time with the commands:

```
C>DEBUG
-N PI.FIL
-L 100
-N E.FIL
-L 110
```

Then, typing:

```
D 100 L 20
```

would display something like:

```
30DD:0100   50 49 3D 33 2E 31 34 31-35 39 32 36 35 00 00 00   PI=3.14159265...
30DD:0110   45 3D 32 2E 37 31 38 32-38 00 00 00 00 00 00 00   E=2.71828.......
```

You really didn't have to specify the address of 100 when you loaded the first PI.FIL file, since DEBUG normally loads files at offset 100. But you did have to tell DEBUG to load the second E.FIL file at offset 110. If you loaded these two files one after the other but forgot to specify addresses, DEBUG would put the second one over the first one. It would look like:

```
C>DEBUG
-N PI.FIL
-L
-D 100 L 20
30DD:0100  50 49 3D 33 2E 31 34 31-35 39 32 36 35 00 00 00   PI=3.14159265...
30DD:0110  00 00 00 00 00 00 00 00-00 00 00 00 00 00 00 00   ................
-N E.FIL
-L
-D 100 L 20
30DD:0100  45 3D 32 2E 37 31 38 32-38 39 32 36 35 00 00 00   E=2.718289265...
30DD:0110  00 00 00 00 00 00 00 00-00 00 00 00 00 00 00 00   ................
```

Note that since the PI.FIL file is longer than the E.FIL file, the contents of the E.FIL file overwrite just the beginning of the PI.FIL file; the end of the PI.FIL string is still visible after DEBUG plunks the E.FIL file on top of it.

In addition, you have to be careful when loading COM files, since DEBUG always loads files ending with COM at offset 100. So if you try to load a COM file at an address other than 100, DEBUG won't let you:

```
C>DEBUG
-N MODE.COM
-L 110
      ^ Error
-L 101
      ^ Error
-L 100
```

If you do need to load two COM files at the same time, you'll have to rename one of them before starting DEBUG, and then load the renamed COM file at an address higher than 100. If you wanted to load two short color-setting COM files called RED.COM and BLUE.COM, you would first rename BLUE.COM to BLUE.TMP. Then you'd load RED.COM into memory without specifying an address (DEBUG will load it at offset 100), and then load BLUE.TMP at a higher address. You can use the RCX command to find out how long the RED.COM file is so you don't overwrite it with the BLUE.TMP file:

```
REN BLUE.COM BLUE.TMP
DEBUG
-N RED.COM
-L
-RCX
```

```
CX 001D
:
-N BLUE.TMP
-L 120
```

The RCX command reported that the RED.COM file was 1D bytes long, which means the last byte in the file was at address 10E. You could have loaded BLUE.TMP directly after it — at address 10E — but it's often easier to work with files that are loaded at even paragraph boundaries, with offsets that end in 0, such as 100, or 120, or FD0.

COM vs. EXE

DEBUG loads different kinds of files in different ways. First, some background.

DOS can execute only three kinds of files, those with BAT, COM, or EXE extensions. Two of these, COM and EXE files, are generally called programs, although frustrated users sometimes call them far more colorful things. (Originally, "COM" stood for "command" and "EXE" stood for "executable" but these names don't mean much these days.) Files that end in BAT are called batch files.

Program files contain long sequences of machine-level commands in binary format that put your CPU through its paces. If you peeked inside one (with the DOS TYPE command) you'd see lots of seemingly meaningless strings of odd-looking characters. Batch files are ASCII files that contain recognizable English-language commands to load and run programs or perform certain DOS functions.

An executable program is simply a collection of instructions (and the data for these instructions) kept in a language your system can readily process. Some programs can be short and simple; others need to span several different 64K segments and do fancy footwork with memory.

Programs that end in COM are exact images of the instructions in memory that make the programs do their magic. And they're relatively short; COM files, their internal data, and their temporary stack storage areas, must all squeeze into 64K. Actually, the largest size of a COM file is 65,278 bytes, rather than the full 64K (65,536), since each COM file must reserve a minumum of two bytes for its stack, and 256 bytes (100 hex bytes) for a Program Segment Prefix that contains certain important addresses and data needed by DOS. (This is why DEBUG loads most files at offset 100.) Since no translation is required when reading them off a disk and putting them into memory, COM files load and start quickly. DOS just copies the block of instructions that constitutes the file to a certain memory address and presses the start button.

Programs that end in EXE, (pronounced "ex-ee"), are not exact duplicates of what ends up in memory. EXE files aren't limited to 64K, and in fact can take up all available memory. Each EXE file is prefaced by a block of information called a *header* that tells DOS how to allocate the proper amount of memory space it needs and then load the various parts of the file into the proper memory areas.

DEBUG is more than just a file editor; as mentioned earlier, it's a programming development and debugging environment. Programmers can work on a file and then run it from inside DEBUG without having to exit to DOS. Because of this, if you load an EXE file directly into DEBUG, DEBUG looks at the header and performs all the necessary memory allocation, segment juggling, and other fancy DOS tricks.

When you load a COM file into DEBUG the first byte of the file is at offset 100, the second at offset 101, etc. When you load a file with an EXE extension into DEBUG, the first few bytes of the actual file are discarded; these tell DOS that it's working with an EXE file, and specify how many sectors long the file is, how big the header is, etc.

If you want to examine or modify an EXE file with DEBUG, you'll have to first make a copy of the file that has an extension other than EXE (or no extension at all). Then when you load this renamed version of the file, the first byte will indeed be at offset 100, and the second at offset 101. (These bytes should be 4D and 5A, which are the EXE "file signature" that tells DOS to give them special treatment.) Working with the non-EXE version of the file will make it easier to modify, but you won't be able to run it while inside DEBUG (no great loss). You can see how differently DEBUG treats the versions by looking at the shortest DOS file that has an EXE extension — SORT.EXE. Copy SORT.EXE to a file named SORT.XXX. Load each into DEBUG and use the RCX command to see how long DEBUG thinks the file is. Then look at the first hex 10 (16 decimal) bytes at offset 0 — the very beginning of each file, and the hex 10 bytes at offset 100 — where DEBUG normally loads all files:

```
C>DEBUG SORT.EXE
-RCX
CX 05B9
:
-D 0 L 10
30F9:0000  CD 20 6A 31 00 9A 10 06-AB FF F4 02 2E 2D 2F 03   . j1.........-/.
-D 100 L 10
30F9:0100  00 00 2F 00 00 00 00 00-B4 30 CD 21 3D 03 1E 74   ../......0.!=..t
-Q


C>DEBUG SORT.XXX
-RCX
CX 07B9
:
-D 0 L 10
30DD:0000  CD 20 00 A0 00 9A EE FE-1D F0 F4 02 2E 2D 2F 03   . ...........-/.
-D 100 L 10
30DD:0100  4D 5A 9D 01 04 00 01 00-20 00 01 00 01 00 3D 00   MZ...... .....=.
-Q
```

Remember, here you're looking at the exact same file with two slightly different names.

If you do have to modify an EXE file, be sure to make a copy of it with a non-EXE extension. Then, when you're done making the changes, rename the changed file back to an EXE file again so DOS will run it. DOS will refuse to execute a file called SORT.XXX, even though it may be a perfectly executable file.

Loading Sectors

Data is data. Whether it's in memory or on your disk, it's just magnetically coded information. But storing this data is very tricky. You could keep it permanently in memory, but you'd need a huge amount of memory to maintain all your programs and data as well as a surefire way to prevent it from disappearing when you turned the power off. (You could actually do it, if you used very expensive *static* or battery backed-up CMOS RAM chips rather than the cheaper but power-hungry *dynamic* RAM chips in most systems.) And while such a storage system would be blazingly quick, it wouldn't let you transport your data easily from machine to machine.

Disks are a far better way to store data; they're vastly cheaper, more transportable, and secure. But you can't just throw data onto the surface of a disk. You have to organize it so storage and retrieval are fast and reliable. You have to know exactly what's on each disk, and which of the different versions of your data is the most recent. And you have to allow frequent modification; users are constantly changing their files — making them bigger, smaller, editing them, and moving the information in them around.

The best way to store data is in chunks. But the chunks have to be a workable size. If the chunks are too small you'll spend all your time figuring out where each is located. Storing just one byte at a time would be a logistical nightmare; the map needed to record where each byte is would take up more space than the data itself. Make the chunks too large, however, and you'll end up with utter inefficiency. If each chunk is 10,000 bytes long and you're storing five 200-byte programs, you'll waste 49,000 bytes of space.

The standard chunk on a PC disk is called a sector, and the standard sector is 512 bytes long. Sectors are actually parts of tracks. Tracks are concentric rings like circles on bull's-eye targets. Each track is divided into wedges shaped like slices of pie. These wedges form the disk sectors.

But your system doesn't always store data in individual sectors. Instead, it uses something called an *allocation unit*, more commonly referred to as a *cluster*. A cluster can be a single sector (as is it on single-sided 5-1/4 inch diskettes, or the godawful AT 1.2 megabyte floppies). Or it can be two sectors long (as with the common 360K diskette), or four (on the original AT 20-megabyte drive), or even eight (on the original ten-megabyte XT hard disk).

Manipulating these sectors directly is an elaborate and tedious process, but DOS does all the dirty work for you, organizing and keeping track of your files. And it also knows where all the little pieces of the file are scattered across your disk.

When you first create a file on a brand new disk, all the sectors that contain the information in that file are in the same contiguous area. But as you add and delete files on the disk, and make existing files bigger and smaller, DOS ends up storing pieces of your files in clusters scattered over the entire disk surface. This kind of fragmentation slows everything down, since DOS has to churn through numerous read and write operations each time you load or save a file. One of the best ways to improve performance of your hard disk is to back up all your files (very assiduously) to floppies, reformat the hard disk, and then copy them back. Doing this will make your files contiguous and do away with fragmentation — until you start chomping away at them again.

DOS uses two tables to keep track of where all the individual clusters in every file are located. The first one is the disk directory itself, which maintains the name, size, creation date and time, and attribute (which is a label that lets you hide files or prevent them from being changed or erased). It also tells DOS where the very first cluster of the file is located. The second one, called a file allocation table (or FAT), takes over after the initial directory entry and keeps track of where all the remaining clusters are stashed.

As we've seen, it's relatively safe and easy to load whole files into DEBUG and then write them back to disk, since DOS takes care of the tricky loading and writing processes for you. However, it's extraordinarily risky to load specific sectors into DEBUG, then modify and write these back to disk, since one little slip could corrupt your directory or FAT. Scramble those two tables (especially the FAT) and you'll make it impossible for DOS to figure out where all the little pieces of your files are located.

The FAT is so important, in fact, that your disks contain two identical versions of it. Actually this is a bit short-sighted. Mariners know to take either one compass or three to sea, but never two. If two don't agree, which one is wrong? DOS should have allocated space for three FATs, on the theory that it's unlikely two will fail spontaneously. Of course, with DEBUG, nothing's impossible.

It's bad enough that you could destroy all the data on a floppy disk with an errant DEBUG command. But the same thick-fingered command could eradicate the key FAT and directory information on your hard disk, leaving you with a funny expression on your face and your foot through the screen.

So while you can load and write disk sectors, don't experiment unless you're totally backed up, and are the kind of belt-and-suspenders type who checks every action five times before he does anything. And be absolutely sure to keep DEBUG away from your hard disk sectors — one little slip and goodbye.

The following examples all apply to floppy disks only. In fact, they all illustrate how to work with the floppy disk in drive A:, for two reasons:

1. Some users with hard disks don't have a floppy disk that's strictly called drive B: (although they can simulate it by temporarily renaming drive A:).

2. Worse, one of the biggest pitfalls in working with sectors is that DEBUG refers to drive A: as drive 0, drive B: as drive 1, drive C: as drive 2, etc. It's easy to forget this late at night and put something on drive 2 when you really wanted to write to drive B:. Accidentally writing a floppy disk FAT sector onto the hard disk FAT will zap your data to dust. Your files will still be on your disk, in lots of little scattered pieces, but with the FAT gone you won't have any way to find where the pieces are located. If you use drive A: exclusively (which DEBUG refers to as drive 0) and you acciden-

tally write something to drive 1 thinking that 1 is A:, you may wreak havoc on the floppy in drive B: but at least your hard disk will still be intact.

So remember:

Drive Letter	What DEBUG Calls It
A:	0
B:	1
C:	2
D:	3

You won't really need to load and write absolute disk sectors very often. But this ability can come in handy. If you do somehow bomb your FATs, you can put the broken disk in drive A: and laboriously go through it sector by sector, loading the information from each sector to figure out where your text and data files are located. Then, once you've mapped out the contents of each sector, you can load the sectors from the bombed-out disk in the proper order and write them sequentially to a blank, formatted disk in drive B:. When you're done, you can load all the sequential sectors from drive B: into higher and higher addresses in memory, then use the N and W commands to name and write a new file containing all these pieces. It's nasty work, but it beats losing all your files. Barely.

This technique won't work with binary files (programs), since you won't be able to tell where all the pieces are, and even if you could, if you're off by even one byte when you put everything together you'll end up with garbage. With text or most data files you can always go into the file with your editor or word processor when you're done and clean things up. Better yet, use a program like the Norton or Mace Utilities to handle all the drudgery for you.

A real problem with this kind of rescue operation is that you may end up hopelessly confused because of all the slightly different versions of your file scattered over the disk. When you create a text file, your word processor generally saves the previous version as a backup (BAK) file. Some programs also create working files with extensions like TMP or $$$ while they're operating; they usually erase these or give them BAK extensions when you save or quit. When you look at your disk with DEBUG you may find several sectors that seem to have nearly identical contents, since they stored temporary or backup versions of your file. Sorting them all out can give you a big headache. The real answer is to back up all your work carefully and often, assuming the worst, since the computer definition of "the worst" is "just a matter of time."

One place where you really can use DEBUG's sector reading and writing abilities is with directories. Remember, however, don't try meddling with absolute sectors on your hard disk!

DOS disks are arranged as follows:

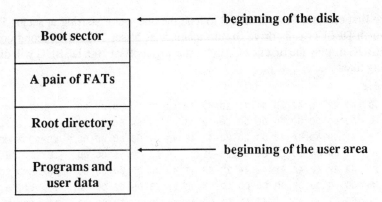

The boot sector does three things: It lets DOS know that the disk is indeed an MS-DOS or PC DOS-formatted disk, and not a disk for an Apple, DEC, or other system. It provides a table (called the BIOS Parameter Block, or BPB) of important values that DOS needs to know, such as the size of the disk's sectors, clusters, and directory. And it runs a bootstrap program that looks for the main operating system files and launches them into action.

The two FATs keep tabs on every cluster on your disk. When DOS needs to store a chunk of information, it looks at the FAT to see where the first available unused cluster is on your disk, and puts the data there. When it later has to retrieve the data it consults the FAT to see which cluster holds the information.

The main directory is called the root directory because it's at the beginning of a "tree-structured" (or hierarchical) system with subdirectories branching off it.

The root directory maintains the name, size, creation (or last modification) time and date, and the initial cluster location for a specified number of files — the number varies depending on the type of system you're using. (DOS limits the number of root directory entries, but lets subdirectories hold as many files as disk space permits.) Finally, the directory maintains a key piece of information about each file called an *attribute*.

A file attribute tells DOS what kind of file it's dealing with. Some files contain such important gut-level utilities and information that erasing them would bring your system to its knees, and DOS prevents you from altering or deleting these. Some files perform special services; the volume label and every subdirectory on your disk are just special kinds of files that can't be copied or deleted using normal DOS file management commands. And DOS lets you "hide" sensitive files from normal directory searches, or stamp them as "read only" so users can examine them but not change or erase them.

Each directory listing takes up 32 (or hex 20) bytes. The file attribute information is kept in the 12th byte (byte number 11, or hex 0B, since the first byte is byte number 0). You can look at the first few directory entries on a 360K floppy disk in drive A: with the command:

```
C>DEBUG
-L 100 0 5 1
-D 100 L C0
```

The first command told DEBUG to load the one sector starting at sector 5 on drive A: (which DEBUG calls drive 0) into memory at offset 100. The second command had DEBUG display the first hex C0 bytes starting at offset 100. DEBUG will display something like:

```
30DD:0100  49 42 4D 42 49 4F 20 20-43 4F 4D 27 00 00 00 00   IBMBIO  COM'....
30DD:0110  00 00 00 00 00 00 00 60-72 0E 02 00 54 56 00 00   .......'r...TV..
30DD:0120  49 42 4D 44 4F 53 20 20-43 4F 4D 27 00 00 00 00   IBMDOS  COM'....
30DD:0130  00 00 00 00 00 00 00 60-71 0E 18 00 CF 75 00 00   .......'q....u..
30DD:0140  43 4F 4D 4D 41 4E 44 20-43 4F 4D 20 00 00 00 00   COMMAND COM ....
30DD:0150  00 00 00 00 00 00 00 60-71 0E 36 00 DB 62 00 00   .......'q.6..b..
30DD:0160  50 43 20 4D 41 47 41 5A-49 4E 45 28 00 00 00 00   PC MAGAZINE(....
30DD:0170  00 00 00 00 00 00 45 6E-5B 0F 00 00 00 00 00 00   ......En[.......
30DD:0180  48 49 44 44 45 4E 20 20-46 49 4C 22 00 00 00 00   HIDDEN  FIL"....
30DD:0190  00 00 00 00 00 00 51 6E-5B 0F 4F 00 29 00 00 00   ......Qn[.O.)...
30DD:01A0  53 55 42 44 49 52 31 20-20 20 20 10 00 00 00 00   SUBDIR1    .....
30DD:01B0  00 00 00 00 00 00 6A 6E-5B 0F 50 00 00 00 00 00   ......jn[.P.....
```

(Obviously the contents will be different on your own system, but the structure will be similar.)

The first 32-byte entry, for IBMBIO.COM, is made up of the following parts:

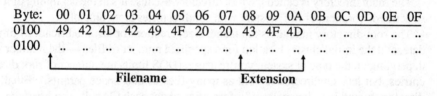

Byte:	00	01	02	03	04	05	06	07	08	09	0A	0B	0C	0D	0E	0F
0100	49	42	4D	42	49	4F	20	20	43	4F	4D	..	..	..	..	..
0100	..	..	..	..	..	..	..	..	..	..	..	..	..	..	..	..

Filename   **Extension**

Byte:	00	01	02	03	04	05	06	07	08	09	0A	0B	0C	0D	0E	0F
0100	..	..	..	..	..	..	..	..	..	..	..	27	..	..	..	..
0100	..	..	..	..	..	..	..	..	..	..	..	..	..	..	..	..

Attribute

Byte:	00	01	02	03	04	05	06	07	08	09	0A	0B	0C	0D	0E	0F
0100	..	..	..	..	..	..	..	..	..	..	..	..	..	..	..	..
0110	..	..	..	..	..	..	00	60	72	0E	..	..	..	..	..	..

Time   **Date**
(in coded form)

Byte:	00	01	02	03	04	05	06	07	08	09	0A	0B	0C	0D	0E	0F
0100	..	..	..	..	..	..	..	..	..	..	..	..	..	..	..	..
0110	..	..	..	..	..	..	..	..	..	02	00	..	..	..	..	..

First cluster in FAT

Byte:	00	01	02	03	04	05	06	07	08	09	0A	0B	0C	0D	0E	0F
0100	..	..	..	..	..	..	..	..	..	..	..	..	..	..	..	..
0110	..	..	..	..	..	..	..	..	..	..	..	..	54	56	00	00

File size

(The area from offset 0C through 15 is "reserved" for future use; all bytes in this part of the entry have a value of zero.)

By looking at the DEBUG display, you can tell this floppy disk is probably bootable, since the first two files in the directory are IBMBIO.COM and IBMDOS.COM. These two files have an attribute value of hex 27, which means that the following bits are "set" to 1 rather than 0:

- Read-Only
- Hidden
- System
- Archive

Most bytes in the directory entry are values that tell DOS what ASCII characters to display, or how big something is, or where in a table to look up something. Some are *coded* values — the date and time words (remember, a word is two bytes) compress a lot of information into a short space.

But the attribute byte is just a collection of bits. Its value depends on which bits happen to be set to 1 and which aren't. If the first (0th), second (1st), third (2nd), and sixth (5th) bits are set:

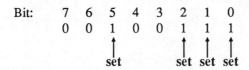

the value of the byte would be $2^0 + 2^1 + 2^2 + 2^5$, or $1 + 2 + 4 + 32$, or decimal 39 (hex 27). The value of hex 27 itself means nothing — it just happens to be a convenient way to store a lot of information, the above bit pattern, in one compressed chunk.

But how can you tell which bits represent which attributes? Just look them up in Figure 8.1:

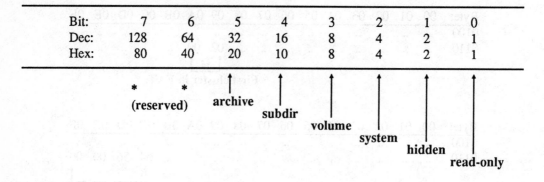

Figure 8.1   Interpretation of Directory Attribute Byte

Bit = number of bit
Dec = decimal value of bit
Hex = hexadecimal value of bit

To use this, you obviously have to be able to know the binary representation of the byte. Hex 27 in binary is:

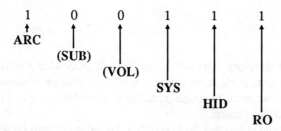

Translating bytes from hex to binary isn't all that hard, if you know how to count from 0 to F (0 to 16 decimal) in binary:

0000 = 0	1000 = 8
0001 = 1	1001 = 9
0010 = 2	1010 = A
0011 = 3	1011 = B
0100 = 4	1100 = C
0101 = 5	1101 = D
0110 = 6	1110 = E
0111 = 7	1111 = F

Notice that the first column (0-7) has the same bit pattern as the second column (8-F), except that on binary numbers lower than 8 the leftmost digit is a 0 and on those from 8 through F this digit is a 1.

Now take the hex digit 27, and divide it in half. Translate each half into binary and then put the two halves together, to see that hex 27 equals binary 00100111:

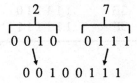

Here's a decimal/hex/binary table for all hex values from 0 to 3F (decimal 0 through 63), if you'd rather look things up than puzzle them out:

Dec Val	Hex Val	Six-Bit Binary Representation	Dec Val	Hex Val	Six-Bit Binary Representation
0	0	0 0 0 0 0 0	32	20	1 0 0 0 0 0
1	1	0 0 0 0 0 1	33	21	1 0 0 0 0 1
2	2	0 0 0 0 1 0	34	22	1 0 0 0 1 0
3	3	0 0 0 0 1 1	35	23	1 0 0 0 1 1
4	4	0 0 0 1 0 0	36	24	1 0 0 1 0 0
5	5	0 0 0 1 0 1	37	25	1 0 0 1 0 1
6	6	0 0 0 1 1 0	38	26	1 0 0 1 1 0
7	7	0 0 0 1 1 1	39	27	1 0 0 1 1 1
8	8	0 0 1 0 0 0	40	28	1 0 1 0 0 0
9	9	0 0 1 0 0 1	41	29	1 0 1 0 0 1
10	A	0 0 1 0 1 0	42	2A	1 0 1 0 1 0
11	B	0 0 1 0 1 1	43	2B	1 0 1 0 1 1
12	C	0 0 1 1 0 0	44	2C	1 0 1 1 0 0
13	D	0 0 1 1 0 1	45	2D	1 0 1 1 0 1
14	E	0 0 1 1 1 0	46	2E	1 0 1 1 1 0
15	F	0 0 1 1 1 1	47	2F	1 0 1 1 1 1
16	10	0 1 0 0 0 0	48	30	1 1 0 0 0 0
17	11	0 1 0 0 0 1	49	31	1 1 0 0 0 1
18	12	0 1 0 0 1 0	50	32	1 1 0 0 1 0
19	13	0 1 0 0 1 1	51	33	1 1 0 0 1 1
20	14	0 1 0 1 0 0	52	34	1 1 0 1 0 0
21	15	0 1 0 1 0 1	53	35	1 1 0 1 0 1
22	16	0 1 0 1 1 0	54	36	1 1 0 1 1 0
23	17	0 1 0 1 1 1	55	37	1 1 0 1 1 1
24	18	0 1 1 0 0 0	56	38	1 1 1 0 0 0
25	19	0 1 1 0 0 1	57	39	1 1 1 0 0 1
26	1A	0 1 1 0 1 0	58	3A	1 1 1 0 1 0

27	1B	0 1 1 0 1 1	59	3B	1 1 1 0 1 1
28	1C	0 1 1 1 0 0	60	3C	1 1 1 1 0 0
29	1D	0 1 1 1 0 1	61	3D	1 1 1 1 0 1
30	1E	0 1 1 1 1 0	62	3E	1 1 1 1 1 0
31	1F	0 1 1 1 1 1	63	3F	1 1 1 1 1 1

The following BASIC ATTRBUTE.BAS program will do all the work for you by looking at which bits are set to 1 in any attribute value you enter, and reporting the appropriate attributes.

```
100 ' ATTRBUTE.BAS
110 SCREEN 0:COLOR 3,0:KEY OFF:CLS
120 S$=STRING$(5,32):PRINT STRING$(56,61)
130 PRINT "Enter hex attribute value ";
140 INPUT "(or just hit Enter to end): ",N$
150 N=VAL("&H"+N$)
160 IF N>63 THEN BEEP:GOTO 130
170 IF N=0 THEN END
180 PRINT "File Attributes are:"
190 IF N AND  1 THEN PRINT S$;"Read-Only"
200 IF N AND  2 THEN PRINT S$;"Hidden"
210 IF N AND  4 THEN PRINT S$;"System"
220 IF N  =  8 THEN PRINT S$;"Volume"
230 IF N AND 16 THEN PRINT S$;"Subdirectory"
240 IF N AND 32 THEN PRINT S$;"Archive"
250 GOTO 120
```

If you examine the attribute byte values for the other files in the above DEBUG display:

Byte:	00 01 02 03 04 05 06 07 08 09 0A 0B 0C 0D 0E 0F		
0100	.. .. 27	IBMBIO	COM'....
0120	.. .. 27	IBMDOS	COM'....
0140	.. .. 20	COMMAND COM	....
0160	.. .. 28	PC MAGAZINE(....	
0180	.. .. 22	HIDDEN	FIL"....
01A0	.. .. 10	SUBDIR1	.....

you can look at Figure 8.1 to figure out which attribute bits are set:

Filename	Hex value	Binary value	Attributes
IBMDOS.COM	27	1 0 0 1 1 1	ARC, SYS, HID, RO
COMMAND.COM	20	1 0 0 0 0 0	ARC
PC MAGAZINE	28	1 0 1 0 0 0	ARC, VOL
HIDDEN.FIL	22	1 0 0 0 1 0	ARC, HID
SUBDIR1	10	0 1 0 0 0 0	SUB

This tells you that IBMDOS.COM, like IBMBIO.COM, has its archive bit set, and is a hidden, system, read-only file. The only bit set in the COMMAND.COM entry is the archive bit. PC MAGAZINE is the disk's volume label (which appears in DIR listings, CHKDSK output, etc.) since its 2^3 bit is set. The archive bit is also set in HIDDEN.FIL, and since the 2^1 bit is set, this is also hidden from normal directory searches. And SUBDIR1, with its 2^4 bit set, is a subdirectory.

Don't start meddling with volume labels or subdirectory entries. And if any file is marked as a system file, keep your hands off that as well. But the other attributes are fair game. For example:

- DOS sets the directory archive bit on (to 1) whenever it creates or modifies a file. When you use the DOS BACKUP or XCOPY commands with a /M switch, DOS unsets (turns off, or sets to 0) this bit after it makes the copy. This lets subsequent backup operations skip over any files that you haven't changed since you last backed up your disk. By setting the read-only bit on (to 1) you can prevent anyone from changing or erasing any file. You'll still be able to read or copy it, but DOS won't let you alter its contents.
- By setting the hidden bit on (to 1) you can keep a file from showing up in DIR searches. Actually, setting the system bit on will exclude it from DIR searches as well. (Since a subdirectory is just a special kind of file, you can even hide whole subdirectories from DIR listings. You'll still be able to change (CHDIR or CD) and remove (RMDIR or RD) and they'll show up if your PROMPT contains a $P.)

Here's where DEBUG's sector-handling ability can be very useful. DOS maintains file attributes in your disk's directory. You can't use the L FILENAME command to load your directory into DEBUG as if it were a file. Instead, you have to tell DEBUG to read specific sectors off your disk and put them into memory.

The problem is that directories aren't all the same length, and they don't start at the same sector on every disk. DOS supports 160K, 180K, 320K, 360K, 720K, 1.2M and 1.44M diskettes. The number of possible listings in the root directories of these diskettes varies from 64 to 224. And since the directories occupy space on the disks after the two FATs of varying sizes, the starting directory sectors vary widely.

To figure out where each directory starts, and how long it is, you can examine the BIOS Parameter Block (BPB) in the boot sector (sector 0 — the first one on the disk).

The root directory is located right after the single boot sector and the two redundant FATs. So if you figure out how many sectors each FAT takes up, multiply this number by 2 (since FATs come in pairs), and then add 1 (for the boot sector), the directory will start at the sector with the very next number.

The BPB uses the single byte at offset 10 (hex) of the boot record to keep track of how many FATs are on the disk — one or two. And it uses the two bytes at offset 16 (hex) to keep track of how many sectors each FAT contains.

To examine the boot sector (sector 0) on a 360K diskette in drive A: load DEBUG without specifying a filename. Then issue a Load command with four parameters:

1. The address in memory where you want DEBUG to load the information (any address will do, but use 100 hex).

2. The drive number. Remember that drive A: is drive number 0, drive B: is drive number 1, drive C: is drive number 2, etc. To avoid disaster, always think twice when specifying DEBUG drive numbers!

3. The first sector you want loaded.

4. How many sectors you want to load — starting with the first sector specified in the previous step. You can't load more than hex 80 sectors (64K) at once, but this shouldn't be a problem.

To load the single sector 0 on drive A: (drive number 0) into address 100, issue the command:

```
-L 100 0 0 1
```

Then display the first hex 20 bytes. To make life easier, display the one byte at BPB offset 10 (which is at offset 110 in memory, since you loaded the file at address 100 rather than address 0), and the two bytes starting at offset 16 (DEBUG offset 116):

```
C>DEBUG
-L 100 0 0 1
-D 100 L 20
30DD:0100  EB 34 90 49 42 4D 20 20-33 2E 33 00 02 02 01 00   .4.IBM  3.3.....
30DD:0110  02 70 00 D0 02 FD 02 00-09 00 02 00 00 00 00 00   .p..............
-D 110 L 1
30DD:0110  02                                                .
-D 116 L 2
30DD:0110                          02 00                             ..
```

The value of 2 at offset 110 specifies that this disk contains two FATs (all DOS disks do). And the value of 2 at offset 16 tells you that each FAT sprawls over two sectors. Armed with this information, you can figure out that the directory on a 360K floppy begins on sector 5:

- The boot sector starts at sector 0 and stops at sector 1
- The pair of FATs start at sector 1 and stop at sector 4
- The directory begins at sector 5

So the formula for figuring out the starting directory sector is:

(number of sectors in FAT x 2) + 1

Since all FATs on floppy disks use fewer than 256 sectors, you can figure out the number of sectors per FAT with the simple DEBUG commands:

```
C>DEBUG
-L 100 0 0 1
-D 116 L 1
```

This would look on drive A:. To look on drive B: change the first line to:

```
-L 100 1 0 1
```

Fine. Now you know where the directory starts; but where does it end? The two-byte value at offset hex 11 gives you the maximum number of entries in the root directory; you can see by looking at the DEBUG display above that the value here is hex 70 (decimal 112).

(Two-byte values can be tricky, since they're stored in "backwords" format. Users gave IBM's storage system this informal name because two eight-bit bytes combine into one 16-bit word and because the low-order byte — the half that's worth less — is at the lower address, which sometimes seems backward. You'll see why in a second.)

This book contains many warnings that caution you against fooling around with hard disk sectors. To make sure you don't try to fiddle with the real thing yourself, here's what one looks like on an old AT:

```
30DD:0100 EB 34 90 49 42 4D 20 20-33 2E 33 00 02 04 01 00
30DD:0110 02 00 02 07 A3 F8 29 00-11 00 04 00 11 00 80 00
```

bytes 11 and 12

The number of root directory entries on an AT is obviously more than 2. Since the bytes are stored in backwards order, flip 00 02 around and you get 02 00, or hex 200 (decimal 512).

The floppy disk directory used in these examples can hold hex 70 (decimal 112) entries, and because each entry is 20 hex (decimal 32) bytes long, this particular directory will take up E00 hex bytes. Sectors are always 200 hex bytes long, so E00 / 200 = 7, which means that the directory will span seven sectors, starting at sector 5.

The formula for figuring out how many sectors the whole root directory takes up is:

Number of root directory entries * hex 20 / hex 200

which translates to:

Number of root directory entries / hex 10

And while you're at it, you can figure out the total number of bytes taken up by the root directory either with:

Number of root directory entries * hex 20

or:

Number of sectors taken up by the root directory * 200

Since the number of root directory entries on a floppy disk is less than 256, you can figure out the number (on drive A:) with the simple DEBUG commands:

```
C>DEBUG
-L 100 0 0 1
-D 111 L 1
```

You could load the entire directory on a 360K floppy disk in drive A: and then display it with the command:

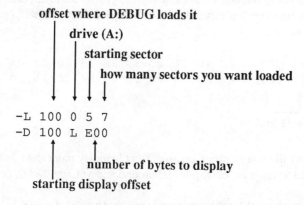

Dumping E00 (3,584 decimal) bytes will scroll the listing quickly off the screen, but you can stop and restart the display by alternately pressing Ctrl-S. You could also press Ctrl-NumLock to halt the display, but you'd then have to press an alphanumeric key to restart it. Or, to end up with a printed copy of the listing, you could turn your printer on and type Ctrl-P or Ctrl-PrtSc before you start. When you're finished, press Ctrl-P or Ctrl-PrtSc again to toggle this printer echoing feature off. And if you want a copy of it on your disk, you could always create a file called DEBUG.SCR that contained the three lines:

```
L 100 0 5 7
D 100 L E00
Q
```

Make sure you press the Enter key after each line, especially the last one with the Q! Then, at the DOS prompt, type:

```
DEBUG < DEBUG.SCR >DIRLIST
```

and DOS will redirect the DEBUG listing into a file called DIRLIST.

To make things easier, Figure 8.2 presents all the necessary DEBUG loading and display addresses:

	Sectors in boot record	Sectors in FATs	Sectors in root DIR	Entries in root DIR	DEBUG commands to see root directory in A
5-1/2 160K	1	2	4	64	L 100 0 3 4 D 100 L 800
5-1/2 180K	1	4	4	64	L 100 0 5 4 D 100 L 800
5-1/2 320K	1	2	7	112	L 100 0 3 7 D 100 L E00
5-1/2 360K	1	4	7	112	L 100 0 5 7 D 100 L E00
5-1/2 1.2M	1	14	14	224	L 100 0 F E D 100 L 1C00
3-1/2 720K	1	6	7	112	L 100 0 B E D 100 L E00
3-1/2 1.44M	1	18	14	224	L 100 0 13 E D 100 L 1C00

Figure 8.2. DEBUG Loading and Display Addresses

Note: All values in decimal format; DEBUG command parameters in hexadecimal

As an example, here's the DIR listing of a 360K floppy in drive A:

```
Volume in drive A is PC MAGAZINE
Directory of  A:\

COMMAND    COM      25307     3-17-87    12:00p
TEST1      FIL         20    10-27-88    10:57p
TEST2      FIL         26    10-27-88    10:58p
TEST3      FIL         30    10-27-88    10:59p
SUBDIR1         <DIR>           10-26-88    12:06a
           5 File(s)     279552 bytes free
```

Since the first file is COMMAND.COM, odds are that it's a formatted disk, which means the first two files on it are the hidden system files IBMBIO.COM and IBMDOS.COM. The disk also has a volume label, which is an additional small file, and one subdirectory called \SUBDIR1. Other than those and three small TEST files, it's fairly empty.

The DEBUG display of this would look something like:

```
C>DEBUG
-L 100 0 5 1
-D 100 L 100
30DD:0100   49 42 4D 42 49 4F 20 20-43 4F 4D 27 00 00 00 00   IBMBIO  COM'....
30DD:0110   00 00 00 00 00 00 00 60-72 0E 02 00 54 56 00 00   .......'r...TV..
30DD:0120   49 42 4D 44 4F 53 20 20-43 4F 4D 27 00 00 00 00   IBMDOS  COM'....
30DD:0130   00 00 00 00 00 00 00 60-71 0E 18 00 CF 75 00 00   .......'q...u..
30DD:0140   43 4F 4D 4D 41 4E 44 20-43 4F 4D 20 00 00 00 00   COMMAND COM ....
30DD:0150   00 00 00 00 00 00 00 60-71 0E 36 00 DB 62 00 00   .......'q.6..b..
30DD:0160   50 43 20 4D 41 47 41 5A-49 4E 45 28 00 00 00 00   PC MAGAZINE(....
30DD:0170   00 00 00 00 00 00 19 B7-5B 0F 00 00 00 00 00 00   ........[.......
30DD:0180   54 45 53 54 31 20 20 20-46 49 4C 20 00 00 00 00   TEST1   FIL ....
30DD:0190   00 00 00 00 00 00 39 B7-5B 11 4F 00 14 00 00 00   ......9.[.O....
30DD:01A0   54 45 53 54 32 20 20 20-46 49 4C 20 00 00 00 00   TEST2   FIL ....
30DD:01B0   00 00 00 00 00 00 58 B7-5B 11 50 00 1A 00 00 00   ......X.[.P.....
30DD:01C0   54 45 53 54 33 20 20 20-46 49 4C 20 00 00 00 00   TEST3   FIL ....
30DD:01D0   00 00 00 00 00 00 60 B7-5B 11 51 00 1E 00 00 00   ......'.[.Q.....
30DD:01E0   53 55 42 44 49 52 31 20-20 20 20 10 00 00 00 00   SUBDIR1    .....
30DD:01F0   00 00 00 00 00 00 DB 00-5A 11 52 00 00 00 00 00   ........Z.R.....
```

Since it's potentially dangerous to alter system files, volume labels, or subdirectory entries, experiment with the others. COMMAND.COM, TEST1.FIL, TEST2.FIL, and TEST3.FIL all have the same attribute — hex 20. Figure 8.1 presented earlier shows that the only bit that's set in all these files is the archive bit.

The first thing to try is hiding a file. To change an attribute, you have to do three things:

1. Read the existing attribute from the directory.
2. Figure out what the new attribute value should be.
3. Very carefully write the new attribute back to the directory.

You already know that the COMMAND.COM attribute is hex 20. So how do you change this so DOS will hide the file? You use logic.

A synopsis of the attribute bit values and the logical operators you'll need to change them is:

Attribute	Bit	Set	Unset
Read-Only	0	OR 1 (hex 1)	AND 254 (hex FE)
Hidden	1	OR 2 (hex 2)	AND 253 (hex FD)
System	2	OR 4 (hex 4)	AND 251 (hex FB)
Volume	3	OR 8 (hex 8)	AND 247 (hex F7)
Subdirectory	4	OR 16 (hex 10)	AND 239 (hex EF)
Archive	5	OR 32 (hex 20)	AND 223 (hex DF)

To set or unset a bit without disturbing any of the other bit values, just look up the applicable logical operation and perform it. It helps if you have a calculator like the one in *SideKick* that can do logical AND and OR operations. But you do have a free one you probably never use — BASIC.

If you want to make sure the hidden bit is set on, all you have to do is have the current byte value handy — let's say it's decimal 53 — then load BASIC (by typing either BASICA or GWBASIC, depending on what system you're using), and type:

```
PRINT 53 OR 2
```

You could even use shorthand and type:

```
? 53 OR 2
```

In either case, BASIC will respond with:

```
55
```

You may be wondering why we didn't just add 2 to 53. Easy answer: If the hidden bit (the 2^1 bit) wasn't already set, adding 2 to the number would work just fine. But if the hidden bit was already set, adding 2 would utterly confuse things.

If you tried this OR operation with a number like 47:

```
PRINT 47 OR 2
```

BASIC would respond with:

47

because the 2^1 bit is in fact already set in the number 47. If you just added 2 to decimal 47 you'd end up with decimal 49. The binary representation of these looks like:

- decimal 47 (hex 2F)   101111
- decimal 49 (hex 31)   110001

The first set of attributes (decimal 47, or binary 101111) would be:

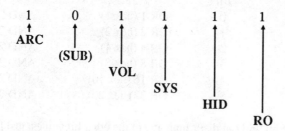

which wouldn't really exist, since a volume label isn't an archived, read-only, hidden system file.

The second set of attributes (decimal 49, or binary 110001) would be:

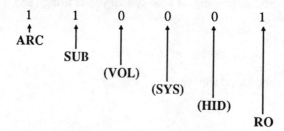

Again, you wouldn't really see this exact configuration. It's meant only to show you that you can't just blindly add a number to an attribute value. You have to first see if the bit you want to set is already set. If it is already set, leave it alone.

Incidentally, BASIC is terrific at handling hex numbers as well as decimal ones. But you have to preface them with an "&H" prefix. Decimal 47 = hex 2F, so you could have gone into BASIC and typed:

```
PRINT HEX$(&H2F OR 2)
```

and BASIC would have responded with:

2F

If you had simply tried:

```
PRINT &H2F OR 2
```

without the HEX$( ), BASIC would have performed the logical OR operation and would have then converted the result to decimal, yielding:

47

You could look up the binary representation of each number, see if the particular bit was set, and leave the value alone if it already was set, or add the proper value (in this case 2^1, or 2) if it wasn't yet set. But this is time-consuming, and you have to have a binary chart handy (or be facile with binary numbers).

Using logical operations is a far better method, since these will automatically do the job you want on a particular bit only if the bit is in the opposite state. Otherwise it will leave things they way they are. It lets you set any bit to 1 if it's 0, but leave the bit alone if it's already 1. And if you want to reverse the process, it will unset a bit to 0 if it's 1, but leave it alone if the bit is already a 0.

Logical operations are pretty straightforward. All you have to know here is that 1 means true and 0 means false, and then learn some simple rules:

1	AND	1	=	1	(true)
1	OR	1	=	1	(true)
1	OR	0	=	1	(true)
0	OR	1	=	1	(true)
0	AND	0	=	0	(false)
1	AND	0	=	0	(false)
0	AND	1	=	0	(false)
0	OR	0	=	0	(false)

Think about it. An AND operation means:

Something will be true only if both the first thing AND the second thing are true.

An OR operation means:

Something will be true if either the first thing OR the second thing is true.

Here's a shortcut:

1. The only AND operation that can be true is if both the first thing AND the second thing are true. So if you AND any number with a 0 you end up with a 0.

2. Any OR operation is true if it has a 1 somewhere in it. So if you OR any number with a 1 you get a 1.

To do the proper logical operation on a single bit you have to isolate the bit you want to change. You can isolate any bit by using a bit *mask* to screen out all other interference. (A bit mask is a number that forces a bit to a desired state without changing any other bit values, when used with a logical operator like AND or OR.) A binary mask to set the hidden bit (the 2^1 bit) on would look like:

```
OR 00000010
```

No matter what binary number you use with this OR mask, when you're done the 2^1 bit will be a 1 and all the other bits will be the way they were originally.

The opposite bit mask to set this bit off would look like:

```
AND 11111101
```

No matter what binary number you use with this AND mask, when you're done, the 2^1 bit will be a 0 and all the remaining bits will remain unchanged.

Try this with the decimal 53 and 47 examples used earlier. The OR 00000010 operation will set the hidden bit in 53 (where it's not set) but leave the bit alone in 47 (where it's already set). The opposite AND 11111101 instruction will unset the hidden bit in 47 (where it's set) and leave it alone in 53 (where it's already unset):

decimal 53:

```
         00110101              00110101
    OR   00000010         AND  11111101
    =    00110111 (55)    =    00110101 (53)
```

        ↑   ↑

   (bit *not* set;this   **(bit *already* unset; this**
        sets it)   **leaves it alone)**

decimal 47:

```
         00101111              00101111
    OR   00000010         AND  11111101
    =    00101111 (47)    =    00101101 (45)
```

        ↑   ↑

   (bit *already* set; this   **(bit *not* unset; this**
    leaves it alone)   **unsets it)**

If you want to change several bits in an attribute just perform successive AND and OR operations unless you're really handy with binary calculations.

You can learn the value by looking at the 12th byte over (byte number 11, or hex 0B) in the directory display DEBUG provides:

attribute byte

```
30DD:0140   43 4F 4D 4D 41 4E 44 20-43 4F 4D 20 00 00 00 00   COMMAND COM ....
30DD:0150   00 00 00 00 00 00 00 60-71 0E 36 00 DB 62 00 00   .......'q.6..b..
```

So here's how you can hide COMMAND.COM:

The value of the COMMAND.COM attribute byte is hex 20. To turn on its attribute byte, you have to OR this value with 00000010, or hex 2. Hex 20 expressed in binary notation is 00100000. So:

```
         00100000   (hex 20)
OR       00000010   (hex 2)
=        00100010   (hex 22)
```

To change the meaning of the drive A: COMMAND.COM attribute byte from "archive only" to "archive and hidden:"

1. Load the sectors containing the directory into DEBUG.
2. Make sure the value that you want to change is indeed at offset 14B (and if it's not, jot down the correct offset).
3. Use the E command to enter the new 22 value in place of the old 20 value.
4. Check your work to make sure everything is correct.
5. *Write the sectors very carefully back to drive A:.*

Here's how the whole process would look:

1. Start DEBUG and load the first directory sector from the 360K floppy in drive A: into memory at address 100:

```
DEBUG
-L 100 0 5 1
```

2. Make sure the attribute byte for COMMAND.COM is at address 14B. Here it's the number surrounded by asterisks (these asterisks won't show up in the actual listing):

```
-D 100 L 60
30DD:0100   49 42 4D 42 49 4F 20 20-43 4F 4D 27 00 00 00 00   IBMBIO  COM'....
30DD:0110   00 00 00 00 00 00 00 60-72 0E 02 00 54 56 00 00   .......'r...TV..
30DD:0120   49 42 4D 44 4F 53 20 20-43 4F 4D 27 00 00 00 00   IBMDOS  COM'....
30DD:0130   00 00 00 00 00 00 00 60-71 0E 18 00 CF 75 00 00   .......'q....u..
30DD:0140   43 4F 4D 4D 41 4E 44 20-43 4F 4D*20*00 00 00 00   COMMAND COM ....
30DD:0150   00 00 00 00 00 00 00 60-71 0E 36 00 DB 62 00 00   .......'q.6..b..
```

3. Change the value of the byte at offset 14B from 20 to 22:

```
-E 14B
30DD:014B   20.22
```

4. Check your typing (again, asterisks are included here to show you where you should be looking; they won't appear in the actual DEBUG display):

```
-D 140 L 20
30DD:0140  43 4F 4D 4D 41 4E 44 20-43 4F 4D*22*00 00 00 00   COMMAND COM"....
30DD:0150  00 00 00 00 00 00 00 60-71 0E 36 00 DB 62 00 00   .......`q.6..b..
```

5. Write the sectors to disk and quit. To write sectors, *use the exact same syntax that you used to load them, but substitute a "W" for the original "L"* — and don't press the Enter key until you've checked your typing to make sure that the parameters you entered for the W command match the L parameters exactly. Also, be absolutely sure that that number following the 100 is 0 so you write to drive A: rather than any other drive:

```
-W 100 0 5 1
-Q
```

Then, when you're done, look at the directory again:

```
DIR A:

        Volume in drive A is PC MAGAZINE
        Directory of  A:\

        TEST1     FIL       20   10-27-88  10:57p
        TEST2     FIL       26   10-27-88  10:58p
        TEST3     FIL       30   10-27-88  10:59p
        SUBDIR1         <DIR>        10-26-88  12:06a
              4 File(s)      279552 bytes free
```

This time, no COMMAND.COM. But you can tell it's still on your disk by executing the command:

```
CHKDSK A: /V
```

The /V switch will display every file on your disk, hidden or not, so you'll see something like:

```
Volume PC MAGAZINE created Oct 27, 1988 10:56p
        Directory A:\
```

```
        A:\IBMBIO.COM
        A:\IBMDOS.COM
        A:\COMMAND.COM
        A:\PC MAGAZ.INE
        A:\TEST1.FIL
        A:\TEST2.FIL
        A:\TEST3.FIL
Directory A:\SUBDIR1

   362496 bytes total disk space
    78848 bytes in 4 hidden files
     1024 bytes in 1 directories
     3072 bytes in 3 user files
   279552 bytes available on disk
   655360 bytes total memory
   471200 bytes free
```

The standard CHKDSK report tells you that the disk contains four hidden files. By comparing the CHKDSK /V report with the DIR listing, you can tell that the hidden files are IBMBIO.COM, IBMDOS.COM, COMMAND.COM, and the volume label, PC MAGAZ.INE (DOS displays a period near the end, since the volume label is actually a small file, and CHKDSK tries to turn the final three characters of the label's name into an extension).

The disk will boot normally, even though no COMMAND.COM appears when you examine the disk with DIR. Hiding COMMAND.COM is not very useful, except that you could theoretically hide all three files you'd normally have in your root directory — COMMAND.COM, CONFIG.SYS, and AUTOEXEC.BAT — as well as your main root-level subdirectories. Everything would work the same, but if you logged into the root directory of such a disk and tried a DIR command you'd see the "File not found" message.

If you're using a variety of security tricks to keep nosy co-workers out of your files, this may help a bit. They'll still be able to figure out what's on the disk by using CHKDSK /V, or by loading DEBUG and looking at the directory the way you did to make the changes. And they can still look at your AUTOEXEC.BAT and CONFIG.SYS files by using the TYPE command.

DEBUG can load hidden files. In fact, if you wanted to copy the three system files from drive A: to a formatted disk in drive B: that didn't contain these files — and you didn't have SYS.COM or FORMAT.COM handy — you could do so by typing:

```
C>DEBUG
-N A:IBMBIO.COM
-L
-N B:IBMBIO.COM
-W
-N A:IBMDOS.COM
```

```
-L
-N B:IBMDOS.COM
-W
-Q
C>COPY A:COMMAND.COM B:
```

(This example is for IBM DOS versions; substitute the generic MS-DOS names for your system files if you're not using PC-DOS.)

If you try this, you'll notice that the newly written IBMBIO.COM and IBMDOS.COM system files on drive B: are no longer hidden. These files don't have to be hidden to boot your system. When DEBUG writes a file to disk, it ignores any previous directory attributes and turns on just the archive bit.

Of course, you now know how to hide those two files. If you put the 360K floppy with the unhidden system files into drive A: you could load the beginning of the directory into DEBUG with the command:

```
C>DEBUG
-L 100 0 5 1
```

The first three files on this disk should be:

- IBMBIO.COM
- IBMDOS.COM
- COMMAND.COM

or their generic MS-DOS equivalents. Check to make sure this is the case with the command:

```
-D 100 L 5F
```

which should produce a listing very similar to:

```
30DD:0100  49 42 4D 42 49 4F 20 20-43 4F 4D 20 00 00 00 00   IBMBIO  COM ....
30DD:0110  00 00 00 00 00 00 38 0D-66 0F 02 00 54 56 00 00   ......8.f...TV..
30DD:0120  49 42 4D 44 4F 53 20 20-43 4F 4D 20 00 00 00 00   IBMDOS  COM ....
30DD:0130  00 00 00 00 00 00 44 0D-66 0F 18 00 CF 75 00 00   ......D.f....u..
30DD:0140  43 4F 4D 4D 41 4E 44 20-43 4F 4D 20 00 00 00 00   COMMAND COM ....
30DD:0150  00 00 00 00 00 00 00 60-71 0E 36 00 DB 62 00      .......'q.6..b.
```

The attribute bytes for the first two files should be at addresses 10B and 12B, and the value should be hex 20 (which means just the archive bit is set). To make sure the hidden bit is set in any attribute byte, simply OR it with 2:

```
20 OR 2 = 22
```

Use the DEBUG E command in interactive mode to enter the new value of 22 in place of the old 20:

```
-E 10B
30DD:010B  20.22
-E 12B
30DD:012B  20.22
```

Then check your work with the same D command that you used earlier:

```
-D 100 L 5F
30DD:0100  49 42 4D 42 49 4F 20 20-43 4F 4D 22 00 00 00 00  IBMBIO  COM"....
30DD:0110  00 00 00 00 00 00 38 0D-66 0F 02 00 54 56 00 00  ......8.f...TV..
30DD:0120  49 42 4D 44 4F 53 20 20-43 4F 4D 22 00 00 00 00  IBMDOS  COM"....
30DD:0130  00 00 00 00 00 00 44 0D-66 0F 18 00 CF 75 00 00  ......D.f....u..
30DD:0140  43 4F 4D 4D 41 4E 44 20-43 4F 4D 20 00 00 00 00  COMMAND COM ....
30DD:0150  00 00 00 00 00 00 00 60-71 0E 36 00 DB 62 00     .......'q.6..b.
```

When you're all done, *very carefully* write the new directory sector back to drive A: by duplicating the Load command you used initially, but substituting a W for the earlier L:

```
-W 100 0 5 1
```

Check your typing before you press the Enter key. When you're sure everything is accurate, press Enter, then type Q and press Enter to quit, and the normally hidden system files will once again be hidden.

Writing Information from Memory to Disk

Format: **W [address [drive sector sector]]**

Write is potentially the most dangerous tool in DEBUG's arsenal. It lets you write information to any part of any disk in your system. If you're not extremely careful, you can destroy good data on your disk by writing bad data over it. Worse, if you accidentally write the wrong data over the two key tables that DOS uses to organize every disk — the pair of FATs and the directory — you can pretty much just kiss your data goodbye.

DEBUG lets you load and write information in two forms — as files and as absolute disk sectors.

Working with files is relatively safe and easy, so long as you always work with *copies* of your important files rather than the originals. This way you can start over again if the DEBUG changes you made weren't exactly right. But working with sectors is *playing with fire.* Once again, a warning:

WARNING!

Unless you know exactly what you're doing, and are sure your disks are completely backed up, and take every possible prudent measure to safeguard your system, and triple-check every command before you execute it, be extraordinarily careful when loading and working with sectors, and utterly paranoid and overcautious when writing them. And be sure you always work on *copies* of all your files, *never* the originals. If you're the least bit nervous or uncertain about this kind of activity, *don't do it.* Just type Q and press the Enter key to Quit.

The easiest way to use the Write command is to load an existing file (either with the N and L commands or by specifying it at the end of the DOS command line), then change it and write the modified file back to the same disk with the simple command:

```
-W
```

You can't write a file to disk unless DEBUG knows the name and size of the file. When you load an existing file 64K or smaller, DEBUG keeps track of the filename at offset hex 82 of the code segment and puts the number of bytes (the file size) into the CX register. If the file is larger than 64K, DEBUG uses the CX and BX registers to store the file size.

To patch version 3.3 of COMMAND.COM so CLS clears the screen to red text on a white background, you could issue just three commands:

```
C>DEBUG COMMAND.COM
-E 2BAD 74
-W
Writing 62DB bytes
-Q
```

Since you specified the name of a file at the end of the DOS command line, after the word DEBUG, DEBUG knows the name of the file and how many bytes to write.

But if you tried to create a file from scratch, you'd have to make sure you gave DEBUG a proper name and size. If you simply typed:

```
C>DEBUG
-E 2BAD 74
-W
```

DEBUG wouldn't know what you wanted to name the file, and would respond with a "(W)rite error, no destination defined" message. And if you specified a brand new filename like XYZ.COM without telling DEBUG how long the file was, either by typing:

```
C>DEBUG XYZ.COM
File not found
-E 2BAD 74
-W
-Q
```

or:

```
C>DEBUG
-E 2BAD 74
-N XYZ.COM
-W
-Q
```

DEBUG would create a directory entry, but wouldn't write anything to the file. You'd see the message "Writing 0000 bytes." A subsequent DIR listing would display the XYZ.COM filename, the correct creation time and date, but a file size of 0.

So when creating a new file, specify both the name (either at the end of the DOS command line after the word DEBUG, or by using the N command), and the size (with the RCX command — and the RBX command if you're creating a real monster). Here's a sample script file:

```
N DRIVE.COM
E 100 B4 09 BA 14 01 CD 21 B4 19 CD
E 10A 21 04 41 88 C2 B4 02 CD 21 C3
E 114 "Current drive is $"
RCX
26
W
Q
```

Type this in using a pure-ASCII word processor or EDLIN, and call the file DRIVE.SCR. Or, if you don't have either of those tools handy, make sure you're at the DOS prompt and insert the line:

```
COPY CON DRIVE.SCR
```

at the very top, and when you're all done, press the F6 function key and then the Enter key at the very end. In either case, be sure to press the Enter key after each line, especially the final one (with the Q). Then put this DRIVE.SCR file in the same directory as DEBUG (unless DEBUG.COM is in a subdirectory that your path knows about) and type:

```
DEBUG < DRIVE.SCR
```

This will create a simple program that reports the current drive. Nothing special. In fact, you could do the same thing with the DOS PROMPT command:

```
PROMPT Current drive is $n$_
```

Note that the script file starts off by naming the file that DEBUG will create. You can put this N command just about anywhere before the W command (except in the middle of a set of continuous Assemble (A) instructions). The RCX command near the end sets the value in the CX register to hex 26 — the length of the file. You always need to specify the length. But you could also have named the file by omitting the:

```
N DRIVE.COM
```

line and instead issuing a:

```
DEBUG DRIVE.COM < DRIVE.SCR
```

command at the DOS prompt. In either case a simple, unadorned W will write the file to disk.

Using a naked W without anything after it tells DEBUG to write the information starting at offset 100 of the code segment. If the information you plan to write starts elsewhere, you can tell DEBUG where to start looking by specifying W and then the appropriate address. So if DRIVE.SCR used the E command to Enter information 100 hex bytes higher than normal, at offset 200, you would type:

```
N DRIVE.COM
E 200 B4 09 BA 14 01 CD 21 B4 19 CD
E 20A 21 04 41 88 C2 B4 02 CD 21 C3
E 214 "Current drive is $"
RCX
26
W 200
Q
```

You'd have to use the W 200 command to tell DEBUG where to look in memory for the information you want it to write to disk. You might want to do this if you have two programs loaded into different places in memory and you wanted to write the one to disk that didn't start at offset 100. Or you might want to write a module of a larger program to disk.

If you do plan to change the contents of an existing file, always make sure you're working on a copy of the file, never the original. Mistakes do happen. Or you might decide you liked the older version better. This is especially necessary when patching files that end in EXE. DEBUG loads EXE files differently from other files. DEBUG doesn't load the first byte of an EXE file at offset 100 the way it does with COM files or virtually every other kind of file. When customizing an EXE file, change the extension to something other than EXE at the same time you're copying it. So if you wanted to patch offset 1A5 of ABCD.EXE, do it this way:

```
C>COPY ABCD.EXE ABCD.XXX
          1 File(s) copied
C>DEBUG ABCD.XXX
-E 1A5 41
-W
Writing 2BC0 bytes
-Q
C>REN ABCD.XXX ABCDNEW.EXE
```

Then experiment with the ABCDNEW.EXE program to make sure you like it before you replace the older ABCD.EXE with it. In any case, save the original ABCD.EXE safely on a floppy disk somewhere. Or name it ABCDOLD.EXE. But don't patch originals. And don't try to write EXE files in DEBUG — it won't let you.

While we're at it, unless you're a programming ace, refrain from using commands like Trace (T), Proceed (P), or Go (G) to run programs from inside DEBUG. Doing this can alter the values in the CX and BX registers. If you're not careful about resetting these registers later so they contain the proper file sizes, DEBUG can end up writing the wrong number of bytes to disk. And it can do very strange things with EXE files, even if you've renamed them. These commands are really for serious programmers only.

If you forget to make a copy of your COM or text file before you start slashing away at it from inside DEBUG, you can prevent DEBUG from overwriting the original. Just use the N command to give a new name to the program currently loaded in memory. So if you're modifying a series of bytes in XYZ.COM and you don't want to obliterate the original version of the program by writing the patched version over it, you could rename the program before you wrote it. Or you could write it to another disk:

```
DEBUG XYZ.COM
-E 111 34
-E 12D C0
-E 20A 4F
-N XYZNEW.COM
-W
Writing 302 bytes
-Q
```

or:

```
DEBUG XYZ.COM
-E 111 34
-E 12D C0
```

```
-E 20A 4F
-N A:XYZ.COM
-W
Writing 302 bytes
-Q
```

The first example gives the file a new name before it writes the file to disk. The second example writes a file with the same name but to a different disk.

Always be sure you're writing the proper number of bytes. If you use the Move (M) command to make a file larger, add instructions to a program, or increase the size of messages that are stuck at the end, be sure to specify the new length with the RCX command. You may have to use the Unassemble (U) and Dump (D) commands to see exactly where the new file ends. Even if you're a single byte too short you can cause problems, especially since the last bytes of a program often jump control of the program back to DOS with code like CD 20 or C3. Truncate those and the program will hang, and you'll have to reboot. It usually doesn't hurt to make programs a bit longer than necessary. And remember when calculating lengths that files generally start at address 100 rather than 101 — so to be on the safe side, add 1 to the length you specify with RCX.

You can't really do much harm when writing entire files, so long as you're working with copies rather than originals. But you can cause devastating heartache if you're not careful when using DEBUG to write absolute sectors.

If you want to create or patch a file, DEBUG will take care of all the dirty DOS work for you. But if you want to alter a directory listing, or work with other fundamental disk underpinnings, you have to manipulate specific sectors directly. And while DEBUG is superb at doing delicate sector surgery, it won't stop you from destroying your disk if you issue a bone-headed or thick-fingered command at the wrong time.

The problem with writing sectors is that it's easy to wipe out or corrupt two key disk structures. DOS relies on two tables — the directory and the duplicate pair of FATs — to tell it where all the little pieces of your file are located. All programs and data are stored in small chunks called clusters, which are in turn made up of disk sectors. On just about all systems where users are constantly making changes to their data, and adding and deleting files, these clusters end up scattered in various places all over the disk surface.

The directory tells DOS where the initial cluster is on your disk, and the FAT maps out where all the remaining clusters (containing the rest of the file) are located. Without these, DOS won't know where to find the pieces of your programs and files. When you ask DOS to load a file, it consults these tables, figures out where the pieces are, and jumps around the disk gathering them all in the correct order and stringing them together properly in memory.

What makes writing sectors especially tricky is that all the parameters have to be in hexadecimal notation, and that DEBUG refers to the first number in any series as 0 rather than 1.

Here's where the trouble happens:

Users sometimes forget what they're doing and mix hex and decimal numbers. Or worse, they forget that DEBUG calls drive A: drive 0 rather than drive 1. If you're trying to write to drive A: and you accidentally specify a 1 when you meant to type a 0, you may damage the disk in drive B:, since DEBUG treats drive 1 as drive B: and will write the sectors to drive B: when you really wanted them to go to drive A:. That's bad, but presumably you have up-to-date backup copies of all your floppy disks, so you won't really lose anything.

However, if you're trying to write sectors to drive B: and you accidentally specify drive 2 when you really meant drive 1, DEBUG will happily oblige and write the sectors to drive C:, since it thinks of drive 2 as drive C:. Unfortunately, drive C: is usually a hard disk. If you're working with sectors from a floppy disk directory, and you inadvertently write these to a hard disk, that one errant keystroke will cost you days or weeks of reconstruction anguish. The data and program pieces will still be on your disk but you won't have any way to find out where they are or be able to assemble them into useful units. To be absolutely safe make sure every last byte of every important file is totally backed up before you start using DEBUG to fiddle with sectors.

Above all, etch into your consciousness how DEBUG refers to drives.

Then, pause whenever you're about to write absolute sectors, and then triple-check your typing and your intentions. Be especially careful if you decide to write to drive B: or your hard disk. If you're at all nervous about it — *don't*. Just erase your Write command (with the backspace or left arrow keys) or press Esc, Ctrl-C, or Ctrl-ScrollLock, then type Q and press Enter to quit.

The following examples all apply to floppy disks *only*. To keep things as safe as possible, they all illustrate how to work with the floppy disk in drive A:.

You don't often need to manipulate absolute disk sectors. One time you do is when you've stupidly destroyed your FATs and are scanning through all your disk sectors one by one looking for the pieces to pick up. This kind of emergency reconstruction is tedious, nasty work, and you'll barely be able to use it to put your text files back together in reasonable form. Splicing your programs or any other binary files together is pretty much out of the question. In fact, doing any work like this is such an arduous undertaking that you're probably better off using commercial utility programs such as Peter Norton's or Paul Mace's to rescue your files.

But if you're adventurous and extraordinarily careful, you can do things like alter your disk directory by patching the relevant sectors. See the Load (L) section for details.

To reduce the risk when working with sectors, use the exact same syntax for loading and writing. So to load an entire directory on a 360K floppy disk in drive A:, you would specify the seven directory sectors starting with sector 5 with the command:

```
L 100 0 5 7
```

You can later write these back to the same disk by changing the initial L to a W:

```
W 100 0 5 7
```

Here's what this particular Write command tells DEBUG:

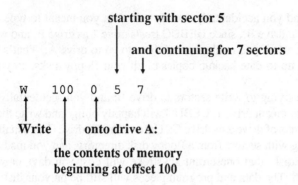

A sector is 512 (hex 200) bytes. When you use the D command without any parameters after it, DEBUG normally displays eight paragraphs, or 128 (hex 80) bytes at a time. So each four times you type D and press the Enter key, you display one sector.

It's a good idea when you're working with sectors to jot down on a notepad the parameters you used to load the sectors, and then refer to your notes and very carefully type the same exact parameters when you're ready to write them back to disk. Then, when you're ready to issue any Write command, always stop and check your typing — and be sure to verify that the disk you've specified is the one you want DEBUG to write to.

You can't write more than hex 80 sectors (64K) at once or write any sectors when using a network drive. And if DEBUG senses a problem when it's trying to write (if a drive door is open, for instance), it will print an error message and halt. If this happens, fix the problem, then press F3 to repeat the previous command and try again to write the file. But the single most important thing to remember is to pause and check all Write commands several times before actually writing any sectors to disk. It may take an extra few seconds. But it sure beats trying to piece together a bombed hard disk.

Quitting DEBUG

Format: **Q**

You can't exit DEBUG and return to DOS unless you issue this simple Quit command. DEBUG doesn't process any commands until you press the Enter key. So if you're using ASCII script files to redirect keystrokes into DEBUG, make sure you press the Enter key after typing in the Q. When you do press Enter after the final Q, the cursor will drop down a line and hover directly below the Q. If you don't do this, your system will freeze and you'll have to reboot.

Quitting does not automatically save your work. If you use the Q command before issuing any W commands, all the work you did in the DEBUG session will be lost. If this happens you may be able to load DEBUG again and hope everything is intact in memory and then use the W command to save — but you can't rely on this technique.

If you realize that you've made a mistake or are afraid you're about to write bad information over good information, you can abandon your work by quitting DEBUG. Or you can use the N command to give the file in memory a different name or write it to a different drive. It's better to redo things than to end up with a mess on your disk.

To wriggle out of a command you're typing, either backspace the command away with the backspace or left arrow keys and press the Esc key to cancel the line, or press Ctrl-C or Ctrl-ScrollLock to cancel everything and return to the DEBUG hyphen prompt. If you're using the Assemble (A) command, once you've cancelled the current line you may have to press the Enter key once to return to this prompt. Then just type Q and press the Enter key to get back to DOS.

It's entirely possible that you'll end up using all 14 of the above DEBUG commands to examine and modify files and parts of your disk — and create brand new files. But unless you're a serious programmer, you probably won't ever need the following five bare-metal commands. So they're included here in abbreviated form just so you know that they exist.

Advanced Commands

Input/Display a Single Byte from a Port

> *Format:* **I portaddress**

and

Output/Send a Single Byte to a Port

> *Format:* **O portaddress byte**

PCs use ports to control and determine the status of various timers, controllers, coprocessors, printer and communications gateways to the outside world, expansion units, and the keyboard. Each port has a unique number. You can read the current values at some (but not all) ports, and can send, or write, new values to some (but not all) ports. In many cases, consecutive ports work together as pairs. First you send a value to the port with the lower address to tell it which function you want to read or write, then you send a value to or read a value from the port with the higher address.

The various AT models (and many newer systems) use a battery-backed-up slice of CMOS memory to store your system's configuration. To see the stored CMOS values you first use the DEBUG O command to tell port hex 70 which function you want to examine, and then use the DEBUG I command to read the specified value from port hex 71.

Type in the following CMOS.SCR script using a pure-ASCII word processor, or EDLIN:

```
E 0 "Century is:"
O 70,32
I 71
E 0 "Year is:"
O 70,9
I 71
E 0 "Month is:"
O 70,8
I 71
E 0 "Day is:"
O 70,7
I 71
Q
```

Note that the first character in the lines with 70s in them is a capital O (although a lower-case one will work just fine) and not a zero. Be sure to press the Enter key after the final Q. You can also create the file at the DOS prompt by adding a line at the very beginning:

```
COPY CON CMOS.SCR
```

Then enter each line as shown — making sure you press the Enter key after the final Q. When you're done, after you typed the last Q and press Enter, press the F6 key, and then Enter one more time.

The E 0 commands are just dummy labels to let you know what's going on. You should see something like:

```
-E 0 "Century is:"
-O 70,32
-I 71
19
-E 0 "Year is:"
-O 70,9
-I 71
88
-E 0 "Month is:"
-O 70,8
-I 71
11
-E 0 "Day is:"
-O 70,7
-I 71
08
-Q
```

This tells you that the date stored in CMOS is 08-11-1988. You can read lots of important information this way, but you'll have to interpret some of it by turning it into binary and looking at which bits are 1 and which are 0.

For instance, the fixed disk type is maintained at CMOS port hex 12. (*Be very careful if you have to examine anything having to do with your fixed disk!* Follow instructions to the letter. And don't experiment unless you truly know what you're doing.) So if you wanted to see your hard disk type you could enter:

```
DEBUG
-O 70,12
-I 71
20
-Q
```

In this case the value stored at this address is hex 20, which doesn't tell you much. To make sense out of it you have to translate the hex 20 into high and low binary *nibbles* (a nibble is four bits, or half a byte):

```
HEX 20 = 0 0 1 0   0 0 0 0
             ↑          ↑
         drive C:   drive D:
```

The high nibble on the left represents the first hard disk (drive C:). The low nibble on the right represents the second hard disk (drive D:). If the value of a nibble is 0000 you don't have the appropriate hard disk installed, or at least your CMOS RAM doesn't know about it.

In this case, a hex 20 means the system contains only one hard disk (since the low nibble is 0000) and that the drive C: hard disk type is type 2 (because binary 0010 = decimal 2).

You could similarly examine the equipment byte at port hex 14 with the commands:

```
DEBUG
-O 70,14
-I 71
43
-Q
```

Again, translate the 43 that DEBUG reported in this case into its binary representation:

43 = 01000011

but split up the binary number as follows:

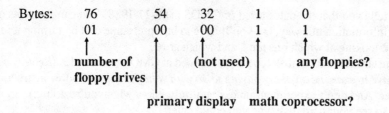

Bytes: 76   54   32   1   0
           01   00   00   1   1
            ↑   ↑   ↑   ↑
      number of   (not used)   any floppies?
      floppy drives   ↑   ↑
                primary display   math coprocessor?

Then consult a table that explains what's going on (like the one in the *Technical Reference* manual):

- Bits 6,7:   A 00 means 1 floppy drive
              A 01 means 2 floppy drives

- Bits 5,4:   A 00 means no monitor or an EGA or better
              A 01 means primary display is 40-column color
              A 10 means primary display is 80-column color
              A 11 means primary display is monochrome

- Bit 1:   A 0 means math coprocessor is not installed
              A 1 means math coprocessor is installed

- Bit 0:   A 0 means no floppy drives installed
              A 1 means floppy drives are installed

So a value of hex 43 means:

- 2 floppy drives are installed.
- Either no monitor or something fancier than a CGA.
- A math coprocessor is installed.

Execute Program in Memory (Go)

Format: **G [=address][address[address...]]**

and

Execute and Show Registers/Flags (Trace)

Format: **T [=address][value]**

and

Execute One Instruction (Proceed)

Format: **P [=address][value]**

DEBUG is really two tools in one. To most power users it's a handy tool for examining and modifying files and parts of disks, as well as for creating new files from scratch. But to programmers it's also a testing and debugging environment. You can load a program into DEBUG and watch it run step by step, which lets you trace the flow of execution from one instruction to the next, and look at the values of all the registers and flags in the process.

Once you've loaded a program (by specifying it at the end of the DOS command line after the word DEBUG, or by using the N and L commands), issuing a Go (G) instruction will execute it. If the program doesn't have any serious programming problems, and is designed to exit gracefully to DOS, DEBUG will print a "Program terminated normally" message onscreen. Don't issue another G at this point, or your system may hang. If you want to execute it a second time, reload the program first by typing:

```
L
```

Then re-enter the G command to run it again.

You may set breakpoints by specifying one, or as many as ten, addresses after the G. If the program execution flow reaches any of these breakpoint addresses while it's running, the program slams on its brakes and DEBUG displays the register and flag settings in force at that instant. You may also tell DEBUG to start the program execution at an address other than the default offset 100 of the code segment. To do so, you would add an equals sign (=) and an address right after the G.

Here's a script for the tiny program BEEP.COM we saw at the beginning of the chapter. (It beeps the speaker by printing a character 7.) Type in the script using any pure-ASCII word processor or EDLIN and call it BEEP.SCR:

```
A
MOV AH,02
MOV DL,07
INT 21
RET

RCX
7
N BEEP.COM
W
Q
```

Make sure you leave the blank line above RCX, and that you press the Enter key after each line (especially the last one with the Q). You could also create the file at the DOS prompt by inserting one line at the very beginning:

```
COPY CON BEEP.SCR
```

Then type in all the lines indicated, and be sure you press the Enter key after each one. When you're done, press the F6 function key, and then tap the Enter key one final time.

Either way, put BEEP.SCR on the same disk as DEBUG (or make sure DEBUG is in a subdirectory that your PATH knows about) and then type:

```
DEBUG < BEEP.SCR
```

To execute BEEP, just type BEEP at the DOS prompt. Then try running it from inside DEBUG. Load BEEP.COM either by typing:

```
DEBUG BEEP.COM
```

or:

```
DEBUG
-N BEEP.COM
-L
```

and then type G and press the Enter key. The program will run and you'll hear a beep. DEBUG will then display the message "Program terminated normally."

At this point if you want to run it again, first type L and press the Enter key to reload it. Then type G and press Enter to re-execute it.

DEBUG lets you trace through a program one or more steps at a time, displaying the state of the registers and flags after each instruction. You can single-step your way through by repeatedly pressing T and then Enter, or can specify a number directly after the T (without an equals sign) that tells DEBUG how many consecutive instructions to execute in a row. If you don't specify a starting address (with an equals sign and an address, just like G) DEBUG will begin tracing through the program at offset 100 of the code segment or at whatever offset address the Instruction Pointer (IP register) is pointing to.

The T command will trace through every single instruction — including those in each interrupt, loop, subroutine, call, etc. If you want to execute these separate processes but not step your way through them one instruction at a time, you can jump to the end of each process with the P command. T will slog through every last step of your program, while P will jump over the repetitive and tangential steps. Some programmers even refer to P as the jumP command.

Using T can get very complicated even in tiny programs, since when it reaches an interrupt, DEBUG will start tracing through the complex code that makes up the actual interrupt instead simply executing it and jumping to the next step in your program. It's useful if you need to see how a particular subroutine or interrupt changes your system's registers. But for nonprogrammers, P is definitely the one to use.

If you took a trip from New York to Portland, Oregon, the P equivalent description of the trip might be:

1. Took cab from home to JFK airport.
2. Took flight to Chicago.
3. Changed planes and took flight to Portland.
4. Took cab from PDX airport to Intel office.

The T instruction would look like:

1. Went out door to hail cab.
2. Located cab.
3. Got in.
4. Told driver to go to JFK.
5. Driver muttered softly and made U-turn.
6. Driver ran first red light.
7. Driver made illegal left turn onto CPW.
8. Driver ran second red light.
9. Driver swerved and narrowly avoided oncoming bus.

and so on. If you need to know the details of each operation, you would use T. If you want just the main points, use P.

Proceed will display the same registers and flags as the Trace command, and let you run the command multiple times by specifying a value after the P (but without an equals sign). Again, if you don't specify a starting address (with an equals sign followed by an address), DEBUG will begin at offset 100 of the code segment. If you try this with BEEP.COM you'll see something like:

```
-P 5

AX=0200  BX=0000  CX=0007  DX=0007  SP=FFFE  BP=0000  SI=0000  DI=0000
DS=3131  ES=3131  SS=3131  CS=3131  IP=0102   NV UP EI PL NZ NA PO NC
3131:0102 B207          MOV     DL,07

AX=0200  BX=0000  CX=0007  DX=0007  SP=FFFE  BP=0000  SI=0000  DI=0000
DS=3131  ES=3131  SS=3131  CS=3131  IP=0104   NV UP EI PL NZ NA PO NC
3131:0104 CD21          INT     21

AX=0207  BX=0000  CX=0007  DX=0007  SP=FFFE  BP=0000  SI=0000  DI=0000
DS=3131  ES=3131  SS=3131  CS=3131  IP=0106   NV UP EI PL NZ NA PO NC
3131:0106 C3            RET

AX=0207  BX=0000  CX=0007  DX=0007  SP=0000  BP=0000  SI=0000  DI=0000
DS=3131  ES=3131  SS=3131  CS=3131  IP=0000   NV UP EI PL NZ NA PO NC
3131:0106 CD20          INT     20


Program terminated normally
-
```

Note that the original BEEP.COM program consisted of the four lines:

```
MOV AH,02
MOV DL,07
INT 21
RET
```

The first line is missing in the P display, and DEBUG added a final INT 20 line.

The first line isn't there because the tracing process didn't kick in until after the first instruction. You can see the first instruction, and the state of things at the very beginning of the process, by typing R. The last INT 20 line is listed because a coded version of this instruction makes up the first two bytes — offset 0 — of the Program Segment Prefix that DOS uses to keep track of important information it needs to run the program properly. Under certain circumstances, such as ending a program with RET, execution jumps to offset 0, which executes INT 20. INT 20 shuts things down and returns to DOS.

If you do find yourself creating short assembly language programs to set colors, change file attributes, handle odd inputs for IF ERRORLEVEL batch tests and the like, you'll invariably end up making mistakes. By loading your ailing (or developing) program into DEBUG — complete with command line parameters — you can use P to step through the code and diagnose the trouble. The P command will usually pause at the right places and ask for input, print any of the executing program's built-in messages onscreen, and execute chores like changing colors.

A program like the screen-clearer mentioned elsewhere in this book accepts color numbers from the user on the command line. If you're writing a program like this, you can watch it read in and process the actual user input. Just enter something like:

```
DEBUG COLOR.COM 4e
```

(with the COM extension) and press P repeated to step through the program, keeping your eyes on the registers that are supposed to be affected. You might have constructed the program to process uppercase letters only and see that the value in a certain register is hex 20 too high, since the hex ASCII value for "e" is 65 while its uppercase version is 45. DEBUG's P command won't fix the problem for you, but it will help you spot it, which is often the hardest part of finishing something.

Chapter 9

ANSI and Other DOS Drivers

You can clear your screen on a color system to a color other than the dull default grey on black by running a short program. Likewise, you can redefine your keys with another set of programs that would, for example, put the Ctrl key back where it belongs on IBM's unpopular 101-key keyboards. And you can switch from one screen width to another with the DOS MODE command, if you happen to have MODE.COM handy.

But DOS provides one direct way to accomplish all these tasks — with ANSI.SYS. And it even tosses in a few special new tricks. ANSI's abilities are a bit cumbersome to work with, and horribly documented, but once you start fiddling with ANSI you may find it hard to stop. We'll present ANSI (and other DOS drivers) in this chapter, and show you how to master all of its commands.

ANSI.SYS is a *device driver*. DOS uses device drivers as bridges between the operating system and the vast array of hardware gadgets on the market. In an ideal world, hardware manufacturers would get together and agree on one set of immutable standards. This way, users would need to learn only one command to set any printer's right margin, or move a cursor on a screen.

But the reverse has occurred. Manufacturers are loathe to tell each other what they're up to. And they often try to widen their markets by producing hardware that can run on dozens of different computers and dozens of operating systems. In addition, many hardware designers simply invent new standards either because they think their way of doing things is better, or because they want to lop off a share of the market and make all other vendors' products incompatible. Even if everyone agreed on one existing set of commands, vendors would undoubtedly slap on brand new features so often that any standard would need frequent and constant upgrading.

DOS couldn't possibly keep up with this perplexing vendor shivaree by maintaining internal tables of codes and instructions. The tables would be huge, and would slow lots of operations down. And they'd be out of date as soon as they were compiled. So the designers of DOS came up with an ingenious solution — they published a specification that all hardware manufacturers could use to develop their own hooks to the operating system. Any vendor who wanted his hardware to plug into DOS would provide a program called a driver that purchasers could copy onto their disks. Then, the user would simply tell DOS which drivers were there, and DOS would attach the driver and sniff out the necessary information.

Device drivers come in two classes — *block drivers* and *character drivers*. Block drivers move data around in relatively large chunks and are used to control random I/O on mass-storage devices such as hard disks, tape drives, and optical disks. Character drivers shuttle data in and out of systems serially (one character at a time), and deal with things like screens, printers, mice, keypads, and modems.

To install such a device all a user has to do is include the name and path of the device's driver in a CONFIG.SYS file. So if you're hooking up a mouse, you need to have a CONFIG.SYS file in the main root directory of your bootup disk that contains a line like (with the correct path for the file, of course):

```
DEVICE=MOUSE.SYS
```

When your computer boots up, your IBMBIO.COM system file (or IO.SYS file in non-IBM systems) checks for a CONFIG.SYS file, and loads the appropriate drivers into memory.

DOS provides several drivers of its own: DRIVER.SYS and VDISK.SYS (aka RAMDRIVE.SYS on some systems), as well as a pair to handle its confounding "code page switching" abilities — DISPLAY.SYS and PRINTER.SYS. We'll introduce these drivers before we get to the most important one of all: ANSI.SYS.

DRIVER.SYS

DRIVER.SYS lets you do for any diskette drive what DOS does automatically for a system with a single floppy. If you need to copy files from one 3-1/2 inch diskette to another, for instance, the best way is to trick your system into thinking you have two logical drives for the same physical drive.

The most common use for this driver is in hooking up an external 3-1/2 inch diskette. You have to tell DOS the drive number. But apart from that, if you don't specify anything to the contrary, the default is:

- 80 tracks per side
- 9 sectors per track
- 2 sides
- no changeline support required

DRIVER.SYS: Format

Here's the form DRIVER.SYS should follow in the CONFIG.SYS file:

```
DEVICE=[d:][path]DRIVER.SYS /D:ddd
[/T:ttt][/S:ss][/H:hh][/C][/N][/F:f]
```

where:

/D:ddd is the drive number, from 0 to 255 (if you're up to 255 we'd like to see your system). A 0 here refers to the first diskette drive (A:), a 1 to the second diskette drive, and a 2 to the third diskette drive. To specify the first hard disk, use a value of 128; to refer to the second hard disk, use 129, etc. (However, it's far easier to use the SUBST command than this mess to reshuffle hard disk designations.)

/T:ttt is the number of tracks on each side, from 1 to 999. If you omit this switch, DOS uses a default of 80 tracks.

/S:ss is the number of sectors per track, from 1 to 99. Omit this and DOS assumes 9 sectors.

/H:hh is the number of read/write heads per drive, from 1 to 99. Leave this out and DOS will use 2 heads. (In virtually all cases the number of heads is the number of disk surfaces, or sides.)

/C means you need changeline support. This is a special hardware feature of AT-class and above systems that knows when you've changed the disk in a particular drive. You don't really have to worry about this.

/N means the drive is not removable. You won't need this since it's best not to use DRIVER.SYS with hard disks.

/F:f tells DOS what type (form factor) of drive you're talking about. Omit this and DOS assumes you want a 720K 3-1/2-inch diskette (type 2). However, you could also specify any one of these values for f, depending on the type of drive:

0	160/180/320/360K 5-1/4" floppy
1	1.2M 5-1/4" AT floppy
2	720K 3-1/2" diskette
7	1.44M 3-1/2" diskette

- removable medium
- 3-1/2 inch 720K diskette

If you need to specify another type of diskette, you should consult the documentation furnished with it.

Since the defaults are set for a 3-1/2 inch 720K external diskette, to hook one up to a system with a single hard disk (assuming you stored the DRIVER.SYS file in your \DOS subdirectory), you would use the simple CONFIG.SYS command:

```
DEVICE=C:\DOS\DRIVER.SYS /D:2
```

You could then treat this external device as drive D:. Some of the more popular laptops on the market come with a cable that attaches to the external floppy disk controller port on a PC or XT. By using a command like the one above, and then running a special program on the laptop, you can temporarily turn the laptop diskette drive into a *slave* drive. Your PC or XT will then use this remote laptop drive as an additional floppy drive, which it will refer to as C: on a PC or D: on an XT. This makes it a snap to move information back and forth from your desktop and laptop systems, and transfer files from 5-1/4 to 3-1/2 inch formats and vice versa.

A generation of original XT users learned that they could treat the single floppy drive as both A: and B:, which made it less of a chore to copy diskettes. DRIVER.SYS makes it possible for users to give any internal or external drive an additional drive letter. If you installed one external 3-1/2 inch 720K diskette and want to refer to it both as drive D: and E: just use the above command twice:

```
DEVICE=C:\DOS\DRIVER.SYS /D:2
DEVICE=C:\DOS\DRIVER.SYS /D:2
```

Your system will bump up the drive letter one notch each time it processes this command. You could then copy files from one 3-1/2 inch 720K diskette to another with a command like:

```
COPY D:*.* E:
```

Similarly, if you're using an AT with a 1.2 megabyte 5-1/4 inch diskette in drive A:, and you want to copy files from one of these dead-end disks to another, you can have the DRIVER.SYS command customize your system so you can refer to this drive both as A: and D:

To do this, you have to use a 0 after the /D: switch to tell DOS to work its magic on the first diskette drive in the system. And remember that the default switch settings are designed for 720K diskettes:

```
/T:80 /S:9 /H:2 /F:2
```

while 1.2M floppies require these settings:

```
/T:80 /S:15 /H:2 /F:1
```

The number of tracks and heads is the same on both, but you'll have to redefine the other parameters. So on an AT with a 1.2M floppy as drive A:, a second floppy, and a hard disk, and all the DOS files in a subdirectory called C:\DOS, you could treat the 1.2M drive both as A: and D: with the command:

```
DEVICE=C:\DOS\DRIVER.SYS /D:0 /S:15 /F:1
```

When DOS assigns drive letters, it always refers to the first diskette drive as A:. If it finds a second internal diskette drive, DOS calls this B:. If it finds only one internal diskette drive it refers to this single drive both as A: and B:. The lowest drive designation for a hard disk is C:, but since you can have such a welter of hard disks, external floppies, RAMdisks, and external block devices of all sorts, once it gets past the floppies, DOS starts checking out your configuration and assigns drive letters in the order in which it finds things. If you're using VDISK.SYS to set up RAMdisks, put the VDISK commands after the DRIVER.SYS commands.

VDISK.SYS

VDISK.SYS is used to create a RAMdisk, by fooling your system into treating part of RAM like a disk. DOS won't install VDISK if it determines that you have less than 65K of memory free. And even if you specify a smaller value (for bbb), the smallest virtual drive it will try to set up is 64K. However, if you're short on memory, DOS may reduce the size of the virtual disk that you specified since it will always leave a minimum 64K of memory free after the VDISK is in place. The size specified for the RAMdisk includes space allocated for normal disk structures (the boot sector, file allocation table (FAT), and directory), so you won't be able to use the entire space you specified for data.

If you have a system with one or two floppies and a single hard disk and low memory to spare, and you keep your DOS files in a \DOS subdirectory on drive C:, and you accept all the defaults by including the line:

```
DEVICE=C:\DOS\VDISK.SYS
```

in your CONFIG.SYS file, DOS will set up a 64K VDISK on drive D: with the following specifications:

Total sectors:	512
Bytes per sector:	128
Sectors per cluster:	1
Bytes per cluster:	128
Reserved (boot record) sectors:	1
Sectors per track:	8
Number of heads:	1

VDISK.SYS: Format

Here's the syntax of VDISK.SYS in the CONFIG.SYS file:

```
DEVICE=[d:][path]VDISK.SYS [bbb][sss][ddd][/E[:m]]
```

where:

bbb is the size of the virtual disk, expressed as the decimal number of kilobytes, ranging from 1 to the maximum amount of free memory in your system. The default is 64K.

sss is the sector size in bytes. The default is 128 bytes, but you can use 128, 256, or 512.

ddd is the number of directory entries, from 2 to 512. The default is 64. Obviously the number of directory entries determines the number of files you can store on this virtual disk (except that one entry is used to store the volume label).

Note: You may stick in "comments" (text such as "buffer size=") before the bbb, sss, and ddd parameters, but why bother?

/E installs the virtual disk in extended memory. The optional **:m** tells DOS how many sectors to transfer in a single gulp, from 1 to 8, with a default of 8.

Tracks per side:	64
Number of FATs:	1
Sectors per FAT:	6 (@ 128 bytes)
Total sectors used by FATs:	6 (@ 128 bytes)
Maximum root directory entries:	64
Sectors used by root directory:	16 (@ 128 bytes)
Total bytes available on disk:	65536 (64K)
Total bytes available for data:	62592

DOS normally uses 512-byte sectors on physical disks, but sets up sectors one-quarter that size on a typical virtual disks created by VDISK. Larger sectors are slightly more efficient for larger files, but are a bit wasteful if you're storing lots of tiny files.

DOS may fiddle with the number of directory entries you specify, since it will fill up directory sectors completely. Each directory entry is 32 bytes long. If the sector size is the default 128 bytes, DOS will create directory entries in multiples of four (128 / 32). It always rounds up to the next higher multiple. Four entries will use one sector. Since five entries require two sectors, DOS has to use a second sector and will set up space for eight entries.

If you specify a tiny VDISK and DOS discovers it can't cram the FAT and directory into it and have two sectors left over, it will try reducing the directory size a sector at a time. If this slimming-down process continues until the directory is a single sector long, and VDISK still has problems, DOS will abort the setup process.

VDISK is one of the only DOS functions that uses extended memory. Most other applications that go past 640K use expanded rather than extended RAM. Extended memory works only on ATs and later hardware with properly configured memory above the 1 megabyte address space. You can use up to 4 megabytes for each VDISK in extended memory. You may have to experiment with the :m setting, reducing it if you discover that interrupts are going unprocessed.

A VDISK operating in extended memory shuts out interrupts when it moves data. The bigger the amount of data that it moves, the longer it ignores interrupts. You can reduce both the sector size (down to 128) and the number of sectors moved at once (down to one) to prevent interrupts from vanishing.

You can't use the DOS DISKCOPY command with a virtual disk created by VDISK. You can't format VDISK's virtual disks, but they come already formatted so you don't have to. And if you create multiple virtual disks, DOS will automatically give them increasingly higher drive letters.

DISPLAY.SYS and PRINTER.SYS

Both DISPLAY.SYS and PRINTER.SYS are for specialized font loading, which IBM perversely calls *code page switching*. You can wrestle with this pair of drivers to add multilingual, Portugese, French-Canadian, or Norwegian touches to your work. As IBM sheepishly points out, "The U.S. user normally does not need" this aggravation. Skip it.

DISPLAY.SYS and PRINTER.SYS: Format

Here's the syntax of DISPLAY.SYS and PRINTER.SYS in CONFIG.SYS.

```
DEVICE=[d:][path]DISPLAY.SYS CON[:]=(type[,[hwcp][,n]])
```

or

```
DEVICE=[d:][path]DISPLAY.SYS CON[:]=(type[,[hwcp][,(n,m)]])
```

where:

type is the display (MONO, CGA, EGA, or LCD).

hwcp is the hardware code page (437, 850, 860, 863, or 865).

n tells how many additional "prepared" code pages you want, from 0 to 12, although on MONO or CGA systems this number has to be 0. The default is 0 for MONO and CGA, and 1 for everything else.

m defines the number of "sub-fonts" per code page. The default is 1 for the LCD screen on IBM's Convertible laptop, and 2 on EGA and VGA screens.

```
DEVICE=[d:][path]PRINTER.SYS LPT#[:]=(type[,[hwcp][,n]])
```

or

```
DEVICE=[d:][path]PRINTER.SYS LPT#[:]=(type[,[(hwcp1,hwcp2,...)][,n]])
```

where:

LPT# is the printer, from LPT1 to LPT3 (you may use PRN instead of LPT1).

type is either 4201 (for the IBM Proprinter) or 5202 (for the IBM Quietwriter III).

hwcp is the hardware code page (437, 850, 860, 863, or 865).

ANSI.SYS

While VDISK.SYS can help you by speeding up disk-intensive operations, and DRIVER.SYS is useful in certain hardware configurations, the one real gem of a DOS device driver is ANSI.SYS. But although users of all types could benefit from the extended screen and keyboard control that ANSI offers, this feature is documented poorly and hard to implement with the meager tools DOS provides. Worse, IBM took its turgid but factual descriptions of how to use this driver out of the DOS manual and put them instead in the *DOS Technical Reference* manual, which few users own.

In some respects DOS hasn't changed much since its early days on tiny 16K single-sided floppy hardware. Even on today's capable color systems the default DOS display is a dingy grey text against a black background. DOS normally doesn't make it easy to use foreign language alphabets, symbols like cents signs, or common characters like 1/2. And its macro abilities are limited to repeating and editing previous commands.

DOS treats screens as TTY (teletype) devices, displaying just one line at a time. It can't handle graphics (apart from clumsy ASCII border characters), or put characters anywhere other than the line the cursor is currently on, and it can't back up past the left margin. In fact, DOS behaves as if it were driving a printer instead of a full-sized screen.

ANSI fixes all that (well, most of it). By installing the ANSI driver, and coming up with an automated method for issuing its thorny commands, you can dress your color screen in a rainbow of attributes, put text anywhere you like, redefine any alphanumeric key on the keyboard (sorry, it won't alter keys like Alt or CapsLock), and even give your system primitive macro powers.

CONFIG.SYS is the place to tell your system that you want to use ANSI.SYS. (You should already have a CONFIG.SYS configuration file on your bootup disk to specify how many disk buffers you want, increase the number of files you can open at one time if you're using a large database, expand the number of drive designations, specify a much larger environment size than the wimpy 160 bytes DOS normally allots, and load drivers for devices like mice or fancy hard disks.) Just include this line in CONFIG.SYS:

```
DEVICE=ANSI.SYS
```

If you're using a hard disk, you should keep all your DOS files — including the DOS device drivers — in their own subdirectory called \DOS. If ANSI.SYS is properly in your \DOS subdirectory on drive C:, the CONFIG.SYS command to load it would actually look like:

```
DEVICE=C:\DOS\ANSI.SYS
```

Be sure to include the SYS extension in this command. If you haven't ever used ANSI, copy the ANSI.SYS file from your DOS diskettes into your \DOS subdirectory. If you're using a floppy disk system (and these days there's little reason to do so), copy ANSI.SYS onto your main system disk — once DOS loads ANSI it will keep it in memory so you can replace your bootup disk with an applications disk if you need to. Either way, if you're changing your CONFIG.SYS file or creating one for the first time, reboot your system when you're done since it has to read the CONFIG.SYS file at bootup to load and set everything properly. If you're using a 2.x version of DOS, and this line is the last (or only) one in your CONFIG.SYS file, be sure to press the Enter key at the end of the line or else DOS may become hopelessly confused, refuse to load ANSI.SYS, and print a garbled message onscreen. (DOS 3.x fixes this problem. It fixes lots of problems. You really should upgrade.)

When you load ANSI.SYS, DOS will grab the module containing the ANSI code, and grow slightly in size. Under version 3.3, DOS by itself takes up 55,200 bytes of system RAM. With ANSI.SYS attached, DOS uses 56,784 bytes (1.5K more).

Once ANSI is hooked up and ready to go, every DOS command will filter through it. The ANSI driver will assiduously look for two special "signature" characters and execute whatever legal ANSI instructions follow.

All ANSI commands must begin with the same two characters:

1. The ESC character — decimal 27, hex 1B
2. The left bracket ("[") — decimal 91, hex 5B

If it doesn't see these two characters it will pass everything on to be processed normally.

Because every ANSI command begins with an ESC, the ANSI commands are sometimes referred to as *escape sequences*. If you don't have ANSI loaded, and you display these escape sequences, you'll see a small arrow pointing left followed by a left bracket and a tangle of other characters. If you do have ANSI loaded, you'll never see these characters since the ANSI driver will intercept them and act on the commands they contain.

The rest of the commands are combinations of upper- and lowercase letters, decimal numbers, text, and punctuation. DOS usually doesn't care whether you type commands in uppercase or lowercase, since it generally turns everything into capital letters. However, ANSI is case-sensitive. If the command calls for a small "u" and a capital "K" you have to type these in exactly as specified or they won't work. Its syntax is precise and a bit jarring, so be careful to type everything in exactly as it appears here.

Since every ANSI command starts off with an ESC character, you can't just type in the appropriate escape sequence at the DOS prompt. This is because DOS interprets any tap on the Esc key as an instruction to abort whatever you happened to be doing. Regardless of what you were typing, as soon as you press the Esc key, DOS will print a backslash (\), cancel the command you were trying to execute, and drop down a line waiting for a new one.

DOS does let you issue an ESC by following its PROMPT command with the *meta-string* $E or $e. (A meta-string is just a fancy name for a sequence of characters beginning with a dollar sign.) But using this technique makes your existing system prompt disappear, leaving you with a blank, promptless screen. And it forces you to work with raw, unfriendly ANSI codes.

It's fairly easy to create COM or BAT files that execute ANSI strings. All the major word processors, including *WordPerfect*, Microsoft *Word*, and *WordStar*, let you insert an ASCII 27 in your text. (To do it in *WordStar*, for instance, type ^P^Esc — hold down the Ctrl key and while you're holding it down, press the P key and then the Esc key. Then release the Ctrl key.) In some cases you'll see a ^[onscreen if you're successful.

Don't be confused by the left bracket following the caret if you do see ^[— this just happens to be one way to display the single ASCII 27 ESC character (another way is a little arrow pointing left). This has nothing to do with the real left bracket character that follows ESC in every ANSI command. If your word processor uses ^[to signify an ESC, it will make the beginning of every ANSI command look like:

```
^[[
```

So on some word processors, an ANSI command to clear the screen, ESC[2J, would actually look like:

```
^[[2J
```

(Remember, the ESC in ESC[2J and all the other examples shown here actually stands for the ASCII 27 escape character, not the letters "ESC.")

With many other word processors, you can insert an ESC character by holding down the Alt key, typing 27 on the number pad while you're holding it down, and then releasing the Alt key. (This technique works only with the numbers on the cursor/number pad, not with the top row number keys.)

You can also use EDLIN or DEBUG to create files that contain ANSI commands, with all the required ESC characters. With EDLIN, type Ctrl-V and then type a left bracket to enter the ESC character. EDLIN will display ^V[if you do this properly. Again, this left bracket is part of the representation of the ESC character; you'll have to type an additional left bracket (without the Ctrl-V this time) to enter the second character of each ANSI command. EDLIN will show the pair of characters as ^V[[. Note that some 3.x versions of EDLIN have trouble displaying this pair.

To execute an ANSI command, you first have to make sure you booted your system with a CONFIG.SYS file that included a line that loaded ANSI.SYS. Then you have to check that the ANSI command you want to issue begins with an ESC character and a left bracket, and that you typed the rest of the command precisely. If you're following instructions that say 2J and you type 2j instead, all that will happen when you execute the command is that DOS will display the erroneous "j."

You then have to print the correct ANSI instruction onscreen for it to take effect. You can use a DOS command like TYPE or COPY or MORE to do this. Or you can put the ANSI command in a batch file and use the ECHO batch command. Or issue a PROMPT command either at the DOS command line or inside a batch file. But doing so will wipe out your normal C> or other customized DOS prompt, so you'll have to follow it with another PROMPT command to reset it.

Creating ANSI Commands with EDLIN and DEBUG

Using the DOS EDLIN.COM utility to create ANSI files is a bit tricky. First, make sure EDLIN.COM is on your disk. If not, copy it from the DOS disk into your \DOS subdirectory. To have EDLIN create a new file, type EDLIN and then the name of the file you want to create. (You can't start EDLIN unless you enter a filename after it on the command line.) This example will produce a small file called CLEAR that clears the screen. So you start off by typing:

```
C>EDLIN CLEAR
```

EDLIN will then respond with a message indicating that it can't find an existing file with the name CLEAR, and then print an asterisk on the next line:

```
New file
*
```

An asterisk hugging the lefthand edge of your screen is EDLIN's prompt, just as A> or C> is DOS's prompt and a hyphen ("-") is DEBUG's prompt. The prompt tells you EDLIN is waiting for a command.

If you don't see the "New file" message, or see something like "End of input file" this means you do have a file called CLEAR on your disk. Abort the process by typing Q (then Enter) and then Y (and Enter). Then pick another filename and start over.

To start entering characters in this file, just type I and press the Enter key. You'll see:

```
*I
        1:*
```

The "1:" tells you that you're working on line 1. EDLIN is a line editor that can work only one line at a time. The asterisk following the 1: is EDLIN's way of indicating the current line — the one it's working on at the moment. (See Chapter 7 for the details on EDLIN.)

Now you start entering characters. The ANSI command to clear the screen is only four characters long:

1. The first character has to be: ESC
2. The second character has to be: [
3. The third character is: 2
4. The fourth character is: J

So the entire command looks like:

```
ESC[2J
```

To enter the ESC character, type ^V and then a left bracket ("["). This combination of ^V[inserts an ESC character into your file. Note however that the left bracket that follows the ^V is different from the actual left bracket character required by ANSI. It just so happens that you create an ESC character by typing ^V and then [. But all that typing ^V[does is put an ESC character in your text. It has nothing to do with the [that DOS requires in all ANSI commands. So you'll have to type a SECOND [character. Then type the remaining 2 and J characters. Be careful to type a capital J rather than a lowercase one, since ANSI is case-sensitive. Line 1 would now look like:

```
1:*^V[[2J
```

This tells you that line 1 contains four characters:

1. ^V[(ESC character)
2. [([character)
3. 2 (2 character)
4. J (J character)

Press the Enter key to enter the four characters. EDLIN won't accept anything you typed on a particular line until you press Enter at the end of that line. Once you press Enter, it will offer you the chance to type in something on line 2:

```
2:*
```

You don't want to, so type Ctrl-C or Ctrl-Break to tell EDLIN both that you're done entering characters and that you want it to go back to command mode. This will look like:

```
    2:*^C

  *
```

To save the text you just created, type E and press Enter:

```
  *E

  C>
```

Then, assuming you had previously loaded ANSI.SYS by including a line in your CONFIG.SYS file that said something like:

```
DEVICE=ANSI.SYS
```

or:

```
DEVICE=C:\DOS\ANSI.SYS
```

you can test the file you just created by typing:

```
TYPE CLEAR
```

If you did everything properly the screen should clear. If DOS simply prints a 2J on the screen, you probably forgot to type the second left bracket character.

If you didn't originally have a DEVICE=ANSI.SYS line in your CONFIG.SYS file, and you just added it, you'll have to reboot for it to take effect. DOS has to see this line in your CONFIG.SYS file when it boots up, or else it won't load ANSI or process ANSI commands.

The whole process looks like:

```
C>EDLIN CLEAR
New file
*I
        1:*^V[[2J
        2:*^C

*E

C>
```

The only problem with using EDLIN is that it automatically puts a carriage return and line feed (as well as ^Z end-of-file marker) at the end of the files it creates. So when you execute an ANSI command created with EDLIN it may bounce the DOS prompt down an extra line. You could fix this by using DEBUG to subtract the last three bytes from the file.

First, make sure the DEBUG.COM file is in the current directory or is in a subdirectory that your PATH knows about. If it's not, copy it from your DOS diskette into your \DOS subdirectory.

Load the CLEAR file into DEBUG with the command:

```
C>DEBUG CLEAR
```

You should see just the DEBUG hyphen prompt. If DEBUG prints a "File not found" message above the hyphen, abort the process by typing Q and then pressing Enter. Make sure CLEAR is in the subdirectory you're currently logged into, and try again.

To have DEBUG report the length of the file in hexadecimal representation, just type RCX and press the Enter key. In this case you should see:

```
-RCX
CX 0007
:
```

Typing RCX instructs DEBUG to display the contents of the CX register. When you load a typically short file like CLEAR into DEBUG, DEBUG looks at the directory entry for this file, figures out how many bytes the file contains, and then puts this number of bytes into the CX register. So typing RCX right after you load the file will display this number (in hex notation).

The 0007 following the CX tells you that the value in CX is hex 7, or that the file is seven bytes long.

The colon on the next line is a special DEBUG prompt that offers you the opportunity to change the value of a register, which is exactly what you want to do.

If you had used the DEBUG Display (D) command to view the seven bytes of the file, you would have seen something like:

```
-D 100 L7
34E5:0100   1B 5B 32 4A 0D 0A 1A                      .[2J...
```

The D 100 L7 command tells DEBUG to display seven bytes starting at memory offset 100. Ignore the 34E5; this number is the segment address and varies from system to system. The 0100 is the starting address of the memory contents DEBUG is displaying. And:

```
1B 5B 32 4A 0D 0A 1A
```

is the hexadecimal representation of all seven bytes in the file, as follows:

1B — ESC character
5B — [character
32 — 2 character
4A — J character
0D — carriage return
0A — linefeed
1A — ^Z end-of-file marker

EDLIN added three extra characters (a carriage return, a linefeed, and an end-of-file marker), so if you subtract 3 from the length of the file, DEBUG will make the file three characters shorter, chopping those extra meddlesome characters off. DEBUG reported that the length of the file (the value in register CX) is 7, and 7 - 3 = 4. So type a 4 to the right of the colon and press the Enter key:

```
CX 0007
:4
_
```

You might want to check your work by examining the new value in the CX register. Just type RCX again and press the Enter key:

```
CX 0004
:
```

Since this is the value you wanted, just press the Enter key again without entering a new number, and you'll return to the DEBUG hyphen prompt. Then, save the truncated file and quit DEBUG by typing W (then Enter) and then Q (and then Enter). The whole process looks like:

```
C>DEBUG CLEAR
-RCX
CX 0007
:4
-W
Writing 0004 bytes
-Q

C>
```

However, if you're going to use DEBUG to trim the extra characters off, you might as well use it to create the whole file.

Remember that DEBUG works exclusively in hex. But once you get the hang of it, you can bang out ANSI commands in seconds. To create the ESC[2J clear-screen instruction in DEBUG you would type everything following the DEBUG hyphen prompts:

```
C>DEBUG
-E 100 1B "[2J"
-N CLEAR
-RCX
CX 0000
```

```
    :4
    -W
    Writing 0004 bytes
    -Q
```

The line:

```
    E 100 1B "[2J"
```

tells DEBUG to enter a group of characters starting at memory offset 100. The characters it enters are 1B (the hexadecimal represention of the ESC character itself), then a left bracket, a 2, and a capital J. Normally you make DEBUG entries in hex as you did with the 1B. But when entering normal letters and numbers, you can put them in quotes and have DEBUG translate them into hex for you.

You specify a filename with the DEBUG N command. The line:

```
    N CLEAR
```

tells DEBUG to name the file that you'll eventually save as CLEAR. You also have to tell DOS how long to make the file. The 1B ESC counts as one character, and the [2J add up to three more, for a total of four. You specify the length by typing:

```
    RCX
```

and then entering:

```
    4
```

when you see the cursor blinking beside a colon. Then, write the CLEAR file to disk and quit DEBUG by typing W and pressing Enter and then typing Q and pressing Enter.

NOTE

All examples presented use the abbreviation "ESC" to represent the decimal ASCII 27 (or hexadecimal 1B) escape character. Don't type in the letters "E-S-C" since this won't do anything except exercise your fingers. Use the techniques mentioned above to insert this ESC character in each command. And remember that each ESC character is always followed by a left bracket ([) character, so every ANSI string begins with the two characters ESC[.

If you're looking at an ANSI string in DEBUG, you'll see that every one begins with 1B 5B, since 1B is the hex value for the ESC character, and 5B the hex value of the left bracket character.

The methods DOS provides are all relatively primitive and cumbersome:

1. Putting the commands in a file (called something like ANSI.FIL, although you can give it any legal filename) and then using any DOS command that displays text, such as one of these:

```
TYPE ANSI.FIL
MORE < ANSI.FIL
COPY ANSI.FIL CON
```

2. Putting the commands after the word ECHO in a batch file, e.g. ECHO ESC[2J (to clear the screen). This ECHOANSI.BAT batch file will make setting colors a bit less painful (remember to substitute the actual escape character for the ESC below):

```
ECHO OFF
IF %1!==! GOTO OOPS
:TOP
ECHO ESC[%1m
SHIFT
IF %1!==! GOTO END
GOTO TOP
GOTO END
:OOPS
ECHO You have to specify at least
ECHO one parameter, eg:
ECHO %0 0 to reset all attributes, or
ECHO %0 34 47 for blue text on white
:END
```

3. Using a $E or $e meta-string with the DOS PROMPT command, in the form $c (where c = meta-string). Remember that meta-strings are not case-sensitive, and you can combine them, so that a sample sequence like:

```
PROMPT $P (Time is $T$H$H$H$H$H$H):
```

at 3:20 PM in directory \DOS on drive C: yields:

```
C:\DOS (Time is 15:20):
```

Here are the meta-strings and their purposes:

Meta-String	DOS Functions
t	Time
d	Date
p	Current directory on default drive
v	DOS version number
n	Default drive letter
	Drawing Characters
$	$ character
g	> character
l	< character
b	I character
q	= character
	Special Characters
h	Backspace (erases previous character)
e	Escape character (ASCII 27 decimal, 1B hex)
_	Carriage return/line feed (drops down one (line and moves to left edge of screen)

As an example, you could reset any previous screen attributes (with ESC[0m), then set the colors to bright (with ESC[1m) cyan text (with ESC[36m) on a blue background (with ESC[44m), then clear the screen (ESC[2J) and reset your prompt to show the current sub-directory, by using:

```
PROMPT $E[0;36;1;44m
PROMPT $E[2J
PROMPT $P:
```

An even better way to use the PROMPT meta-strings is to create and run the following ANSIPROM.BAT batch file:

```
ECHO OFF
IF %1!==! GOTO OOPS
SET OLDPROM=%PROMPT%
ECHO ON
PROMPT $E[%1
ECHO OFF
SET PROMPT=%OLDPROM%
SET OLDPROM=
GOTO END
:OOPS
ECHO You forgot to specify an ANSI string, eg:
ECHO %0 34;47m   (for blue text on white) :END
```

The ANSIPROM.BAT batch file will let you enter ANSI codes without having to worry about the ESC or left bracket characters. And it will reset the PROMPT automatically for you. If does this by using environment variables (%PROMPT% and %OLDPROM%), so be sure your environment can handle the few extra bytes this process requires. You can expand your environment in later versions of DOS with the CONFIG.SYS SHELL command, which will look something like:

```
SHELL=C:\COMMAND.COM /E:512 /P
```

(This particular example expands the default 160-byte environment to 512 bytes.)

To use ANSIPROM.BAT, enter the part of the ANSI command that follows the ESC and left bracket. To clear the screen, just type:

```
ANSIPROM 2J
```

Note: You can't use PROMPT to generate ANSI sequences when ECHO happens to be off. If you remove the:

```
ECHO ON
```

line from the ANSIPROM.BAT batch file above, DOS won't set any colors. Most users routinely set ECHO OFF at the beginning of their batch files so commands in the batch file don't clutter up the screen as they execute. But if one of the commands is a PROMPT that is supposed to set attributes, and ECHO is off, nothing will happen. To set colors with PROMPT when ECHO is off, include an ECHO ON line directly above the PROMPT color-setting line, and an ECHO OFF line right below it.

If you do want to keep ECHO off for the duration of your batch file, have ECHO issue your ANSI commands (just as ECHOANSI.BAT does) instead of using PROMPT.

But it's fairly simple to learn a few simple techniques that can really tame ANSI.

Working with Color

One of the easiest ways to use ANSI is to create a small COM file that writes ANSI escape sequences to standard output (as IBM suggests half-heartedly). Here's a COLOR1.SCR DEBUG script that creates such a file:

```
A
MOV BX,1
MOV CX,E
MOV AH,40
MOV DX,10E
INT 21
RET
DB 1B,"[0;34;47m",1B,"[2J"

N ANSCOLOR.COM
RCX
1C
W
Q
```

Every attribute-setting ANSI command ends with a lowercase "m." You can issue just one color-changing command at a time, or you can stack several together. But you need only one "m" per line. So the command:

```
ESC[34m
```

by itself will change the foreground to blue, while the longer:

```
ESC[0;34;47m
```

will also undo any existing attributes, and set the background to white at the same time.

The COLOR1.SCR DEBUG script will create a file called ANSCOLOR.COM that will set your screen colors to blue text on a white background and then clear the screen. You can substitute other colors by replacing the 34 with the foreground color of your choice, and 47 with the background color of your choice. The line:

```
DB 1B,"[0;31;43m",1B,"[2J"
```

would yield red text (31) on a yellow background (43).

The first 0 in either color version resets all the existing attributes. This is necessary because ANSI adds attributes in layers. If your text is red and blinking, changing the color to green will yield green blinking text; it won't do away with the blink. The 0 will first reset everything before it changes the colors the way you want them. So the string that this program sends to your screen contains three parts:

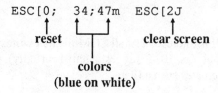

reset colors clear screen
(blue on white)

You can create both a blue-on-white ANSCOLOR.COM and a special black-on-black INVIS.COM with the following COLOR2.SCR DEBUG SCRIPT:

```
E 100 BB 01 00 B9 0E 00 B4 40 BA 0E 01 CD 21 C3
E 10E 1B 5B 30 3B 33 34 3B 34 37 6D 1B 5B 32 4A
N ANSCOLOR.COM
RCX
1C
W
E 104 8
E 110 38
M 117 L5 111
N INVIS.COM
RCX
16
W
Q
```

Type in either of these DEBUG script files with a pure-ASCII word processor, or EDLIN. If you don't have one handy, add a line at the very top of each that says:

```
COPY CON COLOR1.SCR
```

or:

```
COPY CON COLOR2.SCR
```

and then carefully enter the lines at the DOS prompt. When you're all done typing, press the Enter key after the final Q (very important!), then press the F6 function key, then press the Enter key one final time. You should see the message "1 File(s) copied." If you're creating the COLOR1.SCR script, be sure to leave the blank line directly above N ANSCOLOR.COM.

Then put either script file in the same directory as DEBUG.COM (or make sure you have DEBUG in a subdirectory your path knows about) and type:

```
DEBUG < COLOR1.SCR
```

or:

```
DEBUG < COLOR2.SCR
```

If you later want to use DEBUG to substitute your own colors in ANSCOLOR.COM, put the hex ASCII value of the last digit of the foreground color of your choice at address 113 and the hex ASCII value of the last digit of the background color of your choice at address 116. You can figure out the values to patch ANSCOLOR.COM from this table:

Color	*Hex ASCII Value to Use at* *DEBUG Addresses 113 and 116*
Black	of "0" is 30
Red	of "1" is 31
Green	of "2" is 32
Yellow	of "3" is 33
Blue	of "4" is 34
Magenta	of "5" is 35
Cyan	of "6" is 36
White	of "7" is 37

So if the ANSCOLOR.COM you originally created set the colors to blue on white, and you wanted yellow text on a red background instead, you would use DEBUG to put a value of 33 at address 113 and a value of 31 at address 116. Then you'd give the file a new name like REDYEL.COM (so you don't wipe out the existing ANSCOLOR.COM file):

```
C>DEBUG ANSCOLOR.COM
-E 113 33
-E 116 31
-N REDYEL.COM
-W
-Q
```

Or you could do the same thing with:

```
C>DEBUG ANSCOLOR.COM
-E 113 "3"
-E 116 "1"
-N REDYEL.COM
-W
-Q
```

This may seem confusing at first, because you're entering the hex representation of the last digit of the color numbers, and not the value of the numbers themselves. The hex representations of the digits 0 through 7 happen to be 30 through 37 ("0" is ASCII 30, "1" is ASCII 31, etc.). When you patch the original ANSCOLOR.COM file to set new colors, what you're really doing is replacing just the second digit of the foreground and the second digit of the background. The first digits of each remain the same.

Languages like BASIC use the same color numbers for foreground and background, but ANSI has a different set for each. All ANSI color numbers have two digits. The first digit of all foregrounds is "3" and the first digit of all backgrounds is "4" in the ANSI color system. In each case the second numbers specify the color (0=black, 1=red, 2=green, etc.). So a green foreground is 32, and a green background would be 42, for example. These ANSI numbers are slightly different from IBM's standard color values, as is shown here:

Color	IBM	ANSI
Black	0	0
Red	4	1
Green	2	2
Yellow	6	3
Blue	1	4
Magenta	5	5
Cyan	3	6
White	7	7

For high-intensity IBM colors, add 8 to the value of the color. So high-intensity yellow is 6 + 8, or 14 decimal; E hex. For high-intensity ANSI colors the command ESC[1m will do it.

The special INVIS.COM program will turn your colors to black on black and then clear the screen. This is useful when you have to leave your system unattended and you don't want anyone else to look through your directories. When you get up to take a break, just type:

```
INVIS
```

Unauthorized users will still be able to meddle by typing DEL *.* or COPY *.* A: for instance, but they'll have to do it on a totally blank screen. If they're smart, and they know you have a program such as *WordStar* that isn't affected by ANSI color settings, they can use the directory-reporting and file manipulation abilities of the program to poke around.

When you return, type ANSCOLOR (or REDYEL or whatever you've named your real color-setting program to) to unblank the screen. You can use a variation of this technique to keep nosy co-workers from using the TYPE command to examine things like your CONFIG.SYS or AUTOEXEC.BAT files. Just put the INVISIBLE ANSI string itself at the beginning of the file. When your system tries to execute it you'll get either a "Unrecognized command in CONFIG.SYS" message or a "Bad command or filename" message, which won't hurt anything. But if someone tries to use the TYPE command to see what's in your text files, ANSI will intercept the string and turn the display off.

You can create this invisible string with the DEBUG INVIS.SCR script:

```
E 100 1B 5B 38 6D 1B 5B 32 4A
N LINEONE
RCX
8
W
Q
```

(Or just get into DEBUG and type each of the six lines.) This will create a tiny file called LINEONE. You can then blank out your screen with the command:

```
TYPE LINEONE
```

But the trick here is to use your word processor to read the LINEONE file into the beginning of your CONFIG.SYS or AUTOEXEC.BAT or related files. If you do this and you see a string of ^@^@^@^@^@ characters, erase these.

One final variation of this technique will make it very easy to prevent anyone from getting into your hard disk when you're not there. Rename both the color-setting file (ANSCOLOR.COM, REDYEL.COM or whatever you call it) to something innocuous like WRDCOUNT.COM. Put this file in a directory that your PATH knows about (such as \DOS). And rename the INVIS.COM program to an equally uninteresting name like SETMODEM.COM.

Then add a line to your AUTOEXEC.BAT that says something like:

```
SETMODEM /1 /12 /N81
```

When DOS reaches this line of the batch file it will execute SETMODEM (and ignore the innocent-looking parameters after it), which will blank the screen. The only way to unblank it is to type WRDCOUNT, or whatever you named ANSCOLOR.COM to. Remember, WRDCOUNT.COM either has to be in the root directory or a subdirectory that's included in your PATH setting for this to work properly.

This isn't foolproof, since another user could boot off a diskette in the floppy drive and circumvent your AUTOEXEC.BAT file. But, as they say in the locksmith business, it will keep the honest people out.

Okay, okay. Just one more. But you have to promise that you'll check your typing very, very carefully and that you won't try this on your hard disk. And if you haven't read about DEBUG in Chapter 8, you might want to give it a quick scan. The following instructions are designed for a floppy disk in drive A: only.

If you have a hard disk system that loads ANSI.SYS, you can keep prying eyes from seeing what's on your floppies. All you have to do is put the INVIS code into your floppy disk directory. A good place is in the directory entry that holds the disk's volume label.

This example will use a 360K 5-1/4 inch floppy and add the system files to it. This way you can put ANSI.SYS on your diskette along with a CONFIG.SYS file that contains the line:

```
DEVICE=ANSI.SYS
```

Then you can copy your DOS files to the disk and label it "DOS 3.3" (or whatever version you happen to be using). If you've locked intruders out of your hard disk, the first thing they'll probably try to do is boot off a floppy disk with the DOS system files on it. If you leave this disk around they'll find it, try to boot off of it, and end up temporarily stymied. First, format a blank disk, using the:

```
FORMAT A: /S /V
```

syntax, which will copy the system files onto it and then prompt you to enter a volume label. If you're using an AT high-density drive you can either add a /4 switch to the end of the above command, or format the disk in drive B:. IBM admits that the /4 option is unreliable, so format the floppy in drive B: and then switch it into drive A:.

After DOS finishes, it will tell you the format was successful and then ask for a volume label:

```
Format complete
System transferred

Volume label (11 characters, ENTER for none)? PC MAGAZINE
```

As the example illustrates, type in:

```
PC MAGAZINE
```

or any other 11-letter name.

Make sure this formatted disk is in drive A:, and that DEBUG.COM is in a directory that your PATH knows about (if it's not, put it there). Load it by typing:

```
DEBUG
```

Now very carefully load the first four directory entries from drive A: by typing:

```
-L 100 0 5 1
```

(Note: The 0 in this command refers to drive A:. Be very careful not to have anything other than a 0 in this position!)

Tell DEBUG to display these four directory entries by typing:

```
-D
```

You should see something like:

```
3140:0100  49 42 4D 42 49 4F 20 20-43 4F 4D 27 00 00 00 00   IBMBIO  COM'....
3140:0110  00 00 00 00 00 00 00 60-72 0E 02 00 54 56 00 00   .......'r...TV..
3140:0120  49 42 4D 44 4F 53 20 20-43 4F 4D 27 00 00 00 00   IBMDOS  COM'....
3140:0130  00 00 00 00 00 00 00 60-71 0E 18 00 CF 75 00 00   .......'q....u..
3140:0140  43 4F 4D 4D 41 4E 44 20-43 4F 4D 20 00 00 00 00   COMMAND COM ....
3140:0150  00 00 00 00 00 00 00 60-71 0E 36 00 DB 62 00 00   .......'q.6..b..
3140:0160  50 43 20 4D 41 47 41 5A-49 4E 45 28 00 00 00 00   PC MAGAZINE(....
3140:0170  00 00 00 00 00 00 09 B3-74 0F 00 00 00 00 00 00   ........t.......
```

Ignore the first four characters in each row (here they're 3140); these will vary from system to system and don't affect this. Note that the fourth entry is PC MAGAZINE. The 28 in the same row tells you that this entry is the disk's volume label. Use DEBUG's E command to replace all 11 characters in "PC MAGAZINE" with the INVIS string plus three ASCII 7 beep characters. Type this very carefully:

```
-E 160 1B,"[8m",1B,"[2J",7,7,7
```

This will overwrite all the letters in "PC MAGAZINE." Use a variation of the D command to check your work:

```
-D 160 L 10
```

Apart from the 3140 at the beginning of the line, your screen should look exactly like this:

```
3140:0160  1B 5B 38 6D 1B 5B 32 4A-07 07 07 28 00 00 00 00   .[8m.[2J...(....
```

If it doesn't, type Q and press Enter to quit. Then start again.

If it does, write the file to disk. *Be extraordinarily careful and type this exactly as it appears!* Type this in wrong on a hard disk and you could lose everything, so check your typing several times before finally pressing the Enter key. Above all, make sure that the number between the 100 and the 5 is a 0:

```
-W 100 0 5 1
```

Then type Q to quit and press Enter. Make sure you included the line:

```
DEVICE=ANSI.SYS
```

(or a variation with your particular system's path to ANSI.SYS in it) in your CON-FIG.SYS file. Also, be certain you have your ANSI color-setting program (ANSCOLOR.COM or REDYEL.COM) handy. And type DIR A:.

As soon as DOS tries to display the directory and prints the volume label onscreen, ANSI.SYS will intercept the code and blank the screen. Then DOS will beep three times. This should deter any unauthorized user, who's probably wondering if he or she just broke your system. Again, you can get around this by booting up from a factory-fresh DOS disk.

If you want to see the files on drive A:, just be sure the DOS FIND.EXE utility is in a subdirectory your PATH knows about, and type:

```
:DIR A: | FIND "-"
```

This will filter out everything that doesn't have a hyphen in it, which means the volume label won't print onscreen but all the filenames will.

The entire FORMAT and DEBUG process looks like this, for DOS version 3.3:

```
FORMAT A: /S /V

Format complete
System transferred

Volume label (11 characters, ENTER for none)? PC MAGAZINE

    362496 bytes total disk space
     78848 bytes used by system
    283648 bytes available on disk

Format another (Y/N)?n
```

```
C>DEBUG
-L 100 0 5 1
-D
3140:0100  49 42 4D 42 49 4F 20 20-43 4F 4D 27 00 00 00 00   IBMBIO  COM'....
3140:0110  00 00 00 00 00 00 00 60-72 0E 02 00 54 56 00 00   .......'r...TV..
3140:0120  49 42 4D 44 4F 53 20 20-43 4F 4D 27 00 00 00 00   IBMDOS  COM'....
3140:0130  00 00 00 00 00 00 00 60-71 0E 18 00 CF 75 00 00   .......'q....u..
3140:0140  43 4F 4D 4D 41 4E 44 20-43 4F 4D 20 00 00 00 00   COMMAND COM ....
3140:0150  00 00 00 00 00 00 00 60-71 0E 36 00 DB 62 00 00   .......'q.6..b..
3140:0160  50 43 20 4D 41 47 41 5A-49 4E 45 28 00 00 00 00   PC MAGAZINE(....
3140:0170  00 00 00 00 00 00 09 B3-74 0F 00 00 00 00 00 00   ........t.......
-E 160 1B,"[8m",1B,"[2J",7,7,7
-D 160 L 10
```

```
3140:0160  1B 5B 38 6D 1B 5B 32 4A-07 07 07 28 00 00 00 00    .[8m.[2J...(....
-W 100 0 5 1
-Q
```

If you want to do something particularly sensitive in DOS, and you don't want to have it appear on your screen, ANSI can turn off the display if you set the colors to ESC[8m (where ESC represents a decimal 27 or hex 1B character), clear the screen with ESC[2J, and then reset the screen to your default colors when you're done. If you like blue text on a white background, you'd reset them to ESC[34;47m, so the batch file would look like:

```
ECHO ESC[8m;ESC[2J
REM (sensitive things happen here)
ECHO ESC[34;47m
```

Obviously, replace the "REM (sensitive things happen here)" line with the actual sensitive command(s).

If you're not using ANSI, you could get the same basic effect with two small COM programs, BLANK.COM and UNBLANK.COM. Create them both by typing in the following BLANK.SCR with a pure ASCII word processor or EDLIN:

```
A 100
MOV DX,184F        ;80 x 25
MOV CX,0000        ;Top left corner
MOV AX,0600        ;Scroll window up
MOV BH,00          ;00 = black on black
INT 10             ;Do it
MOV AH,02          ;Set cursor position
MOV BH,00          ;Main page
MOV DX,0000        ;Top left corner
INT 10             ;Do it
RET                ;Back to DOS

RCX
17
N BLANK.COM
W
E 10A 71
N UNBLANK.COM
W
Q
```

Omit the semicolons and the text following them. Be sure to leave a blank line above RCX, and to press the Enter key at the end of each line, especially the last one with the Q. Be certain DEBUG.COM is handy and type:

```
DEBUG < BLANK.SCR
```

Then put lines in your batch file that look like:

```
BLANK
REM (sensitive things happen here)
UNBLANK
```

Both of these techniques use the same color settings. BLANK will clear your screen to black on black, and UNBLANK will restore it to blue on white. You may change either of these as follows:

To change the BLANK.COM program, make sure you set the foreground and background to the same color. If you use the BLANK.SCR script, change:

```
MOV BH,00        ;00 = black on black
```

by replacing the 00 with any other pair of digits. Using 11 would give you a solid blue screen, 22 a solid green screen, 33 solid cyan, 44 solid red, 55 solid magenta, 66 solid brown, and 77 solid white.

To change the color of the UNBLANK.COM program, replace the 71 in the BLANK.SCR script line:

```
E 10A 71
```

with any other color you like. The lefthand digit is the background color, and must be in the range 0 to 7. The righthand digit is the text (foreground) color and must be a hex number bewteen 0 and F. Once again, here are the available colors:

Value	Color	Value	Color
0	Black	8	Grey
1	Blue	9	Bright blue
2	Green	A	Bright green
3	Cyan (Lt Blue)	B	Bright Cyan
4	Red	C	Bright red
5	Magenta	D	Bright magenta
6	Brown	E	Yellow
7	White	F	Bright white

⟵ **background only** ⟶

⟵——————— **foreground** ———————⟶

Changing the hex number from 71 to 74 would give you red text on a white background. Changing it to 4E would give you yellow text on a red background. The advantage to using the ANSI method is that typing CLS when the black on black setting is in effect would keep things black on black. However, typing CLS when BLANK.COM had temporarily made things black on black would reset your attributes to the default DOS grey on black, so you'd be able to see what you were doing. If you use BLANK.COM in a batch file, you won't have to worry about this.

A completely different (and more flexible) way to master ANSI is to enter commands via the ESCAPE.COM program below. You can create this program either of two ways. You could type in the following DEBUG ESCAPE.SCR script:

```
A 100
MOV DX,0120           ;point to device name CON at offset 120
MOV AX,3D01           ;open the standard input device
INT 21                ;do it
MOV BX,AX             ;save file handle in BX
MOV SI,0080           ;point to buffer containing inputed string
MOV CL,[SI]           ;get count of characters in string
INC CL                ;adjust count for prefix
XOR CH,CH             ;zero out high byte of count
MOV WORD PTR [SI],5B1B
                      ;put ANSI ESC[ sequence at beginning
MOV DX,SI             ;point to start of string
MOV AH,40             ;output string to the standard input device
INT 21                ;do it
MOV AH,3E             ;close handle
INT 21                ;do it
RET                   ;back to DOS
DB "CON",20,20,20,20,20,0

RCX
N ESCAPE.COM
2B
W
Q
```

While this lets you enter ANSI escape sequences from the command line, it uses a slow and slightly cumbersome trick (writing to standard output). A faster way is simply to have DOS display the string. Here's an adaptation of the above program that uses an undocumented DOS interrupt 29 "Quick TTL" display:

```
A
MOV SI,0080           ;point to buffer containing inputed string
MOV CL,[SI]           ;get count of characters in string
INC CL                ;adjust count for prefix
XOR CH,CH             ;zero out high byte of count
```

```
      MOV WORD PTR [SI],5B1B
                            ;put ANSI ESC[ sequence at beginning
      MOV AL,[SI]           ;put character from string into AL
      INT 29                ;undocumented "quick TTL" interrupt
      INC SI                ;point to next character in string
      LOOP 010D             ;go back and put next character into AL
      RET                   ;return to DOS

      RCX
      15
      N ESCAPE.COM
      W
      Q
```

But since running undocumented commands can be potentially troublesome, try this slightly longer, legal version that's nearly as fast:

```
      A
      MOV SI,0080           ;point to buffer containing inputed string
      MOV CL,[SI]           ;get count of characters in string
      INC CL                ;adjust count for prefix
      XOR CH,CH             ;zero out high byte of count
      MOV WORD PTR [SI],5B1B
                            ;put ANSI ESC[ sequence at beginning
      MOV AH,02             ;DOS'"display output" function
      MOV DL,[SI]           ;put character from string into DL
      INT 21                ;execute main DOS interrupt
      INC SI                ;point to next character in string
      LOOP 010D             ;go back and put next character into AL
      RET
      RCX
      17
      N ESCAPE.COM
      W
      Q
```

If you try any of these ESCAPE.SCR methods, use a pure-ASCII word processor or EDLIN, call the file ESCAPE.SCR, and be sure that you leave a blank line above RCX, and that you press the Enter key after each line — especially the last one with the solitary Q. You may omit the comments following the semicolons and the semicolons themselves. Then put the ESCAPE.SCR script file in the same directory as DEBUG.COM (or be sure DEBUG is in a directory that your path knows about) and type:

```
      DEBUG < ESCAPE.SCR
```

The ESCAPE.COM program that these techniques creates will let you enter ANSI commands without having to worry about the ESC character or the left bracket that follows it. So to clear the screen, just type:

```
ESCAPE 2J
```

or:

```
ESCAPE J
```

To reset all attributes to grey on black:

```
ESCAPE 0m
```

or:

```
ESCAPE m
```

To set the foreground to bright red, type:

```
ESCAPE 31;1m
```

Or to redefine Alt-1 so it prints the Spanish upside-down exclamation point, type:

```
ESCAPE 0;120;173p
```

(To save wear and tear on your typing fingers, you might want to rename ESCAPE.COM to E.COM. Then you could simply type:

```
E 0;120;173p
```

to redefine Alt-1, or:

```
E J
```

to clear the screen, etc.

And if you don't want to deal with ANSI numbers (such as 34 for a blue foreground, or 1 for highlighting) you can use the following FORE.BAT, BACK.BAT, and SPE-CIAL.BAT batch files:

First, FORE.BAT, to change foreground colors. Just type FORE and then a color — black, red, green, yellow, blue, magenta, cyan, or white. You may enter the colors in uppercase, lowercase, or a combination of both:

```
ECHO OFF
REM This is FORE.BAT
IF %1!==! GOTO OOPS
GOTO %1
ECHO ON
:BLACK
ECHO ESC[30m
GOTO END
:RED
ECHO ESC[31m
GOTO END
:GREEN
ECHO ESC[32m
GOTO END
:YELLOW
ECHO ESC[33m
GOTO END
:BLUE
ECHO ESC[34m
GOTO END
:MAGENTA
ECHO ESC[35m
GOTO END
:CYAN
ECHO ESC[36m
GOTO END
:WHITE
ECHO ESC[37m
GOTO END
:OOPS
ECHO You must enter a new text color, eg:
ECHO %0 WHITE  or  %0 red
:END
```

Next, BACK.BAT. This works exactly the same as FORE.BAT except that it lets you set the background color. Again, enter the color you want on the command line after the name BACK:

```
ECHO OFF
REM This is BACK.BAT
IF %1!==! GOTO OOPS
GOTO %1
ECHO ON
:BLACK
ECHO ESC[40m
```

```
GOTO END
:RED
ECHO ESC[41m
GOTO END
:GREEN
ECHO ESC[42m
GOTO END
:YELLOW
ECHO ESC[43m
GOTO END
:BLUE
ECHO ESC[44m
GOTO END
:MAGENTA
ECHO ESC[45m
GOTO END
:CYAN
ECHO ESC[46m
GOTO END
:WHITE
ECHO ESC[47m
GOTO END
:OOPS
ECHO You must enter a new background color, eg:
ECHO %0 WHITE  or  %0 red
:END
```

Finally, SPECIAL.BAT, to give you control over ANSI's other attributes (blinking, underlining on mono systems, high-intensity, etc.). You can also use it reset all your existing attributes back to plain white on black. You'll need to do this if you want to turn off blinking, or high-intensity, or any of the other special features:

```
ECHO OFF
REM This is SPECIAL.BAT
IF %1!==! GOTO OOPS
GOTO %1
ECHO ON
:RESET
:NORMAL
ECHO ESC[0m
GOTO END
:BOLD
:BRIGHT
:HIGHLIGHT
ECHO ESC[1m
```

```
GOTO END
:UNDERLINE
ECHO ESC[4m
GOTO END
:BLINK
ECHO ESC[5m
GOTO END
:REVERSE
 ECHO ESC[7m
GOTO END
:CANCEL
:BLANK
ECHO ESC[8m
GOTO END
:CLS
ECHO ESC[2J
GOTO END
:OOPS
ECHO You must enter a special attribute from this list:
ECHO RESET, NORMAL, BOLD, BRIGHT, HIGHLIGHT, CLS
ECHO UNDERLINE, BLINK, REVERSE, CANCEL, BLANK
ECHO eg:    %0 RESET    or    %0 CLS
:END
```

This trio lets you set attributes by typing in words rather than codes. So to set the foreground to blue, you'd type:

```
FORE blue
```

or:

```
FORE BLUE
```

or even something like:

```
FORE bLuE
```

To set the background to white, type:

```
BACK white
```

or:

```
BACK WHITE
```

And you can use the SPECIAL.BAT batch file to reset everything back to the default grey on black, or make the foreground blink or become bold. To reset everything to normal, just type:

```
SPECIAL reset
```

or:

```
SPECIAL RESET
```

or:

```
SPECIAL normal
```

or:

```
SPECIAL NORMAL
```

The choices are listed at the end of the SPECIAL.BAT file — and they appear onscreen if you simply type SPECIAL with nothing following it. Some definitions are duplicates. Here's the full slate of special ANSI attributes:

Action	Code
Normal grey-on-black (cancels any attributes currently in effect)	0
Bold (bright, or high-intensity; works on foreground only)	1
Underline (on IBM-compatible mono screens only; blue foreground on color systems)	4
Blink (foreground only)	5
Reverse video (white on black)	7
Canceled (black on black; invisible)	8

Most non-ANSI color-setting programs simply invoke one of the two BIOS INT 10 Scroll Window video services (Scroll Up or Scroll Down). But the colors these set aren't "sticky." If you run a program to give yourself bright magenta text on a cyan background, and then type CLS, DOS will reset your colors to grey on black, although you can patch the Scroll Window BIOS routine buried inside COMMAND.COM so that CLS will clear the screen to a predefined set of colors. But when you set colors and then clear the screen with ANSI, any subsequent CLS commands will wipe away existing text while maintaining the attributes you specified.

In fact, when you type a normal CLS command, DOS sends an ESC[2J to your BIOS to clear the screen. You can see this in action by redirecting the output of the CLS command into a file called CLRSCRN:

```
A>CLS > CLRSCRN
```

Then use the DOS TYPE command to display the contents of the file:

```
A>TYPE CLRSCRN
```

and the screen will clear.

Actually, this gives you one more way to create ANSI files that contain the elusive ESC character. Once you've redirected the CLS command into a file, you can edit that file with your word processor or EDLIN and change the command following the ESC[to execute whatever ANSI sequences you like. You can even add an ECHO to the beginning of the line and then rename the file by adding a BAT extension, which will turn it into a batch file that can set your colors or redefine your keys.

You could also have the following ANSICOLR.BAT batch file create individual files called COL.COM that you can run whenever you need to set your screen attributes to the predefined colors that you like. For this to work, your DEBUG.COM utility has to be in the same directory or in a directory that your path knows about:

```
ECHO OFF
IF %1!==! GOTO OOPS
IF EXIST COL.COM GOTO RENAME
ECHO N COL.COM                                    > COL.SCR
ECHO E 100 B4 9 BA 8 1 CD 21 C3 1B "["           >> COL.SCR
IF %4!==! GOTO THREE
ECHO E 10A "%1;%2;%3;%4m$"                        >> COL.SCR
GOTO FINISH
:THREE
IF %3!==! GOTO TWO
ECHO E 10A "%1;%2;%3m$"                           >> COL.SCR
GOTO FINISH
:TWO
IF %2!==! GOTO ONE
ECHO E 10A "%1;%2m$"                              >> COL.SCR
GOTO FINISH
:ONE
ECHO E 10A "%1m$"                                 >> COL.SCR
:FINISH
ECHO RCX                                          >> COL.SCR
ECHO 16                                           >> COL.SCR
ECHO W                                            >> COL.SCR
ECHO Q                                            >> COL.SCR
```

```
DEBUG < COL.SCR
DEL COL.SCR
ECHO Now run COL to set your color(s) to %1 %2 %3 %4
GOTO END
:OOPS
ECHO Enter from one to four ANSI color values after %0
ECHO eg: %0 34    for a blue foreground
ECHO or: %0 34 47 for blue text on a white background
ECHO or: %0 0 1 37 44 to reset the existing attributes
ECHO        then set your colors to bright white on blue
ECHO (And you must have ANSI loaded)
GOTO END
:RENAME
ECHO First rename your existing COL.COM so this
ECHO doesn't write over it, then restart %0
:END
```

Once you've typed in ANSICOLR.BAT, you could create a small program called COL.COM that would set your text color to blue, by typing:

```
ANSICOLR 34
```

The ANSICOLR batch file would redirect a customized script into DEBUG and create the appropriate COL.COM file. Typing:

```
COL
```

at the DOS prompt would set the foreground to blue. The:

```
IF EXIST COL.COM GOTO RENAME
```

in this batch file prevents it from overwriting any COL.COM you may have created previously. If ANSICOLR.BAT finds an existing COL.COM it will print a message telling you to rename the one you already have and then restart.

You may enter from one to four attributes on the command line after the name of the batch file itself. So:

```
ANSICOLR 5 35 42
```

would create a version of COL.COM that sets your colors to blinking magenta on green — a combination so horrid you would immediately erase COL.COM and type something like:

```
ANSICOLR 0 1 37 44
```

to create a COL.COM that would cancel any existing attributes and set the colors to bright white on a blue background.

One nice thing about having a program like COL.COM around is that you can stick it in your AUTOEXEC.BAT startup file and have DOS set your colors automatically. And if something accidentally resets your colors, you can run the COL.COM version you've created to put them back the way you like.

Full Screen Displays

While DOS ordinarily keeps you confined to the single line your cursor is on, ANSI gives you full control over the screen. You can move anywhere you want by issuing either of the commands:

```
ESC[row;columnH
```

or:

```
ESC[row;columnf
```

substituting the row you want for "row" and the desired column for "column." So ESC[13;35f and ESC[13;35H will both position the cursor on row 13, column 35, roughly in the center of the display. This doesn't do much good unless you display something at that location. So you could print a centered "WARNING!" either with:

```
ESC[13;35fWARNING!
```

or:

```
ESC[13;35HWARNING!
```

You can make this even more dramatic by adding:

```
ESC[5m
```

on the previous line to make the message blink. If you do this, you'll later have to get rid of the blink (with ESC[0m) and then reset your colors (with something like ESC[34;47m) on the line following it. Or you could combine the reset and color-setting operations into one line. The whole process would look like:

```
ESC[34;47m
ESC[5m
ESC[13;35fWARNING!
ESC[0;34;47m
```

The first line sets the colors; in this case to blue on white. The second makes the foreground blink. The third positions the message and prints it. The fourth gets rid of the blink by resetting everything back to white on black (with ESC[0), and then resets the colors to blue on white.

Actually, you could put all of these on the same line. The following short batch file would do it:

```
ECHO ESC[34;47mESC[5mESC[13;35fWARNING!ESC[0;34;47m
```

You don't have to put spaces between ANSI commands when you concatenate them like this. In fact, ANSI will print any leading and trailing spaces you specify, and these will show up if you print the message in a color that contrasts with the background. The following variation of the above command would put two spaces on either side of the WARNING message, and print the message in magenta on green:

```
ECHO ESC[34;47mESC[5;35;42mESC[13;35f  WARNING!  ESC[0;34;47m
```

ANSI uses decimal numbers only. If you omit both parameters when using the ESC[row;columnH positioning command, DOS will move the cursor to the home position, in the upper lefthand corner. Include just a single parameter and ANSI will use a default of 1 for either missing value. So:

```
ESC[fWARNING!
```

will print the word WARNING! in the upper lefthand corner, since both the row and column parameters are missing. ANSI treats this as if you entered the command:

```
ESC[1;1fWARNING!
```

If you type:

```
ESC[10;fWARNING!
```

ANSI will fill in a 1 for the missing column and print the message on column 1 of row 10. If you issue the command:

```
ESC[;10fWARNING!
```

ANSI will insert a default value of 1 for the row, and print the message on column 10 of row 1.

The PCMAG.BAT batch file below will put the letters "PC" in all four corners of the screen, and position the word "MAGAZINE" dead center. It will print these in contrasting, blinking, screen colors:

```
ECHO OFF
ECHO ESC[37;44m
ECHO ESC[2J
ECHO ESC[34;47;5m
ECHO ESC[24;2f PC
ECHO ESC[24;76f PC
ECHO ESC[2;2f PC
ECHO ESC[2;76f PC
ECHO ESC[13;35f Magazine
ECHO ESC[0;37;44m
```

To make the text stand out better, put one space on each side of the words " PC " and " Magazine ." The following ANYWHERE.BAT batch file will let you position one word of text anywhere on your screen:

```
ECHO OFF
IF %3!==! GOTO OOPS
IF %4!==! GOTO START
ECHO ESC[2J
:START
ECHO ESC[s
ECHO ESC[%1;%2f%3
ECHO ESC[u
GOTO END
:OOPS
ECHO You must specify three parameters
ECHO (row, column, word) after %0, eg:
ECHO %0 10 15 Hello
ECHO (Adding any 4th parameter clears screen)
:END
```

If you enter:

```
ANYWHERE 10,20,Hello
```

or:

```
ANYWHERE 10  20  Hello
```

it will print the word "Hello" on column 20 of row 10. Include any dummy fourth parameter, to clear the screen first. So:

```
ANYWHERE 10,20,Hello,1
```

or:

```
ANYWHERE 10 20 Hello Sports Fans
```

will print the word "Hello" on row 10, column 20 of a blank screen. This works because DOS scans across the command line when you enter any batch file command and assigns replaceable parameter values to each successive chunk of text separated by a space, comma, colon, or other delimiter. All replaceable parameters begin with percent signs. DOS would assign five of these to the command:

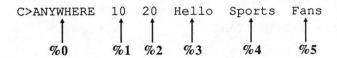

The very first chunk of text DOS sees after the C> or A> prompt is always a command or the name of an executable file, and it gives this special string of characters the parameter %0. The next chunk becomes %1, the one following that %2, etc. If your batch file doesn't use replaceable parameters, DOS ignores this special feature. But whenever it does see a % sign followed by a number from 0 to 9 it will try to replace it with the respective chunk of text from the command line. So if you execute the ANYWHERE batch file using the above command syntax, whenever DOS sees a %0 in the batch file it will replace the %0 and print out "ANYWHERE" instead.

If the batch file included the line:

```
ECHO The password is %0
```

DOS would print:

```
The password is ANYWHERE
```

If the line said:

```
ECHO The password is %1
```

DOS would display:

```
The password is 10
```

since 10 is the second discrete lump of text on the command line, and DOS assigns the second chunk of text on the command line a parameter of %1.

The ANYWHERE.BAT batch file uses a %0 at the bottom to print out the name of the batch file itself. This way if you rename it to something like POSITION.BAT, it will print out the new batch file name. This batch file also uses replaceable parameters %1 through %4. It will replace %1 with the first thing it found after the name of the batch file itself (here this is 10), %2 with the second thing (here it's 20), and %3 with the third thing (Hello). It doesn't really care what %4 is, since it uses this simply to test whether or not you specified any additional parameters after %3. If you did enter a word there like "Sports," DOS will turn the:

```
IF %4!==! GOTO START
```

test into:

```
IF Sports!==! GOTO START
```

The characters "Sports!" are clearly not equal to the single character "!" so the test fails (note that batch file tests like this use double equals signs). Since the test failed, DOS won't execute the command that follows at the end of the line (in this example the conditional command is GOTO START). If you hadn't entered anything on the command line after Hello, %4 would be equal to (nothing), and DOS would have translated the test into:

```
IF !==! GOTO START
```

Sure enough, "!" does equal "!" so DOS will jump to the label named START. (A label is a short word preceded by a colon). So if you didn't enter a parameter for %4, DOS will jump around the line that follows the test and go directly to :START. As illustrated here, this will skip the following clear-screen command.

Before it does anything else, the ANYWHERE.BAT batch file checks to see if the user entered any third parameter. The first two parameters are the row and column, but these won't do much if the user didn't enter anything on the command line to display. So DOS checks to make sure %3 isn't equal to (nothing) with the test:

```
IF %3!==! GOTO OOPS
```

If it finds nothing there, it will jump to the OOPS label and print a message displaying the proper syntax and reminding the user to enter a row, a column, a message, and an optional fourth parameter to clear the screen.

While ANSI's ESC[row;columnH and ESC[row;columnf positioning commands let you print messages at a precise location, there are times when you want to print text at relative locations. For example, if you want to display a message below the prompt, you could position the prompt at a certain predefined place on the screen and then print the message. However, if you didn't want to disturb what was on the screen, you could tell ANSI to figure out where the prompt happened to be at the time, and print the message directly below wherever that location was.

To make such relative positioning commands easy, ANSI lets you move the cursor up, down, left, or right one or more characters at a time with the following commands:

Up	ESC[#A
Down	ESC[#B
Left	ESC[#C
Right	ESC[#D

The # in each command equals the number of rows or columns to move; the default is 1. ANSI will ignore these commands if further movement in the specified direction is impossible. So if the cursor is already at the left edge of the screen, issuing an ESC[2C command won't do anything. If you leave out a number, ANSI will move just one row or column, so ESC[B will move down one row. When ANSI moves the cursor left or right it maintains the original row; when it moves up or down it keeps the original column position.

It's possible to blank a line by moving up and then printing spaces over it. You can use the ECHO command to do this in a batch file if you want to obliterate the initial commands. But you can't just put spaces after ECHO or DOS will think you're asking it whether ECHO currently happens to be set on or off.

The following CLEARSLF.BAT batch file will erase both the command line and the ECHO OFF message it prints. The line of xxxx's represents spaces; if you try this be sure to type a space in place of each x (you may have to vary the number of spaces to suit your screen). You have to use a character like a colon or period directly after the the ECHO for this to work.

```
ECHO OFF
ECHO ESC[2A
ECHO:xxxxxxxxxxxxxxxxxxxxxxxxxxxx
ECHO ESC[4A
ECHO:xxxxxxxxxxxxxxxxxxxxxxxxxxxx
```

Wiping out text with spaces isn't very efficient. ANSI provides two erasing commands to make it far easier. Many of the above examples above use one of these commands, ESC[2J, to clear the entire screen. (Incidentally, the DOS manuals say to use ESC[2J, but ESC[J works just as well; both will clear the screen to the foreground and background colors currently in effect. It doesn't really matter what reasonably sized number precedes the J.) But ANSI gives you finer erasing control than that. It lets you erase any line from and including the cursor position and extending to the right edge of the screen. Just issue the command:

```
ESC[K
```

You might want to position the cursor first and then erase to the end of the line. To get rid of everything to the right of column 40 on row 5, type:

```
ESC[5;41fESC[K
```

or:

```
ESC[5;41HESC[K
```

A better CLEARSLF.BAT batch file that incorporated this technique looks like:

```
ECHO OFF
ECHO ESC[2A
ECHO ESC[K
ECHO ESC[4A
ECHO ESC[K
```

While you're jumping all around the screen printing messages in various places it's handy to return to your original position when you finish. ANSI makes this a snap. Just issue this command:

```
ESC[s
```

to store the current cursor position, and then a:

```
ESC[u
```

command to put it back where it originally was when you stored it.

ANSI provides a set of commands called CPR (Cursor Position Report) and DSR (Device Status Report) that you almost certainly won't ever need. Issuing a DSR:

```
ESC[6n
```

will trigger a CPR in the form:

```
ESC[row,columnR
```

where row and column represent the current cursor position.

Mode-Setting Commands

You probably won't use ANSI's mode-setting commands either, since most users do all their DOS work exclusively in their system's 80 x 25 default text mode. And ANSI is way behind the times, since it offers only seven primitive screen modes. It also lets you disable and enable line wrapping, something most users just don't have a burning desire to do.

To set screen widths and modes, use the similar commands ESC[=#l or ESC[=#h, substituting a number from 0 to 6 in place of the #. Note that the l in the first version is a lowercase L, not a 1.

#	Screen Mode
0	40 x 25 black and white
1	40 x 25 color
2	80 x 25 black and white
3	80 x 25 color
4	320 x 200 color graphics
5	320 x 200 black and white graphics
6	640 x 200 black and white graphics

While the l and h suffixes work exactly the same with values from 0 through 6, they behave very differently when used with a value of 7. To set line wrap off, issue the command:

```
ESC[?7l
```

or:

```
ESC[=7l
```

To turn it back on, type:

```
ESC[?7h
```

or:

```
ESC[=7h
```

If you're typing something long and you reach the right edge of your screen, DOS normally wraps the text down one line and over to the left edge of the screen. Turning line wrap off means that once you reach the right edge of a typical 80-column screen, instead of bouncing down a line, DOS will print each character on the 80th column. Every letter will overlap the previous letter. You won't lose any keystrokes, but you won't really be able to see what you've typed. Turning line wrap off may have made sense once, but it's an anachronism today.

Redefining Keys

ANSI's attribute-handling abilities are extremely welcome on today's increasingly common color screens. But equally handy is its talent for redefining keys.

You can harness ANSI's formidable key definition abilities to:

- create duplicate keys
- switch keys around on the keyboard
- configure or redefine function keys to execute commands and cut down on typing

For example, some people need to type quotation marks far more often than they need the apostrophe that's on the same physical key as the quote mark. Or they may use question marks frequently but never have to type slashes. Normally you have to hold down the shift to have your keyboard gen°rate quotation and question marks. But it's simple for ANSI to swap the uppercase and lowercase versions of these keys.

And some new users keep pressing the forward slash / key when they really mean to type the backslash \ key. ANSI can turn the slash key into a duplicate backslash. Then whenever the user pressed either key his system would think he typed a backslash. The only problem is that this would prevent him from using a normal slash, unless the slash function was moved somewhere else.

Finally, if you're tired of having to issue repetitive, long-winded DOS commands full of tricky syntaxes, you can assign these commands to single keys. This makes it easier to handle daily DOS chores — and far more accurate.

Redefining keystrokes can be dangerous, so be very careful, and think about what you're doing. Users often give their files shorthand names to save typing. If you're writing a massive report on the 1990 plans for the Atlanta regional office, you may temporarily call the file just A rather than ATLOFC90.RPT. This makes it easier to work with, since it's faster to load the file into your word processor by typing:

```
WS A
```

(for *WordStar*) than:

```
WS ATLOFC90.RPT
```

When you're all done with the report, you can rename the file to give it its properly inscrutable but far more descriptive name. These same time-pressured users may also use ANSI to switch the semicolon (which they don't use in DOS) with the colon (which they do use frequently). This way they don't have to hold down the shift key when referring to a drive like C:.

If you have a long file on your C: drive that you've temporarily named A, and you've switched the colon and semicolon keys, and it's late at night, and you're tired, you could wipe out the whole file with an innocent command. How? If you want to copy a small file called C:MEMO to drive A: and you accidentally hold down the shift key, you'll end up with:

```
C>COPY MEMO A;
```

DOS will interpret the semicolon as a space, and copy the short MEMO file on top of the long file you've named A. Okay, maybe it's not a good idea to use single-letter names (especially names you could confuse with disk drive letters), and of course you should have backed up your work, and anyway DOS should alert you when you're about to copy one file onto another one (but it doesn't). These things happen. Back up often and be careful.

ANSI isn't perfect when it comes to redefining keys. It limits the number of keys you can redefine and the amount of information you can assign to them. Most programs come with their own keyboard handlers that bypass DOS, so your macros won't work in all cases. But you can use them at the DOS prompt, in DEBUG, EDLIN, or in certain editors such as IBM's *Personal Editor.*

You also have to make sure you don't reset a key such as Enter or space, or replace a letter of the alphabet that would prevent you from issuing normal DOS commands. You can reassign uppercase letters while leaving the lowercase ones intact (or vice versa), which lets you type practically anything. But if you reassign both the uppercase "I" and lowercase "i" you won't be able to execute commands like PRINT or DIR. And if you fool around with character 13 — the Enter key — you're dead in the water.

Finally, while DOS does let you reset any ANSI key redefinitions back to normal, it doesn't provide any method for listing the current key reassignments or clearing them out of memory to make room for others. Fortunately, you can do it yourself, if you're extremely careful and you follow the directions below.

First, however, move some keys around to see what ANSI can do.

If you never ever use square brackets — the "[" and "]" characters — but you rely heavily on normal parentheses and you hate having to hold the Shift key down to type them, just have ANSI turn the brackets into a duplicate set of parentheses.

You'll still be able to type them the old way, by leaning on Shift and pressing the 9 and 0 keys. But once you've executed a short ANSI script you'll also be able to generate parentheses by tapping the lowercase bracket keys. However, this will temporarily prevent you from putting brackets into your text — a minor drawback if you have to create any new ANSI sequences, since the second character of every ANSI command is a left bracket. Any key redefinitions you make using this technique will stay in effect until you reboot, unless you know the trick below for doing an ANSI lobotomy.

The decimal ASCII codes for the characters involved in this particular redefinition process are:

[= 91
] = 93
(= 40
) = 41

To redefine any key, issue the usual ANSI ESC[prefix, follow it with two ASCII codes separated by a semicolon, and tack a lowercase p onto the end. The first ASCII code is the key you want to press and the second is the character you want that key to produce. To redefine the [and] keys so they'll generate parentheses rather than brackets, for example, run the following two-line batch file:

```
ECHO ESC[91;40p
ECHO ESC[93;41p
```

Remember, this ANSI command has five parts:

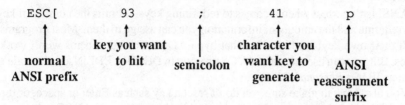

```
ESC [          93          ;          41          p
```
↑ normal ANSI prefix   ↑ key you want to hit   ↑ semicolon   ↑ character you want key to generate   ↑ ANSI reassignment suffix

You can enter the characters themselves in quotes rather than the ASCII codes if you like, but this can look confusing, especially when you're assigning lots of characters to a single key as you will a bit later. The following two lines will do the exact same redefinition as the ones above:

```
ECHO ESC["[";"("p
ECHO ESC["]";")"p
```

If you redefine these keys, and you discover that you do need to type brackets, you can reset the keys back to normal by putting the same ASCII code on both sides of the semicolon. This will do the trick:

```
ECHO ESC[91;91p
ECHO ESC[93;93p
```

You could also reset things by running a batch file that you created previously containing the two lines:

```
ECHO ESC["[";"["p
ECHO ESC["]";"]"p
```

However, you can't create these lines in DOS while the old redefinitions are in effect, because reassigning parentheses to the bracket keys temporarily did away with the brackets. (If you really had to do it, you could run a word processor such as *WordStar* that disregarded any ANSI changes.)

Redefining keys often ends up preventing you from typing certain characters, as it did above with brackets. However, ANSI makes it just as easy to swap one set of characters for another. If you use quotation marks more often than apostrophes, both of which share the same physical key, you can switch them so a tap on the unshifted key generates a quotation mark, while holding down the Shift and pressing the key yields an apostrophe. The ASCII values of these two keys are:

```
" = 34
' = 39
```

So you could run the following two-line batch file:

```
ECHO ESC[34;39p
ECHO ESC[39;34p
```

To switch both characters you have to execute both lines. Running just the first one by itself:

```
ECHO ESC[34;39p
```

would assign the apostrophe character to the shifted version of the key — the one that normally produces a quotation mark. This would cause the key to produce an apostrophe regardless of whether you were holding the Shift key down, which isn't what you want.

Again, you could also use the actual characters themselves in the ANSI command rather than the ASCII codes. But this gets tricky when one of the keys you're trying to redefine is a quotation mark, since you have to use quotation marks to identify the characters you want to change.

DOS can treat pairs of single quotation marks (which are really just apostrophes) the same way it handles pairs of double quotation marks. So you can run the following, two-line batch file to make the swap:

```
ECHO ESC['"';"'"p
ECHO ESC["'";'"'p
```

and then either:

```
ECHO ESC[34;34p
ECHO ESC[39;39p
```

or:

```
ECHO ESC['"';'"'p
ECHO ESC["'";"'"p
```

to reset things to their original state.

Swapping or duplicating alphanumeric keys is straightforward and easy. But ANSI can also assign characters to dozens of special key combinations that generate what IBM calls *extended* codes.

ANSI deals with normal "typewriter" keys like A, a, 1, or $ by manipulating single ASCII values between 32 (a space) and 126 (a Spanish tilde). A capital "A" has an ASCII value of 65, and a lowercase "a" an ASCII value of 97. Refer back to the chart of ASCII values for the typewriter keys in Chapter 5. Any of these values can be plugged into the examples above to move the keys around the keyboard.

ANSI can also handle nonalphanumeric keys such as the F1 function key, the Home key, and the Ins key. And it can work with less common shifted key combinations such as Ctrl-End, Alt-E, or Shift-F1. All of the special key combinations in Figure 9.1 generate a pair of ASCII values rather than just a single value. The first value in the pair is always an ASCII 0, or NUL character. Figure 9.2 is an index of all key combinations and their values.

Miscellaneous Key Combination	Code[*]	Function Key Combination	Code[*]
NUL	0;3	F1	0;59
Shift-Tab	0;15	F2	0;60
Alt-A	0;30	F3	0;61
Alt-B	0;48	F4	0;62
Alt-C	0;46	F5	0;63
Alt-D	0;32	F6	0;64
Alt-E	0;18	F7	0;65
Alt-F	0;33	F8	0;66
Alt-G	0;34	F9	0;67
Alt-H	0;35	F10	0;68
Alt-I	0;23	Shift-F1	0;84
Alt-J	0;36	Shift-F2	0;85
Alt-K	0;37	Shift-F3	0;86
Alt-L	0;38	Shift-F4	0;87
Alt-M	0;50	Shift-F5	0;88
Alt-N	0;49	Shift-F6	0;89
Alt-O	0;24	Shift-F7	0;90
Alt-P	0;25	Shift-F8	0;91
Alt-Q	0;16	Shift-F9	0;92
Alt-R	0;19	Shift-F10	0;93
Alt-S	0;31	Ctrl-F1	0;94
Alt-T	0;20	Ctrl-F2	0;95

continued

Alt-U	0;22	Ctrl-F3	0;96
Alt-V	0;47	Ctrl-F4	0;97
Alt-W	0;17	Ctrl-F5	0;98
Alt-X	0;45	Ctrl-F6	0;99
Alt-Y	0;21	Ctrl-F7	0;100
Alt-Z	0;44	Ctrl-F8	0;101
Alt-1	0;120	Ctrl-F9	0;102
Alt-2	0;121	Ctrl-F10	0;103
Alt-3	0;122	Alt-F1	0;104
Alt-4	0;123	Alt-F2	0;105
Alt-5	0;124	Alt-F3	0;106
Alt-6	0;125	Alt-F4	0;107
Alt-7	0;126	Alt-F5	0;108
Alt-8	0;127	Alt-F6	0;109
Alt-9	0;128	Alt-F7	0;110
Alt-0	0;129	Alt-F8	0;111
Alt--	0;130	Alt-F9	0;112
Alt-=	0;131	Alt-F10	0;113
Home	0;71		
Cursor Up	0;72		
PgUp	0;73		
Cursor Left	0;75		
Cursor Right	0;77		
End	0;79		
Cursor Down	0;80		
PgDn	0;81		
Ins	0;82		
Del	0;83		
Ctrl-PrtSc	0;114		
Ctrl-Cursor Left	0;115		
Ctrl-Cursor Right	0;116		
Ctrl-End	0;117		
Ctrl-PgDn	0;118		
Ctrl-Home	0;119		
Ctrl-PgUp	0;132		

Figure 9.1.   Extended ASCII Codes for Special Key Combinations

[*]In the form ASCII 0;code

Key Combination	Code[*]	Key Combination	Code[*]
NUL	0;3	Shift-F2	0;85
Shift-Tab	0;15	Shift-F3	0;86
Alt-Q	0;16	Shift-F4	0;87
Alt-W	0;17	Shift-F5	0;88
Alt-E	0;18	Shift-F6	0;89
Alt-R	0;19	Shift-F7	0;90
Alt-T	0;20	Shift-F8	0;91
Alt-Y	0;21	Shift-F9	0;92
Alt-U	0;22	Shift-F10	0;93
Alt-I	0;23	Ctrl-F1	0;94
Alt-O	0;24	Ctrl-F2	0;95
Alt-P	0;25	Ctrl-F3	0;96
Alt-A	0;30	Ctrl-F4	0;97
Alt-S	0;31	Ctrl-F5	0;98
Alt-D	0;32	Ctrl-F6	0;99
Alt-F	0;33	Ctrl-F7	0;100
Alt-G	0;34	Ctrl-F8	0;101
Alt-H	0;35	Ctrl-F9	0;102
Alt-J	0;36	Ctrl-F10	0;103
Alt-K	0;37	Alt-F1	0;104
Alt-L	0;38	Alt-F2	0;105
Alt-Z	0;44	Alt-F3	0;106
Alt-X	0;45	Alt-F4	0;107
Alt-C	0;46	Alt-F5	0;108
Alt-V	0;47	Alt-F6	0;109
Alt-B	0;48	Alt-F7	0;110
Alt-N	0;49	Alt-F8	0;111
Alt-M	0;50	Alt-F9	0;112
F1	0;59	Alt-F10	0;113
F2	0;60	Ctrl-PrtSc	0;114
F3	0;61	Ctrl-Cursor Left	0;115
F4	0;62	Ctrl-Cursor Right	0;116
F5	0;63	Ctrl-End	0;117
F6	0;64	Ctrl-PgDn	0;118
F7	0;65	Ctrl-Home	0;119
F8	0;66	Alt-1	0;120
F9	0;67	Alt-2	0;121
F10	0;68	Alt-3	0;122
Home	0;71	Alt-4	0;123

continued

Cursor Up	0;72	Alt-5	0;124
PgUp	0;73	Alt-6	0;125
Cursor Left	0;75	Alt-7	0;126
Cursor Right	0;77	Alt-8	0;127
End	0;79	Alt-9	0;128
Cursor Down	0;80	Alt-0	0;129
PgDn	0;81	Alt--	0;130
Ins	0;82	Alt-=	0;131
Del	0;83	Ctrl-PgUp	0;132
Shift-F1	0;84		

Figure 9.2. Index of Extended ASCII Codes

*In the form ASCII 0;code.

When IBM designed the BIOS support for the enhanced keyboard, it added over 30 new extended keyboard codes starting at 133. However, it did not make these keyboard codes available to programs through the normal BIOS keyboard interface. To do so would have created incompatibilities with some existing programs. For instance, some keyboard macro programs define their own extended keys and these may conflict with the new IBM codes. DOS (and most programs) get keyboard information from the BIOS through interrupt 16H, function calls 0, 1, and 2. For the enhanced keyboard, IBM defined new function calls numbered 10H, 11H, and 12H that duplicated 0, 1, and 2 except that the new calls also return the new extended keyboard codes in addition to the old ones.

Here's a DEBUG script for a NEWKEYS.COM program you can create that allows DOS access to the new codes and lets you use these new keys with ANSI.SYS:

```
N NEWKEYS.COM
A
JMP     013A            ; Jmp Initialize
DW      0,0
CMP     AH,00           ; NewInt16:
JZ      0115            ; Jmp GetKey
CMP     AH,01
JZ      0121            ; Jmp GetStatus
CS:
JMP     FAR [0102]      ; Jmp OldInt16
MOV     AH,10           ; GetKey:
PUSHF
CS:
CALL    FAR [0102]      ; Call OldInt16
CALL    0131            ; Call FixUp
IRET
```

```
        MOV    AH,11          ; GetStatus:
        PUSHF
        CS:
        CALL   FAR [0102]     ; Call OldInt16
        JZ     012E
        CALL   0131           ; Call FixUp
        RETF   0002
        CMP    AL,E0          ; FixUp:
        JNZ    0139
        SUB    AL,AL
        CMP    AL,01
        RET
        MOV    AX,3516        ; Initialize:
        INT    21             ; Get OldInt16
        MOV    [0102],BX      ; Save it
        MOV    [0104],ES
        MOV    DX,0106
        MOV    AX,2516
        INT    21             ; Set NewInt16
        MOV    DX,013A
        INT    27             ; Stay Resident

        RCX
        54
        W
        Q
```

Create NEWKEYS.COM by typing the lines shown into a file called NEWKEYS.SCR. (Don't type the semicolons or the comments that follow them.) Then type:

```
DEBUG < NEWKEYS.SCR
```

to creates the program.

NEWKEYS.COM is a *Terminate and Stay Resident* (TSR) program so you need to load it only once during your PC session. Like most TSRs, it may have some compatibility problems with other programs. If everything seems to work OK once you load it, then you're probably in good shape.

When NEWKEYS is loaded, you can use the extra keyboard codes for ANSI.SYS redefinitions. The new codes are shown in Figure 9.3.

Miscellaneous Key Combination	Code[*]
F11	0;133
F12	0;134
Shift-F11	0;135
Shift-F12	0;136
Ctrl-F11	0;137
Ctrl-F12	0;138
Alt-F11	0;139
Alt-F12	0;140
Ctrl-Up-Arrow	0;141
Ctrl -	0;142
Ctrl-5	0;143
Ctrl-+	0;144
Ctrl-Down-Arrow	0;145
Ctrl-Insert	0;146
Ctrl-Delete	0;147
Ctrl-Tab	0;148
Ctrl-/	0;149
Ctrl-*	0;150
Alt-Home	0;151
Alt-Up-Arrow	0;152
Alt-Page-Up	0;153
Alt-Left-Arrow	0;155
Alt-Right-Arrow	0;157
Alt-End	0;159
Alt-Down-Arrow	0;160
Alt-Page-Down	0;161
Alt-Insert	0;162
Alt-Delete	0;163
Alt-/	0;164
Alt-Tab	0;165
Alt-Enter	0;166

Figure 9.3. IBM 101/102-Key Keyboard Extended Codes

[*]In the form ASCII 0;code.

As an example, if you have ANSI.SYS loaded and want to redefine the F11 key to do a DIR command, just issue the command:

```
ESC[0;133;"DIR";13p
```

(where ESC is a hex 1B or decimal 27 Esc character, not the letters ESC).

You can examine the ASCII values of all the keys on the keyboard — except for the Ctrl, Alt, CapsLock, NumLock, ScrollLock, Sys Req, and Shifts — by running this BASIC KEYCODE.BAS program:

```
100 ' KEYCODE.BAS
110 DEF SEG=0:POKE 1047,PEEK(1047) AND 223   ' turns cursor pad on
120 DEF SEG:KEY OFF:COLOR 2,0:CLS            ' sets screen
130 FOR A=1 TO 10:KEY A,"":NEXT             ' disables function keys
140 PRINT "Press a key (or Enter to end):",  ' instructions
150 I$=INKEY$:IF I$="" THEN 150              ' waits for key to be hit
160 IF I$=CHR$(13) THEN END                  ' ** hit Enter to end **
170 IF LEN(I$)>1 THEN PRINT "ext",:GOTO 190  ' is it extended code?
180 PRINT I$,                                ' print character
190 IF LEN(I$)>1 THEN PRINT "0 +";           ' again, is it extended?
200 PRINT ASC(RIGHT$(I$,1))                  ' print ASCII code
210 GOTO 140                                 ' loop back for new key
```

BASIC has trouble displaying certain characters such as ASCII 7, 10, 11, and 12, since it interprets these as commands to beep, clear the screen, and so on. But you'll be able to see the ASCII values for all the alphanumeric and extended keys.

The ASCII code method for swapping or duplicating extended keys is exactly the same as for normal alphanumeric keys except that you have to include an extra "0;" prefix. To to swap F1 and F3, run the following two-line batch file:

```
ECHO ESC[0;59;0;61p
ECHO ESC[0;61;0;59p
```

In notation that ANSI can understand, the extended ASCII codes for F1 and F3 are 0;59 and 0;61. At the DOS prompt, pressing the F1 key normally repeats the previous DOS command one character at a time, while F3 reproduces the entire previous command with a single tap. But after you run the two-line ANSI command above, the functions will reverse.

You can restore the original functions of these two keys with the two lines:

```
ECHO ESC[0;59;0;59p
ECHO ESC[0;61;0;61p
```

When dealing with extended keys you have to use ASCII codes exclusively since DOS doesn't provide any method for referring to these keys in quotes. You can't make F1 duplicate the function of F3 with a command like:

```
ECHO ESC["F1";"F3"p
```

All this will do is assign the character string "1F3" to the uppercase F key.

You could also have the following ANSICHAR.BAT batch file (similar to the attribute-setting ANSICLOR.BAT file above) create a series of individual files called CHAR.COM that you can run whenever you need to redefine a key. Again, for this to work, your DEBUG.COM utility has to be in the same directory or in a directory that your PATH knows about:

```
ECHO OFF
IF %2!==! GOTO OOPS
IF EXIST CHAR.COM GOTO RENAME
ECHO N CHAR.COM                              > CHR.SCR
ECHO E 100 B4 9 BA 8 1 CD 21 C3 1B "[" >> CHR.SCR
IF %4!==! GOTO THREE
ECHO E 10A "%1;%2;%3;%4p$"              >> CHR.SCR
GOTO FINISH
:THREE
IF %3!==! GOTO TWO
ECHO E 10A "%1;%2;%3p$"                 >> CHR.SCR
GOTO FINISH
:TWO
ECHO E 10A "%1;%2p$"                    >> CHR.SCR
:FINISH
ECHO RCX                                >> CHR.SCR
ECHO 7F                                 >> CHR.SCR
ECHO W                                  >> CHR.SCR
ECHO Q                                  >> CHR.SCR
DEBUG < CHR.SCR
DEL CHR.SCR
ECHO Now run CHAR whenever you want to reset this key
GOTO END
:OOPS
ECHO Enter two ANSI key codes after %0
ECHO eg: %0 126 155   to have the ~ key print a
ECHO cent-sign (And you must have ANSI loaded)
ECHO Remember to use a 0 for extended characters
ECHO eg: %0 0 68 0 61 to make F10 work like F3, or
ECHO     %0 0 67 ""DIR/W"" 13 to make F9 do a wide DIR
ECHO (Note the double quotes around character strings!
```

```
ECHO — and note you CAN'T have spaces in strings, so
ECHO you cannot enter: %0 0 67 ""DIR /W"" 13)
GOTO END
:RENAME
ECHO First rename your existing CHAR.COM so this
ECHO doesn't write over it, then restart %0
:END
```

Once you've typed in ANSICHAR.BAT, you could create a small program called CHAR.COM that would turn your dollar sign into an English pound sterling sign, by typing:

```
ANSICHAR 36 156
```

The ANSICHAR batch file would redirect a customized script into DEBUG and create the appropriate CHAR.COM file. Typing:

```
CHAR
```

at the DOS prompt would redefine your dollar sign key so it printed a pound symbol instead.

As with ANSICOLR.BAT, the:

```
IF EXIST CHAR.COM GOTO RENAME
```

line in this batch file prevents it from overwriting any CHAR.COM you may have created previously. If ANSICHAR.BAT finds an existing CHAR.COM it will print a message telling you to rename the one you already have and then restart. If you're redefining extended keys such as function keys, cursor-pad keys, or Alt-key combinations, be sure to include the 0 prefix that ANSI requires.

So, to turn F8 into an additional Insert key, you'd type:

```
ANSICHAR 0 66 0 82
```

Then you'd run the CHAR program it created to do the actual redefining. Or if you wanted to have DOS print a pi symbol whenever you typed Alt-P, you'd enter:

```
ANSICHAR 0 25 227
```

and then type CHAR to finish the process. If you want to define a function key like F10 so it executes a command such as DIR/W, you'd type:

```
ANSICHAR 0 67 ""DIR/W"" 13
```

(The double quote marks are necessary only because of the way the batch file interacts with DEBUG; if you attach this definition to this key using a technique other than ANSICHAR.BAT you'd use only one set. And if you enter a string, be sure not to insert any spaces in it, so:

```
""DIR/W""
```

will work just fine, while:

```
""DIR /W""
```

won't work at all.)

The 13 at the end of the line represents the Enter key (which has an ASCII value of decimal 13). If you include this at the end of a redefined key command, DOS will print the command out when you press the appropriate key and then execute it. If you leave the 13 off, DOS will simply print out the command without running it.

As with COL.COM, it's handy to have versions of CHAR.COM around to put in your AUTOEXEC.BAT startup file so DOS will redefine your keys automatically each time you boot up. Be sure to rename previous versions of CHAR.BAT each time you create new ones. It's helpful to give them descriptive names like CHARPI.COM if it types a pi symbol, or CHARDIRW if it executes a DIR/W.

Macro Magic

If you want to assign a text string or a command to any key, ANSI will let you if there's room left. DOS maintains an area inside the ANSI.SYS code itself as a table of redefinitions. This table is absurdly small. DOS 2.x provides only 196 bytes of space for this purpose, and DOS 3.x a mere 204 — and some of this space at the end of the table can't be used.

In fact, even in the larger DOS 3.x versions, you can cram in a maximum of 64 redefinitions — assuming you're not using any extended keys (which take up slightly more space) and that each redefinition is only a single key long. Wedging in a 65th starts to create problems.

Worse, if you try using ANSI to attach text messages to your keys you'll run out of space almost before you begin. If you try hard you can define a maximum of 191 characters — by creating two macros, one 127 characters or less, and the other 191 characters minus the length of the first one. For instance, you could define one that turned "a" into 127 capital As:

```
ESC[97;"AAAAAAAAAAAAAAAAAAAAAAAAAAAAAAAAAAAAAAAAAAAAAAAAAAAAAAAA
        AAAAAAAAAAAAAAAAAAAAAAAAAAAAAAAAAAAAAAAAAAAAAAAAAAAAAAAA
        AAAAAAAAAAAAAAAAAAAAAAAAA"p
```

and another that turned "b" into 64 capital Bs:

```
ESC[98;"BBBBBBBBBBBBBBBBBBBBBBBBBBBBBBBBBBBBBBBBBBBBBBBB
       BBBBBBBBBBBBB"p
```

(Obviously you would type these on one long line each, but we can't show that on this page.)

However, if you want a true macro processor, get your hands on a powerful commercial package like *SuperKey*, *ProKey*, *SmartKey*, *KeyWorks*, or any of the other similar products crowding the market. For quick and dirty macro work, ANSI does just fine. If you miss having a cent sign at your fingertips, ANSI can put one there. To define Alt-C so that it prints a cent sign (which is ASCII character 155), run this one-line batch file:

```
ECHO ESC[0;46;155p
```

Or you could define a group of keys at once. The following CHARS.BAT batch file will give you direct keyboard access to the ten characters shown. It's sometimes handy to add text as this batch file does to keep you (or other users you give the file to) informed. ANSI won't start processing commands in a line until it sees an ESC[, so the initial descriptive labels won't affect the definition process:

```
ECHO OFF
ECHO Defining keys as follows:
ECHO ALT+1=square-root radical sign    ESC[0;120;251p
ECHO ALT+2=degree sign                 ESC[0;121;248p
ECHO ALT+3=old-fashioned division sign ESC[0;122;246p
ECHO ALT+4=pi                          ESC[0;123;227p
ECHO ALT+5=infinity                    ESC[0;124;236p
ECHO ALT+6=(squared)^2                 ESC[0;125;253p
ECHO ALT+7=1/2                         ESC[0;126;171p
ECHO ALT+8=1/4                         ESC[0;127;172p
ECHO ALT+9=pound sterling              ESC[0;128;156p
ECHO ALT+0=yen                         ESC[0;129;157p
```

You can, of course, attach more than one character to a key. So after running EINSTEIN.BAT:

```
ECHO ESC[0;18;"E=MC";253p
```

typing Alt-E will display the familiar formula.

A more practical application would give you one-key execution of a complex command that you perform all day long, such as:

```
DIR C: | SORT /R /+14 | FIND "-" | MORE
```

This displays the contents of the current directory on drive C: with the largest files at the top of the list. It also screens out extraneous information about volume labels and bytes free by filtering the output through FIND.EXE, and pauses a screenful at a time. The NEWDIR.BAT batch file:

```
ECHO ESC[0;46;"DIR C: | SORT /R /+14 | FIND ";34;"-";34;" | MORE";13p
```

lets you run this command simply by typing ALT-C.

The pair of 34s on the above line provide the two quotation marks that you need to surround the "-" in the FIND command, since 34 is the decimal ASCII value of ". The 13 at the end is the ASCII representation of a carriage return, which executes the command. If you omitted the 13, ANSI would print the command but not execute it.

What makes this especially handy is that you can add two more lines to the batch file so the three keys Alt-A, Alt-B, and Alt-C, will execute this command on the three drives A:, B:, and C:

```
ECHO ESC[0;30;"DIR A: | SORT /R /+14 | FIND ";34;"-";34;" | MORE";13p
ECHO ESC[0;48;"DIR B: | SORT /R /+14 | FIND ";34;"-";34;" | MORE";13p
ECHO ESC[0;46;"DIR C: | SORT /R /+14 | FIND ";34;"-";34;" | MORE";13p
```

You can attach any text to any key, if there's room. The following ADDRESS.BAT batch file would print a three-line return address each time you typed Alt-P:

```
ECHO ESC[0;25;"PC Magazine";13;"One Park Avenue";13;"New York, NY 10016";13p
```

You won't be able to use this with any word processor that has its own internal keyboard handling routine. But if you create a letter using the DOS COPY CON command, or EDLIN, or a commercial product like IBM *Personal Editor*, tapping Alt-P once will put:

```
PC Magazine
One Park Avenue
New York, NY 10016
```

at the cursor position.

The only real problems with having ANSI assign text and commands to specific keys are that you normally can't see what key assignments you've previously made, and that you run out of space for new commands very quickly. And, while ANSI lets you reset keys to their original values, it doesn't provide a way to clear everything out of memory and start afresh. Fortunately, we do.

Customizing Your Configuration

Actually, the configuration file doesn't have to be called CONFIG.SYS, and it needn't be located in the root directory. If you want to keep your root directory spare and uncluttered, you can name the file something like TESTIT and store it in your \DOS subdirectory.

Part of the process involves changing a DOS directory entry. DOS uses the disk directory to record each file's name, its size, the time and date you created or last modified it, and where the actual data begins on the disk. It also relies on one byte in the directory to keep track of what kind of file each is — so DOS can determine things like whether it will display the filename in directory searches and whether it will let you modify the data in the file.

Try this ONLY on a diskette in drive A: since writing absolute sectors is incredibly dangerous on your hard disk. Follow the directions precisely and check your work carefully as you proceed. The most dangerous command here is Write (W), so when you're ready to execute any lines starting with:

    -W

check your typing and make absolutely sure it matches the example here. Finally, *don't* try this on your hard disk. The instructions below are for a 360K diskette running under DOS 3.3 in drive A: *only!*

Step 1

Format a 360K floppy disk and put the DOS system files on it, using the command:

    C>FORMAT A:/S

Then log onto drive A: and create a subdirectory on it called \DOS:

    A>MD\DOS

Copy DEBUG.COM and ANSI.SYS from your hard disk or main DOS disk into this \DOS subdirectory.

If you type DIR you should see something like:

    A:\:DIR

    Volume in drive A has no label
    Directory of A:\

    COMMAND COM   25307   3-17-87   12:00p
    DOS   <DIR>   11-28-88   4:27p
            2 File(s)   282624 bytes free

Step 2

The DOS utility that sniffs out your CONFIG.SYS is called IBMBIO.COM (or IO.SYS on generic systems). DOS marks the directory entry for this file so it's hidden from normal DIR searches and so you can't alter it. But we will. Load DEBUG into memory and have it load the part of your diskette that stores the beginning of the DOS directory:

```
A>\DOS\DEBUG
-L 100 0 5 1
```

Then display the first hex 10 (decimal 16) bytes of the directory listing with the command:

```
-D 100 L 10
```

You'll see something like:

```
3140:0100   49 42 4D 42 49 4F 20 20-43 4F 4D 27 00 00 00 00   IBMBIO  COM'....
```

If you don't, type Q to quit and then press Enter, and restart. Make sure you're using a 360K diskette in drive A: and that you formatted it with the DOS system files on it. (The 3140 number at the left edge of the screen will vary from system to system and doesn't matter here.)

The 27 to the left of the four pairs of 00s — at memory offset 10B — is the value of the directory attribute byte that tells DOS the file is:

- Read-only   value of hex 1
- Hidden   value of hex 2
- System   value of hex 4
- Archive   value of hex 20

You want to temporarily remove the first three, which will reduce the value there from 27 to 20:

```
-E 10B 20
```

Then, check your typing to make sure the value that used to be a 27 is now a 20:

```
-D 100 L 10
```

You should see:

```
3140:0100   49 42 4D 42 49 4F 20 20-43 4F 4D 20 00 00 00 00   IBMBIO  COM ....
```

(again, ignore the 3140 at the beginning of the line). If you don't, be sure to press Q to quit and then press Enter, because the next line is the one you really have to type extremely carefully.

Write the directory information back to the diskette in drive A: by typing:

```
-W 100 0 5 1
```

Make absolutely sure that the character between the 100 and the 5 is 0!! DEBUG thinks of drive A: as drive 0, so check your typing before you press Enter to make sure there's a 0 after the 100 and not any other number. Then quit DEBUG and get back to DOS:

```
-Q
```

This time if you type DIR you should see:

```
A:\:DIR

Volume in drive A has no label
Directory of  A:\

IBMBIO    COM     22100    3-18-87   12:00p
COMMAND   COM     25307    3-17-87   12:00p
DOS               <DIR>    11-28-88   4:27p
        3 File(s)     282624 bytes free
```

Step 3

Now, look for the mention of CONFIG.SYS inside IBMBIO.COM and change the name and location of the configuration file IBMBIO.COM will look for. Load IBMBIO.COM into DEBUG:

```
A>DEBUG IBMBIO.COM
```

Find out how long the IBMBIO.COM file is by typing RCX and pressing the Enter key twice:

```
-RCX
CX 5654
:
-
```

The number to the right of the CX is the file length in hex notation. This number will differ if you're using a version of DOS other than 3.3. Plug the number that you see into a DEBUG search command:

```
-S 100 L 5654 "CONFIG.SYS"
```

This tells DEBUG to search through the entire length of the IBMBIO.COM file for the characters CONFIG.SYS. It should find several occurrences and report the starting memory address of these character strings:

```
315C:53AC
315C:5612
-
```

(Once again, ignore the 315C to the left of the colon. This number will be different on your own system.)

Next, peek inside the 20 hex (decimal 16) bytes of memory starting at the first address:

```
-D 53A0 L 20
```

DEBUG should display something like:

```
315C:53A0  4F 4E 00 41 55 58 00 50-52 4E 00 5C 43 4F 4E 46   ON.AUX.PRN.\CONF
315C:53B0  49 47 2E 53 59 53 00 41-3A 5C 43 4F 55 4E 54 52   IG.SYS.A:\COUNTR
```

When DOS finishes booting up, it will look at the filename and path specified here for the name and location of the configuration file. As it's delivered from the factory, this information is:

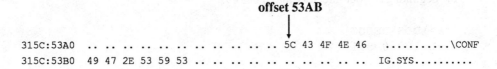

offset 53AB

```
315C:53A0  .. .. .. .. .. .. .. .. .. .. .. .. 5C 43 4F 4E 46   ...........\CONF
315C:53B0  49 47 2E 53 59 53 .. .. .. .. .. .. .. .. .. ..   IG.SYS.........
```

You can change this to anything you want, provided the new name and path are the same length as the existing ones. This example will substitute \DOS\TESTIT:

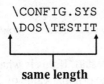

```
\CONFIG.SYS
\DOS\TESTIT
```

same length

You don't have to enter the \ at offset 53AB where \CONFIG.SYS currently starts, since \DOS\TESTIT also begins with a \. So you can start entering the rest of the new characters — DOS\TESTIT — at the following address, 53AC:

```
-E 53AC "DOS\TESTIT"
```

Use the Display (D) command again to check your typing:

```
-D 53A0 L 20
```

and you should now see:

```
315C:53A0  4F 4E 00 41 55 58 00 50-52 4E 00 5C 44 4F 53 5C    ON.AUX.PRN.\DOS\
315C:53B0  54 45 53 54 49 54 00 41-3A 5C 43 4F 55 4E 54 52    TESTIT.A:\COUNTR
```

If you do, save your changes by typing W and pressing Enter, then quit by typing Q and then pressing Enter:

```
-W
Writing 5654 bytes
-Q
```

Step 4

Now you have to give IBMBIO.COM back its original directory attribute of 27. You really don't have to, but the idea was to prevent clutter, and this will hide it. It will also prevent you from inadvertently erasing it.

So reverse the process shown in step 2. Load DEBUG and read the information from the beginning of your directory into memory.

```
A>\DOS\DEBUG
-L 100 0 5 1
```

Display the first hex 10 (decimal 16) bytes:

```
-D 100 L 10
```

which should look like:

```
3140:0100  49 42 4D 42 49 4F 20 20-43 4F 4D 20 00 00 00 00    IBMBIO  COM'....
```

Again, if it doesn't, type Q to quit, then press Enter, and restart. If this is what you see, you want to replace the value of 20 at address 10B with the original value of 27:

```
-E 10B 27
```

Check your typing:

```
-D 100 L 10
```

You should see:

```
3140:0100  49 42 4D 42 49 4F 20 20-43 4F 4D 27 00 00 00 00    IBMBIO  COM ....
```

Very carefully write the directory information back to the diskette in drive A: by typing:

```
-W 100 0 5 1
```

One more time — *be certain the character between the 100 and the 5 is 0!* Check it several times before you press the Enter key.

Finally, quit DEBUG:

```
-Q
```

and execute a DIR command to make sure the IBMBIO.COM doesn't appear:

```
A:\:DIR

Volume in drive A has no label
Directory of  A:\

COMMAND  COM     25307    3-17-87   12:00p
DOS             <DIR>     11-28-88    4:27p
          2 File(s)    282624 bytes free
```

Step 5

Now log into the \DOS subdirectory, and create a file called TESTIT that contains the information you'd normally put into your CONFIG.SYS file:

```
A>CD\DOS
A>COPY CON TESTIT
DEVICE=C:\DOS\CONFIG.SYS
^Z
          1 File(s) copied
```

and issue a DIR command to make sure that the file is there:

```
A>DIR

Volume in drive A has no label
Directory of  A:\DOS

    .           <DIR>       11-28-87    4:27p
    ..          <DIR>       11-28-87    4:27p
ANSI     SYS     1678       3-17-87   12:00p
DEBUG    COM    15897       3-17-87   12:00p
TESTIT            24       11-28-88    4:33p
          5 File(s)    263168 bytes free
```

Then add a MESSAGE.BAT batch file to execute an ANSI command to make sure this worked:

```
ECHO ESC[0;59;"It worked"p
```

Boot your system with this custom-made disk, and then run the MESSAGE.BAT batch file. Press F1 and you should see:

```
It worked
```

Total ANSI Management

DOS sorely needs two ANSI utilities — one to show you what key definitions are currently active, and one to clear out all existing definitions so you can start over.

ANSI stores all its key definitions in a small internal buffer. When you first load it, the buffer is filled with zeros. You can create a pair of tiny utilities that will give you total control over this storage area. One will display the contents of the ANSI buffer, and the other can reset all the entries back to zeros. The utilities are quick and powerful, but because DOS comes in many different versions and can run on so many hardware configurations, you'll have to do some simple detective work to ferret out two important addresses that the utilities need.

If you look inside ANSI.SYS (version 3.3), you can see what an unused buffer looks like:

```
3140:0650   FE 0E 06 01 EB EB 81 C3-5B 05 C3 04 00 72 10 00   ........[....r..
3140:0660   00 00 00 00 00 00 00 00-00 00 00 00 00 00 00 00   ................
3140:0670   00 00 00 00 00 00 00 00-00 00 00 00 00 00 00 00   ................
3140:0680   00 00 00 00 00 00 00 00-00 00 00 00 00 00 00 00   ................
3140:0690   00 00 00 00 00 00 00 00-00 00 00 00 00 00 00 00   ................
3140:06A0   00 00 00 00 00 00 00 00-00 00 00 00 00 00 00 00   ................
3140:06B0   00 00 00 00 00 00 00 00-00 00 00 00 00 00 00 00   ................
3140:06C0   00 00 00 00 00 00 00 00-00 00 00 00 00 00 00 00   ................
3140:06D0   00 00 00 00 00 00 00 00-00 00 00 00 00 00 00 00   ................
3140:06E0   00 00 00 00 00 00 00 00-00 00 00 00 00 00 00 00   ................
3140:06F0   00 00 00 00 00 00 00 00-00 00 00 00 00 00 00 00   ................
3140:0700   00 00 00 00 00 00 00 00-00 00 00 00 00 00 00 00   ................
3140:0710   00 00 00 00 00 00 00 00-00 00 00 00 00 00 00 00   ................
3140:0720   00 00 00 00 00 00 00 00-00 00 00 CD 11 24 30 3C   .............$0<
```

(The 3140: segment address at the right edge of your screen will vary from system to system and doesn't matter here.)

When DOS boots up, it looks inside the CONFIG.SYS configuration file (unless you've renamed this file and the reference to it in your IBMBIO.COM or IO.SYS system files) to see what device drivers to load. If you've included ANSI.SYS in the list, it reads the file off the disk and copies it to the lowest memory segment (segment 0000).

To view or erase the contents of the buffer, you have to know where DOS loaded ANSI.SYS on your particular system. You can use DEBUG's search abilities to find the location.

Make sure that your CONFIG.SYS includes a line that loads ANSI:

```
DEVICE=ANSI.SYS
```

and that ANSI.SYS is indeed on your disk. Then boot up normally.

If you examine the above buffer display you'll see that the last four bytes near the end of the top row before all the 00s are:

```
04 00 72 10
```

You can find where DOS maintains its ANSI buffer by having DEBUG scan through the lowest (0000) segment of RAM for that specific four-byte pattern. Just load DEBUG and issue the command:

```
DEBUG
-S 0:0 L0000 4 0 72 10
```

DEBUG should print one or two addresses. If you're using DOS 3.3 on an AT and the first line of your CONFIG.SYS file is:

```
DEVICE=ANSI.SYS
```

you should see something like:

```
0000:A1DB
```

If you're using DOS 3.3 on a PC, you might see two addresses:

```
0000:9C2B
0000:F9F8
```

The addresses will be different if you're using different versions of DOS. And even if you're using version 3.3 on an AT, if your CONFIG.SYS file loaded other drivers and set up buffers before it loaded ANSI.SYS, the address may vary.

If you do see two addresses, odds are that the lower of the two is the one you're interested in. You can check to see if the address is indeed the ANSI buffer by replacing the rightmost digit of the addresses DEBUG reported with a 0 and then using the Display (D) key to display the contents of memory at that location.

DEBUG handles addresses in the form XXXX:YYYY where XXXX is the segment and YYYY is the offset. In most DEBUG operations you don't have to worry about the segment, but here you do. If you wanted to examine the area of memory at offset A1D0 of segment 0000, and you simply typed:

```
-D A1D0
```

DEBUG would display the contents of whatever segment it happened to be loaded in, rather than the 0000 segment that you wanted. So don't forget the 0: or 0000: before the offset address (0: in this case works just as well as a 0000:).

Since the offset address that DEBUG's Search (S) command found on an AT using DOS 3.3 was 0000:A1DB, replace the rightmost digit — here this is a B — with a 0. DEBUG reported:

```
0000:A1DB
```

change the B at the end to a 0, then type:

```
-D 0000:A1D0
```

or:

```
-D 0:A1D0
```

You should see something like:

```
0000:A1D0   FE 0E 06 01 EB EB 81 C3-5B 05 C3 04 00 72 10 00   ........[....r..
0000:A1E0   02 00 2F 00 00 00 00 00-00 00 00 00 00 00 00 00   ../.............
0000:A1F0   00 00 00 00 00 00 00 00-00 00 00 00 00 00 00 00   ................
0000:A200   00 00 00 00 00 00 00 00-00 00 00 00 00 00 00 00   ................
0000:A210   00 00 00 00 00 00 00 00-00 00 00 00 00 00 00 00   ................
0000:A220   00 00 00 00 00 00 00 00-00 00 00 00 00 00 00 00   ................
0000:A230   00 00 00 00 00 00 00 00-00 00 00 00 00 00 00 00   ................
0000:A240   00 00 00 00 00 00 00 00-00 00 00 00 00 00 00 00   ................
```

The 04 00 72 10 bytes appear at the end of the top row, and are followed by a block of 00s. If you're using different versions of DOS, the 04 00 72 10 numbers will be located in different positions on the line (and at different addresses), but will always be followed by lots of 00s. If you don't see a large block of 00s following them, you're at the wrong address. Try any other offset address that DEBUG's Search (S) command may have reported, or type Q to Quit DEBUG, check your typing, and start again.

You need to figure out and write down the address of the first 00 in that large block of 00s that follows the 04 00 72 10 pattern. The easy way to calculate the address is to add 4 to the actual offset address that DEBUG reported. In this case DEBUG's Search (S) command reported an address of:

```
0000:A1DB
```

(The 0000 on the left is the segment address. The A1DB on the right is the offset address.) Add 4 + A1DB and you get A1DF.

If you're not comfortable adding hex numbers, don't worry. DEBUG can do it for you. Just use the DEBUG Hex Math (H) command and follow it with both numbers:

```
-H A1DB 4
```

DEBUG will respond by printing first the sum and then the difference of the two hex numbers you entered:

```
A1DF   A1D7
```

The sum of the two numbers that you entered is on the left. The difference of your two numbers is on the right:

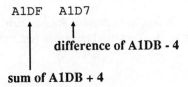

Here you're interested in the sum (AD1F). Jot it down safely and label it "Buffer Start." You'll need this address shortly.

Now calculate the other important address. ANSI maintains a one-byte pointer into its buffer that keeps track of where the next available chunk of free storage space is located. If you tell ANSI to create a macro for F1 that's 15 characters long, and then you have it create a second macro for F2, this pointer tells ANSI where to store the information for F2 so it doesn't write over the data already stored in the buffer for F1.

You can figure out where this pointer address is by looking up a value in Figure 9.4 and subtracting it from the buffer start address you just calculated.

DOS Version	Value to Subtract from Buffer Start Address to Get Pointer Address	Number of Bytes in the Buffer
2.0	44A	C4
2.1	44A	C4
3.0	45E	CC
3.1	468	CC
3.2	468	CC
3.3	464	CC

Figure 9.4. ANSI Memory Display and Clearing Parameters

Again, use the DEBUG Hex Math (H) command to do the calculation. The buffer start address for an AT running DOS 3.3 is AD1F, and the value you have to subtract is 464. So the DEBUG command to figure out the difference is:

```
-H A1DF 464
```

DEBUG will again print the sum and difference of the two hex numbers that you entered after the H:

```
A643   9D7B
```

This time you're interested in the difference (the second of the two numbers DEBUG printed out) — 9D7B.

When you first load ANSI, the value at this pointer address is 4. Use DEBUG's Display (D) command to make sure the value at the pointer address you just calculated is also 4:

```
-D 0:9D7B L1
```

DEBUG should print:

```
0000:9D70                                    04
```

If you don't see this, or you're using a version of DOS that's not on the chart, you can have DEBUG's Search (S) command uncover the pointer address for you. Issue the command:

```
S 0:0 L0000 CF 0 4 0
```

and then add 2 to the offset that DEBUG reports.

Either way, write down the pointer address, then quit DEBUG by typing Q and then pressing Enter.

The whole process for an AT running DOS 3.3 that loaded ANSI.SYS before it loaded any other drivers or set up any other buffers would look like:

```
C>DEBUG
-S 0:0 L0000 4 0 72 10
0000:A1DB
-D 0:A1D0
```

```
0000:A1D0  FE 0E 06 01 EB EB 81 C3-5B 05 C3 04 00 72 10 00    ........[....r..
0000:A1E0  02 00 2F 00 00 00 00 00-00 00 00 00 00 00 00 00    ../.............
0000:A1F0  00 00 00 00 00 00 00 00-00 00 00 00 00 00 00 00    ................
0000:A200  00 00 00 00 00 00 00 00-00 00 00 00 00 00 00 00    ................
0000:A210  00 00 00 00 00 00 00 00-00 00 00 00 00 00 00 00    ................
0000:A220  00 00 00 00 00 00 00 00-00 00 00 00 00 00 00 00    ................
0000:A230  00 00 00 00 00 00 00 00-00 00 00 00 00 00 00 00    ................
0000:A240  00 00 00 00 00 00 00 00-00 00 00 00 00 00 00 00    ................
-H A1DB 4
A1DF  A1D7
-H A1DF 464
A643  9D7B
-D 0:9D7B L1
0000:9D70                                              04
-Q
```

Now you can create two script files that will make it a snap to see what ANSI character definitions are currently active, and to clear all those definitions out of the buffer. But you need one more piece of information — the buffer length (number of bytes in the buffer) — and you can get this from the same chart you used to look up the subtraction value. For all DOS 3.x versions this number is hex CC; for DOS 2.x versions it's C4.

Assuming you've written down the same buffer start, pointer, and buffer length numbers as the ones in the above example, type the following SCRIPT.CLR file:

```
E 0:9D7B 4
F 0:A1DF LCC 0
Q
```

Then type this SCRIPT.SEE file:

```
D 0:A1D0 LE0
Q
```

Be sure to press the Enter key after each line, especially the last ones with the Q. If you don't press Enter after the Q, your system will freeze when you try to execute these.

Now create two one-line batch files that will make working with ANSI a joy. First, CLR.BAT:

```
DEBUG < SCRIPT.CLR
```

Then, SEE.BAT:

```
DEBUG < SCRIPT.SEE
```

Finally, make sure DEBUG.COM and these four files are in the directory you're likely to be using when you work on ANSI. Or put them in a directory that your DOS PATH and (version 3.3 and later) APPEND commands know about.

Running these two batch files will redirect the SCRIPT.SEE and SCRIPT.CLR files into DEBUG and execute DEBUG commands just as if you had typed them from the keyboard. But these files are far faster and more accurate than commands you'd have to type yourself.

The SCRIPT.SEE file simply displays hex E (decimal 14) rows, or paragraphs of memory that contain the buffer. It rounds the buffer start address down to an even paragraph boundary by changing the rightmost digit from an F to a 0, which makes the display look better. If you're using a different version of DOS, replace the rightmost digit with a 0 and substitute it for the A1D0 in this example.

The LE0 command (which could also be written as L E0) specifies the length of the DEBUG display — E0 bytes, which simply means hex E rows (hex 10 bytes in a paragraph or row, so E x 10 = E0). Depending on the where the buffer start address happens to be in the first line of the display, you would want to have DEBUG show either D0 or E0 lines. It's always safer to pick the larger number, E0. (Note: this number is different from the buffer length value that's shown in Figure 9.4.)

The SCRIPT.CLR file is more complicated. It has to change two parts of memory. First, it has to reset the pointer back to the starting value of 4. Then it has to fill the buffer with 00 characters.

SCRIPT.CLR resets the pointer simply by using the DEBUG Enter (E) command to put a value of 4 at the pointer address. Then it uses the DEBUG Fill (F) command to fill the entire buffer with 00s. You tell it where to start putting the 00s by specifying the buffer start address directly after the F command. And you tell it how many 00s to insert at that address by specifying the buffer length number for that particular version of DOS. If you're substituting your own values, remember:

In SCRIPT.SEE:

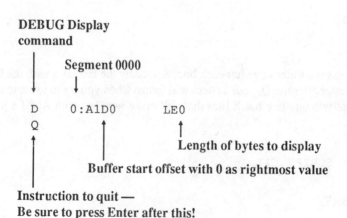

**DEBUG Display
command**

Segment 0000

```
D      0:A1D0      LE0
Q
```

Length of bytes to display

Buffer start offset with 0 as rightmost value

**Instruction to quit —
Be sure to press Enter after this!**

In SCRIPT.CLR:

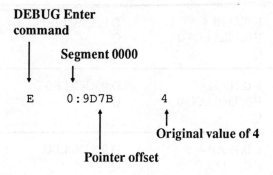

DEBUG Enter command

Segment 0000

E   0:9D7B   4

Original value of 4

Pointer offset

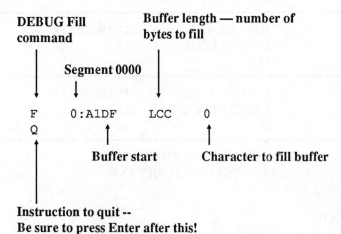

DEBUG Fill command

Buffer length — number of bytes to fill

Segment 0000

F   0:A1DF   LCC   0
Q

Buffer start

Character to fill buffer

Instruction to quit --
Be sure to press Enter after this!

The actual values you enter for these script files can vary for lots of reasons — you might be working with different hardware, different versions of DOS, different loading requirements, and so on. But the following charts show our popular files — SCRIPT.CLR and SCRIPT.SEE — as they would appear for different DOS versions. The files assume the line DEVICE=CONFIG.SYS is the only line in your CONFIG.SYS file. First, for the PC:

DOS Version	SCRIPT.CLR	SCRIPT.SEE
2.0	E 0:519B 4 F 0:55E5 LC4 0 Q	D 0:55E0 LD0 Q

continued

DOS Version	SCRIPT.CLR	SCRIPT.SEE
2.1	E 0:519B 4 F 0:55E5 LC4 0 Q	D 0:55E0 LD0 Q
3.0	E 0:7EEB 4 F 0:8349 LCC 0 Q	D 0:8340 LE0 Q
3.1	E 0:7EAB 4 F 0:8313 LCC 0 Q	D 0:8310 LD0 Q
3.2	E 0:97DB 4 F 0:9C43 LCC 0 Q	D 0:9C40 LD0 Q
3.3	E 0:97CB 4 F 0:9C2F LCC 0 Q	D 0:9C20 LE0 Q

SEE.BAT = DEBUG < SCRIPT.SEE
CLR.BAT = DEBUG < SCRIPT.CLR

Then for the AT:

DOS Version	SCRIPT.CLR	SCRIPT.SEE
2.0	E 0:519B 4 F 0:55E5 LC4 0 Q	D 0:55E0 LD0 Q
2.1	E 0:519B 4 F 0:55E5 LC4 0 Q	D 0:55E0 LD0 Q
3.0	E 0:84EB 4 F 0:8949 LCC 0 Q	D 0:8940 LE0 Q

continued

3.1	E 0:861B 4	D 0:8A80 LD0
	F 0:8A83 LCC 0	Q
	Q	
3.2	E 0:9C9B 4	D 0:A100 LD0
	F 0:A103 LCC 0	Q
	Q	
3.3	E 0:9D7B 4	D 0:A1D0 LE0
	F 0:A1DF LCC 0	Q
	Q	

SEE.BAT = DEBUG < SCRIPT.SEE
CLR.BAT = DEBUG < SCRIPT.CLR

Once you've created the four files: SEE.BAT and SCRIPT.SEE; and CLR.BAT and SCRIPT.CLR, get into DOS and type:

    SEE

This will execute SEE.BAT, which will redirect the SCRIPT.SEE file into DEBUG. You should see something like:

```
C>DEBUG < SCRIPT.SEE
-D 0:A1D0 LE0
0000:A1D0  FE 0E 06 01 EB EB 81 C3-5B 05 C3 04 00 72 10 00   ........[....r..
0000:A1E0  00 00 00 00 00 00 00 00-00 00 00 00 00 00 00 00   ................
0000:A1F0  00 00 00 00 00 00 00 00-00 00 00 00 00 00 00 00   ................
0000:A200  00 00 00 00 00 00 00 00-00 00 00 00 00 00 00 00   ................
0000:A210  00 00 00 00 00 00 00 00-00 00 00 00 00 00 00 00   ................
0000:A220  00 00 00 00 00 00 00 00-00 00 00 00 00 00 00 00   ................
0000:A230  00 00 00 00 00 00 00 00-00 00 00 00 00 00 00 00   ................
0000:A240  00 00 00 00 00 00 00 00-00 00 00 00 00 00 00 00   ................
0000:A250  00 00 00 00 00 00 00 00-00 00 00 00 00 00 00 00   ................
0000:A260  00 00 00 00 00 00 00 00-00 00 00 00 00 00 00 00   ................
0000:A270  00 00 00 00 00 00 00 00-00 00 00 00 00 00 00 00   ................
0000:A280  00 00 00 00 00 00 00 00-00 00 00 00 00 00 00 00   ................
0000:A290  00 00 00 00 00 00 00 00-00 00 00 00 00 00 00 00   ................
0000:A2A0  00 00 00 00 00 00 00 00-00 00 00 CD 11 24 30 3C   ............$0<
-Q
```

Now fill the buffer by executing 64 key redefinitions. Since doing it by hand would take too long, run the following BASIC CASESWAP.BAS program, and type:

    S

when it asks whether you want to switch cases or reset them. It will create a file called SWITCH, then automatically TYPE it for you to trigger the actual ANSI definitions:

```
100 ' CASESWAP.BAS — creates ANSI file to switch/reset cases
110 ' Make sure your DOS CONFIG.SYS file contains line:
120 '              DEVICE=ANSI.SYS
130 DEF FNST$(Y)=RIGHT$(STR$(Y),LEN(STR$(Y))-SGN(Y))
140 PRINT "Switch cases or Reset them (S/R): "
150 I$=INKEY$:IF I$="" THEN 150 ELSE I$=CHR$((ASC(I$) AND 95))
160 IF I$="R" THEN N$="RESET":P=0:ELSE N$="SWITCH":P=32
170 PRINT N$:OPEN N$ FOR OUTPUT AS #1
180 FOR A=65 TO 90
190 PRINT #1,CHR$(27);"[";FNST$(A);";";FNST$(A+P);"p"
200 NEXT
210 FOR A=97 TO 122
220 PRINT #1,CHR$(27);"[";FNST$(A);";";FNST$(A-P);"p"
230 NEXT
240 FOR A=1 TO 12
250 READ B
260 PRINT #1,CHR$(27);"[";FNST$(B);";";
270 IF I$="R" THEN PRINT #1,FNST$(B); ELSE PRINT #1,FNST$(A+45);
280 PRINT #1,"p":NEXT:CLOSE
290 IF I$="R" THEN SHELL "TYPE RESET" ELSE SHELL "TYPE SWITCH"
300 PRINT "(Now type: SYSTEM  and press Enter key)"
310 DATA 62,63,41,33,64,35,36,37,94,38,42,40
```

The SWITCH file turns all the lowercase alphabetic keys into uppercase ones and vice versa. And it also effectively disables the uppercase functions of all the number keys as well as the greater-than and question mark keys. So typing any normal lowercase letter will produce its uppercase version, and typing the top-row number keys, the slash, or the period (the one on the main part of the keyboard, not on the number pad) in either shifted or unshifted states will generate the lowercase versions of those keys.

The actual SWITCH file looks like:

```
ESC[65;97p
ESC[66;98p
ESC[67;99p
    .
    .
    .
ESC[94;54p
ESC[38;55p
ESC[42;56p
ESC[40;57p
```

(The actual file is longer; this shows just the beginning and end of it.)

Try typing some of these keys to make sure ANSI did in fact redefine them. Then run SEE.BAT again and you'll see:

```
C>DEBUG < SCRIPT.SEE
-D 0:A1D0 LE0
0000:A1D0  FE 0E 06 01 EB EB 81 C3-5B 05 C3 04 00 72 10 03   ........[....r..
0000:A1E0  41 61 03 42 62 03 43 63-03 44 64 03 45 65 03 46   Aa.Bb.Cc.Dd.Ee.F
0000:A1F0  66 03 47 67 03 48 68 03-49 69 03 4A 6A 03 4B 6B   f.Gg.Hh.Ii.Jj.Kk
0000:A200  03 4C 6C 03 4D 6D 03 4E-6E 03 4F 6F 03 50 70 03   .Ll.Mm.Nn.Oo.Pp.
0000:A210  51 71 03 52 72 03 53 73-03 54 74 03 55 75 03 56   Qq.Rr.Ss.Tt.Uu.V
0000:A220  76 03 57 77 03 58 78 03-59 79 03 5A 7A 03 61 41   v.Ww.Xx.Yy.Zz.aA
0000:A230  03 62 42 03 63 43 03 64-44 03 65 45 03 66 46 03   .bB.cC.dD.eE.fF.
0000:A240  67 47 03 68 48 03 69 49-03 6A 4A 03 6B 4B 03 6C   gG.hH.iI.jJ.kK.l
0000:A250  4C 03 6D 4D 03 6E 4E 03-6F 4F 03 70 50 03 71 51   L.mM.nN.oO.pP.qQ
0000:A260  03 72 52 03 73 53 03 74-54 03 75 55 03 76 56 03   .rR.sS.tT.uU.vV.
0000:A270  77 57 03 78 58 03 79 59-03 7A 5A 03 3E 2E 03 3F   wW.xX.yY.zZ.>..?
0000:A280  2F 03 29 30 03 21 31 03-40 32 03 23 33 03 24 34   /.)0.!1.@2.#3.$4
0000:A290  03 25 35 03 5E 36 03 26-37 03 2A 38 03 28 39 00   .%5.^6.&7.*8.(9.
0000:A2A0  00 00 00 00 00 00 00 00-00 00 00 CD 11 24 30 3C   .............$0<
-Q
```

Each of the 64 one-character redefinitions takes up a three-space chunk of the buffer:

- one for the key you assigned the new character to
- one for the new character you assigned to the key
- one for a counter that tells ANSI how long the chunk is

The first redefinition assigns "a" to "A" so when you type a capital A you'll end up with a lowercase one. In the buffer this looks like:

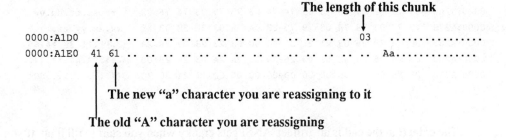

The length of this chunk

```
0000:A1D0  .. .. .. .. .. .. .. .. .. .. .. .. .. .. .. 03   ................
0000:A1E0  41 61 .. .. .. .. .. .. .. .. .. .. .. .. .. ..   Aa..............
```

The new "a" character you are reassigning to it

The old "A" character you are reassigning

Now run the CASESWAP program again, but this time when it asks whether you want to switch cases or reset them, type:

R

CASESWAP will now create a file called RESET, then automatically TYPE it for you to trigger a new set of ANSI definitions that effectively resets things back to normal. The actual RESET file looks like:

```
ESC[65;65p
ESC[66;66p
ESC[67;67p

  .

  .

  .

ESC[94;94p
ESC[38;38p
ESC[42;42p
ESC[40;40p
```

(Again, this shows just the beginning and end of it; the real RESET file is longer.)

Type any letters or the uppercase versions of the top-row keys and you'll see that things are indeed back to normal. Run SEE.BAT again and you'll see:

```
C>DEBUG < SCRIPT.SEE
-D 0:A1D0 LE0
0000:A1D0  FE 0E 06 01 EB EB 81 C3-5B 05 C3 04 00 72 10 03   ........[....r..
0000:A1E0  41 41 03 42 42 03 43 43-03 44 44 03 45 45 03 46   AA.BB.CC.DD.EE.F
0000:A1F0  46 03 47 47 03 48 48 03-49 49 03 4A 4A 03 4B 4B   F.GG.HH.II.JJ.KK
0000:A200  03 4C 4C 03 4D 4D 03 4E-4E 03 4F 4F 03 50 50 03   .LL.MM.NN.OO.PP.
0000:A210  51 51 03 52 52 03 53 53-03 54 54 03 55 55 03 56   QQ.RR.SS.TT.UU.V
0000:A220  56 03 57 57 03 58 58 03-59 59 03 5A 5A 03 61 61   V.WW.XX.YY.ZZ.aa
0000:A230  03 62 62 03 63 63 03 64-64 03 65 65 03 66 66 03   .bb.cc.dd.ee.ff.
0000:A240  67 67 03 68 68 03 69 69-03 6A 6A 03 6B 6B 03 6C   gg.hh.ii.jj.kk.l
0000:A250  6C 03 6D 6D 03 6E 6E 03-6F 6F 03 70 70 03 71 71   l.mm.nn.oo.pp.qq
0000:A260  03 72 72 03 73 73 03 74-74 03 75 75 03 76 76 03   .rr.ss.tt.uu.vv.
0000:A270  77 77 03 78 78 03 79 79-03 7A 7A 03 3E 3E 03 3F   ww.xx.yy.zz.>>.?
0000:A280  3F 03 29 29 03 21 21 03-40 40 03 23 23 03 24 24   ?.)).!!.@@.##.$$
0000:A290  03 25 25 03 5E 5E 03 26-26 03 2A 2A 03 28 28 00   .%%.^^.&&.**.((.
0000:A2A0  28 28 00 00 00 00 00 00-00 00 00 CD 11 24 30 3C   ((...........$0<
-Q
```

The extra ((at the end is an artifact. ANSI gets cranky when you start to fill it up. If you had assigned 65 new definitions and then reassigned them, ANSI would have choked.

To clear all these definitions out of memory, run CLR.BAT. Try typing the keys that were just redefined and you'll notice that they're back to normal. Then run SEE one last time and the screen should look again like:

```
C>DEBUG < SCRIPT.SEE
-D 0:A1D0 LE0
0000:A1D0  FE 0E 06 01 EB EB 81 C3-5B 05 C3 04 00 72 10 00    ........[....r..
0000:A1E0  00 00 00 00 00 00 00 00-00 00 00 00 00 00 00 00    ................
0000:A1F0  00 00 00 00 00 00 00 00-00 00 00 00 00 00 00 00    ................
0000:A200  00 00 00 00 00 00 00 00-00 00 00 00 00 00 00 00    ................
0000:A210  00 00 00 00 00 00 00 00-00 00 00 00 00 00 00 00    ................
0000:A220  00 00 00 00 00 00 00 00-00 00 00 00 00 00 00 00    ................
0000:A230  00 00 00 00 00 00 00 00-00 00 00 00 00 00 00 00    ................
0000:A240  00 00 00 00 00 00 00 00-00 00 00 00 00 00 00 00    ................
0000:A250  00 00 00 00 00 00 00 00-00 00 00 00 00 00 00 00    ................
0000:A260  00 00 00 00 00 00 00 00-00 00 00 00 00 00 00 00    ................
0000:A270  00 00 00 00 00 00 00 00-00 00 00 00 00 00 00 00    ................
0000:A280  00 00 00 00 00 00 00 00-00 00 00 00 00 00 00 00    ................
0000:A290  00 00 00 00 00 00 00 00-00 00 00 00 00 00 00 00    ................
0000:A2A0  00 00 00 00 00 00 00 00-00 00 00 CD 11 24 30 3C    ............$0<
-Q
```

You can use SEE.BAT and CLR.BAT to watch ANSI in action. First, make sure the buffer is empty, by running CLR.BAT. Then create four one-line batch files, 1.BAT, 2.BAT, 3.BAT, and 4.BAT:

```
ECHO This is 1.BAT    ESC[49;"AAAAAAAAAA"p

ECHO This is 2.BAT    ESC[50;"BBBBBBBBBB"p

ECHO This is 3.BAT    ESC[51;"CCCCCCCCCC"p

ECHO This is 4.BAT    ESC[50;"bbbbbbbbbb"p
```

Run 1.BAT, which tells ANSI to reassign character 49 (the digit 1) so pressing it will print a string of ten As onscreen. DOS will first insert a hex 0C (decimal 12) into the buffer to tell itself that it's using up 12 buffer spaces — ten for the AAAAAAAAAA, one for the "1" that it assigns these As to, and one for the length counter (the 0C) itself. Then it will put the reassigned key into the buffer, and finally the characters you're reassigning:

```
C>DEBUG < SCRIPT.SEE
-D 0:A1D0 LE0
0000:A1D0  FE 0E 06 01 EB EB 81 C3-5B 05 C3 04 00 72 10 0C    ........[....r..
0000:A1E0  31 41 41 41 41 41 41 41-41 41 41 00 00 00 00 00    1AAAAAAAAAA.....
0000:A1F0  00 00 00 00 00 00 00 00-00 00 00 00 00 00 00 00    ................
0000:A200  00 00 00 00 00 00 00 00-00 00 00 00 00 00 00 00    ................
0000:A210  00 00 00 00 00 00 00 00-00 00 00 00 00 00 00 00    ................
```

```
0000:A220  00 00 00 00 00 00 00 00-00 00 00 00 00 00 00 00   ................
0000:A230  00 00 00 00 00 EB EB 00-00 00 00 00 00 00 00 00   ................
0000:A240  00 00 00 00 00 00 00 00-00 00 00 00 00 00 00 00   ................
0000:A250  00 00 00 00 00 00 00 00-00 00 00 00 00 00 00 00   ................
0000:A260  00 00 00 00 00 00 00 00-00 00 00 00 00 00 00 00   ................
0000:A270  00 00 00 00 00 00 00 00-00 00 00 00 00 00 00 00   ................
0000:A280  00 00 00 00 00 00 00 00-00 00 00 00 00 00 00 00   ................
0000:A290  00 00 00 00 00 00 00 00-00 00 00 00 00 00 00 00   ................
0000:A2A0  00 00 00 00 00 00 00 00-00 00 00 CD 11 24 30 3C   .............$0<
-Q
```

Next, run 2.BAT, which assigns ten Bs to the 2 key. DOS will use up 12 more characters of buffer space:

```
C>DEBUG < SCRIPT.SEE
-D 0:A1D0 LE0
0000:A1D0  FE 0E 06 01 EB EB 81 C3-5B 05 C3 04 00 72 10 0C   ........[....r..
0000:A1E0  31 41 41 41 41 41 41 41-41 41 41 0C 32 42 42 42   1AAAAAAAAAA.2BBB
0000:A1F0  42 42 42 42 42 42 42 00-00 00 00 00 00 00 00 00   BBBBBBB.........
0000:A200  00 00 00 00 00 00 00 00-00 00 00 00 00 00 00 00   ................
0000:A210  00 00 00 00 00 00 00 00-00 00 00 00 00 00 00 00   ................
0000:A220  00 00 00 00 00 00 00 00-00 00 00 00 00 00 00 00   ................
0000:A230  00 00 00 00 00 00 00 00-00 00 00 00 00 00 00 00   ................
0000:A240  00 00 00 00 00 00 00 00-00 00 00 00 00 00 00 00   ................
0000:A250  00 00 00 00 00 00 00 00-00 00 00 00 00 00 00 00   ................
0000:A260  00 00 00 00 00 00 00 00-00 00 00 00 00 00 00 00   ................
0000:A270  00 00 00 00 00 00 00 00-00 00 00 00 00 00 00 00   ................
0000:A280  00 00 00 00 00 00 00 00-00 00 00 00 00 00 00 00   ................
0000:A290  00 00 00 00 00 00 00 00-00 00 00 00 00 00 00 00   ................
0000:A2A0  00 00 00 00 00 00 00 00-00 00 00 CD 11 24 30 3C   .............$0<
-Q
```

Finally, run 3.BAT, which assigns ten Cs to the 3 key:

```
C>DEBUG < SCRIPT.SEE
-D 0:A1D0 LE0
0000:A1D0  FE 0E 06 01 EB EB 81 C3-5B 05 C3 04 00 72 10 0C   ........[....r..
0000:A1E0  31 41 41 41 41 41 41 41-41 41 41 0C 32 42 42 42   1AAAAAAAAAA.2BBB
0000:A1F0  42 42 42 42 42 42 42 0C-33 43 43 43 43 43 43 43   BBBBBBB.3CCCCCCC
0000:A200  43 43 43 00 00 00 00 00-00 00 00 00 00 00 00 00   CCC.............
0000:A210  00 00 00 00 00 00 00 00-00 00 00 00 00 00 00 00   ................
0000:A220  00 00 00 00 00 00 00 00-00 00 00 00 00 00 00 00   ................
0000:A230  00 00 00 00 00 00 00 00-00 00 00 00 00 00 00 00   ................
0000:A240  00 00 00 00 00 00 00 00-00 00 00 00 00 00 00 00   ................
```

```
0000:A250  00 00 00 00 00 00 00 00-00 00 00 00 00 00 00 00   ................
0000:A260  00 00 00 00 00 00 00 00-00 00 00 00 00 00 00 00   ................
0000:A270  00 00 00 00 00 00 00 00-00 00 00 00 00 00 00 00   ................
0000:A280  00 00 00 00 00 00 00 00-00 00 00 00 00 00 00 00   ................
0000:A290  00 00 00 00 00 00 00 00-00 00 00 00 00 00 00 00   ................
0000:A2A0  00 00 00 00 00 00 00 00-00 00 00 CD 11 24 30 3C   ...........$0<
-Q
```

What happens when you redefine a key? The old 2.BAT batch file assigned BBBBBBBBBB to the 2 key. The 4.BAT batch file reassigns the 2 key so it prints bbbbbbbbbb instead.

DOS will discard the definition for the old 2 key, move everything that followed it up toward the beginning of the buffer to save valuable space (in this example the only definition that followed was the one that assigned CCCCCCCCCC to 3), and then stick the new definition for the 2 key at the end:

```
C>DEBUG < SCRIPT.SEE
-D 0:A1D0 LE0
0000:A1D0  FE 0E 06 01 EB EB 81 C3-5B 05 C3 04 00 72 10 0C   ........[....r..
0000:A1E0  31 41 41 41 41 41 41 41-41 41 41 0C 33 43 43 43   1AAAAAAAAAA.3CCC
0000:A1F0  43 43 43 43 43 43 43 0C-32 62 62 62 62 62 62 62   CCCCCCC.2bbbbbbb
0000:A200  62 62 62 00 00 00 00 00-00 00 00 00 00 00 00 00   bbb.............
0000:A210  00 00 00 00 00 00 00 00-00 00 00 00 00 00 00 00   ................
0000:A220  00 00 00 00 00 00 00 00-00 00 00 00 00 00 00 00   ................
0000:A230  00 00 00 00 00 00 00 00-00 00 00 00 00 00 00 00   ................
0000:A240  00 00 00 00 00 00 00 00-00 00 00 00 00 00 00 00   ................
0000:A250  00 00 00 00 00 00 00 00-00 00 00 00 00 00 00 00   ................
0000:A260  00 00 00 00 00 00 00 00-00 00 00 00 00 00 00 00   ................
0000:A270  00 00 00 00 00 00 00 00-00 00 00 00 00 00 00 00   ................
0000:A280  00 00 00 00 00 00 00 00-00 00 00 00 00 00 00 00   ................
0000:A290  00 00 00 00 00 00 00 00-00 00 00 00 00 00 00 00   ................
0000:A2A0  00 00 00 00 00 00 00 00-00 00 00 CD 11 24 30 3C   ...........$0<
-Q
```

Armed with SEE.BAT and CLR.BAT and any of the above programs that send escape characters directly to DOS, you can do some real screen and keyboard magic.

P A R T   I I I

Power User's Secrets

Chapter 10

Batch Techniques

A batch file is simply a file with a BAT extension that contains a list of DOS instructions you want to execute and programs you want to run. When you execute the batch file, DOS looks at each line and executes the instruction or runs the program specified on that line just as if you had typed it in directly.

Once you master its dozen or so batch commands, you can have DOS automate all your daily chores and chop tedious file management tasks down to size. You can even use these commands to dial your phone, look up names and addresses, or keep track of your appointments. All at the touch of a key or two.

Batch files are really just computer programs, written in DOS. All programming languages share certain basic features. One is the *conditional* ability to execute commands only when the proper conditions are met. Other features are the ability to loop repeatedly, or use variables with changeable values, or divide jobs into small subroutines. Microsoft's batch file language isn't elegant, and it needs a little help. But it packs a wallop into its few commands and gives you astonishing control over your system.

Batch File Basics

To illustrate how a batch file works, you need a program for it to run. The examples that follow will use a program on the accompanying disk called DECIDE.COM.

Batch file creation and operation are complex and exacting. It's a little like trying to write a novel in a language with only a handful of words — or commands. To give you a feel for how the commands work and what you have to do whip them into shape, this section will start out by providing a brief overview of the most important commands. Then it will explore each command in painstaking detail, fleshing out the fundamentals where necessary. Finally, it will provide a slate of useful samples.

Once you have DECIDE.COM handy, run it by typing:

```
C>DECIDE
```

Then type the F3 key and press Enter a few more times. The program simply checks your computer's internal clock, and helps you make decisions based on the numbers it happens to find there, like a high-tech version of the "Magic 8-Ball" many of us owned as kids.

Having to type the six-letter program name DECIDE each time you want your computer to help you select a course of action is tedious. You could rename DECIDE.COM to something shorter like D.COM. Then all you'd have to do to run the program is type:

```
D
```

However, the program would then show up in your DIR listings simply as D.COM, and if you didn't use it for a long time and then happened to see the not-very-descriptive D.COM filename several months later, you might forget what the program did.

You could run it to find out, but some programs don't do anything immediately apparent when you execute them. For instance, try running the DOS GRAPHICS.COM program. Your disk will spin for a second or two and nothing will appear onscreen to tell you what just happened. All programs should at least put a message onscreen to keep you informed, but many don't. In this case the message should have been something like "Graphics print screen function (Shift-PrtSc) now properly configured for IBM compatible printers."

Even worse, a program could have potentially destructive results. That D.COM program could have once been named DESTROY.COM and you may have used it long ago to erase all the files on your disk for security purposes.

Easy Batch File Creation

But you can execute the DECIDE.COM program with a single keystroke without having to rename it. Just create a one-line batch file called D.BAT that will do all the typing for you. You could use your word processor to create this file, but DOS provides two quicker, easier ways — the COPY CON command and EDLIN.

To use the COPY CON technique, type:

```
COPY CON D.BAT
```

and press Enter. The cursor will simply drop down a line. Then type:

```
DECIDE
```

and press the F6 function key, then the Enter key. When you press F6 you'll see a ^Z appear, and when you press Enter you should see a message that says "1 File(s) copied." If you make a mistake while using COPY CON, hold down the Ctrl key, and press either C or ScrollLock to abort the process. Then press the F3 key and then Enter to restart.

To use the EDLIN technique, type:

```
EDLIN D.BAT
```

You should see a message that says:

```
New file
*
```

When EDLIN displays an asterisk hugging the left margin, it means it's waiting for you to enter a command. An asterisk in column 1 like this is the EDLIN "prompt" just as A> or C> is the default DOS prompt.

If you don't see this "New file" message, or you see something that says:

```
End of input file
*
```

this tells you that you're editing an existing file rather than creating a new one, which is definitely not what you want to do. If this happens, type Q to quit, and when you see the message:

```
Abort edit (Y/N)?
```

type Y to confirm that you do indeed want to quit. Then restart the process, but pick a different name, such as A.BAT (which is short for Answer).

However, if you did see the:

```
New file
*
```

message, type an I (or an i) to start Inserting text. EDLIN will indent itself and print:

```
1:*
```

Here EDLIN uses the asterisk to tell you that line 1 is the "current" line. EDLIN can work on only one line at a time (which it refers to as the current line) and it signifies which line is the current one by putting an asterisk beside its line number.

Type in:

```
1:*DECIDE
```

either in uppercase or lowercase; DOS isn't picky when it comes to ordinary batch file commands. Press the Enter key and you should see:

```
1:*DECIDE
2:*
```

Now EDLIN is telling you that line 2 is the current line. But all you wanted to do was create a one-line batch file, so to tell EDLIN you're done inserting text, just hold down the Ctrl key and press either C or ScrollLock while you're holding it down. You should see:

```
1:*DECIDE
   2:*^C
*
```

Then End the EDLIN file creation process by typing:

```
*E
```

(or e).

Whether you used EDLIN or the COPY CON approach, after you get back to the familiar DOS prompt, type D to execute the batch file. DOS executes a batch file one line at a time. The first (and only) line in D.BAT is:

```
DECIDE
```

DOS tries to execute this line by first seeing if DECIDE is an internal DOS command. The instructions to execute common DOS commands such as DIR, TYPE, or COPY are buried inside the DOS COMMAND.COM program, and Microsoft refers to these as internal commands. External commands, like SORT.EXE or CHKDSK.COM, are separate programs, and are not a part of COMMAND.COM at all. You can always execute an internal command like TYPE or DIR, since they're built into COMMAND.COM. But you won't be able to run an external command such as FORMAT unless the FORMAT.COM program happens to be on your disk.

DOS maintains a list of all the internal commands inside COMMAND.COM, and it won't find one called DECIDE there. So it then looks for a program called DECIDE.COM in the current directory. Since you just put this file there, DOS will run it.

Incidentally, if you created the D.BAT file and you happen to have a file in the same directory called D.COM or D.EXE, you'll never be able to run D.BAT. Whenever you enter a command or the name of a file you want to run, COMMAND.COM first checks to see if you entered an internal DOS command. If it doesn't find an internal command that matches what you typed, it next checks for a file with the same name but with a COM extension. If it doesn't find a COM file with the same name, it looks for a similarly named file with an EXE extension. It will run a batch file with the name you typed only if it can't find an internal command, a COM file, and an EXE file with the same filename.

Similarly, don't ever try giving any executable file a name that duplicates an internal command. If you tried to create a file called TYPE.COM or DIR.BAT you'd have a hard time trying to run it, since DOS would see that you wanted to execute something called TYPE or DIR and think you were referring to the internal command with the same name.

Well, okay, DOS provides a tricky way to run a file with a name similar to an internal command, by letting you put a drive letter or pathname in front of it. When you add a drive or path, DOS knows you can't be talking about an internal command. To try it, make a copy of D.BAT called DIR.BAT. Then enter:

```
.\DIR
```

(The ".\" prefix tells DOS that the filename after the prefix is in the current directory.) But spare yourself the trouble and avoid such names.

Turning ECHO Off

Running a batch file like D.BAT really clutters up your screen. You type:

```
D
```

You should see:

```
C>DECIDE

The answer is . . . maybe.
```

When DOS executes the contents of any batch file, it normally prints, or *echoes*, each line onscreen just as if you had typed it. But you can prevent most commands from echoing onto your screen with the batch file command:

```
ECHO OFF
```

So if you enhanced the D.BAT batch file by adding a line at the very beginning, so it looked like this:

```
ECHO OFF
DECIDE
```

when you ran the batch file you'd see:

```
C>ECHO OFF

The answer is . . . no.
```

This is a bit better than the original version, because it suppresses the name of the program the batch file executes when you run it. But you do have to look at the initial ECHO OFF command.

However, if you're using DOS version 3.3 or later, you can prevent any batch file command from appearing onscreen by putting a @ sign at the beginning of the line. So if you're using a later DOS version and you changed D.BAT to read:

```
@ECHO OFF
DECIDE
```

when you ran this version all you'd see is:

```
C>D

The answer is . . . yes.
```

Still, while this prevents the DECIDE filename from appearing onscreen, and suppresses the ECHO OFF command, it makes you stare at the name of the batch file itself, D.BAT. You can get rid of this by clearing the screen with a CLS command. So adding a third line to D.BAT:

```
ECHO OFF
CLS
DECIDE
```

will clear the screen and print:

```
The answer is . . . maybe.
```

in the upper lefthand corner.

You can tell whether or not ECHO is off or on by typing ECHO on a line by itself and pressing Enter. If your batch file ever displays a line that says:

```
ECHO is off
```

or:

```
ECHO is on
```

it means that the batch file either had the command ECHO on a line by itself with nothing following it, or thought it did. Since DOS treats equals signs, tabs, semicolons, and commas as spaces, it will interpret lines such as:

- ECHO =
- ECHO ;
- ECHO ,

simply as ECHO commands with nothing after them other than meaningless spaces, and think you're asking it to report whether ECHO happens to be toggled off or on.

REMinding Yourself

Running the DECIDE.COM program from the D.BAT batch file rather than renaming DECIDE.COM to D.COM does help prevent your disk from filling up with mysterious-sounding programs like A.COM, BB.EXE, and Z.COM that don't really tell you what they do.

However, months from now if you stumble across D.BAT you may forget what DECIDE.COM does. It sounds harmless enough, but if you have a few dozen megabytes of critical information on your hard disk, and, well, one of these days you're definitely going to back up every last file, don't take chances.

To make life easier, use the DOS REM (Remark) batch command to add a nonexecuting comment to D.BAT:

```
ECHO OFF
REM decide.com provides yes/no/maybe answers to questions
CLS
DECIDE
```

Lines beginning with REM can contain up to 123 characters of text. If you turn ECHO off earlier in the batch file they won't appear onscreen. If you don't turn ECHO off, or if you turn ECHO back on before the REM line, DOS will display it onscreen, REM and all. So a batch file such as:

```
REM decide.com provides yes/no/maybe answers to questions
DECIDE
```

or:

```
ECHO OFF
CLS
ECHO ON
REM decide.com provides yes/no/maybe answers to questions
DECIDE
```

would display:

```
C>REM decide.com provides yes/no/maybe answers to questions

C>DECIDE

The answer is . . . yes.
```

The second example above would, of course, clear the screen first. If you don't turn ECHO off, and you indent the lines in your batch file, DOS will maintain the indentation when it displays them. So a batch file that contained the lines:

```
REM Be very
    REM very
        REM very
            REM very
                REM careful
REM when you use the FORMAT command
```

would show up onscreen as:

```
C>      REM Be very

C>          REM very

C>              REM very

C>                  REM very

C>                      REM careful

C>      REM when you use the FORMAT command
```

Since DOS won't display any lines beginning with REM if ECHO is off, adding an ECHO OFF at the beginning of the above batch file would end up spinning your disk but displaying nothing except a blank line or two.

If you wanted to print a warning message like the one above, and you didn't want it cluttered with REMs and DOS prompts and extra spaces, you could use the ECHO command to display it.

Putting the word ECHO at the beginning of a line tells DOS to print onscreen everything that follows it on the same line.

If you included the line:

```
ECHO Hello there
```

in a batch file, DOS would print:

```
Hello there
```

When using ECHO command to display messages, be sure to turn ECHO off before you print the first one. Otherwise you'll end up printing both the words you want displayed and the command to display them. If you didn't first turn ECHO off, the "ECHO Hello there" line would appear as:

```
C>ECHO Hello there
Hello there
```

So a better version of the FORMAT-cautioning batch file would be:

```
ECHO OFF
ECHO Be very
ECHO       very
ECHO             very
ECHO                   very
ECHO                         careful
ECHO when you use the FORMAT command
```

DOS will display:

```
Be very
    very
        very
            very
                careful
when you use the FORMAT command
```

The indentation trick that staggered REM statements across the screen won't work with ECHO commands. To indent text that ECHO displays you'll have to add spaces between the word ECHO and the text that it prints.

ECHO can print boxes and borders onscreen as well as text. The BOXMAKER.BAS program on the accompanying disk will create a BOX.BAT batch file that displays a single-line or double-line box any size you want, and indented wherever you want it. You can use your word processor or EDLIN to add text inside the box.

DOS executes batch files one line at a time. If you have a system with a fast hard disk or RAMdisk, you can get away with using the ECHO command to print a large block of text onscreen. But on a floppy disk system all you'll get is a lot of disk grinding and a painfully slow display as DOS churns the floppy line by line to see what it should ECHO next.

If you don't have a hard disk, set up a RAMdisk and copy your batch files onto it. The DOS VDISK.SYS virtual disk driver supplied with versions 3.0 and later works well, or you can use the program furnished with your system's memory expansion card.

An alternative method is to use the TYPE command to display any really large text blocks. If you want your batch file to print a long involved set of instructions, you could type these into a separate file called INSTRUCS and then insert a line into your batch file at the appropriate place that said:

```
TYPE INSTRUCS
```

While using the TYPE command to display text in a separate file is far faster than ECHOing it to the screen a line at a time, you'll have to remember to keep both the batch file with the TYPE command and the file to be typed together. If you want to give your batch file to a co-worker, you may forget to pass along the text file. Or the co-worker may see the file, not know what it is, and unwittingly erase it. And if your batch file uses TYPE to display the contents of multiple message files, you complicate things even more.

One final problem is that small files take up more space than you think. On an old PC-XT, even a two-line file can waste 4K of disk space.

The best solution in this case (and in just about every other one) is to get yourself a jet-propelled hard disk, and a speedy CPU. Speed is addictive. One of the reasons you started using a computer in the first place was to do more chores in less time, and a neck-snapping system makes this easier. The highly competitive hardware market ensures that hot, muscular new systems are always coming down in price. Or you can purchase an accelerator board. And in any event, stuff your system with memory, then have your start-up AUTOEXEC.BAT file copy your important batch files to a RAMdisk and run them directly out of memory.

Jumping, Skipping, Looping, and Branching

The DECIDE.COM program prints "yes," "no," or "maybe" answers in a fairly even random distribution. If you keep running it you'll see that each response appears about a third of the time.

How does it work? It uses the DOS Read Time function (hex 2C) to sniff out numbers from your system's clock. DOS will report the current time by putting four values — hours, minutes, seconds, and hundredths of seconds — into four registers (CH, CL, DH, and DL). Actually, since this clock "ticks" approximately 18.2 times per second, the finest resolution is about five-hundredths of a second (1/18.2). But all 100 values between 0 and 99 eventually appear in the hundredths register (DL) in even enough proportion that DECIDE.COM can use whatever number happens to be there as a random number.

DECIDE.COM starts dividing this random number into even chunks by first lopping off the top third — any number from 64 to 99. It does this by testing whether the seventh bit in the value it finds is set to 1 (turned on). Since this bit is equal to 2^6, or decimal 64, any number with this bit set has to be equal to or greater than 64. If DECIDE finds the bit set — and it should about a third of the time — it prints the "maybe" message and exits.

If it sees that the seventh bit is not set, the value has to be in the two-thirds of the remaining numbers between 0 and 63. Dividing these numbers in half to yield the two remaining thirds is easy; they're either odd or even. Odd numbers all have their first or 2^0 bit set to 1, while in even numbers this bit is always a 0. DECIDE prints a "yes" or "no" depending on whether or not it sees this first bit set.

If you wanted to test this theory and make sure DECIDE printed out "yes," "no," and "maybe" in roughly equal proportions, you could type DECIDE and press the Enter key and then sit there banging on the F3 and Enter keys to execute the program over and over.

But you could also write a short NONSTOP.BAT batch file to rerun the program automatically until you tell it to stop:

```
ECHO OFF
:TOP
DECIDE
GOTO TOP
```

(Be sure to put a carriage return at the end of the last line, or else the batch file will execute the DECIDE program once and then quit.) Run NONSTOP.BAT and you'll see something like:

```
The answer is . . . yes.

The answer is . . . maybe.

The answer is . . . maybe.

The answer is . . . yes.

The answer is . . . yes.

The answer is . . . no.
```

scrolling endlessly down your screen. The only way to stop it (other than rebooting your system) is to press Ctrl-C or Ctrl-ScrollLock, at which point DOS will print a message that says "Terminate batch job (Y/N)?"

If you type Y or y the batch file will abort and you'll return to the DOS prompt. If you type N or n the batch file will continue doing whatever it was doing. Type anything else and DOS will stubbornly keep printing the same (Y/N) request.

(Obviously you'll have to run the program lots of times to see a fairly even distribution. Very small samples like these can be misleading.)

The mechanism that repeated the NONSTOP.BAT batch file output — a loop — is one of the fundamental computer tools. Remember, computers aren't smart, they're just fast. They're especially good at executing the same basic instruction over and over. This comes in handy more often than you might think, since computer programs are loaded with loops. Even something as simple as figuring out what you typed on the DOS command line is a loop, since what DOS really does is examine and interpret the first character and then move on to examine the next character, and the next, until it's reached the end of the line and processed each one.

Loops are terrific tools. But endless loops that force you to break out of them by typing Ctrl-C or Ctrl-ScrollLock aren't so terrific.

If you know exactly how many times you want part of your batch file to loop, you can control the process with a small utility on the accompanying disk called LOOP.COM.

To use it, first insert a line near the very beginning of your batch file — before the loop actually starts — containing the command:

```
LOOP /S
```

This initializes the loop counter by putting a zero in a certain place in memory, and prevents you from running into trouble if you use the LOOP.COM utility more than once.

Then, simply put the command:

```
LOOP
```

on a line by itself somewhere inside the loop. Then follow this line with another line that says:

```
IF ERRORLEVEL (number) GOTO (label)
```

or:

```
IF NOT ERRORLEVEL (number) GOTO (label)
```

substituting the number of times you want to loop in place of the (number), and the actual LABEL you want the batch file to jump to in place of (label).

Each time the batch file executes it, LOOP.COM will increase a value that DOS can measure with this oddly named IF ERRORLEVEL command. The following version of the NONSTOP.BAT batch file will execute the DECIDE program 15 times and then stop:

```
ECHO OFF
LOOP /S
:TOP
DECIDE
LOOP
IF NOT ERRORLEVEL 15 GOTO TOP
```

Using IF NOT ERRORLEVEL to check a negative (NOT) condition saves steps, but you could accomplish the same exact thing with a non-negative version of NONSTOP.BAT that reads:

```
ECHO OFF
LOOP /S
:TOP
DECIDE
LOOP
IF ERRORLEVEL 15 GOTO END
GOTO TOP
:END
```

LOOP.COM works by storing an ever-increasing value at low memory address 0040:006B. This location is reserved for the cassette recorder and is unused on most systems (unless you're one of the two people in the known universe using a cassette). Each time LOOP runs, it retrieves the counter, increments it, and exits with the new value.

The largest number of repetitions you can specify is 255. If you use a number higher than 255, your system will perform a modulo operation on it, which means it will start over again at 1. So 254 will repeat 254 times, and 255 will repeat 255 times, but 256 and 257 will repeat just one time, 258 will repeat two times, 259 will run three times, and so on.

Incidentally, if you wanted to have DOS count how many times the DECIDE.COM program printed "maybe" vs. "yes" vs. "no" the following COUNTIT.BAT batch file would do it for you automatically:

```
ECHO OFF
ECHO Running DECIDE 255 times...
LOOP /S
:TOP
DECIDE >> DECIDE.LOG
LOOP
IF NOT ERRORLEVEL 255 GOTO TOP
ECHO Counting...
ECHO Number of "maybe" lines:
FIND /C "maybe" DECIDE.LOG
ECHO Number of "yes" lines:
FIND /C "yes" DECIDE.LOG
ECHO Number of "no" lines:
FIND /C "no" DECIDE.LOG
```

For this to work, you'll need to have the DOS FIND.EXE program in the same subdirectory as COUNTIT.BAT, LOOP.COM, and DECIDE.COM, unless it's in a directory that your path knows about. COUNTIT.BAT will use the LOOP.COM utility to run DECIDE.COM 255 times, but instead of printing each:

```
The answer is . . . maybe.
```

response onscreen, it will redirect the output to a file called DECIDE.LOG. Then, when it's all done, it will use the line-counting abilities of the DOS FIND filter and add up exactly how many lines have the words "maybe," "yes," or "no" in them.

Running COUNTIT.BAT may take a minute or two. If you have a fast hard disk system it's not so bad, but if you're using floppies, you're much better off creating a RAMdisk, copying COUNTIT.BAT, FIND.EXE, LOOP.COM, and DECIDE.COM into it, and then running it on the RAMdisk. Otherwise your diskettes will grind for an awfully long time.

One more point—COUNTIT.BAT redirects DECIDE.COM's output into a file called DECIDE.LOG with the line:

```
DECIDE >> DECIDE.LOG
```

This instruction uses a pair of > DOS redirection signs. Using just a single > sign would have created a brand new file each time DOS executed this instruction. This isn't what you want, since DOS would end up writing each new line over each older one (so the second would wipe out the first, the third would wipe out the second, and the 255th would write over the 254th). When you were all done all you'd have is a one-line log file containing just the single 255th line of output.

When DOS sees a >> pair of these signs it adds or appends each new line onto the existing file of older ones. If no older file exists, the first time DOS runs this command it creates a new one, and then appends all subsequent output to it. But if it finds an existing file with the name you specified, it adds the new output onto the end of this existing file.

This means that if you run COUNTIT.BAT once, you'll end up with 255 repetitions. But since the double redirection sign adds new output onto existing output, you can run COUNTIT.BAT several times to increase the number of repetitions to a point where the division of "maybe," "yes," and "no" responses starts to become statistically meaningful. Run COUNTIT.BAT twice and your log file will contain 510 entries, four times and it will hold 1,020, etc.

This technique works like a charm when you know exactly how many times you want the loop to repeat. Just be sure you include a line before the the loop starts that says:

```
LOOP /S
```

and then add the command:

```
LOOP
```

by itself somewhere near the bottom of the loop, and follow it with an IF ERRORLEVEL or IF NOT ERRORLEVEL line. Adjust the value after ERRORLEVEL to reflect the number of repetitions.

ERRORLEVEL — Best Command, Worst Name

Knowing how to use ERRORLEVEL is vital if you want to turn ordinary batch files into screaming power tools. Don't be thrown off by its rotten name; it's the only real method DOS provides for making batch files dynamically interactive. But while the framework is there, it needs a little help. DOS does let you use replaceable parameters to pass information from the command line into a batch file when you first execute it, but this won't let you or your system talk to a batch file while it's running.

The only problem is that while ERRORLEVEL provides the raw muscle, DOS doesn't give you any convenient way to harness it. So you have to create your own tiny assembly language programs to help. It's easy once you get the hang of it. And you'll be amazed at the increased power and flexibility of DOS when you grab the assembly language front-end reins.

We'll explore every aspect of the IF ERRORLEVEL command later on in this chapter. For now, just type in the examples that follow to get a sense of what DOS can do in the right hands. They'll show you how to really make DOS purr when you're trying to create your own menu systems or run a complex series of tasks with lots of options.

The above COUNTIT.BAT batch file assumes you know ahead of time how many loops you want. In cases like these, you want the user to be able to stop the program at the appropriate time by pressing a key. But you don't want the stopping mechanism to interfere with the loop, and you don't want to force the user to press something as awkward as Ctrl-ScrollLock.

To solve this problem, create a tiny KEYSTROK.COM program by typing in the following seven lines:

```
DEBUG
E 100 B8 00 06 B2 FF CD 21 74 04 B4 4C CD 21 C3
N KEYSTROK.COM
RCX
E
W
Q
```

The program it creates looks like this:

```
MOV AX,0600    ;Direct-console I/O function
MOV DL,FF      ;Select input request
INT 21         ;Do it
JZ  010D       ;If no key pressed, exit
MOV AH,4C      ;Otherwise, terminate with code in AL
INT 21         ;Do it
RET            ;Back to DOS
```

Then, create a brand new version of NONSTOP.BAT:

```
ECHO OFF
ECHO Press any key to stop
:TOP
DECIDE
KEYSTROK
IF NOT ERRORLEVEL 1 GOTO TOP
```

Now NONSTOP.BAT will loop continuously until you press any key (other than a shift key such as Ctrl or NumLock). If you don't press a key it will keep looping. If you're familiar with BASIC, this is similar to:

```
100 PRINT "Press any key to stop"
110 REM (The repeating command goes here)
120 IF INKEY$="" GOTO 110
```

You can fine-tune the KEYSTROK.COM program to work only if the user presses a specific key. If you want to limit this process so the user has to press the Esc key to stop, you could create a file called TEST4ESC.COM by typing in the following eight lines:

```
DEBUG
E 100 B8 00 06 B2 FF CD 21 74 0A 3C
E 10A 1B 75 06 B0 FF B4 4C CD 21 C3
N TEST4ESC.COM
RCX
14
W
Q
```

This jazzes up the KEYSTROK.COM program slightly:

```
MOV AX,0600      ;Direct-console I/O function
MOV DL,FF        ;Select input request
INT 21           ;Do it
JZ  0113         ;No key pressed, so exit
CMP AL,1B        ;Key was pressed; was it Esc?
JNZ 0113         ;No, so exit
MOV AL,FF        ;Yes, so put FF in AL for ERRORLEVEL
MOV AH,4C        ;Terminate with code
INT 21           ;Do it
RET              ;Back to DOS
```

Then change the NONSTOP.BAT batch file to read:

```
ECHO OFF
ECHO Press the Esc key to stop
:TOP
DECIDE
TEST4ESC
IF NOT ERRORLEVEL 255 GOTO TOP
```

The version of NONSTOP.BAT that used KEYSTROK.COM let you quit by pressing any key, and required a value of 1 after the word ERRORLEVEL. The new NONSTOP.BAT that uses TEST4ESC won't quit unless you press the Esc key, and needs a value of 255 after the word ERRORLEVEL.

You can change the trigger key from Esc to Enter, space, or tab, or any other single-purpose key that doesn't have different uppercase and lowercase versions, simply by changing one byte. Notice that the TEST4ESC.SCR script contained a line:

```
CMP AL,1B
```

The 1B is the hexadecimal representation of decimal 27, which is the ASCII value of Esc. To change this so a user would have to press the Enter key to stop, substitute an 0D (the hex version of decimal 13) in place of the 1B. To change the trigger to the spacebar, substitute a 20 (the hex representation of decimal 32) in place of the 1B.

If you're typing in the lines that begin with E 100, replace the 1B directly after the E 10A.

The process becomes a bit trickier if you want the user to type a letter, such as Q (for Quit), A (for Abort), X (for eXit), or S (for Stop), since the uppercase and lowercase versions of these letters have different ASCII values. However, by adding an additional logical OR instruction, you can create a program that will recognize both the uppercase and lowercase versions of any alphabetic character.

Type in the following eight lines:

```
DEBUG
E 100 B8 00 06 B2 FF CD 21 74 0C 0C 20 3C
E 10C 61 75 06 B0 FF B4 4C CD 21 C3
RCX
16
N TEST4A.COM
W
Q
```

This produces a TEST4A.COM program that looks like:

```
MOV AX,0600      ;Direct-console I/O function
MOV DL,FF        ;Select input request
INT 21           ;Do it
JZ  0115         ;No key pressed, so exit
OR  AL,20        ;Make sure the letter is lowercase
CMP AL,61        ;Was it an 'a' ?
JNZ 0115         ;No, so exit
MOV AL,FF        ;Yes, so put FF in AL for ERRORLEVEL
MOV AH,4C        ;Terminate with code
INT 21           ;Do it
RET              ;Back to DOS
```

Again, change NONSTOP.BAT to read:

```
ECHO OFF
ECHO Press A to Abort
:TOP
DECIDE
TEST4A
IF NOT ERRORLEVEL 255 GOTO TOP
```

To change the trigger key from A to any other letter key, replace the hex 61 in the TEST4A.SCR script line:

```
CMP AL,61
```

or if you're typing the eight lines directly into DEBUG, replace it in the second line directly after E 10C. To figure out the new values, consult the chart below, which contains the hexadecimal ASCII representation of the lowercase version of each letter. The program converts uppercase values to lowercase ones, and leaves lowercase ones alone.

Hex Lowercase ASCII Values

a - 61	j - 6A	s - 73
b - 62	k - 6B	t - 74
c - 63	l - 6C	u - 75
d - 64	m - 6D	v - 76
e - 65	n - 6E	w - 77
f - 66	o - 6F	x - 78
g - 67	p - 70	y - 79
h - 68	q - 71	z - 7A
i - 69	r - 72	

You may take this even one step further, and allow the user to enter any letter of the alphabet. Type:

```
DEBUG
E 100 B8 00 06 B2 FF CD 21 74 0E 0C 20 3C
E 10C 61 72 08 3C 7A 77 04 B4 4C CD 21 C3
N ANYLETR.COM
RCX
18
W
Q
```

to produce the ANYLETR.COM program:

```
MOV AX,0600     ;Direct-console I/O function
MOV DL,FF       ;Select input request
```

```
INT 21              ;Do it
JZ  117             ;No key pressed, so exit
OR  AL,20           ;Make sure letter is lowercase
CMP AL,61           ;Is letter lower than 'a' ?
JB 117              ;Yes, so exit
CMP AL,7A           ;Is letter higher than 'z' ?
JA 117              ;Yes, so exit
MOV AH,4C           ;Terminate with code
INT 21              ;Do it
RET                 ;Back to DOS
```

Once you've created ANYLETR.COM, type in the following LETTER1.BAT batch file:

```
ECHO OFF
ECHO Type Z to quit
:TOP
ANYLETR
IF ERRORLEVEL 122 GOTO END
IF ERRORLEVEL 0   IF NOT ERRORLEVEL 1 DECIDE
IF ERRORLEVEL 97  IF NOT ERRORLEVEL 98  ECHO You typed A
IF ERRORLEVEL 98  IF NOT ERRORLEVEL 99  ECHO You typed B
IF ERRORLEVEL 99  IF NOT ERRORLEVEL 100 ECHO You typed C
IF ERRORLEVEL 100 IF NOT ERRORLEVEL 101 ECHO You typed D
IF ERRORLEVEL 101 IF NOT ERRORLEVEL 121 ECHO You typed E-Y
GOTO TOP
:END
ECHO Ok, you typed Z; quitting...
```

This will repeat the same old DECIDE.COM program, but will also quit if the user types in a Z (or a z), and will report any other letter he or she types. Each letter requires a separate test on a separate line, so to keep things short, LETTER1.BAT explicitly echoes back A, B, C, or D (or a, b, c, or d) but will lump together E through Y. Otherwise it would have to contain 21 additional lines of tests.

While reporting which letter the user typed may be interesting, it's not really all that practical. But if you want to include a menu in your batch file that gives a user several choices, this technique comes in very handy, as the following LETTER2.BAT batch files suggests:

```
ECHO OFF
:MENU
ECHO Type Q to quit, M for this menu
:TOP
ANYLETR
IF ERRORLEVEL 113 IF NOT ERRORLEVEL 114 GOTO END
```

```
IF ERRORLEVEL 109 IF NOT ERRORLEVEL 110 GOTO MENU
DECIDE
GOTO TOP
:END
ECHO Ok, you typed Q; quitting...
```

LETTER2.BAT will also run DECIDE.COM repeatedly. But it will quit if the user enters Q, or print the menu if the user enters M. Okay, it's a short menu, but you could make it much longer.

All of the above keystroke-sniffing programs — KEYSTROK.COM, TEST4ESC.COM, TEST4A.COM, and ANYLETR.COM — will sit back and let a batch file loop, acting only if the user types a key. This is definitely a plus if you have to run a program continuously and you don't want your batch file stopping at frequent intervals to ask users if they want to continue.

But if you want to create a simple menu system that waits patiently for the user to enter a menu choice, and screens out invalid choices, you'll need a keystroke-sniffer such as WAIT4A-Z.COM that's a bit more sophisticated. Type in these ten lines:

```
DEBUG
E 100 BA 2A 01 B4 09 CD 21 B8 07 0C CD 21 0C 20
E 10E 3C 61 72 F5 3C 7A 77 F1 50 88 C2 B4 02 CD
E 11C 21 B2 0D CD 21 B2 0A CD 21 58 B4 4C CD 21
E 12A 'Enter a letter from A to Z: $'
N WAIT4A-Z.COM
RCX
47
W
Q
```

Since you may want to modify this program later, you could create WAIT4A-Z.COM by turning the assembly language instructions below into a DEBUG script file called WAIT4A-Z.SCR. Type it in exactly as shown (although you may omit the semicolons and the comments following them), being careful to leave a blank line above RCX and to press the Enter key at the end of each line — especially the last one.

```
A
MOV DX,12A      ;Address of 'Enter a letter...'
MOV AH,09       ;Ready to print message
INT 21          ;Do it
MOV AX,0C07     ;Flush buffer then input char
INT 21          ;Do it
OR  AL,20       ;Make sure letter is lowercase
CMP AL,61       ;Is letter lower than 'a' ?
JB 107          ;Yes, so exit
CMP AL,7A       ;Is letter higher than 'z' ?
```

```
JA 107              ;Yes, so exit
PUSH AX             ;Save keystroke
MOV DL,AL           ;Then get ready to
MOV AH,02           ;Print it
INT 21              ;Do it
MOV DL,0D           ;Now print carriage return
INT 21              ;Do it
MOV DL,0A           ;And line feed
INT 21              ;Do it
POP AX              ;Retrieve keystroke
MOV AH,4C           ;Terminate with code
INT 21              ;Do it
DB 'Enter a letter from A to Z: $'

RCX
47
N WAIT4A-Z.COM
W
Q
```

When you're done, put the WAIT4A-Z.SCR file in the same directory as DEBUG.COM, or make sure DEBUG.COM is in a directory your PATH knows about, and at the DOS prompt type:

```
DEBUG < WAIT4A-Z.SCR
```

Then you'll need a batch file like MENU.BAT that handles all the other menu details:

```
ECHO OFF
:TOP
PAUSE
CLS ECHO   *************************
ECHO        A -- Run dBase
ECHO        B -- Run WordStar
ECHO        C -- Run 123
ECHO        Z - Quit
ECHO        *************************
WAIT4A-Z
IF ERRORLEVEL 122 GOTO END
IF NOT ERRORLEVEL 100 GOTO OPTION3
ECHO You typed D - Y; no options here
GOTO TOP
:OPTION3
IF NOT ERRORLEVEL 99 GOTO OPTION2
```

```
ECHO This would run 123
GOTO TOP
:OPTION2
IF NOT ERRORLEVEL 98 GOTO OPTION1
ECHO This would run WordStar
GOTO TOP
:OPTION1
ECHO This would run dBase
GOTO TOP
:END
ECHO Ok, you typed Z; quitting...
```

You could change this to ask the user to type a number between 1 and 9 rather than a letter between A and Z. To do this, replace four lines in the WAIT4A-Z.COM program:

1. **Change:**

```
CMP AL,61          ;Is letter lower than 'a'?
```

   to:

```
CMP AL,31          ;Is number lower than '1'?
```

2. **Change:**

```
CMP AL,7A          ;Is letter higher than 'z'?
```

   to:

```
CMP AL,39          ;Is number higher than '9'?
```

3. **Change:**

```
DB 'Enter a letter from A to Z: $'
```

   to:

```
DB 'Enter a number from 1 to 9: $'
```

4. **Change:**

```
N WAIT4A-Z.COM
```

   to:

```
N WAIT41-9.COM
```

To make the patches, type everything below:

```
DEBUG WAIT4A-Z.COM
E 10F 31
E 113 39
E 132 "numb"
E 13E 31
E 143 39
N WAIT41-9.COM
W
Q
```

If you prefer the WAIT41-9.COM number version to the WAIT4A-Z.COM letter version, you'll have to change the MENU.BAT batch file as well:

```
ECHO OFF                        ECHO OFF
:TOP                            :TOP
PAUSE                           PAUSE
```

```
CLS                                         CLS
ECHO  ************************              ECHO  ************************
ECHO      A -- Run dBase                    ECHO      1 -- Run dBase
ECHO      B -- Run WordStar                 ECHO      2 -- Run WordStar
ECHO      C -- Run 123                      ECHO      3 -- Run 123
ECHO      Z -  Quit                         ECHO      9 -  Quit
ECHO  ************************              ECHO  ************************
WAIT4A-Z                                    WAIT41-9
IF ERRORLEVEL 122 GOTO END                  IF ERRORLEVEL 57 GOTO END
IF NOT ERRORLEVEL 100 GOTO OPTION3          IF NOT ERRORLEVEL 52 GOTO OPTION3
ECHO You typed D - Y; no options here       ECHO You typed 4 - 8; no options here
GOTO TOP                                    GOTO TOP
:OPTION3                                    :OPTION3
IF NOT ERRORLEVEL 99 GOTO OPTION2           IF NOT ERRORLEVEL 51 GOTO OPTION2
ECHO This would run 123                     ECHO This would run 123
GOTO TOP                                    GOTO TOP
:OPTION2                                    :OPTION2
IF NOT ERRORLEVEL 98 GOTO OPTION1           IF NOT ERRORLEVEL 50 GOTO OPTION1
ECHO This would run WordStar                ECHO This would run WordStar
GOTO TOP                                    GOTO TOP
:OPTION1                                    :OPTION1
ECHO This would run dBase                   ECHO This would run dBase
GOTO TOP                                    GOTO TOP
:END                                        :END
ECHO Ok, you typed Z; quitting...           ECHO Ok, you typed 9; quitting...
```

This example will assume you're using the A-Z letter version. Note that in both cases, the MENU.BAT batch file only simulates running programs. To make the batch file useful, substitute the actual commands that execute your programs instead of the messages telling the programs would have run. So where the batch file says something like:

```
ECHO This would run WordStar
```

replace the line with the actual command that runs *WordStar*. Here you'd replace this line with:

```
WS
```

The WAIT4A-Z.COM program works by printing a message on the screen, waiting for the user to enter a keystroke, testing the keystroke to make sure it's in an acceptable range, and then putting the keystroke in a special place when it exits so the DOS IF ERRORLEVEL command can handle it.

The message it prints is "Enter a letter from A to Z:". If you wanted, you could limit the range to something like "Enter a letter from A to H:".

WAIT4A-Z.COM rejects all keystrokes that aren't letters of the alphabet. To modify the range of acceptable inputs, you'll have to change the actual values that the program tests. WAIT4A-Z.COM automatically turns uppercase letters into lowercase ones (and leaves lowercase letters alone) to reduce the number of tests it has to make. The test for the lower limit is the line:

```
CMP AL,61        ;Is letter lower than 'a' ?
```

You probably don't want to change this. If you do, the 61 is the hexadecimal number of a lowercase 'a.' To change this to 'b' you'd replace the 61 with a 62. But again, you probably shouldn't.

The test for the upper limit is:

```
CMP AL,7A        ;Is letter higher than 'z' ?
```

The 7A is the hexadecimal representation of a lowercase 'z.' If you do want to limit the range, and change the program so it rejects anything other than the letters A through H, substitute the hex value of lowercase 'h' (which the chart a few pages back tells you is hex 68):

```
CMP AL,68        ;Is letter higher than 'h' ?
```

You don't have to modify the comments, but it doesn't hurt, and it makes it far easier later to see what you did.

Obviously if you chop the top off the range, you won't be able to have the user type Z to quit. You'll probably want to make the highest letter H the exit key. MENU.BAT tests for a 'z' with the line:

```
IF ERRORLEVEL 122 GOTO END
```

To change this so H quits, replace the 122 (the decimal value of lowercase 'z') with the decimal value for lowercase 'h' — 104. Unfortunately, DEBUG requires hex notation but the DOS IF ERRORLEVEL command works exclusively with decimal numbers. One more thing — if you do limit the range to something like A-H, make sure you modify all references to it. This means changing:

1. The CMP AL,hexvalue test(s) for upper/lower limits in the WAIT4A-Z.SCR script.
2. The DB 'Enter a letter from A to Z: $' message at the bottom of the WAIT4A-Z.SCR script.
3. The decimal number in the MENU.BAT exit test that normally reads ":IF ERROR-LEVEL 122 GOTO END."
4. The "You typed D - Y; no options here" MENU.BAT error message two lines below the test in #3 above.
5. The "ECHO Z - Quit" menu choice itself.

6. And the "ECHO Ok, you typed Z; quitting..." message it triggers at the very end of MENU.BAT

You don't have to patch the program to limit the choices, since the WAIT4A-Z.COM program filters out anything that isn't a letter, and the MENU.BAT batch file "traps" any keystrokes that aren't currently menu choices. Here's how to add another menu option:
First, make the little menu larger by adding a D option:

```
ECHO     ************************
ECHO        A -- Run dBase
ECHO        B -- Run WordStar
ECHO        C -- Run 123
ECHO        D -- Run ProComm
ECHO        Z -  Quit
ECHO     ************************
```

Then, change the message that said D was out of range from:

```
ECHO You typed D - Y; no options here
```

to:

```
ECHO You typed E - Y; no options here
```

Finally, (and this is the only tricky part), add a module near the top of the batch file to accommodate D entries. The top of the batch file currently looks like:

```
    .
    .
    .
IF ERRORLEVEL 122 GOTO END
IF NOT ERRORLEVEL 100 GOTO OPTION3
ECHO You typed D - Y; no options here
GOTO TOP
:OPTION3
IF NOT ERRORLEVEL 99 GOTO OPTION2
ECHO This would run 123
GOTO TOP
:OPTION2
    .
    .
    .
```

Since D (with a lowercase decimal value of 100) is now the highest legal value, you'll have to change the test for invalid entries so it starts at 101 (the decimal value of the lowest new invalid entry — E) rather than 100. And you'll also have to insert the D module directly after the test that executes the menu choice. The code that replaces the above section will look like:

```
      .

      .

      .

IF ERRORLEVEL 122 GOTO END
IF NOT ERRORLEVEL 101 GOTO OPTION4
ECHO You typed E - Y; no options here
GOTO TOP
:OPTION4
IF NOT ERRORLEVEL 100 GOTO OPTION3
ECHO This would run ProComm
GOTO TOP
:OPTION3
IF NOT ERRORLEVEL 99 GOTO OPTION2
ECHO This would run 123
GOTO TOP
:OPTION2

      .

      .

      .
```

Two final cosmetic notes — the MENU.BAT file echoes a very small menu onscreen. You may prefer to use the DOS TYPE command to display a separate, fancier menu file. A tiny program such as MAKESCRN.BAS can create a template called MENU with a little 3-D shadow behind it; you can use your pure-ASCII word processor to add text to it. Actually, EDLIN is terrific at this, once you know how to use the F3 and arrow keys.

```
100 ' MAKESCRN.BAS -- makes MENU
110 ' screen you can TYPE in DOS
120 CLS
130 OPEN "MENU" FOR OUTPUT AS #1
140 S$=STRING$(26,219)
150 T$=S$+STRING$(2,177)
160 U$=STRING$(26,177)
170 FOR A=1 TO 5:PRINT #1,:NEXT
180 PRINT #1,TAB(27);S$
190 FOR A=10 TO 20
200 PRINT #1,TAB(27);T$
210 NEXT
220 PRINT #1,TAB(29);U$
230 FOR A=1 TO 3:PRINT #1,:NEXT
```

```
240 PRINT "Now type TYPE MENU"
250 CLOSE:SYSTEM
```

When you've created the MENU with MAKESCRN.BAS and entered text with EDLIN or your word processor, replace the lines:

```
ECHO    ************************
ECHO        A -- Run dBase
ECHO        B -- Run WordStar
ECHO        C -- Run 123
ECHO        Z -  Quit
ECHO    ************************
```

in MENU.BAT with a single line:

```
TYPE MENU
```

Or use the MAKECOM.BAS program on the accompanying disk. Create a fancy menu or text screen and call it something like SCREEN1 — but make sure it's no larger than 24 rows by 79 columns. Then run the MAKECOM program and when prompted for a filename, enter SCREEN1. MAKECOM will attach an assembly language program to your text screen that makes it leap instantly onto your display. And it retains the existing screen colors.

You could create several text screens, with fancy boxes and borders, and call them HELP1.COM, HELP2.COM, HELP3.COM. Put a centered message at the bottom of each one that says "Press any key for the next screen...." Then add a section to a batch file that looks like:

```
ECHO Instructions follow
PAUSE
HELP1
PAUSE > NUL
HELP2
PAUSE > NUL
HELP3
```

The fancy text screens will flash onto the display one by one. When the user presses a key he'll instantly get the next one. You can also use this to display menus, introductory sign-on screens, etc. Redirecting the output of PAUSE to NUL with the command:

```
PAUSE > NUL
```

will suppress the normal DOS "Strike a key when ready . . ." message in version 3.x. However, version 2.x will display this message even if you try to get rid of it, so if you try this on a 2.x system, allow for this intrusive message.

The MENU.BAT batch file clears the screen each time it displays a menu. If you don't have ANSI.SYS loaded, this will cancel any attribute settings you may have in effect, and turn the screen to a drab grey on black. Issuing the CLS command with ANSI loaded will clear the screen but retain the preset colors.

To avoid this, either load and use ANSI.SYS (see Chapter 9 on ANSI techniques), or replace the CLS line with a line such as BLUWHITE or WHITEBLU and then make sure you have a short COM program handy to clear the screen to the colors you like. The following COLOR.SCR DEBUG script will create both BLUWHITE.COM (blue text on a white background) and WHITEBLU.COM (the reverse):

```
N BLUWHITE.COM
E 100 B8 00 06 B9 00 00 BA 4F 18 B7
E 10A 71 CD 10 B4 02 BA 00 00 B7 00
E 114 CD 10 B0 04 BA D9 03 EE C3
RCX
1D
W
E 10A 17
N WHITEBLU.COM
W
Q
```

Type this in using a pure-ASCII word processor, or EDLIN, or else insert a COPY CON COLOR.SCR script at the very top, then after typing the final line with the Q, press Enter, then the F6 function key, then Enter again.

In any event, make sure you press Enter at the end of each line, especially the last one. Then get into DOS, make sure DEBUG.COM is handy, and type:

```
DEBUG < COLOR.SCR
```

The byte that actually sets the color is at DEBUG offset 10A — the first entry on the second line, directly after E 10A. In the above script this value is 71.

This byte is a two-digit hex number where the first digit is the background color and the second digit is the foreground color. The choices for each are: 0 = black, 1 = blue, 2 = green, 3 = cyan (light blue), 4 = red, 5 = magenta (purple), 6 = brown or yellow, and 7 = white. You can make the foreground number (but not the background) high intensity by using: 8 = grey, 9 = bright blue, A = bright green, B = bright cyan, C = bright red, D = bright purple, E = yellow, or F = bright white as the second digit.

To change the color, either replace the 71 directly after the E 10A on the second line with a different color value, and then change the name in the first line from BLUWHITE.COM to something that reflects your new colors, Or, once you've created the above files, you can change the color by using DEBUG directly. This series of commands would produce a program called YELRED.COM with bright yellow text on a red background:

```
DEBUG BLUWHITE.COM
E 10A 4E
N YELRED.COM
W
Q
```

Breaking Out of a Batch Job

The DECIDE.COM program prints each Maybe, Yes, and No fairly randomly. If you want to verify this you could run it once by typing:

```
DECIDE
```

and then keep pounding away alternately at the F3 and Enter keys to repeat the process. But DOS provides an easier way. Just create a batch file called REPEAT.BAT by typing:

```
COPY CON REPEAT.BAT
ECHO OFF
DECIDE
REPEAT
```

Then press F6 and then the Enter key. Run this new batch file by typing:

```
REPEAT
```

and you should see:

```
The answer is . . . maybe.

The answer is . . . no.

The answer is . . . maybe.

The answer is . . . yes.
```

scroll endlessly down your screen. DOS executes each batch file one line at a time. The first line turns off the ECHO feature to prevent screen clutter. The second line runs the DECIDE program. And the third line starts the whole process all over again by executing its own name.

Once you start REPEAT it will loop endlessly until you turn your system off or "break" out of it. To break out, hold down the Ctrl key and press either the C key or the Scroll-Lock key. DOS will temporarily halt the scrolling, display a ^C onscreen, and then print the message: "Terminate batch job (Y/N)?" If you answer No by typing an N or n, DOS will resume where it left off and continue scrolling. If you tell it Yes by typing a Y or y, DOS will break out of the loop and return to what you were doing previously. (Usually this returns you to the DOS prompt, but since batch files can in turn run other batch files, as you'll see soon, breaking out of the second one will return you to the first one.)

If you type anything other than a Y, y, N, or n, DOS will stubbornly keep repeating the "Terminate batch job (Y/N)?" message.

As it's written above, the REPEAT batch file will keep invoking itself and looping only if you keep its name REPEAT.BAT. If you renamed it to AGAIN.BAT, it would execute normally the first time through until it reached the third line. Then it would try to run a command or file called REPEAT. But since you renamed it, it wouldn't find such a command, and would simply print a "Bad command or file name" error message and crash to a halt.

DOS provides an easy way to solve this problem. Create a new file called ON-CEMORE.BAT containing the three lines:

```
ECHO OFF
DECIDE
%0
```

The %0 is a replaceable parameter. When DOS starts running any batch file, it looks at what you entered on the command line and parses it into as many as ten separate parts separated by the standard DOS delimiters.

A command line delimiter is a character that DOS uses to separate entries that you type at the DOS prompt. You may use spaces, commas, tabs, semicolons, or equals signs as delimiters.

DOS scans through whatever you typed at the DOS prompt and assigns replaceable parameters %0 through %9 to the first ten things it identifies as separate, discrete entries. The first entry on the command line is always the name of a command or file, and DOS assigns a %0 to this. So if you type:

```
A>ONCEMORE
```

DOS will make %0 equal to ONCEMORE. It will execute the first line by turning ECHO off, then will run the DECIDE program specified on the second line, and finally will replace the %0 on the third line with the ONCEMORE that you typed directly after the DOS prompt. Since this is the name of the batch file itself, it will re-execute itself and continue looping until you press Ctrl-C or Ctrl-Break.

If you typed:

```
ONCEMORE INTO THE BREACH G-G-GUYS SAID PFC A121763
```

DOS would assign the following parameters:

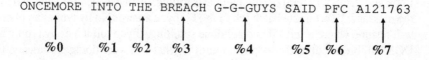

You actually could have typed:

```
ONCEMORE INTO;THE=BREACH,G-G-GUYS,SAID;;;PFC==;;,,A121763
```

and DOS would have assigned the same parameters, since it treats all the delimiters shown above as spaces. And it treats repeating delimiters just the same as single ones.

(If you renamed ONCEMORE.BAT to DOITAGIN.BAT or XYZ.BAT and ran either of those files, they too would repeat endlessly, since DOS would substitute the new DOITAGIN or XYZ names for the %0 on the third line.)

DOS will replace every single occurrence of %0 with the name of the batch file itself, so if you modified ONCEMORE.BAT to contain the lines:

```
ECHO OFF
ECHO This is a batch file called %0.BAT.
ECHO You typed %0 to start it.
ECHO Now %0 is going to run the DECIDE program.
DECIDE
ECHO And %0 will now start over again
%0
```

running it would produce something like:

```
C>ONCEMORE
This is a batch file called ONCEMORE.BAT.
You typed ONCEMORE to start it.
Now ONCEMORE is going to run the DECIDE program.

The answer is . . . maybe.
And ONCEMORE will now start over again
This is a batch file called ONCEMORE.BAT.
You typed ONCEMORE to start it.
Now ONCEMORE is going to run the DECIDE program.

The answer is . . . yes.
```

etc.

If DOS sees a replaceable parameter on any line beginning with an ECHO, it will try to substitute the appropriate parameter that you typed on the command line. If the replaceable parameter following ECHO is %0, something will definitely appear in place of the %0 since you had to enter some filename to run the batch file in the first place, and since %0 always represents that filename.

So the command:

```
ECHO You typed %0
```

will always print something after the word "typed." But it you changed the line to:

```
ECHO You typed %8
```

DOS would replace the %8 with the ninth thing you typed on the command line (remember, the first thing on the command line is %0 rather than %1, so %8 prints the ninth command line entry). If you didn't type nine separate things (and you probably wouldn't have), DOS would print a blank after the word "typed:"

```
You typed
```

Note that DOS replaces the %0 with the actual command you typed, not the whole filename. Since you typed ONCEMORE at the DOS prompt, it makes %0 = ONCEMORE, not ONCEMORE.BAT.

You can tell your batch file to add the BAT extension to an ECHO display by tacking it on after the %0:

```
ECHO This is a batch file called %0.BAT.
```

Technically you could execute the batchfile by typing either:

```
ONCEMORE
```

or:

```
ONCEMORE.BAT
```

However, virtually no one adds the BAT extension when they run a batch file, and there's really no reason to. But if you did enter ONCEMORE.BAT rather than just plain ONCEMORE, and your batch file included the line:

```
ECHO This is a batch file called %0.BAT.
```

DOS would print:

```
This is a batch file called ONCEMORE.BAT.BAT.
```

The %0 parameter will duplicate exactly what you typed. So it you start the ball rolling by typing:

```
OnCeMoRe
```

You'll end up with:

```
This is a batch file called OnCeMoRe.BAT.
You typed OnCeMoRe to start it.
Now OnCeMoRe is going to run the DECIDE program.
```

You can use replaceable parameters to personalize your batch files. If you changed ONCEMORE.BAT so it contained the lines:

```
ECHO OFF
ECHO Well, %1 --
DECIDE
```

then you ran this batch file by typing:

```
A>ONCEMORE Henry
```

DOS would substitute two replaceable parameters:

- %0 = ONCEMORE
- %1 = Henry

This newly modified version of ONCEMORE.BAT doesn't use the %0 parameter, but it does use %1. It will replace the %1 in the second line with Henry, yielding:

```
ONCEMORE
Well, Henry --

The answer is . . . no.
```

You'd run into trouble if you tried adding a %0 at the end of ONCEMORE.BAT:

```
ECHO OFF
ECHO Well, %1 --
DECIDE
%0
```

If you then ran this by typing:

```
A>ONCEMORE Henry
```

DOS would would substitute "Henry" in place of the %1 and "ONCEMORE" in place of the %0 the first time through the batch file:

```
A>ONCEMORE
Well, Henry --

The answer is . . . yes.
```

But once DOS reached the %0, replaced it with ONCEMORE, and executed the batch file a second time, the %1 would no longer be equal to "Henry." When *you* executed the batch file the first time, you entered something ("Henry") on the command line that DOS could use in place of %1. But when DOS re-executed the batch file it didn't enter anything after the %0. So you'd see:

```
C>ONCEMORE Henry
Well, Henry --

The answer is . . . maybe.
Well,  --

The answer is . . . yes.
Well,  --
```

etc. You can remedy this by forcing DOS to enter the same %1 parameter that you did. Just change the ONCEMORE.BAT file to:

```
ECHO OFF
ECHO Well, %1 --
DECIDE
%0 %1
```

When DOS reached the bottom line, instead of just re-executing %0 as ONCEMORE, it would execute %0 %1 as ONCEMORE Henry and you'd end up with the result you wanted:

```
C>ONCEMORE Henry
Well, Henry --

The answer is . . . yes.
Well, Henry --

The answer is . . . maybe.
Well, Henry --
```

etc.

If you want to experiment with replaceable parameters, run the following SHOW-PARM.BAT batch file:

```
ECHO OFF
ECHO Parameter 0 is %0
IF NOT %1!==! ECHO Parameter 1 is %1
IF NOT %2!==! ECHO Parameter 2 is %2
IF NOT %3!==! ECHO Parameter 3 is %3
IF NOT %4!==! ECHO Parameter 4 is %4
IF NOT %5!==! ECHO Parameter 5 is %5
IF NOT %6!==! ECHO Parameter 6 is %6
IF NOT %7!==! ECHO Parameter 7 is %7
IF NOT %8!==! ECHO Parameter 8 is %8
IF NOT %9!==! ECHO Parameter 9 is %9
```

EDLIN makes it easy to create a batch file like this one with so many similar lines. To start the process, type:

```
EDLIN SHOWPARM.BAT
```

When you see the EDLIN "New file" message and asterisk prompt, type:

```
I
```

to start inserting lines, then enter the first three lines. This should look like:

```
New file
*I
        1:*ECHO OFF
        2:*ECHO Parameter 0 is %0
        3:*IF NOT %1!==! ECHO Parameter 1 is %1
```

Then hold down the Ctrl key and press either the C or ScrollLock keys while you're holding it down. You'll see a:

```
4:*^C
```

and you'll return to EDLIN's command mode, where the asterisk is in column 1. Then, make nine more copies of the:

```
3:*IF NOT %1!==! ECHO Parameter 1 is %1
```

line you just typed by issuing the EDLIN command:

```
*3,3,4,8C
```

If you wanted to make sure you had copied line 3 the correct number of times, you could type:

```
*L
```

which would list:

```
 1: ECHO OFF
 2: ECHO Parameter 0 is %0
 3: IF NOT %1!==! ECHO Parameter 1 is %1
 4:*IF NOT %1!==! ECHO Parameter 1 is %1
 5: IF NOT %1!==! ECHO Parameter 1 is %1
 6: IF NOT %1!==! ECHO Parameter 1 is %1
 7: IF NOT %1!==! ECHO Parameter 1 is %1
 8: IF NOT %1!==! ECHO Parameter 1 is %1
 9: IF NOT %1!==! ECHO Parameter 1 is %1
10: IF NOT %1!==! ECHO Parameter 1 is %1
11: IF NOT %1!==! ECHO Parameter 1 is %1
```

Now all you have to do is increase the number references in each of the lines you just copied, so that all the 1s become 2s in line 4, 3s in line 5, and so on. Again, EDLIN makes this surprisingly easy. Actually, the DOS function keys make it easy, and EDLIN is one of the few programs that knows how to use them.

While the arsenal of DOS editing tricks is not exactly overwhelming, its function keys can really cut down on repetitive keystrokes. Most users know that tapping the F3 key once will repeat the previous DOS command. But they rarely use the powers of the F2 key, probably because they'd rather just press F3 and backspace the errant characters away.

While the F3 key will repeat the entire command that you typed previously at the DOS prompt, entering the F2 key followed by a character will repeat just part of the previous command — up to but not including the character you entered. So if the previous command was:

```
A>ONCEMORE abcdefghijklmnopqrstuvwxyz
```

and you pressed the F3 key, you'd end up again with:

```
A>ONCEMORE abcdefghijklmnopqrstuvwxyz
```

But if you pressed the F2 key and then typed a lowercase e you would see:

```
A>ONCEMORE abcd
```

since this tells DOS to display the part of the previous command starting from where the cursor currently is and ending right before the first occurrence of the letter you entered. When you're staring at a bare DOS prompt, the cursor is at column 1, so tapping the F2 key and then typing e at that point will display everything from column 1 right up to (but not including) where the first lowercase e is located.

If you had pressed the F2 key and typed an uppercase E, DOS would have displayed:

```
A>ONC
```

since the F2 key is case-sensitive and will stop right before the first uppercase E it finds.

This technique makes it a snap to replace all the 1s with 2s and 3s and 4s when you're using EDLIN.

Tell EDLIN you want to edit the first line that needs changing — line 4 — by typing:

```
*4
```

EDLIN will respond by printing the current contents of line 4 and then dropping down a line to let you edit it:

```
4:*IF NOT %1!==! ECHO Parameter 1 is %1
4:*
```

If you were to type F3, DOS would fill the lower line with an exact duplicate of the upper one:

```
4:*IF NOT %1!==! ECHO Parameter 1 is %1
4:*IF NOT %1!==! ECHO Parameter 1 is %1
```

But this isn't what you want. Instead, press the F2 key and type a 1. EDLIN will display the beginning of the upper line right up to but not including the first occurrence of a 1:

```
4:*IF NOT %1!==! ECHO Parameter 1 is %1
4:*IF NOT %
```

Now, type in a 2 to replace the 1:

```
4:*IF NOT %1!==! ECHO Parameter 1 is %1
4:*IF NOT %2
```

But don't press the Enter key yet. Instead, repeat the same process to get to the next 1 — press F2 and type a 1. You should see:

```
4:*IF NOT %1!==! ECHO Parameter 1 is %1
4:*IF NOT %2!==! ECHO Parameter
```

Type another 2 and press F2 one more time, so your screen looks like:

```
4:*IF NOT %1!==! ECHO Parameter 1 is %1
4:*IF NOT %2!==! ECHO Parameter 2 is %
```

Add a final 2 and press the Enter key:

```
4:*IF NOT %1!==! ECHO Parameter 1 is %1
4:*IF NOT %2!==! ECHO Parameter 2 is %2
```

Then try this with line 5, this time replacing the 1s with 3s. It looks more complicated than it actually is. All you have to do to fix line 5 is:

1. Type 5 (and press Enter).
2. Press F2 and type 1 then type 3 (do this three times).

It really goes quickly once you get the hang of it. Be sure to press Enter when you're all done and you reach the very end of each line, since EDLIN won't register any changes until you do.

After editing the last line (line 11), type:

```
*E
```

to save and exit. Then type SHOWPARM at the DOS prompt and try following it with different kinds of parameters. First enter SHOWPARM with nothing after it:

```
C>SHOWPARM
Parameter 0 is SHOWPARM
```

Try it with nine other entries on the command line:

```
C>SHOWPARM a b c d e f g h i j
Parameter 0 is SHOWPARM
Parameter 1 is a
Parameter 2 is b
Parameter 3 is c
Parameter 4 is d
Parameter 5 is e
Parameter 6 is f
Parameter 7 is g
Parameter 8 is h
Parameter 9 is i
```

Since SHOWPARM.BAT displays only ten parameters, you'll see the same result as the one directly above if you try:

```
C>SHOWPARM a b c d e f g h i j k l m n o p q r s t u v w x y z
Parameter 0 is SHOWPARM
Parameter 1 is a
```

```
Parameter 2 is b
Parameter 3 is c
Parameter 4 is d
Parameter 5 is e
Parameter 6 is f
Parameter 7 is g
Parameter 8 is h
Parameter 9 is i
```

Various collections of delimiters will have predictable results:

```
C>SHOWPARM a=bb=ccc
Parameter 0 is SHOWPARM
Parameter 1 is a
Parameter 2 is bb
Parameter 3 is ccc


C>SHOWPARM a,,,b====c;;;;;;d       e,=; ;=,f
Parameter 0 is SHOWPARM
Parameter 1 is a
Parameter 2 is b
Parameter 3 is c
Parameter 4 is d
Parameter 5 is e
Parameter 6 is f
```

You may have noticed that SHOWPARM displayed a message like "Parameter 6 is" only when you typed a seventh entry on the command line that required it. The batch file was smart enough to know how many entries you had typed so it could print the appropriate number of "Parameter N is..." messages.

If DOS weren't able to do this, and you had entered just one parameter, the display would have looked something like:

```
C>SHOWPARM a
Parameter 0 is SHOWPARM
Parameter 1 is a
Parameter 2 is
Parameter 3 is
Parameter 4 is
Parameter 5 is
Parameter 6 is
Parameter 7 is
Parameter 8 is
Parameter 9 is
```

The mechanism that prevented this was an IF STRING1==STRING2 test. Each line contains one. The first line with a test is:

```
IF NOT %1!==! ECHO Parameter 1 is %1
```

If you entered:

```
SHOWPARM XXX
```

DOS would make %0 equal to SHOWPARM, and %1 equal to XXX. So when it executed the test it would substitute XXX for %1 and end up with:

```
IF NOT XXX!==! ECHO Parameter 1 is XXX
```

Since XXX! is not equal to !, the test fails. However, it's a negative test, so you want it to fail. Note that you have to use double equals signs in IF tests like these.

If you had entered just:

```
SHOWPARM
```

without anything after it, DOS would have made %0 equal to SHOWPARM, and %1 equal to nothing. So the test would have turned into:

```
IF NOT !==! ECHO Parameter 1 is XXX
```

Here the single ! on the left side of the == is equal to the single ! on the right side. The test passes. The "NOT" in the test means that DOS won't execute the ECHO command that follows the test at the end of the line.

Putting It All Together

By combining environment variables, replaceable parameters, FOR commands, ECHO statements, fancy branching, nested batch file calling, and IF ERRORLEVEL tests you can do something that will make cleaning up cluttered disks a joy.

This CLEANUP process will queue up selected groups of files and present them to you one file at a time with a simple menu that makes it a snap to examine them, delete them, or leave them intact.

For this to work you need four files:

1. A small assembly language program called GETANS.COM that makes your batch files interactive. (You'll create GETANS.COM below.)
2. A main CLEANUP.BAT batch file that screens unwanted files from the cleanup process. (You'll also create CLEANUP.BAT.)
3. A secondary DOIT.BAT batch file loaded by CLEANUP.BAT that does most of the work and is the part the user ends up interacting with.

4. A PEEK.COM file that DOIT.BAT uses to display the beginnings of files. (PEEK.COM is on the accompanying disk.)

You also should make sure the DOS FIND.EXE program is in the same directory as these four files, or is in a directory that your path knows about. If you're using a floppy disk system, copy the FIND.EXE file onto your floppy and make sure COMMAND.COM is also on the diskette if you're running a version of DOS earlier than 3.3.

GETANS.COM is an example of a customized keystroke-sniffing program that returns exit codes that the DOS IF ERRORLEVEL command can process. Power users often end up writing their own variations of programs like this, or customizing similar ones.

To create GETANS.COM, type in the following eight lines:

```
DEBUG
E 100 B8 00 08 CD 21 0C 20 3C 79 74 0C 3C 63 74
E 10E 08 3C 64 74 04 3C 65 75 04 B4 4C CD 21 C3
N GETANS.COM
RCX
1C
W
Q
```

The actual GETANS.COM program looks like:

```
MOV AX,0800        ;Get keystroke
INT 21             ;Do it
OR  AL,20          ;Make sure it's lowercase
CMP AL,79          ;See if it's a 'y'
JZ  0117           ;Yes, so goto exit with code
CMP AL,63          ;See if it's a 'c'
JZ  0117           ;Yes, so goto exit with code
CMP AL,64          ;See if it's a 'd'
JZ  0117           ;Yes, so goto exit with code
CMP AL,65          ;See if it's an 'e'
JNZ 011B           ;No, so go to exit no code
MOV AH,4C          ;Exit with code
INT 21             ;Do it
RET                ;Exit without code
```

You can use PEEK.COM instead of the DOS TYPE command to see the first 22 lines of any file, with the command:

```
PEEK < filename
```

So if you see a file in your directory called BIGRPT8.TXT and you have no idea what it is, you can type:

```
PEEK < BIGRPT8.TXT
```

and you'll see a screenful of it.

You could save typing by using the DOS MORE.COM utility in place of PEEK.COM. However, MORE.COM will display the entire file one screenful at a time rather than just showing you the beginning of the file and then quitting, the way PEEK does.

If you want, you can patch one byte in the DOS MORE.COM utility to display just a single screenful and then quit. In all DOS versions from 2.0 through 3.2, this patching address is 1C4. In version 3.3 it's 1C2. To find this address, type:

```
DEBUG MORE.COM
-
```

You should see the DEBUG hyphen (-) prompt. Look at the following chart and pick the hex representation of the length:

MORE Version	HEX Length
2.0	180
2.1	180
3.0	140
3.1	11A
3.2	127
3.3	139

If you're using a version not listed, type RCX and press the Enter key twice. The number DEBUG prints to the right of the CX is the length.

Plug the hex length into the line:

```
-S 100 L 139 B4 0C
           ↑
        length
```

So if you're using a version like 3.2, change the line to:

```
-S 100 L 127 B4 0C
```

DEBUG should report something like:

```
30FA:01C3
```

Ignore the four hex digits to the left of the colon. Jot down the four rightmost hex digits. This is the address of the byte directly after the one you want to patch, so subtract 1 from the number. For DOS 3.3, 1C3 - 1 = 1C2. For versions 2.0 through 3.2, 1C5 - 1 = 1C4. The number you're left with is the patching address.

Use the DEBUG E command to examine the value at this address:

```
-E 1C2
```

When you press Enter you should see something like:

```
30FA:01C2  21._
```

If you don't, press Enter, type Q and press Enter to quit, then start again. But if you do see a 21 with a period after it, type in a 20 and then press Enter:

```
30FA:01C2  21.20
```

Then rename the file to something like MORENEW.COM:

```
-N MORENEW.COM
```

Write this new file to disk and quit by typing W and pressing Enter and then typing Q and pressing Enter.

Then, when you want to view just the first screenful of any file, type:

```
MORENEW < filename
```

Unfortunately, however, both MORE.COM and its patched MORENEW.COM cousin display files exactly as they appear. If you happen to be using a word processor such as *WordStar* that meddles with the high bit and makes the text unreadable in DOS, MORE and MORENEW will keep it unreadable. But PEEK will straighten it out. So use either PEEK or a patched version of MORE.COM.

In any event, create CLEANUP.BAT next:

```
ECHO OFF
SET VAR=%1
IF %1!==! SET VAR=*.*
FOR %%I IN (%VAR%) DO COMMAND /C DOIT %%I
SET VAR=
:END
```

If you're using DOS version 3.3 or later, you may want to substitute the line:

```
FOR %%I IN (%VAR%) DO CALL DOIT %%I
```

in place of:

```
FOR %%I IN (%VAR%) DO COMMAND /C DOIT %%I
```

shown above. If you do use CALL instead of COMMAND /C the process will run a bit
more smoothly. However, CALL won't work in any version of DOS older than 3.3.
   And finally, DOIT.BAT:

```
ECHO OFF
IF %1!==! GOTO WRONG
:TOP
ECHO [Alt-255 or Character 0]
ECHO Examine/Delete/CheckDIR/Skip %1 (E/D/C/S)?
GETANS
IF ERRORLEVEL 102 GOTO SKIP
IF ERRORLEVEL 101 GOTO EXAMINE
IF ERRORLEVEL 100 GOTO DELETE
IF ERRORLEVEL  99 GOTO DIRLIST
:SKIP
ECHO %1 NOT deleted...
GOTO END
:DELETE
ECHO Are you sure you want to delete %1 (Y/N)?
GETANS
IF ERRORLEVEL 121 IF NOT ERRORLEVEL 122 GOTO DOIT
GOTO SKIP
:DIRLIST
DIR %1 | FIND "-"
GOTO TOP
:DOIT
DEL %1
ECHO %1 deleted...
GOTO END
:EXAMINE
ECHO The first 22 lines (or fewer) of %1 look like:
PEEK < %1
ECHO [Alt-255 or Character 0]
GOTO TOP
:WRONG
ECHO Run the accompanying CLEANUP.BAT first
:END
```

The fourth line from the top and the fifth line from the bottom in DOIT.BAT look like:

```
ECHO [Alt-255 or Character 0]
```

Don't actually type "[Alt-255 or Character 0]" after the ECHO and the space. This simply tells you to put either an ASCII 255 blank character or ASCII 0 null character here; both are impossible to display. By following the word ECHO with a space and then either an ASCII 255 character or an ASCII 0 character you can have DOS print a blank line when the batch file executes.

If you're entering these batch files with a word processor, you're probably better off trying to create a character 255. Most good word processors let you enter ASCII characters by holding down the Alt key, typing the ASCII value (in this case 255) on the number pad — not the top row number keys — and then releasing the Alt key. So type in:

```
ECHO
```

then press the spacebar once, then hold down Alt, tap 255 on the number pad, and then let the Alt key up.

If you're entering the batch files using EDLIN or the DOS COPY CON command, you may use the same technique to insert an ASCII 255, or you may use a simpler trick to put an ASCII 0 in your file. To enter an ASCII 0 in DOS (or EDLIN) just press the F7 function key. Again, remember first to type in the word ECHO, then press the spacebar once, then press F7.

Now that you've got all the files you need, you can clean up any disk. Make sure CLEANUP.BAT, DOIT.BAT, GETANS.COM, PEEK.COM, and FIND.EXE — and COMMAND.COM if you're using a version of DOS older than 3.3 — are handy, and type:

```
CLEANUP [filespec]
```

Omitting filespec and typing simply:

```
CLEANUP
```

has the same effect as typing:

```
CLEANUP *.*
```

If you wanted to clean up all your TXT files, for example, you could type:

```
CLEANUP *.TXT
```

Or if you wanted to clean up all files that began with the letter T you could type:

```
CLEANUP T*.*
```

Once you've entered your choice, the batch files will click into action and start displaying one by one the names of all files that match the filespec you specified. So if you have three BAK files on your disk:

- REPORT88.BAK
- MEMOPC.BAK
- INCOME88.BAK

and you enter:

```
CLEANUP *.BAK
```

DOS will begin by printing:

```
Examine/Delete/CheckDIR/Skip REPORT88.BAK (E/D/C/S)?
```

At this point you have four choices. Press E and DOS will display the first 22 (or fewer) lines of REPORT88.BAK and then print the:

```
Examine/Delete/CheckDIR/Skip REPORT88.BAK (E/D/C/S)?
```

prompt again.

If you want to delete it, type D. You'll get a confirmation message "Are you sure you want to delete REPORT88.BAK (Y/N)?" Here you'll have to type Y or y to erase the file. Typing any other key will abort the deletion process, print a "REPORT88.BAK NOT deleted..." message to keep you posted, and move on to the next file:

```
Examine/Delete/CheckDIR/Skip MEMOPC.BAK (E/D/C/S)?
```

If you have no idea what MEMOPC.BAK was, and you want to see the size of the file or the date you created it, type C to Check the DIR listing:

```
MEMOPC     BAK     6253   12-18-88    2:57a
```

You'll then again see the familiar:

```
Examine/Delete/CheckDIR/Skip MEMOPC.BAK (E/D/C/S)?
```

This process uses environment variables, which won't work in DOS 3.0, and can work erratically in earlier versions. The main CLEANUP.BAT file does only two jobs:

1. It uses a FOR command to execute the DOIT command repeatedly, once for each element in the filespec. If you wanted to look at all the *.BAK files and you had four of these on your disk, the FOR command would execute DOIT four times.

2. It also looks at the filespec you entered, and substitutes *.* if you didn't enter anything. It does this by setting an environment variable — here called VAR — to the filespec you enter, and then testing to make sure you entered something. If you for-

got to enter something it sets the variable to "*.*" and assumes you want to look at all the files on your disk.

If you haven't increased the size of your environment, and you have a long PATH and some other space-eaters, setting a new variable may fill up the environment. It's easy to run out of space, since the default is a paltry ten 16-byte paragraphs, or 160 bytes.

To increase the environment size under DOS 3.0 and 3.1, just put this command in your CONFIG.SYS file:

```
SHELL [d:][path]COMMAND.COM /E:n /P
```

where n represents the number of 16-byte paragraphs. For versions 3.2 and later, use the same SHELL command but specify the actual number of bytes rather than paragraphs. The default in all cases is 160 bytes (ten paragraphs). You can increase it all the way to 32K in DOS 3.2 and 3.3, but are limited to 62 paragraphs (992 bytes) in earlier versions.

If you're using DOS 2.0 or 2.1 these techniques won't work. You'll have to patch COMMAND.COM at hex address ECF to represent the number of 16-byte memory paragraphs that will make up your new environment. (For DOS 2.11 the address is hex DF3.)

Now that you have a taste of what batch files can do, read the list of guidelines below, and then roll up your sleeves and plunge in by learning the nuances of each command. Then when you're done, try the very useful examples provided.

The Batch Commands

This section describes each batch command in detail, with lots of sample programs to show you just how the commands work. The commands are presented roughly in the order in which they are usually crop up in a file.

First, some rules and advice:

- The general format for executing a batch file is:

```
[d:][path]filename[.BAT] [parameters]
```

- Each line in a batch file must be shorter than 128 characters.
- Generally, all lines must end with carriage returns. However, a carriage return may be omitted from the very last line in cases when including it would print a double DOS prompt upon exiting.
- Since DOS processes batch files one line at a time, it's best to run them from fast hard disks or RAMdisks for optimal performance.
- When branching conditionally, batch files will always start searching for labels at the beginning of the file, so duplicate labels are ignored.
- Labels are not case sensitive, but all other aspects of batch file operations are.

- Batch filenames must end in BAT. Make sure that no COM or EXE file shares the same filename as your batch file. If you have a file on your disk called RUN.COM or RUN.EXE, and you create a batch file called RUN.BAT, DOS will always execute the RUN.COM or RUN.EXE file first, and never get around to running the RUN.BAT file.
- DOS processes batch files differently in versions 2.x and 3.x. Earlier versions cannot use IF EXIST tests outside the current subdirectory or redirect PAUSE messages, insist that labels begin in column 1, and become confused if label names are longer than eight characters.
- Versions 3.x and later offer the ability to CALL other batch files without having to run an additional copy of COMMAND.COM, can suppress line displays by prefacing them with @ signs, and in recent editions document the use of environment variables (although these won't work in 3.0).
- Finally, each version of DOS uses slightly different (but overlapping) techniques for generating blank lines with the ECHO command.

ECHO

Format: **ECHO [ON|OFF|message]**

Controls display of onscreen messages and can create files or append data to existing files by redirecting ECHO output.

ECHO ON displays all commands as they execute. This is the normal default.

ECHO OFF suppresses commands (including REM remark statements) from displaying as DOS executes them. But messages and errors will still appear. To prevent screen clutter and suppress as many messages as possible, make ECHO OFF the first line in your batch file.

If you nest batch files by using COMMAND /C to jump back and forth from one to the other, you'll have to put an ECHO OFF at the beginning of each. When COMMAND /C loads a secondary command processor, the new command processor turns ECHO on again, forcing you to turn it off manually. The CALL command introduced in version 3.3 maintains the ECHO state when jumping from one batch file to another.

In versions 3.3 or later, prefacing any command with an @ sign tells DOS not to display the command, as if ECHO were turned off. By starting all your batch files with @ECHO OFF you not only prevent subsequent commands from displaying, but you also keep the ECHO OFF command itself from showing up onscreen.

You probably don't use any programs that begin with a @ character. But if you do, and you want to execute one in a version 3.3 or later batch file, add an extra @ sign to the beginning of the filename, when you refer to it in the batch file.

Following ECHO with up to 122 characters of text displays this text, so that:

```
ECHO Back Up Your Disks Often
```

would print:

```
Back Up Your Disks Often
```

regardless of whether ECHO is currently on or off. If ECHO is off, just the text will appear. If ECHO is on, the actual ECHO command will appear first, followed on a separate line by the message it's printing, so you'll see something like:

```
C>ECHO Back Up Your Disks Often
Back Up Your Disks Often
```

Actually, ECHO can display any printable ASCII character. This lets you print fancy borders and boxes around your text, or display foreign language characters or math symbols. However, DOS doesn't make it easy to generate these characters except by using the Alt-keypad technique or by letting you harness ANSI.SYS to redefine certain shifted keys so they print characters with ASCII values greater than 127.

To ECHO a message with a DOS operator symbol (such as |, <, or >) in it, wrap the symbol between quotation marks, as in:

```
ECHO "|" is the Piping Symbol
```

You may dress up your screen by using ECHO to display fancy box and border high-bit ASCII characters (with values over 127). Some of the accompanying utilities will make it easy to work with such characters, or you can use the Alt + numeric keypad technique or redefine your keyboard using ANSI.SYS or a commercial keyboard macro program.

To create or append data to a file, use:

```
ECHO data > filename
```

which creates a brand new file called filename, or:

```
ECHO data >> filename
```

which appends data to an existing file.

Entering ECHO on a line by itself, or with nothing after it other than spaces, tells DOS to report whether ECHO currently happens to be set ON or OFF.

Be careful when using ECHO to display characters that DOS treats as delimiters (commas, semicolons, or equals signs) to separate parameters and commands. DOS will treat these as blanks and, if nothing else is on the same line other than the word ECHO, will think you're asking for a report on the current ON/OFF state.

Also, since batch files use percent signs to indicate environment variables or replaceable parameters, DOS will display every other one if you try to ECHO a string of them. So a batch file like:

```
ECHO OFF
ECHO ,,,,,,,,,,
```

```
ECHO ==========
ECHO ;;;;;;;;;
ECHO %%%%%%%%%
```

will produce:

```
ECHO is off
ECHO is off
ECHO is off
%%%%%
```

The addition of the message-suppressing @ symbol is welcome, but still won't prevent DOS from printing messages such as "1 File(s) copied." The way to suppress these is to add a NUL after any DOS command that would normally generate a message onscreen:

```
COPY C:\DOS\*.COM D: > NUL
```

The following UPDATE.BAT batch file will change the date and time in the directory listing for any file you specify:

```
ECHO OFF
IF %1!==! GOTO OOPS1
IF NOT EXIST %1 GOTO OOPS2
COPY /B %1 +,,
ECHO %1's date and time now updated.
GOTO END
:OOPS1
ECHO You must specify a filename to update.
GOTO END
:OOPS2
ECHO There is no file called %1 in this directory.
:END
```

If COMMAND.COM is in the current directory and you enter:

```
UPDATE COMMAND.COM
```

you'll see:

```
C>ECHO OFF
COMMAND.COM
        1 File(s) copied
COMMAND.COM's date and time now updated.
```

To clean this up, change the:

```
COPY /B %1 +,,
```

line to read:

```
COPY /B %1 +,,  > NUL
```

Then when you enter UPDATE COMMAND.COM, all you'll see is:

```
C>ECHO OFF
COMMAND.COM's date and time now updated.
```

(And in versions 3.3 or later, you can change the first line in the batch file to @ECHO OFF to suppress the initial ECHO OFF message.)

If you try this yourself, be sure to include the /B in the COPY line. The COPY +,, process actually copies the file onto itself, and updates the directory listing in the process. By adding a /B switch, you tell DOS to copy the entire length of the file specified by the number of bytes in the directory listing. If you don't include this, DOS will stop copying if it sees an ASCII character 26, since it interprets this as an end-of-file marker. Many text files slap on such an end-of-file indicator, but program files treat occurrences of these ASCII 26 characters differently. If you forget to add the /B parameter you'll end up truncating your program files, which makes them utterly worthless — so be careful.

If you really want to shut things down, you can sandwich any potential screen-clutterers between the lines:

```
CTTY NUL
```

and:

```
CTTY CON
```

But if you try this, be very careful, since CTTY NUL effectively disconnects your keyboard and screen from what's going on, and unless you're absolutely certain that the batch file is going to make it back to the restorative CTTY CON line, you're playing with fire.

Assuming you don't have a file in your current directory called !@#$, running the following ERROR.BAT batch file:

```
ECHO OFF
DIRR
DIR !@#$
```

will display two error messages — "Bad command or file name" since DIR is misspelled, and "File not found" since the !@#$ file isn't on your disk. But if you add CTTY NUL and CTTY CON commands:

```
ECHO OFF
CTTY NUL
DIRR
DIR !@#$
CTTY CON
```

nothing will display except ECHO OFF.

The normal DOS default setting is ECHO ON. You can turn ECHO off directly at the command line if you want, which makes the prompt disappear. Executing a subsequent CLS wipes everything off your screen.

Some users patch COMMAND.COM to flip the default to ECHO on. If you aren't comfortable doing this (and there are valid reasons for being squeamish about it), you can suppress initial ECHO OFF commands in batch files several ways. The obvious one is to prefix the command with an @ sign, but this won't work in versions prior to 3.3.

If you have ANSI.SYS loaded, you can follow ECHO off with the ANSI sequence:

```
ESC[1A ESC[K ESC[B
```

on the line below (being sure to substitute an actual ASCII character 27 — hex 1B — in place of the three ESCs in the example). ESC[1A moves up a line, ESC[K erases that line, and ESC[B moves down a line when done.

However, most users don't load ANSI. The alternative is to use the NOECHO.COM program on the accompanying disk, which does essentially the same thing without forcing the user to deal with ANSI codes.

NOECHO.COM moves cursor up one line on the current video page, then erases that line. To use this, make the first line in your batch file ECHO OFF and make the second NOECHO.

Adding blank lines to your batch files is a bit trickier. Under later versions of DOS, you can print blank lines in your batch files by typing any of 35 different characters (ASCII values 0, 1, 2, 3, 4, 5, 6, 7, 8, 11, 12, 14, 15, 16, 17, 18, 19, 20, 21, 22, 23, 24, 25, 27, 28, 29, 30, 31, 34, 43, 46, 47, 58, 91, or 93) right after the word ECHO, without any intervening space (as in ECHO: or ECHO[).

Many of these ASCII values represent *control characters* that you can enter in DOS by using the Alt-keypad method. Just hold down the Alt key, type in the ASCII value on the number pad (not the top row number keys), then release the Alt key. You won't be able to do this with all of them, however. DOS will interpret entries like ASCII 3 as Ctrl-Break, 8 as a backspace, and 27 as Esc. You can enter a character 0 in DOS by pressing the F7 key.

To enter such difficult characters, you could use a BASIC program such as ECHOMAKR.BAS:

```
100 ' ECHOMAKR.BAS -- for blank lines
110 OPEN "ECHOBLNK.BAT" FOR OUTPUT AS #1
120 PRINT #1,"ECHO OFF"
130 FOR A=1 TO 3:READ B
```

```
140 PRINT #1,"ECHO USING CHARACTER";B;"--"
150 PRINT #1,"ECHO";CHR$(B)
160 NEXT:CLOSE
170 DATA 0,8,27
```

Or you could type in dummy characters and use DEBUG to patch them. If you created a file called DUMMY.BAT that looked like:

```
ECHO OFF
ECHO USING CHARACTER 0 --
ECHOa
ECHO USING CHARACTER 8 --
ECHOb
ECHO USING CHARACTER 27 --
ECHOc
```

You could then go into DEBUG and replace the a, b, and c with 0, 9, and 1B (1B is the hexadecimal representation of decimal 27 and DEBUG works exclusively in hex):

```
C>DEBUG DUMMY.BAT
-RCX
CX 0071
:
-D 100 L 71
30DD:0100  45 43 48 4F 20 4F 46 46-0D 0A 45 43 48 4F 20 55   ECHO OFF..ECHO U
30DD:0110  53 49 4E 47 20 43 48 41-52 41 43 54 45 52 20 30   SING CHARACTER 0
30DD:0120  20 2D 2D 0D 0A 45 43 48-4F 61 0D 0A 45 43 48 4F   --..ECHOa..ECHO
30DD:0130  20 55 53 49 4E 47 20 43-48 41 52 41 43 54 45 52   USING CHARACTER
30DD:0140  20 38 20 2D 2D 0D 0A 45-43 48 4F 62 0D 0A 45 43   8 --..ECHOb..EC
30DD:0150  48 4F 20 55 53 49 4E 47-20 43 48 41 52 41 43 54   HO USING CHARACT
30DD:0160  45 52 20 32 37 20 2D 2D-0D 0A 45 43 48 4F 63 0D   ER 27 --..ECHOc.
30DD:0170  0A                                                .
-S 100 L 71 "a"
30DD:0129
-E 129 0
-S 100 L 71 "b"
30DD:014B
-E 14B 8
-S 100 L 71 "c"
30DD:016E
-E 16E 1B
-W
Writing 0071 bytes
-Q
```

You type everything following the DEBUG hyphen (-) prompts; DEBUG prints out all the rest. Typing RCX and pressing the Enter key twice reports how long the file is. The D 100 L 71 command tells DEBUG to display (D) the contents of the file starting at address 100 and continuing for a length (L) of 71 bytes (you have to start at address 100 because DEBUG loads just about all files at that address rather than at address 0).

One way to figure out where the a, b, and c are located is just to eyeball the display, but DEBUG's search (S) command can do it for you automatically. A command like S 100 L 71 "a" tells DEBUG to Search for the character "a" starting at address 100 and continue searching for 71 bytes. In the example above, DEBUG found an "a" at address 30DD:0129. When you're dealing with virtually any batch file you can ignore the four hex digits to the left of the colon; these will vary from system to system and don't matter here. The 0129 number does matter — it's the address of the "a."

To replace the "a" with a character 0, use the Enter command in the form E 129 0. This tells DEBUG to Enter (E) a value of 0 at address 0129.

Remember to use hex notation exclusively. Consult a decimal-to-hex chart if you need to. So when entering decimal ASCII character 27, you have to first convert it to its hex form, 1B. If you tried to enter a 27 rather than a 1B, DEBUG would think you meant a hex 27, which is equal to decimal 39.

When you're all done, use the W and Q commands to write the file to disk and then quit. If you're not an experienced DEBUG user, work on a copy of DUMMY.BAT called DUMMY2.BAT (or whatever). That way if you make a mistake you can always make another copy of the original and try again.

You can type some version 3.x blank-producing characters directly:

```
ECHO"
ECHO+
ECHO.
ECHO/
ECHO:
ECHO[
ECHO]
```

Again, this will work only in 3.x versions. (Under DOS 3.x you can also follow ECHO with a space and then one of the ASCII characters 0, 8, or 255.)

Unfortunately, earlier versions of DOS behave very differently.

Under version 2.x you can print a blank line by following ECHO directly with any of the ASCII characters 0, 1, 2, 3, 4, 5, 6, 7, 8, 9, 10, 11, 12, 14, 15, 16, 17, 18, 19, 20, 21, 22, 23, 24, 25, 27, 28, 29, 30, 31, 32, 34, 43, 44, 47, 58, 59, 61, 91, 92, and 93 — and then adding an extra space. If you forget the extra space at the end this technique won't work at all.

Note that this list is different from the 3.x list above. You can generate a blank line in version 3.x by putting a period (character 46) directly after ECHO, but this won't work with 2.x. However, under version 2.x, putting characters 9, 10, 32, 44, 59, and 61 (tab, line feed, space, comma, semicolon, or equals sign) and then a space after ECHO will display a blank line while these won't do the trick in version 3.x. And version 3.x doesn't really care whether you have an extra space at the end of the line, while 2.x won't budge unless you include this final space. DOS is consistently inconsistent.

You can also generate blank lines by following ECHO with a space, and then one of a short list of characters. In DOS 2.x you can use this method with characters 0, 8, 9, 32, and 255. Under DOS 3.x, characters 9 and 32 won't work. In both cases you don't need to slap on an additional space at the end of the line.

However, the safest way in just about every version is to use ASCII character 0 and a space, in either order. Type:

```
ECHO
(then press the space bar)
(then press the F7 function key)
```

or type:

```
ECHO
(then press the F7 function key)
(then press the space bar)
```

Following ECHO with just a character 0 will work under DOS 3.x but not 2.x.

When you press F7 at the DOS prompt, DOS will display a @ sign. Don't confuse this with the @ character itself, and don't try entering a @ by typing the shifted 2 key.

Some versions of DOS also insist that every line that begins with an ECHO end with a carriage return. Recent editions have gotten around this problem, but if you're using an older version and DOS prints the ECHO command itself as well as the message it's supposed to ECHO, try inserting a carriage return at the end of the offending line.

This is especially true if an ECHO command is the last line of a batch file. If you use the ECHO + space + ASCII 0 technique (which will appear as ECHO @):

```
ECHO OFF
ECHO First line
ECHO @
ECHO Last line
```

If you omit the carriage return after:

```
ECHO Last line
```

DOS 3.x won't mind, but DOS 2.x will become confused and print the "Echo Last line" command onscreen along with the "Last line" message that it's supposed to ECHO. So be sure to include a carriage return at the end of any ECHO command that happens to be on the final line of a batch file.

ECHO can come in very handy when you have to simulate user response in a batch file, or when you want to combine commands. You can delete all your files, for instance, by using ECHO to send DOS a Y as if you had typed it in response to the "Are you sure (Y/N)?" prompt:

```
ECHO Y | DEL *.*
```

Use this command sparingly, since it will wipe out all your files.

A similar trick will print the time or date without any user intervention. Just type:

```
ECHO | MORE | TIME
```

Normally you'd have to press Enter when you just want to print the time or date onscreen, since DOS always asks you if you want to change the current settings. ECHO helps do this for you.

ECHO will trigger the MORE command, which sends a carriage return into the TIME command. Sounds complicated, but it's actually very simple, and it lets you harness TIME and DATE without having to be there to bang on the Enter key. You can use this to redirect the output of TIME and DATE into a log file:

```
ECHO | MORE | DATE | FIND "C" > LOGFILE
ECHO | MORE | TIME | FIND "C" >> LOGFILE
```

The extra FIND command screens out the DOS update requests and cleans up LOG-FILE by looking only for the lines with the word "Current" in them and tossing anything else. Without them you'd end up with a file that looked like:

```
Current date is Sun 1-14-1990
Enter new date (mm-dd-yy):
Current time is 2:47:36.80
Enter new time:
```

REM

Format: **REM [message]**

REM lets you add comments and titles to your batch files.

It will display up to 123 characters of text following the word REM — but only when ECHO is on. When ECHO is off, DOS won't display anything. Under version 2.x, you could put a period in the first column and follow it with a text message to add remarks to your batch files, but Microsoft removed this from version 3.x.

To include a DOS operator symbol (such as |, <, or >) in the remark, enclose the symbol in quotes, e.g.:

```
REM "|" is the Piping Symbol
```

The text following REM may actually be longer than 123 characters, but DOS will display only the first 123 when ECHO is turned ON.

You can also add comments to your batch files by prefacing them with a colon and treating them as unreferenced labels — labels for which there is no corresponding GOTO command (see GOTO). DOS treats any line beginning with a colon as a label, and won't display it or process it regardless of whether ECHO happens to be ON or OFF. (This means you don't have to wrap operators such as | or < inside quotation marks when using them as label-type comments.) Comments can be far longer if you treat them as labels than if you preface them with REMs.

If you do use labels to insert comments, be sure that the first word of the comment is not the same as any of the real labels paired with a GOTO statement. DOS always starts searching for labels at the beginning of a batch file, and will stop as soon as it finds a match. If you have two identical labels in the same batch file, DOS will always jump to the first one and will never get around to any others with the same spelling.

DOS 2.x was fussy about having labels begin at the left edge of the screen, and it insisted that colons be in column 1. DOS 3.x is far more liberal.

Some users include a REM and the name of the batch file in each batch file:

```
ECHO OFF
REM This is DIRSORT.BAT
DIR | SORT
```

Not too many people ever want their REM statements to display, and most generally use colons instead to fool DOS into treating remarks like labels, which never print onscreen.

If you do want to print a message, it's probably better to use ECHO. But if you insist on sticking with REM, you can eliminate the actual word REM from the display. Just add a string of backspaces after the word REM. You can't do this when using COPY CON to create your batch files, since DOS uses the backspace key for making corrections. But any word processor that allows embedded control codes (such as *WordStar*) makes the process a snap. With *WordStar* you can enter a backspace by typing Ctrl-P then Ctrl-H.

If your word processor can't imbed ASCII character 8 backspaces in your file, try running the following BASIC program, which will create a REMLESS.BAT demonstration file:

```
100 ' REMLESS.BAS — creates REMLESS.BAT test batchfile
110 OPEN "REMLESS.BAT" FOR OUTPUT AS #1
120 PRINT #1,"CLS"
130 PRINT #1,"REM this is a remark"
140 PRINT #1,"REM";STRING$(3,8);"this is a REMless remark"
150 CLOSE:END
```

GOTO

Format: **GOTO [:]LABEL**

This is a powerful command that sends control of a batch file (or *branches*) to another location in the batch file identified by a unique *label*.

A batch file label is simply a string of characters with a colon prefix in the leftmost column. (DOS 2.x is fussier than 3.x about what constitutes the leftmost column; under 2.x the colon has to be at the very left edge of the screen. Version 3.x simply wants a colon as the first character, and can handle leading spaces and indentations.) The rules for naming labels are virtually the same as for naming files, except that for some reason, DOS version 3.x accepts question marks as labels. If you ran the following QUES-TION.BAT batch file using version 3.x:

```
ECHO OFF
ECHO This is the first line
GOTO ???
ECHO This middle line won't appear
:???
ECHO This is the bottom line
```

The middle line won't ever appear, since the GOTO ??? command skips around it and jumps execution directly to the :??? label. However, other illegal filename characters such as < >[ ]|;,*=." won't work.

Run QUESTION.BAT under version 2.x, however, and DOS would display the first line onscreen but stumble over the ??? and print a "Label not found" error message. If DOS scans all the way through a batch file and can't locate a label specified by a GOTO command, it prints this message and stops the batch file in its tracks.

If you hadn't exactly matched the NONSTOP.BAT label with the reference in the GOTO command:

```
ECHO OFF         ECHO OFF         ECHO OFF
:TOPP            :TOP             :TOP
DECIDE     or    DECIDE     or    DECIDE
GOTO TOP         GOTO TOPP        GOTO
```

each example would run the DECIDE program once then grind to a halt.

It's smart to give your labels names that help you debug, enlarge, or otherwise adapt them later. So you'd be better off changing QUESTION.BAT to read:

```
ECHO OFF
ECHO This is the first line
GOTO CONTINUE
ECHO This middle line won't appear
```

```
:CONTINUE
ECHO This is the bottom line
```

DOS is fussy about not allowing reserved devices names (such as CON and NUL) in filenames, so it won't let you create a file such as NUL.BAT or PRN.TXT. But you can use these as batch labels. So the RESERVED.BAT file:

```
ECHO OFF
GOTO CON
:NUL
ECHO This is NUL
GOTO PRN
:AUX
ECHO This is AUX
GOTO END
:CON
ECHO This is CON
GOTO NUL
ECHO This is the right place
:PRN
ECHO This is PRN
GOTO AUX
:END
```

would print out:

```
This is CON
This is NUL
This is PRN
This is AUX
```

When DOS hunts for labels it starts at the top of the batch file and works down toward the end. So if you try the following NEVER.BAT batch file with duplicate labels:

```
ECHO OFF
GOTO MAGAZIN1
REM Dummy line
:MAGAZIN1
ECHO It will print this
GOTO END
:MAGAZIN1
ECHO It will never print this
:END
```

when DOS sees the GOTO MAGAZIN1 label it will jump to the first instance of it and never get to the second one. Even if you moved the GOTO command below the first occurrence of the label it specifies:

```
ECHO OFF
REM Dummy line
:MAGAZIN1
ECHO It will keep printing this
GOTO MAGAZIN1
:MAGAZIN1
ECHO It will never print this
:END
```

DOS will still circle back to the beginning of the file and jump to the first :MAGAZIN1 label. In this particular case it would display the "It will keep printing this" line and then loop back endlessly — or at least until you type Ctrl-C or Ctrl- ScrollLock and then Y to stop it.

While you can use very long label names in your batch files, such as:

```
:THIS_IS_WHERE_THE_PROGRAM_WILL_GO_NEXT
```

all that DOS really cares about is the first eight letters, not including the colon, which isn't actually part of the label.

So under version 3.x, running the LONG.BAT batch file:

```
ECHO OFF
GOTO THIS_IS_
GOTO END
:THIS_IS_WHERE_THE_PROGRAM_WILL_GO_NEXT
ECHO Yes, the program did get here.
:END
```

will print out:

```
Yes, the program did get here.
```

since DOS whittles the THIS_IS_WHERE_THE_PROGRAM_WILL_GO_NEXT label down to THIS_IS_.

Unfortunately, different versions of DOS handle long label names differently. While DOS 3.x truncates extra long labels, DOS 2.x doesn't. Under version 2.x, the long

```
:THIS_IS_WHERE_THE_PROGRAM_WILL_GO_NEXT
```

label is totally different from:

```
:THIS_IS_
```

So under 2.x, running the above batch file would simply display "Label not found."

If you tried using long, similar label names, in the following variation of the above NEVER.BAT batch file under 3.x:

```
ECHO OFF
GOTO MAGAZINE1
REM Dummy line
:MAGAZINE2
ECHO This is the wrong place.
GOTO END
:MAGAZINE1
ECHO This is the right place.
:END
```

DOS would print out:

```
This is the wrong place.
```

because it would interpret the GOTO MAGAZINE1 command simply as GOTO MAGAZINE, and truncate the :MAGAZINE2 label (which is nine characters long) to simply MAGAZINE. So to this version of DOS, the NEVER.BAT batch file really looks like:

```
ECHO OFF
GOTO MAGAZINE
REM Dummy line
:MAGAZINE
ECHO This is the wrong place.
GOTO END
:MAGAZINE
ECHO This is the right place.
:END
```

But try to run this new NEVER.BAT batch file under DOS 2.x and all you'll get is a nasty "Label not found" error, since DOS will chop off the end of the instruction "GOTO MAGAZINE1" and turn it into "GOTO MAGAZINE." It will then scan through the batch file looking for a ":MAGAZINE" label but will find only ":MAGAZINE1" and ":MAGAZINE2" and it will consider these to be different from plain old ":MAGAZINE."

If you shortened the labels in NEVER.BAT down to the maximum eight characters long:

```
ECHO OFF
GOTO MAGAZIN1
REM Dummy line
:MAGAZIN2
ECHO This is the wrong place.
GOTO END
:MAGAZIN1
ECHO This is the right place.
:END
```

and then ran it under any version of DOS, you'd see:

```
This is the right place.
```

Be sure to put a colon in the leftmost column when you actually use a label on a line by itself to tell the batch file where to jump. You don't have to attach the colon to the label name in the GOTO command, but it won't hurt. The original NONSTOP.BAT batch file could would work either way:

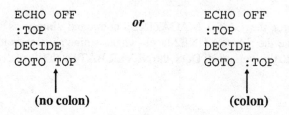

```
ECHO OFF                    ECHO OFF
:TOP          or            :TOP
DECIDE                      DECIDE
GOTO TOP                    GOTO :TOP
```

  (no colon)   **(colon)**

Batch files often boast multiple GOTO commands that share the same label destination. It's common practice to end complex batch files with an ":END" label and include lots of different GOTO END commands that will jump execution there when appropriate.

DOS doesn't mind if you include labels in your batch files that aren't matched with GOTO commands. Such unreferenced labels are treated as REM statements, except that DOS will never display them. (It will display REM statements if ECHO is turned on.)

Labels are not case sensitive, so a batch file such as:

```
:tOp
ECHO This line will keep printing.
GOTO ToP
```

will loop until you press Ctrl-C or Ctrl-ScrollLock. Later you'll see how useful this can be in branching user input to the right label without having to do all sorts of repetitive tests for TOP, top, Top, ToP, TOp, toP, etc.

If your batch file does contain an error such as a missing label, DOS won't detect the mistake unless it tries unsuccessfully to execute it. So a batch file like:

```
ECHO OFF
GOTO END
GOTO ABCD
:END
ECHO This is the end
```

will execute flawlessly, since DOS will never have the chance to see that the :ABCD label is missing.

You may mix GOTO commands with conditional IF commands:

```
IF %1==RED GOTO COLOR
```

or:

```
IF NOT ERRORLEVEL 255 GOTO END
```

This lets you include provisions for many different potential user responses or system configurations in one large batch file, and branch to the one that's appropriate.

You can easily exploit the case-insensitivity of labels. It's common to ask a user to enter information from the command line and then have your batch file process this information so it can branch properly. This is usually done by handling the user input as a replaceable parameter (such as %1 or %2) and then passing it through a series of IF %1==STRING tests. If the user entered a parameter n characters long, you would normally have to set up 2^n tests to trap every possible combination of uppercase and lowercase letters.

Even if the user entered a three-letter parameter from the command line, you'd have to examine eight potential variations. If you were testing for JFK to jump to the :AIRPORT label, this would mean a cascade of tests:

```
IF %1==JFK GOTO AIRPORT
IF %1==JFk GOTO AIRPORT
IF %1==JfK GOTO AIRPORT
IF %1==jFK GOTO AIRPORT
IF %1==jFk GOTO AIRPORT
IF %1==jfK GOTO AIRPORT
IF %1==jfk GOTO AIRPORT
```

And all these tests are for just one possible user parameter. If you had to test for other airports the batch file would quickly grow long and ponderous.

Because labels are case-insensitive, you could eliminate all these tests by having one "dispatcher" line at the beginning of your batch file:

```
GOTO %1
```

You'd then make the label names the same as the parameters that the user might enter. So if you had a :JFK label (or one spelled :jfk or :Jfk, etc.) in a batch file called FLIGHT.BAT, and the user entered:

```
FLIGHT JFK
```

or:

```
FLIGHT jfk
```

or even something like:

```
FLIGHT jFk
```

the GOTO %1 dispatcher would branch immediately to the :JFK label without having to wade through dozens of tests.

However, while the IF %1==STRING method lets you screen out every possible right or wrong entry, a GOTO %1 command won't test for invalid entries or errant keystrokes. If a label exists that exactly matches the letters in the parameter the user entered, the batch file will jump execution to it. But if the user entered a parameter for which there was no matching label, DOS would panic, print a "Label not found" error message, and abort the batch file.

CALL

Format: **CALL [d:][path]filename**

Starting with version 3.3, this lets you execute one batch file from inside another and return execution to the original batch file when the second one finishes. When DOS returns command to the original batch file it will jump to the line immediately following the CALL. Beginning with version 2.x, users had been able to nest batch files by using COMMAND /C to load additional command processors, but this had environment drawbacks, and ate up unnecessary space.

Each time you load another command processor, it makes the default ECHO ON. This means that if you turn ECHO OFF in the first line of a batch file, and then use COMMAND /C to load a second batch file, you'll have to include a second ECHO OFF in the second batch file to keep DOS from cluttering up your display. But when you use CALL the ECHO state is maintained in any nested batch files so you don't have to keep resetting it.

However, COMMAND /C has its uses. While DOS claims you can't nest FOR commands, you can do it by inserting a COMMAND /C at the right place. This technique won't work with CALL.

Both COMMAND /C and CALL let you nest batch files several levels deep. You may have a batch file CALL itself, so long as you're certain you'll be able to exit properly and avoid an endless loop.

If you have a file on your disk called BATCH1.BAT:

```
ECHO OFF
ECHO This is BATCH1.BAT
COMMAND /C BATCH2
ECHO Now you're back to BATCH1
```

and another one called BATCH2.BAT:

```
ECHO OFF
ECHO Now you're in BATCH2.BAT
```

and you run BATCH1.BAT in either DOS 2.x or 3.x, DOS will:

1. Start executing BATCH1.BAT by turning ECHO OFF and printing just the "This is BATCH1.BAT" message.
2. Load a second copy of COMMAND.COM.
3. Have this additional copy of COMMAND.COM start running BATCH2.BAT.
4. Turn ECHO OFF and print just the "Now you're in BATCH2.BAT" message.
5. Exit both BATCH2.BAT and the second copy of COMMAND.COM.
6. Return to BATCH1.BAT.
7. Print the final "Now you're back to BATCH1" message.

This will take a few seconds, since DOS has to find a copy of COMMAND.COM to load, read it off the disk into memory, and then load and run the second batch file. The whole process will look like:

```
C>ECHO OFF
This is BATCH1.BAT

C>ECHO OFF
Now you're in BATCH2.BAT
Now you're back to BATCH1
```

If you're using a DOS version 3.3 or later, you can change BATCH1.BAT to read:

```
ECHO OFF
ECHO This is BATCH1.BAT
CALL BATCH2
ECHO Now you're back to BATCH1
```

This time DOS doesn't have to hunt for a version of COMMAND.COM to load. And it doesn't need the additional ECHO OFF at the beginning of BATCH2.BAT. The process takes far less time and will look like:

```
C>ECHO OFF
This is BATCH1.BAT
Now you're in BATCH2.BAT
Now you're back to BATCH1
```

If you try the COMMAND /C version, be sure you have a copy of COMMAND.COM handy for the batch file to load. And also note that when you load a secondary command processor you have to turn ECHO OFF again in the second batch file.

DOS is very liberal about handling different COMMAND /C syntaxes. All of the following versions will work identically:

- COMMAND /C BATCH2
- COMMAND/C BATCH2
- COMMAND /CBATCH2
- COMMAND/CBATCH2

Don't assume that DOS will be so cavalier about spacing with most other commands. It's not.

Fast Exits

Users often want to have DOS treat direct calls to batch programs the same way it handles other executable commands from within batch files — as subroutines. You can call another batch file by loading a secondary command processor that runs the second batch file and then returns to the first, or you can use CALL to turn batch branches into subroutines (in versions 3.3 or above).

However, calls to executable programs and system commands *always* act as subroutine calls, returning processing to the next line in the batch file. Many times it's necessary for a batch file to branch to one other command after an IF test and then exit. This is usually done with a cumbersome and clutter-producing GOTO command that branches to another part of the batch program, runs the desired command, and then branches again to a common exit point, such as a final line called :END.

All this branching, especially in long batch programs, can be time-consuming and confusing to edit. An quick alternative is to capitalize on DOS's absolute branching feature by calling a batch file that simply runs a program or an internal DOS command and then quits. A tiny DO.BAT batch file can accomplish this for you with just one line:

```
@%1 %2 %3 %4
```

(The initial @ will prevent the line from displaying, and works only in versions 3.3 or later. Omit it if you're using an older version of DOS.)

This technique works very quickly. Just have an IF test (or an IF ERRORLEVEL check) branch to an executable DOS command or COM or EXE program and then quit.

As an example, you could use DO.BAT in a program called #.BAT that displays either a selected phone number or your entire phone list, depending on whether you specify a parameter when you run it. So:

```
# Nixon
```

or:

```
# (212)
```

would find all listings with Nixon or (212) in them, while:

```
#
```

by itself would display the entire list. The batch file looks like:

```
ECHO OFF
REM #.BAT
IF %1!==! DO TYPE C:\DATA\PHONE.DAT
FIND "%1" C:\DATA\PHONE.DAT
```

Of course, #.BAT is short and doesn't really need such a trick. But DO.BAT does save time and space. Without it, the original batch file would have been written:

```
ECHO OFF
REM #.BAT
IF !%1==! GOTO SEELIST
FIND "%1" C:\DATA\PHONE.DAT
GOTO END
:SEELIST
TYPE C:\DATA\PHONE.DAT
:END
```

You can adapt this technique with two other speedy batch files — ABORT.BAT and COMPLETE.BAT — that can branch absolutely. These will quickly quit any batch file after an IF check, with the option of including a message:

```
REM ABORT.BAT
IF NOT %1!==! ECHO %1 %2 %3 %4 %5 %6 %7 %8 %9
ECHO Operation aborted.
```

```
REM COMPLETE.BAT
IF NOT %1!==! ECHO %1 %2 %3 %4 %5 %6 %7 %8 %9
ECHO Operation completed.
```

So you can have a line in your program like:

```
IF NOT EXIST ABC ABORT ABC not found.
```

If DOS doesn't find ABC, the batch file will quit without executing any GOTO statements and display:

```
ABC not found.
Operation aborted.
```

If the words after ABORT had been omitted, then the only closing message would be "Operation aborted."

You can combine the two techniques into one big #.BAT batch file:

```
ECHO OFF
REM #.BAT
IF NOT EXIST ABC ABORT ABC not found.
IF %1!==! DO TYPE C:\DATA\PHONE.DAT
FIND "%1" C:\DATA\PHONE.DAT
```

In this case, whether or not you type anything after the #, the program simply won't proceed if ABC isn't on your disk. If you create a dummy ABC file (that contains just the word REM), the program will bypass this test and look up numbers with aplomb. If you erase ABC, all you'll get is the:

```
ABC not found.
Operation aborted.
```

message and the #.BAT file will grind to a halt.

These examples assume that you have a list of your phone numbers called PHONE.DAT in your C:\DATA directory, and that this file is in a form, with each entry on one line with a carriage return at the end of it, that FIND can handle.

Passing Parameters

You may pass parameters from one batch file to another. Just include a parameter after the filename on the line with the CALL or the COMMAND /C.

If you had a file on your disk called TEST1.BAT:

```
@ECHO OFF
ECHO this is TEST1
CALL TEST2 TESTPARM
ECHO Back to TEST1
```

and another called TEST2.BAT that was called by TEST1.BAT:

```
ECHO This is TEST2
ECHO %1
```

if you ran TEST1, you'd see:

```
This is TEST1
This is TEST2
TESTPARM
Back to TEST1
```

The first batch file passed the parameter TESTPARM to the second by including it after the name of the file it called. The second batch file picked up the parameter with %1.

If you're using a version of DOS earlier than 3.3, substitute COMMAND /C in place of CALL, and add an additional ECHO OFF line at the very beginning of TEST2.BAT.

You can make this process more useful by blitzing out parameters repeatedly with a FOR command.

If you run the following FIL1.BAT batch file:

```
@ECHO OFF
Echo Starting out in FIL1.BAT
FOR %%A in (*.BAK) DO CALL FIL2 %%A
ECHO Back to batch file #1
```

the third line will CALL the next FIL2.BAT batch file:

```
ECHO OFF
ECHO ***********************
ECHO Now you're in FIL2.BAT
ECHO The contents of %1 are:
TYPE %1
ECHO ***********************
PAUSE
```

and pass parameters from FIL1.BAT to FIL2.BAT using the %%A in FIL1.BAT and the %1 in FIL2.BAT.

FIL1.BAT will seek out all the files that have BAK extensions and FIL2.BAT will ECHO the name of each one and then use TYPE to display the contents of each one. After FIL2.BAT has displayed the last *.BAK file, it will stop running and DOS will return command to the line in FIL1.BAT following the line with the CALL. If you try this yourself and you're using an older version of DOS, substitute COMMAND /C for CALL.

Later you'll see how you can construct some very useful disk management utilities by combining FOR commands with CALL or COMMAND /C.

You can also pass values to other batch files without having to first load them with COMMAND /C or CALL. Just use SET to store the value as an environment variable.

You can have your batch files detect whether any specified settings are currently in force with a test like:

```
IF %MONITOR%!==! GOTO NOSETTNG
```

You could test to see if you had previously set any variables, check the validity of the setting, and act on it with a batch file like this:

```
ECHO OFF
IF %MONITOR%!==! GOTO SETMON
IF %MONITOR%==MONO GOTO GREENCOL
IF %MONITOR%==mono GOTO GREENCOL
IF %MONITOR%==COLOR GOTO NORMLCOL
IF %MONITOR%==color GOTO NORMLCOL
ECHO %MONITOR% monitor setting invalid
GOTO END
:SETMON
ECHO No monitor variable in use
GOTO END
:GREENCOL
ECHO Mono attribute setter would go here
GOTO END
:NORMLCOL
ECHO Color setter would go here
:END
```

FOR...IN...DO

This integrated trio allows repeated execution of a command on a specified set of files. The format is :

```
FOR %%variable IN (set) DO command [%%variable]
```

inside batch files, and:

```
FOR %variable IN (set) DO command [%variable]
```

outside of batch files. (Note that you use double %% signs inside batch files and single % signs outside batch files.)

%%variable and %variable are variable names, generally single letters such as %%a or %Z. You can't use the digits 0-9 for variable names, since DOS reserves these for replaceable parameters.

(set) is the filespec or collection of filespecs that DOS will act on, and can be a wildcard such as:

```
(*.*)
```

or:

```
(*.BAK)
```

or a group of files such as:

```
(MORE.ASM MORE.OBJ MORE.COM)
```

So a batch file command such as:

```
FOR %%A IN (*.*) DO DEL %%A
```

would erase all the files in your directory one by one without asking for a confirming:

```
Are you sure (Y/N)?
```

the way DEL *.* does.

However, a batch file that used a FOR command to delete all your files would end up erasing itself, and you'd get a "Batch file missing" error message. To avoid this, put a drive letter or path in front of the *.* and run it from another directory or drive.

To see a directory listing of all you COM and EXE files, you'd type:

```
FOR %%A in (*.COM *.EXE) DO DIR %%A
```

Be sure to add the final %%A. If you leave it off, DOS won't do a DIR *.COM and a DIR *.EXE. Instead it will just do a plain old DIR, since there wouldn't be any parameters after it. When you don't enter any parameters after DIR, DOS assumes you mean:

```
DIR *.*
```

The command:

```
FOR %%A in (*.COM *.EXE) DO DIR
```

would sniff out all the files that ended in COM and EXE, but would end up doing the same repeated DIR *.* listing for each occurrence of a COM or EXE file. So if there are two COM files and three EXE files, DOS will do a DIR *.* command five times. You must add the %%variable command onto the end for the FOR command to act on what you've specified in the (set).

Be sure that the %%variable matches in case at the beginning and end of the line:

```
FOR %%A IN (*.BAK) DO DEL %%A
```

and:

```
FOR %%a IN (*.BAK) DO DEL %%a
```

will erase all your BAK files, but:

```
FOR %%a IN (*.BAK) DO DEL %%A
```

and:

```
FOR %%A IN (*.BAK) DO DEL %%a
```

won't.

If you had a lot of quarterly expense reports on your disk, with names like 88Q1EXP.RPT, 88Q2EXP.RPT, 88Q3EXP.RPT, 88Q4EXP.RPT, 87Q4EXP.RPT, 87Q3EXP.RPT, 87Q2EXP.RPT, and 87Q1EXP.RPT, and you wanted to print out just the ones from the first and second quarters, you could run a batch file with the single line:

```
FOR %%A IN (1 2) DO COPY 8?Q%%AEXP.RPT PRN
```

DOS would replace the ? with the last digit of the year (7 or 8) and replace the %%A with 1 or 2.

One of the simplest and most useful FOR applications can check to see whether you've backed up your files, and will make backup copies only when you haven't. Just create a one-line batch file, called BACKCHEK.BAT:

```
FOR %%A IN (*.*) DO IF NOT EXIST B:%%A COPY %%A B:
```

This is far from the perfect backup tool, since it won't copy newer versions of files over older ones, or pause when your B: diskette is full and prompt you to insert another floppy. And it works within one directory only. But it can come in handy for quick brute-force backups and puts a lot of DOS intelligence into one line.

By adding replaceable parameters you can enhance this one-line backup command to accept filespecs from the command line and copy files to another disk or subdirectory only if they're not already there. The following COPYFAST.BAT batch file will do it:

```
ECHO OFF
IF %2!==! GOTO HELP
ECHO Copying files from %1 that are not already on %2
CTTY NUL
FOR %%A IN (%1) DO IF NOT EXIST %2%%A COPY %%A %2
```

```
CTTY CON
GOTO END
:HELP
ECHO %0 copies files from a source disk or directory to a
ECHO destination if they're NOT already on the destination.
ECHO Syntax: %0 *.* c:
ECHO %0 *.DOC \subdir
ECHO You must be in the directory you want to copy from.
:END
```

This batch file uses CTTY NUL to disconnect the keyboard and screen temporarily so you don't see a long line of "1 File(s) copied" messages. The CTTY CON command puts things back the way they were. Unfortunately, if something goes wrong after the CTTY NUL but before the CTTY CON has a chance to return control to you, you'll be locked out of your system. If you want to avoid this potential problem, without having to concoct a scheme where this batch file loads another batch file, just remove the two lines that begin with CTTY.

You can adapt this technique to help make various directory chores a whole lot easier. For instance, if you want to compare the contents of two disks or a disk with a subdirectory to see which files are in one and not in the other, you can use the UNIQ.BAT batch file:

```
ECHO OFF
IF %2!==! GOTO HELP
ECHO Files on %1 but not on %2
FOR %%A IN (%1*.*) DO IF NOT EXIST %2%%A ECHO %%A
ECHO Files on %2 but not on %1
FOR %%A IN (%2*.*) DO IF NOT EXIST %1%%A ECHO %%A
GOTO END
:HELP
ECHO %0 lists files that are not on both disks
ECHO Syntax: %0 A: C: where C: is the default drive
:END
```

To have UNIQ.BAT tell you what files are on drive C: but not drive B: and vice versa, just type:

```
UNIQ C: B:
```

This won't work with DOS versions earlier than 3.0, since these can't handle IF EXIST searches with paths in them.

If you want to log the list of files reported by UNIQ.BAT to disk rather than just displaying them on the screen, create a small file called LOG.BAT:

```
ECHO OFF
IF !%2==! GOTO OOPS
COMMAND /C UNIQ %1 %2 > LOGFILE
GOTO END
:OOPS
ECHO Syntax: %0 A: C: where C: is the default drive
:END
```

Combining the FOR command with both replaceable parameters and environment variables gives it real power. If your path included the root directory (which is why the NOT test is required) and it specified subdirectories on one disk only, a batch file called PATHDIR.BAT containing the command:

```
FOR %%A IN (%PATH%) DO IF NOT %%A==C:\ DIR %%A\%1
```

would let you find all your COM files in all the subdirectories in your PATH by typing:

```
PATHDIR *.COM
```

DOS would replace the %PATH% variable with the actual list of subdirectories specified by your PATH command, and the FOR command would perform a DIR search through each for any *.COM files. Elements in the set must be separated by delimiters such as spaces, but the semicolons used in path specifications will work admirably.

To use the FOR command directly at the DOS prompt, replace the twin %% signs with single % signs. However, double %% signs are required for use in batch files.

DOS won't normally let one FOR command execute another FOR command. Try it and DOS will print a "FOR cannot be nested" error message. However, you can make an end run around this restriction by having the first FOR load a secondary command processor right before the second FOR.

If you try nesting these without COMMAND /C in a batch file called FORNEST1.BAT:

```
FOR %%A IN (1 2) DO FOR %%B IN (A B) DO ECHO %%A %%B
```

you'll just get a "FOR cannot be nested" error message. But create a file called FORNEST2.BAT that adds a COMMAND /C to invoke a secondary command processor:

```
FOR %%A IN (1 2) DO COMMAND/C FOR %%B IN (A B) DO ECHO %%A %%B
```

and sure enough DOS will execute it, nest the two commands, and print:

```
C>FOR %A IN (1 2) DO COMMAND/C FOR %B IN (A B) DO ECHO %A %B

C>COMMAND/C FOR %B IN (A B) DO ECHO 1 %B
```

```
C>ECHO 1 A
1 A

C>ECHO 1 B
1 B

C>COMMAND/C FOR %B IN (A B) DO ECHO 2 %B
C>ECHO 2 A
2 A

C>ECHO 2 B
2 B
```

You could reduce the clutter a bit by adding an initial ECHO OFF, but this won't suppress the bulk of the display since DOS turns ECHO back on when it loads the second copy of COMMAND.COM. This nesting technique works only with COMMAND /C, so if you're using a DOS version 3.3 or later, don't try replacing the COMMAND /C with CALL.

Commands like COPY and DIR don't take multiple arguments. A way around this is to have DOS execute the command multiple times, each with a different argument. For example, to copy all COM and EXE files to a floppy disk, you could type directly at the DOS prompt:

```
FOR %F IN (*.COM *.EXE) DO COPY %F A:
```

While this works, DOS will grind through the process one file at a time rather than ganging things up as it does with wildcards.

Using a FOR loop on the command line isn't limited to just filenames. Commands can also be used as FOR loop variables as in:

```
FOR %C IN (COPY ERASE) DO %C A:*.EXE
```

to copy .EXE files from a floppy disk, then erase them from the disk.

Another way to do multiple copies on the same command line is to use piping. The following command will copy all your COM and EXE files to drive A:

```
COPY *.COM A: | COPY *.EXE A:
```

PAUSE

Format: **PAUSE** [message]

This momentarily halts execution. Nothing more.

PAUSE is helpful if you have to change disks, turn on a printer, or perform some other time-consuming task, since it puts the batch file on hold until you press a key to continue:

```
ECHO Put a blank formatted
ECHO diskette in drive A:
PAUSE
```

Used on a line by itself, this command temporarily halts the batch file execution, then prints a "Strike a key when ready . . ." message, and waits for the user to press any non-shift key other than Ctrl-C or Ctrl-ScrollLock. If the user presses either of those "break" key combinations the process aborts and DOS displays the usual interruption message "Terminate batch job (Y/N)?".

If you type Y or y DOS will abort the batch file and return you to whatever you were doing before. If you type N or n, DOS will continue running the batch file as if nothing had happened. Press any other key and DOS will stubbornly repeat the "Terminate..." message.

It's possible to put a message after the word PAUSE, but this message displays only when ECHO is off, which means that the user also sees the DOS prompt and the word PAUSE. Very unsightly.

Users of version 3.x can replace the normal "Strike a key when ready" message with an ECHO command and then redirect the normal PAUSE output to NUL with a trio of lines like:

```
ECHO OFF
ECHO Make sure your printer is on, then press any key
PAUSE > NUL
```

but this won't suppress the "Strike" message on older versions. If users of DOS 2.x want to display a message, they can at least prevent the word PAUSE from showing up onscreen by putting five backspaces directly after it. They can add backspace characters using most good word processors (with *WordStar*, for example, they'd simply type Ctrl-P Ctrl-H five times).

An even better method that works under all versions of DOS is to run the NEW-PAUSE.COM program on the accompanying disk, or one of the fancier PAUSE utilities such TICKER.COM.

Use NEWPAUSE either on a line by itself or by following it with text you want displayed. A sample batch file that included just the lines:

```
ECHO OFF
DIR
NEWPAUSE
DIR
```

would display a directory listing, then pause without putting anything onscreen, and then display another directory listing as soon as the user pressed any key.

By adding a message after NEWPAUSE:

```
ECHO OFF
DIR
NEWPAUSE Press any key to see this again:
DIR
```

DOS will display the line:

```
Press any key to see this again:
```

when it pauses after the initial DIR listing.

The TICKER.COM program on the accompanying disk will display a moving ticker-tape display across the bottom of your screen. It's a bit gimmicky, but it's also a way to liven up your batch files.

You can use PAUSE or any of these other utilities to break out of an otherwise endless loop:

```
CD \MEMO
WS
PAUSE
DEL *.BAK
%0
```

This file switches into your MEMO directory and runs *WordStar*. Then when you exit *WordStar* it pauses temporarily. If you want to continue you can press any key and the batch file will erase any BAK backup files, then reload the batch file and start the process all over again. However, if you don't want to continue, you can press Ctrl-ScrollLock or Ctrl-C and answer Y or y to the confirming question it asks and you're back at the DOS prompt.

A better way is to use IF ERRORLEVEL, which is discussed in detail later, and ask the user to press one key to continue or another to abort.

Replaceable Parameters

%0 %1 %2 %3 %4 %5 %6 %7 %8 %9

These handy tools let batch files use text entered on the DOS command line to control how the batch files work or display custom messages and prompts.

When you execute a batch file, DOS scans the command line, looks for delimiters such as spaces, equals signs, semicolons, commas, and tabs that separate what you entered into discrete chunks, and then assigns the text that makes up these chunks to ten variables — %0 through %9.

DOS can handle up to 127 characters typed on the command line. If you enter more than nine separate clumps of text after the name of a batch file, DOS can't immediately assign replaceable parameters to anything past the ninth one. But by using the SHIFT command, you can have DOS gradually work its way through them all.

If you enter fewer than nine discrete parameters after the name of the batch file, DOS assigns *null strings* that are zero characters long to any variables for which there isn't any text.

The first discrete chunk of text is assigned to %0. This is always the name of the batch file itself. The next is assigned to %1, and the one after that to %2, etc.

If you run the simple ENDLESS.BAT batch file, the sole contents of which are the two characters:

```
%0
```

DOS will substitute the name of the batch file itself — ENDLESS — for the %0, and then execute it, which will rerun itself until you press Ctrl-C or Ctrl-ScrollLock and then type Y to stop.

When DOS replaces the variables with the actual text from the command line, it's sensitive about spacing. So if you created a batch file called OVER.BAT:

```
%1%2%3%4 %1 %2 %3 %4
```

and then ran it by typing:

```
OVER O V E R
```

DOS would keep repeating the batch file endlessly since it would concatenate the O, the V, the, E, and the R that you entered after the batch file name itself, and lump them together into OVER.

You can display all the replaceable parameters you entered with the following short SEEALL.BAT batch file:

```
ECHO OFF
FOR %%A IN (%0 %1 %2 %3 %4 %5 %6 %7 %8 %9) DO IF NOT %%A!==! ECHO %%A
```

If you type in just SEEALL, all you'll get is:

```
SEEALL
```

But enter something like:

```
C>SEEALL 12345 abc LMNOP !!!!!!! PC Magazine
```

and the batch file will print out:

```
SEALL
12345
```

```
abc
LMNOP
!!!!!!!
PC
Magazine
```

If you have ANSI.SYS loaded, and you use a color monitor and like white backgrounds, but you sometimes want black text, red text, or blue text, you could create a file called TEXT.BAT:

```
ECHO OFF
IF %1!==! GOTO OOPS
GOTO %1
:OOPS
ECHO Enter %0 BLUE or %0 RED or %0 BLACK
GOTO END
:BLUE
ECHO ESC[0;47;34m
GOTO END
:BLACK
ECHO ESC[0;47;30m
GOTO END
:RED
ECHO ESC[0;47;31m
:END
```

Note: Don't type this in exactly as shown — instead, substitute the actual Esc character, decimal ASCII 27 (or hex 1B) in place of the three occurrences of "ESC." Also, be sure your CONFIG.SYS file includes a line like:

```
DEVICE=ANSI.SYS
```

If you've loaded ANSI.SYS and have inserted actual Esc characters in place of each ESC, you can change your foreground color to red simply by typing:

```
TEXT RED
```

just as shown, or in mixed case or lowercase — it doesn't matter.

Typing TEXT BLACK will give you black text on a white background, and TEXT BLUE will yield blue letters against white. However, if you typed simply:

```
TEXT
```

without any color after it, TEXT.BAT would print out instructions on how to use this file, and quit. You'd see something like:

```
Enter TEXT BLUE or TEXT RED or TEXT BLACK
```

The line that prints the instructions:

```
ECHO Enter %0 BLUE or %0 RED or %0 BLACK
```

uses %0 rather than the name TEXT.BAT, so if you rename TEXT.BAT to something like FOREGRND.BAT or COLORSET.BAT the instructions will always print out the correct new batch filename.

This batch file uses labels that are the same as the replaceable parameters entered by the user. Labels are not case-sensitive, so this technique eliminates the long list of tests normally required to see whether a user entered Red, RED, or ReD, for example.

To see whether you did enter a color on the command line, TEXT.BAT uses the line:

```
IF %1!==! GOTO OOPS
```

If you entered something like:

```
TEXT RED
```

DOS would assign replaceable parameter %1 the value RED. It would then replace each occurrence of %1 in the batch file with RED, so the test would become:

```
IF RED!==! GOTO OOPS
```

Since the characters "RED!" obviously do not equal the single character "!" the test fails and the batch file does not jump execution to the :OOPS label.

However, if the user didn't enter any color, and simply typed:

```
TEXT
```

on the DOS command line, %1 would be equal to (nothing) and the test would become:

```
IF !==! GOTO OOPS
```

Clearly, "!" is equal to "!" so the batch file will execute the command at the end of the line, which jumps execution to the :OOPS label. The commands at this label will print instructions on how to use the program and then quit.

You don't have to use exclamation points; any pair of characters will do. The test could just as easily have been:

```
IF %1@==@ GOTO OOPS
```

If you didn't mind slogging through a cascade of case-sensitive tests, and you were willing to forego tests for unusual capitalizations such as bLuE, you could change the top of the batch file so that TEXT.BAT looked like:

```
ECHO OFF
IF %1!==! GOTO OOPS
IF %1==BLUE GOTO COL1
IF %1==blue GOTO COL1
IF %1==BLACK GOTO COL2
IF %1==black GOTO COL2
IF %1==RED GOTO COL3
IF %1==red GOTO COL3
:OOPS
ECHO Enter %0 BLUE or %0 RED or %0 BLACK
GOTO END
:COL1
ECHO ESC[0;47;34m
GOTO END
:COL2
ECHO ESC[0;47;30m
GOTO END
:COL3
ECHO ESC[0;47;31m
:END
```

In this case if the user entered a color that TEXT.BAT wasn't able to handle, such as:

```
TEXT MAUVE
```

the batch file would pass the first IF %1!==! test, but fail all six IF %1==COLOR tests. Execution would "fall through" this sieve of tests and end up at the :OOPS label, where the batch file would display the message about which colors were allowed, and then exit.

Unfortunately, if the user entered:

```
TEXT Blue
```

the batch file would think this was a disallowed color, since the only versions of color entries that TEXT.BAT is prepared to accept are all uppercase and all lowercase. It would be easy to add an additional test for each color that accepted variations where the first letter was uppercase and all the remaining ones were lowercase. But then if the user entered:

```
TEXT BLue
```

(which is a common typing mistake), the batch file wouldn't recognize this variant.

There is a way to get around this (DOS is nothing if not flexible), but it's preposterous. Add a few lines so the TEXT.BAT file looks like:

```
ECHO OFF
IF %1!==! GOTO OOPS
ECHO :%1 > TEMPFILE
ECHO COPY %0.BAK %0.BAT >> TEMPFILE
ECHO DEL %0.BAK >> TEMPFILE
COPY %0.BAT %0.BAK > NUL
COPY %0.BAT+TEMPFILE > NUL
DEL TEMPFILE
GOTO %1
:OOPS
ECHO Enter %0 BLUE or %0 RED or %0 BLACK
GOTO END
:BLUE
ECHO ESC[0;47;34m
GOTO END
:BLACK
ECHO ESC[0;47;30m
GOTO END
:RED
ECHO ESC[0;47;31m
:END
```

This uses the ECHO command and DOS redirection to create a temporary file called TEMPFILE containing a brand new label that matches whatever you typed in, as well as some commands to copy and delete backup versions of the main file. TEXT.BAT then appends this new file to the end of itself. Since the new file contains a valid label, you won't get a "Label not found" message.

If you typed in an invalid color such as PUCE, you'll end up with a meaningless :PUCE label at the very end that won't change any colors and is there simply to guard against error messages. If you typed in a valid color such as RED, you'll end up with two :RED labels. However, since (1) this process appends the phony label at the end, (2) DOS starts looking for labels at the beginning of the file, and (3) DOS will execute the first occurrence of a label if a batch file contains more than one, TEXT.BAT will jump to the first :RED label and execute the proper command to set the foreground to red.

This enhancement will clean up after itself by making a backup copy of the original file, copying this unblemished backup copy onto the changed one, and then erasing the extra backup. But it's not really worth it. For one thing, DOS 2.x can become confused if you enter a label name that's longer than eight characters. And this won't work with any version of DOS if you enter an invalid label, such as one with a period in it. But it shows what you can do to get around a DOS bottleneck.

If you had a batch file on your disk called READBACK.BAT:

```
ECHO OFF
ECHO %0.BAT is the name of the batch file
ECHO %1
ECHO %2
ECHO %3
ECHO %4
ECHO %5
```

and you entered at the DOS prompt:

```
READBACK This message
```

you'd end up with:

```
C>ECHO OFF
READBACK.BAT is the name of the batch file
This
message
ECHO is off
ECHO is off
ECHO is off
```

DOS would substitute "READBACK" for %0, "This" for %1, and "message" for %2. But since you didn't enter any other text, DOS would make the parameters %3, %4, and %5 equal to nothing. When it got around to executing the lines:

```
ECHO %3
ECHO %4
ECHO %5
```

DOS would turn them into:

```
ECHO
ECHO
ECHO
```

and report the current ON/OFF ECHO state.

To prevent this from happening, you can put an ASCII character 0 at the end of each of the bottom five lines (by using EDLIN to create READBACK.BAT and pressing the F7 key and the end of each line).

Adding a character 0, which will appear onscreen as a blank, to each line will make sure that DOS will ECHO something and not interpret a missing parameter as just an ECHO command on a line by itself.

DOS can handle up to nine replaceable parameters %1 through %9 in one gulp, and will always replace %0 with the name of the batch file itself (just as it was entered at the

DOS prompt). If you want to use more than nine replaceable parameters you have to use the SHIFT command.

SHIFT Parameters

Each time DOS executes the SHIFT command it moves each replaceable parameter down in value one notch. So the value that was stored as %3 moves down and becomes %2, and the value stored at %2 becomes %1, and %1 becomes %0 (which originally held the name of the batch file). Each time you execute SHIFT the old %0 value disappears.

If you had a batch file called SHIFTIT.BAT:

```
ECHO OFF
ECHO %0 %1 %2 %3
SHIFT
ECHO %0 %1 %2 %3
SHIFT
ECHO %0 %1 %2 %3
SHIFT
```

and you typed:

```
SHIFTIT A B C D
```

DOS would print:

```
C>ECHO OFF
SHIFTIT A B C
A B C D
B C D
```

as it shifted all the parameters down one by one.

In the first line DOS replaced %0 with the name of the batch file and printed three of the four letters entered on the command line. After the first shift, the name of the batch file disappears as DOS moves everything down a notch, but this time the batch file prints the fourth parameter entered on the command line (the D) even though the fourth parameter didn't appear the first time.

If you want to preserve the name of the batch file itself when using the SHIFT command, you have to set an environment variable as this new SHIFTIT2.BAT batch file does:

```
ECHO OFF
SET NAME=%0
ECHO %0 %1 %2 %3
SHIFT
ECHO %NAME% %0 %1 %2 %3
```

```
SHIFT
ECHO %NAME% %0 %1 %2 %3
SHIFT
SET NAME=
```

DOS will still wipe out the name of the batch file originally stored as %0 the first time it executes the SHIFT command, but it will still be able to remember and display it since you stored it as an environment variable called NAME with the:

```
SET NAME=%0
```

command, and then dredged it back up when you used the:

```
ECHO %NAME%
```

command. This time, using the same four parameters after SHIFTIT2.BAT:

```
SHIFTIT2 A B C D
```

would yield:

```
C>ECHO OFF
SHIFTIT2 A B C
SHIFTIT2 A B C D
SHIFTIT2 B C D
```

retaining the name of the batch file each time even though the SHIFT command wrote over it. Unfortunately, because of a DOS bug, environment variables won't work in version 3.0.

The SHIFT command can read as many parameters off the command line as you entered, and you can type in only 127 characters including the name of the batch file itself. If your batch file had a name that was just one letter long and you entered only single-character parameters, with spaces between them, you could have SHIFT squeeze out 63 of them. The MAXSHIFT.BAT batch file below:

```
ECHO OFF
:TOP
IF %1!==! GOTO END
ECHO %1
SHIFT
GOTO TOP
:END
```

will keep reading all the parameters off the command line and ECHOing them one by one until they've all been processed. You could enter:

```
MAXSHIFT A B C D E F G H I J K L M N O P Q R S T U V
```

and continue all the way through the uppercase and lowercase alphabets and MAXSHIFT would display every letter. It knows when to stop because it runs a:

```
IF %1!==! GOTO END
```

test each time it shifts. This test will be true (and it will stop displaying characters) only when %1 is finally equal to nothing because all the parameters have been used up. When this happens the test will become:

```
IF !==! GOTO END
```

Until then, %1! will always be equal to A! or B! or z! or whatever variable just shifted over. And something like:

```
IF A!==! GOTO END
```

will not be true, because "A!" is not equal to just "!" by itself.

Environment Variables

Format: **SET ENVVAR=VALUE** (*to create an environment variable*)
ECHO %ENVVAR% *or* **IF %ENVVAR%==PRESET GOTO LABEL**
(*to use it*)

Although it wasn't documented until PC-DOS version 3.3, doesn't always work properly with earlier versions, and doesn't work at all under 3.0, you may use a special section of memory called the environment as a storage area for variables.

You can see what DOS currently stores in your environment by typing SET at the DOS prompt. You'll always see a line beginning COMSPEC= which tells your system where to look for the COMMAND.COM command processor. And you'll probably also see your path, your PROMPT, and possibly an APPEND path and a few variables set by some commercial software (such as *WordPerfect*).

Entering the word SET followed by a variable name of your choice, then an equals sign, then a character string:

```
SET SCREEN=EGA
```

will add:

```
SCREEN=EGA
```

to your environment.

Once you've added a variable to your environment, you can change it simply by using another SET command:

```
SET SCREEN=VGA
```

You can remove the variable from the environment by entering the variable name and an equals sign with nothing after it:

```
SET SCREEN=
```

If you have two screens and you're changing to a monochrome display, the batch file that does the changing can also reset the SCREEN variable:

```
SET SCREEN=MONO
```

Then any other programs and batch files can tell which screen is active by looking at the %SCREEN% variable.

The ability to keep track of a state and pass the information to a batch file can help you debug batch files. When you're creating and testing a batch file you often want ECHO to be ON so you can see where any potential problems are. But when you run the batch file you want ECHO to be off so it doesn't clutter your screen with commands. To solve this, make the first line in your batch file:

```
ECHO %ECHO%
```

Then, at the DOS prompt, type:

```
SET ECHO=ON
```

when you want to see all the commands execute, and:

```
SET ECHO=OFF
```

when you want to suppress them.

Be careful when setting environment variables since they're case-sensitive and space-sensitive. If you set ECHO=ON you'll have to test for:

```
IF %ECHO%==ON GOTO OKAY
IF %ECHO%==on GOTO OKAY
IF %ECHO%==On GOTO OKAY
```

In addition, you should first test to see whether you've given the %ECHO% variable any setting at all, with a test like:

```
IF %ECHO%!==! GOTO NOTSET
```

And watch your typing if you reset environment variables. If you initially set ECHO=ON and you tried to reset the value to OFF by typing:

```
SET ECHO =OFF
```

DOS would think you were trying to establish an additional environment variable with a space as the fifth character, and you'd end up with two variables:

```
ECHO=ON
ECHO =OFF
```

The first one would be %ECHO% and the second would be %ECHO %.

However, while extra spaces are always a concern, you don't have to worry about case on the left side of the equals sign when setting a variable. The three commands:

- SET ECHO=OFF
- SET echo=OFF
- SET eChO=OFF

will all set an environment variable ECHO to OFF.

You can put all these tests into a batch file that would look like:

```
ECHO OFF
IF %ECHO%!==! GOTO NOTSET
IF %ECHO%==ON GOTO OKAY
IF %ECHO%==on GOTO OKAY
IF %ECHO%==On GOTO OKAY
IF %ECHO%==OFF GOTO OKAY
IF %ECHO%==off GOTO OKAY
IF %ECHO%==Off GOTO OKAY
ECHO %ECHO% is an invalid ECHO setting
GOTO END
:NOTSET
ECHO Set your ECHO variable
GOTO END
:OKAY
ECHO ECHO is current set to %ECHO%
:END
```

Note: If you insert too many strings into your environment you can run out of environment space. The default is a paltry ten 16-byte paragraphs, or 160 bytes.

Under DOS 2.0 and 2.1 you can patch COMMAND.COM at hex address ECF to represent the number of 16-byte memory paragraphs that will make up your new environment. (For DOS 2.11 the address is hex DF3.)

For DOS 3.0 and 3.1, there's a much better way. Just put a:

```
SHELL [d:][path]COMMAND.COM /E:n /P
```

command in your CONFIG.SYS file, where n represents the number of 16-byte paragraphs. For versions 3.2 and later, use the same SHELL command but specify the actual number of bytes rather than paragraphs. The default in all cases is 160 bytes (ten paragraphs). You can increase it all the way to 32K in DOS 3.2 and 3.3, but you're limited to 62 paragraphs (992 bytes) in earlier versions.

IF

Format:

```
IF EXIST [d:][path]filename[.ext] command
IF NOT EXIST [d:][path]filename[.ext] command

IF string1==string2 command
IF NOT string1==string2 command

IF ERRORLEVEL number command
IF NOT ERRORLEVEL number command
```

IF allows conditional command execution. It is invaluable for finding files, string handling, and other uses including IF ERRORLEVEL, DOS's undocumented gem.

File Finding

One of DOS's most powerful tools, IF allows batch files to execute specific commands or branch to specific batch routines depending on external conditions. This lets you make your batch files smarter and interactive, with the addition of a tiny utility to process user input (which DOS neglected to provide).

The simplest IF command tests whether a file is present. Under DOS 2.x, you couldn't specify a path, so all tests had to be within the current directory. However, DOS 3.x remedied this glaring oversight. The command:

```
IF EXIST HELP.TXT TYPE HELP.TXT
```

will display a HELP.TXT file only if one exists in the current directory. This can come in handy if you want to create a log file and check that the header in the file says what you want.

A section of a batch file like:

```
IF EXIST LOGFILE GOTO FOUNDIT
ECHO This is a new file > LOGFILE
:FOUNDIT
```

will create a new file and put a line of text in it only if no file with the specified name existed previously. Or, if you've kept a blank LOGFILE file in a subdirectory called C:\MISC, you could copy it to the current directory, if none existed, with the command:

```
IF NOT EXIST LOGFILE COPY C:\MISC\LOGFILE
```

Batch files often use DOS filters like MORE.COM, FIND.EXE, and SORT.EXE. It's simple to have a batch file check whether these happen to be in the current directory. But you can also tell it to see whether these files happen to be in a directory that your path knows about. If these executable files are either in the current directory or one specified by your path, a batch file that needs them will be able to do its job. If they're not in either of those places the batch file will stumble. You can test whether a file is in a directory your path can handle with a CHEKPATH.BAT batch file like:

```
ECHO OFF
IF %1!==! GOTO OOPS
FOR %%A IN (%PATH%) DO IF EXIST %%A\%1 GOTO YES
FOR %%A IN (%PATH%) DO IF EXIST %%A%1 GOTO YES
GOTO END
:YES
ECHO %1 is in a directory your PATH knows about
GOTO END
:OOPS
ECHO Enter a file (with extension) to search for
:END
```

DOS replaces the %PATH% in the FOR commands with your actual path, then has each FOR command execute an IF EXIST check in every directory your path specifies. All elements in a set specified by a FOR command have to be separated by normal DOS delimiters. Usually this delimiter is a space, and you end up with a set like:

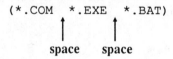

However, a semicolon works just as well as a space, and path directories happened to be separated by semicolons. So DOS translates a (%PATH%) set to something like:

```
(C:\;C:\DOS;C:\DOS\BIN)
```

which is the same as:

```
(C:\ C:\DOS C:\DOS\BIN)
```

You need both versions of the FOR test since your path can include directories that end in a backslash (such as C:\) as well as those that don't (such as C:\DOS). Fortunately, DOS won't choke on the inevitable syntax errors that result from some of the tests. Unfortunately, DOS versions earlier than 3.0 won't do an IF EXIST test outside the current directory. And 3.0 has trouble with environment variables such as %PATH%.

You'd obviously have to adapt this demonstration CHEKPATH.BAT batch file to look for the specific files your particular batch file needs.

If you're writing this for someone else you may want to include a test to make sure that a path does in fact exist. You could do this with a line:

```
IF %PATH%!==! GOTO NOPATH
.
.
.
:NOPATH
ECHO Set up a proper path!
GOTO END
```

The following DIRSORT.BAT batch file will check to make sure that the DOS SORT.EXE utility is either in the current directory or a directory that your path knows about, that you have a path, and that you entered a parameter after the name of the batch file to tell it how to sort. If everything is okay it will then sort your directory by name, size, or extension. If it finds something wrong it will print the appropriate error message:

```
ECHO OFF
IF %1!==! GOTO OOPS1
IF %PATH%!==! GOTO OOPS2
IF EXIST SORT.EXE GOTO YES
FOR %%A IN (%PATH%) DO IF EXIST %%A\SORT.EXE GOTO YES
FOR %%A IN (%PATH%) DO IF EXIST %%ASORT.EXE GOTO YES
ECHO Put SORT.EXE on your disk for this to work
GOTO END
:YES
IF %1==S GOTO SIZE
IF %1==s GOTO SIZE
IF %1==F GOTO FILEN
IF %1==f GOTO FILEN
IF %1==E GOTO EXTEN
IF %1==e GOTO EXTEN
GOTO OOPS1
:SIZE
DIR | SORT /+14
GOTO END
:FILEN
DIR | SORT
```

```
GOTO END
:EXTEN
DIR | SORT /+10
GOTO END
:OOPS1
ECHO Enter %0 S to sort by size, %0 F to sort by
ECHO filename, or %0 E to sort by extension
GOTO END
:OOPS2
ECHO Set up a proper PATH
:END
```

String Handling

You can also use the IF command to compare two sets of character strings. For the comparison to be valid, the strings must be identical in length, content, and case.

One of the most important uses for this type of IF test is in processing replaceable parameters. If you want to protect your hard disk against accidental formatting, you can rename your FORMAT.COM command to something like FMT.COM, and run it out of a batch file called FORMAT.BAT:

```
ECHO OFF
IF %1!==! GOTO OOPS
IF %1==A: GOTO OKAY
IF %1==a: GOTO OKAY
IF %1==B: GOTO OKAY
IF %1==b: GOTO OKAY
ECHO You can't format drive %1 !!
GOTO END
:OKAY
FMT %1
GOTO END
:OOPS
ECHO Enter FORMAT then a drive letter A: or B: only
:END
```

Note that you have to use a double equals sign in a string comparison test.

Since users can enter text in uppercase or lowercase, you need two IF tests (IF %1==A: GOTO OKAY and IF %1==a: GOTO OKAY) to catch both variations of each drive letter.

If the user enters FORMAT B:, DOS will make replaceable parameter %1 equal to B: and then plug this into the IF tests. The test:

```
IF %1==B: GOTO OKAY
```

will become:

```
IF B:==B: GOTO OKAY
```

Since the replaceable parameter string B: is indeed equal to the preset string B:, the batch file will jump to the :OKAY label and run the real FORMAT.COM program — which you've named to FMT.COM — and pass the B: drive letter to it.

FORMAT.BAT will accept only four parameters — A:, a:, B:, and b:. If the user enters anything other than one of these, all four tests will fail and the batch file will eventually reach the error message "ECHO You can't format drive %1 !!". Again, it will replace the %1 with whatever the user entered. If he or she entered FORMAT C:, the batch file will take the C: and replace the %1 with it, producing the message "ECHO You can't format drive C: !!". Then it will exit by jumping to the :END label.

FORMAT.BAT contains an initial IF %1!==! GOTO OOPS test to make sure that the user entered something on the command line after the name of the batch file. If the user didn't enter anything at all after the name of the batch file, the test becomes:

```
IF !==! GOTO OOPS
```

Since ! clearly does equal ! the batch file jumps to a message at the :OOPS label that gives the user instructions. You may use any character on both sides of the double == sign, but make sure it's something unusual such as !, #, or $. So:

```
IF $%1==$ GOTO OOPS
```

is just as valid a test.

DOS offers considerable flexibility in writing batch files like these. For example, you could rephrase the tests to make them negative and nest them all on one line in NEST.BAT if you wanted:

```
ECHO OFF
IF %1!==! GOTO OOPS
IF NOT %1==A: IF NOT %1==a: IF NOT %1==B: IF NOT %1==b:
GOTO NOPE
FMT %1
GOTO END
:NOPE
ECHO You can't format drive %1 !!
GOTO END
:OOPS
ECHO Enter FORMAT then a drive letter A: or B: only
:END
```

Another clever way to allow multiple inputs but screen out invalid keystrokes is to use the FOR command. The FORTEST.BAT batch file will accept A, B, or C, or the lowercase version of each, while rejecting everything else. And it does this all on one line:

```
ECHO OFF
FOR %%A in (A B C a b c) DO IF !%1 == !%%A GOTO OKAY
ECHO No, Enter: %0 A or %0 B or %0 C
ECHO (or the lowercase versions of these).
GOTO END
:OKAY
ECHO Entering %1 is okay
:END
```

It's often necessary to avoid long strings of IF commands, especially on slower systems. EASYAS.BAT tests three conditions in a single line:

```
ECHO OFF
IF NOT %2!==! IF %1==123 IF %2==456 GOTO YES
ECHO Sorry, you entered the numbers wrong
GOTO END
:YES
ECHO Yes, you entered both numbers correctly
:END
```

If you enter just the name of the batch file, the first test, for a missing second parameter (if not %2!==!) will jump execution down to the "Sorry..." line. The same is true if you enter just one number, or any two numbers other than the correct ones, after the name of the batch file. However, if you enter:

```
EASYAS 123 456
```

the file will print the correct "Yes, you entered..." message.

One of the best places to use string tests is in dealing with environment variables. If you have two color-setting routines on your disk, one that uses direct BIOS calls (like the programs on the accompanying disk) and one that uses ANSI.SYS commands, you can have your batch file figure out which color system is active and execute the appropriate setting program.

To do this, make sure you issue a batch file command SET ANSI=OFF (or BIOS=ON) when you configure your system to run without ANSI.SYS. Here it's easier to test for the absence rather than the presence of ANSI.SYS, since you load ANSI through your CONFIG.SYS file and not through a batch file. If you happened to have a batch file that loaded ANSI, it could set ANSI=ON at the same time.

Some users have complex batch file schemes to rename various versions of their CONFIG.SYS and AUTOEXEC.BAT files and then reboot, in an effort to load ANSI or start their systems without it, and it's possible to have the batch file that triggers the whole process create a file called YESANSI when it does this. Then you could use an IF EXIST YESANSI command to detect whether ANSI is loaded. If you did try this, you'd have to make sure you erased YESANSI when you weren't starting your system with ANSI active. A lot of bother.

Once your AUTOEXEC.BAT file executed a line like:

```
SET ANSI=OFF
```

or:

```
SET BIOS=ON  .
```

or:

```
SET ANSI=ON
```

later batch files could include a line like IF ANSI==ON GOTO ANSISET or IF BIOS==ON GOTO BIOSSET. If ANSI was loaded, you could then jump to the ANSI color setter rather than the BIOS color setter. When you weren't using ANSI, the test would look at the environment and see that ANSI was not equal to ON, and branch to the BIOS setter rather than the ANSI one.

Being able to phrase tests using negative conditions adds flexibility. The ANSITEST.BAT batch file could be written:

```
ECHO OFF
IF NOT !%ANSI%==!ON GOTO BIOSSET
:ANSISET
ECHO ANSI color setter goes here
GOTO END
:BIOSSET
ECHO BIOS color setter goes here
:END
```

The exclamation points are needed to prevent a syntax error if no ANSI variable exists in the environment. Without something there (you could use any two other identical symbols such as IF NOT @%ANSI%==@ON) you would end up with a line that translated to

```
IF NOT ==ON
```

which would trigger a syntax error.

Case Insensitivity

DOS is flexible about combinations of uppercase and lowercase text when it processes labels, but it's rigid and inflexible when comparing strings.

This means that if you want to test all the possible ways to enter something as short as a three-letter word you'd have to make eight tests (2^ number of letters). And longer words mean dramatically longer tests.

To speed things up, you can use the COMPARE.COM utility on the accompanying disk. COMPARE.COM compares two strings and ignores the case of the alphabetic characters. On return, it sets ERRORLEVEL 255 if both strings are equal and ERROR-LEVEL 0 if they are not equal or if a syntax error has occurred. After executing COM-PARE.COM, your batch file may take appropriate action with the statement:

```
IF ERRORLEVEL 255 action
```

You can try this out by creating a sample batch file called COMPTEST.BAT:

```
ECHO OFF
IF %2!==! GOTO OOPS
COMPARE %1==%2
IF ERRORLEVEL 255 GOTO MATCH
ECHO The strings are not equal
GOTO END
:MATCH
ECHO The strings are equal
GOTO END
:OOPS
ECHO The format required is:
ECHO COMPTEST STRING1 STRING2
:END
```

Then, at the DOS prompt, type:

```
COMPTEST hello HELLO
```

and it will respond with the message:

```
The strings are equal.
```

But type something like "COMPTEST hello HELLOE" and the batch file will let you know the strings don't match.

IF ERRORLEVEL

One of the single most powerful DOS batch file tools is also one of the most poorly documented — IF ERRORLEVEL.

ERRORLEVEL makes your batch files truly interactive, and lets you create slick, friendly, foolproof menus that can run your whole system — or help a beginner through a complex task.

Before users knew about IF ERRORLEVEL techniques, they'd slap together primitive menu systems that involved lots of little batch files. The main batch file would do nothing other than use the DOS TYPE command to display the contents of a text file like:

```
─────────────── Menu ───────────────

            1 - Spreadsheet
            2 - Wordprocessor
            3 - Database

    Pick a number (1-3) then press Enter
```

Then they'd write short batch files called 1.BAT, 2.BAT, and 3.BAT. Each would contain just the name of the software they wanted to load, and perhaps a CD\ command to jump into the proper subdirectory.

While this worked, it had many drawbacks. After the batch file used TYPE to display the menu, it dropped back to DOS. The user saw a DOS prompt, and wasn't sure whether to type in a number or enter a command. You could get around this by using the PROMPT command to change the DOS prompt itself from C> or A> to:

```
Type a number from 1 to 3 then press Enter ==>
```

But when you were done running a particular program, the prompt would still ask you to pick a number. Then again, you could have the individual 1.BAT, 2.BAT, 3.BAT batch files reset the prompt back to normal, but you might want to make another menu selection.

Worse, if the user entered the wrong kind of response, the menu would scroll up off the screen. In addition, the user had to press the Enter key after typing in the proper response, and some couldn't figure that out. And when the user was finished running the program he or she had chosen, the menu had long since vanished, leaving a bare screen. Again, the individual batch files could redisplay the menu when they finished, but that might be confusing to users who wanted to do something other than what was listed.

Finally, dozens of little menu batch files, each with its own array of program-loading files, can waste a tremendous amount of space, especially on a system like an XT with its greedy 4K clusters.

ERRORLEVEL avoids every one of these problems, and lets you create menus that are smart, easy, and compact.

An ideal menu system would display the options and wait for the user to enter a (preferably) single-digit choice, then execute that choice, without forcing him or her to hit the Enter key.

It would be single-minded, preventing the user from stumbling into some other command. This defect alone makes the primitive 1.BAT, 2.BAT system worthless, since it returns to the DOS command line after displaying its choices. If the user enters a command like DIR, DOS will scroll the menu choices off the screen.

And it would retain control by looping back to the beginning every time a program finished running. One of the menu options would be to exit gracefully, and the menu system would restore the screen back to normal.

IF ERRORLEVEL is one of the worst-named and most powerful of all DOS commands. According to IBM, all it really does is let your batch files know whether DOS successfully completed commands such as BACKUP, KEYB, REPLACE, RESTORE, or FORMAT. These programs set *exit codes* (also called *return codes*) depending on whether the programs were able to work completely or partially. And they can tell if the user or some system error interrupted the program in midstream.

The IF ERRORLEVEL command can read these exit codes and act accordingly. So you could create a batch file to execute BACKUP or FORMAT and have provisions in the batch file to print customized messages onscreen if something goes wrong. IBM spends a lot of space in its manuals on this, and nobody uses it.

On the other hand, IBM doesn't talk at all about how to send user input into batch files, which is something that DOS desperately needs. And DOS doesn't provide any direct utilities for putting IF ERRORLEVEL to work this way.

But it's simple to harness IF ERRORLEVEL and make your batch files truly interactive. All you need is a version of a short assembly language program that reads keystrokes and translates them into exit codes that IF ERRORLEVEL can process. Then you just include the name of the program in your batch file and follow it with tests for the appropriate exit codes. These tests can jump to different labels inside the batch file, or they can execute programs or commands directly if the codes match.

The basic test is in the format:

```
IF ERRORLEVEL number action
```

or:

```
IF NOT ERRORLEVEL number action
```

where number is the decimal value of the exit code, and action is the command to execute.

Note: The tricky part of this is that IF ERRORLEVEL will execute the action if the exit code is equal to — or greater than — the number after the word ERRORLEVEL.

DOS allows 256 possible exit codes from 0 to 255, so the command:

```
IF ERRORLEVEL 0 ECHO True
```

will always work, since all 256 possible exit codes are equal to or greater than 0. So this test will always print the message "True." You don't even need a batch file to test this. Just type it in at the DOS prompt.

At the other end of the spectrum:

```
IF ERRORLEVEL 255 ECHO True
```

will work in only one case — when the exit code happens to be 255.

If you want to isolate a character like a space (which has an ASCII value of decimal 32), you have to first screen out any higher exit codes:

```
IF ERRORLEVEL 33 ECHO Nonspace
IF ERRORLEVEL 32 ECHO Space
```

You can combine such tests into one long line:

```
IF ERRORLEVEL 32 IF NOT ERRORLEVEL 33 ECHO Space
```

The most primitive example of a keystroke processing program is GETKEY.COM, which you can create by making sure DEBUG.COM is handy and then typing these seven lines:

```
DEBUG
E 100 B4 00 CD 16 B4 4C CD 21
N GETKEY.COM
RCX
8
W
Q
```

Here's the assembly language program that this creates:

```
MOV AH,00    ; BIOS read a character and
INT 16       ; puts its ASCII code into AL
MOV AH,4C    ; ready to exit with code
INT 21       ; do it
```

(Both DOS and your system's BIOS can process keystrokes for you. This particular example uses BIOS, but you could just as easily have substituted a DOS function call. In fact, DOS is better for certain applications because it offers several options. It can display the character you entered, or discard it. It can wait for a keystroke — which you usually want to do in menu systems — or process one only if it's there waiting. And it can handle attempts to break out of the operation, or ignore them.)

Then create a batch file called ERRTEST.BAT:

```
ECHO OFF
:TOP
ECHO You may break out of this loop
ECHO by pressing Enter. Or press
ECHO any other key to continue . . .
GETKEY
IF ERRORLEVEL 13 IF NOT ERRORLEVEL 14 GOTO END
GOTO TOP
:END
```

This batch file simply tests to see whether the user pressed the Enter key, which has an ASCII value of decimal 13.

When ERRTEST executes, it will print the three-line message and then run GET-KEY.COM. GETKEY.COM waits for the user to press a single alphanumeric key, and sets the return code to the ASCII value of that key. The single line:

```
IF ERRORLEVEL 13 IF NOT ERRORLEVEL 14 GOTO END
```

in the batch file tests whether the return code was 13, and at the same time screens out any higher values. You could just as easily change the batch file to:

```
ECHO OFF
:TOP
ECHO You may break out of this loop
ECHO by pressing Enter. Or press
ECHO any other key to continue . . .
GETKEY
IF ERRORLEVEL 14 GOTO TOP
IF ERRORLEVEL 13 GOTO END
GOTO TOP
:END
```

The following CASETEST.BAT batch file uses GETKEY.COM to fetch keystrokes and pass the ASCII value for each one to a "cascade" of IF ERRORLEVEL tests:

```
ECHO OFF
:ERR
ECHO Enter a lowercase or
ECHO an uppercase letter
ECHO (Or spacebar to quit)
:TOP
```

```
GETKEY
IF ERRORLEVEL 123 GOTO ERR
IF ERRORLEVEL 97 GOTO LOWER
IF ERRORLEVEL 91 GOTO ERR
IF ERRORLEVEL 65 GOTO UPPER
IF ERRORLEVEL 33 GOTO ERR
IF ERRORLEVEL 32 GOTO END
IF ERRORLEVEL 0 GOTO ERR
:LOWER
ECHO Lowercase
GOTO TOP
:UPPER
ECHO Uppercase
GOTO TOP
:END
```

All lowercase letters have decimal ASCII values from 97 through 122. All uppercase letters have decimal ASCII values from 65 through 90. The chart below shows all the IF ERRORLEVEL ASCII Characters.

Characters	255-224:	math, Greek letters, symbols
Characters	223-219:	blocks
Characters	218-179:	box and border elements
Characters	178-176:	shaded blocks
Characters	175-169:	miscellaneous symbols
Characters	168-155:	miscellaneous currency signs and symbols
Characters	154-128:	various diacritical marks and symbols
Characters	127-123:	miscellaneous exotic punctuation
Characters	122-97:	lowercase alphabet (z=122; a=97)
Characters	96-91:	more miscellaneous exotic punctuation
Characters	90-65:	uppercase alphabet (Z=90; A=65)
Characters	64-58:	punctuation
Characters	57-48:	digits (9=57; 0=48)
Characters	47-33:	punctuation and symbols
Character	32:	space
Character	27:	escape
Character	26:	end-of-file marker (^Z)
Character	13:	enter (^M)
Character	10:	line feed (^J)
Character	9:	tab (^I)
Character	8:	backspace (^H)
Character	7:	beep (^G)
Character	0:	null

CASETEST.BAT first uses a test for 123 to screen out anything higher than the top range of lowercase values. The second test will detect anything from 97 through 122 and jump to the label that identifies this as a lowercase letter. The next test screens out the few odd characters with values from 91 through 96. It's followed by a test that detects anything from 65 through 90 and jumps to a label identifying these as uppercase letters.

Finally, a test for 33 screens out any key with a value greater than a space (remember, a space is 32) but lower than the bottom range of uppercase letters. Then a test for 32 isolates spaces, and a last test for 0 traps any other keystrokes.

Most single keys on your keyboard generate single ASCII codes. But key combinations like Ctrl-End, Ins, or F7 generate two-character values called extended codes, where the first value is always a 0. Key-sniffing programs more sophisticated than GETKEY.COM can detect these; GETKEY thinks all such keys are returning codes of 0. Later you'll see how you can soup up GETKEY to handle such keys.

More sophisticated key-processing programs, like the ones on the accompanying disk, let you print customized onscreen prompts telling the user which of several keys to press. If the program doesn't do this, you have to have an ECHO command display a message prompting the user.

The following PROGMAKR.BAT batch file will actually create a version of GET-KEY.COM that displays its own customized message:

```
ECHO OFF
REM PROGMAKR.BAT
IF %2!==! GOTO ERROR
CTTY NUL
ECHO E 100 B4 09 BA 0F 01 CD 21        > DBG.ZZZ
ECHO E 107 B4 00 CD 16 B4 4C CD 21    >> DBG.ZZZ
ECHO E 10F '%2 %3 %4 %5 %6 %7 %8 %9$' >> DBG.ZZZ
ECHO N %1.COM                         >> DBG.ZZZ
ECHO RCX                              >> DBG.ZZZ
ECHO 100                             >> DBG.ZZZ
ECHO W                                >> DBG.ZZZ
ECHO Q                                >> DBG.ZZZ
DEBUG < DBG.ZZZ
DEL DBG.ZZZ
GOTO END
:ERROR
ECHO The correct syntax is:
ECHO %0 PROGNAME WORD1 [WORD2] . . . [WORD8]
ECHO Where: PROGNAME is the name of the .COM file and
ECHO WORD1 to WORD8 are words the program will print.
ECHO eg: %0 BATCHKEY Enter a number from 1 to 5:
ECHO Notes: 1) DON'T use single quotes (') or dollar signs.
ECHO 2) DON'T put a .COM extension on PROGNAME!
ECHO (%0 will do it for you automatically.)
:END
```

```
CTTY CON
IF NOT %1!==! ECHO Now type %1
```

To use PROGMAKR.BAT, you need to have DEBUG.COM in the current directory or in one your path knows about. It lets you enter a program name (such as GETKEY or BATCHKEY) and then a prompt of up to eight words after it. So if you entered:

```
PROGMAKR BATCHKEY Enter a number from 1 to 5:
```

it will automatically create a small file called BATCHKEY.COM that displays the prompt:

```
Enter a number from 1 to 5:
```

and waits for a key. When you press any normal (nonextended) key, BATCHKEY will turn its ASCII value into an exit code that IF ERRORLEVEL can process.

This is a very powerful little batch file. But if you use it, note:

1. Be sure you have DEBUG.COM handy.
2. It uses a CTTY NUL command to shut off the display temporarily while it's working. If something unexpected happens before the batch file gets to the restorative CTTY CON command at the end, you'll be frozen out of your keyboard. Check your typing carefully and make sure you don't have any unsaved files lurking around when you try this for the first time.
3. You can enter up to eight discrete words or clumps of characters, but don't enter any single quotes or dollar signs, since DOS treats these specially.
4. Type in everything exactly as it appears, and watch for small but important characters like the single quote marks in the ECHO E 10F '%2 %3 %4 %5 %6 %7 %8 %9$' line.
5. Remember that directly below the CTTY NUL the first ECHO line ends with a single > DBG.ZZZ while the others have double >> DBG.ZZZ signs. A single > sign creates a file and a double >> sign appends data to an existing file.
6. Remember to type in the name of the program you want to create before you start entering the message. And be sure to leave off the .COM extension; the batch file will add it for you automatically.

PROGMAKR.BAT will create a file that looks (at least for the sample prompt above) like:

```
MOV AH,09        ; DOS message printer
MOV DX,010F      ; address of the message
INT 21           ; print it
MOV AH,00        ; BIOS read a character and
INT 16           ; puts its ASCII code into AL
```

```
MOV AH,4C      ; ready to exit with code
INT 21         ; do it
DB 'Enter a number from 1 to 5: $'
```

Narrowing the Search

In any IF ERRORLEVEL process something has to screen out erroneous keystrokes. You can have the batch file do it by including a series of IF ERRORLEVEL tests. Or you can have the assembly language program do it, either by refusing to budge unless the user presses certain keys, or by setting one kind of exit code for correct responses and another kind for incorrect keypresses. You can adapt GETKEY.COM to do either.

This version will set a code of 13 if the user presses Enter, and a code of 0 otherwise:

```
DEBUG
E 100 B4 00 CD 16 3C 0D 74 02 30 C0 B4 4C CD 21
N GETKEY2.COM
RCX
E
W
Q
```

You can run this with a shorter version of ERRTEST.BAT called ERRTEST2.BAT:

```
ECHO OFF
:TOP
ECHO You may break out of this loop
ECHO by pressing Enter. Or press
ECHO any other key to continue . . .
GETKEY2
IF ERRORLEVEL 13 GOTO END
GOTO TOP
:END
```

Here you don't need to test for any exit code other than 13, since GETKEY2.COM does all the keystroke screening by making sure that the exit code for every key other than Enter is 0. The assembly language program for this looks like:

```
MOV AH,00      ; BIOS read a character
INT 16         ; puts ASCII code into AL
CMP AL,0D      ; is character an Enter?
JZ 010A        ; yes; skip next step
XOR AL,AL      ; make the exit code a 0
```

```
MOV AH,4C      ; ready to exit with code
INT 21         ; do it
```

The exit code that the program sets doesn't have to be the same as the ASCII code of the key that the user pressed. GETKEY3.COM sets a code of 255 if the user pressed Enter. Create it by typing:

```
DEBUG
E 100 B4 00 CD 16 3C 0D 75 02 B0 FF B4 4C CD 21
N GETKEY3.COM
RCX
E
W
Q
```

This is almost identical to GETKEY2.COM:

```
MOV AH,00      ; BIOS read a character
INT 16         ; puts ASCII code into AL
CMP AL,0D      ; is character an Enter?
JNZ 010A       ; no; skip next step
MOV AL,FF      ; make the exit code a 255
MOV AH,4C      ; ready to exit with code
INT 21         ; do it
```

The ERRTEST3.BAT batch file to use this program might look like:

```
ECHO OFF
:TOP
ECHO You may break out of this loop
ECHO by pressing Enter. Or press
ECHO any other key to continue . . .
GETKEY3
IF ERRORLEVEL 255 GOTO END
GOTO TOP
:END
```

or even simpler:

```
ECHO OFF
:TOP
ECHO You may break out of this loop
```

```
ECHO by pressing Enter. Or press
ECHO any other key to continue . . .
GETKEY3
IF NOT ERRORLEVEL 255 GOTO TOP
```

GETKEY3.COM sets the exit code to 255 if the user presses the Enter key. It leaves all other values intact, so that if the user happened to press the space bar, which has an ASCII value of 32, the exit code would be 32. But testing for an ERRORLEVEL of 255 heads all other lower exit codes off at the pass.

The only problem with this is that if the user happened to enter character 255 (by holding down the Alt key, typing 255 on the number pad, and then releasing the Alt key), ERRTEST3.BAT would treat it as if the user had pressed the Enter key. Both would end up with an exit code of 255. Screening this out would be trivial, but seriously, how many users are going to enter character 255?

You could have the assembly language program do even more work by rejecting any keystrokes other than the ones your batch file is designed to handle. GETKEY4.COM will sit and wait for the user to press a key, and will discard all keypresses other than Enter (with a code of decimal 13, or hex 0D) and Escape (with an exit code of decimal 27, or hex 1B):

```
DEBUG
E 100 B4 00 CD 16 3C 0D 74 04 3C 1B 75 F4 B4 4C CD 21
N GETKEY4.COM
RCX
10
W
Q
```

If you ran the ERRTEST4.BAT batch file:

```
ECHO OFF
:TOP
ECHO Press Esc to loop again
ECHO or Enter to quit . . .
GETKEY4
IF ERRORLEVEL 27 GOTO TOP
```

pressing Esc would loop through the batch file and repeat the message, pressing Enter would quit, and pressing any other key would do nothing. GETKEY4.COM looks like:

```
MOV AH,00      ; BIOS read a character
INT 16         ; puts ASCII code into AL
```

```
CMP AL,0D      ; is character an Enter?
JZ 10C         ; yes; goto exit code
CMP AL,1B      ; is character an Esc?
JNZ 100        ; no; go back and get another
MOV AH,4C      ; exit code
INT 21         ; do it
```

These tiny exit-code setters can really enhance the operation of your system. Earlier a program called FORMAT.COM used string tests to screen out attempts to format any drive higher than B:. You could adapt a batch file like that to use a small drive-sensing program called DRIVE.COM together with a few IF ERRORLEVEL tests to exit automatically if it found that you were on drive C: or D:. To create DRIVE.COM, just type:

```
DEBUG
E 100 B4 19 CD 21 B4 4C CD 21
N DRIVE.COM
RCX
8
W
Q
```

DRIVE.COM is somewhat similar to GETKEY.COM:

```
MOV AH,19      ; get current drive
INT 21         ; do it (A=0, B=1, etc)
MOV AH,4C      ; put drive in exit code
INT 21         ; do it
```

A DRIVER.BAT batch file to show how this worked might look like:

```
ECHO OFF
DRIVE
IF ERRORLEVEL 0 IF NOT ERRORLEVEL 1 ECHO Drive A
IF ERRORLEVEL 1 IF NOT ERRORLEVEL 2 ECHO Drive B
IF ERRORLEVEL 2 IF NOT ERRORLEVEL 3 ECHO Drive C
IF ERRORLEVEL 3 IF NOT ERRORLEVEL 4 ECHO Drive D
IF ERRORLEVEL 4 ECHO Higher than Drive D
```

You could add a DRIVE command at the beginning of your FORMAT batch file, and if the following IF ERRORLEVEL test detected a value of 2 or more, just have it GOTO END.

The easiest way to create IF ERRORLEVEL-based menus is probably to limit yourself to ten choices — the digits 0 through 9. Or you could use letters rather than numbers, since letters offer 26 single-digit choices rather than ten. But you'd have to test for both uppercase and lowercase entries, and all the ASCII characters in between, which means lots of IF tests or a clever assembly language program to do all the work.

You could expand the GETKEY.COM program slightly to handle function keys, which don't have uppercase and lowercase versions. Or, you could limit all your ERRORLEVEL decisions to Yes/No questions. This second method works very well in some cases, but not in menus.

Typing in the following few lines will create a GETFKEY.COM program designed to work with extended key combinations:

```
DEBUG
E 100 B4 00 CD 16 3C 00 74 04 B0
E 109 FF EB 02 88 E0 B4 4C CD 21
N GETFKEY.COM
RCX
12
W
Q
```

The GETFKEY program looks like:

```
MOV AH,00      ; BIOS read a character
INT 16         ; puts ASCII code into AL
CMP AL,00      ; is character extended?
JZ 010C        ; yes; go to register mover
MOV AL,FF      ; no; so make exit code 255
JMP 010E       ; and skip next step
MOV AL,AH      ; make extended code the exit code
MOV AH,4C      ; exit with code
INT 21         ; do it
```

It works just like GETKEY.COM, except that it can handle function keys and shifted key combinations as well as normal alphanumeric keys. When you press an alphanumeric key, BIOS puts the ASCII value of the key in the AL register and the scan code in the AH register. When you trigger an extended key combination, BIOS puts the ASCII code in the AH register and a NUL, or character 0, in the AL register.

GETFKEY.COM waits until the user presses a key, then checks to see if the AL register is set to 0. If not, GETFKEY assumes the key was a normal garden-variety letter or number, makes the exit code 255, and quits. If it does see a 0 in AL it moves the ASCII code down from AH to AL and makes it the exit code. At this point any normal key has an exit code of 255; anything less means the user pressed an extended key combination.

On IBM's old reliable keyboards you actually have a lot of possible extended keys from which to choose (the newer IBM Chinese typesetting version offers even more):

	Function Keys				*Keypad Keys*		
						Unshifted	Ctrl
F1...F10	unshifted	=	59...68				
F1...F10	+ Shift	=	84...93	Home	71	119	
F1...F10	+ Ctrl	=	94...103	Up	72	-	
F1...F10	+ Alt	=	104...113	PgUp	73	132	
				Left	75	115	
				Right	77	116	
	Alt + Regular Key			End	79	117	
QWERTYUIOP		16...25		Down	80	-	
ASDFGHJKL		30...38		PgDn	81	118	
ZXCVBNM		44...50		Ins	82	-	
1234567890-=		120...131		Del	83	-	

A typical batch EXTENKEY.BAT file that used extended keys would look something like this:

```
ECHO OFF
:START
ECHO INS - See a sorted DIR
ECHO DEL - Return to DOS
ECHO *** Hit Ins or Del ***
GETFKEY
IF ERRORLEVEL 84 GOTO START
IF ERRORLEVEL 83 GOTO 2
IF ERRORLEVEL 82 GOTO 1
GOTO START
:1
DIR | SORT
PAUSE
GOTO START
:2
```

This uses the Ins (82) and Del (83) keys, and rejects anything else.

While the previous examples demonstrate how ERRORLEVEL can manage menus, IF ERRORLEVEL can also come in handy when a batch file gives a user a two-way choice — continue or not, load a program or not, echo something to the printer or not, and so on.

In all these cases, the batch file pauses and asks a Yes or No question, and then proceeds with the option only if the user answers with Y or y.

The GETYES.COM program below checks for Y or y and puts an ASCII 255 value into the AL register if it finds one. Batch files that use this technique can get away with just a single IF ERRORLEVEL test — for a value of 255 only.

You can create GETYES.COM by typing:

```
DEBUG
E 100 B4 00 CD 16 3C 59 74 04 3C
E 109 79 75 02 B0 FF B4 4C CD 21
RCX
12
N GETYES.COM
W
Q
```

The program it creates looks like:

```
MOV AH,00      ; BIOS read a character
INT 16         ; puts ASCII code into AL
CMP AL,59      ; is character a 'Y' ?
JZ 010C        ; yes; go to 255 stuffer
CMP AL,79      ; is character a 'y' ?
JNZ 010E       ; if not, skip next step
MOV AL,FF      ; make exit code 255
MOV AH,4C      ; exit with code
INT 21         ; do it
```

You can see this in action by running the following YESNO.BAT batch file:

```
ECHO OFF
:TOP
ECHO Hit y or Y or another key:
GETYES
IF ERRORLEVEL 255 GOTO YES
GOTO NO
:YES
ECHO You said yes.
GOTO CONTINUE
:NO
ECHO You didn't hit y or Y.
:CONTINUE
ECHO Now, want to quit (Y/N)?
GETYES
IF ERRORLEVEL 255 GOTO END
GOTO TOP
:END
```

GETYES.COM checks for Y (hex 59) and y (hex 79). You could substitute 4E (the hex code for N) and 6E (the hex code for n) for 59 and 79 and create GETNO.COM.

Just use DEBUG to patch GETYES.COM and make a new copy of it called GETNO.COM:

```
DEBUG GETYES.COM
E 105 4E
E 109 6E
N GETNO.COM
W
Q
```

Then adapt the above batch file and turn it into NOYES.BAT:

```
ECHO OFF
:TOP
ECHO Hit n or N or another key:
GETNO
IF ERRORLEVEL 255 GOTO NO
GOTO YES
:NO
ECHO You said no.
GOTO CONTINUE
:YES
ECHO You didn't hit n or N.
:CONTINUE
ECHO Now, want to quit (Y/N)?
GETNO
IF ERRORLEVEL 255 GOTO TOP
:END
```

GETYES.COM and GETNO.COM behave quite differently, as you can see from experimenting with the YESNO.BAT and NOYES.BAT batch files. These batch files are designed to do one task if the user presses one specific letter, and another task if he or she presses any other key. If you're asking whether a user is sure he or she wants to FORMAT a hard disk, you'd better be sure you accept only a Y or y answer. Having programs handy that operate only on Y (or y) and only on N (or n) gives you flexibility in phrasing such potentially dangerous questions.

It's simple to turn a handful of IF ERRORLEVEL tests into a menu system. If you want to write your own keyboard processor, one of the easiest ways is to use numeric entries, since you don't have to worry about uppercase and lowercase variations. Of course you're limited to ten entries.

A very simple MENU1.BAT menu system might look like:

```
ECHO OFF
:TOP
```

```
ECHO +----------------------+
ECHO |  1 - Run 123         |
ECHO |  2 - Run WordStar    |
ECHO |  3 - Return to DOS   |
ECHO +----------------------+
:MENU
ECHO Select 1, 2 or 3
GETNUM
IF ERRORLEVEL 52 GOTO MENU
IF ERRORLEVEL 51 GOTO END
IF ERRORLEVEL 50 GOTO STAR
IF ERRORLEVEL 49 GOTO LOTUS
GOTO MENU
:LOTUS
123
GOTO TOP
:STAR
WS
GOTO TOP
:END
```

You could just run a program like GETKEY.BAT that returns an exit code for any key on the keyboard. But it's not much more difficult to create a small program called GET-NUM.COM that rejects all keystrokes other than 0 through 9:

```
DEBUG
E 100 B4 00 CD 16 3C 30 72 F8 3C 39 77 F4 B4 4C CD 21
N GETNUM.COM
RCX
10
W
Q
```

This program looks like:

```
MOV AH,00      ; BIOS read a character
INT 16         ; puts ASCII code into AL
CMP AL,30      ; is character < 0 ?
JB 100         ; yes; get another key
CMP AL,39      ; is character > 9 ?
JA 100         ; yes; get another key
MOV AH,4C      ; exit code
INT 21         ; do it
```

While IF ERRORLEVEL works exclusively in decimal notation, DEBUG handles only hex. The ASCII value for character 0 is 30, and for 9 is 39.

Digit	Decimal	Hex
0	48	30
1	49	31
2	50	32
3	51	33
4	52	34
5	53	35
6	54	36
7	55	37
8	56	38
9	57	39

If you press any number key between 0 and 9, GETNUM.COM transfers its ASCII value to the exit code. If you press any other key GETNUM simply rejects it and goes back for another.

The MENU1.BAT program accepts only the choices 1, 2, or 3. The topmost:

```
IF ERRORLEVEL 52 GOTO MENU
```

bounces any exit code of 52 or higher, screening out any digit from 4 through 9.

You could narrow the test by going into DEBUG and changing the:

```
CMP AL,30    ; is character < 0 ?
```

and:

```
CMP AL,39    ; is character > 9 ?
```

lines so they were more restrictive, but it's really not necessary.

Many users prefer working with letters rather than numbers.

But if you want to create a menu with options A, B, and C you have to worry about uppercase and lowercase entries.

Actually this isn't much of a problem. All you have to do is perform a logical OR operation on the key, which turns uppercase letters into lowercase ones and leaves lowercase ones alone.

The lowercase letters have ASCII values 20 hex (32 decimal) higher than their uppercase counterparts:

Letter	Dec	Hex	Letter	Dec	Hex
A	65	41	a	97	61
B	66	42	b	98	62
C	67	43	c	99	63
D	68	44	d	100	64
E	69	45	e	101	65
F	70	46	f	102	66
G	71	47	g	103	67
H	72	48	h	104	68
I	73	49	i	105	69
J	74	4A	j	106	6A
K	75	4B	k	107	6B
L	76	4C	l	108	6C
M	77	4D	m	109	6D
N	78	4E	n	110	6E
O	79	4F	o	111	6F
P	80	50	p	112	70
Q	81	51	q	113	71
R	82	52	r	114	72
S	83	53	s	115	73
T	84	54	t	116	74
U	85	55	u	117	75
V	86	56	v	118	76
W	87	57	w	119	77
X	88	58	x	120	78
Y	89	59	y	121	79
Z	90	5A	z	122	7A

So to make all letters lowercase, just add the line:

```
OR AL,20
```

to the GETKEY.COM program:

```
MOV AH,0
INT 16
OR AL,20
MOV AH,4C
INT 21
```

You could create the small LOWERIT.COM program by typing:

```
DEBUG
E 100 B4 00 CD 16 0C 20 B4 4C CD 21
N LOWERIT.COM
RCX
A
W
Q
```

Then run the following sample HALFTEST.BAT demonstration batch file:

```
ECHO OFF
ECHO Press any letter key
ECHO Or press spacebar to quit
:TOP
LOWERIT
IF ERRORLEVEL 123 GOTO TOP
IF ERRORLEVEL 110 GOTO BACK
IF ERRORLEVEL 97 GOTO FRONT
IF ERRORLEVEL 33 GOTO TOP
IF ERRORLEVEL 32 GOTO END
:BACK
ECHO N-Z
GOTO TOP
:FRONT
ECHO A-M
GOTO TOP
:END
```

Type in any uppercase or lowercase letter and the batch file will tell you which half of the alphabet it's in.

You could, of course, go the other way and make all letters uppercase. Instead of the line:

```
OR AL,20
```

substitute:

```
AND AL,DF
```

Create UPPERIT.COM by typing:

```
DEBUG
E 100 B4 00 CD 16 24 DF B4 4C CD 21
```

```
N UPPERIT.COM
RCX
A
W
Q
```

The program looks like:

```
MOV AH,0      ; BIOS read a character and
INT 16        ; puts its ASCII code into AL
AND AL,DF     ; uppercase all letters
MOV AH,4C     ; ready to exit with code
INT 21        ; do it
```

And you'll have to change the HALFTEST.BAT demonstration batch file slightly:

```
ECHO OFF
ECHO Press any letter key
ECHO Or press Enter to quit
:TOP
UPPERIT
IF ERRORLEVEL 91 GOTO TOP
IF ERRORLEVEL 78 GOTO BACK
IF ERRORLEVEL 65 GOTO FRONT
IF ERRORLEVEL 14 GOTO TOP
IF ERRORLEVEL 13 GOTO END
:BACK
ECHO N-Z
GOTO TOP
:FRONT
ECHO A-M
GOTO TOP
:END
```

ANDing any ASCII value with 223 (hex DF) will capitalize lowercase letters and leave uppercase letters alone. The logical AND operation works by comparing two values (the example below will compare one bit at a time) and returning a "1" only when both values are nonzero.

- 1 AND 1 = 1
- 1 AND 0 = 0
- 0 AND 1 = 0
- 0 AND 0 = 0

223 equals binary 11011111. Capital A (decimal 65) is binary 01000001, while lower-case a (decimal 97) is binary 01100001. The AND operation on these numbers could be represented as

$$
\begin{array}{ll}
 & 01000001\ (65) \\
\text{AND} & \underline{11011111}\ (223) \\
 & 01000001\ (65)
\end{array}
$$

$$
\begin{array}{ll}
 & 01100001\ (97) \\
\text{AND} & \underline{11011111}\ (223) \\
 & 01000001\ (65)
\end{array}
$$

ANDing either a 0 or a 1 with 1 in effect leaves the value alone, and ANDing both a 0 and a 1 with 0 in effect turns the value into a 0. The binary number 11011111 forces the 2^5 bit — the sixth one from the right — to become a 0 and leaves all the other bits the way they were. (The rightmost bit is 2^0; the leftmost is 2^7.)

The only difference between a lowercase letter and its capital counterpart is that the 2^5 bit is set (equals 1) in the lowercase version. ANDing it with 11011111 unsets the bit, changing it to a 0 and lowering the ASCII value by 32.

To reverse the process and turn capital letters into lowercase ones, use the logical OR operation to OR a value with 32:

- 1 OR 1 = 1
- 1 OR 0 = 1
- 0 OR 1 = 1
- 0 OR 0 = 0

32 equals binary 00100000. Since ORing either a 1 or a 0 with 0 in effect leaves the value alone, and ORing either a 1 or a 0 with 1 in effect turns the value into a 1, the binary number 00100000 forces the 2^5 bit to become a 1 and leaves all the other bits the way they were.

This sets the unset 2^5 bit in an uppercase letter, changing it to a 1 and raising the ASCII value by 32.

$$
\begin{array}{ll}
 & 01000001\ (65) \\
\text{OR} & \underline{00100000}\ (32) \\
 & 01100001\ (97)
\end{array}
$$

$$
\begin{array}{ll}
 & 01100001\ (97) \\
\text{OR} & \underline{00100000}\ (32) \\
 & 01100001\ (97)
\end{array}
$$

One problem with blanket logical operations like the OR AL,20 and the AND AL,DF is that they switch uppercase to lowercase and vice versa, but end up changing the values of many of the nonletter keys as well.

The solution is to test each letter to make sure it's in the right range before performing the logical operation on it. GETLETR.COM does just that:

```
MOV AH,08      ; get a keystroke
INT 21         ; do it
CMP AL,1B      ; is it escape?
JE 11E         ; bye
CMP AL,7A      ; higher than 'z' ?
JA 0102        ; get another one
CMP AL,60      ; lower than 'a' ?
JBE 0114       ; then try next test
AND AL,DF      ; otherwise uppercase it
JMP 011C       ; and jump to subtract
CMP AL,5A      ; higher than 'Z' ?
JA 0102        ; get another one
CMP AL,41      ; lower than 'A' ?
JB 0102        ; get another one
AND AL,3F      ; subtract 64
MOV AH,4C      ; exit with code
INT 21         ; do it
```

GETLETR.COM is on the accompanying disk. But you could create it easily by adding an:

```
A
```

on a line by itself at the very beginning, a blank line, and then the following five lines:

```
RCX
22
N GETLETR.COM
W
Q
```

at the end (don't forget the blank line above RCX).

This won't accept nonletter entries, and is case insensitive. It will generate a code of 1 for A, 2 for B, and 26 for Z. It will also generate a 27 for Esc, which lets you use Esc as an exit.

It takes advantage of a DOS keyboard-reading routine rather than the BIOS interrupt 16H used in the GETKEY.COM series. Either will do.

Then create a sample batch file like MENU2.BAT:

```
ECHO OFF
:TOP
ECHO Enter a letter from A to E (or type Esc to quit):
```

```
:START
GETLETR
IF ERRORLEVEL 27 GOTO END
IF ERRORLEVEL 6 GOTO START
IF ERRORLEVEL 5 GOTO LABELE
IF ERRORLEVEL 4 GOTO LABELD
IF ERRORLEVEL 3 GOTO LABELC
IF ERRORLEVEL 2 GOTO LABELB
:LABELA
ECHO (this simulates menu choice A)
PAUSE
GOTO TOP
:LABELB
ECHO (this simulates menu choice B)
PAUSE
GOTO TOP
:LABELC
ECHO (this simulates menu choice C)
PAUSE
GOTO TOP
:LABELD
ECHO (this simulates menu choice D)
PAUSE
GOTO TOP
:LABELE
ECHO (this simulates menu choice E)
PAUSE
GOTO TOP
:END
```

This example uses only five choices. When you start adding lots more, the tests can become cumbersome.

As mentioned above, it's possible to shorten long cascades of IF ERRORLEVEL tests by using a FOR command to dispatch the branching operation correctly.

The demonstration LEVEL.BAT batch file uses seven programs called ERRTEST0.COM through ERRTEST6.COM that simulate the errors in their filenames. It's a little complicated, but the batch file crams a ton of performance into a relatively small space:

```
ECHO OFF
IF %1!==! GOTO OOPS
FOR %%A IN (0 1 2 3 4 5 6) DO IF %1==%%A GOTO NEXT
GOTO OOPS
:NEXT
ERRTEST%1
```

```
FOR %%E IN (1 2 3 4 5 6) DO IF ERRORLEVEL %%E GOTO LABEL%%E
ECHO Everything is okay
GOTO END
:LABEL1
ECHO ERROR #1
GOTO END
:LABEL2
ECHO ERROR #2
GOTO END
:LABEL3
ECHO ERROR #3
GOTO END
:LABEL4
ECHO ERROR #4
GOTO END
:LABEL5
ECHO ERROR #5
GOTO END
:LABEL6
ECHO ERRORLEVEL GREATER THAN 5
GOTO END
:OOPS
ECHO Enter %0 and then a number from 0 to 6
:END
```

The line:

```
IF %1!==! GOTO OOPS
```

tests to make sure you entered something after the name of the batch file, and the:

```
FOR %%A IN (0 1 2 3 4 5 6) DO IF %1==%%A GOTO NEXT
```

screens out any entries that aren't the digits 0 through 6.
When you enter a valid digit, the line:

```
ERRTEST%1
```

tacks on (concatenates) the appropriate number in place of the %1 replaceable parameter, turning the ERRTEST string into something like ERRTEST2 or ERRTEST4. DOS then executes one of the seven error-simulating files on the disk, and the line:

```
FOR %%E IN (1 2 3 4 5 6) DO IF ERRORLEVEL %%E GOTO LABEL%%E
```

reads the error the small program generated and branches to the appropriate comment line in the batch file.

While LEVEL.BAT simply prints a message and exits, you could easily modify it to include specific actions to be taken for each error type. Also, note that if ERRORLEVEL is some value larger than any in the list, control will transfer based on the last value in the list.

To test this out, make sure DEBUG is handy and type in the following 24 lines. Or use a pure ASCII word processor to type them into a script file called ERR.SCR, and when you're done, get back to the DOS prompt and type:

```
DEBUG < ERR.SCR
```

This creates seven small files, ERRTEST0.COM through ERRTEST6.COM. Substitute them one at a time for the ERRTEST line in the LEVEL.BAT batch file. Each will set an ERRORLEVEL equivalent to the number in its name.

```
E 100 B8 00 4C CD 21
RCX
5
N ERRTEST0.COM
W
E 101 1
N ERRTEST1.COM
W
E 101 2
N ERRTEST2.COM
W
E 101 3
N ERRTEST3.COM
W
E 101 4
N ERRTEST4.COM
W
E 101 5
N ERRTEST5.COM
W
E 101 6
N ERRTEST6.COM
W
Q
```

All of the key-processing programs above discard the keystroke after reading it and setting an exit code. Since batch files execute painfully slowly on a slow system, an impatient user may repeatedly press the key several times until he or she sees something happen. The computer stores these extra keystrokes in the keyboard buffer, and they may cause problems.

You could adapt the basic GETKEY.COM program to display the key entered by changing it to:

```
MOV AH,0     ; BIOS read a character and
INT 16       ; puts its ASCII code into AL
MOV DL,AL    ; ready to display character
MOV AH,02    ; DOS display output
INT 21       ; do it
MOV AH,4C    ; ready to exit with code
INT 21       ; do it
```

Type the following to create it:

```
DEBUG
E 100 B4 00 CD 16 88 C2 B4 02 CD 21 B4 4C CD 21
N GETNEW1.COM
RCX
E
W
Q
```

If you wanted to adapt this to display uppercase letters for any uppercase or lowercase letters you entered, type:

```
E 100 B4 00 CD 16 24 DF 88 C2 B4 02 CD 21 B4 4C CD 21
N GETNEW2.COM
RCX
10
W
Q
```

This creates a program called GETNEW2.COM that will automatically uppercase any lowercase letter you enter while leaving uppercase entries alone. However, it works by performing a logical AND operation on the value in register AL:

```
AND AL,DF
```

If you entered a lowercase "a" (with a hex value of 61), ANDing this value with DF will turn it into 41, which is the hex value of uppercase "A." Enter an uppercase "A" and the AND DF operation will leave it alone.

Since this process forces the 2^5 bit to become unset (turning it into a 0), it will subtract a value of 32 from any number that has its 2^5 bit set, and leave any number that already has a 0 in that bit position alone.

- From 0 to 31   — values remain the same
- From 32 to 63   — it subtracts 32 from the value
- From 64 to 95   — values remain the same
- From 96 to 127   — it subtracts 32 from the value
- From 128 to 159   — values remain the same
- From 160 to 191   — it subtracts 32 from the value
- From 192 to 223   — values remain the same
- From 224 to 255   — it subtracts 32 from the value

So use a program like GETNEW2.COM with care.

Incidentally, as mentioned earlier, DOS offers a variety of key-processing functions, some of which display the key you press and some of which don't. Function 1 of interrupt 21 does. So you could just as easily have used:

```
MOV AH,1    ; DOS read a character and
INT 21      ; displays it
MOV AH,4C   ; ready to exit with code
INT 21      ; do it
```

to echo the keystroke to the screen.

Speeding Things Up

You may notice a lag when running batch files containing long strings of IF ERROR-LEVEL tests on a slow system. The first rule of batch files is to execute them from RAMdisks or fast hard disks.

But you can also streamline the operation by designing your batch files properly. One method for speeding things up is to limit the number of choices. But this isn't really practical for many applications.

The second rule of batch files is that it's always better to do processing outside of the batch file. DOS executes batch files one slow line at a time. But an assembly language program can process keyboard information virtually instantly. You'll be able to take out almost all the potential delays by putting the tests you want in the key-processing program rather than in the batch file. That's why this section included so many examples and provided the assembly language code for each. You should be able to adapt one of the above programs to do all the testing you need.

But if you do have to put a cascade of IF ERRORLEVEL tests in your batch files, you'll find one method is indeed faster than the other. Tests generally work in one of two ways. You either put the muscle on each line or spread it over a dispatching cascade:

To put it on each line, test for a value, and make sure the next higher value isn't valid:

```
ECHO OFF
:TOP
ECHO Type a letter key (A-Z) or Esc to quit:
GETLETR
```

```
IF ERRORLEVEL 27 GOTO END
IF ERRORLEVEL 26 IF NOT ERRORLEVEL 27 ECHO Z
IF ERRORLEVEL 25 IF NOT ERRORLEVEL 26 ECHO Y
IF ERRORLEVEL 24 IF NOT ERRORLEVEL 25 ECHO X
```

and so on. To dispatch the command execution, try something like:

```
ECHO OFF
:TOP
ECHO Type a letter key (A-Z) or Esc to quit:
GETLETR
IF ERRORLEVEL 27 GOTO END
IF ERRORLEVEL 26 GOTO Z
IF ERRORLEVEL 25 GOTO Y
IF ERRORLEVEL 24 GOTO X
    .
    .
    .
:Z
ECHO Z
GOTO TOP
:Y
ECHO Y
GOTO TOP
:X
ECHO X
GOTO TOP
:W
```

etc. The second way is faster.

Two programs on the accompanying disk — OPTION.COM and ASK.COM — add even more power to batch file IF ERRORLEVEL tests.

You supply OPTION.COM with pairs of parameters on the command line. The first character in each pair is the key pressed and the second is the ERRORLEVEL code generated. For example, if you entered:

```
OPTION A1B2
```

OPTION would return an ERRORLEVEL of 1 if you typed A or 2 if you typed B. To allow uppercase and lowercase entries, you would change it to:

```
OPTION A1a1B2b2
```

OPTION can also display onscreen prompts. Follow the parameter pairs with a hyphen and the message to be displayed. For example:

```
OPTION y1Y1n0N0-Enter Y or N:
```

with two spaces at the very end displays the prompt Enter Y or N: and positions the cursor two spaces from the colon.

OPTION also lets you use the Enter key by representing it as a plus sign. So you could enter:

```
OPTION +1 0-Hit Enter for 1, Space for 0
```

Be careful not to insert extra spaces in the string of argument pairs unless you actually want the spacebar to count as a valid key. For more details see OPTION in the manual section of this book.

If OPTION sounds too complicated, just use ASK.COM, which combines ERROR-LEVEL setting and dynamic user prompting in a single command.

ASK.COM, like ECHO, prints the text following it on the same line. However, unlike ECHO, ASK.COM waits for the user to enter a keystroke. It ANDs each input character with DF to turn everything uppercase and make all entries case insensitive, and it echoes the keystroke (in its uppercase version) to the screen. Finally, it handles "y" and "n" specially, displaying "Yes" and "No" in response to single keystrokes.

Use ASK.COM the same way you'd use ECHO. So if your batch file includes the line:

```
ASK Want to back up your files (Y/N)?
```

ASK will display the line:

```
Want to back up your files (Y/N)?
```

onscreen and wait for a reply.

One last BASIC program on the accompanying disk, MAKEMENU.BAS, will create a full-fledged menu system for you automatically, including a custom-made batch file with up to 26 choices, an attractive onscreen display, and an assembly language program to process the keystrokes correctly.

Batch File Applications

The small demonstration programs above were designed to exercise the various batch commands and show you how they operate. But if you really want to put these commands to work, try some of the following batch file applications.

DOS Notepads

Batch files make it easy to harness the DOS COPY CON command and turn it into a quick notepad. One method for doing this is to type in the BUILD.BAT batch file below, and then enter:

```
BUILD filename
```

when you're in DOS (substituting the name of your own file). BUILD.BAT will clear
the screen, display a ruler line, and save all your input in an ASCII file called filename.
When you're finished entering text, simply hit the Z key while holding down the Ctrl key
and then press the Enter key — or just press the F6 function key, which does the same
thing. If a file with the same name as filename already exists, BUILD.BAT will rename
it to have a BAK extension. By specifying PRN as the filename, all text entered is dumped
to your default printer. This is useful for short memos or notes.

Since BUILD.BAT allows only the current line to be edited, it won't replace your word
processor. In fact, even EDLIN leaves it in its dust. But it does allow you to create tiny
batch files or memos quickly and painlessly in DOS. And it's forgiving enough not to
write over an existing file.

```
ECHO OFF
IF %1!==! GOTO OOPS
IF %1==PRN GOTO START
IF EXIST %1.BAK GOTO OOPS2
IF NOT EXIST %1 GOTO START
REN %1 *.BAK
:START
CLS
ECHO ** Press F6 and then the Enter key when you're all done to save %1 **
ECHO    5   10   15   20   25   30   35   40   45   50   55   60   65   70   75
ECHO ----!----!----!----!----!----!----!----!----!----!----!----!----!----!----
COPY CON %1
GOTO END
:OOPS
ECHO Enter a filename after %0
GOTO END
:OOPS2
ECHO You already have a file called %1.BAK
ECHO Rename or erase it so this can proceed
:END
```

Another memo maker, QUIKNOTE.BAT, creates a small memo file and lets you update it automatically without having to use a word processor.

After you've entered any information, typing QUIKNOTE will display it. To update
the information, just type QUIKNOTE followed by up to nine words of text. The next
time you type QUIKNOTE the new text will appear, appended to the old.

QUIKNOTE.BAT also prints instructions even if you don't enter anything after the
filename:

```
ECHO OFF
IF %1!==! GOTO DISPLAY
```

```
ECHO %1 %2 %3 %4 %5 %6 %7 %8 %9 >> %0.DOC
:DISPLAY
CLS
IF NOT EXIST %0.DOC GOTO OOPS
TYPE %0.DOC
GOTO END
:OOPS
ECHO You haven't entered anything yet . . .
ECHO To enter data, type %0 and then type
ECHO up to 9 words on each line
ECHO (You can enter up to 23 lines.)
ECHO ----
ECHO To see what you've typed, just type %0
:END
```

A Date with DOS

You can adapt the above techniques to create a small appointment book that lets you add and delete entries, sorts your appointments for you automatically, and can show you in just a few seconds what you have lined up on any day:

```
ECHO OFF
IF %1!==! GOTO LIST
IF %2!==! GOTO TODAY
ECHO %1 %2 %3 %4 %5 %6 %7 %8 %9 >> NEW.DAT
SORT < NEW.DAT > TODO
ECHO (%1 %2 %3 %4 %5 %6 %7 %8 %9 ADDED)
GOTO DONE
:LIST
IF NOT EXIST TODO GOTO FIRSTIME
ECHO ******* APPOINTMENTS ********
MORE < TODO
:FIRSTIME
ECHO *****************************
ECHO To enter appointments, type:
ECHO ---------------------------
ECHO %0 DATE TIME MEMO
ECHO ---------------------------
ECHO WHERE DATE = MM/DD
ECHO TIME = HH/MM
ECHO MEMO = 7 OR FEWER WORDS
GOTO DONE
:TODAY
ECHO *** TODAY'S APPOINTMENTS ***
IF NOT EXIST TODO GOTO FIRSTIME
```

```
FIND "%1" TODO
:DONE
```

To use APPT.BAT just type:

```
APPT APPTDATE APPTTIME APPTMEMO
```

where APPTDATE is in MM/DD format (and you pad out single digit months and days with zeros), APPTTIME is in HH:MM format (and you pad out single digit hours and minutes with zeros here also), and APPTMEMO is text from one to seven words long.
If you simply type:

```
APPT
```

the batch file will type all your appointments. And if you type:

```
APPT MM/DD
```

(substituting a real date, such as 01/05 for MM/DD), the batch file will display all the appointments for that particular date.
For APPT.BAT to work, you must either have the DOS SORT.EXE, MORE.COM, and FIND.EXE files on your disk or have them properly pathed to. Still, it's not perfect. If you ask it to find 2/1 it will also show any line with a 2/11 or 12/11 date at the beginning, as well as any line with a 2/1 in the memo part of a listing that starts with a totally unrelated date.
However, you can also use it to display all your appointments on all dates with Mr. Jones, by typing APPT Jones (it's case sensitive, so it won't find JONES if you ask for Jones), or all your meetings with different people on the subject of taxes if the word taxes appears in the memo area of several different appointments with those different people. If you try searching for key words rather than dates, remember these have to be single words — you can search for "Jones" but not "John Jones."
You can indeed have DOS remove names as well as add them. APPT.BAT keeps track of things with the files NEW.BAT and TODO. REMOVE.BAT uses the FIND /V command to expunge any date you don't want from these two files:

```
ECHO OFF
IF %1!==! GOTO OOPS
FIND /V "%1" NEW.DAT | FIND /V "-" | FIND " " > TEMP
DEL NEW.DAT
DEL TODO
REN TEMP NEW.DAT
COPY NEW.DAT TODO > NUL
GOTO END
:OOPS
ECHO Enter the date you want removed after
```

```
ECHO the word %0
:END
```

To remove everything on 6/12, type:

```
REMOVE 6/12
```

Or to remove all references to Mrs. Smith, type:

```
REMOVE Smith
```

(observing case sensitivity and remembering that this will also remove any references to Mr. Smith if one exists).

Free Dialer

Now that you have a memo pad and an appointment book, you'll need a telephone dialer. By using features of the Hayes Smartmodem and the output redirection capabilities of DOS, you can turn a simple batch file into your own telephone dialer with its own built-in directory,

DIAL.BAT will automatically dial the phone (with a 1200 baud modem), disconnect the modem, and allow you to continue the call. In addition, it lets you set up an extensive dialing directory by expanding the conditional tests for names within the program. You'll need to have the DOS MODE.COM and FIND.EXE programs in the same directory as the dialer program or in a directory your PATH command knows about.

```
ECHO OFF
MODE COM1:1200 >NUL
IF %1!==! GOTO OOPS
IF %1 == # GOTO LIST
IF %1 == TOM GOTO TOM#
IF %1 == Tom GOTO TOM#
IF %1 == tom GOTO TOM#
IF %1 == DICK GOTO DICK#
IF %1 == Dick GOTO DICK#
IF %1 == dick GOTO DICK#
IF %1 == HARRY GOTO HARRY#
IF %1 == Harry GOTO HARRY#
IF %1 == harry GOTO HARRY#
ECHO ATDT%1; >COM1:
GOTO END
:TOM#
ECHO ATDT111-1111; >COM1:
GOTO END
:DICK#
```

```
ECHO ATDT222-2222; >COM1:
GOTO END
:HARRY#
ECHO ATDT9-333-3333; >COM1:
GOTO END
:LIST
ECHO The %0 batch file currently
ECHO contains numbers for:
FIND "#" %0.BAT | FIND /V "%%"
GOTO BYE
:OOPS
ECHO You have to enter a number or a name that
ECHO you've put in the batch file after %0
ECHO eg %0 555-1212 or %0 TOM
ECHO OR — Type %0 # to see a list of names
ECHO currently in the %0.BAT directory
GOTO BYE
:END
ECHO -------------------------------
ECHO When the dialing is done, press
ECHO any key to disconnect the modem.
ECHO -------------------------------
PAUSE
ECHO ATH >COM1:
:BYE
```

To use DIAL.BAT, just type:

```
DIAL number
```

or:

```
DIAL name
```

where number is the telephone number you wish to dial, and name is the name of someone in the batch file's directory. Listen to the speaker in the modem to determine when
the dialing is done, lift the handset, and then press any key to disconnect the modem and
reconnect the handset. Complete your call as usual.

So if you want to call your friend Tom, and you've put his name in the directory, you
can enter:

```
DIAL TOM
```

(or DIAL Tom or DIAL tom). If you haven't put his name in the directory, but you know
his number is 123-4567, enter:

```
DIAL 123-4567
```

You can see which names are currently included in your DIAL.BAT batch file by typing:

```
DIAL #
```

The names TOM, DICK, and HARRY in the sample DIAL.BAT batch file and the phone numbers that follow are obvious dummies. Replace them with your own entries. Note the following rules, however:

1. You should add three tests for each name, so you can type them in in uppercase, lowercase, or with an initial capital letter.
2. Make sure you put a # at the end of each label, as shown by :TOM# or :DICK#, as well as in the GOTO TOM# or GOTO DICK# commands. This lets the FIND command isolate the names if you enter DIAL # to see which names are currently listed in the batch file.

MODE insures that the right COM port is set to the proper baud rate. If you're using COM2 or a different baud rate, change the values in the program accordingly. MODE usually prints a message to the screen; DIAL.BAT gets rid of this by redirecting it to the NUL device.

When using modems by manufacturers other than Hayes, be sure the RS-232-C lines CTS (clear to send) and DSR (data set ready) from the modem are on, or else you'll get a DOS error. And although some non-Hayes modem options can be set for DSR and CTS on, the lines may be disabled until the "wake up" signal is sent to the modem. DOS, however, aborts the transmission to the modem before it sends any characters at all since the modem does not appear to be ready.

Free Telephone Directory

Hate to look up numbers in your telephone book or Rolodex? You don't ever have to again; DOS can do all the work for you.

The trick is to whip together three batch files — ADD.BAT, REMOVE.BAT, and LOOKUP.BAT. Then create a subdirectory called \PHONES that contains these batch files and room for the NAME.LST list of names.

ADD.BAT is very straightforward:

```
ECHO OFF
IF %1!==! GOTO OOPS
IF %1==# GOTO SEELIST
ECHO %1 %2 %3 %4 %5 %6 %7 %8 %9 >> NAME.LST
SORT < NAME.LST > TEMP
DEL NAME.LST
REN TEMP NAME.LST
```

```
GOTO END
:OOPS
ECHO To add data, enter up to 9 words after %0:
ECHO ------------------------------------------------
ECHO LASTNAME FIRSTNAME PHONENUMBER ADDRESS MEMO
ECHO ------------------------------------------------
ECHO (Try to avoid spaces, so use 212-555-1212
ECHO rather than (212) 555 1212)
ECHO ------------------------------------------------
ECHO ** Or enter %0 # to see the whole list **
GOTO END
:SEELIST
IF NOT EXIST NAME.LST GOTO OOPS
MORE < NAME.LST
:END
```

You either type ADD followed by up to nine words:

```
ADD Cleaver Theodore 312-555-1111 34 Elm, Chicago, IL 34567
```

or:

```
ADD #
```

to see the whole list.

REMOVE.BAT is also simple:

```
ECHO OFF
IF %1!==! GOTO OOPS
FIND /V "%1" NAME.LST | FIND /V "NAME.LST" | FIND " " > TEMP
COPY NAME.LST NAME.OLD > NUL
DEL NAME.LST
REN TEMP NAME.LST
GOTO END
:OOPS
ECHO Enter a key word from the line you want
ECHO removed after the word %0
:END
```

To delete a name, just type:

```
REMOVE Cleaver
```

But be careful, since this will remove any line that has the character string Cleaver in it. However, if you find you've made a mistake, you won't lose anything since REMOVE.BAT creates a backup file each time called NAME.OLD.

LOOKUP.BAT is the simplest of all:

```
ECHO OFF
IF %1!==! GOTO OOPS
IF %1==# GOTO SEELIST
FIND "%1" NAME.LST | MORE
GOTO END
:OOPS
ECHO To look up data, enter %0 then a single key word
ECHO ** Or enter %0 # to see the whole list **
GOTO END
:SEELIST
IF NOT EXIST NAME.LST GOTO OOPS2
MORE < NAME.LST
GOTO END
:OOPS2
ECHO First use ADD.BAT to create your NAME.LST
:END
```

You can retrieve information in all sorts of useful ways. You could, of course, hunt for a name by typing something like:

```
LOOKUP Benway
```

But you could also get a list of all the names and numbers in NY by typing:

```
LOOKUP NY
```

Or if you remember that someone has a telephone number containing a 98 in it, but you can't remember the name or anything else, you could type:

```
LOOKUP 98
```

You can also add "keys" like BB to indicate business, or HH to tell you the listing is a home address.

Obviously this isn't perfect. It's case sensitive, so it wouldn't report Dr. Benway if you typed the lowercase:

```
LOOKUP benway
```

But it would find him if you entered an abbreviated form, like:

```
LOOKUP enwa
```

since it looks for occurrences of character strings. In any event, it's fast and handy, and it can retrieve names and numbers when all you have to go on is a scrap of information such as part of a phone number or a recollection that the person was on the west coast (with a 90xxx Zip code).

Again, to make this work, you have to have FIND.EXE, SORT.EXE, and MORE.COM in the same subdirectory, or in one your path knows about.

Daily Chores

If you need a way to run your systems unattended overnight to reindex data base files, print reports, and get your electronic mail, or if you want to run certain programs on certain days only, you can have batch files do all the dirty work for you.

You need a few small utilities to help. GETDATE.COM returns an ERRORLEVEL of 1 to 31 equal to the current date-of-month. GETMONTH returns an ERRORCODE of 1 to 12, equal to the current month. DOW.COM returns an error code related to the day of the week, where Sunday equals 0 and Saturday equals 6.

To create the three programs, type in the following 15 lines:

```
DEBUG
E 100 B4 2A CD 21 88 F0 B4 4C CD 21 CD 20
N GETMONTH.COM
RCX
C
W
E 105 D0
N GETDATE.COM
W
E 104 B4 4C CD 21 CD 20
N DOW.COM
RCX
A
W
Q
```

Then create the three batch files below: SHOWMON.BAT, SHOWDATE.BAT, and WEEKDAY.BAT. Substitute your own commands in place of the dummy ECHO statements to execute your programs at specified times. First, SHOWMON.BAT:

```
ECHO OFF
REM This is SHOWMON.BAT
GETMONTH
IF ERRORLEVEL 1 IF NOT ERRORLEVEL 2 ECHO Month = Jan
IF ERRORLEVEL 2 IF NOT ERRORLEVEL 3 ECHO Month = Feb
```

```
IF ERRORLEVEL 3 IF NOT ERRORLEVEL 4 ECHO Month = Mar
IF ERRORLEVEL 4 IF NOT ERRORLEVEL 5 ECHO Month = Apr
IF ERRORLEVEL 5 IF NOT ERRORLEVEL 6 ECHO Month = May
IF ERRORLEVEL 6 IF NOT ERRORLEVEL 7 ECHO Month = Jun
IF ERRORLEVEL 7 IF NOT ERRORLEVEL 8 ECHO Month = Jul
IF ERRORLEVEL 8 IF NOT ERRORLEVEL 9 ECHO Month = Aug
IF ERRORLEVEL 9 IF NOT ERRORLEVEL 10 ECHO Month = Sep
IF ERRORLEVEL 10 IF NOT ERRORLEVEL 11 ECHO Month = Oct
IF ERRORLEVEL 11 IF NOT ERRORLEVEL 12 ECHO Month = Nov
IF ERRORLEVEL 12 ECHO Month = Dec
```

Next, SHOWDATE.BAT:

```
ECHO OFF
REM This is SHOWDATE.BAT
GETDATE
IF ERRORLEVEL 1 IF NOT ERRORLEVEL 2 ECHO Date = 1st
IF ERRORLEVEL 2 IF NOT ERRORLEVEL 3 ECHO Date = 2nd
IF ERRORLEVEL 3 IF NOT ERRORLEVEL 4 ECHO Date = 3rd
IF ERRORLEVEL 4 IF NOT ERRORLEVEL 5 ECHO Date = 4th
IF ERRORLEVEL 5 IF NOT ERRORLEVEL 6 ECHO Date = 5th
IF ERRORLEVEL 6 IF NOT ERRORLEVEL 7 ECHO Date = 6th
IF ERRORLEVEL 7 IF NOT ERRORLEVEL 8 ECHO Date = 7th
IF ERRORLEVEL 8 IF NOT ERRORLEVEL 9 ECHO Date = 8th
IF ERRORLEVEL 9 IF NOT ERRORLEVEL 10 ECHO Date = 9th
IF ERRORLEVEL 10 IF NOT ERRORLEVEL 11 ECHO Date = 10th
IF ERRORLEVEL 11 IF NOT ERRORLEVEL 12 ECHO Date = 11th
IF ERRORLEVEL 12 IF NOT ERRORLEVEL 13 ECHO Date = 12th
IF ERRORLEVEL 13 IF NOT ERRORLEVEL 14 ECHO Date = 13th
IF ERRORLEVEL 14 IF NOT ERRORLEVEL 15 ECHO Date = 14th
IF ERRORLEVEL 15 IF NOT ERRORLEVEL 16 ECHO Date = 15th
IF ERRORLEVEL 16 IF NOT ERRORLEVEL 17 ECHO Date = 16th
IF ERRORLEVEL 17 IF NOT ERRORLEVEL 18 ECHO Date = 17th
IF ERRORLEVEL 18 IF NOT ERRORLEVEL 19 ECHO Date = 18th
IF ERRORLEVEL 19 IF NOT ERRORLEVEL 20 ECHO Date = 19th
IF ERRORLEVEL 20 IF NOT ERRORLEVEL 21 ECHO Date = 20th
IF ERRORLEVEL 21 IF NOT ERRORLEVEL 22 ECHO Date = 21st
IF ERRORLEVEL 22 IF NOT ERRORLEVEL 23 ECHO Date = 22nd
IF ERRORLEVEL 23 IF NOT ERRORLEVEL 24 ECHO Date = 23rd
IF ERRORLEVEL 24 IF NOT ERRORLEVEL 25 ECHO Date = 24th
IF ERRORLEVEL 25 IF NOT ERRORLEVEL 26 ECHO Date = 25th
IF ERRORLEVEL 26 IF NOT ERRORLEVEL 27 ECHO Date = 26th
IF ERRORLEVEL 27 IF NOT ERRORLEVEL 28 ECHO Date = 27th
IF ERRORLEVEL 28 IF NOT ERRORLEVEL 29 ECHO Date = 28th
IF ERRORLEVEL 29 IF NOT ERRORLEVEL 30 ECHO Date = 29th
```

```
IF ERRORLEVEL 30 IF NOT ERRORLEVEL 31 ECHO Date = 30th
IF ERRORLEVEL 31 ECHO Date = 31st
```

(This long batch file is actually easy to create using the copy commands of your word processor or EDLIN.) And finally WEEKDAY.BAT:

```
ECHO OFF
REM This is WEEKDAY.BAT
DOW
IF ERRORLEVEL 0 IF NOT ERRORLEVEL 1 ECHO Sun
IF ERRORLEVEL 1 IF NOT ERRORLEVEL 2 ECHO Mon
IF ERRORLEVEL 2 IF NOT ERRORLEVEL 3 ECHO Tue
IF ERRORLEVEL 3 IF NOT ERRORLEVEL 4 ECHO Wed
IF ERRORLEVEL 4 IF NOT ERRORLEVEL 5 ECHO Thu
IF ERRORLEVEL 5 IF NOT ERRORLEVEL 6 ECHO Fri
IF ERRORLEVEL 6 ECHO Sat
```

The sample batch files are based on pairs of IF ERRORLEVEL tests on each line. Since IF ERRORLEVEL tests are true if the exit codes they test are equal to — or greater than — the value after IF ERRORLEVEL, you have to screen out the next higher one to isolate any exit code.

You could put just one test on each line, interspersed with GOTO statements. The following WEEK2.BAT would yield the same results as WEEKDAY.BAT, but it's far longer:

```
ECHO OFF
REM This is WEEK2.BAT
DOW
IF ERRORLEVEL 1 GOTO 1
ECHO It's Sunday
GOTO END
:1
IF ERRORLEVEL 2 GOTO 2
ECHO It's Monday
GOTO END
:2
IF ERRORLEVEL 3 GOTO 3
ECHO It's Tuesday
GOTO END
:3
IF ERRORLEVEL 4 GOTO 4
ECHO It's Wednesday
GOTO END
:4
IF ERRORLEVEL 5 GOTO 5
```

```
ECHO It's Thursday
GOTO END
:5
IF ERRORLEVEL 6 GOTO 6
ECHO It's Friday
GOTO END
:6
ECHO It's Saturday
:END
```

You could also try setting environment variables rather than ECHOing directly. The following WEEKDAY2.BAT batch file will cycle through the choices, resetting the environment variable DAY until the IF test is no longer true, and then retrieve the current setting and ECHO it to the screen.

```
ECHO OFF
REM This is WEEKDAY2.BAT
DOW
IF ERRORLEVEL 0 SET DAY=Sun
IF ERRORLEVEL 1 SET DAY=Mon
IF ERRORLEVEL 2 SET DAY=Tue
IF ERRORLEVEL 3 SET DAY=Wed
IF ERRORLEVEL 4 SET DAY=Thu
IF ERRORLEVEL 5 SET DAY=Fri
IF ERRORLEVEL 6 SET DAY=Sat
ECHO Day is %DAY%
```

The advantage here is that once you've run WEEKDAY2.BAT, other programs and batch files can grab the DAY variable directly from the environment without having to rerun the WEEKDAY2.BAT and DOW.COM. The DAY variable and its value don't take up much environment space, but you should consider expanding your environment just to make sure you don't run out. Or insert a placeholder:

```
SET DAY=XXX
```

command in your AUTOEXEC.BAT file to reserve the few bytes needed.

It's simple to adapt this process to report on anything DOS can sniff out. For instance, create the ID.COM and MODEREAD.COM programs by typing in this MODEID.SCR file:

```
A
MOV AX,F000     ; top segment
MOV DS,AX       ; ready to use it
MOV BX,FFFE     ; ID offset
MOV AX,[BX]     ; ready to read it
```

```
          MOV AH,4C        ; exit with code
          INT 21           ; do it

          RCX
          E
          N ID.COM
          W
          A 100
          MOV AH,0F         ; get video mode
          INT 10            ; do it
          MOV AH,4C         ; exit with code
          INT 21 ; do it

          RCX
          8
          N MODEREAD.COM
          W
          Q
```

Be careful to leave the two blank lines above each RCX, and to press the Enter key at the end of each line — especially the last one. Then, at the DOS prompt, type:

```
DEBUG < MODEID.SCR
```

Or, just type the following 12 lines:

```
DEBUG
E 100 B8 00 F0 8E D8 BB FE FF 8B 07 B4 4C CD 21
N ID.COM
RCX
E
W
E 100 B4 0F CD 10 B4 4C CD 21
N MODEREAD.COM
RCX
8
W
Q
```

Then run HARDWARE.BAT:

```
ECHO OFF
REM This is HARDWARE.BAT
ID
```

```
IF ERRORLEVEL 255 ECHO System = PC
IF ERRORLEVEL 254 IF NOT ERRORLEVEL 255 ECHO System = XT or Portable
IF ERRORLEVEL 253 IF NOT ERRORLEVEL 254 ECHO System = PCjr
IF ERRORLEVEL 252 IF NOT ERRORLEVEL 253 ECHO System = AT
IF ERRORLEVEL 251 IF NOT ERRORLEVEL 252 ECHO System = Model 50, 60 or
new XT
IF ERRORLEVEL 250 IF NOT ERRORLEVEL 251 ECHO System = Model 30
IF ERRORLEVEL 249 IF NOT ERRORLEVEL 250 ECHO System = Convertible
IF ERRORLEVEL 248 IF NOT ERRORLEVEL 249 ECHO System = Model 80
```

or SHOWMODE.BAT:

```
ECHO OFF
MODEREAD
IF ERRORLEVEL 19 IF NOT ERRORLEVEL 20 ECHO 640x480 256 colors
IF ERRORLEVEL 18 IF NOT ERRORLEVEL 19 ECHO 640x480 16 colors
IF ERRORLEVEL 17 IF NOT ERRORLEVEL 18 ECHO 640x480 2 colors
IF ERRORLEVEL 16 IF NOT ERRORLEVEL 17 ECHO 640x350 16 colors
IF ERRORLEVEL 15 IF NOT ERRORLEVEL 16 ECHO 640x350 Mono
IF ERRORLEVEL 14 IF NOT ERRORLEVEL 15 ECHO 640x200 EGA 16 color graphics
IF ERRORLEVEL 13 IF NOT ERRORLEVEL 14 ECHO 320x200 EGA 16 color graphics
IF ERRORLEVEL 10 IF NOT ERRORLEVEL 11 ECHO 640x200 EGA 64 color graphics
IF ERRORLEVEL 9 IF NOT ERRORLEVEL 10 ECHO 50x25 PCjr color
IF ERRORLEVEL 8 IF NOT ERRORLEVEL 9 ECHO 20x25 PCjr color
IF ERRORLEVEL 7 IF NOT ERRORLEVEL 8 ECHO 80x25 Mono B&W text
IF ERRORLEVEL 6 IF NOT ERRORLEVEL 7 ECHO 640x200 CGA B&W graphics
IF ERRORLEVEL 5 IF NOT ERRORLEVEL 6 ECHO 320x200 CGA 4 greys graphics
IF ERRORLEVEL 4 IF NOT ERRORLEVEL 5 ECHO 320x200 CGA 4 color graphics
IF ERRORLEVEL 3 IF NOT ERRORLEVEL 4 ECHO 80x25 CGA 16 color text
IF ERRORLEVEL 2 IF NOT ERRORLEVEL 3 ECHO 80x25 CGA B&W text
IF ERRORLEVEL 1 IF NOT ERRORLEVEL 2 ECHO 40x25 CGA 16 color text
IF ERRORLEVEL 0 IF NOT ERRORLEVEL 1 ECHO 40x25 CGA B&W text
```

to tell your batch files what the current CPU and video mode are.

Obviously these are demonstration programs and not workhorse batch files. To put them to use, you'd have to jump to different system-handling and screen-handling routines instead of just printing messages as these do here.

Time of the Month

Or, you may want to execute a specific program at boot-up on a specific day, perhaps to run CHKDSK.COM once each week and Peter Norton's DISKTEST.EXE once each month to monitor the condition of a fixed drive. Batch files make it easy.

First, create the DATECHEK.COM program by typing in the DATECHEK.SCR script:

```
A
MOV AH,2A      ; get date
INT 21         ; do it
CMP AL,02      ; is it Tues?
JNZ 0113       ; no, AL=2
MOV AL,00      ; yes, AL=0
CMP DL,08      ; first week?
JNB 0115       ; no, AL=0
MOV AL,01      ; yes, AL=1
JMP 0115       ; skip next line
MOV AL,02      ; set level
MOV AH,4C      ; exit with code
INT 21         ; do it

RCX
19
N DATECHEK.COM
W
Q
```

Again, be careful to leave the blank line above RCX and to press Enter after each line, especially the last one. Then get back into DOS and type:

```
DEBUG < DATECHEK.SCR
```

Or just type the following eight lines:

```
DEBUG
E 100 B4 2A CD 21 3C 02 75 0B B0 00 80 FA 08
E 10D 73 06 B0 01 EB 02 B0 02 B4 4C CD 21
N DATECHEK.COM
RCX
19
W
Q
```

Then create a CHKDATE.BAT batch file:

```
ECHO OFF
DATECHEK
IF ERRORLEVEL 2 GOTO 2
IF ERRORLEVEL 1 GOTO 1
ECHO It's Tues (not the 1st)
GOTO END
```

```
:2
ECHO It's not Tuesday
GOTO END
:1
ECHO It's the first Tuedsay
:END
```

DATECHEK program requests the system date via function 2AH, looks for the day of the week and, if it is Tuesday, then checks to see if it is the first Tuesday of the month. The program terminates with function 4CH, which returns a value in AL that the IF ER-RORLEVEL command can test in a batch file.

You can alter the day of the week to be tested by changing the line:

```
CMP AL,02
```

in the listing (00 = Sun, 02 = Tues, 06 = Sat). If you wanted to patch an existing DATECHEK.COM program with DEBUG, change the value at offset 105. So to change it to Wednesday, which has a value of 3, type:

```
DEBUG DATECHEK.COM
E 105 3
W
Q
```

The day of the month is reported in DL. Tuesday was chosen to avoid missing the monthly test due to a holiday (July 1 and January 1 present problems only infrequently).

The CHKDATE.BAT uses the ERRORLEVEL returned by DATECHEK.COM to branch to the appropriate test. It's a dummy file for demonstration purposes; substitute your own commands for the ECHO messages shown.

Current Events

It's usually difficult to give DOS access to the date or time when running batch files. But there's a way to get around this problem.

Assume you want to run a program called ONCEONLY.COM only once a day. Add the following line to your AUTOEXEC.BAT:

```
ECHO | MORE | DATE > READDATE.BAT
```

and make:

```
READDATE
```

the last line in your AUTOEXEC.BAT. Then create a batch file called CURRENT.BAT:

```
ECHO OFF
IF !%TODAY%==!%4 GOTO END
SET TODAY=%4
REM ONCEONLY program goes here
:END
```

You can even arrange that it runs only once a week, say every Friday, by adding a line:

```
IF NOT %3==Fri GOTO END
```

after the line SET TODAY=%4. And as a bonus, you wind up with today's date in the environment.

This works by creating a file READDATE.BAT, containing the output of DATE:

```
Current date is Sun 9-30-1990
Enter new date (mm-dd-yy):
```

DOS tries to run the line beginning with "Current date is" by looking for an executable file (with an extension COM, EXE, or BAT) called CURRENT — and finds the one we created called CURRENT.BAT. DOS then interprets the groups of words and numbers following the word "Current" as parameters for CURRENT.BAT. So it reads "date" as %1, "is" as %2, the day of the week as %3, and the actual numeric date as %4.

One special trick that's worth noting is the use of the MORE command in the middle of the ECHO I MORE I DATE > READDATE.BAT line. All this does is supply the extra carriage return that the DATE command needs to execute properly. (To make this work, MORE.COM has to be in the same directory or be in one your path knows about.) Note also that adding READDATE as the final line in your AUTOEXEC.BAT means that as soon as AUTOEXEC.BAT finishes, DOS will load and execute READDATE.BAT.

You could adapt this process slightly if you didn't have an internal clock but needed to reboot frequently. First, put these lines near the top of your AUTOEXEC.BAT file:

```
ECHO OFF
IF NOT EXIST D.BAT GOTO SETIT
COMMAND /C D
:SETIT
DATE
DATEMAKE
```

and then a final AUTOEXEC.BAT line:

```
DATEMAKE
```

The COMMAND /C allows one batch file to run another batch file and then jump execution back to the first when the second is done. Users of DOS 3.3 could substitute

CALL for COMMAND /C. D.BAT is a short batch file created by DATEMAKE.BAT, containing the lines

```
Current date is Sun 9-30-1990
Enter new date (mm-dd-yy):
```

(or whatever the last set date was).

The DATE command below COMMAND /C D lets you correct the date the first time you run AUTOEXEC.BAT each day. DATEMAKE.BAT contains the single line:

```
ECHO | MORE | DATE > D.BAT
```

Again, MORE.COM has to be in the current subdirectory or in one your PATH knows about. The only other file you need for this to work is a tiny one called, you guessed it, CURRENT.BAT:

```
DATE %4
```

Real-Time Batch File Entries

If you could send a command from the keyboard to a batch file while it was executing, you could enter a switch or a command as needed during execution. To do this, include a line:

```
COPY CON TEST.BAT
```

in your batch file. As soon as DOS reaches this line it will pause and let you enter anything you want. Then when you type Ctrl-Z and press Enter, DOS will resume processing the batch file.

To see this in action, type in the SAMPLE.BAT batch file below:

```
ECHO OFF
REM SAMPLE.BAT
ECHO    To edit or create a file
ECHO    using WordStar, type:
ECHO    WS followed by a filename
ECHO    Then Enter, Ctrl-Z, then Enter
ECHO        example: WS MYFILE.LET
ECHO (then Enter, Ctrl-Z, Enter)
COPY CON TEST.BAT
COMMAND /C TEST
ECHO end of demo
```

The COMMAND /C command (you may substitute CALL if you're using DOS 3.3) executes the new TEST.BAT file that you just created. Then, when TEST.BAT finishes running, DOS returns control to the main SAMPLE.BAT batch file.

This is handy for giving instructions to new users and then executing the commands they type.

You can adapt this technique to create a real-time log that will keep track of who's using your system. Just create the following LOGIT.BAT batch file:

```
ECHO OFF
IF EXIST LOG GOTO NEXT
ECHO === Logfile === > LOG
:NEXT
ECHO This will add your name to the logfile
ECHO Instructions:
ECHO     1. Enter your name
ECHO     2. Hit the Enter key
ECHO     3. Hit the F6 key
ECHO     4. Hit the Enter key again
CTTY NUL
COPY CON ADD
COPY LOG+ADD /B
ECHO | MORE | TIME | FIND "Current" >> LOG
ECHO -------------------------- >> LOG
CTTY CON
MORE < LOG
```

Run it by typing LOGIT. When prompted, enter your name, then press Enter, then press F6, then Enter. Your name and the current time will be added to the log. You may also add comments below your name, on separate lines — just be sure to press Enter, then F6, then Enter when you're done.

More Efficient Copies

DOS doesn't make it easy to copy groups of files from the current directory to another directory or disk with a single command — unless you do it with a batch file. The COPYEASY.BAT batch file lets you use as many as eight shorthand filespecs on a single command line:

```
ECHO OFF
IF "%2" == "" GOTO HELP
ECHO This will copy %2 %3 %4 %5 %6 %7 %8 %9
ECHO from
CD
ECHO to %1
ECHO Hit Ctrl-Break to abort, or
```

```
PAUSE
SET MYVAR=%1
SHIFT
:AGAIN
ECHO Copying %1 to %MYVAR%
FOR %%A IN (%1) DO COPY %%A %MYVAR% > NUL
SHIFT
IF NOT "%1" == "" GOTO AGAIN
SET MYVAR=
GOTO END
:HELP
ECHO To use this %0 utility, enter:
ECHO %0, DESTINATION, and up to 8 filespecs
ECHO in current directory. For example:
ECHO ----------------------------------
ECHO %0 B: *.BAT *.D?? MYFILE.TXT TEST.*
ECHO ----------------------------------
:END
```

This batch utility provides help if it's needed and specific feedback on what to type on the command line; it also requests confirmation before proceeding. This version uses only DOS commands, but you can streamline it by adding IF ERRORLEVEL branching.

COPYEASY really takes advantage of DOS variables. It starts out by using replaceable parameters to read everything off the command line, and then has the DOS SHIFT command process them one by one. Each time the SHIFT command executes it moves all the replaceable parameters up a notch, so %3 becomes %2 and %2 becomes %1 and the old value for %1 is discarded.

So if you entered:

```
COPYEASY D: *.BAT C*.COM ??.EXE
```

- %1 would = D:
- %2 would = *.BAT
- %3 would = C*.COM
- %4 would = ??.EXE

Execute SHIFT once and:

- %1 would = *.BAT
- %2 would = C*.COM
- %3 would = ??.EXE

The old D: value of %1 would vanish, and %4 wouldn't have any value. Remember, the %0 parameter is a special case — it represents the name of the batch file itself.

The %1 parameter originally represents the destination for all the copies, and this is used the whole time the batch file runs. But the first time SHIFT executes, it wipes out the old value of %1 and replaces it with what used to be %2. COPYEASY gets around this by taking the original value of %1 and setting it to an environment variable, with the command:

```
SET MYVAR=%1
```

It can then use this destination at any subsequent time in the batch file by referring to it as %MYVAR% rather than %1. And it cleans up when finished by removing the variable from the environment with the command:

```
SET MYVAR=
```

If you do try this, make sure your environment is large enough to hold the extra variable. Under DOS 2.0 and 2.1 you can patch COMMAND.COM at address ECF to represent the number of 16-byte memory paragraphs that will make up your new environment. (For DOS 2.11 the address is DF3.) For DOS 3.0 and 3.1, use a SHELL [d:][path]COMMAND.COM /E:n /P command in your CONFIG.SYS file, where n represents the number of 16-byte paragraphs. For versions 3.2 and later, use the same SHELL command but specify the actual number of bytes rather than paragraphs. The default in all cases is 160 bytes (ten paragraphs). You can boost it all the way up to 32K in DOS 3.2 and 3.3, but are limited to 62 paragraphs in earlier versions.

AUTOEXEC.BAT

Virtually all users start their systems with AUTOEXEC.BAT files. But there are times when you want to start without all of the various programs your AUTOEXEC.BAT normally loads.

A combination of resident programs loaded by your AUTOEXEC.BAT might cause your machine to hang. Or, you might not want to run a product your AUTOEXEC.BAT installs (for example, you might not want to bring up the *PC Network* before doing backups).

You could simply begin the file with a PAUSE command, but this means you'd have to sit by and watch the disks grind until you reached the PAUSE. And you'd end up just banging the space bar to proceed 99 percent of the time.

Or, you could boot off a floppy disk in your A: drive, or do what most users do — continually press Ctrl-Break while your machine is booting, hoping your AUTOEXEC.BAT will be aborted before the critical instructions occur. Either solution is fine if you only run into the problem once in a while, but neither solution is ideal.

A far better method is to use a small program called KBFLAG.COM to monitor your keyboard as you boot up, and send a code to your AUTOEXEC.BAT file that an IF ERRORLEVEL instruction can trap. Once you install this program, you can press one single key while your machine is booting to avoid running your AUTOEXEC.BAT.

To create KBFLAG.COM, type in the following KBFLAG.SCR script:

```
A
MOV AX,40      ; segment 0040
MOV DS,AX      ; get it ready
MOV AL,[17]    ; get value at offset 17
MOV AH,4C      ; exit with code
INT 21         ; do it

RCX
C
N KBFLAG.COM
W
Q
```

Be sure to leave a blank space above RCX, and press the Enter key at the end of each line, especially the last one. Then get into DOS and type:

```
DEBUG < KBFLAG.SCR
```

Or just type in the following seven lines:

```
DEBUG
E 100 B8 40 00 8E D8 A0 17 00 B4 4C CD 21
N KBFLAG.COM
RCX
C
W
Q
```

Then, add these two lines at the very beginning of your AUTOEXEC.BAT:

```
KBFLAG
IF ERRORLEVEL number GOTO END
```

(replacing "number" with one from the chart below).

You'll also need a label at the end of your batch file that says simply:

```
:END
```

KBFLAG sets the DOS ERRORLEVEL to the value of the KBFLAG in the ROM BIOS area. You can use different keys to trigger KBFLAG. These keys, and the codes read by IF ERRORLEVEL, are:

1	=	Right shift
2	=	Left shift
4	=	Ctrl key

8	=	Alt key
16	=	ScrollLock
32	=	NumLock
64	=	CapsLock
128	=	Insert

For example, you can avoid running AUTOEXEC.BAT if you press and hold a Shift key while your machine boots, or if you simply press NumLock while your CONFIG.SYS is running.

You can add the above key values together. If you wanted the trigger to be the Right and Left Shift keys plus the Ins key (toggled on), you would use an ERRORLEVEL trap of 131 (1 + 2 + 128 = 131).

You could make your batch file test for several ERRORLEVELs, and act differently when different keys are pressed. For example, CapsLock could mean abort the AUTOEXEC.BAT, while NumLock could do everything but load a couple of resident programs. KBFLAG can be used in any BAT file, not just AUTOEXEC.BAT.

A handy way to do this is to use a value of 128. Then you can avoid running your AUTOEXEC.BAT file by toggling the Ins key when you boot up. KBFLAG will send a 128 to the IF ERRORLEVEL trap, which will branch to the :END label.

This is a far more elegant solution to avoiding AUTOEXEC.BAT than pounding on the keyboard, which can generate bootup errors and force you to press the F1 key and then restart the whole operation. Using the Ins (or NumLock, ScrollLock, or CapsLock) toggle means that you can branch out of the program with one simple key press, or start running normally by keeping your fingers off the keyboard.

Chapter 11

The DOS Environment

The DOS environment is a memory pool of information that is available to all batch files or programs in your system. You can place virtually any kind of information in it. The Microsoft C compiler, for example, takes advantage of the environment to pass file handling information from one program to another. And you can put your own variables there to store values or transmit them from one executable file to another.

The actual memory area where the environment information is stored is known as the *master environment block*. Each item there is stored as a series of characters known as a *string*. Environment strings consist of a variable name, an equals sign (=), and a word or phrase of information, in the form:

variable=phrase

As used here, *variable* is the name of an environment variable, and *phrase* is the information stored with that variable.

The environment normally contains the familiar PROMPT and PATH descriptor strings, and the important COMSPEC variable. While DOS creates COMSPEC and PATH by default, you can manipulate all three directly from the DOS command line or from a batch file by using the SET, PATH, or PROMPT commands. You can also use the SET command to create, delete, and modify "user-defined" environment variables. These variables let you store your own information with variable names of your own choosing, and can really supercharge some aspects of batch file operation.

Richard Hale Shaw's series of articles on the DOS environment were among the very first to discuss some of the finer points involved. The updated section here also contains contributions by Charles Petzold and several *PC Magazine* readers.

The SET Command

The most convenient way to modify the environment is via the SET command. You can use SET at the DOS prompt or in a batch file. The full syntax for using SET on the DOS command line is:

```
SET [variable=[phrase]]
```

where variable is the name of the environment variable you want to modify, and phrase is the string of characters you want the variable to refer to.

If you enter SET by itself, DOS will display the current environment strings on the screen. You can redirect these into a file with the command like this one:

```
SET > ENVFILE.TXT
```

which will write a copy of the current environment strings to a file called ENVFILE.TXT.

If you enter SET, then a variable name, then an equals sign with nothing following it, DOS will remove the variable from the environment.

Note that when you use SET to define an environment variable, any spaces between the end of the variable name and the equals sign will become part of the variable name itself. So the command:

```
SET x =y
```

will create a variable called "X ." Similarly, any spaces found after the = sign become part of the phrase, so:

```
SET x= y
```

will set the variable X to the phrase " y." DOS always capitalizes the variable name passed to it by SET, regardless of whether you entered it in upper- or lowercase. But it maintains the case of the variable value exactly as you entered it.

The DOS command line processor limits the length of environment strings entered on the command line or in a batch file to 127 characters. Actually, most environment strings are limited to 123 characters because "SET " takes up four spaces on the command line. Since PATH and PROMPT don't require the use of SET, they alone can use the full 127 characters. An environment variable name or phrase can be any length as long as the entire string's combined length, including the equals sign, does not exceed 127 characters.

To see SET in action, enter:

```
SET PASSWORD=SHERLOCK
```

This will create an environment variable called PASSWORD that is equal to the string "SHERLOCK." You can change the phrase that PASSWORD points to at any time simply by entering the change with SET. So the command:

```
SET PASSWORD=WATSON
```

will change PASSWORD so it's equal to "WATSON." And the command:

```
SET PASSWORD=
```

will remove PASSWORD from the environment altogether. If you're trying to get rid of a variable, be sure not to put any spaces after the equals sign. If you do accidentally include a space there, the variable will remain in the environment, since DOS will think you're trying to make the variable equal to a single space. To verify that you've removed an environment string, just enter SET by itself, which will produce a display like:

```
COMSPEC=D:\COMMAND.COM
PATH=D:\;C:\;C:\BIN;C:\DOS
PROMPT=$p:
```

The PROMPT Environment Variable

One of the first things a serious user learns is how to modify the DOS prompt from C> or A> to something slightly more descriptive. PROMPT is not an independent DOS command; it's actually shorthand for SET PROMPT. You can use either PROMPT or SET PROMPT when customizing the PROMPT variable.

You can create all sorts of different prompts by using symbols that IBM calls meta-strings. Meta-strings all begin with an initial dollar sign, and are immediately followed by the meta-string symbol or character. For example, the default DOS prompt itself is simply the meta-string ng. The $n displays your current drive letter, and the $g displays the greater-than (>) sign.

DOS provides a variety of meta-strings that can be used singly or in combinations to configure your prompt. (See Chapter 9 on ANSI.SYS for the full list.)

DOS will ignore any "null" meta-strings that are created by following the initial dollar sign with a character that's not a meta-string symbol. But DOS will print, as part of the prompt itself, any characters that immediately follow a null meta-string. This gives you an opportunity to include almost anything in the prompt. To print a name or a phrase as part of a prompt, you simply precede it with a null meta-string like "$a." For instance, the PROMPT command:

```
$aGood Morning:
```

will produce the prompt:

```
Good Morning:
```

You don't really need the use null strings however. The command:

```
PROMPT Hi there
```

will turn your DOS prompt from C> or A> into:

```
Hi there
```

You may add an optional SET and an equals sign. These will both produce the same "Hi there" prompt:

```
PROMPT Hi there
SET PROMPT=Hi there
```

To illustrate the use and selection of a variety of prompts, try running SWPROMPT.BAT, which makes it easy to switch among five different DOS prompts. To make it work you first have to run STPROMPT.BAT:

```
ECHO OFF
IF !%PROMPT6%==! SET PROMPT6=%PROMPT%
SET PROMPT1=$$
SET PROMPT2=Date is $d; Time is $t $h$h$h$h$h$h$h:
SET PROMPT3=$p:
SET PROMPT4=This is $v:
SET PROMPT5=$lPC$g
```

This will create five environment variables:

- a single dollar-sign prompt
- a date-and-time prompt
- a prompt that displays the current directory
- a "This is IBM Personal Computer DOS Version 3.30" prompt
- a prompt containing the initials <PC>

Then create SWPROMPT.BAT:

```
ECHO OFF
IF !%1==! GOTO END
IF %1==0 PROMPT=
IF %1==1 PROMPT=%PROMPT1%
IF %1==2 PROMPT=%PROMPT2%
IF %1==3 PROMPT=%PROMPT3%
IF %1==4 PROMPT=%PROMPT4%
IF %1==5 PROMPT=%PROMPT5%
IF %1==6 PROMPT=%PROMPT6%
:END
```

Once you've created SWPROMPT.BAT, and run STPROMPT.BAT (which you need do only once in a DOS session), just enter:

```
SWPROMPT n
```

at the DOS prompt, where n is a number from 0 to 6. If you enter a number from 1 to 5, SWPROMPT will change your prompt to one of the five described above. If you do not enter a number, no change will take place. Entering a 0 brings back the standard DOS A> or C> prompt, and entering a 6 will reset the prompt to what it was when you first ran STPROMPT.

Obviously you should modify STPROMPT.BAT to set up your own series of custom prompts. If you change the number of prompts being initialized, simply modify SWPROMPT to handle the right number.

Since these strings normally begin with a dollar sign, you have to use a pair of dollar signs if you want one to appear in the prompt. Also note that the line of hhhhhh characters after the $t time meta-string will erase the seconds and hundredths of seconds normally reported by DOS.

Unfortunately this won't work under version 3.0. A bug in that version of DOS prevents it from understanding environment variables such as %PROMPT1%..

PC Magazine contributor Ethan Winer points out that apart from the usual custom prompts, such as:

```
PROMPT $p$g
```

which will show the current path, followed by a ">" sign, or something a bit more complex like:

```
PROMPT $d$_$t$_$n$g
```

which will show the current date, time, and drive on separate lines, you can experiment with more frivolous ones. Try:

```
PROMPT ^B$g
```

(Enter the ^B character by holding down the Ctrl key while typing the letter B.) Or, if you want to see something truly strange, type in:

```
PROMPT YoYo$hoo$hoo$hoo$hoo$ho$h$ho$h$ho$h
```

For clarity, all of the repetitions for this PROMPT command are not shown above. After the initial PROMPT YoYo, enter 13 groups of $hoo, followed immediately by 12 groups of hoh.

One of the best uses of PROMPT is in entering escape sequences for ANSI.SYS. See Chapter 9 on ANSI for details.

The COMSPEC Environment Variable

COMSPEC, an acronym for COMmand SPECification, defines the drive, path, filename, and extension of the DOS COMMAND.COM command interpreter.

When DOS initially boots your system, it loads different parts of COMMAND.COM into high and low memory addresses. The portion in high memory controls the use of batch files and internal commands, things your programs don't normally use while they're running. Programs that need the additional memory space can overwrite the part of COMMAND.COM stored in high memory. When such a program terminates, DOS checks to see if the high memory portion of the command interpreter has been overwritten by the program. If so, it reloads that part from the disk. The COMSPEC environment variable tells DOS where to find the COMMAND.COM file.

The DOS default for this variable is:

```
COMSPEC=C:\COMMAND.COM
```

on a system booted from a hard disk, and:

```
COMSPEC=A:\COMMAND.COM
```

on any system initially booted from a floppy disk, regardless of whether a hard disk is attached. This means that the drive and path to the command interpreter can point to any valid copy of COMMAND.COM (or any other command interpreter).

To change the COMSPEC with SET, enter:

```
SET COMSPEC=[d:][path]filename.ext
```

where d: is the drive, path is the directory path and filename.ext is the name of the command interpreter to be used.

Reloading the command interpreter after a program terminates may tie up your system an extra 1 to 4 seconds before the DOS prompt appears. This is a good reason to change COMSPEC. If you're using a RAMdisk under DOS 3.0 or above (for example, as drive D:), you can pare down this time by putting the following two lines in your AUTOEXEC.BAT file:

```
COPY COMMAND.COM D:\
SET COMSPEC=D:\COMMAND.COM
```

Substitute the drive letter of your RAMdisk in place of D: After you make this change, if DOS has to reload a copy of COMMAND.COM it will take it from the RAMdisk, which will be a whole lot faster and quieter than before.

Application programs that let you load DOS without leaving the program itself use COMSPEC to load COMMAND.COM. If your programs take advantage of this, or if you load COMMAND.COM in your batch files, changing COMSPEC will make everything go faster.

If you do change the COMSPEC variable, remember that this is the only way DOS will know where the command processor is located. Be careful that you actually have a copy of COMMAND.COM where you just told DOS to look for it, on the drive pointed to by the new COMSPEC setting. Otherwise, you may get the dreaded "Cannot load COMMAND, system halted" message from DOS, which means you'll have to reboot and lose any data that wasn't saved to disk.

The PATH Environment Variable

The path is a list of directories that DOS searches to find programs or batch files. Although you may occasionally want to try it on a floppy disk system, path is a necessity on any computer with a hard disk.

Path lets you organize your disk by placing your most frequently used programs and utilities in unobtrusive, out-of-the-way subdirectories. It will show DOS exactly where they're located.

To change the PATH variable, enter:

```
SET PATH=[d:]directory[;directory]
```

where d: is an optional drive specification. As with the PROMPT command, the SET and the = need not be entered, saving extra characters if you need a very long path specification.

Whenever you enter anything at the DOS prompt, COMMAND.COM first checks to see if what you typed was an internal command. DOS keeps a table of these common commands (such as DIR, COPY, and TYPE) inside the COMMAND.COM command processor itself.

If it searches all the way through the list and doesn't find a match, it assumes that what you typed is an external command (a program or a batch file). It then searches the current directory first for a file with an extension of COM, then for one that ends with EXE, and finally one with a BAT extension. If it finds one that fits the bill it loads and executes it.

However, if it doesn't find an external command in the current directory with a COM, EXE, or BAT extension, DOS then looks for a PATH variable in the environment. If no PATH variable has been defined, the search ends there and DOS prints its "Bad command or file name" message. But if it does see a PATH variable, DOS will look for COM, EXE, or BAT files with the filename you specified in each of the directories listed in the path.

Since DOS runs COM files before EXE files, if you have two programs called PROG.COM and PROG.EXE in the same directory, DOS won't ever get a chance to run PROG.EXE. And since it runs EXE files before BAT files, if PROG.EXE and PROG.BAT are in the same directory, DOS won't ever get a chance to run PROG.BAT. However, if you have a program in the current directory called PROG.BAT and one called PROG.COM in another directory that your PATH knows about, DOS will run

PROG.BAT, since it always tries to run a COM, EXE, or BAT file in current directory before running any files in other directories.

Some users mistakenly place . or .\ in their PATH list. These symbols represent the current directory. But since the current directory is searched before the PATH is even examined by DOS, they just slow down the search process.

When DOS first creates the environment, the path is initialized to a null (empty) string of characters, just as if you had cancelled your current path by entering:

```
PATH=
```

Your AUTOEXEC.BAT file should contain an appropriate path statement as one of its first commands. Then DOS can find programs this batch file specifies later.

You should put all your most frequently used COM, EXE, and BAT files in a directory called \DOS, \UTILS, or \BIN, and then include this directory in your path. It's often useful to keep your DOS files together in a directory called \DOS, and your non- DOS utilities in one called \BIN. This makes it easy to update from one version of DOS to another.

If you used both of these subdirectories, your path might look like:

```
PATH=C:\;C:\DOS;C:\BIN
```

DOS uses semicolons to separate path directory entries. The first directory on the list (C:\), is simply the root directory. You shouldn't have any visible files in your root directory other than AUTOEXEC.BAT, CONFIG.SYS, and COMMAND.COM.

If you want to speed things up you can set up a RAMdisk (on drive D: if you have a typical one-drive hard disk system) and have your AUTOEXEC.BAT file copy your most frequently used utilities there. In this case, you'd have a PATH that looked like:

```
PATH=D:\;C:\;C:\DOS;C:\BIN
```

You'd put the D:\ first, since it's faster for DOS to look at a RAMdisk than even a speedy hard disk.

This will let DOS load any COM, EXE, and BAT files stored in any of the directories included in your path, no matter which directory you happen to be logged into. Without it you could run only the COM, EXE, and BAT files in the current directory. It's important to use drive letters in your path if you jump around between drives. If you never switch drives, you don't need to specify them.

The SWPATH.BAT batch file below lets you change your path from within a batch file:

```
ECHO OFF
IF !%1==! GOTO EXIT
IF %1==1 PATH=%PATH1%
IF %1==2 PATH=%PATH2%
IF %1==3 PATH=%PATH3%
```

```
IF %1==4 PATH=%PATH4%
:EXIT
```

To switch PATHs, just enter:

```
SWPATH n
```

where n is a number from 1 to 4.

For this to work you first have to run SETPATH.BAT before using SWPATH (you need run SETPATH only once per DOS session). Make sure you modify the examples shown in SETPATH so that PATH1, PATH2, and PATH3 define meaningful paths based on your current subdirectory structure. The subdirectory names used here are just dummies:

```
ECHO OFF
PATH1=C:\WP\LTRS
PATH2=C:\LOTUS\PAYROLL
PATH3=C:\;C:\UTIL;C:\WP
PATH4=%PATH%
```

If you enter a number from 1 to 3 following SWPATH on the command line, your path will be reset to a path pointed to by PATH1, PATH2 or PATH3. If you enter a 4, your path will be reset to its original state at bootup— the way it was before you ran SWPATH.

There are some limits to what path can do, however. It can't find all of your programs. Application programs like *WordStar* (which is really WS.COM) use overlay program files, which usually have OVR or OVL file extensions. If you tell DOS where your *WordStar* files are located, it can find and load the WS.COM file but not the overlay files. Similarly, if your programs create nonexecutable data files, DOS will be able to look at the path and find the program that creates the data but not the data files themselves. paths are designed to work with executable files only.

If you're using DOS version 3.3 you can take advantage of the APPEND command to take care of this limitation. In fact, you may use APPEND with or without putting it in your environment; a /E switch adds the APPEND strings to the environment. APPEND works just like the PATH command except that it helps DOS find nonexecutable files. If you're using a version of DOS earlier than 3.3, you'll have to purchase a PATH extender such as *Filepath* or *File Facility*.

Batch Files and the Environment

You may add to or modify the environment by entering commands directly at the DOS prompt or by including these SET, PROMPT, or PATH commands in batch files. To read environment variables in batch files, you have to wrap them in percent signs (%), as the %PROMPT% variables demonstrated above. You can't use these percent signs directly on the DOS command line.

The batch file FOR command makes it easy to print out parts of environment variables that have been delimited by semicolons. So the single-line batch file:

```
FOR %%I IN (%PATH%) ECHO %%I
```

will produce a list of directories in the PATH. If the PATH variable were PATH=D:\;C:\;C:\BIN;C:\DOS, the batch file would display:

```
D:\
C:\
C:\BIN
C:\DOS
```

One advantage of using environment variables in batch files is that they can be redefined on the fly. For instance, you might have used your AUTOEXEC.BAT file to define environment variable PASSWORD as:

```
SET PASSWORD=ANYONE
```

If a batch file that loads an accounting package contains the lines:

```
ECHO OFF
IF %PASSWORD%==ROSEBUD GOTO START
ECHO INVALID PASSWORD!!
GOTO END
:START
REM This will now run the ACCT.EXE accounting program
ACCT
:END
```

then only users who entered:

```
SET PASSWORD=ROSEBUD
```

prior to running the batch file would be able to get into the accounting system. This isn't much of a security measure for experienced users, but it can keep beginners honest.

If you modify the environment from the DOS command line or from a batch file, the changes you make will be available for all subsequent programs. The exception is with batch files that run under a secondary copy of COMMAND.COM.

It's a common practice to "nest" batch files by having one batch file load a second copy of COMMAND.COM that runs a second batch file. If you wanted A.BAT to run B.BAT and return to A.BAT, you'd just put a line in A.BAT that said:

```
COMMAND /C B.BAT
```

Assuming B.BAT executed without a hitch and didn't load still one more batch file, when B.BAT finished it would exit the second copy of COMMAND.COM and return to the first copy and A.BAT.

However, when you load B.BAT with an additional copy of COMMAND.COM, DOS gives it a copy of the environment. And changes made to that copy are lost when the BAT file terminates.

If you had a line in B.BAT like:

```
SET SIGNAL=OK
```

this won't let B.BAT pass environment information back to A.BAT by putting the environment variable "SIGNAL" in the master environment block. SIGNAL would be set only in B.BAT's copy of the environment. Any modifications that B.BAT makes to the environment copy will be lost on returning to A.BAT. Since it runs under a secondary command processor, B.BAT can't add the variable SIGNAL to the master environment block.

Again, DOS 3.3 solved this by letting you nest batch files by using the CALL command. CALL doesn't have to load a second copy of COMMAND.COM, which means that any nested batch files can create of change environment variables that the original batch file can use.

If A.BAT contained the lines:

```
ECHO OFF
SET > SETOLD
CALL B
SET > SETNEW
TYPE SETOLD
TYPE SETNEW
```

and B.BAT contained simply:

```
SET PC=MAGAZINE
```

when A.BAT finished running it would display two copies of the environment, and the second one (SETNEW) would contain a line:

```
PC=MAGAZINE
```

that the first didn't.

Hard disk users often create a subdirectory for each new project they begin. These can end up being several subdirectory levels deep. After changing to another directory, returning to the deeply buried one means typing (and often mistyping) a long path over and over again.

If you're going to keep a new subdirectory called:

```
\WORK\JOB1\ACCT\SMITH
```

on your hard disk, you can just create a batch file called SMITH.BAT that contains the single line:

```
CD \WORK\JOB1\ACCT\SMITH
```

After you put this small batch file in a \BIN or \BAT subdirectory that was included in your path, you could type:

```
SMITH
```

and DOS would change into that directory.

But you may not want to create a permanent file, especially if you're using an inefficient hard disk like the one on the early XTs that wasted 4K of space for even the smallest files.

By setting a single environment variable and using a two-line batch file called HOME.BAT that's in a directory your path knows about, you can get immediately to your project subdirectory by simply entering:

```
HOME
```

HOME.BAT consists of two lines:

```
ECHO OFF
IF NOT !%HOMEDIR%==! CD %HOMEDIR%
```

Assuming your project directory is C:\LOTUS\PAYROLL\PROJECT, at the DOS command prompt enter

```
SET HOMEDIR=C:\LOTUS\PAYROLL\PROJECT
```

Now whenever you've been working in another directory and want to get back to your project, just enter HOME and DOS will automatically switch to the directory name pointed to by the environment variable HOMEDIR.

When DOS sees an environment variable in a batch file, it tries to find that variable in the environment. If it finds one there, DOS substitutes what's to the right of the equals sign for the variable itself and executes the batch file line.

The IF test makes sure you entered an environment variable. IF you didn't, DOS replaces %HOMEDIR% with (nothing) and turns the line into:

```
IF NOT !==! CD
```

The IF NOT !==! test fails, since ! is indeed equal to !. In this case nothing awful would happen if you omitted the IF test. Changing it to:

```
ECHO OFF
CD %HOMEDIR%
```

would switch to your home directory if you had defined one with the SET command, and would simply execute a CD, which reports the current directory, if you hadn't. You could get fancy (as was done in the batch section of this book) and print a message if no variable was found:

```
ECHO OFF
IF !%HOMEDIR%==! GOTO OOPS
CD %HOMEDIR%
GOTO END
:OOPS
ECHO Enter a HOME directory using the
ECHO SET= command, eg SET HOMEDIR=\DOS\BAT
:END
```

The nice thing about this (apart from saving keystrokes) is that you can redefine the HOMEDIR variable whenever you want, just by typing in another SET HOMEDIR command.

Programs and the Environment

Unlike batch files, which can access the master environment block directly, programs (including memory resident programs) can get only one copy of the environment, either from DOS or from the program that loaded them.

Many popular application programs let users load a second copy of COM-MAND.COM without leaving the program (with commands like *dBASE*'s RUN, BASIC's SHELL, and *1-2-3*'s /S). Any changes made to the environment in this way are made only to the copy of the environment that DOS provides, and are lost as soon as you type EXIT command to return to the application program.

All programs require two important DOS memory structures — a Program Segment Prefix (PSP) and a Memory Control Block (MCB). The PSP provides a program with information like command-line arguments, file-handling data, and the location of the next instruction to execute when the program terminates. The MCB is set by DOS to mark off different parts of memory — specifically the memory allocated to a program.

These memory structures lie directly above a program's copy of the environment. If either one is accidentally altered by a program that is trying to make changes to its copy of the environment, some very serious errors could occur, including damage to data files.

Your program can read the copy of its environment, but it has to be careful about making changes. If changes are made, they will be available to any programs loaded by your program, but they will be lost when the program terminates. And if the changes do not fit precisely into the space allocated to the program's copy of the environment, you face the probable disaster of overwriting a critical portion of memory.

The memory map below shows that a program's copy of the environment is always located below the program, its PSP, and its MCB. This is why the space provided for the copy is limited: only a few bytes higher in memory are areas that are vital to the program. Changes made to a copy of the environment must fit in the space provided.

640K

High memory portion of COMMAND.COM
Current program data space
Current program code space
Current program's PSP, includes: Address of this program's environment at offset 2CH in PSP
DOS memory control block (MCB)
Current program's environment
If the current program was loaded and run by a program other than DOS, the parent program and its environment will reside here. It's possible to have several programs, one loaded on top of the other, in this space. Memory resident programs and their environments will also be here.
Master environment block
Low memory portion of COMMAND.COM
PSP of COMMAND.COM
(Any device drivers loaded from CONFIG.SYS)
BIOS areas

Current program begins here →

Current program's PSP begins here →

0K

To find a program's copy of the environment, you need to look into the PSP. All programs are allocated one or more 64K memory blocks, or segments, for their code. The actual code for a program begins at offset 100H in its first segment. The area from 0 to 100H is reserved for the PSP. Among the many important items of information stored in the PSP is the memory segment address of the program's copy of the environment, stored at offset 2CH in the PSP. You can use the DOS DEBUG utility both to find the address of a program's environment copy and to display the actual environment copy in memory.

To see the contents of your DOS environment, load DEBUG (by typing DEBUG at the DOS prompt). When you see the DEBUG hyphen (-) prompt enter:

```
D2C 2D
```

DEBUG will display something like:

```
-D 2C 2D
37E6:0020                    0B 34              .4
```

When you loaded DEBUG, DOS made a copy of the environment available to it and placed the segment address of the copy at offset 2CH in DEBUG's PSP. Segment addresses like this occupy two bytes of memory (a "word"), and are stored in "back-words" format. You have to reverse the bytes to get a meaningful segment address.

The command you typed told DEBUG to display the contents of memory at offsets 2CH through 2DH (only two bytes). In the example above, the contents are 0BH and 34H. Since these are stored in reverse order, flip them round to make them 340BH. The H suffix just reminds you that you're dealing with hex notation. This is obvious when you're working with a number with a letter like B in it. But it's not so obvious when you see a number like 100. Hex 100 is equal to 256 decimal.

To have DEBUG display the contents of memory at segment 340BH, at the prompt enter

```
D340B:0
```

The ":0" tells DEBUG to treat this as a segment address, starting at offset 0 in the segment. If you use an unusually large environment, you may have to enter D several times to page through the whole environment. The DEBUG display will look something like:

```
-D340B:0
340B:0000 43 4F 4D 53 50 45 43 3D-43 3A 5C 43 4F 4D 4D 41 COMSPEC=C:\COMMA
340B:0010 4E 44 2E 43 4F 4D 00 50-41 54 48 3D 42 3A 5C 3B ND.COM.PATH=B:\;
340B:0020 44 3A 5C 3B 43 3A 5C 3B-43 3A 5C 42 49 4E 00 48 D:\;C:\;C:\BIN.H
340B:0030 4F 4D 45 44 49 52 3D 63-3A 5C 64 73 5C 62 72 5C OMEDIR=c:\ds\br\
340B:0040 6E 65 78 74 62 72 00 50-52 4F 4D 50 54 3D 24 70 nextbr.PROMPT=$p
340B:0050 24 5F 00 00 01 00 43 3A-5C 44 45 42 55 47 2E 43 $_....C:\DEBUG.C
340B:0060 4F 4D 00 43 4D 50 3D 64-3A 5C 63 38 38 2E 65 78 OM.CMP=d:\c88.ex
340B:0070 5A 13 34 ED 6B 3D 64 3A-5C 61 73 6D 38 38 2E 65 Z.4.k=d:\asm88.e
```

As you can see by looking at the ASCII part of the DEBUG display (at the extreme right side of it), each environment string is stored as a series of characters terminated by a null, or zero byte. So the first string, for COMSPEC, actually looks like:

The null byte of the first string, COMSPEC, is on the second line of the center display, at 340B:0016. A string of ASCII characters that ends with an ASCII character 0 is called an ASCIIZ string. When you use SET to modify the environment, the internal DOS procedures invoked by SET supply this terminating null byte automatically.

The 00 appears as a dot, since DEBUG displays any character with an ASCII value higher than 126 or lower than 32 as a period.

Each one of the series of strings in the environment is similarly terminated by a null. The very last string, PROMPT, ends with an additional null byte. The two null bytes together mark the end of the environment.

At the end, DOS places a copy of the complete file specification (drive, path, filename, and extension) of the current program. This is the string "C:\DEBUG.COM" shown at 340B:0056, followed by a NULL terminator. (The address you get will, of course, differ from the one shown.) The remainder is garbage left over in memory from a previous program process.

To end your DEBUG session, just type Q to quit and press the Enter key.

Memory-Resident Programs

Like other programs, the environment block used by a memory-resident program (also called a TSR, for Terminate and Stay Resident) is a copy of the master environment block, made by DOS at the time the memory-resident program is loaded. Since this copy is never updated, a memory-resident program will never see any changes made to the master environment block at a later time.

This has several immediate implications. If a memory-resident program needs to refer to an environment variable to operate properly, that variable should be set before the memory-resident program is loaded.

Furthermore, every memory-resident program gets a complete copy of the environment, so using several memory-resident programs will eat up additional memory. This may be important if you have expanded the size of your environment significantly.

Finally, the DOS manual contains a puzzling warning that DOS cannot expand the environment beyond 127 bytes if you have loaded a memory-resident program, such as MODE or *SideKick*. It implies that if you intend to expand the environment you would have to reserve a larger size and fill that extra memory space with dummy temporary strings before your AUTOEXEC.BAT encountered its first memory-resident command. This isn't correct. Using the techniques explained below you can safely expand your environment space without worrying about how they'll affect any TSR programs your AUTOEXEC.BAT file loads.

Expanding the Environment

You can't really create utilities and batch files that use the environment if your environment doesn't have enough space to add new variables and information. The DOS default limit on environment space is 160 bytes, of which the PATH and COMSPEC variables take up a minimum of 29 bytes. It's easy to expand the size, but the techniques for making your environment larger vary according to DOS version.

DOS did not offer environment capabilities prior to version 2.0. Since then, the default environment block size has been set at 160 characters. DOS sets the environment size in units of 16 bytes each, known as paragraphs, and ten paragraphs (160 bytes) are allocated for the environment.

DOS 3.2

The simplest way to increase the size of the environment past 160 bytes is to use a DOS version 3.2 or later, which lets you make your environment as large as 32K. Simply put a line in your system's CONFIG.SYS file that says:

```
SHELL=COMMAND.COM /E:xxxxx /P
```

where xxxxx represents the size, in bytes, of the master environment block you want to reserve (a number from 160 to 32768), and /P means "load AUTOEXEC.BAT automatically." If you forget to add the /P switch, DOS will not load AUTOEXEC.BAT even if it's in the right place on your startup disk.

If you're using a DOS version older than 3.2, first, consider upgrading. If you have the DOS SETENV utility (Microsoft distributes it with some of its C and some other languages) you can patch COMMAND.COM to reserve an environment from 160 to 992 bytes. If you don't have SETENV, you can use DEBUG to patch your working copy of COMMAND.COM yourself, as described below. It's actually a simple and painless operation.

Warning: While the SETENV technique and the patches presented below have been tested on versions 2.0, 2.1, 3.0, and 3.1 of IBM's PC-DOS version of MS-DOS, and on Compaq's MS-DOS versions 3.0 and 3.1, and should work on MS-DOS for close compatibles, they can't be guaranteed. Some "compatible" vendors have rewritten COMMAND.COM, so the data to be changed with DEBUG or SETENV may not be in the same locations across versions of MS-DOS. So whether you use SETENV or try one of the COMMAND.COM patches described below, try it on a new diskette formatted with the /S option. After you make the changes, run TESTENV.BAT (see below) to make sure that your environment has been expanded as you expected. Then copy the modified COMMAND.COM to your work diskettes or hard disk. Don't overwrite your original copy of COMMAND.COM.

DOS 3.0 and 3.1

If you have DOS version 3.0 or 3.1, you can try an undocumented solution similar to the one described above. To increase the environment under DOS 3.0 or 3.1, add the following line to your CONFIG.SYS:

```
SHELL=COMMAND.COM /E:xx /P
```

where xx refers to the number (from 10 to 62) of 16-byte memory paragraphs to reserve for the environment. Note that this process is slightly different from the one above, since it makes you specify the number of 16-byte memory paragraphs you want, rather than the absolute number of bytes. Again, make sure you add a /P so DOS will load your AUTOEXEC.BAT file when booting up.

DOS 2.0 to 3.1

If you have Microsoft's SETENV.EXE handy, just enter:

```
SETENV COMMAND.COM <size>
```

where <size> is the size (in bytes) of the environment block you want, from 160 to 992. SETENV will round this up to an even paragraph value (a multiple of 16). You can specify a larger number if you wish, but versions 2.0 to 3.1 of DOS limit the environment block size to a maximum of 992 bytes even if you try to exceed that figure.

Patching COMMAND.COM with DEBUG

If you're not using a version of DOS higher than 3.1, and you don't have SETENV, and the other solutions for expanding the environment don't suit your taste, you can use DEBUG to patch COMMAND.COM.

To do this, format a blank diskette with the /S option to add the system files to it. Then copy DEBUG to the diskette, and enter the appropriate command for the version of DOS you're using.

For DOS 2.0 or 2.1 only, enter:

```
DEBUG COMMAND.COM
E ECF 3E
W
Q
```

This will patch DOS 2.0 and 2.1 COMMAND.COM to set the environment size at the maximum 992 bytes. If you'd like a smaller environment, change the last number on the first line to the hexadecimal value of the number of 16 byte paragraphs you want your environment size to be. Refer to this chart:

Decimal Para- graphs	Decimal Bytes	Hex Value to Use	Decimal Para- graphs	Decimal Bytes	Hex Value to Use	Decimal Para- graphs	Decimal Bytes	Hex Value to Use
10	160	0A	28	448	1C	46	736	2E
11	176	0B	29	464	1D	47	752	2F
12	192	0C	30	480	1E	48	768	30
13	208	0D	31	496	1F	49	784	31
14	224	0E	32	512	20	50	800	32
15	240	0F	33	528	21	51	816	33
16	256	10	34	544	22	52	832	34
17	272	11	35	560	23	53	848	35
18	288	12	36	576	24	54	864	36
19	304	13	37	592	25	55	880	37
20	320	14	38	608	26	56	896	38
21	336	15	39	624	27	57	912	39
22	352	16	40	640	28	58	928	3A
23	368	17	41	656	29	59	944	3B
24	384	18	42	672	2A	60	960	3C
25	400	19	43	688	2B	61	976	3D
26	416	1A	44	704	2C	62	992	3E
27	432	1B	45	720	2D			

For DOS 3.0 only, enter:

```
DEBUG COMMAND.COM
E F2C 3E
W
Q
```

For DOS 3.1 only, enter:

```
DEBUG COMMAND.COM
E D11 3E
W
Q
```

If you're using generic MS-DOS 2.11, try:

```
DEBUG COMMAND.COM
E DF3 3E
W
Q
```

If you do patch COMMAND.COM, be sure you don't mix patched and unpatched versions on your disk, since doing so can end up confusing DOS.

To test your changes, reboot your system with the diskette containing the newly modified COMMAND.COM. This removes any programs (including memory-resident programs) from memory that might alter the test results. Then run TESTENV.BAT.

The easiest way to create TESTENV.BAT is to run the TESTENV.BAS program:

```
100 ' TESTENV.BAS - creates TESTENV.BAT
110 OPEN "TESTENV.BAT" FOR OUTPUT AS #1
120 PRINT #1,"ECHO Initializing Test Strings"
130 FOR A=0 TO 15
140 PRINT #1,"SET ";HEX$(A);"=";STRING$(78,A+65)
150 NEXT
160 PRINT #1,"ENVCOUNT"
170 PRINT #1,"PAUSE"
180 FOR A=0 TO 15
190 PRINT #1,"SET ";HEX$(A);"="
200 NEXT
210 PRINT #1,"ECHO Test complete"
220 CLOSE
```

You can run this by entering:

```
BASICA TESTENV.BAS
```

(or GWBASIC TESTENV.BAS if you're using a generic system.) It creates a batch file that looks like:

```
ECHO Initializing Test Strings
SET 0=AAAAAAAAAAAAAAAAAAAAAAAAAAAAAAAAAAAAAAAAAAAAAAAAAAAAAAAAAAAAAAAAAAAAAAAAAAAAAAAA
SET 1=BBBBBBBBBBBBBBBBBBBBBBBBBBBBBBBBBBBBBBBBBBBBBBBBBBBBBBBBBBBBBBBBBBBBBBBBBBBBBBBB
SET 2=CCCCCCCCCCCCCCCCCCCCCCCCCCCCCCCCCCCCCCCCCCCCCCCCCCCCCCCCCCCCCCCCCCCCCCCCCCCCCCCC
SET 3=DDDDDDDDDDDDDDDDDDDDDDDDDDDDDDDDDDDDDDDDDDDDDDDDDDDDDDDDDDDDDDDDDDDDDDDDDDDDDDDD
SET 4=EEEEEEEEEEEEEEEEEEEEEEEEEEEEEEEEEEEEEEEEEEEEEEEEEEEEEEEEEEEEEEEEEEEEEEEEEEEEEEEE
SET 5=FFFFFFFFFFFFFFFFFFFFFFFFFFFFFFFFFFFFFFFFFFFFFFFFFFFFFFFFFFFFFFFFFFFFFFFFFFFFFFFF
SET 6=GGGGGGGGGGGGGGGGGGGGGGGGGGGGGGGGGGGGGGGGGGGGGGGGGGGGGGGGGGGGGGGGGGGGGGGGGGGGGGGG
SET 7=HHHHHHHHHHHHHHHHHHHHHHHHHHHHHHHHHHHHHHHHHHHHHHHHHHHHHHHHHHHHHHHHHHHHHHHHHHHHHHHH
SET 8=IIIIIIIIIIIIIIIIIIIIIIIIIIIIIIIIIIIIIIIIIIIIIIIIIIIIIIIIIIIIIIIIIIIIIIIIIIIIIIII
SET 9=JJJJJJJJJJJJJJJJJJJJJJJJJJJJJJJJJJJJJJJJJJJJJJJJJJJJJJJJJJJJJJJJJJJJJJJJJJJJJJJJ
SET A=KKKKKKKKKKKKKKKKKKKKKKKKKKKKKKKKKKKKKKKKKKKKKKKKKKKKKKKKKKKKKKKKKKKKKKKKKKKKKKKK
SET B=LLLLLLLLLLLLLLLLLLLLLLLLLLLLLLLLLLLLLLLLLLLLLLLLLLLLLLLLLLLLLLLLLLLLLLLLLLLLLLLL
SET C=MMMMMMMMMMMMMMMMMMMMMMMMMMMMMMMMMMMMMMMMMMMMMMMMMMMMMMMMMMMMMMMMMMMMMMMMMMMMMMMM
SET D=NNNNNNNNNNNNNNNNNNNNNNNNNNNNNNNNNNNNNNNNNNNNNNNNNNNNNNNNNNNNNNNNNNNNNNNNNNNNNNNN
SET E=OOOOOOOOOOOOOOOOOOOOOOOOOOOOOOOOOOOOOOOOOOOOOOOOOOOOOOOOOOOOOOOOOOOOOOOOOOOOOOOO
SET F=PPPPPPPPPPPPPPPPPPPPPPPPPPPPPPPPPPPPPPPPPPPPPPPPPPPPPPPPPPPPPPPPPPPPPPPPPPPPPPPP
```

```
ENVCOUNT
PAUSE
SET 0=
SET 1=
SET 2=
SET 3=
SET 4=
SET 5=
SET 6=
SET 7=
SET 8=
SET 9=
SET A=
SET B=
SET C=
SET D=
SET E=
SET F=
ECHO Test complete
```

TESTENV.BAT runs a program that's on the accompanying disk, ENVCOUNT.COM, which counts the number of bytes used in the environment. You could also create ENVCOUNT.COM by assembling the ENVCOUNT.ASM code:

```
; ENVCOUNT.ASM — Counts number of bytes in Environment
CSEG            SEGMENT
                ASSUME CS:      CSEG, DS:CSEG, ES:CSEG, SS:CSEG
                ORG             100H                ; For COM file
ENTRY:
MAX_COUNT EQU 4
BEGIN:
                PUSH            DS                  ; Save DS on stack
                MOV             AX,CS:[2CH]         ; Get Environment address
                MOV             DS,AX               ; into DS
                MOV             DI,0                ; Set DI to offset 0
                XOR             SI,SI               ; Clear SI to 0
NEXT_BYTE:
                CMP             WORD PTR[SI],0000 ; Check for End of Environment
                JE              FOUND_END           ; If found, break out of loop
                INC             SI                  ; Point to next byte
                JMP             NEXT_BYTE           ; Loop back to check next byte
FOUND_END:
                MOV             AX,SI
                ADD             AX,4                ; Add for current bytes
                                                    ; and "word-count"
```

```
              POP           DS                 ; Restore DS from stack
              ; The size of Environment space in use is now in AX
              MOV           CX,MAX_COUNT       ; Length of count into CX
              MOV           DI,OFFSET COUNT+4 ; Point DI to End of string
              MOV           SI,10              ; Set SI to divide AX by 10
              XOR           DX,DX              ; Clear DX
ANOTHER:      DIV           SI                 ; Divide AX by 10, rem. in DX
              ADD           DX,'0'             ; Convert DX to ASCII
              MOV           BYTE PTR [DI],DL   ; Move Ascii value to buffer
              DEC           DI                 ; Decrement Pointer
              XOR           DX,DX              ; Clear DX
              CMP           AX,SI              ; If AX is >= 10
              JAE           ANOTHER            ; Loop back
              ADD           AX,'0'             ; Else Convert DX to ASCII
              MOV           BYTE PTR [DI],AL   ; Move ASCII value to buffer
PRINT_RESULT: MOV           DX,OFFSET MESSAGE ; Load Message address
              MOV           AH,9               ; Function to print message
              INT           21H                ; Call DOS
EXIT:         INT           20H                ; Back to DOS
NOTICE        DB 'Copyright 1988 Ziff-Davis Publishing Co.'
NOTICE2       DB 'Programmed by Richard Hale Shaw'
MESSAGE       DB 'The Environment is currently using: ' ; message to print
COUNT         DB '            bytes,'13,10,'$' ; Place for count
ENDPROG LABEL BYTE ; End of program
CSEG ENDS
              END ENTRY
```

Or, type in the following 14 lines:

```
DEBUG
E 100 1E 2E A1 2C 00 8E D8 BF 00 00 33 F6 83 3C 00 74
E 110 03 46 EB F8 8B C6 05 04 00 1F B9 04 00 BF B0 01
E 120 BE 0A 00 33 D2 F7 F6 83 C2 30 88 15 4F 33 D2 3B
E 130 C6 73 F2 05 30 00 88 05 BA 88 01 B4 09 CD 21 CD 20
E 141 'Copyright 1988 Ziff-Davis Publishing Co.'
E 169 'Programmed by Richard Hale Shaw'
E 188 'The Environment is currently using: '
E 1AB 20 20 20 20 20 20 20 'bytes,'0D,0A,24
RCX
BA
N ENVCOUNT.COM
W
Q
```

TESTENV.BAT creates a series of temporary environment strings in an attempt to fill up environment space. Then it runs ENVCOUNT.COM to report how much space is used (make sure ENVCOUNT.COM is in the current directory or is in one that your path knows about). If you see the "Out of environment space" message, you know you've filled up your environment, which is what you want. If you don't see the message, modify the file to add more strings.

TESTENV will add up to 1,280 bytes of strings to the environment, which will overflow it under DOS versions earlier than 3.2, which can't handle more than 992 bytes. To test larger environments under DOS 3.2 or later, increase the 15 at the end of lines 130 and 180 of the TESTENV.BAS program. Each time you increase this number by 1 you'll take up an additional 80 bytes (or more) of memory. If you want to increase it above 190, change:

```
STRING$(78,A+65)
```

at the end of line 140 to:

```
STRING$(78,65)
```

If you do make the batch file too large, you won't hurt anything by trying to overflow your environment.

ENVCOUNT.COM counts the number of bytes actually occupying the environment. After counting, it prints the message: "The environment is currently using: XX bytes," where XX is the number it counted. You can also run ENVCOUNT as a standalone program at the DOS prompt.

PC Magazine contributor Charles Petzold has another approach. As he points out, COMMAND.COM maintains the environment in an area of memory that you don't have direct access to. Whenever COMMAND.COM loads an executable program into memory, it makes a copy of the environment table for use by that program. The segment address of this copy is stored at offset 2CH in the program's PSP. As mentioned earlier, any changes a program makes to this environment alter this copy and not the original.

If you need to add a new directory path to your existing path string, and you're not using the buggy DOS 3.0 version, you can do so very easily with a one-line batch file called ADDPATH.BAT:

```
PATH=%PATH%;%1
```

You'd execute it like this:

```
ADDPATH C:\SUBDIR
```

where SUBDIR is a subdirectory on drive C: that you want to add to your path string.

It would be better to have full editing capabilities with a path string and not have to load secondary copies of COMMAND.COM. You could do it with a batch file called EDPATHB.BAT (EDPATHB stands for "EDit PATH with Batch file"):

```
ECHO PATH=%PATH% >NEWPATH.BAT
EDLIN NEWPATH.BAT
NEWPATH
```

The first line creates a file called NEWPATH.BAT that contains a PATH command with your current path. (Once again, you can't use this under DOS 3.0.) The second line loads it into EDLIN. Once you're in EDLIN you can press 1 to edit the first (and only) line. You can then use the DOS editing keys (right arrow to recall characters, DEL to delete them, INS to go into insert mode, etc.) and change the path. Then press Enter and E to end EDLIN. EDPATHB then executes the NEWPATH.BAT batch file with your new path. If you don't like EDLIN, you can have this batch file load NEWPATH into the ASCII text editor of choice.

DOS provides another way to change COMMAND.COM's environment from within a program without reloading a secondary copy of COMMAND.COM. However, doing so requires an undocumented and little known DOS interrupt called interrupt 2EH. This interrupt passes a command line addressed by DS:SI to COMMAND.COM. The command line must be formatted just like the unformatted parameter area of a PSP. The first byte must be a count of characters, and the second and subsequent bytes must be a command line with parameters. The whole thing is terminated by a carriage return.

When this command line is passed to interrupt 2EH, COMMAND.COM executes it. If the transient part of COMMAND.COM is not present in memory, the resident part will reload it. However, it does not load a new copy of COMMAND.COM into memory.

Interrupt 2EH is very strange. If interrupt 2EH is called from a program executed from within a batch file, it will abort the batch file. If it's executed in a program run from a "Run a Program" or "Shell" option in an application that has itself been executed from a batch file, it aborts the whole chain and will probably crash your system. Interrupt 2EH is also difficult to use because it destroys the contents of all registers including the stack pointer.

Charles Petzold's EDPATHA.COM ("EDit PATH with Assembly program") program on the accompanying disk uses this interrupt to make changing your path a breeze. Or you could create it with DEBUG by typing the following instructions:

```
A
MOV     BX,0368              ; Above top of program
MOV     SP,BX                ; New stack pointer
ADD     BX,+0F
MOV     CL,04
SHR     BX,CL                ; Convert BX to segment
MOV     AH,4A                ; Deallocate memory
INT     21
PUSH    ES
```

```
MOV      ES,[002C]              ; Points to environment
SUB      DI,DI
MOV      SI,016A                ; Points to "PATH="
CLD
ES:                             ; SEARCH:
CMP      BYTE PTR [DI],00       ; See if end
JZ       0133                   ; JZ TRANSFER
PUSH     SI
MOV      CX,0005                ; 5 bytes ot compare
REPZ                            ; Compare them
CMPSB
POP      SI
JZ       0133                   ; JZ TRANSFER
SUB      AL,AL                  ; Search for next 0
MOV      CX,8000
REPNZ
SCASB
JMP      011B                   ; JMP SEARCH
MOV      BX,016F                ; TRANSFER:
MOV      CL,05                  ; Number of chars already
ES:                             ; TRANSLOOP:
MOV      AL,[DI]                ; Get byte
INC      DI                     ; Kick up pointer
OR       AL,AL
JZ       0147                   ; JZ DONE
INC      CL                     ; Kick up counter
MOV      [BX],AL                ; Save byte
INC      BX
JMP      0138                   ; JMP TRANSLOOP
MOV      BYTE PTR [BX],0D       ; CR at end
MOV      [0169],CL              ; Save count
POP      ES
MOV      DX,0168                ; Let user edit it
MOV      AH,0A
INT      21
MOV      SI,0168                ; Fix it up
MOV      AL,[SI+01]
INC      AL
MOV      [SI],AL
MOV      BYTE PTR [SI+01],20
INT      2E                     ; Execute new path
INT      20                     ; terminate
DB       80,00
DB       "PATH="
RCX
```

```
6F
W
Q
```

EDPATHA searches the environment for a PATH, saves it in an area of memory following the characters "PATH=," and passes this string to DOS function call 0AH. You can then use the DOS editing keys to edit it. For instance, if you want to add something to the end, press F3, which will recall the whole line onscreen and let you type the addition. You could also try normal DOS editing insertions and deletions. When you're done, press the Enter key and EDPATHA will send the string to interrupt 2EH. COMMAND.COM then executes it like a regular PATH command.

Incidentally, if you start experimenting with your environment, you may end up corrupting your PATH or APPEND settings. And if you're working on someone else's system you may want to change the PATH or PROMPT temporarily, but clean up when you're done and put things back to normal.

The solution for both of these problems is to type:

```
SET > RESET.BAT
```

before you make any changes. This puts all the environment settings into a RESET.BAT batch file. When you're done, just type RESET and DOS will put things back the way they were. COMSPEC and other environment variables require SET COMSPEC=xxxx phrasings, so RESET.BAT will produce a brief flurry of harmless error messages as it executes. On the rare occasions when you do need to change these you can always customize RESET.BAT with your word processor.

And if you end up with a long list of space-hogging variables in your environment and want to get rid of them in one operation, you can type:

```
SET > FIX.BAT
```

and then use your word processor to wipe out all the settings like:

```
A=XYZ
B=C:\DOS\UTILS\ADDTO
C=12345
```

by changing these to:

```
SET A=
SET B=
SET C=
```

and then running FIX.

You can also keep your PATH safe if you use a technique like the ADDPATH.BAT batch file mentioned above, by first typing:

```
PATH > OLDPATH.BAT
```

Then, to reset your PATH back to normal, just type OLDPATH.

Chapter 12

Screens and Color

Okay, you've worn the letters off your keytops, and you've ground the heads on your disk drives down to the bare metal, but the one part of your system you probably know better than any other is your screen. If you're like most avid users, you're glued to it hypnotically each day for hours on end. So you might as well make staring at it as pleasant as possible.

The first important thing to learn is that color is a true productivity tool. You can cram 2,000 characters onto a typical 80-column, 25-line screen (and 72 percent more text on newer 43-line displays). With information this dense, you need a way to highlight important information without making it blink or drawing little boxes around it.

The only method DOS provides for setting screen colors is through ANSI.SYS. However, ANSI is cumbersome because it makes you deal with escape characters that DOS normally treats as abort commands, and its color numbering scheme is different from the standard one used by BIOS and BASIC. But without ANSI, DOS consigns users of color systems to a drab grey-on-black existence.

According to insiders, IBM designers considered color frivolous, and were reluctant to produce a color system for the original PC. Colors were for games, they reasoned, and adding color meant handling lots more information — you not only had to put a character at a certain location on the screen, but had to worry about setting its display attribute at the same time.

Anyway, the PC's high-resolution monochrome adapter produced crisp, detailed characters on IBM's rock-solid mono monitor. The cool green persistent phosphor was touted as ergonomic perfection. To sweeten the monochrome deal, IBM threw in a parallel printer port for free.

(Way back then IBM didn't even offer a color display; you had to spend close to a thousand dollars to buy a third-party monitor. And when IBM did eventually advertise one, serious business users dismissed it as a toy. Besides which, coaxing color out of existing software was next to impossible. For users accustomed to the razor-sharp monochrome output, IBM's gritty, flickery color hardware made work on it nearly impossible. It was like reading text through a twitching screen door.)

But the IBM design team caved in at the last minute and offered a board called the CGA (Color Graphics Adapter) that offered several low-resolution color text and graphics modes, and a small selection of available colors. If you knew the right tricks, you could run a few applications in color, and you could use the system's built-in BASIC language to write graphics routines that addressed 320 x 200 pixels (short for "picture elements" — really just dots) in three colors, or 640 x 200 pixels in grey on black.

Trouble is, whether you bought an early CGA card and a grainy color monitor, or one of the newest high-tech color systems on the market, you'll still end up with a grey-on-black DOS. If you set colors with ANSI.SYS, typing CLS will clear the screen to those colors. But without ANSI, COMMAND.COM is hard-wired to use the color attribute number 07 when clearing the screen. The 0 yields a black background, and 7 is IBM's number for grey.

You can use DEBUG to patch COMMAND.COM so that typing CLS will clear the screen to any color you choose. Just pick the background and foreground colors you want, look up their single-digit hex values on the charts below, and combine the individual digits into a two-digit hex number. The background goes on the left and the foreground on the right. If you wanted bright yellow (hex E) text on a red (hex 4) background, for instance, you'd use the number 4E. Bright white text on a dark blue background would be 17. Then pick the appropriate patching address:

DOS Version	*DEBUG Address*
2.0	2346
2.1	2359
3.0	2428
3.1	2642
3.2	282E
3.3	2BAD

To patch version 3.3 so CLS will change your colors to bright yellow text on a red background, just type:

```
DEBUG COMMAND.COM
E 2BAD 4E
W
Q
```

If you're not using version 3.3, substitute the proper addresses in place of the 2BAD. Then either reboot, or load the patched version of COMMAND.COM by typing COMMAND. When you type CLS, DOS should clear your screen and print the prompt in bright yellow on red. Don't pick a background color (lefthand digit) higher than 7 unless you want your screen to blink.

This procedure won't set the border color, however. It's possible to move things around inside COMMAND.COM and add a routine to set the color of the border, but it's really not worth it these days, since the EGA and VGA screens don't support borders. And while patching one attribute byte in COMMAND.COM is really not all that dangerous, moving chunks of instructions around can cause problems. (Remember, if you do try patching COMMAND.COM, don't mix patched and unpatched versions on the same disk, and work only with copies of COMMAND.COM, never your original.)

If you're using a CGA system and you're desperate to set the border color, type in the following 12 lines. Omit the semicolons and the comments that follow them. Be certain to leave a blank line after the RET (just press Enter twice after typing RET), and make sure you press the Enter key at the end of each line, especially the last one with the Q:

```
DEBUG
A
MOV AH,0B          ; set color palette on CGA
MOV BL,4           ; to produce a red (4) border
INT 10             ; have BIOS do it
RET                ; back to DOS

RCX
7
N REDBORDR.COM
W
Q
```

This will create a tiny program called REDBORDR.COM that sets CGA borders to red. To have it use a different color, substitute the hex value of the color you want in place of 4 in the fourth line. So to have a bright cyan border (with a value of hex B), change the fourth line to:

```
MOV BL,B
```

Or you could type in the following 14 lines:

```
DEBUG
A
SUB BH,BH          ; color ID=0
MOV BL,[5D]        ; get paramter from FCB
AND BL,0F          ; keep 4 low bits
MOV AH,0B          ; BIOS palette setter
INT 10             ; do it
INT 20             ; back to DOS

RCX
F
N BORDRSET.COM
```

```
W
Q
```

to create a program called BORDRSET.COM. Again, omit the semicolons and the comments that follow them. Be certain to leave a blank line after the INT 20 (just press Enter twice after typing INT 20), and make sure you press the Enter key at the end of each line, especially the last one.

You can enter the border color you want on the DOS command line directly after the name of the program. So:

```
BORDRSET 1
```

will give you a dark blue border, and:

```
BORDRSET E
```

will produce a bright yellow one.

Even better is to use Charles Petzold's memory-resident KBORDER.COM program on the accompanying disk, which lets you reset border colors on the fly, and works on PC*jr* systems (the above REDBORDR.COM program won't). For more behind-the-scene details, see Chapter 8 on DEBUG. And for advanced techniques involving the EGA and beyond, see Chapter 13.

Even if your color screen can't handle borders, it can use KBORDER to adjust the colors of graphics screens. Just install KBORDER, and load BASIC by typing either BASICA (for IBM systems) or GWBASIC (for generic systems). Then enter:

```
SCREEN 1
```

for medium-resolution graphics, or:

```
SCREEN 2
```

for what IBM laughingly refers to as high-resolution (640 x 200) graphics (real high-resolution is at least 1,000 X 1,000 pixels). Press Ctrl-< and Ctrl-> to change colors. In medium resolution this will change the background; in high res it will modify the foreground.

One last note about ANSI and the CLS command. If you type CLS, DOS will generate the ANSI command to clear the screen — ESC2J (where ESC stands for the decimal 27 or hex 1B escape character and not the letters E-S-C). To see this, type:

```
CLS > SEEIT
```

which redirects the output of the CLS command into a file called SEEIT. If you then examine the SEEIT file by typing:

```
TYPE SEEIT
```

you'll see a little arrow pointing left (the escape character) followed by a 2 and a J. If you have ANSI loaded, using TYPE to display the file will end up clearing the screen instead, since ANSI will see its CLS command onscreen, and process it. If you need to work with ANSI or printer escape sequences, you can use EDLIN or your word processor to customize this SEEIT file, since the hard-to-type ESC character will already be in the file and you can simply add any other non-ESC commands after it.

The first thing most decent programs do these days when they start up is figure out whether or not a color adapter (CGA, EGA, or VGA) is active, and set the screen colors accordingly. Other programs simply use one set of colors that works on both monochrome and color systems.

Basic CGA text screens can use only eight possible colors (including black). IBM assigned the following numbers to these:

Color	Dec	Hex	Binary
Black	0	0	000
Blue	1	1	001
Green	2	2	010
Cyan	3	3	011
Red	4	4	100
Magenta	5	5	101
Brown	6	6	110
White	7	7	111

Cyan is otherwise known as light blue; magenta as purple. Brown is the hardest color to produce on many monitors, and may end up appearing as dingy yellow or purplish orange.

All of these numbers can be expressed in three binary digits (bits) as varying combinations of 0s and 1s. Three of these — red, green, and blue — have just a single 1 in them:

- Red   100
- Green   010
- Blue   001

Early IBM color displays were often referred to as "RGB" monitors since they had three electron guns behind the CRT that handled individual red, green, and blue signals. A binary color 100 meant that only the red gun was active; 001 turned on just the blue gun. By mixing and matching IBM came up with the other five. Black (000) meant that all guns were off, and white (111) that all were on.

Turn the rightmost bit (001) on by itself and you get blue. Turn the middle bit (010) on and you end up with green. Set the leftmost bit to 1 (100) and the screen displays red. Turn both the red and blue bits on (101) and your monitor activates the red and blue guns and ends up with purple (which IBM calls magenta).

By slapping one additional bit of information onto the three other color bits, IBM increased the number of color choices to 16. It named the leftmost bit the "intensity" bit, and when this bit was turned on, the screen displayed a brighter version of the color determined by the other three bits.

Turning this fourth bit on (setting it to 1) is the same as adding 8 to the value of the other three bits. So if the value of a normal color happened to be 5 (binary 101), turning on the intensity bit would add 8 to the color value, yielding 13:

```
   101      (magenta = decimal 5)
+ 1000      setting the intensity bit (adding 8)
  1101      (bright magenta = decimal 13 or hex D)
```

This chart shows the decimal, hex, and binary values for the high-intensity colors:

High-Intensity Color	*Dec*	*Hex*	*Binary*
Bright black	8	8	1000
Bright blue	9	9	1001
Bright green	10	A	1010
Bright cyan	11	B	1011
Bright red	12	C	1100
Bright magenta	13	D	1101
Bright brown	14	E	1110
Bright white	15	F	1111

Bright black turned into grey. Bright red became a sort of salmony pink color, and bright brown emerged as yellow.

Displays that could handle the intensity bit were called "IRGB" monitors. Some displays were blind to this intensity bit and made a color like bright magenta (color 13) look exactly like normal magenta (color 5). Others had trouble with the intensity circuitry and made bright colors too bright or too close to normal colors.

However, by limiting the color information to four bits — half of a byte, or a nibble — IBM could put the color information for both the foreground and background into one byte. It specified that the text or foreground data would be in the rightmost ("low") nibble and the background data in the leftmost ("high") nibble. So bright blue text (1001) on a cyan background (0011) would be coded as:

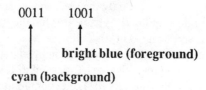

The value of this byte would be 00111001, or decimal 57 (hex 39). This is one case where hex numbering is clearly easier to work with than decimal. The binary number for bright blue text on cyan is 0011 1001. Again, the high nibble is the four bits on the left, while the low nibble is the four bits on the right. (The left half is called high because it's worth more than the right half, just as in the decimal number 57, the 5 is the high half because it's really equal to 5 x 10, or 50, and the 7 is the low half because it's equal to 7 x 1, or 7.)

The high nibble — cyan — is equal to 3. The low nibble — bright blue — is equal to 9. Together the hex value for this byte is 39:

```
0011 1001
 (3)  (9)
```

Each nibble can be one of 16 values, from 0 (0000) to 15 (1111). So a color byte can have 256 possible values, from a low of 0 (0000 0000) to a high of 255 (1111 1111). Incidentally, these examples insert a space between the high and low nibbles for clarity; but your system doesn't. To it, 255 is just 11111111.

But IBM wanted this one byte to store all the attributes, not just the color. By turning on the leftmost bit in the low (foreground) nibble it could highlight text the same way boldface type stands out on a page. And by rotating the foreground and background around, it could produce the reverse of a normal display so that text appeared black against white (or black on green in monochrome).

IBM felt that two other attributes — blinking and underlining — were important. But virtually no room was left in the byte, since three bits in each nibble were taken up by red/green/blue color information, and the remaining bit in the low nibble served as a high-intensity on/off switch.

After puzzling over underlines, IBM's designers gave up and cheated. They realized that the resolution of the original CGA color screen was truly rotten. Every one of the 255 possible displayable characters had to be made up out of a crude box or grid eight dots wide and eight dots high. That's eight rows and eight columns (actually one of the eight columns was left blank in most cases so adjacent letters wouldn't touch, and one of the eight rows was reserved for descenders on lowercase letters, yielding a 7 x 7 box). Try making characters like @, &, and % on such a small grid yourself and see how hard it is.

Worse, the bottom of one 8 x 8 CGA character box touched the top of the one below it. This meant that descenders, like the tails on the letters y or j or p, actually touched the tops of capital letters and ascenders on lowercase letters like l, d, or b. The only way to add an underline would have been to sacrifice one of the eight rows that made up the characters. Things were so tight already that the engineers decided to allow underlining on monochrome screens only, where the character box measured 9 x 14. They assigned the first nonzero value — 0001 — as a switch to turn on underlining. This value of 1 happens to be the setting for blue on a color monitor. So anything designed to appear in blue text on a color monitor ends up underlined on a mono display and vice versa.

Probably after staring at a high-intensity purple background for too long, IBM engineers realized they could sacrifice the high-intensity bit in the background (high) color nibble and use it instead to control blinking. Nobody would want to look at a glaring bright green or pulsing purple background anyway. So the leftmost bit in the low nibble controls intensity, while the leftmost bit in the high nibble controls blinking.

Actually, you can disable blinking and use high-intensity backgrounds. The easiest way to see this is in BASIC. Load BASIC by typing either BASIC (for IBM systems) or GWBASIC (for generic systems). Then type:

```
COLOR F,B
```

substituting a foreground color from 0 to 15 in place of the F, and a background color from 0 to 7 in place of the B. Entering COLOR 15,1 will produce bright white text on a dark blue background. If you add 16 to the foreground color, it will blink. Entering COLOR 31,1 will yield blinking bright white text on a blue background. Now, assuming you're using an 80-character screen, type:

```
OUT &H3D8,9
```

The text should stop blinking, and the background will turn high-intensity blue.

This technique won't work on all color systems or on all color monitors; the older your system the more likely this command will disable blinking and brighten your background. And note that BASIC actually lets you enter three color numbers (COLOR F,G,B) where the B sets the border color — the area between the 80 x 25 screen and the bezel of your monitor. IBM stopped using border colors with the EGA and continued to ignore them with the VGA, so borders are pretty much passé by now.

Since the background nibble is on the left, and the text nibble on the right, this meant that the very leftmost bit — the eighth one — would determine whether or not blinking was turned on. The eighth bit is equal to 128 (2^7 or 1000 0000). So if this bit is on, or set to 1, the text color blinks. Turning this bit on is the same as adding 128 to the existing combination of color and intensity attributes. So the bright-blue-on-cyan hex 39 example above:

```
0011 1001
```

doesn't blink. But adding 128, or binary 1000 0000 to it:

```
   0011 1001
+  1000 0000
   1011 1001
```

would produce a blinking bright blue on cyan display. The decimal value of 1011 1001 is 185. The nonblinking version of this was 57.   57 + 128 = 185.

But again, it's easier to work with hex. 1011 is equal to hex B. 1001 is equal to hex 9. So the hex notation for this is B9. Any hex number with a lefthand digit higher than 7 will blink.

In summary, an attribute byte looks like this:

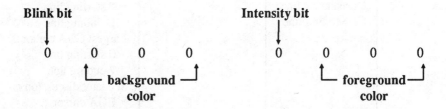

If the value of this byte is over 7F hex (127 decimal), the blink bit will be set and the text color will blink. If the blink bit is 0, it won't. In both cases the lefthand hex digit is the background color and the righthand digit is the foreground (text) color.

Most programs that set colors or clear the screen use BIOS interrupt 10. (Some programs bypass BIOS and go straight to the hardware, but such ill-behaved software won't be discussed here.) DOS doesn't offer any underlying color facilities, and uses the BIOS functions itself. It can write individual characters, or strings of characters, but these will appear in whatever attribute happens to be set at the time.

BIOS INT 10 offers a fat toolkit of character-based functions to handle just about everything you'll need to add sparkle to your display. While IBM enhanced INT 10 when it released the AT, and then jazzed it up even more when it brought the PS/2 series to market, the original services are still very capable. Figure 12.1 summarizes the standard text arsenal available (though it doesn't include pixel-oriented services, and ones that deal with things like light pens).

Since BIOS is your system's hardware specialist, just about all video tools use BIOS interrupt 10. However, DOS gets into the act a bit with a scant few teletype-oriented interrupt 21 routines (Figure 12.2).

Name of Service	What You Specify	What You Get Back	Notes

Set mode (text)	AH=0
	AL=mode
		(nothing)	Modes:
			  0 = 40x25 no color
			  1 = 40x25 color
			  2 = 80x25 no color
			  3 = 80x25 color
			  7 = 80x25 monochrome

Set cursor type and size	AH=1
	CL=starting line
	CH=ending line
		(nothing)	Largest mono cursor is:
			  0 starting line
			  D ending line
			Largest CGA cursor is:
			  0 starting line
			  7 ending line
			See later discussion on
			  EGA cursor
			Default mono is:
			  CH=0B CL=0C
			Default CGA is:
			  CH=06 CL=07
			Setting CH=20 may make
			  the cursor vanish
			A start line larger than
			  its ending line will
			  produce a 2-part cursor.

Set cursor position	AH=2
	DH=row
	DL=column
	BH=page (0)
		(nothing)	Upper lefthand corner is
			  0,0, so DX=0000
			Unless you're really
			  tricky, page is always 0

Read cursor position	AH=3
	BH=page (0)
		DH=screen row
		DL=screen column
		CH=starting line
		CL=ending line
			Again, assume the page
			  is 0, although BIOS
			  maintains positions
			  for each page

Set active page	AH=5
	AL=page
		(nothing)	AL=0-3 for 80-column
			  screens (modes 2,3)
			AL=0-7 for 40-column
			  screens (modes 0,1)

Name of Service	What You Specify	What You Get Back	Notes

Scroll up window	AH=6
	AL=number of lines to scroll
	CH=upper lefthand window row
	CL=upper lefthand window column
	DH=lower righthand window row
	DL=lower righthand window column
	BH=attribute to fill window
		(nothing)	To clear 80x25 screen use:
			  AL=0
			  CH=0
			  CL=0
			  DH=18
			  DL=4F
			  BH=color
			DH and DL are 1 less than 80x25 (hex 4F and 18 since these start at 0, not 1)
			Use AL=0 to clear screen

Scroll down window	AH=7
	AL=number of lines to scroll
	CH=upper lefthand window row
	CL=upperlefthand window column
	DH=lower righthand window row
	DL=lower righthand window column
	BH=attribute to fill window
		(nothing)	To clear 80x25 screen use:
			  AL=0
			  CH=0
			  CL=0
			  DH=18
			  DL=4F
			  BH=color
			DH and DL are 1 less than 80x25 (hex 4F and 18 since these start at 0, not 1)
			Use AL=0 to clear screen

Read attribute, character at cursor	AH=8 BH=page (0)	AL=ASCII value of character AH=attribute	Use 0 for page. This comes in handy for clearing screen to existing color.
Write attribute, character at cursor	AH=9 BH=page (0) CX=number of characters to write AL=ASCII value of character to write BL=attribute of character	(nothing)	Use 0 for page. This can fill an 80x25 screen instantly by putting a hex 7D0 (same as decimal 2000) in RCX. Have to worry about moving the cursor yourself.

Name of Service	What You Specify	What You Get Back	Notes

Write character at cursor	AH=0A
	BH=page (0)
	CX=number of
	   characters to
	   write
	AL=ASCII value of
	   character to
	   write
		(nothing)	Use 0 for page. You can use this without having to worry about getting the existing color or coming up with a new one.

Set color palette (border in text mode)	AH=0B
	BH=0
	BL=border color
		(nothing)	Works on CGAs only
			   Border may be 0-16.
			   (Function 0B has other
			   graphics abilities.)

Write character as TTY (teletype)	AH=0E AL=ASCII value of character to write	(nothing)	Advances cursor automatically but can't handle colors and treats ASCII 7, 8, 10, and 13 characters specially
Get current video state	AH=0F	AL=mode AH=number of columns BH=active page	

Figure 12.1. Original INT 10 Tools

Name of Service	What You Specify	What You Get Back	Notes
Display output	AH=2 DL=character	(nothing)	One character at a time
Display String	AH=9 DS:DX=pointer to output string	(nothing)	Must end string with a $ which means you can't display a $

Figure 12.2. INT 21 Tools

DOS's INT 21 tools are far more feeble than INT 10's. While DOS lets you display single characters, or strings of characters, it doesn't let you set or change the colors. It just displays them in whatever colors happen to be active. And since its Display Output function 9 uses a dollar sign to indicate the end of the string, you can't have function 9 *display* a dollar sign.

You could also use some of the other slightly more exotic DOS services such as the output half of Direct Console I/O function 6, or Write to File or Device function 40, or you could even use Open File 3D and write to the CON (console) device rather than a file. (The discussion of ANSI in Chapter 9 showed how to use the undocumented INT 29 "Fast TTY" function.) But the Display Output (function 2) and Display String (function 9) services, or the speedier BIOS services, can handle just about anything you'll need.

To create a short program that will display the letters "PC" you could try several different approaches. Each of the examples below uses the DEBUG (2.0 or later) mini-assembler. DEBUG works exclusively in hex, so be careful not to mix hex and decimal notation. If you're confused about registers, read the chapters on memory and DEBUG first.

After starting DEBUG (by typing DEBUG) you turn on the assembler by typing A at the DEBUG hyphen (-) prompt. You'll be creating COM files that start at hex offset 100. If you're creating several COM files in succession without leaving DEBUG, use the command:

```
A 100
```

to start each new one at offset 100. After you've created the first one, don't just use A without adding a 100 after it or else you'll end up telling DEBUG to begin the next program at the wrong starting address.

When you're done entering the interrupt 10 BIOS or interrupt 21 DOS instructions, be sure to include an instruction to exit your small program and return to DOS. If you don't, the program will freeze, or "hang" your system. There are all sorts of ways to exit. Most experts tell you that you should use function 4C of interrupt 21, the code for which looks like:

```
MOV AH,4C
INT 21
```

This approach is handy when you have to set an *exit* code (or *return* code) that a batch file can process. Adding a line before the INT 21:

```
MOV AH,4C
MOV AL,FF
INT 21
```

will set an exit code of hex FF (decimal 255). Your batch file can then include a line that says:

```
IF ERRORLEVEL 255 GOTO LABEL1
```

so the batch file jumps, or *branches* to :LABEL1 if your display program worked properly. See Chapter 10 for more information on batch techniques.

However, you can also exit a program and return to DOS with a simple:

```
INT 20
```

And with short programs like the ones below, you can use a still simpler:

```
RET
```

After you enter the final instruction to return your program to DOS, you'll have to press the Enter key twice to exit DEBUG's mini-assembler. Then just give DEBUG a name that ends with a COM extension (by using the N command), tell DEBUG how long the program is (by using the RCX command), write the program to disk (with a W), and quit (by typing Q).

To use DOS service 2 of Interrupt 21, the process would look like:

C>DEBUG	**You type DEBUG to start.**
-A	**Then type A at the hyphen prompt.**
30DD:0100 MOV AH,2	
30DD:0102 MOV DL,50	**Here DEBUG prints the AAAA:BBBB**
30DD:0104 INT 21	**addresses; you type in the instructions**
30DD:0106 MOV DL,43	**like MOV AH,2 or INT 21 and press**
30DD:0108 INT 21	**Enter after each.**
30DD:010A RET	
30DD:010B	**Just press Enter here.**
-N SERVICE2.COM	**You type N and the filename.**
-RCX	**You enter RCX.**
CX 0000	**DEBUG responds with this.**
:B	**And you enter the length (B bytes) here.**
-W	**Then you enter W to write the file.**
Writing 000B bytes	**DEBUG prints this message.**
-Q	**And you type Q to quit.**

The 30DD before the colon on seven of the lines is the segment address, and will probably be different on your system. It doesn't matter here.

Each time you enter an instruction, DEBUG figures out how many bytes it took and offers you a chance to enter an additional instruction at the next available address. When you're all done entering instructions, just press Enter. In the above example, you'd do this when you see the line:

```
30DD:010B
```

To figure out how long your program is, just look at the offset address of this line (the one following your last instruction). Ignore the leftmost four digits. Since DEBUG starts all files at address 100, subtract 100 from the rightmost four digits:

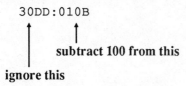

```
30DD:010B
```

subtract 100 from this

ignore this

With small programs, hex subtraction is easy:

```
   010B
 − 100
   ───
     B
```

If even this scares you, use the free hex calculator supplied with DEBUG. Just enter H (for "H math") then the rightmost four digits (here these are 010B) and finally the 100 you want to subtract. The whole command looks like:

```
-H 010B 100          You type everything after the hyphen.
020B 000B            DEBUG responds with this.
```

The first number DEBUG prints is the sum of the two numbers. The second number is the difference. You want the difference (000B). You can skip the leading zeros; 000B is the same as just plain B. Hex numbers are often expressed as pairs of digits, so you'll often see hex B written as 0B.

If you enter everything as it appears above, you'll end up with a small program on your disk called SERVICE2.COM that uses DOS service 2 to display a P and then a C and then exit. Once you've created it, just type SERVICE2 at the DOS prompt.

This program uses service 2 twice — once to print the P (which has a hex value of 50), and once to display the C (with has a hex value of 43). You tell the program you want to use service 2 of interrupt 21 by putting a 2 into the AH register with the MOV AH,2 instruction. Then you put the hex values of the characters you want to display into the DL register one at a time, with the MOV DL,50 and MOV DL,43 instructions. Then you issue an INT 21 to put DOS to work. DOS will look in the AH register to see what you want it to do, figure out that you'd like it to display a character, then get the value in register DL and display the character with that value.

This example used only one:

```
MOV AH,2
```

instruction, but two:

```
MOV DL,50
MOV DL,43
```

instructions. This is a shortcut; the first MOV AH,2 instruction lasts for both of the MOV DL,50 and MOV DL,43 instructions since the program doesn't meddle with the AH register at all after putting the 2 into it. Sometimes this won't work and you'll have to specify the MOV AH,2 twice:

```
MOV AH,2
MOV DL,50
INT 21
MOV AH,2
MOV DL,43
INT 21
RET
```

You could modify this SERVICE2.COM program and turn it into SERVICE6.COM, by repeating the process but changing the line:

```
30DD:0100 MOV AH,2
```

to:

```
30DD:0100 MOV AH,6
```

and then changing the line:

```
-N SERVICE2.COM
```

to:

```
-N SERVICE6.COM
```

Both will work almost identically. About the only difference is that while you can break out of the SERVICE2.COM program by pressing Ctrl-C (very quickly), you can't do this to the SERVICE6.COM program. However, these programs are both so short this doesn't really make any difference.

If you then wanted to see what the actual assembly language instructions looked like, you could use DEBUG's U (Unassemble) command:

```
C>DEBUG SERVICE2.COM
-U 100 LB
30F9:0100 B402     MOV     AH,02
30F9:0102 B250     MOV     DL,50
30F9:0104 CD21     INT     21
```

```
30F9:0106 B243      MOV     DL,43
30F9:0108 CD21      INT     21
30F9:010A C3        RET
```

To use the U command, specify the starting address (on programs like these it will always be 100), then the letter L, then the hex length. If you don't know the hex length of a file you just loaded into DEBUG (with a command like DEBUG SERVICE2.COM), you can have DEBUG tell you — just type RCX and press Enter twice. The number DEBUG prints after the CX is the length. The process will look something like:

```
-RCX
CX 000B
:
-
```

Both SERVICE2.COM and SERVICE6.COM printed one character at a time. If you wanted to print both at once, you could use service 9, which prints a string of characters. Just type:

`C>DEBUG`	**You type DEBUG to start.**
`A`	**Then type A at the hyphen prompt.**
`30DD:0100 MOV AH,9`	
`30DD:0102 MOV DX,108`	**Here DEBUG prints the AAAA:BBBB addresses; you type in the instructions like MOV AH,9 and INT 21 and press Enter after each.**
`30DD:0105 INT 21`	
`30DD:0107 RET`	
`30DD:0108 DB 'PC$'`	
`30DD:010B`	**Just press Enter here.**
`-N SERVICE9.COM`	**You type N and the filename.**
`-RCX`	**You enter RCX.**
`CX 0000`	**DEBUG responds with this.**
`:B`	**And you enter the length (B bytes) here.**
`-W`	**Then you enter W to write the file.**
`Writing 000B bytes`	**DEBUG prints this message.**
`-Q`	**And you type Q to quit.**

When you use service 9 of DOS interrupt 21, all you have to do is:

1. Put a 9 in register AH (with MOV AH,9).
2. Use register DX to point to the address in memory of the string that you want to print (with MOV DX,108 for instance, if the string starts at offset address 108).
3. Make sure the string you want to print starts at the address you specified in step 2, and ends with a $ (a hex 24 character).
4. Issue an INT 21 to have DOS do it for you.
5. Use one of the exit commands (such as RET or INT 20) to return to the DOS prompt once you're done.

When entering a string with the DEBUG A (Assemble) command, put it inside a pair of single or double quotation marks, and precede it with a DB. And be sure you end the string with a dollar sign, which won't appear onscreen when DOS displays the rest of the string.

You could have used the hex value of the dollar sign (24) instead of putting the $ between the quotes. Both:

```
30DD:0108 DB 'PC$'
```

and:

```
30DD:0108 DB 'PC' 24
```

will work the same.

With simple programs like this the dollar sign is often the last character in the file. If you forget to add the dollar sign, or if you specify a file length that's a byte too short so DEBUG doesn't include the final dollar sign when it writes the file to disk, you can run into problems. When you run the file DOS will print the string (in this case, PC), but since there's no dollar sign to tell it to stop it will keep printing whatever characters happen to be loaded in memory after the string until it hits a character 24 by chance. DOS may stumble over a character 24 right away, or it may print a screen or two of beeping, flashing garbage before it finally stops.

Technically, the MOV DX,108 instruction that points to the string skips a step. If you were writing a longer program, you'd have to specify an additional value, for DS, since the address of the string is pointed to by DS:DX, where DS is the segment address and DX is the offset address. (See the discussion of segmented addressing in Chapter 6 for details.) With tiny programs like these you don't have to worry about the DS segment address.

However, this time, if you try to use the DEBUG Unassemble command, you'll see:

```
C>DEBUG SERVICE9.COM
-U 100 LB
30DD:0100 B409          MOV     AH,09
30DD:0102 BA0801        MOV     DX,0108
30DD:0105 CD21          INT     21
30DD:0107 C3            RET
30DD:0108 50            PUSH    AX
30DD:0109 43            INC     BX
30DD:010A 2426          AND     AL,26
```

The first four lines are correct, but the:

```
30DD:0108 DB 'PC$'
```

instruction that specifies the string disappeared and was replaced by three other assembly language instructions:

```
30DD:0108 50          PUSH    AX
30DD:0109 43          INC     BX
30DD:010A 2426        AND     AL,26
```

DEBUG's U command tries to turn everything into instructions. It isn't smart enough to see that you're using a Display String instruction and that you're telling it that the string begins at address 108. So it looks at the bytes that make up the string (and the final dollar sign) and translates these into meaningless instructions rather than identifying them as data.

If you used the DEBUG D (for Dump or Display) command instead of the U command, you'd see your string:

```
-D 100 LB
30DD:0100 B4 09 BA 08 01 CD 21 C3-50 43 24       ......!.PC$
```

The SERVICE2.COM, SERVICE6.COM, and SERVICE9.COM programs all use display services of DOS interrupt 21. They don't meddle with the color settings, and will display the characters you specified in whatever colors happen to be active at the time. They essentially treat your screen like a teletype device (abbreviated as TTY).

In this respect, they're similar to the BIOS Write Character as Teletype service E of interrupt 10. You could adapt the SERVICE2.COM program above very easily to use this BIOS function:

```
C>DEBUG
-A
30DD:0100 MOV AH,E
30DD:0102 MOV AL,50
30DD:0104 INT 10
30DD:0106 MOV AL,43
30DD:0108 INT 10
30DD:010A RET
30DD:010B
-N SERVICEE.COM
-RCX
CX 0000
:B
-W
Writing 000B bytes
-Q
```

Service E of BIOS interrupt 10 lets you use screen *pages* on a color system. In fact, you could add a line before the first INT 10 that says:

```
MOV BH,0
```

This tells your system to write the characters to screen page 0 — the one you normally work with. If you did this you'd have to increase the length of the program that you specified with the RCX command. Fortunately, you shouldn't have to worry about this, since just about nothing takes advantage of screen pages other than page 0.

What's a page?

It's far easier to display a screenful of characters than a screenful of dots. A 25-row, 80-column screen can hold 2,000 characters (25 x 80 = 2,000). It takes one byte to store the value of each character, and one additional byte to store the color of each character. So displaying one complete 25 by 80 screenful of text requires 2,000 bytes of memory to store the characters, plus another 2,000 bytes to store the colors of each character.

However, IBM's original four-color 320 by 200 medium-resolution graphics screen required 16,000 bytes of memory. The system has to keep track of 64,000 dots (320 x 200) and the colors of these dots. It does this by using two bits — a quarter of a byte — to represent the color of each dot (pixel). Two bits yields four possible colors (actually three colors plus color 00, which is the same as the background color):

Bits	Decimal	Result
00	0	no color
01	1	first color
10	2	second color
11	3	third color

These four values (0-3) will produce different colors depending on which "palette" of possible colors is active. You can see this palette by typing in the following PAL-SHOW.BAS BASIC program, using a pure ASCII word processor or EDLIN. Omit the single quotation (') marks and the comments following them

```
100 'PALSHOW.BAS — shows different graphics palettes
110 SCREEN 1                      ' 320 x 200 graphics
120 COLOR 1,0                     ' blue background, palette 0
130 CLS                          ' clear screen
140 FOR A=1 TO 3
150 CIRCLE (60+A*50,50),25,A      ' draw three circles
160 PAINT (60+A*50,50),A,A        ' color them with colors 1, 2, and 3
170 NEXT
180 LOCATE 20,4
190 PRINT "Press any key to switch palettes"
200 LOCATE 21,9
210 PRINT "(or press Esc to end)"
```

```
220 I$=INKEY$:IF I$="" THEN 220
230 IF I$=CHR$(27) THEN END ELSE K=K+1
240 COLOR 1,K                       switch to the other palette
250 GOTO 220
```

Once you've created the program, run it on any color system by typing BASICA PAL-SHOW (or GWBASIC PALSHOW if you're not using IBM hardware). Press any key and you'll see the three circles change from palette 0 (where they're green, red, and brown/yellow) to palette 1 (where they're cyan, magenta, and white). Press the Esc key to quit.

The location of the dot onscreen is simply its relative position in the 16,000 possible bytes of memory. The very first of the 16,000 bytes of display memory represents the first four dots on the screen (since each byte contains eight bits and each dot takes up two bits), starting in the upper lefthand corner. The second byte represents the next four dots, and so on. It actually gets fairly complicated, since the odd-numbered rows and even-numbered rows are maintained separately. More on that later.

Originally, IBM also offered a "high resolution" graphics screen measuring 640 by 200. This meant keeping track of 128,000 dots (640 x 200). Each bit of each of the 16,000 bytes stood for one dot. A dot was either on (white) or off (black), and no color was allowed unless you knew how to program the graphics controller directly.

The total 16,000 bytes x 8 bits per byte = 128,000 bits. In high resolution, all the bits were used up just telling your system whether each of the 128,000 dots was on or off. In medium resolution, you could use two bits to specify one of four colors (with binary values 00, 01, 10, or 11) so 64,000 dots x 2 bits = 128,000. And if you knew how to tweak your system, you could even experiment with a low-resolution screen that displayed 160 x 200 dots in 16 colors.

Each CGA system came with 16K of display memory on the display adapter. Graphics used it all. But a full 80-column screen of text used only 4,000 of the 16,000 bytes. IBM let you use the rest by dividing the 16,000 total bytes into four screen pages each 4,000 bytes long. The default was always page 0. But you could write on any of the four pages and then switch instantly to any of them.

With 40-column screens you could use eight pages. Nobody really ever uses 40-column text screens, which were developed originally so that users could hook up their systems to home television sets. Home TVs didn't have decent enough resolution to display 80-character text, but they could handle 40-character text decently. You can't ordinarily mix 40-character text and 80-character text on the same screen. The following BASIC SIZEMIX.BAS program will do it, however, on most color systems:

```
100 ' SIZEMIX.BAS
110 SCREEN 2:OUT 985,2:CLS
120 LOCATE 5,30:PRINT "This is small type"
130 DEF SEG=0:POKE 1097,4:POKE 1098,40:DEF SEG
140 LOCATE 7,12:PRINT "This is large type"
150 DEF SEG=0:POKE 1097,6:POKE 1098,80:DEF SEG
160 LOCATE 9,30:PRINT "And back to small type"
```

Screen pages are potentially very useful, since you could put things like menus and help screens on pages 1, 2, and 3, and then flip to these instantly without disturbing the contents of your main page 0. Unfortunately, few (if any) programs ever use this. Why? Because users with monochrome screens don't have any extra screen memory, so they don't have any extra pages. And software vendors don't like to create programs that owners of some systems can't use properly.

Also, by putting slightly different images on different screen pages and then switching rapidly from one page to another you can create the illusion of movement or animation.

The DAZZLER.COM program on the accompanying disk uses this technique to produce a fast kaleidoscopic image. When the program starts it creates a pattern onscreen in the first two video pages. Then, alternating between pages 0 and 1, it increments or decrements every character's color on the inactive page, and makes the inactive page the active page. And the HORSE.BAS program on the disk shows how you can put slightly different images on different pages and then riffle quickly through them to produce a very realistic animation.

You could also see how pages work by running the small PAGEDEMO.BAS program below:

```
100 ' PAGEDEMO.BAS — shows color screen pages
110 ' --- set up array of 200 screen positions ---
120 DIM R(200),C(200)
130 FOR A=1 TO 200
140 R(A)=INT(RND*23+1)
150 C(A)=INT(RND*79+1)
160 NEXT
170 CLS
180 LOCATE 12,30
190 PRINT "Building screens . . . "
200 ' --- fill array with arrows ---
210 FOR C=3 TO 0 STEP -1
220 IF C>1 THEN E=C+2 ELSE E=C
230 SCREEN ,,C,0
240 COLOR E,7:CLS
250 FOR D=1 TO 200
260 LOCATE R(D),C(D)
270 PRINT CHR$(24+C)
280 NEXT
290 LOCATE 25,13
300 PRINT "Press any key to switch to ";
310 PRINT "another page (or Esc to end)";
320 NEXT
330 ' --- switch from one page to next ---
340 I$=INKEY$:IF I$="" THEN 340
```

```
350 IF I$=CHR$(27) THEN 380 ELSE K=(K+1) MOD 4
360 SCREEN ,,,K
370 GOTO 340
380 SCREEN 0,1,0,0:SYSTEM
```

PAGEDEMO first figures out 200 random screen coordinates, then puts four different sets of arrows in four different colors on the four 80 x 25 video pages. It lets you flip from one to the next by pressing any key. Pressing Esc sets things back to normal and quits.

Or you could run the PAGE.COM program on the accompanying disk to switch among pages 0 to 3 in DOS on an 80 x 25 color screen. To use it, type PAGE followed by a number from 0 to 3. So entering:

```
PAGE 2
```

will switch you to video page 2. If you want to find out what page you're currently in, type:

```
PAGE ?
```

If you type PAGE without any parameters after it, or with parameters that are out of range, PAGE will print instructions. It also removes the extra space DOS inserts when displaying a new prompt. This is because the only real use for PAGE.COM is to jump to a page other than the default 0, put something on that page (like a directory listing), and then jump back and forth between it and page 0. Each time you execute a command to jump away, DOS will scroll up a line of your display, chopping away at the directory listing or whatever you wanted to put on the alternate pages.

After you switch into any of these pages you can clear the screen by typing CLS. But if you've set the colors previously, and you want to clear the screen to those preset colors, you have to be careful. Many of the programs that set colors and clear the screen assume you want to be in video page 0. To get around this, run the PAGECLS.COM program on the accompanying disk.

This program will clear the screen to the existing colors. If you want to modify it so it will set a specific color while it clears the screen, load the program into DEBUG and change the two values starting at address 109. So to have PAGECLS.COM set the colors to bright yellow on red and then clear the screen to those colors, you would type:

```
DEBUG PAGECLS.COM
E 109 B7 4E
W
Q
```

If you want to change the colors to white on blue, you'd substitute:

```
E 109 B7 17
```

for:

```
E 109 B7 4E
```

Whether you customize PAGECLS.COM to set a specific color, or run it unpatched to clear the screen to the existing colors, the program will refrain from changing the current video page.

After you patch it, part of the PAGECLS.COM program would look like:

```
MOV BH,4E          ;put 4E attribute in BH
MOV AX,0600        ;scroll up and cls
MOV CX,0000        ;starting at 0,0
MOV DX,184F        ;25 x 80
INT 10             ;do it
```

You can have a version of this routine set the colors and clear the screen. This uses service 6 of BIOS interrupt 10 to "scroll up" a window. You specify the upper lefthand row and column of the area you want cleared by putting the row number register CH and the column number in register CL. And you tell it the lower righthand corner of the window you want cleared by putting the row in register DH and the column in DL.

Since most of the time you want to clear an entire 80 x 25 screen, you use the following values:

- CH=0
- CL=0
- DH=18
- DL=4F

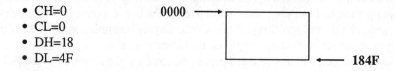

BIOS refers to the upper lefthand corner as row 0 and column 0. You specify 18 and 4F as the row and column numbers of the lower righthand corner, since hex 4F is the same as decimal 79, and hex 18 is equal to decimal 24. The numbering system starts with 0 rather than 1, so subtract 1 from the size of the window you want cleared.

If you want to get fancy, you can read the number of rows from the low-memory BIOS area (at address 40:84) and have service F of interrupt 10 tell you how wide the screen is (it reports the number of columns in register AH), and then move these values into the appropriate registers so the scroll up routine clears the whole screen no matter how it's set.

You don't have to clear the whole screen at once. The WINDOWS.COM demo program on the accompanying disk will clear successively smaller and smaller windows each to a different color.

Once you've run the program (on a color monitor only), enter:

```
DIR /W
```

to produce a wide directory listing, and you'll see that the text in the center blinks, since the background color for the few central windows is higher than 7.

Services 6 and 7 of BIOS interrupt 10 are identical except that service 6 will scroll down and service 7 will scroll up. When clearing windows this really doesn't matter much. Most programs use service 6.

With 16 possible foreground colors and eight possible background colors, you can mix and match 128 color combinations. The COLRSHOW.COM program on the accompanying disk uses service 9 to show them all. (Actually, it shows only 120, since it skips any combinations that have the same background and foreground colors.) When you run it, press the up arrow repeatedly to increase the color value, or the down arrow key to decrease it. Or type in any letter other than a space to jump directly to the color value specified by that key. Pressing Esc will quit. Since it needs to print something in the foreground, it fills the entire screen with the ASCII character that happens to represent each color value.

In the Cards

When the PC was first introduced, just about everyone purchased IBM's monochrome display adapter (MDA), which could be hooked up only to IBM's monochrome display. A handful of pioneers purchased IBM's color graphics adapter (CGA), which they used to drive either an RGB monitor (which cost over $1,000 way back then), or a home television set.

Hooking up a PC to a TV set meant having to purchase a separate RF modulator, or trying to run the signal through the RF circuitry of a video tape recorder. The results were totally unsatisfactory, since the definition was crude. If you were lucky you could just about make out text in 40-column modes. When the CGA was attached to an RGB monitor it used separate outputs for the red, green, and blue (and intensity) signals. When it was attached to a TV, it used a *composite* output that blurred all the information into one signal. The *burst* parameter that turns color on and off with things like BASIC's SCREEN command applies to composite output only.

Composite screens often have trouble displaying colors other than black (0) and white (7 or F). However, if you know what you're doing, you can produce interesting *artifact color* displays by experimenting with different black-and-white line patterns.

PCs use *memory-mapped* displays. The system builds an image of the screen in memory, which the video circuitry reads and turns into recognizable text or graphics. The adapter card translates the information in video memory into signals that control one or more electron guns. These scan beams of electrons onto chemical phosphors painted on the monitor glass that glow when energized.

The CGA had several nasty habits. It occasionally produced a random pattern of interference called "snow" when programs tried to write directly to this video memory memory at the same time that the display electronics was putting the image onscreen. (The MDA and most recent video adapters have *dual-ported* video RAM that lets the

CPU update memory without interfering with the reading process.) Relatively sophisticated programs write data to CGA video memory only during the 1.25 millisecond *vertical retrace interval*.

The electron beam sweeps from left to right and from top to bottom as it zigzags its way across the entire surface of the screen. Each time it reaches the right edge it has to scurry down a line and over to the left edge again. This is the *horizontal retrace*. And each time it reaches the very bottom righthand corner of the screen it has to jump all the way back to the upper lefthand corner and start over. This is the *vertical retrace*. In addition, the beam always overscans each line a hair past the edge, which wastes a tiny bit of time.

CGA screens also flickered when they scrolled up a line, which produced a disturbing strobe effect if you were reading through a long document. The display circuitry was supposed to paint images onto the screen 60 times each second, but the CGA put just 30 images onto the screen and alternated these with all-black screens. This wasn't that noticeable when the image didn't change much, or when the background was black. But if you used a light-colored background and scrolled lines repeatedly, you ended up goggle-eyed.

The CGA was also slower and fuzzier than the MDA. The MDA could handle more dots (720 across and 350 up and down compared to the CGA's maximum 640 x 200 resolution). And it boasted a *long-persistence* phosphor that blurred the individual dots together into solid-looking characters and did away with just about all flicker. The MDA also had a higher *bandwidth* than the CGA, which let the mono adapter pump more information per second to a mono screen than the CGA could send to a color screen.

But while the MDA and CGA could both juggle 2,000 characters on each screen, the CGA could manipulate discrete dots, which let users draw lines, circles, and other graphic images.

One year after the PC hit the market, an independent hardware manufacturer developed a display adapter called the Hercules Graphics Card (HGC) that handled monochrome text on mono monitors just like the MDA but added dot-addressable graphics abilities like those on the CGA. This was followed four years later by an upgraded Hercules Graphics Card Plus (HGC+) that could work with different customized onscreen fonts, and a year after that with a proprietary Hercules InColor Card that could display 16 colors out of a palette of 64 in graphics mode, in 720 x 348 resolution.

In 1985 IBM introduced a display card called the Enhanced Graphics Adapter (EGA) that produced text and dot-addressable graphics on both color and IBM monochrome screens. It could drive a higher resolution color screen than the CGA, could juggle more colors, didn't flicker when it scrolled, and didn't have problems with snow. It could use customizable fonts, and could display a very readable 43 lines of text onscreen, 72 percent more than the CGA or MDA. IBM's original EGA card was expensive, and didn't come with the full complement of memory required. But manufacturers soon began stamping out inexpensive clones with the full 256K of video RAM, and the EGA became an instant standard. See Chapter 13 for details on the EGA.

These early adapters had *digital* outputs. When IBM brought out its PS/2 computer series, it stunned the monitor industry by using *analog* graphics systems. Analog outputs can handle color gradations more adroitly than digital ones. But all of the monitors sold by IBM were digital. Some of the popular *multisynching* monitors sold by companies like NEC and Sony could handle both digital and analog inputs.

IBM's integrated a new standard called Multi-Color Graphics Array (MCGA) — a sort of beefed-up CGA — into the main circuit board of the bottom-of-the-line PS/2 Models 25 and 30. Maximum MCGA resolution was decent (640 by 480 dots) and it could put 256 colors onscreen at once, out of a palette 256K colors wide, in 320 by 200 resolution. And it could produce 64 shades of grey on IBM's newer monochrome displays.

But the MCGA was overshadowed by a more capable system named after a chip called the Video Graphics Array, or VGA. The VGA handled all MDA, CDA, and EGA modes, and tossed in a few new ones of its own. It also worked with an IBM enhancement add-in card with the euphonious name 8514-A that boosted performance even more.

Figure 12.3 compares the various types of monitors.

System	Bandwidth (MHz)	Horizontal Scan Rate (KHz)	Vertical Scan Rate (Hz)	Dot Box (width x height)
MDA	16.257	18.432	50	9x14
HGC	16.257	18.432	50	9x14
CGA	14.318	15.75	60	8x8
EGA color	14.318-16.257	15.75-21.85	60	8x8,8x14
EGA mono	16.257	18.432	50	9x14
MCGA	25.175	31.5	60-70	8x16
VGA	25.175-28.322	31.5	60-70	8x8,8x14, 9x14,9x16

Figure 12.3.   Video Hardware Specifications

The *bandwidth* determines the maximum number of dots each system can handle per second. The relatively slow CGA can push just 14,318,000 dots down the line each second, while the sprintier VGA can shuttle nearly twice than number in the same amount of time. The *horizontal scan rate* tells how many lines each system can display per second. Again, the PS/2 displays can handle double the number of lines (31,500 per second) compared to the older CGA. The *vertical scan rate* is the number of fully refreshed screens each system produces per second. The *dot box* is the dimensions of the box in which a character is formed.

The horizontal scan rate divided by the vertical scan rate yields the maximum displayable lines per screen. (Some of these are used for other things, however, such as vertical retrace intervals and overscan margins.) The bandwidth divided by the horizontal scan rate yields the number of dots per line (although some of these are used for the horizontal retrace and overscan). You can then divide these by the various dot widths and heights to see how many characters each could handle.

You can put combinations of these display adapters into the same system. IBM originally assigned different memory and port addresses to the MDA and CGA cards:

System	Video Memory Address	Port Addresses
MDA	B000	3B0 - 3BF
CGA	B800	3D0 - 3DF

Since an EGA can drive either a color or mono display, you can add it to a system that already has an MDA or CGA attached. You can also mix an MDA with a VGA or MCGA. Hercules monochrome cards will work with just about everything (other than an IBM MDA). However, since Hercules cards use 64K of video RAM starting at address B000:0, 32K of this overlaps memory allotted to the CGA that begins at address B800:0. You can use the two together if you configure the Hercules video memory to avoid conflicts with the CGA.

The EGA (and VGA) can use 32K of video RAM beginning either at the normal mono address of B000:0, or the normal color address of B800:0. Or it can start at A000:0 and use just the 64K A000 segment, or take 128K by spanning both the A000 and B000 segments. The MCGA uses the 64K A000 segment.

Storage Schemes

PCs store text in character/attribute pairs of ASCII values. The position of each character onscreen depends on its position in video memory. Since each 80-column, 25-line screen can display 2,000 characters, it takes 4,000 bytes of memory to hold the characters and attributes for a full screen. The first of the 4,000 bytes in video memory stores the ASCII value of the text character in the upper lefthand corner. The second byte stores the attribute of that character. The third byte stores the ASCII value of the second character on the top line. The fifth byte stores the value of the third character on the top line.

So if you're using a color system with blue text on a white background, and you have the letters ABC in the upper lefthand corner of your screen, the hex representation of the contents of memory starting at address B800 would look like:

Address	Value	Contents
B800:0000	41	the letter A
B800:0001	71	the color for A
B800:0002	42	the letter B
B800:0003	71	the color for B
B800:0004	43	the letter C
B800:0005	71	the color for C

The hex value for "A" is 41, so this is the first value in video memory. This is followed at the very next address by the color in which the "A" appears (71 is blue on white). The third memory address contains a value of 42 ("B") which is again followed by the color (71), and so on.

You can see this better by using DEBUG. If you're using a color system, just clear your screen, make sure DEBUG.COM is handy, and at the DOS prompt, type:

```
DEBUG
D B800:0 LB0
```

Depending on what your prompt looks like, you should see something like:

```
B800:0000 20 07 20 07 20 07 20 07-20 07 20 07 20 07 20 07 . . . . . . . . .
B800:0010 20 07 20 07 20 07 20 07-20 07 20 07 20 07 20 07 . . . . . . . . .
B800:0020 20 07 20 07 20 07 20 07-20 07 20 07 20 07 20 07 . . . . . . . . .
B800:0030 20 07 20 07 20 07 20 07-20 07 20 07 20 07 20 07 . . . . . . . . .
B800:0040 20 07 20 07 20 07 20 07-20 07 20 07 20 07 20 07 . . . . . . . . .
B800:0050 20 07 20 07 20 07 20 07-20 07 20 07 20 07 20 07 . . . . . . . . .
B800:0060 20 07 20 07 20 07 20 07-20 07 20 07 20 07 20 07 . . . . . . . . .
B800:0070 20 07 20 07 20 07 20 07-20 07 20 07 20 07 20 07 . . . . . . . . .
B800:0080 20 07 20 07 20 07 20 07-20 07 20 07 20 07 20 07 . . . . . . . . .
B800:0090 20 07 20 07 20 07 20 07-20 07 20 07 20 07 20 07 . . . . . . . . .
B800:00A0 43 07 3E 07 44 07 45 07-42 07 55 07 47 07 20 07 C.>.D.E.B.U.G. .
```

Then type Q and press the Enter key to quit. (If you're trying this on a mono system, substitute B000 for B800 in the example.) Clearing the screen with CLS on many systems actually puts the DOS prompt on the second line, as is the case here, so the first line is blank. A blank line is made up of 80 spaces, which takes 160 bytes of storage — 80 for the space characters themselves and another 80 for the color of the spaces. The ASCII character for a space is hex 20. The first, third, fifth, etc. characters above are all hex 20 spaces.

When you type CLS, COMMAND.COM normally clears the screen to white (color 7) on black (color 0). The second, fourth, sixth, etc. characters above are all 07 white-on-black attributes.

The command you typed:

```
DEBUG
```

appears hex A0 (decimal 160) characters into the DEBUG display.

Again, each character is followed by its attribute. These show up as dots in the right-hand column of the DEBUG display, since DEBUG uses dots to represent anything with ASCII values lower than hex 20 (decimal 32) or higher than hex 7E (decimal 126).

You can use DEBUG to write information to video memory, which is a lot more interesting than just reading from RAM.

If you're using a color system, type:

```
DEBUG
F B800:0 LA0 41
```

This will put the value hex 41 into the first A0 (decimal 160) bytes of video memory. Each 80-column screen line uses 80 spaces in RAM to store the character values and another 80 addresses to maintain the attributes for these characters, for a total of decimal 160 bytes. So this command will fill the top line of your screen with the hex character 41 — uppercase A. And since the attribute 41 happens to be blue (color 1) on red (color 4), the line of AAAAAAAs will appear in blue on red.

If you enter:

```
F B800:0 LA0 61
```

you'll get a top row of lowercase "a" characters in blue (color 1) on a yellow (color 6) background. If you enter:

```
F B800:0 LA0 FE
```

the top row will fill with blinking bright yellow boxes (character hex FE) on a white background, since the E produces a high-intensity yellow foreground and the F makes the background white and blinks the foreground. Or try:

```
F B800:0 LA0 DD
```

which produces a top line of blinking alternate light and dark purple horizontal stripes. The LA0 in each of these tells DEBUG to fill just hex A0 (decimal 160) bytes, or one line. By expanding this to hex FA0 (decimal 4,000), you can fill the entire screen. The command:

```
F B800:0 LFA0 DD
```

will blanket your entire screen with these blinking purple stripes.

If you type:

```
E B800:0 "aabbccddeeffgghhiijjkkllmmnnooppqqrrssttuuvvwwxxyyzz"
```

you'll end up with a lowercase alphabet in various foreground colors on brown and white backgrounds. The hex ASCII values of the letters "a" through "z" are all between 61 and

7A. The color for brown is 6 and for white is 7, which happens to be the lefthand digits of the character values.

If you tried:

```
E B800:0 "AABBCCDDEEFFGGHHIIJJKKLLMMNNOOPPQQRRSSTTUUVVWWXXYYZZ"
```

you'd see an uppercase alphabet in assorted text colors on a red and purple background, since the hex ASCII values of the letters "A" through "Z" are all between 41 and 5A. The color for red is 4, and the color for purple (magenta) is 5.

Since the position in memory dictates the position onscreen, you could put a string anywhere you want by varying its address. The following three DEBUG commands will put three messages in three colors in three places on screen:

```
E B800:0 "TGOGPG"
E B800:7CA "MVIVDVDVLVEV"
E B800:F94 "BaOaTaTaOaMa"
```

The top command will put the letters "TOP" in white text on a red background in the upper lefthand corner of the screen. The first, third, and fifth characters of "TGOGPG" are the ones that show up onscreen. The second, fourth, and sixth "G" characters don't actually appear; instead, these set the color to white (7) on red (4), since the hex ASCII value of "G" is 47. The 0 address after B800: tells DEBUG to put the "TGOGPG" string at the very beginning of color video memory.

The second command will put the word "MIDDLE" in the middle of your screen. The alternate "V" characters will make the word appear in brown (6) text on a purple (5) background, since the value of "V" is hex 56. And the 7CA offset address after the B800: told DEBUG to insert the "MVIVDVDVLVEV" string hex a little less than halfway through the 4,000 bytes of video memory. Hex 7CA is equal to decimal 1994.

Similarly, the third command will put the word "BOTTOM" in the lower righthand corner of a 25-line, 80-column screen. The lowercase "a" characters in the "BaOaTaTa-OaMa" string set the color to blue (1) on brown (6), since the hex ASCII value of "a" is 61. The F94 offset address following the B800: starts the string near the very end of the 4,000 bytes of video memory, since F94 is equal to 3,988.

The attribute value for blue text on a white background is 71, which is also the hex value of the "q" character. To print "THIS IS A TEST" in the upper lefthand corner of your color screen, just type:

```
DEBUG
E B800:0 "TqHqIqSq qIqSq qAq qTqEqSqT"
```

DEBUG will put the values for all these characters into the beginning of color video memory, which will interpret the hex 71 "q" characters as blue-on-white attributes. Remember that your system stores characters first and then attributes. If you accidentally started the string off with a "q" rather than a text character:

```
DEBUG
E B800:0 "qTqHqIqSq qIqSq qAq qTqEqSqT"
```

all you'd end up with is a multicolored string of qqqqqqs. Memory numbering systems start with 0. Even-numbered addresses contain ASCII values of characters. Odd-numbered addresses store the attribute values for these characters.

This technique provides a quick and dirty way to set the screen attributes while using DEBUG. If you normally prefer blue text on a white background, and you're using DEBUG to trace through a program, you can run into color trouble. Programs often contain routines to clear the screen, and if you stumble over one of these your screen may suddenly turn a dismal grey on black (unless you have ANSI.SYS loaded). To fix it, just issue a command like:

```
F B800:0 LFA0 "q"
```

and your screen will instantly be filled with blue-on-white lowercase "q" characters. Lean on the Enter key until the "q" characters disappear off the top, and you'll be left with a cleared blue-on-white screen. Substitute "t" for "q" if you want a red-on-white screen, since the hex ASCII value for "t" is 74.

If you want to clear your screen to a color such as cyan (3) on dark blue (1), you won't be able to enter a character such as "t" or "q." So just enter the hex number directly:

```
F B800:0 LFA0 13
```

As an added bonus, when you're all done working with DEBUG and you enter Q to return to DOS, the colors this trick set will remain in effect until something else changes them.

Note that you can put a red-on-white "$" character at the very bottom righthand corner of a 25-line, 80-column screen, by typing:

```
E B800:F9E "$t"
```

Since video memory starts at page 0, this will display a red dollar sign character on the default 0 page. And, as mentioned earlier, page 1 follows page 0. You might think that since F9E (the address of the $) and F9F (the address of the red-on-white attribute value) were the last two memory addresses of page 0, you could print a blue-on-white dollar sign at the top of the following video page — page 1 — by using an address two bytes higher:

```
E B800:FA0 "$q"
```

Try this and nothing visible will happen. Page 1 does indeed follow page 0 — but not directly. The second video page starts at the even hex address 1000, which is equal to decimal 4096, not 4000. The:

```
E B800:FA0 "$q"
```

command put the blue dollar sign in an unused area between page 0 and page 1. To put this blue dollar sign at the top of page 1, type:

```
E B800:1000 "$q"
```

To see that the blue dollar sign actually appeared at the top of page 1, use the PAGE.COM program on the accompanying disk. Or create a tiny program called PAGE1.COM by typing:

```
E 100 B4 05 B0 01 CD 10 C3
N PAGE1.COM
RCX
7
W
Q
```

The PAGE1.COM program looks like:

```
MOV AH,5      ; set video page
MOV AL,1      ; to page 1
INT 10        ; have BIOS do it
RET           ; back to DOS
```

You can return to the default page 0 by using the PAGE.COM program or, if you're using a color system, by making sure the DOS MODE.COM utility is handy and typing:

```
MODE CO80
```

The video page map for an 80 x 25 display would look like:

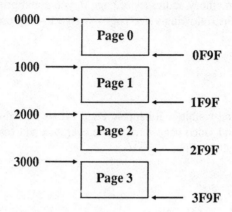

Your system wastes the hex 60 (decimal 96) bytes of memory between each of the pages.

While the focus of this book is on text rather than graphics, it's interesting to note that IBM uses odd-even distinctions in graphics areas as well.

If you run the following BASIC HIRES.BAS program:

```
100 ' HIRES.BAS
110 KEY OFF:SCREEN 2:CLS
120 FOR A=200 TO 1 STEP -2
130 LINE (0,A)-(639,A):NEXT
140 FOR E=1 TO 150
150 A=RND*600+1:B=RND*180+1:C=RND*20+5
160 LINE (A,B)-(A+C,B+C),0,BF
170 LINE (A+4,B+1)-(A+C+4,B+C+1),,BF
180 NEXT
190 DEF SEG=&HB800
200 BSAVE "IMAGE,"0,&H4000
```

BASIC will create a 640 x 200 graphics image, and store it on disk as a 16K file containing a bank of even-numbered lines and a bank of odd-numbered lines.

Once you've run HIRES.BAS, run the short RELOAD.BAS program to load the disk file onto the screen:

```
100 SCREEN 2
110 BLOAD "IMAGE"
```

You'll see BASIC recreate the image in two passes. You can have the HIRES.BAS program store only one bank by changing line 200 to:

```
200 BSAVE "IMAGE,"0,&H2000
```

RELOAD.BAS will then only restore every other line.

Blanking Out the Screen

Of course, black is a color too. And it's very useful. If you're using a CGA, for instance, you can reduce (but not eliminate) the effects of scroll-flicker by using a black background. A black background also makes foreground colors look brighter. But one of the best uses for black is in blanking screens.

It's possible to "burn" a permanent image into the long-persistence phosphor on an IBM monochrome display. If you use one program all day long on a mono system, and the software has certain screen elements in the same place all the time — such as the *1-2-3* grid or the *WordStar* function keys — you can actually etch this element into the screen so you see it even when the monitor is turned off.

Lots of utilities can shut off monochrome displays attached to monochrome adapters if a certain period has elapsed when nothing has been typed on the keyboard. These utilities usually won't work on other video boards such as the EGA. Screen blanking programs for the mono adapter shut off the display by writing a 0 to bit 3 of output port 3B8H, which disables the video signal. Port 3B8H does not exist on boards like the EGA. And although these screen-blanking utilities have no effect on the EGA, some of them have very serious effects when used with a Hercules Monochrome Graphics Adapter.

You can turn an IBM or compatible CGA display off by using the BASIC statement:

```
OUT 984,1
```

To turn it back on, type:

```
OUT 984,41
```

While this works on a CGA, it will run into problems on something like a Hercules Graphics Card, or a regular IBM mono system. This OUT command manipulates the "Mode Control Port Register," which has a different address on color adapters and monochrome adapters (including the Hercules Graphics Card). The control port for monochrome displays is at address 952 rather than 984. (In hexadecimal, these addresses are 3B8 and 3D8.)

You can blank an IBM Monochrome Adapter or Hercules Graphics Card with the statement:

```
OUT 952,1
```

and unblank it with:

```
OUT 952,41
```

but that's not the best way to do it.

The control port address is always four higher than the I/O address of the 6845 video chip. That port address is a word (two bytes) stored at hexadecimal address 0040:0063 in the BIOS data area. So, you can define a variable for the control port with the BASIC commands:

```
DEF SEG=&H40
CTRLPORT = 4 + 256 * PEEK(&H64) + PEEK(&H63)
```

Now you can simply use the variable CTRLPORT instead of 984 or 952.

Or, you can simply clear the screen to black on black. The BLANKINS.COM program on the accompanying disk will:

1. Figure out the existing screen colors and store them.
2. Blank the screen by clearing the display to black on black.
3. Sit there waiting for you to press a certain key (in this case the Ins key).
4. Clear the screen back to the existing colors as soon as the Ins key is pressed.

It's easy to change the key that reactivates things by substituting a new value at address 12C. If you wanted to create a new version of the program called BLNKALTR.COM that used Alt-R to restore the screen, just type:

```
DEBUG BLANKINS.COM
E 12C 13
N BLNKALTR.COM
W
Q
```

You can choose other shifted or nonalphanumeric key candidates from those shown in Figures 12.4a, 12.4b, and 12.4c.

Function Key Combination		Extended Hex Value
F1 through	F10	3B through 44
Shift-F1 through	Shift-F10	54 through 5D
Ctrl-F1 through	Ctrl-F10	5E through 67
Alt-F1 through	Alt-F10	68 through 71
Alt-1 through	Alt-10	78 through 81

Figure 12.4a. Hex Codes for Extended Keys — Function Keys

Key	Hex	Key	Hex
Alt-A	1E	Alt-N	31
Alt-B	30	Alt-O	18
Alt-C	2E	Alt-P	19
Alt-D	20	Alt-Q	10
Alt-E	12	Alt-R	13
Alt-F	21	Alt-S	1F
Alt-G	22	Alt-T	14
Alt-H	23	Alt-U	16
Alt-I	17	Alt-V	2F
Alt-J	24	Alt-W	11
Alt-K	25	Alt-X	2D
Alt-L	26	Alt-Y	15
Alt-M	32	Alt-Z	2C

Figure 12.4b. Hex Codes for Extended Keys — Alt Keys

Miscellaneous Key	Hex
Shift-Tab	0F
Alt -	82
Alt-=	83
Home	47
Cursor Up	48
PgUp	49
Cursor Left	4B
Cursor Right	4D
End	4F
Cursor Down	50
PgDn	51
Ins	52
Del	53
Ctrl-PrtSc	72
Ctrl-Cursor Left	73
Ctrl-Cursor Right	74
Ctrl-End	75
Ctrl-PgDn	76
Ctrl-Home	77
Ctrl-PgUp	84

Figure 12.4c. Hex Codes for Extended Keys — Miscellaneous

Cursor Words

The blinking onscreen cursor is controlled by hardware. Some users would prefer that the cursor be a different size, or refrain from blinking. Changing the size is easy. Turning off the blinking isn't. It's possible to write a routine that continuously figures out where the cursor is, makes the cursor invisible, temporarily stores the value and attribute of the character at the cursor position, writes a solid unblinking block ASCII 219 character over that character, and then restores the old character and attribute when you move the cursor to another position. It's not worth it.

Monochrome display adapters use a 9 x 14 dot box to form all characters. Uppercase letters actually take up a maximum of nine rows and seven columns. The two outside columns provide interletter spacing. Descenders on letters such as y and g use the 10th and 11th lines. The 12th and 13th lines (hex 0C and 0D, since the first line is 00) are used by the cursor. The 14th (bottom) line keeps the lines of text separated from each other.

CGA display adapters use an 8 x 8 dot grid. Uppercase letters take up a maximum of seven rows and seven columns. The rightmost column keeps letters separated. The bottom two lines do double duty — they display descenders on lowercase letters, and also display the cursor.

You can change the size of the cursor by using service 1 of BIOS interrupt 10. And you can read the size of the cursor by using service 3 of interrupt 10. But there's a serious catch with the EGA that's explained in detail in Chapter 13.

When dealing with cursors you have to keep track of two values — the starting line and the ending line. On monochrome systems, the default starting line is hex 0C (decimal 12) and the default ending line is hex 0D (decimal 13). On CGA systems, the default starting line is 6 and the default ending line is 7.

You can make the cursor larger by widening the distance between the starting and ending lines. Using values of 0 (start) and 0D (end) will produce a full-size cursor on mono systems. Settings of 0 (start) and 7 (end) will do the same on CGA systems. You can experiment with different settings by using the BASIC LOCATE statement:

```
LOCATE ,,,S,E
```

where S represents the starting line and E represents the ending line.

Some settings will produce bizarre effects, such as two-part wraparound cursors, or no cursor at all.

IBM's newer hardware is a little trickier. The MCGA doubles the CGA starting line and ending line, then adds 1 to the ending line in an effort to map 8 x 8 settings onto an 8 x 16 box. The EGA and VGA try to scale monochrome and CGA values into settings appropriate to the dot box that happens to be in use — but with slight differences.

The EGA cursor starts at the starting line but ends one line sooner than the specified value of the ending line. This means that you have to specify an ending line that's actually 1 greater than the one you really want. If the ending line is less than the starting line, the cursor wraps around from the bottom to the top and splits into two parts. If the values of the starting and ending lines are the same, the cursor takes up just one line instead of the usual two. And if the ending line is larger than the total number of rows in the dot box, the EGA displays a full-block cursor.

The VGA extends from the specified starting line to the ending line. You don't have to worry about adding 1 to the value of the ending line as you do with the EGA. And if you specify a starting line that's larger than the ending line, the cursor won't wrap.

(The newer PS/2 hardware offers many more options than earlier systems, and the PS/2 BIOS provides a far richer assortment of interrupt 10 tools to handle it all.)

BIOS tries to keep track of the starting and ending lines at offsets 60 and 61 of segment 0040. The CURSREAD.COM program on the accompanying disk will report these values.

If CURSREAD finds a starting or ending value greater than hex F, it gives up. Wouldn't you?

BIOS interrupt 10 service 3 reports the same information. You can patch CURSREAD.COM so it uses this service instead of peeking inside the BIOS data area. Just type:

```
DEBUG CURSREAD.COM
E 107 B4 03 CD 10
F 10B 114 90
W
Q
```

This changes the lines:

```
    PUSH DS          ; save segment
    MOV DX,40        ; new segment is 0040
    MOV DS,DX        ; put this into DS
    MOV BL,61        ; put offset 61
    MOV CH,[BX]      ; into CH
    DEC BX           ; next offset
    MOV CL,[BX]      ; next value into CL
    POP DS           ; restore segment
```

to:

```
    MOV AH,3
    INT 10
    NOP
    NOP
    NOP
    NOP
    NOP
    NOP
    NOP
    NOP
```

```
NOP
NOP
```

You can run the CURSOR.COM and CURSOR2.COM programs on the accompanying disk to experiment with cursors of different sizes. CURSOR.COM lets you enter the start and stop lines as two hex digits on the command line.

CURSOR2.COM lets you use the arrow keys interactively to adjust the start line and the end line. The up-arrow and down-arrow keys will adjust the start line, and the left-arrow and right-arrow keys will change the end line. You'll be able to see the size of the new cursor as you press the keys. When you see a cursor that you like, you can press the Enter key to lock it in. Or, if you press the Esc key, you can exit the program without making any changes.

These programs all assume you're using page 0. BIOS actually keeps track of the different cursor positions on each video page, although it will use the same cursor shape for all pages. But these demonstration program are busy enough without having to worry about other pages.

If you want to try especially large values you can use Charles Petzold's CURSOR3.COM. To create it, type:

```
A
MOV AX,[005D]        ; 1st Parameter
CALL 0116            ; Call ASC2HEX
MOV CH,AL            ; Save in CH
MOV AX,[006D]        ; 2nd Parameter
CALL 0116            ; Call CONVERT
MOV CL,AL            ; Save in CL
MOV AH,01            ; Set Cursor
INT 10               ; through BIOS
INT 20               ; Terminate
CALL 0125            ; ASC2HEX:
XCHG AL,AH           ; Subroutine to
CALL 0125            ; convert ASCII
MOV CL,04            ; digits in AX
SHL AH,CL            ; to one-byte
ADD AL,AH            ; value in AL
RET
OR AL,20             ; ASC2HEX: Converts
SUB AL,57            ; one ASCII digit
JNB 012D             ; to hexadecimal
ADD AL,27
RET

RCX
2E
N CURSOR3.COM
```

W
Q

To use it, enter:

```
CURSOR3 SN EN
```

where SN represents a two-digit hex starting number, and EN represents a two-digit hex ending number. Typing:

```
CURSOR3 05 06
```

will create a normal color cursor that begins on line 5 and ends on line 6. Typing just plain:

```
CURSOR3
```

will make the cursor disappear, since the program will think you entered:

```
CURSOR 00 00
```

It's possible to get rid of the cursor by using large, out-of-range values, or by using a hex 20 as the starting line value. But getting rid of it is easy; trying to put the cursor back later on an EGA can run into trouble.

The best way to get rid of the cursor is to "hide" it by moving it off the screen. Just peek into the BIOS data area, see how long the screen is, and park the cursor on the line below the bottom line. This way it still retains its original shape, but simply isn't visible. To restore it, just use brute-force to move it from its "hidden" location to one that's back on the screen. Unfortunately, this means lots of shifting back and forth from the active screen area to the parking lot.

Clear Colors

Many of the programs on the accompanying disk make it easy to fiddle with your screen's colors. COLOR.COM uses service 6 of INT 10 to set colors while it clears a standard 25-line screen. COLOR2.COM takes advantage of a different technique that changes just the video attribute bytes in memory and leaves the text bytes alone, which lets you set any foreground and background colors without disturbing the text onscreen. (It too is written for a 25-line screen.) The COLORSET.BAS program lets you create programs that set colors and either clear the screen or leave the text on it intact. And it lets you specify just about any screen size.

COLORPIK.COM lets you use the arrow keys to churn through different color settings without altering your text. When you see a color you like you can press Enter to lock it in. And COLRSHOW.COM displays all the available color combinations.

REVERSE.COM will swap the foreground and background colors — very useful on a color system, since CLS will normally set the colors to white on black and you can then use REVERSE to flip them so you'll end up with the kind of "paper-white" system that's growing in popularity these days.

Jeff Prosise's DOSKEY.COM, the swiss-army knife of utilities, will, among other things, let you change foreground and background colors in DOS by pressing function keys. It also prevents the CLS command from resetting your colors to the default DOS grey on black, and makes it operate properly on screens that have more than 25 lines. STICK.COM, another piece of programming wizardry by Jeff Prosise, will lock your screen settings into place and prevent other programs from altering them.

Several other color programs on the disk, mostly written by programming master Charles Petzold, tame the EGA and really show off its abilities. And *PC Magazine* Senior Technical Editor Robert Hummel's popular SPECTRUM.COM gives you total control in remapping the EGA colors. These techniques are all described in Chapter 13.

Chapter 13

EGA and Beyond

IBM's introduction of the Enhanced Graphics Adapter (EGA) and Enhanced Color Display (ECD), in the fall of 1984, came with little warning. Initially, the rest of the industry was slow in providing software support and compatible hardware. After several years, however, the EGA (and its emulation by the newer VGA) finally established itself as the high-resolution color graphics standard for all but specialized applications. And it converted hundreds of thousands of diehard monochrome users who had turned up their noses at IBM's initial CGA (Color Graphics Adapter) standard.

Unfortunately, the documentation IBM supplied with its EGA board didn't cover much more than installation. And most manufacturers of EGA-compatibles didn't do any better. Virtually no EGA boards even came with a single demonstration program. Although the improved resolution of the EGA was obvious to the eye, it was certainly not clear to many users what other magic was packed into the board.

Compared to earlier IBM color systems, the EGA in its normal default modes was impressive enough. But once you understand a few important techniques and have a slate of short assembly language programs handy you'll find it's capable of far more magic than you thought possible. To harness the raw abilities of the EGA, you first have to untangle the confusion of video modes, resolutions, colors, pages, and fonts. Then you need to create a powerful set of utilities that will tailor the EGA's operations to your needs and make the whole process painless.

Many experts feel that Charles Petzold's *PC Magazine* series on the inner workings of the EGA was the most salient and useful ever published on the subject. It's a true classic, and the utilities that accompanied the articles have become industry standards. The edited and updated section here also contains contributions by another *PC Magazine* technical wizard, Jeff Prosise, as well as several sent in by readers.

Virtually all of the programs presented in this chapter use the BIOS interrupt 10H video routines to communicate with the EGA. However, it's possible to incorporate the techniques into programs written in high-level languages, since many of them (such as Turbo Pascal) also support BIOS calls. (BASIC, of course, is the most notable exception.)

Our assembly language programs were designed so that users could type the contents directly into DEBUG, or create script files that they could later redirect into DEBUG.

If you have a macro assembler and some experience in assembly language programming, you may want to convert these SCR listings into ASM programs. To make this easier, the script listings include jump and call labels in the comment sections. However, there are lots of other considerations involved in converting script files to ASM format (such as using SHORT jumps, specifying numbers with the H suffix for hexadecimal, or substituting labels for data references) so try this only if you know what you're doing.

If you have device drivers or memory-resident programs that do things with the display, particularly with colors, try out these EGA utilities first without loading those other programs. You'll see later, for instance, that the EGA has alternative methods for coloring your display.

In particular, try out these utility programs without having ANSI.SYS loaded. ANSI.SYS always assumes that the display is 25 lines long, and one of the EGA's best features is the ability to display nearly twice that many (or half as many in special large-text modes). ANSI.SYS also does not correctly determine the starting address for different video pages.

Changing Video Modes

The Enhanced Graphics Adapter supports a variety of video modes, including all those supported by the original CGA and the Monochrome Adapter. Additional EGA modes provide higher resolution graphics with more colors.

IBM's EGA offers considerably more power and flexibilty than any of its earlier graphics adapters, as shown in Figure 13.1.

The video modes available on your EGA depend upon the type of monitor attached and the amount of memory installed on the adapter board. The "resolution" column in Figure 13.1 indicates the number of displayable scan lines (going down the screen) and the number of displayable dots (going across the screen).

The number of scan lines that the EGA displays is either 200 (which is the same as the CGA) or 350 (which is the same as the Monochrome Adapter). An EGA attached to a regular color display cannot use the 350-line modes. An EGA attached to an ECD can use either 200 or 350 lines. The difference between 200 and 350 scan lines is obvious on the screen: you can count the individual scan lines on your screen in a 200-line display,

Mode	Type	Display	Resolution	Characters	Box	Colors	Pages
0 & 1	Text	CD	200x320	25x40	8x8	16	8
		ECD	350x320	25x40	14x8	16/64	8
2 & 3	Text	CD	200x640	25x80	8x8	16	8
		ECD	350x640	25x80	14x8	16/64	8
4 & 5	Graphics	CD&ECD	200x320	25x40	8x8	4	1
6	Graphics	CD&ECD	200x640	25x80	14x8	2	1
7	Text	Mono	350x720	25x80	14x9	4	8
8		PC*jr* modes not supported by EGA					
9		PC*jr* modes not supported by EGA					
10		PC*jr* modes not supported by EGA					
11		Used internally by EGA for loading fonts					
12		Used internally by EGA for loading fonts					
13	Graphics	CD&ECD	200x320	25x40	8x8	16	2 (64K)
							4 (128K)
							8 (256K)
14	Graphics	CD&ECD	200x640	25x80	8x8	16	1 (64K)
							2 (128K)
							4 (256K)
15	Graphics	MONO	350x640	25x80	14x8	4	1 (64K)
							2 (128K)
16	Graphics	ECD	350x640	25x80	14x8	4/64 (64K)	1 (128K)
						16/64 (128K)	2 (256K)

Figure 13.1. The EGA Video Modes

Note: Modes and other features vary depending on the type of monitor attached to the EGA and the amount of memory on the adapter.

but with 350 lines you cannot. These two basic modes of operation are also very different in ways other than resolution that will be discussed later.

If your screen displays 25 lines of characters (the normal method for using an EGA but definitely not the only way), the "Box" column in Figure 13.1 shows the resolution available for each character. If an ECD (or compatible) attached to an EGA produces only an 8 x 8 character box, the EGA DIP switches are not set correctly. Fortunately, most EGA card manufacturers put these DIP switches on the rear of the circuit board, so you can set or reset them without having to open your system.

The following EGAMODE.COM program will let you switch to any video mode supported by your monitor:

```
N EGAMODE.COM
A 100
JMP    011B                  ; Skip Label
DB     "Current Video Mode is 00$"
MOV    BX,005D               ; Parmeter
MOV    DH,0A                 ; Set DH to 10
SUB    AL,AL                 ; Accumulate number
MOV    CX,0003               ; Up to 3 numbers
MOV    DL,[BX]               ; GETLOOP:
SUB    DL,30                 ; Subtract "0"
JB     0138                  ; Jump if not number
CMP    DL,09                 ; See if over 9
JA     0138                  ; Jump if not number
MUL    DH                    ; Multiply by 10
ADD    AL,DL                 ; Add to accumulation
INC    BX                    ; Point to next one
LOOP   0125                  ; LOOP GETLOOP
CMP    BX,+5D                ; See if no parameter
JZ     0141                  ; JZ SKIPSET
SUB    AH,AH                 ; Set video mode
INT    10                    ; through BIOS
MOV    AH,0F                 ; SKIPSET:
INT    10                    ; Get video mode
AND    AX,007F               ; Wipe out high bit
DIV    DH                    ; Divide by 10
ADD    [0118],AX             ; Save in text
MOV    DX,0102               ; Point to text
MOV    AH,09                 ; Write to screen
INT    21                    ; through DOS
INT    20                    ; Terminate


RCX
57
W
Q
```

The easiest way to create this and all the utility programs that follow is to turn them into script files using a pure-ASCII word processor or EDLIN. Give each file a SCR extension. Make sure you observe the following extremely important rules:

1. Always leave a blank line above the line that says RCX.
2. Press the Enter key at the end of each line, especially the last one with the Q.

Then when you're all done, make sure DEBUG.COM version 2.0 or later is handy (either in the same directory as the script file you just created or in a directory that your path knows about). At the DOS prompt, type:

```
DEBUG < EGAMODE.SCR
```

(substituting different filenames for the EGAMODE.SCR). This will redirect the keystrokes from the script file into DEBUG just as if you had typed them yourself. Using a script file makes a lot of sense since it lets you check your typing, and since you can often adapt one script file slightly and create another similar program without much fuss. After you create EGAMODE.COM, run the program by typing:

```
EGAMODE mode
```

where mode is the video mode (expressed as a decimal number) to which you want to switch. The normal modes for the DOS command level and most programs that use text are 3 for color displays and 7 for monochrome. You can run EGAMODE without a parameter to see what your current mode is.

You can also use the PC DOS MODE command to switch between video modes, but that command is limited to the text modes and uses keywords rather than numbers. The MODE parameters and the corresponding video modes are:

- BW40 (mode 0)
- CO40 (mode 1)
- BW80 (mode 2)
- CO80 (mode 3)
- MONO (mode 7)

Modes 0 through 6 are the CGA modes. Mode 7 is the monochrome adapter mode. All of these modes are supported by the EGA when it is connected to the proper monitor.

Modes 8, 9, and 10 are the additional PC*jr* graphics modes that are not supported by the EGA BIOS. Modes 11 and 12 are used internally by the EGA BIOS to load fonts into the adapter.

You'll notice that Figure 13.1 shows pairs of modes that are the same: 0 and 1, 2 and 3, 4 and 5. On the EGA, both modes in each pair are identical, as they were identical on the CGA if you used its regular, direct drive connector. However, if you used the composite video output on the CGA with a black-and-white monitor, modes 0, 2, and 5 disabled the color-burst signal. The EGA does not support composite monitors.

If you experiment with EGAMODE, you may be surprised that the EGA BIOS allows you to change the mode to one that your monitor doesn't support. If you happen to do this accidently, close your eyes and enter EGAMODE 3 (if you have a color monitor) or EGAMODE 7 (for monochrome) to get things back to normal.

While you can switch to graphics modes at the DOS command level, the screen operations are significantly slower. This is because the BIOS has to construct the dot patterns of each character on the screen instead of just writing the ASCII code of the character to display memory. If you run an application program that does not set the video mode but writes directly to the display, you'll get garbage on your screen if you enter it in a graphics mode.

Normally when the EGA switches to a new mode it clears out all video memory. However, if you add 128 to the mode number when running EGAMODE, the EGA BIOS will set the mode but will retain the contents of the screen memory buffer so the screen will not be cleared. (The PC*jr* BIOS functions similarly.) However, the cursor will be returned to its home position in the upper lefthand corner. If you're in mode 3, try:

```
EGAMODE 131
```

to see what happens. The screen will still have the same contents as before, but the cursor will now be up at the top. For a more interesting effect, try:

```
EGAMODE 144
```

This sets the EGA to mode 16 without clearing memory. You'll see some snowy "garbage" scattered on your display. These are the characters stored in the EGA memory, which are now being interpreted as dots. As you can see, the text and graphics modes are very different. Now go back to mode 3 with:

```
EGAMODE 131
```

The characters from the graphics mode now appear as various colored blocks on the screen.

You shouldn't run other programs after resetting the mode with 128 added to it. When a program reads the mode through the BIOS, the BIOS reports this high-numbered mode. This may completely confuse an application program.

The EGA and Other Adapters

If your EGA is connected to a color monitor, you can still have a Monochrome Adapter in your system as well. Similarly, if your EGA is connected to a monochrome display, you can also have a CGA attached. EGAMODE will not switch between the two adapters, however. Use the MODE command to do that.

If you have a Hercules Graphics Card attached to a monochrome monitor, it, too, can co-exist with an EGA attached to a color display. However, you'll want to use EGAMODE before running any program that uses the "page 1" graphics of the Hercules card. Here's why: Monochrome mode 7 uses memory starting at segment address B000H for the display. Color modes 0 through 6 use memory starting at segment address B800H. No conflict so far. However, the Hercules card can use both "page 0" (starting at B000H) and page 1 (at B800H) for graphics. Many programs that support the Hercules card use page 1 graphics. You may know about this because some of these programs require that you run HGC FULL before you use them to enable this second graphics page. Hercules page 1 graphics would normally conflict with a CGA (and hence an EGA) board. However, the EGA graphics modes 13 through 16 all use display memory beginning at A000H. This allows you to move the EGA out of the way before you use Hercules graphics. To do this, you would enter:

```
MODE CO80
EGAMODE 16
MODE MONO
```

The first program switches to the EGA in mode 3 (in case you're not already there); the second sets the EGA mode to 16 (which uses segment A000H); and the third program switches to the monochrome display. (If your EGA is attached to a regular color display, use EGAMODE 14 instead.) Now you can use Hercules graphics without any restrictions. If you have some batch files with HGC FULL statements, you can add these three lines to the batch file before the HGC FULL line.

After you're done and want to return to the EGA, use:

```
MODE CO80
```

This statement can be placed after an HGC HALF statement in a batch file.

You won't need to do this for all programs that use Hercules graphics. But if you ever see garbage appear on a color display attached to an EGA while graphics appear on a monochrome display attached to a Hercules Graphics Card, it means there's a memory conflict.

Pages and Pages

The column headed "Pages" in Figure 13.1 shows the number of video pages on the EGA for various modes and memory sizes. Particularly in character modes, the display you see on your screen takes up only a small amount of the total EGA memory. The extra memory is used for other video pages.

The EGAPAGE program below lets you change the video page from the DOS command level:

```
N EGAPAGE.COM
A 100
JMP  011A                           ; Jmp BEGIN
DB   "Current Video Page is 0$"
MOV  AL,[005D]                      ; BEGIN: Convert
SUB  AL,30                          ; Parameter
JB   0129                           ; JC GETPAGE
CMP  AL,07                          ; See if above 7
JA   0129                           ; JA GETPAGE
MOV  AH,05                          ; Set page
INT  10                             ; through BIOS
MOV  AH,0F                          ; GETPAGE:
INT  10                             ; through BIOS
ADD  [0118],BH                      ; Store in string
MOV  DX,0102
MOV  AH,09                          ; And display it
INT  21
INT  20                             ; Terminate

RCX
3A
W
Q
```

BIOS keeps track of cursor positions for eight separate video pages. When a video mode is first set, all of the cursors are positioned in the upper lefthand corner. To switch to page 1, type:

```
EGAPAGE 1
```

To go back to page 0, type:

```
EGAPAGE 0
```

The EGAPAGE program doesn't accept page numbers higher than 7, but it doesn't check to see whether the current video mode supports fewer than eight pages. Without a parameter, EGAPAGE tells you the current video page.

EGAPAGE is useful when you have something on your screen that you want to return to later. Just change the video page, do your other task, and then come back to the original video page. Resetting the video mode, however, blanks out the contents of all video pages.

ANSI.SYS users, take note: The EGA uses starting addresses for these video pages that are different from those used by the CGA. Although the starting address is stored in the BIOS data area, ANSI.SYS doesn't use it and will not correctly handle anything other than page 0 on the EGA.

The 64 Color Palette

Notice in Figure 13.1 that the number of available colors for the 350 line modes is 16/64. This means that only 16 colors can be displayed simultaneously on the screen, but these 16 colors may be selected from 64 colors. In the video modes that use 200 scan lines, only 16 colors are possible.

That 64 colors are available only on the ECD in 350-line modes is not a coincidence or the whimsy of the people who designed the EGA. The Enhanced Color Display runs at a faster horizontal sync rate in order to fit in all 350 lines. The display is triggered to use this higher horizontal sync rate by the polarity of the vertical sync signal. At the same time, it uses six color signals on the video connector instead of just the four that the regular color display uses. (The monochrome display uses two signals for color, called "Video" and "Intensity.")

The four-bit color code in 200-line modes is called *IRGB*. The *RGB* part of this stands for red, green, and blue, and *I* stands for Intensity. Thus, 16 colors are available: low and high intensity versions of eight colors.

The six-bit color code in 350-line modes can be represented as *rgbRGB* with both primary (RGB) and secondary (rgb) red, green, and blue signals. The lowercase letters are sometimes referred to as "1/3 intensity" (which are darker) and the uppercase letters are "2/3 intensity" (brighter). In both cases, these are digital signals, either on or off, so the 350-line modes have a total of 64 colors.

To understand how color works on the EGA, and what you can do with it, consider first how IBM handled color on its earlier CGA:

In CGA text modes, each character stored in the adapter memory has a corresponding one-byte attribute that controls the foreground and background colors of the character. The lower four bits of this attribute contain an IRGB code for the foreground color, which is the color of the character.

The next highest three bits of the attribute contain a nonintensified RGB code for the background color. The highest bit controls blinking.

In this respect, the EGA works the same way and uses the same attribute codes. (On the CGA, you could disable blinking, and thus make the higher four bits a full IRGB code for the background, by writing the value 09H to register 3D8H. The EGA does not support this register but you can do the same thing with a BIOS call:

```
MOV AX, 1003H
MOV BL, 0
INT 10H
```

This enables background intensity. A value of 1 in BL enables blinking, as shown in the script for the small EGABLINK.COM program:

```
N EGABLINK.COM
A 100
MOV   BL,[005D]         ; Get Parameter
AND   BL,01             ; Only last bit
```

```
MOV   AX,1003            ; Set Blink/Intensity
INT   10
INT   20

RCX
E
W
Q
```

But there's a big difference between how the CGA and the EGA handle color. On the CGA, the four color bits represented by the IRGB code go directly to the video connector and then the monitor. On the EGA, the four-bit color code passes through an *attribute controller* before going out to the monitor. In 200-line modes, this attribute controller can translate a four-bit IRGB code into any other four-bit IRGB code. In 350-line modes, the attribute controller can translate it into any six-bit rgbRGB code. The attribute controller functions as a lookup array. The translation is controlled by values loaded into the EGA *palette registers*.

Figure 13.2 illustrates the default mapping of the IRGB codes into rgbRGB codes in the EGA 350-line modes. The binary representation is helpful because it shows how the bits correspond directly to the letters in IRGB or rgbRGB. The octal (base 8) representation for the rgbRGB code is actually more useful because the first digit represents the 1/3 intensity rgb signal and the second digit is the 2/3 intensity RGB signal.

Color	IRGB Code			Default rgbRGB Mapping		
	Binary	Octal	Hex	Binary	Octal	Hex
Black	0000	00	00	000000	00	00
Blue	0001	01	00	000001	01	01
Green	0010	02	02	000010	02	02
Cyan	0011	03	03	000011	03	03
Red	0100	04	04	000100	04	04
Magenta	0101	05	05	000101	05	05
Brown	0110	06	06	010100	24	14
White	0111	07	07	000111	07	07
Dark Grey	1000	10	08	111000	70	38
Light Blue	1001	11	09	111001	71	39
Light Green	1010	12	0A	111010	72	3A
Light Cyan	1011	13	0B	111011	73	3B
Light Red	1100	14	0C	111100	74	3C
Light Magenta	1101	15	0D	111101	75	3D
Yellow	1110	16	0E	111110	76	3E
Bright White	1111	17	0F	111111	77	3F

Figure 13.2.   Mapping of IRGB Codes to rgbRGB Codes in the EGA 350-Line Modes

Note that for the intensified colors, the default mapping combines the 2/3 intensity signal with all three 1/3 intensity signals so that, at the bottom of the chart, the "bright white" color has all bits turned on. Note also that the EGA brown is faked: it uses a dark green and light red signal. Forty-eight other possible rgbRGB codes aren't used at all in this default mapping.

On the DOS command level, and in many programs that don't use color, characters are represented with an attribute code of 07H (hexadecimal). This means the background is black (0) and the foreground is white (7). However, the EGA maps these two codes into black and white only by default. By loading different values into the EGA palette registers you can map these drab colors into any other color combinations available. That's what EGACOLOR.COM does:

```
N EGACOLOR.COM
A 100
MOV   AX,[005D]              ; 1st Parameter
CALL  0117                   ; CALL CONVERT
MOV   BL,AL                  ; Save in BL
MOV   AX,[006D]              ; 2nd Parameter
CALL  0117                   ; CALL CONVERT
MOV   BH,AL                  ; Save in BH
MOV   AX,1000                ; Change Palette
INT   10                     ; through BIOS
INT   20                     ; Terminate
SUB   AL,30                  ; CONVERT:
CMP   AH,20                  ; Check if one digit
JZ    0127                   ; JZ ALLDONE
SUB   AH,30                  ; Convert to binary
MOV   CL,03                  ; Three bit shift
SHL   AL,CL
ADD   AL,AH                  ; Put two together
RET                          ; ALLDONE:

RCX
28
W
Q
```

It takes two arguments, both of them octal numbers. The first two-digit number is the IRGB color value from 0 through 17. The second is the rgbRGB color value from 00 through 77 that you want the IRGB code translated into. Leading zeros aren't required.

For instance, entering:

```
EGACOLOR 00 01
EGACOLOR 07 76
```

changes everything normally displayed as black to dark blue, and everything normally white to high-intensity yellow. If you're not using any other program to control color and run these two programs, your screen will suddenly flash into yellow on blue. The color translation is done in the EGA hardware.

If your EGA is connected to a regular color display (which only supports 200 scan lines and 16 colors), you can still use EGACOLOR but only with the four-bit IRGB codes in octal (i.e., 00 through 17) for the second argument.

If you change the video mode with EGAMODE, the colors go back to normal. A mode reset always loads the EGA palette registers with the default mapping. The best thing about using the EGA palette registers to control color is that programs that do not reset the video mode will still use the colors you've set. Later on, you'll see how to load the palette registers even for programs that set the video mode.

By running EGACOLOR 64 times with the command:

```
EGACOLOR 0 XX
```

where XX is an octal number from 00 through 77, you can see all 64 colors as background colors. But don't waste your time. There's a better method.

The EGA 64 Varieties

As mentioned previously, you can't display all 64 colors at once on the EGA. It's just impossible. But with a little "gonzo programming," even the impossible is possible.

The EGAPALET program displays all 64 EGA colors on an ECD. Note — if you're using an AT, substitute a value of 2B for 22 in the line near the top that begins with DB:

```
N EGAPALET.COM
A 100
JMP   0103              ; JMP SHORT BEGIN
DB    22
CLD                     ; BEGIN:
MOV   AX,0003           ; Set Mode to 3
INT   10                ; through BIOS
MOV   AX,B800           ; Set ES to B800
MOV   ES,AX             ; display segment
SUB   DI,DI             ; Start at top
MOV   AL,DB             ; Use block character
MOV   BH,19             ; Number of lines
SUB   AH,AH             ; LOOP2:
MOV   BL,08             ; Colors per line
MOV   CX,000A           ; LOOP1: 10 chars
REPZ                    ; Write to display
STOSW
INC   AH                ; Next color
```

```
DEC   BL              ; Decrement counter
JNZ   0118            ; JNZ LOOP1
DEC   BH              ; Decrement counter
JNZ   0114            ; JNZ LOOP2
MOV   BH,[0102]       ; Get "Count" value
MOV   DX,03DA         ; Status Poîª
MOV   AX,0040         ; Set DS to BIOS
MOV   DS,AX           ; data area
STI                   ; MAINLOOP:
SUB   AH,AH           ; Start colors at 0
MOV   BL,01           ; Temporary "Count"
CLI                   ; VERTWAIT:
IN    AL,DX           ; Wait for vertical
TEST  AL,08           ; retrace
JZ    0138            ; JZ VERTWAIT
IN    AL,DX           ; ENDVERT:
TEST  AL,08           ; Wait for end of it
JNZ   013E            ; JNZ ENDVERT
IN    AL,DX           ; HORIZWAIT:
SHR   AL,1            ; Wait for horizontal
JNB   0143            ; JNB HORIZWAIT
DEC   BL              ; Decrement "Count"
JZ    0153            ; JZ BLITZ
IN    AL,DX           ; ENDHORIZ:
SHR   AL,1            ; Check horiz. retrace
JB    014C            ; JC ENDHORIZ
JMP   0143            ; JMP HORIZWAIT
MOV   CX,0008         ; BLITZ:
MOV   DL,C0           ; Palette register
MOV   AL,AH           ; BLITZLOOP:
AND   AL,07           ; Output palette
OUT   DX,AL           ; number 0 - 7
MOV   AL,AH           ; Output color value
OUT   DX,AL           ; 00 - 3FH
INC   AH              ; Next color
LOOP  0158            ; LOOP BLITZLOOP
MOV   AL,20           ; Enable video
OUT   DX,AL
MOV   DL,DA           ; Reset DX
MOV   BL,BH           ; "Count" value
CMP   AH,40           ; See if end of colors
JNZ   0143            ; JNZ HORIZWAIT
MOV   CX,[001A]       ; Check if key struck
CMP   CX,[001C]
JZ    0133            ; JZ MAINLOOP
```

```
MOV    AX,0003            ; Reset video mode
INT    10
INT    20                 ; Terminate

RCX
81
W
Q
```

When you run the program, you should have eight rows with eight different colors in each. The display is much more stable on an AT; the flickering and wavy lines between the rows of color on a PC or XT is normal. If the bottom row is larger than the rest on your machine, increase the number following DB a bit. If the bottom row is smaller than the rest (or if you don't see rows at all) decrease the number. Make it no bigger than 2BH.

You may have to turn up your contrast and brightness controls to see the full range of colors. Even then, some of the colors may appear very similar. If you have a magnifying glass or camera close-up lens, you can check that they do indeed use different dots. Press any key to leave the program.

The EGAPALET program actually uses only eight color values, 0 through 7, and displays eight columns of blocks using these values. However, every 1/480th of a second, EGAPALET changes these eight palette registers so the colors on your screen change. It controls the timing by counting horizontal scan retraces.

The default EGA color mapping uses the top row and bottom row of EGAPALET's 64 colors, except for brown, which is in the third row, fifth from the left. If you see a color you'd like to use in EGACOLOR, you can determine its octal code in this way: Count down to the row from the top, starting at zero. That's the first digit. Count over to the column from the left, starting at zero. That's the second digit. Octal notation may be confusing to users who have just managed to master hexadecimal numbering, but it is a better way to represent these colors.

BASIC's PALETTE statement lets you map any of the normal 16 attribute codes into any of the 64 colors available on the EGA when attached to an ECD (or compatible) and running in a video mode that uses 350 scan lines. (The 64 colors are not available on the older color display, or with video modes that use 200 scan lines.)

The PALTEST.BAS program below runs under both BASICA 3.x and QuickBASIC 2.0 or later:

```
100 ' PALETTE.BAS — FOR EGAs ONLY
110 DEFINT A-Z:CLS:KEY OFF:COLOR 1
120 LOCATE 23:PRINT " Hit keys to cycle ";
130 PRINT "colors, or enter numbers <64 ";
140 PRINT "(Hit Enter after 1-digit nmbrs)"
150 FOR R=5 TO 20:LOCATE R,6
160 PRINT STRING$(70,219):NEXT:COLOR 7
170 PALCOLOR=(PALCOLOR+1) MOD 64
180 PALETTE 1,PALCOLOR
```

```
190 LOCATE 2,30:COLOR 1
200 PRINT "Color value";PALCOLOR;
210 PRINT "(octal ";OCT$(PALCOLOR);") "
220 I$=INKEY$:IF I$="" THEN 220
230 IF I$=CHR$(13) AND J$<>"" THEN 260
240 IF I$<"0" OR I$>"9" THEN 170
250 J$=J$+I$:IF LEN(J$)<2 THEN 220
260 PALCOLOR=VAL(J$)-1:J$="":GOTO 170
```

PALTEST.BAS draws a large block using attribute code 1 (normally blue), maps that into palette color 0 (black) and waits for you to press a key. Pressing any key increments the palette color through the 64 possible palette colors. Ctrl-Break exits. If you run this program under BASICA 3.x, you'll want to execute CLS and PALETTE statements after you exit the program to return things back to normal.

If many of the colors look identical when you run PALTEST, you may want to adjust the brightness and contrast of your monitor. The colors look most distinct with a brightness level higher than you'll probably find comfortable for normal work. You'll notice that this program does not change the video mode and uses just the default SCREEN 0. The tables in the early QuickBASIC 2.0 manuals were somewhat inaccurate. If your EGA is attached to an ECD you can use the 64 colors with either SCREEN 0 or SCREEN 9. In the other color modes (SCREEN 1, SCREEN 2, SCREEN 7, and SCREEN 8) you can map any of the available attributes to any of 16 palette colors. For instance, in SCREEN 2 (normally 640 by 200 black and white) you can set the background and foreground colors to any of 16 colors.

It's not possible to see more than 16 colors at once. This is rather frustrating if you're trying to compare the colors. To translate the BIOS video mode numbers into the BASIC video modes, use this table:

BIOS Video Mode	BASIC Video Mode
0 & 1	SCREEN 0 : WIDTH 40
2 & 3	SCREEN 0 : WIDTH 80
4 & 5	SCREEN 1
6	SCREEN 2
7	SCREEN 0 (on monochrome)
13	SCREEN 7
14	SCREEN 8
15	SCREEN 10 (on monochrome)
16	SCREEN 9

The EGA Border Problem

In 350-line mode the EGA allows you to set the border (called the *overscan register*) to any of the 64 colors. A program called EGABORD.COM will do this for you:

```
N EGABORD.COM
A 100
MOV  AX,[005D]          ; Get Parameter
SUB  AL,30              ; Convert to binary
CMP  AH,20              ; Check for blank
JZ   0113              ; JZ ALLDONE
SUB  AH,30              ; Convert 2nd digit
MOV  CL,03             ; Shift it 3 spaces
SHL  AL,CL
ADD  AL,AH             ; Stick two together
MOV  BH,AL            ; ALLDONE:
MOV  AX,1001          ; Set border through
INT  10                ; BIOS
INT  20                ; Terminate


RCX
1C
W
Q
```

Run this program by typing:

```
EGABORD XX
```

where XX is the two-digit octal code for an rgbRGB color.

However, the results are pathetic. Not only is the border very skimpy, but using it causes some shading problems in the left two-thirds of the display. (If your EGA is attached to a regular color display, you don't have this problem. But again, you can only set your border to one of the 16 IRGB colors.)

Borders on the EGA are a problem, and the best way to solve the problem is to convince yourself that an EGA cannot display borders in 350-line modes. When you know something is impossible, it may cease to bother you. You may even learn to prefer the black border. The display arithmetic can prove it to you, and you'll be able to relax knowing that you're not missing out on anything.

In 200-line compatibility modes, the EGA (like the CGA) uses the 14.318 MHz clock available on the system bus for the dot clock. At each pulse of the dot clock the adapter sends a color signal to the display. But, in 350-line enhanced modes, the EGA has to write more dots to the display in the same amount of time, so the EGA uses an on-board 16.257 MHz crystal for the dot clock.

This already looks ominous: the EGA displays 75 percent more scan lines with only a 13.5 percent higher dot clock frequency.

In 200-line compatibility modes, the horizontal scan rate is 15.75 KHz. This is the rate at which each scan line of the screen is displayed. Dividing the dot clock (14.318 MHz) by the horizontal scan rate results in 909 dots, the equivalent of 114 characters. The displayable area uses only 640 dots for 80 characters. The horizontal retrace requires about eight characters. The 26 characters left over are in the border area. If you divide the horizontal scan rate (15.75 KHz) by the vertical scan rate (60 Hz) you get 262 lines. The displayable area needs only 200 lines (25 character rows with eight scan lines each). Again, some of the leftovers occur during the vertical retrace (when the signal jumps from the lower right to the upper left corners of the display), but the rest are available for the top and bottom border region.

In 350-line modes on the ECD both the dot clock and the horizontal scan rate are slightly higher. The 16.257 dot clock divided by the 21.85 KHz horizontal scan rate results in 744 dots or 93 characters, of which 80 are displayed and about ten occur during the horizontal retrace. That leaves about three characters for the left and right borders. The horizontal scan rate (21.85 KHz) divided by the vertical scan rate (60 Hz) shows that the EGA can display 364 lines. Three-hundred fifty of them are used in the display and 13 occur during the vertical retrace. That leaves about one scan line for a top and bottom border.

The reason why the EGA can't do borders in 350-line modes is thus very simple: very soon after it finishes a scan line, it begins the horizontal retrace. Almost immediately after completing the last scan line, it makes a vertical retrace. The border area is untouched by the dot gun.

In fact, because of the very tight timing restrictions, the display is not fully blanked during the whole horizontal retrace. That's why you get a faint background shading when you try to display a border. The unwanted shading is actually the border color being displayed during the horizontal retrace. It's faint because it's stretched out.

Now that you know a border is impossible in 350-line modes, you can skip the next section. Unless you're just so accustomed to the CGA border that you can't be swayed.

Sooner or later, you are going to read about a way to do a real border on the EGA, so you might as well read about it here. Opinion is divided over whether this technique can damage your monitor. Enough said? You don't really want a border, do you? Still, if you're nervous, just read along and soak up the theory. Try these tricks at your own risk.

Okay, so you like to take chances. Here's the premise: although the ECD is designed for a horizontal sync rate of 21.85 KHz, it has some tolerances. Most ECDs can run about 5 percent lower. If you program the EGA to do so, you'll be able to fit in enough dots to make a border.

While the ECD normally runs at a vertical sync rate of 60 Hz, it's actually rated for vertical syncs between 50 Hz and 60 Hz. Because of this, it's fairly easy to add a top and bottom border. It's the left and right borders that cause the problem.

The EGATIME program below is designed to be run in mode 3 with an ECD attached, but it does not check to make sure you are doing so:

```
N EGATIME.COM
A 100
JMP  01A3
DW 6000,5602,2003,5604,5C05,8C06,6E10,2B11,6E15,1A16
DW 5F00,5502,3F03,5504,5B05,8C06,6E10,2B11,6E15,1A16
DW 5E00,5402,3E03,5404,5A05,8C06,6E10,2B11,6E15,1A16
DW 5D00,5302,3D03,5304,5905,8C06,6E10,2B11,6E15,1A16
```

```
DW 5C00,5302,3C03,5304,5805,8C06,6E10,2B11,6E15,1A16
DW 5F00,5502,3F03,5504,5B05,7C06,6610,2B11,6615,1216
DW 5D00,5302,3D03,5304,5905,7C06,6610,2B11,6615,1216
DW 5B00,5302,3703,5104,5B05,6C06,5E10,2B11,5E15,0A16
MOV  AL,[005D]          ; Get parameter
AND  AL,07              ; Use lowest 7 bits
MOV  AH,14              ; Multiply by 20
MUL  AH
ADD  AX,0103            ; Add offset of beginning
MOV  SI,AX              ; Make that the source
MOV  DX,03D4            ; CRT Controller Register
MOV  CX,000A            ; 10 words to load
CLD
LODSW                   ; OUTLOOP: Get byte
OUT  DX,AX              ; Output to register
LOOP 01B8               ; Loop OUTLOOP
INT  20                 ; Terminate

RCX
BE
W
Q
```

EGATIME.COM takes a one-digit parameter from 0 to 7 to select from eight sets of possible values to load into the EGA's CRT controller registers. These change the basic timings of the EGA. The lower the number you give to EGATIME, the better the border, but the less chance your ECD can handle it. The parameter of seven loads the normal values.

You can experiment with EGATIME by first running:

```
EGABORD 1
```

to select a blue border. Then try:

```
EGATIME 6
```

and if that doesn't make your screen look like a television that needs a trip back to the shop, try something lower. You can always return to normal with:

```
EGATIME 7
```

If you really want a border, using EGATIME to create one is up to you. But if you do decide to use it, you may also want to add the following EGABORDR.COM program to your AUTOEXEC.BAT file:

```
N EGABORDR.COM
A 100
JMP   013A                 ; JMP SHORT INIT
DB    0
DW    0, 0
PUSH  AX                   ; NEWINT9:
PUSH  BX
CS:
MOV   BH,[0102]            ; Get current color
IN    AL,60                ; Get scan code of key
CMP   AL,1A                ; Check if [
JZ    011C                 ; JZ DECREMENT
CMP   AL,1B                ; Check if ]
JNZ   0133                 ; JNZ SKIPALL
INC   BH                   ; Increment the color
JMP   011E                 ; JMP SHORT CONTINUE
DEC   BH                   ; DECREMENT:
AND   BH,3F                ; Only last six bits
MOV   AH,02                ; Check for ALT key
INT   16
TEST  AL,08
JZ    0133                 ; JZ SKIPALL
MOV   AX,1001              ; Set border
INT   10                   ; through BIOS
CS:
MOV   [0102],BH            ; Save new color
POP   BX
POP   AX
CS:
JMP   FAR [0103]           ; Do old Int. 9
MOV   AX,3509              ; INIT: Get old
INT   21                   ; Int. 9
MOV   [0103],BX            ; Save it
MOV   [0105],ES
MOV   DX,0107              ; Set new Int. 9
MOV   AX,2509
INT   21
MOV   DX,013A              ; Terminate and
INT   27                   ; stay resident


RCX
54
W
Q
```

EGABORDR.COM is a remain-resident program that lets you change your border to any of the 64 colors from your keyboard. Alt-] advances through the 64 colors, and Alt-[goes backwards.

Permanent Color Mapping

The EGACOLOR program maps attribute colors into screen colors, but these color mappings revert to the defaults whenever a program changes the video mode. You may be wondering if there's a way to write a resident program that would intercept interrupt 10H, watch for a mode change, and then set the colors you want right after the BIOS has changed the video mode. But you can use a much better trick to do this.

When the BIOS resets the video mode it loads the EGA registers and sets the values in the BIOS data area based on a set of video parameters that include the default colors. These video parameters are normally located in the EGA BIOS. However, you can direct the BIOS to use an alternate set of video parameters by creating a remain-resident program with the parameters and setting a pointer located in the BIOS data area to point to it. This may sound tricky but it's not: the EGA BIOS is set up to allow you to do things like this legitimately and easily.

The BIOS listing in the *EGA Technical Reference* mentions a pointer called SAVE_PTR stored at memory location 0000:04A8. It points to a set of seven other double word (i.e. segment and offset) pointers, called DWORD_1 through DWORD_7. DWORD_5 through DWORD_7 are reserved for future use.

DWORD_1 points to a 1472 byte location in memory that contains 64 video parameters for each of the 23 video modes supported by the EGA. Twenty-three? Where did 23 video modes come from?

First, there are 17 video modes 0 through 16 that are the same as those in the video mode chart above. Although the EGA does not support modes 8 through 10 (the PC*jr* modes), and uses modes 11 and 12 internally when loading fonts, these are still included in the table. But modes 0 through 3 at the beginning of the table are for the 200-scan line versions when a regular color display is attached to the EGA. Modes 15 and 16 are for EGAs with only 64K of memory. So, after these 17 modes, the table next contains values for modes 15 and 16 when 128K or more is attached to the EGA. Finally, 350-scan line versions of modes 0 through 3 are included when an EGA is equipped with an ECD. That makes 23.

(*Note*: Although the first version of the *EGA Technical Reference* (page 103) indicates in large letters that the Interrupt 43H vector points to the Video Parameters table, this is not so. Interrupt 43H actually points to the Graphics Character Table, which is the font used to construct characters in graphics modes. Interrupt 44H, which the *EGA Technical Reference* mistakenly indicates as pointing to this Graphics Character Table, is not used by the EGA BIOS. This change may seem odd, since interrupt 44H is used by the PC*jr* to point to the Graphics Character Table, but that's the way it is.)

For each video mode, the 64 video parameters include the values loaded into the palette registers. But you can't change the table directly, since these are stored in the EGA ROM BIOS, and you can't write into ROM.

So, what you have to do is use a remain-resident program such as EGAPRMOV.COM ("EGA Parameter Move") that simply moves the set of seven pointers and the entire video parameter table into RAM:

```
N EGAPRMOV.COM
A 100
CLD
SUB   AX,AX
MOV   ES,AX               ; Set ES to 1st segment
ES:
LDS   SI,[04A8]          ; Get SAVE_PTR
MOV   DI,013C            ; Set up for transfer
ES:
MOV   [04A8],DI          ; New SAVE_PTR
ES:
MOV   [04AA],CS
PUSH  CS
POP   ES
MOV   CX,000E            ; 14 Double Words
REPZ
MOVSW
ES:
LDS   SI,[013C]          ; Get DWORD_1 pointer
MOV   DI,0158            ; Set up for transfer
ES:
MOV   [013C],DI          ; New DWORD_1
ES:
MOV   [013E],CS
PUSH  CS
POP   ES
MOV   CX,05C0            ; 23 * 64 bytes
REPZ
MOVSB
MOV   DX,0718            ; Keep resident
INT   27                ; and exit

RCX
3C
W
Q
```

You need to execute EGAPRMOV.COM only once during your PC session.

Once you've loaded EGAPRMOV you can manipulate the video parameters. The following EGACOSET ("EGA Color Set") program replaces the default palette values for video mode 3 (in 350-line mode) with those of your own choosing:

```
N EGACOSET.COM
A 100
CLD
SUB   AX,AX
MOV   ES,AX              ; ES to low memory
ES:
LES   DI,[04A8]         ; Get SAVE_PTR
ES:
LES   DI,[DI]           ; Get DWORD_1
MOV   SI,011B           ; Values to move in
ADD   DI,05A3           ; Offset for mode 3
MOV   CX,0010           ; 16 bytes
REPZ
MOVSB
INT   20
DB    00,01,02,03,04,05,14,07
DB    38,39,3A,3B,3C,3D,3E,3F

RCX
2B
W
Q
```

The two lines near the bottom, beginning with DB, can be customized. For instance, if you use:

```
DB 01, 01, 02, 03, 14, 05, 06, 3E
DB 30, 31, 32, 33, 34, 35, 36, 32
```

the EGA will map color 00 (black) to 01 (blue), color 07 (white) to 3E (bright yellow), and color 0F (bright white) to 32 (bright green). You may find it slightly confusing to go back to hexadecimal after you've mastered the octal representations of EGACOLOR, but DEBUG can't handle octal.

If your EGA is attached to a regular color display, change the line reading ADD DI,05A3 to ADD DI,00E3 and use only color values that range from 00 through 1F in the DB lines.

When you first execute EGACOSET, nothing will happen. But if you then change the video mode with an:

```
EGAMODE 3
```

your screen will display yellow on blue.

Once EGACOSET is executed, the EGA BIOS will load these values into the palette registers whenever mode 3 is set. When a program tries to displays white-on-black characters, yellow-on-blue will show up instead. EGACOSET is not a resident program like EGAPRMOV, so you can experiment by running different versions of it without using additional memory.

If you put both EGAPRMOV and EGACOSET in your AUTOEXEC.BAT file, almost every program that uses black-and-white in video mode 3 will use your colors instead. It's as simple as that. There are exceptions, however. Some "EGA-aware" programs from technologically capable companies like Microsoft and Lotus load the palette registers themselves after they load.

If you've found an EGATIME setting that works for you, here's a utility called EGABOSET that will also adjust the CRT controller registers to these values when mode 3 is set:

```
N EGABOSET.COM
A 100
CLD
SUB    AX,AX
MOV    ES,AX              ; ES to low memory
ES:
LES    DI,[04A8]          ; Get SAVE_PTR
ES:
LES    DI,[DI]            ; Get DWORD_1
ADD    DI,0580            ; Offset for mode 3
MOV    SI,012B            ; Values to move in
MOV    CX,000A            ; 10 bytes first
LODSW                     ; STORELOOP: Get byte
MOV    BL,AL              ; Use low byte
SUB    BH,BH              ; for offset
MOV    AL,AH              ; Use high byte for value
ES:
MOV    [BX+DI+0A],AL      ; Save it
LOOP 0117                 ; Loop STORELOOP
LODSB                     ; Get border color
ES:
MOV    [DI+34],AL         ; Save it
INT    20                 ; Terminate
DW 6000,5602,2003,5604,5C05,8C06,6E10,2B11,6E15,1A16
DB 01

RCX
40
W
Q
```

EGABOSET assumes that EGAPRMOV has been loaded. It's set up for the same values as EGATIME 0 and a blue border. If EGATIME 0 didn't work but something else did, count down the lines of numbers beginning with DW in EGATIME.SCR (starting at 0) and substitute the number in the line beginning with DW in EGABOSET.SCR. If you want a border color other than blue, change the number after the line that begins DB in EGABOSET to the hexadecimal rgbRGB code for the border color you want.

Important warning for people with a regular color display attached to an EGA: do not use EGABOSET. If you want a border color set automatically, go back to EGACOSET. Change the line reading MOV CX,0010 to MOV CX,0012. At the end of the second line of numbers that start with DB, add a comma, 08, another comma, and the color value of the border you want. The line after RCX should be changed from 2B to 2D.

Background on Fonts

As with the old CGA, the EGA supports both text and graphics video modes. In text modes, the ASCII codes of the displayed characters are stored in video memory. The adapter hardware translates these characters into dots through the use of a font table that contains the dot patterns for all 256 characters. In graphics modes the dots themselves are stored in memory, and the adapter hardware simply translates these dots into video signals. For programs that need display only normal text, text modes are preferable because they require less video memory and can be manipulated more rapidly by application programs.

The CGA and the IBM Monochrome Adapter use a font table stored in ROM on the adapter board. This ROM is not accessible from software, and programs may not load a different font in text modes. The only way to change the font is to remove the ROM chip from the adapter board and substitute your own. These adapters are also generally limited to 25 lines of text on the screen. (The 6845 CRT controller chip on these boards can be programmed for a 50 line interlace mode, but it looks awful.)

EGA text modes work a little differently. The adapter memory contains both the font table and the ASCII codes of the displayed characters. The EGA BIOS downloads the appropriate font into the EGA memory when it sets the video mode. The fonts are stored in the EGA BIOS and programs have complete access to them through a BIOS call that returns a pointer to the stored fonts. Following a video mode set, you can also call the BIOS to download your own font into EGA memory. At the same time, you can change the number of displayable character rows on the screen.

(Of course, in EGA graphics modes a program can write whatever dots it wants to the screen and could even create proportionally spaced fonts. In character modes you don't have quite this same flexibility.)

EGA text mode fonts have some limitations. The most severe restriction is that the width of each character is fixed at eight dots. This includes the space between characters, so in most cases characters will be only seven dots wide.

The character height, however, may range from one to 32 scan lines. The maximum number of displayable character rows on the screen is equal to the total number of displayable scan lines (200 for the old color display and 350 for the monochrome display and ECD) divided by the number of scan lines per character. The EGA BIOS contains complete fonts for an 8 x 8 character set (eight scan lines per character) and for an 8 x 14 character set (14 scan lines). You can get the starting address of these fonts in the EGA BIOS by simple interrupt 10H calls.

These fonts are stored in the BIOS in a simple format. The order of the characters is sequential by ASCII code. Each character is defined by a series of bytes, with the number of bytes used in each character equal to the height of the character in scan lines. The first byte contains the dot patterns for the top scan line. The most significant bit of each byte corresponds to the leftmost dot of the character. The least significant bit is usually 0 to allow for the space between characters. So the character box is eight dots wide while the characters are generally seven dots wide. The line- and box-drawing characters (ASCII codes C0H through DFH) are eight dots wide, which lets them connect horizontally to form continuous shapes.

The monochrome display requires separate mention here, as its character box is actually nine dots wide. For most characters, however, the ninth dot will be displayed as background. For the block- and line-drawing characters the EGA makes the ninth dot the same as the eighth dot, so the characters connect horizontally. The EGA BIOS stores what is called a 9 x 14 font, but isn't really a complete font. For all but 20 characters, the EGA uses the same 8 x 14 font used for the ECD. The 9 x 14 font contains alternate dot patterns for these exceptions.

The storage format is different from that of the other fonts: Each character requires a one-byte ASCII code, followed by 14 bytes for the dot patterns. The entire 9 x 14 font is terminated by a zero. This 9 x 14 font allows monochrome characters to be eight dots wide, since the nine-dot width of the character box still leaves a space between characters. If you plan to create your own fonts, you may want to forget about this peculiarity. For greatest versatility, you can use an eight-dot wide character box with a seven-dot wide character for both the ECD and the monochrome display.

In text modes that use 200 scan lines on the screen (video modes 0 through 3 when an EGA is connected to on old color display) the EGA normally uses the 8 x 8 font, putting 25 character rows on the display. Connected to an ECD or monochrome display, the EGA displays 350 scan lines, so the text modes (monochrome mode 7 and color modes 0 through 3) use the 8 x 14 font, again creating 25-character rows.

However, if you use the 8 x 8 font in a 350-scan line video mode, you can display 43-character rows, since 43 times 8 equals 344. A font that is ten scan lines high (which can be the 8 x 8 font with two blank scan lines) allows 35 displayable rows. If you create your own 8 x 6 font, you can fit 58 lines on the screen.

These alternative displays are supported by the EGA BIOS. What this means is very simple: the EGA stores the current number of lines per screen (less 1) at address 0000:0484H. An application can also obtain this information by an interrupt 10H call. The BIOS Teletype routine (interrupt 10H, function call 0FH), which is normally used for screen output at the DOS command level (except when ANSI.SYS is loaded), uses this value to determine when to scroll the screen.

Font Changes Through the BIOS

Even if you're not the type of person who lives to see everything on the screen in italics, try the following EGAITAL program:

```
N EGAITAL.COM
A 100
CLD
MOV   BH,02                    ; Get 8x14 font
MOV   AX,1130
INT   10                       ; Returns ES:BP
PUSH  ES
POP   DS
MOV   SI,BP                    ; DS:SI points to font
PUSH  CS
POP   ES
MOV   DI,0159                  ; ES:DI = destination
MOV   BX,0100                  ; Number of characters
MOV   CL,03                    ; MAINLOOP:
CALL  0147                     ; Call SHIFTRIGHT
CALL  0147                     ; Call SHIFTRIGHT
CALL  0147                     ; Call SHIFTRIGHT
CALL  0150                     ; Call SHIFTLEFT
CALL  0150                     ; Call SHIFTLEFT
CALL  0150                     ; Call SHIFTLEFT
CALL  0150                     ; Call SHIFTLEFT
DEC   BX                       ; Decrement char count
JNZ   0114                     ; Loop if not zero
MOV   BP,0159                  ; Point to font
SUB   DX,DX                    ; Starting character
MOV   CX,0100                  ; Character count
MOV   BH,0E                    ; Bytes per character
CS:
MOV   BL,[005D]
AND   BL,03                    ; Block to load
MOV   AX,1100                  ; Load font
INT   10
INT   20                       ; Terminate
LODSW                          ; SHIFTRIGHT:
SHR   AL,CL
SHR   AH,CL
STOSW                          ; and store
DEC   CL
RET
LODSW                          ; SHIFTLEFT:
```

```
SHL   AL,CL
SHL   AH,CL
STOSW                      ; and store
INC   CL
RET

RCX
59
W
Q
```

Note: because it loads a 14 scan line character font, EGAITAL.COM can be used only with EGAs that are attached to ECD or monochrome displays.

The first EGAITAL INT 10H call (where AX equals 1130H) returns a pointer to the 8 x 14 font stored in the EGA BIOS. You can get a pointer to the 8 x 8 font by setting BL to 3, and to the 9 x 14 font extension by setting BL to 5. This function call also returns the current number of character rows (less one) in register DL and the current scan lines per character (called *points* in the BIOS documentation) in register CX.

Next, EGAITAL transfers the font to local memory and, in the process, shifts each byte to tilt the character to the right. (If you think that doing bit manipulations on existing fonts is a flaky way to create new fonts, that's how Microsoft *Word* does italics in EGA graphics modes, though *Word* uses a different algorithm that is not quite as extreme.) Finally, EGAITAL makes another BIOS call to load the font — function call 11H (in AH), subfunction 00H (in AL), which is used to load a user font when the number of displayable rows does not change. Although you're loading all 256 characters starting at ASCII code 00, you can load only part of a character set by setting registers CX and DX appropriately.

You can go back to the normal font by resetting the video mode with EGAMODE.COM or by executing the tiny EGA8X14 utility below:

```
N EGA8X14.COM
A 100
MOV   AX,1101              ; Load 8x14 font
MOV   BL,0                 ; Block to load
INT   10                   ; Call BIOS
INT   20

RCX
9
W
Q
```

EGA8X14.COM uses another, simpler, BIOS call in which register AH again equals 11H but in which AL equals 01. This loads the normal 8 x 14 font. If AL were 02, the 8 x 8 font would be loaded, but you wouldn't be happy with the way it looks. Since the

EGA is still using 14 scan lines per character, the bottom six scan lines will display the bottom of the 8 x 14 font.

Incidentally, when you execute these programs, you may see a brief contraction of your display (and it may even roll over once) when the font is loaded. This is normal. The EGA BIOS has to change the video mode to one of the internal modes (11 and 12) so it can access the video memory to load the font. Then it must change the mode back to the original mode.

Changing the Displayable Rows

The interrupt 10H function calls used in the previous examples (where AH is 11H and AL equals 00, 01, or 02), simply load the font. When AL equals 10H, 11H, or 12H, BIOS loads the font and recalculates the number of displayable rows on the screen based on the new character height.

BIOS also recalculates the cursor and monochrome underline position, but it does so incorrectly, causing the cursor on an ECD and the underline on the monochrome display to disappear. Most of the EGA-compatible boards seem to duplicate this bug.

Note also that the video page size is recalculated. Programs that directly access video memory of different pages should use the "CRT_LEN" value stored at memory location 0000:044CH for the length of a video page. Programs should not follow the example of ANSI.SYS, which hard codes a page size.

Because of the recalculations the BIOS must make when using these function calls, the IBM documentation recommends you execute them right after a video mode set. That's not really necessary, but you should be using video page 0 (which is normal) and, if you're changing to a smaller number of displayable lines, your cursor should be somewhere near the top of the display, on a row lower than the number of rows you'll be changing to. In any case, if you're fooling around with these programs and your cursor ends up somewhere below the bottom of the displayable screen, just enter EGAMODE 3 (for color) or EGAMODE 7 (for monochrome) to return to normal.

The most popular of the new EGA screen formats is the 43-line mode. The EGA43.COM program implements it:

```
N EGA43.COM
A 100
MOV   AX,1112             ; Load 8x8 Font
MOV   BL,00
INT   10
SUB   AX,AX
MOV   DS,AX
PUSH  [0487]              ; Save INFO byte
OR    BYTE PTR [0487],01
MOV   CX,0600             ; Set cursor size
MOV   AH,01
INT   10
```

```
POP   [0487]          ; Restore INFO byte
MOV   DX,03B4         ; Fix up underline
MOV   AX,0714
OUT   DX,AX
INT   20

RCX
28
W
Q
```

EGA43.COM also fixes the cursor on the ECD and the underline on the monochrome display. If you haven't loaded ANSI.SYS (or some other resident program that messes around with the screen), you'll see that commands such as DIR work fine with 43 rows. Any program that uses DOS for simple teletype screen output (such as EDLIN and DEBUG) will also use the 43 rows, although some of the commands are hard-wired to fill one 25-line screen at a time.

For instance, DIR /P (which pauses after a full screen) assumes the display has 25 rows. Until the EGA, there was no BIOS call that returned the number of displayable rows on the screen, so most programs that need to know the number of rows on the screen still just use 25. If the developers of the original PC BIOS had had the foresight to allow for an adapter capable of more than 25 rows, this would not be a problem.

Because of this deficiency in the original system board BIOS, you'll find that full-screen application programs will react to the 43-line mode in one of three ways. If the program resets the video mode on entry, the display will go back to 25 lines. If the program does not reset the mode, it will probably use only the top 25 lines of the screen. However, EGA-aware programs are starting to appear that will pick up the information from the EGA BIOS and use all 43 lines. Increasing numbers of commercial programs, such as *XyWrite*, Microsoft *Word*, and even *WordStar*, offer an option to use the EGA in its 43-line mode.

If you've loaded ANSI.SYS, you'll see that it assumes the display has 25 rows. ANSI.SYS users might want to look up Hersey Micro Consulting's *Fansi-Console*, version 1.15 which, along with many other features, supports ANSI functions on the EGA in different screen formats.

EGA Aware MORE

PC Magazine reader Johnny Y. Chin pointed out that the DOS MORE filter pauses every 25 lines even though the EGA is capable of displaying more, and discovered how to patch the DOS MORE.COM utility (versions 3.1 or later) to handle this. Just use the EGAMORE.SCR script below:

```
N MORE.COM
L
```

```
A 112              ;use 114 for DOS 3.1 and 3.2
JMP 1EE            ;jmp to patch code
NOP
NOP

A 1EE              ;same for DOS 3.1 and 3.2
MOV AX,1130        ;invoke video BIOS character generator
INT 10             ;routine to return information; current
INC DL             ;number of rows returns in DL
MOV [1E5],DL       ;use [1E7] for DOS 3.1 and 3.2
JMP 117            ;use 119 for DOS 3.1 and 3.2

A 1BA              ;use 1BC for DOS 3.1 and 3.2
JBE 1DC            ;use 1DE for DOS 3.1 and 3.2
MOV DL,7           ;change code to issue beep
MOV AH,2           ;instead of — More —
INT 21
NOP

A 1C9              ;use 1CB for DOS 3.1 and 3.2
MOV DL,D           ;send carriage return only
MOV AH,2           ;to save one line
INT 21
NOP

E 13F 80           ;use 141 for DOS 3.1 and 3.2
N EGAMORE.COM      ;increase buffer size to 32K
W
Q
```

The addresses in this script are for version 3.3 only; for versions 3.1 and 3.2 note the slightly different offsets mentioned after the semicolons on some of the lines.

Type in the script using a pure ASCII word processor, EDLIN, or the DOS COPY CON command (and make sure you're entering the right addresses and values for your particular version of DOS). Press the Enter key after each line, especially the last one with the Q. And be sure to leave the four blank lines; this won't work without them. Then make sure DEBUG.COM is handy, put EGAMORE.SCR in the same directory as your DOS MORE.COM, and type:

```
DEBUG < EGAMORE.SCR
```

The script will create a new version of MORE.COM called EGAMORE.COM.

This patch is useful for EGA systems since it uses the character generator routine provided by INT 10 to figure out the proper number of rows. The patch codes are located where the "— More — " message was. EGAMORE.COM will beep instead of printing this message. Finally, this patch increases the size of the buffer from 4K to 32K.

All utilities should use this technique to sniff out the actual screen size. But few do. Worse, most DOS utilities don't. Shameful. Remember, don't have ANSI.SYS loaded when you try to expand your EGA screen size, since ANSI hardwires the screen size to 25 lines.

You can create an adaptation of Charles Petzold's 43-line setting utility that will clear an EGA screen to blue text on a 43-row white background, by typing in the following 11 lines:

```
DEBUG
E 100 B8 12 11 B3 00 CD 10 29 C0 8E D8 FF 36 87 04 80
E 110 0E 87 04 01 B9 00 06 B4 01 CD 10 8F 06 87 04 BA
E 120 B4 03 B8 14 07 EF B8 00 06 B7 71 31 C9 BA 4F 2A
E 130 CD 10 B4 02 30 FF 31 D2 CD 10 CD 20 74 03 C6 07
E 140 00 A0 67 46 32 06 69 46 22 C5 22 C1 74 03 C6 07
N CLSEGA.COM
RCX
50
W
Q
```

Once you've created it you may patch the color by using DEBUG to change the byte at address 12A. The lefthand digit represents the background and the righthand digit the foreground; changing it from the existing 71 to 25 would produce purple text on a green background. To do so, and create a new file called PURPLE.COM, you'd type:

```
DEBUG CLSEGA.COM
E 12A 25
N PURPLE.COM
W
Q
```

See the EDLIN chapter for another 43-line EGA patch.

Creating Custom Screens

If 43 lines seem too cramped for you, how about 35 lines with EGA35.COM?

```
N EGA35.COM
A 100
CLD
MOV  BH,03            ; 8x8 font pointer
MOV  AX,1130
```

```
        INT   10
        PUSH  ES
        POP   DS
        MOV   SI,BP           ; DS:SI points to font
        PUSH  CS
        POP   ES
        MOV   DI,0152         ; ES:DI to destination
        MOV   BX,0100         ; Number chars
        MOV   CX,0008         ; Bytes per char
        REPZ                  ; Move them
        MOVSB
        SUB   AX,AX           ; Store two zeroes
        STOSW
        DEC   BX
        JNZ   0114            ; Next character
        MOV   BP,0152         ; Points to font
        MOV   DX,0000         ; Starting char
        MOV   CX,0100         ; Number of chars
        MOV   BH,0A           ; Bytes per char
        MOV   BL,00           ; Block to load
        MOV   AX,1110         ; Load user font
        INT   10
        SUB   AX,AX
        MOV   DS,AX
        PUSH  [0487]          ; Fix up cursor
        OR    BYTE PTR [0487],01
        MOV   CX,0800
        MOV   AH,01
        INT   10
        POP   [0487]
        MOV   DX,03B4         ; Fix up underline
        MOV   AX,0914
        OUT   DX,AX
        INT   20

        RCX
        52
        W
        Q
```

EGA35.COM retrieves a pointer to the 8 x 8 font from the BIOS but stores the font in local memory with two blank scan lines at the end of each character. It then loads the font (which is now, since we've changed it, a user-defined font) into the EGA through another BIOS call.

On the other hand, if 43 lines are not quite enough, you may want to try out EGA50.COM:

```
N EGA50.COM
A 100
CLD
MOV  BH,03              ; 8x8 font pointer
MOV  AX,1130
INT  10
PUSH ES
POP  DS
MOV  SI,BP              ; DS:SI points to font
PUSH CS
POP  ES
MOV  DI,0150           ; ES:DI to destination
MOV  BX,0100           ; Number of chars
MOV  CX,0007           ; Bytes per char
REPZ                   ; Move them
MOVSB
INC  SI                ; Skip over last byte
DEC  BX
JNZ  0114              ; Next character
MOV  BP,0150           ; Points to font
MOV  DX,0000           ; Starting char
MOV  CX,0100           ; Number of chars
MOV  BH,07             ; Bytes per char
MOV  BL,00             ; Block to load
MOV  AX,1110           ; Load user font
INT  10
SUB  AX,AX
MOV  DS,AX
PUSH [0487]            ; Fix up cursor
OR   BYTE PTR [0487],01
MOV  CX,0600
MOV  AH,01
INT  10
POP  [0487]
MOV  DX,03B4           ; Fix up underline
MOV  AX,0614
OUT  DX,AX
INT  20


RCX
50
```

```
W
Q
```

EGA50.COM loses the descenders on the lowercase letters and makes commas look like periods, but it's still readable.

Going the other way, perhaps you'd like something a little taller on your screen, such as EGA12.COM:

```
N EGA12.COM
A 100
CLD
MOV   BH,02              ; Get font pointer
MOV   AX,1130
INT   10
PUSH  ES
POP   DS
MOV   SI,BP              ; DS:SI points to font
PUSH  CS
POP   ES
MOV   DI,014C            ; ES:DI is destination
MOV   CX,0E00            ; 14 bytes per char
LODSB                   ; Get bytes
STOSB                   ; Store it twice
STOSB
LOOP  0114               ; Keep going
MOV   BP,014C            ; Points to font
MOV   DX,0000            ; Starting char
MOV   CX,0100            ; Number of chars
MOV   BH,1C              ; Bytes per char
MOV   BL,00              ; Block to load
MOV   AX,1110            ; Load font
INT   10
SUB   AX,AX
MOV   DS,AX
PUSH  [0487]             ; Fix up cursor
OR    BYTE PTR [0487],01
MOV   CX,1619
MOV   AH,01
INT   10
POP   [0487]
MOV   DX,03B4            ; Fix up underline
MOV   AX,1B14
OUT   DX,AX
INT   20
```

```
RCX
4C
W
Q
```

The EGA12.COM program doubles up the dots of the 8 x 14 font and creates a 12-character line display. While its output looks a little strange in an 80-column mode, try executing it after EGAMODE 1, and you'll end up with a 12 line by 40 column display. Once again, commands like DIR are very happy with this format.

Finally, EGA25 returns things to normal:

```
N EGA25.COM
A 100
MOV    AX,1111              ; Load 8x14 font
MOV    BL,00
INT    10
SUB    AX,AX
MOV    DS,AX
PUSH   [0487]               ; Fix up cursor
OR     BYTE PTR [0487],01
MOV    CX,0B0D
MOV    AH,01
INT    10
POP    [0487]
MOV    DX,03B4              ; Fix up underline
MOV    AX,0D14
OUT    DX,AX
INT    20

RCX
28
W
Q
```

You may run the above size-changing programs on EGAs attached to ECD or monochrome displays. If you have your EGA attached to a regular old color display, you have only 200 scan lines to work with. EGA43 will make your display use the normal 25 lines, EGA50 will turn it into a 28-line display, EGA35 will do 20 lines, EGA12 will do seven lines, and EGA25 will do 14 lines.

The Problems of Cursor Emulation

Our size-changing programs required the addition of some code to fix the monochrome underline and the color cursor. The fix to the monochrome underline is necessary because of a simple bug in the EGA BIOS. The fix to the color cursor is necessary because of a more complex bug.

Programs that set a cursor size usually assume that each character in a color mode has eight scan lines; setting the cursor to scan lines 6 and 7 normally creates the familiar underline cursor. On the EGA, however, this would put the cursor in the middle of the character. For this reason, the EGA BIOS uses *cursor emulation* logic to translate a cursor size into something appropriate for a 14 scan line character. (The cursor registers in the EGA also function a little differently from those in the CGA.) This cursor emulation algorithm, however, is based on the presence of an ECD rather than the size of each character. The sample programs above first turn off cursor emulation by flagging a bit in lower memory, then restore the bit when they're done.

You probably won't want to turn off cursor emulation entirely because programs that set the cursor size through the BIOS will then put the color cursor on scan lines 6 and 7 when your normal character set is 14 scan lines high. Even with cursor emulation on, you may see this problem with programs that go directly to CRT registers to set the cursor size.

Once again, this is a problem that could have been avoided had the designers of the original system board BIOS foreseen an adapter that had a variable number of scan lines per character and created a memory location (like the one the EGA BIOS maintains) to store this value.

A New Print Screen Routine

If you tried a Shift-PrtSc while in 35- or 43-line mode you were probably surprised that only the top 25 lines appeared on your printer. That happens because the interrupt 5 print screen routine in effect is still the one in the system board BIOS, which is locked into using 25 lines per screen.

Fortunately, the EGA has its own print screen routine. It's virtually identical to the one in your system board BIOS except that it uses a variable number of lines per screen. However, when the EGA boots up, this new print screen routine is not automatically substituted for the old one.

The following EGAPRTSC.COM utility rectifies this oversight by substituting the EGA print screen routine for the one in your system board BIOS:

```
N EGAPRTSC.COM
A 100
MOV   AH,12      ; Select Alternate
MOV   BL,20      ; Print Screen
INT   10
INT   20

RCX
8
```

```
W
Q
```

If you intend to use regularly the various alternate screen formats presented here, you should make EGAPRTSC.COM a part of your AUTOEXEC.BAT file, and it should be very close to the top. It should be executed early because if you load EGAPRTSC after any resident program that also uses interrupt 5 (e.g. the PC-DOS GRAPHICS program and some print buffers) these other programs will be locked out.

Of course, the EGA print screen routine does not support the printing of graphics screens created in EGA graphics modes. (Neither does the PC-DOS GRAPHICS program.) Nor will you be able to print alternate fonts that you load into the EGA.

EGA Screen Dumps

There is no real standard for implementing graphics on printers. If someone were to write an EGA graphics screen dump program it would have to be for the IBM Graphics Printer and compatibles, because that's as close to a standard as exists right now. This would be fine for people with IBM Graphics Printers but not for everybody else. Even for people with Graphics Printers, that printer is not going to do very well printing 16-color graphics. It does not even have enough resolution to use different dot densities for the different colors. The usual method — printing dots for every color except background — sometimes looks OK and sometimes doesn't.

If you'd rather have a graphics screen dump routine triggered by a Shift-PrtSc, you could use the following EGAGRAF.SCR script file to create EGAGRAF.COM — a remain-resident program that prints EGA 640 by 350 graphics displays on an IBM Graphics Printer or compatible only. Type it in using a pure-ASCII word processor or EDLIN. Omit the semicolons and the comments after them. Make sure you leave the blank line above RCX and that you press the Enter key at the end of each line, especially the last one with the Q:

```
N EGAGRAF.COM
A
JMP    01C2                          ; Jump INITIALIZE
DW     00,00
DB     02,0D,0A
DB     09,09,20,20,20,20,1B,4C,80,02
DB     03,1B,4A,18
PUSH   AX                            ; NEWINT5:
PUSH   BX
PUSH   DS
MOV    AH,0F                         ; Get Video Mode
INT    10
AND    AL,7F                         ; Strip High Bit
CMP    AL,0F                         ; If below 15
```

```
JB    0135                        ; do OLDINT5
CMP   AL,10                       ; If above 16
JA    0135                        ; do OLDINT5
MOV   AX,0050                     ; Print-Screen data
MOV   DS,AX
CMP   BYTE PTR [0000],01
JNZ   013D                        ; If busy, do not
POP   DS                          ; print
POP   BX
POP   AX
CS:
JMP   FAR [0103]                  ; Do OLDINT5
MOV   BYTE PTR [0000],01          ; Set busy
STI
PUSH  CX
PUSH  DX
MOV   BX,0107                     ; Initial String
CALL  0199                        ; Call PRINTSTRING
SUB   DX,DX                       ; Row Register
MOV   BX,010A                     ; Row Beginning String
CALL  0199                        ; Call PRINTSTRING
SUB   CX,CX                       ; Column Register
MOV   BX,0800                     ; Dots per byte
PUSH  BX
SUB   BH,BH
MOV   AH,0D
INT   10                          ; Read dot
POP   BX
CMP   DX,015E                     ; See if above row 350
JNB   0169                        ; If so, no dot
CMP   AL,01                       ; See if dot is black
CMC
RCL   BL,1                        ; Slide in bit
INC   DX                          ; Next row
DEC   BH                          ; 1 less row
JNZ   0158                        ; Do next row
MOV   AL,BL                       ; 8 row byte
CALL  01A8                        ; Call PRINT
SUB   DX,+08                      ; Back 8 rows
INC   CX                          ; Next column
CMP   CX,0280                     ; See if below 640
JB    0155
MOV   BX,0114                     ; End of row string
CALL  0199                        ; Call PRINTSTRING
ADD   DX,+08                      ; Up 8 rows
```

```
        CMP   DX,015E              ; See if above 350
        JB    014D                 ; If not, next 8 rows
        MOV   BYTE PTR [0000],00   ; Not busy
        POP   DX
        POP   CX
        POP   DS
        POP   BX
        POP   AX
        IRET                       ; Return
        CS:                        ; PRINTSTRING:
        MOV   CL,[BX]
        SUB   CH,CH
        INC   BX
        CS:
        MOV   AL,[BX]
        CALL  01A8                 ; Call PRINT
        LOOP  019E
        RET
        PUSH  AX                   ; PRINT:
        PUSH  DX
        SUB   DX,DX
        SUB   AH,AH
        INT   17                   ; BIOS Print Char
        TEST  AH,29
        POP   DX
        POP   AX
        JZ    01C1
        MOV   BYTE PTR [0000],FF   ; Error
        ADD   SP,+02
        JMP   0193                 ; And exit
        RET
        MOV   AX,3505              ; INITIALIZE:
        INT   21                   ; Get Old Int 5
        MOV   [0103],BX            ; Save it
        MOV   [0105],ES
        MOV   DX,0118              ; Set NEWINT5
        MOV   AX,2505
        INT   21
        MOV   DX,01C2              ; Terminate and
        INT   27                   ; remain resident

        RCX
        DC
        W
        Q
```

Then make sure DEBUG.COM is handy and type:

```
DEBUG < EGAGRAF.SCR
```

This creates EGAGRAF.COM. Load EGAGRAF.COM and it will remain resident in memory until you reboot. When you press the Shift-PrtSc combination in video mode 15 (equivalent to BASIC's mode 9 — EGA 640 by 350 graphics on a monochrome display) or 16 (BASIC's mode 10 — EGA 640 by 350 graphics on an ECD), the resident program will print the screen.

EGAGRAF.COM prints a dot for every color except the background. This causes white-on-black graphics (or, in the case of the monochrome display, green-on-black graphics) to be printed as black on white. This reversal of colors is normal for printing graphics. If you want black printed as black and all other colors not printed (which is the way it actually looks onscreen), make a copy of EGAGRAF.COM called EGAGRAF2.COM and use DEBUG to change the value of the byte at address 168 to 90 by typing:

```
COPY EGAGRAF.COM EGAGRAF2.COM
DEBUG EGAGRAF2.COM
E 168 90
W
Q
```

If you need to put an image onscreen, run this sample BASIC program:

```
100 'EGACIRCL.BAS — adapted from Charles Petzold program
110 DEFINT A-Z
120 SCREEN 9              ' Use 10 for EGA on monochrome
130 CLS
140 FOR I=1 TO 75
150 A=INT(640*RND):B=INT(350*RND):C=INT(40*RND)+5:D=INT(16*RND)
160 CIRCLE (A,B),C,D
170 PAINT (A,B),C MOD 15+1,D
180 CIRCLE (A,B),C-5,D
190 PAINT (A,B),0,D
200 NEXT
210 WHILE INKEY$="":WEND
220 SCREEN 0
```

A New Screen Clearer

When using screen lengths of more than 25 lines, you'll find that CLS no longer works right, either. It also suffers from the curse of the original PC, in that it has to assume 25 lines on the screen. A new EGA-aware clear screen program (called CS) fixes this problem:

```
N CS.COM
A 100
MOV  DL,18          ; 24 columns default
SUB  BH,BH          ; Get number of columns
MOV  AX,1130
INT  10
MOV  AH,0F          ; Get video information
INT  10
DEC  AH
MOV  CH,DL
MOV  CL,AH          ; CX = maximum row and col
MOV  AH,00          ; Graphics attribute
CMP  AL,07          ; See if monochrome mode
JZ   011D
CMP  AL,03          ; See if text mode
JA   012D
MOV  DL,20          ; Write space to display
MOV  AH,02
INT  21
MOV  AL,08          ; Backspace
MOV  AH,0E
INT  10
MOV  AH,08          ; Read attribute
INT  10
PUSH BX             ; Save video page
MOV  BH,AH          ; Clear screen
MOV  DX,CX
SUB  CX,CX
MOV  AX,0600
INT  10
POP  BX             ; Get back video page
SUB  DX,DX          ; Home cursor
MOV  AH,02
INT  10
INT  20
RCX
42
W
Q
```

CS.COM program uses the BIOS call to determine the number of lines on the screen (actually one less than the total). To maintain compatibility in case the program is used on a system without an EGA, it first sets DL to 24 before making the call. If an EGA is not installed, the system board BIOS will just return all registers unchanged.

The program is different from CLS in some other ways. It doesn't ignore the screen color attribute currently in effect and doesn't wipe out a border (as CLS does when ANSI.SYS is not loaded) and it doesn't turn the screen white for graphics modes (as the ANSI.SYS CLS does).

Blanking Out the Screen

If you have an EGA attached to a monochrome display and you spend most of your time with the same basic image onscreen — a Lotus grid or a *WordStar* menu, for instance — you may end up with traces of this image permanently burned into the display.

You can avoid this problem by running EGABLANK, a memory-resident program that turns the screen off automatically to prevent this from happening if nothing has been typed for 7.5 minutes. Typing anything on the keyboard will bring it back to normal.

To create EGABLANK.COM, type in the following EGABLANK.SCR script file using a pure-ASCII word processor or EDLIN. Omit the semicolons and the comments following them. Be sure to leave a blank line above RCX and to press the Enter key after each line, especially the last one:

```
N EGABLANK.COM
A
JMP  0153              ; JMP INITIAL
DW   0, 0
DW   0, 0
DW   0
CS:                    ; NEWINT8:
CMP  WO [010A],+00     ; Check COUNTDOWN
JZ   0122              ; If zero, DONOTHING
CS:
DEC  WO [010A]         ; Decrement COUNTDOWN
JNZ  0122              ; If not 0, DONOTHING
PUSH AX
MOV  AL,00             ; Byte to turn off
CALL 0142              ; Call ONOFF
POP  AX
CS:
JMP  FAR [0102]        ; Jmp OLDINT8
CS:                    ; NEWINT9:
CMP  WO [010A],+00     ; Check COUNTDOWN
JNZ  0136              ; If non-zero, OK
PUSH AX
MOV  AL,20             ; Byte to turn on
CALL 0142              ; Call ONOFF
```

```
POP   AX
CS:                           ; OK:
MOV   WO [010A],2000          ; Set COUNTDOWN
CS:
JMP   FAR [0106]              ; Jmp OLDINT9
PUSH  DX                      ; ONOFF:
PUSH  AX
MOV   DX,03BA                 ; Reset flip-flop
IN    AL,DX                   ; for monochrome
MOV   DX,03DA                 ; Reset flip-flop
IN    AL,DX                   ; for color
MOV   DX,03C0                 ; Attribute Port
POP   AX
OUT   DX,AL                   ; Turn on or off
POP   DX
RET
MOV   AX,3508                 ; INITIAL:
INT   21
CS:
MOV   [0102],BX               ; Save OLDINT8
CS:
MOV   [0104],ES
MOV   DX,010C                 ; Set NEWINT8
MOV   AX,2508
INT   21
MOV   AX,3509
INT   21
CS:
MOV   [0106],BX               ; Save OLDINT9
CS:
MOV   [0108],ES
MOV   DX,0127                 ; Set NEWINT9
MOV   AX,2509
INT   21
MOV   DX,0153                 ; Bytes for resident
INT   27                      ; Terminate

RCX
86
W
Q
```

Then be certain DEBUG.COM is handy and type:

```
DEBUG < EGABLANK.SCR
```

You may alter the amount of time EGABLANK waits before blanking the screen, by changing the current hexadecimal delay value of 2000. A value of 1 will blank the screen every 55 milliseconds. Going up to FFFF gives you about an hour before the lights go out.

To change the value to 1000 (3.25 minutes), change the "SET COUNTDOWN" line in the EGABLANK.SCR script file from:

```
MOV        WO [010A],2000
```

to

```
MOV        WO [010A],1000
```

and repeat the above process.

Or, if you've already created EGABLANK.COM and don't have the script file handy (this is one good reason to keep them around on a floppy disk), load the program into DEBUG by typing:

```
DEBUG EGABLANK.COM
```

Then type:

```
A 137
```

and press the Enter key. Enter:

```
MOV WO [10A],1000
```

and press Enter twice. Then type W and press Enter to save the changes to disk, and then type Q and press Enter to quit DEBUG.

Note that this program is for EGA and EGA compatibles only. It will not work with other adapters, but it will not harm them either. Although it is really for the monochrome display (since monochromes are the ones susceptible to phosphor burn), it will also work with a color display attached to an EGA. Under extremely unusual circumstances, it could interfere with a program engaged in setting the EGA palette registers, so use it at your own risk.

EGABLANK will not work well with programs that entirely steal the keyboard interrupt, since it has no way of knowing when keys have been struck. If you have any of these programs, you probably know about this since other resident programs won't work with them either. Some more sophisticated commercially available screen blankers continually check the contents of the screen for changes to get around this problem.

43-Line WordStar

Classic *WordStar* 3.3, of course, is one of the few application programs that can be easily patched for different screen formats. The patch points have been well documented and have remained consistent (in most cases) from version to version. Many *WordStar* users have switched to other word processors or have tried more recent versions of it packaged by MicroPro, but the classic edition of this program still has a huge following.

If you'll be using DOS in a 43-line mode, all you have to do to get *WordStar* to use 43 lines is change the value at offset 248H from 18H (which is 24 decimal) to 2AH (42) or 2BH (43). Using the latter value eliminates the display of the function keys down at the bottom of the screen.

If you'll be using DOS with 25 lines but want to use *WordStar* with 43 lines, it's easy to patch *WordStar* version 3.3 so that it switches to the 43-line mode on entry and restores 25 lines on exit by resetting the video mode. This WS43.SCR patch assumes that nothing else is located in the *WordStar* patch area at offset 2E0H:

```
N WS.COM
L
N WS43.COM
E 248 2A
A 2A4
JMP   2E1                 ; Initialize Screen
NOP
JMP   300                 ; De-Initialize

A 2E1
MOV   AH,0F               ; Get Video Mode
INT   10
MOV   [2E0],AL            ; Save it
SUB   BL,BL               ; Use 43 column mode
MOV   AX,1112
INT   10
MOV   CX,0007             ; Set cursor to block
MOV   AH,1
INT   10
RET

A 300
MOV   AL,[2E0]            ; Get back mode
SUB   AH,AH               ; And re-set
INT   10
RET

W
Q
```

Note: If you create this WS43.SCR script file, be absolutely sure you leave the blank lines where indicated.

To patch your copy of WS.COM and create a version of *WordStar* called WS43.COM, type in the WS43.SCR script and put it, DEBUG.COM, and a copy (never the original!) of WS.COM in the same subdirectory. Properly executed, this script doesn't change the original *WordStar* program (it makes a copy of it that has a new name), but if you make a typing mistake in the process, you'd better be safe than sorry. Then type:

```
DEBUG < WS43.SCR
```

If you'd rather get an extra line of text instead of the function key definitions down at the bottom, change the line reading:

```
E 248 2A
```

to

```
E 248 2B
```

A few editors at *PC Magazine* still use classic (and very highly patched) versions of *WordStar* for both writing and program development. Before we bought EGAs, we used to print things out to do extensive editing or to get a better perspective on program flow. With 43 lines, however, in many cases we have enough information right on our screens to avoid doing this. The increase in productivity with a 43-line mode is very real, and it can save lots of trees, as well.

The 512 Character Set

The font techniques presented above worked by making simple substitutions for the font normally loaded by the BIOS. However, an EGA equipped with 256K can actually store four entire 256-character fonts in its memory. If your EGA has 128K, it can hold two fonts. A 64K EGA is limited to one font. These days virtually all cards come with the maximum amount. Usually only one of these fonts is active at any one time, but you can tell the EGA which one you want to be active by using a simple BIOS call.

In addition, you can select any two of the four fonts to be active at the same time on the same screen. Instead of a normal 256 character set, this lets you use a 512-character set. Since the ASCII code for each character is still limited to one byte, something else outside the character code has to specify which font is to be used for each character.

This "something else" is the attribute bit that normally indicates foreground color intensity. Instead of (or in addition to) making a character high intensity, this bit selects the alternate font. So if your word processor can display all 256 normal characters and can also use high intensity to represent boldface on the screen, you can use boldface instead to select an additional 256 different characters on your screen.

You may have noticed that in the previous font-loading examples, register BL was always set to zero. This register specifies what the EGA BIOS calls the *Block to Load*. You can set it to any value from 0 through 3, and it corresponds to the four fonts you can load into a 256K EGA. If the value of BL is set to 1, the font is loaded into block 1 instead of block 0. Since block 0 is normally used for both low-intensity and high-intensity characters, you won't immediately see any change in your display until you tell the EGA to use the intensity bit to select the alternate font.

An example will make this clearer. The earlier EGAITAL.COM loaded an italic character set. This program can actually take a parameter that specifies the block (0 through 3) into which to load the font. If no parameter is specified, it loads the font into block 0. But now try running:

```
EGAITAL 1
```

Running EGAITAL earlier with no parameter italicized the text onscreen. But when you type EGAITAL 1, nothing happens. The italics font has been loaded into the EGA memory, but in block 1 instead of block 0. Block 0 still contains the normal font.

Now you have to tell the EGA two things:

1. That you want block 0 to be used for low intensity characters and block 1 to be used for high intensity;
2. That we want to suppress the normal use of the intensity bit in the attribute byte.

The EGA512.COM will do this for you automatically:

```
N EGA512.COM
A 100
MOV   BL,[005D]        ; 1st Parameter
AND   BL,03            ; Lower 3 bits
MOV   BH,[006D]        ; 2nd Parameter
AND   BH,03            ; Lower 3 bits
MOV   CX,BX            ; Save in CX
SHL   BH,1             ; Shift BH left
SHL   BH,1
OR    BL,BH            ; Combine with BL
MOV   AX,1103          ; Set block spec.
INT   10
MOV   BX,0F12          ; Enable all planes
CMP   CL,CH            ; but only if
JZ    0124             ; blocks are equal
MOV   BH,07            ; Otherwise low
MOV   AX,1000          ; Enable planes
INT   10
INT   20
```

```
RCX
2B
W
Q
```

EGA512.COM takes two parameters that may range from 0 through 3. The first is the font to use on low-intensity characters, the second the font to use for high-intensity characters. If you enter:

```
EGA512 0 1
```

anything that is high intensity on your screen will become low-intensity italics. Anything that is low-intensity will remain the same.

To prove this, execute TEST512:

```
N TEST512.COM
A 100
MOV  AH,0F          ; Get video page
INT  10
MOV  AH,03          ; Get cursor
INT  10
MOV  BP,0128        ; String 1
MOV  CX,000F        ; Number of chars
MOV  BL,07          ; Attribute
MOV  AX,1301        ; Write String
INT  10
MOV  AH,03          ; Get cursor
INT  10
MOV  BP,0137        ; String 2
MOV  CX,0010        ; Number of chars
MOV  BL,0F          ; Attribute
MOV  AX,1301        ; Write String
INT  10
INT  20
DB "Low Intensity,"0D,0A
DB "High Intensity,"0D,0A

RCX
47
W
Q
```

This program prints two lines, one in low intensity and one in high intensity. The high-intensity line will not be high intensity, but will instead be italics. Now if you type:

```
EGA512 1 0
```

everything in low intensity will be italics (the block 1 font), and everything in high intensity will be the normal font (block 0).

Finally, typing:

```
EGA512 0 0
```

turns everything back to normal. It makes both low intensity and high intensity share the same font. The EGA512 program checks if the two parameters are the same and, if so, restores the meaning of the attribute bit to specify high intensity.

If your word processor works in text mode, does onscreen display of boldface, and doesn't reset the video mode on entry, try entering:

```
EGA512 0 1
```

and see if you can get italics in your word processor instead of boldface. (Of course, then you'll have trouble printing those extra 256 characters on your printer. But that's a whole other problem.)

You may be distressed that you lose a high-intensity character display when you use the 512-character set, but there's a way around that, too.

Earlier, you saw how to use the EGA palette registers to map the four-bit IRGB code into a six-bit rgbRGB code. With this technique you can map the low-intensity IRGB codes (where the "I" intensity bit is 0) into high-intensity rgbRGB codes. The only thing you're really limited to with a 512-character set is eight foreground colors instead of 16 for the two fonts, since only the RGB bits of the attribute (and not the I bit) are used for foreground intensity. Using the palette registers, you can map these into anything you want.

Another alternative to restoring the high intensity-foreground is to invert all the bits of the two fonts and use another BIOS call (AX = 1003H and BL = 0) to enable background intensity instead of blinking. Now, since your characters are really background, you have all 16 colors available for the two fonts. Your background is now limited to eight colors (which is normal) and you can't use hardware blinking.

The underline on the monochrome display presents another problem. If you decide to remap palette registers to give you low and high intensity for each font, you'll only be able to use an underline in low or high intensity, but not both.

The Poor Person's Font Editor

Now that you've seen how you can load fonts into the EGA, you may want to create your own fonts. There are two ways to do it. You could start off with a piece of graph paper, draw each character by coloring in the appropriate blocks, translate each row of dots into a two-digit hexadecimal number, and then type these numbers into a file. This is the long way.

It's easier to use an onscreen "font editor" program. You can then begin with an existing font and make modifications to it. Of course, font editors can be complex, but it's possible to take an inexpensive approach by turning your own text editor into a font editor. You'll be editing an assembly language file that contains a series of assembler "DB" statements. You can then convert this file back into bytes with the IBM or Microsoft Macro Assembler.

The FONT2DB.COM program below retrieves an existing EGA font and translates it into these DB statements:

```
N FONT2DB.COM
A 100
MOV  BH,02                    ; 03 for 8x8 Font!
MOV  AX,1130
INT  10                       ; ES:BP points to font
MOV  CX,0100                  ; Number of characters
MOV  BH,0E                    ; 08 for 8x8 Font!
ES:
MOV  DH,[BP+00]               ; Get Byte
INC  BP                       ; Point to next
MOV  BL,08                    ; 8 bits
MOV  DI,013C                  ; Destination
MOV  BYTE PTR [DI],00         ; Zero it out
RCL  DH,1                     ; Get the bit
ADC  BYTE PTR [DI],30         ; Put in 0 or 1
INC  DI                       ; Next bit
DEC  BL                       ; Bit counter
JNZ  0116                     ; Loop around
MOV  DX,0139                  ; Point to output
MOV  AH,09                    ; And print it
INT  21
DEC  BH                       ; Bytes per character
JNZ  010C                     ; Loop around
MOV  DX,0145                  ; Print out return
MOV  AH,09
INT  21
LOOP 010A                     ; Get next character
INT  20
DB "DB 01234567b,"0D,0A,"$"
RCX
48
W
Q
```

The file that FONT2DB.COM creates is quite long: there are 256 characters and 14 bytes per character (for the 8 x 14 font), and each byte uses one line. The bytes are shown in binary format as 0s and 1s so you get a visual representation of the font on your screen. Although FONT2DB is set up to list the 8 x 14 font, the comments in the FONT2DB.SCR listing shown which values to change to use it for the 8 x 8 font.

If you simply execute:

```
FONT2DB
```

you'll get a listing of the font on your screen. If you use redirection of standard output:

```
FONT2DB > MYFONT
```

the font will be saved in a file called MYFONT. Now you can load MYFONT into your text editor, turn off Insert mode, and make changes to the font by replacing 0s with 1s where you want a dot, and 1s with 0s where you don't want a dot.

To make the font a different height, simply delete or add additional lines. You can use between one and 32 lines per character. Make sure each character has the same number of bytes, however, or your font will look quite strange.

After you've created your own font, the next step requires the IBM or Microsoft Macro Assembler. A shell program called FONTLOAD.ASM will make the process easier:

```
; FONTLOAD.ASM — Loads a customized font
CSEG        Segment
    Assume  CS:CSEG, DS:CSEG, ES:CSEG
    Org     0100H
Entry:      Mov     AX, 1100H        ; Load font
            Mov     BH, 0EH          ; Bytes/Char
            Mov     BL, 00H          ; Block
            Mov     CX, 0100H        ; Number Chars
            Mov     DX, 0000H        ; Start Char
            Mov     BP, Offset Font  ; Address
            Int     10H
            Int     20H


Font                Label    Byte


Include             MYFONT              ; Your font file name goes here
CSEG                Ends
            End     Entry
```

The INCLUDE statement includes your edited font in the assembly. For more versatility, you may want to assemble your fonts independently and rewrite the loader program to load them from disk files.

EGA Underlines

One of the minor annoyances of using a program like *WordPerfect* with an EGA is that underlined characters are displayed on the screen in a color of your choice rather than as characters with a line under them. This forces you to remember which colors are installed as underline, boldface, and underlined-boldface, and turns many popular programs into somewhat less than "What-You-See-Is-What-You-Get."

Using several of Charles Petzold's techniques, Peter N. Howells developed the program UNDERLN.COM, created by the UNDERLN.SCR DEBUG script below, for systems with an IBM (or compatible) EGA:

```
N UNDERLN.COM
A 100
CLD
PUSH   DS
PUSH   ES
MOV    AL,[005D]              ; get first character of parameter
CMP    AL,4F                  ; is it 'O'?
JZ     0118                   ; yes, jmp 2ndChar
CMP    AL,6F                  ; is it 'o'?
JZ     0118                   ; yes, jmp 2ndChar
MOV    DX,0194                ; BADPARM
MOV    AX,0900                ; print message
INT    21
INT    20                     ; exit
MOV    AL,[005E]              ; 2ndChar
CMP    AL,4E                  ; is it 'N'?
JZ     013A                   ; yes, jmp TURNON
CMP    AL,6E                  ; is it 'n'?
JZ     013A                   ; yes, jmp TURNON
CMP    AL,46                  ; is it 'F'?
JZ     012D                   ; yes, jmp 3rdChar
CMP    AL,66                  ; is it 'f'?
JZ     012D                   ; yes, jmp 3rdChar
JMP    010E                   ; no, jmp BADPARAM
MOV    AL,[005F]              ; 3rdChar
CMP    AL,46                  ; is it 'F'?
JZ     013D                   ; yes, jmp TURNOFF
CMP    AL,66                  ; is it 'f'?
JZ     013D                   ; yes, jmp TURNOFF
JMP    010E                   ; no, jmp BADPARAM
STC                           ; TURNON — set carry flag
JMP    013E                   ; jmp FontPointer
CLC                           ; TURNOFF
MOV    BH,02                  ; FontPointer — get 8x14 font
```

```
MOV    AX,1130
INT    10                    ; returns ES:BP
PUSH   ES
POP    DS
MOV    SI,BP                 ; DS:SI points to font
PUSH   CS
POP    ES
MOV    DI,0194               ; ES:DI = destination
MOV    CX,00E0               ; 32 control chars @ 7 word/char = 224 words
LODSW                        ; NEXTWORD1 — get 2 bytes
STOSW                        ; store them, unmodified (not underlined)
LOOP   0151                  ; loop NEXTWORD1
MOV    CX,0060               ; 96 "printable" characters
PUSH   CX                    ; NEXTCHAR — save character counter
MOV    CX,0006               ; get and store 1st 12 bytes of character
LODSW                        ; NEXTWORD2 — get 2 bytes
STOSW                        ; store them
LOOP   015C                  ; loop NEXTWORD2
LODSW                        ; get last 2 bytes
JNB    0165                  ; underlining on? no, jmp STORELASTWORD
MOV    AH,FF                 ; yes, underline the character
STOSW                        ; STORELASTWORD — store last 2 bytes
POP    CX                    ; restore character counter
LOOP   0158                  ; loop NEXTCHAR
MOV    CX,0380               ; 128 "foreign" chars = 896 words
LODSW                        ; NEXTWORD3 — get 2 bytes
STOSW                        ; store them
LOOP   016C                  ; loop NEXTWORD3
MOV    BP,0194               ; point to new font
MOV    CX,0100               ; character count
XOR    DX,DX                 ; starting character
MOV    BX,0E01               ; BH = bytes/char — BL = block to load
MOV    AX,1100               ; load font
INT    10
MOV    BX,0001               ; MOV BX,0004: HIGH INTENSITY UNDERLINE
MOV    AX,1103               ; set block spec
INT    10
MOV    BX,0712               ; enable only low planes
MOV    AX,1000               ; enable planes
INT    10
POP    ES
POP    DS
INT    20
DB 0A 0D 'Type: UNDERLN ON to load the underline font'
DB 0A 0D '      UNDERLN OFF to unload the underline font'
```

```
DB 0A 0D '$'

RCX
F4
W
Q
```

Type this UNDERLN.SCR file in using a pure-ASCII word processor, then create the UNDERLN.COM program by making sure DEBUG.COM is handy and typing:

```
DEBUG < UNDERLN.SCR
```

UNDERLN will generate an underlined character font from the EGA BIOS resident 8 x 14 font and load it as the EGA low-intensity characters. Only the "printable" characters with ASCII values from 32 through 127 will be underlined.

Typing UNDERLN ON from the DOS prompt (or in a batch file) causes any low-intensity characters on the screen to be underlined and any high-intensity characters will not be underlined. Or, if you prefer, changing the line near the bottom of the script from:

```
INT 10                      INT 10
MOV BX,0001      to         MOV BX,0004
MOV AX,1103                 MOV AX,1103
```

will underline the high-intensity characters and use the normal EGA 8 x 14 font with the low-intensity characters.

Typing UNDERLN OFF restores the normal font. Resetting the display mode will also eliminate the underlined characters. The command line parameters, ON and OFF, are not case sensitive. Since *WordPerfect* does not reset the video display mode upon entry into the program, the following batch file will turn on underlining while running *WordPerfect* and turn it off upon exiting.

```
CD\WP
UNDERLN ON
WP
UNDERLN OFF
```

Once in *WordPerfect*, you may define the screen colors using the Ctrl-F3, 4 key. Pick foreground and bold colors from the high- intensity colors, I (dark grey) to P (white); and underline and bold underline colors from the low-intensity colors, A (black) to H (grey). Background A (black), foreground L (bright cyan), underline D (cyan), bold M (bright red), bold underline F (magenta) is a pleasing color scheme.

This patch makes *WordPerfect* magical on EGAs; no one likes to look at one color for bold; another for underlining, and so on. But you can adapt the program to underline the output of any other application that doesn't completely take over the hardware and that lets you give underlined text its own attribute.

A more modest EGA underline program was submitted by reader Brian O'Neill, of Boston, Massachusetts, whose UNDERLN2.COM utility, created by the UNDERLN2.SCR script below, will underline any text with a blue-on-black attribute:

```
N UNDERLN2.COM
A 100
MOV AL,[005D]            ; 1st char of argument, if any
XOR BX,BX
MOV DS,BX
MOV AH,[0485]           ; AH = bytes/char
CMP AL,4E               ; 'N'
JZ 0111                 ; don't underline
DEC AH                  ; underline at last scanline
MOV DX,[0463]           ; DX = port address, video ctrlr
MOV AL,14               ; AL = Underline Loc data register
OUT DX,AX
INT 20

RCX
1A
W
Q
```

You can create this program by redirecting the script into DEBUG:

```
DEBUG < UNDERLN2.SCR
```

Typing UNDERLN2 N or UNDERLN2 n will turn underlining off; typing just UNDERLN2 will toggle it on.

The EGA can display fonts with more or less than 25 lines onscreen, so the number of scan lines per character is not fixed at 14. The scan line that displays the underline depends upon how many "bytes per character" are in the currently displayed font. UNDERLN2.COM fetches this information from 0040:0085H of the BIOS data area.

The program also looks up the port address of the video controller; this address will vary, depending upon whether the EGA card is being used with a color or a monochrome monitor. UNDERLN2.COM will work in either case.

The only attributes that UNDERLN2 will underline are 1 and 9 (blue on black, both normal and high intensity). However, EGACOLOR.COM can be used to change colors 0, 1, and 9 to whatever colors you want. You can see the program in action by using the EGAUNDER.SCR script to create the sample EGAUNDER.COM program:

```
N EGAUNDER.COM
A
MOV AX,0600              ; scroll window up
MOV BH,02               ; green-on-black
MOV CX,0000             ; upper lefthand corner
MOV DX,1950             ; 25 x 80 screen
INT 10                  ; do it
MOV AH,02               ; set cursor
MOV BH,00               ; page 0
MOV DX,0000             ; upper lefthand corner
INT 10                  ; do it
MOV AX,0950             ; write character 'P'
MOV BX,0001             ; page 0; blue on black
MOV CX,0028             ; 40 of them
INT 10                  ; do it
MOV AH,02               ; set cursor
MOV DX,0028             ; after 40th 'P'
INT 10                  ; do it
MOV AX,0943             ; write character 'C'
MOV BL,02               ; green on black
INT 10                  ; do it
INT 20                  ; back to DOS

RCX
31
W
Q
```

Type this using the same pure-ASCII word processor, then enter:

```
DEBUG < EGAUNDER.SCR
```

EGAUNDER.COM will display a string of 40 Ps in blue and 40 Cs in green. Then use UNDERLN2 and UNDERLN2 N to toggle the blue text underlining on and off.

An Introduction to EGA Graphics

All of the examples and techniques we've presented deal exclusively with the EGA's text modes. The EGA is capable of producing some very impressive graphics. But, as Charles Petzold points out, programming your own graphics on the EGA is no picnic.

If you are interested in creating graphics applications for the EGA, you should seriously consider using a *virtual device interface*, such as that found in Microsoft *Windows* or IBM's Graphics Development Toolkit. The Graphics Development Toolkit, for instance, contains routines that can be accessed from IBM Pascal, IBM FORTRAN, the IBM BASIC Compiler, or Lattice C (but not the BASIC interpreter). So far, the BASICA interpreter included with DOS does not support EGA graphics.

If you have lots of time to waste while waiting for your screen to be painted, you could also use the BIOS for graphics. The EGA BIOS supports the same read dot and write dot function calls used by the system board BIOS for CGA graphics. The only difference is that register BH must contain the video page. The BIOS Write Dot call is extremely slow, about 0.5 milliseconds per dot on a normal 4.77 MHz PC or XT, so it takes a little under two minutes to refresh an entire 640 x 350 screen in the simplest case. You can run the WRITEDOT.COM program below to see for yourself how incredibly pokey BIOS is:

```
N WRITEDOT.COM
A 100
MOV  AX,0010          ; Set video mode
INT  10               ; to 16
SUB  BH,BH            ; Page 0
SUB  DX,DX            ; Row 0
SUB  CX,CX            ; Column 0
MOV  AL,01            ; Blue
MOV  AH,0C            ; Write Dot
INT  10
INC  CX               ; Next Column
CMP  CX,0280          ; See if 640
JB   010B             ; If below, loop
INC  DX               ; Next Row
CMP  DX,015E          ; See if 350
JB   0109             ; If below, loop
MOV  AX,0003          ; Set video mode
INT  10               ; to 3
INT  20               ; Terminate
RCX
26
W
Q
```

If none of these methods is good enough and you want to program your own graphics, you'll have to write directly to the video memory and program the EGA registers. There is no better way to learn EGA graphics than to stick your head in the *EGA Technical Reference* and sweat it out. But it's not too difficult to get started once you know a few basics.

You'll get the fastest graphics routines by programming in assembly language. You can also program EGA graphics routines directly in any high-level language that supports BIOS calls, register output commands, and direct access of memory in a far segment.

When you program graphics on the EGA, you write directly to the screen memory. This memory is organized differently from the memory in CGA graphics modes.

In the CGA compatible graphics modes (4 through 6) the display memory occupies 16K of RAM, beginning at segment address B800H. In medium resolution modes (4 and 5), the 320 dots of each scan line require 80 bytes. Each byte represents four pixels, with two bits each for the four colors. In high resolution black-and-white mode 6, where the 640 horizontal dots also require 80 bytes, each byte represents eight pixels. In either case, 200 scan lines require 16,000 bytes of memory. The only complication is that all the even scan lines are at the top of this memory, and are followed by all the odd scan lines.

The display memory in EGA graphics modes 13 through 16 occupies the 64K segment beginning at segment address A000H. In graphics mode 16 (350 scan lines with 640 dots each and 16 colors), one screen's worth of data requires 80 bytes per scan line times 350 scan lines times 4 (for the 16 colors), or 112,000 bytes. Two video pages are available, bringing total memory to 224,000, just below the maximum 256K on the EGA.

IBM wedged this 256K of display memory into a 64K memory space by organizing it into four 64K color planes. The four color planes represent the blue, red, green, and intensity bits that define the 16 colors. Each of the four color planes is addressed the same way: You specify which color plane you want to write to or read from by using the EGA registers accessible through output ports.

The byte at address A000:0000 is the leftmost eight bits in the first scan line of the display. The byte at address A000:0001 is the next eight bits in the top scan line. For graphics modes 14 through 16 the byte at address A000:0050 is the first eight bits in the second scan line. For graphics mode 13, the second scan line begins at address A000:0028. The most significant bit always represents the leftmost dot.

Although the division of EGA graphics memory into identically addressed color planes initially appears clumsy, it has some distinct advantages. Since you can write to all four color planes simultaneously, you can actually write up to 32 bits of data (eight bits of four colors) by writing one byte to the display memory. Partially for this reason, the wrong way to program EGA graphics is to start off with a simple "Write Dot" routine and base all other graphics routines on this one function. You'll speed thing up dramatically if you try to take advantage of the EGA's memory organization rather than work against it.

Video Wrinkles

The EGA BIOS has a bug in it that prevents the interrupt 10H cursor mode function from working reliably. This problem becomes acute in modes that display more than 25 lines onscreen. EGA users who take advantage of the special 35-line and 43-line modes provided by the adapter know all too well that the cursor often vanishes when a TSR window is popped up and back down.

When an EGA is connected to an ECD and 25 lines of text are displayed, each character cell has 14 scan lines. The same EGA running in 43-line mode has eight scan lines per cell. A standard CGA does the same in any text mode. A monochrome adapter gives you 14 lines per character.

However, an EGA supporting 350 scan lines in text mode (14 per line) doesn't default its cursor to scan lines 13 and 14. The characters themselves use lines 1 through 11, so a cursor at the extreme bottom of the block would leave an almost unnoticeable gap of one line between itself and the character above it. Instead, the EGA cursor uses lines 12 and 13, which makes it look pretty much identical to its CGA cousin.

Cursor Registers

Both the CGA and the monochrome display adaptor are designed around Motorola's 6845 CRT controller. This smart chip provides a set of 18 internal registers supporting a wide variety of video modes and video support functions. All 18 registers are accessed through only two ports in PC address space. The first port, located at 3D4H if a CGA is installed (or 3B4H for monochrome), is the address register. The second, found at 3D5H for color (or 3B5H for monochrome), is the data register. Values are written by first OUTing the internal register number (0 through 17) to the address register, then sending the data to be written to the data register.

The BIOS defines cursors by their starting and ending scan lines. (If the starting scan line is greater than the ending one the cursor "wraps around" the character cell and splits into two halves.) The 6845 sets aside an internal register for each of these parameters; the starting scan line is held in register 10 and the ending scan line in register 11. When the BIOS sets a cursor shape by executing interrupt 10H with AH equal to 1 and the cursor definition in CX, it simply transfers the values in CH and CL to the CRT controller's cursor registers.

This was a straightforward process until the EGA was introduced. Both the EGA and the VGA implement a custom CRT controller similar to the 6845. To retain some degree of compatibility with older adapters, the EGA designers arranged the array of CRT controller registers in a manner almost identical to the 6845. The cursor registers are located again at 10 and 11, and are accessed through the same manipulations of the address register and data register that were required with the CGA and MDA. As a result, programmers can deal directly with the hardware cursor registers without having to identify the adapter first.

A problem arises, however, because of the EGA's different interpretation of the ending scan line. With a CGA, MDA, or VGA (which handles the cursor very much like its predecessors), setting the cursor to scan lines 6 and 7 meant writing values of 6 and 7 to the cursor registers. This positioned the cursor on the seventh and eighth scan lines, since the first scan line is numbered zero.

On an EGA, however, you must write the value of the ending scan line plus 1. So if there are eight scan lines per character, the cursor registers are set to 6 and 0 to obtain the standard two-line underline cursor.

You can create a block cursor on a CGA by specifying starting and ending values of 0 and 7 (or 0 and 13 on an MDA). It follows that an EGA would require a value of 0 and 0. Not so. Like the other video adapters, the EGA leaves you with a single scan line cursor if the starting line and ending line are the same. To produce a block cursor when using the EGA, you give the ending line an "out-of-range" value of 1EH.

The VGA behaves much like a CGA, even though its design isn't based on the 6845 chip. Starting and ending scan lines are interpreted the same way, and the cursor registers are located at the same addresses. Setting the starting scan line greater than the ending scan line, however, destroys the cursor. The VGA alone among the video adapters prohibits a wrap-around cursor.

Bug in the BIOS

The built-in BIOS functions have traditionally been a wellspring of help and important information when things start getting overly complex. Video BIOS provides a convenient function for setting the cursor shape that worked very well with the first generation of adapters. Unfortunately, because of good intentions rendered useless by poor execution, this source of ready assistance has proved unreliable with the EGA.

Before the days of the EGA, applications commonly defined their own cursor shape by checking to see whether they were running on a CGA or an MDA, setting values for the starting and ending scan lines accordingly, and either calling interrupt 10H or writing to the 6845 to initialize a cursor. So that existing programs would not have to be rewritten for the EGA, the EGA BIOS authors included cursor emulation logic in their code. These cursor emulation routines checked the values of CH and CL when the cursor mode function was called and made adjustments as necessary to fit the cursor to a 14 scan line block. An application designed to create an underline cursor on the CGA with scan lines of 6 and 7 works quite well on an EGA because the values are transparently remapped to 11 and 12 before being sent on to the CRT controller.

The EGA BIOS makes a valiant if somewhat misguided attempt to maintain software compatibility across the CGA-EGA line. If emulation mode is toggled on (determined by the state of the emulation bit, bit 0 of the EGA information byte at absolute address 0000:0487H), then cursors designed to fit in the eight-line CGA character box are scaled to conform to the EGA's normal 14-line box.

However, there are two flaws in the emulation logic. The first and more serious is that the new BIOS assumed that an EGA connected to an ECD would always have 14 scan lines per character box. Yet the EGA supports programmable modes, including the popular 43-line mode that uses only eight scan lines per character. So a call to set the cursor to scan lines 6 and 7 in 43-line mode destroys the cursor because the BIOS routines blindly intercept it and erroneously increase the values beyond the bounds of the true number of scan lines. This is one reason why *SideKick* often leaves users without a cursor when it pops down in 43-line mode.

The second flaw in the emulation is that the record of the current cursor mode kept in the BIOS data area reflects the values sent by the calling routine, not those that the BIOS actually sets for the cursor. If there are 14 scan lines per character and the BIOS correctly translates a call for a 6-7 cursor into an 11-12 cursor, it stores away the bytes 6 and 7. Since the cursor registers are write-only, an application that comes along at a later time has no way of determining how the cursor really appears.

Making that determination is critical to a TSR as well as to some transient applications. Even programs that aren't memory resident are forced to reset the cursor to an underline because they can't be certain where the cursor's starting and ending scan lines are when they take control. Nor can they assume that the cursor emulation state (which can be enabled and disabled by toggling bit 0 of the byte at absolute address 0040:0087H) is the same as it was the last time the cursor was set.

Going hand-in-hand with the EGA's cursor emulation function is the emulation bit stored in the BIOS data area. The EGA provides its own facility for enabling and disabling cursor fixups by clearing or setting the emulation bit, respectively. Note that setting this bit to 0 turns emulation on. In a reversal of traditional on/off roles, a value of 1 disables the emulation. To maintain compatibility with the EGA BIOS, programs should follow the lead of the emulation bit and refrain from manipulating cursor calls when the bit is toggled on.

If you use an EGA or VGA, cursor emulation is active by default when your machine is powered on (the emulation bit is zeroed). The emulation bit is rarely changed, but a few applications do set it in order to perform cursor shaping without the risk of BIOS interference.

So, while reading the cursor mode from the BIOS data area and following it with a BIOS call to set the same configuration was once a safe and reasonable task, with the advent of the EGA it has become something of a crapshoot. (The VGA BIOS also uses emulation logic, but the details are sketchy.) Because of this BIOS mess, programmers have little choice except to bypass it and go directly to the cursor registers.

An intelligent cursor setter will query the BIOS for the number of scan lines per character (called *points* in BIOS parlance) before scaling the cursor shape. It first examines the specified ending scan line to determine whether or not the call was intended for a CGA. If the value is greater than 7 or is equal to 0 (an ending line of 0 defines a true underline cursor on the EGA), the program assumes that the definition was in fact intended for an EGA. If it doesn't satisfy this criteria and the emulation bit is 0, the program can begin its own scaling process.

First, interrupt 10H is generated with AH set to 11H and AL equal to 30h. The number of points is returned in CX. The difference in the number of scan lines actually allocated to each line and the scan lines indicated in the cursor call is used as an adjustment offset, and the original values of CH and CL passed to set the cursor shape are incremented by that offset. As a result, an underline cursor on the CGA (scan lines 6 and 7) is interpreted to mean lines 12 and 13 on an EGA showing 14 points. At the same time, if there are 43 lines displayed with eight scan lines per character box, the values aren't adjusted at all. Thus, popping a TSR up and down in 35- or 43-line mode will no longer destroy the cursor.

It's important to increment the ending scan line by 1 to satisfy EGA cursor register protocol. If this last operation produces a 0 in both CH and CL, CX is changed to 001EH, representing the EGA's version of a block cursor. And if the end result is a value in CX of 0C00H, the specifier for a true underline cursor in 25-line text modes, CH and CL are decremented to move the cursor up a single scan line (since the normal EGA underline cursor resides on scan lines 11 and 12 rather than 12 and 13).

Identifying Adapters

The new VGA adapter adds still another step to the process of identifying the video adapter installed and active in a system at any given moment.

The BIOS of the IBM Personal System/2 machines retains all of the interrupt 10H video functions of its predecessors and appends a few of its own. Function 1AH returns a display code that reveals, with certain limitations, what kind of video hardware is installed. If calling interrupt 10H with AH set to 1AH and AL set to 0 returns a 0 in AL, it means that the function is not supported and, by inference, that there's no VGA. If AL comes back as 1, BL contains the display code. A display code of 7 means that a VGA is installed, active, and connected to an analog monochrome display. A display code of 8 signals the calling routine that a VGA is linked to an analog color monitor. Like the EGA, a VGA can co-reside with other video adapters, and as a result can be present in the system but not active at the time of detection.

The EGA search method recommended in IBM's Personal System/2 and Personal Computer *BIOS Interface Technical Reference* is to first call the interrupt 10H with AH equal to 12H and BL set to 10H. If this function returns BL unchanged, then it is unsupported and an EGA cannot be present in the system (see the EGATEST.COM program below). If an EGA is detected, the EGA information byte at offset 87H in the BIOS data area (this is the the same byte that holds the cursor emulation status bit) must be consulted to determine whether the EGA is currently active or has yielded control to another adapter. If bit 3 is clear, the EGA is active; a 1 means it's not. You could look at the base address of the CRT controller at offset 63H (a word) to see whether the EGA is connected to a color or monochrome monitor. Or you could read bit 1 of the EGA information byte for the same information.

When both the VGA and the EGA tests fail, a program can assume it's dealing with either a CGA or an MDA. The CRT controller base address provides the answer, just as it reveals whether an EGA is running in monochrome or color. The 6845 address register is mapped into port address 3D4H for a CGA and into 3B4H for an MDA, a difference of one bit. You can examine the single bit with a TEST instruction and ferret out the information you need.

PC Magazine reader Terry P. Sanderson noted that one of the first major programs to take advantage of the EGA, Microsoft *Word* 2.0, used a method that was both awkward and unsupported by IBM to detect whether an EGA was attached. Embedded near the beginning of IBM's EGA ROM BIOS, at location C000:001E, are the letters "IBM." *Word* 2.0 tested for the presence of these letters in the copyright notice, and if it found them assumed an EGA was available.

It's curious that Microsoft chose this method, Sanderson points out, because IBM includes a warning in the *EGA Technical Reference* manual about a similar misuse of its BIOS. At location C000:0000, a two-byte signature appears (AA55H) that identifies a valid adapter ROM module to the POST routine. IBM explicitly states in the documentation that this signature is *not* to be used as an EGA presence test. However, if you were to disassemble the MODE command (which allows the user to, among other things, set the mode of the video adapter or change monitors in a two-monitor system), you would find the following code fragment.

```
MOV    AZ,0C000H              ; move segment address..
MOV    ES,AX                  ; into es register
CMP    WORD PTR ES:0,0AA55H   ; is it the signature ?
JNZ    ...                    ; jump if true
```

Here, IBM disobeyed its own warning and uses the BIOS signature to test for the presence of an EGA card.

As mentioned above, a far more conventional test for the presence of an EGA is to use the extended BIOS features available in the EGA's ROM. When an EGA is present, BIOS video interrupt 10H is vectored to the EGA's ROM, and interrupt 42H is used to revector the old planar ROM video interrupt. This means that the extra EGA features are available through interrupt 10H. One of these extended features is called Alternate Select. Its major function is to select the Alternate Print Screen routine, but another of its functions is to return EGA information. The following assembler code segment can be used to request EGA information.

```
MOV    AH,12H    ; function 12H
MOV    BL,10H    ; subfunction 10H
INT    10H       ; video interrupt
```

This function returns the following information:

Register	Description
BH	mode in effect (color or mono)
BL	memory on EGA (01H=64k, 02H=128k, etc.)
CH	feature bits
CL	EGA switch settings

Note that the BL register is used both on input and to return a value. The standard ROM BIOS interrupt 10H does not have a function 12H, so the BL register is returned intact if there is no EGA. Fortunately, if there is an EGA, the BL register will return a value of 0H, 1H, 2H, or 3H, depending on the memory size, but cannot return a value of 10H. If the BL register has changed, an EGA is present.

This procedure can be used to identify the presence of an EGA, but does not report whether the EGA is active. If the EGA is connected to a color or Enhanced Color Display, you can also have a monochrome adapter and monitor installed. Conversely, if the EGA is connected to a monochrome display, you can also install a CGA and color monitor. If you are going to write any hardware dependent routines, you must take into consideration the possibility of a two-monitor system.

IBM does not provide a video function that lets you determine which adapter is active if there is more than one installed. However, you can use the information in the ROM BIOS data area to determine if the EGA is the active adapter. At absolute location 487H, IBM defines a byte used to store EGA information. Bit 3 of this byte (using the notation that bit 0 is the low-order bit) lets you know if the EGA is the active adapter. If this bit is 0, the EGA has the active monitor; if it is 1, another adapter card is active.

After doing this, look again at the values returned by the previous video function call. Register BH returns a value of 0H if the EGA is connected to a color monitor, and a value of 1H if a monochrome monitor is attached. Combining this information, you can finally determine which adapter is active.

To create Sanderson's EGATEST.COM program that checks for the presence and activity of an EGA, type in the EGATEST.SCR script below:

```
A
PUSH CS               ; data segment = code segment
POP  DS
MOV  AH,12            ; function 12h (alternate select)
MOV  BL,10            ; sub-funct 10h (return ega info)
INT  10              ; video interrupt
CMP  BL,10            ; has bl changed?
JNZ  0113            ; yes, so we have an ega present
LEA  DX,[013E]       ; no, load no-ega message
JMP  0138
MOV  AX,0040         ; move the bios_data segment to ax.
MOV  DS,AX           ; ..and into the data segment
MOV  AH,[0087]       ; get info byte from rom data area
PUSH CS
POP  DS              ; return to data seg = code seg
AND  AH,08           ; isolate+0ga active bit
JNZ  012E            ; ega does not have active monitor
CMP  BH,00           ; is monochrome connected to ega?
JNZ  0134            ; yes, so display mono message
LEA  DX,[0198]       ; no, so display color message
JMP  0138
LEA  DX,[0152]       ; load not-active message
JMP  0138
LEA  DX,[0171]       ; load address of mono message
MOV  AH,09           ; function 9h (print)
INT  21              ; do it
INT  20              ; done
DB 0D,0A,'EGA not present',0D,0A,24
DB 0D,0A,'EGA present but not active',0D,0A,24
DB 0D,0A,'EGA active with monochrome monitor',0D,0A,24
DB 0D,0A,'EGA active with color monitor',0D,0A,24

RCX
BA
N EGATEST.COM
W
Q
```

Programmers can adapt this to put appropriate error codes into AL, terminate with function 4CH, and trigger an IF ERRORLEVEL test. Or they can incorporate this basic code into their own programs. Either way, it's a shame IBM or Microsoft didn't make the process a whole lot easier.

Chapter 14

Favorite Tips

Over the years readers have sent us basketfuls of their favorite tips, and *PC Magazine* editors such as Charles Petzold and Robert Hummel have answered hundreds of reader questions. These thoughtful answers actually receive their own fan mail. We've assembled (and enhanced) the most popular ones below. You'll find tips here on the DOS commands, filters, printers, security, communications, and more.

DOS Commands

RECOVER

Just about everyone knows that the FORMAT command can be dangerous if it's used indiscriminately or carelessly. However, few users know about another potentially destructive DOS command — RECOVER.COM.

The DOS manual says RECOVER.COM is supposed to "recover files." Novice users who have lost or corrupted files may try this command in desperation without fully understanding what it does, and accidentally type RECOVER C: at the DOS prompt. Even though DOS prints a warning message most users will probably type Y to proceed with the recovery.

RECOVER then does the following:

1. Removes the subdirectory structure from the disk.
2. Places all the files into the root directory.
3. Renames all files FILE0001.REC, FILE0002.REC, etc.

You're then forced to back up all of these similarly named REC files, reformat the disk, and then filter through the files to try and discover which file is which. It's nearly impossible to recover from RECOVER.

The description in the DOS manual is truly inadequate, and doesn't provide nearly enough warning about how potentially dangerous the command is is. It's another case of the moronic names in DOS. DEBUG really ought to be called something friendlier like PATCHER or TOOLBOX. The IF ERRORLEVEL command should be called something like TEST. It's no wonder that a panicky and inexperienced user might think a command named RECOVER will fix his disk right up.

RECOVER isn't so bad if you ask it to dig out the pieces of just one file that had a sector go south somewhere. And if you've somehow wiped out your whole directory, laboriously sorting out the puzzle pieces of your text files is better than losing everything. But it's far too easy to wipe out a whole disk with it. Back up often, plod through the manual before trying anything you're not familiar with, and take RECOVER.COM off your hard disk.

CHKDSK

When used with a /V parameter, CHKDSK churns out a long list of all the directories and files on the specified or default disk. This can come in very handy when you have to locate a file or group of files. To see every file with MAG in it, for instance, you could type:

```
CHKDSK /V | FIND "MAG"
```

However, if you start experimenting with this feature, you'll notice that the filenames are sometimes not listed under the directory where they are actually located.

The problem results from the confusing and downright deceptive manner in which CHKDSK lists directories and files. To illustrate this, start with a formatted blank disk in drive A: and run the following four commands:

```
COPY   CHKDSK.COM A:
MD     A:\SUBDIR
COPY   TREE.COM A:\SUBDIR
COPY   BACKUP.COM A:
```

Now execute a CHKDSK A:/V command. You'll probably see the listing shown below:

```
Directory A:\
      A:\CHKDSK.COM
Directory A:\SUBDIR
      A:\SUBDIR\TREE.COM
      A:\BACKUP.COM
```

It sure seems like BACKUP.COM is in the SUBDIR directory, doesn't it? But look closer. The files are listed with the full path name. So A:\BACKUP.COM means that BACKUP.COM is in the root directory, which is absolutely correct. CHKDSK lists the files and directories in the order that it finds them in the directory. Since SUBDIR is the second entry of the root directory, CHKDSK lists all files in the SUBDIR directory and then finishes listing the files of the root directory.

Whenever you do a DIR command and see files listed below directory entries, be aware that CHKDSK /V will list those files after it lists the files in the directory.

On a disk where a lot of deletion and creation of directories and files has taken place, the CHKDSK /F listing may be almost unreadable. Use the TREE /F command instead for seeing what files are in what directories.

CHKDSK can also let you know about potential disk problems. Almost nothing is as terrifying as seeing a list of unfamiliar messages from CHKDSK (except perhaps a zinger such as "General Failure Error Reading Drive C:"). Sometimes CHKDSK messages indicate very serious problems with the data on the disk. Sometimes they don't.

Among other things, CHKDSK checks for consistency between a disk's directory listing and its file allocation tables (FATs) — the critical maps that tell DOS how a disk's clusters are chained together. Files are stored in separate chunks, and the redundant FATs keep track of where these individual pieces are located on the disk.

When you get a message from CHKDSK indicating "lost clusters," it's usually not much to worry about. It simply means that an area on the disk had been allocated for a file, but the file was never properly closed. The lost clusters are "orphaned" — the FAT says they've been allocated, but they don't belong to any file. This sometimes happens if the program creating the file terminates abnormally, or runs out of disk space and doesn't clean up afterwards.

If you run CHKDSK with a /F parameter, it will convert the lost clusters to files with the extension CHK in the root directory. If your normal files are missing something, the data could be in one of the CHK files. You can take a look at the CHK files with the TYPE command, but unless they're in ASCII format and came out of a word processing document, you probably won't be able to do much with them.

If you're missing entire files from your directory, these CHK files may correspond to the missing files. This could result from a damaged directory. The FAT still allocates chained clusters as if they belonged to a file, but the directory doesn't indicate where the chains begin.

Messages from CHKDSK indicating "cross-linked files" are cause for concern. Cross-linking means that the FAT's cluster chain for two or more files intersects at some point, so that some clusters seem to belong to multiple files. In other words, your FAT or directory has probably been badly mangled. Although cross-linking is relatively rare, it could be caused by gremlins (i.e., a power surge or line drop during a disk write operation).

You can easily create a cross-linked FAT and a mangled directory yourself by replacing a diskette before typing an answer to an "Abort, Retry, Ignore" message.

For instance, if you're running a program and you try to save something to a diskette that has a write-protect tab, DOS will try to write to the disk and will end up displaying a "Write Protect Error" message followed by "Abort, Retry, Ignore." If instead of removing the write-protect tab from the disk you insert another disk in the drive and press R for Retry, you can kiss that data goodbye. This often happens when you realize you're trying to save a file on the wrong disk.

The problem is that DOS keeps FAT and directory information in memory, but doesn't check to make sure that it's writing data back to the original disk it thinks is still in the drive. If you switch disks without telling it, it will write the FAT and directory map (or part of it) from the first disk onto the second disk, and you'll end up with an unusable mess.

Sometimes you can salvage chunks of mangled files by using disk surgery programs like the *Norton Utilities* to piece them back together, but it's hard work and you need to know what you're looking for.

To prevent this, don't switch disks in the middle of a program unless you're very careful about it. And if you're about to write data to a floppy and you get an "Abort, Retry" message, choose abort, then make sure the disk you originally read from is in the drive you want to write to. If it's not, try to execute a DIR command to read the new directory information into memory.

COPY

COPY will usually detect when you are trying to copy a file to itself. For instance, if you have a file called MYFILE and you enter:

```
COPY MYFILE MYFILE
```

it will tell you it can't do it. But COPY can be fooled. If MYFILE is located in the root directory and you enter:

```
COPY MYFILE \MYFILE
```

COPY gets confused and doesn't realize you're referring to the same file two different ways. This can be a serious problem if the file is larger than 64K.

Here's what will happen in that second case: COPY will open the first file for reading. It will read 64K of the file into memory (or less if the full 64K is not available). It will then tell DOS to create the second file. If the second file already exists (as it does in this case), the file gets truncated to zero bytes and the space in the FAT is freed up. Then COPY writes the 64K buffer to the second file. Now COPY goes back to read the next chunk of the first file. DOS takes a look at the FAT for the first file and finds out all the clusters have been freed up. It says "Hey, what happened?" and generates an error message.

You can also run into trouble if you try a command like:

```
COPY FILE1 FILE2
```

If FILE2 already exists, but FILE1 is much larger than available disk space, DOS aborts the COPY with an "Insufficient disk space" message, but also deletes FILE2. It may seem like a "Shoot first, ask questions later" approach.

To determine whether enough disk space exists to copy FILE1 to FILE2, COMMAND.COM would have to check if the space available on the disk plus the size of FILE2 is less than or equal to the size of FILE1. Instead, the COPY command creates the destination file FILE2 (erasing the old one in the process) and then tries to copy the contents of FILE1 to it. If this fails, FILE2 is gone. Usually this won't create a serious problem, since you were intending to get rid of the existing FILE2 anyway.

But one other COPY problem can cause heartache. Let's say you're trying to copy all your programs to a subdirectory called SUBDIR, and you issue the two commands:

```
COPY A:*.COM SUBDIR
DEL A:*.COM
```

If you make a mistake and type something like SUBDIT (rather than SUBDIR), which is not an existing directory name, COPY will create a file called SUBDIT and copy all the COM files into it. Since this is an ASCII copy, because the syntax implies you're concatenating the files, it stops copying after the first ASCII end-of-file marker in each on the COM files. Result: garbage.

Here's another COPY quirk — you can display an ASCII file to the screen with:

```
COPY filename CON
```

because the output device CON is the display. This command does basically the same thing as:

```
TYPE filename
```

Likewise, you can copy a file to the printer with:

```
COPY filename PRN
```

The file goes to the printer and a "1 file(s) copied" message appears on the screen. Using redirection of standard output, you can also copy a file to the printer with the command:

```
TYPE filename >PRN
```

So far, so good. Based on this, you might think that the command:

```
COPY filename CON >PRN
```

would copy the file to the printer, because the COPY command is copying it to the screen, and the screen is redirected to the printer. But it doesn't. Instead, it just copies the file to the screen and puts the "file(s) copied" message on the printer.

While the results look a little peculiar, DOS is actually working consistently. To see why, you have to understand the distinction between devices (CON and PRN) and the handles that programs use to refer to these files and devices.

Beginning with version 2.0, DOS adopted a *handle* approach to working with files and devices. When a program such as COMMAND.COM opens a file or device for the COPY or TYPE commands, it tells DOS the filename and DOS returns a handle (which is simply a number) that refers to the file.

DOS maintains two tables that correlate the handles and the files or devices they refer to. The first table is located in the program's Program Segment Prefix starting at offset 18H. The number at address [18H + handle] refers to a second table internal to DOS that contains the file or device name and other information that DOS needs to read from or write to the file. (This is not documented, by the way.)

The restriction of 20 file handles per program derives from the length of this table in the Program Segment Prefix. The maximum number of open files that DOS can maintain depends upon the space allocated for the internal DOS tables and is governed by the FILES statement in a CONFIG.SYS file.

When a program begins execution, five file handles are already defined. Normally, handle 1 (which is defined as standard output) is mapped to the output device CON, which is the display.

The internal workings of the TYPE command are simple. It reads a file and writes it with function call 40H using a handle of 1, so output normally goes to the CON device. However, when you specify on the command line that standard output should be redirected to PRN with the command:

```
TYPE filename >PRN
```

COMMAND.COM opens the PRN device to get a handle for it, and then uses the FORCDUP function call (46H) to make handle 1 refer to the PRN device. So, TYPE is still writing the file using handle 1, but the handle refers to a device other than CON.

When you specify CON or PRN as the destination in a COPY command, COMMAND.COM opens that device through DOS, gets back a handle for it (which will *not* be one of the predefined handles), and uses that handle for writing the file. So, the two commands:

```
COPY filename PRN
```

and:

```
TYPE filename > PRN
```

are not really the same thing. In the first case, the COPY command uses a handle that refers to the device PRN. In the second case, the TYPE command uses handle 1, but this handle has been redirected to the device PRN. Because of this, when COMMAND.COM executes the command:

```
COPY filename CON >PRN
```

it first redirects handle 1 to the PRN device. But then COPY opens the device called CON for the destination and DOS returns a new handle that refers to this device. The file appears on the screen because the COPY command is writing it using this new handle. It then writes the "file(s) copied" message to standard output (the handle 1), but this message goes out to the printer because the handle has been redirected.

Copying files to devices can come in handy when you want to scan through several files one after the other, or peek inside executable files.

If you use the TYPE command on a binary, nontext file like COMMAND.COM, DOS will stop when it reaches the first ASCII character 26, since it will erroneously think this is an end-of-file marker and grind to a halt.

But you can see the whole COMMAND.COM file by typing:

```
COPY /B COMMAND.COM CON
```

The /B (for "Binary" file) tells DOS to look up the length of the file in the disk directory and copy that number of bytes. Using CON as a destination tells DOS to copy these bytes to the console (screen) rather than a file.

Get to know the /B switch. It can prevent lots of COPY problems. For instance, you can use the COPY command to update (or backdate) the time and date in the directory listing of any file. But be extremely careful when using this update feature. If you have a short text file on your disk called OLDFILE that you created a long time ago, you can make the date and time in its directory listing current by typing:

```
COPY OLDFILE +,,
```

However, DOS thinks all files it copies this way are ASCII files unless you tell it otherwise, and will stop copying the contents if it sees an ASCII character 26, which it interprets as an end-of-file marker. If you're not careful, you can end up with a copy of just the beginning of a non-ASCII file.

Most text files don't contain any ASCII 26 characters (except at the very end), but just about every COM or EXE file contains several. You can tell DOS to bypass this problem by making copies based on the file's true length, as reported by the directory listing.

While adding a /B after the word COPY tells DOS to make copies based on file length rather than the detection of an ASCII 26, adding a /A (for "ASCII" file) does the reverse. When you tack on a /B or /A switch, DOS will handle all files listed after the switch in that particular COPY command with these rules in mind.

You can mix-and-match /A and /B switches, file by file, if you are concatenating several smaller ASCII and binary files into one big one. When you don't specify any switches, DOS assumes all concatenations are for ASCII files, while all non concatenating (normal) copies are for binary files.

The "+" sign in the "COPY filename +,," updating command makes DOS treat the process like a concatenation, even though it is really dealing with only one file at a time. Because of this, it is important to add a /B switch to the command.

So the final command to update the directory listing for both ASCII and binary files is:

```
COPY /B filename +,,
```

You can create a one-line batch file called UPDATE.BAT that uses a replaceable parameter:

```
COPY /B %1 +,,
```

Then, you can make the date of any file current by typing:

```
UPDATE filename
```

You can also use this technique to change the date backwards or forwards. Before you run UPDATE.BAT, just reset the DATE (and TIME, if you want) commands.

You can't update all your files using wildcards. The command:

```
COPY /B *.* +,,
```

won't work. But you can bring all your files up to date using FOR...IN...DO. To enter the command directly in DOS, type:

```
FOR %F IN (*.*) DO COPY /B %F +,,
```

To put this into a batch file called REDATE.BAT, substitute a %%F for each %F, and redirect the output to NUL to suppress the one-by-one executions and "1 File(s) copied" messages produced by the FOR...IN...DO command. The contents of REDATE.BAT would be:

```
FOR %%F IN (*.*) DO COPY /B %%F +,, > NUL
```

An even better way is to use the TOUCH.COM program on the accompanying disk.

If you're nervous about making copies, and you want to verify that the backup is indeed valid, don't bother with the /V COPY option. All this does is make sure that DOS can read the copied file; it doesn't check the copy against the original to make sure that every byte is the same. And it slows the whole process down.

A better way is to use the COMP command immediately after you make any copies. Since the actual commands COPY and COMP are the same length and use the same syntax, once you've copied the files you can check the accuracy of the copies by pressing F1 or the right cursor arrow key twice, typing "MP" to replace the "PY" in the word COPY, and then pressing F3 to finish repeating the command. So:

```
COPY *.* B:
```

with just a few keystrokes becomes:

```
COMP *.* B:
```

If you're using XCOPY, just insert an extra space at the beginning, so the process would look like:

```
C>XCOPY *.* B:
C> COMP *.* B:
```

DOS will ignore the space directly after the prompt.

If you want to look at lots of files — such as a collection of your small batch files — in succession, you can adapt this technique with:

```
COPY *.BAT CON
```

Another good way to do this is to create two short batch files called SCANBATS.BAT and READ.BAT. First, SCANBATS.BAT cycles through all the BAT files on your disk:

```
ECHO OFF
FOR %%F IN (*.BAT) DO COMMAND /C READ %%F
```

Then, READ.BAT, which is called by SCANBATS.BAT, does the actual displaying:

```
ECHO OFF
CLS
ECHO %1
MORE < %1
PAUSE
```

If you create these files using EDLIN or the DOS COPY CON command, you may want to add a line before the final PAUSE in READ.BAT that says:

```
ECHO <F7>
```

But instead of actually typing <F7>, press the F7 key. If you're in DOS, this will generate an ASCII 0 null character (unless you've redefined the F7 key). Following ECHO with a null will put a blank line onscreen. You may need this if the files you're trying to display don't end with carriage returns. If they don't, the "Strike a key when ready . . . " message generated by the PAUSE command will appear at the end of the last line of the batch file rather than on a line by itself.

To try SCANBATS and READ, create both batch files, then enter:

```
SCANBATS
```

If you're using a 3.3 or later version of DOS you can make the process slightly more efficient by changing the second line of SCANBATS.BAT to:

```
FOR %%F IN (*.BAT) DO CALL READ %%F
```

If you are using a more recent DOS version, you can also omit the ECHO OFF at the top of READ.BAT. And you'll find that using CALL instead of COMMAND /C makes it easier to break out of the process prematurely if you want.

Users often ask about turning their computers into typewriters. It's hard to have each letter appear on your printer as you type it, but you can harness the COPY command and end up with something halfway close. At the DOS prompt, try typing:

```
COPY CON PRN
```

CON refers to both the keyboard and screen, although here DOS will use the keyboard half of the device. PRN refers to your printer. After you enter this command, start typing. Press the Enter key at the end of each line. If you make a mistake on a screen line, you can use the backspace or left arrow key to correct it, but after you've pressed Enter, or wrapped down to the next screen line, you're stuck with it (which is why it's better to use a word processor or EDLIN). And don't try any lines longer than 127 characters.

The text won't appear on the printer until you're done. To finish, press the F6 key (or Ctrl-Z) and then press Enter one final time. The text will then be printed.

You may have to add a Ctrl-L before the Ctrl-Z to issue a form feed after the text is printed.

One final note — be careful about the order of filenames or devices when making copies. Users of non-DOS systems may be accustomed to listing these in reverse order. If you wanted to send a small file's output to your printer, and typed:

```
COPY LPT1 filename
```

instead of the correct:

```
COPY filename LPT1
```

you'll end up with a "0 file(s) copied" message and a deleted file.

VERIFY

The DOS VERIFY option often confuses users, who wonder whether running their systems with VERIFY on actually does anything. They also want to know if their word processor, data base, and spreadsheet programs take advantage of whatever protection VERIFY provides.

The good news is that because most applications do their file handling by calling DOS functions, the VERIFY option is invoked whenever data is written to the disk. The bad news is that turning the VERIFY option on in DOS actually does little more than slow down your disk operations.

The syntax of the VERIFY switch is easy to understand. You turn it on with the command VERIFY ON, and off with VERIFY OFF. Entering VERIFY with no argument displays the current status. But while the syntax is fairly obvious, the effect of the command isn't.

Common sense would lead you to expect that VERIFY makes sure the correct data had been written to the disk. A logical procedure for the operation might be: write the data to the disk, read it back from the disk, and compare the returned data to the original. If it isn't the same, retry the operation a specified number of times. If the process continues to be unsuccessful, signal an error. Logical as this may seem, in reality, it doesn't happen that way.

One of the reasons for creating DOS was to free applications from the burden of having to include code for handling disk I/O directly. Consequently, most programs interact with the disk by going through DOS. DOS, in turn, accesses the disk hardware through your system's hardware-specific BIOS routines.

Consider what happens when you save a file from inside an application program. The program first calls DOS with the request to save the file. DOS must then move the data, which is stored in a buffer in memory, to the disk. This is accomplished by providing the correct parameters to the BIOS disk write routine. BIOS, in turn, then sends the correct commands to the disk controller. Before the data is written onto the disk, however, some additional information is appended. This extra information is used to detect errors, and it is written to the disk at the same time as the data. The most common addition is called a Cyclical Redundancy Check (CRC), which is a halfway sophisticated type of checksum. The same data will always generate the same CRC value. So, by calculating the CRC and writing it to the disk along with the data, two independent representations of the same data are recorded.

The read function is simply the reverse of the write function. It causes data to be transferred from the disk to a memory buffer. Each time the data is read, however, the CRC is again calculated and compared with the CRC that was recorded when the data was originally written. If the two CRCs match exactly, the data is assumed to be correct, and is copied to the buffer. If not, the operation may be retried several times, but if the old CRC and the new CRC still don't match, the BIOS reports an error and does not return the data. (This discussion uses a little legerdemain by lumping BIOS and the disk controller together. In fact, the disk controller itself can actually detect and correct certain errors, which provides one more level of defense.)

The verify function operates nearly identically to the disk read operation, except that no data is moved to a buffer, even if the read is successful. VERIFY causes the data to be read from the disk and the CRC to be recalculated. The new CRC is compared to the old CRC to ensure that they match. Again, typically, if they don't match, the operation is retried a specified number of times, and then an error is returned. The important thing to note is that at no time is the data itself on the disk compared to anything. Thus, the verify function serves simply to check the continued readability and integrity of the disk, not of the data.

When you turn on the DOS VERIFY switch, a flag is set inside DOS. From then on, each disk write operation that DOS is requested to perform is immediately followed by a similar call to the verify operation. In other words, DOS simply checks to see that the area of the disk it just wrote your data to is readable — not that it wrote the correct data! Excluding bad sections, each normal area of a disk always has a valid CRC. If the data your program tried to write was somehow sidetracked into the Twilight Zone, and never made it to the disk, the verify call would still return a good value, and DOS would never know.

VERIFY has one other effect. The disk drive hardware must always wait for the correct area of the disk to rotate under the head, read the data, and calculate the CRC. The new CRC must then be compared to the recorded CRC. All this takes a certain amount of time. In the case of disk access, an operation that might normally have been accomplished in a single rotation might take three or more to complete. So, VERIFY's most obvious effect is to slow down disk I/O.

DISKCOPY

Many new users make backups of their files by using the DISKCOPY command. This isn't smart. The only times you should use DISKCOPY are when you want to back up a commercial software disk or when you have a data-integrity problem with a diskette. Ironically, what could have caused the problem is DISKCOPY itself.

New users like DISKCOPY because it's faster than COPY *.* and because it formats on the fly. Experienced users know that COPY *.* and the even better XCOPY handle two problems better — fragmentation and bad tracks.

The more you use a disk the more fragmented the files on it become. Ideally your files should be contiguous. Having pieces of your files scattered over the disk results in time-consuming head "churning," or "thrashing" as your system retrieves all the far-flung chunks of each file. This also causes unnecessary wear and tear on the disk and the drive heads and motor.

You should periodically back up any disk you've used for a while onto a freshly formatted one using the COPY *.* or XCOPY *.* commands.

The second, and more troublesome, reason not to use DISKCOPY is that it puts a mirror image of the original disk's contents onto the new one. If the blank disk has internal defects such as bad sectors, especially bad sectors that have bitten the dust after the FORMAT command originally roped off defective areas, DISKCOPY can write a copy of the original disk's data onto these bad areas, rendering such information unusable on the copy.

You should use DISKCOPY when you discover that you're having a data-integrity problem with a floppy, or when you accidentally erase a file on a disk and realize you're going to have to perform surgery with something like the *Norton Utilities* to recover the data. If this happens, you can use DISKCOPY to make a perfect copy of the affected disk, and first try the surgery on the copy. If you make a mistake in the recovery process and end up ruining it, you can make another DISKCOPY of the original and try again.

When you open a fresh package of floppy disks, format them all, without the system files (you can always add these later with SYS). It's always a good idea to have a box of blank formatted disks around, since you somtimes need one when you're in the middle of a program and can't quit to format one then or you'd lose data.

Then use XCOPY (or COPY if you're using an older version of DOS) to make backups onto these blank, formatted disks.

ASSIGN

Sometimes users expect DOS to be a whole lot smarter than it actually is, especially when they try to outfox it. So beware of dangerous collisions when using "alias" commands such as ASSIGN that trick DOS into treating one drive as another.

The ASSIGN program included with PC-DOS is potentially bad news. ASSIGN is a remain-resident program that intercepts most DOS file calls and simply swaps disk drive letters. It was included with DOS 2.0 and later to deal with pre-XT programs that assumed every PC had only drives A: and B: and nothing more. All of the PC-DOS manuals include warnings about using ASSIGN.

If you must use ASSIGN with certain programs, don't issue the ASSIGN commands manually. Put them in a batch file like this:

```
ASSIGN A=C B=C
```

[then execute the program that can't use drive C:]

```
ASSIGN
```

The second ASSIGN undoes all the ASSIGNments so you don't accidently do something dangerous with a command such as COPY. For instance, if you had typed:

```
ASSIGN A=C
```

and then later had tried to copy a hard disk file to a floppy disk with the command:

```
COPY C:filename A:
```

DOS would have attempted to copy the file on top of itself. If the file was larger than 64K you could end up with a "File Allocation Table Error" and a truncated version of the original.

APPEND

Since version 2.0, you've been able to tell the DOS PATH command which subdirectories to check for executable files (ending in COM, EXE, or BAT). But nonexecutable files remained immune to even the most comprehensive search.

DOS executes internal commands such as DIR, VER, or TYPE directly, since the instructions for these are imbedded inside COMMAND.COM. If DOS doesn't recognize the command you typed, it first checks the current directory (if you entered something like CHKDSK), or any directory you may have specified (if you typed something like D:\BIN\CHKDSK). It then looks in each of the subdirectories that you included in your path. So if you added a line to your AUTOEXEC.BAT file that read:

```
PATH C:\;C:\DOS;D:\
```

if DOS didn't immediately find the file you specified it would hunt for one by that name with a COM, EXE, or BAT extension in the root and \DOS subdirectories on drive C:, and on the root directory of drive D:.

However, if you or your program needed to find a file that had an extension other than COM, EXE, or BAT, you had to purchase a path extender program. Or, if you were working with DOS 3.1 or 3.2, you could use the SUBST command to trick DOS into thinking a subdirectory was actually a logical drive with its own drive letter.

For example, the main classic *WordStar* 3.3 WS.COM file always needed to know where you'd stored its two .OVR overlay files. If these files were kept in C:\PROGS you could use DEBUG to patch WS.COM so that it looked on drive E:

```
DEBUG WS.COM
E 2DC 5
W
Q
```

and then tell DOS about it with the command:

```
SUBST E: C:\PROGS
```

(For anything higher than drive E: you also had to add a LASTDRIVE command to your CONFIG.SYS.) If your MEMO file was stored in C:\STAR\WORK and you had used SUBST to turn that subdirectory into F: you could then type WS F:MEMO.

APPEND makes the process relatively easy — and a lot cleaner. Just follow the PATH command in your AUTOEXEC.BAT file with an APPEND command using similar syntax and telling DOS where your important nonexecutable files are located. If you keep overlays in the subdirectory mentioned above, and correspondence with royalty in \KING\LTRS, your APPEND command could be:

```
APPEND C:\PROGS;C:\KING\LTRS
```

DOS gives you two ways to keep tabs on your APPEND list. You can start off with an extra APPEND /E command, which loads APPEND strings into your environment and lets you change them with the SET command, just as with PATH. But, if you or your programs switch command processors (by exiting the one you're currently using) such strings become inaccessible. With long PATH and APPEND strings, you may have to expand your environment size by using the SHELL command. In fact, these days the default 160 byte environment is straining at the seams.

You can also add an additional APPEND /X command to spiff up the way DOS looks for files. Or you can add both /E and /X, but you then have to run APPEND twice — first with any switches, and then with the actual list of subdirectories DOS will search.

The DOS manual contains all sorts of dire warnings on using APPEND with BACK-UP and RESTORE, running it with ASSIGN, or having it anywhere near IBM LAN commands of the same name (hard to believe IBM didn't change the name, but true). And as with any path extender, you have to be careful that you're not accidentally pulling in a long-forgotten file from a distant subdirectory that APPEND knows about but that you don't.

EXE2BIN

When IBM first delivered DOS 2.0 it included some very valuable programs and documentation. But it gradually did away with some key tools. First, it removed all mention of ANSI.SYS from the DOS manual. Then in version 3.3 it got rid of the manual section on DEBUG and replaced it with some turgid prose about using foreign character sets.

And, for some incomprehensible reason, IBM removed the EXE2BIN.EXE program from the DOS program diskettes; to obtain a copy of this program, you have to buy the DOS 3.3 *Technical Reference* manual. If you try using the old 3.2 version under 3.3, you'll just get an "Incorrect DOS Version" message.

EXE2BIN version 3.2 checks the DOS version number right after it's loaded, and exits if it finds itself running under any version of DOS greater than 3.2. Changing the byte at offset 30D converts a JZ instruction to a JMP, causing the program to jump to the right place regardless of what the version test found.

To patch the 3.2 version of EXE2BIN.EXE so it runs under DOS 3.3, copy and rename your 3.2 version of EXE2BIN.EXE to EXE2BIN.XXX. Then patch the byte at address 30D from 71 to EB. Finally, rename the EXE2BIN.XXX file EXE2BIN.EXE. The whole process looks like:

```
COPY EXE2BIN.EXE EXE2BIN.XXX

DEBUG EXE2BIN.XXX
E 30D EB
W
Q
REN EXE2BIN.XXX EXE2BIN.EXE
```

KEYBxx

DOS 3.0 to 3.2 came in five international flavors. By executing the appropriate KEYBxx command you could tweak the keyboard into British, German, French, Italian, or Spanish modes. Actually, since you could toggle back and forth between the standard keyboard and the foreign variants, you could adapt the KEYBxx command to print just about anything onscreen.

For instance, you could patch KEYBUK.COM (the smallest of the five KEYBxx files) so that the:

```
QWE
ASD
ZXC
```

block of keys would produce either a single line box (with lowercase letters) or a double-line box (with capital letters). To try this (with DOS 3.2 on an old AT keyboard), type in the following SCRIPT.KBD file:

```
N KEYBUK.COM
L
E 9AB DA C2 BF
E 9B9 C3 C5 B4
E 9C7 C0 C1 D9
E 9E5 C9 CB BB
E 9F3 CC CE B9
E A01 C8 CA BC
N KEYBOX.COM
W
Q
```

For other 3.x versions of DOS, replace the address column directly after the initial Es as follows:

DOS Version		
3.0	*3.1*	*3.2*
592	662	9AB
5A0	670	9B9
5AE	67E	9C7
5CC	69C	9E5
5DA	6AA	9F3
5E8	6B8	A01

Once you've created the appropriate KEYBOX.COM file, run it. You can toggle back and forth between the normal keyboard and the new one by hitting Ctrl-Alt-F1 and Ctrl-Alt-F2.

With version 3.3, IBM totally revamped the way DOS handles foreign alphabets. But it did so in the most confusing way possible. First, instead of calling the process something clear and simple like "font loading," IBM referred to it as "code page switching." Then, it forced the user to digest three different and seemingly contradictory chunks of the manual — a whole chapter relegated to the rear between Error Messages and EDLIN, an abstruse few pages under "DEVICE" in the CONFIG.SYS section, and several other dense dollops under MODE, NLSFUNC, and CHCP. Manual writers everywhere should be forced to plod their way through these sections to see the ultimate example of how not to explain things. *PC Magazine*'s resident DOS expert Charles Petzold took one long look, shook his head, and said "Thank God we're Americans."

Code page switching will show new fonts only with DOS 3.3 or later and only on EGA/ECD monitors, PS/2 displays, and IBM Convertible LCD screens. (You can print the new character fonts only on IBM Model 4201 Proprinters and Model 5202 Quietwriter IIIs.) If you want to see all the new characters, assuming both that the 3.3 or later DISPLAY.SYS file is in your C:\DOS subdirectory and that you're using an EGA, first include a line in your CONFIG.SYS file:

```
DEVICE=C:\DOS\DISPLAY.SYS CON=(EGA,437,5)
```

Then create a small SHOWFONT.COM file that will display the high-bit ASCII characters DOS tinkers with, by loading DEBUG.COM and typing in:

```
E100 B4 0E B0 84 CD 10 FE
E107 C0 3C FC 75 F8 B0 0D
E10E CD 10 B0 0A CD 10 C3
N SHOWFONT.COM
RCX
15
W
Q
```

Finally, type in the following CODEPAGE.BAT batch file (assuming COUNTRY.SYS is in your C:\DOS subdirectory and that MODE, NLSFUNC, and the SHOWFONT.COM file you just created are in a directory you've included in your path):

```
C:\DOS\COUNTRY.SYS
MODE CON CP PREP=((850,860,863,865) EGA.CPI)
ECHO Hit any key 4 times
MODE CON CP SEL=865 >NUL
SHOWFONT
PAUSE>NUL
MODE CON SP SEL=850 >NUL
PAUSE>NUL
MODE CON SP SEL=860 >NUL
PAUSE>NUL
MODE CON SP SEL=863 >NUL
PAUSE>NUL
MODE CON SP SEL=437 >NUL
```

While code pages 865, 863, and 860 will be interesting only to residents of Norway, French-speaking Canada, and Portugal, Multilingual CP 850 can display some long needed characters, such as ®, ©, ¶, ×, ¢, 3/4, and [1] and [3].

COMP

IBM's COMP.COM DOS utility can use a lot of help. If you try to compare files of different sizes, COMP just shuts down and gives up. And even if you compare files the same exact size, COMP will beep at you and stop in its tracks if it uncovers more than ten mismatches. The generic MS-DOS FC utility is far better than the one provided by IBM.

If you have two identical files with just a handful of words different in each, COMP will give up trying to sort out the differences after just the second or third unidentical word. For all practical purposes, this means that COMP is useless unless the differences in your files are tiny.

But you can use DEBUG to fix COMP so it works far better.

COMP keeps track internally of the number of mismatches it finds, and checks them against a preset limit of ten. You can use DEBUG to change the preset limit from 1 to 255. Or you can do away with the limit entirely.

The assembler instruction for checking the limit looks like:

```
CMP BYTE PTR [0779],0A
```

although the number inside the brackets (here it's 0779) will vary depending on what version of DOS you're using; all examples here apply to version 3.3.

This instruction tells the program to compare the accumulated number of mismatches that COMP.COM stores at offset 779 with the preset limit of hex 0A, or decimal 10. You can have DEBUG search through COMP.COM's code for this instruction.

The actual machine-language code for it is 80 3E 79 07 0A:

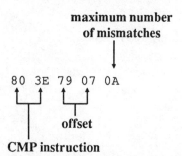

The 0A at the end is the maximum number of mismatches COMP.COM will ordinarily allow before stopping. The 79 07 right before it is the hex offset address 0779 in reverse format. The 80 3E at the beginning represents the actual CMP "opcode" that does the comparison.

To find all occurrences of this opcode, first find out how long the COMP.COM file is. But first make a copy of the COMP.COM file called ZOMP.COM. Then, at the DOS prompt, type:

```
DEBUG ZOMP.COM
```

and when you see the DEBUG hyphen prompt, type:

```
RCX
```

and then press the Enter key twice. Then type Q to quit and press the Enter key again. You should see something like:

```
C>DEBUG ZOMP.COM
-RCX
CX 1076
:
-Q
C>
```

The hex number after the CX is the program's length. Once you know this, you can create a script that will do the actual detective work. Make sure you're using a pure-ASCII word processor, EDLIN, or the DOS COPY CON command, and create a file called ZOMP.SCR that contains the three lines:

```
S 100 L 1076 80 3E
U 100 L 1076
Q
```

(Replace the 1076 in the top two lines with the actual hex number following the CX if the number you uncovered in your version is different.)

Note: Be sure to press the Enter key at the end of each line, especially the last one with the Q, or you'll freeze your system later when you try to use this.

Then make sure you have about 150K of vacant disk space, and that DEBUG.COM, ZOMP.COM, and the ZOMP.SCR you just created are all in the same directory, and type:

```
DEBUG ZOMP.COM < ZOMP.SCR > ZOMP.LST
```

After the disk stops spinning, you'll have a new, long file on your disk called ZOMP.LST. Use a word processor with a search function to examine it. At the top of the ZOMP.LST file you'll see something like:

```
-S 100 L 1076 80 3E
30F9:0235
30F9:0250
```

```
30F9:0269
30F9:02A0
30F9:02EA
30F9:02FB
30F9:07A9
30F9:07C0
30F9:07D8
30F9:07E2
30F9:086A
30F9:0AEF
30F9:0B06
30F9:0C0F
30F9:0DB9
-U 100 L 1076
```

In this example, ignore the four hex numbers to the left of the colon (here they're 30F9). These will differ from system to system and don't matter here.

Use your word processor's search command to search for the rightmost four hex numbers at the top of the list, which in this case are 0235. Your word processor will scan through the ZOMP.LST file and stop when it gets to something like:

```
30F9:0235 803E090100 CMP BYTE PTR [0109],00
```

This isn't the instruction you want, since the final two digits here are 00 and you're looking for 0A. So continue searching down the list. The next address is 0250, and your word processor's search command will find:

```
30F9:0250 803E050100 CMP BYTE PTR [0105],00
```

Wrong again. But after you've worked your way down to the bottom, you'll eventually reach the one you want:

```
30F9:0AEF 803E79070A CMP BYTE PTR [0779],0A
```

(Since this is near the bottom, it's actually smarter and faster to use your word processor to start searching from the bottom of the list and work your way up to the top.) This tells you that the assembly language instruction that prevents COMP.COM from going past ten mismatches is located at the hex offset address 0AEF.

To patch ZOMP.COM so it doesn't care how many mismatches it finds, get rid of this instruction. At the DOS prompt type:

```
DEBUG ZOMP.COM
```

and then when you see the DEBUG hyphen prompt, type:

```
F 0AEF L5 90
```

and press the Enter key. Type W and press the Enter key to write the changed file to disk, and then Q and Enter to quit.

Replace the 0AEF in this example with the address that you found when you used your word processor to search, if the address is different.

To see if this patch worked, create two test files called FORWARD and BACKWARD. FORWARD looks like:

```
ABCDEFGHIJKLMNOPQRSTUVWXYZ
```

and BACKWARD looks like:

```
ZYXWVUTSRQPONMLKJIHGFEDCBA
```

Each file is 26 bytes long. Compare them with COMP.COM and the process will stop at ten mismatches. Then try it with ZOMP.COM and it should find all 26 differences. If you're uncovering lots of differences with ZOMP.COM, it's best to redirect the results into a file, with something like:

```
ZOMP FORWARD BACKWARD > COMPFILE
```

Then examine the COMPFILE file at your leisure. If you want to get rid of all the extra spaces that DOS throws in, try:

```
ZOMP FORWARD BACKWARD | FIND "e" > COMPFILE
```

GRAPHICS and GRAFTABL

If you're working with text and you want a permanent copy of what's on the screen, you can just turn your printer on and press Shift-PrtSc.

But if you're working with a language like BASIC or Pascal and you have a fancy graphics image on your screen and want to send a copy of this image to your printer, you can't just use the Shift-PrtSc technique unless you first run the DOS GRAPHICS utility.

The print screen routine coded in ROM BIOS works only with characters. If the display is in a graphics mode, the routine will print only the ASCII characters that it can recognize, but won't translate the graphics. This is a reasonable restriction, since graphics protocols for printers vary a great deal and the ROM BIOS can't support them all.

The GRAPHICS.COM program (or GRAPHICS.EXE in some versions) supplements the ROM BIOS print screen routines. It remains resident in memory, so you need load it only once during your PC session. Once it's loaded, your system can print 320 x 200 four-color graphics (video modes 4 and 5), and 640 x 200 black and white graphics (video mode 6) on an IBM Graphics Printer or compatible.

GRAPHICS uses different dot densities for the four colors of the 320 x 200 mode to simulate color. More recent DOS versions of GRAPHICS also support various IBM printers that can actually reproduce the colors.

GRAPHICS.COM doesn't support the additional video modes of the IBM Enhanced Graphics Adapter (EGA). Fortunately, Charles Petzold's EGAGRAF.COM program on the accompanying disk provides new screen-dump routine for EGA 640 x 350 graphics displays on an IBM Graphics Printer or compatible.

Petzold's EGAPRTSC.COM program replaces the normal BIOS print screen routine to let you make text screen dumps of EGA displays that use more than 25 lines. EGA and later video adapter ROMs can look in the BIOS data area (at address 0040:0084) to see how large the screen is and how many lines of text to send to the printer.

If you're using a graphics screen on a CGA system and you try to generate ASCII characters with values above 127, you'll end up with a mess unless you first load the DOS GRAFTABL utility.

The PC ROM stores the bit patterns for ASCII characters with values from 0 through 127 starting at address F000:FA6E. Each character is represented by eight successive bytes. Interrupt 1F at the very bottom of memory (address 0000:007C) stores the address of an optional table of bit patterns for the high-bit ASCII characters with values from 128 to 255. GRAFTABL loads such a table into RAM and adjusts the address at 0000:007C to point to this table.

If GRAFTABL isn't loaded, the address at 0000:007C will be 0. If you then try to print an ASCII value over 127 in graphics mode, your system will assume the table of high-bit character patterns is stored at address 0, or 0000:0000. This happens to be where your system stores interrupt vectors, not character patterns, so your system will end up trying to make characters out of vector addresses. The result is junk.

Each new hardware release changes the rules. EGA and later video adapter BIOS provide bit patterns for all 255 characters. In the most recent version of DOS, GRAF-TABL can also load the hodgepodge of foreign language code page data into memory.

Starting with the EGA, IBM made it easy to use alternate character sets. The CGA and monochrome adapter ROMs contained character dot patterns that only the adapter could use. But the EGA and all subsequent adapters put copies of the dot patterns into the normal megabyte of the PC's address space, where they're fairly easy to reach.

(Actually, the CGA contains two sets of dot patterns. The normal one draws characters out of lines that are two pixels wide. If you yank out your CGA adapter, find jumper P3, and connect the jumper's two pins, you can see the alternate single-pixel character set. It's not worth the trouble.)

Chapter 13 on the EGA explains how to load and activate an alternate character set through software control. Two simple programs (again written by Charles Petzold) can switch you back and forth between a pair of different 256-character fonts with ease.

STACKS

If you're stuck using DOS version 3.2, watch out for a nasty but easily correctible bug — an "Internal Stack Error" message. Simply pressing the Pause key on the new IBM keyboard rapidly ten times will produce this message and lock your system, forcing a power-down restart.

The DOS manual states that this error is caused by a "rapid succession of recursive hardware interrupts," and suggests adding the command "STACKS=N,S" to your CONFIG.SYS file. N represents the number of stack frames, where the default is 9 and the range is 8 to 64. S is the size in bytes of each frame, where the default size of each stack frame is 128 bytes and the range is 32 to 512. Using this STACKS statement reduces available memory.

While most users don't pound on the Pause key, a fast typist entering data into a Lotus *1-2-3* spreadsheet can easily trigger the error, halting your system and resulting in lost data, time, and effort.

You can eliminate the problem by adding a line like:

```
STACKS=32,256
```

to your CONFIG.SYS file, which lets you pound on the Pause key about 25 times before causing an error.

XCOPY

Sometimes a new DOS version isn't much of an improvement over the previous one. At other times, however, the new DOS version contains a real gem. One of the most dazzling is the XCOPY command introduced with version DOS 3.2. It's an extended COPY command that includes some of the features of BACKUP, as well.

XCOPY is fast. It reads as many files as will fit into memory from the source disk, then writes the files to the destination disk in one speedy gulp. COPY, on the other hand, reads and writes each file individually, continually switching back and forth between the drives.

When used with its optional /S switch, XCOPY will also copy files from nested subdirectories, creating new subdirectories on the target disk as needed. While subdirectories are more common on hard disks than diskettes, some floppies contain subdirectories to organize the data on them better or to store more than the maximum 112 or 224 files that a diskette root directory can hold. To copy such a diskette type:

```
XCOPY A:*.* B: /S
```

To copy all the diskette files to a subdirectory of your hard disk while maintaining the same directory structure, try:

```
XCOPY A:*.* C:\SUBDIR /S
```

where SUBDIR is a subdirectory of your hard disk.

Similarly, if you need to copy a directory of your hard disk (including subdirectories within just that directory) to a diskette, XCOPY also comes to the rescue:

```
XCOPY C:\SUBDIR\*.* A: /S
```

Sometimes you may want to copy selected files from one disk to another. You could COPY each of these files individually, or you could use the /P (prompt) switch with XCOPY:

```
XCOPY C:\SUBDIR\*.* A: /P
```

In this case, XCOPY will ask file by file whether you want to copy each. You simply type Y or N. And, you can use the /S and /P switches together.

XCOPY is extremely useful for making backups. The /D switch followed by a date copies just those files created or changed on that date or later. So:

```
XCOPY C:\SUBDIR\*.* A: /D:04-15-88
```

copies to A: only those files created or changed on or after April 15, 1988.

Another aid in backing up files is the file archive bit, which is set to 1 when the file is first created and every subsequent time you change it. When you tack on a /M parameter, XCOPY will copy only those files whose archives bit are set to 1. After it copies each file, XCOPY resets the archive bit to 0. The next time you use XCOPY with a /M parameter, XCOPY will skip over any file with an archive bit value of 0, which avoids cluttering up your backup disks with duplicate copies of files that you haven't changed.

You can use XCOPY to back up your C: hard disk with the command:

```
XCOPY C:\*.* A: /S /M
```

When drive A: runs out of space, simply put in a new diskette and rerun the command. Those files already copied will not be recopied to the next diskette.

The advantage of using XCOPY instead of BACKUP for this chore is that the copies on the diskette remain normal useable files. While BACKUP can also copy files selectively, you have to use the RESTORE command on copies made with BACKUP before you can use them. The one advantage of BACKUP is that it can split huge files over several floppy disks. But until version 3.3, BACKUP and RESTORE could create havoc on your hard disk by copying older versions of your DOS system files over newer versions.

COMMAND

If you're like most users, you know that COMMAND.COM is a part of DOS needed to operate your system properly. Erase it from your root directory and you won't be able to boot your system. You may also know that one of COMMAND.COM's roles is to process the commands you type, like DIR, CHKDSK, or 123. But you may not know that COMMAND.COM itself is also a useful command.

To understand how this works, you have to know what the various parts of DOS do. When you make a disk bootable (by formatting it with a /S parameter, or later using SYS and COPY COMMAND.COM), you're adding three files to it:

- IBMBIO.COM
- IBMDOS.COM
- COMMAND.COM

The first two files (which may be called IO.SYS and MSDOS.SYS on non-IBM systems) are "hidden" since they won't show up in normal directory searches, although you can see them by typing CHKDSK /V or running a program on the accompanying disk like DR.COM.

In DOS 2.0 and above, IBMBIO is essentially a series of device drivers that let DOS communicate with the hardware of the PC, including the display, the keyboard, the disk drives, and the printer. In many cases, these IBMBIO.COM device drivers use the ROM BIOS interrupts.

IBMDOS.COM contains the code needed to execute the DOS function calls that actually do the behind-the-scenes file, disk, and basic system work. If a particular function call needs to use a hardware device, it calls a device driver routine in IBMBIO.COM. This is why Chapter 12 on screens deals almost exclusively with BIOS calls rather than DOS calls, since video is hardware-based.

In most cases, programs issue DOS calls to IBMDOS.COM, then IBMDOS.COM issues device driver calls to IBMBIO.COM, then the device drivers issue interrupts to the ROM BIOS, and the ROM BIOS talks to the hardware.

COMMAND.COM is the program that is running when no other program is running. It asks for the date and time when you boot up, displays the DOS prompt, reads in what you type at the DOS prompt, and searches to see if what you typed in is an internal command (DIR, COPY, ERASE, etc.). If so, it will execute that command, often using lots of interrupt 21H DOS function calls. If the command you typed is not an internal command, then COMMAND.COM will search the current directory for a COM, EXE, or BAT file of that name, and then use directory paths set by path to do further searches. COMMAND.COM then loads the program, and takes over when the program is done.

COMMAND.COM also executes batch file programs, including AUTOEXEC.BAT when DOS is first loaded. And it assumes control during critical hardware errors and issues the much-loved "Abort, Retry, Ignore?" message.

To further complicate matters, COMMAND.COM divides itself into two pieces when it is first loaded into memory. The "resident" part of COMMAND.COM, about 3K bytes, sits in the lower end of memory above the other two DOS files. The "transient" part of COMMAND.COM — the bulk of the program — resides up at the very top of user memory.

The transient part of COMMAND.COM interprets and executes the DOS internal commands and does batch file processing. These facilities are not needed when other programs are running. By sitting at the top of memory, the transient COMMAND.COM does not take up valuable memory space. It can be overwritten by other programs if they need the space.

When a program exits, it returns control to the resident part of COMMAND.COM, which performs a simple checksum calculation of the memory area normally occupied by the transient COMMAND.COM. This way it can tell whether the information loaded in that area of memory is indeed its own transient part or whether the transient part was overwritten. If it was overwritten, the resident part then reloads the transient part of COMMAND.COM back into memory.

That's why exiting from a large program can cause a disk access while COMMAND.COM is reloaded into memory. Some programs — like *1-2-3* and many compilers — always use that top area, so this may happen often.

You can execute any DOS internal command (or any COM, EXE, or BAT program for that matter) from within an assembly language program by loading a *secondary* copy of COMMAND.COM and passing to it a parameter containing the command or program name. COMMAND.COM will then handle all the complicated details and return control back to your program.

If you want, you can load a secondary version of COMMAND.COM directly from the DOS command level. First, figure out how much memory is available by typing:

```
CHKDSK
```

Then type:

```
COMMAND /C CHKDSK
```

and you'll see that a smaller amount of memory is available.

Under DOS 3.3 the memory-reporting part of the listing will look something like:

```
C>CHKDSK

    655360 bytes total memory
    471200 bytes free

C>COMMAND /C CHKDSK

    655360 bytes total memory
    467456 bytes free
```

The 3,744-byte difference is the amount of memory used by the second resident portion of COMMAND.COM. When you add a /C and the name of an executable file (such as CHKDSK), COMMAND.COM will execute the file and then terminate just like any other program by returning control to the previously executing program, which in this case is the primary copy of COMMAND.COM.

This can come in very handy with batch files. Normally if a line in one batch file executes a second batch file, control won't return to the first batch file. But if the first batch file contains a line like:

```
COMMAND /C BATFILE2
```

then the second BATFILE2.BAT batch file will be executed by the secondary command processor. When BATFILE2 finishes, DOS returns control to the original copy of COMMAND.COM, which continues processing the initial batch file at a point directly following the COMMAND /C BATFILE2 line.

(The CALL batch command, introduced with version 3.3, handles this task somewhat more efficiently.)

However, if BATFILE2 contains a PROMPT, PATH, or SET command, then this will affect the environment of the secondary COMMAND.COM which will be lost when BATFILE2 completes execution and control is returned to the primary COMMAND.COM.

If you load a secondary copy of COMMAND.COM without the /C you can see how this works, by having the two versions juggle different prompts. Try typing in these four commands, one after the other:

```
PROMPT [LEVEL1]
COMMAND
PROMPT [LEVEL2]
EXIT
```

The first command changes your normal prompt to [LEVEL1]. The second command loads a secondary version of COMMAND.COM. The third command changes the prompt to [LEVEL2]. This [LEVEL2] prompt is effective only for the second copy of COMMAND.COM. Typing EXIT at that point returns you to your original version of COMMAND.COM, so the prompt returns to [LEVEL 1].

Programs often load secondary versions of COMMAND.COM themselves. First, they make sure that enough memory is available for DOS to load another version of COMMAND.COM. When a program first begins executing, all available memory is allocated to it. So, some of this memory must be freed up. Before the memory is freed up, the stack pointer may have to be moved from the area of memory being freed, so the stack isn't destroyed in some way.

Then, the program has to figure out where you've stored COMMAND.COM on your disk. In DOS 2.0 and above, programs have access to your system's environment, which is designed to keep track of things like the current DOS prompt, any path you may have set with the PATH command, and the drive, directory, and filename of your current command processor.

You can see the current environment setting by typing SET. One of the lines displayed will begin with "COMSPEC=" and will show the drive, directory, and filename of the command processor COMMAND.COM. Any program can get at its environment by accessing the memory beginning at the segment address stored in offset 002CH of the Program Segment Prefix.

Once the program that needs to load COMMAND.COM figures out where it's stored, it can perform a PC-DOS EXEC function call 4BH of interrupt 21H, which loads any COM or EXE file, executes it, and then passes control back when finished.

COMMAND.COM can generate slightly confusing errors based on which parts of it are handy and which are not. If you run programs that use disks without DOS on them, you may see one of the following three messages on the screen:

```
Non-system disk or disk error.
Replace and strike any key when ready.
```

or

```
Insert disk with COMMAND.COM
and strike any key when ready.
```

or

```
Insert disk with batch file
and press any key when ready.
```

The first message occurs when the PC is booting and the disk in drive A: does not have a copy of all the required operating system files on it. If you get the first message after you run a program, it means the program is terminating by rebooting your system. That's not very polite, but some primitive programs do it that way.

The transient section of COMMAND.COM that includes all the internal commands is not needed while another program is running. But once a program terminates, your system does need this section, so the resident part of COMMAND.COM performs the checksum calculation mentioned above. If it can't find COMMAND.COM on the disk, it prints the message:

```
Insert disk with COMMAND.COM
and strike any key when ready.
```

Usually, the transient part of COMMAND.COM looks for COMMAND.COM on the disk it was originally loaded from. For a floppy system, this will be drive A:. You can change this, however, if it will later be more convenient to keep COMMAND.COM somewhere else. With DOS 3.x versions you can tell DOS to look for COMMAND.COM elsewhere by changing the COMSPEC variable in the environment string. If you're using a RAMdisk as drive C:, for instance, you can enter:

```
COPY COMMAND.COM C:
SET COMSPEC=C:\COMMAND.COM
```

Under DOS 2.x, this won't work. You have to load a secondary copy of COMMAND and specify the search path as a parameter:

```
COPY COMMAND.COM C:
COMMAND C:\COMMAND.COM
```

Copying COMMAND.COM onto a RAMdisk and then telling your system you've done so can speed up operation significantly after memory-hungry programs have finished.

The third error message from the above list:

```
Insert disk with batch file
and press any key when ready.
```

means that the program was invoked from a batch file and COMMAND.COM needs the rest of the batch file to continue. What's annoying is that you'll get the third message even if the batch file has just executed its last line. But this message is the easiest to get rid of. Just press Ctrl-Break. You'll be asked if you want to terminate the batch file. Answer with a Y.

If you have a batch file called SAMPLE.BAT and you want a permanent record of its execution, you can't get one by redirecting the output with a command like:

```
SAMPLE.BAT > LOGFILE
```

However, 2.x versions of DOS let you use COMMAND.COM to do it. First, add a final line to your batch file that says:

```
EXIT
```

Then type:

```
COMMAND > LOGFILE
```

This will load a second version of COMMAND.COM and redirect all activity into it. You won't be able to see anything on your screen at this point. Type in the name of your batch file very carefully. The batch file will run normally, then execute the EXIT command when it's done and return to the first version of COMMAND.COM. To see what went on, just inspect the LOGFILE file.

With later versions of DOS, you can try:

```
COMMAND /C SAMPLE.BAT > LOGFILE
```

(replacing SAMPLE.BAT with the actual name of the batch file you want to execute and any parameters you want to pass to it).

You can also record batch activity by typing Ctrl-PrtSc or Ctrl-P to toggle on your system's printer echo feature. Press Ctrl-PrtSc or Ctrl-P when you're done to turn this feature off. While it's on, everything that appears onscreen will also be sent to your printer (unless you're doing something tricky that your printer can't figure out).

SYS

These days there's no excuse for doing anything with floppy disks other than using them to back up your data or move information to another system.

However, some diehards still work on floppy-based systems, and some pesky copy-protected software still forces users to boot from floppies. Booting from a diskette means that the floppy has to have the three DOS system files on it. However, each new, improved version of DOS is even more bloated than the one before it. And sometimes there's almost no room left on your floppies for the fat new system files.

To upgrade the DOS version on a bootable disk, you'd normally use SYS to transfer the new IBMBIO.COM and IBMDOS.COM files (or their generic equivalents) to the old disk, then use COPY to install the new version of COMMAND.COM.

But this may not always be so easy.

Each disk contains a tiny single-sector 512-byte boot record that reads IBMBIO and IBMDOS from the disk and loads them into memory. It's handicapped greatly because IBMBIO and IBMDOS know all about using files and the disk, but the boot record can't use them because the files aren't in memory yet.

Because of this handicap, the boot record requires that IBMBIO.COM and IBMDOS.COM be the first two directory entries and that IBMBIO.COM be at the beginning of the disk data area in *contiguous sectors*. (The IBMDOS.COM can be anywhere on the disk.)

The problem is that DOS has grown so much that diskettes prepared for earlier DOS versions do not have enough room for the later IBMBIO files. A floppy containing a once-popular version of *1-2-3* (1A) allocated 1,920 bytes for IBMBIO.COM and 6,400 bytes for IBMDOS.COM. Under DOS version 3.1 IBMBIO.COM grew to 9,564 bytes. For PC-DOS 3.2, it ballooned to 16,368 bytes. The 3.3 version was a whopping 22,100.

To fix a situation like this, you have to get rid of the file temporarily that prevents IBMBIO.COM from being stored in contiguous sectors. In the case of the *1-2-3* (1A) system disk, this file is the first one you see when you do a DIR command, or run 123.EXE.

So you would first use the COPY command to transfer 123.EXE to another diskette. Next (assuming you have the DOS disk in the default drive A: and the *1-2-3* system disk in drive B:) you'd execute the following commands:

```
DEL B:123.EXE
SYS B:
COPY COMMAND.COM B:
```

Finally, you would copy the 123.EXE file back to its old floppy.

The copy protection used in *1-2-3* (1A) is innocuous so you can safely copy files to other diskettes and then copy them back. Other copy-protected software may require that all the files be in certain sectors, and the above technique won't work with those disks.

FDISK

Fooling around with your hard disk can be very dangerous. Don't even think of doing it if you're not totally backed up or if you're the least bit nervous about it. Charles Petzold is a true wizard on these topics, and the following advice of his can be trusted utterly. But because you may have a strange hardware configuration, a funny version of DOS, or some other bizarre and potentially troublesome system quirk, don't try these tricks unless you follow every instruction to the letter and take full responsibility for anything that happens.

When you first turn on your PC or reboot with Ctrl-Alt-Del, ROM BIOS first checks out and initializes your system. BIOS then attempts to load into memory the first sector of the first surface of the first track of the diskette in drive A. The first sector on a diskette contains a single-sector *bootstrap loader* program. If the diskette is bootable, the bootstrap loader loads the rest of the operating system into memory. The operating system is effectively pulling itself up by its own bootstraps, which is why a system reset is called a boot.

On a hard disk system, the BIOS will first attempt to boot from drive A:. If drive A: does not contain a diskette or the drive door is open, the BIOS then attempts to boot from the hard disk. Again, it reads into memory the first sector of the first surface of the first cylinder of the hard disk. If this sector contained a bootstrap loader like the one on a diskette, the hard disk could accommodate only one operating system.

Instead, the first sector on a hard disk contains another small *partition loader* program and some partition information. The format of this partition information is documented in IBM's *DOS Technical Reference* manual. Only 16 bytes are required for each partition. These 16 bytes contain a code to identify the operating system, the starting and ending sectors of each partition on the hard disk, and which partition is bootable.

The partition loader searches through the partition information to determine which partition is marked as bootable. Each partition contains its own bootstrap loader in the first sector of the partition. So, all the partition loader need do is load the bootstrap loader for the bootable partition and then let the bootstrap loader take over.

In summary, for a diskette, the BIOS loads the bootstrap loader and the bootstrap loader loads the operating system. For a hard disk, the BIOS loads the partition loader, the partition loader loads the bootstrap loader for the bootable partition, and the bootstrap loader loads the operating system.

The program that lets you juggle hard disk partitions is FDISK, which can divide a hard disk into one, two, three, or four separate partitions. Each of these partitions can accommodate a different operating system. Most people use the whole hard disk for DOS and thus have only one partition on the hard disk. When you first set up a system with a hard disk, you have to use FDISK to define a DOS partition even before you use FORMAT. (Often this is done by the computer store, so if you're using a hard disk and have never used FDISK, don't worry about it.)

If you use FDISK to define more than one partition on your hard disk, FDISK lets you mark one (and only one) of these partitions as "active," which means that it's bootable. If you boot from the hard disk, the operating system in that partition will be the one that comes up.

For a partitioned hard disk, you have several ways to choose one operating system over another when you boot up your machine:

Even if the DOS partition is not marked as bootable, you can still access the DOS partition if you boot DOS from a diskette. So, if you had two partitions on your hard disk — DOS and something else — you could use the DOS partition if you boot DOS from a diskette and the "something else" partition if you boot from the hard disk. The choice between the two partitions simply depends upon the drive A: door being open or not.

Or, you could boot up DOS from a diskette, use FDISK to change the partition, then reboot from hard disk. This is fairly fast and if you do it a lot, you may want to set up a special disk that calls FDISK from an AUTOEXEC.BAT file.

Be very careful — experimenting with hard disk partitions is best done with a clean hard disk or a hard disk with disposable data. Changing the size of the DOS partition with FDISK wipes out the DOS partition (or at least the FAT and directory information). FDISK will warn you about this. Heed the warning.

If you're using a hard disk that seems to devour more than its share of space, you might be able to make things more efficient by reducing the cluster size. Might. And again, you have to very careful about this.

The entire data area of a hard disk is divided into smaller areas called clusters. Files on a disk are always stored in one or more clusters. If the file does not fill up the last cluster it occupies, then the rest of the space in that cluster is lost. The number of bytes in each file reported by the DIR command is the size of the file when it was created or last modified. The amount of space that file actually requires on the disk is the size of the file rounded up to the next multiple of the cluster size.

On average, you would probably lose about half a cluster for each file on the disk. It might be more if you have a lot of small files less than half the cluster size.

You can easily determine the cluster size for a particular disk. First, do a DIR and note the "bytes free" value. Then create a very small file. The easiest method is with the command:

```
ECHO > SMALLFIL
```

Do another DIR and see how much space you've lost. That's your cluster size.

The cluster size is always a power of 2 and for most normal disks, a multiple of 512. Some RAMdisks may have cluster sizes of 128 or 256, but real disks have cluster sizes of 512, 1,024, 2,048, 4,096, and 8,192 bytes. For a single-sided floppy diskette, the cluster size is 512 bytes. For a double-sided diskette, it's 1,024 bytes. For a ten-megabyte hard disk, the cluster size is 4,096 bytes.

For hard disks larger than ten megabytes, the cluster size is dependent upon the DOS version used when originally configuring the disk using FDISK and FORMAT. A 20-megabyte hard disk originally configured under DOS 2.x has a cluster size of 8,192 bytes.

A cluster size of 8,192 bytes is absurdly large, and is the result of the method introduced way back in DOS 1.0 for storing files on a disk. This method limited the total number of clusters on a disk to 4,078 (4,096 minus a handful of cluster numbers used for special purposes).

With DOS 3.0, the total number of clusters possible on a hard disk was increased to 65,518, which let users make the cluster size on a hard disk smaller. A 20- or 30-megabyte hard disk that has been FDISKed and formatted under DOS 3.x has a cluster size of 2,048 bytes, because DOS 3.x allows cluster sizes on a hard disk to be represented by 16-bit values instead of 12-bit values. However, DOS 2.x can work only with the old 12-bit FAT.

It's a good thing that DOS 2.x doesn't even recognize the 20-megabyte hard disk formatted under DOS 3.x. If it assumed that the FAT contained 12-bit values, it could easily scramble up the FAT beyond recognition. Since the FAT is the most critical part of a disk, this would be a very serious problem.

How does DOS 2.x know enough to leave the disk alone? It's all in the partition table. A hard disk can be divided into one to four partitions, each of which may contain a different operating system. (Most XT and AT users allocate the entire hard disk for a single DOS partition.) A table with the partition information is stored on the first sector of the disk. Each partition has a *system indicator*, which is a one-byte value that denotes the operating system of the partition. DOS 2.x uses a 01 to indicate a DOS partition. DOS 3.x uses a value of 01 for a DOS partition with a 12-bit FAT and 04 for a DOS partition with a 16-bit FAT. So, when DOS 2.x looks at the hard disk partition table and sees only that 04 system indicator, it thinks the partition is non-DOS even though it really is a DOS partition.

You'll experience this DOS 2.x incompatibility only with hard disks greater than ten megabytes formatted under DOS 3.x. A normal PC-XT ten-megabyte disk can be used by either DOS 2.x or DOS 3.x regardless of the formatting.

With 65,518 clusters available, it's theoretically possible to have a cluster size of 512 bytes for a 20- or 30-megabyte disk, but you really don't want a cluster size that small. Since files are stored in noncontiguous areas of a disk, a small cluster size would mean that files could become overly fragmented, which could slow down file access time.

Prior to DOS 3.0 (which was introduced at the same time as the IBM PC-AT) IBM did not sell a hard disk over ten megabytes. The original PC-AT had IBM's first 20-megabyte hard disk. Although it's possible to install a 20- or 30-megabyte drive on a PC or XT running DOS 2.x, nobody working with strict IBM parts ever had a cluster size over 4,096 bytes. The problem of these excessively large cluster sizes was fixed only when IBM introduced a 20-megabyte hard disk. In one sense, it's not even IBM's problem if you have a 8,192 byte cluster size.

So, what can you do about this? If you have a hard disk over ten megabytes originally configured under DOS 2.x, you can usually reconfigure it under DOS 3.x to get a smaller cluster size.

Warning: don't even think of trying the techniques mentioned in this section unless every single one of your files is absolutely currently backed up, and you're working with a brand new blank hard disk, and you know what you're doing, and you take all the responsibility for any bizarre effects. Otherwise, just read along.

This assumes that your C: hard disk is connected to a hard disk controller card that has its own ROM BIOS, that you don't need anything special in a CONFIG.SYS file to use the hard disk, and that you (or somebody at your computer store) originally configured the hard disk by running the normal FDISK and FORMAT command included in IBM's PC-DOS. It also assumes you're using a version of PC-DOS 3.2 or later.

First, you must back up your entire hard disk with BACKUP. Do it twice to play it safe. For your 12 megabytes of files, you'll need about six boxes of diskettes for two backups. Buy high quality diskettes for this. Format them all before you begin. Don't use any that have bad sectors.

The BACKUP command you want is:

```
BACKUP C:\*.* A: /S
```

which backs up everything on drive C: in all subdirectories. BACKUP will prompt you to put in new diskettes. Label them in sequence.

When you're done with the backup, boot up PC-DOS from drive A:, and run FDISK by typing:

```
FDISK
```

One of the FDISK menu options is to delete the existing DOS partition. Do this first. Then create a DOS partition, which is another menu option. You probably want to use the entire hard disk for DOS, so answer yes to that question. Your system will now reboot. Make sure the DOS diskette is still in drive A:.

When you get back to the DOS prompt, format the hard disk with:

```
FORMAT C:/S/V
```

After this is done, you can verify that everything is running smoothly by doing a DIR and a CHKDSK on drive C:. You can try rebooting with the drive A: door open. You machine should boot from the hard disk. At this point, you can create a small file to see if your cluster size is indeed smaller. It should be 2,048 bytes.

Boot up again from the floppy. Now you can proceed to RESTORE the backed-up files onto your hard disk with the RESTORE command:

```
RESTORE A: C:\*.* /S /P
```

This whole process can be very scary and you may encounter some "gotchas" along the way. Here are some of them:

First, some copy-protected programs installed on a hard disk may not work after a BACKUP and RESTORE. Others will. Some of the problem programs (Lotus *1-2-3* Release 2, for instance) can be deinstalled. If you have any of these programs, deinstall them from the hard disk before you begin and reinstall them when you're all done. When in doubt, contact the manufacturer. (After they give you the information you need, tell them what you think about copy protection. Use whatever language you feel appropriate.)

Second, people have sometimes had problems with BACKUP and RESTORE. Sometimes RESTORE chokes in the middle of restoring from a bunch of diskettes. That's why you should do two BACKUPs. You may want to take other precautions: your hard disk probably has a number of purchased programs on it and a number of your own data files in various subdirectories. You can probably recreate those purchased programs from the original diskettes. For your own data files, particularly the ones most valuable to you, use the regular COPY command to copy them to diskettes.

Third, if you're using a version of DOS older than 3.3, BACKUP will back up hidden and read-only files, including the DOS files called IBMBIO.COM and IBMDOS.COM. When you run RESTORE, you want to use the /P switch as shown above, which prompts you when it is about to backup over existing read-only files. When you get the prompt for IBMBIO.COM and IBMDOS.COM, answer NO.

Older versions of RESTORE will copy the old version of COMMAND.COM from the backed up floppies to your hard disk. When you are done with the RESTORE, copy COMMAND.COM from your newest DOS floppy diskette to the root directory of the hard disk with the command:

```
COPY COMMAND.COM C:\
```

If you booted from the newly formatted hard disk before running RESTORE, DOS will try to load the COMMAND.COM from the hard disk after RESTORE is completed. But this would be the old COMMAND.COM. This is why you should boot from your latest DOS floppy before beginning RESTORE. When RESTORE ends, you will be prompted to put the DOS disk in drive A:, so it can find the correct version of COMMAND.COM.

DOS 3.3 solved these system-file problems by modifying RESTORE so it won't restore IBMBIO.COM, IBMDOS.COM, or COMMAND.COM. However, because it won't restore these files, you have to use SYS to put these system files back on your hard disk, and then use the COPY command to put COMMAND.COM back. Nobody said it would be easy.

Fourth, after you're done with the RESTORE, your hard disk will still contain copies of all the external DOS programs (such as CHKDSK and MODE) from your old DOS version. You should replace these with the latest DOS versions. More recent copies of DOS have a command called REPLACE that automates this process.

Fifth, sometimes after all this, funny things happen. For instance, you may not be able to boot from drive C:. If this is the case, boot from a new DOS floppy and get into FDISK again. Choose "Change the Active Partition" in the menu. If the status of the DOS partition is marked "N," it means it's nonactive and you can't boot from it. Make it active. Sometimes just entering and leaving FDISK fixes the problem.

If you think that your hard disk still has the old DOS IBMBIO, IBMDOS, or COMMAND files on it, you can boot from your new DOS floppy and execute the commands:

```
SYS C:
```

and:

```
COPY COMMAND.COM C:\
```

This will reinstall the newest version of DOS on your hard disk.

Sixth, if you have a tape backup unit and you would rather use that instead of BACK-UP and RESTORE, you should determine whether it does a file-by-file backup or an "image" backup. Many tape backup units give you a choice. You want to do a file-by-file backup. If your tape backup unit can only do an image backup, don't use it. The image stored on the tape will include the hard disk's FAT and this will be a different format under DOS 3.x. When you restore the hard disk from the imaged tape, the old File Allocation Table will be copied back to the disk. No good. If you do a file-by-file backup and restore, it will probably copy over the DOS files. Boot your new version of DOS from drive A: and do the SYS command and COPY of COMMAND.COM before you try booting from the hard disk.

Seventh, after you've used DOS 3.x FDISK on a 20-megabyte or bigger disk, you cannot use the hard disk with any DOS version prior to 3.0. If you boot up from a DOS 2.x floppy, DOS simply will not recognize the hard disk. Some people (program developers, mainly) need to test programs under several DOS versions. These people may need to have their hard disks recognizable by DOS 2.x. They shouldn't reconfigure their hard disk.

Finally, this whole discussion is based on the IBM version of MS-DOS (which is called "Personal Computer DOS" by IBM and commonly called "PC-DOS" by the rest of us). Some versions of MS-DOS for other manufacturer's machines may not support the smaller cluster size, so doing this will not have any effect. Again, when in doubt, contact the manufacturer.

DOS Filters

One of the most useful features of DOS versions starting with 2.0 is the ability to *pipe* or *redirect* data.

These later versions of DOS provide five standard input and output devices (standard input, output, error, auxiliary, and printer) and let you reshuffle the way these devices handle their input and output. For instance, while programs normally receive input from the keyboard and display output on the screen, you could easily reroute things so that a program receives input from a disk file and sends output to your printer.

To give you added power, DOS provides three special programs called filters that can comb through the data on its way from one part of your system to another: MORE.COM, SORT.EXE, and FIND.EXE. You can use MORE to display text a screenful at a time, SORT to arrange the contents of your files in sorted order, and the multitalented FIND to hunt through files for specific strings of characters, count the number of lines in your files, and even add line numbers to your text.

The accompanying disk contains several other useful filters that do things like skip certain lines when displaying files, or turn whole text files uppercase or lowercase.

DOS uses three command-line operators to handle redirection and piping: <, >, and |. The command:

```
DIR > DIRLIST
```

redirects output by taking the directory information that would normally appear onscreen and sending it instead into a disk file called DIRLIST. Similarly, the command:

```
SORT < DIRLIST
```

would redirect input by using the contents of the DIRLIST file as input for the SORT filter rather than keystrokes from the keyboard. The output of this process would go to the screen, and you'd see a directory listing sorted in alphabetical filename order.

(You could even combine redirected input and output on the same line, by adapting this command to:

```
SORT < DIRLIST > DIRLIST.SRT
```

DOS would then take the raw, unsorted DIRLIST file, redirect it as input into the SORT program, and redirect the output into a new alphabetically sorted file called DIRLIST.SRT.)

By executing the first two commands one after the other, you could produce a sorted directory listing:

```
DIR > DIRLIST
SORT < DIRLIST
```

However, this would leave a file on your disk called DIRLIST that you'd have to erase later. What you really want to do is combine the two lines into one command. But you can't do it with a command like:

```
DIR > SORT
```

Instead, use the | piping symbol:

```
DIR | SORT
```

When you pipe the output of DIR into SORT, DOS will create its own temporary files in the root directory of your disk to hold the information normally sent to standard output by the DIR command. Then it will redirect standard input so this temporary file feeds into the SORT program. When it's done, DOS will automatically delete the temporary files it created.

If you're in the root directory when you try this, you may see two strange files with names like:

```
0D102A1F       0       6-01-88       1:16p
0D102A25       0       6-01-88       1:16p
```

These zero-length files with eight-digit hexadecimal filenames are the temporary files DOS creates during the redirection process.

DOS 3.x uses the PC's clock to derive names for the temporary files, which is why they look like numbers. DOS 2.x gave the temporary files names with the word PIPE in them, which is at least a hint at what they did:

```
%PIPE1       $$$       0      6-01-88      1:16p
%PIPE2       $$$       0      6-01-88      1:16p
```

All temporary PIPE files have 0 bytes lengths since DOS displays the directory listings after it created the files and opened them for input but before it had a chance to close them.

You can also use piping to execute several programs or commands in sequence. For instance, if you had a \GAMES subdirectory and a program in it called CHESS.COM, you could first change directories and then run CHESS by typing:

```
CD \GAMES | CHESS
```

If you had another game called CHECKERS.COM in the same subdirectory, you could do the above and then run CHECKERS immediately after CHESS by typing:

```
CD GAMES | CHESS | CHECKERS
```

While this doesn't work with all DOS commands, it does let you combine certain operations together into one line. To see how this works, type in the following one-line batch file called THISFILE.BAT that creates a subdirectory called TEMP one level lower than the directory you are currently using, copies itself into this new subdirectory, logs into it, and then does a directory listing:

```
MD TEMP | COPY THISFILE.BAT TEMP | CD TEMP | DIR
```

Actually, DOS provides a fourth redirection operator: >>. When you use the double >> symbol, DOS will create a new file for output if the specified file doesn't already exist, but will append information to an existing file without overwriting any old information already in the file. If you use a single > symbol, DOS will always overwrite any existing information.

So if you don't already have a file called DIRLIST on your disk, both of these commands will work identically:

- DIR I SORT > DIRLIST
- DIR I SORT >> DIRLIST

But if your disk already contains a DIRLIST file, the first command will wipe it out and replace it with the sorted directory listing, while the second command will just tack the new sorted directory listing onto the end of the existing DIRLIST file.

When you issue a command like DIR I SORT without any parameters after it, DOS assumes you want to sort alphabetically starting with the first character on each line. If

SORT finds lines with the same first character, it will look at the second character to break the tie. If these are the same, it will keep looking at the next column until it finds a difference.

SORT arranges text by looking at the ASCII value of each character. The decimal ASCII value of a lowercase "a" is 97 while the value of an uppercase "A" is 65. However, DOS 2.x and 3.x sort characters differently. DOS 2.x was case-sensitive, and would arrange a character string like "AAA" before one like "aaa" since the ASCII value of initial uppercase "A" is lower than its lowercase counterpart. DOS 3.x gives lowercase letters the same value as their uppercase versions. (DOS 3.x also treats high-bit accented foreign-language characters the same as their normal low-bit unaccented cousins.)

So if you asked DOS 2.0 or 2.1 to sort a file called DATA.RAW that contained the three lines:

```
banana
AVOCADO
apple
```

with the command:

```
SORT < DATA.RAW
```

you'd end up with:

```
AVOCADO
apple
banana
```

But if you tried the same command under DOS 3.x, you'd get:

```
apple
AVOCADO
banana
```

You can use two different syntaxes for many identical filter operations. For example, if your disk contains a long text file called LONGTEXT, and you tried to view the contents with the command:

```
TYPE LONGTEXT
```

DOS would scroll the display rapidly off your screen before you had a chance to read it. You could pause and then restart the scrolling process by pressing Ctrl-S repeatedly, but this takes too much concentration and is too imprecise. Instead, just send the output of the TYPE command through the MORE.COM filter with:

```
TYPE LONGFILE | MORE
```

DOS will start displaying information, then pause automatically when the screen fills. If you press just about any key, DOS will then display another screenful, and repeat the process until it reaches what it thinks is the end of the file.

You could do the same thing with the command:

```
MORE < LONGFILE
```

Similarly, if you wanted to sort the above DATA.RAW file, you could do it either with:

```
TYPE DATA.RAW | SORT
```

or:

```
SORT < DATA.RAW
```

But be very careful about which way you point the redirection symbol. While:

```
SORT < DATA.RAW
```

will sort the contents of your DATA.RAW file, turning the symbol around:

```
SORT > DATA.RAW
```

will *wipe out* your DATA.RAW file. This is because DOS thinks you want a new file called DATA.RAW to be the output of the SORT process rather than to serve as the input. So it opens the DATA.RAW file and erases everything already in it.

Similarly, typing:

```
DIR | MORE
```

will display your files a screen at a time (as will DIR /P), but typing:

```
DIR > MORE
```

will create a new file called MORE and redirect your directory listing into it. It won't damage the MORE filter, since its real name is MORE.COM.

When a redirection symbol is pointing *into* a filter, DOS will treat the file on the other side of the symbol as a source of input. When a redirection symbol is pointing *out of*, or away from, a filter, DOS will treat any filename on the other side of the symbol as an output file.

If you're using a redirection symbol rather than a piping symbol, the name of the DOS filter has to be the first thing after the DOS prompt. So:

```
C>SORT < DATA.RAW
```

will work just fine, while:

```
C>DATA.RAW > SORT
```

won't do anything other than generate a "Bad command or filename" error, since DOS will view the period between DATA and RAW as a space, and look for a command or executable file named DATA. If you happened to have a file called DATA.COM, DATA.EXE, or DATA.BAT handy, DOS would run it.

When you have the choice, it's more efficient to use redirection than piping. To see the comparison, try running two slightly different sets of batch files that display the contents of all the batch files in your current subdirectory one at a time. Once you've created all four files, see the difference in speed by first running SCANBAT1 and then running SCANBAT2. The first pair, SCANBAT1.BAT and READ1.BAT, use piping:

```
REM SCANBAT1.BAT
ECHO OFF
FOR %%F IN (*.BAT) DO COMMAND /C READ1 %%F
```

```
REM READ1.BAT
ECHO OFF
CLS
ECHO %1
TYPE %1 | MORE
PAUSE
```

The second pair, SCANBAT2.BAT and READ2.BAT, use redirection:

```
REM SCANBAT2.BAT
ECHO OFF
FOR %%F IN (*.BAT) DO COMMAND /C READ2 %%F
```

```
REM READ2.BAT
ECHO OFF
CLS
ECHO %1
MORE < %1
PAUSE
```

The workhorse line in READ2.BAT:

```
MORE < %1
```

is far faster than its equivalent in READ1.BAT:

```
TYPE %1 | MORE
```

(Again, you can speed things up even more by substituting CALL in place of COMMAND /C for any DOS version 3.3 or later.)

You can have the SORT command start sorting on a column other than the first one. Just add a /+ and a column number after the SORT command.

A normal directory listing looks something like:

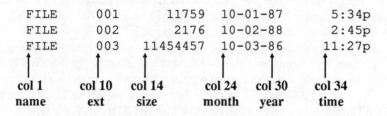

```
FILE        001         11759   10-01-87         5:34p
FILE        002          2176   10-02-88         2:45p
FILE        003      11454457   10-03-86        11:27p

col 1       col 10   col 14        col 24   col 30   col 34
name        ext      size          month    year     time
```

The filename itself starts on column 1. The filename extension begins on column 10, its size on column 14, its date on column 24, and its time on column 34.

To sort this list of files by size, type:

```
DIR | SORT /+14
```

If you wanted to sort them by size, but in reverse order, just add a /R:

```
DIR | SORT /+14 /R
```

or:

```
DIR | SORT /R /+14
```

These numbers are hard to remember. You can create one big SD.BAT (for Sorted Directory) batch file that makes it easy to see any sort of directory listing you want:

```
ECHO OFF
SET DEV=CON
IF %1!==! GOTO OOPS
FOR %%A IN (N n E e S s D d T t) DO IF %1==%%A GOTO OKAY
GOTO OOPS
:OKAY
IF %3!==! GOTO NOTHIRD
SET DEV=%3
IF %2==/r GOTO CHEKNAME
IF %2==/R GOTO CHEKNAME
GOTO OOPS
:CHEKNAME
ECHO This will create a file called %3
```

```
ECHO If this is not what you want, press
ECHO Ctrl-C then answer Y. Otherwise,
PAUSE
GOTO MAIN
:NOTHIRD
IF %2!==! GOTO MAIN
IF %2==/r GOTO MAIN
IF %2==/R GOTO MAIN
ECHO This will create a file called %2
ECHO If this is not what you want, press
ECHO Ctrl-C then answer Y. Otherwise,
PAUSE
SET DEV=%2
:MAIN
GOTO %1
:N
DIR | SORT %2 > %DEV%
GOTO END
:E
DIR | SORT /+10 %2 > %DEV%
GOTO END
:S
DIR | SORT /+14 %2 > %DEV%
GOTO END
:D
DIR | SORT /+24 %2 > %DEV%
GOTO END
:T
DIR | SORT /+34 %2 > %DEV%
GOTO END
:OOPS
ECHO You can sort by name, extension, size, date or time
ECHO by following %0 with a N or E or S or D or T, eg:
ECHO %0 N or %0 n or %0 E
ECHO To sort in reverse order, add a /R, eg:
ECHO %0 N /R or %0 n /r or %0 E /r
ECHO To put the results into a file, add a filename, eg:
ECHO %0 S /R DIRSORTR.FIL or %0 S DIRSORT.FIL
:END
IF %DEV%==CON GOTO BYE
IF %DEV%!==! GOTO BYE
ECHO Now enter: TYPE %DEV%
:BYE
SET DEV=
```

Early versions of DOS may erroneously turn ECHO back on at the end of the batch file. If this happens, stick an ECHO OFF at the offending point.

This batch file is somewhat complicated because it can accept so many different syntaxes and because it tries hard to screen out invalid entries.

If you enter just SD without any parameters, or with invalid parameters, the batch file will jump to the :OOPS label and print instructions. Here's a summary of what the program will do for you:

Sort in Order Of	Syntax
Name	SD N (or) SD n
Extension	SD E (or) SD e
Size	SD S (or) SD s
Date	SD D (or) SD D
Time	SD T (or) SD T
Reverse name	SD N /R (or) SD n /R
Reverse extension	SD E /R (or) SD e /R
Reverse size	SD S /R (or) SD s /R
Reverse date	SD D /R (or) SD D /R
Reverse time	SD T /R (or) SD T /R

(Actually, you could substitute /r in place of /R.)

The %0 variables in the ECHO statements following the :OOPS label will make sure that the instructions accurately reflect the batch file's name if you decide to rename it to something like DIRSORT.BAT.

The long test line:

```
FOR %%A IN (N n E e S s D d T t) DO IF %1==%%A GOTO OKAY
```

screens out any sorting parameters that aren't valid. Then it uses the:

```
GOTO %1
```

command to jump execution to the proper batch label, so if you enter S because you wanted to sort by size, the batch file will jump to the :S label. DOS is normally case-sensitive about everything, but it automatically capitalizes labels, so it will jump to the :S label whether you typed SD S or SD s.

The lines that look like:

```
IF %1!==! GOTO OOPS
```

and:

```
IF %2!==! GOTO MAIN
```

and:

```
IF %3!==! GOTO NOTHIRD
```

test to see how many parameters you entered. When you enter a command at the DOS prompt, DOS sets the value of a replaceable parameter called %0 with the name of the command (or executable file) itself. Then it sees if you typed anything after the name of the command or file and sets additional replaceable parameters values accordingly. So if you entered:

```
SD E /R
```

DOS would set the following parameter values:

```
%0 = SD
%1 = E
%2 = /R
```

SD.BAT gives you two options for handling the results of the various directory sorts. You can either have it display the results onscreen (the default) or redirect the results into a file. If you specify a valid filename as a third parameter, SD.BAT will create a file and redirect the sorted listing into it. You may also skip the /R parameter and add a filename as the second parameter.

To give you the option of sending the sorted results to the screen or to a file, SD.BAT uses an environment variable called %DEV%. It first sets the value of %DEV% to CON. If you didn't enter a filename, DOS will substitute CON for %DEV: and turn the line:

```
DIR | SORT /+14 %2 > %DEV%
```

into:

```
DIR | SORT /+14 %2 > CON
```

Here the CON output device stands for the screen, so redirecting output to CON displays the sorted listing on your monitor.

However, if you stuck a filename onto the end:

```
SD S DIRSORT.FIL
```

or:

```
SD S /R DIRSORT.FIL
```

SD.BAT will redefine %DEV% to the filename you entered. The tricky part is that this filename can either be the second or third thing that you enter on the command like after the SD, since you can add an optional /R as the second parameter.

The %DEV% variable doesn't hog much room in the environment, but if yours is already crammed to the gills you may get an error message telling you you're out of environment space. If so, you'll have to make your environment a bit bigger. See the chapter on environments for details.

You can try the same kind of device switching if you program in BASIC. Many programmers who write routines that send output to the printer first write them to display on the screen. This saves paper and makes debugging a lot easier.

The technique involves using PRINT # instead of the normal PRINT command. Before executing any of these PRINT # statements OPEN the screen (SCRN:) for output (e.g., OPEN "SCRN:" FOR OUTPUT AS #1).

Then, whenever the PRINT # statement executes, the output will go to the screen just as it would if it were using an ordinary PRINT statement. If you want a hardcopy version of the same output, CLOSE the file and OPEN it again using your printer as the output device (e.g., OPEN "LPT1:" FOR OUTPUT AS #1).

If you try this, avoid using commands like LOCATE statements that would confuse your printer. A sample routine might look like:

```
100 ' DEVSHIFT.BAS
110 '
120 PRINT "Where should the output go — "
130 PRINT TAB(10);"1 — Screen"
140 PRINT TAB(10);"2 — Printer
150 I$=INKEY$:IF I$="" THEN 150
160 ON VAL(I$) GOTO 180,190
170 BEEP:GOTO 150
180 OPEN "SCRN:" FOR OUTPUT AS #1:GOTO 230
190 OPEN "LPT1:" FOR OUTPUT AS #1
200 '
210 '   ** program continues here **
220 '
230 PRINT #1, "This is a test"
```

Unfortunately, SORT isn't perfect. The date entry in a directory listing begins on column 24. The U.S. date format is MM-DD-YY, so if you try to sort a directory listing by date:

```
DIR | SORT /+24
```

DOS will put the month and day sequence in the correct order but not the year. You can have DOS sort properly by year with:

```
DIR | SORT /+30
```

but this won't get the month and day columns sorted properly.

Getting a directory listing that's correctly sorted by date requires three steps. First you have to create a temporary file in month/day order:

```
DIR | SORT /+ 24 > TEMPFILE
```

Next you have to use a word processor or EDLIN to remove the time information from the TEMPFILE file. It's best to use a word processor that can delete columns, and have it delete everything after column 31.

Finally, redirect the edited TEMPFILE file into another SORT command that looks at the year column:

```
SORT /+30 < TEMPFILE
```

While it's possible (and common) to combine different filter operations on the same line, if you tried:

```
DIR | SORT /+24 | SORT /+30
```

you wouldn't end up with a listing properly sorted by date. To see how this works, assume you had these four files on your disk:

```
FILE       001     60032   12-14-88    9:00a
FILE       002      1021    6-01-88   12:00p
FILE       003     22528   12-22-87   11:31p
FILE       004    125056    1-16-88    9:17a
```

If you tried either:

```
DIR | SORT /+24
```

or:

```
DIR | SORT /+30 | SORT /+24
```

you'd end up with:

```
FILE       004    125056    1-16-88    9:17a
FILE       002      1021    6-01-88   12:00p
FILE       001     60032   12-14-88    9:00a
FILE       003     22528   12-22-87   11:31p
```

The months and days would be correct, but not the year. And if you tried either:

```
DIR | SORT /+30
```

or:

```
DIR | SORT /+24 | SORT /+30
```

DOS would spit out:

```
FILE    003     22528    12-22-87   11:31p
FILE    001     60032    12-14-88    9:00a
FILE    004    125056     1-16-88    9:17a
FILE    002      1021     6-01-88   12:00p
```

with the entries sorted properly by year but with a 12/88 file arranged before a 1/88 file.

If you do try sorting your files, make sure that similar entries all begin in the same column. SORT will work well with a fixed-field data base but not with a random access file. Fixed field files look like:

```
Allenovitch   Paul      345 Hilltop Lane
Ballmerski    Steve     10 Maple Avenue
Kingstein     Adrian    98612 Hideaway Heights
```

A random-access or comma-delimited version of this might be:

```
Allenovitch,Paul,345 Hilltop Lane
Ballmerski,Steve,10 Maple Avenue
Kingstein,Adrian,98612 Hideaway Heights
```

If you wanted to sort on first names, you'd be able to do it on the fixed-field version.

SORT also won't work on any file longer than 63K. A pity. And it needs to see carriage returns at the ends of the lines it's sorting. Many applications have their own sorting routines that use faster algorithms, but for quick and dirty DOS tasks, SORT works just fine.

FIND is one of the most versatile DOS commands. When combined with other DOS commands and features, it can track down long-forgotten files, scan across hundreds of files in a subdirectory for matching strings, and even give you a rudimentary address book with an automatic lookup feature.

Most users clutter their root directory with dozens of miscellaneous or temporary files. The ideal root directory, however, should contain only your first level of subdirectories and the critical files COMMAND.COM, CONFIG.SYS, and AUTOEXEC.BAT. This way, typing:

```
DIR \
```

will give you an index to the main subdirectory structure of your hard disk.

While DOS will print out a list of subdirectories if you type:

```
DIR *.
```

the list will also include any filename that lacks an extension. The DOS manual provides a better way, using FIND:

```
DIR | FIND "<DIR>"
```

Actually, to prevent wear and tear on your fingers, all you have to enter is:

```
DIR | FIND "<"
```

However, this will show you only the subdirectories in your root directory. For a quick onscreen list of all your subdirectories, type either:

```
TREE | FIND "Path"
```

or:

```
CHKDSK /V | FIND "Dir"
```

For a permanent copy, redirect the output into a SUBDIR.LST file:

```
TREE | FIND "Path" > SUBDIR.LST
```

or:

```
CHKDSK /V | FIND "Dir" > SUBDIR.LST
```

In fact, since CHKDSK /V reports every file on your disk in every subdirectory, along with the full path, you can use it to locate a file buried in a subdirectory many levels deep. The FINDFILE.BAT batch file mentioned in Chapter 3 can find any file on your disk. It's built around the single line:

```
CHKDSK / V | FIND "%1" | MORE
```

FINDFILE.BAT isn't as fast as dedicated assembly language utilities such as WHERE or SEARCH but it's slightly easier to use, since it lets you locate files by entering just a fragment of the filename. FINDFILE will uncover any matches containing the specified fragment, regardless of whether the match is to the left or right of the dot in the filename.

If you normally use FIND to uncover single words or parts of single words, and you hate typing in the required quotation marks, you can create another small batch file called F.BAT:

```
ECHO OFF
IF %2!==! GOTO OOPS
```

```
FIND "%1" %2
GOTO END
:OOPS
ECHO The format is: %0 STRING FILE
ECHO where STRING is the one-word
ECHO string you want, and FILE is
ECHO the file you're searching
:END
```

While this saves typing, it won't let you hunt for any strings with spaces in them, since it will interpret the word after the first space as the name of the file you want to search. Remember, too, that FIND is case-sensitive, so it won't locate "String" if you tell it to find "string" or "STRING."

DOS can't handle wildcards when executing a normal FIND command, although you can tell it to look through several files in one operation. To have it search through the first three chapters of a book for the text "DOS version" you would use a command like:

```
FIND "DOS version" CHAPTER.1 CHAPTER.2 CHAPTER.3
```

You can have FIND snoop through every file on your disk by using a FOR...IN...DO command in a batch file like the following FINDALL.BAT:

```
ECHO OFF
IF %1!==! GOTO OOPS
FOR %%A IN (*.*) DO FIND "%1" %%A
GOTO END
:OOPS
ECHO You must enter a one-word
ECHO string you want to find
:END
```

This batch file will uncover every matching single-word string in every file in the logged subdirectory. Unfortunately, while it will print each match it finds, it will also print the name of every file it checks, along with a "----------" whether or not it locates a match.

You can normally get rid of such unwanted lines by piping text through a FIND command that includes a /V parameter. If you wanted to see a listing of all the files in a particular directory, but didn't want to see any subdirectories, you could type:

```
DIR | FIND /V "<DIR>"
```

or the shorthand version:

```
DIR | FIND /V "<"
```

If you're currently in a subdirectory bursting with files and you want to see all the files with the letters "COM" in them, you can type:

```
DIR | FIND "COM"
```

and you may see something like:

```
COMFILES    <DIR>          6-05-88  7:46p
WELCOME  HOM    21376      8-27-88 11:32a
INCOMING MAL     6925      2-22-88 10:22p
MORE     COM      313      3-17-87 12:00p
COMMON   LST     1561      5-22-88 12:00p
PRINT    COM     9026      3-17-87 12:00p
PROCOMM     <DIR>          6-05-88  7:46p
```

To remove the subdirectories from this list, add a FIND /V command:

```
DIR | FIND "COM" | FIND /V "<"
```

and you'll get:

```
WELCOME  HOM    21376      8-27-88 11:32a
INCOMING MAL     6925      2-22-88 10:22p
MORE     COM      313      3-17-87 12:00p
COMMON   LST     1561      5-22-88 12:00p
PRINT    COM     9026      3-17-87 12:00p
```

(If all you wanted was the COM files, you could of course type:

```
DIR *.COM
```

But this FIND command would do it as well:

```
DIR | FIND " COM"
```

You need the extra space between the quotation marks, since DOS sticks a space between the filename and the extension in all directory listings.)

However, you can't combine FIND commands in a FOR...IN...DO batch command. Changing the third line in FINDALL.BAT to:

```
FOR %%A IN (*.*) DO FIND "%" %%A | FIND /V "---"
```

wouldn't remove the extraneous filenames and "----------" bars. You could do it by adapting FINDALL.BAT so it passes parameters to a second batch file called FA.BAT that does the actual work:

First, the revised FINDALL.BAT:

```
ECHO OFF
IF %1!==! GOTO OOPS
FOR %%A IN (*.*) DO COMMAND /C FA %1 %%A
GOTO END
:OOPS
ECHO You must enter a one-word
ECHO string you want to find
:END
```

Next, FA.BAT:

```
ECHO OFF
FIND "%1" %2 | FIND /V "---"
```

If you're using a DOS version 3.3 or later, you could improve performance slightly by substituting CALL for COMMAND /C.

It's important to time- and date-stamp your files so you'll always know which versions are most current. And by doing so, you can have the DOS FIND filter help locate recent files for you.

If you have a crowded subdirectory that contains an important file you know you created in January, but you can't remember what you named the file, you can isolate all your January files by typing:

```
DIR | FIND " 1-"
```

DOS is finicky about what's inside the quotation marks. FIND "1-" would display dates like "11-23-87" and " 3-21-86" since the "1-" string is part of each. The leading space (directly after the initial quotation mark and before the 1) in " 1-" is unique to January. However, if your subdirectory contains files created over several years, FIND " 1-" may display files created in 1/85, 1/86, 1/87, 1/88, etc. To toss out all but 1/88 files, use FIND twice:

```
DIR | FIND " 1-" | FIND "-88"
```

This pipes the entire directory through the January filter, and then filters out everything that doesn't have an 88 in it. If you suspect that this process would uncover lots of files, you can pause the display a screenful at a time by sending the output through the MORE filter:

```
DIR | FIND " 1-" | FIND "-88" | MORE
```

Piping output through one or two filters in a row doesn't degrade performance very much, but a long chain of successive FINDs could drag on for quite a while. Copy the files to a RAMdisk if you can. And if you try it on a crowded floppy disk, you may as well just go out for lunch.

Directory output contains more information than just a listing of files and subdirectories. If want to see your files without the volume and directory information at the top:

```
Volume in drive A is PC MAGAZINE
Directory of  A:\SUBDIR
```

or the "bytes free" data at the bottom:

```
5 File(s)        295936 bytes free
```

you can type:

```
DIR | FIND /V "e"
```

All three lines of text contain lowercase "e" characters but no filenames can, and the /V will suppress anything with an "e" in it.

One of FIND's least used features is its ability to count your lines. If you were sure every line of all your files contained something common like a space, you could have FIND look for spaces (by specifying " ") and count them. Unfortunately, many files contain lines with nothing on them except carriage returns, or single unspaced words at the end of paragraphs.

However, since presumably no line in any of your files has a ridiculous string like "&@#$" you can use the /V to count how many lines don't contain this. This NUMBER.BAT file will use this trick to give you an accurate line count:

```
ECHO OFF
IF %1!==! GOTO OOPS
ECHO Number of lines:
FIND /C /V "&@#$" %1
GOTO END
:OOPS
ECHO Enter a filename after %0
:END
```

Run this batch file on the revised FINDALL.BAT batch file above and you'll see:

```
Number of lines:
---------- FINDALL.BAT: 8
```

The FIND command can also number all your lines. Again, use the trick of having the /V report all lines without an unlikely string:

```
ECHO OFF
IF %1!==! GOTO OOPS
FIND /V /N "&@#$" %1 | FIND /V "-----"
GOTO END
:OOPS
ECHO Enter a filename after %0
:END
```

Run this batch file on the new FINDALL.BAT and you'll see:

```
[1]ECHO OFF
[2]IF %1!==! GOTO OOPS
[3]FOR %%A IN (*.*) DO COMMAND /C FA %1 %%A
[4]GOTO END
[5]:OOPS
[6]ECHO You must enter a one-word
[7]ECHO string you want to find
[8]:END
```

You can create a brand new file where each line is individually numbered, by redirecting the output to a file (here called NMBRFILE):

```
ECHO OFF
IF %1!==! GOTO OOPS
FIND /V /N "&@#$" %1 | FIND /V "-----" > NMBRFILE
GOTO END
:OOPS
ECHO Enter a filename after %0
:END
```

You can use FIND to clean up many displays and reports. For instance, if you want to see how many bad sectors are on your hard disk and type CHKDSK, DOS will bury this bad-sector information in with a report on the volume name, the amount of free memory, the number of hidden files, etc. But if you filter the output through FIND with:

```
CHKDSK | FIND "bad"
```

all you'll see is how many bytes of bad sectors that DOS uncovered. By putting other strings inside the quotes, you could use this same technique to report just the number of subdirectories, the amount of free space on your disk, the number of files on your disk, etc.

One of the more annoying aspects of DOS is that it won't ordinarily report the time and date without asking you whether you want to reset them. By using FIND, however, you can create two files, T.BAT and D.BAT, that will print the current time and date without any fuss.

T.BAT contains the single line:

```
ECHO ONE | MORE | TIME | FIND "Cu"
```

Similarly, D.BAT is:

```
ECHO ONE | MORE | DATE | FIND "Cu"
```

If you're using a version of DOS 3.3 or later, put a @ at the very beginning of the line so it doesn't display onscreen as it executes. Using the ECHO command starts the whole process, but it doesn't actually print the word ONE. The MORE command supplies the carriage return needed to trigger the DATE and TIME. And the FIND command screens out everything other than the line with the word "Current" on it.

Many RAMdisk users reset their COMSPEC so that DOS looks on the correct drive if it needs to reload COMMAND.COM. What's your current COMSPEC? A single-line batch file called COMSPEC.BAT will let you know:

```
SET | FIND "SP"
```

If you've ever used the TYPE command to snoop inside a COM file to see what text messages it contains, you've probably been annoyed by a profusion of beeps. Whenever TYPE stumbles across an ASCII character 7 it tells DOS to beep the speaker. You can avoid this in examining a beep-filled file like COMMAND.COM, by typing:

```
FIND /V "^G" COMMAND.COM
```

(Note: You don't actually enter the ^G in the above example, although one will show up onscreen when you enter the ASCII 7 bell character. To enter it, after typing in the FIND /V and the initial quotation mark, type Ctrl-G, then type the second quotation mark and the COMMAND.COM filename.)

The above techniques assume you're hunting for single strings only. By piping the output of one FIND command through another FIND command, you can limit your search to the few instances where two specified strings occur in the same line.

Suppose you have a file called NAMEFILE with the following contents:

```
Buddy Jones, 3 Main Street, Boneville, OK
Mary Smith, 1 Park Lane, Washington, DC
Sam Jonesbury, 21 M Street, Washington, DC
```

If you wanted to locate just the Jones who lived in Washington, typing:

```
FIND "Jones" NAMEFILE
```

would report both the Jones you were looking for and the Jonesbury you weren't. You could limit the search to lines containing both "Jones" and "DC" with the command:

```
FIND "Jones" NAMEFILE | FIND "DC"
```

While SORT required fixed-field records, FIND isn't picky. But it is fussy about quotation marks. If you're searching for these you have to wrap each one in its own set of quote marks. Assume you're hunting through a MORETEXT file covering the MORE filter that contains the passages:

```
Unfortunately, the MORE command isn't
really very friendly. After it fills a
screen with text, it prints a terse
message at the bottom: "— More —"
What it really means at this point is
"Hit a key to see additional text."
```

If you want to find occurrences of the string "— More —" you'd have to use a command like:

```
FIND """— More —""" MORETEXT
```

FIND also makes it easy to print a list of files that you've either created or changed on a particular day. If you've been toiling away all day on 12/9/87, and you want to check a particular file you updated early in the morning but have forgotten its name, you can simply type:

```
DIR | FIND "12-09-87" | FIND "a"
```

The first FIND will search for everything created on 12/9 (you must remember to pad single-digit dates with zeros), and the "a" will limit the search only to files created before noon. This assumes, of course, that you properly date- and time-stamp your files.

While you can pipe the output of one FIND search through several others, such repeated FIND sieves can take an awfully long time unless you're working on a fast hard disk or RAMdisk.

The classic use of FIND is to give yourself a lightning-fast address book. First, to build up your NAMEFILE file of names and addresses, create an ADDNAME.BAT batch file with the following contents:

```
ECHO OFF
ECHO Enter up to one line of name
ECHO and address info at a time
ECHO ---
ECHO When all done, press Enter, then
ECHO the F6 key, then Enter again
ECHO ---
ECHO Enter names and addresses now:
COPY NAMEFILE + CON NAMEFILE > NUL
```

Then, whenever you want to add a new name to your master NAMEFILE list, just type ADDNAME and follow the directions onscreen. When you're all done entering new names, be sure to hit the Enter key and then the F6 function key and then the Enter key one last time. The > NUL in ADDNAME.BAT prevents unnecessary text from showing up onscreen.

The actual LOOKUP.BAT batch file that searches through your address book looks like:

```
ECHO OFF
IF %1!==! GOTO OOPS
FIND "%1" NAMEFILE | MORE
GOTO END
:OOPS
ECHO Enter the string to look up after the %0
:END
```

Again, putting quotation marks in the batch file saves you from having to type them in yourself each time you want to look something up, but it also limits you to single-word entries. If you don't mind typing quotation marks from the command line, and you want the ability to search for strings with spaces in them, remove the quotation marks that surround the %1.

If you create your master NAMEFILE properly, you can use this technique to print out the listings for those people living in NY, or with Zip Codes that start with 100.., or who have area codes beginning with 212. And if you add discrete codes to the NAMEFILE listing, such as XM to indicate that the person should be on your Christmas card list, you can sort such listings out easily.

Remember, though, that FIND is case sensitive, and that if you're hunting for Empire State listings by searching for "NY," LOOKUP.BAT would also print out a listing for the "PONY RIDERS ASSOCIATION."

You could create a DELNAME.BAT batch file that used redirection and the /V FIND option to delete names:

```
COPY NAMEFILE NAMEFILE.BAK
FIND /V "%1" NAMEFILE.BAK | FIND /V "---" > NAMEFILE
```

This DELNAME.BAT procedure is far from foolproof, however, since it's all too easy to delete an inadvertent match (which is why the batch file creates an automatic backup file). And this process can pile up extra carriage returns in your files.

One more trick: If you don't want to have to enclose FIND strings between quotation marks you can modify FIND.EXE so that quotes aren't necessary. The only drawback is that this new version of FIND won't be able to search for strings containing spaces. However, the easy way around this is to keep two versions of FIND — an unmodified version called FIND.EXE that needs quotes and can handle several words separated by spaces, and a patched version called FINDNOQ.EXE that just hunts for single words without requiring quotes.

Make a copy of FIND.EXE and be absolutely sure to remove the EXE extension. Just call it FIND. (DEBUG will treat EXE files specially, and you don't want it to in this case.) Then load it into DEBUG:

```
DEBUG FIND
```

Figure out how long the file is by typing:

```
RCX
```

and pressing the Enter key twice. You should see something like:

```
CX 1922
:
```

The 1922 is the length in hexadecimal notation (for version 3.3). This length will vary from version to version. Jot it down to use in the next command.

Search for all occurrences of the pair of bytes 3C 22. This is the code that FIND uses to see if the character you typed is a quotation mark (which has a hex value of 22). Take the length from the previous step and use it in the middle of the commmand, substituting it for 1922 if necessary:

```
S 100 L 1922 3C 22
```

(length goes here)

Again, you'll see different numbers in different versions, but DEBUG should report three addresses:

```
30DD:03AF
30DD:03CD
30DD:03D2
```

Ignore the four digits to the left of the colons; they'll vary from system to system and don't matter here. You have to make three small patches in each of these general areas. On a sheet of paper, mark these addresses 1, 2, and 3:

```
03AF   Address 1
03CD   Address 2
03D2   Address 3
```

Patch 1: Take the four righthand digits from address 1 (03AF in this case, but substitute the one you found if yours is different) and type:

```
U 03AF L4
```
↑
(address 1 goes here)

You should see something like:

```
30DD:03AF 3C22          CMP        AL,22
30DD:03B1 750A          JNZ        03BD
```
↑
(use the address you find here)

The 03BD following the JNZ will vary from version to version, but it doesn't matter, since you're going to change it. Replace the 750A with 4E90. Do this by taking the address directly to the left of the 750A (here it's 03B1, but substitute the one you see if yours is different) and typing:

```
E 03B1 4E 90
```
↑
(plug the address you found into here)

Then press the Enter key to register the change.

Patch 2: Take the four righthand digits from address 2 (03CD in this case, but substitute the one you found if yours is different) and type:

```
U 03CD L2
```

You should see something like:

```
30DD:03CD 3C22          CMP        AL,22
```

You're going to replace the 22 with 20. Do this by taking the address you just entered (here it's 03CD) and typing:

```
E 03CD 3C 20
```
↑
(address 2 goes here)

Press the Enter key to register the change.

Patch 3: Take the four rightmost digits from address 3 (03D2 in this case, but substitute the one you found if yours is different) and subtract 1 from it. This is easy.

3D2 - 1 = 3D1. If you need help with hex math, DEBUG can do the subtraction for you. Type an H, then the address, then a 1, then press Enter:

```
H 03D2 1
03D3   03D1
         ↑
     (difference)
```

DEBUG will print a pair of hex values. The first is the sum of the two numbers you entered, and the second is the difference. You want the difference. Take this difference and plug it into the following command:

```
U 03D1 L6
  ↑
(address 3 [minus 1] goes here)
```

When you press the Enter key you should see something like:

```
30DD:03D1 AC          LODSB
30DD:03D2 3C22        CMP     AL,22
30DD:03D4 740F        JZ      03E5
30DD:03D6 4E          DEC     SI
```

Again, the address after the JZ will be different from 03E5 in different versions, but it doesn't matter since you're going to replace all of this. Do it by taking the address-minus-one that you used in the U 0361 L6 command, and typing:

```
F 03D1 L6 90
  ↑
(address 3 [minus 1] goes here)
```

Press Enter to make the change final. Now save your changes to disk and quit DEBUG by typing:

```
W
Q
```

and pressing Enter after each. When you see the DOS prompt, rename the FIND file you just patched to FINDNOQ.EXE. Then try using it to find a single word, but leave off the quotation marks.

While you're at it, if you hate the ---------- line that FIND.EXE prints out at the top of each report, and you don't like using FIND /V "-----" to screen it out, you can use DEBUG to remove it once and for all.

To do so, before you write the above changed file and quit DEBUG, search for the ---------- line by plugging the length of your FIND.EXE file into the following command:

```
S 100 L 1922 "----------"
```
(length goes here)

Substitute the length of your particular version if it's different from 1922. DEBUG should respond with a single address:

```
30DD:19F7
```
(use this address)

Ignore the numbers to the left of the colon. Plug the four digits to the right of the colon (19F7 in this case, but substitute the one you found if yours is different) into the following command:

```
F 19F7 LA 8
```
(plug it in here)

This replaces the ten hyphens that FIND normally prints with ASCII 8 backspace characters. Then type W and press the Enter key to write the changed file and Q and Enter to quit. When you're all done, rename the file and give it back its EXE extension.

You could, of course, eliminate the need for quotes by creating a batch file called F.BAT containing the one line:

```
FIND "%1" %2
```

Then to find every occurrence of DIR in COMMAND.COM you just type:

```
F DIR COMMAND.COM
```

Printers

When ROM-BIOS tries to send something to your printer, it checks whether the printer is ready to receive characters. If the printer isn't ready, BIOS sits there continually rechecking the status. To avoid getting trapped in an endless loop, BIOS will give up after a predetermined "timeout" interval, and report that the printer is busy. If you're printing from DOS, you'll be greeted with the friendly "Abort, Retry, Ignore" message.

On early PCs, timeouts sometimes occurred during form feeds on the IBM's slow dot matrix printer, so IBM increased the timeout interval starting with version 1.1 of DOS. These delay values are stored in the BIOS data area beginning at hex address 0040:0078. This area contains four-byte values for the four parallel printers that the BIOS (in theory) supports. The current PC ROM BIOS initializes the time-out values to hex 14 (decimal 20).

You can experiment with different timeout values in DEBUG. To double the LPT1 timeout value to 40 (28 hex), for instance, just load DEBUG and enter the following pair of lines at the DOS prompt:

```
E 0040:0078 28
Q
```

Be careful with memory addresses; if you get them wrong, you can write over some other important settings or instructions and get into trouble.

Once you find a value that works well, you can add a line to your AUTOEXEC.BAT file to change it everytime you boot up. Just adapt the two lines shown above and put them into a file called TIMEOUT.SET. Then add the following line to your AUTOEXEC.BAT:

```
DEBUG < TIMEOUT.SET
```

When your system boots up, BIOS sniffs through your hardware trying to figure out, among other things, how many parallel printer adapters are attached. It uses three possible I/O port addresses to communicate with up to three adapters — hex 278, 378, and 3BC.

When it finds a valid printer adapter, it inserts the adapter's port number into a table starting at BIOS data area 0000:0408. The table has room for four 16-bit entries. BIOS puts the first port address at offset 408, the second (if it exists) at 40A, and the third (if there is one) at 40C. Then it encodes the number of printers it found into the high two bits of the BIOS Equipment List word at offset 410.

DOS uses four device names to refer to printers — PRN, LPT1, LPT2, and LPT3. PRN is the default, and is the same as LPT1.

Many commercial applications are designed to work with LPT1. If you have two printers — LPT1 and LPT2 — hooked to your system and want to swap them, all you have to do is exchange the port addresses at offsets 408 and 40A of low memory. Charles Petzold's tiny PRNSWAP.COM on the accompanying disk makes it easy.

Many of the programs on the accompanying disk are designed to tame your printer. Some let you generate form feeds from the keyboard. Others make it easy to send commands to your printer or prevent accidental print-screen attempts.

It's really frustrating to hit Shift-PrtSc accidentally. If your printer is on you have to wait until it finishes typing the contents of the screen, and then readjust the paper to the top of the next page. If it's off, your system will hang until DOS realizes that the printer is not going to respond.

When you type Shift-PrtSc, DOS issues an interrupt 5, which first looks at a location in low memory called STATUS_BYTE to see whether your system is already dumping a screen to the printer. If STATUS_BYTE is equal to 1, DOS thinks a screen dump is taking place, and exits the routine without dumping another screen to the printer. If STATUS_BYTE is equal to 0, the routine sets STATUS_BYTE to 1 so that it cannot interrupt itself, then does the actual dump, and finally resets STATUS_BYTE equal to 0 and exits the routine.

This means you can disable the Shift-PrtSc routine with a simple assembly language routine, DISABLE.COM, that sets STATUS_BYTE to 1. A similar routine, ENABLE.COM, can turn it back on by setting STATUS_BYTE to 0. Both are on the accompanying disk.

Most printers are capable of doing fancy tricks with fonts, spacing, and unusual operating modes of one sort or another. But sending codes to your printer isn't always easy.

First, many printer command codes begin with an escape character (hex 1B, decimal 27). But if you try to issue an escape character in DOS, you won't be successful, since DOS interprets this character as a signal to abort whatever you were trying to do. However, you can use DEBUG, or EDLIN, or a good word processor, or even BASIC to generate these escape sequences. See the chapter on ANSI.SYS for tips on how to do it (ANSI codes also begin with Escape characters).

To make creating custom printer control files easy, you can use the PRCODER.BAT below. You'll need to have DEBUG.COM in your current subdirectory, or in a directory that your PATH knows about.

PRCODER.BAT reads parameters from the command line and inserts them into a DEBUG script (to send the hex values 1BH, 49H, and 03H you would type PRCODER 1B 49 3). You can enter several dozen codes on the same command line; the SHIFT command reads them in and substitutes them one by one for the %1 replaceable parameter in the:

```
ECHO MOV DL,%1 >> PR.SCR
```

line. PRCODER.BAT then loops back and uses the:

```
IF %1!==! GOTO FINISH
```

test to see if there are any more command-line parameters to process. If it finds any, it concatenates them to the existing DEBUG script. If it doesn't find any, it jumps to the :FINISH label, adds the necessary DEBUG instructions to write the file, redirects the script into DEBUG by loading a secondary command processor with:

```
COMMAND /C DEBUG < PR.SCR
```

to create a COM file, and then erases the DEBUG script.

If the user doesn't enter any parameters, PRCODER.BAT prints instructions and then quits. DOS substitutes the actual name of the batch file for the %0, so you can rename PRCODER.BAT to whatever you want. The process will make each PRCODE.COM file 284 bytes long, the maximum length this process can handle. Be sure to rename existing PRCODE.COM files before creating new ones so the older version isn't obliterated by the new.

While some users might argue that it really isn't necessary to rewrite the MOV AH,5 line each time, it's a good idea to do so since you can't always be sure the AX register will remain intact after an INT 21.

Note also that the line:

```
ECHO. >> PR.SCR
```

won't work properly in some versions of DOS. Its purpose in this batch file is to generate a solitary carriage return. If your version of DOS stumbles over this, see the comments on ECHO in the chapter on batch files. If you're creating this batch file in DOS, you can press the F7 key instead of typing the period, which will generate a null.

```
ECHO OFF
IF %1!==! GOTO OOPS
ECHO N PRCODE.COM > PR.SCR
ECHO A >> PR.SCR
:TOP
IF %1!==! GOTO FINISH
ECHO MOV DL,%1 >> PR.SCR
ECHO MOV AH,5 >> PR.SCR
ECHO INT 21 >> PR.SCR
SHIFT
GOTO TOP
:FINISH
ECHO INT 20 >> PR.SCR
ECHO. >> PR.SCR
ECHO RCX >> PR.SCR
ECHO 11C >> PR.SCR
ECHO W >> PR.SCR
ECHO Q >> PR.SCR
COMMAND /C DEBUG < PR.SCR
DEL PR.SCR
ECHO PRCODE.COM created
GOTO END
:OOPS
ECHO Enter %0 and then the HEXADECIMAL
ECHO values (each FF or less) of the
ECHO printer codes you want to send, eg:
```

```
ECHO %0 1B 49 3
:END
```

The DOS PRINT utility, introduced with version 2.0, is a resident program that lets you print out disk files while you're running other programs. It's fundamentally different from other *background* (or spooler) printing programs, since most software print buffers lop off a large chunk of user memory as a holding area for text being sent to the printer. The print buffer program intercepts printer output, stores it in this memory buffer, and then later transfers it to the printer. This frees up the system for other activities.

PRINT, however, transfers disk files to the printer and takes up much less memory than a print buffer program. The size of these files is limited only by disk space. Once a regular print buffer becomes full, printing slows down to the speed of the printer.

Although PRINT can be used with a diskette system (if you don't change the diskette containing the print file while printing is in progress), it's best suited for a hard disk system.

The PRINT.COM program in DOS versions 2.0 and 2.1 had some real problems. You couldn't specify directory paths with the filename or optimize operation for particular printers. PRINT version 3.0 corrected these problems and added a slate of new parameters designed to make the process far more efficient and painless. Unfortunately, the PC-DOS manual discusses these parameters in an obscure and generally unhelpful manner. It took PC wizard Charles Petzold to sort it all out:

PRINT's syntax looks mystifying:

```
[d:] [path] PRINT [/D:device] [/B:buffsiz] [/U:busytick]
[/M:maxtick] [/S:timeslice] [/Q:quesiz] [/C] [/T] [/P]
[[d:] [path] filename[.ext]]
```

The /D (device name) and /Q (queue size) parameters are simple enough. Most of the time you'll just specify /D:PRN or /D:LPT1 to send output to the first parallel printer. /Q can be set to the largest number of files you'll want to print at one time.

The /B parameter specifies the buffer size; its default is 512 bytes. This is the amount of memory PRINT sets aside for reading the disk file. The default value means that the print file will be read 512 bytes at a time. If the buffer is too small, you'll see frequent disk accesses, particularly with a fast printer. If the buffer is too large, the disk accesses will be less frequent but slightly longer, and PRINT will occupy more memory.

For a hard disk system with 640K, the best buffer size is probably something like 4096 or 8192, both of which are multiples of 512.

To understand the /S, /M, and /U parameters, you have to understand how PRINT works.

During operation of the PC, the 8253 timer chip invokes a hardware interrupt (08H) 18.2 times per second, or about once every .055 seconds. This interrupt executes a short routine in ROM BIOS that counts the number of times it's called so DOS can know what time it is. The interrupt 08H routine also invokes an interrupt 1CH, often called the "Timer Tick." PRINT intercepts the Timer Tick interrupt to trigger it into operation.

The /S parameter, which IBM calls the *timeslice*, is the number of timer ticks during which PRINT will do nothing. When PRINT is doing nothing, the rest of the PC system will operate as normal, so the /S parameter should really be called the "System Time Slice."

The /M parameter, which IBM calls the *maxtick*, is the number of timer ticks during which PRINT will attempt to shovel characters out to the printer. This is really the time slice allocated to PRINT. Assuming that the printer is ready for these characters, PRINT will have nearly total control during this period and other programs may do nothing.

The default maxtick and timeslice settings are /M:2 and /S:8, which means that PRINT will be alternately active for 0.11 seconds and inactive for 0.44 seconds (assuming that the printer is always ready to accept characters). Consequently, PRINT will be working 20% of the time; any other program will be working at 80% of normal speed.

The /U parameter, which IBM calls the *busytick*, comes into play only if the printer is busy when PRINT attempts to print a character. The default value is /U:1, which means that PRINT will wait one clock tick (.055 seconds) before giving up its /M time slice. The rest of the system can then work for /S timer ticks before PRINT makes another attempt to print.

PRINT also gives up its time slice if a disk access is in progress. The reason for this is obvious — if PRINT has to get another piece of the file during this time, then real problems could develop if another program is accessing the disk. The time slice is also forfeited if a DOS function call is in progress. If /M is very high in relation to /S, you'll notice a significant degradation of system speed. If /M is too low, printing will not proceed as fast as the printer can manage. If /U is too high, PRINT may spend too much time just checking the printer without actually printing anything if the printer is busy.

However, these parameters may be specified only when PRINT is first loaded. So, unless you like doing little three-finger exercises repeatedly, you would normally have a very difficult time optimizing the parameters for your system.

The IBM Graphics Printer that most print utilities consider to be the standard has an 80-character internal buffer. It will not begin printing until the buffer is full or the printer receives a carriage return or a form feed. When the printer begins printing, it is busy and cannot accept any more characters until the internal buffer is empty.

The optimum parameter settings for this printer are an /M value equal to the number of timer ticks needed for PRINT to fill up the printer's buffer, and a /S value equal to the timer ticks required for the printer to print the contents of the buffer.

For the IBM Graphics Printer printing 80 character lines, the optimal values are /S:20, /M:4, and /U:2. These values caused better performance than the default values, even though for most lines, PRINT is active only 1/6th of total system time. The PRINT command would look like:

```
PRINT /D:PRN /Q:20 /B:8192 /S:20 /M:4 /U:2
```

Unlike the IBM Graphics Printer, many other printers have internal buffers larger than 80 characters. If you attempted to set /M equal to the time it takes for PRINT to fill up a large buffer, you may find it to be something like 20 clock ticks or more. In operation, this would be intolerable, because 20 clock ticks is over one second and the rest of your system would halt during that time.

For printers with large internal buffers, set /U equal to 1, and /M equal to 4 or 5 (about 1/4 second), and experiment with /S. For very fast printers, you may find /S to be low in relation to /M. You may want to deliberately slow down the printing so you can get some work done, or speed up the printing if that's what's important.

You can use PRINT to print any text file, with or without control characters, stored on a disk. It expands tabs and assumes that an ASCII 26 (hex 1A) character represents the end of the file, so you can't use PRINT for graphics. PRINT will be active during any program that does not steal interrupt 1C. (Some compiled BASIC programs do this.)

Programs that let you go to the DOS command level and then return when you're done make this process a lot easier. Be sure, though, to load PRINT before you use it from within another program, because you don't want to make it resident on top of some other application.

Here's the real kicker: On the DOS command level, and during execution of any program using DOS function calls to obtain keyboard input, PRINT operates in a totally different manner, and none of the above information about timer ticks applies.

You could set completely wrong values for PRINT (/S to 255 and /M to 1) and when you jump into DOS, the printer will churn away, printing your text as fast as possible. To understand why this happens, you have to look at the internal guts of PRINT.

PRINT works with disk files, so it must make DOS calls to pull these files into memory. During a DOS function call, DOS switches to an internal stack. DOS actually maintains three stacks — one for function calls 01 through 0C, another for function calls 0D and above (which includes the file accesses), and a third for function calls 01 through 0C when a critical error is in progress.

Because of this internal stack, PRINT (or any other multitasking utility triggered by a hardware interrupt) cannot arbitrarily make DOS function calls to access a disk file. If another program is making a DOS function call, PRINT's function calls may clobber the internal stack and eventually cause the system to crash.

To prevent this, PRINT use the undocumented DOS interrupt 21 function call 34 when it first loads. This function call returns registers ES:BX pointing to a byte in DOS. Whenever this byte is nonzero, a DOS function call is in progress. When PRINT is triggered by a timer tick, it checks this byte. If it's nonzero, PRINT just returns from the interrupt without attempting to print anything.

This creates a real problem, because on the DOS command level, COMMAND.COM executes a DOS function call 0A for keyboard input, and this DOS call is in progress until the user presses the Enter key at the end of a line. Many other DOS programs, such as DEBUG or EDLIN, also use this function call.

So, PRINT takes advantage of another undocumented feature of DOS — interrupt 28. PC-DOS itself continually executes an interrupt 28 whenever it is in a wait state (i.e., when it is waiting for keyboard input) during a function call of 01 through 0C.

When an interrupt 28 is invoked, PRINT knows that a function call of 01 through 0C is in progress. Because a separate stack is used for function calls of 0D and above, which includes all the file access calls, PRINT knows that it's safe to retrieve a file if necessary.

PRINT will always grind to a halt during any disk access. But you'll also see it stop during a TYPE command after the disk has been accessed. This is because TYPE uses function call 40 to write the file to the display, and PRINT cannot use DOS during that time.

Anyone who believes that multitasking is simple to implement in PC-DOS should try dissassembling PRINT.COM and take a look at the backflips and contortions required for simple background printing from disk files.

Security

The more information you can store on your system, the more vulnerable you are to security problems. Hard disks are a treasure of valuable data — about your company, your job, even your personal activities.

It's not bad enough that someone could make unauthorized copies of your important files. What's worse is that he could change or destroy the data. You would certainly know if someone had erased a critical file. But you might never know if someone altered an important record or two.

Starting with its AT, IBM wised up and wired its systems to a lock and key. You don't think IBM added it for show, did you?

Unfortunately, many users are cavalier about security. They leave floppy disks in drawers or plastic disk caddies, and often wouldn't miss a valuable diskette if it vanished. One of the penalties of such portability is that someone could walk out of your office with several file cabinets' worth of confidential information hidden in a pocket or brief-case.

And while you can catalog your floppies and keep sensitive ones locked in a safe, your hard disk is just a sitting duck for anyone who wants to pry. An unbreachable system is certainly not impossible to put together. Legions of government users have to forego the convenience of conventional hard disks for removable mass storage devices that can be locked up at night.

There's even a government standard for erasing files and then writing over them to obliterate any last magnetic trace. The *Norton Utilities* WIPEDISK and WIPEFILE programs use these.

If you really need grade-A security, DOS can't help. And most power users can break into any system in seconds. Encryption is also a possible solution, but a genuine nuisance. However you can keep casual snoops from getting at your files.

Most tricks involve preventing unauthorized users from booting your hard disk. The only drawback with such techniques is that a snoop can start an otherwise unstartable hard disk system by bringing his own diskette along and booting off it. Still, the following tricks are like locks on desk drawers — they keep the honest people out. If someone wants to get in, he or she will.

When DOS boots, it looks to see whether AUTOEXEC.BAT is in your root directory. If it is, DOS passes control to it. So an easy way to keep the honest people out is to patch COMMAND.COM so it looks for another file, especially one that doesn't have a BAT extension. In fact, if you're the cautious type, it shouldn't. (See the "Booting Up With BERNIE" discussion in the hard disk chapter.)

Once you patch COMMAND.COM to start from a hidden AUTOEXEC.BAT file, the AUTOEXEC.BAT clone can then do the magic you want.

An easy example would be to run an IF ERRORLEVEL program that looked for a strange key combination — such as Shift-Tab — to continue. If you press Shift-Tab (or whatever you set the IF ERRORLEVEL test to detect) the program would forge ahead, and would set things up properly.

But if a user typed any other key, like the Enter key, another IF ERRORLEVEL test in the list of IFs would detect it and jump to a batch file command that would execute a small file that reboots your system.

When a PC boots, its BIOS checks a *flag word* at location 0040:0072. (One word equals two bytes; a flag is a part of memory used to keep track of a condition, such as whether something is set off or on.) If the value of the flag is 1234H, BIOS does a warm boot — the fast Ctrl-Alt-Del type. However, if it finds the value of the flag is not 1234H, BIOS does a cold slow boot, going through its tedious memory and equipment checks.

If you use DEBUG to look at low memory addresses 472 and 473 you'll see 34 12 rather than 12 34, since the PC stores words backwards. The high order byte (12) goes into the higher memory address (473), while the low order byte (34) goes into the lower memory address (472). Despite this, the word takes the lower memory address as its own.

You can use the WARMBOOT.COM and COLDBOOT.COM programs on the accompanying disk for this. The effect is the same. Actually, it's probably more infuriating to a data snooper to make him sit through a long memory diagnostic or two.

To further confound unauthorized users, you can do additional mischief. Make sure you've permanently set your COMMAND.COM to ECHO OFF, or use the ECHO-suppressing techniques mentioned in the chapter on batch techniques. Then, since you no longer have a startup file called AUTOEXEC.BAT, create one with the five lines below and leave only it and COMMAND.COM on your root directory:

```
CLS
ECHO ===== Unauthorized Access =====
ECHO Damage to computer will result if
ECHO it is not turned off immediately.
PROMPT Error
```

If the user tries to run this file, he'll get a warning and a blank screen. If he just TYPEs it, he'll know you mean business. The last line — customizing the PROMPT to say "Error" — is a nice touch, since every time the user tries something, the screen will balk and then just print:

```
Error
```

Even more diabolical is preventing the unauthorized user from trying any of the standard DOS commands. The way to do this is simply to rename the important commands inside COMMAND.COM using DEBUG.

COMMAND.COM maintains a table of internal commands for RENAME, ERASE, etc. Two of these, DIR and TYPE, are the ones a snooper would use in trying to figure out what's going on.

If you rename DIR to something like RID or XYZ, and TYPE to EPYT or QRST, whenever the unauthorized user tries the normal version of these, all he'll get is the irritating message "Bad command or file name" since COMMAND.COM will no longer recognize TYPE or DIR.

You can use DEBUG to change the names of the commands stored inside COMMAND.COM. Load COMMAND.COM into DEBUG and find the file length using RCX. Specify a search from 100 to the length reported by RCX for something like "REN" or "TYPE." Use E to replace them, making sure your new commands are the same size as the old ones. Verify with D, write (W), and quit (Q).

You should keep a real copy of COMMAND.COM somewhere on your disk. Once you've gotten past your IF ERRORLEVEL test and screened out the unauthorized users, you can load a copy of the real COMMAND.COM, as a secondary command processor. (If you ever want to, you can drop down to the phony one by entering EXIT.) Using a secondary command processor like this lets you run all the normal DOS commands. But be careful if you try this since DOS sometimes gets mad if you mix different versions of COMMAND.COM.

But the best simple DOS security tip of all lets you hide all your files — including COMMAND.COM, AUTOEXEC.BAT, CONFIG.SYS, and all your subdirectories — with a very short HIDE.COM program that adjusts the directory listing so DIR won't show them. And you can bring them all back just as easily with UNHIDE.COM. This means that you can hide *everything* in your root directory, presenting the snooper with a bare disk. The files are still there, and they still work, but DIR won't report any.

Of course, CHKDSK /V will still be able to see them, but not all users know this, and you can rename CHKDSK.COM to something like CH.COM, which is far easier to type anyway. Still, any serious user can bring his own DOS disk up to your system and figure out what you did.

This lets you hide and rename your key files and subdirectories, pretty much locking out anyone who doesn't know how to unhide files using DEBUG.

You can hide all your files at once with the command:

```
FOR %F IN (*.*) DO HIDE %F
```

But you won't be able to unhide them this way, since global characters like * or ? can't handle hidden files. If you do try the mass-hide technique, remember to keep UNHIDE.COM (preferably a renamed version of it) on a separate disk or subdirectory. You can't use a hidden UNHIDE.COM file to unhide itself.

The HIDE and UNHIDE programs are on the accompanying disk. An even better program is Charles Petzold's ATTR attribute setter.

The *Norton Utilities* (and other similar programs) make it child's play for anyone to "unerase" a file that you've deleted from your disk. With the latest iteration of Norton's software, all you have to do is type QU (for Quick Unerase) and your data is back unless something else has written over it in the interim.

This is because DOS doesn't actually erase the file; it simply changes the first character in the directory listing (to tell itself that the old file's space on the disk is available for new files) and adjusts the disk's internal location tables accordingly.

If you start to overwrite the file before you get a chance to unerase it, you may lose the beginning of the deleted file, and may have to puzzle over the pieces somewhat, but if it was a text file you can usually rescue much of it.

Norton's WIPEFILE and WIPEDISK programs can obliterate any trace of deleted files by writing a new file over their entire length. You can even have these programs write specially designed bit patterns over the old data area, and re-execute themselves multiple times to make sure what's gone is gone.

So once you've used a program like WIPEFILE on your deleted files, you can breathe easy, right? Don't be so sure. Such programs expunge only those files you know about. But what about the secret copies of your files you don't know about?

Many programs, especially word processors, create temporary files during their normal operation. They all erase these files before they shut down in normal use, so you almost never see them.

But if something unexpected happens and you crash out of the program, you may see a file with a similar filename to one you were just working on, but with a $$$ or TMP extension.

The trouble is that your word processor almost certainly isn't going to erase the temp file any better than the DOS ERASE (or DEL) command, which, as we've seen, doesn't do a very thorough job. And unless you know they're there, you can't obliterate them with a WIPEFILE-type program.

The solution is simple. Before using WIPEFILE, try to use an unerase program like QU. You should before someone else does.

This means UNerasing all the little tiny orphan clusters too that end up strewn around your disk. When it's time to use WIPEFILE, do a maximum disk-wide unerase first, and follow it up with a maximum text search (Norton again). Then wipe out all the files you didn't know existed, and all the little leftover pieces.

For maximum hard disk security, periodically copy all your files to floppies or tape, or to a Bernoulli Box, and WIPEDISK the entire disk. Then reformat the hard disk and copy everything back. The added benefits to this time-consuming task make the project worth the effort. First, you end up with current backups, which you obviously should lock in a safe place. Also, you do away with the inevitable disk fragmentation that results when you write pieces of files over each other. Your files will fly on a newly formatted, nonfragmented disk.

Another security technique is to keep a large harmless file around, and copy it over the file you want to erase before you erase it. This way if someone unerases a file with a name like SECRET they'll see the contents of the harmless file that you used to obliterate the actual sensitive one.

To keep the honest people out of your files, hide a Ctrl-Z, or decimal ASCII character 26 end-of-file marker, near the beginning of a file. When a DOS TYPE command trips over one of these, it stops in its tracks, no matter how long the directory listing says the file actually is.

You can try using DEBUG to imbed an end-of-file hex 1A at the beginning of your files; it will always stop the DOS TYPE command, but it also may stop the file from working properly.

A better tip is to give your files bizarre, high-bit names. This will freeze beginners out of your files, since they won't be able to figure out how to enter the characters to TYPE, load, or run the filenames. (You know — just use Alt + the numeric keypad.)

Or you can try something odd like inserting spaces in the middle of your filenames. DOS chokes on these, but you can use BASIC to manipulate them. And in a pinch, you can substitute wildcards for spaces in DOS and rename any spaced-out file.

You can also use DEBUG to substitute high-bit characters for COMMAND.COM internal commands if you really want to confuse snoopers. Carrying this one step further, you can turn your normal DOS messages, like:

```
Volume in drive C is PC Magazine
Directory of  C:\PROGRAM

34 File(s)    1677312 bytes free
```

into the same kind of high-bit gibberish. If someone boots up and sees undecipherable messages and filenames, odds are he'll give up pretty quickly, thinking you're using some sort of very exotic operating system he couldn't possible figure out.

High-bit messages and filenames, coupled with selectively hidden subdirectories and files, wild-goose-chase AUTOEXEC files, renamed DOS commands, and totally obliterated disk surfaces, should let you sleep a tiny bit easier at night. But they can end up being a pain in the neck for you too.

PC users in corporations often live by a simple rule: if the file contains confidential information, it must be stored on a diskette and kept in a locked desk. Typically some paranoia accompanies this rule, requiring users to turn off the PCs after using a confidential file so nobody can DEBUG the data out of memory, but this is a little extreme outside the CIA.

Another potential trouble area is a print spooler or buffer. Some spoolers hang onto copies of the most recently printed file. If you're nervous about this, reboot after printing something sensitive, and turn any hardware buffers off and on again.

While you're at it, be careful about communications programs that store your password or other secret information in plain ASCII. These days most "comm" software encrypts such information, but users often take advantage of keyboard macro programs to put things like bank account numbers and access codes onto single keys to avoid having to type them in when doing electronic banking. Make sure any program you use for this doesn't make it easy for others to learn more about you than you want them to know.

If you're using a sensitive data base that's much too big and complex for diskettes, another solution is a removable storage medium like the one on Iomega's popular Bernoulli Box.

Another possibility is to use an encryption and decryption program. After using a confidential file, you'd run the encryption program with a password, which scrambles up the file. When you want to use it again, you'd run the decryption program with the same password to unscramble it.

Such encryption schemes are very difficult to break without knowing the password, even if you have access to the decryption program. Moreover, if someone maliciously tries to scramble up the encrypted program, it should be obvious when it's decrypted. For such events you should be keeping diskette backups anyway.

Users often want to know how they can install some sort of password protection on their systems. Infortunately, because of the PC's open architecture, password security is very difficult to implement. Unless you put a special ROM in your system, any smart user can defeat just about any password scheme on a hard disk by booting off a floppy.

It is technically possible to install a password program that cannot be circumvented by a drive A: boot. But this program has to be executed before the PC even attempts to boot. Here's how it works:

When the PC is first turned on, it executes a Power-On Self Test (POST) program coded in the PC's ROM BIOS. This program initializes the system, checks memory, and ultimately boots the operating system from a diskette or hard disk. Before the boot, however, the POST program checks memory locations between hex addresses C8000 and F4000 for the presence of additional ROM programs. Generally these programs must perform some extra system initialization before the PC is booted. In fact, the extra BIOS for the XT hard disk is at hex address C8000. You would have to program a small password routine somewhere in that memory space where it wouldn't conflict with anything else. Moreover, the program must stay in memory when the PC is turned off.

Getting the password program encoded in ROM is a bit extreme. An easier approach is to code it into random access memory on a CMOS RAM memory board with battery backup. CMOS RAM uses very little power — almost none at all while inactive — so a rechargeable battery backup should last for many months.

The board's memory address would be set up to begin at D0000, D8000, E0000 or E8000. The program must be in a special format, explained in the ROM BIOS section of the PC or XT *Technical Reference* manuals under the heading "Adapter Cards with System-Accessible ROM Modules." The code must start off with a hex 55 and AA, to tell the BIOS that it is executable. The third byte is the number of 512 byte blocks in the program (probably 1 for a simple password routine). The program itself begins at the fourth byte. It must return to the BIOS with a far return. You should write the program in assembly language and not use any DOS calls (interrupts 20 and up) because DOS will not be loaded when the program runs. You may use all the BIOS resources for the keyboard and display.

The ROM BIOS does a checksum of the bytes of the program and gives you a terse "ROM" message if they don't add up to zero ignoring overflow above 256. So, you're going to have to add up all the bytes in your program, take the negative, and put that byte somewhere in the file.

One final tip — if you have a security system that disables your keyboard when you walk away from it, be sure to lock up any other input devices, like mice. If you're using

Windows, for instance, someone could come along and use the mouse to do all sorts of damage. Be careful out there.

Communications

We don't really end up printing too many communications tips, but Charles Petzold's TINYCOMM program is a real gem.

As Petzold points out, communication software doesn't have to be complex. And his tiny 49-byte assembler program, when coupled to a five-line BASIC program, will let you hook two computers together in a flash.

One reason a communications program can be so small and still pack a punch is that today's smart, programmable modems do the lion's share of the work. But the program still has to handle the I/O details.

To create TINYCOMM, the smallest "functional" assembly language communications program possible, type in the following TINYCOMM.SCR script using a pure-ASCII word processor or EDLIN. Omit the semicolons and the comments following them. Be sure to leave a blank line above RCX, and press the Enter key after each line, especially the last one with the Q:

```
A
MOV     DL,[005D]           ; Get Parameter
AND     DX,0001
MOV     AH,03               ; Get Comm Status
INT     14
TEST    AH,01               ; If nothing, go on
JZ      011F
MOV     AH,02               ; Read character
INT     14
PUSH    DX
MOV     DL,AL
MOV     AH,02               ; Write to display
INT     21
POP     DX
JMP     0108                ; Loop around
MOV     AH,0B               ; Check Keyboard
INT     21
OR      AL,AL
JZ      0108
MOV     AH,08               ; If char, read it
INT     21
MOV     AH,01               ; Send to modem
INT     14
JMP     0108                ; Loop around
```

```
RCX
31
N TINYCOMM.COM
W
Q
```

When you're all done, make sure DEBUG.COM is handy, and type:

```
DEBUG < TINYCOMM.SCR
```

TINYCOMM uses the ROM BIOS interrupt 14H to read incoming data from the modem and to write outgoing data to the modem. It uses DOS interrupt 21H function calls to read what you type at the keyboard and to write to the display.

TINYCOMM first makes a status call to interrupt 14H. If the status word returned in register AX indicates that the modem has received a character, TINYCOMM calls interrupt 14H again to get the character and then displays it to the screen through DOS. If no character has been received yet, TINYCOMM goes on to check if anything has been typed at the keyboard. If so, it sends the typed character to the modem, again by interrupt 14H. Then it goes back to the top. Notice that in both cases (reading the modem and reading the keyboard), TINYCOMM first checks if anything is ready. It doesn't want to get stuck waiting for a character from either source if none is available.

To use TINYCOMM, first turn on your modem and execute the PC-DOS MODE command to set it up for 300 baud, no parity, 8 data bits, and 1 stop bit:

```
MODE COM1:300,N,8,1
```

Don't try 1200 baud just yet. (If your modem is connected to COM2, substitute that in place of COM1 in the MODE command above.) Now run TINYCOMM by entering:

```
TINYCOMM
```

for a modem connected to COM1, or:

```
TINYCOMM 1
```

for COM2. You're not online yet, but you are in direct connection with your modem.

If you have a Hayes SmartModem or compatible, you can now type in any of the AT attention codes documented in the *User's Guide* or *Technical Reference* that came with the unit. For instance, with the SmartModem 1200 or 1200B, you can enter

```
ATI0
```

to see the product's revision number;

```
ATI1
```

for the modem's ROM checksum, and (with the 1200, but not the 1200B):

```
ATI2
```

to check the integrity of its internal memory. This last instruction will return either "OK" or "ERROR."

The "Smart" in "SmartModem" refers to the modem's ability to interpret such AT codes and to send back appropriate responses. If your phone happens to ring while you're experimenting like this, TINYCOMM will display the word "RING." Similarly, when using your normal communications programs, you may have noticed the words "CONNECT" or "NO CARRIER" displayed when you attempt to place a telephone call. These messages are not produced by your communications package; they all come straight from the modem, whose internal programming generates them.

Try making a call to the PC Magazine Interactive Reader Service bulletin board. To do this, enter:

```
ATD 1-212-696-0360
```

on the east coast, or:

```
ATD 1-415-598-9100
```

on the west coast.

If you have touch-tone service, you can use ATDT instead of ATD. (Even if you have pulse dialing, you might try this command anyway.)

If you're using an external modem, you'll see your modem's OH (Off Hook) light go on and you'll hear the dialing. If the PC-IRS has a free line, you'll hear the PC-IRS carrier signal, quickly followed by your modem answering that carrier signal with its own. The CD (Carrier Detect) light on your modem will go on, you'll see the word CONNECT on the screen, and then the modem will go silent. You're online. When you eventually want to get out of TINYCOMM, just press Ctrl-Break.

If you get a busy signal, eventually your modem will give up and you'll get a NO CARRIER message. You can redial by typing A/, which is the only Hayes control sequence that does not require a preceding AT.

Notice that TINYCOMM is really doing very little in establishing this connection. Almost everything is handled by the modem itself. After you enter ATD and the phone number, the modem waits a couple of seconds for the dial tone before dialing the number and, if it doesn't detect a carrier, it waits another period of time before sending back the NO CARRIER message and placing the phone back on the hook.

You can set these two timings, and many other variable aspects of the SmartModem, with modem control sequences. ATS6, followed by the time in seconds, controls the dial tone wait; ATS7 similarly controls the carrier detect wait. If you want to listen continuously to the carrier signals while you're online, you can enter ATM2 before making the call.

You can't enter these AT codes directly while you're online, because the modem has no way of determining that you want to talk to it instead of to the remote computer. To issue commands while online, you first enter the Hayes escape sequence — three plus signs (+++) in a row — typed quickly. You must wait a second before typing in the first plus sign, and wait a second afterwards before typing anything else. (The modem uses these brief pauses to distinquish its escape sequence from three plus signs that may occur in transmitted data.) If you entered the +++ code properly, you'll get an OK from the modem, indicating that you're in the command state instead of online. After you're done giving commands, ATO returns the modem online.

If you want to use an escape sequence other than three plus signs, that too is programmable, as the Hayes manual explains.

TINYCOMM uses the DOS function call 08H for reading your keystrokes. According to the *DOS Technical Reference* manual, this function call does not echo keystrokes to the screen. So why then can you see your keystrokes as you type them?

Some of the characters you enter at the keyboard will be modem AT control sequences. The modem itself "echoes" these characters back, so TINYCOMM reads them as characters coming from the modem. (You can turn off this modem echoing with the command ATE0. Then when you type an AT code, you won't see it on the screen. Turn this type of modem echoing back on with ATE1.)

When you get online with a remote computer, however, whether it's an information service (such as CompuServe or Dow Jones News Retrieval) or with a bulletin board such as *PC Magazine*'s IRS, the host computer echoes back most of the characters it receives. That's why you'll sense a slight delay between the time you type characters and their display on the screen.

This echoing is often inaccurately referred to as full-duplex communication. A better term is remote-echo or echoplex. It requires that the two computers handle data differently. On your end, your communications program is reading the keyboard and sending the characters out to the modem without echoing them to the display. The host computer to which you are connected sends most of these characters back to you (with a few exceptions) in addition to sending you its own data.

On your receiving end, your program really can't tell whether a particular character was sent by the remote computer or echoed. If you also echoed back to the host computer everything you received, you'd really be thrown for a loop, because the characters would continually be tossed back and forth between the two computers.

When you use a modem to communicate with another PC or some other small computer, you'll probably want to use local echo (often inaccurately called half-duplex). With local echo, each communications program handles the data the same way, by echoing keyboard characters to the screen as they are being typed and sending them out to the modem at the same time.

If you're online but find that you can't see what you type, it simply means that your software is set up for remote echo, but the computer you're talking with thinks you're using local echo. If you see two of every character you type, the cause is just the opposite.

To connect with another PC over the telephone lines, you'll probably want to use local echo. You can do this in one of two ways. First, you can change TINYCOMM to use function call 01 instead of function call 08 for reading from the keyboard. A better way, however, is to instruct the modem itself to echo what you type by entering the control sequence ATF0. (You can later return to remote-echo with ATF1.)

Communicating modems use two separate sets of carrier frequencies, called "Answer" and "Originate," which are independent of which modem is making the phone call. When you call an information service or bulletin board, by convention your modem uses the Originate frequencies. When you connect with another PC, however, you must decide which PC will use Answer and which will use Originate.

The easiest way to establish a connection between two PCs over the telephone lines is to first establish a voice communication. After you decide upon a common baud rate, data bits, parity, and stop bit and have everything set up, the person using Originate frequencies enters:

```
ATD
```

and the other person (using Answer frequencies) enters:

```
ATA
```

The Answer carrier will sound first, followed by the tone from the Originate modem. Now hang up the phones and start typing.

You also must consider how you're going to handle line feeds. When you press the Enter key, you generate only one character, ASCII 13, the carriage return. When your screen receives this character its proper response is simply to move the cursor to the beginning of the current line. The Carriage Return code does not tell the cursor to move down to the beginning of the next line, as well. You need an additional character — a line feed (ASCII 10) — to move the cursor down one line.

Most real communications programs will add the extra line feed, but TINYCOMM will not. Unless you want to change TINYCOMM to do this, you can get around it by typing a Ctrl-J (line feed) after every Enter. Or, instead of pressing Enter, you can press Ctrl-M Ctrl-J. Yes, you can get accustomed to it.

When you use TINYCOMM to go online with another microcomputer, you'll have the opportunity to try out CTTY, one of DOS's most interesting commands. TINYCOMM is ideal for CTTY for two reasons. First, TINYCOMM will not break the modem connection when you leave it by using Ctrl-Break. Many other communications programs will. Second, unlike other communications programs, TINYCOMM just uses interrupt 14H instead of doing anything fancy. (You'll see later this is a deficiency when it comes to more serious communications work.)

To try out CTTY, first use TINYCOMM to establish a modem connection with another microcomputer operated by a friend you trust. This friend does does not need to be using TINYCOMM or even an IBM PC.

Now, instruct your friend to turn off his or her local echo. Then, exit TINYCOMM with Ctrl-Break, and at the DOS command level simply enter:

```
CTTY COM1
```

(or COM2 if that's where your modem is). Your DOS prompt will then appear on your friend's screen and not on yours. If your friend enters DIR, you won't see it but your disk drives will whirr, and the directory listing will appear on the other computer's display. (Now you see why this person should be someone you trust. That DIR could just as easily be a DEL *.*.)

After your friend has been fully amused by using your PC over the telephone line, he or she can enter:

```
CTTY CON
```

At this point, your DOS prompt will appear back on your screen and you can re-enter TINYCOMM to continue your online communication.

CTTY allows another device (in this case the communications port) to be substituted for DOS's normal standard input device (the keyboard) and standard output device (the screen). Any program that uses DOS function calls for keyboard and screen display will then use this alternate device instead of the default CON device. Any of the DOS internal commands (with the exception of CLS) will work, as well as most of the DOS programs such as CHKDSK, EDLIN, and DEBUG.

If your friend tries to run Lotus *1-2-3*, however, it will appear on your screen and accept input from your keyboard. This is because *1-2-3* (like most spreadsheet and word processing programs) does not use DOS for keyboard input and screen output. The BASIC interpreter also does not use DOS for keyboard and screen activities and will not work with CTTY.

For a real treat, if your friend's communications program supports terminal emulation (ANSI or VT-100, for example) you can patch *WordStar* to tell it that it's not running on an IBM PC. *WordStar* will then use DOS for the keyboard and screen function, and you can customize it to use screen control sequences for positioning the cursor and anything else the terminal emulation program allows. Your friend can then use *WordStar* over the telephone lines, even on a Macintosh. To work with *WordStar* at a 300 baud screen update rate is a fascinating experience and one that will allow you to catch a few winks after every Page Down.

TINYCOMM will produce some problems. If you've been using it to communicate with information services or bulletin boards, you've probably already noticed some of these oddities already.

Although TINYCOMM is programmed in assembler and thus, in theory, is very fast, you can't use it at 1200 baud. Try it out by changing the baud rate with MODE and connecting to an information service or bulletin board. If you start at the top of the screen, things seem to go fairly well, but once you get down to the bottom of the screen, you'll notice that TINYCOMM starts missing the first few letters of each line sent from the remote computer.

Communications programs do not normally use interrupt 14H, as TINYCOMM does. This is because interrupt 14H is missing two very important ingredients of normal communication software: buffering and interrupt control. Instead, TINYCOMM simply polls the serial port for data, and if it can't do its polling fast enough, it misses characters. This is what happens when the screen scrolls at 1200 baud. During the time it takes the screen to scroll, several characters at the start of the line are coming through. Real communications programs don't have this problem because they use the serial port's interrupts and buffer all the data.

The interrupt 14H code in the ROM BIOS is not very big as assembly language goes — just a bit over two pages in IBM's *Technical Reference* manual. It works by accessing the 8250 UART (Universal Asynchronous Receiver Transmitter) through I/O ports. These ports are at address 3F8H through 3FFH for COM1 and 2F8H through 2FFH for COM2.

Where you can find documentation on these serial I/O ports depends upon what type of modem you have. The Hayes 1200B internal board modem comes with a hardware reference manual that discusses the ports in detail, since the UART is part of the board. The standalone modem connects by cable to an asynchronous communications port, and the registers involved are also discussed in the documentation for the serial board in any of the technical reference manuals for the PC.

If you are new to UART programming and want to learn how to do it right (instead of using interrupt 14H), be prepared to spend many hours with these few pages of documentation, with the interrupt 14H code (until you understand every line), and in doing lots of experimentation.

The greatest advantage to programming the UART directly through the I/O ports is the ability to enable its interrupts. Instead of polling the UART status, as TINYCOMM does, a real communications program is hardware interrupt driven. The UART can be programmed to generate an interrupt whenever it receives a character or is ready to send another character.

A real communications program will also buffer outgoing and incoming data. When a new character is received, the interrupt routine stores it in a circular buffer. When the main communications program accesses incoming data, it retrieves it from this buffer instead of from the port. Similarly, typed keyboard input goes into another circular buffer. As the UART sends this data, it generates a hardware interrupt when it's done with one and ready for another. That way, the main program can shovel a lot of data to the buffer and not wait for the UART to transmit it all.

If you want to try programming something like this, you might also benefit from looking at the code for keyboard interrupts 9 and 16H, in the ROM BIOS listing. That will show you how circular buffers work. You could add direct UART programming, interrupt control, and buffering to TINYCOMM. But it wouldn't be tiny for long.

Instead, you could try using software supplied with PC-DOS that already has builtin data buffering and interrupt-driven communications logic. You didn't know you already had such software? Sure you do. It's all there in the BASIC interpreter.

Type in the following BASCOMM.BAS program, using a pure-ASCII word processor. Be sure to press the Enter key at the end of each line:

```
100 ' BASCOMM.BAS — Charles Petzold
110 OPEN "COM1:300,E,7,1" AS #1
120 OPEN "SCRN:" FOR OUTPUT AS #2
130 IF NOT EOF(1) THEN PRINT #2,INPUT$(1,1);
140 A$=INKEY$:IF A$ <> "" THEN PRINT #1,A$;
150 GOTO 130
```

Or, load BASIC by typing GWBASIC (if you're using an IBM system) or BASICA (if you're not). Then type in the lines as shown. When you're finished, type:

```
SAVE "BASCOMM,"A
```

to store the program on your disk in ASCII format.

BASCOMM also has a few deficiencies, some of which are repeated from TINYCOMM and some of which are new. Otherwise, it works in almost the same way as TINYCOMM. You enter the modem control sequences directly and press Ctrl-Break when you want to get out.

The new problem you'll encounter is double spacing of all incoming lines of data. This is BASIC "helping" you out by sticking a line feed onto each carriage return. Unfortunately, in remote-echo communications, you don't want that extra line feed.

You'll also notice (as you probably did with TINYCOMM) that at various times you'll see two odd characters appear on your display, the double exclamation point (ASCII 19 or Ctrl-S) and the left pointing triangle (ASCII 17 or Ctrl-Q). These characters have formal ASCII names of DC3 and DC1. The DC stands for Device Control, but in modem communications they are more commonly referred to as XOFF and XON.

When your communications program receives a Ctrl-S (XOFF) character, it interprets this as a signal to stop sending data. The computer you are connected to is telling you (by sending XOFF) that it is doing something else and may suffer a buffer overflow if you continue. Likewise, when the remote computer sends a Ctrl-Q (XON), it is signaling that it can resume receiving data from you.

Your communications program might also want to send XOFF and XON to the remote computer. With the simple BASCOMM program, you can do that yourself simply by pressing Ctrl-S and Ctrl-Q. Generally you stop the flow of data to give yourself time to read it.

XOFF and XON become more important during ASCII file transfers. For instance, if you add some file transfer logic to the BASCOMM program, you must send XOFF when beginning a disk access. This prevents a buffer overflow while you are using the disk. When you are done with the file access and have read enough characters from the buffer to deplete it, you can then send an XON to signal that data transfer may be resumed.

BASIC has several other built-in functions that will help you manage the input buffer. These include LOC (which tells you the number of characters in the input buffer) and LOF (the free space in the buffer). Check out Appendix F of IBM's BASIC 2.0 manual or Appendix C of the BASIC 3.0 manual. Under the heading "An Example Program," you'll find a 20-line BASIC program (documented with lots of comments) that handles both the line feed problem and the XON/XOFF protocol.

Although it's tough to beat the power of several recent (and large) communications programs, you may find a smaller communications program is sometimes preferable, for the same reasons that people sometimes prefer riding a bicycle to driving a car. You're more in control, closer to the ground, unsheltered, and feel every bump.

Chapter 15

When It All Goes Wrong

Funny, isn't it. You get up one perfect morning and the air is crisp and clear, you're full of energy, bubbling with ideas and enthusiasm. You roll up your sleeves and snap on your PC to get some real work done. Along about half a disk later you notice a faint odor of toasting plastic. Nothing to worry about, right? The citizens of Pompeii and Herculaneum probably shrugged it off too, when they caught the first slight whiff of sulphur hissing down the slopes of Vesuvius.

Unlike the ancient Romans, however, you have some control over your fate — at least when it comes to your computer. You can protect yourself from obvious problems simply by exercising some care. The following pages contain some important common sense rules.

Don't erase files blindly. And avoid unnecessary shortcuts. If you want to erase the BAK backup files that are cluttering up your disk, typing:

```
DEL *.B*
```

will take all your BAT batch files and BAS basic files with it. Whenever you're using wildcards to delete files, make it a two-step process. First do a directory listing, with something like:

```
DIR *.B*
```

or whatever the wildcard filespec happens to be. If you see any surprises you can make the filespec more specific (*.BAK for instance) and try again. But if everything is fine, just type:

```
DEL
```

and press the F3 function key. DOS will fill in the wildcard filespec from the previous DIR command.

If you're trying to delete all EXE files with names ending with ABC and you accidentally issue the command:

```
DEL *ABC.EXE
```

DOS will get rid of all your EXE files. This is because DOS stops looking at characters after a wildcard, and interprets the command as:

```
DEL *.EXE
```

If you entered:

```
DEL *ABC.*XE
```

DOS would read this as:

```
DEL *.*
```

You'd know you were in trouble when it prompted you with "Are you sure (Y/N)?" which is the sign it's about to get rid of everything.

Back up every day. There are three kinds of backups: the perfectly organized, meticulously verified kind that nobody does; the adequate "throw it all on a disk and sort it out later" kind that's a lot more common; and the "I'll definitely back up everything tomorrow" lie that freezes you in your seat when you see the inevitable "General failure error reading drive C:" message instead of the DOS prompt.

Remember, even expensive hard disks are just aluminum coated with iron oxide. Would you trust your future to a rusty pie plate? You can purchase lots of fancy commercial backup packages to automate the process. Or you could use the BAC.COM utility on the accompanying disk. And the sensational PC-DOS XCOPY command first introduced with version 3.2 is a real treasure.

XCOPY is speedy and powerful. While the older COPY command reads files from the source disk and then writes them laboriously to the target disk one at a time, XCOPY soaks up as many files as memory can handle, and blasts them onto your backup disk *en masse*.

If you add an /S switch it can copy all the files from all your buried subdirectories, and will duplicate any subdirectory structure on the fly so you don't have to sit there and fumble with MD and CD commands.

Adding a /P will automate the decision-making process by pausing at each file and asking whether you want to copy it. Type a Y and it will make the copy, type a N and it will prompt you for the next file. You can use the /S and /P switches in tandem.

Best of all, by adding a /D switch followed by a date you can have it copy only those files created or changed on the specified date or later. And, of course, it can make backups based on whether the archive bit is set, which lets you skip over files that you haven't changed since the last backup.

DOS has gradually improved the BACKUP and RESTORE commands over the years (so they work faster and won't do idiotic things like write old system files back onto your hard disk over newer ones). And BACKUP is ideal when you're copying files to diskettes that are bigger than the diskette, since it can break them up and have RESTORE put them back together later. But BACKUP stores files in a format that's nonexecutable; you have to run them through RESTORE before you can use them again. XCOPY doesn't change a bit; it keeps files in executable form. The astonishing thing is that XCOPY was written by IBM, which is not noted for producing wonderful PC software. This one is a winner, however. Use it every day.

Don't experiment with original copies of files. If you feel adventurous and want to reformat a data file with unusual margins, or replace carriage returns with something else, or if you decide to see just what DEBUG can do to a program, do it to a copy. Originals are sacred.

Be extremely wary of DOS commands like ASSIGN, FORMAT, and RECOVER. Everyone knows that you have to be careful when using the FORMAT command on a hard disk, and DOS has grown more careful over the years, by asking you to enter volume labels, refusing to proceed unless you enter a drive letter, and printing scary boldface warnings in the manuals.

But if you get fancy and start shuffling your drive letters with ASSIGN, JOIN, and SUBST, and then try to run BACKUP, RESTORE, or PRINT, or if you change the configuration of your system drives frequently by putting RAMdisks in odd places, you're just asking for trouble.

Always stop before you FORMAT and check your intentions, especially late at night or when you've been pounding away at the keyboard for so long you're starting to hear voices from the speaker. And if any beginners ever share your system, use one of the tricks described elsewhere in this book to give yourself added protection. One of the slickest tricks is to patch COMMAND.COM so it thinks FORMAT is an internal command, which will head off any FORMAT requests at the pass unless someone boots your hard disk system off a floppy.

And avoid the RECOVER command entirely. It's nothing but trouble, and can turn every file and subdirectory on your hard disk into an undecipherable puzzle piece that will take you days to reconstruct. If you absolutely must use it, make sure you enter a filename after it. Otherwise, pray your backups are current. To be safe, remove it from your system altogether.

DOS makes it almost too easy to delete files, but there's always the Norton Utilities *to bring your files back from the netherworld.* If you discover that you've just erased a key file or used too broad a wildcard and expunged a whole slate of files, be absolutely sure you don't create or change any other files. Immediately stop what you're doing and drag out your Norton disk (or equivalent), and "unerase" the temporarily lost files.

An innocent-looking command like COPY can also do real damage if you're not careful. First, you could copy an older version of a file over a newer one. Second, if you're concatenating several small files into one big one, and you try combining binary and ASCII files, you can end up mangling the result. You can also end up wiping out a smaller file you're trying to join with others if you use its filename as the name of the final big file. Third, if you're trying to copy a list of program files into another directory (like \BACKUP) and you make a typing error (like COPY *.COM \BAKUP), you may end up concatenating them into one useless mess of a file. Fourth, if you try copying a file over itself and the process somehow gets interrupted, you can end up with garbage where your file used to be. Fifth, if you've been making backup copies of a file to a floppy disk, and the original grows larger than the amount of available space, and you try to copy the oversized file anyway, DOS will erase the previous copy on the floppy. Sixth, if you've forgotten you have an old file on your disk with the same name as the one you're giving to the copy of a file you're about to make, you'll lose the contents of the old file. Seventh, if you try copying a file to another drive with a command like COPY MYFIL B: and you accidentally type a semicolon rather than a colon after the B, you'll end up with a copy on the same drive as MYFIL called B. Think before you copy.

You may think this one's obvious, but guard against stupid power problems. Don't plug your system into a rat's nest of cubetaps and four-way plugs that are so heavy they're falling out of the wall socket. Don't string your power cord across the room. Don't plug into a circuit shared with power-greedy appliances like air conditioners and heating elements. And don't put a power director or power strip on the floor beneath your desk where your toe is going to tapdance on the on/off switch.

Don't ever change add-in boards with the power on. And be careful about static electricity — touch your stereo, a radiator, or a lamp when you shuffle over to your system after petting the cat in the winter. A spark may not seem like much, but those hundreds of thousands of volts can really do damage when they're hurtling down pathways a micron or two wide.

Don't buy floppy disks that are so cheap you can't believe the price. Your data is worth the extra few cents. If you format them and see "bad sector" messages, throw them out, or use them for emergencies. One of the worst sounds known to mankind is the noise of a cheap sandpaper disk grinding down your drive heads.

Watch out when redirecting commands and files. The command:

```
SORT < DATA.FIL
```

will sort the contents of the DATA.FIL file on column one and display the results onscreen. But:

```
SORT > DATA.FIL
```

will trash your DATA.FIL and give it a length of 0. Be careful when using MORE (which, when used backwards, will wipe out your file and replace it with a two-byte file containing just a solitary carriage return and line feed) or any other filter. Redirection is a powerful tool. But learn the rules first — so you can avoid doing things like using the TYPE command to redirect the contents of a file that contains an ASCII 26 somewhere in it, since this tells TYPE to screech to a halt. Also, don't use >, <, or | signs in batch files. If you put a line in your batch file that says:

```
ECHO ----> Enter a key:
```

DOS will think you are asking it to create a file called Enter and use ECHO to redirect text from that line into the file. Even something as innocent as:

```
REM Now returning to the C> prompt
```

ends up generating a file called PROMPT. In later DOS versions you can include such signs in batch files if you put quotes around them:

```
ECHO The "|" is a pipe sign
```

Caveats are usually given for a reason. When you see a program listed somewhere that says "use this on color monitors only" you might as well place the call to your insurance agent before you try it on your monochrome display. Contrary to popular belief, software can indeed destroy hardware. You can break a hard disk activator arm by slamming it into a place where it wasn't supposed to go, or burn out a monitor in an instant by fiddling with the video controller.

If you ever see the message "Are you sure (Y/N)?" when you don't expect it, the answer is always NO. If you're trying to erase a file and you make a typing mistake you can accidentally be telling your operating system to erase everything in a subdirectory. That's what these warnings are for.

Don't mix hex and decimal. The single easiest mistake to make when working with DEBUG is to slip in a decimal value, or subtract 1 from a number like 100 and think the result is 99 when it's really FF. Work with copies of your files, never originals. Educate your fingers so they type only in hex.

And, whenever you're using DEBUG to work with absolute sectors rather than files, and you're about to use the W command — pause and stare at what you're about to enter before going near the Enter key. Remember too that DEBUG treats drive A: as 0 rather than 1. One little slip here, especially when you're fooling with something like the FAT or directory, and it's time to hunt for the backup disks.

Be extremely careful when trying new memory-resident software, especially when you already have other resident software loaded. These things can be tricky and unpredictable enough by themselves; throwing a few together in memory and watching them fight for the same interrupts is not a pretty sight. It's also a recipe for a power-switch reboot. Don't work with any unsaved data files when you're testing out resident software interactions. And to be really safe, use a TSR manager like the INSTALL/REMOVE duo on the accompanying disk, or any of the similar commercial packages available.

Don't mix utilities from different DOS versions, and avoid having different, patched versions of COMMAND.COM on your disk. One of the most chilling messages you can see is "Cannot load COMMAND, system halted." And you're a lot more likely to see it when you mix and match DOS parts.

If you use a RAMdisk, stop working at least once or twice an hour and copy your work to a more tangible medium. RAMdisks are fast. But they can also lose data in the blink of an eye if you bump the power cord, or if the generator at your local power company burps, or if your software just decides to lock up. RAMdisk software ought to come with a little clock that beeps every 15 minutes to remind you to back up your ephemerall files.

Treat hard disks as if they contained little booby-trapped bottles of nitroglycerine. Don't bang, drop, nudge, tap, stomp, poke, jostle, smack, shove, whack, thump, pound, or otherwise knock into any system with a humming hard disk. One little bump is all it takes to send the drive heads plowing into the disk surface. From then on you can just kiss your data goodbye. Be especially careful with systems that are mounted on the floor, since these tend to attract a disproportionate share of kicks, hammer blows from vacuum-cleaners, and other miscellaneous assaults.

Don't mix high-density and low-density floppies, especially when dealing with 720K and 1.44M diskettes. It shouldn't be a problem, but because of the way these disks are formatted, it is. Label potentially confusing disks after you format them, and don't intermingle high- and low-density formats.

Take care in using the CTTY NUL command in batch files. This disconnects your keyboard until the batch file sees a restorative CTTY CON command. If something unexpected happens in the interim, all you can do is reach for the power switch.

It's a great convenience to redirect keystroke scripts into DEBUG rather than having to type each command. This lets you check your typing before you proceed, and modify long, previous DEBUG instructions just by changing the file. But be sure to include blank lines where indicated (after ending A commands) and to include a carriage return at the end of each line, especially the last one that quits.

If you have sensitive files on your disk, don't leave words like "CONFIDENTIAL" or "SECRET" in them if any other users have access to your system. It's easy to scan across the disk for such text, which lets anyone pinpoint such files. And give any sensitive files or subdirectories innocent-sounding names, not names like SECRET.1 or CONFDNTL.

While you shouldn't make it too easy for someone to get at your confidential files, don't make it too hard. If you encrypt your files, don't use keys like F$J#DV!N&1E@ unless you're sure you can remember them later.

If you erase sensitive files, make sure they're gone. Use a utility like Norton's WIPEFILE, or else someone may use Norton's UNERASE utilities to bring the files back to life. And while you're at it, tell Norton's program to wipe out all erased files. You may get rid of the latest version of a confidential report, but if you're not careful, you can end up leaving previously erased BAK or $$$ copies lurking on the disk. Some word processors create backup or temporary work files without your knowledge, and erase them before you exit the program. A snooping co-worker can revive these just as easily as any other "erased" file.

If you lock your system and you have mouse attached, hide the mouse or lock it up too. A mouse is simply an alternate input device, and a knowledgeable user can use it instead of the locked keyboard to change or examine your files.

If you have to print a sensitive document, turn off the printer when you're done, and reset your system as well. It's possible that parts or all of the file are still buffered in memory when you finish.

Be careful when "unerasing" hidden files left by commercial software. Some benighted software, in an effort to be as greedy and hostile as possible, scrambles your disk sectors and then hides a file in these sectors. If you have software like this installed in a subdirectory, and you want to get rid of it, and you try deleting all the files and then using the RD command to remove the subdirectory, you'll get some version of a:

```
Invalid path, not directory,
or directory not empty
```

message. You can see the file by running CHKDSK /V or by using some of the utilities on the accompanying disk. And you can unhide it and delete it. But the sectors will remain scrambled, which can bring your operating system to its knees later. If commercial software comes with a deinstallation program, use it instead of trying to erase all the files yourself. It will usually repair any damage it's caused during installation.

Assume any software that you download from any source other than one that rigorously tests everything, such as Compuserve or PC Magazine's Interactive Reader Service, is dangerous until proven otherwise. You can use some of the utilities on the accompanying disk to peek inside any just-downloaded programs and look for messages such as "Gotcha!" Or you can run it on a floppy disk system with a RAMdisk configured as drive C: and watch what it does.

If someone wants to corrupt your system, and you like to experiment with downloaded software, you really can't protect yourself entirely. Most bulletin boards are careful to screen out such potentially dangerous software, and much of the electronically distributed software available today is sensational. But nasty "virus" software and "trojan horse" programs do get around. Unless you trust your source implicitly, watch out for programs that intentionally wipe out the files on your hard disk.

Don't use DISKCOPY except in two cases — when you're making a backup copy of a new commercial software disk, or when you've somehow damaged a disk and want to work on it with DEBUG or Norton Utilities-*type products.* For all other copies, format a blank disk and use the COPY *.* or XCOPY command to make the backups.

Except when copy protection schemes are involved, DISKCOPY will make an exact replica of the original disk. This is bad for two reasons:

When you put a lot of wear and tear on a a diskette — erasing, adding, and changing data frequently — you end up fragmenting your files. DOS ends up chopping them into small pieces and pigeonholes the pieces in lots of different locations. Then when it has to load or write a fragmented file, DOS takes a long time to sort everything out. In fact, if you use floppies extensively, you should periodically format a blank disk and copy the files from the older disk to the newly formatted one to enhance performance. Copying them gets rid of the fragmentation — at least until you start slicing and dicing them again.

Also, while DOS is supposed to protect against it, it's possible when using DISKCOPY to copy good information from one disk onto a magnetically unsound area on another without knowing it. The disk formatting process guards against this, but DISKCOPY won't reformat a disk unless it has to. If a sector has gone bad since the disk was formatted, it's possible to write good information onto a bad sector and lose it.

Using DISKCOPY to make exact replicas of commercial disks is certainly a good idea. And if you somehow mangle a disk and want to dig beneath the surface and try to fix it, you should use DISKCOPY to duplicate the broken disk and try to repair the copy. This way if you make matters worse, you can always create another DISKCOPY and try the process again.

It's not always smart to set BREAK to ON. The default DOS setting is OFF, which means DOS will check to see if you pressed Ctrl-C or Ctrl-ScrollLock only during a handful of routine screen, output, and keyboard operations. If you're running a program that chews data all day long and doesn't do much I/O, and you have to break out of it periodically, you may want to set BREAK to ON so DOS will check for Ctrl-C or Ctrl-Scroll-Lock presses far more frequently.

But this can have a down side as well, since a break signal can grind certain programs to a halt. If you're running *WordStar*, for instance, and you pound incessantly on Ctrl-C you can crash out of the program without saving the file you were working on. Since Ctrl-C happens to be a *WordStar* command to scroll the screen up (same as a PgDn), this can be dangerous when you're paging through a long file. Worse, this may bypass the program's normal cleanup operations (such as resetting interrupt vectors), which can clobber subsequent programs you try to run.

Don't assume you've copied files correctly just because the VERIFY command is active. DOS lets you add a /V switch to the COPY and XCOPY commands, or issue a VERIFY ON command, that supposedly ensures data integrity by verifying that the original and copy are the same.

Unfortunately, this process uses a CRC check, which can catch gross errors but is not utterly foolproof. The COMP command, on the other hand, compares both files byte-by-byte and is more reliable. Unfortunately, COMP.COM is crude and slow, and will stop working if it stumbles over a scant ten mismatches. The generic DOS FC.EXE File Compare utility is vastly better, and it's a real mystery why IBM gave users the pathetic COMP command instead of the far superior FC.

In any event, if you're validating copies, COMP should work just fine, and will uncover potential problems that can fool /V or VERIFY.

Using your computer in a thunderstorm is a bit risky, since lightning strikes can foul up the power lines. If you're nervous about direct lightning hits and you put a lightning arrester in the power circuit, don't forget to isolate the phone line to your modem. A wire's a wire.

Never switch diskettes in the middle of an aborted operation. If you try to copy files to a floppy and DOS for some reason interrupts the process and pauses, and you realize you put the wrong diskette in the drive, don't just remove the wrong floppy and put in the right one. DOS may still think the old one is there and copy data to the wrong place on the new one, which will damage it. Instead, to be safe, stop what you were doing and issue a nonwriting command for that drive like DIR to let DOS know you've switched disks.

PART IV

The Utilities DOS Forgot

Over the past few years, *PC Magazine* has published one or more sophisticated assembly language utilities in each issue. While many of these are extremely powerful (and even rival commercial software packages in some cases) they were meant to be educational as well as useful. Each utility is accompanied by detailed text explaining how a particular aspect of the PC works, and revealing how each program was constructed. And a profusely commented copy of the assembler code for each is normally published along with the article.

The editors put every program through an extensive testing and refining process before it's published. Each utility is commissioned because it fills a specific need that DOS (and sometimes even commercial software packages) can't handle. Readers download over 15,000 copies of these utilities each day, seven days a week, from *PC Magazine*'s electronic Interactive Reader Service. And the number is constantly climbing.

While the programs are powerful, useful, and extremely popular, space limitations in the magazine prevent us from adding things like fancy opening screens and extensive help systems. And while we torture-test them on a wide range of hardware running all important versions of the operating system, we can't possibly try these on every last clone and every possible configuration.

In addition, new hardware and software releases occasionally do unexpected things that step on these programs' toes. Some of these utilities make assumptions based on information that is reliable at the time they are developed, but may later change. And since they can't devote huge sections of code to handling some of the more ill-behaved memory-resident programs, be sure to try our programs on your system with all your normal resident programs and utilities in place, and no data files open, to make sure everything will coexist smoothly before you install them permanently.

Many of these programs — such as DR, RN, CO, BROWSE, SPECTRUM, VTREE, ATTR, KEY-FAKE, NO, SWEEP, DOSKEY, SETUP, BAC, and INSTALL/REMOVE — have become instant classics and are collectively hard at work on millions of systems today. (And they've made celebrities out of *PC Magazine* programmers like Charles Petzold, Michael Mefford, Jeff Prosise, Robert Hummel, and John Dickinson.) They really are, as one grateful user put it, "the utilities that DOS forgot."

This disk contains the most popular programs from the magazine's Programming, Utilities, and Lab Notes columns, as well as a few from other technical sections, and some never published before. (Many of the manual entries for the larger programs from *PC Magazine*'s Programming and Lab Notes columns were written by *PC Magazine* Technical Editor Craig Stark.)

The disk also contains lots of smaller, single-purpose programs from *PC Magazine*'s User-to-User and PC Tutor columns. Many of these are designed to attack one specific problem and provide effective, often ingenious solutions. We've collected the very best of these compact, power-packed utilities, tweaked them to work even a bit better, and put them into a handy toolkit that will help boost your productivity through the roof. And we've added a slate of new ones never before published to fill in the gaps.

Some of these utilities are very slick indeed, and show a lot of polish and dazzle. Others aren't so fancy — it's hard to put glittery opening screens or miles of menus in something that's 200 bytes long. Some are tiny and rely on DOS or BIOS to do all the hard work. But each one gets a specific job done. Once you try these power tools you'll end up using some of them every day and wondering how you ever worked productively without them.

We've tested and refined these program over the years, but again, as with any new utilities, test them first before you start using them with unsaved files floating around in RAM. You wouldn't plug a dozen electric saws and drills into the same outlet, and you shouldn't blindly use these software tools without testing them with the software that you use every day. Strange interactions sometimes take place, especially if you're working with memory-resident software. Take special pains if you're running a program like *Side-Kick* that takes over your system, or if you're trying a lot of the memory-resident programs from this disk at the same time. You can use INSTALL and REMOVE to juggle any memory-resident programs, and PCMAP to see what's loaded where.

These utilities were all written before DOS 4.0 was released. The vast majority of them will work just fine under any version of DOS from 2.0 through 4.0. However, a few of them use undocumented tricks that version 4.0 just doesn't understand. RN, for instance, relies on a clever technique to read the contents of your hard disk far faster than DOS would normally allow. DOS 4.0 doesn't support this trick — but you don't really need RN with later versions since DOS 4.0 provides a utility much like RN in its Shell. PCMAP works a bit differently as well, but again, users of version 4.0 can rely on the DOS MEM/DEBUG command instead. SCROLL2/WAITASEC, WINDOWS, and BOOTREC.PCM also chafe under version 4.0.

If some of the programs don't seem to work, odds are that it's either because you have other TSR programs already resident in memory, or because you're using a non-IBM system with a fussy BIOS. You can't do anything about the second problem, but INSTALL and REMOVE can help you sort out most memory conflicts.

Summary of Programs

Chapter 17: BASIC Programs

Chapter 16

Assembly Language Programs

APPBK **Command**	Michael J. Mefford

Purpose: Reminds you of appointments at the times you specify; provides additional optional hourly chime and continuous on-screen date/time display.

Format: [d:][path]APPBK

or

[d:][path]APPBK [f,][b,][s,][h,][a]

Remarks: APPBK is a memory-resident utility that is normally loaded through your AUTOEXEC.BAT file. It must be loaded after any system time/date setting routines, and before loading *SideKick* (if used).

Pressing Alt-R opens the onscreen APPBK window, in which you enter your appointments. Enter times as 2:00, not 02:00, and include the A or P before the M in the window. You can edit your appointment list using the F1 and F3 keys, by overstriking letters, and with the deleting backspace key. F2 toggles an hourly chime on and off; F4 similarly toggles a continuous onscreen display of the time and date.

An alarm will sound at the appointment times specified. Additionally, should you be away from your desk and not hear the reminder, your first keystroke following the alarm will pop up the reminder window. To close the window, press Esc or the Alt-R (default) APPBK trigger key.

At the time it is loaded, APPBK may be given alternative parameters for its color (f), border color (b), trigger-key scan code (s), hourly chime frequency (h), and alarm frequency (a). The default values are 7,112,19,2217,2960. Tables of acceptable alternative parameter values are contained on the following pages. In entering parameters, separate each with a comma. Commas alone may be used for initial parameters you do not wish to change.

Examples: `APPBK ,,,1760`

would change only the frequency (tone) of the hourly chime (the h parameter).

Parameter Tables

Color Codes (f and b Parameters)

Foreground	Background	Color Adaptor Color	Foreground	Color
0	0	Black	8	Grey
1	16	Blue	9	Light blue
2	32	Green	10	Light green
3	48	Cyan	11	Light cyan
4	64	Red	12	Light red
5	80	Magenta	13	Light magenta
6	96	Brown	14	Yellow
7	112	White	15	Bright white

Foreground	Monochrome Adaptor Background	Color
0	0	Black
7	112	White
15	na	Bright white

Notes:

1. Add foreground color to the background color to arrive at parameter number. For example, blue letters on cyan (light blue) would be 48 + 1 = 49.

2. Defaults are 7 (white on black) for the reminder field (foreground) and 112 (black on white) for the frame (border).

Scan Codes for ALT-KEY Combinations (s Parameter)

Code	Key	Code	Key	Code	Key	Code	Key
16	Q	30	A	44	Z	120	1
17	W	31	S	45	X	121	2
18	E	32	D	46	C	122	3
19	R	33	F	47	V	123	4
20	T	34	G	48	B	124	5
21	Y	35	H	49	N	125	6
22	U	36	J	50	M	126	7
23	I	37	K			127	8
24	O	38	L			128	9
25	P					129	0
						130	-
Default is 19 (Alt R)						131	=

Tone/Frequency (h and a Parameters)

A	55	110	220	440	880	1760	3520	1740	14080
A#	58	117	233	466	932	1857	3714	7428	14856
B	62	123	247	494	988	1976	3952	7904	15808
C	65	131	262	523	1046	2093	4186	8372	16744
C#	69	139	277	554	1109	2217	4434	8868	17736
D	74	149	294	587	1175	2349	4698	9396	18792
D#	78	156	311	622	1245	2489	4978	9956	19912
E	82	165	330	659	1319	2637	5274	10548	21096
F	87	175	349	698	1397	2794	5588	11176	22352
F#	93	185	370	740	1480	2960	5920	11840	23680
G	98	196	392	784	1568	3136	6272	12544	25088
G#	104	208	415	831	1661	3322	6644	13288	26576

Note: Middle C is 262. The defaults are 2217 (C#) for the hourly chime and 2960 (F#) for the alarm chime.

Notes: While APPBK is compatible with most applications programs and resident utilities, complete compatibility cannot be assured. It cannot, for example, be used with *XyWrite*.

ASC   Jeff Prosise
Command

Purpose: Provides a pop-up ASCII chart showing decimal, hexadecimal, and character equivalents for the full IBM character set.

Format: `[d:][path]ASC`

Remarks: ASC.COM is a memory-resident utility that is normally loaded at bootup, via your AUTOEXEC.BAT file. Once loaded, pressing Alt-A pops up the first page (32 ASCII codes) of the display window over any currently active applications program. The Up- and Down-Arrow, PgUp and PgDn, and Home and End keys access the remaining ASCII display pages. Pressing Esc closes the window, restoring the original screen display.

In operation, ASC.COM requires approximately 2.5K of RAM. It is compatible with most applications and TSR (terminate and stay resident) programs that do not themselves require the Alt-A key combination, and it may be used with monochrome, color, or EGA monitors.

Notes: You may use DEBUG to modify the default border, text, and header colors of ASC.COM. These values, initially 0FH, 1FH, and 1EH, respectively, are located at offsets 014D through 014F in the .COM file. For use with a composite monochrome display, the values 70H, 07H, and 07H are suggested.

ASK   Yan Seiner
Batch file command

Purpose: Combines a keyboard input facility that returns ERRORLEVEL codes with automatic prompting, in a single command.

Format: `[d:][path]ASK prompt_string`

Remarks: Many users take advantage of keyboard input routines that control IF
ERRORLEVEL batch branching. However, in virtually all cases, the
input routines need to be preceded by an ECHO statement prompting the
user to strike a particular key.

ASK.COM combines ERRORLEVEL setting and user prompting in a
single command. Like ECHO, ASK prints the text following it on the
same line. However, unlike ECHO, ASK.COM waits for the user to
enter a keystroke. It ANDs each input character with DF to turn everything uppercase and make all entries case INsensitive, and it echoes the
keystroke (in its uppercase version) to the screen.

In addition, ASK gives "y" and "n" entries special treatment, by printing
out the full words "Yes" and "No."

Examples: Use ASK.COM the same way you'd use ECHO. So if your batch file includes the line:

`ASK Want to back up your files (Y/N)?`

ASK will display the line:

`Want to back up your files (Y/N)?`

onscreen and wait for a reply. You can then test the ERRORLEVEL in a
series of IF statements. The CHECK.BAT batch file below shows how
to stack the IF ERRORLEVEL tests, with the largest numbers at the top.

```
ECHO OFF
:BADCHAR
ASK Do you want to run CHKDSK (Y/N)?
IF ERRORLEVEL == 90 GOTO BADCHAR
IF ERRORLEVEL == 89 GOTO RUNCHK
IF ERRORLEVEL == 79 GOTO BADCHAR
IF ERRORLEVEL == 78 GOTO GOODCHAR
GOTO BADCHAR
:GOODCHAR
ECHO You didn't want to run it
GOTO END
:RUNCHK
CHKDSK
:END
```

This batch file will ask if you want to run CHKDSK; if you answer N or n it will echo No to the screen and jump to the message saying you didn't want to run it. If you answer Y or y it will jump to the CHKDSK command near the bottom and run it.

Notes: ASK.COM won't check to see if a keystroke is valid; it will happily munch on anything you feed it from the keyboard. To modify the program so that it's case sensitive, replace the:

```
AND AL,DF
```

at location 11E with two NOPs (the code for a NOP is 90):

```
DEBUG ASK.COM
E 11E 90 90
W
Q
```

ATSIZE (and SIZE) Command(s)   Art Merrill

Purpose: Calculates the storage requirements of a file or group of files, based on the number of DOS clusters necessary to make floppy disk and hard disk copies. This uses a value of 2K for AT cluster size.

See SIZE.

ATTR (Attribute) Command   Charles Petzold

Purpose: Lets you display and modify archive, system, hidden, and read-only file attributes.

Format: `[d:][path]ATTR`

or

`[d:][path]ATTR *.*`

or

```
[d:][path]ATTR [+A|-A] [+S|-S] [+H|-H] [+R|-R]
[d:][path]filename[.ext]
```

Remarks: Entering ATTR without any parameters, as in the first format shown above, produces a help display (essentially identical to the third form above) that shows which file attributes can be changed.

ATTR.COM permits the use of the global ? and * characters (as in the second format above). Entering ATTR *filename* displays a specific file's attributes. For example:

```
ATTR IBMBIO.COM
```

returns the display:

```
IBMBIO.COM      Arc      Sys Hid R-O
```

showing that the Archive, System, Hidden, and Read-Only bits of the attribute byte are set for this file.

When wildcards are used to list the attributes of all the files in a directory, subdirectory names are shown as Dir (between the Arc and Sys in the example above). Unlike the DOS DIR command, ATTR lists hidden files, whether sought by specified filename or through a *.* listing. However, ATTR does not show volume names or the dot and double-dot entries in subdirectories.

The syntax for changing file attributes is indicated in the third format above. After typing ATTR (and a space) you simply precede the file specification with a plus or minus sign, followed by the letter A (Archive), S (System), H (Hidden), or R (Read-Only). A plus sign turns on the specified attribute; a minus sign turns it off. More than one attribute can be changed at once, and the attribute-designating letters may be entered in any order and in upper- or lowercase. No space may be used between the plus or minus and the letter that follows it, however.

Examples: To convert the file 88TAX.WKS to hidden and read-only, you would enter:

```
ATTR +H +R 88TAX.WKS
```

Since DOS itself normally sets the Archive bit, entering:

```
ATTR 88TAX.WKS
```

would produce the display:

```
88TAX.WKS        Arc      Hid R-O
```

Since the Hidden attribute has been set, however, the DIR command will produce the message, "File not found." And since the Read-Only flag has also been set, a DEL command will produce the message, "Access denied."

BAC   John Dickinson
Command

Purpose: Backs up all (or selected) files in a directory to hard or floppy disks, permitting disk changes when target disks become full.

Format: `[d:][path]BAC [d:][path]filename[.ext] [d:][path]`

Remarks: Unlike the DOS COPY command, BAC.COM permits you to change (formatted) target disks when backing up files to disk. Furthermore, it backs up only files whose date stamp is later than those of identically named files on the target disk. Unlike BACKUP, BAC does not change the setting of the archive bit. Also, files copied with BAC.COM are fully usable at all times; they do not need to first go through a RESTORE process.

BAC.COM supports the use of global (* and ?) characters in filenames and extensions. It does not, however, permit you to REName files during copying.

Examples: You are working at a PC AT with a hard disk drive (C:) on which you keep your copy of BAC.COM, and you want to back up all the .DOC files stored on a 1.2-Mb floppy disk (drive A:) onto regular 360K disks (drive B:). Since these .DOC files will require approximately 600K, you must have two formatted blank floppy disks ready to use in drive B:. From the C> prompt, you enter:

```
BAC A:*.DOC B:
```

When the first target disk in drive B: is full, you will be prompted to change disks.

Notes: BAC.COM compares the date stamps of identically named files and will not overwrite a newer version with an older one. This may cause files to be skipped if you don't keep your date/time current. Also, for best results, keep the number of files in any directory under 255.

BIOS   Robert L. Hummel
Command

Purpose: Displays the values that BIOS returns for each keypress or key combination.

Format: `[d:][path]BIOS`

Remarks: When you press any key, the keyboard controller tells your system BIOS which physical key was struck by reporting its scan code (a proprietary number assigned by IBM to identify the physical key layout).

However, scan codes don't directly tell your system what you had in mind when you pressed a particular key. When you typed an A, you might have been trying to enter a lowercase a, or an uppercase A, or a Ctrl-A, or an Alt-A. It's up to your system's BIOS to interpret everything properly.

BIOS interrupt 9 normally retrieves the scan codes from the keyboard, looks at the status of the various shift keys, and figures out what you were trying to type. Certain keys and key combinations (such as Ctrl-3 or the 5 on the numeric keypad when it's in cursor mode) aren't recognized by the BIOS, and any program that depends on BIOS keyboard services can't use these.

However, if you typed something simple — like a lowercase a — that translates to a normal ASCII character, the BIOS places the single-byte ASCII code for it in the keyboard buffer, followed by the "make" scan code for that key. (When you press a key the keyboard controller identifies which physical key it was by generating a make code; when you release it the controller generates a "break" code with a value hex 80 (decimal 128) higher than the make code.)

If BIOS determines that the character is not ASCII, it puts an extended ASCII code in the keyboard buffer, followed by a zero. BIOS.COM will display the hexadecimal values that BIOS returns for each key. Pressing the space bar will exit the program and return to DOS, so it won't report what BIOS returns each time you tap a space (3920H).

Notes: Enhanced keyboard users face an additional problem. To access the added keys (like F11 and F12), the new BIOS keyboard functions (10H, 11H, and 12H) must be used in place of 0, 1, and 2. The NEWKEYS program by Charles Petzold in this section lets programs take advantage of these new functions.

(See Robert Hummel's SCAN program in this section for more details on scan codes.)

The BIOS.COM program was originally written to display codes continuously on the same line, which saved space if you wanted to examine a lot of keys in a row. However this version inserts carriage returns to put each code on a line by itself, which makes them easier to examine. If you want to remove the carriage returns and display everything continuously, use DEBUG to make the following patch:

```
DEBUG BIOS.COM
F 136 LA 90
W
Q
```

BLANKINS   Jozef H. Khoe and Paul Somerson
Command

Purpose: Blanks the screen temporarily by turning the colors to black-on-black without changing the onscreen text. Pressing the Ins key restores the original colors (see note) and text.

Format: [d:][path]BLANKINS

Remarks: You can use this to prevent an image from burning itself into the phosphor, or to blank the screen temporarily if you have to walk away from your system and you don't want anyone to see what's on your screen.

You can change the key that reactivates things by patching address 12C. To change the restorative key to Shift-Tab and make a copy of the program called BLNKSHTB.COM, you'd type:

```
DEBUG BLANKINS.COM
E 12C 0F
N BLNKSHTB.COM
W
Q
```

The lists of possible reactivation keys and their hex codes are shown in the charts below.

Function Key Combinations		Extended Hex Value
F1 through	F10	3B through 44
Shift-F1 through	Shift-F10	54 through 5D
Ctrl-F1 through	Ctrl-F10	5E through 67
Alt-F1 through	Alt-F10	68 through 71
Alt-1 through	Alt-10	78 through 81

Key	Hex	Key	Hex
Alt-A	1E	Alt-N	31
Alt-B	30	Alt-O	18
Alt-C	2E	Alt-P	19
Alt-D	20	Alt-Q	10
Alt-E	12	Alt-R	13
Alt-F	21	Alt-S	1F
Alt-G	22	Alt-T	14
Alt-H	23	Alt-U	16
Alt-I	17	Alt-V	2F
Alt-J	24	Alt-W	11
Alt-K	25	Alt-X	2D
Alt-L	26	Alt-Y	15
Alt-M	32	Alt-Z	2C

Miscellaneous Key	Hex
Shift-Tab	0F
Alt--	82
Alt-=	83
Home	47
Cursor Up	48
PgUp	49
Cursor Left	4B
Cursor Right	4D
End	4F
Cursor Down	50
PgDn	51
Ins	52
Del	53
Ctrl-PrtSc	72
Ctrl-Cursor Left	73
Ctrl-Cursor Right	74
Ctrl-End	75
Ctrl-PgDn	76
Ctrl-Home	77
Ctrl-PgUp	84

Notes: 1.   When you press Ins (or any other key you've used to restore the screen) BLANKINS.COM will reset the colors to the ones in effect at the cursor when you started the program. If you use lots of different colors on the screen at once this won't restore them all.

If you want to adapt this so it will clear the screen after you press the restorative key, you can create a variation of it called BLANKCLS.COM, by typing:

```
DEBUG
E 100 30 FF B4 08 CD 10 50 30
E 108 FF E8 10 00 30 E4 CD 16
E 110 3C 00 75 F8 80 FC 52 75
E 118 F3 58 88 E7 B8 00 06 31
E 120 C9 BA 4F 18 CD 10 B4 02
E 128 30 FF 31 D2 CD 10 C3
N BLANKCLS.COM
RCX
```

```
2F
W
Q
```

To patch BLANKCLS so it uses a different restorative key, change the byte at address 116.

2.   BLANKINS.COM is hard-wired for 25 x 80 screens only. It restores the color by filling every other byte in video memory with the desired attribute value. Don't use this on screens longer than 25 lines.

BLOAD   Michael J. Mefford
Command

Purpose: Loads graphics images previously saved by BSAVE.COM onto the screen.

See DRAW.

BOOTREC.PCM   Charles Petzold and Robert L. Hummel
New boot record

> **Warning:** this is a potentially dangerous command. Read instructions carefully before trying it. If you're at all nervous, DON'T try it. If you do try it, check your typing very carefully!.

Purpose: You can't legally distribute a bootable DOS disk, since Microsoft (and its customers such as IBM) won't allow you to sell or give away the three system files that every disk needs to start operating. Users who try to boot disks without these system files will simply see a message:

```
Non-System disk or disk error
Replace and strike any key when ready
```

In most cases users can make such disks bootable by putting their own copies of the system files onto these disks, but the terse error message above doesn't explain how. And it's so unfriendly that it can create a bad impression.

BOOTREC.PCM is a brand new boot record that lets a diskette without the DOS system files display a complete screenful of information instead of those two nasty lines. If you're distributing a legal disk without the system files on it you can have BOOTREC.PCM load an entire, attractive screenful of information welcoming users and telling them how to proceed.

Format: Assuming you're working with a double-sided 5-1/4 inch diskette in drive A:, to use this new boot record, you have to do the following:

1.   Take a brand new disk from out of the box and format it with a /B parameter:

```
FORMAT A: /B
```

2.   Add a volume label to the disk:

```
LABEL A:
```

(Then when DOS prompts you for one, type in whatever volume label is appropriate. At *PC Magazine* we often just make the label PC MAGAZINE. The LABEL command works with any version of DOS 3.0 or later.)

3.   Copy your introductory screen — which *must* be called BOOTSCRN — onto the disk:

```
COPY BOOTSCRN A:
```

BOOTSCRN must be the first file to appear in the directory listing, and it must be an ASCII text file. You may want to copy and edit the sample BOOTSCRN file on this disk.

4.   Make sure the BOOTREC.PCM file and DEBUG.COM are handy, load DEBUG by entering:

```
DEBUG
```

at the DOS prompt, and then type (very, very carefully) the four lines:

```
N BOOTREC.PCM
L
W 100 0 0 1
Q
```

being sure to press the Enter key at the end of each one. However, check your typing several times before entering the line that begins with the W.

5. Once you've completed steps 1 through 4, test it by making sure the new disk is in drive A: and pressing Ctrl-Alt-Del to reboot. If you see your BOOTSCRN screen you've done everything properly. If not, start over.

6. Then copy all the files that you want to distribute onto this disk. Write "MASTER" on a pressure-sensitive diskette label, and attach the label to the diskette. Use only the DISKCOPY command to make distribution copies; don't try making distribution copies with COPY or XCOPY.

Warning: *Be extremely careful when typing the DEBUG instructions in step 4!*

These instructions copy the BOOTREC.PCM file onto the diskette that you just formatted with the /B parameter. If you type it exactly as it appears, you'll be safe. But if you have a hard disk system, and you don't enter the precise numbers that are shown, you could potentially copy it onto the wrong place on the wrong disk and end up damaging your files. So be extremely careful.

Also, this technique won't work if you change or skip any of the above steps. The diskette must be in drive A:, and you have to format it with the /B paramater and then immediately add a volume label to the disk and then copy a file named BOOTSCRN onto it. (Actually, you could switch the order of steps 3 and 4 without affecting anything adversely.)

If you're using an AT with a two floppy disks, a 1.2M and a 360K, and you want to use the 360K drive to make your copies, you could adapt the above instructions to work with drive B: instead of drive A:. If you do, when you get to step 4 above, change the DEBUG commands to:

```
N BOOTREC.PCM
L
W 100 1 0 1
Q
```

But again, be *very, very careful* when you type the line starting with the W.

Remarks: The very first sector on every DOS-formatted diskette is called the *boot sector* or the *boot record* regardless of whether the three system files that DOS needs to boot up are present.

At the very beginning of this tiny (512 byte) boot record is an instruction that identifies the diskette as a DOS disk. If your system doesn't see this instruction, it can tell it's dealing with something other than a properly formatted DOS disk.

Right after this instruction is an "OEM identification" space where the Original Equipment Manufacturer that licensed your version of DOS can put an abbreviated form of its name. Next, all disks other than ones formatted with ancient DOS versions contain a coded chunk of information that holds the BIOS Parameter Block (BPB) — a table that furnishes data on things like how many sectors the disk contains, and the maximum number of entries allowed in the root directory.

Finally, after an additional few bytes of configuration data, is the *bootstrap program* that sees if the necessary DOS system files are on the disk in the right place. If they are, it loads them into memory and gets you up and running. If they're not on the disk in the exact right location, this bootstrap program displays the two line "Non-System disk..." message.

The boot record is normally written to the first disk sector by the DOS FORMAT.COM program when you format the disk.

BOOTREC.PCM is a 512-byte file that replaces the existing boot record. Like the normal boot record, it contains an initial instruction that tells your system it's dealing with a DOS disk. The OEM ID says:

```
"  PC-MAG  "
```

(with a space at each end) but you may use DEBUG to replace this by putting your own eight-character label at offset 103H. And the BOOTREC.PCM BPB tells DOS it's working with an eight-sector/track 320K floppy rather than the standard nine-sector/track 360K diskette.

The bootstrap loader in BOOTREC.PCM is totally different from the DOS version. It first loads the disk's directory into memory and makes sure the fourth directory entry is called BOOTSCRN. If the fourth entry isn't BOOTSCRN, the loader prints an message that says:

```
This is not a bootable disk
Put a bootable DOS disk in drive A:
and press any key when ready
```

If BOOTSCRN is the fourth directory entry, BOOTREC.PCM reads the four sectors starting at track 7, sector 3, on side 0 of the disk.

DOS refers to sectors sequentially, starting at 0 and going to:

- 319 for 160K diskettes
- 359 for 180K diskettes
- 639 for 320K diskettes
- 719 for 360K diskettes
- 2,399 for 1.2M diskettes
- 1,439 for 740K diskettes
- 2,879 for 1.44M diskettes

However, BIOS maps disk using three coordinates — tracks (sometimes called cylinders), sides (often referred to as heads), and sectors:

Size	Sides	Sectors	Tracks
160K	0	0-8	0-39
180K	0	0-9	0-39
320K	0-1	0-8	0-39
360K	0-1	0-9	0-39
1.2M	0-1	0-15	0-79
740K	0-1	0-9	0-79
1.44M	0-1	0-18	0-79

The equivalent of BIOS track 7, sector 3, side 0 is DOS sector 114. You can make sure the BOOTSCRN file actually starts at DOS sector 114 by putting the disk containing BOOTSCRN in drive A:, then loading DEBUG and typing:

```
L 100 0 72 4
```

This loads four sectors (a 25 x 80 text screen filled with 2,000 characters requires four 512-byte sectors) starting with sector 72H (the hex equivalent of decimal 114) on drive A: (which DEBUG calls 0). Then type:

```
D 100 L 800
```

and you should see your BOOTSCRN file. See the SECTOR.BAS program on this disk if you need to translate sector numbers back and forth from DOS to BIOS.

Remember, this new BOOTSCRN file is simply a replacement for the old two-line "Non-System disk..." message. If you later use the SYS command to put the system files onto this disk, and copy COM-MAND.COM onto it, DOS won't display BOOTSCRN again. It's there only to provide a friendlier, more helpful, and more attractive display when users try to boot the disk without first putting the system files on it.

Notes: 1.   When you format a disk using the:

```
FORMAT /B
```

option to leave space allocated for the two system files, DOS idiotically turns all such disks into eight-sector/track, 320K floppies. This wastes 40K of precious disk space, considering that virtually everybody uses nine-sector/track 360K floppies as the preferred distribution medium.

2.   The image in your BOOTSCRN file can't be the full 25 rows tall by 80 columns across. The new BOOTREC.PCM loader will in fact display all 2,048 characters in the four sectors it loaded unless it sees an ASCII 0 character or a character 26 (hex 1A) end-of-file marker.

(This means that you need to put one of these characters at the end of your BOOTSCRN file. If you're creating it with a decent ASCII word processor, the word processor will probably handle this for you.)

However, the BIOS "Write teletype to active page" or "Write TTY" 0EH function of INT 10 that displays these characters will always move the cursor to the next screen position after writing each one, and will scroll down one line after it's written a character at the right edge of the screen. So you can't display all 2,000 characters on a 25 x 80 screen, since the last one would be in the 80th column, forcing BIOS to scroll up one line, which would push the top line of your text off the screen.

If you want to create a border that looks as if it goes all the way around the screen, you can do it one of three ways:

- Make the box that the border creates 80 columns across but only 24 rows tall.
- Make the box 25 rows tall but only 79 columns across.
- Put small "notches" in the corners of your screen and hide a character 0 or character 26 in the lower righthand corner (the 2,000th character):

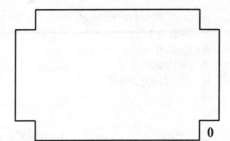

0

Also, be careful if you create the screen with a word processor, since some put both a carriage return (CR) and a line feed (LF) — decimal 13 and 10; hex 0D 0A — at the end of each line. Function 0EH of INT 10 treats the carriage return (the character 13 or 0D) as a command to wrap the display down a line, and won't actually print this character. But it will interpret a line feed as an additional character that can throw off the display.

You can create the BOOTSCRN file either as one long 2,000-character line (actually a 1,999 character line) with no carriage returns whatsoever, since BIOS will wrap the lines automatically for you. Or you can put a carriage return without a line feed at the end of each line, which makes the image easier to create. If you want your lines to be 79 columns across you don't have to worry about this, since the line feed can sit invisibly in the 80th column of each row. But if you want your image to span the full 80 columns, the best way to handle it is to construct it with your ASCII word processor by entering carriage return/line feeds the way you normally would, and then use your word processor's search-and-replace command either to remove the CR/LF pair entirely or change the CR/LF into just a CR.

3.   As written, BOOTREC.PCM displays the BOOTSCRN text in bright yellow (color 0EH). If you want to change this, patch the byte at address 183. Changing the value at 183 to 2 will print the screen in green; changing it to a hex value above 7 will make it high intensity (so that putting a C at this address will display the text in bright red).

4.   You may not need or want to leave room on the disk for DOS. For instance, the accompanying disk contains so many programs that there's just no room left for the DOS system files.

By omitting the space reserved for DOS you can cram more of your own files onto the disk. To do this, use DEBUG to make a modified version of BOOTREC.PCM called BOOTREC.BIG:

```
DEBUG BOOTREC.PCM
E 14F 74
E 15E 01
E 161 00
N BOOTREC.BIG
W
Q
```

Then, follow these instructions very carefully:

1.   Format a brand new floppy disk in drive A: by typing:

```
FORMAT A: /8
```

Note that in this case you're adding a /8 switch after the FORMAT command rather than the /B switch used earlier. This earlier /B parameter left room for DOS files. The /8 parameter that you use in this case simply formats the disk for 8 sectors per track without setting aside room for DOS.

2.   Then, before doing anything else, copy your BOOTSCRN file — the 2,048-byte screen you want to display — onto this formatted floppy disk. It must be the very first file to appear in the disk directory, so be sure you don't add any volume labels or other files to the disk before copying BOOTSCRN onto it.

3.   Then transfer the BOOTREC.BIG file onto the floppy in drive A: by typing:

```
DEBUG
N BOOTREC.BIG
L
W 100 0 0 1
Q
```

4.   Once you've completed the above steps, you can copy any other files onto the disk. Again, *be extremely careful* when typing the DEBUG instructions directly above.

This revised BOOTREC.BIG boot record checks to see if BOOTSCRN is the very first directory entry, and if so, loads the actual BOOTSCRN file stored at DOS sector 10 (BIOS sector 3, track 0, side 1).

BORDER
Command

Paul Somerson

Purpose: Sets border color from the command line on CGA or CGA-compatible screens.

Format: `[d:][path]BORDER n`

where *n* is the hex value of a border color from 0 to E.

Examples: Type:

`BORDER 4`

to set the CGA border to red, or:

`BORDER E`

(or BORDER e) to set it to bright yellow.

Remarks: IBM doesn't support border colors on any systems other than the CGA. However, if you are using a CGA you may choose any border color from 0 (black) to F (bright white).

Value	Color	Value	Color
0	Black	8	Grey
1	Blue	9	Bright blue
2	Green	A	Bright green
3	Cyan (Light Blue)	B	Bright cyan
4	Red	C	Bright red
5	Magenta	D	Bright magenta
6	Brown	E	Yellow
7	White	F	Bright white

BOXDRAW
Command

Tapio K. Vocadlo

Purpose: Lets you create boxes and borders directly by typing on the cursor/number pad.

Format: `[d:] [path]BOXDRAW`

to load it, then Alt-B to toggle it on and off. (The CapsLock and Num-lock keys must be on for it to work.)

Once you've toggled the program on, you can select among four separate palettes of border characters by typing the capital letters A, B, C, or D. Each lets you work with a different character set:
- A = all single-line borders
- B = all double-line borders
- C = double horizontals, single verticals
- D = single horizontals, double verticals

To print the actual characters, make sure:

1.   The CapsLock and NumLock keys are both on.

2.   You've toggled Alt-B on.

Then use the number pad and the plus and minus signs to draw the boxes. The upper lefthand corner of the number pad (key 7/Home) will draw the upper lefthand corner of a box on your screen. The lower righthand corner of the number pad (3/PgDn) will produce the lower righthand box character onscreen, etc. The minus sign will draw a horizontal bar and the plus a vertical bar.

Remarks: Drawing borders with IBM's high-bit character set can take forever, especially when you're in the middle of an application program. To produce each character directly onscreen, you have to hold down the Alt key, type in the three-digit ASCII value of the border character on the number pad, and then release the Alt key. A simple box can take several minutes to draw.

You can use keyboard macro programs or ANSI.SYS to redefine your keyboard, but these each have drawbacks. BOXDRAW.COM is a memory-resident program that specializes in making it easy to draw four different sets of box and border characters. It replaces the normal BIOS keyboard-support routine so it can check on characters being transferred from the input buffer to any application in use during keystroke requests.

Load it before any of your application programs. You can then toggle BOXDRAW on and off by pressing Alt-B (holding down the Alt key and pressing B). To disable BOXDRAW, just press Alt-B when you're done to toggle it off. This works with many — but not all — commercial applications. But make absolutely sure you test it first with your applications before you start working with unsaved data files. And as with any resident programs, watch out for strange interactions with programs such as *SideKick*. Test thoroughly before you use it.

You can change the characters it draws by using DEBUG to substitute others (shading characters, Greek letters, etc.):

Palette 1: Trigger is A
Addresses: Hex 1FB through hex 205
Characters: 192, 193, 217, 195, 197, 180, 218, 194, 191, 196, 179

Palette 2: Trigger is B
Addresses: Hex 206 through hex 210
Characters: 200, 202, 188, 204, 206, 185, 201, 203, 187, 205, 186

Palette 3: Trigger is C
Addresses: Hex 211 through hex 21B
Characters: 212, 207, 190, 198, 216, 181, 213, 209, 184, 205, 179

Palette 4: Trigger is D
Addresses: Hex 21C through hex 226
Characters: 211, 208, 189, 199, 215, 182, 214, 210, 183, 196, 186

BROWSE Command   Charles Petzold

Purpose: Permits scrolling forward and backward throughout a file without use of a word processing program.

Format: `[d:][path]BROWSE [d:][path]filename[.ext] [/W]`

Remarks: The DOS TYPE command does not permit you to scroll ahead or go back to previously displayed material in a file. It also exits at the first instance of Ctrl-Z (ASCII 26, conventionally used as an end-of-file marker), making it impossible to scan binary (e.g. .COM) files for error messages, copyright notices, and the like.

BROWSE.COM overcomes these limitations, giving you the chance to go immediately to the top or the end of a file (the Home and End keys, respectively), to the succeeding or previous screen (PgUp and PgDn), or to move up or down a line at a time (Up Arrow or Down Arrow). To return to DOS, simply press the Esc key or Ctrl-Break.

Wide displays, e.g., a spreadsheet file, are not broken at 80 columns, as with TYPE. BROWSE ignores carriage returns (ASCII 13), breaking lines only on line feeds (ASCII 10). The Right Arrow key scrolls the display to the right in eight-character increments (see note 3 below) to view wide displays; the Left Arrow key returns you immediately to column zero.

BROWSE expands tab characters (ASCII 9) to the next eight-character boundary, but does no other character processing unless the /W parameter is specified. Use of the /W option permits using BROWSE with *WordStar* files.

Notes: 1.   BROWSE can run under *TopView* or *Windows*; specify "writes directly to screen" in the .PIF and use the default 52K memory requirement. (The program actually requires only approximately 33K to run.) For the *TopView* PIF, specify that the program intercepts interrupt 23H.

2.   BROWSE is compatible with the IBM monochrome, CGA, VGA, and EGA displays, and will even run in the EGA 43-line mode. Files prepared with word-processors that employ a one-line-per-paragraph format (such as Microsoft *Word* and *XyWrite*) may require excessive right-scrolling, however.

3.   You can patch BROWSE.COM with DEBUG at address 10F so that its right-scroll jumps by more than the default eight characters.

Replace the existing value of 8 at that address with any other reasonable hex number. So for a 40-column jump, enter hex 28. For an 80-column jump, enter hex 50. For a 1-column jump, enter 1. This will change the increment from the default 8 to decimal 80 and rename the program to BROWSE2.COM:

```
DEBUG BROWSE.COM
E 10F 50
N BROWSE2.COM
W
Q
```

4.   If *WordStar* users want to patch BROWSE so the high bit is already toggled off when they begin, and they have to use a /N switch for non-*WordStar* text, they can create a version called BROWSE3.COM by typing:

```
DEBUG BROWSE.COM
E 16A 7F
```

```
E 1DB 6E
E 1E2 FF
N BROWSE3.COM
W
Q
```

5. BROWSE attempts to figure out your current screen color to use when displaying the file. If you'd rather use a unique color for BROWSE, you can patch the byte at address 108 so BROWSE works in a predefined color. You must use a 2-digit hex number for the color. The lefthand digit is the background and can be any value between 0 and 7. The right digit is the foreground, and can be any digit between 0 and F. Any background color from 8 through F blinks.

Value	Color	Value	Color
0	Black	8	Grey
1	Blue	9	Bright blue
2	Green	A	Bright green
3	Cyan (Light Blue)	B	Bright cyan
4	Red	C	Bright red
5	Magenta	D	Bright magenta
6	Brown	E	Yellow
7	White	F	Bright white

← **background only** →

← **foreground** →

So to create a new version called BROWSE4 that always appears in bright red text (C) on a dark blue background (1), type:

```
DEBUG BROWSE.COM
E 108 1C
N BROWSE4.COM
W
Q
```

BSAVE Command

Michael J. Mefford

Purpose: Saves graphics images to disk so you can load them later with BLOAD.

See DRAW.

CALC
Command
Douglas Boling

Purpose: A pop-up programmer's calculator with base conversion, bit-shifting, logical operator, mod functions, and 32-bit number representation that also supports a two-decimal place integer arithmetic calculations.

Format: `[d:] [path]CALC`

Remarks: CALC is a memory resident program that you can load either at the DOS command line or as a part of an AUTOEXEC.BAT file.

Pressing Alt-S pops up a six-line window for calculations; pressing Esc exits the calculator and restores the screen to its previous condition. The program automatically accommodates monochrome, CGA, or EGA displays.

Any number on CALC's entry line can be successively converted to hexadecimal, binary, octal, or decimal (default) notion by pressing F1. Mixed-base calculations are supported, and the +, -, *, and / functions conventionally so long as it is realized that CALC operates in integer, not floating point mode. (Fixed two-decimal place calculations can be made by pressing F2 before entering the numbers.) In integer mode the mod function (e.g., 25 mod 8 = 1) is also supported, using either the % or the \ sign as the operator.

CALC uses full 32-bit number representation and so can be used for address calculations. The function keys F3, F4, and F5 perform logical AND, OR, and XOR operations between two numbers. F6 performs a NOT (invert) function on the number entered. F7 shifts bits left and F8 shifts right. F9 is a change-sign key, and F10 clears the entry line. To clear the calculator field, press Shift-F10.

CAMERA
Command
Phillip Cheng

Purpose: Grabs screens and saves them to disk so you can later load them into a slide show or poor man's presentation-graphics demonstration.

Format: `[d:] [path]CAMERA`

Once CAMERA.COM is loaded into memory, you can save any text or graphics screen to disk by simply pressing the Ctrl, Alt, and Right Shift keys simultaneously. The first time the program is invoked, it will create a file named "A" on the logged disk drive with one of the following extensions, depending upon the mode under which the screen was saved:

- .40T forty-column text
- .80T eighty-column text
- .MRG medium resolution graphics
- .HRG high-resolution graphics

The next images will be saved using the filenames "B," "C," etc., with the appropriate extensions. To view any image, simply set the correct screen mode in BASIC and BLOAD the file. Assembly language programmers who wish to save files without a BLOAD header should delete the lines at DEBUG hex addresses 107-10D and 17B-188.

Remarks: This makes it very easy to capture screen images and save them to disk while a program is running. However, it works only with modes supported by the CGA (and any later displays such as the EGA that can emulate CGA). And for the sake of simplicity, it saves only the first page when dealing with text screens (although the program can easily be changed to save all the pages in one file).

Important: This will conflict with some memory-resident programs, and programs that use interrupt 9, such as *SideKick*. So test it carefully before you have any unsaved data files in memory.

You can easily combine different screen modes in one slide show by using a BASIC program like CAMLOAD.BAS on the accompanying disk.

First, run CAMERA.COM. Type in the sample programs below, or write your own in each of the four modes it can handle. Capture screens in different modes by hitting Ctrl-Alt-Right Shift when you see ones you like. Then get back into DOS and create a batch file called CAM.BAT that consists of the three lines:

```
DIR ?.* > CAMERA.FIL
[d:][path]BASICA [d:][path]CAMLOAD
DEL CAMERA.FIL
```

(Substitute GWBASIC in place of BASICA if you're using a generic system.) CAM.BAT will create a file called CAMERA.FIL consisting of the names of the screens captured by CAMERA.COM, and then run

CAMLOAD. CAMLOAD asks how many seconds you want to view each slide, then sets the proper mode and BLOADs the screens automatically.

If you don't have your own sample images, you can use the short 40TEXT.BAS, 80TEXT.BAS, MEDRES.BAS, and HIRES.BAS BASIC programs created by the SAMPLE.BAS program on the accompanying disk. Then use the CAMLOAD.BAS "slide show" program to display them.

See CAMLOAD.BAS, SAMPLE.BAS.

CAPSLOCK
Command

Todd M. Lewis

Purpose: Automatically turns the CapsLock key off when you forget to.

Format: [d:] [path] CAPSLOCK

Remarks: If you've ever forgotten that your CapsLock key is on, then you've invariably created phrases like "dEAR sIRS," DOS thinks you really need a feature that lets you press the Shift key and get lowercase letters, but it usually results in a lot of wasted time. You have to delete, retype, and then recover your train of thought. This is one of those cases when your computer really should have known what you meant.

CAPSLOCK.COM gives your CapsLock key enough common sense to know when you're thinking in CapsLock Off mode. Any time you use the Shift key with a letter key, the CapsLock turns off. Shifting nonalphabetic keys has no effect on CapsLock, so you can still get to all the special characters and punctuation marks.

You have to run CAPSLOCK only once for it to operate. Again, test this first with any other programs you may be running that act on the keyboard.

CAPSOFF
Command
Mike Cohn

Purpose: Turns CapsLock Shift off.

Format: `[d:][path]CAPSOFF`

Remarks: See KEYLOCK, NUMON, NUMOFF, CAPSON, SCROLLON, SCRLLOFF, LOCK, and LOX.

CAPSON
Command
Mike Cohn

Purpose: Turns CapsLock Shift on.

Format: `[d:][path]CAPSON`

Remarks: You can create a version of this program called CAPSFLIP.COM that alternately toggles the CapsLock shift on and off every other time it executes.

Simply type:

```
DEBUG CAPSON.COM
E 108 34
N CAPSFLIP.COM
W
Q
```

See KEYLOCK, NUMON, NUMOFF, CAPSOFF, SCROLLON, SCRLLOFF, LOCK, and LOX.

CAPTURE   **Tom Kihlken**
Command

Purpose: Saves the text and attribute bytes on the screen to a 4,000-byte file that
the *PC Magazine* HELP.COM utility can pop up either from within an
application or at the DOS prompt. CAPTURE instantly turns the custom
help menus, tables, or anything you type on your screen into files you
can pop up.

Format: [d:][path]CAPTURE

Remarks: CAPTURE is a memory-resident screen-saving program. Its default hotkey is Alt-C, although you can change it. The program takes no
parameters and saves to filenames with the names SCREEN.000,
SCREEN.001, etc. It will not overwrite existing filenames, but instead increments the number in the extension. Filenames stored by CAPTURE
can then be renamed for use by HELP.COM. CAPTURE files may also
be combined into multiple-page help screens (up to the 14-screen limit
of HELP.COM), by using the DOS COPY /B option for copying binary
files.

Examples: To combine the first three CAPTUREd help screens into the file,
HELP.HEP (which might be one of the files in a \HELP subdirectory):

```
COPY /B SCREEN.000+SCREEN.001+SCREEN.002 HELP.HEP
```

The Alt-C trigger key may be changed with DEBUG, by entering the following commands:

```
DEBUG CAPTURE.COM
E 268 SS     ;Your Scan code
E 27D MM     ;Your Shift mask
W
Q
```

(Substitute the actual hex values from the following tables for the SS and
MM in the above example.)

Shift-mask Value Table

Value	Alt	Ctrl	L-Shft	R-Shft
00				
01				X
02			X	
03			X	X
04		X		
05		X		X
06		X	X	
07		X	X	X
08	X			
09	X			X
0A	X		X	
0B	X		X	X
0C	X	X		
0D	X	X		X
0E	X	X	X	
0F	X	X	X	X

Note: X means key is pressed

Scan-Code Value Table (in Hex)

Key	Code	Key	Code
Esc	01	Z	2C
!1	02	X	2D
@2	03	C	2E
#3	04	V	2F
$4	05	B	30
%5	06	N	31
^6	07	M	32
&7	08	<,	33
*8	09	>.	34
(9	0A	?/	35
)0	0B	Right-Shift	36
_-	0C	PrtSc*	37
+=	0D	Alt	38

Backspace	0E	Space	39
Tab	0F	CapsLock	3A
Q	10	F1	3B
W	11	F2	3C
E	12	F3	3D
R	13	F4	3E
T	14	F5	3F
Y	15	F6	40
U	16	F7	41
I	17	F8	42
O	18	F9	43
P	19	F10	44
{[	1A	NumLock	45
}]	1B	ScrollLock	46
Enter	1C	7 Home	47
Ctrl	1D	8 Up	48
A	1E	9 PgUp	49
S	1F	-	4A
D	20	4 Left	4B
F	21	5	4C
G	22	6 Right	4D
H	23	+	4E
J	24	1 End	4F
K	25	2 Down	50
L	26	3 PgDn	51
:;	27	0 Ins	52
"'	28	. Del	53
~`	29	SysReq	54
Left Shift	2A	F11	57
\	2B	F12	58

CARDFILE
Command

Jeff Prosise

Purpose: Combines a data base of names, addresses, phone numbers, and memo-IDs with a Hayes-compatible autodialer.

Format: `[d:][path]CARDFILE [d:][filespec]`

Remarks: You normally load CARDFILE with a specific database (*filespec*) by listing it as a line in your AUTOEXEC.BAT file. You can switch to another database by repeating the command with a different filespec at the DOS prompt.

The Alt-Right Shift key combination pops up the CARDFILE window, and Esc returns you to your application. Within the window, the function keys are assigned as follows:

- F1 Begin/save a new or edited card
- F2 Edit the card currently displayed
- F3 Delete the card currently displayed
- F4 Search all cards for a text string
- F5 Save datafile to disk
- F6 Dial the phone number currently displayed

All card data entry and editing is done in overstrike mode. The backspace key deletes the previous character and the four cursor keys can position the cursor anywhere in the record area. Enter moves the cursor to the start of the next line.

You can page through all of the cards with the PgUp, PgDn, and Enter keys. The Home and End keys let you jump quickly to the first or last card, respectively.

To search the database, press F4 and enter a text string. Pressing Enter resumes the search (which is not case-sensitive) after a match; Esc cancels the search. An alternate way to find a name quickly is to press Alt and a letter key. To find "Smith," for example, press Alt-S, then use PgDn or Enter to skip past "Sagamore" and "Siddhartha."

When used with Hayes-compatible modems, F6 dials the number currently displayed. At the prompt, pick up the phone and press the spacebar to break the modem connection. The CARDFILE autodialer ignores all nonnumeric characters except the comma, which inserts a pause sometimes needed to access an outside line.

Because CARDFILE is a memory-resident program, it must assume rather than change the modem parameters. By default, CARDFILE is initially configured for a 1200-baud modem connected to the COM1. Using DEBUG you can change the value at 182 from 0 to 1 to change from COM1 to COM2, to 2 for COM3, etc. Similarly, to change to a different baud (bps) rate, change the value at 184 from the default 83H, as follows:

- 300 baud 43H
- 1200 baud 83H
- 2400 baud A3H

- 4800 baud C3H
- 9600 baud E3H

The "ATDT" (dial) and "ATH0" (hangup) strings are at addresses 185 and 18A, respectively. While they can be changed (especially substituting a "P," ASCII 80 for the "T" in the dialing command), note that each sequence must be four bytes long. The dial string must be delimited by a zero byte, and the hangup string must end with 0DH and 00.

To save memory, the card capacity may be lowered from the default 255 (FFH) at 169. Each record takes 192 bytes. And if the Alt-Right Shift hotkey conflicts with other software, change the default value 09 at address 36A to a combination of the following:

- Right-Shift   1
- Left-Shift   2
- Ctrl   4
- Alt   8

Notes: While CARDFILE will operate under DOS 2.x, its critical error handler is only fully effective with DOS 3.x.

CFPRINT
Command

Jeff Prosise

Purpose: Companion program to send output of CARDFILE.COM name, address, and phone files to your printer.

Format: `[d:][path]CFPRINT [d:][path]filename[.ext]`

where filename is the CARDFILE data file that you want printed.

Remarks: CARDFILE uses an unusual method of storing ASCII data without end-of-line markers. This thwarts conventional methods of reading and interpreting its files. However, its file structure is simple:

The first byte in the file holds a binary value that represents the number of records stored (where one card corresponds to one record). This is followed by the ASCII text of the cards themselves.

Each record is composed of six 32-byte lines.

There are no carriage returns; instead, each line is delimited by its known 32-byte length. Thus a file created by CARDFILE consists of a single-byte value followed by groups of text 192 bytes in length.

Examples: To print out a CARDFILE data file called CFDATA.FIL in the \NUMBERS directory on drive C:, using the default LPT1 printer, enter:

```
CFPRINT C:\NUMBERS\CFDATA.FIL
```

Notes: Output is routed by default to LPT1 (with a zero at offset 103). To alter the program for other printer ports, use DEBUG to change this byte. A value of 0 corresponds to LPT1, 1 to LPT2, and 2 to LPT3. A DEBUG script to modify CFPRINT to use a printer configured as LPT2 looks something like this:

```
DEBUG CFPRINT.COM
E 0103 01
W
Q
```

CHANGE   Michael J. Mefford
Command

Purpose: Performs a rapid search-and-replace operation for text strings and/or ASCII decimal codes throughout a file of maximum 40,000-byte length.

Format: `[d:][path]CHANGE filespec findstring replacestring`

Remarks: The *filespec* parameter may include a drive letter and a path in addition to the designated filename.

Findstring and *replacestring* may consist of text characters enclosed within (double) quote marks or ASCII decimal codes whose numbers are separated by commas. Note that the format requires that each parameter be separated by a single space. Text strings in quotes and ASCII values in numerals may be combined in either string if separated by commas.

Example: To change all references to Miss Jones to Mrs. Smith in the file NOGOSSIP.ART on the current directory, you would enter:

```
CHANGE NOGOSSIP.ART "Miss Jones" "Mrs. Smith"
```

To strip out all carriage return-line feeds (i.e. replace them with a null string) in the file MCI.B16 in the \COMM subdirectory, enter:

```
CHANGE \COMM\MCI.B16 13,10 ""
```

Notes: In the second example you might want to use a space between the quote marks rather than a null string to keep the words from running together. Observe that by putting the number of the month in hexadecimal (B=November) you can fit both month and day within the three-character DOS filename extension.

CHD   Stephen Barsky
Command

Purpose: Adds intelligence and ease-of-use to the DOS CD (CHDIR) directory changing command.

Format: `[d:][path]CHD path`

Remarks: CHD.COM is almost identical to CHDIR except that it relaxes the requirements for specifying paths.

If you omit the leading " \ " CHD first tries to find the specified directory relative to where you are in the tree structure, just as CHDIR does. Unlike CHDIR, however, if CHD fails to find the subdirectory immediately below your current position, it makes a second attempt to find it just below the root directory.

As an added feature, you may change the current directory to the root by entering CHD followed by at least one space and then a carriage return.

Yet another feature is that CHD generates a return code that can be used by an IF ERRORLEVEL test in a batch file to determine whether that directory change actually worked. A return code of 0 means the directory change worked, while a return code of 1 means that the change failed.

Most users have very few (if any) identically named subdirectories, and are not interested in having to tell DOS exactly where to find everything. But they are interested in making subdirectory management far easier and less irritating. CHD.COM helps.

Example: If you are in \MAIN\DBASE and you enter:

```
CHD FORM
```

CHD will first try to change the current directory to
\MAIN\DBASE\FORM. If this fails, it will then try to set the current
directory to \FORM. If this second attempt fails, it will print the familiar
"Invalid directory" message. Entering CHD followed immediately by a
carriage return displays the current directory, just as with CHDIR.

Notes: Don't use this program unless you have a $P somewhere in your DOS
prompt so that you know at all times exactly which directory you're in,
or you'll end up very confused. In fact, every hard disk user should use
at least a $P: or a PG prompt to help navigate through the maze of sub-
directories and backslashes.

CHECK
Batch file command

Jeff Prosise

Purpose: Increases the usefulness of batch files by letting them report a variety of
parameters that range from free disk space to installed hardware to the
time and date. Your batch programs can make intelligent decisions based
on the results reported by CHECK through the DOS IF ERRORLEVEL
code.

Format: `[d:][path]CHECK keyword [parameter1 parameter2 ...]`

The 16 *keywords* are divided into three classes.

1. Disk-related keywords: DISKSPACE, FILESIZE, FILEFOUND,
and FILETEXT.

2. Hardware-related keyswords: MEMORY, VIDEOCARD, MODEL,
8087, and 80287.

3. Miscellaneous keywords: TIME, DAY, MONTH, VIDEOMODE,
VERSION, KEYBOARD, KEYPRESS.

(Although they're mentioned exclusively in uppercase here, you may
enter keywords in any case or mixture of cases in a batch file — so
DAY, day, Day, and DAy are all acceptable.)

Function	Return Code
FILESIZE filespec	Length of file in K
FILEFOUND filespec	0: File found 1: File not found
FILETEXT filespec 'string'	0: String found 1: String not found
DISKSPACE [d:]	Number of whole 16K blocks free on indicated or default drive
MEMORY	Number of 16K RAM modules
VIDEOCARD	0: Mono Display Adapter 1: Color Graphics Adapter 2: Enhanced Graphics Adapter
MODEL	Machine ID byte
8087	0: 8087 or 80287 installed 1: 8087/80287 not installed
80287	0: 8087 or 80287 installed 1: 8087/80287 not installed
TIME	Current hour (0-23)
DAY	Current day (1-31)
MONTH	Current month (1-12)
VIDEOMODE	Current video mode (0-16)
VERSION	DOS version (major number e.g., 3 for 3.1 or 3.2)
KEYBOARD	0: Keyboard buffer empty 1: Entry awaiting processing
KEYPRESS	ASCII code of key pressed

Remarks: CHECK can come in very handy when you want to create a batch file to run a certain program, but you have two versions of that program, one for an EGA and one for a CGA, or one that needs a math coprocessor, or one that requires a certain version of DOS or even a certain type of computer. And it can safely perform disk operations like COPY or DEL only when the proper amount of disk space is available.

1.   Disk-related keywords: DISKSPACE, FILESIZE, FILEFOUND, and FILETEXT. DISKSPACE returns the amount of free disk space on the specified or default drive, in terms of whole 16K blocks. If there is 70K of room, DISKSPACE returns a value of 4 to ERRORLEVEL, indicating there are four blocks free. FILESIZE reports the length of a given file in kilobytes. A value of 255 means that the length is 255K or greater. FILEFOUND is essentially a duplicate of the operating system's IF EXIST conditional test and returns 0 if a file exists, 1 if it does not. FILETEXT searches for a given text string inside a file and is invoked like this:

```
CHECK FILETEXT C:TEXT.DOC 'Once upon a time'
```

In this case, the file TEXT.DOC is opened on drive C: and is searched for any occurrence of the string "Once upon a time." If the string is found, a 0 is returned; if it's not, or if an error is encountered (invalid syntax or the failure to find the file, for example) a 1 is returned. When using this function, you must enclose the string to be searched for in single quotes or a syntax error will be reported. FILETEXT is included in CHECK for a couple of reasons: first, because it serves a legitimate purpose on its own; and second, because it provides an example of how user-written functions can make use of a third command line parameter (in this case the text string) even though the automatic parsing routine built into the program acts only on the first two.

2.   Hardware-related keywords: MEMORY, VIDEOCARD, MODEL, 8087, and 80287. These let batch files check the amount of memory installed in the system, the type of display adapter, the computer type, and whether or not an 8087 or 80287 math coprocessor chip is installed. The 8087 and 80287 keywords can be used interchangeably; both detect the presence or absence of a math coprocessor, regardless of whether it's an 8087 or an 80287. MODEL returns the machine's ID byte. An IBM PC is identified by the value 255, an XT by 254, a PC*jr* by 253, an AT by 252, and the PC Convertible by 249. There is some uncertainty inherent in using this function because of IBM's assignment of the same internal ID code to systems such as the XT and the now-defunct Portable PC, and because of the lack of standardization among the compatible manufacturers. VIDEOCARD assumes that either an MDA, a CGA, or an EGA is being used and returns a value from 0 to 2 correspondingly.

3.   Miscellaneous keywords: TIME, DAY, MONTH, VIDEOMODE, VERSION, KEYBOARD, KEYPRESS.   TIME, DAY, and MONTH return the current hour (0-23), day of the month (1-31), and month (1-12), respectively. VIDEOMODE returns the current video mode (0-16) and VERSION reports the major number of the version of DOS being used. The major number for DOS 3.2, for example, is 3. Versions 1.00 and 1.10 cannot be reported because these earliest releases of DOS didn't incorporate service 4CH. CHECK must be used with version 2.00 or higher. KEYBOARD checks the keyboard buffer and returns a 1 if a keycode is awaiting retrieval or a 0 if the buffer is empty. Finally, KEYPRESS returns the ASCII code of any key pressed. For those keys that produce an extended code like the function keys and the cursor keys, ERRORLEVEL will be set to 0. Together, the last two functions single-handedly enhance a batch file's capability to query the user for keyboard input.

Examples: TIMEODAY.BAT prints a greeting message appropriate for the time of day:

```
ECHO OFF
CHECK TIME
IF ERRORLEVEL 18 GOTO EVENING
IF ERRORLEVEL 12 GOTO AFTERNOON
ECHO GOOD MORNING!
GOTO END
:AFTERNOON
ECHO GOOD AFTERNOON!
GOTO END
:EVENING
ECHO GOOD EVENING!
:END
```

HITSPACE.BAT pauses and waits until the user presses the space bar, endlessly looping while other keys are pressed:

```
ECHO OFF
ECHO PRESS SPACE BAR TO CONTINUE
GOTO START
:ERROR
ECHO NO, I SAID HIT THE SPACEBAR
:START
CHECK KEYPRESS
IF ERRORLEVEL 33 GOTO ERROR
IF NOT ERRORLEVEL 32 GOTO ERROR
```

48K-LEFT.BAT proceeds with file deletion only if free disk space is less than 48K:

```
ECHO OFF
CHECK DISKSPACE B:
IF NOT ERRORLEVEL 3 DEL B:*.OBJ
```

32K-FILE.BAT accepts a filename and deletes that file only if its length exceeded 32K:

```
ECHO OFF
CHECK FILESIZE %1
IF ERRORLEVEL 33 DEL %1
```

FILEDUPE.BAT decides whether or not to copy a given file based on its presence or absence on the target disk (here you could do the same thing with the DOS IF EXIST command):

```
ECHO OFF
CHECK FILEFOUND B:SAMPLE.DOC
IF ERRORLEVEL 1 COPY A:SAMPLE.DOC B:
```

NEED256K.BAT loads and executes a certain program (called NEWPROG here) only if the PC being used has a minimum of 256K of RAM:

```
ECHO OFF
CHECK MEMORY
IF NOT ERRORLEVEL 16 GOTO SHORT
NEWPROG
GOTO END
:SHORT
ECHO MINIMUM 256K REQUIRED TO RUN
:END
```

NEEDVER3.BAT aborts loading a program (here called NEWPROG) if the user has a DOS version lower than 3.0:

```
CHECK VERSION
IF ERRORLEVEL 3 GOTO CONTINUE
ECHO DOS 3.00 OR HIGHER REQUIRED
GOTO END
:CONTINUE
NEWPROG
:END
```

MONITOR1.BAT runs one version of a program (here called PROG1) on a monochrome system and another version (here called PROG2) on a color system, assuming an EGA isn't being used with a mono display:

```
ECHO OFF
CHECK VIDEOCARD
IF ERRORLEVEL 1 GOTO COLOR
PROG1
GOTO END
:COLOR
PROG2
:END
```

MONITOR2.BAT determines explicitly which video mode is currently active, since modes 7 and 15 are the only two mono modes among the 17 (numbered 0-16) supported:

```
ECHO OFF
CHECK VIDEOMODE
IF ERRORLEVEL 16 GOTO COLOR
IF ERRORLEVEL 15 GOTO MONO
IF ERRORLEVEL 8 GOTO COLOR
IF ERRORLEVEL 7 GOTO MONO
:COLOR
ECHO THIS IS A COLOR SYSTEM!
GOTO END
:MONO
ECHO THIS IS A MONOCHROME SYSTEM!
:END
```

COPROCSR.BAT runs one version of a program (here called PROG1) that needs a math coprocessor only if one is installed, and another (here called PROG2) that doesn't use a math chip:

```
ECHO OFF
CHECK 8087
IF ERRORLEVEL 1 GOTO NOMATH
PROG1
GOTO END
:NOMATH
PROG2
:END
```

NOPCJR.BAT aborts if it finds it's running on a PC*jr*:

```
ECHO OFF
CHECK MODEL
IF ERRORLEVEL 254 GOTO OK
IF NOT ERRORLEVEL 253 GOTO OK
ECHO DIFFERENT VERSION REQUIRED FOR PCJR
GOTO END
:OK
RUNIT
:END
```

Notes: Because DOS is limited to one eight-bit return code, in some cases it is impossible to pass back an indication of whether or not the function itself failed or succeeded. The FILESIZE command, for instance, can return a value anywhere from 0 to 255 to define the length of the file in question, but it must somehow raise a flag if the file cannot be found. In such situations, CHECK sends an error message to the display and attempts to end with an exit code that is indicative of the worst case. Thus, FILESIZE returns a 0 if DOS cannot open the file for one reason or another. This philosophy is implemented consistently throughout the utility, but it once again represents the need to compromise to live within the DOS resources provided.

CLICK Command John P. Sohl

Purpose: Lets you toggle an audible keyboard click on and off.

Format: `[d:][path]CLICK`

Remarks: The PC*jr* had a lot of problems, but it did offer a few interesting features. One of these was the ability to turn the keyboard click on and off.

The memory-resident CLICK.COM program can add this feature to any system. Once it's installed, alternately pressing Ctrl-Alt-Ins will turn it on and off.

When it's active, CLICK will make a sound only when you press an alphanumeric key. The program intercepts interrupt 9 and toggles the speaker bit every time a key is newly pressed. It does not click on either of the Shift keys, the Ctrl key, or the Alt key, and it passes all keys through unaltered.

Since the Ins key is right next to the Del key, there's an obvious risk in pressing Ctrl-Alt-Del and rebooting your system when you just want to turn off clicking. To change the hotkey from Ctrl-Alt-Del to Ctrl-Alt-something-else, patch the value at address 18C with the scan code for the new hotkey you want.

To make it Ctrl-Alt-Esc, type:

```
DEBUG CLICK.COM
E 18C 1
W
Q
```

since the scan code for the Esc key is 1. However, since CLICKER starts clicking as soon as it is installed, you may never need to use the hotkey toggle.

CLICKER does not check to see if it is installed already, so it's possible to invoke it more than once. Interestingly, the click timbre changes depending on whether it's been installed an odd or even number of times.

PC Magazine receives lots of keyclick programs, but this one's different since you can toggle it on and off. Be careful if you use it with *SideKick* or any other program that's greedy about interrupt 9; test it thoroughly before using these TSRs with unsaved data floating around in RAM.

CLSEGA Command   Charles Petzold and Paul Somerson

Purpose: Provides a combination mode-setting, color-setting, cursor-setting, and screen-clearing program for the EGA 43-line screen.

Format: [d:] [path]CLSEGA

Remarks: The CS.COM command sets the mode properly, but has a few snags. CLSEGA sets the EGA screen mode to 43-lines, sets the colors (in this case to bright yellow on red), sets the cursor properly, and clears the entire screen.

If you want to use colors other than high-intensity yellow on red, use DEBUG to patch the byte at address 12A.

To pick a new color, use a two-digit hex number where the lefthand digit is a background color number from 0 to 7 and the righthand digit is a text color number from 0 to F. Any text value greater than 7 becomes high-intensity. So entering 1F would give you bright white text (F) on a blue background.

If you wanted to patch CLSEGA.COM to set high-intensity white on blue, type:

```
DEBUG CLSEGA.COM
E 12A 1F
W
Q
```

CMOSGET   Robert L. Hummel
Command

Purpose: Saves the CMOS configuration settings on AT and later systems so you can reload them instantly after changing batteries and avoid having to reconfigure your entire system from scratch.

Format: `[d:][path]CMOSGET`

Remarks: IBM keeps its configuration information for the AT and later machines in a CMOS memory chip that's maintained by battery even when the machine is turned off. A failing battery can cause errors at bootup and trigger bad configuration record or failed battery messages. Typical batteries have a useful life of about three years. However, when you remove the battery, you lose all the configuration information and have to run the SETUP program to restore the configuration.

To make matters worse, many systems were configured originally by dealers or MIS staffers who are no longer available. IBM hid the configuration program on the diagnostics disk, and makes users answer questions they can't possibly remember, like what numerical hard disk type they're using.

CMOSGET and CMOSPUT make this far easier. CMOSGET reads the contents of the CMOS memory chip and writes it to standard output; redirecting this output to a file saves 64 bytes of information. CMOSPUT performs the complementary function. It reads from standard input and loads the CMOS chip with the saved data. It again uses redirection to read the data file created by CMOSGET.

You can't simply restore all the old data, however, since you'd end up resetting the time and date that were active when you saved the 64 bytes, and would have to use SETUP to update them. CMOSPUT avoids this by getting the current time and date from DOS and using the BIOS to update the real-time clock (RTC).

Example: The complete procedure is as follows: First, create a bootable diskette by using the FORMAT command with the /S option. Onto this diskette, copy the SETUP program used by your machine and the CMOSPUT.COM program you created. (Later, if the BIOS detects that the data in the CMOS is not reliable, it will boot only from the A: drive and refuse to access the hard disk at all. So this process will create the proper bootable diskette.)

Run CMOSGET to save the CMOS memory in a file on the diskette, with the command:

```
CMOSGET > A:CMOS.DAT
```

Change the battery. Boot the computer from the floppy and ignore the error messages. Set the date and time with the DOS TIME and DATE commands. Run CMOSPUT to load the CMOS memory with the command:

```
CMOSPUT < CMOS.DAT
```

Now, remove the diskette and reboot the computer. If everything works, you should get no errors and the correct time and date. (If there is a problem, you can reboot using the diskette and run the SETUP program.)

Notes: As an added feature, if you're using a version of DOS older than 3.3, you may run the programs to update the time and date in the real-time clock without resorting to the SETUP program.

CMOSPUT
Command   **Robert L. Hummel**

Purpose: Retrieves the CMOS configuration settings on AT and later systems saved by CMOSGET so you can reload them instantly after changing batteries and avoid having to reconfigure your entire system from scratch.

Format: `[d:] [path]CMOSPUT`

See CMOSGET.

CO   Michael J. Mefford
Command

Purpose: Copies, moves, or deletes files individually or in tagged groups from directory listings sorted by name, extension, size, or date.

Format: `[d:][path]CO [d:][\directory][/E][/S][/D][/T][/O]`

Remarks: Entered without any of its optional parameters and switches, CO displays an alphabetized listing of the current directory with a menu of function key commands on the right. The file attributes (archive, hidden, read-only, and system) are shown by the appropriate letters to the right of each listed file.

The Up Arrow and Down Arrow keys move the file-selection highlighted bar one line at a time. Ctrl-PgUp and Ctrl-PgDn move to the top and bottom of the current display page (21 files), while PgUp and PgDn allow you to scroll through the entire directory listing. The Home and End keys go to the beginning and end of the listing, respectively. Pressing a letter moves the highlighted bar to the first (then subsequent) filename(s) beginning with that letter.

Multiple files are tagged for group copying, moving, or deleting by pressing the grey plus (+) key; the grey minus (-) key unmarks a mistagged file.

The optional /E, /S, /D, /T, and /O command-line switches sort the initial directory listing by Extension, Size, DaTe (/D and /T operate identically), or by Original DOS order. Once CO is running, function keys F7 (Name), F8 (Extension), F9 (Size), and F10 (Date) can be used for subsequent sorts. F1 initiates the Copy process for the highlighted (or marked) file(s). F6 toggles the Copy Verify option (comparable to DOS /V). F2 and F3 are used for Move and Delete. You are prompted for the appropriate destination for Copy and Move: different drives and paths are supported, as is the use of the DOS ? and * wildcards. Renaming while copying is permitted.

When a marked (tagged) file is successfully copied, its marker arrow is replaced by an asterisk. If a floppy disk becomes filled, CO automatically attempts to find other marked files that will fit, but backup will then halt with some files remaining to be copied. Replace the full diskette with another, press F1 again, re-enter the correct destination drive, and the remaining marked files will be copied.

To divide the contents of a directory into two parts, mark and copy the first set of files, as above, so that all have the "copied" asterisk. Then press F5 to mark the previously untagged files and repeat the copying process for the second group.

Notes: CO functions can alternately be performed by Ctrl-letter commands: ^C (Copy), ^D (Delete), ^M (Move), ^V (Verify), ^N (sort by Name), ^E (sort by Extension), ^S (sort by Size), and ^T (sort by Date).

COLDBOOT
Command
Charles Petzold

Purpose: Performs a full power-on reboot, complete with initial self-test diagnostics.

Format: `[d:] [path] COLDBOOT`

Remarks: Put this in batch files to discourage unauthorized users. Include a test that jumps to this command if the snooping user doesn't answer it properly.

Running this makes your system act as if you had turned the main power switch off and then on again.

For a faster reboot that skips the initial tests, see WARMBOOT. For a flexible utility that allows both kinds of rebooting and lets the user abort the process, see REBOOT.

COLOR
Command

Paul Somerson

Purpose: Sets foreground and background colors from the command line and clears the screen to those colors.

Format: `[d:] [path]COLOR bf`

where *f* is a hex foreground color and *b* is a hex background color.

Remarks: You must enter two different hex numbers from 0 through F, where *f* is the foreground and *b* is the background. Enter anything else and COLOR.COM will simply print instructions on how to use it.

You may enter alphabetical hex digits in either uppercase or lowercase. Digits may be separated by spaces, commas, or any other characters, or entered next to each other.

Entering a background higher than 7 will make the foreground blink. See BROWSE for a color chart.

Example: Entering:

`COLOR 71`

(or COLOR 7,1 or COLOR 7 1) will set the colors to blue text on a white background, and clear the screen.

Notes: This will set the foreground and background colors (on a color system) but not the border, since IBM doesn't support border colors on any systems other than the CGA. However, if you're using a CGA and want to set the border, run the companion BORDER.COM program.

See COLOR2 for a program that sets colors but doesn't clear the screen.

COLOR2   **Jozef H. Khoe and Paul Somerson**
Command

Purpose: Sets foreground and background colors from the command line but leaves the contents of the screen intact.

Format: `[d:][path]COLOR2 bf`

where *f* is a hex foreground color and *b* is a hex background color.

Remarks: While the companion program COLOR.COM program clears the screen when it sets the colors, this doesn't disturb the screen contents. It does so by writing to the attribute bytes in video memory, and assumes a 25 x 80 screen at segment B800H.

As with COLOR.COM, you must enter two different hex numbers from 0 through F, where *f* is the foreground and *b* is the background. Enter anything else and COLOR2.COM will simply print instructions on how to use it.

You may enter alphabetical hex digits in either uppercase or lowercase. Digits may be separated by spaces, commas, or any other characters, or entered next to each other.

Entering a background higher than 7 will make the foreground blink. See BROWSE for a color chart.

If you want to patch the program so it colors more than a 25 x 80 screen, change the word at address 146. The default value there is 7D0H (for a 2,000-byte screen), and it's stored in "backwords" order. The easiest way to change it is to use the DEBUG:

```
A 145
```

command and plug in a whole new MOV instruction to replace the existing:

```
MOV CX,07D0
```

COLORPIK
Command
Jozef H. Khoe and Paul Somerson

Purpose: Lets you change screen colors by pressing arrow keys.

Format: [d:] [path]COLORPIK

Remarks: Pressing the Left and Right Arrow keys cycles through all available colors. Pressing the Up and Down Arrow keys cycles through the eight available background colors — without clearing the screen.

When you see the color combination you want, just press the Enter key to lock it in and exit.

If you want to abort the process and restore your original colors, press Esc. Since the program lets you use the same foreground and background colors, which makes any text on the screen invisible, pressing Esc will put everything back to normal.

Notes: This program is hard-wired for an 80 x 25 screen.

COLORSET
Command
Charlie Butrico

Purpose: Memory-resident utility that sets the foreground, background, and border colors on color systems, and prevents attempts by applications software to reset these colors to grey on black.

Format: [d:] [path]COLORSET FG/BG BORD

Remarks: While dozens of small programs can set your screen colors, many popular programs (such as *dBASE II*) will reset them to a drab grey on black. The first time you execute COLORSET, it will set your colors, remain in memory, look for such resetting instructions, and will instead set the colors to the ones you specified. Later executions of COLORSET will update the attributes only.

FG/BG is the foreground and background color (a decimal number from 0 to 255). To calculate *FG/BG*, multiply the number of the background color by 16 and add the number of the foreground color to it.

BORD is the border number (a decimal number from 0 to 15).

Examples: The FG/BG number for blue text on a white background is 113, i.e., ((7*16) + 1).

The number for red text on a cyan background is 52, i.e., ((3*16) + 4).

Keying just one number or using COLORSET on an EGA will change only the foreground and background colors.

After running COLORSET, the DOS CLS command will clear the screen to the colors you chose rather than to the default DOS grey on black.

Notes: DOS does not permit you to use bright background colors; trying a FG/BG number higher than 127 will produce text that blinks.

COLRSHOW   Paul Somerson
Command

Purpose: Shows all possible foreground-background color combinations on color systems.

Format: `[d:][path]COLRSHOW`

Remarks: With 16 possible foreground colors and eight possible background colors, you can mix and match 128 color combinations. COLRSHOW.COM uses BIOS INT 10 service 9 to show them all. (Actually, it shows only 120, since it skips any combinations that have the same background and foreground colors.)

Because it needs to print something in the foreground, it fills the entire screen with the ASCII character that happens to have the same value as the color attribute shown.

When you first run it, COLRSHOW will fill the screen with ASCII character 01 smiling faces. Since the color attribute that has the same value as the character shown — 01 — is blue (color 1) on black (color 0), the screenful of faces will appear in blue on black.

You can press the Up Arrow repeatedly to increase the value of the character shown (as well as the color it's shown in), or the Down Arrow key to decrease this value. Or you can type in any letter other than a space to fill the screen with that character in the color that matches its ASCII value. (Typing in a space wouldn't show anything other than a green background.)

Examples: Typing a "t" will fill the screen with red lowercase "t" characters on a white background, since the hex value of "t" is 74, and the color attribute 74 is red (4) on white (7).

Pressing the Up Arrow repeatedly will fill the screen with blue ASCII 01 characters, then green ASCII 02 characters, then cyan ASCII 03 characters, etc. Pressing the Down Arrow key repeatedly will display these characters in descending order. If you reach the top or bottom of the list of possible values, the program will let you cycle through them all again.

Pressing Esc will quit. The screen will remain set in the color you last selected.

COMPARE
Batch file command

Vytenis Markevicius

Purpose: Provides a simple technique for processing user input in batch files without having to worry about testing lots of uppercase and lowercase variations.

Format: `[d:] [path]COMPARE string1 string2`

Remarks: DOS makes it easy to control branching by passing parameters into batch files from the command line. You can then use IF statements to compare such parameters and branch accordingly. But DOS is case sensitive, so a string n characters long requires 2^n IF statements to compare all of the possible uppercase and lowercase variations.

A string containing the three characters ABC would require eight IF statements (testing for aBc, ABc, aBC, etc.) to exhaust every possible combination. Anything longer than two or three characters becomes impractical to test, and ends up frustrating users who are typing in the right string but in the wrong case.

COMPARE.COM speeds up the process dramatically by comparing two strings and ignoring the case of the alphabetic characters. On return, it sets ERRORLEVEL 255 if both strings are equal and ERRORLEVEL 0 if they are not equal or if a syntax error has occurred. After executing COMPARE.COM, your batch file may take appropriate action with a statement like:

```
IF ERRORLEVEL 255 (do something)
```

Example: The following sample COMPTEST.BAT shows how the program works:

```
ECHO OFF
IF %2!==! GOTO OOPS
COMPARE %1==%2
IF ERRORLEVEL 255 GOTO MATCH
ECHO The strings are not equal.
GOTO END
:MATCH
ECHO The strings are equal.
GOTO END
:OOPS
ECHO The format required is:
ECHO %0 string1 string2
:END
```

Once you create this batch file, type:

```
COMPTEST hello HELLO
```

or:

```
COMPTEST hello HeLlO
```

and it will respond with the message "The strings are equal."

Change any letter in either string to another character, or make one string longer than the other, and the batch file will print:

```
The strings are not equal.
```

CONFIRM
Command

Jeff Siegel

Purpose: Intercepts any Shift-PrtSc commands to send a screen dump to the printer, asks for confirmation, and aborts the process if desired.

Format: `[d:][path]CONFIRM`

Remarks: While the Shift-PrtSc instant screen dump is a terrific feature, at one time or another just about everyone has pressed these keys by mistake, wasting much time and paper.

If your printer is on you have to wait until it finishes grinding out the contents of the screen, and then readjust the paper to the top of the next page. If it's off, your system will hang until DOS realizes that the printer is not going to respond.

CONFIRM.COM pops up a small window and lets you confirm or cancel each print screen attempt before it has a chance to tie up your system.

Try installing CONFIRM.COM after all other memory-resident programs (TSRs) like GRAPHICS.COM. CONFIRM takes up approximately 512 bytes when resident, and modifies the print screen interrupt (hex 5) to point to itself. Test this program out with your other resident programs loaded before you start using it with unsaved data files in RAM.

If you find that this conflicts too much with other TSRs, try the smaller DISABLE and ENABLE nonresident programs included in this package.

You may need to modify CONFIRM to work with certain IBM compatibles that have a different keyboard layout or numbering system. CONFIRM reads the keyboard port directly to ensure that it will work with programs that modify the keyboard interrupt vector. If it doesn't respond to Y and N, and if your computer uses a different keyboard format, try changing the scan code for the Y and N keys.

(If you have to switch keys, use DEBUG's U Unassemble command and hunt down lines that look like CMP AL,15. The scan code for the Y key on a PC is hex 15; for the N key it's hex 31.)

Notes: Most other tricks for preventing unwanted Shift-PrtSc dumps work by disabling the print screen function more or less permanently. CONFIRM gives you total control over screen dumps.

Here are two short, but very effective alternate techniques:

1.   When you press Shift-PrtSc, DOS issues an interrupt 5, which first looks at a location in low memory called STATUS_BYTE to see whether your system is already dumping a screen to the printer. If STATUS_BYTE is equal to 1, DOS thinks a screen dump is taking place, and exits the routine without dumping another screen to the printer. If STATUS_BYTE is equal to 0, the routine sets STATUS_BYTE to 1 so that it cannot interrupt itself, then does the actual dump, and finally resets STATUS_BYTE equal to 0 and exits the routine.

This means you can temporarily disable the Shift-PrtSc routine with a simple assembly language routine that sets STATUS_BYTE to 1. A similar routine can turn the function back on by setting STATUS_BYTE to 0. The DISABLE and ENABLE programs in this package will do just that.

If you rarely use the Shift-PrtSc function but have a habit of activating it when you don't want to — and you don't want to install yet another memory-resident program like CONFIRM — you can put DISABLE in your AUTOEXEC.BAT file and leave it more or less permanently off.

2.   You could also deal with errant Shift-PrtSc commands by replacing the ROM INT 5 routine with a one-instruction routine in RAM that passes control back to the program that was running as if nothing had happened.

Robert Hummel used this technique in his NOINT5.COM program, (which is included in this package) by changing the vector for INT 5 so it points to a dummy routine rather than the one in ROM.

See ENABLE, DISABLE, and NOINT5.

CONTROL
Command

Richard Kihlken

Purpose: Reads decimal values from the command line and sends them to your printer.

Format: [d:] [path]CONTROL n [, n, n...]

where *n* is a decimal value from 0 to 255

Remarks: Many users like to configure their printers automatically from within batch files, or on the fly at the DOS prompt. While it's possible to write lots of different COM files for each control code you want to send, it's far easier to create one master print control program that reads codes off the command line.

CONTROL.COM reads any decimal arguments you enter and sends them to your printer. You can use any legal delimiters between the numbers.

The limit on the number of codes you can send is 127, which is the maximum number of arguments DOS will transfer into the Program Segment Prefix (PSP).

CONTROL.COM is designed to send codes to LPT1. If you need to change this, use DEBUG to alter the word at address 13B.

Example: To send a CHR$(12) form feed, for instance, you'd simply type:

CONTROL 12

Or to send the IBM Esc+G command to turn on double-strike printing, type:

CONTROL 27 71

since 27 is the ASCII value of Esc, and 71 the ASCII value of "G."

Littering your disk with dozens of tiny COM files can really eat up space. But while this technique lets one utility dispatch all your printer control code chores, you have to remember the actual codes. A batch file like PRINTER.BAT below will handle up to nine control codes, and prompt you if you forget them and enter just the name of the batch file:

```
ECHO OFF
IF %1!==! GOTO OOPS
CONTROL %1 %2 %3 %4 %5 %6 %7 %8 %9
GOTO END
:OOPS
ECHO Enter decimal control codes after the
ECHO word %0 on the DOS command line:
ECHO --------------------------------------
ECHO 10 CPI=18 12 CPI=27 58 17 CPI=15
ECHO DP=27 73 0 DRAFT=27 73 3 NLQ=27 73 1
ECHO WIDE=27 87 1 CANCEL WIDE=27 87 0
:END
```

COPYSAFE
Command

Michael J. Mefford

Purpose: Prevents accidentally overwriting files when using the COPY command.

Format: [d:] [path] COPYSAFE

Remarks: COPYSAFE is a memory-resident utility that displays the filename(s), drive, and directory of any file that will be overwritten if a COPY command is executed. After being warned, you are given the opportunity either to terminate the COPY procedure or to continue, and so overwrite the file.

COPYSAFE should be loaded only once per session. The best procedure is to include it in an AUTOEXEC.BAT file. Be sure, however, to load COPYSAFE after any commands (such as DATE or TIME) that pause for user input.

Notes: 1. Because of the way DOS processes commands in a batch file, COPYSAFE cannot warn against accidental overwriting if you run COPY as part of a .BAT file. Similarly, it is not designed to handle instances in which the COPY command is used to concatenate files.

2. COPYSAFE is highly compatible with other memory-resident programs (TSRs), but because absolute compatibility among all possible

TSR utilities cannot be guaranteed, you should check its operation on your system thoroughly.

CPU-NDP
Command
Baron L. Roberts

Purpose: Identifies the main CPU and any math coprocessor chips installed in any PC or compatible.

Format: [d:][path]CPU-NDP

Remarks: There are now eight types of CPUs and three types of NDPs (Numeric Data Processors) in use. These CPUs and NDPs span a wide range of instruction set capabilities and performance differences. As the capability and performance gap widens between the low-end Intel 8088 and NEC V20 CPUs and the state-of-the-art Intel 80386, it becomes increasingly wasteful to write code to the low-end chips. And the same is true with NDPs as the chip has grown from the 8087 to the 80387.

Most routines can identify only a few CPU or NDP types and usually cannot distinguish between the eight-bit external data bus CPUs (Intel 8088, 80188 and NEC V20) and the 16-bit external data bus models (Intel 8086, 80186, NEC V30). These differences become especially important in critical timing loops.

CPU-NDP.COM individually identifies Intel 8088, 8086, 80188, 80186, 80286, 80386, as well as NEC V20, V30 CPUs, and Intel 8087, 80287, 80387 NDPs.

CS
Command
Charles Petzold

Purpose: Clears the screen when using displays of more than 25 lines.

Format: [d:][path]CS

Remarks: The DOS CLS command is hard-coded for 25-line displays, and so does not fully clear the screen when using 43-line (or similar) EGA displays. CS is a simple replacement for CLS in such cases.

CTRLLOCK
Command

Joe Dorner

Purpose: Temporarily disables the Ctrl key.

Format: `[d:] [path]CTRLLOCK`

Remarks: Once this is installed it will prevent users from breaking out of programs by typing Ctrl-C or Ctrl-ScrollLock, and from rebooting by typing Ctrl-Alt-Delete.

The only way to remove it from memory is to reboot (or install it using INSTALL/REMOVE). This means you either have to turn the main power switch off or run a simple program like WARMBOOT.COM or REBOOT.COM (both of which are included in this package).

Notes: 1.   This program makes using *WordStar*, with its heavy reliance on the Ctrl key, nearly impossible. If you accidentally happen to load *WordStar* while CTRLLOCK is active, you can save and exit by simulating Ctrl-KX. To do this, hold down the Alt key, type 11 on the number pad (not the top row number keys), and then release the Alt key. Then type X.

2.   Be careful if you try using this with a memory-resident program like *SideKick* that takes over the keyboard. Since this program uses INT 9, it may end up in a battle with other memory-resident programs over the INT 9 keyboard interrupt.

See WARMBOOT, COLDBOOT, and REBOOT.

CTYPE
Command

Jeff Prosise

Purpose: Recovers the cursor when it disappears upon leaving an application, and lets you customize the cursor shape.

Format: `[d:] [path]CTYPE [/xy]`

Remarks: The optional */xy* command line parameter, which can also be used in an AUTOEXEC.BAT file, consists of two letters ranging from A to the letter that represents the maximum number of scan lines in the current video mode character box. This is N for an MGA or an EGA in 25-line mode (14 scan lines), and H for an EGA in 43-line mode or a CGA in text mode (eight scan lines).

Entered without the /xy parameter, CTYPE brings up a selection frame. As you use the arrow keys to move the cursor inside the frame, the cursor size and shape gradually changes. Pressing the spacebar at this point alternately shows the cursor against a sample line of text and returns to the selector frame. Pressing Enter selects the cursor shape shown and returns to the command line prompt.

When the cursor is temporarily lost, as when exiting from *SideKick* (or some other TSR utilities) while in a 43-line EGA mode, entering CTYPE will restore the cursor.

Notes: Many applications programs reset the cursor internally for their own purposes. These settings will supercede those of CTYPE. To restore the CTYPE cursor on exit, run such programs from a batch file whose last line resets the desired CTYPE parameters. Or, just use this in combination with STICK.

CURSOR   Paul Somerson
Command

Purpose: Sets cursor shape.

Format: `[d:][path]CURSOR se`

where *s* is the cursor starting scan line and *e* is the cursor ending scan line, in hex notation.

Remarks: A monochrome display uses 14 scan lines for each character, 0 - 13. A CGA (and, for all practical purposes an EGA) uses eight scan lines, 0 - 7.

While the EGA character box has 14 lines, most programs designed to work on color systems assume an eight-line box. Using the default color scan lines 6 and 7 on an EGA would normally result in a cursor blinking somewhere in the middle of the character box. The EGA BIOS's built-in "cursor emulation" logic translates the normal cursor size into something more appropriate for a 14 scan line character.

The CURSOR.COM number to enter for the default monochrome cursor is BC (starting at scan line hex 0B, or decimal 11, and ending at scan line hex 0C or decimal 12). The number for the default CGA cursor is 67 (starting at scan line 6 and ending at scan line 7).

You can change the size and shape of the cursor by specifying new starting and ending values. A low starting line and a high ending line yields a block cursor. You can also end up with unusual shapes by making the starting line higher than the ending line.

Entering the default values will bring the cursor back to normal.

Example: To set a block cursor on a color system type:

CURSOR 07

To put it back to normal, type:

CURSOR 67

To set a block cursor on a mono system, type:

CURSOR 0C

Notes: The EGA has a BIOS bug that can do strange things with the cursor. Running this program with the parameters 67 can usually put things back to normal.

If you want to use larger numbers than single hex digits to specify the starting and ending scan lines you can try Charles Petzold's CURSOR3.COM program. Type everything below to create it:

```
DEBUG
A
MOV AX,[005D]              ; 1st Parameter
CALL 0116                 ; Call ASC2HEX
MOV CH,AL                 ; Save in CH
MOV AX,[006D]             ; 2nd Parameter
CALL 0116                 ; Call CONVERT
MOV CL,AL                 ; Save in CL
MOV AH,01                 ; Set Cursor
INT 10                    ; through BIOS
INT 20                    ; Terminate
CALL 0125                 ; ASC2HEX:
XCHG AL,AH                ; Subroutine to
```

```
CALL 0125                ; convert ASCII
MOV CL,04                ; digits in AX
SHL AH,CL                ; to one-byte
ADD AL,AH                ; value in AL
RET
OR AL,20                 ; ASC2HEX: Converts
SUB AL,57                ; one ASCII digit
JNB 012D                 ; to hexadecimal
ADD AL,27
RET

RCX
2E
N CURSOR3.COM
W
Q
```

Be sure to leave the blank line above RCX and to press Enter at the end of each line. To use it, follow CURSOR3 with a two-digit hex start line and a two-digit hex stop line. Then, if you want to try something strange like a starting line of 99 and an ending line of F3, enter:

```
CURSOR3 99 F3
```

You can usually see the current cursor setting by typing:

```
DEBUG
D 40:60 L2
Q
```

CURSOR2   **Paul Somerson**
Command

Purpose: Lets you create any cursor shape you want interactively by pressing the arrow keys.

Format: [d:] [path] CURSOR2

Remarks: CURSOR2 gives you an easy way to see what cursor shapes are possible, with the option of changing your current cursor.

When you first load the program, the current cursor drops down one line.

Pressing the arrow keys will change the cursor shape as follows:

- Up Arrow: increase starting line
- Down Arrow: decrease starting line
- Left Arrow: increase ending line
- Right Arrow: decrease ending line

Each time you press an arrow key, the value changes by 1 in the direction indicated.

If you like what you see, you can press the Enter key, which will lock in the currently displayed value and then exit.

However, since many values will either make your cursor disappear entirely or will produce something that you can't possibly use, you may press Esc to abort the process and the program will usually restore your original cursor.

If you load CURSOR2 and then press Enter without making any changes, the program will display a set of instructions.

CURSREAD
Command

Paul Somerson

Purpose: Reports the starting and ending cursor lines as maintained by BIOS low memory.

Format: [d:] [path] CURSREAD

Remarks: BIOS tries to keep track of the cursor size — the starting and ending lines — by maintaining two bytes in low memory at addresses 0040:0060 and 0040:0061. This program simply reports the values stored there.

If any value is larger than hex F (decimal 15), the program quits.

The values maintained by BIOS aren't always the actual cursor starting and ending line values. But if you use the accompanying CURSOR.COM utility to set legal values, this will tell you what they are.

You can also use service 3 of BIOS interrupt 10 to obtain the same information. To adapt CURSREAD.COM so it uses this service instead of dredging the values out of low memory, type:

```
DEBUG CURSREAD.COM
E 107 B4 03 CD 10
F 10B 114 90
W
Q
```

DATECHEK   Patrick R. McClintock
Batch file command

Purpose: Lets a batch file execute a program on a specified day of the week and optionally run it only once each month.

Format:
```
[d:][path]DATECHEK N
IF ERRORLEVEL 2 GOTO NO
IF ERRORLEVEL 1 GOTO YES
```

where *N* is a number from 1 to 7 (Sunday = 1, Monday = 2, ... Saturday = 7), and where the first IF ERRORLEVEL message screens out wrong days of the week, and the second screens out wrong weeks of the month.

Remarks: Users often want to do a certain job on a certain day of the week or the first week of each month — pay bills, do a complete hard disk backup, test a hard disk thoroughly for errors, etc. But DOS doesn't provide a direct way to accomplish this.

DATECHEK.COM, when run inside a batch file such as CHKDATE.BAT (below), makes the process simple.

The program requests the system date via function 2AH, and looks for the day of the week. If it discovers that the current date is indeed the day of the week specified by the user, it then checks to see if the weekday happens to be the first one of these in the current month. This would let you check to see if it's a Friday, and if so, whether it happens to be the first Friday of the month. You can test for one or both events with IF ERRORLEVEL.

The sample CHKDATE.BAT file demonstrates how this works:

```
ECHO OFF
IF %1!==! GOTO OOPS
GOTO %1
:1
SET DAT=Sun
GOTO NEXT
:2
SET DAT=Mon
GOTO NEXT
:3
SET DAT=Tues
GOTO NEXT
:4
SET DAT=Wednes
GOTO NEXT
:5
SET DAT=Thurs
GOTO NEXT
:6
SET DAT=Fri
GOTO NEXT
:7
SET DAT=Satur
:NEXT
DATECHEK %1
IF ERRORLEVEL 2 GOTO NO
IF ERRORLEVEL 1 GOTO YES
:YESBUT
ECHO It's %DAT%day (not the first one)
GOTO END
:NO
ECHO It's not %DAT%day
GOTO END
:YES
ECHO It's the first %DAT%day
GOTO END
:OOPS
ECHO Enter a day number:
ECHO (1=Sun, 2=Mon, 7-Sat)
:END
```

To run CHKDATE.BAT make sure DATECHEK.COM is in the same directory. If you enter just:

```
CHKDATE
```

the batch file will print a message reminding you to enter a number from 1 to 7 representing the weekday you want to test (where 1 = Sunday and 7 = Saturday).

If the current day is a Friday in the middle of the month, and you enter:

```
CHKDATE 6
```

the batch file will print:

```
It's Friday (not the first one)
```

However, if the current day does happen to be the first Friday of the month, the batch file will print:

```
It's the first Friday
```

If the current day is Friday, but you enter:

```
CHKDATE 3
```

which represents Tuesday, the batch file will print:

```
It's not Tuesday
```

All of these messages are just placeholders. Put the name of the program(s) that you want to run once a week under the :YESBUT label. Or insert the name of the program(s) you want to run once a month under the :YES label.

DATECHEK returns an IF ERRORLEVEL code of 2 if the day you specified isn't the current day of the week. It returns an IF ERROR-LEVEL code of 0 if the day you specified does match the current day but doesn't happen to be the first one of these in the current month. And it returns a code of 1 if the days match and it *is* the first one that month.

Notes: You have to specify a numeric day of the week for DATECHEK.COM to work. If you enter anything other than a number from 1 through 7, the program will exit and print a short set of instructions.

However, if you're running CHKDATE.BAT and you enter a number that's out of range, or something that's not a number, you'll get a "Label not found" error message generated by DOS in this sample batch file. This happens because the batch file uses the numeric day of the week both as a parameter for DATECHEK.COM and as a label to translate the number into a word.

CHKDATE.BAT uses %VAR% environment variables. These were first documented under DOS 3.3, but they worked in earlier versions. (However, DOS 3.0 had trouble with them.) You don't need them to make DATECHEK.COM work; they're included in the sample CHKDATE.BAT batch file only to demonstrate the process.

Environment variables consume ennvironment space. If the CHKDATE.BAT batch file doesn't work, it could be because you haven't specified enough enviroment space.

Under DOS 2.0 and 2.1 you can patch COMMAND.COM at address ECF to represent the number of 16-byte memory paragraphs that will make up your new environment. (For DOS 2.11 the address is DF3.)

For DOS 3.0 and 3.1, put a:

```
SHELL [d:][path]COMMAND.COM /E:n /P
```

command in your CONFIG.SYS file, where n represents the number of 16-byte paragraphs (from 10 to 62). Using ten paragraphs gives you the standard 160 bytes; pushing it to 62 yields 992 bytes of environment space.

For versions 3.2 and later, use the same SHELL command but use n to specify the actual number of bytes (from 160 to 32768) rather than paragraphs. The default in all cases is 160 bytes.

DAZZLER   Paul W. Carlson
Command

Purpose: Exercises color systems.

Format: `[d:][path]DAZZLER`

Remarks: DAZZLER.COM is an example of a self-modifying program that saves a lot of code. It will run on color systems only.

When the program starts it creates a pattern onscreen. Pressing the spacebar toggles an opcode from INC to DEC (or vice versa) which reverses the direction of the pattern's movement. Pressing Esc exits the program.

The program works by creating a pattern in the first two video pages. Then, alternating between pages 0 and 1, it increments or decrements every character's color on the inactive page, and makes the inactive page the active page. The program would have been considerably shorter without so much page swapping, but this method prevents CGA flicker.

Readers send lots of "gee whiz" color demo programs to *PC Magazine*, but most of them use nonstandard techniques that refuse to work on certain kinds of systems. DAZZLER should work on any color screen.

Notes: You may increase or decrease the speed by patching the value at address 1A8. Making it smaller (all the way down to 0) speeds things up. Increasing the value at this address slows things down.

DDIR
Command
Charles Petzold

Purpose: Displays all (or selected) directory entries in double columns, sorted in alphabetical order.

Format: `[d:][path]DDIR [d:][path][filename[.ext]]`

Remarks: If no parameters are specified, DDIR will list all files in the current directory. Use of the global characters ? and * in the filename and extension parameters is supported.

If more than one screenful (48 entries) is required, the display pauses at the bottom, showing the message, "Press any key to continue."

Notes: Because DDIR.COM loads a secondary command processor, it will not operate under the Run option of *WordStar* and possibly with some other programs that normally allow calling up external programs. For the same reason, it cannot be automatically reinvoked using the F3 key when at the DOS command level.

DECIDE
Sample program
Paul Somerson

Purpose: This is included here because it's used as an example earlier in the book, and having it on disk spares you from typing it in.

Format: `[d:][path]DECIDE`

Remarks: This small program simply reads the hundredths value returned by the DOS Get Time function (hex 2C) of interrupt 21 and prints one of three statements in an approximate random pattern.

The clock actually ticks about 18.2 times a second (based on the output of the system's 1.190 MHz timer / 64K), so the finest available clock resolution is about .055 of a second rather than .01 of a second. However, the numbers that end up in the DL hundredths register are random enough to use here.

DELETE
Command
R. Andrew Killinger

Purpose: Deletes any file or group of files in any legal path and, unlike DOS, produces a tally of the files it erased.

Format: `[d:][path]DELETE filespec`

where *filespec* is any legal filename or wildcard specification.

Remarks: DOS is sometimes too taciturn. If you want to erase just a few BAK files and you accidently type:

`DEL *.BA*`

you'll take all your BAT and BAS files with it too. Since DOS doesn't report how many files it erased, you won't know until the next time you type DIR and see a whole lot fewer files than you expected. You could have put things back together at the time by using a package like the *Norton Utilities*, but once you start writing new files and changing old ones, unerasing becomes impossible.

DELETE works just like the DOS DEL or ERASE command, except that it provides a count of the files it deleted.

It also respects directories. If you have a subdirectory called \WORK, and a file called WORK1 and you're in the root directory and type:

```
DEL WORK
```

DOS will think you're telling it:

```
DEL \WORK\*.*
```

and prompt you with:

```
Are you sure (Y/N)?
```

If this has happened to you before, you know it's trying to tell you — in its own terse way — that it's about to erase all the files in a directory. Type Y and everything is gone. But DELETE won't let this happen.

DELETE won't delete files with hidden, system, or read-only directory attributes.

Examples: To erase OLDFILE.BAK, type:

```
DELETE OLDFILE.BAK
```

To erase all your BAK files in the \WORK subdirectory, type:

```
DELETE \WORK\*.BAK
```

DIRCOMP
Command

Charles Petzold

Purpose: Lets you compare the contents of two directories in alphabetical order, with the options of redirecting the screen display either to a file or to a printer.

Format: `[d:][path]DIRCOMP directory1 directory2`

Remarks: The directories to be compared do not need to be on the same drive. Use the normal DOS backslash (\) character in specifying the path to a desired directory. The DOS wildcard characters (* and ?) may be used to limit the filenames displayed.

Identically named files are shown side by side to facilitate comparison of their size, date, and time. Other filenames are presented alphabetically in their respective directory columns. Use Ctrl-NumLock to halt the display scrolling temporarily; striking any key thereafter causes scrolling to resume.

In comparing large directories it is frequently desirable to redirect the output of DIRCOMP either to a file (which you can then call up with your word processor) or to a printer.

Examples: To create a file called COMPARE.TMP in the root directory of your currently active drive that compares the listings in your \LETTERS subdirectory with the files contained on a floppy disk in drive A: you would enter:

```
DIRCOMP \LETTERS A: > \COMPARE.TMP
```

To print out the same comparison without creating a file, you would enter:

```
DIRCOMP \LETTERS A: > PRN
```

Notes: DIRCOMP does not provide forward/backward scrolling capabilities. If these are desired as an alternative to alphabetical listings, use SCAN-DIR, which is also contained on this disk.

DIRNOTES
Command

Michael J. Mefford

Purpose: Presents an alphabetically sorted DOS-format directory listing in the left portion of the display, together with a coordinated, 38-character field on the right side of the screen in which you can enter descriptive comments about the file contents, hotkeys, etc. Your notes are automatically saved when the Esc key is pressed, in a file called DIRN-abc.DAT, where abc represents the first three letters of the directory name.

Format: `[d:] [path]DIRNOTES [d:] [path] [directory]`

Remarks: Use the cursor Up Arrow and Down Arrow keys to scroll the coordinated directory listings and notes line by line. PgUp and PgDn scroll by screenful, and Home and End go to the beginning and end of the listings. The DIRNOTES editor operates in overstrike mode and incorporates a backspace delete. The Left Arrow and Right Arrow keys can be used to move the cursor without deleting characters beneath it.

A "U" immediately after the directory listing indicates that that file has been updated since the last time the DIRNOTES data file was updated, so the file description may need to be changed.

The DAT file created by DIRNOTES is in standard ASCII format, which means you can examine the contents by using the DOS TYPE or MORE commands.

Do not attempt to edit the DAT file with a word processor, however, as the record field lengths are fixed and any changes made other than by DIRNOTES itself may render the file unrecoverable.

DISABLE
Command
Steve Dozier

Purpose: Disables Shift-PrtSc function. Running ENABLE will turn it back on.

See CONFIRM.

DISKPREP
Command
Jeff Prosise

Purpose: Lets you make a floppy disk self-booting even if the DOS "system" files were omitted when the disk was formatted and program files have subsequently been added to it.

Format: `[d:] [path]DISKPREP [d:]`   (followed by:)

`SYS [d:]`   (a DOS command)
`COPY COMMAND.COM [d:]`   (a DOS command)

Remarks: In addition to having a copy of COMMAND.COM, diskettes formatted with the /S (system) option contain the two hidden files, IBMBIO.COM and IBMDOS.COM, as the first two entries in the disk directory. (The clusters for IBMBIO.COM must be continuous.) A nonsystem disk stores regular files in the areas where the system files must reside if the disk is to be self-booting.

DISKPREP relocates clusters currently used by nonsystem files to other areas on the disk, updating the disk directory and file allocation table accordingly. After running DISKPREP, the DOS SYS command can install the hidden system files in their proper locations, and the DOS COPY command can be used to put COMMAND.COM on the disk.

DISKPREP does not support high-density (1.2 megabyte) diskettes, 3–1/2 inch disks, or hard disks. However, provided sufficient room remains on the disk, DISKPREP can be used to upgrade the DOS version on a self-booting disk. Attempting to replace a later DOS version with an earlier (lower numbered) one is not recommended.

Notes: 1.   DISKPREP should not be used on floppy disks that already contain subdirectories.

2.   Since copy-protected disks often employ nonstandard sectoring for their own purposes, DISKPREP is not recommended for use on such disks.

DISKSCAN   Charles Petzold
Command

Purpose: Locates and identifies disk errors on hard and floppy disks, Bernoulli boxes or other similar storage devices.

Format: `[d:][path]DISKSCAN [d:]`

Remarks: The DOS "Abort, Retry, Ignore?" and the CHKDSK "x lost clusters found" messages tend to appear after it is too late to save possibly valuable data. Regular use of DISKSCAN will show when a hard disk is beginning to go bad— for example, when a specific sector or two in an as-yet unallocated cluster has become unusable since the disk was formatted. (DOS marks and does not use bad clusters it finds while formatting. DISKSCAN reports these "Flagged as bad.")

DISKSCAN error messages include:

CRC Error: Data checksum as recalculated during read does not agree with checksum stored on disk when written.

Sector Not Found: Sector boundary created during formatting is no longer readable.

File Alloc. Table and Can't Read FAT: Very serious error: Back up what you can with COPY and then reformat disk before trying to put files back on it.

Boot Sector: If this sector of a hard disk goes bad, put a DOS disk in drive A: and issue SYS C: command. Then COPY COMMAND.COM C:. This will put a fresh copy of the system files on drive C:. If this does not work, boot up again from the external DOS floppy disk, back up all hard disk files, and reformat the hard disk.

Root Directory: Errors here could keep you from later being able to load a file or save updates to it. CHKDSK will probably indicate unallocated cluster chains or cross-linked files, and you may have to use CHKDSK/F to save what you can.

Unallocated: As yet, not serious, as the bad sector is not being used. When it is, though, and you try to save a file with this sector, you'll get an "Abort, Retry, Ignore" message. Select "Ignore" to save what you can, then REName the file and save again under the new name. Use RECOVER *filename* with the original file; this will cause DOS to flag its cluster(s) as bad. (DISKSCAN does not enter the bad cluster numbers in the File Allocation Table; FORMAT and RECOVER do.) Then delete the original (RECOVERed) filename and check the second version you saved (under the new name) to see how much (if any) of it is usable.

Used by file: While DISKSCAN reports the bad sector number, it does not do a cross-check to see which of your files is using that sector. You may be able to identify this by issuing the command:

```
SWEEP COPY *.* NUL
```

When COPY encounters the file with the bad sector it will report "Abort, Retry, Ignore." Note the bad file and press "I" to continue.

Read Fault and General Failure: The sectors so designated are bad, but the errors reported don't fall into any of the above categories.

DOS-EDIT
Command

Charles Petzold

Purpose: Lets you move to, edit, and reenter onscreen DOS commands without retyping.

Format: [d:][path]DOS-EDIT

then

<Up Arrow>	(enables DOS-Edit keys)
<Left Arrow>	(cursor left)
<Right Arrow>	(cursor right)
<Up Arrow>	(cursor up)
<Down Arrow>	(cursor down)
<Backspace>	(destructive backspace)
<Ins>	(insert/overwrite toggle)
<Del>	(delete character)
<PgDn>	(delete to end of line)
<PgUp>	(cursor to column 1)
<Home>	(cursor to initial column #)
<Esc>	(exit edit mode, no changes)
<End>	(transfer text line right of cursor to end of original line)
<Enter>	(like <End>, plus execute command)

Remarks: When loaded, normally through your AUTOEXEC.BAT file, an initial Up Arrow keypress activates the DOS-EDIT mode. (Thereafter, the Up Arrow functions as a normal cursor arrow key.) If you move the cursor down to the original line, you will leave the DOS-EDIT mode (e.g., the Left Arrow key will once again delete characters).

Examples: A typical use of DOS-EDIT is to correct a long command line in which you made a typing error. Simply move the cursor up to the mistyped line, correct the mistake (using the appropriate keys listed under Format), press Home (to position the cursor to pick up the whole line), then Enter.

A less obvious example occurs if you have just done a DIR listing and want to run a program. Move the cursor up and just to the right of the program name. Press PgDn to delete the extension and the rest of the line, PgUp to position the cursor to pick up the whole command name, then Enter.

Notes: DOS-EDIT is a memory-resident program, and so may cause conflicts with some other memory-resident software programs. Such problems can frequently be solved by changing the order in which the several memory-resident programs are loaded. DOS-EDIT should be loaded before ASSIGN.COM and before *SideKick*, for example.

DOSKEY Command

Jeff Prosise

Purpose: DOSKEY is multitalented memory-resident utility that:

1. Lets you change foreground and background colors in DOS by pressing function keys.

2. Includes a command stack that holds up to 15 of your most recent commands and lets you scroll through the stack and re-execute them easily.

3. Provides macro abilities for DOS function keys F3 through F12.

4. Gives you enhanced editing functions on the DOS command line.

5. Enhances the the CLS (Clear Screen) command by preventing it from resetting your colors to the default DOS grey on black, and lets it operate on displays of more than 25 lines.

Format: `[d:][path]DOSKEY`

Remarks: DOSKEY is normally loaded through a line in your AUTOEXEC.BAT file, but you may load it at any time from the command line.

After you load the program, pressing the F1 key will successively cycle through all 16 foreground (text) colors, while pressing F2 will cycle through the eight available background colors. Pressing the Shift key with either F1 or F2 reverses the direction of the cycling. CLS remembers the last-set color scheme and will clear screens of varying sizes to that color setting.

If you type a space between CLS and Enter, the color will revert to the DOS defaults (grey on black).

Function keys F3 through F12 are assigned by default to the following command macros:

F3	dir
F4	type
F5	copy
F6	delete
F7	chdir
F8	path
F9	browse
F10	cls
F11	backup
F12	restore

Use the Up Arrow and Down Arrow cursor keys to bring previously issued commands from the command stack back to the command line so you can re-execute them.

The new command line editor supports Left Arrow and Right Arrow cursor motion without deletion, lets you move to the ends of the line with Home and End, and allows character deletion with Del and backspace. Pressing Esc clears the command line, and pressing Ins toggles between insert and overwrite modes.

You may change any of these assignments by using DEBUG. The BROWSE command (F9) is another *PC Magazine* utility, written by Charles Petzold, that lets you scan quickly through files. Use of the F11 and F12 keys requires an enhanced keyboard and appropriate BIOS support.

To change the default macro strings assigned to the function keys, note that:

1.   Each string consists of the text of the string preceded by a byte indicating the string length.

2.   The total length of the string (including the length byte) cannot exceed 32 bytes. You may end a string with ASCII 13 (carriage return) but this isn't required.

The offset addresses corresponding to the beginning of each string, together with the associated commnd, are as follows:

Key	Address	Default
F3	148	dir
F4	168	type
F5	188	copy
F6	1A8	delete
F7	1C8	chdir
F8	1E8	path
F9	208	browse
F10	228	cls
F11	248	backup
F12	268	restore

To install a new string just overwrite the text of the old one. If you want the command string to be executed automatically when you press the function key, terminate the string with a byte of value FFH. Do not include the FFH delimiter in the string's character count. If you omit the FFH, the string will be output but you'll have to press Enter yourself to execute it. The default settings for the function keys F3-F9 illustrate this. When you press F4 for "type", for example, you have to enter a filename after it. Without the file specifier, the command is meaningless.

To change the F10 macro so it executes "CHKDSK" (with an FFH added to produce automatic execution), make sure that DOSKEY.COM is in your current directory and that DEBUG.COM is in the current subdirectory or in one that your PATH knows about. Then, at the command line, enter:

```
DEBUG DOSKEY.COM
E 0228 06 "CHKDSK" FF
W
Q
```

DOSKEY initially assumes you want to use the drab DOS default grey on black. But you can have DEBUG reassign the initial color selection to anything you want. If you prefer white text on a blue background, for instance, DOSKEY can be modified to set that combination the first time CLS is issued. The advantage is that you aren't forced to pound on the F1 and F2 keys every time you boot up. A simple CLS will do.

Two bytes inside DOSKEY define the startup color selection. The byte at offset 142 determines the text color (07, or white). And the one following it at 143 is the initial background color (00, or black). You can put any value from 0 through hex F (decimal 15) at the first byte, and any value from 0 through 7 at the second. See BROWSE for a summary of available colors.

DOSLEVEL   **Phillip A. Smith**
Batch file command

Purpose: Lets you test for different DOS versions from inside a batch file.

Format: `[d:][path]DOSLEVEL`
                `IF ERRORLEVEL n result`

where *n* is the two most signficant digits of a DOS version number with the period removed (e.g., 33 for DOS 3.30) and *result* is the command or program to execute if the test is true.

Remarks: DOS behaves so differently in its many versions that you often have to make special provisions in your batch files for users with older versions.

For instance, in more recent versions of DOS the IF EXIST command can test whether files exist outside of the current directory. However, DOS 2.x can't handle searches outside the default directory. If you want to include a test for a faraway file, you have to find a way to tell what version of DOS is being used, and then jump around the test if the version is old.

DOSLEVEL makes it easy to test for different DOS versions. It returns a two-digit exit code equal to ten times the two leftmost digits of the DOS version (so the code contains the same major and minor version numbers but without a period in the middle). It will report DOS 3.3 as 33, DOS 2.1 as 21, etc.

Examples: The following VERSTEST.BAT batch file reports which version you're using:

```
ECHO OFF
DOSLEVEL
IF ERRORLEVEL 40 IF NOT ERRORLEVEL 41 ECHO Version 4.0
IF ERRORLEVEL 33 IF NOT ERRORLEVEL 34 ECHO Version 3.3
IF ERRORLEVEL 32 IF NOT ERRORLEVEL 33 ECHO Version 3.2
```

```
IF ERRORLEVEL 31 IF NOT ERRORLEVEL 32 ECHO Version 3.1
IF ERRORLEVEL 30 IF NOT ERRORLEVEL 31 ECHO Version 3.0
IF ERRORLEVEL 21 IF NOT ERRORLEVEL 30 ECHO Version 2.1
IF ERRORLEVEL 20 IF NOT ERRORLEVEL 21 ECHO Version 2.0
```

Obviously this exact batch file is not necessary, since you can use the DOS VER command to report the current version. You can, however, modify it to branch around commands that older versions can't handle.

DOWN Command   Charles Petzold

Purpose: Changes the logged directory downward, in the direction away from the root.

Format: `[d:][path]DOWN`

Remarks: If you keep a lot of deeply nested subdirectories on your hard disk you can jump easily from a one several levels down to one closer to the root by entering CD .. (or Charles Petzold's companion program UP) repeatedly.

However, DOS doesn't provide an easy way to move in the other direction. DOWN.COM does. Just enter:

```
DOWN
```

and you'll be whisked to the next lower directory.

This obviously works best if your directories are "skinny" rather than full of branches, since each time DOWN goes down a level it has to decide which of the several branches there to traverse. But if you're clever about the way you set up your subdirectory tree, you can have DOWN shuttle you gracefully down any path.

Notes: DOWN is part of a trio of subdirectory navigation aids. See also UP and NEXT.

DR
Command

Michael J. Mefford

Purpose: Provides an integrated set of file management facilities for sorting, viewing, renaming, deleting, and moving files to another directory.

Format: `[d:][path]DR [d:][directory]`

Remarks: The default filename display (21 per page, to a maximum of 721) is sorted alphabetically. Various switches may be added to sort by other criteria:

/E (sort by Extension)
/S (sort by Size)
/D or /T (sort by DaTe)
/O (sort by current DOS DIR Order)

When a DR listing is onscreen, a menu is displayed showing additional options. A highlight bar illuminates a single filename, and the Up and Down Arrow keys move the highlight bar a line at a time. The PgUp and PgDn keys move the bar a page at a time, and Ctrl-PgUp and Ctrl-PgDn move it to the top and bottom of the current page. Home and End move to the beginning and end of the directory listing. Pressing (and repressing) a letter moves the bar to the first (and successive) filenames beginning with that letter.

The highlighted file may be brought onscreen for viewing by pressing F1 (or Enter or Ctrl-V). The Up and Down Arrows, PgUp and PgDn, and Home and End work within the file, as well. Esc, Enter, or F1 return you to the menu and directory listing. When pressed at the menu level, Esc terminates the program.

Within DR, the following function keys (and alternatively, the indicated Ctrl-letter) combinations are used:

F1	Ctrl-V (or Enter)	View file
F2	Ctrl-D	Delete file
F3	Ctrl-R	Rename file
F4	Ctrl-M	Move file
F5	(none)	CONFIRM Delete On/Off
F6	Ctrl-W	WordStar hi-bit On/Off
F7	Ctrl-N	Sort files by Name

F8	Ctrl-E	Sort files by Extension
F9	Ctrl-S	Sort files by Size
F10	Ctrl-T	Sort files by daTe

Successive sorts can be used to arrange files, e.g., in order of size and then, additionally, by extension.

Files can be renamed and may be moved from one directory to another within DR, but they cannot be renamed and moved in a single step. Files cannot be copied from within DR.

Examples: To sort the initial display of the C:\PROG directory of the default drive by size:

```
DR C:\PROG /S
```

If you were already logged into C:\PROG you could load DR simply by typing:

```
DR
```

Once DR was loaded, you could arrange the files by size either by pressing the F9 key or Ctrl-S.

Notes: One of the best features of DR is that you can instantly figure out which file in a directory was created most recently. Just load DR with the /T or /D option (or load it without any options and then press the F10 function key or Ctrl-T), and then press End.

See DRNEW.

DRAW
Command

Michael J. Mefford

Purpose: Provides low-resolution (320 x 200) color or high-resolution (640 x 200) monochrome drawing capabilities on a color, enhanced color, or (with some MGA boards) a monochrome display, without the need to work in BASIC.

Format:

`[d:][path]DRAW[/K]`	(Option I)
`[d:][path]DRAW string[/K]`	(Option II)
`[d:][path]DRAW filespec/F[/K]`	(Option III)

Remarks: Entered at the DOS prompt with no arguments on the command line (Option I), DRAW looks in the current directory for a file named DRAW.DAT and executes the commands in that file. A sample DRAW.DAT file is included on this disk. The file can be examined, and similar files created, with a regular ASCII word processor.

Alternatively, DRAW can be entered with a string of commands (Option II, for a simple graphic) or with the name of a file consisting of commands (Option III). Any legal DOS filename may be used, and full path support is provided, but a /F terminator must be appended to the filename. An optional /K may be added to prevent a keystroke from halting execution.

Example: You can get a feel for how DRAW operates by entering, at the DOS prompt:

```
DRAW X0 C2 BU50 M+40,70 L80 M+40,-70 BD5 P2,2
```

This will create a red triangle in the middle of your screen. You can trace the specific steps in this command sequence by referring to the DRAW Command Set table, presented in the following pages.

The DRAW Command Set

Xn Change to low resolution 320 x 200 color graphics.

If X is not found, the default is 640 x 200 high resolution black and white graphics. X must be the first character of the command line or the first character in a file.

The palette will be changed to n, where n can be either zero or one. See C (color) command below for the color of each palette.

K Do not poll the keyboard while drawing. If K is not found, any keystroke terminates the program.

Sn Flood the screen color to pattern n. The n must be a decimal number in the range 0-255, and represents an eight-bit pattern. Normally this command is issued immediately after the X command (if present), to clear the screen with a background color other than black. For example, to clear to color red (2) in low resolution, the command is S170 (binary 10101010).

color	320 x 200	640 x 200
0	0	0
1	85	255
2	170	NA
3	255	NA

Pattern colors may also be used. For example, a pattern of half green and half black would be S68 (binary 01000100). In high resolution, each bit represents a dot, eight dots per byte. This is why only two colors (black or white) are available. In low resolution, there are two bits per dot, so four combinations can be represented. In the example here the sequence is 01 (green), 00 (black), 01 (green), 00 (black). See C (color) command below for complete coding of the colors.

U,D,L,R,   These commands, followed by a number, will move in one of the follow-
E,F,G,H   ing compass directions:

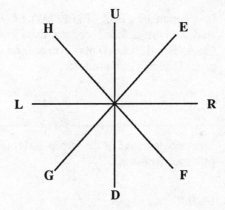

Mx,y   Move x,y units either relative to the current position or to the absolute coordinates, x,y. If the x coordinate is prefaced with either a plus sign or minus sign, the move is relative. Otherwise, the move is absolute. Note, you do not need to include a plus sign in front of the y coordinate in a positive y move.

Pp,b   Paint the color p until the border color b is found. The paint originates from the current position.

B   Blank move. The move following a B will move the desired units without plotting points. The next command will then continue drawing.

N   No update. The draw command following an N command will plot
                points, but the position will not be updated. The next draw command
                will start at the same position as the last.

Cn   Change the color to n. All draws after a C command will be in color n.
                The n can be 0 (black) or 1 (white) in high resolution and 0 to 3 in low
                resolution. In low resolution, the color is dependent on the palette.

	320 x 200		640 x 200
color	palette 0	palette 1	–
0	black	black	black
1	green	cyan	white
2	red	magenta	NA
3	yellow	white	NA

Related Commands

Four commands, BSAVE, BLOAD, LOWRES, and HIGHRES, are included on this disk to speed the display of pictures created by DRAW.
(BSAVE and BLOAD may also be used with text screens for instant
presentation.) The command:

```
BSAVE filespec
```

saves a byte image of the screen buffer to a file (with optional drive and
path specifications).

```
BLOAD filespec
```

writes the saved image back to the screen buffer.

LOWRES and HIGHRES are used in batch files with BLOAD to set the
appropriate display resolution.

Examples: Create the following batch file, SAVE.BAT, using an ASCII word
             processor, EDLIN, or COPY CON:

```
ECHO OFF
DRAW
BSAVE PICTURE
```

Now, similarly create a second batch file, INSTANT.BAT:

```
ECHO OFF
LOWRES
BLOAD PICTURE
PLAY
PAUSE > NUL
MODE CO80
```

If you now enter INSTANT at the DOS prompt the picture you saved previously will appear, with a musical background. Pressing any keystroke will clear the display.

Notes: The PAUSE > NUL line in INSTANT.BAT prevents the DOS prompt from intruding on the picture, but will not work on DOS versions prior to DOS 3.0.

DRIVES
Command

Gerald A. Monroe

Purpose: Reports which drives are active in your system.

Format: `[d:][path]DRIVES`

Remarks: Knowing out which drives are active can be very useful if you're using lots of DOS alias commands (SUBST, JOIN, and ASSIGN).

DRIVES.COM will scan the entire alphabet to report all valid drives, logical and physical, while ignoring any gaps. (It's easy for gaps to result since DOS allows drive configurations such as A:, B:, C:, W: and Z:.)

DRIVES, like COMMAND.COM, employs DOS interrupt 21 function call 29H to check valid drives.

DRIVSPEC
Command

John D. Haluska

Purpose: Reports the characteristics and status of the default or selected drive.

Format: `[d:][path]DRIVSPEC [d:]`

Remarks: DRIVSPEC reports the number of bytes per sector, sectors per cluster, total clusters, total bytes capacity on drive, minimum bytes required for each file, available clusters, and available bytes on the selected drive. It obtains this information from DOS Current Drive service 19H and DOS Drive Free Space service 36H.

Typing:

```
DRIVSPEC B:
```

will produce a report similar to:

```
Characteristics/status of drive B

   512 bytes per sector
     2 sectors per cluster
   354 total clusters
362496 total bytes capacity on drive
  1024 bytes minimum required for each file

    34 available clusters
 34816 available bytes on drive

   FORMAT: DRIVSPEC [d:]
```

(The number of free clusters and available bytes will obviously vary from disk to disk.) Typing DRIVSPEC without any parameters after it will report on the default drive.

Users often confuse sectors, tracks, and clusters. This program should help straighten things out. It's also useful in showing how wasteful some hard disks (such as ten meg XTs running under DOS 2.1) can be.

DRNEW
Command

Michael J. Mefford

Purpose: DRNEW provides some slight enhancements to the existing features of the original program. However, it runs a bit more slowly than the older version.

Remarks: See the DR text above for the list of basic features and key controls. DRNEW also maintains dynamic counts of the amount of free space on the disk. When you delete files, DRNEW updates the number.

While DR does not display subdirectories (including the . and .. directory entries), DRNEW does. And it lets you log into those other directories by moving the highlighted bar to them and then pressing Enter.

The other significant addition is that when you run DRNEW you can execute programs by positioning the highlighted bar on the COM or EXE file you want to run, and then pressing Ctrl-Enter.

See DR.

ECOH   **Tom Kihlken**
Batch file command

Purpose: ECHOes batch file messages in reverse video.

Format: `[d:][path]ECOH text`

where *text* is the message (127 characters or fewer) you want to display.

Remarks: The DOS ECHO command provides a simple way to display messages from within a batch file. ECOH.COM is similar, except it displays the message in reverse video.

ECOH.COM works by first obtaining the screen color attribute at the current cursor position. It then performs a bit rotation on the attribute to exchange the background and foreground colors. This creates a new attribute that is the true reverse of any color combination. It then displays the message one letter at a time, using a ROM-BIOS routine that writes a character / attribute pair. Since this routine doesn't automatically advance the cursor, a second BIOS function call is required to advance it after each character is written.

Notes: By using ECOH.COM in combination with the LOCATE.COM message positioning utility included in this package you can make a message flash onscreen. Since ECOH looks at the existing color and reverses it, each subsequent time you execute it the color will reverse. So to flash a message, just repeat several ECOH statements at the same cursor position:

```
LOCATE 8,36
ECOH This is a test
LOCATE 8,36
ECOH This is a test
LOCATE 8,36
ECOH This is a test
```

EDPATHA   Charles Petzold
Command

Purpose: Lets you edit the DOS PATH directly.

Format: `[d:][path]EDPATHA`

When you type EDPATHA the cursor will drop down a line, but nothing else will happen, At this point you can use the normal DOS editing tools to edit the path. Pressing F3 will summon the entire existing PATH. Using F1 or the Right Arrow key will write it to your screen character by character. Press Enter when done to register your changes.

Remarks: COMMAND.COM maintains a section of memory called the DOS environment, but doesn't give you direct access to it. The environment will always contain a variable called COMSPEC that indicates the disk and directory where COMMAND.COM is stored. If you've used the PATH and PROMPT commands, the environment will contain those also. You can examine the environment contents by entering SET without any parameters after it at the DOS prompt, and can use the SET command to add or delete entire new environment strings. But you can't edit existing ones.

Whenever COMMAND.COM loads an executable program into memory, it makes a copy of the environment table for use by that program. The segment address of this copy is stored at offset 2CH in the program's Program Segment Prefix (PSP). Any changes a program makes to this environment alter this copy and not the original.

If you only need to add a new directory path to your existing path string, you can do so very easily with a one-line batch file called ADDPATH.BAT:

```
PATH=%PATH%;%1
```

You'd execute it like this:

```
ADDPATH C:\SUBDIR
```

where SUBDIR is a subdirectory on drive C: that you want to add to your path string.

If you try this, first type:

```
PATH > OLDPATH.BAT
```

This will put the contents of your existing path into a batch file called OLDPATH.BAT. If you make a mistake, or just want your old path back, simply type:

```
OLDPATH
```

at the DOS prompt and everything will be restored.

The use of environment variables (like %PATH%) isn't documented until version 3.3, although it works in many earlier editions. Batch files now let you use an environment variable name as a replaceable parameter by surrounding the name with percent signs. When COM-MAND.COM executes the batch file it replaces %PATH% with the existing directory path from the environment. In ADDPATH.BAT, this is followed by a semicolon and the parameter on the ADDPATH command line. When COMMAND.COM runs this batch file, it's as if a whole new PATH command were being executed.

The only real problem is that a bug in DOS 3.0 can't handle the %PATH% construction. ADDPATH.BAT won't work under DOS 3.0. And while being able to add subdirectories to the end of an existing path is welcome, it's far from enough.

EDPATHA.COM ("EDit PATH with Assembly program") searches the environment for a path and saves it in an area of memory following the characters "PATH=." The program then passes this string to DOS function call 0AH which lets you use the DOS editing keys to change it.

You can change COMMAND.COM's environment from within a program by reloading a secondary copy of COMMAND.COM, but ED-PATHA uses a much easier method involving an undocumented and little known DOS interrupt called interrupt 2EH. This interrupt passes a command line addressed by DS:SI to COMMAND.COM. The command line must be formatted just like the unformatted parameter area of a PSP.

The first byte must be a count of characters, and the second and subsequent bytes must be a command line with parameters. The whole thing is terminated by a carriage return.

When this command line is passed to interrupt 2EH, COMMAND.COM executes it. If the transient part of COMMAND.COM is not present in memory, the resident part will reload it. However, it does not load a new copy of COMMAND.COM into memory.

Interrupt 2EH is very strange. If interrupt 2EH is called from a program executed from within a batch file, it will abort the batch file. If it's executed in a program run from a "Run a Program" or "Shell" option in an application that has itself been executed from a batch file, it aborts the whole chain and will probably crash your system. Interrupt 2EH is also difficult to use because it destroys the contents of all registers including the stack pointer.

Example: If you want to add something onto the end, press F3. This recalls the whole line on screen and lets you tack on the addition. You could also do normal inserts and deletions. When you're done, press Enter and ED-PATHA will send the string to interrupt 2EH. COMMAND.COM then executes it like a regular PATH command.

You may use the following DOS editing keys to change the PATH string:

Key	DOS Editing Function
F1*	Copies characters one by one from old template to new.
F2	Copies up to specified character from old template.
F3	Copies all remaining characters from old template.
F4	Skips up to specified character from old template.
F5	Replaces old template with existing one.
Esc	Interrupts and cancels changes in current line.
Ins	Switches DOS from overwrite mode into Insert mode.
Del	Erases character at cursor and skips over it in template.
Bksp**	Erases one character to the left.

*Same as Right Arrow key.
**Same as Left Arrow key.

Notes: Heavy use of the DOS environment, particularly from within an AUTOEXEC.BAT file, can cause it to become full. Under DOS 3.1, you can expand the amount of memory COMMAND.COM reserves for the environment by putting the following line in your CONFIG.SYS file:

```
SHELL COMMAND.COM /E:n /P
```

where n is a number between 10 and 62 indicating the number of paragraphs to allocate for the environment. The default is 10 paragraphs. Each paragraph is 16 bytes, so this allows you to set the environment to anything between 160 bytes and 992 bytes. This feature was not documented in DOS 3.1.

In DOS 3.2, the /E parameter was documented but it was also changed. You use the same syntax:

```
SHELL=COMMAND.COM /E:n /P
```

but now x refers to the number of bytes reserved for the environment and may range from 160 to 32768.

EGA12   **Charles Petzold**
Command

Purpose: Resets number of screen rows to 12 when used with an EGA and a 350-line Enhanced Color or monochrome monitor.

Format: [d:][path]EGA12

Remarks: EGA12 can be used in DOS and with EGA-aware applications programs. Applications that reset the video mode on entry will revert to 25 lines per page.

When used together with EGAMODE 1 (a 40-column mode), EGA12 produces a more normal aspect ratio with large-size characters.

When entering the 12-line mode the screen may momentarily contract or roll once. This is normal and will cause no harm. You can return to the normal 25-line mode by entering either of the following:

EGAMODE 3 (EGAMODE 7 for monochrome)
EGA25

These commands are included on this disk. The DOS MODE CO80 (or MODE MONO) commands will also restore normal 25-line operation.

To clear the screen in 12-line mode, use the CS command contained on this disk. (The DOS CLS command is hard-coded for 25 lines.) See also EGAPRTSC in this manual — an EGA-aware print screen command.

The IBM EGA BIOS loses the cursor on the Enhanced Color Display and the underscore on the monochrome display when it has to recalculate the number of displayable rows, and this bug is normally duplicated by other EGA boards. The bug is fixed in EGA12.

Notes: 1.   ANSI.SYS should not be used with EGA12.

2.   Because EGA12 uses an 8 x 14 pixel character box size, it can show only seven lines per page when used with a regular, 200-line color display.

EGA25 Command   Charles Petzold

Purpose: Resets the EGA default font and 25-row display after using programs (several of which are on this disk) that change these conditions when using an EGA and a 350-line Enhanced Color or monochrome monitor.

Format: `[d:][path]EGA25`

Remarks: When reentering the 25-line mode the screen may momentarily contract or roll once. This is normal and will cause no harm. Alternate ways of returning to the normal 25-line mode include issuing the command EGAMODE 3 (color) or EGAMODE 7 (monochrome). These commands are included on this disk. The DOS MODE CO80 (or MODE MONO) commands will also restore normal 25-line operation.

Notes: Because EGA25 uses an 8 x 14 pixel character box size, it can show only 14 lines per page when used with a regular 200-line color display.

EGA35
Command

Charles Petzold

Purpose: Resets number of screen rows to 35 when used with a 350-line Enhanced Color or monochrome monitor and an EGA.

Format: `[d:][path]EGA35`

Remarks: EGA35 can be used in DOS and with EGA-aware applications programs. Applications that reset the video mode will revert to 25 lines per page; some others may write only to the top 25 of the 35 displayable lines.

When entering the 35-line mode the screen may momentarily contract or roll once. This is normal and will cause no harm. You can return to the normal 25-line mode by entering either of the following:

EGAMODE 3 (EGAMODE 7 for monochrome)
EGA25

These commands are included on this disk. The DOS MODE CO80 (or MODE MONO) commands will also restore normal 25-line operation.

To clear the screen in 35-line mode, use the CS command contained on this disk. (The DOS CLS command is hard-coded for 25 lines.) See also EGAPRTSC in this manual — an EGA-aware print screen command.

The IBM EGA BIOS loses the cursor on the Enhanced Color Display and the underscore on the monochrome display when it has to recalculate the number of displayable rows, and this bug is normally duplicated by other EGA boards. The bug is fixed in EGA35.

Notes: 1. ANSI.SYS should not be used with EGA35.

2. Because EGA35 uses an 8 x 14 pixel character box size, it can show only 20 lines per page when used with a regular, 200-line color display.

EGA43	**Charles Petzold**
Command	

Purpose: Resets number of screen rows to 43 when used with an EGA and a 350-line Enhanced Color or Monochrome monitor.

Format: `[d:][path]EGA43`

Remarks: EGA43 can be used in DOS and with EGA-aware applications programs. Applications that reset the video mode on entry will revert to 25 lines per page; some others may write only to the top 25 of the 43 displayable lines.

When entering the 43-line mode the screen may momentarily contract or roll once. This is normal and will cause no harm. You can return to the normal 25-line mode by entering either of the following:

EGAMODE 3 (EGAMODE 7 for monochrome)
EGA25

These commands are included on this disk. The DOS MODE CO80 (or MODE MONO) commands will also restore normal 25-line operation.

To clear the screen in 43-line mode, use the CS command contained on this disk. (The DOS CLS command is hard-coded for 25 lines.) See also EGAPRTSC in this manual — an EGA-aware Print Screen command.

The IBM EGA BIOS loses the cursor on the Enhanced Color Display and the underscore on the monochrome display when it recalculates the number of displayable rows, and this bug is normally duplicated by other EGA boards. The bug is fixed in EGA43.

Notes: 1.   This is one of the most potentially useful utilities for an EGA user, since it puts the screen into the popular 43-line mode. But it needs a little help.

The accompanying CLSEGA.COM utility will set the EGA screen mode to 43-lines, set the colors (in this case to bright white on dark blue), set the cursor properly, and clear the entire screen.

2.   ANSI.SYS should not be used with EGA43. Also, because EGA43 uses an 8 x 14 pixel character box, 200-line color monitors will show only 25 lines.

EGA50
Command   Charles Petzold

Purpose: Resets number of screen rows to 50 when used with an EGA and a 350-line Enhanced Color or monochrome monitor.

Format: `[d:] [path]EGA50`

Remarks: EGA50 can be used in DOS and with EGA-aware applications programs. Applications that reset the video mode on entry will revert to 25 lines per page; some others may write only to the top 25 of the 50 displayable lines.

When entering the 50-line mode the screen may momentarily contract or roll once. This is normal and will cause no harm. You can return to the normal 25-line mode by entering either of the following:

EGAMODE 3 (EGAMODE 7 for monochrome)
EGA25

These commands are included on this disk. The DOS MODE CO80 (or MODE MONO) commands will also restore normal 25-line operation.

To clear the screen in 50-line mode, use the CS command contained on this disk. (The DOS CLS command is hard-coded for 25 lines.) See also EGAPRTSC in this manual — an EGA-aware print screen command.

The IBM EGA BIOS loses the cursor on the Enhanced Color Display and the underscore on the monochrome display when it has to recalculate the number of displayable rows, and this bug is normally duplicated by other EGA boards. The bug is fixed in EGA50.

Notes: 1.   ANSI.SYS should not be used with EGA50.

2. Because EGA50 uses an 8 x 14 pixel character box size, it can show only 28 lines per page when used with a regular, 200-line color display.

EGA512 Command   Charles Petzold

Purpose: Lets you switch between two loaded EGA fonts when used on a 350-line Enhanced Color or monochrome monitor and with software that supports display of bold characters.

Format: `[d:][path]EGA512 x y`

Remarks: The values of *x* and *y* may range from 0 through 3, and correspond to the EGA memory blocks into which fonts can be loaded. The *x* parameter corresponds to the font that will be displayed with normal (low intensity) characters. The *y* parameter accesses the font that will be displayed with high-intensity (boldface) characters.

Examples: Load the italic font into EGA memory block 1 with the command:

```
EGAITAL 1
```

Then enter the command:

```
EGA512 0 1
```

If your word processor supports onscreen boldface and does not reset the video mode on entry, regular characters will now appear normally and boldface characters will appear in italics.

To restore the normal display, enter:

```
EGA512 0 0
```

Notes: The chapter on EGA contains suggestions for remapping the EGA palette registers to use other attributes (e.g. blinking, underline) instead of the intensity attribute.

EGABLANK
Command

Charles Petzold

Purpose: Automatically turns off screens connected to EGA cards at preset intervals to prevent "phosphor etching" or "burning."

Format: `[d:][path]EGABLANK`

Remarks: It's possible to etch a permanent image into the green phosphor used on IBM monochrome displays. Users who spend endless hours with one screen element in the same place — a *1-2-3* grid or a *WordStar* menu, for instance — may end up with traces of this element permanently burned into the display.

EGABLANK is a memory-resident utility that turns the screen off automatically to prevent this from happening if nothing has been typed for 7.5 minutes. Typing anything on the keyboard will bring it back to normal.

You can alter the amount of time EGABLANK waits before blanking the screen by changing the current hexadecimal delay value of 2000. A value of 1 will blank the screen every 55 milliseconds. Going up to FFFF gives you about an hour before the lights go out.

To change the value to 1000 (3.25 minutes), load the program into DEBUG by typing:

`DEBUG EGABLANK.COM`

Then type:

`A 137`

and press the Enter key. Enter:

`MOV WO [10A],1000`

and press Enter twice. Then type W and press Enter to save the changes to disk, and then type Q and press Enter to quit DEBUG.

Notes: 1. This program is for EGA and EGA compatibles only. It will not work with other adapters, but it will not harm them either. Although it is really for the monochrome display (since monochromes are the ones susceptible to phosphor burn), it will also work with a color display attached to an EGA. Under extremely unusual circumstances, it could interfere with a program engaged in setting the EGA palette registers.

2.   EGABLANK will not work well with programs that entirely steal the keyboard interrupt, since it has no way of knowing when keys have been struck. If you have any of these programs, you probably know about this since other resident programs won't work with them either. Some more sophisticated commercially available screen blankers continually check the contents of the screen for changes to get around this problem.

EGACOLOR   Charles Petzold
Command

Purpose: Permits temporary remapping any of the 16 default colors displayable on a 200-line CGA monitor to any of the 64 colors displayable on a 350-line Enhanced Color Display connected to an Enhanced Graphics Adapter.

Format: `[d:][path]EGACOLOR XX YY`

Remarks: The parameters *XX* and *YY* are two-digit octal (base 8) numbers derived from the table shown below. Values for XX may range from 00 to 17; values for YY may range from 00 to 77.

Color	IRGB Code			Default rgbRGB Map		
	Binary	Octal	Hex	Binary	Octal	Hex
Black	0000	00	00	000000	00	00
Blue	0001	01	00	000001	01	01
Green	0010	02	02	000010	02	02
Cyan	0011	03	03	000011	03	03
Red	0100	04	04	000100	04	04
Magenta	0101	05	05	000101	05	05
Brown	0110	06	06	010100	24	14
White	0111	07	07	000111	07	07
Dark grey	1000	10	08	111000	70	38
Light blue	1001	11	09	111001	71	39
Light green	1010	12	0A	111010	72	3A
Light cyan	1011	13	0B	111011	73	3B

Light red	1100	14	0C	111100	74	3C
Light magenta	1101	15	0D	111101	75	3D
Yellow	1110	16	0E	111110	76	3E
Bright white	1111	17	0F	111111	77	3F

The first digit in the two-digit octal number represents the 1/3-intensity rgb signal; the second is the 2/3-intensity RGB signal.

Example: To change black to blue and white to yellow (yellow letters on a black screen), execute:

```
EGACOLOR 00 01
EGACOLOR 07 76
```

Notes: Changing modes resets the default EGA colors. To create more permanent mappings, use the EGAPRMOV and EGACOSET utilities on this disk.

EGACOSET (and EGAPRMOV) Commands
Charles Petzold

Purpose: Loads a customizable 16- (of 64) color palette that is reloaded each time video mode 3 is set.

Format: `[d:] [path] EGAPRMOV`
`[d:] [path] EGACOSET`

Remarks: EGAPRMOV (parameter move) is a memory-resident program that moves the EGA ROM BIOS parameter table and seven pointers into RAM, where it can be accessed by EGACOSET (color set). EGAPRMOV is run once each session, normally through your AUTOEXEC.BAT file.

Running EGACOSET maps a color scheme of your choice to each of the 16 EGA registers. These color settings are then activated by entering the EGAMODE 3 command (described elsewhere in this manual) or by issuing the DOS MODE CO80 command. Thus, to bring up your color scheme each time you boot up, you would put the following three lines in your AUTOEXEC.BAT file:

```
EGAPRMOV
EGACOSET
EGAMODE 3
```

The EGACOSET.COM program on this disk contains the default EGA settings for a 350-line monitor. These are, sequentially (in hex):

Black	00	Dark grey	38
Blue	01	Light blue	39
Green	02	Light green	3A
Cyan	03	Light cyan	3B
Red	04	Light red	3C
Magenta	05	Light magenta	3D
Brown	14	Yellow	3E
White	07	Bright white	3F

Entering:

```
DEBUG EGACOSET.COM
```

```
D 100 L2B
```

displays the offsets and hex values of the entire 43-byte program:

```
100 FC 29 C0 8E C0 26 C4 3E-A8 04 26 C4 3D BE 1B 01
110 81 C7 A3 05 B9 10 00 F3-A4 CD 20 00 01 02 03 04
120 05 14 07 38 39 3A 3B 3C-3D 3E 3F
```

Entering E 11B returns the first color value (00), followed by a period (.). Type in the hex value of the desired color after the period and press Enter. After changing as many values as desired, use the W and Q commands, pressing Enter after each, to write the changes to disk and end the DEBUG session.

Examples: To remap black (00) to blue (01), white (07) to bright yellow (3E), and bright white (0F) to bright green (32), make a copy of EGACOSET.COM and enter:

```
DEBUG EGACOSET.COM
E 11B 01
E 122 3E
E 12A 32
W
Q
```

Notes: To use EGACOSET.COM with a regular 200-line color monitor, change the byte (A3) at offset 112 to E3 and the byte (05) at 113 to 00. In this configuration, restrict the colors selected to the 16 values from 00 through 0F.

EGAGRAF
Command

Charles Petzold

Purpose: Provides new screen-dump routine for EGA 640 x 350 graphics displays on an IBM Graphics Printer or compatible only.

Format: [d:][path]EGAGRAF

Remarks: It's difficult to write a universal screen dump program for EGA graphics, since there are no real standards for implementing graphics on printers, and since even the common IBM Graphics Printer won't do a good job handling the 16 different possible colors. Most printers don't have enough resolution to use different dot densities for the different colors. The usual method — printing dots for every color except the background sometimes works and sometimes doesn't.

EGAGRAF.COM is a remain-resident program that prints EGA 640 x 350 graphics displays on IBM Graphics Printers or compatibles only. Load EGAGRAF.COM and it will remain resident in memory until you reboot unless you use INSTALL/RECOVER. When you press the Shift-PrtSc combination in video mode 15 (equivalent to BASIC's mode 9 — EGA 640 x 350 graphics on a monochrome display) or 16 (BASIC's mode 10 — EGA 640 x 350 graphics on an Enhanced Color Display), the resident program will print the screen.

The program prints a dot for every color except the background, which generates white-on-black graphics (or, in the case of the monochrome display, green-on-black graphics) to be printed as black on white. This reversal of colors is normal for printing graphics. If you want black printed as black and all other colors not printed (which is the way it actually looks onscreen), make a copy of EGAGRAF.COM called EGAGRAF2.COM and use DEBUG to change the value of the byte at address 168 to 90 by typing:

```
COPY EGAGRAF.COM EGAGRAF2.COM
DEBUG EGAGRAF2.COM
E 168 90
```

W

Q

If you need to put an image onscreen, run the following BASIC
EGACIRCL.BAS program:

```
100 ' EGACIRCL.BAS — C. Petzold
110 ' (c) 1988 Ziff Communications Co.
120 '
130 DEFINT A-Z:SCREEN 9:CLS
160 FOR I=1 TO 75
170 A=INT(640*RND):B=INT(350*RND)
180 C=INT(40*RND)+5:D=INT(16*RND)
190 CIRCLE (A,B),C,D
200 PAINT (A,B),C MOD 15+1,D
210 CIRCLE (A,B),C-5,D
220 PAINT (A,B),0,D
230 NEXT
240 WHILE INKEY$="":WEND
250 SCREEN 0
```

EGAITAL
Command

Charles Petzold

Purpose: Produces an displayable italic font from the default EGA font when used
with a 350-line Enhanced Color or monochrome monitor.

Format: `[d:][path]EGAITAL`

or

`[d:][path]EGAITAL n`

Remarks: EGAITAL can be executed directly from the DOS prompt. The slanting
algorithm employed is similar (but not identical) to that used by
Microsoft *Word* to display italics in graphics mode. The normal character display can be restored by executing one of the DOS MODE commands, by issuing the EGAMODE 3 (color), EGAMODE 7
(monochrome) commands on this disk, or by executing EGA25.COM
(also on this disk).

The *n* parameter shown in the second format above accepts values from 0 (the default) through 3. It specifies the EGA memory block into which the italic font is loaded. An EGA with 256K memory can hold up to four fonts simultaneously; a 128K EGA, up to two fonts. A 64K EGA board is limited to one font. The EGA512 command, described elsewhere in this manual, allows two fonts to be active simultaneously when using software capable of showing onscreen bold characters.

EGAMODE Command   Charles Petzold

Purpose: Reports/changes the current video mode.

Format: `[d:] [path]EGAMODE [M]`

Remarks: Entered without the optional *M* parameter, EGAMODE displays the current video mode. In text modes, the commands EGAMODE 03 and EGAMODE 07 have the same practical effect as the DOS MODE CO80 and MODE MONO commands, respectively. The chart below lists the M (mode) parameters to which EGAMODE can be switched.

Mode	Type	Display	Resolution	Characters	Box	Colors	Pages
0&1	Text	CD	200x320	25x40	8x8	16	8
		ECD	350x320	25x40	14x8	16/64	8
2&3	Text	CD	200x640	25x80	8x8	16	8
		ECD	350x640	25x80	14x8	16/64	8
4&5	Graphics	CD&ECD	200x320	25x40	8x8	4	1
6	Graphics	CD&ECD	200x640	25x80	14x8	2	1
7	Text	MONO	350x720	25x80	14x9	4	8
8,9,10		PC*jr* modes not supported by EGA					
11&12		Used internally by EGA for loading fonts					
13	Graphics	CD&ECD	200x320	25x40	8x8	16	2(1)
							4(2)
							8(3)
14	Graphics	CD&ECD	200x640	25x80	8x8	16	1(1)
							2(2)
							4(3)

15	Graphics	MONO	350x640	25x80	14x8	4	1(1)
							2(2)
16	Graph	ECD	350x640	25x80	14x8	4/64(1)	1(2)
						16/64(2)	2(3)

Notes: (1) = 64K memory;
(2) = 128K memory;
(3) = 256K memory

Notes: 1.   Users of a Hercules graphics card can activate "page 1" graphics when an EGA is installed with the command sequence:

```
MODE CO80
EGAMODE 16
MODE MONO
```

Use EGAMODE 14 if your EGA is connected to a conventional color monitor.

2.   Should you switch to a mode not supported by your monitor, you can recover by blindly entering EGAMODE 3 (color) or EGAMODE 7 (monochrome).

3.   By adding 128 to the mode number desired you can change modes without clearing the screen (though the cursor is reset to the upper left). These high numbered modes may confuse some applications programs, however.

EGAPAGE   Charles Petzold
Command

Purpose: Reports/changes the current video page.

Format: `[d:][path]EGAPAGE [P]`

Remarks: Entered without the optional *P* parameter, EGAPAGE reports which video page is currently active. The chart presented in this manual for EGAMODE.COM shows which video pages (*P* parameters, beginning with 0) can be used by each EGA mode.

EGAPAGE can be useful when you have material on your screen to which you want to return later. Entering EGAPAGE 1 activates a new screen while retaining the contents of the default EGAPAGE 0 in memory. The previous display can subsequently be recalled by issuing the EGAPAGE 0 command.

Notes:

1. When using an alternate video page do not change video modes, or the previous display contents will be lost.

2. ANSI.SYS cannot be used with other than video page 0.

EGAPALET
Command

Charles Petzold

Purpose: Displays all 64 EGA colors simultaneously on a 350-line color monitor.

Format: `[d:][path]EGAPALET`

Remarks: If a number of the color squares look the same at first glance, adjust the contrast and brightness controls and inspect the screen at close range to confirm that different pixels are being lit.

Starting with the upper left square as row 0, column 0, the octal values for each color can be determined directly from the screen. Brown, for example, is octal 24 (row 2, column 4), a value you might enter in the EGACOLOR.COM utility included on this disk.

Since the EGA is theoretically limited to simultaneous display of only 16 of 64 colors, EGAPALET employs the unorthodox technique of remapping eight color registers every 1/30th of a second. A certain amount of jitter and flickering must therefore be accepted on a PC or XT. The display is more stable on an AT, but the bottom row of squares is elongated. If you are using an AT, this can be cured with DEBUG, as follows:

```
DEBUG EGAPALET.COM
E 102
```

The value 22. will appear. After the period, enter 2B and press Enter. Then write the modified EGAPALET.COM to disk and quit DEBUG by entering the following commands, each terminated by a carriage return:

W

Q

Notes: Only 16 colors are available on monitors displaying 200 lines.

EGAPRMOV   Charles Petzold
Command

Purpose: Moves the EGA ROM BIOS parameter table and pointers into RAM,
where the EGACOSET program also on this disk can find it.

See EGACOSET.

EGAPRTSC   Charles Petzold
Command

Purpose: Replaces the normal print screen BIOS routine to permit using the Shift-
PrtSc command with EGA displays with more than 25 rows.

Format: `[d:] [path] EGAPRTSC`

Remarks: Although the EGA BIOS contains a new print screen routine usable for
screen dumps of displays with 43, 50, 35, or other 25-plus line displays,
this routine is not automatically loaded when you boot up with the EGA
installed.

EGAPRTSC is a memory-resident utility that installs the updated print
screen routines. If you intend to make more than occasional use of a 43-
line display, you should load EGAPRTSC from your AUTOEXEC.BAT
file.

Notes: EGAPRTSC should be loaded early in the AUTOEXEC.BAT file,
before any printer buffers, commands such as PC-DOS GRAPHICS, or
other programs that use interrupt 5.

EGATEST
Command

Terry P. Sanderson

Purpose: Detects presence of EGA in any system and reports which monitors are active.

Format: `[d:] [path] EGATEST`

Remarks: With so many EGAs installed, programmers now have to test for them in addition to MDAs and CGAs. Unfortunately, IBM has not made it easy to identify the presence (and more important, the activity) of an EGA.

Version 2.0 of Microsoft *Word* was one of the first programs to take advantage of the EGA. However, the method it used to detect the presence of an EGA was both awkward and unsupported by IBM. Embedded near the beginning of IBM's EGA ROM BIOS, at location C000:001E, are the letters "IBM". *Word* 2.0 tested for the presence of these letters in the copyright notice, and assumed that an EGA was available if it found them.

It's curious that Microsoft chose this method, as IBM includes a warning in the *EGA Technical Reference* manual about a similar misuse of its BIOS. At location C000:0000, a two byte signature appears (AA55H) that identifies a valid adapter ROM module to the POST routine. IBM explicitly states in the documentation that this signature is *not* to be used as an EGA presence test. However, if you were to disassemble the MODE command (which allows the user to, among other things, set the mode of the video adapter or change monitors in a two-monitor system), you would find the following code fragment:

```
MOV AZ,0C000H          ; move segment address..
MOV ES,AX              ; into es register
CMP WORD PTR ES:0,0AA55H ; is it the signature ?
JNZ                    ; jump if true
```

Here, IBM disobeys its own warning and uses the BIOS signature to test for the presence of an EGA card.

A far more conventional test for the presence of an EGA is to use the extended BIOS features available in the EGA's ROM. When an EGA is present, interrupt 10H (the video interrupt) is vectored to the EGA's ROM, and interrupt 42H is used to revector the old planar ROM video interrupt. The extra EGA features are then available through interrupt 10H.

One of these extended features is called Alternate Select. Its major function is to select the Alternate Print Screen routine, but another of its functions is to return EGA information. The following assembler code segment can be used to request EGA information:

```
MOV AH,12H   ; function 12H
MOV BL,10H   ; subfunction 10H
INT 10H      ; video interrupt
```

This function returns the following information:

Register	Description
BH	mode in effect (color or mono)
BL	memory on EGA (01H=64K, 02H=128K, etc.)
CH	feature bits
CL	EGA switch settings

Note that the BL register is used both on input and to return a value. The standard ROM BIOS interrupt 10H does not have a function 12H, so the BL register is returned intact if there is no EGA. Fortunately, if there is an EGA, the BL register will return a value of 0H, 1H, 2H, or 3H, depending on the memory size, but cannot return a value of 10H. If the BL register has changed, an EGA is present.

This procedure can be used to identify the presence of an EGA, but does not report whether the EGA is active. If the EGA is connected to a color or enhanced color display, a monochrome adapter and monitor can also be installed. And if the EGA is connected to a monochrome display, a CGA and color monitor can also be in the system. Any hardware-dependent routines must take into consideration the possibility of a two-monitor system.

IBM does not provide a video function that determines which adapter is active if more than one is installed. However, the information in the ROM BIOS data area can help ferret out whether the EGA is the active adapter. At absolute location 487H, IBM defines a byte used to store EGA information. Bit 3 of this byte (using the notation that bit 0 is the low-order bit) is the important one here; if this bit is 0, the EGA has the active monitor; if it is 1, another adapter card is active.

Then, by looking again at the values returned by the previous video function call, EGATEST can pinpoint which monitor is active. Register BH returns a value of 0H if the EGA is connected to a color monitor, and a value of 1H if a monochrome monitor is attached. Fortunately, EGATEST does all the dirty work for you and prints the appropriate message onscreen.

EGAUNDER
Command
Paul Somerson

Purpose: A demonstration program for the UNDRLIN2 EGA underlining utility.

Format: `[d:] [path] EGAUNDER`

Remarks: EGAUNDER will display a string of 40 Ps in blue and 40 Cs in green. Then use UNDRLIN2 and UNDRLIN2 N to toggle the blue text underlining on and off when using an EGA.

See UNDRLIN2.

ENABLE
Command
Steve Dozier

Purpose: Turns Shift-PrtSc function back on after you've turned it off temporarily with DISABLE.

See CONFIRM.

ENTER
Batch file command
Frank Tracy

Purpose: Lets you send an Enter character to simulate entering a command in a batch file.

Format: `[d:] [path] ENTER`
`DOS_CMND`

where *DOS_CMND* is a DOS command that won't do anything unless you (or the ENTER utility) send a carriage return through the keyboard.

Remarks: Users have spent much time and aggravation trying to find ways to execute DOS commands such as TIME and DATE remotely in batch files.

The usual trick is to create a small file called CR that contains nothing but a carriage return and an end-of-file marker, and then to redirect the contents of this tiny file into the command. So if they wanted to add the current date to a file, they could do it with a line like:

```
DATE < CR >> LOGFILE
```

This would redirect the output of CR (which was just a carriage return) into DOS to kick the DATE command into action, which would in turn have its output redirected and appended to the LOGFILE file. Whew.

Users later discovered that the MORE.COM command, which was available on every system that had a hard disk, generated a carriage return when it was executed. The chic new way to send the TIME into a file was to include a line in a batch file that said:

```
ECHO One | MORE | TIME >> LOGFILE
```

The "One" that the ECHO command was supposed to display somehow disappeared into the ether, and ended up just moving the whole process along.

The ENTER.COM utility replaces all those tricks. It places the scan code for the Enter key into the first memory location of the keyboard buffer.

To use it, just precede a command that needs a carriage return, such as DATE, with a line that says ENTER. This batch file will append the output of the DATE command to a LOGFILE file:

```
ENTER
DATE >> LOGFILE
```

One common application for this is to do something (log, set, reset, etc.) the DATE and TIME commands together. You can either use the ENTER command twice:

```
ENTER
DATE
```

```
ENTER
TIME
```

or you can use a special version of ENTER.COM called ENTER2.COM that puts a pair of Enter characters into the keyboard buffer rather than just a single one.

See ENTER2.

ENTER2
Batch file command

Frank Tracy

Purpose: Lets you send a pair of Enter characters to simulate entering two commands in a batch file.

Format:
```
[d:] [path]ENTER2
DOS_CMD1
DOS_CMD2
```

where *DOS_CMD1* and *DOS_CMD2* are two DOS commands that won't do anything unless you (or the ENTER utility) send two carriage returns through the keyboard.

Remarks: The common application for this is to follow ENTER2 in a batch file with DATE and TIME and redirect the results into a usage log:

```
ENTER2
DATE >> LOG
TIME >> LOG
```

Obviously you could do this with two individual ENTER commands as well.

ENVCOUNT
Command

Richard Hale Shaw

Purpose: Counts the number of bytes currently used in the DOS environment.

Format: `[d:] [path]ENVCOUNT`

Notes: DOS uses a special section of memory called the environment to do
things like store information on where your main command processor is
located, or what subdirectories to search when you try to run a program
that's not in the current directory. Some programs also use the environment to store variables, and you can adapt this technique in your own
batch files.

The default environment space is a tiny 160 bytes, which can fill up
quickly if you use long PATH and APPEND strings.

Under DOS 2.0 and 2.1 you can patch COMMAND.COM at address
ECF to represent the number of 16-byte memory paragraphs that will
make up your new environment. (For DOS 2.11 the address is DF3.)

For DOS 3.0 and 3.1, use a:

```
SHELL [d:][path]COMMAND.COM /E:n /P
```

command in your CONFIG.SYS file, where n represents the number of
16-byte paragraphs. For versions 3.2 and later, use the same SHELL
command but specify the actual number of bytes rather than paragraphs.
The default in all cases is 160 bytes (ten paragraphs). You can increase it
all the way up to 32K in DOS 3.2 and 3.3, but are limited to 62
paragraphs in earlier versions.

Be sure to add the /P switch or DOS won't run your AUTOEXEC.BAT
file when it boots up.

ENVCOUNT will report how many bytes in your environment space are
currently being used. To fill it, run the TESTENV.BAS program:

```
100 ' TESTENV.BAS — creates TESTENV.BAT
110 OPEN "TESTENV.BAT" FOR OUTPUT AS #1
120 PRINT #1,"ECHO Initializing Strings"
130 FOR A=0 TO 15
140 PRINT #1,"SET ";HEX$(A);"=";STRING$(78,A+65)
150 NEXT
160 PRINT #1,"ENVCOUNT"
170 PRINT #1,"PAUSE"
180 FOR A=0 TO 15
190 PRINT #1,"SET ";HEX$(A);"="
200 NEXT
210 PRINT #1,"ECHO Test complete"
220 CLOSE
```

You can run this by entering:

```
BASICA TESTENV.BAS
```

(or GWBASIC TESTENV.BAS if you're using a generic system). This will create a batch file called TESTENV.BAT that loads a series of temporary environment strings into your environment, then runs ENVCOUNT, and finally erases the temporary strings. If you see the "Out of Environment Space" message, you know you've filled up your environment, which is what you want. If you don't see the message, modify the file to add more strings.

TESTENV adds over 1,200 bytes of strings to the environment, which will overflow it under DOS versions earlier than 3.2 since these can't handle more than 992 bytes. To test larger environments under DOS 3.2 or later, increase the 15 at the end of lines 130 and 180 of the TESTENV.BAS program. Each time you increase this number by 1 you'll take up an additional 80 bytes (or more) of memory. If you want to increase it above 190, change the:

```
STRING$(78,A+65)
```

at the end of line 140 to:

```
STRING$(78,65)
```

If you do make the batch file too large, you won't hurt anything by trying to overflow your environment.

FASTATKB   Robert Patenaude
Command

Purpose: Dramatically speeds up programmable keyboards starting with PC-ATs.

Format: `[d:][path]FASTATKB nn`

where *nn* is a two digit hex number from 00 to 7F.

Remarks: One reason mice are becoming increasingly popular is that keyboards seem so slow. Until the IBM PC-AT, they were slow. But IBM made the AT and all subsequent keyboards programmable. You can change both the delay (the period between the time you press the key and the time the cursor starts to jump) and the typematic rate (how fast the cursor moves if you hold it down).

Unfortunately, IBM didn't provide any decent mechanism for making the changes. As a result, users with high-performance machines ended up dragging their feet (or at least their fingers) unnecessarily.

FASTATKB lets you enter a two-digit hex number that represents a combination of the typematic rate and delay. To figure out the appropriate number, consult the table below.

The higher you go on the chart, the faster the typematic rate, from an incredibly pokey two characters a second at the very bottom to a neck-snapping 30 at the top. You can match each typematic rate setting with one of four delays ranging from a quarter-second to a full second.

The default for an IBM AT is 2C — 20 characters per second and a delay of half a second. In many cases the maximum setting is so extreme that it becomes unusable, but this isn't the case here. The very fastest setting, with a value of 00 (30 characters per second and a quarter-second starting time) is perfectly acceptable. The first time you try it you won't believe how fast it seems. Then after a few days you'll wonder if you can find a way to make it just a tiny bit speedier . . . .

Typematic	Delay (in seconds)			
Rate(/sec)	0.25	0.50	0.75	1.00
30.0	00	20	40	60
26.7	01	21	41	61
24.0	02	22	42	62
21.8	03	23	43	63
20.0	04	24	44	64
18.5	05	25	45	65
17.1	06	26	46	66
16.0	07	27	47	67
15.0	08	28	48	68
13.3	09	29	49	69
12.0	0A	2A	4A	6A
10.9	0B	2B	4B	6B
10.0	0C	2C	4C	6C
9.2	0D	2D	4D	6D
8.6	0E	2E	4E	6E
8.0	0F	2F	4F	6F
7.5	10	30	50	70
6.7	11	31	51	71

6.0	12	32	52	72
5.5	13	33	53	73
5.0	14	34	54	74
4.6	15	35	55	75
4.3	16	36	56	76
4.0	17	37	57	77
3.7	18	38	58	78
3.3	19	39	59	79
3.0	1A	3A	5A	7A
2.7	1B	3B	5B	7B
2.5	1C	3C	5C	7C
2.3	1D	3D	5D	7D
2.1	1E	3E	5E	7E
2.0	1F	3F	5F	7F

The program works by using the OUT command to send a value of F3H to port 60H, which tells the keyboard's processor that the next byte it receives will establish new rate/delay values. This next byte is divided into three parts as follows:

Bit 7, the most significant bit, is always zero. Bits 6 and 5 determine the delay — which will be 1 plus the binary value of bits 6 and 5 times 250 milliseconds.

Bits 4 thru 0 determine the typematic rate. The formula is 8 plus the binary value of bits 2, 1, and 0; times 2 to the power of the binary value of bits 4 and 3; times .00417 seconds; all divided into 1. Got it?

Example: Entering:

```
FASTATKB 00
```

will slam you back into your seat it's so fast. On the other hand:

```
FASTATKB 1F
```

(or anything with a letter in it) will seem brain-damaged. Once you're accustomed to the fastest speed, just for laughs reset it to the IBM default:

```
FASTATKB 2C
```

It'll be so slow you won't be able to type.

Notes:

1. This works on IBM ATs and later systems (and clones) with programmable keyboards only. It won't work on PCs, XTs, and systems without programmable keyboards.

2. You may change speeds on the fly as often as you want.

3. If you enter a number over hex 7F the program will subtract 80 from it.

FASTOFF   **Tom Kihlken**
Command

Purpose: Speeds up floppy disk use on IBM hardware by reducing the length of time it takes for a disk to stop spinning.

Format: `[d:][path]FASTOFF`

Remarks: If you use your PC's floppy disk drives frequently, you probably spend a lot of time waiting for the disks to stop spinning so you can safely switch them. The memory-resident FASTOFF.COM program turns off the drive motor much more quickly than the standard IBM PC does.

The disk motor normally turns off 37 ticks (about two seconds) after the last disk access. FASTOFF reduces this time by decrementing the elapsed time counter twice as fast as normal.

A single byte located in the ROM data area is used to maintain the number of ticks remaining before the motor will be turned off. Part of the system timer's job is to decrement this byte and turn off the drive motor when the counter reaches zero. FASTOFF uses the timer tick interrupt, which occurs 18.2 times each second, to decrement this same counter.

Notes:

1. Since this program addresses the ROM-BIOS data area, it will work on an IBM or a very close compatible only. Don't try it on a system that's had compatibility problems. To be absolutely safe, don't try it on anything but IBM hardware.

2. You have to run FASTOFF only once each session. And you have to reboot to make it inactive unless you install it with INSTALL/REMOVE.

FFEED
Command

Tom Kihlken

Purpose: Lets you send optional form feeds following Shift-PrtSc screen dumps, and prevents systems from locking up when printers are not online.

Format: [d:][path]FFEED

Remarks: For many users, the next step after doing a screen dump is always to take the printer off line and press the form feed to eject the page. The memory resident FFEED program will add a form feed character automatically after the print screen operation is complete.

However, since there are times when you don't want to generate a form feed — such as when you want several screen dumps on the same printed sheet — FFEED adds it only if you use the RIGHT Shift key with PrtSc.

The program works by intercepting interrupt 5, which is generated by Shift-PrtSc. It then tests the keyboard status to see which shift key is being held down. If it was the right one, then it automatically sends a form feed character to the printer when the screen dump finishes.

FFEED is also smart enough to check to see if the printer is online and ready before beginning the screen print. If the printer is not ready the screen dump is aborted to prevent the keyboard from locking up. This is done by making a printer status call before giving control to the ROM routine. It's odd that such a simple check was not included within the standard ROM routine.

Notes: 1. You need to install FFEED only once each session. And the only way to remove it from memory is to reboot unless you install it with INSTALL/REMOVE.

2. If you don't like having to remember which key activates the Shift-PrtSc and which doesn't, you might prefer using the companion FFEED2 utility that follows. This version checks for printer time-outs, however, which gives it an edge.

FFEED2   **Ethan Winer**
Command

Purpose: Lets you send form feeds to your printer at any time by pressing Alt-PrtSc.

Format: `[d:][path]FFEED2`

Remarks: Print spoolers can knock out a batch of documents or program listings while you're doing something else, but it's a constant struggle to get each new document to start at the top of its own page. Once the memory-resident FFEED2.COM program is installed, you can send form feeds into the print queue with a simple keypress.

FFEED2 sends a decimal ASCII 12 form feed character to the printer whenever you press Alt-PrtSc. It works by intercepting keyboard interrupt 9, and coexists nicely with such other memory-resident programs as *SideKick* and *SuperKey* — if you run it first.

This tiny utility is extremely useful even if you're not queueing up a batch of printing jobs. It can line up paper properly for single jobs, kick single sheets out of laser printers, and clear out the last page of a print job that sometimes stays hidden inside — all from the keyboard.

Notes: 1.   This version is easier to use than the companion FFEED utility, since you don't have to remember which shift key does what.

2.   Just for the record, Charles Petzold published an almost identical routine in *PC Magazine* before this one.

FILL   **Dung Quoc Vu**
Command

Purpose: Sets the attributes of any parts of a color screen without disturbing the text; can create small overlapping differently colored "windows" for batch files.

Format: `[d:][path]FILL x,y,w,h,b,f`

where *x,y* are the coordinates of the upper left corner of the area to fill, *w* is the width of the area to fill, *h* is the height of the area to fill, *b* is the background fill color and *f* is the foreground fill color. Be sure to enter colors in hex. See BROWSE for a color chart.

Entering FILL without any arguments will print a syntax reminder onscreen. You can run FILL from DOS or within any program that can load a secondary command processor.

Examples: A sample DOS batch file might look like:

```
ECHO OFF
CLS
DIR/W
FILL 2,3,30,6,2,4
FILL 4,5,9,13,3,9
FILL 5,13,46,6,6,E
FILL 8,32,39,10,5,B
```

A sample *dBASE* file would look like:

```
SET TALK OFF
@ 5,3 SAY 'Fill 30 x 15 box with'
@ 6,3 SAY 'yellow on red.'
COMMD = 'FILL 4,6,30,15,4,E'
! &COMMD
SET TALK ON
RETURN
```

Users with monochrome monitors can use FILL to turn the intensity of text on and off with the color codes F and 7 respectively. FILL can come in handy in all sorts of situations, such as blanking out an area of the screen where users will input passwords.

This can produce some truly eye-popping effects, especially with over-lapping blocks of color. And it can be attention-getting. For instance, if you use a background color higher than 7 you can make any text blink in DOS.

FREE
Command

Art Merrill

Purpose: Reports the number of unallocated bytes on a floppy or hard disk.

Format: `[d:][path]FREE [d:]`

Remarks: FREE is in many respects a companion program to SIZE.COM: the latter tells you how much storage space you must have to make your copies; the former tells you how much you do have.

The information provided by FREE.COM is, of course, available with the DOS commands CHKDSK and DIR. Where a large group of files is involved, however, the DOS commands are very slow in operation; FREE is almost instantaneous.

FREEZE
Command

Jeff Prosise

Purpose: Ensures confidentiality of in-memory data when it is necessary to leave a PC running without storing the data to a removable medium or encrypting it. FREEZE temporarily suspends program operation, blanks the screen, and disables the Ctrl-Alt-Del reboot sequence until a user-entered password (up to 64 characters) is reentered.

Format: `[d:][path]FREEZE`

Remarks: FREEZE is a memory-resident utility, normally loaded by an AUTOEXEC.BAT file. After loading, the machine is "locked" by pressing Alt-NumLock and then entering the passphrase of choice. The passphrase may include any characters except Esc and Enter. Pressing the Esc key aborts password entry, and pressing Enter initiates the lockdown.

The backspace key may be used to correct incidental mistakes, but care must be exercised, as the characters are not echoed on the screen during entry. To unlock the machine, simply reenter the same password and press Enter. Again, the backspace and Esc keys can be used to correct or abort password entry.

Notes: 1.   The password is never stored and may be changed each time FREEZE is invoked with Alt-NumLock. If an attempt is made to load FREEZE.COM more than once an error message will result.

2.   While FREEZE is believed to be compatible with most other memory-resident programs, because of the importance of data with which it is expected to be used, it should be thoroughly checked out in your specific configuration. In particular, FREEZE should be loaded before *SideKick*.

GETCLOCK
Command
                                                           Michael J. Vanek

---

Purpose: Resets the CMOS clock on systems using versions of DOS earlier than 3.3.

Format: [d:][path]GETCLOCK

Remarks: Users frequently change the DOS time and date when doing something like using a batch file to reset time and date stamps on directory entries. With an aftermarket clock/calendar installed, it's simple to have the batch file end with a command, such as PWRUPCLK or ASTCLOCK, to reset the time.

However, starting with the AT, IBM provided a CMOS realtime clock to initialize the DOS time and date automatically each time you boot up. Under DOS 3.0, 3.1, and 3.2, changing the normal time-of-day clock didn't affect the CMOS clock. This meant that you could reset the time-of-day clock with a single command if you only had a way to transfer the time maintained by the CMOS clock to the time-of-day clock.

GETCLOCK.COM will do this for all pre-3.3 users. It won't do anything in version 3.3 or later, since IBM modified the TIME command with that DOS edition so it automatically reset the CMOS clock every time you changed the time-of-day lock. This was a welcome fix, since users of older versions have to drag out the diagnostics disk and plod through it just to fix the time, and this happens at least twice a year in most places.

If you are using version 3.0, 3.1, or 3.2, just type GETCLOCK to reset the date and time maintained in the CMOS clock.

Notes: GETCLOCK.COM uses the AT BIOS functions to read the CMOS clock and DOS functions to set the DOS clock. The process was complicated since the realtime CMOS clock and the DOS clock store their values in different formats, BCD and hexadecimal, respectively.

HELP
Command

Michael J. Mefford

Purpose: Pops up help or reference screens of the user's choice and design either in the middle of an application or at the DOS prompt. Screens suitable for use with HELP are saved in the required file format by the *PC Magazine* CAPTURE utility.

Format:
```
[d:][path]HELP filespec
[...filespec][/Nn][/Hn][/P] | [/U]
```

Remarks: Filespec is the filename, preceded if necessary by a drive name and path, of a user-customized help or reference file that has been saved using CAPTURE. Multiple help screens may be loaded for successive display by entering more than one filespec on the command line, separating each with a space, tab, comma, or semicolon.

By default, HELP will accept four screen pages, each of which is 4,000 bytes in length. The optional /Nn parameter may be entered to change this default n (4) to values from 1 through 14 pages. The PgUp, PgDn, Home, and End keys are used to display the various help screens. HELP remembers the last help screen accessed and will return to it immediately the next time the program is called up.

HELP is a memory-resident program and is normally loaded by being listed as a line in your AUTOEXEC.BAT file. Its default hotkey is Alt-H. Other Alt-key combinations may be substituted for the default hotkey by entering the optional /Hn parameter. You may use any alphanumeric key, the minus, or the equals keys for n, and the substitution may be made either when the program is loaded or by entering HELP /Hn at a subsequent DOS prompt. Pressing Esc or pressing the hotkey a second time returns you to your application or to DOS.

The optional /P parameter causes the program to pop-up immediately, and the /U parameter unloads it from memory if no other resident program has been loaded after HELP.

Notes: To change the number of screen pages reserved for pop up it is necessary to uninstall HELP or to reboot. Up to the limit of the reserved pages, however, you can change the help screens to be accessed simply by entering the command, together with a new filespec, at the DOS prompt.

HEX   **Charles Petzold**
Command

Purpose: A demonstration of self-modifying assembly language code that doubles as a hexadecimal calculator.

Format: `[d:][path]HEX O:NN MM`

where *O* is an operation represented by one of the letters A:, B:, E:, F:, or G: (with a colon immediately after it), as follows:

A: Add
B: OR
E: AND
F: Subtract
G: XOR

and *NN* and *MM* are each two-digit hex numbers.

Example: To add two hex numbers (such as 43 and C8) enter:

`HEX A:43 C8`

and HEX will return 0B. (The 1 that was carried out of the high digit is discarded.) To do a logical AND operation on these same two hex numbers, use the command:

`HEX E:43 C8`

and the program will return 40. If you use a number less than 10, turn it into a two-digit hex number by padding it with a 0. So to subtract 1 from hex A0, enter:

`HEX F:A0 01`

and HEX will print 9F.

Enter just HEX without anything after it, or with too few parameters, and the program will print out a detailed series of instructions.

Remarks: The term "self-modifying code" refers to programs that change their own instructions. Self-modifying code is most common in assembly language to do certain things that are technically referred to as "neat tricks."

HEX.COM is both a demonstration of self-modifying code and a genuinely useful program. It can add, subtract, AND, OR, or XOR (Exclusive Or) a pair of two-digit hexadecimal numbers. You enter HEX and then a letter from A through G that denotes the operation, followed immediately by a colon, then the first two-digit hexadecimal number, a space, and the second two-digit hexadecimal number. HEX.COM displays the result also as a two-digit hex number.

HEX is a relatively tiny assembly language program that doesn't seem to have enough code to do what it's doing. The entire program, without its messages, looks like:

```
0100 MOV AL,[005C]      ; Get "drive" (1,2...)
0103 DEC AL             ; Make it 0,1...
0105 MOV CL,03          ; Shift left 3 bits
0107 SHL AL,CL
0109 INC CL             ; Make CL 4 for later
010B OR [011D],AL       ; Modify an ADD
010F MOV AX,[006D]      ; Get 2nd parameter
0112 CALL 0137          ; Call ASC2BIN
0115 MOV BL,AL          ; Save in BL
0117 MOV AX,[005D]      ; Get 1st parameter
011A CALL 0137          ; Call ASC2BIN
011D ADD AL,BL          ; MODIFIED !!!!!
011F MOV BL,AL          ; Save result in BL
0121 SHR AL,CL          ; Get high 4 bits
0123 CALL 012A          ; Call BIN2ASC
0126 MOV AL,BL          ; Get lower 4 bits
0128 AND AL,0F
012A ADD AL,90          ; BIN2ASC:
012C DAA                ; (4 line routine)
012D ADC AL,40
012F DAA
0130 MOV DL,AL          ; Write to DOS
0132 MOV AH,02
0134 INT 21
0136 RET                ; Return or Exit
0137 CALL 0144          ; ASC2BIN: Call ASC2BIN2
```

```
013A XCHG AL,AH          ; Now lower byte
013C CALL 0144           ; Call ASC2BIN2
013F SHL AH,CL           ; Shift higher 4 bits
0141 ADD AL,AH           ; Stick them together
0143 RET
0144 ADD AL,C0           ; ASC2BIN2:
0146 JB 014A             ;
0148 ADD AL,07           ; Numbers 0-9
014A ADD AL,09           ; 0-9 and A-F
014C AND AL,0F           ; Low 4 bits only
014E RET
```

The whole bottom half of the program is devoted to routines that convert the ASCII values you type into binary values and then from binary back to ASCII for the final display. But where's all the branching logic depending on the first letter you type in? And where's the code to do subtraction, ORs, ANDs, and XORs?

When you type in the HEX command line, DOS treats the initial letter as a drive indicator. It converts it to a number (where 1 represents drive A:) and stores it at address 5CH. HEX.COM picks up that number, decrements it, and shifts it three bits left. It then adds it to the first machine code byte of the instruction shown in the line with the comment "MODIFIED." This changed the ADD into an OR, AND, SUB, or XOR, depending on the letter you use.

The program changes itself. What you see in the above listing is not what you get when you run it.

Self-modifying code is discouraged partially because it is difficult to maintain and debug. The only real advantage of doing this program with self-modifying code is that it's small. Back in the days when 16K was considered a lot of memory, self-modifying code was often helpful. It just doesn't make much sense any more.

The 8088 and 80286 microprocessors used in the PC and AT can also get you into trouble with self-modifying code. These processors fetch machine code instructions into the processor's "instruction queue" faster than it can execute them. If you change a byte in an instruction that has already been read into the microprocessor, the change will have no effect on the code that the microprocessor executes.

The ultimate in self-modifying code is a program that generates its own code and just keeps on going. Load DEBUG and type in the following lines:

```
A
CLD
MOV SI,107
MOV DI,10B
MOVSW
MOVSW
JMP 10B
```

followed by a blank line.

Now start entering T to trace through the program. You'll find that the last three instructions keep repeating over and over at ever higher addresses. The two MOVSW instructions copy the four bytes of machine code that comprise these three instructions into the higher address. The JMP flushes the instruction queue to avoid problems. Although the JMP instruction will keep jumping to a higher address, it really uses the exact same machine code. That's because it's jumping to a relative address instead of an absolute instruction.

You can keep tracing through this program but after you finish up about 16,000 repeated cycles, the generated instructions will be getting close to the top of the 64K segment. They will run into the stack and you'll crash. If you're using an 8088 machine and enter a G (Go command) in DEBUG, the program will wrap around the segment and just keep on running (although it's possible that a timer tick interrupt will interfere with it). You'll have to reboot to get control back. If you enter a G on an 80286 machine, one of the MOVSW instructions will eventually attempt to write a word at the destination address FFFF. That type of segment wrap is illegal in the 80286 chip and causes the chip to generate an interrupt 0DH. IBM's AT will ignore that interrupt but some AT compatibles will report the violation.

Now that OS/2 is here programmers may start abandoning the real mode of the 80286 microprocessor and start writing programs for 80286 protected mode. In protected mode, the 80286 chip itself prohibits a program from writing over its own code. This is part of what "protection" means. Programs can only write to data segments. If a program tries to write to a code segment, the 80286 generates an interrupt 0DH. Interrupt 0DH is the "General Protection Violation Interrupt" of the 80286 chip. Almost every instruction can cause an interrupt 0DH under certain circumstances.

A protected mode operating system will not ignore this interrupt like the AT BIOS does. A protected mode operating system will toss that program out of memory and make it stand in a corner wearing a dunce cap.

Actually, there is a way for the 80286 working in protected mode to allow a program to write over its own code. The operating system would have have to define an *alias* data segment at the same physical area of memory as the code segment. It's not pretty but it works.

HIDE Command   R. Chung and V. K. Taylor

Purpose: Hides files so they don't appear in directory searches. (You can unhide them later with the companion UNHIDE.COM utility.)

Format: `[d:][path]HIDE [d:][path]filename`

Remarks: Various attribute-setting programs, including the DOS ATTRIB command and Charles Petzold's far better ATTR.COM utility — can set and reset a file's attributes (although the DOS version won't let you hide files, wasn't around before version 3.0, and didn't let you do anything other than change the read-only bit until version 3.2). But they involve complex syntaxes with switches, minus and plus signs, etc.

HIDE.COM simply hides files. It's easy to use because you just type HIDE and the name of the file you want to keep out of sight.

Hidden files are still on your disk, but most DOS functions will ignore them. By hiding a file you prevent casual snoopers from seeing that it exists, and you make it impossible to delete.

You can see the names of all the files on your disk, including the hidden files, by typing:

`CHKDSK /V`

Unfortunately, CHKDSK /V won't tell you which files are hidden and which aren't.

A better way is to have Charles Petzold's ATTR.COM handy and type ATTR *.* to see the status of all your files. Michael Mefford's DR.COM will also show you the settings of each file's attribute byte.

It's common these days for software to come with installation programs that ask (or try to figure out) what kind of hardware you're using, and then install the necessary commands in your AUTOEXEC.BAT and CONFIG.SYS files. Well-behaved installation programs try to append their instructions to any that you're already using. But some rude installation modules just copy whole files onto your disk, obliterating your own files.

In addition, someone who is using your system may get carried away when he cleans up his files and take some of yours with them. If you have a long and complex AUTOEXEC.BAT file and a CONFIG.SYS file filled with all sorts of arcane switches and settings, and someone accidentally deletes your whole root directory, you'd better hope you have backups.

A smart way to get around this is to hide your copies of CONFIG.SYS and AUTOEXEC.BAT, or make them read-only. If a new program tries to write over these files it won't be able to. You can then make sure you have backup copies handy, unhide your files, and let the new program at them. And this will prevent other users from accidentally erasing your key files. Most recent versions of DOS will execute CONFIG.SYS and AUTOEXEC.BAT files that are hidden.

Another safety technique is simply to create a \ROOTBACK subdirectory one level down from the root and copy all your important root directory files into it. When something changes the files in the root directory, or if you somehow erase them, you can log into the root directory and type:

```
COPY ROOTBACK
```

If you do try this, make sure that if you ever change your AUTOEXEC.BAT or CONFIG.SYS files you copy the new versions into \ROOTBACK.

All hiding a file does is change the value of its attribute byte — a specially coded single byte storage flag in the disk directory.

These four files use function 43H of INT 21 to first check the existing attribute byte, and change only the bits that need modification. ORing the existing value with 1 makes it read-only; ORing it with 2 makes the file hidden. ANDing it with FE takes away the read-only attribute; ANDing it with FD unhides the file. This way it leaves other attributes (system or archive) as they were.

Unfortunately, you can't have function 43 change the attribute byte of subdirectories or volume labels, so this won't let you meddle with those. Use Michael Mefford's RN.COM (included in this package) if you want to hide or unhide subdirectories.

Be careful when hiding files *en masse*. If you issued a command such as:

```
FOR %A in (*.*) DO HIDE %A
```

you'd end up with a whole directory of hidden files. You won't be able to use a similar command to unhide them, since DOS won't see any files to unhide. You'll have to unhide all your files individually, since wildcards don't work with hidden files. The safest thing to do if you hide lots of files is first create a master file listing all the filenames, and put this master file in some other directory or on some other disk. If you're on drive C: you could use a command like:

```
DIR > B:C-HIDDEN.LST
```

Making all your root directory files hidden may look interesting, but it can confuse anyone else who tries to work with your system. Making them read-only will prevent other programs from changing (or deleting) them, but you'll still see them in normal DIR searches.

Notes: You can adapt HIDE.COM to create RO.COM (which will make files read-only) and UNRO.COM (which will remove the read-only status). To do so, have DEBUG handy and type:

```
DEBUG HIDE.COM
E 120 C9 01
N RO.COM
W
E 120 E1 FE
N UNRO.COM
W
Q
```

A file can have multiple attributes.

See UNHIDE.

HIGHRES
Command

Michael J. Mefford

Purpose: Sets video mode on color systems to 640 x 200 monochrome graphics.

See DRAW.

HIGRAF-L
Command

Charles Petzold

Purpose: Generates large, fast, compact high-resolution graphics screen dumps that are properly right side up, not on their sides the way DOS produces them. Because of the way this program is written, HIGRAF-L will not work properly on a wide-carriage printer; use HIGRAF-S instead.

Format: `[d:][path]HIGRAF-L`

Remarks: See HIGRAF-S.

HIGRAF-S
Command

Charles Petzold

Purpose: Generates fast, compact high-resolution graphics screen dumps that are properly right side up, not on their sides the way DOS produces them.

Format: `[d:][path]HIGRAF-S`

Remarks: The DOS GRAPHICS.COM utility lets you do Shift-PrtSc screen dumps of high-resolution (640 x 200-dot SCREEN 2) BASIC graphics. But it takes forever (the manual admits that you might have to wait up to three minutes for each one) — and DOS prints the image sideways.

HIGRAF-S (S for "Small") is a memory-resident utility that you run after loading GRAPHICS.COM. Once HIGRAF-S is loaded, it will make your printer sprint through SCREEN 2 graphics dumps, producing images that are small but properly oriented on the page.

Epson graphics (as implemented in the IBM Graphics Printer) are for practical purposes limited to 72 dots per inch (dpi) vertical resolution. The three available printer graphics modes can print 480, 960, or 1,920 dots across an eight-inch page. These correspond respectively to 60, 120, and 240 dots per inch horizontal resolution. The 60 dpi mode is not wide enough for the 640 horizontal dots of the hi-res screen.

If you use the 120 dpi mode to dump a high resolution graphics screen, you'll get an image 5-1/3 inches wide. But with the printer's 72 dpi vertical resolution, you're stuck with printing the 200 scan lines either 2-3/4 inches high, which will make your circles look like watermelons, or, by doubling up the dots, 5-1/2 inches high, which will produce the opposite effect.

The first method looks decidedly better. It yields a tiny image but one that's very clear and attractive. The image that HIGRAF-S prints is indented 12 spaces so it's centered on an 8-1/2 inch page.

The 240 horizontal dpi graphics mode prints 1,920 dots across an eight-inch page. This is exactly three times the dot width of a high resolution display. Since this graphics mode can only print every third dot, it seems ideal. By doubling up the vertical dots, you can create an image eight inches wide by 5-1/2 inches high, which is fairly close to the 4:3 aspect ratio of the screen.

You can print high-resolution graphics in this larger mode by running a companion program, HIGRAF-L, (L for "Large"). Since each line of graphics is exactly eight inches across, the program relies on the printer to do a carriage return and line feed at the end of each line. Because of this, the program will not work on a wide-carriage printer.

Neither HIGRAF-S or HIGRAF-L is optimized the way the PC-DOS GRAPHICS program is, so they may be a bit slower for certain kinds of starkly simple images. GRAPHICS (at least in the more recent DOS versions) checks if each line has any printable graphics data and skips the line if it doesn't. The HIGRAF programs will just keep shoveling zeroes out to the printer on blank lines.

Both HIGRAF-S and HIGRAF-L will print a negative image, so the white on black of the screen will be translated to black on white on the paper. This is normal for printer screen dumps. If you'd prefer to have the images printed as they appear on the screen, you can patch the programs. To change HIGRAF-S.COM, type:

```
DEBUG HIGRAF-S.COM
E 158 F5
W
Q
```

To patch HIGRAF-L.COM, type:

```
DEBUG HIGRAF-L.COM
E 156 F5
W
Q
```

Notes: 1.   This is designed to work on IBM Graphics Printers and Epson workalikes, and anything that claims it's compatible.

2.   Be sure to load these programs after you load the DOS GRAPHICS.COM utility.

3.   HIGRAF-L won't work on wide-carriage printers.

4.   If you want to generate a BASIC SCREEN 2 image, see the short SAMPLE.BAS program on the disk.

IBMFIX   Michael J. Mefford
Command

Purpose: Fixes the blunder IBM made with its enhanced keyboard when it switched the Ctrl and the CapsLock keys.

Format: [d:][path]IBMFIX

Remarks: IBM's 101-key keyboard puts the CapsLock next to the A key instead of the Ctrl key, so *WordStar* users and anyone else accustomed to having a Ctrl key beneath his or her pinkie ends up totally fingerlocked.

IBMFIX switches the Ctrl and CapsLock keys back to where they belong. Instead of training your left little finger to grope for the new Ctrl key, you can use IBMFIX.COM to relocate the two keys closer to their old familiar positions.

IBMFIX intercepts INT 9H, the keyboard hardware interrupt. Every time you press a key, IBMFIX examines the keystroke to see if it is either the Ctrl or CapsLock key. If it's not, IBMFIX passes control on to the original INT 9H to interpret the keystroke normally. Otherwise, IBMFIX changes the keyboard flag byte at 40:17H to reflect the toggle of the CapsLock key or the depressing or release of the Ctrl key.

Notes: Be sure to load IBMFIX before *SideKick*. And you'll have to reboot if you wish to return the meaning of keys to the new IBM assignments, unless you install INSTALL/REMOVE.

INSTALL (and REMOVE) Command(s)   Jeff Prosise

Purpose: This pair of utilities lets you load and unload Terminate-and-Stay-Resident (TSR) programs in and out of memory to avoid potential conflicts and excessive memory use.

Format: `[d:][path]INSTALL [namelist]`

where *namelist* is the name of the TSR program or group of TSR utilities that you want to load. The namelist parameter is an optional descriptor containing up to 119 characters; it does *not* have to match the TSR filenames. The descriptor is used in the list of installed utilities presented when you ask REMOVE to perform a deinstallation.

Remarks: Normally, TSR utilities are loaded simply by entering their names at the DOS prompt or by including them in your AUTOEXEC.BAT file.

However, running the INSTALL program before each TSR (or group of TSRs) is loaded will store pertinent information that the REMOVE program can use to unload them later.

The INSTALL utility is really a kind of "bookmark" used by the operating system. When you invoke INSTALL, it records the current state of the system. Each time you run REMOVE, it restores the system to the state it was in just before the last INSTALL, disabling any TSRs loaded since the last INSTALL.

You can docket up to 32 system states using this technique. If you want the ability to delete TSRs individually, you must run INSTALL before loading each TSR. At the other extreme, you could run INSTALL only once, right after the system power-up, then load all the resident utilities your system can hold. Then a single call to REMOVE would purge them all.

INSTALL is itself a short memory-resident utility. Every time it's called it consumes about 1,600 bytes of memory, but, more important, it inserts a resident "wedge" in memory that contains a complete copy of the PC's interrupt vector table. A utility not preceded somewhere in memory by one of these wedges cannot be removed. REMOVE recovers both the memory used by the programs it unloads and the memory dedicated to their identifying wedge.

Examples: The following sequence (which might be included in an AUTOEXEC.BAT file) installs four resident programs. TIMEKEY and FREEZE, a pair of *PC Magazine* utilities, are each preceded by IN-STALL, so they can be deleted one at a time. *SuperKey* and *SideKick*, the venerable Borland utilities, are loaded consecutively so that they will be erased as a group:

```
INSTALL TIMEKEY
TIMEKEY
INSTALL FREEZE
FREEZE
INSTALL SUPERKEY SIDEKICK
KEY
SK
```

To eliminate the most recently installed group of TSRs, simply run REMOVE. REMOVE displays the list of utilities currently installed (by echoing the descriptive names you typed in on INSTALL's command line), and prompts you to verify the deinstallation by pressing the Enter key. If you had installed the four utilities as shown above, running REMOVE would produce the following display:

```
Number of installations: 3

TIMEKEY
```

```
FREEZE
SUPERKEY SIDEKICK

Press ENTER to remove, ESC to abort
```

If you press the Enter key, REMOVE will release the last group, *Super-Key* and *SideKick*, from memory. However, you can abort the process by pressing the Esc key, which terminates the deinstallation harmlessly. Successive utilities may be deleted through successive calls to REMOVE. Running REMOVE a second time in the example above would show only two installations recorded, with FREEZE the topmost TSR next in line to be deleted.

Notes:
1.   It's perfectly legitimate to load more TSRs than was indicated in the namelist parameter. REMOVE will still delete everything entered since the last INSTALL. REMOVE's list of installed utilities, however, only reflects those designated on INSTALL's command line. If you choose, you can even leave the command line empty. It's usually convenient, however, to have an accurate list of TSRs presented every time you run REMOVE.

2.   It's also legal to run REMOVE immediately after INSTALL, with no TSRs loaded in between. The wedge left by INSTALL will be erased. In fact, although there's no obvious reason to do so, you can run IN-STALL several times in succession, then reverse the action a layer at a time. You may also run other applications, if you prefer, between the time INSTALL is invoked and a TSR is loaded.

3.   INSTALL answers the command to load additional groups beyond the limit of 32 with the message "No room for more." Likewise, when REMOVE is executed with no TSRs installed, it responds with the warning "None installed." Resident programs can be freely INSTALLed and REMOVEd as many times as you wish. In addition, there's no limit to the number of TSRs you can place in a group.

4.   You can delete programs (or groups of programs) only in the *reverse* order in which you installed them. The removal of an intermediate one would create all sorts of problems, one of which would be the tricky proposition of moving all resident routines above it down in memory to fill the hole, rerouting all appropriate interrupt vectors to the modified addresses, and altering any references to absolute addresses — a task that's next to impossible. If you have to purge a set other than the one most recently loaded, run REMOVE as many times as necessary to regress to the one targeted, then reinstall the ones above it.

5.   In the unlikely event that you encounter a "Deinstallation failed" warning in the course of removing a TSR, you should probably reboot the system. It's possible that you might be able to run your system with no adverse side effects without the reset, but it's also possible that down the road somewhere (and at the worst possible time) execution might skid to a halt with a critical memory allocation error.

KBORDER   Charles Petzold
Command

Purpose: Provides a memory-resident utility that can change and reset CGA border colors on the fly and do interesting color tricks with BASIC graphics screens on all color systems.

Format: `[d:] [path]KBORDER`

Remarks: If you want to exploit DOS's built-in color abilities, you should try using ANSI.SYS. A real advantage of ANSI is that it will not wipe out the border on a CGA when you use CLS to clear the screen. However, most programs seem to reset the video mode and wipe out the border when they load. The memory-resident KBORDER program can fix this by letting you change the border color with a few quick keystrokes.

KBORDER.COM will remain resident in memory until you reboot, unless you install it with a program such as INSTALL/REMOVE. It won't work on EGA or later systems that have trouble with border, but it's one of the few border-setting programs that will work on all older color systems, including the PC*jr*, which used nonstandard ports on its video controller.

After KBORDER.COM is loaded, you can hold down Ctrl and press the < key to step through all the 16 border colors. Ctrl > steps backwards through these border colors. It will work within most programs, but not those that hog the keyboard interrupt.

If a PC display is in medium-resolution graphics mode, KBORDER changes the background color. In high-resolution mode on a PC (normally white on black), KBORDER changes the foreground color. This is handy if you're running a program like *Word* that uses high-resolution graphics.

If something does clobber your border, KBORDER makes it easy to return the border to the color you like best. Just type Ctrl < and Ctrl > quickly in succession.

Notes: On EGA and PS/2 systems, when the color ID (BH register) is 0, KBOR-DER will set different high-resolution background colors, which can add real sparkle to otherwise drab hi-res graphics.

KBX   Jeff Prosise
Command

Purpose: Allows entering extended-ASCII line-drawing, foreign language, math, and science symbols from within word processing programs and editors that would not otherwise support them.

Format: [d:][path]KBX

Remarks: KBX is a memory-resident utility that is normally loaded by including it in a line in your AUTOEXEC.BAT file. At any point after you've loaded it, pressing Alt-Space pops up a window that displays the normal PC keyboard layout. While this window is onscreen, pressing NumLock shows the key locations for one of the two extended-ASCII sets; pressing ScrollLock similarly displays the other extended-ASCII set. Esc closes the display and returns to any active applications program.

To enter the extended-ASCII characters, hold down the NumLock (or ScrollLock) key and press the key at the appropriate position. Note that the single-line (NumLock) and double-line (ScrollLock) box-drawing characters are arranged around the outside of the numeric keypad.

Using the NumLock and ScrollLock keys as additional "shift" keys avoids conflicts with applications programs that normally use Alt-key and Ctrl-key combinations. The normal Ctrl-NumLock (pause) and Ctrl-ScrollLock (break) combinations continue to work without change. When KBX is loaded, however, Shift-NumLock and Shift-ScrollLock are used to toggle the NumLock and ScrollLock states.

KBX is not compatible with word processors that normally make use of the eighth ("high") bit for their own purposes (e.g., *WordStar*) or that utilize their own keyboard handlers (e.g., *XyWrite*). Only experimentation will show whether the program will work with a given editor.

Notes: Since different printers vary in the characters they output when presented with extended-ASCII codes, you must determine either from your manual or by experiment whether your printer's character set is compatible with that PC.

KEY-FAKE   **Charles Petzold**
Command

Purpose: Supplies the series of keystrokes needed to initialize an application program on boot-up.

Format:
```
[d:][path]KEY-FAKE ["xyz"] [nn] [0] [@F]
Programname
```

Characters typed within a pair of single or double quotes (*"xyz"*) are normal ASCII-character keystrokes. Numbers (*nn*) not in quote marks are ASCII decimal codes, e.g., 13 (Enter), 26 (Ctrl-Z), or 27 (Esc). Numbers preceded by @ are the extended ASCII decimal codes (128 through 255) generated by the Alt keys, cursor keys, Ins and Del keys, and the function keys (e.g., @61 is the F3 keystroke). The *0* is used with programs that check the keyboard buffer (it tells such programs the buffer is clear, so the programs will treat the succeeding keystroke separately).

Remarks: KEY-FAKE is of greatest use in batch files used to call up application programs. For example, to enter Lotus *1-2-3* and set it for File Retrieve, the following BAT file would be appropriate:

```
CD \LOTUS
KEY-FAKE 0 13 0 13 0 13 0 13 0 13 "/FR"
LOTUS
```

This takes you past the necessary initial carriage returns and /FR command without having to type them in each time.

Similarly, if each time you enter BASICA you want to have a blue border, blue background, and yellow letters, you would create a batch file, B.BAT, containing the lines:

```
KEY-FAKE "COLOR 14,1,1" 13 "CLS" 13
BASICA
```

Notes: 1.   The keystroke sequence stored by KEY- FAKE is limited to 124 characters and must be on one continuous command line. Keystrokes not supported by PC BIOS (e.g., Alt-Home) cannot be stored.

2.   Programs such as *XyWrite* that get keyboard information directly from the hardware keyboard interrupt may bypass KEY-FAKE. KEY-FAKE will also not work well when you are online using a communications program.

3.   KEY-FAKE is memory resident, but can be executed multiple times in the same session without reloading. However, if nested batch files cause it to be reinvoked before its initially stored keystroke sequence has been exhausted, the remaining initial keystrokes will be lost.

KEYLOCK
Command

Kenneth C. Gibbs Jr.

Purpose: Disables the CapsLock, NumLock, and ScrollLock keys to prevent them from being changed unintentionally.

Format: `[d:] [path] KEYLOCK`

Remarks: It's maddening when you try entering a column of numbers with your eyes glued to a ledger book only to find that the NumLock key has mysteriously switched off and all you've done is scooted the cursor around. Or tried to move the cursor to the top of the page and gotten nothing but a row of 8888888888s. Or ended up typing a whole paragraph in uppercase.

KEYLOCK.COM fixes this once and for all by disabling the the Caps-Lock, NumLock, and ScrollLock keys. You can still change the shift states, but you have to do it with software rather than hardware.

Just run KEYLOCK.COM to lock out those three shift keys, then run your favorite shift state toggler, such as LOCK.COM.

If you don't have one handy, you can create six small COM programs to toggle the keys you've disabled. The programs are pretty much the same, with one line changed. This assembler code will turn CapsLock on:

```
MOV    DX,0040
MOV    DS,DX
```

```
MOV   AL,[0017]
OR    AL,40
MOV   [0017],AL
RET
```

By changing the fourth line you can adapt this basic program to create
the other five versions. The replacement lines are as follows:

	ON	*OFF*
CapsLock	ORAL,40	AND AL,BF
NumLock	OR AL,20	AND AL,DF
ScrollLock	OR AL,10	AND AL,EF

The six tiny NUMON.COM, NUMOFF.COM, CAPSON.COM,
CAPSOFF.COM, SCROLLON.COM, and SCRLLOFF.COM utilities included in this package, which turn individual shift states on and off, use
this code.

You may prefer using toggle programs that can flip shift states alternately back and forth each time the programs execute. If so, try running the
NUMFLIP.COM, CAPSFLIP.COM, or SCRLFLIP.COM programs you
can create by using DEBUG to patch the NUMON.COM,
CAPSON.COM, and SCROLLON.COM programs.

Notes: 1.   Once you've loaded KEYLOCK you'll have to reboot to remove it
from memory unless you install it with INSTALL/REMOVE.

2.   Disabling the ScrollLock key means you won't be able to use Ctrl-
ScrollLock to break out of an operation. However, Ctrl-C is not affected
by this program and will still work.

See NUMON, NUMOFF, CAPSON, CAPSOFF, SCROLLON,
SCRLLOFF, LOCK, and LOX.

KEYPRESS
Batch file command   Louis J. Cutrona, Jr.

Purpose: Provides an easy way to create flexible IF ERRORLEVEL tests in batch
files.

Format: [d:][path]KEYPRESS A [B C D...]

Remarks: Most keystroke-reporting utilities designed for IF ERRORLEVEL tests are inflexible and report the same codes (either 0 and FF, or the ASCII character of the keystroke). And most utilities don't usually end up screening out invalid characters very well.

KEYPRESS lets you tell it how many characters to accept, and what those characters are. The program is case insensitive, so it treats uppercase and lowercase letters identically.

Examples: To allow the letters a, b, and c (in either uppercase or lowercase versions):

```
KEYPRESS a b c
```

or

```
KEYPRESS A B C
```

Spaces are optional, so:

```
KEYPRESS ABC
```

will work just as well as KEYPRESS A B C. And you may mix letters, numbers, and even legal punctuation:

```
KEYPRESS 12#Q
```

In this example, if the user types a #, KEYPRESS will generate a return code of 3, since the # is the third character in the list.

Remarks: KEYPRESS will wait for a key to be entered, screen out all invalid entries, and generate an IF ERRORLEVEL code based on any valid character's position on the command line. So in the KEYPRESS 12#Q example directly above, entering a 1 will generate a return code of 1. Entering a Q will produce a return code of 4.

If the user types a character that is not in the legal list, KEYPRESS generates a return code of 0.

A sample batch file using KEYPRESS might look like:

```
ECHO OFF
:TOP
ECHO   SELECT ONE
ECHO   1.      123
```

```
ECHO  D.      DBASE
ECHO  Q.      QUIT
ECHO YOUR CHOICE (1/D/Q) ?
KEYPRESS 1DQ
IF ERRORLEVEL 3 GOTO EXIT
IF ERRORLEVEL 2 GOTO B
IF ERRORLEVEL 1 GOTO A
ECHO INVALID REPLY...
GOTO TOP
:A
123
PAUSE
GOTO TOP
:B
dBase
PAUSE
GOTO TOP
:EXIT
```

As with any series of IF ERRORLEVEL tests, the return codes generated by KEYPRESS must be checked from highest to lowest (right to left in the list of valid characters). IF ERRORLEVEL n succeeds if the return code is greater than or equal to n.

KEYSUB   Robert L. Hummel
Command

Purpose: Lets you redefine your keyboard key layout.

Format: [d:][path]KEYSUB

Remarks: Few computer topics generate as much passion as keyboard layout. Everyone has his or her own quirky feelings about what keys should go where. IBM is the standard setter, but it has changed the standard several times in the brief history of the PC.

As an example, the configuration of the IBM numeric keypad makes it difficult to enter long DATA strings in BASIC programs, since the comma key is so far away. KEYSUB.COM can fix this by letting you turn the period on the Del key into a comma.

When you type a key, the keyboard controller generates a unique scan code that identifies the key. Your system's BIOS translates the scan code into the more familiar ASCII code. KEYSUB let you remap these codes. However, a few keys (like the shift keys) have no ASCII equivalents or, like SYS REQ, are ignored by the BIOS, and KEYSUB can't handle these.

To have KEYSUB change the period key on the numeric pad into a comma, first make sure that NUMLOCK is on; the same key doubles as a period and a Del, and you have to make sure it's in the proper state. Enter KEYSUB to start the process, then press the period/Del key on the keypad when it prompts you with "Change which key?" (Be sure you press the period on the Del key, not the one on the greater-than key.) When KEYSUB asks you to "Press new value," just press the normal comma key. From then on, each time you press the period/Del key, BIOS will generate a comma rather than a period. You can remove key substitutions by rebooting or by first loading them by using a TSR manager such as Jeff Prosise's INSTALL/REMOVE.

Be careful in assigning new keys, since BIOS is very picky about key combinations. Left Shift-A, Right Shift-A, and both Shifts-A generate different codes, and KEYSUB follows them very literally.

LOCATE   Tom Kihlken
Batch file command

Purpose: Positions batch file text anywhere that you want it onscreen (just like the BASIC LOCATE command), and lets you erase text anywhere onscreen.

Format: `[d:][path]LOCATE R,C`

where *R* is the screen Row and *C* is the screen Column expressed as decimal numbers. (The upper lefthand corner of the screen is row 0, column 0 — not row 1, column 1.)

If you enter just:

`LOCATE R`

the text will appear on column 1 of the row specified. If you enter:

```
LOCATE ,C
```

the text will appear on the following line starting in the column specified.

Remarks: One of BASIC's most useful screen controls is its LOCATE command. LOCATE.COM does the same thing for batch programs. It lets you position the cursor anywhere on the screen for subsequent ECHO or ECOH commands. Be sure to begin your batch file with ECHO OFF, and use a separate LOCATE statement for each new line. Also, just as with BASIC, don't LOCATE to row 24 (the bottom line on a normal 25 x 80 display — remember, the top row is row 0), since the screen will automatically scroll up one line if you do.

LOCATE also lets you erase text from the screen. Just enter the LOCATE row and column parameters for the text you want to get rid of, then ECHO a string of spaces the length of the text you want erased, and follow this with an ASCII character 255 or an ASCII 0. To create a character 255, hold down the Alt key, type 255 on the number pad (not the top row number keys), then release the Alt key.

The only real way to create a character 0 is to type the F7 key when you're in DOS. So if you're using EDLIN or the DOS COPY CON command to create a batch file, just insert as many spaces as you need after the word ECHO, then press the F7 function key. DOS is quirky about such characters, and different versions may behave differently.

So if you want to get rid of the first 20 characters on line 5, you'd enter:

```
LOCATE 4,0 xxxxxxxxxxxxxxxxxxxxy
```

or just:

```
LOCATE 4 xxxxxxxxxxxxxxxxxxxxy
```

(where each x represented a space and the y represented an ASCII character 0 or 255 — don't actually type Xs and Ys).

Examples: To print the words "It works" in the middle of your screen (at row 13, column 36), enter:

```
ECHO OFF
LOCATE 12,35
ECHO It works
```

If you want to print the word "Note — " on column 70 of the following line, type:

```
ECHO OFF
LOCATE ,69
ECHO Note —
```

To print "Note — " at the beginning of line 11, enter:

```
ECHO OFF
LOCATE 10
ECHO Note —
```

Notes: By using LOCATE.COM in combination with the ECOH.COM reverse-color text printer included in this package you can make a message flash onscreen. Since ECOH looks at the existing color and reverses it, each subsequent time you execute it the color will reverse. So to flash a message, just repeat several ECOH statements at the same cursor position:

```
LOCATE 8,36
ECOH This is a test
LOCATE 8,36
ECOH This is a test
LOCATE 8,36
ECOH This is a test
```

If you enter something other than numbers, LOCATE will think you wanted the text positioned at 0,0. And if you enter a row that's too high, LOCATE may put the text on another screen page, which can make everything onscreen disappear. If this happens, try entering CLS.

If you enter a column that's out of range, DOS may wrap it around to the next row, but the following command may obliterate it.

LOCK
Command

Terje Mathisen

Purpose: Toggles shift states off and on from the command line.

Format: `[d:] [path]LOCK N+|-  C+|-  S+|-`

where *N* represents NumLock, *C* represents CapsLock, and *S* represents ScrollLock; a + toggles each shift state while a - toggles it off.

Remarks: You may toggle all three shift states at the same time, or just one. LOCK.COM accepts uppercase and lowercase input, and can turn shift states on and off in the same command. And if you're issuing multiple commands on one line you may enter them in any order.

This lets you toggle shift states on and off from within batch files. Since IBM's 101-key keyboards have separate number and cursor pads, IBM decided to turn NumLock on when the system boots. Users who want to turn NumLock off at bootup so they can use the classic cursor can put a:

```
LOCK N-
```

in their AUTOEXEC.BAT file.

Example: The command:

```
LOCK C+
```

turns CapsLock on. And the command:

```
LOCK C-
```

turns CapsLock off. Entering:

```
LOCK N+ C- S+
```

turns NumLock and ScrollLock on, and turns CapsLock off.

LOCK isn't as powerful as LOX, but many users prefer it because it lets them enter the + or - after the letter representing the Shift key, which somehow seems more natural than entering it before the letter.

See KEYLOCK, NUMON, NUMOFF, CAPSON, CAPSOFF, SCROLLON, SCRLLOFF, and LOX.

LOOP   **Tom Kihlken**
Batch file command

Purpose: Controls the number of loops inside a batch file.

Format: `[d:] [path] LOOP /S`

                    .

                    .

                    .

             `[d:] [path] LOOP`

                    .

                    .

                    .

             `IF ERRORLEVEL (number) GOTO (label)`

Remarks: While DOS lets you loop inside batch files by entering something like:

```
:TOP
REM Something happens repeatedly here
GOTO TOP
```

It doesn't provide a method for looping a certain number of times and then jumping out of the loop. If you know exactly how many times you want part of your batch file to loop, you can control the process with LOOP.COM.

To use it, you must insert a line near the very beginning of your batch file — before the loop actually starts — containing the command:

```
LOOP /S
```

This "initializes" the loop counter by putting a zero in a certain place in memory, and prevents you from running into trouble if you use the LOOP.COM utility more than once.

Then, simply put the command:

```
LOOP
```

on a line by itself somewhere inside the loop. Follow this line farther down in the batch file with another line that says either:

```
IF ERRORLEVEL (number) GOTO (label)
```

or:

```
IF NOT ERRORLEVEL (number) GOTO (label)
```

substituting the number of times you want to loop in place of the (number), and the actual LABEL you want the batch file to jump to in place of (label).

Each time the batch file executes it, LOOP.COM will increase a value that DOS can measure with IF ERRORLEVEL.

Example: The following LOGIT.BAT will run a program called DISKTEST.COM (or DISKTEST.EXE) 50 times and log the results to a file called DISKTEST.LOG:

```
ECHO OFF
LOOP /S
:TOP
DISKTEST >> DISKTEST.LOG
LOOP
IF NOT ERRORLEVEL 50 GOTO TOP
```

Using IF NOT ERRORLEVEL to check a negative (NOT) condition saves steps, but you could accomplish the same exact thing with a non-negative version of LOGIT.BAT that reads:

```
ECHO OFF
LOOP /S
:TOP
DISKTEST >> DISKTEST.LOG
LOOP
IF ERRORLEVEL 50 GOTO END
GOTO TOP
:END
```

Notes: The largest number of repetitions you can specify is 255. If you use a number higher than 255, your system will perform a modulo operation on it, which means it will start over again at 1. So 254 will repeat 254 times, and 255 will repeat 255 times, but 256 and 257 will repeat just one time, 258 will repeat two times, 259 will run three times, etc.

LOOP.COM works by storing an ever-increasing value at low memory address 0040:006B. This location is reserved for the cassette recorder and is unused on most systems (unless you're one of the few people who use a cassette). Each time LOOP runs it retrieves the counter, increments it, and exits with the new value.

LOWER
Command
Michael J. Mefford

Purpose: Converts any text file (except overly large ones) to all lowercase.

Format: `[d:][path]LOWER [d:][path]filename`

where *filename* is the file you want entirely lowercased.

Remarks: LOWER.COM will convert any ASCII text file, including *WordStar* document files, to all lowercase. Use LOWER to change a file received in all uppercase to conventional lowercase.

LOWER will leave the first character of a sentence and the singular character "I" capitalized. But it's not perfect; you'll have to edit the file and return the initial character in any proper names and any other special case-sensitive words to uppercase. Still, that's a lot easier than having to edit the entire file.

Notes: Don't try LOWER.COM with files that approach 64K or more.

See UPPER.

LOWRES
Command
Michael J. Mefford

Purpose: Sets video mode on color systems to 320 x 200 color graphics.

See DRAW.

LOX
Command
Grinnell Almy

Purpose: Lets you toggle shift states from the command line and makes it easy to set or reset all toggles at once.

Format: `[d:][path]LOX -|+ CNSI`

where *C* represents CapsLock, *N* Numlock, *S* ScrollLock, and *I* Insert.

Remarks: LOX.COM gives you software control over the CapsLock, NumLock, ScrollLock, and Insert status. These four status bits are located in the high nibble of byte 417 of the BIOS data area, at segment 0. The program can set or clear any of the four bits.

To use it, enter LOX followed by any combination of the characters +, -, C, I, N, or S. The four letters stand for the four status bits: Caps, Insert, Num, and Scroll. The + tells the program to set the bits for all following parameters, while the - tells the program to clear the bits for all following parameters. If it finds parameters at the beginning of the command tail, before any plus or minus signs, it treats them as set parameters.

Examples: LOX C sets CapsLock; LOX -N clears NumLock; LOX S-C sets Scroll-Lock and clears CapsLock, LOX -N+IC clears NumLock and sets Insert and CapsLock; and LOX CNIS sets all four locks. The program can handle shift states in any order, and in uppercase or lowercase. And it ignores illegal parameters.

Notes: It begins by moving the keyboard status bit to AL, and the command tail length to CX, to control the loop. Then it reads each byte in the command tail. It maintains AH as a set/clear flag; if it finds a plus sign it sets AH to one; if it finds a minus sign it sets AH to zero.

If it finds anything else, it first converts it to uppercase if necessary, and then checks to see if it is one of the four valid parameters. If it is, it moves the appropriate code into DH, and then ORs DH with AL to set the bit, or else NOTs and then ANDs it with AL to clear the bit, depending on the status of AH. The program then loops back to read another byte from the command line. When the command line is exhausted, it moves AL back to the keyboard status byte.

LOX is more powerful than LOCK, but some users don't like putting the - or + signs before the letter representing the shift key. LOCK.COM lets them add the + and - afterward.

See KEYLOCK, NUMON, NUMOFF, CAPSON, CAPSOFF, SCROLLON, SCRLLOFF, and LOCK.

MEM512
Command

Barry Herbert

Purpose: Adjusts the amount of available RAM downward to accommodate older and public domain programs.

Format: `[d:] [path]MEM512`

Remarks: Some older or public domain programs misinterpret today's large RAM configurations and refuse to load.

One possible cause is the program's use of a signed compare and jump where an unsigned compare and jump in checking memory size is appropriate. You can address up to 512K with 19 address bits, and need a 20th bit to go any higher. A signed comparison will interpret this as a negative value and report insufficient memory.

Once installed, MEM512.COM looks at the memory size variable set by the diagnostic code during bootup. If this variable says your system has more than 512K installed, the program sets it to indicate that only 512K is available. It then performs a special reboot (Int 19) that bypasses system diagnostics to avoid the memory-sizing routine. The system will load normally except that it will think it has only 512K of RAM.

If you run MEM512.COM on a system with 512K or less, it will display a message indicating the amount of RAM and then quit without rebooting.

Notes: As written, the program will trick your system into thinking it has only 512K of RAM, If you want to change this amount, patch the value of 200 (the hex representation of decimal 512) at addresses 112/113 and 118/119. Remember, the PC stores numbers in "backwords" order, so the hex value of 200 actually looks like 00 02 in DEBUG. An unassembled partial listing looks like:

```
0111 3D0002     CMP     AX,0200
0114 761A       JBE     0130
0116 C7070002   MOV     WORD PTR [BX],0200
```

To make the system think it had only 256K (100 hex), change the single bytes at offsets 113 and 119, so the unassembled code would look like:

```
0111 3D0001    CMP    AX,0100
0114 761A      JBE    0130
0116 C7070001  MOV    WORD PTR [BX],0100
```

MEMORY   Michael J. Mefford
Command

Purpose: Instantly reports the amount of available memory in your system.

Format: [d:][path]MEMORY

Remarks: With all the memory-resident programs and different ways that you can
               configure these programs as well as your own system with buffers, it's
               important to know how much available memory is left for your applica-
               tion programs.

               MEMORY.COM returns the current free RAM in Ks (1,024s), while the
               DOS CHKDSK.COM utility reports them in 1,000s. And CHKDSK is
               painfully slow, especially on a big hard disk, since it has to plod through
               a long disk test just to report the amount of free memory. By running
               MEMORY you can get the answer instantly.

Notes: You must have DOS 2.0 version or later for MEMORY.

MID$ Michael J. Mefford
Batch file filter

Purpose: Provides string-handling and editing abilities in batch files; imitates the
               similarly named BASIC command.

Format: [d:][path]MID$ n,m

               where *n* and *m* are decimal numbers in the range 1 to 255.

Remarks: This powerful filter processes strings of characters. It takes an original
               string and produces a smaller copy of it m characters long beginning at
               an offset of n characters from the start of the string. If n is omitted,
               MID$ defaults to the start of the string. If m is omitted, all rightmost
               characters starting from n are returned.

Be sure to leave only one space between MID$ and the first argument. MID$ is not smart enough to scan off leading spaces, but it's short, fast, and effective.

As with other DOS filters such as SORT and FIND, MID$ is designed to work in combination with the other DOS commands, especially the piping and redirection features. However, you can enter MID$ by itself at the prompt for a quick demonstration of how it works. Enter:

```
MID$ 5,3
```

and then enter:

```
1234567890
```

The command will print:

```
567
```

because the parameters 5,3 mean "take the original 1234567890 string and make a copy of it that is 3 characters long starting with character 5."

You can use MID$ to clean up irritating long-winded DOS messages, and do all sorts of DOS magic.

For instance, if you've ever wanted to use the DOS clock to time an event, you either have to set it to zero and then reset it manually, or you have to show the starting time and ending time and ask the user to subtract one from the other. But not with MID$.COM.

To try this, create three files: CR, ZERO, and TIMER.BAT.

CR is simply a carriage return. Type:

```
COPY CON CR
```

and press the Enter key *twice*, then press the F6 key and then the Enter key a third time.

ZERO is not much bigger than CR. Type:

```
COPY CON ZERO
```

and then press the Enter key, then type:

```
0:0
```

and press the Enter key again, press hit F6, and the Enter key a third time.

TIMER.BAT is a bit longer:

```
ECHO OFF
TIME < CR | FIND "C" | MID$ 18 > HOLDER
ECHO The time is now
TYPE HOLDER
TYPE CR
COPY HOLDER+CR HOLDER > NUL
TIME < ZERO > NUL
ECHO Wait a few seconds then hit a key
PAUSE > NUL
ECHO You paused for
TIME < CR | FIND "C" | MID$ 18
TYPE CR
ECHO seconds ...
ECHO Now resetting the time to...
TYPE HOLDER
TIME < HOLDER > NUL
DEL HOLDER
```

Most people will find MID$.COM to be a truly welcome utility. You'll find dozens of uses for it every day.

Notes: 1.   The PAUSE > NUL in TIMER.BAT won't suppress the normal PAUSE message in older DOS versions.

2.   If you want to avoid using little empty text files like ZERO and CR, you can have the ENTER.COM program included in this package trigger the commands, and use the small RESET.COM program to reset the clock to 0:0:0.

See ENTER and RESET.

MOUSEKEY
Command

Jeff Prosise

Purpose: MOUSEKEY lets your system's mouse stand in for the four cursor keys, the PgUp key, and the PgDn key, within applications that normally don't support a mouse.

Format: `[d:][path]MOUSEKEY`

Remarks: The left mouse button will emulate the PgUp key and the right button will mimic the PgDn key. You can simulate a press of any arrow key by moving the mouse in the corresponding direction. MOUSEKEY works in conjunction with the BIOS keyboard driver and doesn't impede normal operation of the keys it emulates. It's the perfect alternative to sluggish keyboard typematic rates that make a lengthy cursor move seem to last an eternity.

MOUSEKEY will work with either of the Microsoft mice (bus version or serial version) or with any mouse that emulates these.

NEWKEYS
Command

Charles Petzold

Purpose: Gives DOS access to the new codes generated by IBM's 101-key enhanced keyboard.

Format: `[d:][path]NEWKEYS`

Remarks: When IBM designed the BIOS support for its enhanced keyboard, it added 31 additional extended keyboard codes with values starting at 133. However, it didn't make these keyboard codes available to programs through the normal BIOS keyboard interface. To do so would have created incompatibilities with some existing programs. For instance, some keyboard macro programs define their own extended keys, which could conflict with the new IBM codes.

DOS (and most programs) get keyboard information from the BIOS through interrupt 16H, function calls 0, 1, and 2. For the enhanced keyboard, IBM defined new function calls numbered 10H, 11H, and 12H that duplicated 0, 1, and 2 except that the new calls also return the new extended keyboard codes in addition to the old ones.

NEWKEYS.COM is a TSR program so it need only be loaded once during your PC session. Like most TSRs, it may have some compatibility problems with other programs. Test it carefully with your other resident programs before you start using it regularly.

When NEWKEYS is loaded, you could use the extra codes to provide extended ANSI.SYS redefinitions. For instance, the ANSI sequence for redefining the F11 key to do a DIR command is:

```
ESC[0;133;"DIR";13p
```

(where ESC represents the Esc character hex 1B or decimal 27, and not the letters E-S-C).

New Extended Keyboard Codes for IBM Enhanced Keyboard

Extended Code	Key	Extended Code	Key
133	F11	149	Ctrl-/
134	F12	150	Ctrl-*
135	Shift-F11	151	Alt-Home
136	Shift-F12	152	Alt-Up Arrow
137	Ctrl-F11	153	Alt-Page-Up
138	Ctrl-F12	155	Alt-Left Arrow
139	Alt-F11	157	Alt-Right Arrow
140	Alt-F12	159	Alt-End
141	Ctrl-Up Arrow	160	Alt-Down Arrow
142	Ctrl- -	161	Alt-Page Down
143	Ctrl-5	162	Alt-Insert
144	Ctrl-+	163	Alt-Delete
145	Ctrl-Down Arrow	164	Alt-/
146	Ctrl-Insert	165	Alt-Tab
147	Ctrl-Delete	166	Alt-Enter
148	Ctrl-Tab		

NEWPAUSE
Batch file command

Mike Cohn

Purpose: Provides an improved version of the DOS PAUSE command that displays an optional message of your choice and waits for you to press a key.

Format: `[d:] [path]NEWPAUSE [message]`

Remarks: Used by itself, NEWPAUSE will simply put a batch file temporarily on hold until the user presses any non-Shift key.

By following the command with a message, you can have NEWPAUSE display a prompt while it waits.

It's possible to put a message after the DOS PAUSE command, but this message displays only when ECHO is off, which means that the user also sees the DOS prompt and the word PAUSE.

Users of version 3.x can replace the normal "Strike a key when ready" message with an ECHO command and then redirect the normal PAUSE output to NUL:

```
ECHO OFF
ECHO Turn on your printer then press a key
PAUSE > NUL
```

However, this won't suppress the "Strike" message on older versions. Users of DOS 2.x can prevent the word PAUSE from showing up onscreen by using a word processor to put five backspaces directly after it.

NEXT
Command

Charles Petzold

Purpose: Changes the logged directory to the next available one at that level or higher in the subdirectory tree.

Format: `[d:][path]NEXT`

Remarks: DOS lets you move upward from a directory toward the root by typing CD .. and pressing Enter. To move in the other direction it forces you to enter explicit subdirectory names. But it offers no method for meandering across your entire subdirectory structure. NEXT.COM does.

Notes: NEXT is part of a trio of subdirectory navigation aids. See also UP and DOWN.

NO   Charles Petzold
Command

Purpose: Excludes specified files in a subdirectory from the action of a command.

Format: `[d:][path]NO filespec Command [parameter]`

Remarks: NO.COM is designed for situations in which you want to apply a command such as DELete or COPY to all the files in a directory except one or two (or a class of) files. For example,

`NO *.BAS COPY *.* A:`

copies all the files in your current subdirectory to drive A: except for those that have a BAS extension.

To exclude more than one file (or category) you must use a separate NO command for each on the command line. Thus,

`NO *.ASM NO *.COM DEL *.*`

deletes all files in the current directory except those with ASM or COM extensions.

Notes: 1.   NO.COM should not be used in conjunction with the PC-DOS BACKUP and RESTORE commands. This is because NO operates by temporarily setting the "hidden" file attribute bit on the files to be excluded from the main command, then unhiding the files after the main command has been executed. Since the DOS BACKUP/RESTORE operation acts on hidden and unhidden files alike, NO.COM cannot be used to exclude files from BACKUP/RESTORE. RESTORE, indeed, will restore the supposedly excluded files as hidden, overwriting the originals.

2.   While NO.COM provides full path support (and so requires the use of DOS 2.0 or later), it is a good policy when using NO to use CHDIR to make the directory that contains the files on which you wish to operate the current directory.

For example, suppose you are in your root directory, one of whose subdirectories is \BASIC. If you were to enter the command:

```
NO *.BAS DEL \BASIC\*.*
```

you would not delete all the files in the \BASIC subdirectory except those with a BAS extension, as you might have intended to do. To do this from the root directory you would have had to enter:

```
NO \BASIC\*.BAS DEL \BASIC\*.*
```

This complete filespec would tell NO that it had to protect files in the \BASIC, not in the current (i.e., root) directory.

If you follow our recommendation and enter:

```
CD \BASIC
NO *.BAS DEL *.*
```

thus making \BASIC your current directory before you start deleting, you will then clean out all but the BAS files, just as you intended.

3.   Should a parity check error, power outage, or system crash occur during the brief period between the times NO hides and subsequently unhides the protected files, those files will subsequently seem to have disappeared. They are not lost; only hidden from a DIR listing. Use ATTR (included in this set of utilities) to change their hidden status.

NOBOOT
Command

Ethan Winer

Purpose: Disables ability to reboot by pressing Ctrl-Alt-Del.

Format: `[d:][path]NOBOOT`

Remarks: Most good programs provide some type of protection against inadvertent operator errors. For example, pressing Ctrl-Break in an accounting program could cause it to end before important information has been written to disk. But one action that's difficult to guard against is rebooting with Ctrl-Alt-Del.

Trapping Ctrl-Break is easy, because the address for this routine is kept in low memory. All a program has to do is poke a new address there, which usually points to a return instruction located somewhere in ROM. But Ctrl-Alt-Del is handled entirely by the PC's BIOS, so another approach is needed.

NOBOOT is a memory-resident program that intercepts keyboard interrupt 9. Once NOBOOT has been loaded, it will receive control every time a key is pressed. If the key is anything but Ctrl-Alt-Del, then it passes on to the original interrupt 9 handler in ROM. Otherwise, it simply ignores the request and returns.

Once you've run NOBOOT, it will normally be impossible to reboot without turning off the power. You could however run a program like WARMBOOT to do it.

Some programs that take over INT 9, such as *SideKick*, will steal the interrupt back, so test it first with such other interrupt- greedy programs.

NOECHO   F. M. de Monasterio, M.D.
Batch file command

Purpose: Supresses display of initial ECHO OFF in batch files.

Format: `[d:][path]ECHO OFF`
`NOECHO`

Remarks: The DOS default setting for batch file displays is ECHO ON. Most users don't want the individual commands of their batch files to display as they execute, and insert an initial ECHO OFF line as the first line of their batch file. Unfortunately, this initial ECHO OFF command, whose purpose is to prevent screen clutter, ends up cluttering the screen itself.

Users of DOS versions 3.3 and later can add a @ prefix to suppress the display of any line. So they may achieve the same effect by making the first line:

```
@ECHO OFF
```

Similarly, ANSI.SYS users may make the first line of their batch files ECHO OFF and then follow it with a second line:

```
ESC[1A ESC[K ESC[B
```

(where the ESC in the example represents the decimal 27, or hex 1B, Esc character, not the letters E-S-C.) This moves the cursor up a line, blanks that line, then moves the cursor down to the line where it started.

NOINT5 Command   Robert L. Hummel

Purpose: Disables Shift-PrtSc function.

Format: [d:] [path]NOINT5

Remarks: Many users want to disable the Shift-PrtSc screen dump feature so they don't accidentally press those keys and freeze their system when the printer is not online.

The many solutions for this problem include the ones used in CONFIRM.COM and DISABLE.COM. But this program relies on a different technique.

It replaces the ROM INT 5 routine with a one-instruction routine in RAM that passes control back to the program that was running as if nothing had happened. Once you run it, the interrupt 5 vector will point to a dummy routine rather than the one in ROM.

The program uses DOS interrupt 21H "Set Interrupt Vector" subfunction 25H. NOINT5 simply points the vector to an IRET instruction — a special form of the RET (RETurn) used with interrupts — that causes execution to pick up exactly where it was interrupted.

If you use NOINT5, load it from your AUTOEXEC.BAT file, before any other memory-resident programs and before any strings are added to your environment.

See ENABLE, DISABLE, and NOINT5.

NOPRINT   **Charles Petzold**
Command

Purpose: Disables both the Shift-PrtSc screen dump and Ctrl-PrtSc printer echo functions.

Format: `[d:][path]NOPRINT`

Remarks: It's relatively easy to disable Shift-PrtSc either by fooling it into thinking it's already in the middle of a screen dump, or by disabling interrupt 5. Both of these techniques make it easy to turn the Shift- PrtSc off and then of again as you need it.

But disabling Ctrl-PrtSc is more difficult, since this keystroke combination is interpreted by DOS and works quite differently from Shift-PrtSc. The only way to handle it is by intercepting the interrupt 9 keyboard handler.

Because of this, NOPRINT program can't be turned off unless you reboot or load it from a TSR manager such as INSTALL/REMOVE.

As it's written, NOPRINT.COM disables both the Shift-PrtSc and Ctrl-PrtSc functions. If you like the on/off feature of other Shift-PrtSc disablers (such as ENABLE and DISABLE) because you usually leave your printer turned off, you can continue to use these separate Shift-PrtSc handling utilities and patch NOPRINT.COM so the only thing it disables is Ctrl-PrtSc.

To do so, change the value at offset 113 from 7 to 4 by typing:

```
DEBUG NOPRINT.COM
E 113 4
W
Q
```

If you need to echo something to your printer, Ctrl-P will continue to work with either version.

Notes: Under DOS 3.X, Ctrl-PrtSc is not the problem it used to be. It's relatively easy to recover by pressing Ctrl-PrtSc again, and then pressing other keys until DOS comes to its senses. When it finally prints the "Abort, Retry, Ignore?" message, just press A to continue.

NOREPEAT   Tom Kihlken
Command

Purpose: Disables the keyboard auto-repeat feature.

Format: [d:] [path]NOREPEAT

Remarks: For a young child or an inexperienced typist, the auto-repeat feature of most keyboards may cause lots of unwanted duplicate keystrokes. The memory-resident NOREPEAT.COM program eliminates the auto-repeat no matter how long a key is held down.

It works by using interrupt 9 to examine each keystroke. Normally this detects when each key is depressed and when it's released. When a key is held down long enough to repeat, the keyboard simulates the key's being depressed again and again without being released. NOREPEAT senses these duplicate keys and prevents them from being inserted into the keyboard buffer. When the key is finally released, new keystrokes are again allowed to occur normally.

Notes: You have to install NOREPEAT.COM only once each session. And the only way to disable it is to reboot or use INSTALL/REMOVE.

NOSCROLL   William G. Hood
Command

Purpose: Lets you pause and restart scrolling displays by pressing the ScrollLock key.

Format: [d:] [path]NOSCROLL

Remarks: It's awkward to have to use two keys, Ctrl and NumLock (or Ctrl and S) to pause scrolling screen output, and then a third key to resume scrolling. Using the MORE filter, when applicable, is not much better.

NOSCROLL.COM is a resident program that, once installed, will alternately pause and restart scrolling when the ScrollLock key is pressed.

The program works by servicing keyboard interrupt 9. When it sees that the ScrollLock has been pressed, it sets a flag, enables interrupts, then waits until the flag is cleared after another press of the ScrollLock key. Since the routine waits with interrupts enabled, all hardware interrupts will continue to be serviced including the keyboard interrupt. Normal keystrokes will continue to be placed in the keystroke buffer; however, they will not be echoed until screen output is resumed.

Notes: *Important* — since this works by intercepting interrupt 9, don't use it with other memory-resident programs like *SideKick* that also intercept interrupt 9, or your system may lock up.

The only way to deinstall NOSCROLL is to reboot your system or use INSTALL/REMOVE.

NUMCLICK   Kevin Miller
Command

Purpose: Generates audible tones when the NumLock key is on and any key on the cursor/number pad is typed.

Format: `[d:][path]NUMCLICK`

Remarks: Some users are happy to enter numbers into spreadsheets all day long, and keep the NumLock key toggled on. Others spend their time writing or programming, and would be just as happy if the cursor pad had nothing to do with numbers.

Too often non-number-crunchers accidentally turn the NumLock key on and end up typing a row of numbers when they wanted to move the cursor to the top of the screen or the middle of a line.

The memory-resident NUMCLICK.COM program guards against this. Once you've installed it, if you type any of the number pad numbers, or the grey plus or minus key, while NumLock is toggled on, the speaker will beep.

The only way to remove it from memory is to reboot, or install it with a program like INSTALL/REMOVE.

Notes: NUMCLICK.COM contains several smart tests to make sure it doesn't beep at the wrong time. However, if your keyboard is too quiet for you, and you want it to beep at every keypress — not just the ones NUMCLICK was designed for — make a copy of NUMCLICK.COM called simply CLICKALL.COM and then jump around all the tests by putting CLICKALL.COM on the same directory as DEBUG.COM and typing:

```
DEBUG CLICKALL.COM
E 10A EB 20
W
Q
```

If you install CLICKALL.COM, every single key, including shifts, function keys, and toggles, will beep when you type them or hold them down.

NUMOFF   Mike Cohn
Command

Purpose: Turns NumLock shift off (sets it to cursor state rather than numeric state).

Format: `[d:][path]NUMOFF`

Remarks: See KEYLOCK, NUMON, CAPSON, CAPSOFF, SCROLLON, SCRLLOFF, LOCK, and LOX.

NUMON   Mike Cohn
Command

Purpose: Turns NumLock shift on (sets it to numeric state rather than cursor state).

Format: `[d:][path]NUMON`

Remarks: You can create a version of this program called NUMFLIP.COM that alternately toggles the NumLock shift from numeric to cursor state and back to numeric every other time it executes.

Simply type:

```
DEBUG NUMON.COM
E 108 34
N NUMFLIP.COM
W
Q
```

See KEYLOCK, NUMOFF, CAPSON, CAPSOFF, SCROLLON, SCRLLOFF, LOCK, and LOX.

ONCL   Philip J. Erdelsky
Command

Purpose: An all-purpose file character-display and file-creation utility designed to handle otherwise tricky characters such as those with ASCII values below decimal 32.

Format: `[d:][path]ONCL n [n n...]`

or:

`[d:][path]ONCL n [n n...] > newfil`

or:

`[d:][path]ONCL n [n n...] > device`

where each *n* is a decimal value of an ASCII character, *newfil* is an optional filename created by redirecting the ONCL output, and *device* is a DOS device such as PRN.

Remarks: It's difficult to send just a few control characters to your printer on the fly, or create a small file to use as input to another program from within a batch file, without operator intervention. Many text editors won't handle control characters without a struggle, and using full-fledged word processors to create a file a few bytes long is like using a pile driver to pound in a carpet tack. Using BASIC or DEBUG is not much easier.

ONCL.COM (which stands for Output Numbers from Command Line) handles all these chores by sending any characters you specify to standard output, from which they can be redirected to a file, an output device, or another program.

ONCL makes it very easy to generate printer escape codes or ANSI escape sequences.

Example: To set an Epson-compatible printer to its elite (12-character per inch) pitch, enter:

```
ONCL 27 77 > PRN
```

(since the code for this is ESC+"M"). To reset the printer to its standard settings, (ESC+"@") type:

```
ONCL 27 64 >PRN
```

The 27 represents the decimal ASCII value of the Escape character. The decimal ASCII character for M is 77 and for @ is 64.

To generate ANSI escape sequences, you must have ANSI loaded (with the line DEVICE=ANSI.SYS in your CONFIG.SYS file). Then, on a color system, you can issue a command like:

```
ONCL 27 91 51 55 59 52 52 109
```

to set the colors to blue text on a white background, or:

```
ONCL 27 91 51 52 59 52 55 109
```

to set them to white text on a blue background, or:

```
ONCL 27 91 74
```

to clear the screen to those colors. This works because:

```
ONCL 27 91 51 55 59 52 52 109
```

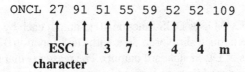

and the command to set colors to white on blue is (the ASCII 27 escape character) plus [37;44m.

You can also use ONCL.COM to create small nontext files. If the ASCII characters won't fit on the command line, you can split them over several lines of a batch file. Add a single > redirection sign and a filename to the end of the first line, and a double >> sign and a filename to all the other lines. The single > sign creates a new file and wipes out any existing files with the same name, and the double >> sign appends all the rest of the lines to the file. The following batch file will create a DECIDE.COM program that helps you make decisions:

```
ONCL 180 9 186 43 1 205 33 180        > DECIDE.COM
ONCL 44 205 33 180 9 246 194 64      >> DECIDE.COM
ONCL 116 7 186 66 1 205 33 235       >> DECIDE.COM
ONCL 17 246 194 1 116 7 186 75       >> DECIDE.COM
ONCL 001 205 33 235 5 186 81 1       >> DECIDE.COM
ONCL 205 33 195 13 10 84 104 101     >> DECIDE.COM
ONCL 032 97 110 115 119 101 114      >> DECIDE.COM
ONCL 32 105 115 32 46 32 46 32       >> DECIDE.COM
ONCL 46 032 36 109 97 121 98 101     >> DECIDE.COM
ONCL 46 13 10 36 110 111 46 13 10    >> DECIDE.COM
ONCL 036 121 101 115 46 13 10 36     >> DECIDE.COM
```

If you don't redirect the ONCL output, it will go to CON (the screen). For example, the command:

```
ONCL 7
```

will beep. You might want to put this at the end of a long batch file so the computer will call you when it's done.

This can come in handy when you're trying to create a COM file and all you have is a list of DATA statements in a BASIC program. If the list is made up of hex numbers you can use the DEBUG E command to enter them directly. But if the numbers in the DATA statements are decimal, adapt the technique used to create the DECIDE.COM above.

Notes: ONCL.COM uses DOS function 40 to output each byte, when it would have been much simpler to do it with DOS function 02 (which sends the contents of DL to standard output). The reason is that DOS function 02 does some meddlesome things like expanding tabs.

OPTION
Batch file command

Edward Morris

Purpose: Provides very sophisticated all-purpose keyboard handling for IF ER-RORLEVEL tests.

Format: `[d:][path]OPTION Aa [BbCc...][-text]`

where *Aa, Bb* etc. are character/code pairs and *-text* is an optional prompt.

Remarks: Lots of short COM programs can read the keyboard and set the ERROR-LEVEL accordingly to allow batch file branching, but most look for one or two predefined keys and set the same ERRORLEVELs each time.

OPTION lets you specify a wide range of parameters in easy-to-remember pairs, as well as an optional custom prompt, directly from the command line. The first character in each pair is the key pressed and the second is the ERRORLEVEL code generated.

Examples: If you entered:

`OPTION A1B2`

OPTION would return an ERRORLEVEL of 1 if you hit A or 2 if you typed B. To allow uppercase and lowercase entries, you would change it to:

`OPTION A1a1B2b2`

OPTION can also display onscreen prompts. Follow the parameter pairs with a hyphen and the message to be displayed. For example:

`OPTION y1Y1n0N0-Enter Y or N:`

with two spaces at the very end displays the prompt:

`Enter Y or N:`

and positions the cursor two spaces from the colon.

OPTION lets you use the Enter key by representing it as a plus sign. So you could enter:

```
OPTION +1 0-Hit Enter for 1, Space for 0
```

(Be careful not to insert extra spaces in the string of argument pairs unless you actually want the spacebar to count as a valid key.)

If you include an odd number of keypress arguments, OPTION uses the last character as the ERRORLEVEL it returns if any key other than the one in the previous valid pair is pressed. So if you try:

```
OPTION +10
```

the program will generate an ERRORLEVEL of 1 if Enter is pressed or 0 for any other key.

If you need ERRORLEVEL values greater than 9 you can use the ASCII characters immediately following 9.

```
OPTION J:L=
```

will return a 10 if J is pressed or a 13 if L is pressed, since in the ASCII sequence the : character immediately follows 9 and the = sign is four characters after 9. Consult the ASCII chart in the front of this book or the back of your BASIC manual for help.

Notes: OPTION prompts the user for a keypress by beeping. It also beeps when it stumbles over an illegal key, discards such characters, and loops back for another key. To get rid of these beeps, put OPTION.COM on the same disk as DEBUG and type:

```
DEBUG OPTION.COM
E 12A 90 90
W
Q
```

When OPTION detects a legal keypress, it clears the screen and puts the cursor in the upper lefthand corner. If you'd rather have it display the key and move the cursor to the next line down, type in the following DEBUG script using a pure ASCII word processor or the DOS COPY CON command, and call the file PATCH.

```
E151 B4 02 CD 21 B2 0D CD 21 B2
E15A 0A CD 21 58 B4 4C CD 21
```

```
RCX
62
W
Q
```

Then get into DOS and type:

```
DEBUG OPTION.COM < PATCH
```

Most ERRORLEVEL generators are rigid and inflexible, and force you to use slightly different COM programs for each set of tests. OP-TION.COM lets you use one all-purpose program with different arguments in all your batch files. And it not only lets you print a customized prompt, but gives you choices about whether or not to beep and clear the screen.

Be careful in using some of the ASCII characters above 9, however, since DOS will try to execute some — such as > redirection symbols.

PAGE Command
Paul Somerson

Purpose: Switches between text pages 0 - 3 on a color system and identifies the current video page.

Format: `[d:][path]PAGE n|?`

where *n* is an 80 x 25 text mode video page number, and *?* is a parameter that reports the current page. Only one of these may be used at a time.

Remarks: Entering a page number from 0 to 3 will make that video page active. Entering a ? will display the current page. The BIOS default page (the one most users commonly work in) is page 0. Entering a page number out of range won't do anything.

Example: To switch to page 2, enter:

```
PAGE 2
```

To switch back to the normal default page, type:

```
PAGE 0
```

To see what page is currently active, type:

```
PAGE ?
```

Entering:

```
PAGE
```

by itself with no spaces after it will print brief instructions.

Notes: 1.   This will work only only color systems and only in the 80 x 25 color text mode.

2.   You can use alternate pages to store information — such as directory listings — and treat these other pages almost as text windows.

3.   *PC Magazine*'s COLOR.COM color-setting program is page aware, and can change the colors of individual 25 x 80 pages. The first time you switch into a non-0 page you may see an odd color pattern. Running COLOR.COM will correct this.

4.   If you want to clear a page to the existing color, you need to have a page-aware CLS program such as PAGECLS.COM handy.

See PAGECLS.

PAGECLS   **Paul Somerson**
Command

Purpose: Clears any 80 x 25 screen to the existing screen colors and on the current video page.

Format: `[d:][path]PAGECLS`

Remarks: Most CLS utilities assume you want to clear the screen to preset colors and on video page 0. This looks at the existing colors and maintains those colors when it clears the screen — and it will clear whatever page happens to be active without disturbing any other video pages.

See PAGE.

PAINT	Jeff Prosise
Command	

Purpose: Edits or creates custom help or reference screens that can be popped up over an application program or at the DOS prompt with the *PC Magazine* HELP.COM utility. Also provides full control of character and video attribute bytes and permits insertion of single-line, double-line, or pattern characters from the extended-ASCII PC text-graphics set.

Format: `[d:][path]PAINT [filespec]`

Remarks: The optional *filespec* is the filename (plus drive and path, if needed) of a help or screen previously saved for HELP.COM by means of the related *PC Magazine* CAPTURE program. If filespec is omitted, PAINT allows you to create and save a new screen in the appropriate format. HELP files are 4,000-byte screen buffer images, and as many as 14 may be chained together for successive display. The PgUp and PgDn keys in PAINT move through multiple-screen files.

The Ins key toggles the PAINT editor between overstrike (the default) and insert modes. The Del key deletes the character under the cursor and closes up the text. In overstrike mode, the backspace key moves the cursor left without moving any text characters to its right. In insert mode, the backspace drags characters with it. The cursor can be moved anywhere within the viewing area by means of the cursor keys. Home and End move the cursor to the ends of the text line, and Enter performs the usual carriage return/line feed.

Function key F1 lists the menus presented by each function key, and Esc deselects any active menu. F3 toggles between text-only and text-plus-attribute modes, which are also reflected in the operation of the back-space and Del keys. Attributes are selected by number(s) after pressing F2, which presents 16 foreground and eight background color choices (color systems) or normal, reverse, boldface, or underline (monochrome systems). By positioning the cursor on any displayed character and pressing F2 twice, that video attribute can be selected without using the menu numbers. Pressing Enter defaults to the current selection. Selected attributes remain in effect until changed.

You can "paint" small or irregular screen areas with the current attribute by holding down the Ctrl key and pressing the desired cursor arrow keys. Large screen areas may be defined by locating the cursor at one corner and pressing F5, then moving to the diagonal corner and pressing F5 again. The program then presents a menu choice either to clear the defined block of text characters or to paint them all with the current video attribute. Pressing F5 twice without moving the cursor defines the entire screen and presents the same choice.

Function key F4 permits selection of single-line, double-line, patterns, or asterisks that the program then writes to the screen when you hold down the Alt key and press the appropriate Up, Down, Left, or Right Arrow keys. Where lines cross, PAINT substitutes the appropriate junction symbols. F6 asks for a filename under which the file is to be saved (it supplies the original filename as a default) and saves the file. And it automatically applies compensation to adjust for differences in display size. Pressing F7 returns to DOS.

Notes: 1.   While PAINT is intended primarily for use with screens that use the HELP program, it can be used to advantage in prototyping screens for application programs and in the design layout of other pop-up windows.

2.   PAINT is compatible both with traditional PCs and with the PS/2 line.

PARSE Command   Michael J. Mefford

Purpose: Displays the number of characters, words, and sentences in ASCII text files.

Format: `[d:][path]PARSE [d:][path]filename`

Remarks: PARSE also calculates and reports the averages of the numbers of characters per word, words per sentence, and "long" words (eight or more characters). It uses these to calculate and display an approximation of the Fog Index grade-level readability rating.

The accuracy of the various counts may be affected, though usually not significantly, by the presence of formatting and printing codes included in the file by non-ASCII word processors. PARSE does ignore the high-bit codes produced by *WordStar* and similar programs, but "dot commands" and the like will be counted.

Notes: For further information on the Fog Index see Robert Gunning's *The Technique of Clear Writing* (McGraw-Hill, 1952, 1968).

PCMAP
Command

Robert L. Hummel

Purpose: Displays a list of the programs currently loaded in memory, and the amount of RAM each program uses.

Format: [d:] [path] PCMAP

Remarks: The DOS CHKDSK command will report how much of your system's memory is free, but it won't tell you what programs happen to be loaded in RAM or the amount of memory allocated to each.

This is especially important if your system is crammed with TSR programs. Whenever you load a TSR it ropes off a section of memory that no other application can use. If you want to run a program that needs a lot of memory, or juggle the selection of TSRs to accommodate one more resident utility, PCMAP will tell you exactly how much RAM each has snagged.

Most full-fledged commercial TSR programs try to behave politely. Once you install them, they'll leave a "signature" in memory to prevent you from inadvertently installing them again during the same session and eating up unnecessary RAM. However, some less sophisticated resident software (like a few of the bare-bones demo utilities included in this package) weren't designed to guard against such problems, and may let you load additional copies into memory as many times as you like. PCMAP will identify these for you.

The program works by tracing the chain of Memory Control Blocks (MCBs) employed by DOS to divide up memory efficiently for different processes. Each 16-byte MCB operates like a bookmark to keep track of how much memory follows it, identify which process "owns" the particular chunk of memory, and tell whether it happens to be the last MCB in use.

If the block isn't the last MCB in the chain, byte 0 will contain M. If it is the final block, byte 0 will be a Z. Bytes 1 and 2 form a four-digit hex number called the Process ID (PID) that identifies the owner of the memory following the MCB. Under current DOS versions, the PID is simply the Program Segment Prefix (PSP) segment address of the program that allocated the memory. Bytes 3 and 4 contain the number of 16-byte memory paragraphs that follow the MCB. (The MCB itself is not included in the number.) The remaining 11 bytes aren't used by current DOS versions, and may contain values left over in memory from other programs.

PCMAP can display the names of some of the resident programs loaded in memory. When DOS loads a program, it gives the program a copy of the DOS environment. (The segment address of the evironment copy is stored in the two bytes beginning at offset 2CH in the program's PSP.) Starting with version 3.0, DOS tacks the full path name of the program onto the end of the environment. PCMAP checks to see if the environment block is owned by the program, and if so, displays the name. If you run PCMAP on an older DOS version you'll simply see "(Unknown)" instead of the program's name.

PCPARK   Robert L. Hummel
Command

Purpose: Parks the heads on hard drives (for PC-ATs and later systems only).

Format: `[d:][path]PCPARK`

Remarks: The comments included here are long and detailed for two reasons:

1.   Robert Hummel does a very good job of explaining a complicated question that's one of the most frequently asked by hard disk users.

2.   Most users are so terrified by the fragility of hard disks in general and the published accounts of specific hard disk disasters that they're nervous about running any kind of program that does more to their hard disks than read from them and write to them. And if they're not, they should be.

While PCPARK uses a very conventional technique (nothing fancy, just two BIOS calls), manufacturers sometimes do insane, nonstandard things. If you are at all squeamish about running a program that moves your disks heads, don't. We tested it thoroughly, but it's impossible to know how it will work on every system. So if you're the least bit apprehensive, or you're not sure how your particular hard disk would handle it, skip this utility.

In any event, if you're thinking about trying it, read everything here first. It will explain what the program does and help you decide if your system is standard enough to be safe. And it's downright fascinating.

Background

A floppy contains only one magnetic disk, called a platter, while a hard disk can contain several platters that are mounted on a single central spindle. Each platter has two surfaces, called sides, on which information can be stored. Sides are numbered consecutively beginning with side 0.

The device that reads and writes data is called a head and is somewhat similar to the recording head in an audio tape recorder. Each recording surface has its own dedicated read/write head, and like disk sides, these are also numbered consecutively beginning with side 0. The term "side" may become confusing when there are more than two, so sides are traditionally referred to by their head number. The terms "side 3" and "head 3" both refer to the fourth recording surface.

All the heads are mounted together on one single movable arm called a servo positioner. This arm moves the heads from the outer edge of the platter to the center, somewhat like a phonograph arm. But while a phono arm moves smoothly, disk heads move in discrete predefined steps, driven either by what is called (logically enough) a stepper motor or by a magnetic coil that performs the same function. This movement creates a series of concentric rings of data known as tracks. A 360K diskette has 40 tracks, while a large hard disk may have over 1,000.

To a programmer, all the tracks on all the sides at any one particular head location are collectively known as a cylinder. The terms track and cylinder are easy to confuse, and are generally used interchangeably. Because the heads are tied together, telling the disk to move head 3 to track 5 has the same effect as telling it to move all the heads to track 5 of their respective sides.

Each track is further divided into packets of data called sectors. Typical hard disks, using standard controllers, use 17 sectors per track. Other controllers, such as the RLL variety, use special techniques to store up to 30 sectors per track. Unlike cylinders, tracks, heads, and sides, sectors are numbered from 1.

To address any packet of data on a hard disk, you must know three coordinates: the cylinder, head, and sector. Changing cylinders is the only process that requires physical movement across the disk, and is the most time consuming. (When you hear a disk called a "40 millisecond drive" this refers to the average time needed to switch among cylinders.) Because the heads are selected electronically, switching among them is virtually instantaneous. Finding the right sector is simply a matter of waiting for the platter to rotate under the head — which can also be a major cause of delay.

Landing Zone

In a floppy disk drive the heads actually ride on the physical surface of the disk. This isn't dangerous, since the floppy disk surface is flexible. The heads and the disk are subject to the same kind of wear as you might find in a VCR. But in a hard disk, the heads ride on a cushion of air, separated from the surface of the disk by less than the width of a human hair. One drive manufacturer has compared the situation to that of a jumbo jet flying at 600 mph just six inches off the ground.

Some of the popular and inexpensive hard disks on the market today lack a critical feature called "Park and Lock." When you turn off the main power at the end of a session, the disk heads on these just drop onto the surface of the disk wherever they happened to be positioned. Extending the analogy of the jumbo jet, the picture is horrible. The heads plow into the relatively soft coating of the disk causing physical damage and possible loss of data. Unfortunately, damage isn't limited only to the crash site. Magnetic particles, sheared off by the impact, settle over the disk causing random contamination and corruption of data. Move one of these disks while the heads are sitting on the surface and the damage increases.

Hard disks that employ more advanced technology (and generally carry a higher price tag) have special built-in "Park and Lock" hardware to prevent this disaster. Powerful springs hold the disk heads away from the platters. When the disk is turned on, the heads are forced down near the surface. When power is turned off, the springs snap the heads back into a parked position and lock them to prevent further movement.

If you have a disk that doesn't park the heads automatically, you can protect your system by parking them manually each time you're ready to shut things down. PCPARK can do this for you.

Working with BIOS

Data on a hard disk is written starting at cylinder 0, and moves toward the higher cylinder numbers as the disk fills. The highest numbered cylinder on the disk will be the last one to be written. Unless your disk is nearly full, therefore, chances are that the last cylinder will be unused and will be a good place to position the heads for parking. Parking the heads is something like a controlled crash landing. By restricting contact to one cylinder on the disk, the potential for loss of data is minimized.

To park the heads on any drive you must know the number of cylinders in the disk, and you can get this information by making a BIOS Return Current Drive Parameters (often called Get Parameters) function call. Despite its name, it doesn't return the parameters of the current drive. And the description published in many popular books of the parameters returned is incorrect. To call the function, load the registers as follows:

AH   =   8

DL   =   physical drive number for which information is requested
(0 = first floppy)
(80H = first hard disk)

Then execute an interrupt 13H. On return, the registers will hold the following:

DL   =   number of drives responding

DH   =   maximum head number
(# heads - 1)

CH   =   maximum cylinders or track number
(# cylinders - 1)
(high two bits are stored in CL)

CL   =   maximum sector number
(lower 6 bits only)

The maximum cylinder number supported by the BIOS is 1023. In binary notation, this would be 1111111111, or ten bits long. Since only eight bits can be stored in the CH register, the leftmost two bits are placed in the leftmost bits of the CL register.

Once you know the number of the last cylinder, you can tell BIOS to move the heads to that cylinder by calling the BIOS Seek service. The registers are assigned the same general meanings as for the Get Parameters function. So, in the same way, load the registers with:

AH   =   0CH

DL   =   physical drive number on which to move heads
(0 = first floppy)
(80H = first hard disk)

DH   =   head number to select

CH = cylinder number to select
(high two bits are stored in CL)

CL = maximum sector number
(lower 6 bits only)

Then execute an interrupt 13H, as before.

Fortunately you don't have to worry about unpacking the cylinder number. The Seek routine expects to see it in the same format as it is returned by the Get Parameters function.

If you're really curious about this, you may follow along by using the DEBUG unassemble command. PCPARK first loads the DX register with 80H, the drive number assigned to the first hard disk installed in the computer. Note, that since only the DL register is checked for the drive number, the instruction could have been MOV DL,80. This would have resulted in a two-byte instruction instead of a three-byte instruction, reducing program size by one byte. But there is an ulterior motive for using this instruction, which will become clear later in the program.

The program then performs a subroutine call to offset 109H. This is another method of reducing code size. Because the CALL places the address of the next instruction on the stack, the RET instruction at the end of the program will cause the same code to be executed twice. The second time, however, the RET instruction will return to DOS, terminating the program.

The next step is to determine the drive parameters. This is done by loading AH with 8 and executing an interrupt 13H. If, on return, the carry flag is set, it means that this function is not supported, and the PCPARK program will not work. A message is displayed to that effect. Early versions of the PC and XT BIOS do not support this function call.

The Get Parameters function returns a lot of information you don't need for this particular operation. Since all the heads move together, it doesn't matter what head or sector we seek to as long as it's on the last cylinder. The Get Parameters call returns the number of drives installed in DL, destroying the drive number that was loaded in the first instruction. The PUSH DX/POP DX instruction pair solves this by loading the drive number (0080H on the first call, 0081H on the second pass) back into the register. Only full-size registers may be pushed and popped, so the 00 was placed in DH to provide a valid head number.

PCPARK then calls the Seek routine. The registers contain the maximum cylinder and sector number as returned by Get Parameters, and the head has been forced to 0. If the call fails, the carry flag will be set, and the program prints a short message onscreen. If successful, a message to that effect is printed, indicating the number of the drive that has been parked. The RET instruction sends the program back to the MOV DX,0081 instruction, and the process is repeated for the second physical drive, if one is installed.

You should always park your hard disk's heads before turning off your computer. It also helps to park them when you leave your computer on, but will be away from it for a while. For those who have never heard a hard disk seek across its width, the sound can be somewhat disconcerting. Even though the heads are moving a large distance (relative to a single track), the stepper motor still moves a track at a time. This rapid on/off movement of the motor causes a "beeping" or "buzzing" sound that you may associate more with floppy drives. Some hard disk are very loud, and others nearly silent. This noise is natural and nothing to worry about.

Should you decide not to shut off your computer after parking the heads, the next disk access will cause the heads to travel just as far to get back to the data as they did to leave it. The result will be more buzzing. And if you hear a "clunk" as the heads find the last cylinder, relax— you're parked safe and sound.

Notes:

1. Manufacturers are correct when they warn you not to use their park programs on other hard disks, however. Because the programs were meant to be sold with a single drive, the last cylinder number is usually hard-coded into the program. Using a park program designed for a drive with 100 cylinders on a disk that has 200 cylinders will place the heads in the middle of the disk and in a position to do some damage.

2. If you're sure your hard disk already parks its heads automatically, you don't need to use this utility.

3. Also, because of the BIOS services the program uses, as mentioned earlier, it won't work on older PCs and XTs.

PEEK   Mike Cohn
Filter

Purpose: Lets you quickly examine the first screenful of any file.

Format: `[d:][path]PEEK < [d:][path]filename`

Remarks: You could use the DOS MORE.COM utility in place of PEEK.COM:

```
MORE < filename
```

However, MORE.COM will display the entire file one screenful at a time rather than just showing you the beginning of the file and then quitting, the way PEEK does.

If you want, you can patch one byte in the DOS MORE.COM utility to display just a single screenful and then quit. In all DOS versions from 2.0 through 3.2, this patching address is 1C4. In version 3.3 it's 1C2. To find this address, type:

```
DEBUG MORE.COM
-
```

You should see the DEBUG hyphen (-) prompt. Look at the following chart and pick the hex representation of the length:

MORE Version	HEX Length
2.0	180
2.1	180
3.0	140
3.1	11A
3.2	127
3.3	139

If you're using a version not listed, type RCX and press the Enter key twice. The number DEBUG prints to the right of the CX is the length.

Plug the hex length into the line:

```
-S 100 L 139 B4 0C
```
↑
length

So if you're using a version like 3.2, change the line to:

```
-S 100 L 127 B4 0C
```

DEBUG should report something like:

```
30FA:01C3
```

Ignore the four hex digits to the left of the colon. Jot down the four rightmost hex digits. This is the address of the byte directly after the one you want to patch, so subtract 1 from the number. For DOS 3.3, 1C3 - 1 = 1C2. For versions 2.0 through 3.2, 1C5 - 1 = 1C4. The number you're left with is the patching address.

Use the DEBUG E command to examine the value at this address:

```
-E 1C2
```

When you press Enter you should see something like:

```
30FA:01C2 21._
```

If you don't press Enter, type Q and press Enter to quit, then start again. But if you do see a 21 with a period after it, type in a 20 and then press Enter:

```
30FA:01C2 21.20
```

Then rename the file to something like MORENEW.COM:

```
-N MORENEW.COM
```

Write this new file to disk and quit by typing W and pressing Enter and then typing Q and pressing Enter.

Then when you want to view just the first screenful of any file, type:

```
MORENEW < filename
```

Unfortunately, however, both MORE.COM and its patched MORENEW.COM cousin display files exactly as they appear. If you happen to be using a word processor such as *WordStar* that meddles with the high bit and makes the text unreadable in DOS, MORE and MORENEW will keep it unreadable. But PEEK will straighten it out.

| **PLAY** | **Michael J. Mefford** |
| **Command** | |

Purpose: Provides many of the music-producing functions of the BASIC PLAY statement without the need to work in BASIC.

Format:
```
[d:][path]PLAY[/K]
```
   (Option I)
```
[d:][path]PLAY string[/K]
```
   (Option II)
```
[d:][path]PLAY filespec/F[/K]
```
   (Option III)

Remarks: Entered at the DOS prompt with no arguments on the command line (Option I), PLAY looks in the current directory for a file named PLAY.DAT and executes the commands in that file. The PLAY.DAT file included on this disk is "Greensleeves." The file can be examined, and similar files created, with a regular ASCII word processor.

Alternatively, PLAY can use either a command-line string (Option II) or any legal DOS filename (Option III) to supply the music command arguments. Filenames may include a path designation, but must include the /F terminator.

Pressing any key while PLAY is executing will terminate operation unless the /K switch has been added.

The command set used with PLAY is shown on the following page and is used in the PLAY.DAT file.

The PLAY Command Set

K   Keyboard. K will cause PLAY not to poll the keyboard during play. If K is not found, any keystroke will exit.

On   Octave. *n* is a decimal number between 0 and 6. Middle C starts 03. The default is 04.

Ln   Length of time the notes will be played until the next L command is encountered. *n* is a decimal number between 1 and 64. For example, L4 = quarter-note and L8 = eighth note.

Tn	Tempo is the pace at which the music is played. *n* is a decimal number between 32 and 255. The larger the number, the faster the pace. The default is T120.
A-G	Letter names corresponding to the notes of the scale. The letter name may be followed by either a # or + for a sharp, or a - for a flat. O3C = middle C.
Nn	Note to be played. *n* is a decimal number between 1 and 84. Each increment is 1/12 of an octave. N can be used as an alternative to defining a note by a letter and an octave. For example, N37 = middle C.
Pn	Pause, or rest, for a length defined by *n*. P works in the same way as the L command above. For example, P2 = a half rest.
MN	Music Normal. The note is played 7/8 of its specified time, and 1/8 is a rest between notes. This is the default.
ML	Music Legato. The note is played the full length of time specified.
MS	Music Staccato. The note is played 3/4 of the time specified, and 1/4 is a rest between notes.
.	Dot. A dot can follow a letter note or a pause. A dotted note increases play time by half the duration of the note or pause. More than one dot may be used.

POP-CAL Command
Leo Forrest

Purpose:	Pops up a calendar window for any month from January, 1583 to December, 9999.
Format:	`[d:][path]POP-CAL` (loads command into memory)

`Alt-C`	Toggles calendar on/off
`Right-Arrow`	Advance one month
`Left-Arrow`	Back one month
`Up-Arrow`	Advance one year
`Down-Arrow`	Back one year

Remarks: POP-CAL is a memory-resident utility and should be loaded into memory before you call up any applications programs. Normally, you would simply enter POP-CAL as one line in your AUTOEXEC.BAT file.

POP-CAL takes the current month and year as its initial value. It subsequently remembers your last-used calendar, facilitating repeated references.

Notes: 1. You may use DEBUG to change the hotkey from Alt-C by replacing the Alt-key scan code value at offset 0174. To change the hotkey to Alt-Q (scan code 10), enter:

```
DEBUG POP-CAL.COM
E 174 10
W
Q
```

The hex values for the various scan codes are given in Appendix E of the IBM BASIC manual (3.0) and also in the "Scan Code Value Table" in connection with CAPTURE, elsewhere in this manual.

2. While POP-CAL has been tested for compatibility with a number of other memory-resident programs, be careful when using it with other TSR programs.

POPDIR (and PUSHDIR) Command(s)

John Friend

Purpose: Provides a way to return automatically to your current directory after running programs that require directory changing.

See PUSHDIR.

PR Command

John Dickinson

Purpose: Prints the standard ASCII files of program listings according to a standard formatted style.

Format: `[d:][path]PR [d:][path]filename[.ext]`

Remarks: PR.COM formats the program listing into 80 columns, expands ASCII tabs, adds a seven-line header and a blank footer, and prints 55 lines of the listing on each 66-line page. The header contains the filename, page number, and date and time the program was last saved.

Notes: The listings photoreproduced in *PC Magazine*'s Programming/Utilities column are often printed using PR.

PRN2FILE   Tom Kihlken
Command

Purpose: Intercepts and captures any output directed to your printer and instead sends it to a file that you can edit or print later.

Format: `[d:][path]PRN2FILE [d:][path]filename [/Pn] [/Bn] [/U]`

Remarks: PRN2FILE is a memory-resident program that is normally loaded as part of your AUTOEXEC.BAT file. It should be installed before other print utilities, such as a print spooler or the DOS MODE command. Once you install it, you may run the program multiple times to change the filename (the drive and path default to the current directory unless specified) designated to receive the printer output.

Unless the filename is changed, successive print operations are appended to the created file, to prevent overwriting it. To disable the printer output redirection, simply omit specifying a filename.

The optional */Pn* parameter designates the printer number (the default is LPT1) to be redirected. Note that output to a non-existent printer (/P2 in a one-printer system) is supported. This is another way to permit normal printing while PRN2FILE remains resident. Legal values for Pn range from 1 through 3.

The optional */Bn* parameter sets the buffer size. The default value is 4,096 bytes, and values up to 64K may be specified. The buffer repeatedly empties when partially full in order to minimize the chance of buffer overflow even when DOS may be called on for other activities than writing the buffer to disk. If the buffer overflows the program will print an error message, but you may lose some data. If this happens, rewrite the file using a larger buffer.

The optional */U* parameter is used to unload PRN2FILE from memory. If other memory-resident utilities have been loaded after PRN2FILE and have chained onto the same interrupts, it will not be possible to unload the program, and a message to this effect will be displayed.

All optional parameters may be entered in any order, but must each be separated by a single space character that acts as a delimiter.

PRNBYLIN   Russell W. Powell
Command

Purpose: Memory-resident Shift-PrtSc enhancer that lets you send sections of the screen rather than the entire display to your printer; also lets you exit from accidental Shift-PrtScs.

Format: [d:] [path] PRNBYLIN

Remarks: When you're debugging a program or working on a spreadsheet, you often need to use the DOS Shift-PrtSc function to print out just a few lines of code or some current figures. More often than not this results in a large amount of wasted paper.

PRNBYLIN.COM gives you control over the normal DOS print screen function.

Once you load it, you may select the exact lines you want printed without having to print the entire screen. When in the 80-column mode, you can move the selection bar by using the + and - keys on the number pad and mark your position by pressing Enter. The program uses DOS's normal print screen function when not in the 80-column mode.

It also lets you escape out of an accidental Shift-PrtSc by hitting Esc. And you can hit Esc if you realize you marked the wrong area and want to start over.

Notes: While PRNBYLIN.COM works from inside most applications, some programs may override it by providing their own PrtSc routines. And since this is a memory-resident program, be careful when using it with other TSR software. As with all the resident programs presented here, test it first in your current system configuration before using it with unsaved files.

PRNSWAP   Charles Petzold
Command

Purpose: Alternately swaps printer ports LPT1 and LPT2.

Format: [d:] [path] PRNSWAP

Remarks: This tiny program (five assembly language instructions) flip-flops the first two parallel printer ports.

Running it once will swap ports LPT1 and LPT2. Running it again will put things back the way they were.

PRNSWAP actually switches the printer I/O port address stored in the BIOS data area. The BIOS uses these to determine where to send LPT1 and LPT2 output. PRNSWAP may not work if you've previously loaded a software print buffer, since print buffers often grab the port address when they first load.

PRSWAP   John Dickinson
Command

Purpose: Converts IBM text-graphics characters into ASCII characters that can be printed by nongraphics printers.

Format: [d:] [path] PRSWAP

Remarks: Many printers can't handle the IBM text-graphics characters (nonstandard ASCII 176-223 and 254) programmers often use to make their screen displays look more attractive. PRSWAP.COM is a memory-resident program that translates these characters into presentable-looking ASCII substitutes.

PRSWAP should be loaded only once until you power down or hit Ctrl-Alt-Del. If you intend to use it regularly, the best place to put it is in your AUTOEXEC.BAT file.

PRT2SCR   **Dean Perry**
Command

Purpose: Redirects all printer output to the screen.

Format: `[d:][path]PRT2SCR`

Remarks: Even the fastest printers are slow, and most are noisy and cumbersome. It's easy to waste a lot of paper while trying to align rows and columns correctly, or when you issue an accidental screen dump. And some programs insist on having a printer hooked up, which makes them difficult to use on a laptop 35,000 feet above Missouri.

PRT2SCR is a memory-resident utility that solves these problems by redirecting all normal printer output to the screen.

It works by intercepting printer services interrupt 17H. When a character is sent to the printer via function 0, that character is teletyped to the screen using a simulated interrupt call to video services function 0EH. If any of the other function calls is sent to printer services, the status code is set to PRINTER OK and the calls are ignored. PRT2SCR remains active until the computer is rebooted.

This program is also great for users who do not have a printer or whose printer is on the fritz. Now you can run those programs that require a printer to be present and not worry about those "Printer not ready" errors.

Unless you're using an extremely rude word processor, PRT2SCR lets you print output to the screen so you can see how things will look before wasting a box of paper.

Notes: 1.   You have to run PRT2SCR only once each session, and the only way to remove it from memory is to reboot unless you use INSTALL/REMOVE.

2.   Since this is a resident program, test it first with the other applications you normally run to prevent trouble.

PRTSCRFF
Command

Gary Khachadoorian

Purpose: Adds an automatic form feed each time you do a Shift-PrtSc screen dump.

Format: `[d:][path]PRTSCRFF`

Remarks: One of the major irritations in doing a series of Shift-PrtSc screen dumps is that every time one finishes you normally have to take the printer offline, press the form-feed button, then put the printer back online.

Once you run the memory-resident PRTSCRFF.COM program, however, your system will automatically add a form feed to each screen dump. You won't have to contend with the front panel printer switches, and you won't accidentally leave the last screen dump in the printer.

PRTSCRFF.COM simply calls the original BIOS print screen routine (interrupt 05H), and follows it up by sending a form feed to the printer. This is especially useful for the Hewlett-Packard Laser Jet printer. The Laser Jet's standard print screen is held in a buffer until you take the printer offline and press the form-feed button. But with PRTSCRFF the page is automatically printed and fed through the system.

You have to run this program only once, so it may be convenient to put a PRTSCRFF line in your AUTOEXEC.BAT batch file.

PUSHDIR (and POPDIR)
Command(s)

John Friend

Purpose: Provides a way to return automatically to your current directory after running programs that require directory changing.

Format: `[d:][path]PUSHDIR`
`[CD \AltDir\ProgName]`
`POPDIR`

Remarks: While PUSHDIR and POPDIR can be entered directly from the DOS prompt, their primary application is in batch files. For example, suppose you create a file named 12.BAT that consists of the following four lines:

```
PUSHDIR
CD\LOTUS
123
POPDIR
```

Suppose also that 12.BAT, PUSHDIR.COM, and POPDIR.COM are either in your root directory or in a subdirectory on the path specified in your AUTOEXEC.BAT file. Assume, finally, that you are currently in your word processing subdirectory (\WP), but need some information from a *1-2-3* spreadsheet. If you now enter:

```
12<CR>
```

from the DOS prompt, PUSHDIR stores the \WP (your current directory) on its stack and DOS changes to the \LOTUS subdirectory and runs *1-2-3*. When you exit from *1-2-3*, you would normally be left in the \LOTUS subdirectory. A DOS CD command in 12.BAT after the 123 line could return you to a specified directory every time you terminated *1-2-3*, of course. But POPDIR returns you to whatever subdirectory you were in when you invoked *1-2-3* — in this case, to your \WP subdirectory.

PUSHDIR can accommodate up to six levels of directories on its stack, permitting considerable programming flexibility in constructing batch files.

QUICKEYS   Leo Forrest
Command

Purpose: Accelerates the "typematic" repeat rate of a PC or XT keyboard. A built-in subprogram is included that instantly clears the keyboard buffer to prevent sending excess accumulated keystrokes to the display.

Format: `[d:] [path]QUICKEYS`   (loads memory-resident program)

`<Alt-Shift>`   (clears keyboard buffer)

Remarks: While the keystroke repetition rate of the AT is adjustable, that of the XT and the PC is fixed at approximately nine keystrokes per second. When QUICKEYS is loaded (normally through your AUTOEXEC.BAT file), the repetition speed is approximately doubled. Successive loadings of QUICKEYS (each requires about 672 bytes of memory) can be used to increase the keyboard speed still further, if desired.

Notes: QUICKEYS is a memory-resident program that inserts itself both into the timer tick and keyboard interrupt routines. It is not compatible with some other memory-resident software and with programs that appropriate the keyboard interrupts.

REBOOT
Command

Paul Somerson

Purpose: Let you select a warm boot or a cold boot, or abort the rebooting process.

Format: `[d:] [path] REBOOT`

Remarks: This is a very simple program that prints a short message onscreen and gives you three options. You can:

1. Press C or c for a cold boot.

2. Press W or w for a warm boot.

3. Press Esc to abort and return to DOS.

The program ignores any other keypresses.

REBOOT is handy when you're there to answer the prompt interactively. But you may want to put a cold/warm rebooting program into a batch file. If so, run the REBOOTB.COM program also included in this package.

While REBOOTB.COM was written for batch files, you can use it directly at the DOS prompt as well. But it's better to use the main REBOOT.COM program, since REBOOT lets you abort the process if you want, and won't do anything if you accidentally press the Enter key or press any key other than C or W.

Notes: 1.   Warm boots and cold boots are virtually identical, except that a cold boot performs an additional power-on-self-test (POST) as if you had turned the main power switch on and off, while a warm boot skips these tests just as if you had pressed Ctrl-Alt-Del.

2.   When a PC boots, its BIOS checks a flag word (two bytes) at location 40:72. If the value of the flag is hex 1234, BIOS does a warm boot. If the flag is not 1234, BIOS does a cold boot. Once you boot up, it puts a 1234 there so subsequent Ctrl-Alt-Del warm boots can skip the POST.

3.   If you use DEBUG to look at addresses 40:72 and 40:73 you'll see 34 12 rather than 12 34, since the PC stores words in "backwords" order. The high order byte (12) goes into the higher memory address (40:73), while the low order byte (34) goes into the lower memory address (40:72). Despite this, the word takes the lower memory address as its own.

See WARMBOOT, COLDBOOT, and REBOOTB.

REBOOTB   Paul Somerson
Command

Purpose: Lets you include a line in a batch file that performs either a cold or warm reboot.

Format: `[d:][path]REBOOTB [C]`

Remarks: REBOOTB.COM lets you perform a warm boot by entering just:

`REBOOTB`

If you add an uppercase or lowercase *C* after it:

`REBOOTB C`

or:

`REBOOTB c`

it will do a cold boot. (Actually, the program will do a warm boot if you enter anything else on the command line other than an uppercase or lowercase C.)

While REBOOTB.COM was written for batch files, you can use it directly at the DOS prompt as well. But it's better to use the main REBOOT.COM program, since REBOOT lets you abort the process if you want, and won't do anything if you accidentally press the Enter key or press any key other than C or W.

See WARMBOOT, COLDBOOT, and REBOOT.

RED (Redirect) Command   John Dickinson

Purpose: Transfers one or more files from one subdirectory to another without requiring the use of COPY and ERASE.

Format: [d:][path]RED [d:][path]filename[.ext] [d:][path]

Remarks: Like the DOS COPY command, RED.COM supports the use of the global characters ? and * in specifying the desired source files.

Unlike COPY, however, RED.COM does not permit renaming a file during the transfer process. (This is why it is unnecessary to supply a target filename.) Furthermore, RED requires that the source and target drives be the same. You cannot, therefore, remove a set of files from drive C: by trying to REDirect them to drive A:.

Example: Before submitting your income tax you calculated it under several different methods, contained in files named ROUGH1.DAT through ROUGH6.WKS. These are all in the subdirectory \IRS on drive C:, and you want to move them all to a sub-subdirectory (which you have created) called \1988TAX\DRAFTS. From the C> prompt enter:

RED \IRS\ROUGH?.* \1988TAX\DRAFTS

and all six files will be moved out of \IRS and into \1988\DRAFTS.

REMOVE (and INSTALL)   Jeff Prosise
Command(s)

Purpose: This pair of utilities lets you load and unload programs in and out of
memory to avoid potential conflicts and excessive memory use.

See INSTALL.

RENDIR   John Dickinson
Command

Purpose: Permits renaming subdirectories directly, without creating a new directory, moving the contents of the old one into it, and then removing the
old directory.

Format: `[d:][path]RENDIR [d:][path]oldname[.ext] newname[.ext]`

Remarks: PC-DOS has always provided a REName command for filenames, but
not for directories. A bug in DOS 3.0 permits you to use the immediate
mode of BASIC to:

```
NAME olddir AS newdir
```

but this bug has been removed from subsequent DOS versions. REN-
DIR.COM permits renaming directories in DOS 3.0 and later.

While RENDIR allows you to change the name of a directory on another
drive than your current one, it does not permit you to transfer a directory
to another drive by RENDIRing it. Thus, for example, if you are on
drive C: and have a directory on drive D: named \TAXES, from the C>
prompt you can:

```
RENDIR D:\TAXES \TAXES88
```

You cannot, however:

```
RENDIR D:\TAXES C:\TAXES88
```

Furthermore, you should not use RENDIR to try to change the name of the subdirectory you are currently in.

Notes: 1.   Unlike RENAME, RENDIR does not support use of the ? and * wildcard characters.

2.   Requires DOS 3.0 or higher.

REPEATS
Command
Michael J. Mefford

Purpose: Checks all directories on a drive and reports all duplicate filenames.

Format: `[d:][path]REPEATS [d:][/P]`

Remarks: While not all duplicate files on a disk are unnecessary, most are. If a hard disk has been in use for some time it is astonishing how many out-dated versions or outright copies of the same file are currently wasting space.

REPEATS lists all identical filenames, together with their directory, size, date, and time information, so you can decide which files to delete. The optional /P switch directs the program output simultaneously to the screen and to a printer. As an alternative, you could redirect output to a file, DUPS.FND, by using the DOS redirection command, thus:

`REPEATS > DUPS.FND`

Notes: During the time it operates, REPEATS requires 128K of available memory. The program can be terminated prematurely by pressing Ctrl-Break.

RESET
Command
Paul Somerson

Purpose: This tiny program resets the clock to 0:0:0.

Format: `[d:][path]RESET`

Remarks: It's often necessary to reset the time-of-day clock to 0 so you can use it to time the duration of an event or log an activity. While you can redirect a text file containing "0:0" into the TIME command, this does it cleanly.

See MID$.

REVERSE   **Jozef H. Khoe and Paul Somerson**
Command

Purpose: Lets you flip your foreground and background screen colors without clearing the screen.

Format: `[d:] [path] REVERSE`

Remarks: This is handy if you're using a color system and type CLS, which normally makes the screen white on black. To flip the colors to black on white, just run this program. Running it a second time will restore things the way they were.

If you're using a color screen with highlighted (bright) text, running this program will make the text blink. To fix this, just press F3 and Enter to run it again.

Notes: This program is hard-wired for an 80 x 25 screen.

RFD   **J. S. Redmond**
Command

Purpose: Removes all files in a directory and the directory itself with a single command either in direct or batch mode.

Format: `[d:] [path] RFD [d:]path [/Y]`

where *[d:]path* is the subdirectory you want to erase, and the optional */Y* bypasses a confirmation prompt and suppresses messages.

Remarks: DOS lacks a utility that in one step deletes all of the files in a specified directory and then removes the directory. RFD.COM (Remove Files and Directory) lets you do this either directly at the DOS prompt or unattended inside a batch file. And it reports on the success or failure of the process.

In interactive mode the program asks the user whether or not to proceed, with the prompt:

```
** WARNING ** - All Files Will Be Deleted !
Do You Wish to Proceed (Y/N) ?
```

Entering anything other than a Y or y at this point terminates the program and prints a message to that effect.

Adding a /Y at the end of the command puts the program into batch mode, which bypasses this prompt and supresses all of RFD's normal messages. However, RFD can tell a batch file exactly what happened by returning an exit code that the batch file can sniff out with an IF ERROR-LEVEL test.

RFD terminates with one of five return codes for IF ERRORLEVEL:

99 — Syntax Error
98 — Program Terminated By Operator
05 — Access Denied — Found Protected File
03 — Specified Path Not Found
00 — Normal Termination — Removed

When RFD encounters a read-only, hidden, or a system file it stops, since such files are usually marked that way for good reason. RFD will delete all files it finds until it encounters a protected file. If the protected file is the first directory entry, no files will be deleted and RFD will exit with a 05 return code.

Like the RD command, RFD will not remove the directory that it is in. But it will delete all of the files in the current directory. This is easier than typing:

```
ECHO Y | DEL *.*
```

or:

```
FOR %A in (*.*) DO DEL %A
```

both of which will wipe out all your files.

When you use the /Y option be absolutely certain that you've entered the correct directory. RFD, like the RD command, will not allow you to remove the root directory, or delete the files in it.

Before DOS will allow the deletion of a subdirectory, it checks to see if the subdirectory has any entries (files). If the subdirectory is empty, it may be deleted. If not, all entries must be eliminated prior to deleting the subdirectory. RFD does this task in one step.

Neither DOS nor RFD will let you remove a directory if it contains another subdirectory. You'll have to use RFD to delete the lowest level (farthest from the root) subdirectories first and then move up the tree.

RFD scans the command line for the switch indicator to see whether or not it's in batch mode. Once the mode has been established, the requested path name and its length are noted and stored. Command line parsing was kept to a minimum, and as a result RFD does not trim any leading blanks from the requested path name. If you specify the root directory as the path name, RFD will issue a syntax error. If you try to place a blank before the \ to bypass this feature, you'll get a "Path Not Found" error.

Notes: RFD makes it very easy to delete a lot of work — especially when you add a /Y switch at the end. Be very careful in typing in any RFD command, and be sure you want to wipe out everything in the specified directory.

RHCTRL
Command

Johnny Y. Chin

Purpose: Turns the 5 key on the cursor/number pad into a second Ctrl key (for the right hand).

Format: `[d:] [path] RHCTRL`

Remarks: The old AT keyboards have one Ctrl key on the left. The new ones have Ctrl keys on left and right sides. RHCTRL.COM puts Ctrl keys at both ends of the keyboard by turning the number pad 5 key into a second Ctrl shift.

The number pad 5 key is a perfect choice, since it isn't affected by Num-Lock shifts the way the other number pad keys are. This additional Ctrl key can come in very handy for *WordStar* users with small handspans. But don't try using it with *SideKick* or other interrupt 9 hogs, unless you like cold restarts.

The best way to load this is to use INSTALL / REMOVE, which will let you juggle it and *SideKick* amiably.

RN Command

Michael J. Mefford

Purpose: Simplifies creating, removing, renaming, hiding, unhiding, and changing from one subdirectory to another. It sets and resets the read-only and archive bits of all files within a directory, and reports the filecount and space allocated. It also can run the *PC Magazine* DR.COM program for handling individual files.

Format: `[d:][path]RN [d:][/I]`

Remarks: You may enter RN either as an immediate command at the DOS prompt, or can install it on a hard drive (using the /I option) with a memory-resident database of directory information that speeds up its subsequent operations. If no drive *(d:)* is specified, the current drive is assumed.

If installed, RN should be loaded before *SideKick* and any other uninstallable memory-resident programs. (RN cannot be deinstalled without rebooting.) The program requires 128K RAM operating room; the database, if used, occupies approximately 14K. RN cannot be called up from within an application with a hotkey; it can be accessed only from the DOS prompt. Pressing Esc terminates RN's operations.

When issued, RN.COM brings up an alphabetized directory tree with the current directory highlighted and a menu listing the function keys used for its various directory services. You can move the highlighted directory bar one entry at a time by the Up Arrow and Down Arrow keys, and in larger increments with the Ctrl-PgUp and Ctrl-PgDn, PgUp and PgDn, and Home and End keys. The highlighted bar should be placed on the directory to be affected by the subsequent function key.

When renaming (F2) and creating (F3) directories, do not enter the backslash (\) character. However, be sure to include it in figuring the maximum path length (63 characters). If you select and confirm RMDIR (F4), RN will delete all files within the directory (unless they are marked read-only) before removing the directory. Hide/Unhide (F5) affects the directory name only, not the individual files inside it. F6 and F7 (mark/unmark as read-only and set/reset the archive bit) toggle these bits on all files within the directory. F8 updates the directory data base if changes are made outside RN, and F9 gives a file count together with the space allocated to a directory's files. F10 calls DR.COM.

Note:

1. F2 (Rename Directory) requires DOS 3.x.

2. To reduce or expand the RAM requirements of an installed RN you can change the offset directly with DEBUG. First decide how many directories you'll ever expect to need and add another 50 directories or so as a buffer. (*Caution*: RN does not check to see if there are more directories than it has room to store, so you need to be a little generous.) Multiply your directory requirements by 20 (there are 20 bytes per record), add 4541 (the length of RN's code plus some string space) and convert the result to hex. *SideKick*'s calculator is handy for this type of addition and conversion. Then enter:

```
DEBUG RN.COM
E 676 yz wx
W
Q
```

Note that wxyz is the number you calculated above (in hex), but that the word must be stored in byte-reversed order, yz wx.

ROMINFO   Paul Somerson
Command

Purpose: Reports the date, copyright notice, and ID byte embedded in your ROM BIOS chip.

Format: [d:][path]ROMINFO

Remarks: IBM changes the BIOS with each new system. Some older BIOS chips had serious problems. For instance, the BIOS in an original PC prevents it from booting off a hard disk. And most systems have gone through several revisions (see chart).

Fortunately, IBM socketed its ROM chips to let you upgrade them. Unfortunately, it also stopped selling some of the upgrade ROMs. If you're trying to install a hot new piece of hardware on an old system and it doesn't work, one reason could be a ROM that needs upgrading.

You can use ROMINFO.COM to detect the date (which IBM calls the "release marker"), the copyright notice, and the machine ID byte. If it tells you that you're using an older ROM, you might be able to have your dealer switch ROM chips with someone who doesn't need the newer one.

If you're using an IBM system you'll probably see some of the following information:

ROM date	ID	System
04/24/81	FF	IBM PC (collector's item)
10/19/81	FF	IBM PC (bugs fixed)
08/16/82	FE	IBM XT (first one)
10/27/82	FF	IBM PC handling hard disk and 640K
11/08/82	FE	IBM Portable PC, XT
06/01/83	FD	IBM PCjr
01/10/84	FC	IBM AT
06/10/85	FC	IBM AT (revision 1)
09/13/85	F9	IBM PC Convertible
11/15/85	FC	IBM AT with speed governor, 30-meg hard disk, enhanced keyboard (submodel 1)
01/10/86	FB	IBM XT (revision 1)
04/21/86	FC	IBM XT-286 (submodel 2)
05/09/86	FB	IBM XT (revision 2)
09/02/86	FA	IBM PS/2 Model 30
N/A	FC	IBM PS/2 Model 50 (submodel 4)
N/A	FC	IBM PS/2 Model 60 (submodel 5)
N/A	F8	IBM PS/2 Model 80

The ID byte in the center column is a single value at the very top of memory (address F000:FFFE) that some software uses to determine the kind of hardware it's dealing with.

Examples: Executing ROMINFO.COM on an early AT would report:

```
ROM date at address F000:FFF5 is 01/10/84.
(C) notice at address F000:E005 is COPR. IBM 1984.
ID Byte at address F000:FFFE is FC.
```

Notes: This looks at the hard addresses mentioned above. The ID byte should be at the same place in most systems, but the copyright notice and perhaps even the ROM release marker may not. If not, the program will print whatever characters happen to be at those addresses and you may just see garbage.

RUN
Command

Michael J. Mefford

Purpose: Executes COM, EXE, or BAT files from any disk directory without requiring changing directories or specifying a path to the file.

Format: `[d:][path]RUN [/C|/S][d:][directory]filename [args]`

Remarks: Unless you specify the optional directory parameter, RUN will search the entire default disk for the file you want to execute. You may add any additional arguments *[args]* that you would normally specify on the DOS command line after the filename. You must specify a drive letter *[d:]* if the file to be run is not on the current drive. During its search, any keypress will abort the operation of RUN.COM.

RUN can either operate from the current directory (its default mode, designated by the optional */S* switch) or it can change to the directory (*/C*) in which it finds the desired program before executing it. The /C option is required by programs such as *WordStar*, which can find their overlay files only when loaded from within the directory in which they are stored. The /C option is also required to run BAT files under DOS 2.x (see Notes below).

Notes: RUN overcomes the inability of DOS 2.x to handle COM and EXE files that are prefixed with a path. Batch files under DOS 2.x, however, still require RUN's /C option. If desired, the /C option can be made the RUN default mode, with /S as its selectable alternative. To make the change, put a copy of RUN in the same directory with DEBUG.COM, and enter the following commands:

```
DEBUG RUN.COM
E 15B 1
E 1E8 "C"
W
Q
```

If you later upgrade your version of DOS and wish to reverse the process, use the same procedure with the following commands:

```
DEBUG RUN.COM
E 15B 0
E 1E8 "S"
W
Q
```

SAY   **Serge Couture**
Command

Purpose: Extends the capabilities of the DOS ECHO command by letting you display any character or combination of characters.

Format: [d:][path]SAY "text" | n [, n, n...]

where *text* is any text enclosed in double quotation marks, and each *n* is the ASCII value of a character from 0 to 255.

You may enter text, characters — or more commonly — combinations of both.

Remarks: ECHO is a powerful command but stumbles over nonprintable ASCII characters, and has other drawbacks. SAY.COM is far more flexible.

SAY will print any text characters from the command line that you enclose inside double quotes ("). If you want to echo the quotation mark character itself, use a pair of quotes. If the quotation mark is the first character to be echoed, triple the quote marks.

SAY will handle nonprintable characters if you type in their decimal ASCII code value on the command line without embedding them between quotes. If you want to print the redirection or piping characters (<, >, and |), just use their ASCII values (60, 62, and 124) since DOS will try to redirect or pipe your command when it sees the actual symbols on a command line.

Example: If you enter:

```
SAY "He: ""Compaq?""" 13 10 "She: ""PC AT.""" 13 10
```

the command will print:

```
He: "Compaq?"
She: "PC AT."
```

If you want to send an escape sequence such as ESC &16D to your
printer, do it with:

```
SAY 27 "&16D" > PRN
```

And if you use ANSI.SYS, you can redefine F10 to do a clear screen and
a DIR /P by issuing the command:

```
SAY 27 "[0;68;""CLS"";13;""DIR /P"";13p"
```

You could even use SAY to automate your DOS chores. Entering:

```
SAY 13 "DISK1" 13 "N" 13 | FORMAT B: /S /V
```

would let you format and name a floppy disk without any user intervention.

SCAN   Robert L. Hummel
Command

Purpose: Displays the make/break scan code for any key.

Format: `[d:][path]SCAN`

Remarks: Each time you press a key, the keyboard controller generates an eight-bit
value called a *make* code. When you release the key, it generates another
eight-bit value called a *break* code. The value of the break code is equal
to the value of the make code plus hex 80 (decimal 128). These values
are called scan codes, and memory-resident programs often monitor
these to see if you happened to type the hot key that will activate a particular TSR.

SCAN.COM will display the make/break code in hexadecimal notation
for any key you type. Holding a key down will cause the make code to
auto-repeat. Pressing the spacebar will exit the program and return to
DOS. Because of this, the program cannot be used to find the
make/break codes for the spacebar (which are 39H and B9H).

Each key on the keyboard — including keys such as Ctrl, CapsLock, and every function key — has its own scan code. These are really just proprietary numbers assigned by IBM to identify the physical keys being struck. When you press the A key, you could be typing a lowercase a, or an uppercase A, or a Ctrl-A, or an Alt-A. Your system's BIOS figures all this out.

See Robert Hummel's BIOS program in this section for more details on how BIOS handles keys.

The SCAN.COM program was originally written to display codes continuously on the same line, which saved space if you wanted to examine a lot of keys in a row. However this version inserts carriage returns to put each code on a line by itself, which makes them easier to examine. If you want to remove the carriage returns and display everything continuously, use DEBUG to make the following patch:

```
DEBUG SCAN.COM
F 146 LA 90
W
Q
```

SCANDIR Command

Michael J. Mefford

Purpose: Permits side-by-side comparison of the contents of two directories using either separately controllable or synchronized forward/backward scrolling.

Format: [d:][path]SCANDIR [d:]directory1 [d:]directory2

Remarks: The directories to be compared do not have to be on the same drive. Use the normal DOS backslash (\) character in specifying the path to a desired directory. The DOS wildcard symbols (* and ?) may be used to limit the filenames displayed.

The two directory listings are presented in the normal DOS order and format. A status line at the bottom of the screen shows whether the right or the lefthand column will be scrolled. Use the Left or Right Arrow keys to set scrolling on for the alternate column, or use the ScrollLock key to toggle synchronized movement on or off. The Up and Down Arrow keys control forward and backward scrolling of the listing(s) one line and a time. The PgUp and PgDn keys move the listing(s) one full screen (20 filename lines) at a time. In the forward direction, if scrolling continues beyond the last filename in a directory, the listing commences again at the beginning.

Notes: 1. SCANDIR is an onscreen program: its display cannot be saved to a file or redirected to a printer. If you require these capabilities, use DIR-COMP.COM, which is also included on this disk.

2. Because SCANDIR loads a secondary command processor, a copy of COMMAND.COM must be available on the boot-up drive (floppy or hard disk).

SCLEAN
Command

Michael F. Roberts

Purpose: Searches an entire disk for specific filenames (or wildcards) and offers you the chance to erase or retain files selectively.

Format: `[d:][path]SCLEAN [d:]filename`

Remarks: It's easy to fill up a hard disk with files that may no longer be needed. DOS doesn't let users delete files globally across subdirectories, but SCLEAN.COM will.

SCLEAN (named for its Selective Cleaning ability) begins its search in the root directory and then scans any subdirectories it finds. Whenever it sees a filename that matches the one you specified, SCLEAN will print out the filename and its path and then wait for you to enter a Y or an N. A Y will automatically delete the match, while an N will leave it alone. If any other key is pressed, the question will be repeated.

Example: To have SCLEAN.COM find all the extra copies of COMMAND.COM that have somehow migrated into various subdirectories, type:

`SCLEAN COMMAND.COM`

Answer N when it asks if you want to delete the one in the root directory, but Y to all the other prompts.

To have SCLEAN.COM find all the files in every subdirectory on your disk that begin with the letter Q and offer you the opportunity to delete them one by one, type:

```
SCLEAN Q*.*
```

SCRLLOFF
Command

Mike Cohn

Purpose: Turns ScrollLock shift off.

Format: `[d:][path]SCRLLOFF`

Remarks: See KEYLOCK, NUMON, NUMOFF, CAPSON, CAPSOFF, SCROLLON, LOCK, and LOX.

SCROLL
Command

Tom Kihlken

Purpose: Lets you control the portion of the screen that scrolls.

Format: `[d:][path]SCROLL n`

where *n* is the number of lines that will be scrolled.

Remarks: It's frustrating when text scrolls off the top of the screen while it's still needed. SCROLL.COM can limit the part of the screen that scrolls.

You could use SCROLL.COM to prevent a title message from disappearing from the top of the screen in a batch file. Or you could keep a directory listing at the top of the screen while you clean up your files.

Example: To have only the bottom ten lines of your display scroll while the top 15 lines stay firmly in place, enter:

```
SCROLL 10
```

To reset things to normal so all lines again scroll (on a 25-row screen), enter:

```
SCROLL 25
```

Notes: 1.   Only programs that do teletype (TTY) output, such as DOS, will be affected. Programs that write directly to video memory, such as most word processors, continue to operate normally.

2.   SCROLL works by intercepting the BIOS scroll function. Normally during teletype output, all 25 lines are scrolled. With SCROLL installed, the top boundary of the scroll region is changed so that only the lower lines move upward.

SCROLL2   Charles Petzold
Command

Purpose: When used with WAITASEC, saves the current display and scrolls it off the screen.

Format: `[d:][path]SCROLL2`

Remarks: To use this, enter SCROLL2 before beginning WAITASEC, and everything on the screen will scroll off the top and be captured in the WAITASEC buffer.

See WAITASEC.

SCROLLON   Mike Cohn
Command

Purpose: Turns ScrollLock shift on.

Format: `[d:][path]SCROLLON`

Remarks: You can create a version of this program called SCRLFLIP.COM that alternately toggles the ScrollLock shift on and off every other time it executes.

Simply type:

```
DEBUG SCROLLON.COM
E 108 34
N SCRLFLIP.COM
W
Q
```

See KEYLOCK, NUMON, NUMOFF, CAPSON, CAPSOFF, SCRLLOFF, LOCK, and LOX.

SEARCH Command

Michael J. Mefford

Purpose: Searches all or specified directories on a disk for either designated filenames or the first occurrence of character strings within files.

Format: `[d:][path]SEARCH [filespec] [string][/P][/C][/B]`

Remarks: SEARCH defaults to a diskwide search of all subdirectories on the current disk. You can specify a different drive and/or a pathname as part of the optional *filespec* parameter. Filename searches support the DOS * and ? wildcards. Character *strings* within files are identified by putting them in quotation marks. (The strings may themselves include a pair of quotation marks.) Pressing either Ctrl-Break or Ctrl-C terminates SEARCH manually.

To redirect the output of the SEARCH command to a printer, add */P* to the command line, as shown in the first example below. Adding a similar */C* switch will make the search for a character string case-sensitive.

When searching for a character string, SEARCH normally ignores COM and EXE files. While this saves time, there may be occasions when you want to find copyright notices, error messages, *et al.* in an executable file. To include binary files in the search, add the */B* parameter on the command line.

Examples: To print out a list all the COM files in the \PROG subdirectory of your current drive, you would enter:

```
SEARCH \PROG\*.COM/P
```

To find which of the files in your \LETTERS subdirectory contained the salutation Dear Miss Jones, enter:

```
SEARCH \LETTERS "Dear Miss Jones"
```

Notes: SEARCH returns a line number, based on the number of previous carriage returns in the file, when it finds a string. It reports only the first occurrence of the string in each file.

SETUP
Command
Jeff Prosise

Purpose: Permits menu-oriented selection and immediate transmission of printer control codes from within a running application program.

Format: `[d:][path]SETUP` (loads command into memory)

```
<Ctrl-Right Shift>                      (activates menu)
<[Shift]<Fx>                    (selects [deselects] mode)
<Esc>                           (activates selection(s) and
                              returns to application program)
```

Fx is a function key (F1 through F10) that sends the required control sequence to the printer. Shift-Fx toggles the selected printer mode off.

Remarks: After loading SETUP (normally via your AUTOEXEC.BAT file), press the Ctrl-Right Shift key combination for a menu. This can be done from within application programs that do not take over the keyboard interrupts; the application is simply suspended until you leave SETUP by pressing the Esc key. (Application programs such as *XyWrite* that do take over the keyboard interrupts can be used with SETUP.COM if they themselves provide the option of temporarily returning to DOS control.)

Printer permitting, more than one mode can be selected at once by pressing additional function keys. The default printer choices are for the Epson RX/FX series. Option 1 shows how to modify the program for other printers.

Notes: 1. SETUP.COM is a memory-resident program (approximately 3K in length), and so is subject to conflicts with other memory-resident software. Several users have reported that it is incompatible with *Pro-Key*, for example. Similarly, while SETUP.COM is compatible with

SideKick, the combination of *SuperKey* and *SideKick* has been reported to be incompatible.

2.   To modify SETUP for other printers (or to use LPT2: or LPT3: instead of LPT1:), use DEBUG.

The following offset addresses, not those originally published in *PC Magazine*, should be used:

The menu color attributes (4F and 70) are at offsets 13F and 140.

To change the port number from LPT1: to LPT2: (or LPT3:) change the default 00 at C7A and at C84 to 01 (or 02).

The start of the menu text table (532 bytes, beginning with C9) is at offset 151. The "P" in "PRINTER SETUP MENU" is at 0172.

The printer control strings themselves begin at 9A1. Each function key (and each shifted function key, with the exception of F19 and F20) can be assigned a string up to 16 bytes long. Each string must include a delimiter of FF (255 decimal) that marks the end of the string. The beginning of the string for each successive function key starts at an address that is a multiple of 16 bytes above the base address (9A1) of the table. You must pad the strings with zeros for any locations that are not used by actual control codes, so that each string begins on a 16-byte boundary.

SHOWCHAR Command   Paul Somerson

Purpose: Displays all 255 ASCII characters.

Format: [d:] [path] SHOWCHAR

Remarks: You could use BIOS service hex 0E of interrupt 10 to write characters, since this treats the screen like a teletype, advancing the cursor automatically each time it prints a character, and wrapping text down to the next line when necessary.

However, this service gives special treatment to four ASCII characters:

decimal 7 — beep
decimal 8 — backspace

decimal 10 — linefeed
decimal 13 — carriage return

If you use it to print these four characters, you won't see their character symbols onscreen. Try to write an ASCII 7 with service 0E, for instance, and instead of displaying the small centered dot character that IBM assigned to a character 7, all you'll get is a beep.

BIOS services 09 and 0A will print the characters IBM assigned to all 256 ASCII values, including the troublesome four above. All three services, 09, 0A, and 0E, will display three ASCII characters as blanks:

decimal 0 — null
decimal 32 — space
decimal 255 — blank

The difference between services 09 and 0A is that service 09 can change the attribute as it writes each character, while service 0A can't. But with both of these you have to advance the cursor yourself, since BIOS won't do it for you.

SHOWCHAR.COM will first use BIOS service 08 to read the attribute at the current cursor position, and will then use service 06 to clear the screen to that position. Then it will display all 256 characters in rows of 32.

Displaying the ASCII characters in rows of 32 shows that the lowercase alphabet letters have values that are decimal 32 (hex 20) higher than their uppercase cousins.

You can experiment with this program to change the way it displays characters. For instance, once you've created it, you can type:

```
DEBUG SHOWCHAR.COM
E 115 D0 07
E 123 EB 0A
N SHOWFULL.COM
W
Q
```

The normal SHOWCHAR.COM program displays only one of each character at a time. SHOWFULL.COM will display 2000 (decimal 7D0) characters at a time — a full 25 x 80 screenful. BIOS will flash through all 256 full screens of characters in a few seconds.

Or, to see the difference between services 09 and 0A, first use a pure-ASCII word processor or EDLIN to create the following ADDCOLOR.SCR script file. Be sure to press the Enter key at the end of each line, especially the last one with the Q:

```
E 11D 88 C3 B4 09 CD 10 FE C0 80 C2 01 80 FA
E 12A 40 75 04 FE C6 30 D2 3C FF 75 E2 C3
N SHOWCOLR.COM
RCX
36
W
Q
```

Then, at the DOS prompt, type:

```
DEBUG SHOWCHAR.COM < ADDCOLOR.SCR
```

and you'll end up with a variation of SHOWCHAR.COM called SHOW-COLR.COM that displays each character using the ASCII value of the character as the attribute. If you're using a color monitor, you'll see all 256 possible attributes.

SHOWCOLOR.COM will display four rows of characters, rather than the eight produced by SHOWCHAR.COM. All four rows will be in color, and because of the BIOS color numbering system, the foreground colors in bottom two rows will be blinking. The four rows will be divided into four chunks of background colors that are each 16 characters wide. Within each of these chunks, each of the 16 characters will have a different foreground color. The leftmost eight will appear in normal colors, while the rightmost eight will appear as high intensity (bright) colors.

It's easiest to see how this works by using the hex value of each attribute. All attributes can be expressed as two-digit hex numbers. The lefthand and righthand digits can each range from 0 to F, which yields decimal 256 possible values from 00 through FF.

The lefthand digit represents the background color, and the righthand digit the foreground color. So on a color system a number like 71 will produce blue (1) text on a white (7) background, while 17 will yield white text on a blue background.

However, a value like 4E will produce bright yellow text (E) on a red (4) background, while E4 will produce bright blinking yellow text on a red background. Any value that has a lefthand digit higher than 7 will blink. So a number like 71 won't blink, while a number like 81 will.

Any value that has a righthand digit higher than 7 will appear as a high intensity color. So a number like 47 will produce a normal, low-intensity color, while 48 will display something in high intensity.

SETCLOCK   Arthur Rothstein
Command

Purpose: Sets the CMOS clock on PC-AT and later IBM systems for users who are still using a version of DOS prior to 3.3.

Format: TIME
            [d:] [path] SETCLOCK

            First set the time with the DOS TIME command, then just type SETCLOCK to make it stick.

Remarks: Prior to DOS 3.3, users of IBM systems with CMOS real-time clocks had problems when the CMOS battery failed or weakened. (DOS 3.3 was the first version that upgraded the TIME command to set the CMOS clock directly.)

            First, they'd have to set the time manually at every power-up. Second, if they restarted with Ctrl-Alt-Del, BIOS would read the wrong time from the AT clock and they'd be back where they started.

            The only way to reset the clock was to drag out the original setup program supplied with the *Guide to Operations* manual, but many users don't know that, can't figure out how to use it, or can't locate it.

            SETCLOCK.COM reads the current time and date from DOS and uses these values to update the AT's clock.

            This short but very useful utility also comes in awfully handy in the fall and spring when the time changes backward or forward an hour in most places.

Notes: This works on PC-ATs and subsequent hardware with CMOS real-time clocks only.

SIZE (and ATSIZE)   **Art Merrill**
Command(s)

Purpose: Calculates the storage requirements of a file or group of files, based on the number of DOS clusters necessary to make floppy disk and hard disk copies.

Format: `[d:][path]SIZE [d:]`   (all files, default directory)

            or

            `[d:][path]SIZE [d:][path]filename[.ext]`

Remarks: DOS stores files in fixed-length allocation units called clusters. For floppy disks, the cluster size is 1,024 bytes (two 512-byte sectors); for the original PC-XT 10Mb hard disk the cluster size is 4,084 bytes. On such a hard disk, whether a file is one byte or 4Kb in actual length (as reported by DIR), it requires the same amount (one cluster) of storage space. The PC AT's 20Mb hard disk is less wasteful in handling small files; its minimum set-aside (cluster size) is 2,048 bytes. AT users should use AT-SIZE.COM.

Entered without parameters, SIZE (or ATSIZE) returns the number of bytes used by all files in the current directory, the amount of space required to copy them to a standard (360K) floppy disk, and the amount of space required for hard disk storage.

Entering SIZE B: returns the same information for a disk in drive B:. Pathnames and wildcards are supported, so you could enter:

`SIZE \PROG\*.COM`

to learn the number of COM files contained in your \PROG subdirectory, and their total size and storage requirements.

SKIPLINE   **Tom Kihlken**
Filter

Purpose: Lets you display or print a range of lines rather than an entire file.

Format: `TYPE filename | [d:][path]SKIPLINE n,m`

or:

`[d:][path]SKIPLINE n,m < filename`

to display a section of a file, and either:

`TYPE fil.1 | [d:][path]SKIPLINE n,m > fil.2`

or:

`[d:][path]SKIPLINE n,m < fil.1 > fil.2`

to create a file called fil.2 that contains a section of fil.1

In all cases, lines numbers in the range of *n* to *m* will not be displayed. If either of the parameters is omitted, the program uses defaults of 0 and 65,535. Be sure to use a comma as a delimiter.

Remarks: All the traditional file functions (COPY, TYPE, etc.) operate on the entire file. If you want to see or print just a few lines, you can filter everything else out by using SKIPLINE.

Example: To see just the first ten lines and the last 5 lines of a 25-line file called MEMO:

`SKIPLINE 11,19 < MEMO`

To copy just lines 1-10 and 20-25 of the MEMO file into a new file called MEMO.LIL:

`SKIPLINE 11,19 < MEMO > MEMO.LIL`

To view just the first ten lines of MEMO:

`SKIPLINE 11, < MEMO`

To view everything in the file called MEMO except the first five lines:

`SKIPLINE ,5 < MEMO`

Remarks: SKIPLINE counts lines of input by watching for the carriage return character (ASCII 13). While in the range of lines being skipped, it ceases to write characters to the output device while continuing to read. After the unwanted lines have passed, it resumes echoing data.

SLOWDOWN Command   Charles Petzold

Purpose: Slows down a fast system to make it simulate a more lethargic system or give you a fighting chance with games written for the PC.

Format: `[d:][path]SLOWDOWN value`

where *value* is a number from 0 through 65535. This is the value SLOW-DOWN uses for the loop. The higher the number, the slower your AT will run. A value of 20000 or 25000 will slow down an 8 MHz AT to about the speed of a 4.77 MHz PC or XT. (It's not possible to mimic a PC or XT exactly because the 80286 microprocessor has different speed advantages depending upon the instruction mix.)

Remarks: Most of the time users are looking for every possible way to speed up their systems. But if you're producing software on a speedy computer and you want to see how it would perform on a slower one, if you just can't keep up with games designed to run on pokier systems, or if you're an old-timer and you just feel nostalgic, it's easy to bring things to a crawl.

SLOWDOWN.COM is a resident program that intercepts interrupt 8, the timer interrupt. The timer interrupt occurs every 55 milliseconds. Normally, interrupt 8 doesn't do very much, so it doesn't significantly alter the speed of your computer. SLOWDOWN, however, executes a small loop every 55 milliseconds to slow down the overall speed of the machine.

You may execute SLOWDOWN more than once, in which case the loop values will accumulate. For instance:

```
SLOWDOWN 10000
SLOWDOWN 10000
SLOWDOWN 5000
```

is the same as:

```
SLOWDOWN 25000
```

To get back to normal speed, you'll have to reboot, unless you use it with a TSR manager like INSTALL/REMOVE.

With a high enough loop value, SLOWDOWN's loop will itself take 55 milliseconds. As soon as the loop completes, another interrupt 8 will start it all over again. This will slow down the machine to almost a dead crawl. (Users of TSO on IBM mainframes will experience some *deja vu* when this happens.) On an 8 MHz AT, this happens with a loop value of about 36300.

With loop values higher than this, the 8 MHz AT will start to speed up again, but it will be jumpy and do things in rhythmic spurts. This is because the loop takes longer than 55 milliseconds and the AT will start skipping interrupt 8s. Your PC's clock will also start losing time.

Notes: 1.   You can't use SLOWDOWN with programs that must be booted from diskettes. Note also that some programs may disable interrupts for a while, grab interrupt 8 themselves, and even reprogram the 8254 timer chip. SLOWDOWN won't work right with programs that do nasty things like this.

2.   If you write your own software and need to do game-like animation in your programs, don't use delay loops. Poll the timer values to pace the program, or grab interrupt 1CH and make the program timer-driven.

SNIPPER   Tom Kihlken
Command

Purpose: Copies any portion of a text screen to a printer or saves it to a file, or acts as an interapplication clipboard and inserts it as keyboard input into an applications program.

Format: `[d:][path]SNIPPER [rows,columns]`

Remarks: SNIPPER is a memory-resident program that is normally loaded as part of your AUTOEXEC.BAT file. The *rows,columns* parameter is required for EGA displays with more than the normal 25 rows and 80 columns. The default hotkey is Alt-W. Esc returns you to your application.

When SNIPPER is popped up, it creates its own cursor, which you can navigate around the screen with the normal arrow keys. To create the window, first press Enter to anchor the upper lefthand corner. The cursor keys then open and size the window, which appears in reverse video. It is not necessary to press Enter again to anchor the lower right corner. In fact, doing so will pop up a help menu showing the options described below.

When the desired area is shown, pressing P dumps its contents to your printer, adding carriage return/line feed characters at the end of each line. SNIPPER then automatically terminates. Pressing F with the window open prompts for a filename, which may include drive and path. If no filename is entered, SCREEN.CUT is used as a default. Pressing Enter writes the marked screen contents to the file. SNIPPER then terminates, but remembers the filename. Successive saves to the same filename are appended to and do not overwrite that file.

Pressing S while a portion of the screen is marked saves the window contents to an internal buffer. Another application program can then be called up, and its cursor positioned at the point where the saved window contents should be inserted. Alt-W then activates SNIPPER, and G gets its stored contents and dumps them into the keyboard buffer as if they had been typed in by hand. Note that G must be the first SNIPPER command used in this case (any other erases its internal, stored buffer). Note, too, that G can be used without S to reenter marked material (e.g., a complex DOS command sequence) on the same screen page.

Examples: Pop up the window by pressing Alt-W. Move the SNIPPER cursor to the position onscreen where you want the upper lefthand corner of the window to appear. Then use the cursor keys to adjust the size of the window you want (but don't hit Enter unless you want a menu of options).

At this point, pressing:

P

would dump the contents of the window to your printer, and then quit SNIPPER when it was done. If you pressed:

F

instead, SNIPPER would ask you to name a file, and would then save the contents of the window to this file. (Omitting a name saves the file as SCREEN.CUT.)

You may also use the window contents as a clipboard to be pasted into another application, by typing:

S

and then loading the new application. Then summon the SNIPPER window back by pressing Alt-W, and feed the window text into the application through the keyboard by typing:

G

If you use SNIPPER as a clipboard, be careful not to issue any other SNIPPER commands while a window already contains text in the process of being moved. Any other command will wipe out the window contents.

Notes: The default hotkey can be changed using DEBUG by substituting the scan code and shift mask values shown in the entry for CAPTURE. The address of the scan code byte is 56B, and that of the shift mask is 57B.

SPECTRUM   **Robert L. Hummel**
Command

Purpose: Provides existing software with a selectable 16-color palette (from among 64 displayable colors) when used with an Enhanced Graphics Adapter and an Enhanced Graphics (or similar) monitor.

Format: `[d:][path]SPECTRUM`

or

`[d:][path]SPECTRUM xx xx xx xx xx xx xx xx xx`
`xx xx xx xx xx xx xx`

Remarks: SPECTRUM is a memory-resident utility that is normally loaded as part of your AUTOEXEC.BAT file. Once loaded, pressing Ctrl-' (the Ctrl key and the grave [reverse] accent key) pops up a display of 16 color boxes, each of which may be set, onscreen, to any of the 64 displayable values. The cursor pad keys are then used, as described in the display, to select any of the boxes and their two-digit color codes. Pressing the End key saves the current color selections and returns you to your application. Home resets the color palette to its default values, and Esc aborts any changes made, restoring your previous color settings.

For loading or changing the SPECTRUM palette without using the pop-up window (e.g., as part of a batch file), the second format above may be used. The values for x may range from 0 through 7 and must be entered in pairs on a single line (not on two lines, as shown). A single space must separate each of the 16 pairs of digits, and a single space must also separate the number-pairs from the command name. Use the pop-up window to determine the proper number-pairs initially.

Notes: 1. Software programs that write directly to the EGA registers will override the SPECTRUM color selections. The SPECTRUM colors may be restored, if lost, by activating the display window (Ctrl-') and then pressing the Esc key.

2. EGACOSET, also on this disk, is an alternative program to SPECTRUM.

STATLINE Command   John Socha

Purpose: Displays 26th-line status indicators for the NumLock, CapsLock, and ScrollLock toggle keys on IBM monochrome, CGA, and Compaq monitors.

Format: `[d:][path]STATLINE`

Remarks: STATLINE converts the normal 25-line text mode display into 26 lines, using the additional line to show a # sign for NumLock, an Up Arrow for CapsLock, and a double-pointed arrow for ScrollLock.

On a monochrome display, where insufficient memory is available for a full 26th line, two-thirds of that line is used by STATLINE; the remainder echoes the first portion of the top line of the regular display.

This utility is not compatible with the IBM EGA and is best suited for use with the CGA and with Compaq displays.

Notes: STATLINE is a memory-resident utility and is known to be incompatible with a number of keyboard macro programs.

STATUS
Command

Michael J. Mefford

Purpose: Reads and reports the system configuration information from a machine's switch settings and/or low memory addresses.

Format: `[d:][path]STATUS`

Remarks: STATUS is entered at the DOS prompt and produces a single-screen display of information that includes: the configuration switch settings of an IBM PC or XT (or the equivalent data contained in the AT equipment byte); number of disk drives installed; presence or absence of a math coprocessor; amount of memory installed on the system board (PC and XT only); number of parallel, series, and game ports installed; initial video mode; total amount of main memory and amount of currently free memory; amount (if any) of extended and/or expanded memory; DOS version in use; and machine BIOS version.

Notes: Readers have reported that on some models of the IBM XT the configuration switch settings are wired upside down with respect to the STATUS graphic display. The basic information presented is correct, however. Also, on some non-IBM "compatibles" some information may not be presented.

STICK
Command

Jeff Prosise

Purpose: Locks and unlocks the cursor size and shape set with *PC Magazine*'s CTYPE utility; similarly locks and unlocks a choice of EGA foreground and background colors; and permits selective replacement of the EGA BIOS code for CGA emulation.

Format: `[d:][path]STICK [/L+|-] [/E+|-] [/B+|-] [/C-| fg bg]`

Remarks: STICK is a memory-resident (560 bytes) program that eliminates several recurring problems connected with the EGA and display. A nonresident utility such as CTYPE.COM can set a cursor size and shape in DOS, and it can prevent the cursor loss frequently encountered when exiting from utilities such as *SideKick* while using a 43-line EGA display.

CTYPE alone can do nothing when applications reset the cursor, however, as they normally do. The STICK */L+* option locks in the cursor shape for all but applications (such as *1-2-3*) that bypass the PC BIOS cursor routines altogether. To permit some applications (such as word processors) to manipulate the cursor shape themselves, the STICK /L- option disables cursor locking.

The STICK */C fg bg* option sets EGA foreground and background colors respectively, using the hex digits shown below:

0	Black	8	Grey
1	Blue	9	Bright blue
2	Green	A	Bright green
3	Cyan	B	Bright cyan
4	Red	C	Bright red
5	Magenta	D	Bright magenta
6	Brown	E	Yellow
7	White	F	Bright white

The foreground color (fg) may range from 0 through F; background (bg) values are limited to 0 through 7. A single space must separate each parameter. The /C- option disables the color selection locking.

The STICK */E+* option substitutes STICK's own cursor emulation BIOS code for the bug-ridden IBM emulation routines. By default, or by using the /E- option, the IBM code is restored. Since the EGA provides an emulation bit whose setting is stored in the BIOS data area, STICK provides an option to set or reset this bit directly. If the /E+ option is active (emulation on), STICK */B+* sets the bit value to 1 (disabling the EGA routines); STICK /B- reenables them.

Entered with no parameters, STICK reports the current settings of its functions. Any or all optional parameters can be entered on a single command line in either upper- or lowercase. The /L and /C options are implemented on all video adapters; the /E switch is limited to EGA systems; /B is functional on EGA and VGA-based machines.

STRIP
Filter   **Phillip Cheng**

Purpose: Filters out high bits and turns *WordStar*-type files into DOS text files.

Format: `[d:][path]STRIP < [d:][path]filename`

Remarks: Certain programs such as *WordStar* adjust the ASCII value of characters at the ends of words by turning on the characters' high bits (adding 128 to the ASCII value). DOS stumbles over these high bits, and can't properly execute commands littered with these high-bit characters or use TYPE to display them.

STRIP.COM is a filter that gets rid of high bits in files, and lets you send the cleaned-up output either to the screen or to a new, clean, pure-DOS file.

Some filters process a single byte or a few hundred bytes at a time, but STRIP.COM can blast up to 63K in and out in a single gulp.

Examples: If you have a *WordStar*-type file on your disk called HIGHBIT.TXT, and you try to use the DOS TYPE command to display it, you'll end up with a barely readable mess. To filter out the high bits and read the file normally, you could type:

`STRIP < HIGHBIT.TXT`

If you want to give a *WordStar*-type file to someone who doesn't have a word processor that can handle it, or if you want to turn a *WordStar*-type file into a batch file or program listing that needs to be cleaned up, just redirect the output into a new file (here called CLEAN.TXT):

`STRIP < HIGHBIT.TXT > CLEAN.TXT`

STRIP.COM is so efficient that it can strip the high bits out of huge files and create cleaned-up versions in a second or two.

SUGGEST
Command

Michael J. Mefford

Purpose: Flashes a message on the screen at selected rates and durations ranging from many minutes to a brevity approaching the limit of subliminal perception.

Format: `[d:][path]SUGGEST message[/Fn][/Dn]`

Remarks: The message may be up to 80 characters in length; longer messages are truncated. The optional /F (frequency) and /D (duration) switches accept a user-entered integer n from 1 through 9. (0 is their default value and need not be entered.) These correspond to the following approximate timings:

/F9=0:05	/D9=0.170
/F8=3:05	/D8=0.153
/F7=6:05	/D7=0.136
/F6=9:05	/D6=0.119
/F5=12:05	/D5=0.102
/F4=15:05	/D4=0.085
/F3=18:05	/D3=0.068
/F2=21:05	/D2=0.051
/F1=24:05	/D1=0.034
/F0=27:05 (default)	/D0=0.017

Examples: You might enter the following:

```
SUGGEST SAVE YOUR WORK/F6/D9
```

as a useful reminder.

Notes: 1. SUGGEST is a memory-resident utility. You may load several messages, but you must reboot to clear the program.

2. Even at its briefest duration the SUGGEST message is still visible, so the program is not intended for scientific investigation of truly subliminal experimentation.

SWEEP Command   Charles Petzold

Purpose: Causes a command to be successively executed in every subdirectory on a hard disk.

Format: `[d:][path]SWEEP Command [parameter(s)]`

Remarks: SWEEP starts from the current directory. In order to use SWEEP to extend the range of a command to all the subdirectories on a disk, use CD (if necessary) to make the root directory your current directory. From the root directory, the command:

```
SWEEP DIR
```

will display the listings, by subdirectory, of every nonhidden file on the disk. To erase all the BAK files on a disk you need only get into the root directory and issue the command:

```
SWEEP DEL *.BAK
```

SWEEP itself will not accept parameters other than its command. Thus, if you are on drive C: and wish a directory of all files on drive D: to be sent to your printer, you must first make drive D: the current drive before you issue the command:

```
SWEEP DIR > LPT1
```

(In this case you would either need a copy of SWEEP.COM on drive D: or else drive D: would have to be listed on your path.)

SWEEP can execute BAT file commands (and even non-DOS commands, such as LOCATE.COM). A useful file called CLEAN.BAT might consist of the three lines

```
DEL *.BAK
DEL *.TMP
DEL *.OBJ
```

From the root directory, if you then enter:

```
SWEEP CLEAN
```

all BAK, TMP, and OBJ files will be erased from the disk.

TEST1980   **Charles Petzold**
Command

Purpose: Tests to see if the user has set the system clock to prevent files from being dated 1-1-1980.

Format: `[d:] [path] TEST1980`

Remarks: Most users have battery-powered real-time clocks in their systems that keep the date and time current. But users of older systems and some compatibles don't. And batteries eventually give out.

It's important to stamp your files with the proper date (and time). If you don't you can end up writing older files over newer ones, or erasing final versions of files, or handing other workers versions that aren't the most recent.

If you start your system with an AUTOEXEC.BAT file, and you don't include the commands DATE and TIME, and you don't have a battery-powered clock, your system will give any files that you create or change a date of 1-1-1980.

If you don't start things each day with an AUTOEXEC.BAT file, or if your AUTOEXEC.BAT file contains the DATE and TIME commands, you can bypass them when prompted to set the date and time by simply pressing the Enter key. Same 1-1-1980 result.

Running the TEST1980 program will beep and print a message onscreen if it sees that the year is 1980. It also sets the exit code to FF, so you can process the information with an IF ERRORLEVEL test. A batch file like DATETEST.BAT won't let you proceed until you've made sure the date is something other than 1980:

```
ECHO OFF
:TOP
TEST1980
IF NOT ERRORLEVEL FF GOTO OK
ECHO You forgot to set the date
DATE
GOTO TOP
:OK
ECHO Date is fine
```

You can put this at the end of your AUTOEXEC.BAT startup file if you want (and remove the "ECHO Date is fine" line). If the year isn't set to 1980 nothing will happen. However, if the year is 1980, it will keep looping back until you change it.

You could change the date to 1981 or any other noncurrent year and fool the test, but if you go that much trouble you might as well set the date properly.

This is very useful in detecting dead or dying clock batteries before you accidentally stamp a lot of files with the wrong date.

TICKER   Hal Shearer
Command

Purpose: Provides the most attention-getting variation of a PAUSE prompt that you'll ever see.

Format: `[d:][path]TICKER text`

where *text* is up to 40 characters of text that you want to display.

Remarks: The DOS PAUSE command is dull and drab. In later versions of DOS you can redirect its output to NUL and use ECHO to substitute your own message with:

```
ECHO Okay, now press a key
PAUSE > NUL
```

but this doesn't work with DOS 2.x and it's only slightly less dull.

TICKER.COM is anything but drab. It accepts a 40-character (or less) message at the command line and displays this message like a ticker tape until any key is pressed.

If you don't enter a custom-made message, TICKER.COM will substitute one of its own.

Examples: To put a rolling ticker-tape message in your batch file that says "Ok, so hit a key already" just include a line in the batch file that says:

```
TICKER Ok, so hit a key already
```

If you simply want TICKER.COM's standard (but eyebrow-raising) message to serve as your prompt, just add the line:

```
TICKER
```

where you would have used PROMPT before, and TICKER.COM will display its ticker-tape "Attention: Please press a key to continue" message.

Notes: As delivered, the TICKER.COM prompt begins on column 19 of row 24. You can change this by patching the bytes at 22E (for the row) and 230 (for the column). You probably won't want to meddle with the column setting since it's centered onscreen. But you may want to adjust the row. To put the display in the middle of the screen (row hex 0D), you'd use DEBUG to make the patch:

```
DEBUG TICKER.COM
E 22E 0C
W
Q
```

(Remember, rows start at 0, not 1, so you have to subtract 1 from 0D.)

TIMEKEY   Jeff Prosise
Command

Purpose: Inserts the date and/or time into documents being created by other applications programs.

Format: [d:][path]TIMEKEY

Remarks: TIMEKEY is a memory-resident utility and must be loaded after the system date and time have been initialized. Subject to this limitation, it may be loaded either at the command line or as part of an AUTOEXEC.BAT file.

Once loaded, TIMEKEY uses the following keystrokes:

Alt-L inserts a long-form date (e.g., June 10, 1987)
Alt-S inserts a short-form date (e.g., 6-10-87)
Alt-T inserts the time (e.g., 12:21 PM)

Notes: 1.   Once loaded, TIMEKEY keeps track of the time automatically, but it does not change the current date at midnight unless the system is manually rebooted.

2.   TIMEKEY is compatible with BASICA (which also uses the timer tick) and with many memory-resident utilities (e.g., *SideKick*), but compatibility with all TSR programs cannot be assured.

TINYCOMM   **Charles Petzold**
Command

Purpose: TINYCOMM is the smallest "functional" assembly language communications program possible.

Format: `[d:][path]MODE COMn:300,N,8,1`

`[d:][path]TINYCOMM [1]`

where *n* is the COM port you want to use, and a 1 follows TINYCOMM if you're using COM2. If you're using COM1, after entering the MODE command, just type:

`[d:][path]TINYCOMM`

on a line by itself.

Remarks: TINYCOMM uses ROM BIOS interrupt 14H to read incoming data from and write outgoing data to your modem. It then uses DOS interrupt 21H function calls to read what you type at the keyboard and to write to the display.

To run TINYCOMM, first turn on your modem and execute the DOS MODE command to set up your system for 300 baud, no parity, 8 data bits, and 1 stop bit:

`MODE COM1:300,N,8,1`

If your modem is connected to COM2, substitute COM2 in place of COM1 in the MODE command above.

(You can't use TINYCOMM at 1,200 baud. See the note below for an explanation.)

Now run TINYCOMM by entering just:

`TINYCOMM`

for a modem connected to COM1, or:

`TINYCOMM 1`

for COM2. The cursor will drop down a line and sit there waiting for a command. At this point you're not yet online, but are in direct connection with your modem.

If you have a Hayes SmartModem or compatible, you can now type in any of the AT attention codes documented in the *User's Guide* or *Reference Manual* that came with the unit. For instance, with the Smart-Modem 1200 or 1200B, you can enter:

```
ATI0
```

to see the product's revision number:

```
ATI1
```

for the modem's ROM checksum, and (with the 1200, but not the 1200B):

```
ATI2
```

to check the integrity of its internal memory. This last instruction will return either "OK" or "ERROR."

The "Smart" in "SmartModem" refers to the modem's ability to interpret such AT codes and send back appropriate responses. If your phone happens to ring while you're experimenting like this, TINYCOMM will display the word "RING." Similarly, when using your normal communications programs, you may have noticed the words "CONNECT" or "NO CARRIER" displayed when you attempt to place a telephone call. These messages are not produced by your communications package; they all come straight from the modem, whose internal programming generates them.

To call the *PC Magazine Interactive* Reader Service bulletin board, enter:

```
ATD 1-212-696-0360
```

on the east coast, or:

```
ATD 1-415-598-9100
```

on the west coast.

If you have touch-tone service, you can use ATDT instead of ATD. (Even if you have pulse dialing, you might try this command anyway.)

If you're using an external modem, you'll see your modem's OH (Off Hook) light go on and you'll hear the dialing. If the PC-IRS has a free line, you'll hear the PC-IRS carrier signal, quickly followed by your modem answering that carrier signal with its own. The CD (Carrier Detect) light on your modem will go on, you'll see the word CONNECT on the screen, and then the modem will go silent. You're now online.

If you get a busy signal, eventually your modem will give up and you'll get a NO CARRIER message. You can redial by typing A/, which is the only Hayes control sequence that does not require a preceding AT.

You can set these two timings, and many other variable aspects of the SmartModem, with modem control sequences. ATS6, followed by the time in seconds, controls the dial tone wait; ATS7 similarly controls the carrier detect wait. If you want to listen continuously to the carrier signals while you're online, you can enter ATM2 before making the call.

You can't enter these AT codes directly while you're online, because the modem has no way of determining that you want to talk to it instead of to the remote computer. To issue commands while online, first enter the Hayes escape sequence — three plus signs (+++) in a row — typed quickly. You must wait a second before typing in the first plus sign, and wait a second afterwards before typing anything else. (The modem uses these brief pauses to distinquish its escape sequence from three plus signs that may occur in transmitted data.) If you entered the +++ code properly, you'll get an OK from the modem, indicating that you're in the command state instead of online. After you're done giving commands, ATO returns the modem online.

When you're online with a remote computer, whether it's an information service (such as CompuServe or Dow Jones News Retrieval) or with a bulletin board such as the *PC Magazine*'s IRS, the host computer echoes back most of the characters it receives. Because of this, you'll sense a slight delay between the time you type characters and their display on the screen.

When you eventually want to exit TINYCOMM, just press Ctrl-Break.

Notes: 1.   Although TINYCOMM is written in assembler and (at least in theory) is very fast, you can't run it at 1,200 baud. Try it by changing the baud rate with MODE and connecting to an information service or bulletin board. Things will go fairly well when you're at the top of the screen, but once you get down to the bottom you'll notice that TINYCOMM starts missing the first few letters of each line sent from the remote computer.

2. Communications programs do not normally use interrupt 14H, as TINYCOMM does. This is because interrupt 14H is missing two very important ingredients of normal communication software: buffering and interrupt control. Instead, TINYCOMM simply polls the serial port for data, and if it can't do its polling fast enough, it misses characters — which is what happens when the screen scrolls at 1,200 baud. During the time it takes the screen to scroll, several characters at the start of the line are coming through. Real communications programs don't have this problem because they use the serial port's interrupts and buffer all the data.

TOUCH Command   Michael J. Mefford

Purpose: Changes the DOS date and/or time designation of a file or group of files either to the current date and time or to one designated by the user.

Format: `TOUCH filespec [/D date] [/T time]`

Remarks: If you enter TOUCH without any arguments, the program will display a help screen showing the proper syntax. If you enter a filespec but neither of the optional switches (/D or /T), TOUCH will update the designated file to the current system date and time. Note that the standard DOS filename wild cards (* and ?) are supported, so TOUCH can operate on groups of files.

The optional /D date switch lets you enter a date in the customary DOS mm-dd-yy format. If you want, you may replace the hyphen delimiters with forward slashes (/), and you may enter the year either in full form (e.g. 1988) or in abbreviated (88) form.

TOUCH checks that each of the three fields is filled with a nonzero value, but does not check the validity of a date (e.g., 2/31/88). Legal DOS years are from 1980 to 2099.

The optional /T time switch lets you enter a user-specified time in hours:minutes:seconds. If the minutes and/or seconds parameters are omitted TOUCH will set them to 0. Hours should be entered in military (24-hour) format.

Notes: The following batch file, TEST.BAT, can be used to cause a DIR listing to leave the time field blank:

```
TIME 0
TOUCH TEST.BAT
DIR TEST.BAT
```

TYPEA   **Tom Kihlken**
Command

Purpose: Lets you look inside program files to examine all the messages, prompts, text, etc.

Format: `[d:][path]TYPEA [d:][path]filename`

Remarks: It's often a good idea to peek inside COM or EXE files to hunt for hidden messages and instructions. Unfortunately, the DOS TYPE and COPY /B CON commands can't properly handle the nonprintable characters inside such files.

TYPEA.COM displays just the ASCII characters in any file (including hidden files). All non-ASCII data are displayed as dots.

The program works by reading the file into an internal buffer and examining each individual byte. It then replaces each non-ASCII code with a dot, and displays the entire file onscreen without any confusing control characters.

While *PC Magazine* programs such as Charles Petzold's BROWSE and Michael Mefford's DR let you examine the contents of program files, this short program will also do the job. It's especially handy for looking at potentially dangerous "Trojan Horse" programs downloaded from bulletin boards. If you run a brand new program through it and see something like "Gotcha!" you can erase it before it does any damage.

Executable files invariably contain Ctrl-Z end-of-file markers that can stop the normal DOS TYPE command in its tracks. Try using the TYPE command to display COMMAND.COM, for instance, and the process will stop after a beep or two. TYPEA.COM will work all the way through any file. And it'll even let you look at the contents of hidden files such as IBMBIO.COM and IBMDOS.COM.

You can view the contents of any file in DOS with the command:

```
COPY /B filename CON
```

but the COPY command is too easily confused by control characters and ends up beeping and blinking. In addition, you can't break out by pressing Ctrl-ScrollLock or Ctrl-C while COPY is scrolling out the contents. You can interrupt TYPEA.COM.

TYPEA substitutes a dot for each low-order nonprintable character it finds. If you want it to simply discard such characters, create the file, get into DOS, and type:

```
DEBUG TYPEA.COM
E 148 A
E 14C 6
W
Q
```

Making this patch can dramatically shorten the amount of text that TYPEA prints, but it will also jam together all of the ASCII text that it finds, which makes the screen harder to read.

UNCRASH   Neil Stahl
Command

Purpose: Safeguards your system against ending up in an endless loop when you're experimenting with new software or writing tricky programs.

Format: [d:][path]UNCRASH

Remarks: If you've ever found yourself hopelessly locked inside an infinite loop, you've probably experienced the frustration of having to reset your computer to get out of it. This can be especially distressing when you're using a volatile RAMdisk and the most recent version of the program that caused that infinite loop evaporates with it. You might think that hitting Ctrl-Break will get you out of such a situation, but this works only if a DOS function is called during the loop. UNCRASH.COM cures this problem.

Your PC executes an interrupt about 18.2 times each second to update DOS time of day clock. The BIOS routine that performs this service also performs another interrupt, called the Timer Tick, that allows other applications, such as a print spooler, to gain control at regular intervals.

UNCRASH takes advantage of this DOS feature; it loads its own address into the location called by the Timer Tick interrupt and gets control 18 times a second. When the Ctrl-Break key is pressed, the BIOS keyboard interrupt servicer sets the highest bit of byte 71H in data segment 40H.

When UNCRASH finds this bit set, it resets the high bit at 71H to zero, sends an end of interrupt signal to the interrupt controller at port 20H, and causes the application to terminate by calling DOS function 4CH. UNCRASH saves and passes control to the address that was previously located at interrupt 1CH, so it shouldn't preempt any other programs that use this service.

Notes:
1. Although UNCRASH works well with all the software we use, it will *not* work in IBM BASIC, and will cause the machine to hang if it is used while in BASIC.

2. To test how well the program breaks out of an assembler routine, before you load UNCRASH, create a tiny endless assembler loop called ENDLESS.COM by making sure DEBUG.COM is on your disk and typing:

```
DEBUG
N ENDLESS.COM
A 100
NOP
JMP 100

RCX
3
W
Q
```

Press the Enter key at the end of every line, and press it twice after typing JMP 100. Run it by typing ENDLESS and try to break out of it by hitting Ctrl-Break. After satisfying yourself that it can't be done, switch your system off and on again, and run UNCRASH.COM. Then run END-LESS and you'll see that you now can indeed Ctrl-Break to safety. However, don't leave UNCRASH in memory and later load BASIC or you'll crash. The moral behind all this, of course, is save everything early and often.

UNDERLN
Command

Peter N. Howells

Purpose: Allows underlining on EGA color screens.

Format: `[d:][path]UNDERLN ON|OFF`

Remarks: One of the minor annoyances of using most of today's popular word processors on color EGA systems is that underlined characters are displayed in a color of your choice rather than as characters with a line under them. This forces you to remember which colors are installed as underline, boldface, and underlined-boldface, and turns many popular programs into somewhat less than "What-You-See-Is-What-You-Get."

UNDERLN.COM will generate an underlined character font from the EGA BIOS resident 8 x 14 font and load it as the EGA low intensity characters. Only the "printable" characters with ASCII values from 32 through 127 will be underlined.

Typing UNDERLN *ON* from the DOS prompt (or in a batch file) will underline all low intensity characters onscreen but leave the high intensity characters alone. Or, if you prefer, you may use DEBUG to patch UNDERLN.COM so it underlines the high intensity characters and uses the normal EGA 8 x 14 font with the low intensity characters.

To make this change, type:

```
DEBUG UNDERLN.COM
E 181 4
W
Q
```

Typing UNDERLN *OFF* restores the normal font. Resetting the display mode will also eliminate the underlined characters. The command line parameters, ON and OFF, are not case sensitive.

If you use UNDERLN.COM with a product like *WordPerfect* that doesn't reset the video display mode upon entry into the program, the following batch file will turn on underlining while running *WordPerfect* and turn it off upon exiting.

```
CD\WP
UNDERLN ON
WP
UNDERLN OFF
```

Once in *WordPerfect* you may define the screen colors using the Ctrl-F3, 4 key. Pick foreground and bold colors from the high intensity colors, I (dark grey) to P (white); and underline and bold underline colors from the low intensity colors, A (black) to H (grey). The background A (black), foreground L (bright cyan), underline D (cyan), bold M (bright red), and bold underline F (magenta) color scheme is pleasing.

This patch makes *WordPerfect* magical on EGAs; no one likes to look at one color for bold; another for underlined, etc. But you can adapt the program to underline the output of any other application that doesn't completely take over the hardware and that lets you give underlined text its own attribute.

If you want to experiment with this, you can work with the slightly more modest EGA UNDRLIN2 program included in this package, which is shorter and easier to adapt.

UNDRLIN2   Brian O'Neill
Command

Purpose: Allows underlining on EGA screens.

Format: `[d:][path]UNDRLIN2 [N]`

Typing UNDRLIN2 *N* or UNDRLIN2 *n* will turn underlining off; typing just UNDRLIN2 will toggle it on.

The EGA can display fonts with more or less than 25 lines onscreen, so the number of scan lines per character is not fixed at 14. The scan line that displays the underline depends on how many "bytes per character" are in the currently displayed font. UNDRLIN2.COM fetches this information from 0040:0085H of the BIOS data area.

UNDRLIN2 also looks up the port address of the video controller; this address will vary, depending on whether the EGA card is being used with a color or a monochrome monitor. UNDRLIN2.COM will work in either case.

The only attributes that UNDRLIN2 will underline are 1 and 9 (blue on black, both normal and high intensity). However, you may use the EGACOLOR.COM program included in this package to change colors 0, 1 and 9 to whatever colors you want. You can see the program in action by running the small EGAUNDER.COM demonstration program also on the disk.

EGAUNDER.COM will display a string of 40 Ps in blue and 40 Cs in green. Then use UNDRLIN2 and UNDRLIN2 N to toggle the blue text underlining on and off.

See the companion UNDERLN underliner.

UNHIDE **Command**	**R. Chung and V. K. Taylor**

Purpose: Unhides files that have been hidden from normal DOS directory searches by programs like HIDE.COM or ATTR.COM.

Format: `[d:][path]UNHIDE [d:][path]filename`

Remarks: Various attribute-setting programs, including the DOS ATTRIB command and Charles Petzold's far better ATTR utility — can set and reset a file's attributes (although the DOS version doesn't let you hide files, wasn't around before version 3.0, and didn't let you do anything other than change the read-only bit until version 3.2). But they involve complex syntaxes with switches, minus and plus signs, etc.

UNHIDE.COM simply unhides any files that you've hidden previously with a utility like ATTR.COM or HIDE.COM.

You can see the names of all the files on your disk, including the hidden files, by typing:

`CHKDSK /V`

Unfortunately, CHKDSK /V won't tell you which files are hidden and which aren't.

A better way is to have Charles Petzold's ATTR handy and type ATTR *.* to see the status of all your files. Michael Mefford's DR will also show you the settings of each file's attribute byte.

Notes: Some software packages hide one or two files as crude copy protection
devices. If you get tired of the software and try to erase all the files from
a hard disk subdirectory and then remove the directory, you won't be
able to. The directory will look empty, but it will still contain a hidden
file or two, and DOS won't remove a directory unless it's truly empty.
You can use CHKDSK/V or ATTR or DR to find out if any hidden files
are still there, and then UNHIDE to take away their hidden status. Then
just erase them normally.

However, some software, in a madcap scheme to cause users grief,
scrambles disk sectors when it hides files. So before you start unhiding
and unerasing files, read the documentation carefully and see if there are
any special deinstallation procedures you have to follow.

See HIDE.

UP   **Charles Petzold**
Command

Purpose: Changes the logged directory to the parent subdirectory.

Format: `[d:][path]UP`

Remarks: If you use lots of multilevel hard disk subdirectories, and you want to
wind your way up toward the root directory from one several levels
deep, you have two options. You could type either:

`CD \`

to move all the way to the root directory in one jump, or:

`CD ..`

and keep pressing the Enter key and then the F3 key.

Jumping directly to the root directory with CD\ is certainly efficient, unless you want to stop along the way.

Typing CD .. repeatedly works well also, except that if you go too far
you eventually get an "Invalid directory" message. When UP.COM

reaches the root directory it just sits there silently. And it's only two characters long, so it's easy to type.

Notes: UP is part of a trio of subdirectory navigation aids. See also DOWN and NEXT.

UPPER Command
Michael J. Mefford

Purpose: Converts any text file, except overly large ones, to all uppercase.

Format: `[d:][path]UPPER [d:][path]filename`

where *filename* is the file you want entirely uppercased.

Remarks: UPPER.COM will convert any ASCII text file, including *WordStar* document files, to all uppercase. Use UPPER if you receive an assembly language source file, for example, that is all or partial lowercase, if you prefer having it all uppercase.

Notes: Don't try UPPER with files that approach 64K or more.

See the companion LOWER utility.

VTREE Command
Charles Petzold

Purpose: Provides a visual representation of the tree-structured subdirectories on a hard or floppy disk.

Format: `[d:][path]VTREE [d:]`

Remarks: VTREE can display up to the full DOS limit of 32 levels of nested subdirectories. Its output may be redirected to a printer, but it employs IBM "text-graphics" characters that many printers cannot properly handle. With such printers, run PRSWAP (included in these utilities) before VTREE.

WAIT   Tom Kihlken
Batch file command

Purpose: Delays batch file execution a specified number of seconds or until any key is struck.

Format: `[d:][path]WAIT S`

where *S* is a decimal number of seconds up to 59.

Remarks: WAIT.COM lets you insert a pause into your batch program. For example, WAIT 5 will pause for five seconds or until you strike any key. This lets you keep a screen displayed long enough to read it before proceeding.

Since WAIT uses DOS's clock to time the delay interval, it works accurately on any machine. Simpler methods that use delay loops are at the mercy of the processor speed and won't give consistent results. The longest single wait interval you can request is 59 seconds. For longer pauses use multiple WAIT statements.

You can easily terminate a wait interval by pressing any key. WAIT detects this by continually checking the keyboard buffer while it loops. If a keystroke is detected, the pause state terminates and the input key is discarded.

Examples: To have a batch file display two opening screens (that you've put in two files called OPENING1.SCR and OPENING2.SCR) for ten seconds each, type:

```
ECHO OFF
CLS
TYPE OPENING1.SCR
WAIT 10
CLS
TYPE OPENING2.SCR
WAIT 10
CLS
```

You may want to put a message at the bottom of each of these screens that says: "(Press any key to continue)."

If you use an indexing program called SORTIT.EXE to sort a file called DATA.FIL, and you wanted it to run from a batch file and beep when it's done, but you didn't want it to beep for two minutes to give yourself time to discover that the job was done, you could type:

```
ECHO OFF
SORTIT DATA.FIL
WAIT 59
WAIT 59
ECHO ^G
```

(where the ECHO ^G line was created by typing ECHO, then pressing the spacebar, then holding down Ctrl and typing G).

WAITASEC Command   Charles Petzold

Purpose: Uses the single-keystroke ScrollLock key to halt a fast-scrolling display; then allows you to scroll backwards, recalling previous screens.

Format: `[d:] [path]WAITASEC`

`<ScrollLock>`

Remarks: WAITASEC is a memory-resident program that is normally loaded through your AUTOEXEC.BAT file. Thereafter, alternately pressing and releasing the ScrollLock key will halt and restart a scrolling display, e.g., a lengthy DIR listing.

While holding down the ScrollLock key to freeze the display, if you also press one of the cursor movement keys (Home, Up Arrow, PgUp, End, Down Arrow, or PgDn), the display will not resume scrolling when you release the ScrollLock key. Thereafter, the Up and Down Arrow keys move the display by one line, the PgUp and PgDown move it by 25 lines, and the Home and End keys take you to the beginning and end of the stored screen memory. Pressing any noncursor key at this point deactivates the stored mode, and the original scrolling resumes.

Notes: 1.   WAITASEC will not work with an 80-column color/graphics display if an unmodified PC-DOS ANSI.SYS has been loaded. (The ANSI.SYS that comes with various versions of MS-DOS does not cause problems with WAITASEC.) To run with IBM's ANSI.SYS, make a copy (MODANSI.SYS) of the original ANSI.SYS and use DEBUG to patch the copy as follows:

```
DEBUG MODANSI.SYS
E 29D 90 90
E 2A1 90 90
W
Q
```

Put the modified MODANSI.SYS in your CONFIG.SYS file in place of ANSI.SYS.

2.   Because of the way they handle TTY output, certain EGA cards will not permit WAITASEC to scroll backwards. This problem can often be cured by adding MODANSI.SYS, as above.

3.   WAITASEC does not save your current display screen. To save your current display, enter the complementary SCROLL2 command before beginning a scroll, and everything on the screen will scroll off the top and be captured in the WAITASEC buffer.

4.   While WAITASEC has been found compatible with *XyWrite* (XYKBD.COM loaded) on a PC AT, as with other memory-resident programs, unforeseen hardware and software incompatibilities may be encountered.

See SCROLL2.

WARMBOOT   Charles Petzold
Command

Purpose: Performs a fast reboot, bypassing initial power-on self tests, as if the user had pressed Ctrl-Alt-Del.

Format: `[d:][path]WARMBOOT`

Remarks: Use this if you've installed a program that disables the Ctrl key, or if you simply have to reboot and want to skip the initial diagnostics.

For a slower reboot that slogs through the initial tests, see COLDBOOT. For a flexible utility that allows both kinds of rebooting and lets the user abort the process, see REBOOT.

WHERE
Command

Kiyoshi Akima

Purpose: Searches all directories on a particular drive and lists the paths of entries that match the specified filename.

Format: `[d:][path]WHERE [filename[.ext]]`

Remarks: WHERE uses normal DOS filename specifications to locate files. Omitting a filename and extension after the command defaults to WHERE *.* and will list all nonhidden files on your disk.

Examples: The command WHERE *.BAT will find all your batch files. WHERE MO*.* would uncover MODE.COM and MORE.COM and any other filenames that begin with MO.

Notes: Although submitted to us by Mr. Akima, this program has its roots in one originally written by John Socha.

WINDOWS
Command

Paul Somerson

Purpose: Demonstration program that shows BIOS window-clearing abilities on color systems.

Format: `[d:][path]WINDOWS`

Remarks: Programmers usually use service 6 of BIOS interrupt 10 to clear the entire screen. This short demonstration program clears successively smaller and smaller centered windows, each to a different color.

Once you've run the program (on a color monitor only), enter:

```
DIR /W
```

to produce a wide directory listing, and you'll see that the text in the center blinks, since the background color for the few central windows is higher than 7.

If you're ambitious, you could adapt this program to produce a kaleido-scopic effect by changing the starting color and looping back to the beginning again.

XDEL
Command

Ronald Czapala

Purpose: Successively presents each filename in your current directory for single-keystroke file deletion or retention.

Format: `[d:][path]XDEL [d:][file.ext]`

Remarks: If no parameters are specified with XDEL, the default filename *.* is used. Both the global characters ? and * may be used in selecting the files to be presented.

The program produces an onscreen menu of keystroke choices, as follows:

<F1> — deletes current file displayed
<PgDn> — skips current file displayed
<Home> — restarts file display
<Esc> — returns to DOS

Notes: Although XDEL.COM requires DOS 2.0 or later, you must use CHDIR (CD) to log into the proper directory.

XDIR
Command

Jeff Prosise

Purpose: XDIR.COM is a memory-resident utility that allows you to display the filenames in any drive/directory even when you are running another applications program.

Format: `[d:][path]XDIR`

Remarks: Once loaded (normally as an entry in your AUTOEXEC.BAT file), pressing the Alt-. (the Alt and the period key combination) causes a blank window to pop up on the screen. Pressing Enter then displays the first 40 filenames of your current directory in the window. Pressing Esc once clears the display, and pressing it a second time returns you to your previous application.

To view other directories, simply enter their appropriate path designation (including drive, if different) before pressing Enter when the window is blank.

The PgUp and PgDn keys are used to display files beyond the initial 40 shown in the window. Up to 360 files in any one directory may be displayed.

Notes: 1. You may use DEBUG to change some of the XDIR.COM defaults. Remember always to make changes to a copy of the program, not to your original. After entering DEBUG XDIR.COM, the following addresses and initial values may be of interest:

Offset	Value	Parameter
13C	4F	Border color attribute
13D	0F	Text color attribute
14D	00	File type (see Note 2)
186	34	Period key scan code
18E	08	Alt-key shift code

2. By default, XDIR displays only normal filenames (00 at 14D). To show hidden files, the value here should be 02. System files are 04, and subdirectories are 10H. These values are additive. To display subdirectories and files marked both hidden and system (e.g. IBMBIO.COM) you would enter the value 16H at offset 14D in place of the default 00.

3. While no TSR program can be guaranteed compatible with all other memory residents, its special interrupt handling should make XDIR.COM coexist even with most "difficult" TSRs.

Chapter 17

BASIC Programs

Ever since IBM started plunking personal computers on desktops, new users have wondered why they received a khaki manual labeled "BASIC." Few of them bought computers to learn how to program, and most mistakenly thought programming was just for wimpy math majors and overweight nerds. But a lot of them ended up typing in the examples in the manual, and quickly discovered that this new language could actually help them work better. Although it would never win any awards for speed, BASIC was easy to learn, surprisingly powerful, and free.

Users found they could load BASIC to do quick hexadecimal math, or perform a trigonometric calculation, or see what ASCII character 178 looked like. Then they discovered its file-handling and graphics abilties, and began producing some very helpful little programs. DOS was so bad at processing strings of characters that it often became necessary to redirect a DOS command into a file and then use BASIC to put the file into shape.

One of the nicest things about BASIC is that if you suddenly find yourself with a problem BASIC can tackle, you can load it, stumble your way through a program, and emerge with a solution a few minutes later. So maybe your program wasn't the most elegant display of programming virtuosity; who cares so long as it worked?

The implementation of BASIC usually packaged with DOS had one very important thing going for it — you didn't need any fancy editors or compilers to get up and running. You just typed away and then pressed the "RUN" key and saw right away whether or not your program was operating properly. BASIC was very forgiving.

Over the last few years interest in programming has skyrocketed. Microsoft and Borland, two leading software packagers, have flooded the market with increasingly powerful versions of several popular languages at irresistably low prices. Millions of users who never thought they'd write a single line of code are now pounding away at updated versions of Pascal, C, and even BASIC.

Assembly language programs have always been the most popular of those published in *PC Magazine*. They can do things in a few bytes of code that would take other languages forever. They run incredibly fast, and take up a fraction of the disk space required by many higher-level programs. All of the utilities in the first part of the accompanying disk are written in 8088 Assembler.

However, the garden variety edition of BASICA (or GWBASIC on compatibles) can do some tricks of its own in a few lines of code that would take an assembly language programmer far longer. This is because BASIC has certain graphics "primitives" and file-handling abilities built in. It's a lot easier to draw a circle with a one-line BASIC command than to have to start worrying about writing complex trigonometric routines from scratch in assembly language.

Some of the following BASIC programs help produce files and screens that demonstrate the abilities of assembly language programs presented in Chapter 16. Others do interesting tricks on their own.

If you haven't ever tried working with BASIC, it's easier than you think. Once you learn the few fundamentals you'll find yourself often writing little routines to help you work. And you may become interested enough to plunge in and learn the fine points of BASIC or one of today's other popular languages.

BATMAKR1.BAS / BATMAKR2.BAS   Paul Somerson

Purpose: Makes it incredibly easy to switch between subdirectories on a hard disk.

Format: `[d:][path]BASICA [d:][path]BATMAKR1`

(Substitute GWBASIC instead of BASICA on generic systems.)

Remarks: Before you run either of these programs, get into DOS and create a file called TEMPFILE that contains a list of every subdirectory on your disk. A single command will do it:

`CHKDSK / V | FIND "Dir" > TEMPFILE`

Then run either BATMAKR1.BAS or BATMAKR2.BAS. Make sure that you put the batch files that these programs create into a directory that your PATH command knows about. This way you'll be able to execute them from anywhere on your disk.

BATMAKR1.BAS will create dozens of individual small files that will switch quickly to any subdirectory, but will take up a lot of real estate on your disk. BATMAKR2.BAS creates one long file called S.BAT that takes up a lot less room but works more slowly than the individual files created by BATMAKR1.BAS.

If you have a fast hard disk and you're not pressed for space, use BAT-MAKR1. It will look at all the subdirectories on your hard disk and create batch files with the name of the lowest level directory. So it will take a subdirectory like:

\DOS\UTILITY\PCMAG\NUM1

and create a file called NUM1.BAT. To switch into this subdirectory, all you have to do is type:

NUM1

DOS can handle similarly named subdirectories, but BATMAKR1 and BATMAKR2 can't. So if you have directories like:

\DOS\UTILITY\PCMAG\NUM1

and:

\DBASE\TAXES\NUM1

both BATMAKR files will use just one.

If you're using a slow hard disk, or a full one, you might be better off with BATMAKR2.BAS, which creates one big switcher file. An XT hard disk can waste 4K per file even if the file is a tiny batch file. If you have 50 subdirectories on an XT hard disk, using BATMAKR1.BAS will take up 50 x 4K, or 200K of disk space. The single S.BAT batch file created by BATMAKR2.BAS will take up just 4K.

If you do use BATMAKR2.BAS, load S.BAT onto a RAMdisk for best performance. Then to switch into:

\DOS\UTILITY\PCMAG\NUM1

(assuming it's the only directory called NUM1), just type:

S NUM1

You could also type:

S num1

since the S.BAT that BATMAKR2.BAS creates can handle all uppercase or all lowercase entries. But it can't deal with mixed uppercase and
lowercase ones.

Notes: 1.   Either of these programs will let you jump around from one subdirectory to another without having to type in long cumbersome pathnames. But they're designed to work on one disk only. If you're logged
into a floppy disk in drive A:, and all your BATMAKR batch files are on
drive C:, log into drive C: before using any of them, since they all assume you want to change directories on the default hard drive.

2.   If you can spare the space, the small individual files created by BAT-
MAKR1 work a lot better than the potentially huge and slow single
S.BAT file created by BATMAKR2. Batch files execute one line at a
time and DOS always starts scanning through them from the beginning
of the file. A subdirectory-switching command stuck at the end of a
string of 50 tests isn't going to work very quickly. But the tiny files
generated by BATMAKR1 will change directories in an instant.

If you do create the many tiny batch files with BATMAKR1, put them
all in their own subdirectory and include the name of this directory in
your path. Keeping them all together makes it easy to erase them and
create new ones when you erase or create new subdirectories.

BOOTREC.BAS   Paul Somerson

Purpose: Uses DEBUG to read the BIOS Parameter Block (BPB) from the boot
track, and then produces a report on the configuration of any disk in your
system.

Format: `[d:][path]BASICA [d:][path]BOOTREC`

(Substitute GWBASIC instead of BASICA on generic systems.)

Remarks: On all but the earliest DOS versions, the DOS FORMAT.COM program
puts a small table of information at the very beginning of the first disk
sector.

After loading the program, just enter the drive letter you want to examine.

BOOTREC uses DEBUG to read this information, does a few necessary
calculations, and produces a report that will look something like:

```
===================== Drive B: =========================

OEM Name and version:                 IBM 3.0
Total sectors:                        720
Bytes per sector:                     512
Sectors per cluster:                  2
Bytes per cluster:                    1024
Reserved (boot record) sectors:       1
Sectors per track:                    9
Number of hidden sectors:             0
Number of heads (sides):              2
Tracks per side:                      40
Number of File Allocation Tables:     2
Sectors per File Allocation Table:    2
Total sectors used by FATs:           4
Maximum root directory entries:       112
Sectors used by root directory:       7
Total bytes available on disk:        368640 — 360K
Total bytes available for data:       362496
Media descriptor byte:                5-1/4 inch, 2 Sides,
                                      9 Sectors/Track
```

Notes: See Chapter 2 for a discussion of how DOS handles disks, what all the terms used in the BOOTREC.BAS report mean, and how you can use this information productively.

BOXMAKER   Paul Somerson

Purpose: Creates a batch file that displays a single- or double-line box in practically any size you want.

Format: [d:][path]BASICA [d:][path]BOXMAKER

(Substitute GWBASIC instead of BASICA on generic systems.)

Remarks: You can spruce up the appearance of your batch files dramatically by putting things like comments, titles, and instructions inside boxes. Unfortunately, DOS doesn't provide any simple way to create such boxes.

BOXMAKER.BAS asks you the dimensions of the box you want to create, the number of spaces you want it indented onscreen, and the type of box (single-line or double-line). It then produces a batch file called

BOX.BAT with the actual box you specified plus all the ECHO statements needed to display it properly.

Use a pure-ASCII word processor to enter text inside the box, then incorporate the filled-in box in your batch files.

You can have batch files print menus and messages either by using the ECHO command to display a line at a time (as is done here), or by putting the menu or message in a separate file and using the TYPE command to display it in one gulp.

The ECHO technique works well on a fast hard disk or a RAMdisk, but may take forever on a floppy-based system. However, it lets you put everything you need in one place, and doesn't require any additional files.

The TYPE method is far faster on all systems, but it forces you to have one batch file refer to another file that contains the text you want displayed. Even small files can take up lots of room — on an old ten-megabyte XT even a one-byte file hogged 4K of disk space. The MAKESCRN.BAS program on the accompanying disk creates a sample MENU file that your batch file can TYPE.

Notes: 1.   Earlier versions of DOS may not handle indentations properly, but they'll still display the box.

2.   If you use this program more than once, be sure to rename any older BOX.BAT file on your disk so the newer one doesn't obliterate it.

See MAKESCRN.BAS.

CAMLOAD   Paul Somerson

Purpose: Works with Philip Cheng's CAMERA.COM program to produce a "slide show" by loading screen images in succession.

Format: Run this program by creating a three-line batch file called CAM.BAT:

```
DIR ?.* > CAMERA.FIL
[d:][path]BASICA [d:][path]CAMLOAD
DEL CAMERA.FIL
```

(Substitute GWBASIC instead of BASICA on generic systems.)

Remarks: The CAMERA.COM program on the accompanying disk lets you save four kinds of images to disk:

- 40-column text
- 80-column text
- 320 x 200 "medium" resolution graphics
- 640 x 200 "high" resolution graphics

You can use CAMLOAD.BAS to load these images onto the screen one after the other. CAMLOAD lets you specify how many seconds each will appear, from 1 to 59. And it will automatically handle the different screen modes required to display the different kinds of image CAMERA.COM can store.

CAM.BAT creates a file called CAMERA.FIL that lists the single-letter names of the image files captured by CAMERA.COM. It assumes that any file with a single-character filename (and any extension) in the current subdirectory is one created by CAMERA.COM. If you have single-character filenames in the current directory that were not created by CAMERA.COM, or if you want to rearrange the order of the slide show, you can edit the CAMERA.FIL file. If you do, omit the last line in CAM.BAT to prevent DOS from erasing the edited CAMERA.FIL file.

The SAMPLE.BAS program on the accompanying disk will create several kinds of images.

Notes: 1.   If you want to modify the program so it loads each successive slide only when you press a key, and not at a timed interval, make two changes.

First, add a line 171 that says:

```
171 GOTO 200
```

Second, replace line 390 with a new one that says:

```
390 WHILE INKEY$="":WEND
```

2.   This process may not be able to reproduce all background colors exactly as they were created.

See CAMERA, SAMPLE.BAS.

COLORSET.BAS   Paul Somerson

Purpose: Creates small COM files that set your display colors, with or without first clearing the screen.

Format: [d:] [path] BASICA [d:] [path] COLORSET

(Substitute GWBASIC instead of BASICA on generic systems.)

Remarks: If you use a color system, you need a way to set your screen colors, and clear the screen to those preset colors.

COLORSET.BAS will create a program called PCCOLOR.COM that sets the foreground and background colors (and the border on CGA screens.) It makes it a snap to choose the colors you want. And it asks whether you want the new PCCOLOR.COM program to clear the screen before it sets the colors. Most users prefer to have such programs clear the screen, but this gives you the option of keeping the image intact and just changing the underlying colors.

COLORSET will also ask you if you're using a screen with more than 25 lines, and adjust the program automatically to reflect the proper screen size.

If you run COLORSET.BAS more than once to create several different versions of the PCCOLOR.COM program, be sure to rename the existing version so the new one doesn't write over the old one.

COLORSET.BAS will ask you to pick a border color. If you're using a CGA, the border color you selected will appear. If you're using any other kind of color system, the border won't appear, but it won't hurt to pick a border color.

Notes: 1.   It's best to rename the PCCOLOR.COM program once you've created it. Obvious choices are the names of the colors themselves (BLUEWITE.COM, REDYELOW.COM etc.). But it's easier to keep the name short, since this saves typing. We usually give such programs names like C.COM or CL.COM. You can't really name a program CLS.COM, since CLS is an internal DOS command. DOS will think you're trying to execute the normal CLS command and give its command preference over yours.

Technically you could create a program called CLS.COM. But you'd have to run it each time by putting a drive letter or path in front of it:

```
C:CLS
```

You could, of course, execute it by typing:

```
.\CLS
```

(which is shorthand for telling DOS you want to run the program in the current directory).

FROG.BAS   Paul Somerson

Purpose: Demonstrates character-animation techniques in a short but energetic game.

Format: `[d:][path]BASICA [d:][path]FROG`

(Substitute GWBASIC instead of BASICA on generic systems.)

Remarks: With a little ingenuity you can use the high-bit ASCII character set (the foreign language, math, and box/border characters) to draw charts, tables, graphs, and even animated pictures.

FROG.BAS is a primitive game that uses a wide variety of these ASCII characters to draw a jumping frog, a flying bug, and a long frog tongue. You play by hitting the F10 function key to launch the tongue so it can catch the bug. You can launch the tongue only when the frog has landed on the ground. If you want to alter the rules, change the numbers indicated in lines 160 and 170. And if the action is too slow, reduce the number in line 470.

Obviously this isn't going to displace your kids' favorite arcade games. It's included here to demonstrate two things — first, that the ASCII characters can create reasonable images on your screen (for bar charts, graphs, etc.), and second, that BASIC is a powerful tool that can pack a wallop in just a few lines.

GRAFPRNT.BAS   Paul Somerson

Purpose: Displays bit patterns for all ASCII characters with values greater than 127.

Format: `[d:][path]BASICA [d:][path]GRAFPRNT`

(Substitute GWBASIC instead of BASICA on generic systems.)

Remarks: DOS version 3.0 offered a new utility called GRAFTABL.COM that made it possible to display the high-bit characters (with ASCII values between 128 and 255). All you had to do was type in GRAFTABL before loading BASIC, and DOS would create a memory-resident lookup table containing the proper values.

GRAFTABL.COM remained the same in versions 3.1 and 3.2, but when IBM introduced its confounding foreign language features in version 3.3 it made GRAFTABL.COM five times larger to accommodate slight differences in foreign character sets.

GRAFPRNT.BAS looks inside GRAFTABL.COM, reads the character patterns into an array, and uses ROMPRINT's binary pattern printer to display an enlarged version of any ASCII character from 128 through 255. It checks to make sure you have a proper version handy, and automatically detects whether it's dealing with an older GRAFTABL.COM or a fat new one, since the internal structures are different.

Examples: If you want to see the cents sign that's missing from the IBM keyboard, just run GRAFPRINT and type in 155. If you want to see the IBM border characters just type in the numbers between 179 and 218.

See ROMPRINT.BAS for a program that displays the lower 128 ASCII character dot patterns.

HORSE.BAS   Paul Somerson

Purpose: Demonstrates screen-page animation (on color systems only).

Format: `[d:][path]BASICA [d:][path]HORSE`

(Substitute GWBASIC instead of BASICA on generic systems.)

Remarks: This program uses the BASIC GET and PUT commands, and a few binary decoding tricks, to put four very realistic galloping horses on any color screen. When it's running, you can press the F9 and F10 function keys to change the colors. Pressing Esc will end the program and drop you back into DOS.

The horse images are patterned after Eadweard Muybridge's stop-action photographs. The digitization first appeared in the *Computer Animation Primer*, a terrific book on animation by David Fox and Mitchell Waite, published by McGraw Hill.

MAKECOM.BAS   Larry Zimmerman

Purpose: Turns your text files into tiny assembly language programs that pop onto the screen.

Format: `[d:][path]BASICA [d:][path]MAKECOM`

(Substitute GWBASIC instead of BASICA on generic systems.)

Remarks: You can display text in DOS several different ways. The most common is to use the ECHO command in batch files:

```
ECHO ==============================
ECHO            ** MENU **
ECHO        1. Run WordStar
ECHO        2. Run dBase
```

A faster way is to put the text you want to display in a file of its own and then use the DOS TYPE or MORE command. If the file were called MENU.TXT, you could do it with:

```
TYPE MENU.TXT
```

If MENU.TXT happened to be longer than 25 lines, you could substitute:

```
MORE < MENU.TXT
```

But these methods just don't look professional. It's much speedier and more impressive to have text flash instantaneously onto your display. MAKECOM.BAS makes it easy to create individual COM files that will do this for you.

Examples: To use this program, first create a text file that's no wider than 79 characters, and no deeper than 24 lines. Use a pure-ASCII word processor, or EDLIN, since you don't want any control characters or distracting word processor formatting commands to appear.

Then load MAKECOM.BAS by typing BASICA MAKECOM or GWBASIC MAKECOM. The program will ask for the name of your text file. Type in the filename (adding a drive and path if necessary). MAKECOM will then tell you that it will create a similarly named version of the text file, but with a COM extension.

If this is acceptable, just press the Enter key. Otherwise, enter a different filename. If you don't include a COM extension, the program will add one for you.

When MAKECOM is done it will tell you the new file has been created. Type:

```
SYSTEM
```

and press the Enter key to return to DOS. Then type in the name of the new program. The text should flash onto your screen.

Notes:

The COM program created by MAKECOM.BAS will not change your display colors when it prints the text. If you do want to have the COM program set new colors, you can do it one of two ways.

You can use DEBUG to patch just the single COM program that MAKECOM.BAS creates. Or you can make a copy of MAKECOM.BAS called MAKECOM2.BAS that will always create screens that appear in one preset color combination of your choice.

Changing single COM files one at a time lets you pop up differently colored screens. Changing the main MAKECOM.BAS program to MAKECOM2.BAS means that every .COM file created by MAKECOM2.BAS will be the same color. But if you want all your screens to be blue on white, you may prefer this method.

To change just a single COM file called MENU.COM, first figure out the two-digit hex value for the color you want to use. (See the note on color at the end of this entry.) If you wanted to make the screen bright yellow on a red background, you would use 4E. Type:

```
DEBUG MENU.COM
E 147 B7 4E
W
Q
```

Now run MENU.COM by typing MENU at the DOS prompt and it should appear in yellow on red. The:

```
E 147 B7
```

in the second line is always the same. But change the 4E to any other color value you want.

To give yourself a copy of MAKECOM.BAS called MAKECOM2.BAS that creates COM files that display screens in the preset colors you want, use your pure-ASCII word processor (or the BASIC editor itself) and make the following change:

In line 430 of the program, replace the two numbers:

```
88,E7
```

with:

```
B7,4E
```

Make sure you put a B7 first, and follow it with a comma. But replace the 4E with any other color value you'd like. The 4E will produce screens that are bright yellow on red. And make sure you don't put a comma after the color number — only one comma should be on that line.

How to Pick a Color Number

The BIOS video attribute numbering system relies on two-digit hex numbers to specify foreground (text) and background colors.

The lefthand digit is the background color. The righthand digit is the foreground color. Select these numbers from the color chart in the BROWSE entry.

Values from 0 to 7 are normal intensity. Values from 8 to F are high-intensity (bright) versions of the normal colors. You can use all 16 values from 0 through F for foreground (text) colors — the righthand digit. But background colors — the lefthand digit — are restricted to values from 0 to 7. If you use a background color higher than 7, the text will blink annoyingly.

Example: The two-digit color number:

```
71
```

will create blue text (1) on a white (7) background. The number:

17

will produce white text on a blue background. To keep the background blue but make the white text high-intensity (bright), use a value of F instead of 7:

1F

For something attention-getting you could always try a combination like bright green (A) on magenta/purple (5) = 5A.

MAKEMENU.BAS   Paul Somerson

Purpose: Automatically creates a custom DOS menu system.

Format: `[d:][path]BASICA [d:][path]MAKEMENU`

(Substitute GWBASIC instead of BASICA on generic systems.)

Remarks: This program really shows what you can do with a short BASIC program.

It asks the user a few questions, and creates a complete DOS menu system that will list the precise number of menu choices specified by the user, wrap these choices in an attractive menu screen, and produce a customized batch file that runs the whole affair.

MAKEMENU.BAS even creates a small assembly language routine called GETLETR.COM that handles the user input when the batch file is operating in DOS.

You can have it create a menu screen surrounded by a single-line or double-line box, and containing from two to 26 menu choices. Each choice is triggered by a letter of the alphabet.

MAKEMENU.BAS creates a batch file called MENU.BAT that prints rows of XXXXXXXs for each menu choice. When you're done, load the MENU.BAT program into your pure-ASCII word processor or EDLIN and replace the XXXXXXs with real choices (such as "A. Run Word-Star"). Then replace the dummy ECHO statements under each label with the actual commands you want the letter choices to execute.

The program also generates the necessary GETLETR.COM file to interpret the user keystroke choices into menu selections so MENU.BAT can branch to the proper place and execute the desired command. Once you've run the program the first time, you don't have to keep recreating the GETLETR.COM routine. You may remove everything in the program from line 760 to the end, but it won't hurt anything if you leave all those lines intact.

Examples: The smallest possible MENU.BAT file you could generate would look something like:

```
ECHO OFF
:TOP
ECHO +-----------------------------------------------------+
ECHO |                    ** MENU **                       |
ECHO |                                                     |
ECHO | A XXXXXXXXXXXXXXXXXXXX   B XXXXXXXXXXXXXXXXXXXXXX |
ECHO |                                                     |
ECHO | Enter a letter from A to B (or type Esc to quit) |
ECHO +-----------------------------------------------------+
:START
GETLETR
IF ERRORLEVEL 27 GOTO END
IF ERRORLEVEL 3 GOTO START
IF ERRORLEVEL 2 GOTO LABELB
:LABELA
ECHO (this simulates menu choice A)
PAUSE
GOTO TOP
:LABELB
ECHO (this simulates menu choice B)
PAUSE
GOTO TOP
:END
```

Once you've run MAKEMENU.BAS and created this sample MENU.BAT file, change the XXXXXXs so they read something like:

```
ECHO +-----------------------------------------------------+
ECHO |                    ** MENU **                       |
ECHO |                                                     |
ECHO |A - Run 25-line WordStar  B - Run 43-line WordStar|
ECHO |                                                     |
ECHO | Enter a letter from A to B (or type Esc to quit) |
ECHO +-----------------------------------------------------+
```

Then change the lines below the appropriate labels in the lower half of the batch file, by replacing the dummy "ECHO (this simulates menu choice A)" lines put there by MAKEMENU.BAS to demonstrate how the system works:

```
:LABELA
WS
PAUSE
GOTO TOP
:LABELB
WS43
PAUSE
```

This example replaced the:

```
ECHO (this simulates menu choice A)
```

line with:

```
WS
```

which runs a normal 25-line version of *WordStar*. Then it replaced the:

```
ECHO (this simulates menu choice B)
```

line with:

```
WS43
```

which runs a special 43-line version of *WordStar*. You could just as easily have inserted another program name such as:

```
123
```

in one of these places to run 123. Or you could have placed a DOS command like

```
DIR | SORT | MORE
```

and changed one of the choices in the menu to:

```
B — Print a sorted directory listing
```

You might want to get rid of the PAUSE that follows each of your commands. This will pause the batch file when the command or the program at each label finishes executing. One tap on the spacebar or any other key and MENU.BAT will redisplay the menu.

You may also want to insert a:

```
CLS
```

command on a line by itself directly below the :TOP label at the very beginning of MENU.BAT. This will clear the screen each time something finishes executing, so the MENU displays on a clean screen.

Once you've created the MENU.BAT file and used your word processor or EDLIN to enter your own menu choices, run it by typing:

```
MENU
```

Be sure the GETLETR.COM program also created by MAKEMENU.BAS is in the same directory, or is in a directory specified by your PATH command.

Typing any menu letter at that point should execute that particular command or program. When it's done, you should see the main menu again. If you've left the PAUSE commands intact, you'll have to press a key to see the menu again.

MENU.BAT screens out erroneous entries, and it's case insensitive so you may enter an uppercase or lowercase A to pick the first menu item. To quit, simply press the Escape key.

MAKESCRN.BAS   Paul Somerson

Purpose: Produces an attractive, simulated-3D menu that you can display in your batch files by using the TYPE command.

Format: [d:][path]BASICA [d:][path]MAKESCRN

(Substitute GWBASIC instead of BASICA on generic systems.)

Remarks: Batch files can display menus and messages either by using the ECHO command to print them line by line, or by using the TYPE command to print the whole thing at once. See BOXMAKER.BAS for a discussion of the merits of each technique.

MAKESCRN.BAS produces a file that contains a centered, reverse-video slab in just about any size you want, complete with a shadow under it that makes it look three-dimensional. It also prints the word "MENU" at the top of it.

You can use your pure-ASCII word processor to add menu items to it. Then just add a line in your batch file that says:

```
TYPE MENU
```

Notes: If you use this program more than once, be sure to rename any existing copies of the MENU file so the new one doesn't obliterate the old one.

See BOXMAKER.BAS.

ROMPRINT.BAS   Paul Somerson

Purpose: Snoops inside your BASIC ROM and prints the bit patterns for the characters there.

Format: [d:] [path]BASICA [d:] [path]ROMPRINT

(Substitute GWBASIC instead of BASICA on generic systems.)

Remarks: ROMPRINT.BAS looks at absolute memory address F000:FA6E, reads the values stored there and interprets them as light and dark blocks on your screen. The main ROM maintains the patterns for each character as a sequence of eight binary numbers, one per row. ROMPRINT retrieves the decimal value of each number and translates it into the binary pattern for each row.

To tell ROMPRINT which character dot patterns you want it to display, either press keys from the keyboard, or enter ASCII values between 0 and 127. If you want to see the dot patterns for the digits 0-9, enter their ASCII values (0 = 48, 1 = 49...9 = 57). If you do type in ASCII numbers, press the Enter key after entering any values with fewer than three digits. When you're all done, press the F10 function key to end the program.

The program also displays the actual life-size character beneath the enlarged dot pattern. It won't display the whole character set, since the system uses some with values like 7, 10, 12, and 13 to control the position of the cursor, clear the screen, beep, and manage other display chores.

But ROMPRINT will show you the actual patterns stored in ROM for every single one.

Examples: To see the patterns for A or #, just press the appropriate keys. Certain characters, such as % and @, are hard to draw in the small 8 x 8 character box your ROM uses.

See GRAFPRNT.BAS for a program that displays characters with ASCII values between 128 and 255.

SAMPLE.BAS   Paul Somerson

Purpose: Generates sample screens in 40-column text, 80-column text, 320 x 200 graphics, and 640 x 200 graphics modes that you can use to demonstrate CAMERA.COM and CAMLOAD.BAS.

Format: `[d:][path]BASICA [d:][path]SAMPLE`

(Substitute GWBASIC instead of BASICA on generic systems.)

Remarks: The images produced by SAMPLE.BAS aren't fancy, but they do use the four modes supported by CAMERA.COM.

The program will pause after generating each screen. Assuming you've loaded CAMERA.COM previously, activate it at that point by pressing Ctrl-Alt-Right Shift to capture each image. Then press any key to generate the next image. After capturing the last (high-resolution) image, type SYSTEM and press Enter to return to DOS.

See CAMLOAD.BAS, CAMERA.

SECTORXL.BAS   Paul Somerson

Purpose: Translates differing BIOS and DOS sector numbers back and forth.

Format: `[d:][path]BASICA [d:][path]SECTORXL`

(Substitute GWBASIC instead of BASICA on generic systems.)

Remarks: BIOS uses a three-dimensional notation system (track/side/sector) for referring to disk sectors. DOS uses a single linear system. Converting from one to the other can be confusing.

What makes it even worse is that track and side numbers start with 0, but sector numbers start with 1.

You might use this if you decide to customize the disk boot record. The boot record uses BIOS calls and the BIOS sector-numbering system exclusively, since one of the things it does is start the process of loading DOS. But the tools you'll use to move files around are probably DEBUG or something like the *Norton Utilities*, both of which use the DOS numbering system.

SECTORXL takes the sting out of the translation process, and prevents you from entering any out-of-range numbers. And it prompts you for all the necessary entries.

SOUNDER.BAS   Paul Somerson

Purpose: Demonstrates the kind of unusual sounds you can have BASIC generate with a tiny amount of code.

Format: `[d:][path]BASICA [d:][path]SOUNDER`

(Substitute GWBASIC instead of BASICA on generic systems.)

Remarks: One thing that drives lots of users crazy is the unvarying DOS beep. If you're writing a batch file that runs a long, slow program, and you want to alert the user when it's done, or if you want to warn users when they're about to do something potentially dangerous, you can insert a:

`ECHO ^G`

line in the batch file (where the ^G is generated by holding down the Ctrl key and pressing G). When DOS executes this line it will beep.

It's possible to write assembly language programs to beep and twitter differently, but BASIC makes the process a whole lot easier. The BASIC manual demonstrates how to do this with the SOUND and PLAY commands. SOUNDER mixes a hnadful of SOUND commands with some OUT commands that manipulate the speaker directly.

You could, for instance, adapt one of the small sound modules in SOUNDER.BAS and dash off a quick program like ALARMER.BAS:

```
100 ' ALARMER.BAS
110 ' (c) 1987 Ziff Communications Co.
120 IF TIME$<>"17:00:00" THEN 120
130 FOR A=1 TO 15
140 FOR B=1 TO 450 STEP 200
150 SOUND 400+B, .3
160 NEXT:NEXT
170 FOR C=1 TO 5000:NEXT
180 IF INKEY$<>"" THEN 200
190 GOTO 130
200 SYSTEM
```

When you run this it will sit there testing the time and do nothing until 5 PM (17:00:00 in BASIC's 24-hour syntax). Then it will produce a repeating sound sort of similar to an electronic telephone ring until you press a key to stop it.

You could adapt this simple ALARMER.BAS program, as Charles Petzold once mentioned in a column of his, to run a process at a certain time. Just remove lines 170 to 190, and change the time in line 120 if necessary.

Then put a line in your batch file that says:

```
BASICA ALARMER
```

(or GWBASIC ALARMER) and follow this line with the command or program you want to execute at that time. The batch file will load BASIC and run the program, then do nothing until the proper time. When the time you entered finally rolls around, it will warble the alarm, jump back into DOS and resume executing the batch file at the following line, running the program you specified there.

Michael Mefford's PLAY utility on the accompanying disk can also make lots of interesting sounds.

PART V

Quick Reference

Chapter 18

The PC-DOS Commands

The chapter covers all the DOS 3.3 commands, including CONFIG.SYS and batch file commands. Some of the following ones, such as APPEND or FASTOPEN, don't exist in previous editions of DOS. Some, such as ATTRIB, BACKUP, RESTORE, or TIME and DATE, work differently in earlier versions. One, XCOPY, isn't on generic DOS disks since it was written by IBM rather than Microsoft. And some terrific Microsoft commands, such as FC, aren't included here since they're not on the standard IBM DOS disk.

See Figures 1.3 and 1.4 in Chapter 1 for a list of new and modified commands in all PC-DOS versions from 1.0 through 3.3.

For more hints and explanations on some of the most powerful DOS commands, such as PRINT or XCOPY, see Chapter 14.

When part of a command's format is specified in brackets ([d:]) it means the part is optional. When two choices are separated by a vertical bar (ON | OFF) it means you should enter one or the other. An *or* means DOS allows multiple syntaxes.

The label *[external command]* means that a separate file with the name of the command and ending in EXE or COM must be on the disk in the current directory or one that your PATH command knows about. If this label does not appear after the name of the command in the listing below, the command is "internal," which means you don't have to have a separate file handy to execute it. The mechanisms for internal commands are contained inside the main DOS COMMAND.COM file.

The number below the line containing the name of the command is the DOS version in which the command was introduced. Many of the commands have gone through extensive revision — for instance, DISKCOPY changed in versions 1.1, 2.0/2.1, 3.0, and 3.2 — so the syntaxes and features listed are for version 3.3 only.

Primary DOS 3.3 Commands

APPEND [external command]
3.2

Searches a specified list of drives and directories for non-executable files and overlays needed by your programs; the PATH command does the same thing for executable files.

Format: `APPEND d:path[;[d:]path...]`

or

`APPEND [/X] [/E]`

or

`APPEND [;]`

[d:] [path] = path to search
/X = process Search First, Find First, and EXEC calls
/E = store APPEND path in environment
; = resets the APPEND path to null when used alone

ASSIGN [external command]
2.0

Gives a drive a new name.

Format: `ASSIGN [ a[=] b [...]]`

a = drive to get new name
b = new name

ASSIGN without parameters clears all assignments

Notes: 1.   Don't use colons after the drive letters. With a single assignment you don't have to use the equals sign.

2.   Never use commands like BACKUP, RESTORE, JOIN, LABEL, SUBST, or PRINT while ASSIGN is active. FORMAT, DISKCOPY, and DISKCOMP commands ignore ASSIGN I/O reroutings.

3.   The best way to use ASSIGN is from inside a batch file where the first batch file line makes the new assignment, the second line runs the program requiring the assignment, and the third resets things the way they originally were. In fact, if you can use SUBST instead of ASSIGN, do it.

ATTRIB [external command]
3.0

Modifies some but not all file attributes.

Format: ATTRIB [+R|-R] [+A|-A] [d:][path]filename[.ext] [/S]

+R = make read-only
-R = make not read-only
+A = set archive bit
-A = reset archive bit
[d:] [path]filename.ext = file(s) to change
/S = do all lower-level subdirectories too

When you enter just a filespec after it, ATTRIB will display the status of the archive and read-only settings by printing an A and/or R before the filename if appropriate.

Notes: 1.   Since ATTRIB lets you use wildcards, you may examine the status of all the files in the current directory by entering ATTRIB *.*

2.   By making a file read-only you can prevent it from being changed or erased. Commands like BACKUP and XCOPY can use the archive bit to figure out whether or not the file has changed since you last backed it up. If you use the /M switch with these commands you can make back-ups more efficient by copying only files that have been modified in the interim.

3.   The ATTR program on the accompanying disk displays *all* attributes, not just a few, and lets you modify additional ones not allowed by ATTRIB.

BACKUP [external command]
2.0

Backs up files; can split large files over several floppy disks. Use the RESTORE command to put files back.

Format: BACKUP s:[path][filename[.ext]] t: [/S] [/M] [/A]
[/D:mm-dd-yy] [/T:hh:mm:ss] [/F]
[/L[:[d:][path][logname.[ext]]]

s: [path] [filename[.ext]] = source drive and/or file(s) to back up
t: = target drive
/S = do files in subdirectories also
/M = back up files changed since last BACKUP
/A = add files to backup disk overwriting same files already on it
/D = back up files changed on or after date
/T = back up files changed on or after time on date
/F = format backup disk if necessary (FORMAT.COM must be handy)
/L = create a log file (default is BACKUP.COM)
[d:] [path] [logname.[ext]] = drive/path and filename for log file

Notes: 1.   BACKUP stores files in a special format; you must use the RESTORE command to put them back in their original condition. Version 3.3 stores backup files in one large chunk; earlier versions maintained individual backup files for each file.

2.   Since early BACKUP and RESTORE versions erroneously let you write system files from earlier versions onto disks containing newer versions, be careful when using older versions to restore files.

Version 3.3 can run the DOS FORMAT command (if it's accessible) when you're backing up files onto unformatted disks. Older versions wouldn't, which forced you to have a tall stack of formatted disks handy before you began. Be careful when using the /F option, since the source and target drive sizes must be identical. And don't use BACKUP when drive or directory mixing commands such as JOIN are in effect.

BREAK
2.0

Lets you specify more or less frequent Ctrl-Break checking, or display the current BREAK status.

Format: BREAK [ON | OFF]

ON = break on demand (for programs with little I/O)
OFF = check for break only during I/O functions (default)

BREAK without parameters displays BREAK status.

CD
2.0

See CHDIR.

CHCP
3.3

Selects DOS code page.

Format: CHCP [nnn]

nnn = number of desired code page

Note: You must load NLSFUNC before using CHCP. May need to have COUNTRY.SYS handy.

CHDIR (CD)
2.0

Changes or displays current directory.

Format: CHDIR [d:][path]

or

CD [d:][path]

d: = drive with path to change
path = new path

CHDIR without parameter displays name of current directory.

Notes: 1.   Specifying a directory name without a backslash (\) in front of it
tells DOS to switch into a subdirectory one level lower than the current
directory. So if the current directory is \DOS, the command CD UTILS
will log into \DOS\UTILS. But if you typed CD \UTILS, DOS would
log into a subdirectory called \UTILS one level down from the root directory that had no relation to the \DOS subdirectory.

2.   Entering CD \ will return to the root directory. Entering CD .. will
change to the parent directory one level up toward the root from the current subdirectory. Since the double dot (..) is shorthand for the parent
directory, if you're logged into \DOS\UTILS\PCMAG and you want to
change to \DOS\UTILS\NORTON you could type CD ..\NORTON.

CHKDSK [external command]
1.0

Checks and repairs disks, reports on memory use and file fragmentation,
and can show names and locations of all files on disk.

Format: CHKDSK [d:][path][filename.[ext]] [/F] [/V]

[d:] = drive to check
[path] [filename.[ext]] = file(s) for fragmentation report
/F = fix errors
/V = show all files and paths on disk

CHKDSK *.* will produce a file fragmentation report for all files. To fix
fragmented files (which slow DOS down), copy them to another disk,
erase the originals, then copy them back.

Notes: 1.   Using CHKDSK /V | FIND "FILE.TXT" will locate all occurrences of a file called FILE.TXT on the specified disk.

2.   When CHKDSK reports that it found hidden files, it usually means the two hidden system files (IBMBIO.COM and IBMDOS.COM or their generic MSDOS.SYS and IO.SYS equivalents) and the hidden volume label. If it reports other hidden files that you don't know about, these are probably sneaky copy protection devices. Don't try using ATTR or DEBUG to unhide such files hidden as copy-protection devices; instead try to uninstall the program that hid them. This is necessary because some nasty copy-protection schemes scramble the underlying disk structure before hiding a file, and will put things back to normal only when you use the authorized deinstallation program that came with software.

3.   Don't use CHKDSK on a drive involved with an active alias command such as SUBST, JOIN, or ASSIGN.

CLS
2.0

Clears a 25-line screen.

Format: `CLS`

Notes: 1.   On a color system this will always clear the screen to grey on black (attribute 07) unless ANSI.SYS is active.

2.   Yes, it's hard to believe, but CLS wasn't a part of DOS until version 2.0.

COMMAND
1.0

Loads and runs an additional copy of the COMMAND.COM command processor.

Format: `COMMAND [d:][path] [/P] [/C string] [/E:xxxxx]`

[d:] [path] = drive/path for command processor to start
/P = make new processor permanent
/C = pass command string to new processor
string = any valid DOS command line
/E:xxxxx = number of bytes for environment (160 to 32768)

Notes: 1. You can use COMMAND /C to load a second batch file when running a first batch file and return to the original one when the additional batch file EXITs. And you can use it to pass parameters to the additional batch file. In versions 3.3 or later you can have the more efficient CALL command use other batch files as subroutines.

2. DOS versions earlier than 3.3 used slightly different methods of increasing the environment size. It's a good idea to increase the size past the trifling default of 160 bytes.

COMP
1.0

Compares files (only if both are same size; stops after ten mismatches).

Format:
```
COMP [a:][path][filename[.ext]]
[b:][path][filename[.ext]]
```

[a:][path][filename[.ext]] = primary file(s)
[b:][path][filename[.ext]] = secondary file(s)

Notes: 1. The generic MS-DOS 2.0 FC command is much better than COMP; unfortunately IBM never included FC in PC-DOS versions.

2. Fortunately, this command accepts wildcards. And, if you want to refer to the current directory, you can use the single period (.) shorthand.

COPY
1.0

Copies, updates, and concatenates files, and can copy to devices as well as files.

Format: `COPY [/A] [/B] [a:][path][filename[.ext]] [/A] [/B]`
`[b:][path][filename[.ext]] [/A] [/B] [/V]`

or

`COPY [/A] [/B] [a:][path][filename[.ext]] [/A] [/B]`
`[+[a:][path][filename[.ext]] [ /A] [/B]...]`
`[b:][path][filename[.ext]] [/A] [/B] [/V]`

/A = ASCII; stop at first Ctrl-Z end-of-file marker in source; add Ctrl-Z
   to target
/B = binary; don't treat any Ctrl-Z as an end-of-file marker; instead use
   file length specified by directory
[a:] [path] [filename[.ext]] = source file(s)
[b:] [path] [filename[.ext]] = destination
/V = use primitive CRC verification
+,, /B = when used at end of line for single file updates date and time

Notes: 1.   You can COPY to devices as well as files, so that COPY TEXT.FIL
CON would display the contents of a file called TEXT.FIL onscreen and
COPY TEXT.FIL PRN would print it on the first parallel printer at-
tached to your system.

2.   It's possible to erase or truncate files if you're not careful about
using the COPY command, especially when dealing with long pathnames or concatenating files.

CTTY
2.0

Lets you change the way DOS handles standard I/O.

Format: `CTTY device-name`

device-name = AUX, COM1, COM2, COM3, COM4 to set new console; CON to restore to screen and keyboard.

CTTY NUL = disconnects keyboard and screen; use with care only in
batch files that have a subsequent CTTY CON command or you won't
be able to regain control.

DATE
1.0 as external command; 1.1 as internal command

Reports and sets the system date.

Format: DATE [mm-dd-yy] | [dd-mm-yy] | [yy-mm-dd]

mm = month (1-12)
dd = day (1-31)
yy = year (80-99 or 1980-1999)

DATE without parameters displays the current date (and day of the week). Pressing the Enter key after typing DATE by itself will leave the date unchanged.

Notes: 1. You can use a period, dash, or slash to separate elements; various orders of entry are based on the active COUNTRY selection.

2. DOS won't let you enter a year earlier than 1980 or later than 2079. You may enter two numbers for the year from (19)80 through (19)99 but you'll need four digits and DOS 3.0 or later to go from 2000 to 2079.

3. While DOS will display the day of the week, don't enter the name of the day yourself.

4. Believe it or not, DATE and TIME were external commands in DOS version 1.0. In version 3.3 these will permanently set the CMOS clock in ATs and later systems.

DEL
1.1

Deletes files. [Same as ERASE]

Format: DEL [d:][path]filename[.ext]

[d:][path]filename[.ext] = file(s) to delete

Notes: 1. Global *.* summons a confirming prompt; type N or n if you don't want to erase everything. Be careful if you specify a directory after DEL (e.g., DEL \SUBDIR) since DOS will assume you mean DEL \SUB-DIR*.*

2. Take care when using * wildcards, since DOS stops reading characters on each side of the period when it sees an asterisk. It will interpret the command:

```
DEL *FIL.*NM
```

as DEL *.* which is probably not what you had in mind. Similarly, the command:

```
DEL .
```

tells DOS to erase all files in the current directory.

Use RD or RMDIR to remove subdirectories after deleting all files in them.

3. Be careful when using DEL while a directory or drive alias command such as SUBST, ASSIGN, or JOIN is active. DOS won't let you erase read-only files, so use the ATTRIB command first to remove the read-only attribute.

4. Utilities like Peter Norton's or Paul Mace's can usually recover inadvertently erased files so long as you use these utilities immediately after the erasure.

DIR
1.0

Lists files, sizes, and creation/modification dates and times, as well as branching subdirectories.

Format: DIR [d:][path][filename[.ext]] [/P] [/W]

[d:] [path] [filename[.ext]] = files to list
/P = pause when screen full (23 entries)
/W = wide format (lists filenames without size, time, or date)

Default is DIR *.*

Notes: 1.   While DOS will display all the files with names that begin with S if you type DIR S* it won't copy or delete them all unless you use COPY S*.* or DEL S*.*

2.   DOS identifies subdirectories by putting a <DIR> in the size column. Typing DIR *. will display all such directory entries as well as any files without extensions. These <DIR> entries, including the current subdirectory (which is listed as a single .), are added to the total file count report produced by DIR.

DISKCOMP [external command]
1.0

Compares two entire diskettes for content differences.

Format: `DISKCOMP [a: [b:]] [/1] [/8]`

a: = source drive
b: = target drive
/1 = compare the first side only
/8 = use only eight sectors per track

Note: DOS won't let you DISKCOMP a VDISK, and is picky about which physical disks you can DISKCOMP. And don't use DISKCOMP while drive- or directory-mixing commands such as JOIN, SUBST, or AS-SIGN are in effect.

DISKCOPY [external command]
1.0

Copies an entire diskette and formats the copy if necessary.

Format: `DISKCOPY [a: [b:]] [/1]`

a: = source drive
b: = target drive
/1 = copy the first side only

Entering DISKCOPY without any parameters tells DOS to use the same drive as the source and target, and prompt you when to remove and insert the appropriate disks into this single drive.

Notes: 1.   DOS won't let you DISKCOPY to a VDISK, and is picky about which physical disks you can DISKCOPY from and to. And don't use DISKCOMP while drive- or directory-mixing commands such as JOIN, SUBST, or ASSIGN are in effect.

2.   DISKCOPY is the fastest way to copy similar-sized disks (and it formats on the fly if necessary), but XCOPY is almost as fast and avoids potential fragmentation headaches.

ERASE
1.0

Deletes files. [Same as DEL]

Format: `ERASE [d:][path]filename[.ext]`

[d:][path]filename[.ext] = file(s) to delete

Notes: 1.   Global *.* summons a confirming prompt; type N or n if you don't want to erase everything. Be careful if you specify a directory after ERASE (e.g., ERASE \SUBDIR) since DOS will assume you mean ERASE \SUBDIR*.*

Take care when using * wildcards, since DOS stops reading characters on each side of the period when it sees an asterisk. It will interpret the command:

`ERASE *FIL.*NM`

as ERASE *.* which is probably not what you had in mind. Similarly, the command:

`ERASE .`

tells DOS to erase all files in the current directory.

Use RD or RMDIR to remove subdirectories after deleting all files in them.

2.   Be careful when using ERASE while a directory or drive alias command such as SUBST, ASSIGN, or JOIN is active. DOS won't let you erase read-only files, so use the ATTRIB command first to remove the read-only attribute.

3.   Utilities like Peter Norton's or Paul Mace's can usually recover inadvertently erased files so long as you use these utilities immediately after the erasure.

FASTOPEN [external command]
3.3

Remembers location on disk of recently accessed files/directories for speedier access the next time you need them.

Format: `FASTOPEN c:[=nnn]...`

c: = fixed disk drive
nnn = # entries to remember for c: (10 to 999; default is 34)

Note: Don't use FASTOPEN while directory or drive alias commands such as SUBST, ASSIGN, or JOIN are active. Use FASTOPEN only once each session and be sure you've defined all your active drives before running it. Each additional entry consumes 35 bytes of system memory. Experiment to find the most efficient value; don't just assume the largest one is best.

FDISK [external command]
2.0

Lets you set up, switch, and otherwise manipulate hard disk partitions.

Format: `FDISK`

Note: In version 3.3 and later, FDISK lets you create "extended" partitions to handle drives larger than 32 megabytes.

FIND [external command]
2.0

Locates specific strings of characters in files; can count lines and number them.

Format: `FIND [/V] [/C] [/N] "string"`
`[[d:][path]filename[.ext]...]`

/V = select lines not containing string
/C = display count of matching lines; ignores /N if both /C and /N specified
/N = display line number of matching lines
"string" = search string enclosed in double quotation marks; DOS interprets two quotes in a row as a single quote mark.
[[d:] [path]filename[.ext]...] = file(s) to search

Notes: 1.   Wildcards are not allowed (so you have to use FOR...IN...DO for global searches). However, you can specify several filenames at once at the end of the command.

2.   To count or number all lines, specify a string after the /V option (such as "$#@&") that doesn't occur at all in the file.

3.   Searches are case-sensitive and stop at the first occurrence of a Ctrl-Z end-of-file marker.

FORMAT [external command]
1.0

Prepares a new disk and locks out defective disk areas, then reports the total space, amount of defective space, and available space; optionally adds system files and volume label.

Format: `FORMAT a:[/S] [/1] [/8] [/V] [/B] [/4] [/N:xx]`
`[/T:yy]`

a: = drive with disk to format
/S = copy system files to new disk
/1 = single-sided (5-1/4 inch floppies only)

/8 = eight sectors per track (5-1/4 inch floppies only)
/V = add volume label
/B = eight sectors per track, reserves space for system files later
/4 = format single/double-sided 5-1/4 inch floppy in 1.2M drive
/N:xx = xx sectors per track
/T:yy = yy tracks on the disk

Default is nine or 15 sectors per track depending on the type of diskette. Use /N:9 /T:80 for 720K disk in 1.44M drive.

Notes:

1.   Formatting can destroy the contents of your files. While later DOS versions guard against accidental hard disk formatting, exercise care when using this command, and consider renaming it if beginners use your system. Utilities like Peter Norton's or Paul Mace's can recover most data stored in subdirectories on an inadvertently formatted hard disk.

2.   FORMAT /S will put the three system files, IBMBIO.COM, IBMDOS.COM (or their generic equivalents), and COMMAND.COM on a disk you can boot from. The SYS command by itself will copy the first two system files only, so you'll have to use the COPY command to put COMMAND.COM on the disk.

3.   FORMAT /B will leave room for users to add the hidden system files later, but will format diskettes with eight sectors per track only. This means the maximum size of a 5-1/4 inch diskette formatted with the /B option will be 320K (rather than 360K) minus the room allotted for system files. Actually FORMAT will create nine or 15 sectors per track but tell DOS to use only eight.

4.   The FORMAT command technically performs "high-level" formatting on hard disks; a special kind of "low-level" formatting is performed by the manufacturer.

5.   FORMAT ignores ASSIGN drive and directory shufflings, but be careful not to try it when SUBST or JOIN are active.

GRAFTABL [external command]
3.0

Loads high-bit ASCII graphics table (characters with values above decimal 128) into memory for CGA mode only; supports code pages.

Format: `GRAFTABL [437 | 860 | 863 | 865 | /STATUS]`

437 = United States code page (default)
860 = Portugal code page
863 = Canada (Fr.) code page
865 = Norway/Denmark code page
/STATUS = show current code page

GRAPHICS [external command]
2.0

Allows Shift-PrtSc screen "dump" of graphics image to IBM-compatible graphics printer.

Format: `GRAPHICS [printer type] [/R] [/B] [/LCD]`

[printer type] =
COLOR1 — IBM Color Printer with black ribbon
COLOR4 — IBM Color Printer with red, green, blue, black
COLOR8 — IBM Color Printer with black, cyan, magenta, yellow
COMPACT — IBM Compact Printer
GRAPHICS — IBM Graphics Printer or Proprinter
THERMAL — IBM Convertible Printer
/R — reverse black and white
/B — print background color (COLOR4, COLOR8 only)
/LCD — print from IBM Convertible LCD display

JOIN [external command]
3.1

Joins a disk drive with a directory on other drive.

Format: `JOIN`

or

`JOIN a: c:\directory`

or

```
JOIN a: /D
```

a: = drive to join
c:\directory = directory to join to (at root only and only one level deep
    maximum)
/D = disconnect a JOIN

JOIN without parameters displays JOIN status.

Note: Be careful when using commands like SUBST or ASSIGN while drive
or directory alias commands like this are active. Don't use BACKUP,
RESTORE, FORMAT, DISKCOPY, or DISKCOMP while JOIN is active.

KEYB [external command]
3.3

Loads a non-U.S. keyboard template.

Format: `KEYB [xx[,[yyy],[[d:][path]filename[.ext]]]]`

xx = keyboard code
yyy = code page for character set
[d:] [path]filename[.ext] = location of KEYBOARD.SYS

Notes: 1.   This replaces individual commands such as KEYBUK and KEYBIT
introduced in DOS version 3.0.

2.   DOS lets you shift back and forth between the standard keyboard
and any new one specified by KEYB by pressing Ctrl-Alt-F1 for the
U.S. version and Ctrl-Alt-F2 for the foreign version.

LABEL [external command]
3.0

Sets, changes, or deletes a disk's volume label

Format: `LABEL [d:][volume label]`

d: = drive to label
volume label = 1 to 11 characters

Notes: 1.   You can also create a volume label when you first format a disk by using the FORMAT /V option. It's important to add a label to hard disks, since this provides an added layer of protection against accidentally formatting the hard disk.

2.   Earlier versions allowed lowercase labels, but DOS now automatically capitalizes them. And it lets you insert spaces in the volume name, although in most other respects it follows the same rules (no *, >, or + etc. characters) as with filenames.

3.   Don't use LABEL when drive alias commands such as SUBST or ASSIGN are active.

MD
2.0

See MKDIR.

MKDIR (MD)
2.0

Creates a subdirectory.

Format: MKDIR [d:]path

or

MD [d:]path

[d:] = drive for new subdirectory
path = subdirectory to make (total 63-character limit including backslashes)

Notes: 1.   Be careful when creating directories if drive alias commands such as JOIN, ASSIGN, or SUBST are active.

2.   Specifying a new directory name without a backslash (\) in front of it tells DOS to create a subdirectory one level lower than the current directory. So if the current directory is \DOS, the command MD UTILS will create a subdirectory called \DOS\UTILS. But if you typed MD \UTILS, DOS would create a subdirectory called \UTILS one level down from the root directory that had no relation to the \DOS subdirectory.

MODE [external command]
1.0 (with lots of upgrades)

---

1.   Sets the printer mode.

Format: MODE LPT#[:] [n] [,[m] [,P]]

       # = printer number (1, 2, or 3)
       n = characters per line (80 or 132)
       m = vertical lines per inch (6 or 8)
       P = continuous retry on timeout errors

2.   Sends parallel printer output to a serial port.

Format: MODE LPT#[:]=COMx

       # = printer number (1, 2, or 3)
       x = COM adapter number (1, 2, 3, or 4)

Note: You must first initialize your COM port with the following version of the MODE command, including ,P at the end.

3.   Sets the serial communication mode (protocols).

Format: MODE COM#[:] baud [,[parity] [,[databits]
        [,[stopbits] [,P]]]]

       # = COM adapter being set (1, 2, 3, or 4)
       baud = baud rate (110, 150, 300, 600, 1200, 2400, 4800, 9600, 19200; only first two digits of each rate are required)
       parity = N, O, or E (for None, Odd, Even; default is Even)
       databits = 7 or 8 (default is 7)
       stopbits = 1 or 2 (default is 2 if 110 baud, 1 if not)

P = indicates COM port is being used for printer; continuously retries on timeout errors

Note: You must first initialize your COM port with this version of the MODE command, including ,P at the end, before sending parallel printer output to a serial port.

4. Sets the video mode.

Format: MODE n

or

MODE [n],m[,T]

n = video mode (40, 80, BW40, BW80, CO40, CO80, MONO)
m = R or L; shift display right or left one or two characters
T = shows test pattern for aligning display

Note: MODE doesn't support any of the newer EGA and VGA video modes.

5. Prepares code pages (foreign fonts)

Format: MODE device CODEPAGE PREPARE=((cplist)
[d:][path]filename[.ext])

or

MODE device CODEPAGE PREPARE=((cp)
[d:][path]filename[.ext])

device = CON, PRN, LPT1, LPT2, or LPT3
cp = a single code page number
cplist = code page number or list of numbers; a list must be surrounded by parentheses
[d:] [path]filename[.ext] = CPI file containing code pages

Note: You may substitute CP for CODEPAGE and PREP for PREPARE.

6. Selects code pages.

Format: MODE device CODEPAGE SELECT=cp

device = CON, PRN, LPT1, LPT2, or LPT3
cp = code page (437, 850, 860, 863, 865)

Note: You may substitute CP for CODEPAGE and SEL for SELECT.

7. Displays the active code page.

Format: `MODE device CODEPAGE [/STATUS]`

device = CON, PRN, LPT1, LPT2, or LPT3

Note: You may substitute CP for CODEPAGE and STA for STATUS.

8. Refreshes the code page.

Format: `MODE device CODEPAGE REFRESH`

device = CON, PRN, LPT1, LPT2, or LPT3

Note: You may substitute CP for CODEPAGE and REF for REFRESH.

MORE [external command]
2.0

Displays files one 25-line screenful at a time.

Format: `MORE < FILE.NAM`

or

`TYPE FILE.NAM | MORE`

where FILE.NAM is the file you want to examine one 25-line screenful
at a time. If the entire file hasn't yet been displayed, DOS will print the
message — More— . Press any key at this point to have it display
another screenful.

NLSFUNC [external command]
3.3

Lets you use the CHCP command to pick code pages.

Format: `NLSFUNC [[d:][path]filename[.ext]]`

[d:] [path]filename[.ext] = COUNTRY.SYS file or equivalent
must load before using CHCP

PATH
2.0

Tells DOS to extend its normal search so that it includes a specified list of drives and directories when trying to run an executable program entered at the command line.

Format: `PATH [[d:]path[[;[d:]path...]]]`

or

`PATH ;`

[d:]path = drive/path for search list; separate multiple paths with semi-colons
; = resets the search path to null (so DOS will not include any additional drives or directories in the search) when used as PATH ;

PATH without parameters displays the current PATH list of drives and directories to search for executable files.

Note: PATH works with COM, EXE, or BAT files only; the APPEND command lets DOS search for nonexecutable files.

PRINT [external command]
2.0

Prints files; can handle background printing and groups (queues) of files.

Format: `PRINT [/D:device] [/B:buffsiz] [/U:busytick]`
`[/M:maxtick] [/S:timeslice] [/Q:quesiz] [/C] [/T]`
`[/P] [[d:][path][filename][.ext]...]`

/D:device = print device (default is PRN; must be first one specified)
/B:buffsiz = bytes for internal buffer (default is 512)
/U:busytick = ticks to wait for printer to be available (default is 1)
/M:maxtick = ticks to use for printing (1-255, default is 2)
/S:timeslice = ticks to use for system, not printer (1-255, default is 8)
/Q:quesiz = number of files in print queue (1-32, default is 10)
/C = lets you cancel file(s) in queue
/T = terminate; cancel entire print queue
/P = print preceding file and add all files to queue until a /C or Enter
[d:] [path] [filename] [.ext] = file(s) to print; wildcards are okay

PRINT without any parameters displays the list of filenames currently in the queue. "Tick" means one .055 second clock cycle.

Notes: 1.   Disables Shift-PrtSc and Ctrl-PrtSc while PRINT is printing.

2.   PRINT adds a formfeed command after each print job to start each new file at the top of a page, and expands tabs (by inserting spaces) to eight-column boundaries.

3.   If you don't use a /D option the first time you execute the command, PRINT will pause and ask which printer you want to use. While you can specify PRN (or LPT1) by pressing Enter at this point, using the /D switch saves a step.

4.   See Chapter 14 for an explanation of how this works and what settings are best.

PROMPT
2.0

Sets the DOS prompt; transmits strings to ANSI.SYS.

Format: PROMPT [prompt-text]

PROMPT without parameters resets the default DOS A> or C> prompt. To see the active PROMPT string, type SET.

prompt-text can contain the following meta-string characters, preceded by a $ sign:

$ $ character
T   time
D   date
P   current directory
V   version number
N   default drive letter
G   > character
L   < character
B | character
Q   = character
H   backspace (erases previous character)
E   Escape character
_   CR/LF sequence (jumps to next lower line on screen)

DOS treats all other characters not on the above list as nulls.

Notes: 1.   Every hard disk user should use PROMPT $P: or PROMPT PG to display the current subdirectory.

You can use the PROMPT command to send otherwise hard-to-type Escape sequences to ANSI.SYS for extended screen and keyboard control. However, doing so will change any custom prompt you may have assigned. To avoid this, first type:

```
SET | FIND "PROMPT" > RESET.BAT
```

to store your prompt, then have PROMPT issue the ANSI escape sequence, then enter RESET to restore your original prompt, and finally erase RESET.BAT. Or have batch file store it as environment variable, with SET OLDP=%PROMPT% then later use SET PROMPT=%OLDP%.

2.   To use ANSI.SYS you must include a line in the CONFIG.SYS file that was active when you booted that says DEVICE=\DOS\ANSI.SYS (if you store ANSI.SYS in your \DOS subdirectory). See Chapter 9.

3.   You may use either the uppercase or lowercase versions of the above meta-strings (so that $P works just as well as $p). However, ANSI is picky about the case of its special commands.

RECOVER [external command]
2.0

Recovers individual defective files or every file and subdirectory on a disk. But don't use it to recover entire disk unless as last resort.

Format: RECOVER [d:] [path]filename[.ext]

or

RECOVER d:

[d:][path]filename[.ext] = file(s) to recover
d: = recover all files on d: [*Use with extreme caution!*]

Notes: 1.   *Beware* — Don't use this for a whole disk! Use it on specific files only unless there's no hope left for the disk. If you try it without specifying a single filename, RECOVER will turn your entire disk structure into mush.

2.   In addition, RECOVER puts its recovered files in the root directory. Since a typical 5-1/4 inch 360K floppy disk root directory can hold a maximum of 112 files, you may have to repeat the process several times, delete files from the damaged disk, etc. Use only as an absolute last resort.

REN
1.1

See RENAME.

RENAME (REN)
1.0

Renames files.

Format: RENAME [d:][path]filename[.ext] filename[.ext]

[d:] [path]filename[.ext] = file(s) to rename
filename[.ext] = new name

Note: You can use wildcards in the filename. If by chance an application (or a program such as BASIC) has created a filename with a space in it, you can use a wildcard to remove the space. So if your directory contains a file called FILE 1.TXT you can type:

REN FILE?1.TXT FILE1.TXT

REPLACE [external command]
3.2

Selectively copies or adds/updates files.

Format: REPLACE [a:][path]filename[.ext] [b:][path]
[/A] [/P] [/R] [/S] [/W]

[a:] [path]filename[.ext] = source file(s)
[b:] [path] = target drive/path
/A = copy source files that don't exist on target
/P = prompt you when a similar file is found on the target
/R = replace read-only files on target
/S = search all directories on target for source matches
/W = wait for you to insert source disk

Note: You can't use /S and /A at the same time.

RESTORE [external command]
2.0

Restores files saved by the BACKUP command.

Format: RESTORE a: [c:][path]filename[.ext] [/S] [/P]
[/B:mm-dd-yy] [/A:mm-dd-yy] [/M] [/N] [/L:time]
[/E:time]

a: = drive with BACKUP source

[c:] [path]filename[.ext] = destination

/S = restore all files in subdirectories too

/P = prompt before restoring files changed since last backup or marked read-only; respond with Y or N

/B = restore if changed on or before date specified

/A = restore if changed on or after date specified

/M = restore if changed or deleted since backup

/N = restore if no longer on target

/L = restore if changed at or after time specified

/E = restore if changed at or before time specified

Notes: 1.   Don't use /B, /A, and /N at the same time. And the DOS manual warns against using RESTORE when a drive or directory alias command such as SUBST, JOIN, or ASSIGN was active when you ran BACKUP. So what are you supposed to do then?

2.   Since early BACKUP and RESTORE versions erroneously let you write system files from earlier versions onto disks containing newer versions, be careful when using older versions to restore files.

3.   BACKUP stores files in a special format; you must use the RESTORE command to put them back in their original condition. Version 3.3 stores backup files in one large chunk; earlier versions maintained individual backup files for each file.

RD
2.0

See RMDIR.

RMDIR (RD)
2.0

Removes a directory.

Format: `RMDIR [d:]path`

or

```
RD [d:]path
```

[d:] = drive to remove from
path = directory to remove

Notes: 1.   DOS won't let you remove a directory if it contains any files (including hidden ones) or lower-level directories.

2.   If DOS tells you that the directory is not empty when you try using RD or RMDIR to remove a subdirectory, and you've already erased all the files in it and used RD to remove any lower-level directories, the culprit is probably a hidden file inside the subdirectory. If the subdirectory contained a program that used a copy-protection scheme, try to uninstall the program. If you're sure that no copy protection scheme was employed, use the ATTR program on the accompanying disk to unhide the file, then erase it. RD or RMDIR should now work.

SELECT [external command]
3.0

Sets up DOS on a new disk.

Format: `SELECT [[A: | B:] [d:][path]] xxx yy`

A: or B: = source drive (default is A:)
[d:] [path] = target drive and path (default is B: root directory)
xxx = country code
yy = keyboard code

Note: Use this command only on brand new disks (if at all) since it runs the DOS FORMAT command as part of its overall operation.

SET
2.0

Puts strings into the environment; displays environment strings.

Format: `SET [name=[parameter]]`

name = environment variable (automatically uppercased)
parameter = value for environment variable
SET with just name (and equals sign) clears name from environment
SET without name or parameters displays environment settings

Notes: 1.   The environment always contains COMSPEC= and probably
PATH= and PROMPT= variables. Many applications can store and read
environment variables. Batch files in later versions of DOS can read
them by sandwiching them between single % signs (e.g., %PROMPT%).

2.   DOS uses a paltry 160 bytes (or 127 bytes under certain circumstances) for the environment size. See COMMAND [/E:xxxxx] for instructions on increasing the default size.

SHARE [external command]
3.0

Supports file sharing.

Format: SHARE [/F:filespace] [/L:locks]

/F: = bytes to allocate for sharing information (default is 2048); each
    open file takes length of filename plus 11 more bytes
/L:locks = locks to allocate (default is 20)

SORT [external command]
2.0

Sorts lines of text inside files starting at the column specified.

Format: SORT [/R] [/+ n]

/R = sort in reverse order
/+ n = sort starting with column n

Notes: 1.   DOS treates lowercase letters the same as uppercase ones in version
3.x; but earlier versions assumed uppercase letters came before lowercase ones. And DOS 3.x can treat accented high-bit foreign-language
characters the same as their unaccented cousins.

2. SORT doesn't expand tabs (it treats them as single characters) and can't handle files longer than 63K.

SUBST [external command]
3.1

Assigns a drive letter to a path.

Format: SUBST e: c:path

or

SUBST e: /D

or

SUBST

e: = drive letter to refer to path
c:path = drive/path referred to (nicknamed)
/D = deletes substitution of e:

SUBST without parameters displays list of substitutions in effect.

Notes: 1. Since SUBST lets you use short drive letters to refer to long paths, you can use it to extend a PATH or APPEND command past the normal character limit.

2. The default number of drives is five (A: through E:). To use a SUBST drive letter higher than E: you must first include a LASTDRIVE= command in the CONFIG.SYS file that was active when you booted.

3. DOS commands such as CHDIR (and CD), MKDIR (and MD), RMDIR (and RD), APPEND, and PATH can work differently when SUBST is active. And all sorts of DOS commands, such as ASSIGN, FORMAT, BACKUP, RESTORE, LABEL, JOIN, DISKCOPY, DISKCOMP, and FDISK have trouble with SUBST, so don't use them while SUBST is in effect.

SYS [external command]
1.0

Puts the two hidden system files onto disk.

Format: `SYS d:`

where d: is the disk you want to contain the IBMBIO.COM and
IBMDOS.COM system files (or their generic equivalents).

Notes: 1.   SYS doesn't transfer COMMAND.COM; you must use COPY
COMMAND.COM d: to do so. On the other hand, FORMAT /S will
transfer both the pair of hidden system files and COMMAND.COM.

2.   DOS is picky about where certain system files are located on the
disk. Since software vendors aren't allowed to give away the DOS system files on the diskettes they sell, many vendors leave space on the disk
for you to use SYS to copy these system files to the proper place on the
disk.

TIME
1.0 as external command; 1.1 as internal command

Reports and sets the system time.

Format: `TIME [hh:mm[:ss[.xx]]]`

hh = hours (0-23)
mm = minutes (0-59)
ss = seconds (0-59)
xx = hundredths of a second (0-99)

TIME without parameters displays the current time. Pressing the Enter
key after typing TIME by itself will leave the time unchanged.

Notes: 1.   So long as you enter at least the hour after the TIME command, you
can skip all the rest of the settings. So entering TIME 8 will set the time
to 8:00:00.00.

2.   TIME uses a 24-hour clock, so 8 p.m. is actually 20:00:00.00. Also, while you can enter hundredths of seconds, your system's clock is actually not that accurate, since it divides each second into just over 18 slices rather than 100.

3.   You may use a period or colon to separate hours, minutes, and seconds. And you may use a period or a comma to separate seconds from hundredths, depending on whether you're using U.S. or foreign settings.

4.   Believe it or not, DATE and TIME were external commands in DOS version 1.0. In version 3.3 these will permanently set the CMOS clock in ATs and later systems.

TREE [external command]
2.0

Displays all the directory paths.

Format: TREE [c:] [/F]

[c:] = drive to display
[/F] = show file names in all directories

Notes: 1.   Use the MORE command (TREE I MORE) to pause the display a screenful at a time.

2.   A picture is worth a K of words, especially here. Use the VTREE or RN utilities on the accompanying disk instead of TREE, since they'll provide a graphical representation of your disk structure rather than just a long list of names. And use CHKDSK /V rather than TREE /F to display all your files, especially if you're redirecting the output of the process to a file.

TYPE
1.0

Displays a file by sending it to standard output (default is the screen).

Format: TYPE [d:] [path]filename[.ext]

[d:][path]filename[.ext] = file to display

Notes: 1.   TYPE wraps long lines after 80 columns and expands tab characters to eight-column boundaries. It stops when it reaches any Ctrl-Z end-of-file marker.

2.   You can't use wildcard characters in type commands but can type several files one after the other by using a FOR...IN...DO command. Or you could use the COPY /B filespec CON command to display several files in succession (substituting the particular wildcard construction for filespec in this example). COPY /B also lets you display a file past a Ctrl-Z character.

3.   You can redirect the output of TYPE to another file (which is sometimes handy in batch files) or to a device such as a printer.

VER
2.0

Reports the DOS version.

Format: VER

Note: DOS refers to the single digit to the left of the period as the major version number, and the pair of digits to the right of the period as the minor version number.

VERIFY
2.0

Verifies disk writes (in a primitive way).

Format: VERIFY [ON | OFF]

ON = verify that data was written correctly
OFF = do not verify (default)

VERIFY without parameters displays VERIFY status.

Note: This performs a CRC check only, which indicates whether or not DOS wrote something to the disk. It doesn't perform the byte-by-byte comparison that COMP does. COPY /V performs the same primitive checking process.

VOL
2.0

Display the disk's volume label (set by FORMAT /V or LABEL).

Format: `VOL [d:]`

[d:] = display label of which drive

XCOPY [external command]
3.2

Copies and backs up files selectively.

Format:
```
XCOPY [a:][path]filename[.ext]
[b:][path][filename[.ext]] [/A] [/D] [/E] [/M]
[/P] [/S] [/V] [/W]
```

or

```
D XCOPY [a:]path[filename[.ext]]
[b:][path][filename[.ext]] [/A] [/D] [/E] [/M]
[/P] [/S] [/V] [/W]
```

or

```
D XCOPY a:[path][filename[.ext]]
[b:] [path][filename[.ext]] [/A] [/D] [/E] [/M]
[/P] [/S] [/V] [/W]
```

[a:] [path] [filename[.ext]] = source
[b:] [path] [filename[.ext]] = target

/A = copy only if archive bit set
/D:mm-dd-yy = copy if date same or later
/E = create subdirectories on target even if they end up empty
/M = copy modified files and reset archive bit
/P = prompt before copying each; respond with Y or N
/S = copy files in current directory and all lower subdirectories and
    create directories on target only if not empty
/V = verify
/W = wait for source disk

Notes: 1.   XCOPY is vastly better than COPY, since it avoids the repetitive
disk churning exhibited by COPY. XCOPY uses all available low
memory and reads lots of files in one gulp before writing them to disk.
Even better, it can reproduce the subdirectory structure of the source
disk onto the target disk, and can thread its way down a long line of subdirectories while it works.

2.   While most DOS utilities were created by Microsoft, this one was
written by IBM, so it's not on some generic DOS disks.

3.   DISKCOPY is the fastest way to copy similar-sized disks (and it formats on the fly if necessary), but XCOPY is nearly as fast and avoids
potential fragmentation headaches.

4.   The /M option lets you use XCOPY as superior backup utility.

DOS 3.3 CONFIG.SYS Commands

The following commands are used only in the main CONFIG.SYS system configuration
file. They have to be in the file when you boot, so you can't change them after starting
up and expect DOS to know about them unless you reboot after the change.
    To take advantage of these, use the form:

```
DEVICE[=]number
```

or

```
DEVICE[=]status
```

or

```
DEVICE[=][d:][path]filename.ext
```

You may substitute a DOS delimiter such as a space or semicolon in place of the equals sign. The CONFIG.SYS file must be a text (pure-ASCII) file containing nothing other than the letters, numbers, and punctuation that you can type directly from the keyboard. And unless you really know what you're doing, your CONFIG.SYS file must be in the root directory of your startup disk.

As with other DOS commands, the syntax and available features differ for versions earlier than 3.3.

BREAK
2.0

Allows extended Ctrl-Break checking.

Format: BREAK = [ON | OFF]

ON = check during any DOS function
OFF = check only during I/O functions

Note: Use BREAK=ON for processes with little I/O; avoid it when using applications that have their own use for Ctrl-C.

BUFFERS
2.0

Sets the number of disk buffers.

Format: BUFFERS = x

x = number of buffers (1-99)

Notes: 1. Each buffer adds 528 bytes to the size of the resident portion of DOS. Don't use BUFFERS if you're running a commercial disk cache program.

2. The default number of buffers is 2 to 15 depending on hardware configuration. You'll have to experiment to see what's best for your own system, but you should try numbers like 20 or 30 for newer, more powerful systems.

COUNTRY
3.0

Specifies country-specific data.

Format: `COUNTRY = xxx, [yyy], [d:] [path]filename[.ext]`

or

`COUNTRY = xxx, [yyy]`

xxx = international telephone country code
yyy = code page; each country has two
[d:][path]filename[.ext] = name of COUNTRY data file

Note: The default country code is 001 for U.S. systems (and the default code page is 437). The number of the country is the international telephone dialing prefix (001 to 999 in recent versions).

DEVICE
3.0

Installs the five device drivers given below.

Format: `DEVICE=[d:] [path]filename[.ext]`

[d:][path]filename[.ext] = file containing device driver

1.   ANSI.SYS — Extended keyboard and screen device driver (2.0)

Format: `DEVICE=[d:] [path]ANSI.SYS`

2.   DISPLAY.SYS — Display code page switching device driver (3.3)

Format: `DEVICE=[d:] [path]DISPLAY.SYS`
`CON[:]=(type[, [hwcp] [,n]])`

or

```
DEVICE=[d:][path]DISPLAY.SYS
CON[:]=(type[,[hwcp][,(n,m)]])
```

type = MONO, CGA, LCD, EGA (use EGA for PS/2)
hwcp = hardware code page (437, 850, 860, 863, or 865)
n = number of prepared code pages (0-12) For MONO and CGA,
    n must be 0
m = number of subfonts per page (U.S. users don't need this (whew))

3. DRIVER.SYS — Disk device access-provider device driver (3.2)

Format:
```
DEVICE=[d:][path]DRIVER.SYS /D:ddd[/T:ttt][/S:ss]
[/H:hh][/C][/N][/F:f]
```

/D:ddd = physical drive number of (diskette 0-127, fixed 128-255); 0 is
    A:; 2 must be external; first physical hard disk must be 128
/T:ttt = tracks per side (1-999, default is 80)
/S:ss = sectors per track (1-99, default is 9)
/H:hh = number of heads/sides (1-99, default is 2)
/C = changeline support required on AT and later only
/N = nonremovable block device (hard disk)
/F:f = form factor (0=160K–360K; 1=1.2M; 2=720K; 7=1.44M)
(Use SUBST rather than DRIVER.SYS for IBM hard drives.)

4. PRINTER.SYS — Printer code page switcher device driver (3.3)

Format:
```
DEVICE=[d:][path]PRINTER.SYS
LPT#[:]=(type[,[hwcp][,n]])
```

or

```
DEVICE=[d:][path]PRINTER.SYS LPT#[:]=
(type[,[(hwcp1,hwcp2,...)][,n]])
```

LPT# = printer 1, 2, or 3
type = 4201 (IBM Proprinter) or 5202 (IBM Quietwriter III)
hwcp = hardware code page (437, 850, 860, 863, or 865)
n = number of additional prepared code pages (0-12)

5. VDISK.SYS — Virtual disk (RAMdisk) device driver (3.0)

Format:
```
DEVICE=VDISK.SYS [comment][bbb][comment][sss]
[comment][ddd][/E[:m]]
```

comment = string of ASCII characters 32-126 except slash /
bbb = disk size in Kbytes (default is 64)
sss = sector size in bytes (128 (default), 256, 512)
ddd = maximum directory entries (2-512, default is 64)
/E = use extended memory
m = extended memory sectors transferred at once (1-8)
(You can't use DISKCOPY on this virtual disk.)

FCBS
3.0

Specifies the number of concurrently open files using file control blocks (FCBs).

Format: FCBS = m,n

m = maximum number of files opened by FCBs at once (1-255, default is 4)
n = files protected from auto-closing if program tries to open more than m files (0-255, default is 0)

(Used primarily with SHARE or networks.)

FILES
2.0

Specifies the maximum number of file handles open at once.

Format: FILES = x

x = 8-255 (default is 8)

Note: DOS uses two methods for file access — file control blocks (FCBs) and file handles. The CONFIG.SYS FCBS command deals with file control blocks (the older system). The FILES command deals with handles (the newer and preferable method).

LASTDRIVE
3.0

Specifies the largest usable drive letter.

Format: `LASTDRIVE = x`

x = letter A-Z (default is E)

Note: Colons aren't required after the drive letter. This command is especially handy when used with SUBST. Each additional drive above E: takes up 81 bytes of RAM.

SHELL
2.0

Specifies substitute for COMMAND.COM, and allows modification of environment size.

Format: `SHELL = [d:][path]filename[.ext] [parm1] [parm2]`

Parameters for COMMAND.COM:

/E:xxxxx = number of bytes in environment (160-32768; default is 160 — different syntax in earlier versions)
/P = keeps COMMAND.COM loaded and runs AUTOEXEC.BAT

STACKS
3.2

Sets stack resources, allowing multiple interrupts to keep interrupting each other without crashing the system.

Format: `STACKS = n,s`

n = stack frames (0, 8-64)
s = frame size in bytes (0, 32-512)

0 means no dynamic STACK support. Defaults are 0,0 for PC, XT, Portable; 9,128 for rest.

DOS 3.3 Batch File Commands

The following commands are used primarily in batch files, although some (such as FOR...IN...DO) may also be used in slightly different format directly at the DOS prompt.

Because DOS batch file commands provide the muscle of a small, powerful, and slightly complex programming language, a detailed batch command help section follows this section.

Replaceable Parameter

Format: %n

n = 0 to 9 (refers to position of parameter on command line)

%0 is always the DOS command itself; %1 is first parameter after the command. Use SHIFT for more than %9 parameters.

Environment Variable

Format: %name%

name = environment variable

This lets batch files work with variable values stored in the DOS environment. See the DOS SET command in the main command section for details on inserting such values into the environment.

@

Prevents following command on that one line from displaying.

Format: @command

batch-line = command to execute without display when ECHO is ON

The most common use for this is starting a batch file with @ECHO OFF (in version 3.3 and later) to suppress command displays without having this command itself appear onscreen.

CALL

Runs another batch file and then returns to first batch file.

Format: CALL [d:][path]filename

[d:][path] = drive/path for additional batch file

This is similar to COMMAND /C but is more efficient in that it retains the ECHO state, is easier to break out of, and executes faster. It also makes it easier to work with environment settings.

ECHO

Controls message display.

Format: ECHO [ON | OFF | message]

ON = show lines as they execute
OFF = do not show lines
message = message to display

ECHO without any parameters after it displays the current display state.

You can use ECHO to redirect output into a new file called FILE.NAM by tacking on > FILE.NAM.

FOR

Lets you execute DOS commands repeatedly.

Format: FOR %%variable IN (set) DO command [%%variable]

%%variable = variable name
(set) = list of files; wildcards will work
command = DOS command optionally using %%variable

If you use this command outside of a batch file (directly at the DOS prompt), use single % signs rather than the double %% signs required by the batch processor.

GOTO

Transfers control of execution to an area of the batch file starting with the label specified.

Format: `GOTO [:]LABEL`

LABEL = a text string similar to a filename but starting with a colon. You may include the colon here as well but it's not necessary.

See the "LABEL" entry.

IF

Executes commands conditionally.

Format: `IF [NOT] EXIST [d:][path]filename[.ext] command`

or

`IF [NOT] string1 == string2 command`

or

`IF [NOT] ERRORLEVEL n command`

NOT = reverses logical condition
EXIST = TRUE if the specified file exists
string1 = = string2 = TRUE if two strings are identical
ERRORLEVEL n = TRUE if previous program's exit code >= n
command = DOS command line, executed only if TRUE

This is one of the most powerful (and complex) batch commands, and one requiring the most explanation and help. For instance, while IF ER-RORLEVEL allows user intervention in batch files, DOS doesn't provide any direct method for processing user entries. See the longer batch help section that follows for details.

Note that string comparisons require double = = signs.

LABEL

Place marker for GOTO.

Format: :STRING

STRING = 8 characters significant

Label names generally follow the same kinds of rules as DOS filenames, except that a period (.) is not allowed. However, different DOS versions have their own peculiarities, so be sure to read the following help section for details.

PAUSE

Pauses execution and waits for a keypress.

Format: PAUSE [remark]

remark = message to display at pause

If you don't enter a new remark, DOS will print its familiar "Strike a key when ready . . . " message. Press any key at this point to proceed.

REM

Remark or comment.

Format: REM [remark]

remark = text up to 123 characters

Lines beginning with REM don't display when ECHO is OFF.

SHIFT

Allows over standard ten %-parameters %0 through %9.

Format: `SHIFT`

This also lets you move the value of a replaceable parameter down one step at a time (e.g., from %4 to %3 to %2). When you do this you'll lose the value of the lowest replaceable parameter, %0. If you need to retain a lower value you can use the SET command to store it in the DOS environment as %VAR% variable before executing SHIFT.

Batch File Help

To do the following in a batch file:	*Use the following command:*
Prevent commands from displaying as they execute	Preface all the commands you want not to display with an initial line in your batch file: ECHO OFF In DOS 3.3 or later, you can prevent any line from displaying by prefacing it with a @ sign. If for some reason you want to execute a program that has a name beginning with an @ sign, be sure to add an extra @ in front of it when you refer to it in the batch file. ECHO OFF will also suppress the DOS prompt if you execute this command outside of a batch file.
Make sure commands display as they execute	Preface any commands you want to display with ECHO ON (ECHO ON is the default state)
Display a message	ECHO *message* Enter ECHO, a space, and then up to 122 characters including letters, numbers, punctuation, and

any "high-bit" ASCII characters with values over 127. These high-bit characters can dress up your screen by adding boxes and borders. You may enter these characters by holding down the Alt key and then typing in the 3-digit ASCII code for each on the number pad (not the top row number keys), and then releasing the Alt key. Or you can use ANSI.SYS to redefine certain shifted keys to produce these box and border characters.

If you want to use a character that has a special DOS meaning, such as < or |, enclose that character inside quotation marks. If you don't, DOS will think you're trying to pipe or redirect something in the middle of the batch file and become confused.

DOS treats certain characters as delimiters that separate parameters and commands. So be careful when using ECHO to display strings of commas, equals signs, or semicolons, which batch files treat as spaces. In such cases DOS will think you're following the word ECHO with nothing but spaces and that you want to know whether ECHO is set to OFF or ON.

In addition, it treats percent signs as part of environment variables or replaceable parameters, and tosses every other one. So if you try running a batch file like:

```
ECHO OFF
ECHO Watch out for --
ECHO commas:
ECHO ,,,,,,,,,,
ECHO equals signs:
ECHO ==========
ECHO semicolons:
ECHO ;;;;;;;;;;
ECHO percent signs:
ECHO %%%%%%%%%%
```

you'll get:

```
Watch out for --
commas:
ECHO is off
equals signs:
ECHO is off
semicolons:
ECHO is off
percent signs:
%%%%%
```

Display a blank line

Unfortunately this varies from system to system. And the "rules" are maddeningly haphazard:

Under later versions of DOS, you can print blank lines in your batch files by entering any of the characters with ASCII values 0, 1, 2, 3, 4, 5, 6, 7, 8, 11, 12, 14, 15, 16, 17, 18, 19, 20, 21, 22, 23, 24, 25, 27, 28, 29, 30, 31, 34, 43, 46, 47, 58, 91, or 93 right after the word ECHO, without any intervening space (as is ECHO: or ECHO[ ).

Many of these characters are difficult to enter from the keyboard, but under many versions of DOS 3.x you may follow ECHO directly with these blank-producing characters:

```
" + . / : [ ] |
```

Under DOS 3.x you can also follow ECHO with a space and then one of the ASCII characters 0, 8, or 255.

Under version 2.x you can follow ECHO directly with any of the ASCII characters 0, 1, 2, 3, 4, 5, 6, 7, 8, 9, 10, 11, 12, 14, 15, 16, 17, 18, 19, 20, 21, 22, 23, 24, 25, 27, 28, 29, 30, 31, 32, 34, 43, 44, 47, 58, 59, 61, 91, 92, and 93 — and then add an extra space. If you forget the extra space at the end this technique won't work at all.

You can also generate blank lines by following ECHO with a space, and then one of a short list of characters: 0, 8, 9, 32, and 255. Under DOS 3.x, characters 9 and 32 won't work. In both cases you don't need to slap on an additional space at the end of the line.

The safest way in most versions is to use ASCII character 0 and a space, in either order. You can generate a character 0 in DOS by pressing the F7 key.

See the current ECHO ON or OFF state	ECHO

Entering ECHO on a line by itself will produce an "ECHO is ON" or "ECHO is OFF" message. DOS may interpret other ECHO commands, such as:

```
ECHO =======
```

as similar requests for the current state of ECHO, since it interprets characters like equals signs, spaces, commas, and semicolons as blanks to ignore under certain circumstances.

Create a new file containing a line of text	ECHO *yourtext* > *newfile*

where *newfile* is a brand new file that will contain the text *yourtext*.

Append text to an existing file	ECHO *yourtext* >> *oldfile*

where *oldfile* is an existing file and *yourtext* is the text you want to add to this file.

Let users enter commands or strings of characters at the command line that DOS translates into variables called replaceable parameters	BTCHFILE *param1 param2 param3* (etc.) where BTCHFILE.BAT is the name of the batch file and *param1, param2, param3,* etc. are values or strings of characters entered at the DOS prompt directly after the name of the batch file itself.

DOS will replace any %1 it sees in the batch file with the first parameter entered on the command line and any %2 it sees with the second parameter, etc. It will replace any %0 it sees with the name of the batch file itself exactly as it was typed in at the DOS prompt.

It will try to replace all the single-digit parameters %1 through %9. If you enter fewer than nine discrete elements after the batch file name on the command line DOS will assign a null value (zero characters long) to any unused parameters. If you type more than nine elements, DOS won't immediately assign a parameter to anything past nine, but it will preserve any temporarily unused ones and let you get at them later with the SHIFT command.

So if you had a batch file on your disk called READBACK.BAT:

```
ECHO OFF
ECHO %0 is the batch file itself
ECHO %1
ECHO %2
ECHO %3
ECHO %4
ECHO %5
```

and you put an ASCII character 0 at the end of each of the bottom five lines (by using EDLIN to create READBACK.BAT and pressing the F7 key at the end of each line), and you entered:

```
READBACK This is a test
```

DOS would print:

```
READBACK is the batch file itself
This
is
a
test
```

Notice that the READBACK.BAT batch file contained tests for five parameters (%1 through %5) but the user entered only four parameters. You need something like the ASCII character 0 at the end of every line in the above batch file, otherwise if no parameter exists for a particular line DOS will make that replaceable parameter equal to nothing. So DOS would have turned the bottom ECHO %5 line into just:

```
ECHO
```

Then DOS would have interpreted this lonely ECHO without anything after it as a command to report the current ECHO ON or OFF state.

By adding a character 0 (which will appear onscreen as a blank) to each line, you make sure that DOS will ECHO something and not interpret a missing parameter as just an ECHO command on a line by itself.

DOS can handle up to nine replaceable parameters %1 through %9 in one gulp, and will always replace %0 with the name of the batch file itself (just as it was entered at the DOS prompt). If you want to use more than nine replaceable parameters you have to use the SHIFT command

You may use the %0 parameter to re-execute the same batch file in an endless loop:

```
DIR
%0
```

will keep doing directory listings and then reloading the same batch file and starting over again.

Use more than nine replaceable parameters so your batch file can read more than nine discrete user-entered characters or character strings off the DOS command line.

SHIFT

Each time DOS executes the command SHIFT it moves each replaceable parameter down in value one notch. So the value that was stored as %3 moves down and becomes %2, the value stored at %2 becomes %1, and %1 becomes %0 (which originally held the name of the batch file).

If you had a batch file called SHIFTIT.BAT:

```
ECHO OFF
ECHO %0 %1 %2 %3
SHIFT
ECHO %0 %1 %2 %3
SHIFT
ECHO %0 %1 %2 %3
SHIFT
```

and you typed:

```
SHIFTIT A B C D
```

DOS would print:

```
C>ECHO OFF
SHIFTIT A B C
A B C D
B C D
```

as it shifted all the parameters down one by one.
Notice that in the first line DOS replaced %0
with the name of the batch file and printed three
of the four letters entered on the command line.
After the first shift, the name of the batch file
disappears as DOS moves everything down a
notch, but this time the batch file prints the
fourth parameter entered on the command line
(the D) even though the fourth parameter didn't
appear the first time.

If you want to preserve the name of the batch
file itself when using the SHIFT command, you
have to set an environment variable as this new
SHIFTIT2.BAT batch file does:

```
ECHO OFF
SET NAME=%0
ECHO %0 %1 %2 %3
SHIFT
ECHO %NAME% %0 %1 %2 %3
SHIFT
ECHO %NAME% %0 %1 %2 %3
SHIFT
SET NAME=
```

DOS will still wipe out the name of the batch file originally stored as %0 the first time it executes the SHIFT command, but it will still be able to remember and display it since you stored it as an environment variable called NAME with the:

```
SET NAME=%0
```

command, and then dredged it back up when you used the:

```
ECHO %NAME%
```

command. This time, using the same four parameters after SHIFTIT2.BAT:

```
SHIFTIT2 A B C D
```

would yield:

```
C>ECHO OFF
SHIFTIT2 A B C
SHIFTIT2 A B C D
SHIFTIT2 B C D
```

retaining the name of the batch file each time even though the SHIFT command wrote over it.

The SHIFT command can handle as many parameters off the command line as you entered (and you can type in only 127 characters including the name of the batch file itself. If your batch file had a name that was just one letter long and you entered only single-character parameters (with spaces between them) you could have SHIFT squeeze out 63 of them.) The MAX-SHIFT.BAT batch file below:

```
ECHO OFF
:TOP
IF %1!==! GOTO END
ECHO %1
SHIFT
```

```
GOTO TOP
:END
```

will keep reading all the parameters off the command line and ECHOing them one by one until they've all been processed. You could enter:

```
MAXSHIFT A B C D E F G
```

etc. all the way through the uppercase and lowercase alphabets and MAXSHIFT would display every letter. It knows when to stop because it runs a:

```
IF %1!==! GOTO END
```

test each time it shifts. This test will be true only when %1 is finally equal to nothing because all the parameters have been used up, and the test will become:

```
IF !==! GOTO END
```

Until then, %1! will be equal to A! or B! or z! so something like:

```
IF A!==! GOTO END
```

will not be true, because A! is not equal to just !.

Store and retrieve variables in the DOS environment

```
SET ENVVAR=VALUE
ECHO %ENVVAR%
IF %ENVVAR%==PRESET GOTO LABEL
```

Although it wasn't documented until DOS version 3.3, and doesn't always work properly with earlier versions, and doesn't work at all under 3.0, DOS lets you set and use batch file variables in a special section of memory called the environment.

You can see what DOS currently stores in your environment by typing SET at the DOS prompt. You'll always see a line beginning COMSPEC= which tells your system where to look for the

COMMAND.COM command processor. And you'll probably also see your PATH, your PROMPT, and possibly an APPEND path and a few variables set by some commercial software (*WordPerfect*, for instance).

Entering the word SET followed by a variable name of your choice, then an equals sign, then a character string:

```
SET SCREEN=EGA
```

will add:

```
SCREEN=EGA
```

to your environment. If you have two screens and you're changing to a monochrome display, the batch file that does the changing can also reset the SCREEN variable:

```
SET SCREEN=MONO
```

Then any other programs and batch files can tell which screen is active by looking at the %SCREEN% variable.

A very handy use for this is in debugging batch files. When you're creating and testing them you often want ECHO to be ON so you can see where any potential problems are. But when you run them you want ECHO to be off so they don't clutter your screen with commands.

To solve this, make the first line in your batch file:

```
ECHO %ECHO%
```

Then, at the DOS prompt, type:

```
SET ECHO=ON
```

when you want to see all the commands execute, and:

```
SET ECHO=OFF
```

when you want to suppress them.

Be careful when setting environment variables. Spacing matters. If you type:

```
SET ECHO=OFF
```

and then try to change it by typing:

```
SET ECHO =ON
```

instead of changing %ECHO% to ON, DOS will establish a second environment variable with a trailing space called %ECHO % and make it equal to ON, and you'll end up with:

```
ECHO=OFF
ECHO =ON
```

To avoid problems, before testing the value of an environment variable make sure the variable has been set with a preliminary command such as:

```
IF %ECHO%!==! GOTO NOTSET
```

Environment variables are case-sensitive, so you should test for the obvious variations and trap against invalid entries that fall through the tests:

```
IF %ECHO%!==! GOTO NOTSET
IF %ECHO%==ON GOTO OKAY
IF %ECHO%==on GOTO OKAY
IF %ECHO%==On GOTO OKAY
IF %ECHO%==OFF GOTO OKAY
IF %ECHO%==off GOTO OKAY
IF %ECHO%==Off GOTO OKAY
ECHO %ECHO% is invalid
GOTO END
```

Note: If you insert too many strings into your environment you can run out of environment space. The default is a paltry ten 16-byte *paragraphs,* or 160 bytes.

Under DOS 2.0 and 2.1 you can patch COM-MAND.COM at address ECF to represent the number of 16-byte memory paragraphs that will make up your new environment. (For DOS 2.11 the address is DF3.)

For DOS 3.0 and 3.1, there's a much better way. Just put a:

```
SHELL=[d:][path]COMMAND.COM /E:n /P
```

command in your CONFIG.SYS file, where n represents the number of 16-byte paragraphs. For versions 3.2 and later, use the same SHELL command but specify the actual number of bytes rather than paragraphs. The default in all cases is 160 bytes (ten paragraphs). You can jack it all the way up to 32K in DOS 3.2 and 3.3, but are limited to 62 paragraphs in earlier versions.

Execute one batch file from within another batch file ("chain" batch file execution together)

```
CALL [d:][path]BTCHFILE
COMMAND /C [d:][path]BTCHFILE
```

where BTCHFILE is the name of the additional batch file to run. (CALL works only in DOS 3.3 or later.)

Examples: Depending on the version, including the lines:

```
COMMAND /C NEXTFILE
```

or:

```
CALL NEXTFILE
```

in a batch file called ORIGFILE.BAT will jump execution to NEXTFILE.BAT. When NEXTFILE.BAT finishes running, execution will generally return to the line after the COM-MAND /C or the CALL command in ORIG-FILE.BAT.

If you want to run another batch file but you don't need to return to the first, you don't need COMMAND /C or CALL. Just end the first batch file with the name of the next one you want to run next.

CALL uses less memory and executes quickly, but COMMAND /C can do some tricks CALL can't. (See the section below on FOR nesting, for instance.)

Execute a DOS command repeatedly

FOR %%var IN (set) DO command [%%var]

inside batch files, and:

FOR %var IN (set) DO command [%var]

outside of batch files.

Note that you use double %% signs inside batch files and single % signs outside batch files.

%%var and %var are variable names, generally single letters such as %%a or %Z.

(set) is the filespec or collection of filespecs that DOS will act on, and can be a wildcard such as (*.*) or (*.BAK), or a group of files such as:

```
(MORE.ASM MORE.OBJ MORE.COM)
```

Examples: to perform a directory listing on EXE and COM files:

```
FOR %%A in (*.COM *.EXE) DO DIR %%A
```

If you leave off the final %%A:

```
FOR %%A in (*.COM *.EXE) DO DIR
```

DOS will do the same repeated DIR listing on the entire directory one time for each occurrence of an EXE or COM file. So if there are two COM files and three EXE files DOS will do a DIR *.* command five times. You must add the

%%var command onto the end for the FOR command to act on what you've specified in the (set). If you don't, DOS will simply repeat the specified command the same number of times that there are matching elements in the set. Also, make sure the %%var matches in case at the beginning and end of the line.

```
FOR %%A IN (*.BAK) DO DEL %%A
```

and:

```
FOR %%a IN (*.BAK) DO DEL %%a
```

will erase all your BAK files, but:

```
FOR %%a IN (*.BAK) DO DEL %%A
```

and:

```
FOR %%A IN (*.BAK) DO DEL %%a
```

won't.

The DOS manual claims that you can't combine (or "nest") FOR commands on the same line. Try this with a command on one line such as:

```
FOR %%A IN (1 2 3) DO FOR %%B IN (A B C) DO ECHO %%A %%B
```

and you'll get a "FOR cannot be nested" error message. However, you can nest FOR commands if you use COMMAND /C (again, all on one line):

```
FOR %%A IN (1 2 3) DO COMMAND /C FOR %%B IN (A B C) DO ECHO %%A %%B
```

This technique won't work with CALL. You have to use COMMAND /C.

DOS isn't picky about COMMAND /C syntax. All of the following constructions will work:

... COMMAND /C FOR ...
... COMMAND/C FOR ...

Pass parameters from one batch file to another

The easiest way is simply to include a parameter after the filename on the line with the CALL or the COMMAND /C.

If you had a file on your disk called TEST1.BAT:

```
ECHO OFF
ECHO This is TEST1
CALL TEST2 TESTPARAM
ECHO Back to TEST1
```

and another called TEST2.BAT that was called by TEST1.BAT:

```
ECHO This is TEST2
ECHO %1
```

If you ran TEST1, you'd see:

```
This is the TEST1
This is TEST2
TESTPARAM
Back to TEST1
```

The first batch file passed the parameter TESTPARAM to the second by including after the name of the file it called. The second batch file picked up the parameter with %1.

Combine CALL or COMMAND /C with FOR %%var IN (set) DO command %%var for added power.

Running the following FIL1.BAT batch file:

```
ECHO OFF
ECHO Starting out in FIL1.BAT
FOR %%A in (*.BAK) DO CALL FIL2
%%A
ECHO Back to batch file #1
```

will CALL the next FIL2.BAT batch file:

```
ECHO OFF
ECHO ***********************
ECHO Now you're in FIL2.BAT
ECHO The contents of %1 are:
MORE < %1
ECHO ***********************
PAUSE
```

and pass the parameter (*.BAK) from FIL1.BAT to FIL2.BAT using the %%A in FIL1.BAT and the %1 in FIL2.BAT.

So FIL1.BAT will hunt down all the files with BAK extensions and FIL2.BAT will ECHO the name of each one and then use MORE.COM to display the contents of each one. After FIL2.BAT has displayed the last *.BAK file, it will stop running and DOS will return command to FIL1.BAT.

You may pass values to other batch files without having to load these batch files directly with COMMAND /C or CALL. Just use SET to park these values in memory as environment variables. This way one batch file can switch monitors, or turn ECHO OFF or ON, or swap printers, and leave status indicators in the environment for other batch files to examine.

A batch file can determine the current state of an environment variable by using string tests like:

```
IF %MONITOR%==MONO GOTO GREENCOL
```

And it can see if no environment variable happens to be set yet, with a test like:

```
IF %MONITOR%!==! GOTO SETMON
```

Jump (branch) to a designated line   GOTO [:]LABEL

will jump to the line beginning with :LABEL. You don't need the colon in the line with the

GOTO, but it won't hurt. You do need to put a colon as the first character in the line with the label. To be safe, make sure all labels are eight or fewer characters long (various versions of DOS treat longer labels differently) and stick to letters and numbers when naming them. And DOS can't handle periods in label names.

In the following batch file:

```
ECHO OFF
GOTO SKIPLINE
ECHO This line will not print
:SKIPLINE
ECHO But this one will
```

the batch file will do exactly what it says.

Labels are *not* case sensitive, so if you have a label:

```
AaAaA
```

and your batch file contains a line that says:

```
GOTO aaaaa
```

or:

```
GOTO AAAAA
```

or:

```
GOTO AAAaa
```

the batch file will jump to the :AaAaA label each time. That same label could have been :AAaaA or :AAAAA or :aaaaA and the batch file still would have jumped to it.

DOS looks for labels starting at the top of each batch file. If the same label is in a batch file twice, DOS will always jump to the first one and will never reach the second one.

Labels work well with replaceable parameters, since labels are not case sensitive. If you wanted to test for JFK and jump to AIRPORT you would have to test all combinations of uppercase and lowercase letters.

```
IF %1==JFK GOTO AIRPORT
IF %1==JFk GOTO AIRPORT
IF %1==JfK GOTO AIRPORT
IF %1==jFK GOTO AIRPORT
IF %1==jFk GOTO AIRPORT
IF %1==jfK GOTO AIRPORT
IF %1==jfk GOTO AIRPORT
```

But you could simplify things simply by jumping to the label:

```
GOTO %1
```

However, when you test all of the IF %1== possibilities, you can screen out typographical errors and invalid entries. Jumping directly to a label bypasses all such tests and is far faster if a valid label exists. But if one doesn't exist, all that will happen is that you'll get a "Label not found" error.

Labels have to start at the very left edge of the screen (with the colon in column 1) in DOS 2.0 versions; later editions are more flexible.

Execute a command only if a certain file exists

IF EXIST *filename action*

where *filename* is the name of the file it's looking for, and *action* is the command DOS will execute only if it finds the file first.

Example:

```
IF EXIST MENU TYPE MENU
```

will use the DOS TYPE command to display a MENU file only if this MENU file is in the current directory. With DOS 3.x you can specify a path and have DOS look outside the current directory, but DOS 2.x won't let you search outside the current directory.

Execute a command only if a certain file does NOT exist

IF NOT EXIST *filename action*

where *filename* is the name of the file it's looking for, and *action* is the command DOS will execute only if that file is not present in the current directory. Again, DOS 3.x lets you specify a path in front of the filename so DOS can look outside the current directory; DOS 2.x does not.

Example:

```
IF NOT EXIST MORE.COM GOTO ERROR
          .
          .
          .
:ERROR
ECHO You need to have MORE.COM in
ECHO this directory for the batch
ECHO file to work properly
GOTO END
```

Execute a command only if a string of characters matches a preset string of characters exactly

IF *string1*= =*string2 action*

where *string1* and *string2* are strings of characters, and action is the command the batch file will execute if both strings are exactly equal. Note the double equals sign. DOS insists that both strings match exactly for the test to work, which means that uppercase and lowercase variations of the same text won't match.

So the tests:

```
IF test1==test1 GOTO NEXTSTEP
```

and:

```
IF TEST1==TEST1 GOTO NEXTSTEP
```

and:

```
IF tEsT1==tEsT1 GOTO NEXTSTEP
```

will all work, and DOS will jump to the
:NEXTSTEP label in all cases. But the tests:

```
IF TEST1==test1 GOTO NEXTSTEP
```

or:

```
IF Test1==TEST1 GOTO NEXTSTEP
```

or:

```
IF TEST==TEST1 GOTO NEXTSTEP
```

will not work because the strings don't match
precisely.

This kind of test is most often used with replaceable parameters to let a user enter a string of
characters (usually a word or someone's name)
at the DOS prompt after the filename and then
have the batch file behave a certain way depending on what the user's character string was.

Example:

```
ECHO OFF
REM SORTDIR.BAT
IF %1==EXT GOTO EXTEN
IF %1==ext GOTO EXTEN
IF %1==Ext GOTO EXTEN
IF %1==SIZE GOTO SIZE
IF %1==Size GOTO SIZE
IF %1==size GOTO SIZE
DIR
GOTO END
:EXTEN
DIR | SORT /+ 10
GOTO END
:SIZE
DIR | SORT /+ 13
:END
```

If the user enters:

```
SORTDIR EXT
```

The first test in the above SORTDIR batch file
will turn into:

```
IF EXT==EXT GOTO EXTEN
```

and the test will be true, so the batch file will
jump execution to the :EXTEN label. The
second and third IF %1==ext and IF %1==Ext
tests will check for uppercase and lowercase
variations of EXT. If the user enters EXt,
however, none of the top three tests will recognize it.

So if the user enters one of these:

```
SORTDIR EXT
SORTDIR Ext
SORTDIR ext
```

the batch file will branch to the :EXTEN label
and execute the command below it that produces
a directory listing sorted by extension.

Similarly, the bottom three tests will detect
whether the user entered SIZE or Size or size,
and if so, will jump to the :SIZE label and execute the command below it that produces a
directory listing arranged in size order.

If all six tests fail, execution will reach the normal DIR command and the batch file will
produce a normal unsorted DIR listing.

String tests are very useful when performed on
environment variables. For instance, you may
have two color setting routines on your disk, one
that uses direct BIOS calls (like the programs on
the accompanying disk) and one that uses
ANSI.SYS commands. When you configured
your system to run ANSI.SYS, you could issue a
batch file command SET ANSI=ON. Then all
later batch files could include a line IF
ANSI==ON GOTO ANSISET. If ANSI was

loaded, the %ANSI% variable in your environment would be equal to ON, and a test like this would be able to jump to the ANSI color setter rather than the BIOS color setter. When you weren't using ANSI, the test would look at the environment and see that ANSI was not equal to ON, and branch to the BIOS setter rather than the ANSI one. (See following entry.)

Execute a command only if a string of characters does not exactly match a preset character string

IF NOT *string*1= =*string*2 *action*

This works just like the

```
IF string1==string2 action
```

test except that the test will succeed only if the two character strings do *not* match precisely. This command is not really all that useful, since it's generally safer to see whether a user entered a particular string, and not whether he or she didn't.

Still, being able to phrase tests using negative conditions adds flexibility. The ANSITEST.BAT batch file could be written:

```
ECHO OFF
IF NOT !%ANSI%==!ON GOTO BIOSSET
:ANSISET
ECHO ANSI color setter goes here
GOTO END
:BIOSSET
ECHO BIOS color setter goes here
:END
```

The exclamation points are needed to prevent a syntax error if no ANSI variable exists in the environment. Without something there (you could use any two other identical symbols such as IF NOT @%ANSI%==@ON) you would end up with a line that translated to:

```
IF NOT ==ON
```

which would trigger a syntax error.

Execute a command only if a special number called an "exit code" or a "return" code matches a preset number

```
IF ERRORLEVEL number action
```

where *action* is the command DOS will execute if the return code is the same as or greater than the decimal *number* specified.

This is one of the most useful and worst-named commands in the entire DOS arsenal. For best results it requires that you use a version of a keyboard-processing program not supplied with DOS. And it's a bit cumbersome to use. But it's the only way to make batch files truly interactive.

IF ERRORLEVEL was originally used by DOS to check the performance status of commands such as BACKUP, KEYB, REPLACE, RESTORE, or FORMAT. These DOS utilities set different *exit codes* or *return codes* that DOS could use to see if the commands were able to work completely or partially, or tell whether the user or some system error interrupted the process.

But few users ever take advantage of this aspect of return codes. Most power users, on the other hand, exploit these codes to the hilt with IF ERRORLEVEL tests in batch files.

DOS lets programmers use several different techniques for ending programs that are not going to remain resident in memory. They can use an interrupt 20H, or a RET (return instruction) that triggers an INT 20H, or function 0 of INT 21H. These simply tell the operating system to reset several things, make the memory used by the program available again to DOS, and pass control back to COMMAND.COM.

But if they use function 31H or, more commonly, 4CH of INT 21H, they can have the program set a code that DOS can later decipher either inside another program (with function 4DH of INT

21H), or inside a batch file with IF ERROR-LEVEL.

The easiest way to process an exit code is to create a tiny program called GETKEY.COM. To do so, make sure DEBUG is handy and type in the following seven lines:

```
DEBUG
E 100 B4 00 CD 16 B4 4C CD 21
N GETKEY.COM
RCX
8
W
Q
```

Be sure to press the Enter key at the end of each line. When you're done you'll have the eight-byte long GETKEY.COM program on your default drive.

Running the program by itself won't do anything other than pause and wait for you to press a key. But when you invoke this program in a batch file, it will pause, wait for you to press a non-Shift key, then pass along the ASCII value of that keystroke to any IF ERRORLEVEL tests that follow.

IF ERRORLEVEL can then act on the keystroke accordingly, jumping to an appropriate label based on what the user entered.

The basic test is in the format:

```
IF ERRORLEVEL number action
```

where *number* is the decimal value of the exit code, and *action* is the command to execute.

The trickiest part of all this is that IF ERROR-LEVEL will execute the action if the exit code is equal to — *or greater than* — the number after the word ERRORLEVEL. DOS allows 256 possible exit codes from 0 to 255, so the command:

```
IF ERRORLEVEL 0 ECHO True
```

will always work and will always print the message "True" since the code will always be equal to or greater than 0.

At the other end of the spectrum:

```
IF ERRORLEVEL 255 ECHO True
```

will work only in one case — when the exit code happens to be 255.

If you want to isolate a character like a space (which has an ASCII value of 32) you have to first screen out any higher exit codes:

```
IF ERRORLEVEL 33 ECHO Nonspace
IF ERRORLEVEL 32 ECHO Space
```

You can combine these into one long line:

```
IF ERRORLEVEL 32 IF NOT ERRORLEVEL 33 ECHO Space
```

The following sample ERRTEST.BAT batch file uses GETKEY.COM to fetch keystrokes and pass the ASCII value for each to a "cascade" of IF ERRORLEVEL tests:

```
ECHO OFF
:ERR
ECHO Enter a lowercase or
ECHO an uppercase letter
ECHO (Or spacebar to quit)
:TOP
GETKEY
IF ERRORLEVEL 123 GOTO ERR
IF ERRORLEVEL 97 GOTO LOWER
IF ERRORLEVEL 91 GOTO ERR
IF ERRORLEVEL 65 GOTO UPPER
IF ERRORLEVEL 33 GOTO ERR
IF ERRORLEVEL 32 GOTO END
```

```
IF ERRORLEVEL 0 GOTO ERR
:LOWER
ECHO Lowercase
GOTO TOP
:UPPER
ECHO Uppercase
GOTO TOP
:END
```

All lowercase letters have ASCII values from 97 through 122. All uppercase letters have ASCII values from 65 through 90.

ERRTEST.BAT first uses a test for 123 to screen out anything higher than the top range of lowercase values. The second test will detect anything from 97 through 122 and jump to the label that identifies this as a lowercase letter. The next test screens out the few odd characters with values from 91 through 96. It's followed by a test that detects anything from 65 through 90 and jumps to a label identifying these as uppercase letters.

Finally, a test for 33 screens out any key with a value greater than a space (remember, a space is 32) but lower than the bottom range of uppercase letters. Then a test for 32 isolates spaces, and a last test for 0 traps any other keystrokes.

One note — most single keys on your keyboard generate single ASCII codes. But key combinations like Ctrl-End or Ins or F7 generate two-character codes, where the first code is always a 0. Key-sniffing programs more sophisticated than GETKEY.COM can detect these; GETKEY thinks all such keys are returning codes of 0.

More sophisticated programs often print onscreen prompts telling the user which of several keys to press. If the program doesn't do this, you have to insert an ECHO command such as:

```
ECHO Press Y for Yes, N for No:
```

to provide the appropriate prompt.

Fancier customized programs also may screen out entire ranges of unacceptable keys. If you want the user to enter Y for Yes, or N for No, you can write a program to screen out all other keystrokes. If the program does this it can spare you from having to use lots of IF ERROR-LEVEL tests to weed out such errant keys.

If you use a fancier program to detect something like Y or N, it's important to make sure the program is case-insensitive so Y will produce the same result as y.

Many GETKEY.COM-type programs detect keystrokes and return something other than the key's ASCII code. This can also save on tests. If you ask the user to press Y (or y) to confirm a process that follows, and any other key to abort it, you could have the GETKEY-type program set a code of 255 only if the user entered a Y or y. This would let you branch properly with just a single test:

```
IF ERRORLEVEL 255 GOTO DOIT
```

See Chapter 10 for lots of other IF ERROR-LEVEL tips and techniques.

Execute a command only if a special number called an exit code or a return code does not *match a preset number*

IF NOT ERRORLEVEL number action

This works just like the above command but only if the numbers don't match.

Halt execution temporarily

PAUSE

This command is helpful if you have to change disks, turn on a printer, or perform some other time-consuming task, since it puts the batch file on hold until you press a key to continue:

```
ECHO Make sure your printer is
ECHO on then press Shift-PrtSC
PAUSE
```

DOS will print a "Strike a key when ready . . ." message onscreen and wait patiently for you to press any non-Shift key. As soon as you press a key, DOS will jump to the next command in the batch file.

If you want to abort what you're doing you may press Ctrl-ScrollLock or Ctrl-C instead. DOS will print a " Terminate batch job (Y/N)?" message onscreen. If you type Y or y DOS will abort the batch file and return you to whatever you were doing before. If you type N or n DOS will continue running the batch file as if nothing had happened. Press any other key and DOS will stubbornly repeat the "Terminate..." message.

PAUSE is also a clunky but effective way to break out of an otherwise endless loop:

```
CD \MEMO
WS
PAUSE
DEL *.BAK
%0
```

This file switches into your MEMO directory and runs *WordStar*. Then when you exit *WordStar* it pauses temporarily. If you want to continue you can press any key and the batch file will erase any BAK backup files, then reload the batch file and start the process all over again. However, if you don't want to continue, you can press Ctrl-ScrollLock or Ctrl-C and answer Y or y to the confirming question it asks and you're back at the DOS prompt.

A better way is to use IF ERRORLEVEL and ask the user to press one key to continue or another to abort.

Under DOS versions 3.x you can suppress the "Strike a key when ready . . ." message but still have PAUSE bring your batch file to a temporary halt by redirecting its output to NUL:

```
PAUSE > NUL
```

You may precede it with an ECHO command
supplying your own message:

```
ECHO (Okay, now press a key)
PAUSE
```

This won't work on older versions.

Add comments to your batch files   REM comment

or

:comment

You may enter REM, then a space, then up to
123 characters. When ECHO is *off*, nothing in
the line beginning with REM will appear
onscreen. When ECHO is ON, DOS will display
the REM and the comments that follow. You
may actually make the comments longer than
123 characters, but DOS will display only that
many when you have ECHO turned ON.

Another way to add comments is to preface
them with a colon (make sure the colon is in
column 1 if you're using an older DOS version).
DOS will treat anything beginning with a colon
as a label, and won't display anything in that
line regardless of whether ECHO is ON or OFF.
Since DOS won't try displaying such comments
you can make them as long as you want. If you
do this, be sure the first word in the line isn't the
same as a real label, or you may confuse a
GOTO statement.

As with ECHO statements, if you want to use a
character in a REM statement such as |, <, or >
that DOS treats as an operator, put the character
between a pair of quotation marks. You don't
have to worry about this if you're using a label
as a comment.

Chapter 19

EDLIN, DEBUG, and ANSI Commands

EDLIN

To do the following in EDLIN:	*Use the following commands:*
Load and begin EDLIN	EDLIN filename [/B]
Start entering text	I
Stop entering text	Ctrl-Break or Ctrl-C
Edit an existing line	[line] (See note)
Delete existing line(s)	[line][,line]D
Move line(s) to another location	[line],[line],lineM
Copy line(s) to another location	[line],[line],line[,count]C
Display part of your text	[line][,line]L *or* [line][,line]P
Search for a specified string	[line][,line][?]S[string]
Replace one string with another	[line][,line][?]R[oldstring][<F6>newstring]

EDLIN, continued

Merge disk file into current one	[line]T[d:]filename
Write part to disk and load more	[n]W *then* [n]A
Quit and save any changes	E
Quit without saving any changes	Q *then* Y

Note: Substitute the appropriate line number in place of [line] above. And note that [line][,line] and [line],[line] really mean "enter the beginning and ending line numbers of the range of lines you want to work on."

DEBUG

To do the following in DEBUG:	*Use the following commands:*
Load and begin DEBUG	DEBUG *or* DEBUG FILENAME
Name file for loading/writing	N [d:][path]filename[.ext]
Load disk information into memory	L [address [drive sector sector]]
Display memory contents	D [address][address] *or* D address length
Display register/flag contents	R [registername]
Enter new memory contents	E address [list]
Fill block of memory	F range list
Move block of memory	M range address
Compare two blocks of memory	C range address
Perform hexadecimal arithmetic	H value value
Search for characters	S range list
Assemble ASM instructions	A [address]
Unassemble instructions	U [address] *or* U [range]
Input/display 1 byte from port	I portaddress
Output 1 byte to port	O portaddress byte
Execute program in memory (Go)	G [=address][address[address...]]
Execute one main instruction	P [=address][value]
Execute and show registers/flags	T[=address][value]
Write data to disk	W [address [drive sector sector]]
Quit (without saving)	Q

ANSI.SYS

Note: In all examples, ESC represents decimal ASCII character 27 and not the letters E-S-C.

Cursor Movers

Move the cursor to a specific position:	ESC[#1;#2H *or* ESC[#1;#2f

#1 = row
#2 = column

Default is 1. Omitting all parameters moves the cursor to row 1, column 1 (upper lefthand corner of the screen). All numbers are in decimal format, and the upper lefthand corner is row 1, column 1.

Example: ESC[5;8H moves the cursor to row 5, column 8.

Move the cursor up: ESC[#A

= number of lines to move

Default is 1. Maintains the current column position. If the cursor is already on the top line, nothing changes.

Example: ESC[3A moves the cursor up three rows.

Move the cursor down: ESC[#B

= number of lines to move

Default is 1. Maintains the current column position. If the cursor is already on the bottom line, nothing changes.

Example: ESC[6B moves the cursor down six rows.

Move the cursor right: ESC[#C

ANSI.SYS, *continued*

	# = number of columns to move
	Default is 1. Maintains the current row position. If the cursor is already at the right edge of the screen, nothing changes.
	Example: ESC[40C moves the cursor 40 columns to the right.
Move the cursor left:	ESC[#D
	# = number of columns to move
	Default is 1. Maintains the current row position. If the cursor is already at the left edge of the screen, nothing changes.
	Example: ESC[25D moves the cursor 25 columns to the left.
Device Status Report (Report Current Cursor Position)	ESC[6n
	Issuing this command (you can't do it via PROMPT) triggers a Cursor Position Report in the form:
	ESC[#1,#2R
	where #1 is the current row and #2 is the current column.
	Example: ESC[6n (if the cursor is at row 3, column 7) will generate a ESC[3,7R string.
Save current cursor position:	ESC[s
	Stores most recent cursor position so you can later restore it with the ESC[u sequence.
	Example: ESC[s (if cursor is at row 6, column 7) will save these coordinates to be restored later.
Restore saved cursor position:	ESC[u

ANSI.SYS, continued

Restores the current row and column previously stored by the ESC[s sequence.

Example: ESC[u (if ESC[s had previously stored the cursor position as row 6, column 7) will reposition the cursor at those coordinates.

Erasing and Screen Clearing

Clear the screen:	ESC[2J *or* ESC[J This erases everything and positions the cursor in the upper lefthand corner of the screen — row 1, column 1. Actually, you don't need the 2 before the J. Just about any number there will work. So will just a J by itself: ESC[J Example: ESC[2J clears the screen to the existing colors.
Erase to end of line:	ESC[K Erases from the current cursor position to the end of the line — including the current column. Examples: ESC[K (if you're using an 80-column screen and the cursor is on column 8) will erase from column 8 through to column 80 on that row. ESC[5;8fESC[K will first move the cursor to column 8 of row 5, and will then erase everything from column 8 through column 80 on that line.

Color and Attribute Setting

Set one or more screen attributes:	ESC[#;...;#m

ANSI.SYS, *continued*

#s are the attributes

Also called Set Graphics Rendition (SGR), the attributes that it establishes remain in place until reset by a subsequent SGR command.

Miscellaneous Attributes:

0	All attributes off (resets everything)
1	High intensity (bright/bold) on
4	Underline on (mono screens only; blue otherwise)
5	Blink on
7	Reverse video on (black on white)
8	"Cancelled" (invisible)

Color Attributes:

Color:	(IBM value)	As background:	As foreground:
Black	(0)	40	30
Red	(4)	41	31
Green	(2)	42	32
Yellow	(6)	43	33
Blue	(1)	44	34
Magenta	(5)	45	35
Cyan	(3)	46	36
White	(7)	47	37

Examples:

ESC[0m resets all attributes to normal (white on black).

ESC[m also resets all attributes to white on black.

ESC[8m blanks the screen (black on black).

ESC[5m blinks the current text color.

ESC[1m makes the current text color bold.

ANSI.SYS, continued

ESC[5;1m blinks current text color and makes it bold.

ESC[44m sets background to blue.

ESC[44;37m sets colors to white text on blue background.

ESC[44;37;1m sets colors to bright white text on blue background.

ESC[44;37;1;5m sets colors to blinking bright white text on blue background.

Mode Controls

Set screen widths/modes:

ESC[=#h
or ESC[=#l

When used with values from 0 to 6 ESC[=#h (SET MODE) and ESC[=#l (RESET MODE) work identically to change screen modes on appropriate displays. (Note that the l is a lowercase L rather than a 1.)

Mode settings (values for #)		(DOS MODE)
0	40x25 black and white	(BW40)
1	40x25 color	(CO40)
2	80x25 black and white	(BW80)(MONO)
3	80x25 color	(CO80)
4	320x200 color graphics	
5	320x200 black and white graphics	
6	640x200 black and white graphics	

Examples: ESC[=3h and ESC[=3l will each set the screen mode on a color system to 80x25 color.

Set line wrap on:

ESC[?7h
or ESC[=7h

ANSI.SYS, *continued*

Anything typed past the rightmost column of the screen will wrap down one line to the leftmost column.

Example: ESC[?7h will make text wrap normally around from right to left and down one line.

Set line wrap off:

ESC[?7l
or ESC[=7l

If you reach the right edge of the screen DOS will lock the cursor there and overlap any additional text you type meaninglessly on the one rightmost column. However, it won't discard any keystrokes, even though it has trouble displaying them. (Note that the l character is a lowercase L and not a 1.)

Example: ESC[?7l will make text disappear once it reaches the rightmost column of the screen.

Keyboard Controls

Redefine one key as another:

ESC[#1;#2p
or ESC[0;#1;#2p
or ESC[#1;0;#2p
or ESC[0;#1;0;#2p

#1 is the ASCII code of the key to be redefined
#2 is the ASCII value of the new definition
If using an extended key, its ASCII value is two characters long; the first character is 0

ANSI can juggle the definitions of any non-Shift keys. (It can't change keys without ASCII values such as Shift or Ctrl or Alt.) To redefine one alphanumeric key (like A or a or 1), first specify the decimal ASCII value of the key you want to redefine and follow it with its new ASCII value. If you're using an "extended" key (like F7, Alt-U, or Ins) either as the key you

ANSI.SYS, *continued*

want redefined or as the new definition, specify this extended key by preceding it with a 0.

To reset a key to its original value, redefine it as itself (put its ASCII value on both sides of the semicolon).

Examples:

ESC[65;90p turns an uppercase A (65) into an uppercase Z (90) while leaving the lowercase a, and both the upper- and lowercase Z alone. (You would be able to type an uppercase Z by holding down the shift key and typing either A or Z.)

ESC[65;90p and ESC[90;65p will switch uppercase Z and A but leave the lowercase versions of each alone.

ESC["A";"Z"p and ESC["Z";"A"p will also switch uppercase A and Z and leave everything else alone.

ESC[65;65p will reset the uppercase A key so it again prints and uppercase A.

ESC[65;65p and ESC[90;90p will put the uppercase A and the uppercase Z back they way they were originally.

ESC[34;39p and ESC[39;34p will swap the " and ' keys.

ESC["'";"""p and ESC['"';"""p will also swap the " and ' keys.

ESC[0;46;155p will turn Alt-C (an "extended" key with an ASCII value two characters long — 0 46) into a cent sign (which has an ASCII value of 155).

ESC[0;59;0;60p and ESC[0;60;0;59p will switch function keys F1 (0 59) and F2 (0 60).

ANSI.SYS, *continued*

ESC[0;59;0;59p and ESC[0;60;0;60p will restore function keys F1 and F2 to their original
settings.

Assign multiple characters to keys: ESC[#1;"text"p
ESC[0;#1;"text"p
ESC[#1;#2;...;#127p
ESC[#1;#2;"text";#100p

#1 is the ASCII code of the key to be redefined.

"text" is the text you want to assign to this key.

If using an extended key, its ASCII value is two
characters long; the first character is 0.

#2 through #100 or #127 are the ASCII values of
the new definitions.

"text" is ASCII text between quotes.

ANSI lets you turn any alphanumeric (nonshift)
key on the keyboard into a "macro" key that can
enter commands, print messages, etc. You may
enter up to 127 characters as the new definition
for each key, by specifying the ASCII value(s)
of the key(s) in the new definition, or by specifying text (between quotation marks) for the new
definition, or by combining both decimal ASCII
values and text into the new definition.

To reset a key to its original value, redefine it as
itself (put its ASCII value on both sides of the
semicolon).

Examples:

ESC[65;66;67;68;69;70p will assign the letters
BCDEF to the capital A, so that typing an A will
print out BCDEF. This will leave the lowercase
"a" alone.

ANSI.SYS, *continued*

ESC[65;65;66;67;68;69;70p will assign the letters ABCDEF to capital A.

ESC[65;65p will restore the capital A back to normal.

ESC["A";"A"p will also restore the capital A to normal.

ESC[0;59;"DIR "p will put the letters DIR followed by a space on the command line whenever you press the F1 key. It won't actually execute the command, so you'll be able to add a drive letter and then press the Enter key.

ESC["~";"DIR C:";13p will assign the command DIR C: to the tilde (~). Adding a 13 at the end before the p will make DOS execute the command instead of just printing it out, because 13 is the ASCII value of the Enter key, and this will simulate pressing Enter. This will leave the lowercase character on the tilde key alone.

ESC[126;"DIR C:";13p will assign the same DIR C: and Enter command to the tilde.

ESC[0;25;"Name: ";13;"Rank: ";13;"Serial Number: ";13p will have AH-P trigger:

Name:
Rank:
Serial Number:

with a carriage return and a space after each. At the DOS prompt this will produce error messages since DOS will think you're trying to execute files called Name:, Rank:, and Serial. But you can use this when creating files with EDLIN or the DOS COPY command or certain text editors such as IBM PE.

ESC[0;15;"DIR | FIND ";34;"-88";34;13p will turn the little-used Shift-Tab key combination into a command that will list all the 1988 files in the current subdirectory (assuming the DOS FIND.EXE utility is handy). The two 34s are needed because 34 is the ASCII value of the quotation marks needed for the FIND command.

Index

IBM PS/2-Compatible 3.5" Diskettes

This Bantam software product is also available in IBM PS/2- compatible 3.5"/720K format. If you'd like to exchange this software for the new 3.5" format, please:

- Package your original 5.25" diskette in a mailer.

- Include a check or money order for US $7.95 ($9.95 Canadian) to cover media, postage and handling (California and Massachusetts residents add sales tax). Foreign orders: please send international money orders; no foreign checks accepted.

- Include your completed warranty card.

Upon receipt Bantam will immediately send your replacement disk via first class mail.

Mail to:

Bantam Electronic Publishing
666 Fifth Avenue
New York, NY 10103
Attn: PCM/3.5 Disk